W9-BVX-856

The Porter Sargent Handbook Series

THE DIRECTORY FOR
EXCEPTIONAL
CHILDREN

PUBLISHER'S STATEMENT

Esteemed educational and social critic Porter Sargent established *The Handbook of Private Schools* in 1914, with the aim "to present a comprehensive and composite view of the private school situation as it is today. No attempt has been made at completeness. The effort on the contrary has been to include only the best, drawing the line somewhat above the average."

Today, **The Porter Sargent Handbook Series** continues its founder's mission: to serve parents, educators and others concerned with the independent and critical evaluation of primary and secondary educational options, leading to a suitable choice for each student.

The Handbook of Private Schools, Guide to Summer Camps and Summer Schools (1924) and *Schools Abroad of Interest to Americans* (1959) provide the tools for objective comparison of programs in their respective fields. *The Directory for Exceptional Children,* first published in 1954, broadens that mission and service to parents and professionals seeking the optimal educational, therapeutic or clinical environment for special-needs children.

THE DIRECTORY FOR
EXCEPTIONAL
CHILDREN

A COMPREHENSIVE LISTING OF
SPECIAL-NEEDS SCHOOLS,
PROGRAMS AND FACILITIES

15TH EDITION
2004-05

PORTER SARGENT PUBLISHERS, INC.
Editorial Office:
11 Beacon Street, Suite 1400
Boston, Massachusetts 02108
Tel: 617-523-1670   Fax: 617-523-1021
info@portersargent.com   www.portersargent.com

Copyright © 2004 by the Estate of J. Kathryn Sargent
Previous editions copyrighted 1954-2001

PRINTED IN CANADA

LIBRARY OF CONGRESS CATALOG CARD NUMBER 54-4975

ISBN 0-87558-150-1
ISSN 0070-5012

R03011 69698

All information as reported to Porter Sargent Publishers, Inc., as of September 3, 2004. Schools and facilities should be contacted for updated information.

All rights reserved. No part of this book may be reproduced or transmitted in any form or by any means, electronic or mechanical, including photocopying, recording, or by any information storage and retrieval system, without permission in writing from the publisher.

Cost: US$75.00 + $7.00 shipping and handling in the USA. Additional copies are available from booksellers, or from the Publisher's customer service center: 300 Bedford St., Ste. 213, Manchester, NH 03101. Tel: 800-342-7470. Fax: 603-669-7945. orders@portersargent.com. www.portersargent.com.

TABLE OF CONTENTS

*This index assists the reader in quickly identifying appropriate pro-
grams by grouping special-needs conditions into broader categories.
The reader can then advance to the geographically organized editorial
listings to learn more about potentially suitable programs.*

Blindness

Deafness

Diabetes

Emotional Disturbances
*(includes Anorexia Nervosa, Anxiety Disorders, Behavioral
Disorders, Bulimia, Conduct Disorder, Mood Disorder, Obsessive/
Compulsive Disorder, PTSD, Prader-Willi Syndrome, Psychosis,
Schizophrenia, School Phobia, Tourette's Syndrome)*

HIV/AIDS

Learning Disabilities
(includes ADD, ADHD, Dyscalculia, Dysgraphia, Dyslexia)

Mental Retardation
(includes Down Syndrome)

Orthopedic/Neurological Disorders
*(includes Apraxia, Arthritis, Asthma, Brain Injury, Cardiac
Disorder, Cerebral Palsy, Cystic Fibrosis, Epilepsy,
Infantile Paralysis, Multiple Sclerosis, Muscular Dystrophy,
Neurofibromatosis, Spina Bifida, Tuberculosis)*

Pervasive Developmental Disorders
(includes Asperger's Syndrome, Autism)

Speech Impairments
(includes Aphasia)

PROGRAM DESCRIPTIONS *(listed alphabetically by program name
within each state)*

Table of Contents

THE DIRECTORY FOR EXCEPTIONAL CHILDREN

Senior Editor	Daniel P. McKeever
Production Manager	Leslie A. Weston
Editor	Adam G. Reich
Development Coordinator	Kirsten M. Macdonald
Editorial Assistant	Heather Lane Savage

PORTER SARGENT PUBLISHERS, INC.

President	John P. Yonce
Directors	Keith L. Hughes
	Cornelia E. Sargent

Publishers

1914-1950	Porter E. Sargent
1951-1975	F. Porter Sargent
1976-1999	J. Kathryn Sargent

PREFACE

Unique among single-volume resources, the 2004-05 *Directory for Exceptional Children* is a survey of approximately 2500 schools, facilities, organizations and associations that serve children and young adults with developmental, emotional, physical and medical disabilities. *Directory* listings provide comprehensive data on programs throughout the United States that serve individuals under age 21 who have special needs. Because of the nature of special-needs programs, many institutions provide programming for adults as well.

In this 15th edition of the *Directory,* our editors have endeavored to increase the utility of our special-needs resource for parents and placement professionals. This edition includes a thorough Index by State, City and Special Needs Addressed, followed by a state-by-state listing of programs. Under each state heading, programs are presented alphabetically by name. This new organization of listings will enable the reader to more readily locate suitable programs, as he or she can review the Index by State, City and Conditions to identify potential programs, then learn more about these programs by advancing to the geographically organized editorial listings.

This new book structure has effectively minimized the duplication of listings that often occurred in previous editions, when chapter placement was determined by special need(s) addressed. Instead of providing one or more additional listings for programs that address more than one special need, our editors have opted to provide additional listings only for programs that operate at other locations more than 100 miles from the primary site. Branches operating within 100 miles of the main site are referenced by city in the statistical portion of the editorial listing under the heading "Nearby locations." When a program's administrative contact city differs from that of the program described, the city of operation appears first, followed by the contact coordinates.

In order to present as many facts as possible in a concise format, it has been necessary to abbreviate statistical information that appears throughout the *Directory.* In all cases, we have attempted to use simple and straightforward abbreviations. The Key to Abbreviations, on pages 19-23, assists the reader in gaining familiarization with these abbreviations.

Detailed information describing each program is presented at no cost or obligation to the facilities. Statistics are printed as supplied in response to our questionnaire, enabling smooth and rapid processing of data. From an aggregate of information, aspects that impartially and objectively depict programs and services are selected for paragraph descriptions.

Programs that sponsor a distinct Illustrated Announcement are able to emphasize those program features they consider to be most significant. A personalized statement of the facility's philosophy and goals afforded through an Illustrated Announcement is a valuable complement to the objective account given in editorial listings.

Although we strive for maximum information in each editorial listing, length and content of entries are solely dependent on the material elicited from each facility. The quality of a facility therefore should not be measured by the length of its listing; nor does a facility's purchase of space in the Illustrated Announcements section affect the length or content of its free editorial listing.

Associations and Organizations, a section that follows the Illustrated Announcements, presents entities dedicated to special-needs children and their families. Included here are state and Federal agencies, as well as organizations relating to advocacy, accreditation, special-needs professionals, recreation, rehabilitation and welfare.

Parents should view this book as a preliminary source for appropriate programs for their children's special needs. Finding the right environment for each person is an individual search, and inclusion in the *Directory* does not constitute an endorsement. It is vitally important to gather as much firsthand information as possible before a decision is made. Visit the facilities and talk with administrators and staff. The more thorough your research, the more likely you are to choose the proper setting for the individual's growth and development.

We hope this *Directory* will enjoy the popularity and wide usage that it has received in past editions, and that it may serve to meet the requirements of those concerned with special-needs children. Our readership's comments on facilities listed in this volume and notification of those closed, omitted or newly established will be invaluable in ensuring that forthcoming editions may continue to present the most complete and accurate data on facilities for exceptional children, adolescents and young adults.

In closing, we wish to thank the many program administrators who updated their listings by completing our questionnaire. Their responses to our queries for new information enabled our editors to make all necessary revisions to their listings.

READING THE
PROGRAM DESCRIPTIONS

The information presented in the Directory *is arranged in a standardized format to facilitate ready comparison of programs. In searching for programs to fulfill special needs, one should first consult the Index by State, City and Special Needs Addressed.*

The Directory *is organized alphabetically by state. The listing of facilities within a state is arranged alphabetically by program name.*

Due to the failure of certain facilities to provide updated data by press time, some listings include basic information only. In such instances, our editors have verified that the facility still operates at the listed address and continues to serve a special-needs population. These concise listings appear alongside the full entries.

1. ## PORTER SARGENT CENTER
    Res and Day — Coed Ages 12-18
    Clinic: All Ages. M-F 8-5; Eves M T Th 5-8.

2. **Boston, MA 02108. 11 Beacon St, Ste 1400.**
    Tel: 617-523-1670. TTY: 617-523-0000. Fax: 617-523-1021.
    www.portersargent.com E-mail: info@portersargent.com.

3. **Bill Covaleski,** BA, MA, Dir. **Garrett Oliver,** MD, Med Dir. **Greg Koch,** Adm.

4. **Focus:** Spec Ed. **Conditions:** Primary—ED BD. Sec—ADD ADHD Dx LD. **IQ 80 and up.**

5. **Gen Acad.** Gr 7-12. Courses: Reading Math Lang_Arts. Man_Arts & Shop.

6. **Therapy:** Hear Lang Music Phys Speech. **Psychotherapy:** Fam Group. **Counseling:** Educ.

7. **Enr:** 106. Res Males 20. Res Females 30. Day Males 25. Day Females 31. **Staff:** 30 (Full 15, Part 15). Pro 3. Educ 24. Admin 3.

8. **Rates 2004:** $25,000/sch yr (+$600). Day Rate $14,250/sch yr (+$450). Clinic $86/hr. Schol 9 ($58,000). State Aid.

9. **Summer Prgm.** Res & Day. Educ Rec Ther. 6 wks.

10. **Est 1914.** Private. Nonprofit. **Spons:** National Association for Special-Needs Children.

11. PSC serves adolescents with emotional and related learning problems. Prescriptive treatment plans are designed for each student and are incorporated into the total therapeutic educational process. Facilities include a multimedia learning resource center, a science laboratory, and a vocational and expressive arts center. The program's goal is to prepare each student for reentry into the educational mainstream as soon as he or she is capable.

A psychiatric and guidance clinic for members of the community operates daily. Counseling and family support services are integral to the program.

12.   **See Also Page 1000**

1. FACILITY NAME and TYPE. Gender and age range of individuals accepted are provided here. For facilities with clinics, ages treated and days and hours of operation are given.

2. CITY or TOWN; STATE; ZIP CODE; STREET/MAILING ADDRESS; TELEPHONE, TTY and FAX NUMBERS; and E-MAIL and WEB SITE ADDRESSES. If the physical location differs from the administrative address, both the full administrative address and the location city and state are listed. Facilities with branch locations include references to the city or cities in which these branches operate.

3. DIRECTOR(S) OF FACILITY. One or more program directors may be listed, depending upon who is directly responsible for the administration of the facility. Academic degrees and relevant licenses held by the director(s) are often noted.

Where appropriate, the MEDICAL DIRECTOR follows. The ADMISSIONS or INTAKE DIRECTOR is then cited, unless a previously listed administrator performs admissions duties.

4. FOCUS is represented by one or more of the following terms: special education, rehabilitation, training and treatment. CONDITIONS ACCEPTED. Disorders of primary concern for treatment or diagnosis appear first, followed by secondary conditions. The INTELLIGENCE QUOTIENT RANGE of children eligible for acceptance is often given.

For a complete Key to Abbreviations, see pages 19-23.

5. ACADEMIC ORIENTATION, GRADES OFFERED and CURRICULUM. For program with an educational or vocational component, the basic curriculum is described as college preparatory, general academic, prevocational or vocational. If a program is ungraded, a notation appears; otherwise, the facility's grade range is listed. Notable academic courses and vocational offerings follow.

6. THERAPY, PSYCHOTHERAPY and COUNSELING OFFERINGS are cited where applicable. See the Key to Abbreviations for further details.

7. ENROLLMENT. The total number of individuals enrolled is followed by the number of residential males and females, then the number of day males and females.

STAFF figures are detailed as follows: total staff members, then number of members full- and part-time. The distribution of professional, educational and administrative staff members often follows.

8. RATES and FINANCIAL ASSISTANCE. When both residential and day departments are maintained, both rates are given, unless the facility failed to provide this data.

   Rates ranges (i.e. $8000-10,500/sch yr) show the fee span from the lowest to the highest grade or age range or level of care. The facility's estimate of extra expenses incurred by the average child follows in parentheses.

   In many instances, sliding-scale rates are reported, indicating that a fee schedule is based on each family's ability to pay. Clinical rates are generally given per session or per hour.

   Availability of scholarship aid and state aid follows rates. When the facility supplies the number of scholarship recipients and the total monetary value of the scholarships, this information is detailed.

9. SUMMER PROGRAM. The type and orientation are given for facilities operating distinct summer sessions. This information does not appear in the listings of clinics or year-round programs.

10. ESTABLISHMENT and ORGANIZATIONAL STRUCTURE. The date of establishment, the organizational nature, the religious affiliation and the sponsoring organization follow.

11. PARAGRAPH DESCRIPTION. Additional information about programs, unique aspects, limitations and other features not adaptable to abbreviated presentation is compiled by our editors on the basis of information provided by the facility.

12. PAGE CROSS-REFERENCES TO ILLUSTRATED ANNOUNCEMENTS. Some facilities supply their own appraisals of ideals and objectives in the Illustrated Announcements section following the editorial listings. A bold-face cross-reference is appended to the paragraph description of each such program.

KEY
TO
ABBREVIATIONS

KEY TO ABBREVIATIONS
CONDITIONS ACCEPTED

ADD	Attention Deficit Disorder	**ED**	Emotional Disturbances
ADHD	Attention Deficit Hyperactivity Disorder	**Ep**	Epilepsy
		HIV	HIV/AIDS
AN	Anorexia Nervosa	**IP**	Infantile Paralysis
Anx	Anxiety Disorders	**LD**	Learning Disabilities
Ap	Aphasia	**MD**	Muscular Dystrophy
Apr	Apraxia	**Mood**	Mood Disorder
Ar	Arthritis	**MR**	Mental Retardation
As	Asthma	**MS**	Multiple Sclerosis
Asp	Asperger's Syndrome	**Nf**	Neurofibromatosis
Au	Autism	**OCD**	Obsessive-Compulsive Disorder
B	Blindness	**ODD**	Oppositional Defiant Disorder
BD	Behavioral Disorders	**ON**	Orthopedic/Neurological Disorders
BI	Brain Injury		
Bu	Bulimia	**PDD**	Pervasive Developmental Disorder
C	Cardiac Disorder		
CD	Conduct Disorder	**Psy**	Psychosis
CF	Cystic Fibrosis	**PTSD**	Posttraumatic Stress Disorder
CP	Cerebral Palsy	**PW**	Prader-Willi Syndrome
D	Deafness	**S**	Speech Impairments
Db	Diabetes	**SB**	Spina Bifida
Dc	Dyscalculia	**SP**	School Phobia
Dg	Dysgraphia	**Sz**	Schizophrenia
DS	Down Syndrome	**TB**	Tuberculosis
Dx	Dyslexia	**TS**	Tourette's Syndrome

GENERAL ABBREVIATIONS

Acad	Academic
Actg	Acting
ADL	Activities of Daily Living
Adm	Admissions, Director of Admission(s)
Admin	Administration, Administrator
Anat	Anatomy
Appt	Appointment
Assoc	Associate
Asst	Assistant
Bus	Business
CEO	Chief Executive Officer
Clin	Clinical

Chair	Chairperson
Chemo	Chemotherapy
Chrm	Chairman
Coed	Coeducational
Col	College
COO	Chief Operating Officer
Coord	Coordinator
Crse	Course
Ctr	Center
Dept	Department
Dev	Development, Developmental
Dir	Director
Ec, Econ	Economics
Ed, Educ	Education, Educational
Eng	English
Enr	Enrollment
Enrich	Enrichment
Environ	Environmental
Est	Established
Exec	Executive
Fam	Family
Fr	French
GED	General Equivalency Diploma
Gen	General
Geog	Geography
Ger	German
Govt	Government
Gr	Grades
Head	Headmaster/Headmistress, Head of School
Hear	Hearing
Hist	History
Hr	Hour
Indiv	Individual
Int	Interim
IQ	Intelligence Quotient
Japan	Japanese
Journ	Journalism
K	Kindergarten
Lang	Language
Lat	Latin
LD	Learning Disabilities
Lib	Library

Man	Manual
Med	Medical
Mo	Month
Neuro	Neurological
Occup	Occupational
On-Job	On-the-Job
PG	Postgraduate
Photog	Photog
Phys	Physical
Physiol	Physiology
Prep	Preparatory
Pres	President
Pre-Voc	Prevocational
Prgm	Program
Prim	Primary
Prin	Principal
Prof	Professional
PS	Preschool
Psych	Psychological, Psychology
Rec	Recreational
Relig	Religion
Rem	Remedial
Res	Residential
Rm	Room
SAT	Scholastic Aptitude Test
Sch	School
Sci	Science
Sec	Secondary
Sem	Semester
Shelt	Sheltered
Soc	Social
Span	Spanish
Ste	Suite
Stud	Studies
Supt	Superintendent
Supv	Supervisor
Ther	Therapy, Therapeutic
Trng	Training
Univ	University
Voc	Vocational
Wk	Week
Yr	Year

DEGREES AND PROFESSIONAL TITLES

ACSW	Academy of Certified Social Workers
BA	Bachelor of Arts
BBA	Bachelor of Business Administration
BD	Bachelor of Divinity
BEd	Bachelor of Education
BFA	Bachelor of Fine Arts
BS	Bachelor of Science
BSN	Bachelor of Science in Nursing
BSOT	Bachelor of Science in Occupational Therapy
CB	Bachelor of Surgery
CCC	Certificate of Clinical Competence
CSW	Clinical Social Worker
DMD	Doctor of Dental Medicine
DMH	Doctor of Mental Health
DO	Doctor of Osteopathy
DPA	Doctor of Public Administration
DPH	Doctor of Public Health
DSW	Doctor of Social Work
EdD	Doctor of Education
LCSW	Licensed Certified Social Worker
LCSW-C	Licensed Certified Social Worker-Clinical
LICSW	Licensed Independent Clinical Social Worker
LISW	Licensed Independent Social Worker
LPT	Licensed Physical Therapist
LSW	Licensed Social Worker
MA	Master of Arts
MAT	Master of Arts in Teaching
MB	Bachelor of Medicine
MBA	Master of Business Administration
MD	Doctor of Medicine
MDiv	Master of Divinity
MEd	Master of Education
MFA	Master of Fine Arts
MHA	Master of Hospital Administration
MPA	Master of Public Administration
MPH	Master of Public Health
MPS	Master in Personnel Service
MS	Master of Science
MSEd	Master of Science in Education
MSN	Master of Science in Nursing
MSP	Master of Science in Planning
MSSA	Master of Science in Social Administration

MSSW	Master of Science in Social Work
MSW	Master of Social Work
OD	Doctor of Optometry
OTR	Registered Occupational Therapist
PhD	Doctor of Philosophy
PSW	Psychiatric Social Worker
PsyD	Psychology Doctorate
RN	Registered Nurse
RPT	Registered Physical Therapist
ScD	Doctor of Science
STM	Master of Sacred Theology

PROGRAM EMPHASIS INDEX

USING THE PROGRAM EMPHASIS INDEX

The index that follows assists the reader in quickly identifying appropriate programs by grouping special-needs conditions into broader categories. The reader can then advance to the geographically organized editorial listings to learn more about potentially suitable programs. See the list below for special-needs abbreviations and categorization.

Blind	Blindness
Deaf	Deafness
Diabetes	Diabetes
Emot Disturb	Emotional Disturbances *includes Anorexia Nervosa, Anxiety Disorders, Behavioral Disorders, Bulimia, Conduct Disorder, Mood Disorder, Obsessive/Compulsive Disorder, PTSD, Prader-Willi Syndrome, Psychosis, Schizophrenia, School Phobia, Tourette's Syndrome*
HIV/AIDS	HIV/AIDS
LD	Learning Disabilities *includes ADD, ADHD, Dyscalculia, Dysgraphia, Dyslexia*
MR	Mental Retardation *includes Down Syndrome*
Ortho/Neuro	Orthological/Neurological Disorders *includes Apraxia, Arthritis, Asthma, Brain Injury, Cardiac Disorder, Cerebral Palsy, Cystic Fibrosis, Epilepsy, Infantile Paralysis, Multiple Sclerosis, Muscular Dystrophy, Neurofibromatosis, Spina Bifida, Tuberculosis*
P	Primary—indicates that a category is accepted as a primary condition
PDD	Pervasive Developmental Disorders *includes Asperger's Syndrome, Autism*
S	Secondary—indicates that a category is accepted as a secondary condition
Speech	Speech Impairments *includes Aphasia*

Program	Town	Females Res	Females Day	Males Res	Males Day	Clinic	Blind	Deaf	Diabetes	Emot Disturb	HIV/AIDS	LD	MR	Ortho/Neuro	PDD	Speech	Page
ALABAMA																	
AUBURN SPEECH HEAR	Auburn					All Ages		P								P	114
HORIZONS SCH	Birmingham	19-26		19-26						S	S		S	S	S	S	116
UCP OF GR BIRMINGHAM	Birmingham		Birth-4		Birth-4		S	S		S		P	S	P	S	S	119
WORKSHOPS	Birmingham		16+		16+		S	S					P	S	S	S	123
N CAL- EARLY CHILD	Decatur		Birth-3		Birth-3		S	S		S		S	P	P	P	S	115
WIREGRASS REHAB CTR	Dothan	16+	16+	16+	16+								P				122
PATHWAY-AL	Enterprise	10-18								P		P	S	P			118
RIVERBEND MENT HLTH	Florence		2+		2+					P							118
TRI-WIL/PORTA CRAS	Green Pond	6-21		6-21				S	P	P		P	P	P		P	119
ARC OF MADISON CNTY	Huntsville		Birth-3		Birth-3		P	P		P		P	P	P	P	P	113
HUNTSVILLE ACHIEVE	Huntsville		5-16		5-16							P	P	P	P	P	116
MHC OF MADISON CTY	Huntsville		5-21		5-21					P		P	P	S			117
MOBILE ARC	Mobile		3+		3+								P				117
WILMER HALL-MURRAY	Mobile	11-18		11-18						P		P	P				122
U OF MONTEVALLO	Montevallo					All Ages		P		P		S	S	S	P	P	121
CHILDRENS-MONTGOMERY	Montgomery		Birth-21		Birth-21								P	P			115
E AL MENTAL HLTH MR	Opelika					All Ages				P			P		S		115
VIVIAN B ADAMS SCH	Ozark		All Ages		All Ages		S			S		S	P	S	S	S	121
CAHABA MHC-EI PRGM	Selma		Birth-3		Birth-3		P	P		P		P	P	P	S	P	114
AL INST DEAF & BLIND	Talladega	3-21	3-21	3-21	3-21		P	P		S			S				113
HELEN KELLER SCH-AL	Talladega	3-21	3-21	3-21	3-21		S	S		S		S	P	S	S	S	116
RISE SCH TUSCALOOSA	Tuscaloosa		Birth-6		Birth-6					P			P	P			118
U AL BREWER PORCH	Tuscaloosa	6-13	6-13	6-13	6-13					P							120

Facility	City	Ages	Emphasis	Page
U AL PSYCH CLINIC	Tuscaloosa	All Ages	P P P S P	120
U AL SPEECH & HEAR	Tuscaloosa	All Ages	P P	120
PARTLOW DEVELOPMENT	Tuscaloosa	All Ages / All Ages	P	122

ALASKA

Facility	City	Ages	Emphasis	Page
AK SCH FOR DEAF/HOH	Anchorage	3-21 / 3-21 / 3-21	P S S S S S	124
HOPE COMM RESOURCES	Anchorage	All Ages / All Ages	P S P	124
SOUTHCENTRAL COUN	Anchorage	3-17	P	125
RESIDENTIAL YOUTH	Ketchikan	10-18 / 10-18	S P P	125

ARIZONA

Facility	City	Ages	Emphasis	Page
CHINLE VALLEY SCH	Chinle	5+ / 5+ / 5+	S S S S P P S	131
AZ BAPTIST CHILDRENS	Glendale	5-18 / 5-18	P P	126
CHILD'S CTR-NEURODEV	Glendale	3-21 / 3-21	S P P P P	130
LIFE DEV INSTITUTE	Glendale	18+ / 16+ / 16+	S P S S S	135
ANASAZI	Mesa	12-25 / 12-25	P S P	126
AZ COUNSELING	Peoria	3-18	P P	126
AZ CHILD ASSOC-PHNX	Phoenix	5-18 / 5-18 / 1-18	P P S P S	129
BETHANY RANCH HOME	Phoenix	18+ / 18+ / All Ages	S P S P P S	129
FLORENCE CRITTENTON	Phoenix	12-21	P S S	132
GOMPERS CTR	Phoenix	5+ / 5+	S S P P S	133
LATCH SCH	Phoenix	2-22 / 2-22	S S S P P S	135
PHOENIX DAY SCH-DEAF	Phoenix	3-22 / 3-22	P P	136
ST PAUL'S PREP	Phoenix	14-18 / 14-18	P P	138
UPWARD FOUNDATION	Phoenix	Birth-22 / Birth-22	P P	139
YOUTH EVAL & TREAT	Phoenix	7-17 / 7-17 / 7-17	S P S	140
AZ CHILD ASSOC-PRESC	Prescott	5-18 / 5-15 / 5-15	S P P	127
DEVEREUX AZ-SCOTTS	Scottsdale	3-21 / 3-21 / 3-21 / All Ages	S P S P S	131

Program	Town	Females Res	Females Day	Males Res	Males Day	Clinic	Blind	Deaf	Diabetes	Emot Disturb	HIV/AIDS	LD	MR	Ortho/Neuro	PDD	Speech	Page
AZ HOWARD GRAY ED PRGM	Scottsdale		11-21		11-21					P	S	P	S	S	P		134
NEW WAY LEARNING	Scottsdale		6-19		6-19					S	S	S	S	S	S	S	136
STERLING RANCH	Skull Valley	18+								S		S	P	P	S	S	138
ST MICHAELS ASSOC	St Michaels	Birth-30	Birth-21	Birth-30	Birth-21								P	P		P	137
EASTER SEALS AZ-EIP	Tempe					Birth-3	S	S		P		P		P	P		132
AZ SCHS DEAF & BLIND	Tucson	5-22	Birth-22	5-22	Birth-22		P	P				S				P	127
AZ CHILD ASSOC-TUCS	Tucson	5-18	5-15	5-18	5-15	1-18				P		P	S	P			128
BLAKE CHILDRENS CTR	Tucson		Birth-5		Birth-5								P	P			130
DEVEREUX AZ-TUCSON	Tucson	3-17	6-21	3-17	6-21	All Ages				P		P		P			132
GRUNEWALD-BLITZ	Tucson					All Ages									P	P	133
PROVIDENCE SERVICE	Tucson	5-18	5-18	5-18	5-18					P		P		P			137
TURNING POINT SCH	Tucson	6-15	6-15	6-15	6-15							P			P		139
VISIONQUEST	Tucson	12-21		12-21						P							140
HENRY OCCUPATIONAL	Youngtown					Birth-19				S		P	S	S	S		134
AZ CHILD ASSOC-YUMA	Yuma	5-18	5-15	5-18	5-15	1-18				P		P	S	S			128
ARKANSAS																	
ARKADELPHIA DEVELOP	Arkadelphia	6+	6+	6+	6+					P			P	P			141
U OF THE OZARKS	Clarksville	18+	18+	18+	18+							P					146
CONWAY HUMAN DEV CTR	Conway	9+		9+			S	S				S	P	S	S	S	143
MILLCREEK OF AR	Fordyce	5-18	5-18	5-18	5-18	All Ages				P		S	P	S	S	S	145
HOT SPRINGS REHAB	Hot Springs	16+	16+	16+	16+	16+	P	P	S	S		P	P	P	P	P	143
JONESBORO HUMAN DEV	Jonesboro	12+		12+			S			S		S	P	S	S	S	144
AR LIGHTHOUSE	Little Rock	18+	18+	18+	18+		P										141
AR SCH FOR THE BLIND	Little Rock	6-21	6-21	6-21	6-21	6-21	P	S				S	S	S		S	141

Facility	Location	Age Range							Page
AR SCH FOR THE DEAF	Little Rock	4-21	S	S	S	S	S	S	142
CTRS FOR YOUTH & FAM	Little Rock	6-18 / 2½-18 / All Ages	S	P	S	P	S	S	142
LIONS WORLD SERVCS	Little Rock	16+	P						144
U OF AR-LR SPCH LANG	Little Rock	All Ages	S	S	S	S	S	P	145
YOUTH HOME	Little Rock	12-18	S	S	P	S	S	S	146
JENKINS CENTER-AR	Pine Bluff	Birth-21 / All Ages			P	P	P	S	144

CALIFORNIA

Facility	Location	Age Range							Page
MHS-ALMEDA SUPPORT	Alameda	3-18	S	S	P	S	S	S	190
REACH FOR LEARN	Albany	All Ages			P	P			205
HENRIETTA WEILL	Bakersfield	Birth-18	P			P			177
STOCKDALE LEARNING	Bakersfield	5+			P	S	S	S	218
ETTIE LEE	Baldwin Park	8-18	P		P				170
MID VALLEY LEARN CTR	Baldwin Park	5-22	S	P	P	P	P	P	190
KEYSTONE EDUCATION	Barstow	5-22	S	S	P	S	P	S	184
CHARLES ARMSTRONG	Belmont	6-14			P	P			159
ALTA BATES-SMALL VOI	Berkeley	1½-6	S	S	S	P	P	P	151
CTR FOR INDEPENDENT	Berkeley	14-22	P	P	P	P	P	P	158
SPECTRUM CTR	Berkeley	3-22	S		P	P	P	S	215
VIA CTR	Berkeley	6-21	S		P	S	P	P	224
SLD CTR-BUENA PARK	Buena Park	Birth-21 / 9-18	S		S	P	S	P	216
DAVIS DYSLEXIA	Burlingame	7+			P	S	S	S	165
CHILDREN THERAPY CTR	Camarillo	Birth-12	S		S	S	P	P	162
LEARNING CLINICS	Camarillo	4+	S		P	S	S		186
EMQ CHILD & FAMILY	Campbell	5-18 / All Ages	P		P	P	S	S	169
CTR FOR COMM DISORD	Canoga Park	13+	S			S	P	P	158
COLLEGE HOSP	Cerritos	2-17	P			S	P	P	163

Program	Town	Females Res	Females Day	Males Res	Males Day	Clinic	Blind	Deaf	Diabetes	Emot Disturb	HIV/AIDS	LD	MR	Ortho/Neuro	PDD	Speech	Page
CA BRISLAIN LEARNING	Chico					4+										S	156
SPECTRUM CTR VALLEY	Concord		4-22		4-22		P	P	P	P	P	P	P	S	P	P	216
FAIRVIEW DEVELOPMENT	Costa Mesa	All Ages		All Ages									P				171
ECHO CTR	Culver City		3-12		3-12			P									168
EXCEPTIONAL CHILDREN	Culver City	18+	Birth-3	18+	Birth-3					S				P	S		171
KAYNE ERAS CTR	Culver City		3-22		3-22	All Ages				P		P	S	S	P	P	183
STOWELL LEARNING CTR	Diamond Bar					5+						P					219
RANCHO-REHAB CTR	Downey					Birth-21		P		P			P	P	P	P	203
RANCHO-SCH	Downey		3-22		3-22		P	P		P		P	P	P	P	P	204
RINCON LEARNING CTR	El Cajon					5+			S	S		P	S	S	S		207
SONOMA DEV CTR	Eldridge	All Ages		All Ages			S	S					P	S		S	215
LEARNING CTR-ENCINO	Encino					2+				P		P	P	P	P		185
N COUNTY LEARNING	Escondido					4+						P	P	P	P	S	194
CALIFORNIA ELWYN	Fountain Valley					All Ages	P			S		P	P			S	156
OPTOMETRIC CTR-FULL	Fullerton	18+	18+	18+	18+	All Ages						P					196
ST JUDE HOSP REHAB	Fullerton					All Ages								P	P	P	210
GLENDALE ADVENTIST	Glendale					All Ages	S	P		S		P	S	P	P	P	174
ONE-TO-ONE READING	Granada Hills					5+						P	P	S	S	S	196
UCP OF C CA-HANFORD	Hanford		Birth-3		Birth-3					P		S	P	P	P	P	222
HAWTHORNE ACAD	Hawthorne		6-22		6-22					P		P	P	S		S	175
BRIDGE SCH	Hillsborough		5-12		5-12		S						S	P		S	155
RADING CTR OF BRUNO	Huntington Beach					4½+						P					205
UCP OF ORANGE COUNTY	Irvine		Birth-18		Birth-18		S	S					P	P		S	223
HILLSIDE SCH & LEARN	La Canada		12-18		12-18	4-30				S		P		S			178

Program	Location	Age	Age									Page
HELP FOR BRAIN/CLETA	La Habra	3-22	3-22	S	S		S		P	P	P	S	176
OPTOMETRIC VISION	La Jolla		All Ages	P		S		P	S	S	S	S	196
SPRINGALL ACAD	La Jolla	5-18	5-18			S		P	S	P	S	S	217
LEROY HAYNES CTR	La Verne	7-18 7-17	7-18		S	P		P	S	P	S	S	186
MELMED LEARNING CLIN	Lafayette		All Ages					P			P	P	189
LA MONTE ACADEMIE	Laguna Hills	5-18	5-18	S	P	P		P	S	P	S	S	184
GUIDING HANDS	Lakeside	17+	5+	S		S			S	S	S	S	178
LOMA LINDA U MED CTR	Loma Linda	5+	5+					P	S	P	P	P	188
TOTALLY KIDS	Loma Linda	Birth-21	Birth-21	S	S				P	P		S	221
CSLB SPCH & HEARING	Long Beach		All Ages								P	P	157
GUIDANCE CTR	Long Beach		1-18			P	S	P	S		S		174
IRLEN INST	Long Beach		7+					P			S	S	180
ACADEMIC GUIDANCE	Los Angeles	3+	3+			P		P	P		P	P	148
BLIND CHILDRENS CTR	Los Angeles	Birth-5	Birth-5	P									154
BOOTH MEMORIAL HS	Los Angeles	14-22						P	P				155
BRAILLE INST LA	Los Angeles	Birth-19	Birth-19	P									155
FOUNDATION JR BLIND	Los Angeles	5+	Birth-21	P				S	S	S		S	172
HOUSE EAR CLINIC	Los Angeles		All Ages	P									179
INDEPENDENCE CTR-LA	Los Angeles	18-30	18-30		S	S		P	S	P	P	S	179
JOHN TRACY CLINIC	Los Angeles	Birth-5	Birth-5		P							P	182
JULIA ANN SINGER SCH	Los Angeles	3-10	3-10					P		P	P	P	182
JULIA HOBBS SPEECH	Los Angeles		All Ages									P	183
LA SCOTTISH RITE	Los Angeles		3-18					S				P	188
MARLTON CHARTER SCH	Los Angeles	3-22	3-22	P	P					P	P	P	189
PARK CENTURY	Los Angeles	6-14	6-14					P				P	198
REISS-DAVIS	Los Angeles	3-21	3-21			P		P		S	P	S	206

CA

Program	Town	Females Res	Females Day	Males Res	Males Day	Clinic	Blind	Deaf	Diabetes	Emot Disturb	HIV/AIDS	LD	MR	Ortho/Neuro	PDD	Speech	Page
SHRINERS-LOS ANGELES	Los Angeles		Birth-18		Birth-18	Birth-18								P			214
UCLA INTERVENTION	Los Angeles		Birth-3		Birth-3		S	S				S	P	P	S	P	222
VISTA DEL MAR	Los Angeles	10-17	7-18	10-17	7-18	Birth-21				P		P	P		P	P	226
WESTVIEW SCH-CA	Los Angeles		11-18		11-18							P					227
WHITE PEDIAT REHAB	Los Angeles					Birth-18				P						P	227
MID-PENINSULA	Menlo Park	14-18	14-18		14-18					P		P					191
PENINSULA ASSOCIATES	Menlo Park					All Ages		S		S		S	S	S	S	P	200
NEWPORT LANGUAGE	Mission Viejo					All Ages		S		S		P	S	P	P	P	194
SIERRA VISTA	Modesto	6-17	5-14	6-17	5-14	Birth-14				P		S					214
MERCI	Monterey Park	18+	6+	18+	6+								P	P	P		190
ORION ACAD	Moraga	13-19	13-19		13-19					S		S					197
ALDEA CHILDREN & FAM	Napa	12-18	12-18	12-18	12-18	All Ages	P	P		P		P	S	P	P	P	150
NAPA VALLEY PSI	Napa	18+	18+		18+								P				192
NEWPORT BEACH DEV	Newport Beach					All Ages	P		S	P		P	P	P	S		193
COUNTRYSIDE PREP	Northridge	5-18	5-18	5-18	5-18					P		P		P	P		164
NATIONAL CTR ON DEAF	Northridge	18+		18+		All Ages		P		P		P	P	P	P		192
LANE'S LEARNING CTR	Novato					All Ages				P		P	P	P	P		185
WIDE HORIZONS RANCH	Oak Run	9-18		9-18						P		P	P	S	S		228
CHILDREN'S HOSP-OAKL	Oakland					1-18										P	162
CLAUSEN HOUSE	Oakland	18+	18+	18+	18+								P				163
EAST BAY AGENCY	Oakland	5-12	5-12	5-12	5-12					P		S		P			167
EASTER SEAL BAY AREA	Oakland		All Ages		All Ages								P	P			167
FRED FINCH YOUTH CTR	Oakland	12-18	12-18	12-18	12-18					P		P		S			172
LINCOLN CHILD CTR	Oakland	6-13	6-13	6-13	6-13					P		P					187

Facility	City	Ages	Emphasis (P/S)	Page
RASKOB	Oakland	All Ages	S, P	204
SALEM CHRISTIAN HOME	Ontario	18-62	P	211
PROVIDENCE SPEECH	Orange	2-6	S, S, S, S	203
ODYSSEY LEARNING CTR	Orangevale	3-22	S, P, S, S	195
GATEWAY CTR-MONTEREY	Pacific Grove	18+	S, P, S	174
RETARDED OF DESERT	Palm Desert	18+	S, S, P, S, S	172
ACHIEVE KIDS-PALO AL	Palo Alto	10-18 / 3-22 / All Ages	P, P, S, P, S	148
CHILDRENS HEALTH	Palo Alto	7-17 / Birth-17	P, P, P, S, S, S	161
LUCILLE PACKARD	Palo Alto	Birth-21	P, S, S	188
PENINSULA CTR	Palo Alto	Birth-22	P, S, S, S, S	200
FROSTIG CTR	Pasadena	6-18 / 6+	S, P, S, S	173
HEAR CTR	Pasadena	All Ages	P, P	175
HUNTINGTON PEDIATRIC	Pasadena	Birth-16		179
SYCAMORES	Pasadena	6-14 / 2-21	P, S, S, P	220
VILLA ESPERANZA	Pasadena	1½-15	S, S, P, P	225
SPEECH LANG-MARIN	Petaluma	All Ages	S, P, P, P, P	217
ANN MARTIN	Piedmont	6-22	P, P, P	151
PORTERVILLE DEV CTR	Porterville	All Ages	S, S, S, S, S	201
KEYSTONE ACAD-CA	Ramona	13-18	P, P, P	183
BENCHMARK YOUNG ADLT	Redlands	18-28	P, S, S, S	153
U OF REDLANDS	Redlands	All Ages	P, P, P	223
JEAN WEINGARTEN-ORAL	Redwood City	Birth-8 / All Ages	P, P, S, S	181
BIG SPRINGS	Riverside	5-12 / All Ages	P, P	153
CHILD CTR-RIVERSIDE	Riverside	Birth-6	S, S, P, P, P	160
CEDU	Running Springs	12-17	P, P	157
ALDAR ACAD	Sacramento	11-22	P, P, P	150

Program	Town	Females Res	Females Day	Males Res	Males Day	Clinic	Blind	Deaf	Diabetes	Emot Disturb	HIV/AIDS	LD	MR	Ortho/Neuro	PDD	Speech	Page
CA RIVER OAK CTR	Sacramento	5-14	5-14	5-14	5-14	2-21			S	P		P	S	S	P	P	207
SACRAMENTO CHILDREN	Sacramento	6-18	5-18	6-18	5-18					P		P	S	P	P	P	209
SHRINERS-CA	Sacramento	Birth-18		Birth-18										P	P		213
SUNNY HILLS	San Anselmo	4-18	4-18	4-18	4-18					P		P				P	219
ASELTINE SCH	San Diego		6-19		6-19					P		P				P	152
CHILDRENS HOSP HLTH	San Diego	Birth-25	Birth-19	Birth-25	Birth-19	Birth-19				P		P		P	P	P	161
CHILDREN'S H-SAN DIE	San Diego		All Ages		All Ages	All Ages		P				P		P	P	P	161
CHILDRENS WORKSHOP	San Diego		3-10		3-10					P		P			P	P	162
EXCELSIOR ACAD	San Diego		7-19		7-19		S	S	S	S		P		P	P	P	170
SAM & ROSE STEIN ED	San Diego		3-22		3-22		S	S	S	P		P	S	S	S	S	211
SD CTR FOR CHILDREN	San Diego	6-18	5-13	6-18	5-13			S		P		P			P		211
SAN DIEGO REGION CTR	San Diego					All Ages							P	P	P	P	212
CA PACIFIC MED CTR	San Francisco					Birth-18				P		P	S	S	S	S	156
EDGEWOOD CTR-CA	San Francisco	6-14	3½-14	6-14	3½-14	6-14				P		S		S	S	S	168
HEARING SOCIETY-SF	San Francisco		Birth-17		Birth-17	Birth-17		P		S		S		S	S	S	176
MISSION LEARNING CTR	San Francisco					7-11						P		P			191
OAKES CHILDRENS CTR	San Francisco		3-16		3-16					P			S				195
ROSE RESNIK	San Francisco		All Ages		All Ages		P										208
SAN FRANCISCO HEAR	San Francisco	1½-8	1½-8	1½-8	1½-8	1½-18		P				P		P	P	P	212
STERNE SCH	San Francisco	11-18	11-18	11-18	11-18							P					218
AGNEWS DEV CTR	San Jose	All Ages	All Ages	All Ages	All Ages		S	S		S		S	P	S	P	S	149
BEACON SCH-CA	San Jose	10-22	10-22	10-22	10-22					P		P	S	S	P	S	152
FAMILY & CHILDREN-SJ	San Jose		All Ages		All Ages	All Ages				P	P	P		P	P	P	171
PINE HILL SCH	San Jose	6-21	6-21	6-21	6-21					P		P			P	P	201

Facility	City	Age	Age									Page
SAN JOSE ST U-COMM	San Jose		All Ages	P				P	P	P	P	212
VISION SANTA CLARA	San Jose		All Ages	S	S		S	P	P	S	S	226
ALAMEDA MED CTR	San Leandro		5+	P				P			P	149
EDEN CHILDREN'S CLIN	San Leandro	2½-17	2½-17	S			P		P		P	168
LINDAMOOD BELL	San Luis Obispo		5+	P							P	187
SLO COUNTY EDUCATION	San Luis Obispo	3-22	3-22	P				P	P		P	213
COUNTRY SCH-CA	San Marcos	9-18	3-22				P	S	P	P	P	164
ED RESOURCE-CA	San Marino		All Ages	P			P	P			P	169
DEV THERAPY PRGM-CA	San Mateo		Birth-10	S		S	S	P	P	P	S	165
RUSSELL BEDE SCH	San Mateo	7-12	7-12	S		S	S	S	S	S	S	208
WINGS LEARNING CTR	San Mateo	5-12	1-12	P				P	P		P	228
LEARNING CTR-SAN RAF	San Rafael		All Ages			S	S	S	P		S	186
TIMOTHY MURPHY SCH	San Rafael	7-17	7-17	P			P					221
BLIND CHILDREN'S CTR	Santa Ana	6mos-6	6mos-6	P	S		S					154
CHILD GUID CTR-CA	Santa Ana	6-14	Birth-17	P			S		S		S	160
PRENTICE SCH	Santa Ana	6-14	6-14	P		S	S	S	S	P	S	202
REGIONAL CTR-ORANGE	Santa Ana		All Ages				P	P	P		P	206
THERAPEUTIC ED CTR	Santa Ana	12-18	12-18	P			P	P	S	S	S	220
DEVEREUX CA	Santa Barbara	8+	8+	P			P	S	P	P	S	165
DUBIN LEARNING CTR	Santa Barbara		All Ages	P			S	S			S	166
MORGAN CTR	Santa Clara	3-22	3-22				S		P		P	191
VIA REHAB SERVS	Santa Clara		All Ages	P		P	S	S	S	S	S	225
SANTA CRUZ LEARNING	Santa Cruz		5+	P			S	S			S	213
ST JOHN'S CHILD-FAM	Santa Monica	Birth-50	Birth-50	S	S		P	P	P	P	P	210
HELP GROUP	Sherman Oaks	2¾-22	2¾-22	P			P	P	P	P	P	177
CHILD DEV CTR-SIMI	Simi Valley	Birth-12	Birth-17	P	S		P	P	P	P	P	159

Program	Town	Females Res	Females Day	Males Res	Males Day	Clinic	Blind	Deaf	Diabetes	Emot Disturb	HIV/AIDS	LD	MR	Ortho/Neuro	PDD	Speech	Page
CA ALMANSOR CTR	South Pasadena		All Ages		All Ages					P		P	S	S	S	S	150
UPAC SCOTTISH RITE	Stockton					3-18										P	224
COMMUNITY SPCH/HEAR	Tarzana					1-Adult		P		P		P	S	P	P	P	163
PARKER HEARING INST	Torrance					All Ages	S	P		S		S		S	S	S	199
SWITZER SCH	Torrance		5-19		5-19	3+				P		P					219
JAMESON SCH	Ventura		6-22		6-22								P	P	P	P	181
VENTURA COLLEGE EDUC	Ventura		16+		16+		P	P		P		P	P	P			224
NEW HAVEN YFS	Vista			8-18						P		P		S		S	193
YGNACIO LEARNING CTR	Walnut Creek					All Ages				P		P					229
YOUTH HOMES-WALNUT	Walnut Creek	6-17		6-17						P							229
PARKHILL	West Hills		5½-18		5½-18					P		P	S	S		S	199
POSEIDON SCH	West Los Angeles		12-18		12-18					S		P		S			202
INTERCOMMUNITY CHILD	Whittier		9-13		9-13	Birth-18				P		P		S			180
ORALINGUA SCH-HEARIN	Whittier		Birth-10		Birth-10			P									197
PACIFIC LODGE	Woodland Hills			13-17						P		S		S			198
COLORADO																	
SAN LUIS VALLEY MHC	Alamosa					All Ages				P		P	S		S		240
EXCELSIOR YOUTH CTRS	Aurora	11-18								P		P	S	S			235
AIM HOUSE	Boulder			17½-25					S	P		P	S	P		S	230
BRECKENRIDGE OEC	Breckenridge	8+		8+			S	S		P		P	P	P	P	S	231
CO SCH-DEAF & BLIND	Colorado Springs	5-21	3-21	5-21	3-21		P	P		S		S	P	S		S	233
PIKES PEAK MHC	Colorado Springs					1-18	S	S		P		P	P		S		239
ANCHOR CTR FOR BLIND	Denver		Birth-5		Birth-5		P										230
CTR HEAR/SPCH/LAN-CO	Denver					All Ages		P				S				P	231

Facility	City	Age	Age	Age										Page
CEREBRAL PALSY OF CO	Denver	Birth-5	Birth-5	Birth-5	S	S	S			P	P	P	P	231
CHILDREN'S H-DENVER	Denver	Birth-21					P		P	P	P	P		232
NEURO REHAB CTR-CO	Denver	Birth-21							P	P				232
DAYBREAK GIRLS' HOME	Denver	12-19					P	S						234
DENVER ACAD	Denver	6-18	6-18					P						234
GOODWILL INDUSTRIES	Denver	18+	18+		S	P	S	S	S	P	P	S		236
HOPE CTR-CO	Denver	2½+	2½+				P			P				237
LARADON	Denver	9+	All Ages	All Ages	S	S	S	S	S	P	S	S		238
MOUNT ST VINCENT	Denver	6-13	3-13	3-13	S		P	P	S	S				238
NBA TENNYSON CTR	Denver	5-12	5-12	5-12			P	S						239
FOREST HEIGHTS LODGE	Evergreen	4-14	All Ages				P	S		S				236
TRAILHEAD WILDERNESS	Georgetown	12-18	12-18				P		S					240
GRAND JCT REGION CTR	Grand Junction	All Ages	All Ages				P		P					237
U N CO SPEECH LANG	Greeley		All Ages	All Ages		P	P					P		241
HAVERN CTR	Littleton	5-13	5-13				P							237
NAMAQUA CTR	Loveland	3-13	3-13	3-13			P	S	S					239
EL PUEBLO	Pueblo	10-18	10-18				P		S					235
COMMUNITY REACH CTR	Thornton		All Ages	All Ages			P							233
DEVEREUX CLEO WALLAC	Westminster	5-21	5-21				P			P				234
CONNECTICUT														
AHLBIN REHAB	Bridgeport		All Ages				S		P					242
CHILD GUID-BRDGEPORT	Bridgeport		Birth-18				P		S					245
TUT & COUNSEL OF CT	Bridgeport		4+				P	S	P			S		262
COMM MENTAL HEALTH	Bristol		Birth-18				P		P					247
LEARNING CLINIC	Brooklyn	6-21	6-21	6-21			P			P				258
CHILDREN HM CROMWELL	Cromwell	9-18	8-18	8-18			P	S	P			P		246

Program	Town	Females Res	Females Day	Males Res	Males Day	Clinic	Blind	Deaf	Diabetes	Emot Disturb	HIV/AIDS	LD	MR	Ortho/Neuro	PDD	Speech	Page
CT UNITED SERVICES CT	Dayville					Birth-18	S	S		P			S	S			263
LK GROVE DURHAM	Durham	8-21		8-21						P		S	S	S	S	S	258
ARC GREENWICH	Greenwich		Birth-3		Birth-3		S	S		S			P	P	P	P	242
EAGLE HILL-GREENWICH	Greenwich	10-16	6-16	10-16	6-16	All Ages						P					251
GREENWICH HOSPITAL	Greenwich					All Ages		P				P	S	S	S	P	255
SARAH	Guilford		16+		16+		S	S		S		S	P	S	S	S	261
CEDARHURST SCH	Hamden		13-21		13-21					P		S					244
CHILDREN'S CTR-CT	Hamden	7-18	12-18	7-18	12-18					P		P	S	S		S	246
CT MED SPEECH LANG	Hartford					Birth-21		P				P		P		P	248
CT INT BLIND-OAKHILL	Hartford	6-21	6-21	6-21	6-21		P	S		P		P	S	S	P	S	248
GRAY LODGE	Hartford	12-18								P		P					255
GRACE S WEBB SCH	Hartford		5-18		5-18		S	S		P	S	S	S	S	P	S	257
ST FRANCIS CARE	Hartford	4-21	4-21	4-21	4-21					P		S					260
CT JUNIOR REPUBLIC	Litchfield			12-16	12-16					P		P					249
FORMAN	Litchfield	13-20	13-20	13-20	13-20							P					253
GROVE SCH	Madison	12-18	12-18	12-18	12-18					P		S			P		256
COMMUNITY CHILD	Manchester		3-13		3-13	Birth-18				P		S	P		P		247
GESELL INSTITUTE	New Haven					2½-9				S		P					254
ST FRANCIS HOME	New Haven		6-15	8-18	6-15					P		P		S			260
S CT ST U CTR	New Haven					All Ages	S	S		S	S	S	P	P	P	P	262
CT COL CHILDREN'S	New London		Birth-6		Birth-6		P	P		P		S	P	P	P	P	248
ELIZABETH IVES SCH	North Haven		5-21		5-21					P		P	P	S	S	S	252
MID-FAIRFIELD CHILD	Norwalk					Birth-18				P		P	S	P	P	P	259
FOUNDATION SCH	Orange		3-21		3-21							P					254

Organization	City	Age Ranges	Emphasis	Page
WATERFORD COUNTRY	Quaker Hill	10-18, 10-18, 10-18, 10-18	P, S, S, S	264
EAGLE HILL-SOUTHPORT	Southport	6-16, 6-16	S, P, S	251
CHILD GUIDANCE-S CT	Stamford	Birth-18	P, P, S, S, S	245
VILLA MARIA ED CTR	Stamford	5-14, 5-14, 5-14	P, P	263
C HUNGERFORD PSYCH	Torrington	2-17	P, S	245
ST VINCENT-FEROLETO	Trumbull	3-21, Birth-21, 3-21, Birth-21	S, S, S, S, P, P	252
HIGH RD LEARN CTR	Wallingford	5-21, 5-21, 5-21	S, S, P, P, P	256
DEVEREUX GLENHOLME	Washington	5-18, 5-18, 5-18, 5-18	P, S, S, P, S	250
EASTER SEAL WATERBUR	Waterbury	Birth-5, Birth-5	P, P, P	252
COUNTY HEARING	Waterford	All Ages	P	250
AM SCH FOR THE DEAF	West Hartford	8-21, 3-21, 8-21, 3-21	P, P, P	242
BEN BRONZ ACAD	West Hartford	7+, 7-21, 7-21	S, S, S	243
GENGRAS CTR	West Hartford	3-21, 3-21, 3-21	S, S, P, P, P	254
INTENSIVE EDUCATION	West Hartford	6-21, 6-21	P	258
SETON ACAD	Westport	11-21, 11-21, 11-21	P, S, S, S	261
CHAPEL HAVEN	Westville	18+, 18+, 18+	S, P, P, P	244
DELAWARE				
ADVOSERV	Bear	8+, 8+, 8+, 8+	P, S, P, S, P	265
CEDARS ACAD	Bridgeville	10-18, 10-18, 10-18	S, P, S	265
CENTREVILLE	Centreville	4-14, 4-14	P, P	266
JOHN S CHARLTON SCH	Dover	3-21, 3-21	P	268
JOHN G. LEACH SCH	New Castle	3-21, 3-21, 3-21	P, P, P	267
MARGARET STERCK SCH	Newark	6-21, Birth-21, Birth-21	P	268
DE GUIDANCE SERVS	Wilmington	3-18	P, S, S	266
EDUCATIONAL SERVICE	Wilmington	3-18	S, P, S	267
MARY CAMPBELL CTR	Wilmington	16+, 3+, 16+, 3+	P, P	268

Program	Town	Females Res	Females Day	Males Res	Males Day	Clinic	Blind	Deaf	Diabetes	Emot Disturb	HIV/AIDS	LD	MR	Ortho/Neuro	PDD	Speech	Page
DE OPPORTUNITY CTR	Wilmington		18+		18+								P				269
PILOT	Wilmington	5-14	5-14	5-14	5-14							P					269
						DISTRICT OF COLUMBIA											
ARMY AUD & SPEECH	Washington					All Ages										P	270
COLUMBIA LIGHTHOUSE	Washington					All Ages	P										270
DEVEREUX-DC	Washington	6-12	6-12	6-12	6-12				P	P		P					270
EPISCOPAL CTR FOR CH	Washington	5½-12	5½-12	5½-12	5½-12					P		P					271
HOSP SICK CHILDREN	Washington		Birth-21		Birth-21		P	P					P	P	P	P	271
HOWARD U CHILD DEV	Washington					Birth-18	P	P					P	P		P	272
KENDALL DEMO SCH	Washington	Birth-15	Birth-15	Birth-15	Birth-15			P					P				272
KINGSBURY CTR	Washington	5-16	5-16	5-16	5-16	All Ages				S		P		S			272
LAB SCH	Washington	5-19	5-19	5-19	5-19							P					273
JOSEPH P. KENNEDY-DC	Washington	Birth-21	Birth-21	Birth-21	Birth-21	All Ages	P	S		S		S	P	P		P	274
MODEL SEC SCH-DEAF	Washington	14-21	14-21	14-21	14-21		P	P									274
NATL CHILDREN'S CTR	Washington	8+	1+	8+	1+			S		S		S	P	S	S	S	275
ST JOHNS COMM SVCS	Washington	18+	All Ages	18+	All Ages								P	P	P		275
SCOTTISH RITE	Washington					Birth-18										P	275
U OF DC SPEECH-HEAR	Washington					All Ages		P					P			P	276
WALTER REED ARMY	Washington				Birth-18	Birth-18	S	S		P		P	S	S		S	276
						FLORIDA											
ARC RIDGE AREA	Avon Park	18+	16+	18+	16+								P				277
ECKERD YOUTH-FL	Brooksville	10-17		10-17	10-17					P		S					287
HARBOR SCH	Casselberry	6-15	6-15	6-15	6-15							P					289
BARRETT REHAB CTR	Clearwater					All Ages		P				P				P	296

Program	Location	Ages	Ages								Page
VANGUARD-COCONUT	Coconut Grove	16+	6-14					P			306
CONKLIN CTRS	Daytona Beach	Birth-6	Birth-6		P	S	S	S	S	S	283
PALADIN ACAD	Delray Beach	5-18	5-18				P		S		298
HENDERSON MHC	Fort Lauderdale	7-18	7-18	Birth-21	P		P				290
NOVA U-BAUDHUIN	Fort Lauderdale	2-5	2-5		S	S		P			297
U OF FL SPEECH-HEAR	Gainesville			All Ages	P		P	P	S	P	304
DUVALL HOME	Glenwood	All Ages	All Ages		S	S		P	S	S	285
LEARNING TO ACHIEVE	Hudson	6-12	6-12				P				293
DANIEL	Jacksonville	5-17	5-17			P	S				283
DEPAUL SCH OF NE FL	Jacksonville	6-14	6-14				P				284
HOPE HAVEN	Jacksonville			Birth-21			S	P	S	S	291
MORNING STAR-JAVILLE	Jacksonville	5-16	5-16		S		P	S	P	S	295
SPCH/HEARING CTR-JAX	Jacksonville			All Ages		P			P		301
VANGUARD	Lake Wales	11-18	12-18	11-18 12-18			P		S		305
PALM BEACH HABILITAT	Lake Worth	18+	16+	18+ 16+	P	P	S	P	P	S	298
C FL SPEECH/HEARING	Lakeland			All Ages		P	S	S	S	P	282
DORIS A SANDERS CTR	Lakeland	5-22	5-22		P	P	P	P	P	P	285
ROYAL PALM SCH	Lantana	3-22	3-22		P	P	S	P	P	P	300
BEACON COLLEGE	Leesburg	18+	18+				P				279
LIGHTHOUSE PT ACAD	Lighthouse Point	6-17	6-17		P	P	P	P			293
PACE-BRANTLEY HALL	Longwood	5-18	5-18				P				297
LA AMISTAD RES CTR	Maitland	6-18	6-18		P	P	P		P		292
BREVARD LEARN CLIN	Melbourne			5+	S		P				281
SEA PINES REHAB	Melbourne	Birth-18	Birth-18			P	P	P	P	P	289
ATLANTIS	Miami	5-18	5-18		S		P		S		278
BERTHA ABESS	Miami	3-21	3-21		P		P				279

Program	Town	Females Res	Females Day	Males Res	Males Day	Clinic	Blind	Deaf	Diabetes	Emot. Disturb.	HIV/AIDS	LD	MR	Ortho/Neuro	PDD	Speech	Page
FL EASTER SEALS MIAMI	Miami		Birth-22		Birth-22	All Ages		P				P	P	P	P	S	286
HEARING & SPEECH FL	Miami					All Ages		P								P	289
HOPE CTR-FL	Miami	18+	18+	18+	18+								P	S			290
KILLIAN OAKS	Miami		5-13		5-13							P				S	291
MAILMAN CTR	Miami		Birth-3		Birth-3	Birth-21		P				P	P	P	P	P	294
SUNRISE COMMUNITY	Miami	All Ages	21+	All Ages	21+		S	S		S		S	P	P	P	S	301
UCP OF SOUTH FLORIDA	Miami	All Ages	All Ages	All Ages	All Ages			S					P	P	P	P	303
DAVID LAWRENCE CTR	Naples	12-17	5-18	12-17	5-18	All Ages				P		P	P	P	P	S	284
STEP BY STEP EARLY	Naples		Birth-5		Birth-5		S	S		P		S	P	P	P	S	301
COMMUNITY LANDMARK	Opa Locka	18+	18+	18+									P				282
MARIAN CTR SERVICES	Opa Locka	6+	2+	6+	2+								P	S			295
GATEWAY SCH-FL	Orlando		11-21		11-21			P		P		S	S				288
PRIMROSE CENTER	Orlando		18+		18+								P				299
BAPTIST HOSPITAL	Pensacola					All Ages						S		S	S	P	278
NORTHVIEW COMMUNITY	Pensacola	All Ages		All Ages										P			297
UCP OF NW FL	Pensacola	18+	18+	18+	18+		P					P	P	P	P	P	303
CENTER ACAD	Pinellas Park		8-19		8-19	4-21						P					281
PERSONAL ENRICHMENT	Pinellas Park	6-17	13-17	6-17	13-17		S			P		P	S	S	S	S	299
TAMPA BAY ACAD	Riverview	4-18	4-18	4-18	4-18			P		P		P					302
FL SCH-DEAF & BLIND	St Augustine	5-21	3-21	5-21	3-21		P	P		S		S	S	S		S	287
ALL CHILDRENS SPEECH	St Petersburg					All Ages										P	277
FSU SPEECH & HEARING	Tallahassee					All Ages		P				P				P	288
WOODLAND HALL ACAD	Tallahassee		6-20		6-20							P					306
BARBARA KING CENTRE	Tampa					All Ages				S		P					279

Program	City	Age Range	Age Range							Page
BISHOP ETON SCH	Tampa	5-18	5-18		S		P		S	280
BOLESTA CTR	Tampa	Birth-14	Birth-14	P	P			S	P	280
LAVOY EXCEPTIONAL	Tampa	3-22	3-22	S	S			P	S	293
MACDONALD TRAINING	Tampa	18-59	18-56				P	P		294
MORNING STAR-TAMPA	Tampa	6-15	6-15		S		P	S	S	296
TAMPA DAY SCH	Tampa	5-14	5-14				P	P	S	302
U OF S FL–COMM SCI	Tampa	All Ages	All Ages	P			S	S	P	304
U OF S FL–GENETICS	Tampa	All Ages	All Ages	P	P	S	P	P	P	305
DEVEREUX FL	Viera	5-17	5-19		P	P	P	P	P	285
ALPERT JEWISH FAMILY	West Palm Beach	6-21	6-21		P	P	P	S	S	277
PROGRESSIVE SCH	West Palm Beach	4-14	4-14			S	P	S	S	300
KURTZ CTR	Winter Park	5+	5+	P	P	P	P	S	S	292
THRESHOLD	Winter Park	All Ages 3-5	All Ages 3-5		P	P	P	P	P	303
GEORGIA										
MILL SPRINGS ACAD	Alpharetta	6-18	6-18		P	P	P		P	319
U OF GA SPEECH-HEAR	Athens	All Ages	All Ages	P	P	S	P	P	P	323
ATLANTA SPEECH-ORAL	Atlanta	Birth-10	Birth-10	P	S		S		S	309
ATLANTA SPEECH SCH	Atlanta	5-12	5-12	P	P		P	S	S	310
BRANDON HALL	Atlanta	10-19	10-19	P	P				P	311
CTR FOR VISUALLY IMP	Atlanta	Birth-18 5+	Birth-18 5+	P	S	S	S	S	S	312
FRAZER CTR	Atlanta	Birth-5	Birth-5	S	S		P	P	S	315
HILLSIDE HOSPITAL	Atlanta	7-18	7-18	S	S	P	S	S	S	317
HOWARD SCH	Atlanta	3-18	3-18	P	P		P			318
SCHENCK	Atlanta	6-14	6-14	P	P					321
FULTON MENTAL HEALTH	Atlanta	All Ages	All Ages		P			P		322
AUGUSTA SCH	Augusta	6-14	6-14	P					P	310

Program	Town	Females Res	Females Day	Males Res	Males Day	Clinic	Blind	Deaf	Diabetes	Emot Disturb	HIV/AIDS	LD	MR	Ortho/Neuro	PDD	Speech	Page
GA ECKERD YOUTH-GA	Blakely			10-17								S					314
SPEECH COASTAL GA	Brunswick					All Ages		P		P						P	323
GA SCH FOR THE DEAF	Cave Spring	4-21	3-21	4-21	3-21			P		S			S	S		S	316
ATLANTA AREA SCH-DEA	Clarkston		3-21		3-21			P				S	S	S	S		309
ACHIEVEMENT ACAD	Columbus		6-15		6-15							P					308
LULLWATER SCH	Decatur		5-15		5-15					S		P	S	S		S	319
BEDFORD SCH	Fairburn		7-14		7-14				S	S		P	S	S			311
NORTHEAST GA SPEECH	Gainesville		3-5		3-5	All Ages	S	S				S	S	S	S	P	320
GRACEWOOD STATE SCH	Gracewood	All Ages		All Ages									P				317
DEVEREUX GA	Kennesaw	10-21		10-21					S	P		P	S	S		S	313
SHEPHERD'S HILL FARM	Martin	13-17		13-17					S	P	S	P		S	P		322
READING SUCCESS	Martinez					4+				P		P		P	P	P	320
LEARNING CTR-GA	Milledgeville		3-22		3-22					P				P	P		318
NW GA REGIONAL HOSP	Rome	5+		5+									P				320
COTTAGE SCH	Roswell		11-18		11-18							P					313
CHATHAM ACAD	Savannah		6-18		6-18							P					312
RIDGEVIEW INSTITUTE	Smyrna	6+	6+	6+	6+					P		S					321
GABLES ACAD-GA	Stone Mountain	12-18	9-18	12-18	9-18							P		P	P		315
GOTTLIEB VISION	Stone Mountain					All Ages	P					S	S	S			316
ANNANDALE VILLAGE	Suwanee	18+	18+	18+	18+			S		S		S	P	P	S		308
VALDOSTA ST U-SPEECH	Valdosta					All Ages		P								P	323
HAWAII																	
HORIZONS ACAD-MAUI	Haiku		6-17		6-17					P		P	S	S	S		326
ASSETS	Honolulu		5-18		5-18					S		P		S	S	S	325

Program	Location	Ages	Page
EASTER SLS HI-SULTAN	Honolulu	9-20 / Birth-3	325
HI CTR-DEAF & BLIND	Honolulu	3-20 / 3-20	326
U HI SPEECH HEARING	Honolulu	All Ages	327
VARIETY SCH OF HI	Honolulu	5-13 / 5-13	327
IDAHO			
ID ELKS REHAB	Boise	1+ / 1+	331
IDAHO YOUTH RANCH	Boise	12-18 / 13-18	332
WARM SPRINGS	Boise	All Ages	334
ECHO SPRINGS STUDY	Bonners Ferry	18-24 / 18-24	330
ELK MTN ACAD	Clark Fork	14-18 / 14-18	330
ID SCH-DEAF & BLIND	Gooding	9-21 / 9-21 / 3-21 / Birth-21	332
ADULT/CHILD DEV CTR	Idaho Falls	Birth+ / Birth+	328
DEV DISABILITIES-ID	Lewiston	Birth+ / Birth+	329
COMMUNICARE-ID	Meridian	18+	329
ID STATE SCH & HOSP	Nampa	All Ages	332
ASCENT	Naples	13-17 / 13-17	328
ROCKY MTN	Naples	14-17 / 14-17	333
CLEARVIEW HORIZON	Sandpoint	13-20	329
GLACIER MTN ACAD	Sandpoint	13-17 / 13-17	331
SUWS ADOL & YOUTH	Shoshone	11-17 / 11-17	333
ADULT & CHILD DEV-ID	Twin Falls	Birth-3 / Birth-3	328
ILLINOIS			
CLEARBROOK	Arlington Heights	18+ / 18+	342
KEMMERER VILLAGE	Assumption	8-18 / Birth-21 / 8-18 / Birth-21	353
CLARE WOODS ACAD	Bartlett	3-21 / 3-21 / 3-21	341
MARKLUND	Bloomingdale	Birth-21 / Birth-21	356

Program	City	Age Range	Emphasis	Page
SWEDISH COVENANT-SLP	Chicago	All Ages	P	364
U OF CHICAGO CHILD	Chicago	Birth-18	S S S P S S	365
U IL CHILD HABILITAT	Chicago	Birth-21	P P P	366
UIC INSTITUTE	Chicago	4-18 / Birth-18	S P S P	367
WALTER S CHRISTOPHER	Chicago	7-13	S S S	367
EASTER SEALS CENT IL	Decatur	All Ages	P P P P	344
N IL SPEECH-LANG	DeKalb	All Ages	S S S S P	358
JACK MABLEY DEV CTR	Dixon	18+	S S S S	351
RAY GRAHAM ASSOC	Downers Grove	3+	P P P	359
SUMMIT SCH-IL	Dundee	6-21	P S	364
WILLIAM W FOX	Dwight	14+	S S S	368
CTR FOR SPEECH/LANG	Elmhurst	1½+	S P P	338
GOOD SHEPHERD-IL	Flossmoor	Birth-3	P	349
GLEN ELLYN	Glen Ellyn	5+	P S	347
PHILIP J. ROCK CTR	Glen Ellyn	3-21	P P	359
BEVERLY FARM	Godfrey	18+	S S S P P S	337
CHILDRENS HABIL	Harvey	Birth-22	P P	341
LEARNING CLINIC-IL	Homewood	All Ages	P P	354
IL SCH FOR THE DEAF	Jacksonville	6-21 / Birth-21	P S S	350
IL SCH VISUALLY IMP	Jacksonville	5-21	P S	351
ACHIEVEMENT CTRS-IL	La Grange	3-18	S P S	335
LIGHTED WAY	La Salle	Birth-21	S S P	355
LAMBS FARM	Libertyville	18+	P	353
W IL U SPEECH LANG	Macomb	All Ages	P P	368
TRINITY SCH-IL	Mokena	3-21	S P S	365
JOSEPH ACAD	Niles	8-21	P P S	352

Program	Town	Females Res	Females Day	Males Res	Males Day	Clinic	Blind	Deaf	Diabetes	Emot Disturb	HIV/AIDS	LD	MR	Ortho/Neuro	PDD	Speech	Page
IL																	
CTR ON DEAFNESS	Northbrook	6-21	6-21	6-21	6-21			P		S		S	S			S	339
COVE SCH	Northbrook		5-21		5-21			S	S	S		P	S	S	S	S	342
EASTER SEALS-LASALLE	Ottawa		Birth-21		Birth-21	All Ages	S	S		S		S		P	S	S	345
ELIM CHRISTIAN SCH	Palos Heights	3-21	3-21	3-21	3-21							P	P	P	P	P	347
EASTER SEALS-UCP	Peoria					All Ages	P	P		P	S	P	P	P	P	P	346
PEORIAREA BLIND CTR	Peoria					1+	P	S		S		S	P	S	S	S	358
CHADDOCK	Quincy	12-21		12-21						P		S					339
QUINCY SCH	Quincy		3-21		3-21		S	S				S	S	S	S	S	359
EASTER SEAL-ROCKFORD	Rockford		Birth-12		Birth-12		S			S		S	S	P	S	S	344
ROCVALE CHILDREN'S	Rockford	6-21		6-21			S	S	S	S		S	P	S	P	P	360
GOLDIE B FLOBERG CTR	Rockton	1+	1+	1+	1+					S		S	S	S	S	S	348
HOPE SCH	Springfield	5-21	5-21	5-21	5-21		S	S	S			P	P	P	P	S	350
MENTAL HLTH CENT IL	Springfield	3-17	3-17	3-17	3-17					P							356
U OF IL-CHICAGO-SPEC	Springfield					Birth-21	P	P					S	S		S	366
STREAMWOOD BEHAV	Streamwood	12-21		12-21									S				363
HOWE CENTER	Tinley Park	18+		18+						P			P				350
JOSEPH P. KENNEDY-IL	Tinley Park	6+	3-21	6+	3-21							S	P	P	P	S	355
CARLE CLIN ASSOC	Urbana					Birth-21	P			S		P	P	P	P	P	338
READING GROUP	Urbana					All Ages						P					360
EASTER SEALS DUPAGE	Villa Park					Birth-21	S	S		P			S	P	P	P	345
PAULSON REHAB	Willowbrook					All Ages	P	P					P	P	P	P	358
THERAPLAY INST	Wilmette					Birth-12	S	S		P			S	P	P		364
CHILD'S VOICE SCH	Wood Dale	3-9	3-9	3-9	3-9			P								S	341
ADULT & CHILD REHAB	Woodstock					All Ages						P	P	P	S	S	335

INDIANA

Program	City	Ages Served	Emphasis / Index
RISE	Angola	16+, 16+, 16+	S ... P P S / 386
CHILDREN FIRST CTR	Auburn	Birth-5, Birth-5, Birth-5	P P / 373
NEW HORIZONS REHAB	Batesville	18+, 18+, Birth+	P ... S S P P S / 383
STONE BELT ARC	Bloomington	4+, 18+, 18+, Birth-3	S S ... S P P P P / 387
S IN RESOURCE SOLS	Boonville	Birth-3, Birth-3, Birth-3	P / 387
BRIDGEPOINTE GOODWIL	Clarksville	2-11	S ... S S P / 372
BARTHOLOMEW COOP	Columbus	5-18, 5-18	P ... P / 370
DEVELOPMENT SERVS-IN	Columbus	16+, 16+	S ... S P P S / 374
RAINBOWS END	Corydon	Birth-12, Birth-12, Birth-12	P ... P / 385
ABILITIES SERVICES	Crawfordsville	Birth-3	P ... P / 369
EVANSVILLE ARC	Evansville	Birth-5, Birth-5, Birth-5	P ... P / 376
MARIAN DAY SCH	Evansville	6-14, 6-14	S P / 381
SW IN MENTAL HEALTH	Evansville	5-12, 5-12	P P / 387
CROSSROAD	Fort Wayne	6-21, 6-21, 6-21	S S S P S / 374
LEAGUE BLIND DISABLE	Fort Wayne	Birth-18, Birth-18	P / 379
TRADEWINDS REHAB CTR	Gary	20-35, All Ages, All Ages	P P P P P / 388
CHILD ADULT RESOURCE	Greencastle	Birth-5, Birth-5	P ... P / 373
ARC OPPORTUNITIES	Howe	Birth+, Birth+	P ... S / 370
KIDS KAMPUS	Huntington	6wks-12, 6wks-12, All Ages	S ... S P P S / 379
ANN WHITEHILL	Indianapolis	Birth-18, Birth-18	S S S S / 369
CHILDRENS BUREAU	Indianapolis	6-21, 6-21	P ... P / 373
EASTER SEALS CROSSRD	Indianapolis	All Ages, All Ages, All Ages	S P P P S / 375
IN SCH FOR THE BLIND	Indianapolis	3-21, 3-21, 3-21	P P / 378
IN SCH FOR THE DEAF	Indianapolis	3-21, 1-21, 1-21	P / 378
LUTHERWOOD	Indianapolis	6-21, 6-21, 6-21	P ... P / 380

Program	Town	Females Res	Females Day	Males Res	Males Day	Clinic	Blind	Deaf	Diabetes	Emot Disturb	HIV/AIDS	LD	MR	Ortho/Neuro	PDD	Speech	Page
IN																	
NOBLE OF INDIANA	Indianapolis		All Ages		All Ages	All Ages	S						P				384
RILEY HOSP AUDIOLOGY	Indianapolis					All Ages		P						P		P	385
WORTHMORE ACAD	Indianapolis		5-19		5-19				S	P		P	P	P	P	P	389
NEW HOPE SERVICES	Jeffersonville									S		S	P	S		S	382
BONA VISTA REHAB CTR	Kokomo	18+		18+		All Ages	S	S		S		S	P	P	P	S	371
FOUR RIVERS	Linton		Birth+		Birth+		P	P		P		P	P	S	S	P	376
JAYNE ENGLISH	Logansport	14+		14+						P		P	P	P	P		380
PEAK COMMUNITY	Logansport	Birth-5	**,**	Birth-5	**,**		S	S		S		P	P	S		S	384
CAREY SERVICES	Marion	18+	Birth-21	18+	Birth-21	Birth-18	S	S		S		P	P	P		P	372
NEW HORIZONS YOUTH	Marion	13-17		13-17					S	S		P	P	P			383
BALL STATE U SL & A	Muncie					All Ages		P								P	370
SILVERCREST	New Albany	Birth-22		Birth-22			S	S		S		S	S	P	S	S	386
BONA VISTA	Peru	18+		18+		Birth+	P	P		P		S	P	P		P	371
MARSHALL STARKE	Plymouth		Birth+		Birth+					P		P	P	P	P	P	382
DUNN MH CTR	Richmond	18+		18+		All Ages				P							375
WERNLE CHILDREN'S	Richmond	6-21		6-21					P	P		P					388
MANITOU CTR	Rochester		18+		18+					P							381
HEAR/SPCH OF ST. JOE	South Bend					All Ages		P					S	P	S	P	377
LOGAN	South Bend	18+	Birth-18	18+	Birth-18+								P				380
MEMORIAL HOSP REHAB	South Bend		All Ages		All Ages							P		S		P	382
GIBAULT	Terre Haute	12-18	8-18	8-18	8-18					P		P		S			377
HAMILTON CTR	Terre Haute		Birth-18		Birth-18					P							377
ISU COMM DISORDERS	Terre Haute					All Ages										P	379
OPPORTUNITY ENTERPRI	Valparaiso		Birth-3		Birth-3		S	S				P	P	S	S	S	384

Organization	City																Page
PORTER STARKE	Valparaiso						All Ages				P						385
CHRISTIAN HAVEN	Wheatfield	6-18	10-18	6-18	11-19	5-17	10-18	All Ages	S	S	P	S	S	P	P	S S	374

IOWA

Organization	City																Page
HOPE HAVEN DEV FOUND	Burlington	6+	6+					S S	S S	S	S	P	P	P			392
RIVER HILLS SCH	Cedar Falls	Birth-21	Birth-21									P					395
UNIA SPEECH HEARING	Cedar Falls			Birth-21		All Ages		P						P			396
ST LUKE'S HOSP ORC	Cedar Rapids					All Ages		S		S	P	P	P				395
COMPREHENSIVE SYSTMS	Charles City	All Ages	All Ages	All Ages	All Ages		S S	S	S	P	S S						391
EASTER SEALS IOWA	Des Moines	Birth-5	Birth-5								P	P					391
ORCHARD PLACE	Des Moines	5-18	5-18	5-18	5-18		S S	S	S	P	P	S					394
SMOUSE SCH	Des Moines	Birth-12	Birth-12							P							395
AREA RESIDENTIAL	Dubuque	11+	27+	11+	27+					P							390
N CENTRAL HUMAN SVCS	Forest City	6mos+	3-26	6mos+	3-26		S S	S		S	P	S					394
GLENWOOD RESOURCE	Glenwood	All Ages	All Ages	All Ages						P							392
U IA SPEECH HEARING	Iowa City				All Ages		P			P							396
CHILDSERVE	Johnston	Birth-21	Birth-21	Birth-21			S S	S	S	P	P	P	S				390
CTR ASSOCIATES	Marshalltown	All Ages								P	P						390
MENTAL HEALTH N IA	Mason City	All Ages								P	P						393
IA BRAILLE SIGHT SCH	Vinton	5-21	Birth-21	5-21	Birth-21		P										393
LUTHERAN SERVICES-IA	Waverly	10-18	7-18						P	P							393
ED RESOURCE-IA	West Des Moines			2+					P	P							392
WOODWARD RESOURCE	Woodward	All Ages	All Ages				S S	S	S	S	P	S	S				396

KANSAS

Organization	City																Page
ARROWHEAD W CHILD	Dodge City	Birth-3	Birth-3					S S	S	S	S	P	P	P			398
MENT HLTH E CENT KS	Emporia	9-17	9-17	Birth-17						P	P	P					404
SUNFLOWER DIVERSIF	Great Bend	Birth-5	Birth-5	Birth-17	Birth-5		P P	P	P	P	P	P	P				405

Program	Town	Females Res	Females Day	Males Res	Males Day	Clinic	Blind	Deaf	Diabetes	Emot Disturb	HIV/AIDS	LD	MR	Ortho/Neuro	PDD	Speech	Page
KS IROQUOIS CTR	Greensburg					5-18	S	S	S	P		S	S	S	P	S	401
GENEVA HERNDON SLHC	Hays					All Ages	S	P	S	S		S	S	S	S	P	400
HIGH PLAINS MENT HTH	Hays					All Ages				P							401
KS STATE SCH	Kansas City	3-21	Birth-21	3-21	Birth-21		P										402
U OF KS MED CTR	Kansas City		Birth-3		Birth-3			P									406
WYANDOT CTR	Kansas City					All Ages				P		S	S				407
LARNED STATE HOSP	Larned	6-17		6-17						P		S	S				404
BERT NASH	Lawrence					All Ages				P		P	S		S		398
U OF KS SPEECH-LANG	Lawrence					All Ages						S	S	S	S	P	406
KANSAS STATE U-SPCH	Manhattan					All Ages		P		S		S	S	S	S	P	403
PAWNEE MENTAL HEALTH	Manhattan					All Ages				P		S					405
YOUTHVILLE	Newton	10-18		10-18						P							406
KS ST SCH FOR DEAF	Olathe	3-21	3-21	3-21	3-21			P				S	P	S			402
LAKEMARY CTR	Paola	6-21		6-21					S	P		S	P	S	P	S	403
PARSONS STATE HOSP	Parsons	All Ages		All Ages									P	P			404
CRAWFORD MENTAL HLTH	Pittsburg		3+		3+	All Ages				P		P					399
ST FRANCIS ACAD-KS	Salina	8-20		8-20						P			S				405
CAPPER FOUNDATION	Topeka		All Ages		All Ages		S	S				S	S	P	S		399
KS NEUROLOGICAL	Topeka	3+	3+	3+	3+								P				402
HEARTSPRING	Wichita	5-21	3+	5-21		All Ages	S	P		S		S	P	P	P	P	400
KS ELKS TRAINING CTR	Wichita	18+	18+	18+	18+							P	P	P			401
WICHITA GUIDANCE	Wichita					Birth-18				P							407
KENTUCKY																	
BELLEFONTE SPCH LANG	Ashland					All Ages		P								P	417

Program	Town	Females Res	Females Day	Males Res	Males Day	Clinic	Blind	Deaf	Diabetes	Emot Disturb	HIV/AIDS	LD	MR	Ortho/Neuro	PDD	Speech	Page
KY MURRAY ST U-SPEEC	Murray					All Ages		P								P	417
WENDELL FOSTER'S	Owensboro	6+		6+		All Ages		S		P		S	P	P	P	S	420
EASTER SEALS W KY	Paducah		1-5		1-5	All Ages	P	P		P		P	P	P	P	P	412
E KY U SPEECH-LANG	Richmond					All Ages		P				S	S	P	S	P	412
LOUISIANA																	
MHC OF CENTRAL LA	Alexandria					6-17				P		P			S		429
ST MARY'S RES TRNG	Alexandria	3-21		3-21			S	S		S		S	P	S		S	431
BRIGHTON ACAD	Baton Rouge		5-14		5-14							P					422
GABLES ACAD-LA	Baton Rouge		6-21		6-21					S		P			S		424
LA SCH FOR THE DEAF	Baton Rouge	3-21	Birth-21	3-21	Birth-21			P					S				426
LA SCH-VISUALLY IMP	Baton Rouge	3-21	3-21	3-21	3-21		P			S		S	S	S		S	427
LA ST U SPEECH-HEAR	Baton Rouge					All Ages				S				P	P	S	428
MCMAINS	Baton Rouge					Birth-18						P	P	P	S	P	428
PARKMEADOW HS	Baton Rouge		13-19		13-19					P		P	P			P	430
METRO DEVELOPMENTAL	Belle Chasse	11-64		11-64								P				P	429
EVERGREEN PRESB	Bossier City	14+		14+								P		P			424
NW LA DEVELOPMENTAL	Bossier City	Birth+		Birth+								P					430
COLUMBIA DEV CTR	Columbia	3-21		3-21			S					P	P	P		P	423
EVANGELINE CHRISTIAN	Lafayette	12-17							S	P	S	P		P			424
LA PHYSICAL THERAPY	Lafayette					All Ages								P			426
U OF LA-LAFAYETTE	Lafayette					All Ages		P		S		P		P	P	P	432
WOMEN & CHILD HOSP	Lake Charles					Birth-18	P	P		S	P	S	P	S	P	P	432
LEESVILLE DEVEL CTR	Leesville		21-59	12-59	18-59					P		S	P	S			425
CHINCHUBA INSTITUTE	Marrero		1½-18		1½-18	All Ages		P								P	423

LOUISIANA (continued)

Facility	City	Age Ranges	Program Emphasis	Page
CHILDREN'S HOSP-NO	New Orleans	Birth-21 / Birth-21	P P / P / P / P P / P P	422
DEPAUL BEHAVIORAL	New Orleans	5-17 / 5-17	P	423
DAVIS DEVELOPMENTAL	New Orleans	6-65 / 6-65 / 6-65	P	426
LSU-HEALTH SCI CTR	New Orleans	All Ages	S S / S / S S	427
NEW ORLEANS SPEECH	New Orleans	All Ages	P / S / S / P S	430
LA TECH SPEECH-HEAR	Ruston	All Ages	S S / S / S S	428
RUSTON DEV CTR	Ruston	12+ / 12+	S S / P / P S	431
HOLY ANGELS-LA	Shreveport	14-25 / 14-25	P / P	425
SHRINERS-LA	Shreveport	Birth-18 / Birth-18	P	432

MAINE

Facility	City	Age Ranges	Program Emphasis	Page
TRI COUNTY MHS	Auburn	Birth-21 / Birth-21	S S / P / S S	437
ELIZABETH LEVINSON	Bangor	Birth-20 / Birth-20	S S / P / S P / S S	434
UCP OF ME	Bangor	7-12 / Birth-20 / 7-12	P P S / P / P P / P S	438
WARREN COMM LEARNING	Bangor	Birth-21	P / P / P S	439
MAY CTR-CHILD DEVEL	Freeport	2-8 / 2-8	P / P / P	435
U ME SPEECH HEARING	Orono	All Ages	S S / P / P / P	438
NEW HORIZONS WILDERN	Orrington	13-18 / 13-18	S S / P / S S	435
ELAN SCH	Poland Spring	12-20 / 12-20	S / P	434
SPURWINK SCH	Portland	4-20 / 4-20	S / P / S / P S	436
MID-COAST SPEECH	Rockport	All Ages	P / S / P P	435
SWEETSER	Saco	5-20 / 5-20 / 3-18	P / S	437
SUMMIT ACHIEVEMENT	Stow	13-17 / 13-17	P / P	436
KENNEBEC MENTAL HLTH	Waterville	All Ages	S / S	434

MARYLAND

Facility	City	Age Ranges	Program Emphasis	Page
HARBOUR SCH	Annapolis	6-21 / 6-21	P / P / P P	447
ASSOC CATHOLIC CHAR	Baltimore	Birth-14 / Birth-14 / Birth-4 / Birth-4	P / P	440

Program	Town	Females Res	Females Day	Males Res	Males Day	Clinic	Blind	Deaf	Diabetes	Emot Disturb	HIV/AIDS	LD	MR	Ortho/Neuro	PDD	Speech	Page
MD CHILDRENS GUILD	Baltimore		3-21	12-18	3-21					P		S				S	442
CHIMES SCH	Baltimore		6-21		6-21					S	S	S	P	S	S	S	442
GATEWAY SCH-MD	Baltimore		3-12		3-12			P	S	S	S	S	S	P	P	P	445
JEWISH FAMILY SERVCS	Baltimore					All Ages				P		P	S	S	P	P	448
LOYOLA SPEECH HEAR	Baltimore					10mos+										P	450
MD SCH FOR THE BLIND	Baltimore	7-21	Birth-21	7-21	Birth-21	All Ages	P	S		S		S	S	S	S	S	450
MCKUSICK-NATHANS INS	Baltimore					All Ages	P	P	P			P	P	P	P	P	451
MT WASHINGTON PEDIAT	Baltimore		Birth-18		Birth-18	Birth-18	S	S		P*		S	S	P	P	P	452
ST. ELIZABETH SCH	Baltimore		11-21		11-21					S		S	P		P	S	455
SYLVAN LEARNING CTR	Baltimore					5-18						P					456
UCP CENTRAL MD	Baltimore		2-21		2-21									P		S	458
WOODBOURNE CTR	Baltimore	9-16		8-18						P					P	S	459
RIDLEY AND FILL	Bethesda					All Ages						P				P	455
REGIONAL INSTIT-S MD	Cheltenham	12-17	11-17	12-17	11-17					P		P					454
SUMMIT SCH-MD	Edgewater	6-15	6-15		6-15							P					456
NORBEL SCH	Elkridge	4-18	4-18		4-18							P					453
LINWOOD CTR	Ellicott City	7-21	7-21	7-21	7-21	7-21									P		450
TAYLOR HEALTH	Ellicott City	5-17	12-17	5-17	12-17	All Ages				P		S	S	S			456
FREDERICK READING	Frederick					5+				S		P	S				444
MD SCH FOR THE DEAF	Frederick	4-21	Birth-21		Birth-21			P				S	S				451
ANNE ARUNDEL CTY MHC	Glen Burnie					5-18				P							440
LAUREL HALL SCH-MD	Hagerstown		6-21		6-21					P		P	S	P			449
GOOD SHEPHERD-MD	Halethorpe	13-18	13-18							P		S					445
JEMICY SCH	Owings Mills		6-14		6-14							P					448

Facility	Location														Page
HANNAH MORE SCH	Reisterstown					S	S	S	P	S		P	S		446
BENEDICTINE SCH	Ridgely	5-21	5-21	5-21	5-21		S		P	S	S	S	S	S	441
ARC-MONTGOMERY CTY	Rockville	All Ages	All Ages	All Ages			S	S	P		S	S	S	S	440
FROST SCH	Rockville	6-21	6-21	6-21	6-21		P		P	S	S	S		S	444
IVYMOUNT SCH	Rockville	4-21	4-21	4-21			P	S	S	P	P	S	S	S	447
JEWISH SOCIAL SERV	Rockville	All Ages			P	P	P								449
RIDGE SCH-MONTGOMERY	Rockville	12-18	12-18	12-18			P	P	P						454
TREATMENT & LEARNING	Rockville	2-14	2-14	2-14	All Ages	S	S	S	P	P	P	P	P	P	457
CHELSEA	Silver Spring	10-18	10-18				P	P					S		441
PATHWAYS SCHS	Silver Spring	9-21	9-21	9-21			P	S	P	S		S	S		453
FRANCIS X. GALLAGHER	Timonium	5-19	5-19	5-19						P					444
VILLA MARIA SCH	Timonium	3-14	3-14	3-14			P	S	P			S		S	458
FORBUSH SCH	Towson	3-21	3-21	3-21			P	S	S		P	P	P		443
NEW HEIGHTS	Towson			6+			P	S	P		P	P	P		453
TOWSON U-SPEECH LANG	Towson		All Ages				S	S	S	S	S	P		457
EDGEMEADE	Upper Marlboro	12-18	12-18	12-18			P	S	S	S	S	S	S		443
MASSACHUSETTS															
BOUNDARIES THERAPY	Acton	All Ages					P	P	P	P					465
CONCORD FAMILY YOUTH	Acton	12-19	12-19	12-19			P	P	P						472
HORACE MANN SCH	Allston	Birth-22	Birth-22	Birth-22		P									485
TRAUMA CTR	Allston		All Ages	All Ages			P	P							514
UMASS AMHERST CTR	Amherst		All Ages	All Ages								P			515
PROF CTR-CHILD DEVEL	Andover	3-7	3-7			S	S	S	P	P			S		508
DEARBORN ACAD	Arlington	5-22	5-22				P	P	P				S		475
MAY CTR-EARLY CHILD	Arlington	3-12	3-12				S	S	S	P		P			497
CRYSTAL SPRINGS SCH	Assonet	3-22	3-22	3-22		S	S	S	P	S	S	S	S		475

Program	Town	Females Res	Females Day	Males Res	Males Day	Clinic	Blind	Deaf	Diabetes	Emot Disturb	HIV/AIDS	LD	MR	Ortho/Neuro	PDD	Speech	Page
MA AUBURN FAMILY INST	Auburn					3-21	S	S	S	P	P	P	S	S	P	S	461
COTTAGE HILL ACAD	Baldwinville	13-19			10-17				S	S		P	S		P		473
STETSON SCH	Barre			8-18					S	P		S	S	S			512
MIDDLESEX COMM COL	Bedford		18+		18+					P		P			P		501
ARLINGTON SCH	Belmont		12-20		12-20					P		P			P		460
SE ALTERNATIVE HS	Berkley		13-18		13-18					S		P					512
BEVERLY SCH FOR DEAF	Beverly		3-22		3-22			P		S		S	S	S		S	464
BOSTON INST FOR ARTS	Boston					All Ages	S	S		P		P	S	S	P	P	465
EMERSON COL-ROBBINS	Boston					All Ages		P						P		P	477
JUDGE BAKER	Boston		5-15		5-15					P		P					487
MGH LANG DISORDERS	Boston					All Ages				P		P					496
NU SPEECH LANGUAGE	Boston					All Ages		P							P	P	506
TUFTS-NEMC-CTR/CHILD	Boston					Birth-22	S	S		P		P	S	P	P	P	514
TUFTS-NEW ENGLAND	Boston	Birth-18	Birth-18	Birth-18	Birth-18	All Ages	S	S		P		P	S	P	P	P	515
CARDINAL CUSHING CTR	Braintree		8-22		8-22					S			P	S	P	S	467
MAY CTR FOR EDUC/VOC	Braintree	11-22	5-22	11-22	5-22							S	S		P		499
LATHAM SCH	Brewster	8-22								P		P	P	S	S		491
FRANCISCAN-KENNEDY	Brighton		3-22		3-22					S		S	S	P	S	S	480
FRANCISCAN-PEDIATRIC	Brighton	3-16		3-16		Birth-18								P	S		480
FRANCISCAN-ED CTR	Brighton		5-18	5-18		5-18				S							481
MCLEAN-FRANCISCAN	Brighton	5-18		5-18						P		P	P		P		499
BEACON HS	Brookline		15-22		15-22					P		P	P				462
IVY STREET SCH	Brookline	13-22	5-22	13-22	5-22					P		S	P	P	P		487
FARR ACAD	Cambridge	12-19	12-19		12-19					P		P	P		P		479

Program	Location	Ages		Page
LESLEY U-THRESHOLD	Cambridge	18-26	18-26	494
MA HOSPITAL SCH	Canton	3-21 / 5-22 / 3-21 / 5-22	All Ages	496
HOLDEN SCH	Charlestown	12-21	12-21	485
MAY CTR	Chatham	3-22	3-22	497
BOSTON COLLEGE SCH	Chestnut Hill	3-21	3-21	465
AVKO DYSLEXIA	Clio	6+		462
NORTHEASTERN FAMILY	Danvers	12+ / 0-18	12+ / 0-18	506
WHITNEY ACAD	East Freetown	10-22		519
RIVERVIEW	East Sandwich	12-23	12-23	509
FALL RIVER DEACONESS	Fall River	13-18		478
MAY CTR-FALL RIVER	Fall River	All Ages	All Ages	497
HEALTHALLIANCE SPCH	Fitchburg	All Ages	All Ages	484
LEARN CTR-DEAF CHILD	Framingham	4-21	4-21	492
REED ACAD	Framingham	7-13		508
WAYSIDE YOUTH NETWK	Framingham	12-17	12-17	518
CADMUS LIFESHARING	Great Barrington	18+	18+	467
CLIN & SUPPORT OPTS	Greenfield	All Ages	All Ages	471
FRANKLIN MED CTR	Greenfield	All Ages	All Ages	481
CARDINAL CUSHING	Hanover	8-21	8-21	468
EAGLE HILL-MA	Hardwick	13-19 / 13-19	13-19	477
NEARI SCH	Holyoke	8-22	8-22	503
LEDGES	Hopedale	18+	18+	493
BERKSHIRE MEADOWS	Housatonic	All Ages	All Ages	464
NAUSET	Hyannis	18+ / 18+	18+	502
CORNERSTONES SCH	Ipswich	6-12 / 6-13	6-12 / 6-13	473
ITALIAN HOME	Jamaica Plain	4-14 / 4-14	4-14 / 4-14	487

Program	Town	Females Res	Females Day	Males Res	Males Day	Clinic	Blind	Deaf	Diabetes	Emot Disturb	HIV/AIDS	LD	MR	Ortho/Neuro	PDD	Speech	Page
MA LANG COGNITIVE DEV	Jamaica Plain		3-13		3-13					S		S	S				490
DR FRANKLIN PERKINS	Lancaster	3+	4-16	3+	4-16					P		P	S	S	S		476
ROBERT F KENNEDY ACT	Lancaster			6-17								P		S			510
BERKSHIRE CTR-CIP	Lee	18-28		18-28				S	S	S		P	S	S	P	S	463
MCAULEY NAZARETH	Leicester		6-13	6-13	6-13				S	P	S	P	P	P	P		499
VALLEYHEAD	Lenox	10-22								P		P	S	S	S		516
LIPTON CTR	Leominster		12-19		12-19	All Ages				P		P			S		495
COTTING SCH/HOPE	Lexington	19-26	3-22	19-26	3-22		S	S	S			P	S	P	S	S	474
INST-LEARN & DEVEL	Lexington					6+						P					486
CARROLL	Lincoln		7-15		7-15							P					469
WILLIE ROSS SCH	Longmeadow		3-22		3-22			P		S			S				519
N SHORE INFANT/TODD	Lynn		Birth-3	Birth-3	Birth-3	Birth-3	P	P		P	P	P	P	P	P	P	505
AMEGO	Mansfield	11+	11+	11+	11+							S	P	S	P		460
ST ANN'S HOME	Methuen	6-17	6-17	6-17	6-17	All Ages				P		P	P	S			510
F.L. CHAMBERLAIN SCH	Middleboro	11-18	11-18	11-18	11-18					P		P		S	P		482
EVERGREEN CTR	Milford	6-22		6-22			S	S		P		P	P	S	P	S	478
GOULD FARM	Monterey	18+		18+						P							483
BRANDON RES CTR	Natick	7-16		7-16	7-16					P		P					466
METROWST CHILD DEVEL	Natick	3-15		3-15	3-15					P							500
COMMONWEALTH	Needham					6+						P					472
WALKER HOME & SCH	Needham	6-13	6-13	6-13	6-13				S	P	S	S	P	S	S	S	517
I H SCHWARTZ REHAB	New Bedford		3-21		3-21		S	S				S	P	S	S	P	486
KENNEDY-DONOVAN CTR	New Bedford		3-22		3-22		P	P		P		S	P	S	P	P	488
KOLBURNE SCH	New Marlborough	8-22		8-22						P		S	S	S	P	S	488

Program	Location										Index
OPPORTUNITY WORKS	Newburyport	16+	16+						P		507
ACAD PHYS SOCIAL DEV	Newton	5-16	5-16			P	S	S	S	S	460
CARROLL CTR	Newton	14+ 3+	14+ 3+	P S	P S					S S	468
FAMILY COUNSELING	Newton	All Ages	All Ages	P		P			P		479
NEW ENGLAND NEURO	North Andover	All Ages	All Ages	P		P		P	P	P	504
NORTHEAST REHAB	North Andover	All Ages	All Ages					P	P	P	506
NEW ENGLAND PEDIATRI	North Billerica	Birth-22 3-22	Birth-22 3-22	P P	P P	P		P	P	S	504
VALLEY VIEW	North Brookfield	11-16	11-16	P		P					516
LIGHTHOUSE SCH	North Chelmsford	3-22	3-22	P		P		P	P		494
CLARKE SCH	Northampton	5-18 4-18	5-18 4-18	P	P	P		P	P		471
LINDEN HILL	Northfield	9-16	9-16			P					495
MAY CTR FOR ED/NEURO	Norwood	5-22 5-22	5-22 5-22					P			498
LAKESIDE SCH	Peabody	8-16 8-16	8-16 8-16	P		P					489
NEW ENGLAND VILLAGE	Pembroke	18+ 18+	18+ 18+	S S	S S	P		S	S		505
BRIEN CTR	Pittsfield	All Ages	All Ages	P		P					466
HILLCREST EDUC CTRS	Pittsfield	6-14 6-18	6-14 6-18	P		P					484
PEDIATRIC DEV CTR-MA	Pittsfield	Birth-3 Birth-3	Birth-3 Birth-3	P P	P P	S		P	P	P	507
BAIRD CTR	Plymouth	10-15 10-15	10-15 10-15			P		P	S	P	462
LANDMARK	Prides Crossing	14-20 7-20	14-20 7-20			P					490
CP OF MA	Quincy	3-7 3-7	3-7 3-7	S S	S S	S		P	S	S	469
SOUTH SHORE MHC	Quincy	All Ages	All Ages	S S	S S	P		S	P	S	511
DEVEREUX MA	Rutland	13-22 6-22	6-22	P		P	S	P	S	S	475
GLAVIN REGIONAL CTR	Shrewsbury	18+	18+			P		P	P		483
BERKSHIRE HILLS MUS	South Hadley	18-30	18-30	S S	S S	S		P	P		463
NEW ENGLAND CTR	Southborough	3-22 1½-12	3-22 1½-12	P		P		P	P	S	503
ASSOC COMM LIVING	Springfield	All Ages	All Ages	P					P		461

Program	Town	Females Res	Females Day	Males Res	Males Day	Clinic	Blind	Deaf	Diabetes	Emot Disturb	HIV/AIDS	LD	MR	Ortho/Neuro	PDD	Speech	Page
MA CHILDREN'S STUDY HOM	Springfield	13-18	6-18	6-18	6-18					P		P	P				470
SHRINERS-MA	Springfield	Birth-18		Birth-18													511
WELDON REHAB	Springfield					Birth-16	P	P						P	P	P	518
RIVERBROOK RESIDENCE	Stockbridge	18+					S		S	S	S	S	P	S		S	509
NEW ENGLAND SINAI	Stoughton					All Ages								P			504
CORWIN-RUSSELL	Sudbury		11-19	11-19					S	S		P			P		473
WILLOW HILL	Sudbury		11-19	11-19								P			P		520
STEVENS TREATMENT	Swansea			12-18						P		S					513
SWANSEA WOOD SCH	Swansea	13-22		13-22						P		P	P	S			513
MORTON HOSP-HEARING	Taunton					All Ages		P				S	S	P	P	P	501
LEAGUE SCH BOSTON	Walpole	3-22	3-22	3-22	3-22								S		P		491
E KENNEDY SHRIVER	Waltham	3-22	3-22	3-22	3-22	All Ages				P		P	P	P			478
LEARNING CTR	Waltham	6-22	6-22	6-22	6-22								P		P		492
NAT'L BIRTH DEFECTS	Waltham					Birth-21	P	P				P	P	P	S	P	502
PERKINS SCH BLIND	Watertown	3-22	3-22	3-22	3-22		P	S									507
LEARN & DEV DISABIL	Wellesley					All Ages				S		P	P	P	P	P	492
LAKE GROVE MAPLE	Wendell			13-21						P		P	P				489
CLEARWAY SCH	West Newton	9-18	9-18		9-18					S		P	P	S	S	S	471
LEARNING PREP SCH	West Newton	8-22	8-22		8-22				S	S		P	P	S	P	S	493
BRIGHTSIDE	West Springfield	5-12		5-17		All Ages				P		S					467
MAY CTR-EARLY INTERV	West Springfield		Birth-5		Birth-5					P		P	P	P	P	P	498
GIFFORD SCH	Weston	8-22	8-22		8-22					P		P	S	S	P		482
WINCHENDON	Winchendon	13-20	13-20	13-20	13-20							P					520
MERCY CENTRE	Worcester	6-22	6-22		6-22					S			P		S	S	500

Facility	City	Ages											Page
MILL SWAN COMM SKILL	Worcester										P		501
YOU INC.	Worcester	12-18	3-21	12-18	12-21	All Ages	P	P	P	P	P		521
					MICHIGAN								
MONTCALM SCH	Albion	12-18						P					530
STARR COMMONWEALTH	Albion	10-17						P		P	P		534
U OF MI-COM DISORDER	Ann Arbor			3+				P		P	P	P	535
CENTER FOR HUMAN DEV	Berkley					All Ages		P		S	P	S	523
BLOSSOMLAND CTR	Berrien Springs	3-26	3-26		S	S	S	P		S	P		522
ETON	Birmingham	6-19	6-19					P					526
CARO CTR	Caro	1+	1+							P	P		522
ST LOUIS CTR	Chelsea		6-18					S			S		533
VISTA MARIA	Dearborn Heights	11-17					S	P		S	P	P	S	535
DETROIT INSTITUTE	Detroit			Birth-21	S	S		S		P			524
DON BOSCO HALL	Detroit	16-20	12-20	7-20				P		P			524
LUTHERAN SPEC ED-MI	Detroit	5-14	5-14					P		S			528
NE GUIDANCE CTR	Detroit			Birth-17				P		P			531
REHAB INST OF MI	Detroit			Birth-21				P		P			532
WAYNE ST SPEECH LANG	Detroit			All Ages						P			536
MI ST U-HERBERT OYER	East Lansing			All Ages	S	P		S			S	P	530
ST VINCENT/S FISHER	Farmington Hills	4-17	12-21	12-23		P		P		S		P	533
MI SCH FOR THE BLIND	Flint	Birth-26	Birth-26	All Ages	P	S		S		S		S	529
MI SCH FOR THE DEAF	Flint	6-26	Birth-26	6-26	Birth-26	S	P	S	S		S	S	529
ARBOR CIRCLE	Grand Rapids			All Ages		P		P		P			522
LINCOLN SCH-MI	Grand Rapids	5-26	5-26							P		P	528
CHILDRENS HM DETROIT	Grosse Pointe	1-8	1-8							P		P	526
COLEMAN FOUNDATION	Hudson	18+	18+							P		P	524

Program	Town	Females Res	Females Day	Males Res	Males Day	Clinic	Blind	Deaf	Diabetes	Emot Disturb	HIV/AIDS	LD	MR	Ortho/Neuro	PDD	Speech	Page
MI STARFISH FAMILY SVCS	Inkster					All Ages				P							534
MANOR FOUNDATION	Jonesville	6-18		6-18						P		P	P	S	P		528
SLD LEARNING CTR	Kalamazoo					All Ages						P					534
FAMILY CHILD MIDLAND	Midland					All Ages				P							526
CMU SPEECH HEARING	Mount Pleasant					All Ages		P					S	S		P	523
MT. PLEASANT REG CTR	Mount Pleasant	All Ages		All Ages						P			P				531
HAWTHORN CTR	Northville	5-17		5-17		5-17				P							527
ERICKSON LEARNING	Okemos					5+			S	S		P	S	S	S		525
JUDSON CTR	Royal Oak	9-17		9-17						P		S					527
WILLIAM BEAUMONT	Royal Oak					1-14							P	P	P	S	536
PENRICKTON CTR-BLIND	Taylor	1-12	Birth-6	1-12	Birth-6		P	S					S	S	S		532
CHILD GUIDANCE	Traverse City	7-17		7-17		Birth-17				P							523
MUNSON MED CTR	Traverse City					All Ages	S	P		S		S	S	S	S	P	531
E MI U SPEECH & HEAR	Ypsilanti					All Ages		P		P				S		P	525
MINNESOTA																	
BAR NONE RES CTR	Anoka	10-18		10-18						S	S	S	S	S	P		538
GERARD TREATMENT	Austin	10-18		10-18						P		S	S	S	S		542
ARCHDEACON GILFILLAN	Bemidji	6-18	6-18	6-18	6-18		S	S		P		S	S	S	S	S	538
BISHOP MCNAIRY	Bemidji	11-17		11-17						P		S					539
EDITH HATCH EVAL CTR	Bemidji	5-17		5-17						P		P					541
NORTHWOOD CHILDREN'S	Duluth	1½-17	1½-17	5-17	1½-17		S	S		P		P	P	P	P	S	546
WOODLAND HILLS-MN	Duluth	12-20	12-17	12-20	12-17				S	P		S		S	S		549
MN STATE ACAD	Faribault	3-21	3-21	3-21	3-21		P	S				S	S	S	S	S	544
MN ST ACAD FOR DEAF	Faribault	5-21	2-21	5-21	2-21			P									545

Facility	City	Age	Page
COURAGE CTR	Golden Valley	All Ages	540
FAIRVIEW U PEDIATRIC	Minneapolis	All Ages	541
FRASER SCH	Minneapolis	6wks-6	541
SAINT JOSEPH'S HOME	Minneapolis	6-17 / 6-12	546
U OF MN-CLEFT PALATE	Minneapolis	All Ages	547
VISION LOSS RESOUR	Minneapolis	16+	548
WASHBURN CHILD GUID	Minneapolis	3-10	548
MN ST-MOORHEAD SPCH	Moorhead	3-21	545
LAURA BAKER	Northfield	4-22 / 4+	544
GROVES ACAD	St Louis Park	3-18	543
BUSH CHILDRENS RES	St Paul	5-17	539
GILLETTE CHILDREN'S	St Paul	All Ages	542
SOLTREKS	Two Harbors	13-25	547
WOODLAND CTRS	Willmar	9-18 / 6-16	548
HOME CREATIVE LIVING	Windom	All Ages	544
DSTRCT FIVE EIGHTEEN	Worthington	6-21	540
MISSISSIPPI			
U OF S MS DUBARD SCH	Hattiesburg	3-14	555
U S MS SPEECH HEAR	Hattiesburg	All Ages	556
EDUCATION CTR SCH-MS	Jackson	5-21	550
MAGNOLIA SPEECH SCH	Jackson	Birth-14	552
MS SCH FOR THE BLIND	Jackson	5-20 / Birth-5	553
MS SOCIETY-DISABILIT	Jackson	Birth-18	553
SOUTH MS REG CTR	Long Beach	5+	554
MILLCREEK BHS	Magee	5-21 / 5-17	552
MERIDIAN SPCH & HEAR	Meridian	All Ages	552

Program	Town	Females Res	Females Day	Males Res	Males Day	Clinic	Blind	Deaf	Diabetes	Emot Disturb	HIV/AIDS	LD	MR	Ortho/Neuro	PDD	Speech	Page
MS N MS REGIONAL CTR	Oxford	5+		5+			S	S	S	S		S	P	S	S	S	554
HERITAGE SCH	Ridgeland	5+	6-15	5+	6-15		S	S	S	S		P	P	S	S	S	551
BADDOUR CTR	Senatobia	18+		18+									P				550
U OF MS-SPEECH/HEAR	University					All Ages		S				P	P	S	P	P	555
HUDSPETH REG CTR	Whitfield	5+		5+			S	S					P			S	551
MISSOURI																	
RAINBOW CTR DAY SCH	Blue Springs		3-21		3-21					S		P	P	P	P	P	569
SE MO ST-SPEECH	Cape Girardeau					All Ages		P		S		S	S	S	S	P	573
ST. JOSEPH INSTITUTE	Chesterfield	5-15	Birth-15	5-15	Birth-15	Birth-3		P				S					570
ST LOUIS CTY FAM MHC	Clayton					All Ages			P	P		P	P			P	571
MIDMO MENTAL HEALTH	Columbia	6+	6-18	6+	6-18					P							567
U OF MO-SPCH/HEARING	Columbia					All Ages		P				P	S	S	P	P	575
CAPITAL REGIONAL	Jefferson City					All Ages	S	S				P	P	P	P	P	557
AREA HEARING & SPCH	Joplin					All Ages		P						P		P	557
COLLEGE VIEW ST SCH	Joplin		5-21		5-21								P				561
CHILDREN'S CTR-VISUA	Kansas City		Birth-8		Birth-8		P	S				S	S	S	S	S	560
CHILDRENS MERCY HEAR	Kansas City					Birth-21		P				S		S		P	560
CHILDREN'S TLC-MO	Kansas City		Birth-8		Birth-8			P				P	P	P	P	P	561
MARILLAC	Kansas City	5-16	5-16	5-16	5-16	5-16				P	S	P	P	S	P	S	566
OZANAM HOME	Kansas City	12-18	12-18	12-18	12-18		S	S		P		S	P	S	P	S	569
SHERWOOD CTR	Kansas City	21+	3-21	21+	3-21			S		S		S	P	S	P	P	572
SPOFFORD	Kansas City	4-12		4-12					P	P		S	P	P	S	S	573
TNC COMMUNITY	Kansas City	18+		18+			S	S		S		S	P	S	S	S	574
KIRKSVILLE REGIONAL	Kirksville					All Ages		S				S	P	S	S	S	565

Program	Location	Age	Program Emphasis (left→right)	Page
TRUMAN ST U-SHC	Kirksville	1+	S P S S S P S S P P	574
AUDRAIN MED SPEECH	Mexico	All Ages	P P S P P	557
CTR FOR HUMAN SERVS	Sedalia	Birth-3	S P P P	558
DEVELOPMENT CTR-OZAR	Springfield	All Ages	S S P P P P P P	562
RIVENDALE INST	Springfield	3-18	P P P P	570
CENTRAL INST-DEAF	St Louis	Birth-12	S P P P	558
CHILD CTR-OUR LADY	St Louis	5-14	P P S S S	559
CHURCHILL SCH	St Louis	8-16	P P	561
EDGEWOOD CTR-MO	St Louis	3-17	P S S	562
EVANGELICAL CHILDREN	St Louis	7-17	P P P P P P P P	562
GALLAUDET HEARING	St Louis	5-16	P S	563
GOOD SHEPHERD	St Louis	Birth-6	P P S S P	563
HAWTHORN CHILDREN'S	St Louis	6-18	P P S S S	564
HOPEWELL CTR	St Louis	3-17	P P S	564
JUDEVINE CTR	St Louis	3+	S S S P P P	564
LOGOS	St Louis	11-21	S S P P S P S	565
LUTHERAN ASSOC	St Louis	6-16	S S P S S S	566
METROPOLITAN	St Louis	10-21	S S P P S P S	567
MO SCH FOR THE BLIND	St Louis	5-21	P S S S S S	568
R JORDAN PED REHAB	St Louis	Birth-16	P P P	570
ST LOUIS ARC	St Louis	All Ages	S S P S S	571
SHRINERS-ST LOUIS	St Louis	Birth-18	P P	572
C MO ST U-WELCH/SCHM	Warrensburg	All Ages	S P S S P	559
MIRIAM SCH	Webster Groves	4-14	S P S S S	568

MONTANA

Program	Location	Age	Program Emphasis (left→right)	Page
THREE RIVERS MT	Belgrade	13-18	S P P S S P	580

Program	Town	Females Res	Females Day	Males Res	Males Day	Clinic	Blind	Deaf	Diabetes	Emot Disturb	HIV/AIDS	LD	MR	Ortho/Neuro	PDD	Speech	Page
MT COR ENTERPRISES	Billings		16+		16+	Birth-21	S	S	S			P	P	P	P	S	577
MONTANA CTR	Billings							S						P	P		579
YELLOWSTONE RANCH	Billings	12-18	10-18	6-18	6-18					P		P		S	S		581
MT DEVELOPMENTAL CTR	Boulder	All Ages		All Ages									P				579
DANCING MOON RANCH	Chinook	11-20								P		P					577
MT SCH-DEAF & BLIND	Great Falls	5-21	2-21	5-21	2-21		P	P		S		S	S	S		S	579
CHILD DEV CTR-MT	Missoula					Birth-21	S	S				P	P	P	P		576
AFFINITY FOUND	Proctor	13-18		13-18						P		P	P	P	S		576
EXPLORATIONS-MT	Trout Creek	12-18		12-18					P			P	P				577
HOPE RANCH	Whitefish	12-18		12-18						P		P					578
STAR MEADOWS ACAD	Whitefish	13-17					S	S	P	P		P	P	P			580
						NEBRASKA											
U NE SPEECH LANGUAGE	Kearney					All Ages		P								P	585
CHILD GUID CTR-NE	Lincoln					Birth-21		S		P		P	S	S	P		582
U OF NE-LINCOLN BARK	Lincoln					All Ages	P		S	P		P	P	P	P		586
NEBRASKA CTR FOR EDU	Nebraska City	5-21	Birth-21	5-21	Birth-21		P										584
ALEGENT HEALTH REHAB	Omaha	All Ages		All Ages		All Ages				P				P			582
BOYS TOWN NATL HOSP	Omaha					All Ages		P				P				S	582
DOCTOR J P LORD SCH	Omaha		5-21		5-21									P	P		583
MADONNA SCH	Omaha		5-21		5-21					S		P	S	P	P	S	584
MUNROE MEYER	Omaha					All Ages	S	S		S		P	S	P	P	S	584
OMAHA HEARING SCH	Omaha		Birth-8		Birth-8			P		S			S	S		S	585
UTA HALEE	Omaha	12-18	12-18							P		S		S			586
VILLA MARIE SCH	Waverly	6-18		6-18									P				587

NEVADA

Program	City	Age Range(s)	Emphasis (P/S)	Page
EPWORTH VILLAGE	York	7-19 / 8-19 / 7-19	S P S P S S	583
NEW HORIZONS ACAD-NV	Las Vegas	6-18 / 6-18	P P	588
SPECIAL CHILDRENS-LV	Las Vegas	Birth-3 / Birth-3 / Birth-3	S S S S S S S	588
VARIETY SCH	Las Vegas	3-22 / 3-22	P P	589
U OF NV-RENO SPEECH	Reno	All Ages / All Ages	S P S S S S	589

NEW HAMPSHIRE

Program	City	Age Range(s)	Emphasis (P/S)	Page
ECKERD YOUTH-NH	Colebrook	10-17	P S P	593
SECOND START ALT HS	Concord	14-18 / 14-18	P P S	598
SPECIAL MED SVCS	Concord	Birth-20	P P P	599
COMMUNITY PARTNERS	Dover	All Ages	P P	591
NEW ENGLAND SPEECH	Dover	All Ages	P P	596
LAKEVIEW NEURO REHAB	Effingham Falls	8-21 / 8-21 / 8-21	S S S P P P	594
CROTCHED MTN REHAB	Greenfield	6-21 / 6-21 / 6-21	S S P P S	591
CEDARCREST	Keene	Birth-16 / 3-16	S S P P	590
DARTMOUTH-HITCHCOCK	Lebanon	All Ages / All Ages	S S S S P	592
EASTER SEALS-NH	Manchester	All Ages / All Ages / All Ages	P P	592
MANCHESTER PRGM	Manchester	3-21 / 3-21	S P S S S	595
MENTAL HLTH MANCH	Manchester	18+ / All Ages	P P	596
HAMPSHIRE COUNTRY	Rindge	8-18 / 8-18	S S P	593
HUNTER SCH	Rumney	5-15 / 5-15	P P	594
NEW ENG SALEM CHILD	Rumney	6-18 / 6-18	P P P	596
CLM BEHAVIORAL	Salem	All Ages	P S	590
RICHIE MCFARLAND CTR	Stratham	Birth-3 / Birth-3	P P P P P	597
PINE HAVEN BOYS CTR	Suncook	6-15	P S S	597
LUKAS COMMUNITY	Temple	18+ / 18+	P P P P	595

Program	Town	Females Res	Females Day	Males Res	Males Day	Clinic	Blind	Deaf	Diabetes	Emot Disturb	HIV/AIDS	LD	MR	Ortho/Neuro	PDD	Speech	Page
NH SPAULDING YOUTH-ED	Tilton			6-16	6-16					P		P					598
SPAULDING YOUTH-NEUR	Tilton	6-21	6-21	6-21	6-21					P		S	S	P	P	P	599
NEW JERSEY																	
RANCH HOPE	Alloway	14-17	14-17	9-16½	9-16½					P							635
ARCHWAY PRGMS	Atco	3-21	3-21	3-21	3-21		S	S		P		S	P	P	P	S	601
LORD STIRLING SCH	Basking Ridge	9-20	9-20		9-20					P		S					628
OCEAN MENTAL HEALTH	Bayville	11-17	12-25	11-17	12-25					P							634
EAST MOUNTAIN DAY	Belle Mead	12-19	12-19		12-19					P							615
1ST CEREBRAL PALSY	Belleville	Birth-21	Birth-21		Birth-21	All Ages						S	S	P		S	617
GREEN BROOK ACAD	Bound Brook	11-21	11-21		11-21					P		S	S				621
DEVEREUX NJ-AUTISM	Bridgeton	14+	5-21	14+	5-21			S		S			S	S	P		614
HUNTERDON LEARN CTR	Califon	12-18	12-18		12-18					P		P	S	S	S	S	623
COOPER U HOSP-SPEECH	Camden					All Ages		P				S	S	S		P	612
BROOKFIELD SCHS	Cherry Hill	5-21	5-21		5-21					P	S	P	S	P	P	P	604
PASSAIC COUNTY ELKS	Clifton	3-21	3-21		3-21		S	S		S		S	S	P	S	S	634
HUNTERDON DEV CTR	Clinton	18+		18+			S	S		S		S	P	S	S	S	623
VANTAGE HEALTH	Dumont			13-17		All Ages				P		S					642
HARBOR SCH-NJ	Eatontown	3-21	3-21		3-21		S			S		P	S	P	P	P	622
JFK JOHNSON REHAB	Edison	Birth-16	Birth-16		Birth-16	All Ages	S	P		P		P	S	P	P	P	625
LAKEVIEW SCH	Edison	3-21	3-21		3-21	All Ages							S	P	P	P	626
CP CTR-BERGEN COUNTY	Fair Lawn	1½-8	1½-8		1½-8	All Ages							P	P		P	606
BANYAN SCH	Fairfield	6-14	6-14		6-14							P					602
GLENVIEW ACAD	Fairfield	6-21	6-21		6-21					P		P		S		S	620
GRAMON SCH	Fairfield	13-21	13-21		13-21					P		S	S	S	S	S	620

Facility	Location	Ages	Emphasis (P/S)	No.
ARTHUR BRISBANE	Farmingdale	11-17, 11-17	P	601
HUNTERDON CHILD DEV	Flemington	Birth-21, Birth-21, All Ages	S, S, P, S, S, P, P	624
HUNTERDON MED CTR	Flemington	Birth-21	P, P, P	624
MONTGOMERY ACAD	Gladstone	5-21, 5-21, 5-21	P, P, P, S	631
FD U PSYCH SVCS	Hackensack	All Ages, All Ages	S, S, P, S	616
HACKENSACK U-JUDY	Hackensack	All Ages, All Ages	P, P	621
HOLLEY CHILD CARE	Hackensack	6-12, 6-12	P, P	622
BANCROFT NEUROHEALTH	Haddonfield	All Ages, All Ages, All Ages	S, P, P, S, P	602
KINGSWAY LEARNING	Haddonfield	5-21, 5-21, Birth-3	S, S, S, P, P, S	626
BERGEN CTR-CHILD DEV	Haworth	5-21, 5-21	P, S, S, S, P	602
CP CTR-GLOUCESTER	Hurffville	Birth-21, Birth-21	S, S, S, P, S	606
ST JOSEPH'S-BLIND	Jersey City	5-21, 3-21, 3-21	P, S, S, P, S	638
ALPHA SCH	Lakewood	3-21, 3-21	S, S, P, P, P	600
ARC EMPLOYMENT CTR	Lakewood	16+, 16+	S, S, P, S, S, S	600
LEHMANN SCH & TECH	Lakewood	3-21, 3-21	S, S, S, P	627
BONNIE BRAE	Liberty Corner	11-18, 11-18	S, P, P, P	604
FELICIAN SCH	Lodi	5-21, 5-21	S, S, S	617
MIDWAY SCH	Lumberton	5-21, 5-21	P, P	630
ARC SOMERSET COUNTY	Manville	Birth-6, Birth-6	P, P, P	601
CEREBRAL PALSY OF NJ	Maplewood	21+, Birth-21, Birth-21	S, S, S, P, S	607
SOMERSET HILLS	Middlesex	7-14, 7-14	S, P, S, P, P, S	640
MILLBURN REGIONAL	Millburn	3-21, 3-21	P, P, P, S	630
CUMBERLAND GUIDANCE	Millville	5-17, 5-17, All Ages	P, P	613
MORRISTOWN MEMORIAL	Morristown	All Ages, All Ages	P, P, P	631
CHILDREN'S HOME-BURL	Mount Holly	11-17, 11-17, 11-17	P, P, P	609
GITHENS CTR	Mount Holly	3-21, 3-21, All Ages	S, S, S, P, S	619

| | | Females | | Males | | | | | | | | | | | | | Page |
Program	Town	Res	Day	Res	Day	Clinic	Blind	Deaf	Diabetes	Emot Disturb	HIV/AIDS	LD	MR	Ortho/Neuro	PDD	Speech	
NJ CRAIG SCH	Mountain Lakes											P					613
CHILDRENS SPECIALIZE	Mountainside	Birth-21		Birth-21						P				P			610
CHILDREN'S-MONMOUTH	Neptune		3-21		3-21							P	P	P	P	P	609
CPC BEHAV HEALTHCARE	Neptune	12-21	5-21	12-21	5-21					P		P	P	P	P	P	612
NEW LISBON DEV CTR	New Lisbon	13+		13+				S	S			S	P	S		S	633
SUMMIT SPEECH SCH	New Providence		Birth-5		Birth-5			P								S	641
MIDLAND SCH	North Branch		5-21		5-21		S	S	S	S			P	S	P	P	629
SEARCH DAY PRGM	Ocean	21+	3-21	21+	3-21								P		P		639
BERGEN COUNTY SERVS	Paramus		3-21		3-21			P		P			P	P	P	S	603
BERGEN BEHAV HEALTH	Paramus	5-17	5-17	5-17		5-17				P				P			603
CHILD CENTER-NJ	Paramus		Birth-3		Birth-3								P	P	P	P	608
MATHENY SCH & HOSP	Peapack	3+	3-21	3+	3-21		S		S				S	P	S	S	629
CAMBRIDGE SCH-NJ	Pennington		5-14		5-14							P					605
RARITAN BAY MH CTR	Perth Amboy					All Ages				S		S	S	S	S		636
CHANCELLOR ACAD	Pompton Plains		13-18		13-18					P				S			608
NEW BRIDGE SVCS	Pompton Plains					All Ages				P				P			632
EDEN INSTITUTE	Princeton		3-21		3-21										P	S	616
LEWIS SCH & CLINIC	Princeton	5+	5+	5+		All Ages						P	S				627
PRINCETON CHILD DEV	Princeton	7+	2+	7+	2+										P		635
HOLMSTEAD SCH	Ridgewood		13-18		13-18					P							622
PINELAND LEARN CTR	Rosenhaym		5-21		5-21			S	S	S		P	S	P	P	S	634
WINSTON SCH-NJ	Short Hills		6-14		6-14							P	S				642
FAMILY RESOURCE	Shrewsbury					Birth-8						P	P	P	P	P	616
ROCK BROOK SCH	Skillman		5-12		5-12	Birth-12		P				P	S	P	P	P	636

Facility	City	Age	Age	Emphasis	Index
COMMUNITY SCH-NJ	Teaneck	14-21	14-21	P	610
COMMUNITY ELEM-NJ	Teaneck	5-14	5-14	S P S S S S S	611
SINAI SPECIAL NEEDS	Teaneck	5-21	5-21	S S P P	639
JCC THERAPEUTIC NURS	Tenafly	3-5	3-5	S P P P	625
DOROTHY B HERSH HS	Tinton Falls	14-21	14-21	S S S S S	614
TITUSVILLE ACAD	Titusville	5-18	5-18	P P P S S	641
MT ST JOSEPH CHILD	Totowa	6-14	6-14	P S	632
NORTH JERSEY DEVELOP	Totowa	All Ages	All Ages	P	633
MARIE KATZENBACH SCH	Trenton	Birth-21	Birth-21	S P S S S S S	628
MERCER SPEECH	Trenton	All Ages	All Ages	P	629
NEWGRANGE	Trenton	8-18	8-18	P S	633
SR GEORGINE SCH	Trenton	5-21	5-21	P P S S	640
CEREBRAL PALSY LEAGU	Union	6mos+	6mos+	P S P S	607
MONTCLAIR ST PSYCH	Upper Montclair	Birth-12	Birth-12	P P P	631
VOORHEES PEDIATRIC	Voorhees	Birth-21 / Birth-21 *	Birth-20	S S S S P	642
FORUM SCH	Waldwick	3-16	3-16	P S P S P P	618
RUGBY SCH-WOODFIELD	Wall	5-21	5-21	P P S P	637
WOODCLIFF ACAD	Wall	10-18	10-18	P P S P P	643
SAINT PATRICK'S SCH	West Orange	5-12	5-12	P P S	638
COMMUNITY SCH-FC	West Paterson	7-21	7-21	P S S	611
ST JOHN GOD COMM SVC	Westville	All Ages	All Ages	P P	637
CALAIS SCH	Whippany	6-21	6-21	S P S S	605
COLLIER HS	Wickatunk	13-18	13-18	P	610
GARFIELD PARK ACAD	Willingboro	5-20	5-20	P S P P	618
E CHRISTIAN CHILDREN	Wyckoff	8+	8+	P P	615

NEW MEXICO

Program	Town	Females Res	Females Day	Males Res	Males Day	Clinic	Blind	Deaf	Diabetes	Emot Disturb	HIV/AIDS	LD	MR	Ortho/Neuro	PDD	Speech	Page
NM NM SCH VISUAL HANDIC	Alamogordo		Birth-21		Birth-21		P										646
ALBUQUERQUE HEARING	Albuquerque					1+	S	P				P	P	P	P	P	644
MANDY'S SPECIAL FARM	Albuquerque	18+		18+											P		645
RCI	Albuquerque		Birth-3		Birth-3	All Ages	S					P	P	P	P	P	647
U OF NM-TINGLEY HOSP	Albuquerque	Birth-21		Birth-21		Birth-21	S	S	S			P	P	P	P	P	648
U NM CHILDRENS PSYCH	Albuquerque	Birth-17	Birth-17	Birth-17	Birth-17		S	S		P							648
U OF NM COMM DIS	Albuquerque					All Ages		P						P	P	P	649
U NM CHILD PSYCH	Albuquerque					2-18				P							649
LAS CUMBRES LEARNING	Espanola	18+		18+						P			P		P		645
LOS LUNAS COMM PROG	Los Lunas		All Ages		All Ages								P				645
E NM U SPEECH LANG	Portales					All Ages						P				P	645
NM SPEECH/LANGUAGE	Roswell					All Ages									P	P	646
NM SCH FOR THE DEAF	Santa Fe	Birth-22	Birth-22		Birth-22			P				S					646
SOUTHWEST NM SVCS	Silver City	18+	Birth-3	18+	Birth-3		P	P				P	P	P	P	P	647
BRUSH RANCH	Tererro	12-19		12-19					P	S		P	P	P			644
						NEW YORK											
CTR FOR THE DISABLED	Albany	6+	All Ages	6+	All Ages	All Ages						S	S	P			659
SAINT ANNE INST	Albany	12-18	12-18	12-18						P		S	S	S		S	710
HENRY VISCARDI SCH	Albertson		3-21		3-21									P			677
COBB MEMORIAL SCHOOL	Altamont	5-21	5-21	5-21	5-21								P				666
KILDONAN	Amenia	11-19	7-19	11-19	7-19							P					683
MAPLEBROOK	Amenia	11-21	11-21	11-21	11-21							P		S		P	692
CAYUGA HOME	Auburn	11-17		11-17					P	P	S	P	S	S		S	657
NY STATE SCH-BLIND	Batavia	5-21	5-21	5-21	5-21		P	S		S		S	S	S	S	S	699

Facility	Location	Age Range				Emphasis (P/S)						Index
ANIBIC NEW YORK	Bayside	18+	5+	18+	5+				P	S	P	653
ST. MARY'S HOSP-NY	Bayside	Birth-19	Birth-19	18+	5+	S	S	S	P	P	P	712
SUNY INST CHILD DEV	Binghamton	10mos-1	10mos-1			P		P	S	P		716
GREEN CHIMNEYS	Brewster	6-17	6-17	5-17		P	S	S	S	P	S	674
CLEAR VIEW SCH	Briarcliff Manor	3-21	3-21	3-21		P		S	S	S	S	664
ALBERT EINSTEIN COL	Bronx	Birth-21				P	P	P	P	P	P	651
CHILDRENS EVAL-BRONX	Bronx	Birth-21				S	S		P	P	P	661
LAVELLE SCH	Bronx	3-21	3-21			P					P	685
MORRISANIA DIAGNOST	Bronx	Birth-18	Birth-18			P		S		S	P	695
MT ST URSULA SPEECH	Bronx	3-18								P	P	696
NY INST SPECIAL ED	Bronx	5-21	3-21	5-21	3-21	P		P	P	S	P	698
ST. JOSEPH'S DEAF	Bronx	Birth-14	Birth-14	5-21		P		P	S	P	S	712
BLOCK INST	Brooklyn	Birth-21	Birth-21	Birth-21		S	S	P	P	P	S	655
CONNIE LEKAS SCH	Brooklyn	14-21	14-21	14-21		S			P	P		656
HEBREW ACAD-SPECIAL	Brooklyn	Birth-21	5-21	Birth-21	5-21			S	S	S	S	676
KINGSBROOK	Brooklyn	Birth-18	Birth-18	Birth-18	Birth-18	P	P	P	P	P	P	684
LEAGUE TREATMENT	Brooklyn	2½-21	2½-21					P	S	S	S	686
LI COL HOSP-LAMM	Brooklyn	All Ages				P	P	P	P	P	P	690
MAIMONIDES MED CTR	Brooklyn	All Ages				S	S	S	P	P	P	692
MARY MCDOWELL CTR	Brooklyn	5-12	5-12			S		S	S	S	S	693
OHEL CHILDREN'S HOME	Brooklyn	7-18	7-18	10-21		P		P	S	S	P	703
ST FRANCIS DE SALES	Brooklyn	Birth-14	Birth-14	Birth-14		P			P	P		711
BUFFALO ST COL-SLHC	Buffalo	All Ages	All Ages			S		S		S		656
CANTALICIAN CTR	Buffalo	Birth-21	Birth-21	Birth-21		P	S		P	P	P	657
CHILD ADOLESCENT	Buffalo	Birth-21	Birth-21					P				661
ROBT WARNER REHAB	Buffalo	Birth-22	Birth-22			P			P	P	P	662

Program	Town	Females		Males		Clinic	Blind	Deaf	Diabetes	Emot Disturb	HIV/AIDS	LD	MR	Ortho/Neuro	PDD	Speech	Page
		Res	Day	Res	Day												
NY ST MARY'S SCH DEAF	Buffalo	5-21	Birth-21	5-21	Birth-21			P									713
WOMEN/CHILDREN'S-BUF	Buffalo					Birth-21	S	P		S		P	S	P	P	P	727
ONTARIO COUNTY MHC	Canandaigua					All Ages				P		P					704
EDWIN GOULD ACAD	Chestnut Ridge	12-20		12-20						P							669
SAGAMORE CHILDREN'S	Dix Hills	8-18	8-18	8-18	8-18	8-18				P		S					709
CHILDREN'S VILLAGE	Dobbs Ferry			5-15						P		P					663
ST CHRISTOPHERS	Dobbs Ferry	12-21	12-18	12-21	12-18					P		S					711
PATHFINDER VILLAGE	Edmeston	5+	5-21	5+	5-21								P				704
LONG ISLAND COUNSEL	Elmont					All Ages				P		P					691
LOWELL SCH	Flushing		5-21		5-21					S		P				P	691
QUEENS COL-SPCH LANG	Flushing					All Ages										P	706
HENRY YOUNGERMAN CTR	Fredonia					All Ages				S		S	S	S		P	717
WOODWARD CHILDREN'S	Freeport		5-21		5-21	5-21							S	S		S	727
GEO JR REPUBLIC	Freeville	12-18		12-18						P		P		S			673
ADELPHI UNIV LD PRGM	Garden City	17+	17+	17+	17+							P					650
LOCHLAND SCHOOL	Geneva	18+		18+									P				690
SCH FOR LANGUAGE/COM	Glen Cove	2-12	2-12		2-12			S		P		P	P	P	P	P	715
FAMILY FOUNDATION	Hancock	13-19		13-19						P		P					670
CTR FOR DISCOVERY	Harris	5+	3+	5+	3+		P	P					P	P			658
LANGUAGE & LEARNING	Harrison					3-21				S		P	S			P	685
CHILDREN'S SCH-HAWTH	Hawthorne		Birth-5		Birth-5								P	P	P	S	663
HAWTHORNE CDS	Hawthorne		Birth-21		Birth-21					P			P	P	P		676
HOFSTRA U SPEECH	Hempstead					All Ages										P	678
ACHIEVEMENT CTR-NY	Horseheads					4+						P					650

Facility	Location	Age	Age	Emphasis	Index
COARC-STARTING PLACE	Hudson	3-5	3-5	S P S	665
FRANZISKA RACKER	Ithaca	Birth-5	Birth-5	P P P P P S S	672
ITHACA COL-SIR ALEX	Ithaca		Birth-21	P P S S	681
LEXINGTON SCH DEAF	Jackson Heights	Birth-21	Birth-21	S S S S	687
QUEENS CTRS PROGRESS	Jamaica	All Ages	All Ages	P P	706
UCP OF QUEENS	Jamaica	Birth-21	Birth-21	S S P P P P	723
SUMMIT-JAMAICA	Jamaica Estates	7-21	7-21	P P P	720
WCA HOSPITAL	Jamestown	All Ages	All Ages	P S S P	727
HANDICAPPED OF S NY	Johnson City	4-21	Birth-5 4-21	P S P S P P	675
FOUR WINDS WESTCHEST	Katonah	5+	5+	P P	672
UCP OF ULSTER COUNTY	Kingston	5+	Birth-21 5+	P S P P	721
ULSTER COUNTY	Kingston		Birth-18	P P P	722
LAKE GROVE SCH	Lake Grove	10-21	10-21	P P S	684
LD ASSOCIATES	Latham		All Ages	S S S P	686
N SHORE U NEUROPSYCH	Manhasset		Birth-5	P P P	702
N SHORE SPEECH HEAR	Manhasset		All Ages All Ages	P P P	702
EDUC LEARN EXPER	Middletown	5-21	5-21	S S S S S P P	669
MILL NECK MANOR SCH	Mill Neck	Birth-21	Birth-21	P S S	695
KARAFIN SCH	Mount Kisco	13-21	13-21	P P	682
LIVINGSTON-WYOMING	Mount Morris	6-16		P	690
ST URSULA LEARN CTR	Mount Vernon	6-16	6-16	P P S	713
ST AGATHA HOME	Nanuet	8-18	8-18	P P	710
CLEARY SCH FOR DEAF	Nesconset	Birth-21	Birth-21	P S	665
JAWONIO	New City	Birth-21	Birth-21	P S S	681
LI JEWISH MED-HEAR	New Hyde Park	Birth-21	Birth-21	P S S P	691
SCHNEIDER HOSP	New Hyde Park	Birth-5	3-21	P P P P	714

Program	Town	Females Res	Females Day	Males Res	Males Day	Clinic	Blind	Deaf	Diabetes	Emot Disturb	HIV/AIDS	LD	MR	Ortho/Neuro	PDD	Speech	Page
NY SUNY-NEW PALTZ SHC	New Paltz					All Ages										P	717
HALLEN SCH	New Rochelle		5-21		5-21		P			S		S	P	P	P	P	675
ASSOC HELP-RETARDED	New York	9+	All Ages	9+	All Ages	All Ages	S	S		S		S	P	P	P	S	653
BETH ISRAEL PSYCHIAT	New York					All Ages				P		P	S	S	S	S	655
CHILDREN'S HEARING	New York					2-18		P				S				S	662
CHURCHILL	New York		5-21		5-21							P				P	664
HERBERT G. BIRCH	New York	4+	Birth-16	4+	Birth-16					S		S	P	P	P	S	678
HUNTER COL CTR	New York					All Ages						P		S	P	P	680
INTL CTR-DISABLED	New York					2½-18		P		P		P		S	P	P	680
KENNEDY CHILD STUDY	New York		Birth-5		Birth-5	Birth-21				S			P	S			682
HARD OF HEARING-NY	New York					All Ages	S	P								P	685
LENOX HILL COMM DIS	New York					All Ages		P				P			P	P	687
LIFESPIRE	New York	18+	18+	18+	18+								P				688
LIGHTHOUSE INTL	New York		All Ages		All Ages		P										689
MT SINAI PSYCHIATRY	New York					5-18	S		S	P		P	S	S	S	S	696
MT SINAI COMM DIS	New York					All Ages		P				P		S	S		696
NYCORNELL HEAR SPCH	New York					All Ages		P							P	P	698
NY PRESBY MED CTR	New York					All Ages		P		S		S			S	P	698
NYU CHILD STUDY CTR	New York					Birth-24				P		P					700
NORTHSIDE CHILD DEV	New York		9mos-8		9mos-8	5-17				P		P			P	P	702
PARKSIDE SCH	New York		5-11		5-11					P		P			P	P	704
RITA & STANLEY	New York			16-21						P		P					707
ROBT L STEVENSON-NY	New York		12-18		12-18					S		P					707
ST VINCENT'S MED CTR	New York					3-18				P		P		S	S		714

Program	Location	Ages	Index
STEPHEN GAYNOR	New York	5-13	719
UCP OF NEW YORK CITY	New York	All Ages	721
WINSTON PREP	New York	11-19	726
YAI NATIONAL	New York	21+ / All Ages	728
WESTCHESTER EXCEPT	North Salem	5-21	725
REHABILITATION CTR	Olean	6wks+ / 5+	706
UPSTATE HOMES	Oneonta	5-21 / 3-21	724
ROCKLAND PSYCH CTR	Orangeburg	11-18 / 5-18	709
ADVOCACY & RESOURCE	Plattsburgh	All Ages	651
BEHAV HEALTH SVCS N	Plattsburgh	4-12 / 5-17	654
SUNY-PLATTSBURGH-SPE	Plattsburgh	All Ages	718
EDENWALD CTR	Pleasantville	6-18	668
PLEASANTVILLE COTTGE	Pleasantville	7-15	705
MARYHAVEN CTR-HOPE	Port Jefferson	5-21	694
ST CHARLES HOSP	Port Jefferson	Birth-18	711
NASSAU LEARNING CTR	Port Washington	15-21 / 15+	697
HUDSON VALLEY LEARN	Poughkeepsie	6+	679
LIFELINE CENTER	Queens Village	2-18	688
DIAGNOSTIC LEARN CTR	Queensbury	All Ages	668
PROSPECT CHILD & FAM	Queensbury	2-21	705
DEVEREUX-NY	Red Hook	5-21	667
ASTOR HOME	Rhinebeck	5-12 / 2-12 / Birth-18	654
CP ROCHESTER	Rochester	Birth-5 / Birth-18	666
CRESTWOOD CHILD CTR	Rochester	5-17 / 3-21 / Birth-21	666
HILLSIDE CTR	Rochester	3-21	678
NORMAN HOWARD SCH	Rochester	11-18	700

Program	Town	Females Res	Females Day	Males Res	Males Day	Clinic	Blind	Deaf	Diabetes	Emot Disturb	HIV/AIDS	LD	MR	Ortho/Neuro	PDD	Speech	Page
NY RIT INSTIT FOR DEAF	Rochester	18+		18+				P									708
ROCHESTER MENT HLTH	Rochester					Birth-18				P							708
ROCHESTER SCH-DEAF	Rochester	Birth-21	Birth-21	Birth-21	Birth-21			P		S		S	S	S		S	708
ST JOSEPH'S VILLA	Rochester	13-17	14-18	11-17	14-18					P		P	P	P			712
HOLY CHILDHOOD	Rochester		5+		5+	All Ages							P		P		715
CENTRAL NY DEV DISAB	Rome	All Ages	All Ages	All Ages	All Ages	All Ages	S			S		S	P	P	P	S	660
NY STATE SCH-DEAF	Rome	5-21	3-21	5-21	3-21		S	P	S			S	S	S		S	700
UCP-NASSAU COUNTY	Roosevelt		All Ages		All Ages	All Ages				S			P	P	P	P	722
CHILD SCH/LEGACY HS	Roosevelt Island	5-21	5-21		5-21					P		P		S		P	661
NORTH SHORE CHILD-NY	Roslyn Heights					Birth-24				P		P	P	P		P	701
N SHORE LEARN ASSOC	Roslyn Heights					6-21				S		P		S			701
UCP-WESTCHESTER CTY	Rye Brook	3-21	3-21		3-21		P	P		P		P	P	P	P	P	723
ADIRONDACK LEADERS	Saranac	13-18		13-18						P		P		S			650
FOUR WINDS SARATOGA	Saratoga Springs	5+		5+		5+				P							671
LEEWAY SCH	Sayville		Birth-14		Birth-14					S		P	S			P	687
SUNNYVIEW REHAB	Schenectady	All Ages	All Ages	All Ages	All Ages								P		P	721
OAK HILL SCH	Scotia	7-14	7-14		7-14				P								703
LITTLE VILLAGE SCH	Seaford		Birth-12		Birth-12		S	S		S		P	P	P	P	P	689
SILVER CREEK	Silver Creek		Birth-5		Birth-5			P		S		P	S	S	P		716
DEVEL DISABIL INST	Smithtown	5-21	13-21	5-21	13-21								P		P		667
GOW	South Wales			12-18								P					674
MARTIN DE PORRES SCH	Springfield Gardens	7-21		7-21						P		P	P	S	P		693
ANDERSON SCH	Staatsburg	5-21	5-21	5-21	5-21		S	S		S		S	S	S	P	S	652
GELLER HOUSE	Staten Island	11-15	11-15	11-15						P	S	P					673

Program	City	Ages	Emphasis	Page
STATEN ISLAND MH SOC	Staten Island	5-18 / Birth-18	P S S S	719
VARIETY CHILD LEARN	Syosset	Birth-7	P P P P	724
ENABLE	Syracuse	All Ages	S P S S P	670
SUNY-UPSTATE MED	Syracuse	All Ages	P P P	718
SUMMIT-NYACK	Upper Nyack	14-21	P S	720
ARC-ONEIDA LEWIS	Utica	18+ / All Ages	S S S S	652
CENTRAL ASSOC-BLIND	Utica	3-5	P S S S S S	660
HOUSE-GOOD SHEPHERD	Utica	6-18 / 6-17	S S P S S	679
MERCY NORTHERN NY	Watertown	All Ages	P S	694
HELEN HAYES HOSPITAL	West Haverstraw	All Ages	P P P	677
ST CABRINI HOME	West Park	12-21	P P	710
W NY CHILDRENS PSYCH	West Seneca	4-18	P P	725
BURKE REHAB HOSPITAL	White Plains	All Ages	P P P	657
NY SCH FOR THE DEAF	White Plains	10-21 / 3-21	P S S	699
WINDWARD-NY	White Plains	6-15	P P	726
GATEWAY LONGVIEW	Williamsville	9-21 / Birth-12	P P	672
CTR FOR DEV DISABIL	Woodbury	5-21	P P	658
NEW INTERDISCIPLINAR	Yaphank	Birth-5	S P S S	697
FERNCLIFF MANOR	Yonkers	Birth-21	S S S S S S	670
JULIA DYCKMAN ANDRUS	Yonkers	5-14	P P P	681
NORTH CAROLINA				
DEV EVAL CTR-ASHEVIL	Asheville	Birth-5	P P P S P P	734
OLSON HUFF CHILD DEV	Asheville	Birth-18	S S P P P P	743
ORTON ACAD	Asheville	10-18	P P S P	743
SOAR-NC	Balsam	8-18	P P	746
STONE MTN SCH	Black Mountain	11-16	P S P	745

Program	Town	Females Res	Females Day	Males Res	Males Day	Clinic	Blind	Deaf	Diabetes	Emot Disturb	HIV/AIDS	LD	MR	Ortho/Neuro	PDD	Speech	Page
NC ECKERD YOUTH-NC	Boomer	10-17		10-17						P		S					738
APPAL ST U-COMM DIS	Boone					All Ages		P		S		S	S	S		P	729
JOHN UMSTEAD HOSP	Butner	6+		6+						P							741
DIV AUTISTIC & COMM	Chapel Hill		All Ages		All Ages	All Ages									P		734
U NC DEVELOPMENT	Chapel Hill		Birth-20		Birth-20	All Ages						P	P	P			747
ALEXANDER YOUTH	Charlotte	5-18	5-18	5-18	5-18					P		S					729
CHILD FAMILY DEVELOP	Charlotte					Birth-18		S		P		P	S	P	S		731
COMPREHENSIVE ED	Charlotte		6-18		6-18	6-18				P		P	S	S	S		732
THOMPSON CHILDREN'S	Charlotte	6-12	6-14	6-12	6-14	Birth-18				P		P	P	P		S	747
GASTON DAY CTR	Dallas	2-21	2-21		2-21								P				738
CONCERN OF DURHAM	Durham	12-18		12-18						P		P		P	P		732
DUKE U MED CTR-AUD	Durham					Birth-21		P		P	P		P	P	P	P	735
DUKE U MED CTR-SLP	Durham					1-18				P	P			P	S	P	735
HILL CTR	Durham		5-19		5-19							S				S	740
CHILDREN'S DEV SERVS	Fayetteville					Birth-5	S	S		P		S	S	S		S	731
GATEWAY EDUC CTR	Greensboro		Birth-22		Birth-22			S					P	P		S	739
GUILFORD CTR	Greensboro	13+	All Ages	13+	All Ages		S	S		S		S	P	S		S	739
GUILFORD DAY SCH	Greensboro		6-20		6-20					S		P		S			740
UNC-GREENSBORO S & H	Greensboro					All Ages		S		S		P	S	S		P	748
ECU DEVELOPMENTAL	Greenville					Birth-6	S	S				P	P	S		P	736
ECU SPEECH-LANG/HEAR	Greenville					All Ages		P				S	S	S		P	736
PITT COUNTY MEMORIAL	Greenville					All Ages	P	P		P		P	P	P		P	744
MHS OF CATAWBA CNTY	Hickory	Birth-18	Birth-18		Birth-18	All Ages	P			P		P	P	P		P	741
PIEDMONT SCH	High Point	6-13			6-13							P					743

Facility	Location	Age Range										Page
CAROBELL	Hubert	All Ages		S	S		S		S		S	730
CASWELL CTR	Kinston	16+		S	S	S	P	P	S	P	S	730
SE REGIONAL MHC	Lumberton	Birth-18		S	S	P	P		S	S	P	745
NC SCH FOR THE DEAF	Morganton	5-21 / Birth-21		P	S			S	P			742
WESTERN CAROLINA CTR	Morganton	3+ / Birth-5	Birth-5	S	S	P	P		S	P	S	748
SUWS-CAROLINAS	Old Fort	13-18	13-18		P	P	P		P	P	P	746
ACHIEVEMENT SCH	Raleigh	6-20	6-20			P	S					729
DOROTHEA DIX	Raleigh	2-18			P	S	P		S			734
EASTER SEALS UCP-NC	Raleigh	Birth-18	Birth-18	Birth-18	S	P	P	P	P	P	P	737
KANT & ASSOC	Raleigh	5-18		P	P			P				741
NCSU DIAGNOST TEACH	Raleigh	3-18		P	P			P				742
SILBER PSYCHOLOGICAL	Raleigh	2-26		P	P			P	S			744
COVE CREEK CTR	Sugar Grove	18-25	16-25		S	P	S	P	S	S	S	733
E NC SCH FOR DEAF	Wilson	5-21	5-21	S	S	P	S		S	S	S	737
CHILDREN'S CTR-DISAB	Winston-Salem	Birth-11	Birth-11	S	S		S		P	P	S	731
NORTH DAKOTA												
ND SCH FOR THE DEAF	Devils Lake	Birth-21	Birth-21	Birth-21	P	S		S	S		S	752
ALTRU PEDIATRIC	Grand Forks	Birth-21		S	S	S	P	P	P	P	P	750
ND VISION SERVCS SCH	Grand Forks	All Ages	All Ages	P			P					752
U ND SPEECH LANG	Grand Forks	All Ages		P			P			P		753
ANNE CARLSEN CTR	Jamestown	Birth-21	Birth-21	Birth-21	P	P	P	P	P	P	P	750
SPCH/HEAR-JAMESTOWN	Jamestown	All Ages	All Ages	P	S		S	S	P	S	P	753
DAKOTA RANCH	Minot	10-18	10-18		P		P					751
MINOT INFANT DEVEL	Minot	Birth-3	Birth-3	P			P	P	P	P	S	751
MINOT ST U COMM DIS	Minot	All Ages		S	S		S	S	S	S	S	751
NORTHWEST HUMAN SVC	Williston	All Ages	All Ages	P	P		P	P	S	P	P	752

OHIO

Program	Town	Females Res	Females Day	Males Res	Males Day	Clinic	Blind	Deaf	Diabetes	Emot Disturb	HIV/AIDS	LD	MR	Ortho/Neuro	PDD	Speech	Page
AKRON SPEECH & READ	Akron					All Ages				S		P	S	S		P	756
BLICK CLINIC	Akron	18+	18+	18+	18+	All Ages	S	S		P		P	P	P	P	P	758
CHILD GUIDANCE & FAM	Akron					Birth-18				P		P	S	P	P		760
OH U SPEECH HEARING	Athens					All Ages		P						P		P	778
LOGAN COUNTY BOARD	Bellefontaine		All Ages		All Ages		S	S		S		S	P	S		S	772
BEREA CHILDRENS HOME	Berea	Birth-18	Birth-18	Birth-18	Birth-18					P							758
BOWLING GREEN U-SPCH	Bowling Green					All Ages		P					S	S		P	759
LAWRENCE SCH	Broadview Heights		6-17		6-17							P					771
N COAST TUTORING	Chagrin Falls		5-18		5-18	5-18				P		P	S	P		P	776
CAMP ALLYN	Cincinnati		18mos+		18mos+	All Ages						P	P	P			760
CHILDRENS HM CINCINN	Cincinnati		2-18		2-18					P							761
CHMC PSYCH DIV-CINCI	Cincinnati					All Ages				P		P	P				762
CINCI ASSOC-BLIND	Cincinnati		All Ages		All Ages		P	S						S	S	S	763
CINCI CHILDREN'S HOS	Cincinnati		Birth-7		Birth-7	Birth-21	P	P		S		P	P	P	P	P	763
CINCI CHILD HOSP-ORT	Cincinnati					Birth-21	P	P				P	P	P	P		764
CINCINNATI OT INSTIT	Cincinnati					All Ages	S	S		S		P	P	P	P		764
HEARING SPEECH-CINCI	Cincinnati		All Ages		All Ages	All Ages		P				S	S	S		S	770
OLYMPUS CTR	Cincinnati					5+						P		P			778
ST RITA SCH-DEAF	Cincinnati	6mos-21	6mos-21	6mos-21	6mos-21			P						S		S	780
SPRINGER SCH & CTR	Cincinnati		6-14		6-14							P					782
U CINCINNATI-MED CTR	Cincinnati					All Ages		P				S		S		P	783
ACHIEVEMENT CTRS-OH	Cleveland		Birth-21		Birth-21		S	S		S		S	P	P	P	P	754
AG BELL	Cleveland		3-12		3-12	All Ages	P	P					P	P		P	756

Organization	City											Page
BEECH BROOK	Cleveland	5-12	5-12	5-12	5-12			P			S	757
CHILDRENS AID SOC	Cleveland	5-14	5-14	5-14	5-14		P	P			P	761
CLEVELAND CLINIC	Cleveland	Birth-18	Birth-18							P		764
CLEVELAND HEARING	Cleveland			All Ages		P	S			S	S	765
CLEVELAND SIGHT CTR	Cleveland	Birth-5	Birth-5	All Ages					P			765
CLEVELAND ST U-SHC	Cleveland			All Ages		S	S	S		S	S	765
CUYAHOGA COUNTY MR	Cleveland	13+	All Ages	All Ages	13+	S	S	P	S	P	P S	766
ELEANOR GERSON SCH	Cleveland	13-21	13-21				P	P				767
HELP FOUNDATION	Cleveland	9-22	3-12	3-12	9-22	S	S	S	S	P	S	770
METROHEALTH MED CTR	Cleveland			Birth-18					P			774
TOWNSEND LEARNING	Cleveland			All Ages			P	P	P		P	783
CHILDHOOD LEAGUE CTR	Columbus	Birth-6	Birth-6			P	P	P			P	761
COLUMBUS HEARING	Columbus	Birth-21	Birth-21			P						766
GRANT/RIVERSIDE CTRS	Columbus			All Ages			S	P	S		S	768
HANNAH NEIL	Columbus	8-12					P	P				769
MARBURN	Columbus	6-18	6-18				P	P				772
OH SCH FOR THE DEAF	Columbus	5-22	5-22			P	P	P				777
OH STATE SCH-BLIND	Columbus	8-21	5-21	3-18		P	S	S	S		S	778
OSU MEDICAL CTR	Columbus	3-18	12-18	All Ages		S S	S	P	S		S	779
ST VINCENT FAMILY	Columbus	6-12	3-12	Birth-18		P	S	P	S		S	781
AIM FOR HANDICAPPED	Dayton	All Ages	All Ages			P	P	P	P		P	755
CHILDREN'S MED CTR	Dayton		4-18					P				762
MARY MAVEC SCH	Euclid	5+	5+				P					774
BUCKEYE RANCH	Grove City	10-18	13-18	6-18		P	P	P	P		S	759
WARRENSVILLE DEV CTR	Highland Hills	19+	19+			S	S	S	S		S	783
KENT ST U-SPEECH	Kent			Birth-18		P	P	P	P		P	771

Program	Town	Females Res	Females Day	Males Res	Males Day	Clinic	Blind	Deaf	Diabetes	Emot Disturb	HIV/ AIDS	LD	MR	Ortho/ Neuro	PDD	Speech	Page
OH FAIRFIELD CENTER	Lancaster													P			767
LIMA SPEECH HEARING	Lima		18+		18+	All Ages		P						P		P	772
MARIMOR SCH	Lima		6-22		6-22					S			P	S			773
ST RITA'S MED CTR	Lima					Birth-18						P	S	P	P	S	780
JULIE BILLIART SCH	Lyndhurst		6-14		6-14							P		S	P	P	771
REHAB SERVCS-N C OH	Mansfield		Birth-6		Birth-6	All Ages	S	S		S		S	S	P	S	S	779
HATTIE LARLHAM	Mantua	Birth-26		Birth-26								P	P	P		S	769
SUNSHINE CHILDREN'S	Maumee	Birth-23		Birth-23			S	S		S		S	P	P			782
SOCIETY FOR REHAB	Mentor					All Ages		P				P		P		P	782
MIDDLEBURG EARLY EDU	Middleburg Heights		1½-6		1½-6					S		P	P	P	P	P	775
MT VERNON CENTER	Mount Vernon	14-22		14-22									P	P		P	775
FILLING	Napoleon	All Ages		All Ages									P	P			768
MT ALOYSIUS	New Lexington			18+									P	P			775
FAIRHAVEN	Niles		All Ages		All Ages								P	P		P	767
MIAMI U SPEECH HEAR	Oxford					All Ages		P						P		P	774
NICHOLAS SCH	Piqua		5-14		5-14							P	S	P	P		776
BELLEFAIRE JCB	Shaker Heights	12-23		12-23						P		S	S			S	757
YOUTH DEV CORP	South Point	Birth-18		Birth-18						P							784
OESTERLEN SVCS	Springfield	12-18		12-18		5-20				P		S					777
BETTY JANE	Tiffin	3-5		3-5		All Ages				P		S	S	P	P		758
MARY IMMACULATE SCH	Toledo	6-14		6-14						S		P		S	P		773
CHILDRENS REHAB	Warren		Birth-18	Birth-18								S	S	P		P	762
ADRIEL SCH	West Liberty	11-18	5-18	11-18	5-18					P		S	P	P	P		755
HALLENBECK PSYCHOED	Willoughby					All Ages				P		P	S	S			768

OKLAHOMA

Facility	City	Age Range	Program Emphasis (P/S marks, left→right)	Page
ACLD SCH & LEARN CTR	Youngstown		S … S S S … P S S … S	754
CHILDREN'S CENTER-OK	Bethany	Birth-18 / Birth-18	S S … S P S S	785
GATESWAY FOUNDATION	Broken Arrow	18+ / 18+	P … P	786
JANE BROOKS SCH-DEAF	Chickasha	3-14 / 6mos-14 / 3-14 / 6mos-14	P	787
JOHN A MORRIS	Chickasha	All Ages	P … S S … P	787
THAYNE A. HEDGES	Enid	All Ages	S S … S S … P	790
LOGAN CTY GUIDANCE	Guthrie	Birth-18	P … P P … P	788
CARL ALBERT COMM MHC	McAlester	8-18	P S … P	785
OK SCH FOR THE BLIND	Muskogee	3-21 / 2-21 / 3-21	P … S S S … S S	788
JD MCCARTY CTR	Norman	Birth-21 / Birth-21	S S … S P P P P	786
OKLAHOMA YOUTH CTR	Norman	5-18 / 5-18	P … P	789
DALE ROGERS	Oklahoma City	18+ / 18+	P … P	785
PAULA STANFORD'S HRN	Oklahoma City	6+	S S … S P S	790
U OF OK HEALTH SCI	Oklahoma City	Birth-14	S S … P P P P	791
U OK HEALTH SCI CTR	Oklahoma City	All Ages	P … P P P P	791
EDWIN FAIR MH CTR	Ponca City	Birth-18	P … P P S	786
OK ST SPEECH-LANG	Stillwater	All Ages	P … P S	789
OK SCH FOR THE DEAF	Sulphur	2½-21 / 2½-21 / 2½-21	P … P	789
TOWN & COUNTRY SCH	Tulsa	5-18 / 5-18	P … P	791
U OF TULSA-MARY CHAP	Tulsa	All Ages	S P … S S … S P	792
NORTHWEST BEHAV HLTH	Woodward	8+	P … P	788

OREGON

Facility	City	Age Range	Program Emphasis (P/S marks, left→right)	Page
CLATSOP BEHAVIORAL	Astoria	All Ages	P … P	794
RIGGS INSTITUTE	Beaverton	5+	P	800
BRIDGES ACAD	Bend	13-17	P … P	793

Program	Town	Females Res	Females Day	Males Res	Males Day	Clinic	Blind	Deaf	Diabetes	Emot Disturb	HIV/AIDS	LD	MR	Ortho/Neuro	PDD	Speech	Page
OR NORTHSTAR CTR	Bend	18-24		18-24					S	P	S	P			S	S	796
EUGENE HEARING	Eugene					All Ages		P						P	P	P	795
JOSEPHINE CTY CLINIC	Grants Pass					All Ages			S					P	P		796
SCAR/JASPER MTN	Jasper	4-12	6-12	4-12	6-12			S		P		P	S	P	P	P	800
DRAGONFLY ADVENTURES	Klamath Falls	18+		18+						P	P	P					794
CHRISTIE SCH	Marylhurst	8-18		8-18						P		P		S			793
HEARING & SPEECH INS	Portland	2-5	2-5	2-5	2-5	Birth-18		P		S			S	P		P	795
MUSCULAR DYSTROPHY	Portland					All Ages								P	P		796
OPEN MEADOW ALT SCHS	Portland		10-18		10-18								P		P		797
PORTLAND HABILITAT	Portland		18-65		18-65								P	S			799
PORTLAND ST U-SHC	Portland					All Ages		P					S	S		S	799
RANCH HOUSE	Portland			14-17					S	P		S	S				799
SHRINERS HOSP-OR	Portland	Birth-21		Birth-21		Birth-21								P			801
THOMAS A EDISON HS	Portland	13-18	13-18	13-18	13-18					S		P		S			801
WAVERLY CHILDREN'S	Portland	6-18	3-12	6-18	3-12	Birth-18				P			S	S			802
OR SCH FOR THE BLIND	Salem	5-21	5-21	5-21	5-21		P			S			S	S		S	797
OR SCH FOR THE DEAF	Salem	5-21	5-21	5-21	5-21			P		P			S	S			798
OR STATE HOSP-CHILD	Salem	14-18		14-18			S	S		P		P	S			S	798
EDGEFIELD CHILD CTR	Troutdale	6-12	6-12	6-12	6-12					P		S					795
PENNSYLVANIA																	
EASTER SEALS E PA	Allentown	Birth-10	Birth-10	Birth-10	Birth-10	Birth-21			S				P	P	P	S	819
MERCY SPEC LEARN CTR	Allentown	1½-21	1½-21	1½-21	1½-21							S	S	S	S	S	836
CTR FOR PSYCH SRVCS	Ardmore					All Ages				P		S		P			809
MAIN LINE ACAD	Bala Cynwyd		5-21		5-21							P	P		P		834

Facility	City	Age Ranges	Program Emphasis (P/S)	Code
MELMARK HOME	Berwyn	4+, 4+, 4+, 4+, 6-21	S, S, P, S, P, S, P, S	835
LEHIGH U CENTENNIAL	Bethlehem	6-21	P, S, S, S	831
BLOOMSBURG U-SLHC	Bloomsburg	All Ages	P, P, P, P	806
BRYN MAWR CHILD STUD	Bryn Mawr	All Ages	P, P, S, P	807
BRYN MAWR HOSP YOUTH	Bryn Mawr	Birth-18	P	807
COMMUNITY CARE CONN	Butler	6-21, 6-21, 6-21, 6-21	P, P, P, P, S, P	812
IRENE STACY CENTER	Butler	6-18, 6-18	P, P, P, P	828
ROSEHILL SCHOOL	Chester Heights	10+, 10+	P, P	842
CLARION UNIV-SHC	Clarion	All Ages	P, S, S, P	811
LOURDESMONT	Clarks Summit	12-17, 12-17, 12-17	S, P, S, S	832
LANCASTER PREP SCH	Columbia	5-13, 5-13	S, P	830
ALLEGHENY VALLEY SCH	Coraopolis	6+, 21+, 6+, 21+	S, S, S, S, S	804
LENAPE VALLEY	Doylestown	All Ages	P, P	832
ELWYN	Elwyn	6+, All Ages, 6+, All Ages	S, S, S, P, P, S	820
ACHIEVEMENT CTR-ERIE	Erie	Birth-21, Birth-21	S, S, P, P, S, P	804
COMMUNITY CO DAY SCH	Erie	6-20, 6-20	P, S, S	813
DR GERTRUDE A BARBER	Erie	Birth-21, Birth-21	S, P, S, P, S	817
ERIE HOMES	Erie	All Ages, All Ages	P, P, S, P, P, S, P, S	821
SARAH REED CHILDRENS	Erie	5-18, 5-18, 3-18	P, P	845
SHRINERS-PA	Erie	Birth-18, Birth-18	P, P	847
CARSON VALLEY SCH	Flourtown	12-18, 9-18, 7-18	P, P	808
WORDSWORTH ACAD	Fort Washington	5-21, 5-21, 5-21	S, S, S	854
CAMPHILL SPECIAL SCH	Glenmoore	5-21, 5-21, 5-21	S, P, S, P, S	808
CLELIAN HEIGHTS SCH	Greensburg	5-25, 5-25, 5-25	S, P, S, S	812
FAMILY BEHAVIORAL	Greensburg	4-18	P, P, S, S, S	821
UCP OF WESTERN PA	Greensburg	Birth-3, Birth-3	P, P, P, P, P, P	850

Program	Town	Females Res	Females Day	Males Res	Males Day	Clinic	Blind	Deaf	Diabetes	Emot Disturb	HIV/AIDS	LD	MR	Ortho/Neuro	PDD	Speech	Page
PA GEORGE JUNIOR	Grove City			9-18										P			823
HAMBURG CTR	Hamburg	18-84		18-84						P		P		P			825
PINNACLEHEALTH SHC	Harrisburg					All Ages		P					P		P	P	840
STRATFORD FRIENDS	Havertown		5-13		5-13							P					848
HELPING HANDS SOC	Hazleton		Birth-6		Birth-6	6-12						P	S	P	P	P	825
COMM COUNSELING CTR	Hermitage					All Ages				P							813
QUAKER SCH-HORSHAM	Horsham		6-14		6-14							P				S	841
LANCASTER CLEFT PAL	Lancaster					All Ages							S	P	P	P	830
MARGARET J KAY	Lancaster					All Ages				P	S	P	P	P	P	P	834
SCHREIBER PEDIATRIC	Lancaster					Birth-21	S	S				P	P	P	P	P	846
WOODS SERVICES	Langhorne	5+		5+			S	S		P		P	P	P	P	S	853
QUDC SCH	Levittown		4½-16		4½-16								P		P		841
HILLSIDE SCH	Macungie		5-13		5-13					S		P					826
DEVEREUX BENETO CTR	Malvern	4-18	6-17	4-18	6-17					P		S	S				816
PHELPS	Malvern	12-18			12-18							P				S	840
CHILD GUID RESOURCE	Media		Birth-21		Birth-21					P							810
DIVERSIFIED HUMAN	Monessen		Birth-3		Birth-3								P		P		817
JANUS SCH	Mount Joy		6-19		6-19							P	P				828
MCGUIRE MEMORIAL	New Brighton	3+	3+	3+	3+		S	S		S			P	S	S	S	835
HUMAN SVCS CTR	New Castle					All Ages				P			P				827
C MONTGOMERY MH/MR	Norristown					All Ages				P					S		809
PATHWAY-PA	Norristown		5-21		5-21					P		P		P	P	S	838
ARCHBISHOP RYAN SCH	Norwood		Birth-14		Birth-14			P				P					805
KIDSPEACE	Orefield	6-18	10-18	6-18	10-18	All Ages				P		P	S	P	P	S	830

Program	Location					Emphasis							Page
CROSSROADS-PA	Paoli			5-15						P			814
DE VALLEY FRIENDS	Paoli	5-21	12-19	12-19						P			815
ROYER GREAVES SCH	Paoli	5-21	5-21	5-21		P	P		S	S	S	S	842
VANGUARD SCH/PEDIAT	Paoli	3-21	3-21	3-21	All Ages				S	P	P	P	851
BRIDGE	Philadelphia	14-18	All Ages	All Ages						P			807
DELTA SCH	Philadelphia	4-21	4-21	4-21						P	P	P	815
EASTER SEALS SE PA	Philadelphia	2-8	2-8	2-8	All Ages	S	S		S	S	P	P	819
GREEN TREE SCH	Philadelphia	3-21	3-21	3-21						P	S	P	824
HMS SCH	Philadelphia	2-21	2-21	2-21		S	S		S	S	S	P	826
MILL CREEK SCH	Philadelphia	12-20	12-20	12-20					P				837
NORTHWESTERN HS-PHIL	Philadelphia	Birth-5	Birth-5							P			837
WOODHAVEN CTR	Philadelphia	10+	10+	10+						P			837
OVERBROOK SCH BLIND	Philadelphia	7-21	3-21	3-21		P				P			838
PA SCH FOR THE DEAF	Philadelphia	2-21	2-21	2-21			P						839
SHRINERS-PHILLY	Philadelphia	Birth-18	Birth-18	Birth-18	Birth-18				P				847
TEMPLE U SPEECH HEAR	Philadelphia				All Ages							P	849
AC-ACLD/TILLOTSON	Pittsburgh	7-21	7-21	7-21				S		P	S	S	803
ACHIEVA EARLY INT	Pittsburgh	Birth-3	Birth-3	Birth-3					P		P		803
BRADLEY CTR	Pittsburgh	10-17½		6-17½		P	P	P	P	P	S	P	806
CHILDREN'S HOSP-PITT	Pittsburgh		Birth-18		Birth-18		P			S	S	P	810
CHILDREN'S INSTITUTE	Pittsburgh	1-40	1-40	2-21	All Ages	S	S		S	P	S		811
CRAIG ACAD	Pittsburgh	6-21	6-21						P				814
DEPAUL INSTITUTE	Pittsburgh	Birth-21	Birth-21	Birth-21			P		S		P		816
EASTER SEAL-W PA	Pittsburgh	2-8	2-8	2-8		S			S		P	S	818
FAMILYLINKS	Pittsburgh	13-18	8-18	3-18	3-18				P	P	P	P	822
LIFES WORK WEST PA	Pittsburgh	13-18	16+	16+	All Ages				P		P		832

Program	Town	Females Res	Females Day	Males Res	Males Day	Clinic	Blind	Deaf	Diabetes	Emot Disturb	HIV/AIDS	LD	MR	Ortho/Neuro	PDD	Speech	Page
PA																	
MERCY HOSP SPEECH	Pittsburgh					All Ages						P				P	836
REHAB SPECIALISTS	Pittsburgh					All Ages		S				S	S	S	S	P	842
ST ANTHONY SCH PRGMS	Pittsburgh		5-21		5-21								P	S	P		843
SOUTHWOOD PSYCH HOSP	Pittsburgh	5-18	8-18	5-18	8-18					P			P		P	S	848
THREE RIVERS YOUTH	Pittsburgh	12-21		12-21						P							849
UPMC-JOHN MERCK PRGM	Pittsburgh	3+	6-16	3+	6-16	All Ages	S	S		P			P	S	P	S	850
WESLEY ACAD	Pittsburgh		9-21		9-21					P		P					851
W PA SCH-BLIND	Pittsburgh	2-21	2-21	2-21	2-21		P							S	P	S	852
W PA SCH FOR DEAF	Pittsburgh	2-21	2-21	2-21	2-21			P					S	S			853
ST JOSEPH CTR	Pottsville		5-21		5-21					P		P	P	P	P	P	843
DICKINSON MENT HLTH	Ridgway					All Ages				P							817
HILL TOP PREP	Rosemont		11-21		11-21							P					825
SAINT EDMOND'S HOME	Rosemont	Birth-21		Birth-21			S	S					P	S		S	843
ALLIED DE PAUL SCH	Scranton		6-15		6-15					P		P	P	S			805
FRIENDSHIP HOUSE	Scranton	6-18	3-15	6-18	3-15					P							823
KEYSTONE COMMUNITY	Scranton	9-18	9-18	9-18	9-18					P		S	P	S	P		829
ST JOSEPH'S CTR-PA	Scranton	All Ages	21+	All Ages	21+	All Ages	S	S		S		S	P	S	P	S	844
SCRANTON COUNSELING	Scranton					All Ages				P		P	P	S	P		846
SCRANTON SCH-DEAF	Scranton	5-21	Birth-21	5-21	Birth-21			P				S	S	S			847
PENN FOUNDATION	Sellersville					All Ages				P		P	S		P		839
EDUC CTR-WATSON INST	Sewickley		3-21		3-21									P	P		820
LAUGHLIN CHILDREN'S	Sewickley					1½-18		S	S	P			S	S	P	S	831
JOHN PAUL II CTR	Shillington		3-21		3-21					P			P	P	P		829
DON GUANELLA SCH	Springfield	6-21		6-21						S		S	P	S	S	S	818

Program	City	Ages	Ages									Page
CP ASSOC-DE COUNTY	Swarthmore	2-21	2-21					P	P	P	P	810
MARTHA LLOYD	Troy	15+	15+	S	S	S	P	P	P	P	S	S	834
ST LUCY DAY SCH	Upper Darby	Birth-14	Birth-14		P		S					845
WEST CHESTER U-SPCH	West Chester	All Ages		P		P	S		S		P	852
WHITE HAVEN CENTER	White Haven	9+	9+					P				853
HOPE ENTERPRISES	Williamsport	All Ages 3+	All Ages 3+			P		P		P		827
LYCOMING COUNTY CCS	Williamsport	3-6	3-6	S			S		S	P	S	833
OUR LADY-CONFIDENCE	Willow Grove	5-21	5-21				S		P	P		838
INSTS-HUMAN POTENT	Wyndmoor	Birth-20	Birth-20	P	P	S	P		P	P	P	827
ST. KATHERINE DAY	Wynnewood	4½-21	4½-21				S		P	S	S	844
FAMILY GUIDANCE CTR	Wyomissing	All Ages	All Ages	S	S	P	S			S	822
GLADE RUN LUTHERAN	Zelienople	6-21	6-21			P	P		S		823
RHODE ISLAND												
HARMONY HILL SCH	Chepachet	8-18	8-18			P	S		S		857
MEETING ST	East Providence	Birth-21	All Ages	S	S	S	P		P	P	859
ECKERD YOUTH-RI	Exeter	10-17				P	S			856
GRODEN CTR	Providence	12-21	3-21			S	S		P	856
HAMILTON SCH	Providence	6-14	6-14			P		P		857
HASBRO CHILDREN'S	Providence	Birth-21	Birth-21	P	P	S	P		P	P	858
RI SCH FOR THE DEAF	Providence	3-21	3-21		P	S	S		S	S	859
KENT COUNTY ARC	Warwick	All Ages	All Ages			P	S		P	S	858
SARGENT REHAB CTR	Warwick	3-21	Birth-21	S		S	P		P	P	860
SOUTH CAROLINA												
ANDERSON OCONEE	Anderson	All Ages	All Ages	P		S	S		S	P	861
CHARLES WEBB CENTER	Charleston	Birth-10	Birth-10				P		P	861
SC SCH-DEAF/BLIND-CH	Charleston	4-21 2½-21	2½-21	P	P	P	S		S	S	867

Program	Town	Females Res	Females Day	Males Res	Males Day	Clinic	Blind	Deaf	Diabetes	Emot Disturb	HIV/AIDS	LD	MR	Ortho/Neuro	PDD	Speech	Page
SC MIDLANDS REGIONAL	Columbia	1+		1+		All Ages							P	P		P	864
SANDHILLS SCH	Columbia		6-15		6-15							P	P	P		P	866
PINE GROVE	Elgin	5-18		5-18						P				P	P	P	866
PEE DEE REGIONAL CTR	Florence	All Ages		All Ages		All Ages							P		P		865
PEE DEE SHC	Florence					All Ages		P		S		P		S		P	865
GEORGETOWN COUNTY	Georgetown		Birth-6		Birth-6			P					P		P	P	863
CAMPERDOWN ACAD	Greenville		5-14		5-14							P					861
HOLLIS CENTER	Greenville		Birth-5		Birth-5								P	P			864
SPEECH, HEAR & LEARN	Greenville					All Ages		P							P	P	868
COASTAL CTR SCDDSN	Ladson	All Ages		All Ages			S	S		S		S	P	S	S	S	862
TRIDENT	Mount Pleasant		5-19		5-19							P		P			869
EDUCATION RX ASSOC	Myrtle Beach					All Ages				S		P	S	S			862
KAPABLE KIDS	Orangeburg		Birth-6		Birth-6					S			P	S	P	P	865
SCSU SPEECH-LANGUAGE	Orangeburg					All Ages		P					S	S	S	P	868
SC SCH-DEAF/BLIND-SP	Spartanburg	4-21	2½-21	4-21	2½-21		P	P	S	S		S	S	S		S	867
HIDDEN TREASURE	Taylors		5-20	5-20	5-20		S	S	S	P		P	P	P	P	P	864
GLENFOREST SCH	West Columbia		6-18		6-18							P					863
CHEROKEE CREEK SCH	Westminster			12-15						P		P	P				862
YORK PLACE	York	6-14		6-14						P		P	P		S		869
						SOUTH DAKOTA											
NORTHEAST MENT HLTH	Aberdeen					All Ages				P							871
SD SCH FOR THE BLIND	Aberdeen	5-21	Birth-21	5-21	Birth-21		P			S		S	S	S	S	S	873
SKY RANCH FOR BOYS	Camp Crook			10-18						P		P	P				872
COMMTY COUNSELING-SD	Huron					All Ages				P		P	P	P	P	P	870

Program	City	Ages						Emphasis						Page
BLACK HILLS CHILDREN	Rapid City	4-13	4-13	4-13	4-13	4-13					P	P		870
SD DEVELOPMENTAL CTR	Redfield	10+	10+				S	S	S	S	S	S	S	872
CHILDRENS CARE HOSP	Sioux Falls	Birth-21	Birth-21	Birth-21	Birth-21			S	P	P	P	P		870
SIOUX FALLS CHS	Sioux Falls	4-13	4-13	4-13	4-13		P		P					871
SIOUX VOCATIONAL	Sioux Falls	14+	14+	14+	14+		P	S	S	P	P	S		871
SD SCH FOR THE DEAF	Sioux Falls	2½-21	Birth-21	2½-21	Birth-21	Birth-21	S	P	S	S	S	S	S	873
USD SPEECH & HEARING	Vermillion	All Ages					P			P				874
TENNESSEE														
CURREY INGRAM ACAD	Brentwood	6-17	6-17					P		P	P			878
HIGH HOPES	Brentwood	Birth-6	Birth-6	Birth-6			S	S	P	P	P	P		881
ADVENT HOME YOUTH	Calhoun	12-16					P		P	P				875
SCENIC LAND SCH	Chattanooga	4-14	4-14	4-14		P	P	P	P	P	P			886
FORTWOOD MENTAL HLTH	Chattanooga	All Ages					P		P					881
ORANGE GROVE CTR	Chattanooga	14+	5+	14+	5+	S	S	S	S	P	S			884
HARRIETT COHN CTR	Clarksville	All Ages	All Ages	All Ages	All Ages			P	P					881
KING'S DAUGHTERS	Columbia	7-22	7-22	7-22	7-22		S	S	P	S	P			882
ECKERD YOUTH-TN	Deerlodge	10-17					P	S	P					880
BILANDY ACAD	Dickson	7-17					P	P	P					876
TN SCH FOR THE BLIND	Donelson	3-21	3-21	3-21	3-21	P	S	S	S	S	S	S		887
BENTON HALL SCH	Franklin	6-19	6-19	6-19			P	P	P	P	P			876
WAVES EARLY INT PRGM	Franklin	Birth-3	Birth-3		P	P	P	P	P	P	P			889
BODINE SCH	Germantown	6-18	6-18	6-18			P	P	P	P				876
BEACON SCH-TN	Greeneville	6-22	6-22	6-22		S	P	S	P	S	P			875
KIWANIC CTR	Jackson	Birth-3	Birth-3	Birth-18		S	S	S	S	S	P	P	S	882
PATHWAYS CHILD/YOUTH	Jackson	3-18					P		S					885
W TN SCH FOR DEAF	Jackson	3-13	3-13	3-13	Birth-21	P		P	P	P				890

Program	Town	Females Res	Females Day	Males Res	Males Day	Clinic	Blind	Deaf	Diabetes	Emot Disturb	HIV/AIDS	LD	MR	Ortho/Neuro	PDD	Speech	Page
TN E TN U SPEECH LANG	Johnson City					All Ages										P	879
CAMELOT SCHS-TN	Kingston	5-17	5-17	5-17	5-17				P	P	P	P		P	P	P	877
CHILD AND FAMILY TN	Knoxville	12-18		12-18		All Ages				P		S					878
E TN CHILDREN'S HOSP	Knoxville					Birth-21	P	S	S	P	S	P	P	P	P	P	879
TN SCH FOR THE DEAF	Knoxville	4-21	4-21	4-21	4-21			P									888
U OF TN-KNOX HEARING	Knoxville		9mos-18		9mos-18	All Ages		P		P			P	P	P	P	889
PENINSULA VILLAGE	Louisville	13-18		13-18						P		P					885
MEMPHIS ORAL SCH	Memphis		Birth-8		Birth-8			P									883
MIDSOUTH ARC	Memphis					All Ages							P	P	P		884
SOUTHEAST MH CTR	Memphis					5-18	S	S		P		P	S	S	S	S	886
U OF TN-BOLING CTR	Memphis					All Ages	P	P		P		P	P	P	P	P	888
MTSU-SLH CLIN	Murfreesboro					All Ages		P		P		P	P	P	P	P	883
EASTER SEALS-MCWHORT	Nashville		Birth-5		Birth-5	Birth-18						P	P	P	P	P	880
REG INTERVENTION	Nashville		Birth-5		Birth-5		S	S		S		S	S	S	S	S	885
SUSAN GRAY SCH	Nashville		Birth-3		Birth-3		S	S					P	P	P	P	887
						TEXAS											
ABILENE STATE SCH	Abilene	6+		6+									P				891
W TX REHAB CTR	Abilene					All Ages	S	S		S		S	S	P		S	933
SW ACAD LEARNING CTR	Allen		3-14		3-14							P					925
AMARILLO COL-ACCESS	Amarillo		16+		16+					P		P		P			891
GATEWAY SCH-TX	Arlington		12-19		12-19							P					905
JEAN MASSIEU ACAD	Arlington		3-22		3-22			P								P	909
AUSTIN CHILD GUIDNCE	Austin					Birth-17				P		P					892
AUSTIN CHILD PSYCH	Austin	4-18		4-18				S		P		S	S				892

Program Emphasis Index

Facility	City	Ages	Program Codes	Index
EASTER SEALS-CENT TX	Austin	All Ages	S, P, S, P	902
MARY LEE FOUNDATION	Austin	5-12 / 18+	P, P, S, S, P, P, P, P, S, P	913
OAKS TREATMENT CTR	Austin	5-17	P, S, S, S	918
SETTLEMENT HOME	Austin	7-17	P	923
TEXAS NEUROREHAB CTR	Austin	8+ / 3-21	P, S, S, S, P, P, P, S, S	928
TX SCH FOR THE BLIND	Austin	6-21	P, S, S, S, S, S, S, S, S	928
U TX SPEECH HEARING	Austin	All Ages	S, S, P	931
VIP EDUC SERVICES	Austin	5+ / 16+	P, P, P, P, S, P, P	932
BAYTOWN CTR	Baytown	16+	P, P	894
HEALTHSOUTH REHAB	Beaumont	All Ages	S, S, S, P, S, P	907
LAMAR U SPEECH-HEAR	Beaumont	All Ages	P, P	910
SHORKEY CTR	Beaumont	Birth-21	P, P, P, P	924
READ & GUIDANCE CTR	Bellaire	5+	P, P	920
UCP-GREATER HOUSTON	Bellaire	All Ages	S, S, P, S, S	930
BRENHAM STATE SCH	Brenham	6+	S, S, S, S	895
BRAZOS VALLEY REHAB	Bryan	All Ages	S, S, S, P, S	894
EXCEL ACAD	Conroe	13-18	P, P, P, P	904
C CHRISTI STATE SCH	Corpus Christi	6+	P, P	899
ARBOR ACRE PREP SCH	Dallas	4-14	S, S, S	891
AUTISTIC TREATMT CTR	Dallas	3+ / 4+	P, P, S, S, S, P, S	893
BURTIS & NOEL CTR	Dallas	1½-18	S, S, P, S, P, P	896
CALLIER COMM DISORD	Dallas	All Ages	P, P, S, P	896
CHILD & FAMILY GUID	Dallas	All Ages	P	898
DALLAS ACAD	Dallas	13-19	P, P	900
FAIRHILL SCH	Dallas	6-18	P, P	905
LUTHERAN SPEC ED-TX	Dallas	5-18	S, S, P, P, P, P, P	912

Program	Town	Females Res	Females Day	Males Res	Males Day	Clinic	Blind	Deaf	Diabetes	Emot Disturb	HIV/AIDS	LD	MR	Ortho/Neuro	PDD	Speech	Page
TX NOTRE DAME SCH-DALL	Dallas		6-21		6-21								P				917
OAK HILL ACAD-DALLAS	Dallas		3-12		3-12	3-12						P				P	918
SHELTON	Dallas		3-18		3-18	3+		S	S	S		P		S		S	923
TX SCOTTISH RITE	Dallas	Birth-18		Birth-18		Birth-18						S		P			929
UCP-DALLAS	Dallas		All Ages		All Ages								S	S	S		931
WINSTON SCH-TX	Dallas		6-19		6-19							P					934
TEXAS WOMAN'S U-SLHC	Denton					All Ages	P	P		S		S	P	P	P	P	930
U OF N TX-SPCH/HEAR	Denton					All Ages		P				S	S	S	S	P	931
EL PASO BRIDGES ACAD	El Paso		6-14		6-14							P		S			904
UTEP-SLP PRGM SHC	El Paso					All Ages		P		S		S	S		P	P	932
HIGH FRONTIER	Fort Davis	12-18		12-18													907
CHILD STUDY CTR	Fort Worth		1-7		1-7	Birth-21				P		P	P	P	P	P	899
EASTER SEALS NW TX	Fort Worth					3+			S			S	P	P		P	903
HILL SCH OF FT WORTH	Fort Worth		7-18		7-18					P		P		P			907
KEY SCH	Fort Worth		4-18		4-18			S				P					910
OVERTON S & L CTR	Fort Worth					All Ages						P	S	P	P	P	919
PSYCH CLINIC-FT WORT	Fort Worth					10-25				P		P					920
TCU-MILLER SHC	Fort Worth					All Ages		P		S		S	S	S			927
TCU STARPOINT SCH	Fort Worth		6-12		6-12							P					927
U OF TX-AUDIOLOGY	Galveston					All Ages		P		S		S	S	S	S	P	932
NEW HORIZONS	Goldthwaite	7-17		7-17						P		S					917
HAPPY HILL FARM ACAD	Granbury	5-18		5-18						P		P		S			906
LONE STAR EXPEDITION	Groveton	13-17		13-17						P		P		S			911
AVONDALE HOUSE	Houston	4-30	3-22	4-30	3-22		S	S		S		S	P		S		893

Facility	Location	Ages	Program Emphasis (P = Primary, S = Secondary)	Page
BATTIN CLINIC	Houston	All Ages	P P P S P	894
BRIARWOOD SCH	Houston	5-21	P P S P	895
CTR HEARING & SPEECH	Houston	2-6 / Birth-18	P P	897
CTR SERVING PERSONS	Houston	18+ / 3-21	S S S P S S	898
CLIFFWOOD SCH	Houston	5-20	P P P	899
ECI KEEP PACE	Houston	Birth-3	P P P P P	903
HOUSTON LEARN ACAD	Houston	13-18	S S P	908
INSTITUTE FOR REHAB	Houston	6mos-17	S S S P P	909
MENNINGER CLIN	Houston	14-18	S S	914
MONARCH SCH	Houston	4-18	P P S P P	916
PARISH SCH	Houston	1½-9	P P P	919
SHRINERS-TX	Houston	Birth-18	P S	924
SPCH & LANG REM CTR	Houston	All Ages	S P S P P	925
WESTVIEW SCH-TX	Houston	2-12	S P P P	933
STAR RANCH	Ingram	7-17	S S S	926
RUTHE B. COWL	Laredo	2-14	P P P P P	921
DEVEREUX TX-LEAGUE	League City	13-22	P P	901
MERIDELL ACHIEVE CTR	Liberty Hill	5-17	S S S S P S	915
CRISMAN PREP	Longview	5-14	P S P	900
SABINE VALLEY CTR	Longview	All Ages	P P P P P	922
MILAM CTR	Lubbock	Birth-21	P P	916
TX TECH U SPEECH	Lubbock	Birth-21	S P S S P	929
MARBRIDGE	Manchaca	18+	S S S S	912
EASTER SEALS RIO	McAllen	All Ages	P P P	903
MEADOWVIEW SCH	Mesquite	6-15	P P	913
MEXIA STATE SCH	Mexia	6+	S S S P S S	915

| | | Females | | Males | | | | | | | | | | | | | |
Program	Town	Res	Day	Res	Day	Clinic	Blind	Deaf	Diabetes	Emot Disturb	HIV/AIDS	LD	MR	Ortho/Neuro	PDD	Speech	Page
TX CAPLAND CTR	Port Arthur					All Ages		S		S			S	S		P	897
HUGHEN CENTER	Port Arthur	5-21	5-21	5-21	5-21	All Ages				P		P	S	P			908
SABER ACAD	Richardson		14-17		14-17				P					P			922
RICHMOND STATE SCH	Richmond	6-65	18-65	6-65	18-65								P				921
CTR FOR HEALTH CARE	San Antonio		All Ages		All Ages			P						P			897
DIAG & REM READING	San Antonio					All Ages						P					901
EASTER SEAL REHAB-TX	San Antonio		Birth-3		Birth-3	All Ages	P	P		P		P	P	P	P	P	902
LAUREL RIDGE TREAT	San Antonio	5-18	5-18	5-18	5-18				S	P		P	S	S	P	P	911
MISSION ROAD DEV CTR	San Antonio	3-18		3-18			S	S				S	P	P			916
HARRY JERSIG CTR	San Antonio					All Ages				S		S	S	S	S	P	919
RIVER CITY CHRISTIAN	San Antonio		4-19		4-19		S	S	S	P	S	P	S	P	P	P	921
SUNSHINE COTTAGE SCH	San Antonio		Birth-19		Birth-19			P					P				926
WINSTON SCH-SANANTON	San Antonio		5-19		5-19							P					934
SAN MARCOS TREATMENT	San Marcos	11-17	11-17	11-17						P		S	S	S	S		923
DEVEREUX TX-VICTORIA	Victoria	6-16	6-16	6-16						P		S					901
GULF BEND MH/MR CTR	Victoria	22+	22+	22+		All Ages				P		P	P	P			906
UTAH																	
INTEGRITY HOUSE	Cedar City	12-17		12-17						P		P		P			938
YOUTH CARE	Draper	11-17	11-17	11-17	11-17					P		S			S		946
TURNING PT-GRANITE	Duchesne	12-18		12-18					S	P		P		P	P		943
TURNABOUT RANCH	Escalante	12-18		12-18						P		P		P			943
SORENSON'S RANCH SCH	Koosharem	14-18		14-18					S	P		P		S			941
WALKABOUT TREATMENT	Lehi	13-17		13-17						P		P		P	P	P	945
ASPEN ACHIEVE ACAD	Loa	13-17		13-17						P		P		P			936

Facility	City	Age	Age										Page
ASPEN RANCH	Loa	13-18	13-18						S			S	936
UT ST U SLHC	Logan	5-21	All Ages	S	P	S	P	S	S	S	S	P	945
UT SCHS-DEAF & BLIND	Ogden	5-21	5-21	P	P	S	S		S		S	S	944
PROVO CANYON	Orem	12-18	12-18			P			P				939
SUNRISE FAMILY SERVS	Orem	12-17				P			P				942
DISCOVERY ACAD	Provo	12-17	12-17	S		P		S	P		S		937
HERITAGE SCHS-UT	Provo	12-18	12-18			P			P				938
CEDAR RIDGE	Roosevelt	13-17	13-17		S	P			P		S		937
CHILDRENS CTR	Salt Lake City	2-7	2-5			P			P				937
REID LEARN CTR	Salt Lake City	8-20	8-20	5-15	S	S	S		P	S	S		940
SEPS LEARN CTR	Salt Lake City	All Ages	5-25	S	S	S	P	P	P	S	P	P	940
U UTAH REHAB	Salt Lake City	All Ages	All Ages			P			P		P		944
U OF UT SPEECH-LANG	Salt Lake City	All Ages	All Ages		P	P			S	S	P	S	944
SUNHAWK ACAD	St George	13-17	13-17			P			P		P		942
MTN HOMES YOUTH	Vernal	12-25	12-25			P			P	S	S		939

VERMONT

Facility	City	Age	Age										Page
BENNINGTON SCH	Bennington	9-21	9-21			P			P		P		947
UNITED COUNSELING	Bennington	All Ages	All Ages			P			P	P	P		952
ECKERD YOUTH-VT	Benson	10-17	10-17			P			S				948
AUSTINE SCH & CTR	Brattleboro	5-21	5-21		P	S			S				947
BRATTLEBORO RETREAT	Brattleboro	6-18	6-18	All Ages	S	S			P	S	S	S	948
WINSTON L PROUTY CTR	Brattleboro	Birth-6	Birth-6		P	P			P	P	P	P	953
BAIRD CENTER	Burlington	6-13	6-17	Birth-21		P			P			S	947
SPRING LAKE RANCH	Cuttingsville	17+	17+			P			S	S	S	P	951
GREENWOOD	Putney	9-15				P			P				949
VT ACHIEVEMENT CTR	Rutland	6wks-18	6wks-18		P	P			S	S	S	S	952

Program	Town	Females Res	Females Day	Males Res	Males Day	Clinic	Blind	Deaf	Diabetes	Emot Disturb	HIV/AIDS	LD	MR	Ortho/Neuro	PDD	Speech	Page
VT NORTHWESTERN COUNSEL	St Albans					Birth-22				P		P		P	P		950
KING GEORGE	Sutton	14-19		14-19						P		P	P	P	S		950
PINE RIDGE	Williston	13-18	13-18	13-18	13-18							P					951
STERN CTR	Williston					5+				S		P	S	P	P	S	952
VIRGINIA																	
LEARY SCH	Alexandria		5-21		5-21					P		P					961
ST. COLETTA-WA	Alexandria		4-22		4-22			S		S		S	P	P	S	S	969
OAKWOOD SCH-VA	Annandale		6-14		6-14							P	P	P			966
PHILLIPS SCHS	Annandale		5-21		5-21					P		P	P	P			967
CHILD DEV CTR-VA	Arlington					Birth-21		S		S.		P	S	S	P	P	956
STRATFORD PRGM	Arlington		11-22		11-22			S		S		S	P	S	S	S	972
MORRISON SCH	Bristol		6-18		6-18							P					962
LEARNING CTR-CHARLOT	Charlottesville		6-21		6-21	6-21				S		S	P	S	S	S	960
REGION TEN COMM SVCS	Charlottesville		16+		16+	All Ages	P	P		P		P	P	P	P	P	968
UVA CHILDREN'S	Charlottesville	Birth-21		Birth-21		Birth-21	P	P		S		S	P	P	P	S	973
UVA CHILD PSYCH	Charlottesville					Birth-18				P		P					974
RIVERVIEW LEARN CTR	Chesapeake		5-17		5-17							P					969
SE VA TRAINING CTR	Chesapeake	2+		2+			S	S					P	S		S	971
TIMBER RIDGE SCH	Cross Junction			11-17						P		P					973
NEW DOMINION SCH	Dillwyn	11-17		11-17						P		P					963
N VA TRAINING CTR	Fairfax	6+		6+		6+	S	S		S			P	S		S	965
EASTER SEALS HOME	Falls Church		Birth-5		Birth-5	Birth-21				S		P	S	P	P	P	957
WOODROW WILSON REHAB	Fishersville	15½+	15½+	15½+	15½+	All Ages	P	P		S		P	S	P	P	P	977
PARENT EDUCATION	Fredericksburg					Birth-3	P	P		P		P	P	P	P	P	967

Facility	Location	Age	Age	Age										#
FAITH MISSION HOME	Free Union	2-15	2-15						P		P			958
ELK HILL FARM	Goochland	13-17	13-17					P	P	P	P			957
ARC VA PENINSULA	Hampton	All Ages	All Ages					P		P				954
HAMPTON U-SLHC	Hampton		2+		S			S	S	S	P			959
VA SCH FOR THE DEAF	Hampton	8-21	3-22	6-22	P	P		S	S	S	S			976
HARRISONBURG-ROCKING	Harrisonburg		3+				P	P	P	P				960
LITTLE KESWICK	Keswick		10-17					P	S	P	S			961
OAKLAND	Keswick	8-14	8-14	8-14			S	P	S	P				965
GRAYDON MANOR	Leesburg	13-17	11-17	All Ages			P	P		S				959
CENTRAL VA TRNG CTR	Lynchburg	All Ages	All Ages					P		P				955
NEW VISTAS SCH	Lynchburg	5-19	5-19				S	P		S				964
SLC OF NORTHERN VA	McLean	2-6	2-6	2-6				P		P	P			972
BLACKWATER OUTDOOR	Midlothian	14-28	14-28				P	P		P				954
CUMBERL& HOSP	New Kent	2-22	2-22		P	P	P	P	P	P				956
BARRY ROBINSON CTR	Norfolk	6-17	6-17				P	P	S	S				954
ST. MARY'S HOME	Norfolk	Birth-18	Birth-18				P	P	P	P				970
TIDEWATER CHILD DEV	Norfolk			Birth-21	P	P	P	P	P	P	P			972
THE PINES RES TREAT	Portsmouth	5-21	5-21				S	S	S	P				967
CHARTERHOUSE SCH	Richmond	11-17	11-17				P	P	S	S				955
INFANT TODDLER CONN	Richmond	Birth-3	Birth-3				P	P		P				960
MEMORIAL CHILD	Richmond			Birth-18			P	P	S					962
NEW COMMUNITY	Richmond	11-18	11-18				P	P		P				963
RIVERSIDE SCH	Richmond	6-13	6-13			P		P	P					968
DOOLEY SCH	Richmond	5-21	5-21	5-21			P	P	P	P				970
VA HOME FOR BOYS	Richmond	12-18	12-18		S	S	P	P	S	P				974
VA REHAB CTR	Richmond	14+	14+	14+	S	S	P	S	S	S	S			975

Program	Town	Females Res	Females Day	Males Res	Males Day	Clinic	Blind	Deaf	Diabetes	Emot Disturb	HIV/ AIDS	LD	MR	Ortho/ Neuro	PDD	Speech	Page
VA VA TREATMENT CTR	Richmond	5-17	5-17	5-17	5-17	All Ages				P		P					977
SOUTHSIDE REGIONAL	South Boston			13-18						P							971
VALLEY COMM SERVICE	Staunton					All Ages				P			P				974
VA SCH-DEAF-STAUNTON	Staunton	5-22	Birth-22	5-22	Birth-22		P	P				P			P	P	975
LEARNING RESOURCE	Virginia Beach					5+						P	P		P	P	961
GRAFTON SCH	Winchester	3-21	3-21	3-21	3-21		S	S		P		P	S	S	S	S	958
NEW LIFESTYLES	Winchester	18-26		18-26					S	P		P	S	S	S		964
ZUNI PRESBYTERIAN	Zuni	18+		18+			S	S	S	S	S	S	S	S	S	S	978
WASHINGTON																	
SECRET HARBOR SCH	Anacortes	11-17		11-17		All Ages				P		P		P			985
HOPE CLINIC-WA	Bellevue					All Ages						P		P			982
FRANCES HADDON	Bremerton	19-35		19-35			S	S		S		S	S	S	P	S	980
HOLLY RIDGE CTR	Bremerton		Birth-3		Birth-3	Birth-3	P	P				P	P	P	S	P	982
LIFE DESIGNS	Cusick	18-26		18-26			S	S	S	P		P	S	S		S	983
PROVIDENCE CHILDRENS	Everett					Birth-14								P	P		984
LAKELAND VILLAGE	Medical Lake	16+		16+									P		P		982
CHILDREN'S INST-WA	Mercer Island		4-15		4-15	4-15			S	P		P	P	P	P	P	979
WASHINGTON ST U-SHC	Pullman					All Ages						P	P	P	S	P	988
BENTON FRANKLIN	Richland		Birth-3		Birth-3		S	S		S		P	S	P	P	P	979
BOYER CLINIC	Seattle					Birth-15						P	P	P	P	P	979
HAMLIN ROBINSON SCH	Seattle	6-14	6-14		6-14							P					980
HEAR SPEECH DEAF CTR	Seattle		Birth-3		Birth-3	Birth-3	S	P	S	S	S	S	S	S	S	S	981
NW SCH HEARING	Seattle	3-14	3-14		3-14			P									984
ST. CHRISTOPHER ACAD	Seattle	13-19	13-19	13-19	13-19							P		S		P	984

Facility	Location	Ages	Program Emphasis	Page
U OF WA EXPERIMENTAL	Seattle	Birth-7 / Birth-7 / Birth-7	S S P S S P P	987
U OF WA-SPEECH/HEAR	Seattle	All Ages	S P S S S P	987
YAKIMA VALLEY SCH	Selah	21+ / 21+	P P	989
MORNING STAR	Spokane	10-18 / 10-18 / 10-18	P P	983
SHRINERS HOSPITAL-WA	Spokane	Birth-18 / Birth-18	P P	985
TAMARACK CTR	Spokane	12-17 / 12-17 / 12-17	P P	986
TYLER RANCH	Spokane	6-18	S P	986
WA ST U HEAR-SPEECH	Spokane	All Ages / All Ages	P S S	988
MARY BRIDGE CHILDREN	Tacoma	Birth-18	P P P P P	983
WA SCH FOR BLIND	Vancouver	3-21 / 3-21 / 3-21 / 3-21	P P P P P	988
WEST VIRGINIA				
ALLDREDGE ACAD	Davis	13-18 / 13-18 / 13-18 / 13-18	S P P S S P	990
DEV THERAPY CTR	Huntington	All Ages	P S S	990
MARSHALL U-SHC	Huntington	All Ages	S S S	991
PRESTERA CTR	Huntington	13+ / All Ages / All Ages	P P	991
WV REHABILITATION	Institute	15+ / 15+	P P	992
WV UNIV-SPEECH/HEAR	Morgantown	All Ages	S S P	992
WESTBROOK HEALTH	Parkersburg	3-18	S S P S S S	993
WV SCHS-DEAF & BLIND	Romney	3-21 / 3-21 / 3-21	P P P P	992
EASTER SEAL REHAB-WV	Wheeling	All Ages	P P S P P P	990
WISCONSIN				
CTR FOR DEAF-KELLOGG	Brookfield	Birth-3 / Birth-3	P S P S	994
WI SCH FOR THE DEAF	Delavan	5-21 / 3-21 / 5-21	S P S S S S	1011
LAD LAKE	Dousman	12-21 / 10-18 / 10-21	P P S S	998
EAU CLAIRE ACAD	Eau Claire	10-18 / 10-18	P P S	997
NW READING CLIN	Eau Claire	All Ages	P P P S P S	1000

Program	Town	Females Res	Females Day	Males Res	Males Day	Clinic	Blind	Deaf	Diabetes	Emot Disturb	HIV/AIDS	LD	MR	Ortho/Neuro	PDD	Speech	Page
WI WI-EAU CLAIRE CTR	Eau Claire					All Ages		P					S	S	S	P	1006
VOCATIONAL INDUST-WI	Elkhorn		16+		16+		S	S		S		S	P	S	S	S	1009
WI CTR FOR THE BLIND	Janesville	5-21	5-21	5-21	5-21		P					S	S	S	S	S	1011
ST COLETTA SCH-WI	Jefferson	18+	18+	18+	18+								P				1003
CHILEDA HABILITATION	La Crosse	6-18	6-18	6-18	6-18		S	S		S		S		P	P	S	996
GUNDERSEN LUTHERAN	La Crosse					All Ages	P	P		P		P	P	P	P	P	997
CENT WI DEVELOPMENT	Madison	All Ages		All Ages									P				995
CHILD & FAM PSYCH	Madison					All Ages				P		P	P	P	P		995
MENDOTA MENTAL HLTH	Madison	Birth-12		Birth-12						P							999
MERITER HOSP	Madison					All Ages	S	S				S	S	P	P	P	1000
U OF WI-CHILD PSYCH	Madison					All Ages				P							1007
U OF WI-MADISON SPCH	Madison					All Ages		P				P	P	P	P	P	1007
WAISMAN CTR	Madison					All Ages	S	S		P		P	P	P	P	P	1009
WALBRIDGE SCH	Madison		7-14		7-14					S		S			S		1010
MARSHFIELD CLINIC	Marshfield					Birth-21	P	P		P		P	P	P	P	P	999
MENOMONEE FALLS CTR	Menomonee Falls		Birth-3		Birth-3							P	P	S	S	P	999
CHILDREN'S HOSP-WI	Milwaukee					Birth-21		P				S	S	S	S	P	995
EASTER SEALS SE WI	Milwaukee		Birth-3		Birth-3		S				S	S	P	P	P	P	996
MARQUETTE U-SHC	Milwaukee					2+										P	998
SACRED HEART REHAB	Milwaukee					Birth-18		P				P	P	P	S	P	1002
ST AEMILIAN LAKESIDE	Milwaukee		4-18	6-15	4-18					P		P	P				1002
SAINT CHARLES YOUTH	Milwaukee	6-17	6-17	6-17	6-17	All Ages				P		P	P	S	P	P	1002
ST COLETTA-WI	Milwaukee		8-16	8-16	8-16							P	P	P	P		1003
ST. FRANCIS CHILDREN	Milwaukee		Birth-8	Birth-8	Birth-8				S	P		P	P	P	P	S	1003

Program	City	Ages	Ref.
SAINT ROSE YOUTH CTR	Milwaukee	8-18, 12-18	1004
U OF WI-MILW SPEECH	Milwaukee	All Ages	1007
WILLOWGLEN ACAD	Milwaukee	10-21, 6-21, 10-21, 6-21	1010
OCONOMOWOC	Oconomowoc	4-21, 4-21, 4-21	1001
WYALUSING ACAD	Prairie du Chien	10-18, 10-18	1012
TAYLOR HOME	Racine	13-16	1005
U OF WI-RF SLH CLIN	River Falls	All Ages, All Ages	1008
REHAB SHEBOYGAN EIP	Sheboygan	Birth-3, Birth-3	1001
SHEBOYGAN COUNTY OUT	Sheboygan	5-18, 5-18	1004
U OF WI-STEVENS CTR	Stevens Point	All Ages, All Ages	1008
BETHESDA LUTHERAN	Watertown	8-18, 8-18	994
TOMORROW'S CHILDREN	Waupaca	5-18, 5-18	1006
THRESHOLD EARLY INT	West Bend	Birth-3, Birth-3	1005
WYOMING			
WYOMING SCH DEAF	Casper	Birth-21, Birth-21	1015
LARAMIE TREATMNT SVC	Cheyenne	All Ages, All Ages	1013
STRIDE LEARNING CTR	Cheyenne	Birth-5, Birth-5	1013
WY ST TRAINING SCH	Lander	All Ages, All Ages	1015
U OF WY-SPEECH/HEAR	Laramie	All Ages, All Ages	1014
TRINITY WILDERNESS	Powell	12-17	1014
COMMUNITY ENTRY SVCS	Riverton	16+, 14+, 16+, 14+	1013

PROGRAM DESCRIPTIONS

ALABAMA

ALABAMA INSTITUTE FOR DEAF AND BLIND
Res and Day — Coed Ages 3-21

Talladega, AL 35160. 205 E South St, PO Box 698.
Tel: 256-761-3200. Fax: 256-761-3344.
www.aidb.org   E-mail: info@aidb.org
Terry Graham, Pres. **Shirley Hamer,** Adm.
  Focus: Spec Ed. Rehab. Trng. **Conditions:** Primary—B D. Sec—BD MR.
  Col Prep. Gen Acad. Pre-Voc. Voc. Ungraded. Courses: Read Math Lang_
    Arts Sci. Man_Arts & Shop. Shelt_Workshop. On-Job Trng.
  Therapy: Hear Lang Phys Recreational Speech Visual. **Psychotherapy:**
    Fam Group Indiv.
  Rates 2003: No Fee.
  Summer Prgm: Res & Day. Educ. Rec. Res Rate $0. Day Rate $0. 2 wks.
  Est 1858. State. Nonprofit.

The institute, with its affiliated schools and centers, seeks to provide practical and academic training for deaf and blind students. In addition to offering the same academic subjects in the schools for the deaf as are available in public schools, the institute provides speech and auditory training, as well as courses emphasizing vocational and life skills training. The course of study at the school for the blind includes literary subjects in braille and large-print classes, as well as orientation and mobility techniques through grade 12.

The multi-handicapped program offers readiness classes in which students develop basic banking and language skills, while the motor development program includes special equestrian riding as a part of physical therapy. The institute teaches independent living skills to students requiring such instruction.

The technical school provides training for any person over age 16 in need of additional educational and vocational training. Trade areas include printing, commercial sewing, business office education and a business enterprise program. Classes in the use of assistive devices are also available.

THE ARC OF MADISON COUNTY
INFANT & TODDLER PROGRAM
Day — Coed Ages Birth-3

Huntsville, AL 35811. 312-A Cahill Dr, Ste A.
Tel: 256-533-7829. Fax: 256-533-1854.
E-mail: itparc@hiwaay.net
Sandra H. Frank, MA, Prgm Coord.
  Focus: Spec Ed. **Conditions:** Primary—ADD ADHD Ap As Asp Au B BD
    BI C CD CP D Dc Dg DS Dx ED Ep IP LD MD MR MS Nf OCD ON PDD
    Psy PW S SB Sz TB.
  Therapy: Hear Lang Music Occup Percepual-Motor Phys Speech. **Psycho-
  therapy:** Fam Group Indiv.

Enr: 40. **Staff:** 11 (Full 3, Part 8). Educ 2. Admin 1.
Rates 2003: No Fee.
County. Nonprofit.

Children with known developmental delays participate in this year-round, family-centered early intervention program. The center detects handicapping conditions, assists and supports families in coping with their children's needs, attempts to speed the child's rate of developmental progress, detects and prevents secondary handicaps, and seeks to reduce future medical, educational, and social service costs to the family and the community. Services facilitate the development of cognitive, communicational, adaptive/self-help, physical/motor and social/emotional skills.

AUBURN UNIVERSITY SPEECH AND HEARING CLINIC

Clinic: All Ages. M-F 8-5.

Auburn, AL 36849. 1199 Haley Ctr.
Tel: 334-844-9600. Fax: 334-844-4585.
http://frontpage.auburn.edu/communication_disorders/screen/default.asp
  E-mail: moltlaw@auburn.edu
William O. Haynes, PhD, Dir.
  Conditions: Primary—D S.
  Therapy: Hear Lang Speech.
  Staff: Prof 9.
  Est 1947.

CAHABA MENTAL HEALTH CENTER
EARLY INTERVENTION PROGRAM

Day — Coed Ages Birth-3

Selma, AL 36701. 1017 Medical Center Pky.
Tel: 334-875-2100. Fax: 334-418-6509.
  Focus: Trng. **Conditions:** Primary—Au B BI CD CP D ED Ep IP MD MR MS ON S SB.
  Therapy: Hear Lang Occup Phys Speech. **Psychotherapy:** Fam Group Indiv.
  Enr: 78. **Staff:** 9 (Full 7, Part 2).
  Est 1984. Private. Nonprofit.

This center provides sensorimotor training, prelinguistics, and cognitive, social and self-help skills training for infants and toddlers from Dallas, Perry and Wilcox counties. Developmental physical management assists children having motor delays. An incidental learning approach is used to teach developmental skills individually. Staff arrange consultations with specialists as needed, and special instruction in the home is also available.

CENTERS FOR THE DEVELOPMENTALLY DISABLED
NORTH CENTRAL ALABAMA EARLY CHILDHOOD SERVICES

Day — Coed Ages Birth-3

Decatur, AL 35602. 1602 Church St NE, PO Box 2091.
Tel: 256-353-1591. Fax: 256-350-1485.
Brad Romine, Chair.
    Focus: Treatment. Conditions: Primary—Au Bl C CP Ep IP MD MR MS ON SB. Sec—ADD ADHD Ap As B BD CD D Dx ED LD OCD Psy S Sz TB.
    Therapy: Hear Occup Phys Speech. Psychotherapy: Parent.
    Enr: 55. Staff: 12 (Full 2, Part 10).
    Rates 2004: No Fee.
    Private. Nonprofit. Spons: United Way.

Serving north-central Alabama, this early intervention program enrolls young children with delays in one or more of the following areas: motor, cognitive, language, self-help and social. After administering a multidisciplinary evaluation, the interdisciplinary team develops and implements an individualized plan for the child that features a description of specific goals and objectives. Services include therapy, developmental intervention and parent training.

CHILDREN'S CENTER OF MONTGOMERY

Day — Coed Ages Birth-21

Montgomery, AL 36107. 310 N Madison Ter.
Tel: 334-262-4850. Fax: 334-262-5155.
www.mps.k12.al.us/board/childrens
Chris Henderson, Prin.
    Conditions: Primary—CP MD MR OH.
    Gen Acad. Ungraded. Courses: Read Math Lang_Arts.
    Therapy: Occup Phys Speech.
    Est 1949. State. Nonprofit.

EAST ALABAMA
MENTAL HEALTH-MENTAL RETARDATION CENTER

Clinic: All Ages. M-F 8-4:30.

Opelika, AL 36801. 2506 Lambert Dr.
Tel: 334-742-2700. Fax: 334-742-2707.
www.eastalabamamhc.org
Anne Penney, EdD, Exec Dir.
    Conditions: Primary—ED MR. Sec—Au PDD.
    Municipal.

HELEN KELLER SCHOOL OF ALABAMA

Res and Day — Coed Ages 3-21

Talladega, AL 35160. Fort Lashley Ave, Hwy 21 S, PO Box 698.
Tel: 256-761-3251. Fax: 256-761-3377.
www.aidb.org/helenkeller
Erminel Love-Trescott, EdD, Prin. **Sharian Gooden,** Educ Dir.
   Focus: Spec Ed. **Conditions:** Primary—MR. Sec—As B C CP D ED Ep LD
    S SB. **IQ 30-89.**
   Pre-Voc. Ungraded. Courses: Read Math Lang_Arts.
   Therapy: Art Hear Phys Speech.
   Enr: 91. Res Males 36. Res Females 40. Day Males 9. Day Females 6.
    Staff: 104.
   Rates 2004: No Fee.
   State. **Spons:** Alabama Institute for Deaf and Blind.

This school provides an educational program for sensory-impaired multi-disabled students. The program includes functional living and work skills training. Out-of-state residents may attend the school for a fee; Alabama residents pay no fee.

THE HORIZONS SCHOOL

Res — Coed Ages 19-26

Birmingham, AL 35233. 2111 University Blvd.
Tel: 205-322-6606. Fax: 205-322-6605.
www.horizonsschool.org   E-mail: mcelheny@horizonsschool.org
Jade K. Carter, EdD, Dir. **Marie H. McElheny,** Adm.
   Focus: Spec Ed. **Conditions:** Primary—ADD ADHD Dc Dg Dx LD. Sec—
    Ap Asp Au BI CP Ep HIV MR ON PDD S SB TS. **IQ 70-85.**
   Gen Acad. Gr PG. On-Job Trng.
   Enr: 34. Res Males 18. Res Females 16. **Staff:** 12 (Full 8, Part 4). Admin 3.
   Rates 2004: Res $20,475-22,955/sch yr. Schol 9 ($58,000).
   Summer Prgm: Res. Educ. 8 wks.
   Est 2000. Private. Nonprofit.

Horizons' nondegree transition program seeks to prepare young adults with specific learning disabilities and mild learning problems to live self-sufficient and productive lives. The peer living environment helps students learn to face the challenges of independent living. Programming emphasizes decision making, communicational skills and effective self-management. An academic advisor monitors the development of each pupil, and families receive a progress report each term.

HUNTSVILLE ACHIEVEMENT SCHOOL

Day — Coed Ages 5-16

Huntsville, AL 35801. 406½ Governors Dr.
Tel: 256-539-1772. Fax: 256-539-1772.

E-mail: hsvachievement@comcast.net
Carol Heard, BS, Dir.
    Focus: Spec Ed. **Conditions:** Primary—ADD ADHD Anx Asp Au BD CD
    DS Dx ED LD MD Mood MR ON PDD S SP. **IQ 60 and up.**
    Gen Acad. Ungraded. Courses: Read Math Lang_Arts.
    Therapy: Hear Movement Music Play Speech.
    Enr: 35. Day Males 16. Day Females 19. **Staff:** 5. (Full 5).
    Rates 2003: Day $400/mo (+$300/yr). Schol avail.
    Est 1963. Private. Nonprofit.

This school operates 10 months a year and offers a structured program that includes academics and sensorimotor development.

MENTAL HEALTH CENTER OF MADISON COUNTY
CENTER FOR LEARNING ACADEMICS AND SOCIAL SKILLS

Day — Coed Ages 5-21

Huntsville, AL 35802. 4040 Memorial Pky SW.
Tel: 256-533-1970. Fax: 256-532-4112.
www.mhcmc.org
Gary W. Porier, PhD, Exec Dir. **Dave Rush,** Clin Dir. **James Hancock,** MD,
    Med Dir.
    Focus: Spec Ed. Treatment. **Conditions:** Primary—ADD ADHD Anx Asp
    ED Mood OCD Psy PTSD Sz TS. Sec—BI LD.
    Gen Acad. Pre-Voc. Gr K-12. Courses: Read Math Lang_Arts Studio_Art.
    Therapy: Chemo Recreational Speech. **Psychotherapy:** Fam Group Indiv.
    Staff: 11. (Full 11). Educ 3. Admin 1.
    Rates 2003: Day $10,500/sch yr.
    Est 1969. County. Nonprofit.

CLASS provides elementary, middle and high school placements for students unable to function appropriately in the public school system. Most students eventually return to their public school classrooms. Educational, parental and personal counseling is available within this day treatment program.

MOBILE ASSOCIATION FOR RETARDED CITIZENS

Day — Coed Ages 3 and up

Mobile, AL 36617. 2424 Gordon Smith Dr.
Tel: 251-479-7409. Fax: 251-473-7649.
www.mobilearc.org   E-mail: jzoghby@mobilearc.org
Jeff Zoghby, Exec Dir.
    Conditions: Primary—MR.
    Gen Acad. Pre-Voc. Voc. Ungraded. Courses: Read Math Lang_Arts. Man_
    Arts & Shop. Shelt_Workshop. On-Job Trng.
    Est 1956. Private. Nonprofit.

PATHWAY

Res — Males Ages 10-18

Enterprise, AL 36331. PO Box 311206.
Tel: 334-894-5591. Fax: 334-894-5264.
www.pathway-inc.com   E-mail: info@pathway-inc.com
Norman G. Hemp, CEO. **Robert Sheddon,** DO, Med Dir. **Arielle Hemp,** Adm.
  Focus: Treatment. **Conditions:** Primary—ADD ADHD As BD CD ED LD
    OCD PTSD. Sec—MR. **IQ 65 and up.**
  Gen Acad. Gr 4-12. Courses: Read Math Lang_Arts Soc_Stud. Man_Arts &
    Shop.
  Therapy: Milieu Play Recreational Speech. **Psychotherapy:** Fam Group
    Indiv Substance_Abuse.
  Enr: 70. Res Males 70. **Staff:** 52. (Full 52). Prof 12. Educ 5. Admin 6.
  Rates 2003: Res $165/day. State Aid.
  Est 1982. Private. Inc.

Pathway offers a highly structured program of professional intervention for boys with
a range of emotional and behavioral difficulties. The campus-style environment supports
comprehensive services and various experiential learning opportunities.

THE RISE SCHOOL OF TUSCALOOSA

Day — Coed Ages Birth-6

Tuscaloosa, AL 35487. 600 4th St E.
Tel: 205-348-7931. Fax: 205-348-9611.
www.riseschool.org/tuscaloosa
Martha Cook, Dir.
  Focus: Spec Ed. **Conditions:** Primary—CP DS MR OH.
  Therapy: Hear Music Occup Phys Speech.
  Est 1974. State. Nonprofit. **Spons:** University of Alabama.

RIVERBEND CENTER FOR MENTAL HEALTH

Day — Coed Ages 2 and up

Florence, AL 35630. 635 W College St, PO Box 941.
Tel: 256-764-3431. Fax: 256-766-4672.
www.rcmh.org
  Conditions: Primary—ED.
  Gen Acad. Gr PS.
  Psychotherapy: Fam Group Indiv.
  Staff: Prof 6.
  Est 1950. State.

TRI-WIL
PORTA CRAS SCHOOL

Res — Coed Ages 6-21

Green Pond, AL 35074. PO Box 77.
Tel: 205-938-7855. Fax: 205-938-3647.
James Brown, MA, Dir.
Focus: Spec Ed. Treatment. **Conditions:** Primary—As BD CD Db ED Mood MR OCD. Sec—Anx D Psy PTSD PW SP Sz TS. **IQ 70-110.**
Gen Acad. Gr K-12. Courses: Read Math Lang_Arts.
Therapy: Art Recreational.
Enr: 40. Res Males 30. Res Females 10. **Staff:** 50. Prof 7. Educ 2. Admin 10.
Rates 2003: Res $143/day. $70 (Therapy)/hr. State Aid.
Summer Prgm: Res. Educ. Rec. 6 wks.
Est 1984. Private. Inc.

Students enrolled at Porta Cras receive individual instruction designed to promote academic success and improve behavioral and social skills. The therapeutic treatment program consists of milieu and recreational therapy, as well as the formulation of individualized treatment plans. The school's experiential education program teaches creativity, teamwork, leadership and effective communication and listening skills. Among the program's challenge opportunities are an Alpine tower, hiking, orienteering, horsemanship and ropes courses.

UCP OF GREATER BIRMINGHAM

Day — Coed Ages Birth-4

Birmingham, AL 35211. 120 Oslo Cir.
Tel: 205-944-3939. Fax: 205-944-3933.
www.ucpbham.com
Gary Edwards, PhD, Exec Dir. **Tina Shaddix,** Prgm Dir. **Mark Cohen,** MD, Med Dir.
Focus: Treatment. **Conditions:** Primary—CP OH. Sec—As Au B D Db DS Ep IP MR PDD S SB.
Therapy: Hear Lang Music Phys Play Speech. **Psychotherapy:** Fam Group. **Counseling:** Nutrition.
Staff: 180 (Full 170, Part 10). Prof 56. Educ 32. Admin 8.
Est 1948. Private. Nonprofit. **Spons:** United Cerebral Palsy Associations.

This center provides services for individuals with cerebral palsy or similar problems for which no other community program exists. An infant stimulation program and a preschool program are provided.

Services include daycare for children, physical and speech therapies, an educational program with general academic and remedial courses, a school readiness program and parental counseling.

UNIVERSITY OF ALABAMA
BREWER-PORCH CHILDREN'S CENTER

Res and Day — Coed Ages 6-13

Tuscaloosa, AL 35487. College of Arts & Sciences, Box 870268.
Tel: 205-348-7007. Fax: 205-348-9368.
www.as.ua.edu/as/faculty/manual/organization/supportunits.html
   Conditions: Primary—BD.
   Gen Acad. Pre-Voc. Courses: Read Math Lang_Arts.
   Staff: Prof 70.
   Est 1970. State. Spons: University of Alabama.

UNIVERSITY OF ALABAMA
PSYCHOLOGY CLINIC

Clinic: All Ages. M-F 8-5; Eve W 5-6:30.

Tuscaloosa, AL 35487. 251A Gordon Palmer Hall, Box 870356.
Tel: 205-348-5000. Fax: 205-348-5002.
http://psychology.ua.edu
Jean Spruill, PhD, Dir.
   Focus: Treatment. Conditions: Primary—ADD ADHD Asp Au CD Dx ED
   LD MR OCD PDD. Sec—BI.
   Psychotherapy: Fam Group Indiv Sex Marital.
   Staff: 23 (Full 17, Part 6). Admin 3.
   Rates 2003: Sliding-Scale Rate $1-55/hr.
   Est 1948. State. Nonprofit.

This mental health center provides diagnostic and treatment services. Graduate students from the university assist on the staff as counselors. Therapeutic and counseling services include marital counseling, psychotherapy, play therapy and behavior modification.

UNIVERSITY OF ALABAMA
SPEECH AND HEARING CENTER

Clinic: All Ages. M-F 8-4:45.

Tuscaloosa, AL 35487. Box 870242.
Tel: 205-348-7131. Fax: 205-348-1845.
www.as.ua.edu/comdis
Karen F. Steckol, Supv.
   Focus: Rehab. Treatment. Conditions: Primary—Ap D S.
   Therapy: Hear Lang Speech.
   Staff: 12.
   Est 1938. State. Nonprofit.

The center provides a full range of diagnostic and rehabilitative services for the individuals with communicative disorders. A hearing aid dispensary operates in conjunction with the audiological services program. The facility provides outreach services (offered on a contractual basis) ranging from industrial hearing screening programs to language intervention programs for private and public organizations.

UNIVERSITY OF MONTEVALLO
SPEECH AND HEARING CENTER

Clinic: All Ages. M-F 8-4:30.

Montevallo, AL 35115. Communication Sciences & Disorders, Sta 6720.
Tel: 205-665-6720. Fax: 205-665-6721.
www.montevallo.edu/csd/services.shtm
Mary Beth Armstrong, PhD, Supv. **Dana Boyd,** MS, Coord.
   Focus: Treatment. **Conditions:** Primary—Asp Au D PDD S. Sec—ADHD
   Ap As Bl C CP Ep MR ON SB.
   Therapy: Hear Lang Phys Speech.
   Staff: 10.
   Rates 2003: Sliding-Scale Rate $0-6/ses.
   Est 1954. State. Nonprofit.

The clinic treats speech, hearing and language problems. Academic work, therapies, social skills, a classroom for the hearing-impaired, tutoring and recreation are offered. Diagnostic services provide pure-tone threshold testing, speech audiometry and site-of-lesion testing. Referral services and parental education are available.

VIVIAN B. ADAMS SCHOOL

Day — Coed All Ages

Ozark, AL 36360. 2047 Stuart Tarter Rd.
Tel: 334-774-5132. Fax: 334-774-3436.
www.vivianbadams.org
Patti Martin, Dir. **Amy Herring,** RN, BSN, Med Dir. **Kathy Brooks,** Adm.
   Focus: Spec Ed. Trng. **Conditions:** Primary—MR. Sec—ADD ADHD Ap As
   Au B BD Bl C CP D DS Dx ED Ep IP LD MD MS OCD ODD ON PDD S
   SB. **IQ 0-70.**
   Pre-Voc. Voc. Ungraded. Courses: Read Math Lang_Arts Life_Skills. Shelt_
   Workshop. On-Job Trng.
   Therapy: Hear Lang Occup Phys Speech.
   Enr: 225. Day Males 132. Day Females 93. **Staff:** 70 (Full 68, Part 2). Prof
   22. Educ 20. Admin 8.
   Rates 2003: No Fee.
   Est 1971. County. Nonprofit.

Special education and training programs provided at this school include behavior modification, learning skills, language, prevocational and vocational training, music and crafts, self-help and independent living classes, social skills and economic self-sufficiency training. Field trips, home visits and entertainment activities supplement the programs.

WILLIAM D. PARTLOW DEVELOPMENTAL CENTER

Res — Coed All Ages

Tuscaloosa, AL 35403. University Blvd E, PO Box 1730.
Tel: 205-553-4550. Fax: 205-554-4120.
www.mh.state.al.us
Allen Fortson, Dir.
  Focus: Trng. Treatment. **Conditions:** Primary—MR.
  Pre-Voc. Voc. Ungraded. Shelt_Workshop.
  Therapy: Hear Lang Occup Phys Speech. **Psychotherapy:** Indiv.
  Est 1923. State.

WILMER HALL CHILDREN'S HOME
THE MURRAY SCHOOL

Res — Coed Ages 11-18

Mobile, AL 36608. 3811 Old Shell Rd.
Tel: 251-342-4931. Fax: 251-342-4466.
www.wilmerhall.org   E-mail: msumlin@wilmerhall.org
William A. Chambers, Exec Dir. **Margie Sumlin,** MA, Prin. **George Hamilton,** Adm.
  Focus: Spec Ed. **Conditions:** Primary—ADD ADHD Anx BD CD Dc Dg Dx
  ED LD MR OCD ODD. **IQ 75-113.**
  Gen Acad. Gr 6-12. Courses: Read Math Lang_Arts Sci Soc_Stud.
  Therapy: Art.
  Enr: 20. Res Males 10. Res Females 10. **Staff:** 5.
  Est 1864. Private. Nonprofit. Episcopal.

This school for children who reside at the Wilmer Hall Children's Home offers an individualized academic program that prepares students for mainstreaming into public school. The curriculum includes core academic subjects such as reading, math, science, social studies and language arts, as well as elective courses. The school's behavioral management program involves counseling and art therapy.

WIREGRASS REHABILITATION CENTER

Res and Day — Coed Ages 16 and up

Dothan, AL 36302. 805 Ross Clark Cir NE, PO Box 338.
Tel: 205-792-0022. Fax: 205-712-7632.
www.dothannow.com/resources/houston_co_res_dir/wiregrass_
    rehabilitation.htm
Jack Sasser, Admin.

Conditions: Primary—MR. **IQ 60-110.**
Voc. Shelt_Workshop. On-Job Trng.
Est 1959. Private. Nonprofit.

WORKSHOPS

Day — Coed Ages 16 and up

Birmingham, AL 35222. 4244 3rd Ave S.
Tel: 205-592-9683. TTY: 205-592-8006. Fax: 205-592-9687.
www.workshopsinc.com
James E. Crim, MEd, MBA, Exec Dir.
    Focus: Trng. **Conditions:** Primary—MR. Sec—ADD ADHD Ap As Au B BD BI C CD CP D Dx ED Ep IP LD MD MS OCD ON Psy S SB Sz TB.
    Gen Acad. Pre-Voc. Voc. Ungraded. Courses: Read Math Lang_Arts. Man_ Arts & Shop. Shelt_Workshop. On-Job Trng.
    Therapy: Occup. **Psychotherapy:** Fam Indiv Parent.
    Enr: 200. Day Males 125. Day Females 75. **Staff:** 40 (Full 38, Part 2).
    Est 1890. Private. Nonprofit. **Spons:** United Way.

This training and employment center specializes in assisting people with disabilities in their vocational development. Depending on individual need, training is available in work adjustment, job skills, literacy, job-seeking skills and other areas. Additional services include job development and placement, supported employment and sheltered employment.

Fees vary according to services provided, and certain services incur no fee. A branch facility is located at 240 Commerce Pky., Pelham 35124.

ALASKA

ALASKA STATE SCHOOL FOR DEAF
AND HARD OF HEARING

Res and Day — Coed Ages 3-21

Anchorage, AK 99519. PO Box 196614.
Tel: 907-742-4243. Fax: 907-742-4299.
www.educ.state.ak.us   E-mail: lee_dennis@asdk12.org
Dennis A. Lee, Dir.
    Focus: Spec Ed. Treatment. **Conditions:** Primary—D. Sec—Ap As Au BD
    Bl C CP ED Ep IP LD MD MR MS ON S SB TB.
    Col Prep. Gen Acad. Pre-Voc. Voc. Gr PS-12. Courses: Read Math Lang_
    Arts. Man_Arts & Shop. On-Job Trng.
    Therapy: Hear Lang Occup Phys Speech. **Psychotherapy:** Fam Group
    Indiv.
    Enr: 45. Res Males 6. Res Females 2. Day Males 21. Day Females 16.
    Staff: 44.
    Est 1972. State. Nonprofit.

The program at this school emphasizes speech and language development in its educational services for deaf students. Support services include audiology, speech therapy, counseling and complete diagnostic evaluations. Classes are held in several Anchorage schools, and the school offers foster and group home placements for out-of-district students. Mainstreaming opportunities consist of interpreter services, academic placements, and social and athletic participation.

Also available is the infant program, a home-based educational service available to children below age 3 with a suspected hearing impairment.

Both programs offer parental education and training.

HOPE COMMUNITY RESOURCES

Res — Coed All Ages

Anchorage, AK 99518. 540 W International Airport Rd.
Tel: 907-561-5335. Fax: 907-564-7429.
www.hopealaska.org
Stephen P. Lesko, Exec Dir.
    Conditions: Primary—MR.
    Therapy: Hear Occup Phys Speech. **Psychotherapy:** Fam Group Indiv.
    Est 1968. Private. Nonprofit.

RESIDENTIAL YOUTH CARE

Res — Coed Ages 10-18

Ketchikan, AK 99901. 2514 1st Ave.
Tel: 907-225-4664. Fax: 907-247-4664.
E-mail: ryc@kpunet.net
Jack Duckworth, BA, Dir.
   Focus: Rehab. Treatment. **Conditions:** Primary—ADD ADHD CD ED Mood PTSD. Sec—BD Bu Db Dx OCD Sz TS.
   Col Prep. Gen Acad. Pre-Voc. Voc. Gr 5-12. Courses: Read Math Lang_ Arts. Man_Arts & Shop.
   Psychotherapy: Fam Group Indiv Parent.
   Enr: 12. Res Males 9. Res Females 3. **Staff:** 17. Prof 14. Admin 3.
   Rates 2003: Res $211/day. State Aid.
   Est 1993. Private.

Youth Care provides emergency shelter care and specialized residential treatment for children and
   adolescents. Treatment typically lasts between six months and a year.

SOUTHCENTRAL COUNSELING CENTER

Clinic: Ages 3-17. M-F 8-5.

Anchorage, AK 99523. 4020 Folker St, PO Box 230687.
Tel: 907-563-1000. Fax: 907-563-2045.
www.southcentralcounseling.org   E-mail: sccinfo@alaska.net
Jerry A. Jenkins, MAC, MEd, Exec Dir. **Jeanne Bereiter,** Med Dir.
   Conditions: Primary—ED. Sec—BD.
   Shelt_Workshop.
   Psychotherapy: Fam Group Indiv.
   Est 1985. Private. Nonprofit. **Spons:** Anchorage Community Mental Health Services.

ARIZONA

ANASAZI OUTDOOR BEHAVIORAL HEALTHCARE PROGRAM
Res — Coed Ages 12-25

Mesa, AZ 85204. 1424 S Stapley Dr.
Tel: 480-892-7403. Fax: 480-892-6701.
www.anasazi.org   E-mail: info@anasazi.org
Lester W. B. Moore, CEO. David J. Jecman, PhD, Clin Dir. LuAnne Endres, Adm.
  Focus: Treatment. Conditions: Primary—CD Mood. Sec—ADD ADHD BD Dx ED LD OCD.
  Gen Acad. Gr 7-12. Courses: Read Math Lang_Arts Sci.
  Psychotherapy: Fam Group Indiv Parent.
  Enr: 40. Staff: 30 (Full 24, Part 6).
  Rates 2004: Res $385-435/. Schol avail.
  Est 1988. Private. Nonprofit. Spons: ANASAZI Foundation.

This program provides treatment for adolescents with emotional, behavioral or substance abuse problems. Participants take part in a rigorous wilderness expedition, during which attitudes and behaviors are examined. Staff attempt to find the source of the adolescent's anger and subsequently strengthen parent-child relationships.

ARIZONA BAPTIST CHILDREN'S SERVICES
Res — Coed Ages 5-18

Glendale, AZ 85302. 6015 W Peoria Ave.
Tel: 623-349-2227. Fax: 623-776-0343.
www.abcs.org
  Conditions: Primary—ED LD.
  Gen Acad. Gr K-12. Courses: Read Math Lang_Arts.
  Therapy: Music. Psychotherapy: Fam Group Indiv.
  Staff: Prof 15.
  Est 1960. Private. Nonprofit.

ARIZONA COUNSELING RESOURCES
Clinic: Ages 3-18. M-F 7-5; Eves M-F 5-8.

Peoria, AZ 85345. 10559 N 99th Ave.
Tel: 623-974-0357. Fax: 623-974-0399.
E-mail: bedoc@msn.com
Bud Leikvoll, MA, Dir.
  Focus: Treatment. Conditions: Primary—ADD ADHD Anx BD BI Bu CD Dc Dx ED Mood OCD Psy PTSD PW SP Sz TS. IQ 90 and up.

Psychotherapy: Fam Indiv Parent.
Staff: 9 (Full 8, Part 1).
Rates 2003: Clinic $95/ses.
Est 1996. Private.

Arizona Counseling offers mental health services to children and adults. Services include assessment, counseling and support.

ARIZONA STATE SCHOOLS
FOR THE DEAF AND THE BLIND

Res — Coed Ages 5-22; Day — Coed Birth-22

Tucson, AZ 85754. PO Box 85000.
Tel: 520-770-3700. Fax: 520-770-3711.
www.asdb.state.az.us
   Conditions: Primary—B D. Sec—LD.
   Col Prep. Gen Acad. Pre-Voc. Voc. Ungraded. Courses: Read Math Lang_
      Arts. On-Job Trng.
   Est 1912. State. Nonprofit.

ARIZONA'S CHILDREN ASSOCIATION

Res — Coed Ages 5-18; Day — Coed 5-15
Clinic: Ages 1-18. M-S 8-5; Eves M-Th by Appt.

Prescott, AZ 86301. 302 W Willis St, Ste 103.
   Nearby locations: Flagstaff.
Tel: 928-443-1991.
www.arizonaschildren.org
Fred J. Chaffee, MA, MSW, Pres. **Ann Lettes,** MD, Med Dir. **Ann McKenna,**
   Adm.
   Focus: Treatment. **Conditions:** Primary—ADD ADHD BD CD ED OCD
      ODD Psy PTSD SP Sz. Sec—Dx LD MR. **IQ 65 and up.**
   Gen Acad. Gr K-12. Courses: Read Math Lang_Arts.
   Therapy: Chemo Milieu Recreational. **Psychotherapy:** Fam Group Indiv
      Parent.
   Rates 2003: Res $250/day. Day $55/day. State Aid.
   Est 1912. Private. Nonprofit.

The agency offers therapy, counseling and special education to severely emotionally disturbed children. Parents are involved in the therapeutic process and the average length of residential treatment is four and a half months.

AZCA offers a continuum of care including prevention, preservation, adoptions, foster care, in-home and office therapy, psychiatric services, family support and unwed teen parent support. This regional center serves individuals in Coconino, Yavapai, Navajo and Apache counties. Other regional centers are located in Tucson, Yuma and Phoenix.

ARIZONA'S CHILDREN ASSOCIATION

Res — Coed Ages 5-18; Day — Coed 5-15
Clinic: Ages 1-18. M-S 8-5; Eves M-Th by Appt.

Yuma, AZ 85365. 3780 S 4th Ave Ext, Ste I.
Nearby locations: Bullhead City; Kingman; Lake Havasu City; Parker.
Tel: 928-344-8800.
www.arizonaschildren.org
Fred J. Chaffee, MA, MSW, Pres. **Ann Lettes,** MD, Med Dir. **Ann McKenna,** Adm.
Focus: Treatment. **Conditions:** Primary—ADD ADHD BD CD ED OCD ODD Psy PTSD SP Sz. Sec—Dx LD MR. **IQ 65 and up.**
Gen Acad. Gr K-12. Courses: Read Math Lang_Arts.
Therapy: Milieu Recreational. **Psychotherapy:** Fam Group Indiv Parent.
Rates 2003: Res $250/day. Day $55/day. State Aid.
Est 1912. Private. Nonprofit.

The agency offers therapy, counseling and special education to severely emotionally disturbed children. Parents are involved in the therapeutic process and the average length of residential treatment is four and a half months.

AZCA offers a continuum of care including prevention, preservation, adoptions, foster care, in-home and office therapy, psychiatric services, family support and unwed teen parent support. This regional center serves individuals in Mohave, La Paz and Yuma counties. Other regional centers are located in Tucson, Prescott and Phoenix.

ARIZONA'S CHILDREN ASSOCIATION

Res — Coed Ages 5-18; Day — Coed 5-15
Clinic: Ages 1-18. M-S 8-5; Eves M-Th by Appt.

Tucson, AZ 85725. 2700 S 8th Ave, PO Box 7277.
Nearby locations: Benson; Bisbee; Globe; Safford; Sierra Vista.
Tel: 520-622-7611. Fax: 520-624-7042.
www.arizonaschildren.org
Fred J. Chaffee, MA, MSW, Pres. **Ann Lettes,** MD, Med Dir. **Ann McKenna,** Adm.
Focus: Treatment. **Conditions:** Primary—ADD ADHD BD CD ED OCD ODD Psy PTSD SP Sz. Sec—Dx LD MR. **IQ 65 and up.**
Gen Acad. Gr K-12. Courses: Read Math Lang_Arts.
Therapy: Chemo Milieu Recreational. **Psychotherapy:** Fam Group Indiv Parent.
Rates 2003: Res $250/day. Day $55/day. State Aid.
Est 1912. Private. Nonprofit.

The agency offers therapy, counseling and special education to severely emotionally disturbed children. Parents are involved in the therapeutic process and the average length of residential treatment is four and a half months.

AZCA offers a continuum of care including prevention, preservation, adoptions, foster care, in-home and office therapy, psychiatric services, family support and unwed teen parent support. This regional center serves individuals in Pima, Santa Cruz,

Graham, Greeley and Cochise counties, as well as in parts of Pinal and Gila counties. Other regional centers are located in Yuma, Prescott and Phoenix.

ARIZONA'S CHILDREN ASSOCIATION

Res — Coed Ages 5-18; Day — Coed 5-15
Clinic: Ages 1-18. M-S 8-5; Eves M-Th by Appt.

Phoenix, AZ 85004. 2833 N 3rd St.
  Nearby locations: Chandler; Surprise; Tolleson.
Tel: 602-234-3733. Fax: 602-234-0139.
www.arizonaschildren.org
Fred J. Chaffee, MA, MSW, Pres. **Ann Lettes,** MD, Med Dir. **Ann McKenna,** Adm.
  Focus: Treatment. **Conditions:** Primary—ADD ADHD BD CD ED OCD ODD Psy PTSD SP Sz. Sec—Dx LD MR. **IQ 65 and up.**
  Gen Acad. Gr K-12. Courses: Read Math Lang_Arts.
  Therapy: Chemo Recreational. **Psychotherapy:** Fam Group Indiv Parent.
  Rates 2003: Res $250/day. Day $55/day. State Aid.
  Est 1912. Private. Nonprofit.

The agency offers therapy, counseling and special education to severely emotionally disturbed children. Parents are involved in the therapeutic process and the average length of residential treatment is four and a half months.

AZCA offers a continuum of care including prevention, preservation, adoptions, foster care, in-home and office therapy, psychiatric services, family support and unwed teen parent support. This regional center serves individuals in Maricopa County, as well as in parts of Pinal and Gila counties. Other regional centers are located in Tucson, Yuma and Prescott.

BETHANY RANCH HOME

Res and Day — Coed Ages 18 and up
Clinic: All Ages. M-S 8-5.

Phoenix, AZ 85016. 6130 N 16th St.
Tel: 602-279-5448. Fax: 602-279-3691.
E-mail: naturopathicdr@msn.com
Barbara Oxley, BSN, RN, MD, Co-Exec Dir. **John Oxley,** BA, RN, MD, Co-Exec Dir.
  Focus: Rehab. Treatment. **Conditions:** Primary—Ar Au Bl CP Db DS Ep MR OH. Sec—ADD ADHD AN Anx Ap As D Dx ED Mood OCD S Sz. **IQ 40-80.**
  Voc. Shelt_Workshop. On-Job Trng.
  Therapy: Recreational Speech.
  Enr: 20. Res Males 9. Res Females 9. Day Males 1. Day Females 1. **Staff:** 12 (Full 10, Part 2). Admin 2.
  Rates 2003: Res $1800/mo. Day $1500/mo. Clinic $150/hr.
  Est 1966. Private. Nonprofit. Nondenom Christian.

This facility provides residential and day training care for developmentally disabled adolescents and adults in a compassionate Christian environment. The program's main goal is to maintain a healthy, home-like atmosphere and a productive work experience along with education and rehabilitation. Residents interact on a daily basis with staff and family members, as well as with children and animals. Training is provided in the areas of work and daily living skills, as well as functional academics. Subcontracts with local industry provide work for which a client is paid.

Recreational and social activities are offered along with counseling and outpatient services. Individuals with severe behavioral problems cannot be accepted, and the length of treatment varies.

THE BLAKE FOUNDATION
CHILDREN'S ACHIEVEMENT CENTER
Day — Coed Ages Birth-5

Tucson, AZ 85716. 3825 E 2nd St.
Tel: 520-325-1517. Fax: 520-327-5414.
www.blakefoundation.org
   Conditions: Primary—BI CP Ep IP MR ON SB TB.
   Therapy: Hear Lang Occup Phys Speech.
   Est 1950. Private. Nonprofit.

THE CHILDREN'S CENTER FOR
NEURODEVELOPMENTAL STUDIES
Day — Coed Ages 3-21
Clinic: Ages 3-21. M-F 8-5.

Glendale, AZ 85301. 5430 W Glenn Dr.
Tel: 623-915-0345. Fax: 623-937-5425.
www.thechildrenscenteraz.org   E-mail: info@thechildrenscenteraz.org
Lorna Jean King, CEO.
   Focus: Spec Ed. **Conditions:** Primary—Anx Ap Asp Au DS ED OCD ON Psy PW. Sec—Apr As BD BI CP D MR Nf SP Sz TS.
   Pre-Voc. Ungraded. Courses: Read Lang_Arts. On-Job Trng.
   Therapy: Art Dance Hear Movement Music Occup Percepual-Motor Play Recreational Speech.
   Staff: 75 (Full 60, Part 15). Educ 9.
   Rates 2004: Clinic $55/hr. State Aid.
   Summer Prgm: Day. Educ. Rec. Ther. Day Rate $0. 8 wks.
   Est 1978. Private. Nonprofit.

The Children's Center offers learning opportunities for children in preschool through high school who have been diagnosed with autism, moderate or severe mental retardation, emotional disabilities, or multiple disabilities with severe sensory impairment or traumatic brain injury. The center focuses on the use of sensory integration as the primary therapeutic approach.

Services are offered to those in the Phoenix area and in central Arizona. The center offers a state-certified special education school (typically paid for by the sending school district), as well as individual therapy services for children who are attending public school but are in need of therapeutic intervention. Auditory integration training is available off site.

CHINLE VALLEY SCHOOL
FOR EXCEPTIONAL CHILDREN
Res and Day — Coed Ages 5 and up

Chinle, AZ 86503. PO Box 159.
Tel: 928-674-2700. Fax: 928-674-2717.
Andrew Benallie, Exec Dir. **Bobby H. Brown,** Adm.
  Focus: Spec Ed. **Conditions:** Primary—Au CP DS Ep MR OH. Sec—Anx Ap Apr B BD Bl CD D Db ED MS S SB.
  Pre-Voc. Ungraded. Courses: Read Math.
  Therapy: Occup Phys Speech. **Psychotherapy:** Indiv.
  Enr: 37. **Staff:** 80 (Full 70, Part 10). Prof 6. Educ 3. Admin 8.
  Private. Nonprofit.

Chinle provides year-round educational services for individuals with developmental disabilities. The day and residential programs are centrally located on the remote Navajo Nation in Chinle. CVS provides services through funding agencies such as the Navajo Nation Division of Social Services, the Arizona Department of Economic Security and local public schools.

DEVEREUX ARIZONA
Res and Day — Coed Ages 3-21
Clinic: All Ages. M-S 8-6; Eves M W 6-9.

Scottsdale, AZ 85259. 11000 N Scottsdale Rd, Ste 260.
Tel: 480-998-2920. Fax: 480-443-5587.
www.devereuxaz.org   E-mail: az@devereux.org
Jim Cole, BS, MA, Exec Dir. **Nasser Djavadi,** MD, Med Dir.
  Focus: Treatment. **Conditions:** Primary—ADD ADHD Asp Au BD Dx ED LD OCD Psy. Sec—Bl CD D S. **IQ 70 and up.**
  Gen Acad. Pre-Voc. Ungraded. Courses: Read Math Lang_Arts Computers.
  Therapy: Chemo Hear Lang Occup Phys Speech. **Psychotherapy:** Fam Group Indiv Parent.
  Enr: 72. **Staff:** 140.
  Est 1967. Private. Nonprofit. **Spons:** Devereux Foundation.

An operating unit of The Devereux Foundation, which was founded in 1912 by Helena T. Devereux, this year-round center provides a variety of psychiatric residential, day and outpatient services for children and adults with moderate to severe emotional and behavioral disabilities. Residential services range from an intensive treatment unit to a transitional psychiatric program.

Devereux utilizes a multidisciplinary team approach to maximize opportunities for therapeutic change. Master's-level therapists and psychologists provide individual, group and family psychotherapy. Psychiatric services include assessments, medication monitoring and, when appropriate, individual therapy. The center aims to eventually return each child to his or her home and community.   **See Also Page 1025**

DEVEREUX ARIZONA

Res — Coed Ages 3-17; Day — Coed 6-21
Clinic: All Ages. M-S 8-6; Eves M W 6-9.

Tucson, AZ 85712. 6140 E Grant Rd.
Tel: 520-296-5551. Fax: 520-296-8244.
www.devereuxaz.org
Jim Cole, Exec Dir.
   Focus: Treatment. **Conditions:** Primary—ADD ADHD Anx Asp Au BD CD Dx ED LD Mood OCD Psy. **IQ 70 and up.**
   Gen Acad. Ungraded. Courses: Read Math Lang_Arts.
   Psychotherapy: Fam Group Indiv.
   Est 1967. Private. Nonprofit. **Spons:** Devereux Foundation.

See Also Page 1025

EASTER SEALS ARIZONA
EARLY INTERVENTION PROGRAM

Clinic: Ages Birth-3. M-F 8-4:30.

Tempe, AZ 85004. 2075 S Cottonwood Dr.
Tel: 480-222-4100. Fax: 480-222-4123.
www.az.easterseals.com
J. Magdaleno, Dir.
   Focus: Treatment. **Conditions:** Primary—Ap Au BI CP ED IP LD MD MR MS ON S SB. Sec—As B C D Dx Ep.
   Therapy: Hear Lang Occup Phys Play Speech.
   Staff: 14.
   Est 1928. Private. Nonprofit.

This facility offers a program designed to improve developmental skills in young children. Services address communication, motor, thinking, social/emotional and self-help areas. Parents participate in the program, acquiring skills to use in working with the child at home. Fees are determined along a sliding scale.

FLORENCE CRITTENTON SERVICES OF ARIZONA

Res — Females Ages 12-21

Phoenix, AZ 85013. 715 W Mariposa St.

Tel: 602-274-7318. Fax: 602-274-7549.
www.flocrit.org
Linda Volhein, Exec Dir.
  Focus: Treatment. **Conditions:** Primary—BD CD ED OCD. Sec—ADD
    ADHD Dx LD. **IQ 75 and up.**
  Gen Acad. Pre-Voc. Ungraded. Courses: Read Math Lang_Arts.
  Psychotherapy: Fam Group Indiv.
  Enr: 22. **Staff:** 15 (Full 12, Part 3).
  Est 1896. Private. Nonprofit.

Prevention/intervention and residential services include emergency shelter care, crisis intervention, independent living skills training, parental skills classes, teen and family counseling, and foster home recruitment. A long-term treatment plan is provided for pregnant and nonpregnant girls who are unsuitable for immediate foster home placement. All girls residing at the center must attend the on-site school.

GOMPERS CENTER

Day — Coed Ages 5 and up

Phoenix, AZ 85017. 6601 N 27th Ave.
Tel: 602-336-0061. Fax: 602-336-0249.
www.gomperscenter.org   E-mail: gompers@doitnow.com
Donald P. Zella, Exec Dir.
  Focus: Treatment. **Conditions:** Primary—Asp Au DS MR PDD. Sec—Ap
    Apr B Bl CP Db ED Ep MD Mood MS Nf OCD ON SB TS.
  Pre-Voc. Ungraded. Courses: Functional Curriculum. Shelt_Workshop. On-
    Job Trng.
  Therapy: Hear Hydro Occup Phys Speech.
  Staff: 24.
  Rates 2003: Day $129/day. $55 (Therapy)/ses.
  Summer Prgm: Day. Educ. Day Rate $107. 8 wks.
  Est 1947. Private. Nonprofit.

Gompers provide children and adults with disabilities and their families with professionally organized and implemented programs of special education, rehabilitative therapy, vocational training, employment placement and community education.
The center also offers dental services, transportation services and recreational options.

GRUNEWALD-BLITZ CLINIC

Clinic: All Ages. M-F 8-5.

Tucson, AZ 85721. 1131 E 2nd St, PO Box 210071.
Tel: 520-621-7070.
http://w3.arizona.edu/~gbc   E-mail: gbc@w3.arizona.edu
Anthony B. DeFeo, PhD, CCC-SLP, Dir.
  Focus: Treatment. **Conditions:** Primary—S.
  Therapy: Lang Speech.

Est 1960. State. **Spons:** Univ of Arizona.

This clinic offers individual diagnostic speech and language evaluations, in addition to group and individual therapies for articulation, language, voice and stuttering problems. Clients must have speech-language difficulties as a primary diagnosis, but the clinic can accommodate individuals with various secondary conditions and IQ levels.

HENRY OCCUPATIONAL THERAPY SERVICES

Clinic: Ages Birth-19. M-F 10-5.

Youngtown, AZ 85363. PO Box 145.
Tel: 623-933-3821. Fax: 623-933-3821.
www.ateachabout.com   E-mail: rick@henryot.com
Diana A. Henry, MS, OTR, Pres.
  Focus: Trng. **Conditions:** Primary—ADHD LD. Sec—Asp Au BD BI CP Dx MR.
  Therapy: Occup.
  Staff: 4 (Full 3, Part 1). Prof 2. Admin 2.
  Rates 2003: Clinic $60/ses. Schol avail. State Aid.
  Est 1984. Private.

This clinic provides in-service training and workshops on sensory integration throughout the US and Canada. Sensory-integrative treatment is also offered to persons with sensory-regulatory disorders. Most clients have also been diagnosed with a learning disability, attention deficit disorder or a motor communication disorder. Treatment generally lasts six months to two years.

HOWARD S GRAY EDUCATION PROGRAM
SAMARITAN BEHAVIORAL HEALTH

Day — Coed Ages 11-21

Scottsdale, AZ 85251. 7575 E Earll Dr.
Tel: 480-941-7558. Fax: 480-994-5558.
E-mail: rand.lane@bannerhealth.com
Rand Lane, MA, Prin.
  Focus: Spec Ed. **Conditions:** Primary—ADD ADHD Anx Asp Dc Dg Dx ED LD Mood OCD Psy Sz TS. Sec—AN Apr As Au BD BI Bu C CD Ep HIV MD MR MS Nf ON PTSD PW SB SP TB. **IQ 80 and up.**
  Gen Acad. Gr 5-12. Courses: Read Math Lang_Arts.
  Enr: 48. Day Males 36. Day Females 12. **Staff:** 10 (Full 9, Part 1).
  Rates 2003: Day $85/day (+$30/ses). Schol 3 ($10,000).
  Est 1985. Private. Nonprofit. **Spons:** Banner Health.

An on-site special function day school for adolescents with learning disabilities, attention deficits, emotional handicaps or a combination thereof, the school seeks to develop the student's intellect, self-discipline and self-esteem, with the aim of returning boys and girls to their home schools.

Classrooms contain personal computers with Internet access and integrate videocassette units, thereby facilitating individualized instruction. Educational and recreational activities take place in the arts and crafts center, the outdoor sports court, open fields, landscaped patios and, for group discussions, in lounges.

LATCH SCHOOL

Day — Coed Ages 2-22

Phoenix, AZ 85051. 8145 N 27th Ave.
Tel: 602-995-7366. Fax: 602-995-0867.
www.latchschool.org   E-mail: latchinc@aol.com
Connie Laird, MS, Exec Dir. **Nancy Molder,** MAEd, Prin. **Donald Coe,** Adm.
　Focus: Spec Ed. **Conditions:** Primary—Au BI CP DS MD MR ON SB.
　　Sec—As B C D ED Ep OCD S.
　Pre-Voc. Voc. Ungraded. Courses: Read Math Lang_Arts. Man_Arts &
　　Shop. On-Job Trng. Horticulture.
　Therapy: Art Hear Lang Movement Music Occup Phys Recreational
　　Speech Aqua. **Psychotherapy:** Equine.
　Enr: 215. Day Males 160. Day Females 55. **Staff:** 189 (Full 188, Part 1).
　　Prof 32. Educ 27. Admin 22.
　Rates 2003: Day $26,000-29,000/sch yr. State Aid.
　Summer Prgm: Day. Educ. Rec. Ther. Day Rate $2800-3200.
　Est 1980. Private. Nonprofit.

LATCH school provides an individualized curriculum with an appropriate balance of academic, vocational and daily living skills. Intense programming in small classrooms with a low student/staff ratio helps each student to reach his or her potential. Vocational programs are designed to teach students work skills and prepare them socially and emotionally for a productive life. Both on-site and off-site employment opportunities provide real-life situations intended to develop confidence, responsibility and independence. Therapy services, which include horseback riding and swimming programs, aim to enhance motor development, sensory awareness, language development, and social and emotional growth.

LIFE DEVELOPMENT INSTITUTE

Res — Coed Ages 18 and up; Day — Coed 16 and up

Glendale, AZ 85308. 18001 N 79th Ave, Ste E-71.
Tel: 623-773-2774. Fax: 623-773-2788.
www.life-development-inst.org   E-mail: ldiinariz@aol.com
Rob Crawford, MEd, Pres.
　Focus: Spec Ed. Trng. **Conditions:** Primary—ADD ADHD Dx LD. Sec—Au
　　BI CP D ED Ep ON S SB.
　Col Prep. Gen Acad. Pre-Voc. Voc. Gr 9-PG. Courses: Computers.
　Enr: 53. Res Males 14. Res Females 14. Day Males 18. Day Females 7.
　　Staff: 13 (Full 11, Part 2).
　Est 1982. Private. Nonprofit.

This program offers secondary and postsecondary education and training and employment services for individuals with learning disabilities. The program aims to enable students to satisfy requirements leading to graduation from LDI's high school, college and technical school programs, begin careers, obtain independent living status and gain financial self-sufficiency.

NEW WAY LEARNING ACADEMY
Day — Coed Ages 6-19

Scottsdale, AZ 85257. 1300 N 77th St.
Tel: 480-946-9112. Fax: 480-946-2657.
www.newwayacademy.org
John Phin, Exec Dir. **Dawn Gutierrez,** MEd, Head.
   Focus: Spec Ed. **Conditions:** Primary—ADD ADHD Dx LD. Sec—ED OCD S. **IQ 80 and up.**
   Col Prep. Gen Acad. Pre-Voc. Gr K-12. Courses: Read Lang_Arts Sci Hist Adaptive_Phys_Ed. On-Job Trng.
   Therapy: Art Lang Music Occup Speech. **Psychotherapy:** Fam Group Indiv Parent.
   Enr: 120. **Staff:** 35.
   Rates 2003: Day $15,750/sch yr. Schol avail.
   Est 1968. Private. Nonprofit.

New Way provides counseling and remediation of specific learning disabilities. The academy designs individualized programs for each student, with an emphasis on both academics and social and emotional development. Other integral aspects of the program are Orton-Gillingham dyslexia training, speech therapy and occupational therapy. The vast majority of pupils go on to earn their high school diploma, and most later attend college.

PHOENIX DAY SCHOOL FOR THE DEAF
Day — Coed Ages 3-22

Phoenix, AZ 85021. 1935 W Hayward Ave.
Tel: 602-336-6800. TTY: 602-336-6800. Fax: 602-336-6944.
www.hawbaker.cx/pdsd
Joseph DiLorenzo, Dir. **Cathie Devers,** Adm.
   Focus: Spec Ed. **Conditions:** Primary—D.
   Col Prep. Gen Acad. Pre-Voc. Voc. Gr PS-12. Courses: Read Math Lang_Arts Sci Computers Studio_Art Speech Home_Ec Bus. Man_Arts & Shop. On-Job Trng.
   Therapy: Hear Lang Occup Phys Speech. **Psychotherapy:** Indiv.
   Enr: 266. Day Males 140. Day Females 126. **Staff:** 142 (Full 105, Part 37).
   Rates 2004: No Fee.
   Est 1967. State.

A comprehensive educational program is offered by the school to deaf and hearing-impaired children. The hearing handicap must be to such an extent as to warrant full-time special services. In addition, vocational, educational, personal and parental counseling is available.

PROVIDENCE SERVICE CORPORATION

Res and Day — Coed Ages 5-18

Tucson, AZ 85711. 5524 E 4th S.
Tel: 520-747-6600. Fax: 520-747-6605.
www.provcorp.com
Fletcher Jay McCusker, CEO.
    Conditions: Primary—ADD ADHD BD CD ED LD OCD. **IQ 70 and up.**
    Gen Acad. Pre-Voc. Courses: Read Math Lang_Arts Sci Hist Studio_Art.
    On-Job Trng.
    Therapy: Occup Recreational Speech. **Psychotherapy:** Fam Group Indiv.
    Enr: 120. **Staff:** 59 (Full 41, Part 18).
    Est 1972. Private. Inc.

Providence conducts year-round, community-based, open-setting facilities that emphasizes behavior control and behavior development using process therapy and insight, reality-oriented therapy. Comprehensive evaluation, assessment and diagnosis, in addition to individual psychotherapy and group, recreational and milieu therapies, are provided in a homelike atmosphere. Family counseling and parental skills training, as well as prevocational and independent living skills training, are also provided.

Also available is the Monitor Prime In-Home Program, which offers in-home crisis intervention in addition to individual and family therapy. It is conducted by a team of therapists assigned to the family.

Recreational opportunities include swimming, horseback riding, tennis, basketball, football, and arts and crafts. Children attend an on-grounds school during their stay, the length of which is usually six to eight months. Nonambulatory, blind and psychotic children are not appropriate for enrollment in this program.

Affiliated programs are located in Florida and Tennessee.

ST. MICHAELS ASSOCIATION
FOR SPECIAL EDUCATION

Res — Coed Ages Birth-30; Day — Coed Birth-21

St Michaels, AZ 86511. PO Box 1000.
Tel: 928-871-2800. Fax: 928-871-4873.
Eugene Thompson, Exec Dir.
    Focus: Spec Ed. Trng. **Conditions:** Primary—CP MR S.
    Pre-Voc. Voc. Ungraded. Courses: Read Math. Shelt_Workshop.
    Therapy: Hear Lang Occup Phys Speech.
    Est 1968. Private. Nonprofit.

ST. PAUL'S PREPARATORY ACADEMY

Res and Day — Males Ages 14-18

Phoenix, AZ 85064. 2645 E Osborn Rd, PO Box 32650.
Tel: 602-956-9090. Fax: 602-956-3018.
www.stpaulsacademy.com   E-mail: lions@stpaulsacademy.com
Lowell E. Andrews, BS, MS, CEO. **Harold Elliot,** Med, Prin. **Julie Vaughan,** Adm.

> **Focus:** Spec Ed. **Conditions:** Primary—ADD ADHD ED. Sec—BD. **IQ 115-120.**
> **Col Prep.** Gr 9-12. Courses: Read Math Lang_Arts Computers Sci Soc_ Stud Life_Skills.
> **Psychotherapy:** Fam Group Indiv.
> **Enr:** 75. Res Males 50. Day Males 25. **Staff:** 37 (Full 33, Part 4). Prof 16. Educ 12.
> **Rates 2003:** Res $31,400/sch yr (+$1500). Day $12,000/sch yr (+$1000). Schol avail.
> **Summer Prgm:** Res & Day. Educ. Rec. Res Rate $3750. Day Rate $1250. 5 wks.
> **Est 1962.** Private. Nonprofit. Episcopal.

This boarding and day school offers young men with low motivation or initial behavior difficulties a rigorous college preparatory program. Students assessments, which occur prior to admission, comprise a review of past academic performance and testing, the identification of strengths and weaknesses, a review of social history, and input from the pupil and his parents. The academy provides enrichment and group therapy sessions designed to build self-esteem and increase motivation. Other features of St. Paul's program are SAT and ACT tutoring and testing, in addition to assistance with college selection and the application process.

Clubs address such student interests as weightlifting, rock climbing, golf, poetry, yearbook, chess, choir, drama, the environment, politics and art. Pupils may take part in regularly scheduled outings to cultural and professional sporting events in the city. In addition, course work incorporates excursions to musicals, plays, the symphony and the opera.

STERLING RANCH

Res — Females Ages 18 and up

Skull Valley, AZ 86338. Old Skull Valley Rd, PO Box 36.
Tel: 928-442-3289. Fax: 928-442-9272.
Trent D. Nickels, BA, BS, Dir.

> **Focus:** Trng. **Conditions:** Primary—BI CP MD MR MS OH. Sec—ADD ADHD Ap Apr Ar As Asp Au CF Dx ED Ep LD PDD S SB Sz. **IQ 35 and up.**
> **Pre-Voc.** Ungraded. Courses: Read Math Lang_Arts ASL Crafts Dance Speech.
> **Therapy:** Lang Occup Phys. **Psychotherapy:** Group.
> **Enr:** 14. Res Females 14. **Staff:** 10 (Full 9, Part 1).
> **Rates 2003:** Res $1500/mo. Schol 2.

Est 1947. Private. Nonprofit.

An outgrowth of Skull Valley Ranch School, Sterling Ranch provides mentally handicapped women with minimally restrictive, family-like residential care. A secure, controlled environment and private rooms give residents the opportunity to develop their natural abilities and assert their independence.

The Ranch's schoolhouse serves as a special training workshop to provide individualized education. Creative activities, such as crafts, music, reading and drama, are important parts of group interaction. Field trips, summer picnics and swimming, and short recreational hikes make up the outdoor experience.

TURNING POINT SCHOOL

Day — Coed Ages 6-15

Tucson, AZ 85705. 200 E Yavapai Rd.
Tel: 520-292-9300. Fax: 520-292-9075.
www.turningpointschool.com
Nancy C. Von Wald, MEd, Dir.
  Focus: Spec Ed. **Conditions:** Primary—ADD ADHD Asp Au Dc Dg Dx LD. IQ 85-120.
  Gen Acad. Gr 1-8. Courses: Read Math Lang_Arts Sci Hist.
  Therapy: Art Music. **Psychotherapy:** Parent.
  Enr: 60. Day Males 42. Day Females 18. **Staff:** 9 (Full 7, Part 2).
  Rates 2003: Day $5,700/sch yr (+$60). Sliding-Scale Rate $4000-4500/ sch_yr. Schol 40.
  Summer Prgm: Day. Educ. Day Rate $475. 4 wks.
  Est 1992. Private. Nonprofit.

Turning Point offers a full day school, a summer session and educational testing to students with average to above-average intelligence who have learning differences. The goal of the school is to remediate and return students to mainstream schools as soon as possible. Students with severe behavioral problems may not enroll.

UPWARD FOUNDATION

Day — Coed Ages Birth-22

Phoenix, AZ 85014. 6306 N 7th St.
Tel: 602-279-5801. Fax: 602-279-0785.
www.upwardfoundation.org   E-mail: info@upwardfoundation.com
  Conditions: Primary—MR.
  Gen Acad. Gr PS-K.
  Therapy: Hear Lang Music Occup Phys Speech. **Psychotherapy:** Indiv.
  Est 1958. Private. Inc.

VISIONQUEST

Res — Coed Ages 12-21

Tucson, AZ 85732. 600 N Swan Rd, PO Box 12906.
Tel: 520-881-3950. Fax: 520-881-3269.
www.vq.com   E-mail: visionquest@vq.com
  Conditions: Primary—BD.
  Gen Acad. Ungraded. Courses: Read Math Lang_Arts. Man_Arts & Shop.
    On-Job Trng.
  Psychotherapy: Fam Group Indiv.
  Est 1973. Private. Inc.

YOUTH EVALUATION AND TREATMENT CENTERS

Res — Coed Ages 7-17
Clinic: Ages 7-17. M-F 8:30-5; Eves M-Th 5-8:30.

Phoenix, AZ 85015. 4414 N 19th Ave.
Tel: 602-285-5550. Fax: 602-285-5551.
www.youthetc.org   E-mail: nmerrick@youthetc.org
Jim Oleson, CLSW, CEO.
  Focus: Treatment. **Conditions:** Primary—BD CD ED. Sec—ADD ADHD Dx
    LD. **IQ 70 and up.**
  Gen Acad. Pre-Voc. Ungraded. Courses: Read Math Lang_Arts Life_Skills.
  Therapy: Milieu Speech. **Psychotherapy:** Fam Group Indiv.
  Est 1974. Private.

The center works with severely emotionally disturbed youths and their families to develop integrity in personal relationships. Treatment is extensive, focusing on group and family unity. Instruction is provided in both individualized and group settings to provide personal attention and to teach appropriate classroom behavior. Short-term crisis shelter and prevention services are also available.

ARKANSAS

ARKADELPHIA HUMAN DEVELOPMENT CENTER

Res and Day — Coed Ages 6 and up

Arkadelphia, AR 71923. PO Box 70.
Tel: 870-246-8011. Fax: 870-246-3864.
www.state.ar.us/dhs   E-mail: margo.green@mail.state.ar.us
Margo Green, Supt.
   Conditions: Primary—MR.
   Courses: Read Math Lang_Arts. Man_Arts & Shop. On-Job Trng.
   Therapy: Hear Lang Occup Phys Speech. **Psychotherapy:** Group Indiv.
   Est 1968. State.

ARKANSAS LIGHTHOUSE FOR THE BLIND

Day — Coed Ages 18 and up

Little Rock, AR 72201. 69th & Murray Sts.
Tel: 501-562-2222. Fax: 501-568-5275.
   Focus: Trng. **Conditions:** Primary—B.
   Est 1940. Private. Inc.

ARKANSAS SCHOOL FOR THE BLIND

Res and Day — Coed Ages 6-21
Clinic: Ages 6-21. T 8-12.

Little Rock, AR 72201. 2600 W Markham St.
Tel: 501-296-1810. Fax: 501-296-1831.
www.arkansasschoolfortheblind.org
Jim Hill, Supt. **Sharon Berry,** Adm.
   Focus: Spec Ed. **Conditions:** Primary—B. Sec—BI CP D ED Ep MR ON S.
   Gen Acad. Pre-Voc. Voc. Gr PS-12. Courses: Read Math Lang_Arts. Man_
     Arts & Shop. Shelt_Workshop. On-Job Trng.
   Therapy: Hear Lang Occup Phys Speech. **Psychotherapy:** Indiv.
   Enr: 94. **Staff:** 73.
   Rates 2004: No Fee.
   Summer Prgm: Res & Day. Educ. Rec. Res Rate $0. Day Rate $0. 3 wks.
   Est 1859. State.

ASB places blind children in grades PS-12 in academic and vocational tracts. The school's Exceptional Unit provides care for blind and visually impaired multi-handicapped students. The facility attempts to teach students self-sufficiency while integrating them more fully into the community.

ARKANSAS SCHOOL FOR THE DEAF
Res — Coed Ages 4-21; Day — Coed 3-21

Little Rock, AR 72203. 2400 W Markham St, PO Box 3811.
Tel: 501-324-9506. TTY: 501-324-9707. Fax: 501-324-9559.
www.arkansas.gov/asd
Marcella Dalla Rosa, EdD, Int Supt. **Marsha Opauski,** Adm.
  Focus: Spec Ed. **Conditions:** Primary—D. Sec—ADD ADHD AN Anx Ap
    Apr As Asp Au B BD Bl Bu C CD CP Db Dc Dg DS Dx ED Ep HIV IP LD
    MD Mood MR MS Nf OCD ODD ON PDD Psy PTSD PW S SB SP Sz TB
    TS.
  Col Prep. Gen Acad. Pre-Voc. Voc. Gr PS-12. Courses: Read Math Lang_
    Arts. Man_Arts & Shop. Shelt_Workshop.
  Therapy: Hear Lang Occup Percepual-Motor Phys Recreational Speech.
  Enr: 153. Res Males 48. Res Females 48. Day Males 28. Day Females 29.
    Staff: 152 (Full 110, Part 42). Prof 49. Educ 38. Admin 8.
  Rates 2004: No Fee.
  Summer Prgm: Res & Day. Educ. Rec. Ther. Enrichment. Res Rate $0. Day
    Rate $0.
  Est 1850. State. Nonprofit.

ASD has an outreach program for deaf and hearing-impaired students that operates throughout the state with teachers and staff in public schools. School staff includes a coordinator, educational audiologists and a consulting sign language interpreter.
  Applicants must be Arkansas residents.

THE CENTERS FOR YOUTH AND FAMILIES
Res — Coed Ages 6-18; Day — Coed 2½-18
Clinic: All Ages. M-F 8:30-5; Eve Th 5-8.

Little Rock, AR 72225. 5905 Forest Pl, PO Box 251970.
Tel: 501-666-8686. Fax: 501-663-6503.
www.youthandfamilies.org
Doug Stadter, MPA, CEO.
  Focus: Treatment. **Conditions:** Primary—ADD ADHD Anx BD CD ED
    Mood OCD Psy Sz. Sec—Au B D Dx LD MR. **IQ 80 and up.**
  Gen Acad. Ungraded. Courses: Read Math Lang_Arts.
  Therapy: Speech. **Psychotherapy:** Fam Group Indiv Parent.
  Enr: 130. Res Males 20. Res Females 20. Day Males 45. Day Females 45.
  Est 1987. Private. Nonprofit.

The centers treat emotionally disturbed learning-disabled children and adolescents through residential, day and outpatient programs. Milieu therapy is combined with behavior modification and reality, transactional analysis and attitudinal therapies. Activity and individualized educational therapies are also conducted.

CONWAY HUMAN DEVELOPMENT CENTER

Res — Coed Ages 9 and up

Conway, AR 72032. 150 E Siebenmorgen Rd.
Tel: 501-329-6851. Fax: 501-336-0508.
Calvin Price, Supt.
  Focus: Spec Ed. Treatment. **Conditions:** Primary—MR. Sec—Au B D LD S.
    IQ 0-68.
  Pre-Voc. Voc. Ungraded. Courses: Read Math Lang_Arts. Shelt_Workshop.
    On-Job Trng.
  Therapy: Hear Lang Occup Phys Speech. **Psychotherapy:** Fam Indiv.
  Enr: 606. Staff: 146.
  Est 1959. State.

This center provides habilitation and educational opportunities for multi-handicapped individuals with a primary diagnosis of mental retardation. Individualized programs emphasize growth and development in social and physical environments consistent with the client's needs. The center emphasizes functional programming.

Clients reside in small living units with other individuals of similar age, sex, and intellectual and functional levels. Medical services include nursing, dentistry and various forms of therapy.

HOT SPRINGS REHABILITATION CENTER

Res and Day — Coed Ages 16 and up
Clinic: Ages 16 and up. M-F 9-4.

Hot Springs, AR 71901. 105 Reserve St.
Tel: 501-624-4411. Fax: 501-620-4311.
http://hotsprings.dina.org/education/hsrc.html
  E-mail: cmtapp@ars.state.ar.us
Tim Milligan, MA, Dir. **Patricia Lang,** MD, Med Dir. **Charles Tapp,** Adm.
  Focus: Rehab. Trng. **Conditions:** Primary—Ap As Asp Au B BI C CP D DS
    Ep LD MD MR MS ON S SB. Sec—Anx BD CD Db ED Mood TS. **IQ 50-**
    120.
  Voc. Man_Arts & Shop. Shelt_Workshop. On-Job Trng.
  Therapy: Hear Lang Occup Percepual-Motor Phys Recreational Speech.
    Psychotherapy: Fam Group Indiv.
  Enr: 300. Staff: 300.
  Rates 2003: Res $549/wk. Day $55/day. Clinic $45/ses. Schol avail. State
    Aid.
  Est 1960. State. Nonprofit.

Located on 21 acres in Hot Springs National Park, the center assists individuals with physical and mental disabilities. Services are offered in specialized areas such as orthopedics, neurosurgery and ophthalmology. The Employability Services Program focuses on basic skills for employment, offering personal counseling, guidance and functional knowledge. A full recreational schedule is offered, and bus transportation is available.

JENKINS MEMORIAL CHILDREN'S CENTER

Day — Coed Ages Birth-21
Clinic: All Ages. M-F 8-4.

Pine Bluff, AR 71603. 2410 Rike Dr.
Tel: 870-534-2035. Fax: 870-534-2058.
Zelda Hoaglan, Exec Dir.
 Focus: Spec Ed. Trng. Conditions: Primary—OH.
 Pre-Voc. Voc. Ungraded. Courses: Read Math Lang_Arts. Shelt_Workshop.
  On-Job Trng.
 Therapy: Hear Lang Occup Phys Speech. Psychotherapy: Fam Group
  Indiv.
 Est 1968. County. Nonprofit. Spons: Society for Crippled Children.

JONESBORO HUMAN DEVELOPMENT CENTER

Res — Coed Ages 12 and up

Jonesboro, AR 72404. 4701 Colony Dr.
Tel: 870-932-5230. Fax: 870-932-4043.
Forrest Steele, BA, Supt.
 Focus: Trng. Treatment. Conditions: Primary—MR. Sec—Ap As Au B BD
  BI C CP Dx ED Ep IP LD MD ON S SB TB. IQ 0-55.
 Gen Acad. Courses: Life_Skills. Shelt_Workshop. On-Job Trng.
 Therapy: Hear Occup Phys Speech. Psychotherapy: Indiv Parent.
 Enr: 128. Res Males 80. Res Females 48. Staff: 67 (Full 62, Part 5).
 Est 1974. State.

This facility provides habilitation and training based upon the individual client's
needs as it aims at increasing the level of independence. Programming emphasizes self-
help training, daily living and prevocational skills, and supported employment.

LIONS WORLD SERVICES FOR THE BLIND

Res — Coed Ages 16 and up

Little Rock, AR 72214. 2811 Fair Park Blvd.
Tel: 501-664-7100. Fax: 501-664-2743.
www.lwsb.org   E-mail: training@lwsb.org
Ramona Sangalli, MEd, Exec Dir. Sherill Wilson, Adm.
 Focus: Spec Ed. Trng. Conditions: Primary—B.
 Col Prep. Gen Acad. Pre-Voc. Voc. Ungraded. Courses: Read Math Lang_
  Arts. Man_Arts & Shop. On-Job Trng.
 Therapy: Speech. Psychotherapy: Group Indiv.
 Staff: 64.
 Est 1939. Private. Nonprofit. Spons: Lions Club.

A rehabilitation center for blind and visually impaired individuals, this facility's services include evaluation, comprehensive personal adjustment, and prevocational and selected vocational training. Educational instruction focuses on communication. College preparatory training includes a class in freshman English that acquaints students with lecture procedure, note taking, theme writing and use of a library. A low-vision clinic provides evaluation and optical aids for sight improvement. The usual duration of training is six months.

MILLCREEK OF ARKANSAS

Res — Coed Ages 5-18
Clinic: All Ages. M-F 8-5.

Fordyce, AR 71742. Hwy 79 N, PO Box 727.
Tel: 870-352-8203. Fax: 870-352-5311.
www.yfcs.com/millcreek_ar.htm
Scott Kelly, Admin. **Hugh A. Nutt**, MD, Med Dir. **Wendy Clay**, Adm.
  Focus: Rehab. Treatment. **Conditions:** Primary—Anx BD CD ED Mood MR OCD Psy PTSD Sz. Sec—ADD ADHD As BI C CP Dx Ep LD ON S SB TB. **IQ 40 and up.**
  Therapy: Art Hear Lang Music Occup Phys Recreational Speech. **Psychotherapy:** Group Indiv Parent.
  Enr: 120. **Staff:** 279.
  Rates 2003: Res $300-350/day.
  Est 1988. Private. Inc. **Spons:** Youth and Family Centered Services.

Millcreek provides mental health services to children and adolescents through two residential programs. The Mental Retardation Treatment Facility program specializes in treating children who are dually diagnosed with mental retardation and an emotional or behavioral disorder. The Psychiatric Treatment Facility program provides services and treatment to children with severe emotional and behavioral disturbances in a structured, therapeutic environment. Millcreek can accommodate any IQ score above 40.

UNIVERSITY OF ARKANSAS-LITTLE ROCK
SPEECH, LANGUAGE AND HEARING CLINIC

Clinic: All Ages. M-F 8-5.

Little Rock, AR 72204. Speech Communication Bldg, Rm 120, 2801 S University Ave.
Tel: 501-569-3155. Fax: 501-569-3157.
www.ualr.edu/~audiology/_backup/clinic.html
Terri Hutton, Coord.
  Focus: Treatment. **Conditions:** Primary—Ap S. Sec—BI CP Dx ED Ep IP LD MD MR MS SB. **IQ 50 and up.**
  Therapy: Hear Lang Speech.
  Staff: 13.
  Est 1971. Federal. Nonprofit.

This training program, which prepares University of Arkansas at Little Rock graduates for positions in a variety of professional settings, provides limited community services. These services include a preschool group for language-disordered children and a group for the hearing-impaired elderly.

UNIVERSITY OF THE OZARKS
THE HARVEY AND BERNICE JONES LEARNING CENTER

Res — Coed Ages 18 and up

Clarksville, AR 72830. 415 N College Ave.
Tel: 479-979-1403. Fax: 479-979-1429.
www.ozarks.edu   E-mail: jlc@ozarks.edu
Julia Frost, MS, Dir. Debby Mooney, Adm.
  Focus: Spec Ed. **Conditions:** Primary—ADD ADHD Dc Dg Dx LD. **IQ 90 and up.**
  Gen Acad. Gr Col-Col. Courses: Read Math Lang_Arts Study_Skills.
  Enr: 80. Res Males 58. Res Females 22. **Staff:** 19 (Full 15, Part 4).
  Rates 2003: Res $30,174/sch yr. Schol 30 ($49,000). State Aid.
  Summer Prgm: Res & Day. Educ. 6 wks.
  Est 1971. Private. Nonprofit. Presbyterian.

The Jones Learning Center provides comprehensive college-level support for students with specific learning disabilities and attention deficit disorder. Developmental services at the center incorporate various services and strategies to help pupils improve basic skills in reading, writing and math. In addition, staff teach three developmental courses: study skills, writing and beginning algebra.

JLC also offers various services that allow students to compensate for their special learning needs. The center provides one-on-one testing accommodations as needed. A technology unit enables pupils to dictate material directly into a computer and subsequently hear the data read back. In addition, an auxiliary services unit provides access to peer tutors, classroom notes and taped material. Tutors work closely with program coordinators to tailor tutoring to the pupil's particular learning style.

Entrants must have a high school diploma or a GED; must possess at least average intelligence; and must have a learning disability or ADD or ADHD as a primary condition. Students complete a two-day psycho-educational evaluation and interview process prior to acceptance.

YOUTH HOME

Res and Day — Coed Ages 12-18
Clinic: All Ages. M-F 8:30-5; Eves by Appt.

Little Rock, AR 72210. 20400 Colonel Glenn Rd.
Tel: 501-821-5500. Fax: 501-821-5580.
www.youthhome.org   E-mail: info@youthhome.org
Beth Cartwright, MSW, Exec Dir. Mark Andersen, MD, Med Dir. Karen Cornwell, Adm.
  Focus: Treatment. **Conditions:** Primary—ADD ADHD Anx BD ED Mood

OCD Psy PTSD SP Sz TS. Sec—Ap As Asp B C CD D Db Dc Dg Dx Ep
HIV LD S SB. **IQ 70 and up.**
Gen Acad. Gr 7-12. Courses: Read Math Lang_Arts.
Therapy: Chemo Milieu Play Recreational Speech. **Psychotherapy:** Fam
Group Indiv.
Enr: 90. Res Males 30. Res Females 20. Day Males 20. Day Females 20.
Staff: 186 (Full 168, Part 18).
Rates 2003: Res $350/day. Day $51/day. Sliding-Scale Rate $11-110/ses
(Clinic). Schol 2. State Aid.
Summer Prgm: Day. Educ. Rec. Ther. 6 wks.
Est 1968. Private. Nonprofit.

The center serves adolescents with severe emotional disturbances or behavior disorders who have a borderline or higher IQ. Services at the home include residential treatment; a special education school that enrolls up to 90 students; foster care group homes; and counseling for various psychiatric problems.

The outpatient office, which provides services for patients and their families, is located at 2 Innwood Cir., Ste. A, 72210 (501-954-7470).

CALIFORNIA

ACADEMIC GUIDANCE SERVICES

Day — Coed Ages 3 and up
Clinic: All Ages. M-F 8:30-5; Eves M-F 5-7:30.

Los Angeles, CA 90035. 1232 S La Cienega Blvd, Ste 204.
Tel: 310-659-8549.
www.addtreatment.com   E-mail: davidhung8@cs.com
David W. Hung, PhD, Dir.
   Focus: Spec Ed. Trng. **Conditions:** Primary—Ap Au BD Dx ED LD MR.
   Col Prep. Gen Acad. Pre-Voc. Voc. Ungraded. Courses: Read Math Lang_
      Arts Writing. On-Job Trng.
   Therapy: Lang Speech. **Psychotherapy:** Fam Indiv.
   Enr: 48. Day Males 26. Day Females 22. **Staff:** 22 (Full 4, Part 18). Prof 20.
      Admin 2.
   Rates 2003: Day $11,000/sch yr. Clinic $95/hr.
   Summer Prgm: Day. Educ. Ther.
   Est 1960. Private.

Academic Guidance Services offers a therapeutic program for children and their families that aims to improve academic performance and behavior. A school curriculum includes credit courses; intensive individual tutoring at all grade levels; remedial work in reading, math and language; study skills development; and test preparation. Counseling on learning problems and family relationships, psycho-educational evaluations and vocational training for adults, and school and career placement are important program concerns.

The facility serves both Orange and Los Angeles and provides distance consultation nationwide.

ACHIEVEKIDS

Res — Coed Ages 10-18; Day — Coed 3-22
Clinic: All Ages. M-F 8-5; Eves M-F 5-8.

Palo Alto, CA 94303. 3860 Middlefield Rd.
Tel: 650-494-1200. Fax: 650-494-1243.
www.achievekids.org
   Focus: Spec Ed. Treatment. **Conditions:** Primary—ADD ADHD Au BD CD
      ED OCD Psy Sz. Sec—BI CP Dx Ep LD MR ON S. **IQ 50-120.**
   Gen Acad. Pre-Voc. Voc. Ungraded. Courses: Read Math Lang_Arts Sci
      Soc_Stud. Man_Arts & Shop. Shelt_Workshop. On-Job Trng.
   Therapy: Lang Occup Speech. **Psychotherapy:** Fam Group Indiv Parent.
   Enr: 82. **Staff:** 110 (Full 45, Part 65).
   Est 1960. Private. Nonprofit.

This program provides educational remediation, gross-motor and sensorimotor training, and therapies in order to integrate children into the public school system. Vocational education is available to adolescents for whom public school placement is not appropriate. An extension program for young adults with severe acting-out behavior emphasizes daily living skills, appropriate community behavior and vocational skills. The residential home provides a structured living environment for children and young adults who have developmental disorders, autism and behavioral difficulties. Clinical fees are determined along a sliding scale according to income. Parent groups, counseling and workshops are also available.

AGNEWS DEVELOPMENTAL CENTER

Res — Coed All Ages

San Jose, CA 95134. 3500 Zanker Rd.
Tel: 408-451-6000. TTY: 408-432-0942. Fax: 408-432-0960.
www.dds.ca.gov/agnews   E-mail: rrichey@agnews.dds.ca.gov
Harold Pitchford, Exec Dir. **Norma Betron,** MD, Med Dir.
　　Focus: Treatment. **Conditions:** Primary—DS MR PDD. Sec—ADD ADHD
　　Ap As Au B BD BI C CD CP D Dg Dx ED Ep IP LD MD MS OCD ON Psy
　　PW S SB Sz TB. **IQ 0-70.**
　　Gen Acad. Pre-Voc. Voc. Ungraded. Courses: Read Math Lang_Arts.
　　Shelt_Workshop.
　　Therapy: Chemo Hear Lang Movement Occup Percepual-Motor Phys Play
　　Recreational Speech. **Psychotherapy:** Group Indiv.
　　Enr: 420.
　　Est 1888. State. **Spons:** California Department of Developmental Services.

Agnews provides prevocational and vocational experiences for the developmentally disabled. While the center can accept clients with a wide range of disorders, mental retardation must be the primary condition. In addition to a wide range of therapies, counseling is available. Applicants must obtain a referral from the San Andreas Regional Center or another regional center.

ALAMEDA COUNTY MEDICAL CENTER
DEPARTMENT OF SPEECH PATHOLOGY AND AUDIOLOGY

Clinic: Ages 5 and up. M-F 8-4:30.

San Leandro, CA 94578. 15400 Foothill Blvd, H Bldg, 1st Fl.
Tel: 510-667-7800.
　　Conditions: Primary—Ap D LD S.
　　Therapy: Hear Lang Speech.
　　Staff: Prof 5.
　　County.

ALDAR ACADEMY

Day — Coed Ages 11-22

Sacramento, CA 95821. 4436 Engle Rd.
Tel: 916-485-9685. Fax: 916-485-1569.
www.aldaracademy.org
   Conditions: Primary—LD S.
   Col Prep. Gen Acad. Pre-Voc. Voc. Gr 6-12. Courses: Read Math Lang_
      Arts. On-Job Trng.
   Therapy: Hear Lang Speech. **Psychotherapy:** Fam Group Indiv.
   Private.

ALDEA CHILDREN AND FAMILY SERVICES

Res and Day — Coed Ages 12-18
Clinic: All Ages. M-F 9-5.

Napa, CA 94559. 1831 1st St, PO Box 841.
Tel: 707-224-8266. Fax: 707-224-8628.
www.aldeainc.org   E-mail: napaadmin@aldeainc.org
Allen Ewig, MSW, LCSW, Exec Dir. **Joseph M. Sholders,** MD, Med Dir. **Chuck
Hall,** Intake.
   Focus: Spec Ed. Treatment. **Conditions:** Primary—ADD ADHD Au B BD
      CD CP D ED LD OCD ON Psy Sz. Sec—BI MD MR MS.
   Gen Acad. Gr 7-12. Courses: Read Math Lang_Arts. On-Job Trng.
   Therapy: Art Milieu Music Play Speech. **Psychotherapy:** Fam Group Indiv
      Parent.
   Enr: 48. Res Males 12. Day Males 28. Day Females 8. **Staff:** 175. Prof 32.
      Educ 4. Admin 4.
   Est 1972. Private. Nonprofit.

   This organization provides community-based treatment programs, including long-
term residential, foster care (for those ages birth-18), nonpublic schools, day treatment,
outpatient programs, drug and alcohol treatment, HIV/AIDS education and prevention,
youth diversion, kinship, a child-abuse prevention program, and a supported living services program for developmentally disabled adults age 18 and up living independently.

THE ALMANSOR CENTER

Day — Coed All Ages

South Pasadena, CA 91030. 1955 Fremont Ave.
Tel: 323-257-3006. Fax: 323-257-0284.
www.almansor.org   E-mail: tacadmin@aol.com
Carmen Silva, MA, Co-Coord. **Tammy Jones-Garcia,** MA, Co-Coord.
   Focus: Spec Ed. Treatment. **Conditions:** Primary—Ap BD CD Dx ED LD S.
      Sec—ADD ADHD As Au BI Ep MR OCD ON Psy Sz.
   Gen Acad. Gr K-12. Courses: Read Math Lang_Arts Adaptive_Phys_Ed.

Man_Arts & Shop. On-Job Trng.
Therapy: Lang Speech. **Psychotherapy:** Fam Group Indiv Parent.
Enr: 250. Day Males 200. Day Females 50. **Staff:** 121 (Full 103, Part 18).
Educ 65. Admin 30.
Rates 2004: Day $113/day. State Aid.
Summer Prgm: Day. Educ. Rec. Ther. 6 wks.
Est 1974. Private. Nonprofit. **Spons:** Institute for the Redesign of Learning.

Almansor serves children, adolescents and adults with learning, developmental and emotional disabilities. Programs include early childhood education, a specialized day school, community outreach services, a speech and language pathology department, and transition and adult services.

ALTA BATES MEDICAL CENTER
SMALL VOICE PROGRAM

Day — Coed Ages 1½-6
Clinic: Ages 1½-6. M-F 8-5.

Berkeley, CA 94704. 2001 Dwight Way.
Tel: 510-204-4599. Fax: 510-204-4557.
www.altabatessummit.org/clinical/rehabpediatric.html
Focus: Treatment. **Conditions:** Primary—Au BI CP MD MR ON S. Sec—
ADD ADHD B C D Dx ED Ep LD SB.
Therapy: Hear Lang Occup Phys Speech.
Enr: 18.
Est 1953. Private. Nonprofit. **Spons:** Sutter Health.

The Small Voice Program offers children with various developmental disorders physical therapy, occupational therapy, complete speech and language evaluations, hearing screenings and full hearing evaluations. The early intervention portion of the program addresses the overall developmental needs of the child and family, with an emphasis on communication. The center also offers comprehensive pediatric outpatient therapy services.

Three-quarters of the children enrolled in the early intervention program receive financial assistance from Small Voice's scholarship fund.

ANN MARTIN CHILDREN'S CENTER

Clinic: Ages 6-22. M-S 8-5; Eves M-F 5-8.

Piedmont, CA 94610. 1250 Grand Ave.
Nearby locations: Oakland.
Tel: 510-655-7880. Fax: 510-655-3379.
www.annmartin.org   E-mail: davidtheis@annmartin.org
David S. Theis, DMH, Exec Dir. **Robert Schreiber,** MD, Med Dir.
Focus: Treatment. **Conditions:** Primary—ADD ADHD AN Anx BD CD Dc
Dg Dx ED LD Mood OCD ODD PTSD TS. **IQ 90 and up.**
Psychotherapy: Fam Group Indiv.

Staff: 45.
Rates 2003: Sliding-Scale Rate $0-80/hr.
Est 1963. Private. Nonprofit.

This center offers a combination of clinical and learning programs for children with learning, emotional, social and behavioral problems. The Learning Program has three components: learning assistance, educational testing and school placement planning. Learning problems and disabilities served include dyslexia; poor school performance; test anxiety; reading, writing, language and math problems; and attentional disorders. Training and supervision are integral parts of the program, and parental education and participation are emphasized. Ann Martin also operates an educational clinic located in the Montclair District of Oakland.

ASELTINE SCHOOL

Day — Coed Ages 6-19

San Diego, CA 92103. 4027 Normal St.
Tel: 619-296-2135. Fax: 619-296-3013.
www.aseltine.org   E-mail: aseltinedev@aol.com
Hayden W. Thomas, BA, MS, PhD, Exec Dir.
   Conditions: Primary—ED LD.
   Gen Acad. Pre-Voc. Gr 1-12. Courses: Read Math Lang_Arts. Man_Arts & Shop.
   Therapy: Lang Occup Speech.
   Est 1968. Private. Nonprofit.

BEACON SCHOOL

Day — Coed Ages 10-22

San Jose, CA 95124. 5670 Camden Ave.
Tel: 408-265-8611. Fax: 408-265-7324.
Teresa Malekzadeh, BA, Dir. Lesley Bryan, Prin.
   Focus: Spec Ed. **Conditions:** Primary—ADD ADHD Asp Au BD ED. Sec— AN Anx Apr As BI CP Dc Dg Dx Ep Mood MR OCD PTSD PW SP TS. **IQ 50 and up.**
   Gen Acad. Pre-Voc. Voc. Gr 5-12. Courses: Read Math Lang_Arts Sci Computers Studio_Art Drama Woodworking Culinary_Arts. Man_Arts & Shop.
   Therapy: Art. **Psychotherapy:** Group Indiv.
   Enr: 60. Day Males 42. Day Females 18. **Staff:** 16 (Full 10, Part 6).
   Summer Prgm: Day. Educ. Rec. 6 wks.
   Est 1970. Private. Inc.

The school prepares adolescents with emotional disorders and other mild disabilities for transition into public school and the workplace by providing special education classes and vocational training. Students receive individualized instruction in the core academic courses, and also explore topics of interest through an elective program. Individual and group counseling sessions cover issues such as social skills, anger management and conflict resolution.

BENCHMARK YOUNG ADULT SCHOOL
Res — Coed Ages 18-28

Redlands, CA 92374. 10444 Corporate Dr, Ste E.
Tel: 909-792-7818.
www.benchmarkeducation.net
  E-mail: admissions@benchmarkeducation.net
Jayne S. Longnecker, MEd, CEO. **Richard Brimhall,** Adm.
  Focus: Spec Ed. **Conditions:** Primary—ADD ADHD AN Anx BD Bu CD Dc Dg Dx ED LD Mood OCD PTSD SP TS. Sec—Apr As Asp BI C CP Db Ep Psy. **IQ 75 and up.**
  Col Prep. Gen Acad. Pre-Voc. Voc. Gr 12-Col. Courses: Read Math Lang_ Arts Life_Skills. Man_Arts & Shop. On-Job Trng.
  Psychotherapy: Group Indiv Parent.
  Enr: 52. Res Males 35. Res Females 17. **Staff:** 29. (Full 29).
  Rates 2003: Res $54,000/yr. Schol avail.
  Est 1993. Private. Inc.

Benchmark offers a community-based program for troubled young adults who require specialized assistance to become healthy, productive and independent. A majority of students complete their program within 12 months, although duration of stay varies according to severity of the individual's problems. Clients who are willing to live in a structured environment stand to benefit most from the program. Students live in a supervised apartment with a small group of their peers. Benchmark's vocation program features training in such areas as framing, electrical, plumbing, furniture building and welding.

Those dealing with drug- or alcohol-related issues must adhere to a program of sobriety.

BIG SPRINGS EDUCATIONAL THERAPY CENTER AND SCHOOL
Day — Coed Ages 5-12
Clinic: All Ages. M-S by Appt; Eves M-Th by Appt.

Riverside, CA 92507. 190 E Big Springs Rd.
Tel: 909-787-0408. Fax: 909-784-5643.
www.bigspringscenterandschool.com
  E-mail: bigspringscenter@msn.com
Regina G. Richards, MA, Dir.
  Focus: Spec Ed. Treatment. **Conditions:** Primary—Dx LD. Sec—ADD ADHD. **IQ 80 and up.**
  Gen Acad. Gr K-6. Courses: Read Math Lang_Arts.
  Therapy: Lang Occup Speech.
  Staff: 9.
  Est 1980. Private. Inc.

Big Springs' day school program offers remediation in the basic skill areas to children with learning differences. Individual educational programs utilize multisensory and multidisciplinary techniques to provide reading and math remediation, perceptual-motor and sensorimotor training, occupational therapy, and auditory and visual perceptual skills. The goal is to provide the skills necessary for a return to regular school programs.

The Richards Educational Therapy Center, located on the Big Springs campus, provides individualized therapy at all age levels for those with learning differences.

BLIND CHILDRENS CENTER

Day — Coed Ages Birth-5

Los Angeles, CA 90029. 4120 Marathon St.
Tel: 323-664-2153. Fax: 323-665-3828.
www.blindchildrenscenter.org   E-mail: info@blindchildrenscenter.org
Midge Horton, BA, Exec Dir. **Fernanda Armenta-Schmitt,** Adm.
 Focus: Spec Ed. **Conditions:** Primary—B.
 Gen Acad. Gr PS.
 Therapy: Lang Occup Speech. **Psychotherapy:** Group.
 Enr: 110. Day Males 70. Day Females 40. **Staff:** 39 (Full 13, Part 26).
 Rates 2004: No Fee.
 Est 1938. Private. Nonprofit. **Spons:** Delta Gamma Fraternity.

The center offers an infant development program, a preschool program, parental counseling and community outreach programs. Parents receive counseling on the use of tactile, auditory and kinesthetic stimulation modalities, among others. The classroom experience develops language, self-help, socialization, physical and cognitive skills.

BLIND CHILDREN'S LEARNING CENTER
EARLY CHILDHOOD CENTER

Day — Coed Ages 6mos-6

Santa Ana, CA 92705. 18542-B Vanderlip Ave.
Tel: 714-573-8888. Fax: 714-573-4944.
www.blindkids.org   E-mail: kathy.goodspeed@blindkids.org
Stacey M. Proctor, BS, MSEd, Pres. **Kathy Goodspeed,** Dir.
 Focus: Spec Ed. **Conditions:** Primary—B. Sec—CP D.
 Gen Acad. Gr PS. Courses: Music.
 Therapy: Occup Play Speech. **Psychotherapy:** Fam Indiv Parent.
 Enr: 67. **Staff:** 45. Prof 14. Educ 12. Admin 5.
 Est 1962. Private. Nonprofit.

The center provides therapy and special education services—regardless of the family's ability to pay—for blind and multi-handicapped infants and children. In the early childhood program, blind and visually impaired children learn and play alongside nondisabled children, thus learning to adapt to the sighted world both academically and socially.

The program, which emphasizes physical maturation and psychological development, includes weekly field trips, orientation and mobility, music, early computer instruction, fine- and gross-motor skills training, and pre-braille and pre-academic activities. Counseling and home training are available.

BOOTH MEMORIAL CENTER HIGH SCHOOL

Day — Females Ages 14-22

Los Angeles, CA 90031. 2670 Griffin Ave.
Tel: 323-225-5929. Fax: 323-225-2558.
Ruth M. Dickens, MA, Prin.
   Focus: Spec Ed. **Conditions:** Primary—ADD ADHD BD Dx ED LD Mood PTSD.
   Gen Acad. Pre-Voc. Gr 8-12. Courses: Read Math Lang_Arts. On-Job Trng.
   Psychotherapy: Indiv.
   Private. Nonprofit. **Spons:** Salvation Army.

BRAILLE INSTITUTE
LOS ANGELES SIGHT CENTER

Day — Coed Ages Birth-19

Los Angeles, CA 90029. 741 North Vermont Ave.
Tel: 323-663-1111. Fax: 323-663-0867.
www.brailleinstitute.org/Centers/LosAngeles.htm
   E-mail: info@brailleinstitute.org
Adama Dyoniziak, Dir.
   Conditions: Primary—B.
   Psychotherapy: Indiv.
   Est 1919. Private. Nonprofit.

THE BRIDGE SCHOOL

Day — Coed Ages 5-12

Hillsborough, CA 94010. 545 Eucalyptus Ave.
Tel: 650-696-7295. Fax: 650-342-7598.
www.bridgeschool.org
Vicki R. Casella, EdD, Exec Dir. **Catherine Sementelli,** Adm.
   Focus: Spec Ed. **Conditions:** Primary—CP OH. Sec—Apr B Bl Ep MR S.
   Gen Acad. Gr PS-8. Courses: Read Math Lang_Arts.
   Therapy: Movement Speech.
   Enr: 14. **Staff:** 10. Prof 4. Admin 1.
   Est 1987. Private. Nonprofit.

The school's educational program serves children with severe speech and physical impairments through the use of augmentative and alternative means of communication and assistive technology applications. An outreach program provides information to parents and professionals interested in these applications. Programming emphasizes communication, recreation, academics, community involvement, self-reliance, independence and lifelong learning.

BRISLAIN LEARNING CENTER

Clinic: Ages 4 and up. M-F 8-5; Eves M-F 5-7.

Chico, CA 95928. 1550 Humboldt Rd, Ste 3.
Tel: 530-342-2567. Fax: 530-342-2573.
Judy Brislain, EdD, Dir.
   Conditions: Primary—Dx ED LD MR. Sec—BD BI CP Ep ON S. **IQ 85 and up.**
   Gen Acad. Pre-Voc. Voc. Ungraded. Courses: Read Math Lang_Arts.
   Therapy: Hear Lang Percepual-Motor Play Speech. **Psychotherapy:** Fam Group Indiv Parent.
   Staff: 7 (Full 3, Part 4).
   Rates 2003: Clinic $40/ses.
   Est 1977. Private.

Brislain conducts a program featuring individual and group instruction for the remediation of educational and behavioral problems in children and adults. Language, reading, perceptual and sensorimotor skills are developed, with attention given to writing and study practices. Counseling sessions strive to produce for the individual more effective communication techniques. Parental seminars, professional workshops and consultations are available.

CALIFORNIA ELWYN

Day — Coed Ages 18 and up

Fountain Valley, CA 92708. 18325 Mt Baldy Cir.
Tel: 714-557-6313. Fax: 714-963-2961.
www.caelwyn.org   E-mail: info@caelwyn.org
Joan McKinney, Exec Dir.
   Conditions: Primary—BI MR.
   Pre-Voc. Voc. Shelt_Workshop. On-Job Trng.
   Est 1974. Private. Nonprofit.

CALIFORNIA PACIFIC MEDICAL CENTER
CHILD DEVELOPMENT CENTER

Clinic: Ages Birth-18. M-F 8:30-5.

San Francisco, CA 94120. 3700 California St, 1st Fl, PO Box 7999.
   Nearby locations: San Mateo.
Tel: 415-750-6200. Fax: 415-752-9068.
www.cpmc.org/advanced/pediatrics/services/child_development.html

Suzanne Giraudo, EdD, Dir. **Karen K. Norman,** OTR, Mgr. **Barbara Bennett,** MD, Med Dir.
  Focus: Spec Ed. Treatment. **Conditions:** Primary—Dx ED LD PDD. Sec—
    Ap BD BI CP Ep MR.
  Therapy: Hear Lang Occup Percepual-Motor Phys Speech. **Psychother-
    apy:** Fam Indiv.
  Staff: 60 (Full 15, Part 45). Prof 50. Educ 4. Admin 4.
  Private. Nonprofit.

A multidisciplinary team provides evaluation and treatment for children with learning differences, as well as developmental delays and disabilities. Standardized testing and clinical examination determine areas of dysfunction. The staff utilizes a variety of therapies during treatment. Individual and group therapy sessions are available for parents, and the usual length of treatment is six to nine months.

A satellite clinic offers service weekly at 210 Baldwin Ave., San Mateo 94401.

CALIFORNIA STATE UNIVERSITY-LONG BEACH
SPEECH AND HEARING CLINIC

Clinic: All Ages. M-F 8-5.

Long Beach, CA 90840. Language Arts Bldg, Rm 112.
Tel: 562-985-4583. Fax: 562-985-4584.
www.csulb.edu/depts/comm-disorders/clinic.html
Carolyn Conway Madding, Dir.
  Conditions: Primary—Ap S.
  Therapy: Hear Lang Speech.
  Est 1970. County.

CEDU SCHOOLS

Res — Coed Ages 12-17

Running Springs, CA 92382. PO Box 1176.
Tel: 909-867-2722. Fax: 909-867-7084.
www.cedu.com   E-mail: info@cedu.com
George P. Condas, PhD, Exec Dir. **Paula Riggs,** Adm.
  Focus: Spec Ed. **Conditions:** Primary—BD ED LD.
  Col Prep. Gen Acad. Pre-Voc. Gr 7-12. Courses: Read Math Lang_Arts.
    Man_Arts & Shop.
  Therapy: Speech. **Psychotherapy:** Group Indiv.
  Enr: 100. **Staff:** 53.
  Rates 2004: Res $5500/mo. Schol avail.
  Est 1967. Private. Nonprofit. **Spons:** CEDU Educational Services.

With both its middle school and its high school campuses located in a heavily forested mountain area high in the San Bernardino National Forest, CEDU offers a program for adolescents with special emotional and educational needs. The CEDU student may have experienced poor interpersonal relationships, failure in school or family problems and may have experimented with drugs or alcohol. CEDU's structured and supportive environment fosters the development of self-confidence, healthy values, life skills and self-respect.

A comprehensive, year-round curriculum integrates counseling, academics, vocational training and a wilderness challenge program. CEDU's 76-acre campus also includes a farm, art studios, and athletic and recreational facilities. Opportunities for travel and study abroad are available for upper school students.

CENTER FOR COMMUNICATION DISORDERS

Clinic: Ages 13 and up. M-F 9-6.

Canoga Park, CA 91303. 7349 Topanga Canyon Blvd.
Tel: 818-883-1381. Fax: 818-883-3583.
E-mail: bsccd@earthlink.net
Barbara Samuels, MA, Dir.
  Focus: Treatment. **Conditions:** Primary—Ap Au Bl Dx LD S. Sec—ADD
    ADHD Apr CP D MD MR MS Nf OH.
  Therapy: Lang Speech.
  Staff: 2 (Full 1, Part 1). Prof 1. Admin 1.
  Est 1974. Private. Inc.

The center provides speech and language services for adolescents and adults who have a wide range of disabilities. Individuals served include persons with learning disabilities, mild autism, traumatic brain injuries, aphasia, and voice and fluency problems. Treatment typically lasts between six weeks and three years.

CENTER FOR INDEPENDENT LIVING
YOUTH SERVICES DEPARTMENT

Day — Coed Ages 14-22
Clinic: Ages 14-22. M-F 9-5.

Berkeley, CA 94704. 2539 Telegraph Ave.
Tel: 510-841-4776. TTY: 510-841-3101. Fax: 510-841-6168.
www.cilberkeley.org
Jan Garrett, JD, Exec Dir. **Sue Yasuko Abe,** MA, Coord.
  Focus: Trng. **Conditions:** Primary—ADD ADHD As Au B Bl C CP D Db Dc
    Dg Dx Ep IP LD MD MR MS ON S SB.
  Enr: 140. **Staff:** 4 (Full 2, Part 2).
  Est 1972. Federal. Nonprofit.

The department provides various services for adolescents with disabilities and their families. Services—which are available on individual, group and in-class bases—include peer counseling, educational and transitional advocacy, independent living skills training, disability awareness training, and information and referral. Also available through the department are support services for special education teachers, workshops and support groups for parents, and technical assistance for the accommodation of children with disabilities in standard classroom settings.

CHARLES ARMSTRONG SCHOOL

Day — Coed Ages 6-14

Belmont, CA 94002. 1405 Solana Dr.
Tel: 650-592-7570. Fax: 650-592-0780.
www.charlesarmstrong.org   E-mail: info@charlesarmstrong.org
Rosalie Whitlock, PhD, Head.
  Focus: Spec Ed. **Conditions:** Primary—Dx LD.
  Gen Acad. Gr 1-8. Courses: Read Math Lang_Arts Hist Sci Soc_Stud
    Studio_Art Music Theater.
  Enr: 230. **Staff:** 60.
  Est 1968. Private. Nonprofit.

CAS conducts an academic program that specializes in serving the dyslexic learner. Classes are designed to address learning-style differences while helping students develop competence in reading, writing and spelling skills. In addition to academics, the program also emphasizes the development of improved social skills and self-esteem. The school attempts to return the pupil to a traditional mainstreamed program as soon as possible.

CHILD DEVELOPMENT CENTER

Day — Coed Ages Birth-12
Clinic: Ages Birth-17. M-F 8-6.

Simi Valley, CA 93065. 2975 N Sycamore Dr.
Tel: 805-955-8120. Fax: 805-527-7183.
Robin P. Millar, BS, Dir.
  Focus: Treatment. **Conditions:** Primary—ADD ADHD Ap Apr Asp Au BI
    CP DS Dx ED Ep IP LD MR ON PW S TS. Sec—As B C D MD MS SB.
  Therapy: Hear Lang Occup Phys Speech.
  Enr: 512. **Staff:** 45 (Full 23, Part 22).
  Est 1979. Private. Nonprofit. **Spons:** Simi Valley Hospital and Health Care
    Services.

The center provides three programs for children with various developmental and physical problems. The early intervention program, which serves infants and toddlers up to age 3, assesses gross- and fine-motor, learning, personal and social, and language skills. Therapists and parents take evaluation results and formulate specific goals for the child in the areas of movement, language and learning. Children up to age 12 who have inadequate sensory processing resulting in learning, attentional, activity-level, motor coordination, language development and behavioral problems receive one-on-one treatment through the facility's sensory integration program. Outpatient services, the third component of the center, consist of follow-up therapy sessions conducted in a one-on-one setting.

CHILD GUIDANCE CENTER

Clinic: Ages Birth-17. M-F 8-5; Eves M-Th 6-8.

Santa Ana, CA 92701. 1440 E 1st St, Ste 100.
   Nearby locations: Fullerton.
Tel: 714-953-4455. Fax: 714-542-2793.
www.cgcoc.org
Henry J. Paris, MSW, LCSW, Exec Dir. **Jeannette Hanna,** MD, Med Dir. **Elizabeth Sobral,** Adm.
   Focus: Treatment. **Conditions:** Primary—ADD ADHD BD ED Mood Psy PTSD SP Sz TS. Sec—BI Dx LD MR S. **IQ 80 and up.**
   Therapy: Chemo. **Psychotherapy:** Fam Group Indiv.
   Staff: 76 (Full 60, Part 16). Prof 60. Admin 5.
   Rates 2003: Sliding-Scale Rate $0-90/ses.
   Est 1967. Private. Nonprofit.

The clinic provides services for children who are emotionally disturbed or who have been victims of child abuse. Treatment involves working with the families of such children. Therapies include both dynamic and behavioral approaches, as well as chemotherapy. In addition, a modified day treatment program is offered to severely dysfunctional children and their families. The program is aimed at minority populations and provides all programs in Spanish as well as English.

A branch office operates at 2050 Youth Way, Fullerton 92635.

THE CHILDREN'S CENTER OF RIVERSIDE

Day — Coed Ages Birth-6

Riverside, CA 92504. 7177 Potomac St.
Tel: 909-784-0020. Fax: 909-784-7062.
E-mail: childctr@pe.net
Joseph Dunn, MBA, PhD, Exec Dir. **Tanja Williams,** Adm.
   Focus: Spec Ed. **Conditions:** Primary—Au CD CP DS ED LD Mood MR ON PDD S. Sec—Ap As B BD BI D Ep MD MS SB TS.
   Therapy: Hear Lang Occup Phys Speech. **Psychotherapy:** Indiv Parent.
   Enr: 200. Day Males 120. Day Females 80. **Staff:** 102 (Full 90, Part 12). Prof 13. Admin 9.
   Est 1976. Private. Nonprofit.

The center's developmental curriculum provides structured activities in sensorimotor and perceptual-motor learning, with opportunities for socialization and peer interaction. Individual tutoring, home teaching and classes for infants, toddlers and preschool children are among the services offered. The parent program includes discussion groups, training and parental education groups. Developmental assessments are available.

THE CHILDREN'S HEALTH COUNCIL

Day — Coed Ages 7-17
Clinic: Ages Birth-17. M-F 8-6, S 9-1; Eves M-Th 6-7;.

Palo Alto, CA 94304. 650 Clark Way.
Tel: 650-326-5530. Fax: 650-688-0206.
www.chconline.org   E-mail: intake@chconline.org
  Conditions: Primary—BD ED LD MR. Sec—ADHD Asp Au CP S.
  Pre-Voc. Voc. Ungraded. Courses: Read Math Lang_Arts.
  Therapy: Lang Occup Speech. **Psychotherapy:** Fam Group Indiv.
  Staff: Prof 75.
  Est 1953. Private. Nonprofit.

CHILDREN'S HOSPITAL AND HEALTH CENTER

Res — Coed Ages Birth-25; Day — Coed Birth-19
Clinic: Ages Birth-19. M-F 8-5.

San Diego, CA 92123. 3020 Children's Way.
Tel: 858-576-1700. Fax: 858-576-7134.
www.chsd.org   E-mail: refsvc@chsd.org
  Conditions: Primary—ADHD As Au BD C CF CP ED LD ON S.
  Courses: Read Math Lang_Arts.
  Therapy: Chemo Hear Occup Phys Recreational Speech. **Psychotherapy:**
    Fam Group Indiv.
  Est 1954. Private. Nonprofit.

CHILDREN'S HOSPITAL AND HEALTH CENTER
DEVELOPMENTAL SERVICES

Clinic: All Ages. M-F 7-6.

San Diego, CA 92123. 3020 Children's Way.
Tel: 858-495-7715. Fax: 858-278-6627.
www.chsd.org
  Focus: Treatment. **Conditions:** Primary—Au D LD ON S.
  Therapy: Hear Lang Occup Phys Speech.
  Staff: 55.
  Est 1998. Private. Nonprofit.

  Through the Developmental Services department, children, adolescents and—in some cases—adults with multiple disabilities or developmental concerns receive evaluation and intervention services. The program consists of evaluations and treatment by specialists in the following areas: physical, occupational and speech therapy; psychology; audiology; and school rehabilitation. An autism center assists children ages 1-5 who have autistic spectrum disorders. A preschool and parent training and research are part of the autism program.

CHILDREN'S HOSPITAL AND RESEARCH CENTER AT OAKLAND

Clinic: Ages 1-18. M-S 8:30-5.

Oakland, CA 94618. 5275 Claremont Ave.
  Nearby locations: Pleasanton; Walnut Creek.
Tel: 510-428-3179. Fax: 510-601-3952.
www.childrenshospitaloakland.org
  Focus: Rehab. **Conditions:** Primary—Ap S.
  Therapy: Lang Speech.
  Staff: 4. (Full 4).
  Rates 2003: Clinic $109/hr.
  Private. Nonprofit.

Evaluations and therapy are provided for speech and language disorders. Branches offering subspecialty services operate at 106 La Casa Via, Ste. 220, Walnut Creek 94598, and 5820 Stoneridge Mall Rd., Ste. 210, Pleasanton 94588.

CHILDREN'S THERAPY CENTER

Clinic: Ages Birth-12. M-F 9-5; Eves T-Th 5-8.

Camarillo, CA 93010. 770 Paseo Camarillo, Ste 120.
Tel: 805-383-1501.
  Focus: Treatment. **Conditions:** Primary—Ap Au Bl IP LD S. Sec—ADD
    ADHD B BD CD D Dx ED MR OCD.
  Therapy: Hear Lang Occup Phys Speech. **Psychotherapy:** Fam Group
    Indiv Parent.
  Staff: 8 (Full 4, Part 4).
  Est 1987. Private. Inc.

CTC provides therapy for children with sensory integration and speech and language disorders. Evaluations are videotaped for parents to review with the examiner. Counseling services are available, and all children who come for evaluations take part, along with their families, in an interview given by a social services consultant. Treatment generally lasts one to two years.

CHILDREN'S WORKSHOP

Day — Coed Ages 3-10

San Diego, CA 92100. 4055 Camino Del Rio S.
Tel: 619-243-1325. Fax: 619-233-8409.
  Conditions: Primary—Ap BD LD S.
  Therapy: Lang Occup Speech. **Psychotherapy:** Indiv.
  Private.

CLAUSEN HOUSE

Res and Day — Coed Ages 18 and up

Oakland, CA 94610. 88 Vernon St.
Tel: 510-839-0050. Fax: 510-444-5790.
www.clausenhouse.org   E-mail: info@clausenhouse.org
Nan Butterworth, Exec Dir.
  Conditions: Primary—MR.
  Pre-Voc. Courses: Read Math Lang_Arts. Man_Arts & Shop. On-Job Trng.
  Est 1967. Private. Nonprofit.

COLLEGE HOSPITAL

Res — Coed Ages 2-17

Cerritos, CA 90703. 10802 College Pl.
Tel: 562-924-9581. Fax: 562-809-0981.
www.collegehospitals.com/c/cservice.html   E-mail: collegeh@gte.net
  Conditions: Primary—BD ED Psy.
  Gen Acad. Courses: Read Math Lang_Arts. Man_Arts & Shop.
  Staff: Prof 34.
  Est 1973. Private.

COMMUNITY SPEECH AND HEARING CENTER

Clinic: Ages 1 and up. M-F 8-5; Eves M-F 5-7.

Tarzana, CA 91356. 18740 Ventura Blvd.
Tel: 818-774-0224. Fax: 818-774-1935.
www.communityspeech.com   E-mail: info@communityspeech.com
Howard A. Grey, PhD, Dir. **Josie LeDoux,** Adm.
  Focus: Treatment. **Conditions:** Primary—ADD ADHD Anx Ap Apr Au BD
    BI CD D Dx LD Mood OCD PTSD S SP. Sec—CP DS ED MR MS OH.
  Therapy: Hear Lang Percepual-Motor Play Speech. **Psychotherapy:** Fam
    Group Indiv Parent.
  Staff: 17 (Full 13, Part 4).
  Rates 2003: Sliding-Scale Rate $120-160/hr.
  Est 1969. Private. Nonprofit.

A rehabilitative outpatient facility for the diagnosis and the treatment of communicative disorders, the center accepts young children who fail to develop language at the proper time, preschoolers with pronunciation problems, adults with speech and hearing defects, and stroke victims.

Evaluation services compare the patient's responses with the norms for children of the same age. Individual needs for adequate communication are criteria for adults. The center also provides lip-reading, auditory and hearing aid training, hearing aid testing and referrals. Measurement of pure-tone and speech-reception thresholds and otoscopic visualization are employed in audiological evaluations. Patients may also receive services in hospitals or in their homes. Counseling and psychotherapy services are available.

THE COUNTRY SCHOOL

Day — Coed Ages 9-18

San Marcos, CA 92078. 1145 Linda Vista Dr, Ste 105.
Tel: 760-744-4870. Fax: 760-510-6866.
E-mail: bettypca@nctimes.net
Krysti DeZonia, MA, Dir. **Elizabeth Parker,** BS, MA, Prin.
   Focus: Spec Ed. **Conditions:** Primary—ADD ADHD Anx Asp Au Bl LD
      Mood Nf OCD ODD PDD S. Sec—Apr Ar As BD CP Dc Dg Dx ED Ep
      MR ON SP TS. **IQ 70-130.**
   Gen Acad. Pre-Voc. Gr 4-12. Courses: Read Math Lang_Arts Sci Computers Soc_Stud Hist Studio_Art Music.
   Therapy: Lang Occup Speech.
   Enr: 27. Day Males 17. Day Females 10. **Staff:** 11 (Full 6, Part 5).
   Rates 2004: Day $13,330/yr. $80 (Therapy)/hr.
   Summer Prgm: Day. Educ. Rec. Day Rate $665. 4 wks.
   Est 1980. Private. Nonprofit. **Spons:** TERI.

The school provides individualized special education classes for students with learning disabilities. Core academic courses such as reading, math, science and social studies are taught at both remedial and accelerated levels. On-site therapeutic options include speech, language and occupational therapies, as well as therapeutic horseback riding. After acquiring the necessary skills (typically about two years), the student returns to a mainstream educational setting.

COUNTRYSIDE PREPARATORY SCHOOL

Day — Coed Ages 5-18

Northridge, CA 91325. 8756 Canby Ave.
Tel: 818-885-5872. Fax: 818-885-1663.
Christopher R. Faucher, MA, Prin.
   Focus: Spec Ed. **Conditions:** Primary—ADD ADHD Asp Dc Dg Dx ED LD
      OCD SP TS. **IQ 78 and up.**
   Col Prep. Gen Acad. Pre-Voc. Gr 1-12. Courses: Read Math Lang_Arts Sci
      Computers Hist Study_Skills. Man_Arts & Shop.
   Therapy: Art Lang Music.
   Enr: 62. **Staff:** 13. Educ 11. Admin 2.
   Rates 2003: Day $8000-12,000/sch yr. $50 (Tutoring)/hr. Schol avail.
   Summer Prgm: Day. Educ. 5 wks.
   Est 1979. Private. Nonprofit.

Countryside provides a full elementary and secondary special education program for children with mild to moderate learning disabilities or emotional disturbances.

DAVIS DYSLEXIA CORRECTION CENTER

Clinic: Ages 7 and up. M-F 9-5.

Burlingame, CA 94010. 1601 Bayshore Hwy, Ste 260.
Tel: 650-692-8990. Fax: 650-692-8997.
www.davisdyslexia.com   E-mail: info@davisdyslexia.com
Fatima Ali, PhD, CEO. **Ronald Dell Davis,** Exec Dir. **Dee Weldon White,** MA,
    Dir. **Richard A. Blasband,** MD, Med Dir.
    Focus: Spec Ed. **Conditions:** Primary—ADD ADHD Dc Dg Dx LD. Sec—
        Ap MR. **IQ 70 and up.**
    Therapy: Lang Movement Percepual-Motor Play Speech. **Psychotherapy:**
        Fam Indiv Parent.
    Staff: 8 (Full 3, Part 5). Educ 5. Admin 3.
    Rates 2003: Clinic $3500/wk.
    Summer Prgm: Day. Educ. Ther.
    Est 1982. Private. Inc.

The center provides a short-term therapy program with long-term follow-up for the correction of dyslexia and related learning disabilities. The short-term program provides one-on-one instruction and runs for five consecutive six-hour days. Emphasis is on integrating reading, writing and language skills with perceptual control. Children also acquire self-help skills during their stay at the clinic. Parent and teacher support training is available.

DEVELOPMENTAL THERAPY PROGRAM

Clinic: Ages Birth-10. M-Th 9-5.

San Mateo, CA 94401. 205 E 3rd Ave, Ste 307.
Tel: 650-579-4908.
Michele Casari, MDT, Dir.
    Focus: Treatment. **Conditions:** Primary—ADD ADHD Apr Asp Au BI CP
        Dc Dg DS Dx IP LD MR ON PDD. Sec—Ap B C D Db ED Ep.
    Gen Acad. Pre-Voc. Ungraded. Courses: Read Math Lang_Arts.
    Therapy: Movement Percepual-Motor Recreational.
    Staff: 3 (Full 1, Part 2).
    Rates 2003: Clinic $75/ses. Sliding-Scale Rate $60-70/ses. State Aid.
    Est 1987. Private.

Developmental Therapy works on improving a child's ability to use the body to learn. Therapy sessions seek to identify the student's developmental level, develop a program to remediate weaknesses, and stimulate perceptual and cognitive growth. Special emphasis is placed on visual-motor and auditory processing skills.

DEVEREUX CALIFORNIA

Res and Day — Coed Ages 8 and up

Santa Barbara, CA 93160. PO Box 6784.

Nearby locations: San Diego.
Tel: 805-968-2525. Fax: 805-968-3247.
www.devereuxca.org
David Dennis, Exec Dir.
   Focus: Treatment. **Conditions:** Primary—Au ED OH. Sec—ADD ADHD BD
      BI CP LD MR S. **IQ 40-100.**
   Gen Acad. Pre-Voc. Voc. Ungraded. Courses: Read Math Lang_Arts. Man_
      Arts & Shop. Shelt_Workshop. On-Job Trng.
   Therapy: Art Hear Lang Music Occup Phys Speech. **Psychotherapy:** Fam
      Group Indiv.
   Est 1945. Private. Nonprofit. **Spons:** Devereux Foundation.

   Established in 1945, this branch of The Devereux Foundation provides year-round services for adolescents and adults with emotional, behavioral and learning disorders. The 33-acre oceanfront facility is located 15 miles north of Santa Barbara.
   Devereux provides a therapeutic milieu using a wide variety of treatment modalities. Individualized programs, developed after comprehensive evaluations, emphasize behavior management. All residents participate in recreational therapy, social activities and therapeutic educational programs according to their needs.
   Course work offered at all academic levels leads to a high school diploma or a certificate of completion. In addition to individualized classroom programming, Devereux offers vocational assessments, work activity programs and industrial arts experiences. Also, programs are available to meet the needs of emotionally disturbed and developmentally disabled youths ages 10-21 who require intensive care and treatment in a structured residential setting.
   The facility provides a complete physical plant including residential units, off-campus group homes and apartments, and a recreation center with a gymnasium, a swimming pool and a work activity center. The usual length of treatment is one to four years.
   In addition to the Santa Barbara center, Devereux California operates a nonpublic school and a group home in San Diego-Vista. Boys and girls ages 12-17 with emotional disturbances and developmental delays may participate in the Puente Program, which seeks to return residents to their home communities and to the least-restrictive living environment possible. Participants develop basic self-care skills receive other training as appropriate. The program, which is conducted at four single-gender neighborhood homes, includes recreational and instructional activities both in the home setting and in the surrounding community.   **See Also Page 1025**

THE DUBIN LEARNING CENTER
Clinic: All Ages. M-F 8-5; Eves M-F 5-7:30.

Santa Barbara, CA 93101. 112 W Cota St.
Tel: 805-962-7122. Fax: 805-962-3502.
www.dubinlearningcenter.com
Barry Dubin, MS, Co-Dir. **Deidre Dubin,** MS, Co-Dir.
   Focus: Treatment. **Conditions:** Primary—ADD ADHD Dx LD. Sec—BD BI
      ED. **IQ 90 and up.**
   Staff: 6 (Full 3, Part 3).
   Est 1979. Private.

Daily two-hour morning sessions at the center provide remediation in reading, writing, spelling and math for students with learning differences. The student spends the remainder of each day in school. Sensorimotor, language, perceptual and cognitive skills training is emphasized. Afternoon educational therapy sessions are also available.

EAST BAY AGENCY FOR CHILDREN

Day — Coed Ages 5-12
Clinic: Ages 5-12. M-F 8:30-4:30.

Oakland, CA 94602. 2540 Charleston St.
Tel: 510-531-3666. Fax: 510-531-0691.
www.ebac.org   E-mail: ebac@ebac.org
Susan Corlett, MA, Exec Dir. **Barbara Saler,** LCSW, Prgm Dir. **Micheline Beam,** PhD, Clin Dir.
Focus: Spec Ed. Treatment. **Conditions:** Primary—ED. Sec—BD LD.
Gen Acad. Ungraded. Courses: Read Math Lang_Arts. Man_Arts & Shop.
Therapy: Art Lang Milieu Occup Play Recreational Speech. **Psychotherapy:** Fam Group Indiv Parent.
Staff: 100. Educ 6.
Rates 2001: Day $124/day. Schol avail. State Aid.
Summer Prgm: Day. Ther.
Est 1953. Private. Nonprofit.

East Bay Agency administers four-day treatment programs in Alameda County. All of the children in these programs have been identified as having serious emotional and behavioral problems that prevent their success in a traditional school setting. Day treatment programs provide academic support, in addition to individual psychotherapy; group, parental and family therapy; medication evaluation and monitoring; recreational activities; and crisis management.

EASTER SEALS BAY AREA

Day — Coed All Ages

Oakland, CA 94612. 180 Grand Ave, Ste 300.
Tel: 510-835-2131. Fax: 510-835-1847.
www.eastersealsbayarea.org
Michael Pelfini, Pres.
Conditions: Primary—MR OH.
Gen Acad. Gr PS.
Therapy: Hear Lang Occup Phys Speech.
Staff: Prof 5.
Private. Nonprofit.

ECHO CENTER

Day — Coed Ages 3-12

Culver City, CA 90232. 3430 McManus Ave.
Tel: 310-838-2442. TTY: 310-202-7201. Fax: 310-838-0479.
www.echohorizon.org   E-mail: info@echohorizon.org
Norma F. Roberts, Exec Dir. **Vicki C. Ishida,** MSEd, Dir. **Paula R. Dashiell,**
  Prin.
  Focus: Spec Ed. **Conditions:** Primary—D.
  Gen Acad. Gr K-6. Courses: Read Math Lang_Arts Sci Computers Studio_
    Art Music.
  Therapy: Hear Lang Speech.
  Enr: 18. **Staff:** 34. (Full 34).
  Rates 2004: Day $13,400/sch yr. Schol avail.
  Est 1970. Private. Nonprofit.

This center for elementary-age children with hearing impairments primarily employs an oral-auditory approach. In addition to receiving specialized training in listening, speech and language skills, hearing-impaired pupils are integrated into mainstream classes on-site at Echo Horizon School. As communication skills are considered the primary need, the center provides frequent opportunities for each child to develop useful language skills and to listen, speak and interact with adults and other children.

EDEN CHILDREN'S CLINIC

Clinic: Ages 2½-17. M-F 8:30-5.

San Leandro, CA 94546. 2045 Fairmont Dr.
Tel: 510-667-7540. Fax: 510-618-3434.
  Focus: Treatment. **Conditions:** Primary—ADD ADHD Au BD CD ED Mood
    OCD Psy Sz. Sec—D Dx LD.
  Therapy: Hear Lang Play. **Psychotherapy:** Fam Group Indiv Parent.
  County.

Eden provides treatment and therapy for children with severe mental health needs. Services include individual and group therapy, as well as psychiatric medication evaluation, prescription and monitoring services. Fees are based on a sliding scale.

EDGEWOOD CENTER
FOR CHILDREN AND FAMILIES

Res — Coed Ages 6-14; Day — Coed 3½-14
Clinic: Ages 6-14. M-F 9-5.

San Francisco, CA 94116. 1801 Vicente St.
Tel: 415-681-3211. Fax: 415-681-1065.
www.edgewoodcenter.org   E-mail: info@edgewoodcenter.org
Nancy Rubin, MSW, Exec Dir. **Robin Randall,** MD, Med Dir. **Monika Green,**
  Adm.

Focus: Treatment. **Conditions:** Primary—BD ED. Sec—Ap Bl Dx LD S. **IQ 60-120.**
Gen Acad. Ungraded. Courses: Read Math Lang_Arts.
Therapy: Art Dance Lang Occup Play Recreational Speech. **Psychotherapy:** Fam Group Indiv.
Enr: 78. Res Males 24. Res Females 24. Day Males 27. Day Females 3.
  Staff: 75. Prof 40.
Rates 2001: Res $185/day. Day $97/day.
Est 1851. Private. Nonprofit.

Edgewood specializes in intensive, highly individualized inpatient care for children with emotional and behavioral disorders. A level system, designed to promote personal responsibility and greater independence, defines expectations and outlines privileges based upon progress toward treatment objectives. The aim for each child is to return him or her to adaptive functioning in school, family and community.

The center's day treatment program offers treatment to emotionally disturbed children with multiple learning problems. The school consists of individualized educational programs, recreational activities, various modes of therapy, and counseling for children and parents. The daycare program runs year-round except for August, offering after-school care and full-day vacation care. No daycare fees are assessed to families.

EDUCATIONAL RESOURCES

Clinic: All Ages.

San Marino, CA 91104. 1000 Huntington Dr.
Tel: 626-308-0313.
www.educationalresourcescenter.com
James C. Dorman, BS, MA, Dir.
  Conditions: Primary—LD.
  Gen Acad. Courses: Read Math Lang_Arts.
  Est 1970. Private.

EMQ CHILDREN & FAMILY SERVICES

Res and Day — Coed Ages 5-18
Clinic: All Ages. M-F 8:30-5; Eves M-Th 5-9.

Campbell, CA 95008. 251 Llewellyn Ave.
Tel: 408-379-3790. Fax: 408-364-4013.
www.emq.org   E-mail: csc@emq.org
F. Jerome Doyle, MSW, Pres. **David Arredondo,** MD, Med Dir. **Larry Hanville,** Adm.
  Focus: Treatment. **Conditions:** Primary—ADD ADHD ED Mood OCD ODD Psy PTSD SP Sz TS. Sec—Asp BD.
  Gen Acad. Pre-Voc. Gr K-6. Courses: Read Math Lang_Arts.
  Therapy: Art Milieu Movement Music Play Speech. **Psychotherapy:** Fam Group Indiv.
  Enr: 168. Res Males 76. Res Females 19. Day Males 63. Day Females 10.

Est 1964. County. Nonprofit.

EMQ uses a family systems therapy approach to treat children with mental or emotional disturbances and their families. Programs include residential treatment (130 beds); school-based day treatment programs; and in-home programs for adolescents and physically and sexually abused children. These programs, which are publicly funded, are offered at 12 sites throughout Santa Clara County.

ETTIE LEE
YOUTH AND FAMILY SERVICES

Day — Males Ages 8-18

Baldwin Park, CA 91706. 5146 Maine Ave, PO Box 339.
Tel: 626-960-4861. Fax: 626-337-2621.
www.ettielee.org   E-mail: info@ettielee.org
Clayton L. Downey, MA, Pres.
   Focus: Treatment. **Conditions:** Primary—BD CD ED.
   Psychotherapy: Fam Group Indiv.
   Enr: 88. **Staff:** 160 (Full 140, Part 20).
   Est 1950. Private. Nonprofit.

Serving individuals from throughout southern California, Ettie Lee provides a continuum of care for children and families in need. Services comprise nine residential care facilities, a treatment foster family agency, an adolescent substance abuse treatment program and various community programs.

The residential care centers serve boys in the communities of Azusa, Baldwin Park, Bloomington, Fontana, North Hollywood, Redlands, Santa Ana and San Jacinto. All located in residential neighborhoods, these homes have accommodations for six to twelve youngsters. The h0mes provide 24-hour supervision, and Ettie Lee maintains a 4:1 staff-resident ratio at each location. Staff members have extensive training in such fields as child development, behavioral science, social work and residential care. Boys have access to a range of therapeutic and other support services, such as individual and group counseling, academic and vocational assistance, psychological testing, psychiatric services, independent living skills and recreational programs.

EXCELSIOR ACADEMY

Day — Coed Ages 7-19

San Diego, CA 92120. 7202 Princess View Dr.
Tel: 619-583-6762. Fax: 619-583-6764.
www.excelsioracademy.com
Frank Maguire, Co-Dir. **Nance Maguire,** Co-Dir.
   Focus: Spec Ed. **Conditions:** Primary—ADD ADHD Asp Dc Dg Dx LD.
      Sec—Anx B D Db ED OCD PW SP TS. **IQ 85-130.**
   Col Prep. Gen Acad. Gr 1-12. Courses: Read Math Lang_Arts Study_Skills.
      On-Job Trng.
   Therapy: Lang Occup Speech.
   Enr: 80. Day Males 65. Day Females 15. **Staff:** 25 (Full 20, Part 5).

Rates 2004: Day $17,280/sch yr.
Est 1988. Private. Nonprofit.

The academy serves students of average to above-average intelligence whose needs fall within the areas of processing, memory, language, attention and socialization.

EXCEPTIONAL CHILDREN'S FOUNDATION

Res — Coed Ages 18 and up; Day — Coed Birth-3

Culver City, CA 90232. 8740 W Washington Blvd.
Tel: 310-204-3300. Fax: 310-845-8001.
www.ecf-la.org
Scott D. Bowling, PsyD, Pres.
    Conditions: Primary—BI MR. Sec—Au CP ED.
    Est 1946. Private. Nonprofit.

FAIRVIEW DEVELOPMENTAL CENTER

Res — Coed All Ages

Costa Mesa, CA 92626. 2501 Harbor Blvd.
Tel: 714-957-5000. TTY: 714-957-5512. Fax: 714-957-5510.
www.dds.cahwnet.gov/fairview/fairview.cfm
Karen Larson, Exec Dir.
    Conditions: Primary—MR.
    Pre-Voc. Shelt_Workshop.
    Staff: Prof 1285.
    Est 1959. State. Nonprofit.

FAMILY AND CHILDREN SERVICES

Clinic: All Ages. M-F9-5; Eves M-F 5-9.

San Jose, CA 95112. 950 W Julian St.
    Nearby locations: Campbell; Palo Alto.
Tel: 408-292-9353. Fax: 408-287-3104.
www.fcservices.org
Jeanne C. Labozetta, MBA, Pres.
    Focus: Treatment. **Conditions:** Primary—ADD ADHD AN Anx BD Bu CD ED HIV LD Mood OCD Psy SP Sz.
    Psychotherapy: Fam Group Indiv Parent.
    Staff: 100 (Full 45, Part 55).
    Rates 2004: Sliding-Scale Rate $35-95/ses.
    Est 2000. Private. Nonprofit.

This human service agency serves individuals and families throughout San Mateo and Santa Clara counties. Programs and services include abuse and violence prevention;

intervention and treatment; crisis management; deaf and hard-of-hearing programming; early childhood services; family support; HIV/AIDS treatment; mental health counseling; school-based services; and substance abuse treatment.

The agency serves the community at agency locations, as well as at schools, daycare sites, corporations, in homes and in jails. Other agency locations are 1 W. Campbell Ave., Ste. D40-41, Campbell 95008, and 375 Cambridge Ave., Palo Alto 94306.

FOUNDATION FOR THE JUNIOR BLIND

Res — Coed Ages 5 and up; Day — Coed Birth-21

Los Angeles, CA 90043. 5300 Angeles Vista Blvd.
Tel: 323-295-4555. Fax: 323-296-0424.
www.fjb.org   E-mail: info@fjb.org
Robert B. Ralls, MS, Pres.
   Conditions: Primary—B. Sec—Au BD BI CP DS ED Ep OH.
   Pre-Voc. Ungraded. Courses: Read Lang_Arts.
   Therapy: Occup Phys Recreational.
   Est 1953. Private. Nonprofit.

FOUNDATION FOR THE RETARDED OF THE DESERT

Day — Coed Ages 18 and up

Palm Desert, CA 92260. 73-255 Country Club Dr.
Tel: 760-346-1611. Fax: 760-773-0933.
www.desertarc.org   E-mail: info@desertarc.org
Richard B. Farmer, PhD, Exec Dir.
   Focus: Trng. **Conditions:** Primary—MR OH. Sec—ADD ADHD Ap As Au B BI CP D Dx Ep IP LD MD MS S SB. **IQ 0-70.**
   Voc. Shelt_Workshop. On-Job Trng.
   Enr: 61. Day Males 27. Day Females 34. **Staff:** 21.
   Est 1959. Private. Nonprofit.

This facility offers year-round adult developmental and work training programs and is concerned with its participants' integration into the community. Clients may participate in work activity or supported employment programs. In addition, the foundation offers community-based programs that emphasize community awareness, personal hygiene and the ongoing development of functional proficiency.

Special services include in-home respite care (for up to six hours), individual counseling and, on a very limited basis, adult residences with 24-hour supervision.

FRED FINCH YOUTH CENTER

Res — Coed Ages 12-18

Oakland, CA 94602. 3800 Coolidge Ave.
Tel: 510-482-2244. Fax: 510-530-2047.

www.fredfinch.org
John Steinfirst, MSW, LCSW, Exec Dir. **Andrea Beil,** Adm.
>   **Focus:** Treatment. **Conditions:** Primary—ADHD Anx BD CD ED Mood
>   OCD ODD Psy PTSD SP Sz. Sec—As Ep LD. **IQ 71 and up.**
>   **Gen Acad. Pre-Voc. Voc.** Gr 7-12. Courses: Read Math Lang_Arts. On-Job
>   Trng.
>   **Therapy:** Occup Speech. **Psychotherapy:** Fam Group Indiv.
>   **Enr:** 48. Res Males 29. Res Females 19. **Staff:** 85. Prof 15. Educ 6.
>   **Rates 2003:** Res $5613-6371/mo (+$150/day). State Aid.
>   **Est 1891.** Private. Nonprofit. United Methodist.

The Youth Center treats adolescents with mild to severe emotional problems through therapy, counseling and special education. The usual length of treatment is 12 to 20 months. The mentally retarded and the physically handicapped are not accepted.

THE FROSTIG CENTER

Day — Coed Ages 6-18
Clinic: Ages 6 and up. M-S 8-5; Eves M-F 5-8.

Pasadena, CA 91107. 971 N Altadena Dr.
Tel: 626-791-1255. Fax: 626-798-1801.
www.frostig.org   E-mail: admissions@frostig.org
Bennett Ross, PhD, Exec Dir. **Tobey Shaw,** MA, Prin. **Bruce Hirsch,** PhD, Clin
Dir. **Kelly Carlton,** Adm.
>   **Focus:** Spec Ed. **Conditions:** Primary—Dc Dg Dx LD. Sec—ADD ADHD
>   Anx Ap Apr Asp Au Bl CP ED Mood OCD PDD S SP TS. **IQ 80 and up.**
>   **Gen Acad. Pre-Voc.** Gr 1-12. Courses: Read Math Lang_Arts Sci Comput-
>   ers Soc_Stud Studio_Art Music Drama Adaptive_Phys_Ed.
>   **Therapy:** Lang Speech. **Psychotherapy:** Fam Group Indiv.
>   **Enr:** 110. Day Males 70. Day Females 40. **Staff:** 75 (Full 45, Part 30).
>   **Rates 2003:** Day $20,425/sch yr. Clinic $105/ses. Sliding-Scale Rate $0-50
>   (Clinic). Schol 10 ($85,000). State Aid.
>   **Summer Prgm:** Day. Educ. Day Rate $3405. 6 wks.
>   **Est 1951.** Private. Nonprofit.

This center utilizes an interdisciplinary team approach in diagnosing learning disabilities, making recommendations, and planning and conducting appropriate educational programs. Frostig, which focuses on the needs of the whole child, provides educational and therapeutic services through a day school program and an outpatient division. Individualized interventions are integrated with academic teaching in small classes for children at all grade levels. Mainstreaming is a primary goal, and some students attend regular school classes for part of their curriculum.

Two intensive, six-week summer programs operate annually: one for currently enrolled day school students, and another serving pupils who attend other schools during the academic year.

GATEWAY CENTER OF MONTEREY COUNTY

Res and Day — Coed Ages 18 and up

Pacific Grove, CA 93950. 850 Congress Ave.
Tel: 831-372-8002. Fax: 831-372-2411.
www.redshift.com/~gcinc
Duane Burnell, CEO.
   Focus: Treatment. **Conditions:** Primary—MR. Sec—Au CP ED Ep.
   Gen Acad. Courses: Life_Skills. Shelt_Workshop. On-Job Trng.
   Therapy: Phys Speech. **Psychotherapy:** Indiv.
   Enr: 49. **Staff:** 70.
   Est 1956. Private. Nonprofit.

Gateway provides a variety of programs for mildly to profoundly retarded persons who may have other handicapping conditions. Services include residential and day activities, semi-independent living arrangements, an adult development center, a sheltered workshop and supported employment.

GLENDALE ADVENTIST MEDICAL CENTER
PEDIATRIC THERAPY CENTER

Clinic: All Ages. M-F 8-5.

Glendale, CA 91206. 1502 E Chevy Chase Dr, Ste 120.
Tel: 818-409-8306. Fax: 818-546-5691.
www.glendaleadventist.com
Donna Beaver, BS, PT, Supv.
   Focus: Rehab. **Conditions:** Primary—ADD ADHD Ap Au BI CP D Dx Ep IP
   LD MD ON S SB. Sec—As B BD C ED MR OCD.
   Therapy: Hear Lang Occup Phys Speech. **Psychotherapy:** Fam Indiv.
   Summer Prgm: Day. Rec. Ther.
   Private. Nonprofit. Seventh-Day Adventist.

Glendale offers full rehabilitative services. The range of handicaps accepted includes physical disabilities, moderate retardation, aphasia and autism. Programs include a six-week sensorimotor summer day camp, sports groups, infant massage and special groups for cooking and crafts during the holidays. The rates vary according to services provided, and limited scholarships are available.

THE GUIDANCE CENTER

Clinic: Ages 1-18. M-F 8-6; Eves M-Th 6-8.

Long Beach, CA 90807. 3711 Long Beach Blvd, Ste 600.
   Nearby locations: Avalon; Compton; North Long Beach; San Pedro.
Tel: 562-485-3085. Fax: 562-981-7569.
David K. Slay, PhD, Exec Dir. **Jill Morgan,** PhD, Clin Dir. **Anne C. Welty,** MD,
   Med Dir.
   Focus: Treatment. **Conditions:** Primary—ADD ADHD Anx BD CD ED

Mood OCD ODD Psy PTSD PW SP Sz. Sec—AN Asp Au Bu HIV MR.
Therapy: Art. **Psychotherapy:** Fam Group Indiv Parent.
Staff: 160. (Full 160). Prof 140. Admin 20.
Est 1946. Private. Nonprofit. **Spons:** Miller Children's Hospital.

TGC offers diagnosis and treatment for children and adolescents with mild to severe emotional disturbances. Parental and personal counseling is part of the program. The clinic has branches in San Pedro, Avalon, North Long Beach and Compton. In addition, the center provides services to 40 school campuses.

HAWTHORNE ACADEMY
Day — Coed Ages 6-22

Hawthorne, CA 90250. 12500 Ramona Ave.
Tel: 310-644-8841. Fax: 310-644-8910.
  Focus: Spec Ed. **Conditions:** Primary—ADD ADHD Dx ED LD MR. Sec—
  OCD ON Psy S Sz.
  Gen Acad. Gr K-12. Courses: Read Math Lang_Arts Adaptive_Phys_Ed.
  On-Job Trng.
  Therapy: Lang Speech. **Psychotherapy:** Group Indiv.
  Enr: 130. Day Males 80. Day Females 50. **Staff:** 38. (Full 38).
  Est 1999. Private. Inc.

An individualized curriculum is designed to provide the required courses of study as well as electives for enrichment and remediation in a variety of areas. Where appropriate, students may enroll concurrently in prevocational and vocational training programs or participate in classes at public schools. High school diplomas are awarded to students who meet the requirements. Counseling, speech and language therapy, and adaptive physical education are provided as needed.

HEAR CENTER
Clinic: All Ages. M-Th 8-5:30.

Pasadena, CA 91101. 301 E Del Mar Blvd.
Tel: 626-796-2016. Fax: 626-796-2320.
www.hearcenter.org   E-mail: auditory@mindspring.com
Josephine F. Wilson, BA, MA, Exec Dir.
  Focus: Rehab. **Conditions:** Primary—D S.
  Therapy: Hear Lang Speech.
  Staff: 9 (Full 5, Part 4).
  Rates 2003: Clinic $70-95/ses.
  Est 1954. Private. Nonprofit.

HEAR Center offers a program for persons with audiological and speech impairments that emphasizes early identification and amplification. Diagnostic evaluations are available for various speech and language disorders. Hearing aid evaluations, trial selection and recommendations are made for children and adults, and therapy is provided for those with hearing impairments and multiple handicaps. Parental counseling is also available.

HEARING SOCIETY FOR THE BAY AREA
Day — Coed Ages Birth-17
Clinic: Ages Birth-17. M-F 9-5.

San Francisco, CA 94102. 49 Powell St, Ste 400.
Tel: 415-693-5870. TTY: 415-834-1005. Fax: 415-834-1538.
www.hearingsociety.org   E-mail: info@hearingsociety.org
Helen Sloss Luey, MSW, LCSW, Supv.
   Focus: Treatment. **Conditions:** Primary—D. Sec—Au ED LD MR ON S.
   Therapy: Hear Lang. **Psychotherapy:** Fam Group Indiv Parent.
   Staff: 22 (Full 11, Part 11). Prof 15. Admin 7.
   Est 1915. Private. Nonprofit.

The Hearing Society offers a full range of services for individuals who are deaf or hard-of-hearing. Direct services include hearing aid loans, assistive device display and demonstration, aural rehabilitation, communication therapy, social work and mental health counseling, work readiness training, consultations for those with hearing and vision losses, and consultations for multicultural families with deaf children.

The agency also offers such community services as information and referral, advocacy, community education, hearing outreach and program planning. In addition, the youth program includes after-school and weekend activities, family support services and direct services for deaf and hard-of-hearing youth.

HELP FOR BRAIN INJURED CHILDREN
THE CLETA HARDER DEVELOPMENTAL SCHOOL
Day — Coed Ages 3-22

La Habra, CA 90631. 981 N Euclid Ave.
Tel: 562-694-5655. Fax: 562-694-5657.
www.hbic.org   E-mail: hbiccleta@aol.com
Cleta J. Harder, Exec Dir. **John G. Miller,** MD, Med Dir.
   Focus: Spec Ed. **Conditions:** Primary—ADD ADHD Asp Au BI CP MR OH.
      Sec—As B BD C D Dx ED Ep IP LD S SB.
   Gen Acad. Voc. Ungraded. Courses: Read Math Lang_Arts. On-Job Trng.
   Therapy: Hear Lang Movement Occup Phys Speech. **Psychotherapy:**
      Indiv.
   Enr: 50. **Staff:** 25 (Full 20, Part 5). Prof 6. Educ 3. Admin 2.
   Summer Prgm: Day. Educ. Rec. Ther. Day Rate $105.
   Est 1967. Private. Nonprofit.

HBIC provides educational and rehabilitative services for children, adolescents and young adults who have a brain injury or dysfunction. Named for the center's founder, the Cleta Harder Developmental School offers an individualized academic program for the pupil who has the potential to move to a higher level of functioning, but who requires a small, controlled environment to do so. Within a highly structured and disciplined environment, the school maintains an individualized motor development regime and a student-faculty ratio of no greater than 2:1.

Another program, Kids Unlimited, provides after-school developmental motor-skills training designed to meet the needs of children who are experiencing school difficulties. Activities include physical, visual and auditory exercise, as well as assistance with academics and social skills.

THE HELP GROUP

Day — Coed Ages 2¾-22

Sherman Oaks, CA 91401. 13130 Burbank Blvd.
Tel: 818-779-5262. Fax: 818-779-5295.
www.thehelpgroup.org   E-mail: admissions@thehelpgroup.org
Barbara Firestone, PhD, Pres. **Thomas Komp,** Adm.
   Focus: Spec Ed. **Conditions:** Primary—ADD ADHD AN Anx Ap Apr Asp Au BD BI CD Dc Dg DS Dx ED LD Mood MR OCD ODD ON PDD Psy PTSD SP Sz TS. **IQ 50 and up.**
   Col Prep. Gen Acad. Voc. Gr K-12. Courses: Read Math. On-Job Trng.
   Therapy: Art Chemo Lang Milieu Occup Speech. **Psychotherapy:** Fam Group Indiv.
   Enr: 984. Day Males 632. Day Females 352. **Staff:** 400. Prof 210. Educ 115. Admin 45.
   Rates 2003: Day $138/day.
   Summer Prgm: Day. Ther. 6 wks.
   Est 1953. Private. Nonprofit.

Through various educational and therapeutic programs, this organization serves children with special needs related to autism, Asperger's syndrome, learning disabilities, emotional development, mental retardation, and abuse and neglect. Within an individualized environment, schools provide academic programs at the elementary, middle school and secondary levels that are designed to improve the student's socialization and communicational skills.

The following schools operate at both the Sherman Oaks location and 4160 Grand View Blvd., Los Angeles 90066: Village Glen School, Sunrise School, Bridgeport School and Young Learners Therapeutic Preschool. Another day school, the Pace Program, is conducted in Sherman Oaks, while Summit View School has locations at 6455 Coldwater Canyon Ave., North Hollywood 91606, and 12101 W. Washington Blvd., Los Angeles 90066. Coldwater Canyon Prep serves students with learning disabilities and accompanying attentional disorders or social or emotional issues at the Coldwater Canyon address. Located at 15339 Saticoy St., Van Nuys 91406, Pacific Ridge School provides an intensive therapeutic educational day program for pupils with emotional and behavioral difficulties.

HENRIETTA WEILL MEMORIAL CHILD GUIDANCE CLINIC

Clinic: Ages Birth-18. M-F 8-5; Eves M-Th 5-7.

Bakersfield, CA 93309. 3628 Stockdale Hwy.
Tel: 661-322-1021. Fax: 661-322-7334.
www.hwmcgc.org
David L. Camara, LCSW, Exec Dir.

Conditions: Primary—BD ED.
Gen Acad. Courses: Read Math Lang_Arts.
Psychotherapy: Fam Group Indiv.
Est 1946. Private. Nonprofit.

HILLSIDE SCHOOL AND LEARNING CENTER

Day — Coed Ages 12-18
Clinic: Ages 4-30. M-F 8-5; Eves M-F 5-8.

La Canada, CA 91011. 4331 Oakgrove Dr.
Tel: 818-790-3044. Fax: 818-790-4225.
www.hillside4success.org   E-mail: hillsidedlc@mindspring.com
Robert A. Frank, BS, MS, Exec Dir. **Pat Ramos,** MS, Prin.
  Focus: Spec Ed. Treatment. **Conditions:** Primary—ADD ADHD Dc Dg Dx.
    Sec—Anx Bl CP ED Mood. **IQ 90-125.**
  Col Prep. Gen Acad. Gr 7-12. Courses: Read Math Lang_Arts. Man_Arts &
    Shop. On-Job Trng.
  Therapy: Lang Speech. **Psychotherapy:** Fam Group Indiv Parent.
  Enr: 72. Day Males 47. Day Females 25. **Staff:** 18 (Full 11, Part 7).
  Rates 2003: Day $8800/sch yr (+$300). Sliding-Scale Rate $50-100/hr
    (Clinic). Schol 5 ($38,000).
  Summer Prgm: Day. Educ. Ther. 6 wks.
  Est 1972. Private. Nonprofit. **Spons:** Parent Advisory League.

The facility specializes in the identification and the treatment of learning disorders as
they relate to developmental medicine and environmental factors. The center's primary
goal is to foster independence and self-reliance in learning-disabled children and adolescents. Related services are available on an adjunctive basis for students who require
intensive one-on-one educational or psychological therapy.

Hillside also provides an outreach program for community schools and services, as
well as travel programs for students. A computer system for career and vocational counseling allows students to explore interests in a wide variety of careers.

HOME OF GUIDING HANDS

Res — Coed Ages 17 and up; Day — Coed 5 and up

Lakeside, CA 92040. 10025 Los Ranchitos Rd.
Tel: 619-448-3700. Fax: 619-448-7208.
www.guidinghands.org
Carol A. Fitzgibbons, MS, Exec Dir. **John James,** MD, Med Dir.
  Focus: Trng. **Conditions:** Primary—MR. Sec—Ap As Au B CP D ED Ep
    ON S Sz. **IQ 0-70.**
  Therapy: Hear Lang Occup Phys Speech. **Psychotherapy:** Indiv.
  Enr: 228. Res Males 88. Res Females 75. Day Males 39. Day Females 26.
    Staff: 292 (Full 204, Part 88). Prof 245. Admin 47.
  Rates 2003: No Fee.
  Est 1967. Private. Nonprofit.

Guiding Hands offers individualized programs, enabling children and adults with developmental disabilities to achieve greater levels of independence in mainstream society. In-home respite and community living services, as well as 24-hour residential services, are provided.

HOUSE EAR CLINIC

Clinic: All Ages. M-F 8-5.

Los Angeles, CA 90057. 2100 W 3rd St.
  Nearby locations: Huntington Beach; Orange; Santa Monica.
Tel: 213-483-9930. TTY: 213-483-5706. Fax: 213-989-7473.
www.houseearclinic.com
William H. Slattery III, MD, Dir.
  Focus: Treatment. **Conditions:** Primary—D.
  Therapy: Hear Speech.
  Staff: 55 (Full 50, Part 5).
  Est 1947. Private. Nonprofit. **Spons:** House Ear Institute.

HEC provides diagnosis and treatment of ear diseases, hearing loss, and disorders related to the skull base, the facial nerve, otologic allergy, acoustic tumors and the balance system. Services include therapy, surgery, hearing aid fittings and a cochlear implant program.

HUNTINGTON MEMORIAL HOSPITAL PEDIATRICS UNIT

Clinic: Ages Birth-16. M-F 8:30-4.

Pasadena, CA 91105. 100 W California Blvd.
Tel: 626-397-8688. Fax: 626-397-2947.
www.huntingtonhospital.com
  Conditions: Primary—As BI C CP Ep IP LD MD MS ON SB TB.
  Therapy: Occup Phys Speech.
  Est 1892. Private. Nonprofit.

INDEPENDENCE CENTER

Res — Coed Ages 18-30

Los Angeles, CA 90034. 3640 S Sepulveda Blvd, Ste 102.
Tel: 310-202-7102. Fax: 310-202-7180.
www.independencecenter.com   E-mail: judym@independencecenter.com
Judy Maizlish, Exec Dir. **Gloria Ogletree,** Admin Dir.
  Focus: Trng. **Conditions:** Primary—ADD ADHD Anx Asp Au BD Dc Dg
      Dx LD PDD SP. Sec—Ap Apr As BI C CP D Db ED Ep Mood OCD ON
      PTSD S TS. **IQ 80 and up.**
  Therapy: Milieu. **Psychotherapy:** Indiv.

Enr: 30. Res Males 21. Res Females 9. **Staff:** 14 (Full 6, Part 8).
Rates 2003: Res $27,500/sch yr. Schol avail.
Est 1985. Private. Nonprofit.

The center offers a mainstreamed transitional apartment living program for young adults with learning disabilities. The program focuses on increasing independent living, vocational social and social/communication skills. The staff includes licensed therapists and credentialed educators. Program participants, who come from all over the country, typically possess low-average to above-average intellectual ability, but they lack the social maturity and skills needed to become successful independent adults.

INTERCOMMUNITY CHILD GUIDANCE CENTER

Day — Coed Ages 9-13
Clinic: Ages Birth-18. M-Th 8-5, F 8-1; Eves M-Th 5-7.

Whittier, CA 90606. 8106 Broadway Ave.
Tel: 562-692-2038. Fax: 562-692-0380.
www.intercommunity.org   E-mail: icgc@vfnet.com
Sandra J. Klein, LCSW, MSW, Exec Dir. **Albert H. Arenowitz,** MD, Med Dir.
   Focus: Treatment. **Conditions:** Primary—ADD ADHD Anx BD ED Mood
      Psy PTSD SP Sz TS. Sec—AN Bu CD OCD.
   Therapy: Art Milieu Play. **Psychotherapy:** Fam Group Indiv Parent.
   Staff: 64 (Full 38, Part 26). Prof 23. Educ 2. Admin 16.
   Rates 2003: Sliding-Scale Rate $0-95/ses. State Aid.
   Est 1957. Private. Nonprofit.

The primary focus of the center is diagnosis and short-term treatment of emotional disturbances and psychological problems through individual and group counseling. Walk-in emergency service is available, as is parent education.

IRLEN INSTITUTE FOR PERCEPTUAL
AND LEARNING DEVELOPMENT

Clinic: Ages 7 and up. M-F 9-5.

Long Beach, CA 90808. 5380 Village Rd.
Tel: 562-496-2550. Fax: 562-429-8699.
www.irlen.com   E-mail: irleninstitute@irlen.com
Helen L. Irlen, MA, Dir.
   Focus: Treatment. **Conditions:** Primary—ADD ADHD Dx LD. Sec—Asp Au.
   Est 1983. Private. Inc.

The clinic uses the Irlen Method to treat individuals with learning, reading, behavior and attention difficulties due to Irlen syndrome/scotopic sensitivity, which is a type of visual perception problem related to the neurological system. The institute employs colored overlays and tinted lenses worn as glasses or contact lenses to reduce or eliminate perception difficulties due to light sensitivity.

The institute maintains clinics around North America and throughout the world.

JAMESON SCHOOL

Day — Coed Ages 6-22

Ventura, CA 93002. 1718 E Main St, PO Box 2179.
Tel: 805-648-2400. Fax: 805-648-3218.
E-mail: jamesonnps@dock.net
Hector Alvarez, MS, Admin.
    Focus: Spec Ed. **Conditions:** Primary—ADD ADHD Asp Au BD CD ED
    Mood MR S. **IQ 75-110.**
    Gen Acad. Gr K-12. Courses: Read Math Lang_Arts Sci.
    Therapy: Speech. **Psychotherapy:** Indiv.
    Enr: 30. Day Males 20. Day Females 10. **Staff:** 12 (Full 11, Part 1). Prof 5.
    Rates 2003: Day $148/day.
    Est 1992. Private. Inc.

The school provides education, child guidance, counseling and vocational training in a highly structured and supportive learning environment for students with learning and developmental disabilities who cannot be served adequately in public schools. Each student follows an Individualized Education Program, while also developing the skills essential for school and society.

JEAN WEINGARTEN PENINSULA ORAL SCHOOL FOR THE DEAF

Day — Coed Ages Birth-8
Clinic: All Ages. M-F 8-4.

Redwood City, CA 94062. 3518 Jefferson Ave.
Tel: 650-365-7500. TTY: 650-365-7500. Fax: 650-365-7557.
www.oraldeafed.org/schools/jwposd   E-mail: jwposd@jwposd.org
Kathleen Daniel Sussman, MA, Dir. **Kathy Berger,** Adm.
    Focus: Spec Ed. **Conditions:** Primary—D. Sec—LD S.
    Gen Acad. Gr PS-2. Courses: Read Math Lang_Arts.
    Therapy: Hear Lang Speech. **Psychotherapy:** Fam Parent.
    Enr: 69. Day Males 34. Day Females 35. **Staff:** 30 (Full 27, Part 3).
    Rates 2003: Day $125/day. $90 (Clinic)/ses. Schol avail.
    Est 1969. Private. Nonprofit.

JWPOSD offers educational and developmental services to deaf and hearing-impaired children and their families through a program that develops spoken communication skills. The program goal is to prepare children to return to their home schools as soon as possible with academic and communication skills that will allow them to function at grade level with their peers. The school's curriculum emphasizes the development of speech, language and audition through a cognitive approach to learning, with a focus on literacy at all levels.

Additional offerings include a parent-infant program, a toddler program, mainstream support services, diagnostic services, a parent education program, and counseling and bilingual services.

JOHN TRACY CLINIC

Day — Coed Ages Birth-5
Clinic: Ages Birth-5. M-F 8-4; Eve T 7-9.

Los Angeles, CA 90007. 806 W Adams Blvd.
Tel: 213-748-5481. TTY: 213-747-2924. Fax: 213-749-1651.
www.jtc.org   E-mail: mmartindale@jtc.org
Barbara F. Hecht, PhD, Pres.
   Focus: Spec Ed. Trng. Conditions: Primary—D S.
   Gen Acad. Gr PS.
   Therapy: Hear Lang Speech. Psychotherapy: Fam Parent.
   Staff: 65 (Full 58, Part 7).
   Rates 2003: No Fee.
   Summer Prgm: Day. Educ. 3 wks.
   Est 1942. Private. Nonprofit.

An audiological testing and educational center for preschool children with hearing loss and their parents, the clinic stresses the education of parents working with their children. The Demonstration Home assists parents in the development of everyday techniques to aid their child in listening skills and language acquisition. The preschool enrolls parents and children in a program that helps the child utilize his or her residual hearing, speech reading, and, eventually, expressive language skills.

Classes for parents include child development, communicational skills and education of preschool children. The clinic also maintains parental support groups. Major services include correspondence courses in English and Spanish and a three-week summer school for parents and hearing-impaired children and their siblings. Audiological outreach services are also performed throughout Los Angeles and contiguous counties.

The clinic also offers a master's program and credential program through the USC Rossier School of Education and Distance Learning for professionals over the Internet.

JULIA ANN SINGER THERAPEUTIC SCHOOL

Day — Coed Ages 3-10

Los Angeles, CA 90064. 3321 Edith Ave.
Tel: 310-202-0669. Fax: 310-839-4158.
www.vistadelmar.org
Susan Schmidt Lackner, MD, Med Dir.
   Focus: Spec Ed. Conditions: Primary—ADD ADHD Anx Ap Apr Asp Au
      BD CD Dc Dg Dx ED Mood MR OCD PDD S. Sec—As Bl CP PTSD. IQ
      80-120.
   Gen Acad. Pre-Voc. Gr PS-5. Courses: Read Math Lang_Arts.
   Therapy: Art Dance Movement Occup Play Speech. Psychotherapy: Fam
      Indiv.
   Staff: 32 (Full 23, Part 9).
   Summer Prgm: Day. Day Rate $0. 6 wks.
   Est 1916. Private. Nonprofit. Spons: Vista Del Mar Child and Family Services.

The Therapeutic School serves children with severe emotional disturbances, learning disabilities, autistic spectrum disorders and developmental delays. A team of educational therapists and mental health professionals prepares Individual Education Plans incorporating play therapy, sensory and motor skill integration, and speech and language therapy for each student. Parent involvement is required, and the goal is to return the child to a community setting as soon as possible.

JULIA HOBBS SPEECH PATHOLOGY

Clinic: All Ages. M-F 9-6.

Los Angeles, CA 90064. 11835 W Olympic Blvd, Ste 250.
Tel: 310-996-8900. Fax: 310-996-8909.
   Conditions: Primary—S.
   Est 1978. Private. Inc.

KAYNE-ERAS CENTER

Day — Coed Ages 3-22
Clinic: All Ages. M-S 8-6.

Culver City, CA 90230. 5350 Machado Rd.
Tel: 310-737-9393. Fax: 310-737-9344.
www.erascenter.com
Barbara Cull, Exec Dir.
   Focus: Spec Ed. Treatment. **Conditions:** Primary—ADD ADHD Anx Ap Au Dx LD. Sec—As ED Ep MR OCD. **IQ 65 and up.**
   Col Prep. Gen Acad. Pre-Voc. Voc. Gr PS-12. Courses: Read Math Lang_ Arts Studio_Art Music Drama.
   Therapy: Lang Occup Phys Speech. **Psychotherapy:** Fam Group Indiv Parent.
   Staff: 173.
   Est 1980. Private. Nonprofit.

Kayne-ERAS offers a day school program to children and youth with speech impairments, as well as a residential program for adults. Outpatient services serve appropriate clients of all ages.

KEYSTONE ACADEMY

Res and Day — Coed Ages 13-18

Ramona, CA 92065. 1130 D St, Ste 13.
Tel: 760-788-9124. Fax: 760-788-7226.
E-mail: bparks@keystoneyouth.com
Brad Parks, BS, MSEd, Dir.
   Focus: Spec Ed. **Conditions:** Primary—ADD ADHD Anx BD CD Dc Dg Dx ED LD Mood OCD PTSD SP Sz TS. **IQ 85-128.**

Col Prep. Gen Acad. Gr 7-12. Courses: Read Math Lang_Arts Sci Soc_Sci.
Enr: 50. Res Males 18. Res Females 18. Day Males 4. Day Females 10.
　Staff: 17 (Full 16, Part 1).
Private. Inc. **Spons:** Keystone Education & Youth Services.

Keystone enrolls children and adolescents with serious emotional, behavioral and learning difficulties who have not succeeded in the traditional public school setting. The highly structured curriculum features daily elective choices, as well as transition services. Therapy and speech and language services round out the program.

KEYSTONE EDUCATION
BARSTOW CAMPUS

Day — Coed Ages 5-22

Barstow, CA 92311. 561 E Rimrock Rd.
Tel: 760-252-5159. Fax: 760-252-2505.
www.keystoneyouth.com   E-mail: nfreedland@keystoneyouth.com
Nancy Freedland, Dir.
　Focus: Spec Ed. **Conditions:** Primary—ADD ADHD Anx Asp Au BD CD
　　ED LD Mood MR OCD PDD Psy. Sec—AN As Bu C D Db Dc Dg Dx Ep
　　HIV PTSD S SP Sz TS.
　Gen Acad. Pre-Voc. Gr K-12. Courses: Read Math Lang_Arts Sci Comput-
　　ers Hist. On-Job Trng.
　Therapy: Art Play. **Psychotherapy:** Fam Group Indiv Parent.
　Enr: 15. Day Males 14. Day Females 1. **Staff:** 8. (Full 8). Educ 5. Admin 2.
　Rates 2004: No Fee.
　Summer Prgm: Day. Educ. Rec. Day Rate $0. 6 wks.
　Private. **Spons:** Keystone Education and Youth Services.

Keystone education programs serve children and adolescents who are in need of behavioral and psychiatric interventions. Barstow services include social skills training, life skills education, cooperative challenge activities, tolerance instruction, play therapy, anger management and intervention reading.

School districts refer pupils and pay their tuition fees. Keystone offers door-to-door transportation.

LA MONTE ACADEMIE

Day — Coed Ages 5-18

Laguna Hills, CA 92653. 23092 Mill Creek Dr.
Tel: 949-455-1270. Fax: 949-455-1271.
www.lamonteacademie.org   E-mail: lamonteacademie@hotmail.com
Laura Bonnecaze, Co-Dir. **Jenafer Ricker,** Co-Dir.
　Focus: Spec Ed. **Conditions:** Primary—ADD ADHD AN As Bu Db Dc Dg
　　Dx LD. Sec—Asp Au B DS ED Mood MR MS S. **IQ 90-130.**
　Gen Acad. Gr K-12. Courses: Read Math Lang_Arts Fr Sci Computers
　　Soc_Stud Studio_Art.
　Therapy: Lang Movement. **Psychotherapy:** Group Indiv.

Enr: 40. Day Males 20. Day Females 20. **Staff:** 8.
Rates 2003: Day $6000-8500/yr (+$780).
Summer Prgm: Day. Educ. 2-8 wks.
Est 1976. Private. Nonprofit.

At La Monte, students with learning difficulties receive one-on-one and small-group instruction enabling each individual to reach their educational peak. The educational program, which begins with a developmentally oriented kindergarten that emphasizes language, sensorimotor, pre-academic and social skills, extends through grade 12.

LANE'S LEARNING CENTER

Clinic: All Ages. M-F 8-7:30.

Novato, CA 94947. 1 Gustafson Ct.
Tel: 415-893-1960. Fax: 415-893-1960.
E-mail: michlane@aol.com
Michele Lane, MS, Dir.
   Focus: Treatment. **Conditions:** Primary—ADD ADHD As Au Dx ED LD MR OCD.
   Summer Prgm: Day. Rec. Ther.
   Est 1981. Private. Nonprofit.

This center's services include educational assessment; individual instruction; consultation with parents, schools and agencies; integration of academics with movement; and swimming instruction during the summer. The usual duration of treatment is six months.

THE LEARNING CENTER

Clinic: Ages 2 and up. M-S 9-6.

Encino, CA 91316. 16944 Ventura Blvd.
Tel: 818-783-6633. Fax: 818-783-6029.
www.learningcenter.net
   Conditions: Primary—ADD ADHD BD BI Dx LD MR. **IQ 60 and up.**
   Therapy: Speech. **Psychotherapy:** Fam Indiv Parent.
   Staff: 14. Educ 9. Admin 3.
   Rates 2001: Clinic $55/hr.
   Est 1967. Private. Nonprofit.

This center seeks the remediation of dyslexia and learning disabilities. The program includes both educational and counseling services for children and adults in the Los Angeles area. All services are provided on a one-on-one basis, with services involving one credentialed teacher or psychologist per student. In addition to educational evaluations, the facility conducts emotional evaluations to determine whether or not psychological counseling is necessary.

THE LEARNING CENTER

Clinic: All Ages. M-Th 9-5; Eves M-Th 5-9.

San Rafael, CA 94903. 819 Hacienda Way.
Tel: 415-472-6212.
Pamela Wilding, MS, Dir.
   Focus: Spec Ed. Conditions: Primary—Dc Dg Dx LD. Sec—ADD ADHD
      ED MR.
   Gen Acad. Ungraded. Courses: Read Math.
   Staff: 6 (Full 1, Part 5).
   Rates 2003: Clinic $75/hr. Schol avail.
   Est 1976. Private. Nonprofit.

Children and adults with learning disabilities receive a variety of year-round services at the center. Comprehensive educational evaluations allow the staff to assess the educational needs of each student, to formulate an individualized learning program, and to arrange one-on-one or small-group assistance for the client. Educational therapy facilitates the remediation of reading, writing, spelling and mathematics problems, as well as the development of improved language, perceptual, cognitive and study skills.

THE LEARNING CLINICS

Clinic: Ages 4 and up. M-Th 9:30-5; Eves M-Th 5-7:30.

Camarillo, CA 93010. 484 Mobil Ave, Ste 12.
   Nearby locations: Ventura.
Tel: 805-482-3730.
   Focus: Spec Ed. Conditions: Primary—ADD ADHD Dc Dg Dx LD. Sec—
      Asp Au B MR PDD.
   Gen Acad. Ungraded. Courses: Read Math Lang_Arts.
   Psychotherapy: Indiv.
   Staff: 14.
   Est 1962. Private.

The clinic utilizes an individualized approach to educational therapy for the learning disabled. An affiliated clinic operates at 2950 Johnson Dr., Ste. 111, Ventura 93003.

LEROY HAYNES CENTER
FOR CHILDREN AND FAMILY SERVICES

Res — Males Ages 7-17; Day — Coed 7-18

La Verne, CA 91750. 233 W Baseline Rd.
Tel: 909-593-2581. Fax: 909-593-5241.
www.leroyhaynes.org   E-mail: info@leroyhaynes.org
Darrell T. Pauck, BA, MS, LCSW, Pres. Sheree Barbee, Intake.
   Focus: Spec Ed. Treatment. Conditions: Primary—ADD ADHD Anx BD Dx
      ED LD Mood OCD PTSD SP. Sec—Ap Asp Au CD Db HIV Psy S Sz TS.
   Gen Acad. Gr K-12.

Therapy: Art Milieu Music Play Recreational. **Psychotherapy:** Fam Group
  Indiv Parent.
Enr: 140. **Staff:** 200 (Full 178, Part 22). Prof 66. Educ 50. Admin 10.
Est 1946. Private. Nonprofit.

LeRoy Haynes Center consists of Haynes Education Center, a nonpublic school, and
LeRoy Boys Home, a group living situation for abused and neglected children. Boys in
the residential program live in one of six cottages, each of which houses 12 children.
Individualized treatment, structured therapeutic activities and therapy are main components of residential life; substance abuse treatment, social skills development, psychiatric and psychological assessment, medical care and parental training are also available.
The program seeks to return the boy to his family or, if this is not possible, place him in
a less restrictive setting.

Founded as a companion to the group home facility, Haynes Education Center started
as a school for residents of the home. The year-round center now also serves the community as a whole, with boys and girls from 10 area school districts enrolling. Within a
highly structured environment, staff members teach a full curriculum that addresses the
needs of students with learning disabilities and behavioral problems. Other aspects of
the curriculum are a vocational program and an after-school day treatment program that
emphasizes life and social skills.

LINCOLN CHILD CENTER

Res and Day — Coed Ages 6-13

Oakland, CA 94602. 4368 Lincoln Ave.
Tel: 510-531-3111. Fax: 510-531-8968.
www.lincolncc.org   E-mail: info@lincolncc.org
Richard T. Clarke, PhD, Pres.
  Focus: Treatment. **Conditions:** Primary—ADD ADHD BD ED Mood ODD
    PTSD. Sec—LD. **IQ 90 and up.**
  Gen Acad. Ungraded. Courses: Read Math Lang_Arts.
  Therapy: Art Milieu Play Speech. **Psychotherapy:** Fam Group Indiv.
  Enr: 85. **Staff:** 71 (Full 54, Part 17). Educ 42. Admin 4.
  Rates 2004: No Fee.
  Est 1883. Private. Nonprofit.

This center provides 24-hour treatment for children with severe emotional and behavioral problems. Services include consultation and referral, residential and day treatment,
and an on-grounds school program. Family, group and individual therapies are available,
and the center requires parental or family involvement. The average length of treatment
is 14-18 months.

LINDAMOOD-BELL LEARNING PROCESSES

Clinic: Ages 5 and up. M-F 8-5.

San Luis Obispo, CA 93401. 416 Higuera St.
Tel: 805-541-3836. Fax: 805-543-0264.
www.lblp.com/learningcenters/slo.shtml

Conditions: Primary—Dx LD. **IQ 60 and up.**
Courses: Read Math.
Therapy: Lang.
Est 1972. Private.

LOMA LINDA UNIVERSITY MEDICAL CENTER
SPECIAL KIDS INTERVENTION PROGRAM

Clinic: All Ages. M-F 8-5; Eves M-F 5-7.

Loma Linda, CA 92354. 11406 Loma Linda Dr.
Tel: 909-558-6144. Fax: 909-668-6002.
  Focus: Treatment. **Conditions:** Primary—ADD ADHD Ap Au Bl C CP LD
    ON S. Sec—Dx Ep IP MD MR MS SB.
  Therapy: Hear Lang Occup Phys Speech. **Psychotherapy:** Fam Group
    Indiv.
  Private. Nonprofit. Seventh-Day Adventist.

SKIP provides speech and language pathology services for nonvocal, severely
handicapped patients who require sophisticated, computerized communicational aids to
supplement or replace oral communication. The program stresses an interdisciplinary
team approach.

LOS ANGELES SCOTTISH RITE
CHILDHOOD LANGUAGE DISORDERS CENTER

Clinic: Ages 3-18. M-F by Appt.

Los Angeles, CA 90048. 6310 San Vincente Blvd, Ste 300.
Tel: 323-936-2153. Fax: 323-937-3742.
Debra Hamlin, BA, MA, CCC, Dir.
  Focus: Treatment. **Conditions:** Primary—S. Sec—ADD ADHD.
  Therapy: Speech.
  Staff: 3. Prof 2. Admin 1.
  Rates 2004: No Fee.
  Est 1977. Private. Nonprofit.

Children who exhibit delays or disorders in speech, language or comprehension skills
receive individual speech and language services through this program. Treatment usually lasts approximately 18 months.

LUCILLE PACKARD CHILDREN'S HOSPITAL
AT STANFORD AUDIOLOGY CLINIC

Clinic: Ages Birth-21. M-F 8:30-4:30.

Palo Alto, CA 94304. 725 Welsh Rd.

Tel: 650-498-2565. Fax: 650-498-2734.
Jody Winzelberg, MA, Dir.
   Focus: Treatment. **Conditions:** Primary—D. Sec—Au MR ON S.
   Therapy: Hear.
   Staff: 7 (Full 4, Part 3).
   Private. Inc.

This clinic specializes in the diagnosis and the treatment of hearing loss. Audiologists with training in sign language are equipped to give such specialized tests as the Auditory Brainstem Response (ABR) and Otoacoustic Emissions (OAES). The facility also dispenses and repairs hearing aids.

MARLTON CHARTER SCHOOL

Day — Coed Ages 3-22

Los Angeles, CA 90008. 4000 Santo Tomas Dr.
Tel: 323-296-7680. TTY: 323-296-7680. Fax: 323-290-1794.
www.lausd.k12.ca.us/Marlton_EL
Cecilia Perea, Prin.
   Focus: Spec Ed. **Conditions:** Primary—B D.
   Gen Acad. Pre-Voc. Voc. Gr PS-PG. Courses: Read Math Lang_Arts. Man_
      Arts & Shop. Shelt_Workshop. On-Job Trng.
   Therapy: Lang Speech. **Psychotherapy:** Indiv.
   Enr: 410.
   Rates 2004: No Fee.
   Summer Prgm: Day. Educ. Rec. Ther.
   State.

This facility offers speech and language therapy and provides personal, educational and vocational counseling.

MELMED LEARNING CLINIC

Clinic: All Ages. M-F 9-6.

Lafayette, CA 94549. 3182 Old Tunnel Rd, Ste A.
Tel: 925-283-6777.
www.melmedlearning.com   E-mail: paul@melmedlearning.com
Paul J. Melmed, MA, PhD, Dir.
   Focus: Treatment. **Conditions:** Primary—ADD LD S.
   Therapy: Lang Speech.
   Staff: 7 (Full 5, Part 2).
   Est 1970. Private.

The clinic provides diagnosis, evaluation and therapy for speech and language problems, in addition to academics for the learning disabled. Distinct programs deal with math and accelerated reading and writing skills. Mentally retarded and emotionally disturbed children cannot attend.

MENTAL HEALTH SERVICES ALAMEDA SUPPORT CENTER

Clinic: Ages 3-18. M-F 8:30-5.

Alameda, CA 94501. 2226 Santa Clara Ave.
Tel: 510-522-4668. Fax: 510-521-6729.
John Brown, LCSW, Supv.

> **Focus:** Treatment. **Conditions:** Primary—ADD ADHD AN Anx BD Bu CD
> ED Mood OCD ODD Psy PTSD SP Sz. Sec—Ap Apr Ar As B CF CP D
> Db Dc Dg Dx Ep HIV IP MS ON S SB.
> **Psychotherapy:** Fam Indiv.
> County.

The center assists children, adolescents and adults who are experiencing a psychiatric crisis or who have significant emotional or behavioral problems. Among the available services are crisis intervention, a behavioral health program, and psychiatric medication evaluation, prescription and monitoring.

MERCI

Res — Coed Ages 18 and up; Day — Coed 6 and up

Monterey Park, CA 91754. 525 N Chandler Ave, PO Box 676.
> **Nearby locations:** Alhambra.
Tel: 626-289-8817. Fax: 626-289-8843.
www.merci.org
Rosemary Cervantes, Exec Dir.

> **Focus:** Trng. **Conditions:** Primary—Au CP Ep MR PDD.
> **Est 1955.** Private. Nonprofit.

MID VALLEY LEARNING CENTERS

Day — Coed Ages 5-22

Baldwin Park, CA 91706. 13940 Merced Ave.
Tel: 626-813-2055. Fax: 626-813-2051.
www.midvalleyschool.com
> **E-mail: drstephensmith@midvalleyschool.com**
Kenneth A. Smith, MEd, Supt. **Nancy R. Smith,** MA, Prin. **Becky Smith,** Dir.

> **Focus:** Spec Ed. **Conditions:** Primary—ADD ADHD AN Anx Ap As Asp
> Au BD Bu CD D Db Dc Dg DS Dx ED Ep IP LD Mood MR OCD ON PDD
> PTSD S SP TS. Sec—Apr B BI CP MD MS Nf SB TB.
> **Gen Acad. Pre-Voc.** Gr K-12. Courses: Read Math Lang_Arts Sci Hist.
> **Psychotherapy:** Indiv.
> **Enr:** 75. Day Males 56. Day Females 19. **Staff:** 37. (Part 1). Prof 15. Admin
> 4.
> **Rates 2003:** No Fee.
> **Est 1977.** Private. Inc.

Enrolling children who have been referred by their home school districts, Mid Valley provides educational and counseling services for students with various special needs. Field trips, as well as athletics and other activities, complement academics.

MID-PENINSULA HIGH SCHOOL

Day — Coed Ages 14-18

Menlo Park, CA 94025. 1340 Willow Rd.
Tel: 650-321-1991. Fax: 650-321-9921.
www.mid-pen.com   E-mail: info@mid-pen.com
Douglas C. Thompson, PhD, Head. **Heidi Moore,** Adm.
    Focus: Spec Ed. **Conditions:** Primary—Dx ED LD. Sec—BD.
    Col Prep. Gen Acad. Gr 9-12. Courses: Read Math Lang_Arts.
    Psychotherapy: Parent.
    Enr: 150. Day Males 87. Day Females 63. **Staff:** 30.
    Est 1980. Private. Nonprofit.

MPHS offers a comprehensive program catering to students with a variety of learning needs. The program includes remediation and college preparation for pupils who require a personalized learning environment. The school encourages parental involvement in the learning process.

MISSION LEARNING CENTER

Clinic: Ages 7-11. M-F 3-5.

San Francisco, CA 94103. 474 Valencia St.
Tel: 415-575-3535. Fax: 415-558-9363.
Loretta Kruger, Exec Dir.
    Conditions: Primary—LD.
    Gen Acad. Pre-Voc. Gr 2-5. Courses: Read Math Lang_Arts.
    Est 1972. Private. Nonprofit.

THE MORGAN CENTER

Day — Coed Ages 3-22

Santa Clara, CA 95050. 400 N Winchester Blvd.
Tel: 408-241-8161. Fax: 408-241-8231.
www.morgancenter.com   E-mail: themorgancenter@aol.com
Jennifer Sullivan, Dir.
    Focus: Spec Ed. **Conditions:** Primary—Au PDD. Sec—MR.
    Gen Acad. Pre-Voc. Ungraded.
    Therapy: Lang Occup Speech.
    Enr: 50. **Staff:** 71 (Full 61, Part 10).
    Rates 2003: Day $232/day.
    Est 1969. Private. Nonprofit.

The Morgan Center provides educational and rehabilitative services for autistic and developmentally disturbed individuals. The nongraded academic program includes remediation in reading, math and language arts. Therapy addresses fine- and gross-motor, prevocational, self-care and socialization skills. Length of stay varies by individual.

NAPA VALLEY
PRODUCTS, SERVICES AND INDUSTRIES

Day — Coed Ages 18 and up

Napa, CA 94559. 651 Trabajo Ln, PO Box 600.
Tel: 707-255-0177. Fax: 707-255-0802.
Jeanne C. Fauquet, Exec Dir.
  Focus: Trng. **Conditions:** Primary—MR. **IQ 19 and up.**
  Pre-Voc. Voc. Courses: Read Math Lang_Arts. Shelt_Workshop. On-Job Trng.
  Therapy: Lang Speech.
  Est 1972. Private. Nonprofit.

NATIONAL CENTER ON DEAFNESS

Res — Coed Ages 18 and up

Northridge, CA 91330. California State Univ-Northridge, 18111 Nordhoff St.
Tel: 818-677-2054. Fax: 818-677-7192.
http://ncod.csun.edu   E-mail: ncod@csun.edu
Merri C. Pearson, EdD, Dir.
  Focus: Spec Ed. Trng. **Conditions:** Primary—D.
  Gen Acad. Gr PG.
  Therapy: Hear Speech.
  Est 1962. State. **Spons:** California State University-Northridge.

Situated on a 350-acre campus, NCOD provides comprehensive mainstream college programs for students who are deaf or hard of hearing. The center offers services such as interpreting, note taking, tutoring, counseling, and hearing and speech therapies. Because of the students' diverse communicative backgrounds, signed English, American Sign Language and deaf-blind interpretation are available. In addition, the center is equipped with Telecommunication Devices for the Deaf (TDDs) throughout campus.

The university's proximity to Los Angeles provides for a wide range of occupational, recreational and cultural opportunities. Social activities include clubs, sports and homecoming events.

NEW HAVEN YOUTH
AND FAMILY SERVICES

Res — Males Ages 8-18

Vista, CA 92083. 216 W Los Angeles Dr, PO Box 1199.
Tel: 760-630-4035. Fax: 760-630-4030.
www.newhavenyfs.org   E-mail: info@newhavenyfs.org
Doreen Quinn, CEO. **Michelle Benjelloun,** Clin Dir.
   Focus: Spec Ed. **Conditions:** Primary—ADD Anx BD CD ED LD Mood
     OCD ODD PTSD SP Sz. Sec—OH Psy S TS. **IQ 70 and up.**
   Gen Acad. Pre-Voc. Gr 3-12. Courses: Read Math Lang_Arts. Man_Arts &
     Shop. On-Job Trng.
   Therapy: Art Hear Lang Music Phys Play Recreational Speech. **Psycho-
     therapy:** Fam Group Indiv Parent.
   Enr: 72. Res Males 72. **Staff:** 170 (Full 150, Part 20). Prof 13. Educ 10.
     Admin 20.
   Rates 2004: Res $5682/mo.
   Est 1967. Private. Inc.

Serving youth with a range of special needs, New Haven treats boys who have failed
to succeed in family or school settings due to mental illness or an abusive family environment. Staff work with residents on issues relating to hopelessness, violence, delinquency, depression and emotional dysfunction during a stay that averages one year.

Residential treatment, which includes 24-hour care, takes place at ten homes in the
Vista area. Boys follow an Individualized Educational Plan, developed in concert with
parents, school district representatives, teachers, residential staff, social workers and the
student himself, that is put into use at New Haven's school. Components of the educational program include instruction in the basic subjects, integrated therapy, after-school
enrichment, vocational assessment and education, computer instruction, substance abuse
prevention and a school-to-work program.

NEWPORT BEACH
DEVELOPMENTAL OPTOMETRY GROUP

Clinic: All Ages. T-S 9-5.

Newport Beach, CA 92660. 901 Dover Dr, Ste 100.
Tel: 949-642-0292. Fax: 949-640-0106.
www.optometrists.org/California   E-mail: 4vision@pcmagic.net
Amanda Dawe, BS, OD, Dir. BS, OD, BS, OD, **Joanne Valentine,** Adm.
   Focus: Treatment. **Conditions:** Primary—ADD ADHD B BD Bl CP DS Dx
     IP LD MD MR MS Nf SB. Sec—Anx Apr As Asp Au Db Dc Dg PDD PW
     TS.
   Therapy: Visual.
   Staff: 15.
   Rates 2003: Clinic $115-125/hr.
   Summer Prgm: Day. Educ. Ther. Day Rate $115.
   Est 1978. Private.

Remediation of visually related conditions contributing to learning disabilities is available at this facility. Comprehensive visual evaluations and subsequent visual perceptual and visual rehabilitative services are available to all patients, with special attention given to stroke-afflicted, developmentally delayed, communicatively impaired, motorically challenged and cognitively handicapped populations. Programs are conducted in a one-on-one setting, and monthly monitored home or out-of-office arrangements are also possible. Treatment usually lasts three to six months.

NEWPORT LANGUAGE AND SPEECH CENTERS
Clinic: All Ages. M-F 8-5.

Mission Viejo, CA 92691. 26137 La Paz Rd, Ste 104.
   Nearby locations: Cerritos; Fountain Valley; Yorba Linda.
Tel: 949-581-8239. Fax: 949-859-0928.
www.newportlanguage.com   E-mail: speak2us@newportlanguage.com
Sharlene Goodman, MA, CCC, Exec Dir. **Mary Ellen Hood,** MS, CCC, Clin Dir.
   Focus: Treatment. **Conditions:** Primary—ADD ADHD Ap Apr Asp Au Bl CP Dx Ep LD PDD S SB. Sec—D ED MR OH. **IQ 80 and up.**
   Therapy: Hear Lang Occup Speech.
   Staff: 25 (Full 15, Part 10).
   Rates 2004: Clinic $50-100/ses.
   Est 1970. Private. Inc.

NLSC provides speech, language and occupational therapy services. The pediatric clinic features individual and group treatment programs that address the needs of children and adolescents with impairments in such areas as articulation, stuttering, cognition, delayed language, learning disabilities, auditory processing, swallowing difficulties and sensory integration. Developmental assessment and stimulation services are available for infants at high risk. Newport provides diagnoses of communicative disorders and rehabilitative services for adults as well.

In addition to the Mission Viejo site, NLSC offers individual and group pediatric services in Yorba Linda (4811 Eureka Ave., Ste. A, 92686), Fountain Valley (18120 Brookhurst St., Ste. 54, 92708) and Cerritos (11385 183rd St., 90703).

NORTH COUNTY LEARNING
Clinic: Ages 4 and up. M-F 10-5; Eves M-F 5-8.

Escondido, CA 92025. 332 S Juniper St, Ste 201.
Tel: 760-489-6066.
   Focus: Treatment. **Conditions:** Primary—ADD ADHD Au Bl Dx LD MR. Sec—Ap ED Ep OCD S. **IQ 70 and up.**
   Gen Acad. Courses: Read Math Lang_Arts Study_Skills.
   Therapy: Lang.
   Staff: 3 (Full 1, Part 2).
   Schol avail.
   Est 1978. Private.

This facility provides year-round psycho-educational assessments and educational therapy for individuals with learning problems that are affecting their school or work performance. The clinic seeks to remediate reading, math, writing, attention span, motivational, organizational and study skill problems while also assisting underachievers and those with low self-esteem and a lack of confidence. Other aspects of the program include school placement assistance, specialized vocational counseling, and parent and teacher workshops.

OAKES CHILDREN'S CENTER

Day — Coed Ages 3-16

San Francisco, CA 94122. 1348 10th Ave.
Tel: 415-564-2310. Fax: 415-564-2313.
http://home.mindspring.com/~oakessf
   E-mail: oakessf@mindspring.com
Richard Geimer, Exec Dir.
   Conditions: Primary—Au ED PDD. Sec—MR.
   Gen Acad. Ungraded. Courses: Read Math Lang_Arts.
   Therapy: Dance Lang Movement Play Speech. **Psychotherapy:** Fam Group.
   Est 1963. Private. Nonprofit. **Spons:** Community Effort for Disturbed Children.

ODYSSEY LEARNING CENTER

Res and Day — Coed Ages 3-22

Orangevale, CA 95662. 7150 Santa Juanita Ave.
Tel: 916-988-0258. Fax: 916-988-0423.
www.odysseylearningcenter.com
   E-mail: info@odysseylearningcenter.com
Cheryl Daly, Exec Dir. Cindee Shapton, Prin.
   Focus: Spec Ed. **Conditions:** Primary—Au. Sec—ADD ADHD CP MS OCD.
   Pre-Voc. Voc. Gr K-12. Courses: Read Math Lang_Arts. Shelt_Workshop. On-Job Trng.
   Therapy: Lang Occup Speech. **Psychotherapy:** Fam.
   Enr: 28. Res Males 8. Res Females 6. Day Males 7. Day Females 7. **Staff:** 45 (Full 40, Part 5).
   Est 1979. Private. Nonprofit.

Odyssey specializes in language-based behavior modification for children with autism. In addition to the educational program, services include motor planning, self-help and socialization skills, parent training, vocational education, community access and medical care. The program operates year-round.

ONE-TO-ONE READING AND EDUCATIONAL CENTER
Clinic: Ages 5 and up. M-S 2-5; M-S 5-8:30.

Granada Hills, CA 91344. 10324 Woodley Ave.
Tel: 818-891-3090. Fax: 818-891-3612.
Paul A. Klinger, MA, EdD, Dir.
  Focus: Spec Ed. Conditions: Primary—ADD ADHD Dx LD. Sec—Ap As
    Asp ON S. IQ 80 and up.
  Gen Acad. Ungraded. Courses: Read Math Lang_Arts.
  Staff: 4 (Full 1, Part 3). Prof 4. Educ 4.
  Rates 2003: Clinic $60/hr.
  Est 1972. Private. Nonprofit.

The center provides year-round educational therapy for the remediation of learning problems, particularly in the areas of reading and mathematics. Complete psycho-educational diagnostic testing is available. After the initial screening evaluations take place, one-on-one sessions are conducted, with instruction being systematic, pattern oriented and, when appropriate, multisensory. Emphasis is placed on oral and recreational reading, and an incentive program is part of the therapy. Attention is given to the improvement of an individual's self-image.

Communication with relevant professionals and school personnel is integral to many students' programs. Additional services include educational counseling, as well as behavior and family therapy. The usual length of treatment is one to three years.

OPTOMETRIC CENTER OF FULLERTON
EYE CARE CLINIC
Clinic: All Ages. M-S; Eves W Th.

Fullerton, CA 92631. 2575 Yorba Linda Blvd.
Tel: 714-449-7400. Fax: 714-992-7811.
www.scco.edu/ecc/home/ecchome.html
Michael W. Rouse, OD, MSEd, Dir.
  Focus: Treatment. Conditions: Primary—B LD.
  Therapy: Percepual-Motor Visual.
  Est 1904. Private. Nonprofit. Spons: Southern California College of Optom-
    etry.

The center provides diagnostic, therapeutic and preventative services to visually impaired individuals. Comprehensive care addresses binocular vision and visual/perceptual-motor development problems. Electro-diagnosis for objective evaluation of visual function is available. This center also serves individuals who have physical, emotional or psychological disabilities in addition to visual disabilities.

OPTOMETRIC VISION DEVELOPMENT CENTER
Clinic: All Ages. M-F 8-6.

La Jolla, CA 92037. 8950 Villa La Jolla Dr, Ste B 128.

Tel: 858-453-0442.
www.optometrists.org/drvalenti   E-mail: cvalenti3@mac.com
Claude A. Valenti, BS, OD, Dir.
  Focus: Treatment. **Conditions:** Primary—ADD ADHD B Dx LD. Sec—Au
    BD BI CP MR.
  Therapy: Visual.
  Staff: 7.
  Est 1980. Private. Inc.

This center specializes in the remediation of visual problems and related learning disabilities.

ORALINGUA SCHOOL FOR THE HEARING IMPAIRED

Day — Coed Ages Birth-10

Whittier, CA 90602. 7056 S Washington Ave.
Tel: 562-945-8391. Fax: 562-945-0361.
www.oralingua.org   E-mail: info@oralingua.org
Jane Freutel, MEd, Admin.
  Focus: Spec Ed. **Conditions:** Primary—D. **IQ 90 and up.**
  Gen Acad. Ungraded. Courses: Read Math Lang_Arts Sci Soc_Stud.
  Therapy: Hear Lang Movement Occup Speech. **Psychotherapy:** Group
    Parent.
  Enr: 52. Day Males 30. Day Females 22. **Staff:** 24.
  Rates 2004: Day $22,000/yr.
  Est 1969. Private. Nonprofit.

Oralingua's aural-oral program is based on the belief that a deaf child can learn to function effectively in a hearing environment. Through the development of residual hearing, meaningful language, understandable speech and strong cognitive skills, deaf children are successfully mainstreamed into regular classrooms in their neighborhood schools. Classes are small (the student-teacher ratio is 3:1).

Full parental participation is encouraged. A parent-infant tutorial program for children from birth to age 3 is also conducted.

ORION ACADEMY

Day — Coed Ages 13-19

Moraga, CA 94556. 350 Rheem Blvd.
Tel: 925-377-0789. Fax: 925-377-2028.
www.orionacademy.org   E-mail: orionacademy@att.net
Kathryn Stewart, PhD, Dir.
  Focus: Spec Ed. **Conditions:** Primary—Asp. Sec—ADD Dc Dg OCD TS.
    IQ 100 and up.
  Col Prep. Gen Acad. Gr 9-12. Courses: Read Math Lang_Arts Lat Sci Hist
    Studio_Art Drama.
  Therapy: Occup Speech. **Psychotherapy:** Group Indiv.
  Enr: 34. Day Males 30. Day Females 4. **Staff:** 13 (Full 7, Part 6). Educ 8.

Admin 3.
Rates 2003: Day $23,000/yr. Schol 1 ($23,000). State Aid.
Summer Prgm: Day. Educ. 4 wks.
Est 2000. Private. Nonprofit.

Orion offers adolescents with Asperger's syndrome and nonverbal learning disorders an academically challenging secondary curriculum that integrates social skill development into daily activities. Students develop academic and social skills in preparation for college or employment upon graduation.

PACIFIC LODGE BOYS' HOME

Res — Males Ages 13-17

Woodland Hills, CA 91364. 4900 Serrania Ave.
Tel: 818-347-1577. Fax: 818-883-5452.
www.plys.org   E-mail: info@plys.org
Frank Linebaugh, Pres.
   Focus: Trng. Treatment. **Conditions:** Primary—BD CD. Sec—ADD ADHD
      As ED LD. **IQ 75 and up.**
   Psychotherapy: Fam Group Indiv Parent.
   Enr: 68. Res Males 68. **Staff:** 85.
   Est 1923. Private. Nonprofit.

Within a homelike environment, court-referred boys who need residential care and treatment learn basic living skills, complete regular chores and participate in an educational program. They may also earn money and gain vocational training through work experience programs, play individual and team sports, and join in social activities and camping experiences.

Boys reside at the year-round facility for nine to twelve months. Upon completing their stay, boys move back in with their family or go to a foster home or an independent living situation.

PARK CENTURY SCHOOL

Day — Coed Ages 6-14

Los Angeles, CA 90025. 2040 Stoner Ave.
Tel: 310-478-5065. Fax: 310-473-9260.
www.parkcenturyschool.org   E-mail: parkcentur@aol.com
Genevieve Shain, MA, Co-Dir. **Gail Spindler,** MA, Co-Dir.
   Focus: Spec Ed. **Conditions:** Primary—ADHD Dx LD.
   Gen Acad. Gr 2-8. Courses: Read Math Lang_Arts Sci Computers Soc_
      Stud Studio_Art Music Drama.
   Therapy: Lang Speech.
   Enr: 57. **Staff:** 30 (Full 21, Part 9).
   Est 1968. Private. Nonprofit.

This program integrates academic learning, social skills, family relationships and physical education. Individual tutoring is provided in reading and math. Small-group instruction in social studies and science parallels that found in local public and private schools. Individualized movement education and perceptual-motor therapy are available as needed, and students may also receive speech and language therapy for an additional hourly fee. A transitional program utilizes materials from local schools.

See Also Page 1042

PARKER HEARING INSTITUTE

Clinic: All Ages. M-F 8:30-5:30.

Torrance, CA 90503. 4201 Torrance Blvd, Ste 140.
   Nearby locations: Manhattan Beach; Marin del Ray; San Pedro.
Tel: 310-540-4327. Fax: 310-316-2685.
www.parkerhearing.com   E-mail: info@parkerhearing.com
William Lee Parker, PhD, Pres.
   Focus: Treatment. **Conditions:** Primary—D. Sec—ADD ADHD Ap As Au B BD BI CP Dx ED LD S. **IQ 72 and up.**
   Therapy: Hear.
   Staff: 6.
   Private.

This center provides hearing tests, evaluations and therapies. Parker Hearing also addresses the fitting, orientation, repair and maintenance of hearing instruments. In addition, the institute offers workshops for the hearing professional. Fees vary according to services provided.

PARKHILL SCHOOL

Day — Coed Ages 5½-18

West Hills, CA 91307. 7401 Shoup Ave.
Tel: 818-883-3500. Fax: 818-883-1519.
E-mail: parkhillone@hotmail.com
Gil Freitag, PhD, Exec Dir. **Bernard Sosner,** MD, Med Dir.
   Focus: Spec Ed. Trng. Treatment. **Conditions:** Primary—Dx ED LD. Sec—ADD ADHD Anx Ap As Asp Au BD Ep Mood MR OCD ON PTSD SP Sz TS. **IQ 80-115.**
   Gen Acad. Pre-Voc. Voc. Gr K-12. Courses: Read Math Lang_Arts. On-Job Trng.
   Therapy: Speech. **Psychotherapy:** Group Indiv Parent.
   Enr: 90. Day Males 80. Day Females 10. **Staff:** 45 (Full 33, Part 12).
   Rates 2003: Day $25,000/sch yr. State Aid.
   Summer Prgm: Day. Educ. Ther. Day Rate $3000. 4 wks.
   Est 1965. Private. Nonprofit. **Spons:** Foundation for Perceptual and Psycholinguistic Development.

Parkhill administers complete diagnostic evaluations to determine the nature of the student's academic or learning problem. Only those of at least potentially average intellectual ability are accepted. One-on-one educational therapy is provided on an adjunctive basis for children who are able to maintain themselves in regular school classes.

This process involves the following: intensive specific training in those areas of learning difficulty; an individual supportive therapeutic relationship; and an integration of remedial training into the academic program.

PENINSULA ASSOCIATES

Clinic: All Ages. M-F 8-5.

Menlo Park, CA 94025. 401 Burgess Dr.
   Nearby locations: San Mateo.
Tel: 650-324-0648. Fax: 650-324-9880.
www.paspeech.com   E-mail: postmaster@paspeech.com
Maureen M. O'Connor, MS, Dir.
   Focus: Treatment. **Conditions:** Primary—S. Sec—ADD ADHD Ap Apr Asp Au BI CP D Dx ED Ep LD MR ON PDD. **IQ 50-110.**
   Therapy: Lang Speech.
   Staff: 17 (Full 13, Part 4).
   Rates 2003: Clinic $100/hr.
   Summer Prgm: Day. Educ. Rec. Ther. 2 wks.
   Est 1978. Private.

PA offers individual and group speech and language therapy. Specialists also work with school readiness, reading and writing, and academic skills. Goals and treatment are coordinated with school personnel. PA operates long-term therapy substitute programs for public and private schools.

The facility maintains a second office at 760 Polhemus Rd., San Mateo 94402.

PENINSULA CENTER FOR THE BLIND AND VISUALLY IMPAIRED

Day — Coed Ages Birth-22

Palo Alto, CA 94306. 2470 El Camino Real, Ste 107.
Tel: 650-858-0202. Fax: 650-858-0857.
www.pcbvi.org   E-mail: center@pcbvi.org
Pam Brandin, MPH, MS, Exec Dir.
   Focus: Trng. Treatment. **Conditions:** Primary—B. Sec—Ap As BI CP D Dx ED Ep LD MR MS ON S SB.
   Therapy: Speech. **Psychotherapy:** Fam Group Indiv.
   Enr: 35.
   Rates 2004: No Fee.
   Est 1936. Private. Nonprofit.

Blind and visually impaired individuals are taught orientation and mobility and daily living skills at this facility. Most instruction is conducted within students' homes or local neighborhoods, and parental support and education are provided. A low-vision clinic also operates at the center. Enrollment is restricted to residents of San Mateo and Santa Clara counties.

PINE HILL SCHOOL

Day — Coed Ages 6-21

San Jose, CA 95124. 3002 Leigh Ave.
Tel: 408-979-8210. Fax: 408-979-8223.
www.pinehillschool.com   E-mail: blancar@secondstart.org
L. E. Boydston, Exec Dir. **David Gerster,** Prin. **Terry Reynolds,** Adm.
   Focus: Spec Ed. **Conditions:** Primary—ADD ADHD Au BD Dx LD S. **IQ 70 and up.**
   Gen Acad. Pre-Voc. Gr 1-12. Courses: Read Math Lang_Arts. On-Job Trng.
   Therapy: Lang Speech. **Psychotherapy:** Group Indiv.
   Enr: 60. Day Males 50. Day Females 10. **Staff:** 29. (Full 29).
   Rates 2003: Day $9000-13,500/sch yr. Schol avail.
   Summer Prgm: Day. Educ. Rec. 6½ wks.
   Est 1976. Private. Nonprofit.

Pine Hill conducts individualized therapeutic programming for students with learning handicapped, emotionally disturbances or both. Prescriptive academics, behavioral planning, speech and language therapy, counseling and vocational training are integral parts of the experiential, language-based program. Pupils incur additional fees for speech and language therapy.

PORTERVILLE DEVELOPMENTAL CENTER

Res — Coed All Ages

Porterville, CA 93258. 26501 Ave 140, PO Box 2000.
Tel: 559-782-2286. TTY: 559-781-7822. Fax: 559-784-5630.
David Freehauf, Exec Dir. **R. Srinivasan,** MD, Med Dir. **Michael Januse II,** Adm.
   Focus: Treatment. **Conditions:** Primary—MR. Sec—Ap B BD Bl CP D Dx ED Ep LD ON S SB.
   Pre-Voc. Voc. Ungraded. Man_Arts & Shop. Shelt_Workshop. On-Job Trng.
   Therapy: Chemo Hear Lang Occup Phys Speech. **Psychotherapy:** Fam Group Indiv.
   Enr: 837. Res Males 593. Res Females 244. **Staff:** 1970. (Full 1970).
   Est 1953. State. Nonprofit.

Serving residents of California, the center provides care and treatment for physically and mentally handicapped individuals of all ages. Continuous skilled nursing is available to children and adults. Generally nonambulatory and severely to profoundly physically and mentally disabled, these individuals participate in therapeutic exercises designed to promote motor abilities. Behavior modification and off-unit and off-grounds activities provide sensory stimulation and serve as motivation for exercising developmental skills.

Residents with sensory handicaps undergo evaluation and receive training. Emphasis is placed on the development of total communication and mobility, as well as on daily living skills and vocational and body awareness training. Audiological screening, testing, training and diagnostic teaching are coordinated through the Sensory Development Program.

The Social Development Program promotes personality development and the refinement of self-care skills. Staff employ behavior modification techniques emphasizing positive reinforcement to teach self-help skills and modify maladaptive behavior. Language development training and adult education are also available.

Those with moderate to profound levels of retardation may participate in the Behavior Adjustment Program, which aims to reduce the frequency of asocial behavior. The program implements behavior modification techniques in small-group settings designed to enhance self-help, interpersonal relationships, and basic pre-educational and prevocational skills. Certain residents may enroll in adult education classes.

The center also provides comprehensive 24-hour treatment, care and training programs for children with mental retardation. Therapy and activity programs seek to develop the client's self-care skills, social interaction abilities, psychological and physical development, and leisure and vocational skills.

THE POSEIDON SCHOOL

Day — Coed Ages 12-18

West Los Angeles, CA 90064. 11811 W Pico Blvd.
Tel: 310-477-1268. Fax: 310-478-5166.
www.poseidonschool.com   E-mail: mail@poseidonschool.com
Joanne D. Saliba, Exec Dir. **Penny Spector,** Adm.
   Focus: Spec Ed. **Conditions:** Primary—ADHD LD. Sec—BD Dx ED.
   Gen Acad. Pre-Voc. Gr 7-12. Courses: Read Math Lang_Arts Studio_Art
      Drama. On-Job Trng.
   Therapy: Speech. **Psychotherapy:** Fam Group Indiv.
   Enr: 43. Day Males 32. Day Females 11. **Staff:** 20.
   Rates 2004: Day $12,000/sch yr. Schol avail. State Aid.
   Summer Prgm: Day. Educ. Ther. 6 wks.
   Est 1971. Private. Nonprofit.

Poseidon formulates an Individualized Education Plan to assist students in remediating their learning handicaps. In addition to the individualized counseling required by the plan, students participate in weekly group counseling sessions, as well as crisis and problem-solving counseling when appropriate. Each student's program is individually planned to meet his or her particular needs in academic, social, emotional and vocational skills.

THE PRENTICE SCHOOL

Day — Coed Ages 6-14

Santa Ana, CA 92705. 18341 Lassen Dr.
Tel: 714-538-4511. Fax: 714-538-0273.
www.prentice.org   E-mail: pdadmin@prentice.org
Carol H. Clark, MA, Int Exec Dir. **Grace Diaz,** Adm.
   Focus: Spec Ed. **Conditions:** Primary—Dg Dx LD. Sec—ADD ADHD Ar As
      Asp CP Db Dc. **IQ 90 and up.**
   Gen Acad. Gr 1-8. Courses: Read Math Lang_Arts Sci Computers Soc_

Stud Studio_Art Music Drama.
Therapy: Art Lang Music Phys Play Recreational Speech.
Enr: 205. Day Males 137. Day Females 68. **Staff:** 52 (Full 37, Part 15).
Rates 2004: Day $15,000/sch yr. Schol avail.
Summer Prgm: Day. Educ. Ther. Day Rate $650. 4 wks.
Est 1986. Private. Nonprofit.

Prentice offers individualized elementary programming for students with dyslexia and language-based learning disabilities. Speech and language therapy, tutoring and workshops are among the available specialized support services.

PROVIDENCE SPEECH AND HEARING CENTER
Day — Coed Ages 2-6
Clinic: Ages 2-6. M-F 7-6.

Orange, CA 92868. 1301 Providence Ave.
Tel: 714-639-4990. Fax: 714-744-3841.
www.pshc.org   E-mail: pshc@pshc.org
Mary Jo Hooper, MA, CCC-SLP, CEO.
   Focus: Rehab. **Conditions:** Primary—Ap Asp Au D PDD S. Sec—ADD ADHD BI CD CP ED LD MD MR MS OH.
   Gen Acad. Gr PS-K. Courses: Read Lang_Arts.
   Therapy: Hear Lang Occup Phys Speech. **Psychotherapy:** Fam Group Indiv Parent.
   Staff: 41.
   Rates 2004: $110 (Therapy)/hr. Schol avail. State Aid.
   Est 1966. Private. Nonprofit.

PSHC provides comprehensive diagnostic speech and hearing testing. Early identification and intervention function as primary factors for rehabilitation. Peer-to-peer support groups and training programs for patients and their families are provided as part of therapy. Two school programs operate within the facility: a mainstreaming preschool and a clinical preschool/kindergarten for children with communicative or learning disabilities. The center also provides complete, on-site audiological services.

RANCHO LOS AMIGOS
NATIONAL REHABILITATION CENTER
COMMUNICATION DISORDERS DEPARTMENT
Clinic: Ages Birth-21. M-F 7-5.

Downey, CA 90242. 7601 E Imperial Hwy.
Tel: 562-401-7687. Fax: 562-401-6690.
Wendy Burton, MA, Dir. **Robert Waters,** MD, Med Dir.
   Focus: Rehab. **Conditions:** Primary—Ap BI D. Sec—IP.
   Therapy: Hear Lang Occup Phys Recreational Speech. **Psychotherapy:** Fam Group Indiv Parent.
   Staff: 35.

Est 1948. County. Nonprofit.

This facility services a variety of neurologically and developmentally impaired children, adolescents and young adults with communicational disorders. Programs include parent-infant stimulation, cleft palate evaluation therapy, nonoral augmentative communication systems, multi-handicapped comprehensive team evaluations and a pediatric head-injury program.

RANCHO LOS AMIGOS SCHOOL
Day — Coed Ages 3-22

Downey, CA 90242. 7601 E Imperial Hwy.
Tel: 562-904-3579. Fax: 562-904-3222.
http://rla.dusd.net
Gary Ratzke, Prin.
  Focus: Spec Ed. Treatment. **Conditions:** Primary—Ap As Au B Bl CP D Dx ED Ep LD MR ON S SB.
  Gen Acad. Ungraded. Courses: Read Math Lang_Arts Life_Skills.
  Therapy: Lang Occup Speech. **Psychotherapy:** Indiv.
  Enr: 28. **Staff:** 16. (Full 16).
  Rates 2004: No Fee.
  State.

Rancho Los Amigos provides services for multi-handicapped children, in addition to an academic program.

Preschool children with patterns of developmental delay, neuromuscular or communicative problems receive therapies and treatment through the pediatric department. Stimulation of speech, language development and psychosocial well-being are emphasized within the school's treatment for individuals with congenital or traumatic oro-facial deformities.

Inpatients and orthopedically handicapped students referred from the surrounding area receive services at the school. Staff members provide assessments in the areas of educational achievement and self-mobility. The program comprises a curriculum of individual and group therapy, medical care, remedial physical education, music and bedside instruction.

RASKOB DAY SCHOOL
AND LEARNING INSTITUTE
Day — Coed Ages 9-14
Clinic: All Ages. M-F 8-5; Eves M-F 5-8.

Oakland, CA 94619. 3520 Mountain Blvd.
Tel: 510-436-1275. Fax: 510-436-1106.
www.raskobinstitute.com　E-mail: raskobinstitute@hnu.edu
Rachel Wylde, Exec Dir.
  Focus: Spec Ed. **Conditions:** Primary—Dx LD. Sec—ADD ADHD ED. **IQ 80 and up.**
  Gen Acad. Gr 4-8. Courses: Read Math Lang_Arts Studio_Art.

Therapy: Speech. **Psychotherapy:** Group Indiv.
Enr: 52. Day Males 32. Day Females 20. **Staff:** 37 (Full 23, Part 14). Prof 17. Educ 13. Admin 3.
Rates 2003: Day $13,900/sch yr. Schol avail.
Summer Prgm: Day. Educ. Day Rate $1730. 6 wks.
Est 1973. Private. Nonprofit.

The academic program at Raskob utilizes a multisensory approach to educating children with learning differences. The curriculum places emphasis on reading/language arts, mathematics and physical education. The program adheres to a strict enrollment limit, and the usual length of stay is two to four years.

The Learning Institute provides remedial tutorials for both children and adults.

REACH FOR LEARNING

Clinic: All Ages. M-S 8-5; Eves M-S 5-7.

Albany, CA 94706. 1221 Marin Ave.
Tel: 510-524-6455. Fax: 510-524-5154.
E-mail: reach1971@yahoo.com
Corinne Gustafson, MEd, Dir.
    Focus: Treatment. **Conditions:** Primary—Dc Dg Dx LD. Sec—ADD ADHD.
    Gen Acad. Ungraded. Courses: Read Math Lang_Arts.
    Staff: 14 (Full 2, Part 12).
    Est 1971. Private. Nonprofit.

The clinic provides individual and small-group educational remediation and diagnostic assessment for individuals with learning disabilities. Educational programs are modified to conform to individual learning styles, and REACH works with parents, school personnel and community services to increase the program's effectiveness.

READING CENTER OF BRUNO

Clinic: Ages 4½ and up. M-S 10-7.

Huntington Beach, CA 92649. 4952 Warner Ave, Ste 243.
Tel: 714-377-7910. Fax: 714-842-9767.
www.readingcenter.info   E-mail: readingct@aol.com
Walter C. Waid, BA, Dir.
    Focus: Trng. **Conditions:** Primary—ADD ADHD Dx LD.
    Est 1961. Private.

This center works with students who have dyslexia and related reading problems. Services include evaluation, testing and remediation.

REGIONAL CENTER OF ORANGE COUNTY

Clinic: All Ages. M-F 8-5.

Santa Ana, CA 92702. 801 Civic Center Dr W, Ste 100, PO Box 22010.
Tel: 714-796-5100. TTY: 714-667-6021. Fax: 714-973-0336.
www.rcocdd.com
William J. Bowman, Exec Dir. **Arleen Downing,** MD, Med Dir.
  Focus: Treatment. **Conditions:** Primary—Au CP Ep MR.
  Therapy: Occup Phys Speech.
  Staff: 350.
  Rates 2003: No Fee.
  Est 1969. Private. Nonprofit.

RCOC coordinates diagnosis and evaluation of developmental disabilities, as well as prevention resources and information and referral, for Orange County residents. Services are contracted with 21 area nonprofit agencies, each of which covers a different geographic region. Through these centers, RCOC coordinates and monitors services for residents who have a disability due to mental retardation, cerebral palsy, epilepsy, autism or a condition similar to mental retardation; whose disability began before age 18; whose disability is likely to continue indefinitely; and whose disability is substantially handicapping.

Prior to receiving services, each client undergoes an individual assessment that includes a social skills evaluation; a review of the individual's medical and psychological history; other medical and psychological evaluations, as needed; and specialized assessments by other professionals, as necessary to determine eligibility. Service coordinators then work with family members to formulate an appropriate program plan. Early intervention is an important service at RCOC.

REISS-DAVIS CHILD STUDY CENTER

Clinic: Ages 3-21. M-F 8:30-5, S 9-2; Eves M-F 5-7.

Los Angeles, CA 90034. 3200 Motor Ave.
Tel: 310-204-1666. Fax: 310-838-2791.
www.vistadelmar.org
James A. Incorvaia, MD, Dir.
  Focus: Treatment. **Conditions:** Primary—ADD ADHD Anx Asp BD ED
    Mood OCD PTSD SP. Sec—Ap As Au BI CD TS.
  Psychotherapy: Fam Group Indiv Parent.
  Staff: 24 (Full 6, Part 18). Prof 21. Admin 3.
  Rates 2003: Sliding-Scale Rate $25-125.
  Est 1950. Private. Nonprofit. **Spons:** Vista Del Mar Child and Family Services.

Reiss-Davis assists children, adolescents and young adults who are experiencing mild to severe emotional, behavioral or learning problems. The center employs a team approach, with psychiatrists, psychologists, clinical social workers, psychoanalysts and educators combining to help children and their families.

The center offers diagnostic and psychotherapeutic services to children and adolescents on a sliding fee scale. Psychotherapeutic services include psychodynamically oriented long-term and short-term individual and family therapy. Parent counseling is an integral part of the therapeutic intervention program.

Through the PEDS program, the center provides comprehensive psycho-educational diagnostic services for children who may have a learning disability. Additionally, the program includes a comprehensive assessment for children and adolescents who are suspected of having an attentional disorder. The evaluation leads to the establishment of an accurate diagnosis with specific treatment recommendations, including cognitive, behavioral, pharmacological and alternative methods of interventions.

RINCON LEARNING CENTER

Clinic: Ages 5 and up. M-F 9:30-5; Eves M-F 5-7:30.

El Cajon, CA 92020. 594 N Westwind Dr.
Tel: 619-442-2722. Fax: 619-442-1011.
www.rinconlearningcenter.net   E-mail: lodots@earthlink.net
Lois R. Dotson, BA, MBA, Dir.
Focus: Spec Ed. **Conditions:** Primary—ADD ADHD Dg Dx LD. Sec—As Asp BD Bl C CD CP Db ED Ep IP MD MR MS ON SB TS. **IQ 50 and up.**
Gen Acad. Ungraded. Courses: Read Math Lang_Arts SAT_Prep.
Staff: 7 (Full 1, Part 6). Educ 7.
Rates 2003: Clinic $32/ses. Schol 1 ($650).
Est 1966. Private.

Rincon offers year-round individual tutoring to moderately retarded and learning-disabled adults and children. Services include diagnostic testing, Slingerland testing for dyslexia, and post-testing to measure the student's progress. The center works cooperatively with the child's regular school and serves as a liaison between parents and schools.

RIVER OAK CENTER FOR CHILDREN

Res and Day — Coed Ages 5-14
Clinic: Ages 2-21. M-F 8-5; Eves M-F 5-8.

Sacramento, CA 95841. 4330 Auburn Blvd, Ste 2000.
Tel: 916-609-5100. Fax: 916-609-5160.
www.riveroak.org   E-mail: info@riveroak.org
Mary Hargrave, PhD, Pres. **Harry Wang,** MD, Med Dir.
Focus: Spec Ed. Rehab. Treatment. **Conditions:** Primary—ADD ADHD Anx Asp BD ED LD Mood OCD PDD Psy PTSD SP Sz TS. Sec—AN As Au Bl Bu CD CP Db Dc Dg Dx Ep MR ON PW SB. **IQ 50 and up.**
Gen Acad. Gr PS-8. Courses: Read Math Lang_Arts.
Therapy: Art Lang Milieu Occup Percepual-Motor Phys Play Recreational Speech. **Psychotherapy:** Fam Group Indiv Parent.
Rates 2003: Res $6371/mo. Day $116-151/day. Clinic $70-106/hr. State Aid.
Est 1966. Private. Nonprofit.

This multi-service behavioral healthcare agency provides a continuum of care for special-needs children and their families. River Oak seeks to treat severe emotional or behavioral problems that have resulted from abuse or mental health issues, to prevent out-of-home placements whenever possible, and to return children to their homes or to the safest and most normalized possible living environment.

The agency conducts three main programs. Residential treatment, which is based at 5445 Laurel Hills Dr., serves boys and girls ages 6-12. Mace School, River Oak's educational component, enrolls students ages 5-14 at 1150 Eastern Ave., 95864. Thirdly, an outpatient division for children, adolescents and young adults operates at 4325 Auburn Blvd., Ste. 100. Typical duration of treatment ranges from six months in the residential program to two years at Mace School. Participants in the residential and day programs must be ambulatory.

ROSE RESNIK LIGHTHOUSE FOR
THE BLIND AND VISUALLY IMPAIRED

Day — Coed All Ages

San Francisco, CA 94102. 214 Van Ness Ave.
Tel: 415-431-1481. TTY: 415-431-4572. Fax: 415-863-7568.
www.lighthouse-sf.org   E-mail: info@lighthouse-sf.org
Anita Shafer Aaron, Exec Dir.
   Focus: Trng. Treatment. **Conditions:** Primary—B.
   Est 1902. Private. Nonprofit.

The LightHouse accepts individuals with visual deficiencies and provides programs through four area divisions. The Education-Recreation Center offers classes in braille, typing, dramatics and communicational skills, frequently in conjunction with San Francisco Community College. Assistance in letter writing, reading and counseling are also available. In addition to educational resources, the Lighthouse has the largest stock of blind aids and appliances in northern California.

Training and employment for blind, deaf-blind and visually impaired adults are available within the Employment Center. Enchanted Hills Camp for Blind Children and Adults is a 311-acre coeducational residential camp located 50 miles from San Francisco. This program stresses independence within a supervised program of swimming, hiking, crafts, horseback riding, boating and bowling.

Another division, Deaf-Blind Services, features interpreting and referral aid for individuals with a combination of deafness and blindness in any degree. The LightHouse also conducts an outreach program throughout the Bay Area and northern California. Fees are determined along a sliding scale based on the family's ability to pay.

RUSSELL BEDE SCHOOL

Day — Coed Ages 7-12

San Mateo, CA 94401. 446 Turner Ter.
Tel: 650-579-4400. Fax: 650-579-4402.
www.russellbedeschool.com   E-mail: russellbedeschool@sbcglobal.net
John Piper, PhD, Prin.
   Focus: Spec Ed. **Conditions:** Primary—LD. Sec—AN Anx Ap Apr As Asp B
   Bl Bu C CP Db Ep MS ON PDD S SP TB. **IQ 75-130.**

Gen Acad. Gr 2-5. Courses: Read Math Lang_Arts.
Enr: 15. Day Males 8. Day Females 7. **Staff:** 6 (Full 3, Part 3).
Rates 2003: Day $15,000-18,000/sch yr.
Summer Prgm: Day. Educ. Day Rate $1000. 4 wks.
Est 1983. Private. Nonprofit. **Spons:** Myers Learning Center.

Typical students at Russell Bede have average to above-average intelligence, but must cope with communication difficulties, specific learning disabilities or an alternative learning style. The school uses an instructional model that focuses on individualized instruction and material for each student, small class sizes, development of self-esteem, development of positive character traits, partnership with parents and daily physical education.

SACRAMENTO CHILDREN'S HOME

Res — Coed Ages 6-18; Day — Coed 5-18

Sacramento, CA 95820. 2750 Sutterville Rd.
Tel: 916-452-3981. Fax: 916-454-5031.
www.kidopolis.net   E-mail: pr@kidopolis.net
Roy Alexander, LCSW, CEO. **Richard Hill,** MSW, LCSW, MFT, Prin.
  Focus: Spec Ed. **Conditions:** Primary—ADD ADHD Anx As Asp Au BD
    Dc Dg Dx ED LD Mood OCD Psy PTSD PW SP Sz TS. Sec—MR. **IQ 60
    and up.**
  Gen Acad. Pre-Voc. Gr K-12. Courses: Read Math Lang_Arts Sci. Man_
    Arts & Shop. On-Job Trng.
  Therapy: Art Dance Lang Movement Music Play Recreational Speech. **Psy-
    chotherapy:** Fam Group Indiv.
  Enr: 43. Res Males 11. Res Females 5. Day Males 25. Day Females 2.
    Staff: 21 (Full 3, Part 18). Prof 11. Educ 6.
  Rates 2003: Day $132/day. Schol ($2500). State Aid.
  Summer Prgm: Res & Day. Educ. Rec. Ther. Day Rate $132. 6 wks.
  Est 1867. Private. Nonprofit. **Spons:** Sacramento Children's Home.

Children who have been victims of abuse or neglect receive various residential and educational services through SCH. Capable of accommodating 80 children, the residential program provides therapy, guidance, support and care for survivors of traumatic childhoods. Most residents have lived in one or more foster homes prior to admittance. They also participate in day services and take part in individual and group therapy.

The Pat Anderson Education Center, SCH's educational program, combines academic instruction and therapy for emotionally troubled and mentally ill boys and girls, as well as those with major learning disabilities, in kindergarten through high school. (Students incur additional fees for speech and language therapy.) Emphasis at the school is on returning the child to a neighborhood school with the skills necessary for success.

ST. JOHN'S CHILD AND FAMILY DEVELOPMENT CENTER

Day — Coed Ages Birth-50
Clinic: All Ages. M-F 8-5.

Santa Monica, CA 90404. 1339 20th St.
Tel: 310-829-8588. Fax: 310-829-8455.
www.stjohns.org/cfdcweb/cfdc   E-mail: mayra.mcdermott@stjohns.org
Rebecca Refuerzo, LCSW, Dir. **Mayra Mendez McDermott,** PhD, Clin Coord.
   Tom Ciesla, MD, Med Dir.
   Focus: Treatment. **Conditions:** Primary—ADD ADHD AN Anx Ap Apr Asp
      Au BD Bu CD D DS Dx ED LD Mood OCD PDD Psy PTSD S SP Sz TS.
      Sec—As B BI C CP Db Dc Dg Ep IP MD MR MS Nf ON PW SB TB.
   Therapy: Art Hear Lang Movement Occup Phys Play Recreational Speech.
      Psychotherapy: Fam Group Indiv Parent.
   Enr: 65. **Staff:** 37.
   Est 1963. Private. Nonprofit. Roman Catholic. **Spons:** St. John's Health
      Center.

CFDC provides a range of services for a population with diverse special needs. Mental health services, however, are the center's primary focus. The following mental health offerings are available on an outpatient basis: short-term family therapy, crisis intervention for children and their families, an attention deficit disorders clinic, psychological testing and psycho-educational evaluations, parent education and community outreach.

CFDC also operates a special mental health program for deaf and hard-of-hearing individuals, as well as a therapeutic preschool that provides intensive early intervention services for young children with severe behavioral or emotional problems or both. This program also features community outreach, research and consultative services.

In addition to its mental health services, the center also offers other specialized services. For persons with developmental disabilities, St. John's provides a therapeutic nursery and infant enrichment, individual and parent-child groups, and long-term daily living support groups. Children and adolescents with learning disabilities may receive educational therapy and tutoring. In response to community needs, outreach services such as consultation, education and prevention are also available. The center places significant emphasis on research and ongoing evaluation of all program activities.

ST. JUDE HOSPITAL AND REHABILITATION CENTER

Clinic: All Ages. M-F 8-4:30.

Fullerton, CA 92835. 101 E Valencia Mesa Dr, PO Box 4138.
Tel: 714-871-3280.
www.stjudemedicalcenter.org/frontpage/default.htm
   Conditions: Primary—Ap BI ON S.
   Therapy: Hear Lang Occup Phys Speech. **Psychotherapy:** Fam Indiv.
   Est 1957. Private.

SALEM CHRISTIAN HOME
FOR THE HANDICAPPED

Res — Coed Ages 18-62

Ontario, CA 91761. 1056 E Philadelphia St.
Tel: 909-947-3761.
Dan Copeland, Exec Dir.
  Focus: Trng. Treatment. **Conditions:** Primary—MR.
  Voc.
  Est 1961. Private. Nonprofit.

THE SAM & ROSE STEIN EDUCATION CENTER

Day — Coed Ages 3-22

San Diego, CA 92120. 6145 Decena Dr.
Tel: 619-281-5511. Fax: 619-281-0453.
www.vistahill.com/newsite/programs/stein/stein.htm
Elizabeth McInnis, PhD, Dir. **Mark Chenven,** MD, Med Dir.
  Focus: Spec Ed. **Conditions:** Primary—ADHD Au BD CD ED MR PDD.
    Sec—Ap B Bl CP D Db DS Ep Mood OCD ON Sz TS. **IQ 10-100.**
  Pre-Voc. Voc. Ungraded. On-Job Trng.
  Therapy: Occup Speech.
  Enr: 200. Day Males 155. Day Females 45. **Staff:** 198 (Full 73, Part 125).
    Prof 33. Educ 23. Admin 10.
  Rates 2004: No Fee.
  Est 1957. Private. Nonprofit. **Spons:** Vista Hill Foundation.

The center provides programs for children and adults with developmental disabilities: autism, epilepsy, cerebral palsy, mental retardation and various neurological conditions. Services are tailored to the special needs of each client, with emphasis placed on individual instructional relationships. On-site psychiatric consultation and medication support services also take place on campus.

The student's home school district typically covers tuition fees.

SAN DIEGO CENTER FOR CHILDREN

Res — Coed Ages 6-18; Day — Coed 5-13

San Diego, CA 92111. 3002 Armstrong St.
Tel: 858-277-9550. Fax: 858-279-2763.
www.centerforchildren.org
Edwin Kofler, CEO. **Eve Dreyfus,** MD, Med Dir.
  Conditions: Primary—BD ED LD.
  Gen Acad. Gr K-7.
  Staff: Prof 74.
  Est 1887. Private. Nonprofit.

SAN DIEGO REGIONAL CENTER
FOR THE DEVELOPMENTALLY DISABLED

Clinic: All Ages. M-F 8-4:30.

San Diego, CA 92123. 4355 Ruffin Rd, Ste 205.
Tel: 858-576-2996. TTY: 858-292-5821. Fax: 858-576-2873.
www.sdrc.org
Raymond M. Peterson, MD, Exec Dir. **Howard L. Wolfinger,** MD, Med Dir.
   Focus: Treatment. **Conditions:** Primary—Au CP Ep MR.
   Est 1969. State. Nonprofit.

SDRC provides central points for developmentally disabled individuals and their families to obtain or be referred to needed services. Diagnosis and coordination of resources, which include education, health, welfare, rehabilitation and recreation, are provided for California residents. Individual programming may include educational and vocational planning, speech therapy, day or residential care, behavior intervention, sensorimotor training, medical and dental care, genetic counseling and specialized medical treatment.

SAN FRANCISCO HEARING AND SPEECH CENTER

Day — Coed Ages 1½-8
Clinic: Ages 1½-18. M-F 8:30-5.

San Francisco, CA 94115. 1234 Divisadero St.
Tel: 415-921-7658. TTY: 415-921-8990. Fax: 415-921-2243.
Rayford Reddell, PhD, Exec Dir.
   Focus: Spec Ed. **Conditions:** Primary—Ap Apr D.
   Gen Acad. Ungraded. Courses: Read Math Lang_Arts.
   Therapy: Hear Lang Speech.
   Enr: 20. Day Males 10. Day Females 10. **Staff:** 45. Educ 7. Admin 4.
   Rates 2003: Day $21,600/sch yr. Clinic $120/hr. State Aid.
   Private. Nonprofit.

The center offers full-service speech therapy and audiology services, as well as newborn screening follow-up.

SAN JOSE STATE UNIVERSITY
CENTER FOR COMMUNICATION DISORDERS

Clinic: All Ages. M-Th 8-5; Eves M-Th 5-7.

San Jose, CA 95192. 1 Washington Sq.
Tel: 408-924-3688. Fax: 408-924-3713.
Jean M. Novak, PhD, Supv. **Patti Solomon,** MS, Coord.
   Focus: Rehab. **Conditions:** Primary—Apr Asp Au BI D LD PDD S.
   Therapy: Hear Lang Speech.
   Staff: 6.
   State.

Education of speech and hearing clinicians is the primary function of the center, which provides diagnosis and treatment for language, speech and hearing disorders. An assessment is made by the clinic, followed by a treatment recommendation for the twice-weekly therapy sessions. Fees are determined along a sliding scale.

SAN LUIS OBISPO COUNTY OFFICE OF EDUCATION

Day — Coed Ages 3-22
Clinic: Ages 3-22. M-S 8:30-4.

San Luis Obispo, CA 93405. 3350 Education Dr.
Tel: 805-543-7732. Fax: 805-541-1105.
www.slocoe.org   E-mail: info@slocoe.org
Julian D. Crocker, Supt.
   Conditions: Primary—OH.
   Pre-Voc. Gr PS-PG. Courses: Read Math Lang_Arts. Shelt_Workshop. On-Job Trng.
   Therapy: Hear Lang Speech. **Psychotherapy:** Indiv.
   Est 1946. County. **Spons:** Chris Jespersen Society.

SANTA CRUZ LEARNING CENTER

Clinic: Ages 5 and up. M-F 7-5; Eves M-F 5-7.

Santa Cruz, CA 95062. 720 Fairmount Ave.
Tel: 831-427-2753.
E-mail: sclrngcntr@yahoo.com
Eleanor F. Stitt, MA, MLS, Dir.
   Focus: Spec Ed. **Conditions:** Primary—ADD ADHD Dx LD. Sec—Asp Au Dc Dg MR. **IQ 85 and up.**
   Gen Acad. Ungraded. Courses: Read Math.
   Therapy: Lang.
   Staff: 1. (Full 1).
   Rates 2003: Clinic $50/hr.
   Est 1981. Private. Nonprofit.

The center provides individualized educational remediation and therapy for learning-different individuals and for those with attentional disorders. Gifted children and pre-delinquents with social readjustment problems also may receive treatment. Other aspects of the program are custom-designed test preparation for high school entrance examinations, the SAT and the ACT, and advocacy for individuals with dyslexia and other learning differences.

SHRINERS HOSPITAL

Res — Coed Ages Birth-18

Sacramento, CA 95817. 2425 Stockton.

Tel: 916-453-2000. Fax: 916-453-2352.
www.shrinershq.org
Margaret Bryan, Admin.
   Conditions: Primary—OH. Sec—CP SB.
   Therapy: Occup Phys Recreational.
   Est 1923. Private. Nonprofit.

SHRINERS HOSPITAL

Day — Coed Ages Birth-18
Clinic: Ages Birth-18. M-F 8-5.

Los Angeles, CA 90020. 3160 Geneva St.
Tel: 213-388-3151. Fax: 213-387-7528.
www.shrinershq.org   **E-mail:** edever@shrinenet.org
G. Frank LaBonte, Admin. **Colin F. Moseley,** MD, Med Dir. **Faviola Ramirez,**
  Intake.
   Focus: Treatment. **Conditions:** Primary—CP ON SB.
   Therapy: Art Hear Hydro Music Occup Phys Recreational. **Psychotherapy:**
   Indiv.
   Staff: 260. Prof 146. Admin 20.
   Rates 2003: No Fee.
   Est 1952. Private.

   Professionals make medical and surgical treatment plans for orthopedically handicapped children at Shriners. In addition, program specialists provide genetic counseling and a wide range of individual and group therapies. Clinical follow-ups are part of the program.
   The city school system sponsors an educational program.

SIERRA VISTA CHILD & FAMILY SERVICES

Res — Coed Ages 6-17; Day — Coed 5-14
Clinic: Ages Birth-14.

Modesto, CA 95354. 1400 K St.
Tel: 209-523-4573. Fax: 209-550-5866.
www.sierravistacc.org
Judy Kindle, Exec Dir.
   Conditions: Primary—BD ED. Sec—LD.
   Gen Acad. Gr K-8.
   Psychotherapy: Fam Group Indiv.
   Est 1972. Private. Nonprofit.

SONOMA DEVELOPMENTAL CENTER

Res — Coed All Ages

Eldridge, CA 95431. 15000 Arnold Dr.
Tel: 707-938-6000. TTY: 707-938-6548. Fax: 707-938-3605.
www.dds.cahwnet.gov/sonoma/sonoma.cfm
Loretta Vlaardingerbroek, Actg Exec Dir.
   Focus: Trng. Treatment. **Conditions:** Primary—MR. Sec—As B Bl C CP D Ep IP MD MS ON S SB TB.
   Pre-Voc. Ungraded. Courses: Lang_Arts. Shelt_Workshop.
   Therapy: Hear Lang Occup Phys Recreational Speech. **Psychotherapy:** Indiv.
   Enr: 900.
   Est 1891. State.

This center provides habilitation, medical and other professional services for persons with developmental disabilities. Programming seeks to help the individual reach his or her potential and achieve maximum growth. Training is conducted in perceptual-motor control and language, as well as self-help, academic, prevocational and socialization skills.

Sonoma serves as a diagnostic and treatment center that strives for community cooperation and interaction.

SPECTRUM CENTER FOR EDUCATIONAL AND BEHAVIORAL DEVELOPMENT

Day — Coed Ages 3-22

Berkeley, CA 94705. 2855 Telegraph Ave, Ste 312.
   Nearby locations: Concord; Fairfield; Oakland; Pittsburg; San Pablo.
Tel: 510-845-1321. Fax: 510-845-7841.
www.spectrumcenter.org
Randy Keyworth, MSW, MA, Co-Exec Dir. **Jack States,** MA, Co-Exec Dir.
   Focus: Spec Ed. **Conditions:** Primary—Au Bl CP ED MR PDD. Sec—B D ON S.
   Gen Acad. Pre-Voc. Voc. Ungraded. Courses: Read Math Life_Skills. On-Job Trng.
   Therapy: Lang Occup Percepual-Motor Recreational Speech. **Psychotherapy:** Indiv.
   Enr: 370. Day Males 296. Day Females 74. **Staff:** 360 (Full 319, Part 41). Admin 18.
   Rates 2004: Day $174/day. State Aid.
   Est 1975. Private. Nonprofit.

Spectrum Center operates five nonpublic schools for students with challenging behaviors and educational needs, each located on a separate campus. Schools operate in San Pablo (16330-16396 San Pablo Ave., 94806), Oakland (6325 Camden St., 94605), Concord (1026 Oak Grove Rd., 94518), Pittsburg (135 E. Leland Rd., 94565), and Fairfield (720 Link Rd, 94534).

The programs provide highly structured and supportive learning environments, low student-staff ratios, nonaversive behavior strategies, individualized student assessment and program design, community-based instruction and an interdisciplinary staff of professionals. Training in social problem solving, self-control, language, life skills, travel, leisure skills, vocational skills and functional academics is included in the curriculum, and the center seeks to facilitate the student's successful return to public school.

See Also Page 1052

SPECTRUM CENTER VALLEY SCHOOL
Day — Coed Ages 4-22

Concord, CA 94518. 1026 Oak Grove Rd, Ste 1.
Nearby locations: Concord; Oakland; Pittsburg; San Pablo; Suisun.
Tel: 925-685-9703. Fax: 925-685-5950.
www.spectrumcenter.org
Marilyn Coronado, Dir.
Focus: Spec Ed. **Conditions:** Primary—ADD ADHD AN Anx Ap Apr Ar As Asp Au B BD Bl Bu C CD CP D Db Dc Dg DS Dx ED Ep HIV IP LD MD Mood MR MS Nf OCD ON PDD Psy PTSD PW S SB SP Sz TB TS.
Voc. Ungraded. Courses: Life_Skills. On-Job Trng.
Therapy: Lang Occup Phys Play Speech.
Enr: 58. Day Males 48. Day Females 10. **Staff:** 43 (Full 40, Part 3). Admin 8.
Est 1975. Private. Nonprofit.

Spectrum Center specializes in helping students with severe handicaps or learning disabilities, among them challenging behaviors, learning handicaps, developmental disabilities, physical disabilities and emotional disturbances. The center has utilizes an educational and behavioral improvement model that emphasizes assessment of student motivational variables, positive and proactive teaching strategies, the improvement of student-teacher interaction, and strategies for successful collaboration between all participants in a child's educational environment (peers, teachers, parents, administrators and support staff).

Campuses operate in Oakland, Concord, San Pablo, Suisun and Pittsburg, California. In addition, Spectrum Center conducts a vocational program and three satellite classrooms in the San Francisco Bay Area.

SPEECH AND LANGUAGE DEVELOPMENT CENTER
Res — Males Ages 9-18; Day — Coed Birth-21

Buena Park, CA 90620. 8699 Holder St.
Tel: 714-821-3620. TTY: 714-821-3628. Fax: 714-821-5683.
www.sldc.net   E-mail: info@sldc.net
Aleen Agranowitz, MA, EdD, CCC, Dir. **Jeannine Michaud,** RN, Med Dir.
Dawn O'Connor, Adm.
Focus: Spec Ed. Treatment. **Conditions:** Primary—ADD ADHD Ap Au DS LD S. Sec—As B BD Bl C CD CP D Dx ED Ep MD MR MS OCD ON SB.
Gen Acad. Pre-Voc. Voc. Ungraded. Courses: Read Math Lang_Arts. On-

Job Trng.

Therapy: Hear Lang Occup Phys Speech. **Psychotherapy:** Fam Group Indiv.

Enr: 311. Res Males 31. Day Males 180. Day Females 100. **Staff:** 200.

Est 1955. Private. Nonprofit.

The center offers a daily school program for students with speech, language, learning and behavioral problems. Additional services include diagnosis and treatment; adaptive physical education; a computer lab; full-inclusion classes; a transition program; and vision and audiology services. The residential program, located in the San Jacinto Mountains, is for language- and learning-handicapped teenagers with behavioral problems.

Near Idyllwild, the center operates the affiliated Morning Sky Residential Program (P.O. Box 379, Mountain Center 92561).

SPEECH, LANGUAGE AND LEARNING SERVICES OF MARIN-SONOMA

Clinic: All Ages. M-F 8:30-5.

Petaluma, CA 94954. 1456 Professional Dr, Ste 403.
 Nearby locations: San Rafael.
Tel: 707-763-6419. Fax: 707-763-2537.
www.speechlanguage.info   E-mail: joycee@svn.net
Elaine Stevick, MA, CCC-SLP, Co-Dir. **Robin Rossman,** MA, CCC-SLP, Co-Dir.
 Focus: Treatment. **Conditions:** Primary—ADD ADHD Ap Apr Asp Au Bl CP D DS Dx LD MD MS Nf PDD PW S SB TS. Sec—B ED MR OCD OH.
 Therapy: Hear Lang Speech.
 Staff: 15 (Full 9, Part 6). Admin 4.
 Rates 2003: Clinic $82/hr. State Aid.
 Est 1980. Private. Inc. **Spons:** Speech Pathology Services of Marin-Sonoma.

The clinic provides comprehensive speech pathology services, as well as treatment for learning disabilities and central auditory processing disorders. The clinic also offers dialect modification, public speaking, and treatment for professional singers and speakers who develop vocal problems such as laryngitis, nodules or loss of pitch range.

A branch clinic operates at 30 N. San Pedro Rd., Ste. 265, San Rafael 94903.

SPRINGALL ACADEMY

Day — Coed Ages 5-18

La Jolla, CA 92037. 6550 Soledad Mountain Rd.
 Nearby locations: Lakeside.
Tel: 858-459-9047. Fax: 858-459-4660.
www.springall.org   E-mail: springall@springall.org
Arlene S. Baker, EdD, Exec Dir.
 Focus: Spec Ed. **Conditions:** Primary—ADD ADHD Asp Bl Dc Dg Dx LD

OH. Sec—BD CP ED Ep MR S.
Gen Acad. Pre-Voc. Gr K-12. Courses: Read Math Lang_Arts Adaptive_
Phys_Ed. On-Job Trng.
Therapy: Lang Occup Speech Visual. **Psychotherapy:** Fam Group Indiv
Parent.
Enr: 125. Day Males 100. Day Females 25. **Staff:** 72. Prof 35. Educ 18.
Admin 5.
Rates 2003: Day $135/day. State Aid.
Est 1972. Private. Nonprofit.

The academy provides highly individualized developmental education for students with learning disabilities and behavioral problems. A full program of basic education in mathematics, reading and language arts is augmented by special services in adaptive physical education, sensorimotor training, behavior development, language and speech therapy, and independent living skills. Extracurricular activities, such as field trips, community wrestling, yearbook, chess club and student council, aid in the development of self-esteem and the building of social skills.

Springall also provides services at 10025 Los Ranchitos Rd., Lakeside 92040.

STERNE SCHOOL
Day — Coed Ages 11-18

San Francisco, CA 94115. 2690 Jackson St.
Tel: 415-922-6081. Fax: 415-922-1598.
www.sterneschool.org   E-mail: sterne@sirius.com
Lisa Graham, Dir. MA, **Deanna Gumina,** Adm.
Focus: Spec Ed. **Conditions:** Primary—Dc Dg Dx LD. Sec—ADD ADHD.
Gen Acad. Pre-Voc. Gr 6-12. Courses: Read Math Lang_Arts Sci Comput-
ers Hist.
Enr: 60. Day Males 35. Day Females 25. **Staff:** 15 (Full 12, Part 3).
Rates 2003: Day $14,000-15,700/sch yr. Schol avail.
Est 1976. Private. Nonprofit.

Sterne provides an educational community where young people with specific learning disabilities realize their individual academic potential. Students are assisted with the mastery of basic skills.

STOCKDALE LEARNING CENTER
Clinic: Ages 5 and up. M-S 8-5; Eves M-Th 5-8.

Bakersfield, CA 93301. 1701 Westwind Dr, Ste 104.
Tel: 661-326-8084. Fax: 661-326-8084.
www.stockdalelearningcenter.net   E-mail: slc@igalaxy.net
Andrew J. Barling, MA, Admin.
Focus: Treatment. **Conditions:** Primary—ADD ADHD Dx LD. Sec—Ap MR.
IQ 90 and up.
Therapy: Lang. **Psychotherapy:** Parent.
Staff: 3 (Full 1, Part 2).

Est 1984. Private.

The center neurologically retrains individuals who have learning disabilities that affect visual perception, auditory perception or both. The facility's multisensory approach to phonics and perceptual training incorporates elements of the following methods: Orton-Gillingham/Slingerland, Frostig and Zweig. Children's classes meet twice weekly after school during the academic year and four mornings per week during the summer. The clinic teaches speech reading, sentence-writing strategies and study skills. Students must possess average to above-average intelligence to be admitted.

STOWELL LEARNING CENTER

Clinic: Ages 5 and up. M-F 8-5; Eves M-F 5-8.

Diamond Bar, CA 91765. 20955 Pathfinder Rd, Ste 332.
Tel: 909-598-2482. Fax: 909-598-3442.
Jill Stowell, MS, Educ Dir.
  Focus: Treatment. **Conditions:** Primary—ADD ADHD Dx LD.
  Staff: 20. (Full 20).
  Est 1984. Private. Inc.

Stowell Learning Center is a year-round diagnostic teaching facility for the treatment of learning and attentional disorders, including dyslexia. The center seeks to remediate educational problems through the development of thinking processes and skills. The program stresses fluency and comprehension.

SUNNY HILLS CHILDREN'S GARDEN

Res and Day — Coed Ages 4-18

San Anselmo, CA 94960. 300 Sunny Hills Dr.
Tel: 415-457-3200. Fax: 415-456-4679.
www.shcg.org   E-mail: contactus@shcg.org
Joseph M. Costa, CEO.
  Conditions: Primary—ED. Sec—BD.
  Col Prep. Gen Acad. Pre-Voc. Voc. Gr K-12. Courses: Read Math Lang_
    Arts. Man_Arts & Shop. Shelt_Workshop. On-Job Trng.
  Psychotherapy: Group Indiv.
  Staff: Prof 37.
  Est 1895. Private. Nonprofit.

SWITZER CENTER SCHOOL & CLINICAL SERVICES

Day — Coed Ages 5-19
Clinic: Ages 3 and up.

Torrance, CA 90501. 1110 Sartori Ave.
Tel: 310-328-3611. Fax: 310-328-5648.

www.switzercenter.org   E-mail: administration@switzercenter.org
Rebecca Foo, PhD, Exec Dir.
   Conditions: Primary—BD ED LD.
   Gen Acad. Pre-Voc. Ungraded. Courses: Read Math Lang_Arts.
   Therapy: Lang Speech. **Psychotherapy:** Fam Indiv.
   Est 1968. Private. Nonprofit.

THE SYCAMORES

Res and Day — Coed Ages 6-14
Clinic: Ages 2-21. M-F 8-6, S Su 10-2:30; Eves Th F 6-8.

Pasadena, CA 91105. 210 S DeLacey Ave, Ste 110.
Tel: 626-395-7100. Fax: 626-395-7270.
www.sycamores.org   E-mail: info@sycamores.org
Wiliam P. Martone, Pres. **Allan McDonald,** MD, Med Dir.
   Focus: Spec Ed. Rehab. **Conditions:** Primary—ADD ADHD Asp BD CD
     ED LD Mood OCD ODD Psy PTSD PW SP Sz TS. Sec—As BI Dx MR
     OH. **IQ 70 and up.**
   Gen Acad. Pre-Voc. Voc. Gr K-12. Courses: Read Math Lang_Arts Hist
     Computers Sci. On-Job Trng.
   Therapy: Art Dance Hear Lang Milieu Movement Music Occup Play Recre-
     ational Speech. **Psychotherapy:** Fam Group Indiv Parent.
   Enr: 234. Res Males 78. Res Females 8. Day Males 108. Day Females 40.
     Staff: 530 (Full 500, Part 30). Prof 200. Educ 40. Admin 58.
   Rates 2004: No Fee.
   Est 1902. Private. Nonprofit. **Spons:** Pasadena Children's Training Society.

  This facility utilizes the cognitive behavioral approach with an emphasis on developing problem-solving skills. Specialized educational programs are provided through an
on-site coeducational school that includes one-on-one tutoring and a computer laboratory.
  Boys live in cottages of 14 while receiving therapy and counseling services in a structured setting. Also available are family-oriented group homes. In addition to preparing
children to function in the community, clinical services seek family reunification.

THERAPEUTIC EDUCATION CENTER

Day — Coed Ages 12-18

Santa Ana, CA 92705. 2212 E 4th St.
Tel: 714-543-5437. Fax: 714-245-2110.
Julie Lucas, MAEd, Prin. **Lisa Grabowski,** Adm.
   Focus: Spec Ed. **Conditions:** Primary—ADD ADHD BD ED MR. Sec—Anx
     CD Mood PDD S SP TS.
   Gen Acad. Pre-Voc. Gr 7-12. Courses: Read Math Lang_Arts.
   Therapy: Speech. **Psychotherapy:** Group.
   Enr: 83. Day Males 58. Day Females 25.
   Rates 2004: No Fee.

Est 1996. County. Nonprofit. Evangelical. **Spons:** Olivecrest.

The center address the academic, emotional and behavioral needs of special-needs students through individualized educational programs. Programming focused on the mastery of basic academic skills, critical thinking skills, social skills, vocational skills, and the development of independence and confidence. Small class sizes and weekly treatment meetings allows for remediation in areas of delay in basic psychological processes and academic skills.

Sending school districts cover tuition costs.

TIMOTHY MURPHY SCHOOL

Res and Day — Males Ages 7-17

San Rafael, CA 94903. 1 St Vincent Dr.
Tel: 415-499-7616. Fax: 415-499-0252.
Brett Sklove, Exec Dir. **Liz Gremillion,** Adm.
    Focus: Spec Ed. **Conditions:** Primary—ADD ADHD BD ED LD.
    Gen Acad. Pre-Voc. Gr 2-12. Courses: Read Math Lang_Arts Sci Hist. On-Job Trng.
    Therapy: Art Music Speech.
    Enr: 75. Res Males 54. Day Males 21. **Staff:** 46 (Full 41, Part 5). Prof 17. Admin 3.
    Rates 2004: Day $162/day.
    Est 1985. State. Nonprofit.

TMS serves boys who have serious emotional and learning disabilities. In addition to providing special education, which includes academic, social skills, physical education and vocational experience, the school also provides health and nursing services, speech, language and hearing services, a learning center program, a behavior management program and a transition high school class.

Boarders typically reside at St. Vincent's Home for Boys.

TOTALLY KIDS SPECIALTY HEALTHCARE

Res — Coed Ages Birth-21

Loma Linda, CA 92354. 1720 Mountain View Ave.
Tel: 909-796-6915. Fax: 909-799-6205.
www.totallykids.com
Doug Padgett, Pres. **Joy Berkompas,** Adm.
    Focus: Treatment. **Conditions:** Primary—As BI C CP Ep IP MD MR MS ON SB TB. Sec—Ap B D S.
    Therapy: Music Occup Phys Recreational Speech. **Psychotherapy:** Indiv.
    Enr: 48. Res Males 30. Res Females 18.
    Est 1953. Private. Inc.

This licensed nursing facility provides pediatric subacute care for medically fragile and technology-dependent children. A nurse case manager formulates an individual care plan for each child. Subsequently, staff members carefully monitor and review the child's progress at regularly scheduled care plan meetings. The program's goal is to enable children who require long-term care due to chronic conditions to achieve the highest possible level of physical, mental and social independence.

UCLA INTERVENTION PROGRAM
FOR CHILDREN WITH DISABILITIES

Day — Coed Ages Birth-3

Los Angeles, CA 90024. 1000 Veteran Ave.
Tel: 310-825-4821. Fax: 310-206-7744.
www.healthcare.ucla.edu   E-mail: children@mednet.ucla.edu
Judy Ann Howard, MD, Med Dir.
   Focus: Rehab. Treatment. **Conditions:** Primary—Ap C CP Ep IP MD MR
     ON S SB. Sec—ADD ADHD Au B BI D Dx LD MS.
   Therapy: Hear Lang Occup Phys Play Speech.
   Enr: 40. Day Males 30. Day Females 10. **Staff:** 16.
   Rates 2004: No Fee.
   Est 1952. Private. Nonprofit.

Affiliated with the UCLA Medical School, this program provides treatment for handicapped children. The facility aims at helping parents gain confidence in their handling and knowledge of their children. Transitional in nature, intervention prepares children and parents for programs available in the community. Three divisions constitute the total facility: a home intervention program in which infants whose developmental age is under nine months are seen at home with occasional center-based visits; an infant program, serving infants whose developmental age is between nine and eighteen months with two weekly afternoon sessions (one and a half hours each); and a toddler program for children between 18 and 36 months that is held for three hours five mornings a week.

The facility utilizes a multidisciplinary approach in parent-child interaction and educational intervention. Each child's education/therapy focuses on the four developmental areas: motor, adaptive, language and personal/social. Emphasis is placed on spontaneous play. A research program in mother-child interaction helps define what changes occur as a result of intervention. The UCLA Intervention Program is supported by fees, private donations and research grants.

UCP OF CENTRAL CALIFORNIA
HANFORD PARENT/CHILD DEVELOPMENT PROGRAM

Day — Coed Ages Birth-3

Hanford, CA 93230. 606 W 6th St.
Tel: 559-584-1551. Fax: 559-584-6757.
www.ccucp.org
Laurie Alves, Exec Dir. **Judy Newton,** Prgm Dir.
   Focus: Treatment. **Conditions:** Primary—Au CP DS MR ON PW S SB.
     Sec—ED LD.
   Therapy: Occup Phys Speech Massage. **Psychotherapy:** Group.
   Enr: 95.

Est 1954. Private. Nonprofit.

This year-round program works with developmentally delayed and at-risk children while providing support and information for their parents. Self-help, socialization and pre-academic skills, as well as recreation therapy and language stimulation, are offered. In addition, consultation and referrals for speech therapy, physical therapy and occupational therapy are available. At age 3, most children receive a more appropriate placement within the public school system.

UNITED CEREBRAL PALSY OF ORANGE COUNTY

Day — Coed Ages Birth-18

Irvine, CA 92602. 230 Commerce, Ste 190.
Tel: 714-200-2600. Fax: 714-200-2640.
www.ucp-oc.org   E-mail: info@ucp-oc.org
Paul Pulver, Exec Dir.
    Focus: Treatment. **Conditions:** Primary—CP DS ON SB. Sec—B BI C D IP S.
    Therapy: Lang Occup Phys Speech.
    Enr: 195. Day Males 95. Day Females 100. **Staff:** 66. Prof 14. Educ 11. Admin 5.
    Rates 2004: No Fee.
    Est 1953. Private. Nonprofit.

UCP of Orange County conducts an infant development program and child care support services that includes special education and occupational, physical and speech therapies. Community health nursing, as well as nutritional and behavioral consultations, are available. Following an evaluation, an individual program aimed at meeting specific needs is designed by an interdisciplinary team together with the child's parents.

The center also provides a home visit program for infants from birth to age 3. This program, combined with classroom sessions, gives parents the emotional support and professional techniques necessary to help their children achieve developmental skills.

UNIVERSITY OF REDLANDS
TRUESDAIL CENTER
FOR COMMUNICATIVE DISORDERS

Clinic: All Ages. M-F 9-6.

Redlands, CA 92373. 1200 E Colton Ave, PO Box 3080.
Tel: 909-335-4061. Fax: 909-335-5192.
Christopher Niles Walker, PhD, Chrm. **Jovita Nuno,** Adm.
    Focus: Trng. **Conditions:** Primary—Ap Apr Asp Au BI CP D DS IP MD ON PDD S. Sec—MR SB.
    Therapy: Hear Lang Speech. **Psychotherapy:** Group.
    Staff: 12 (Full 10, Part 2). Educ 1.
    Rates 2003: Sliding-Scale Rate $0-12/ses.
    Est 1922. Private. Nonprofit.

Truesdail provides diagnosis and remediation of speech, language and audiological disorders. Fees are determined along a sliding scale.

UNIVERSITY OF THE PACIFIC
STOCKTON SCOTTISH RITE LANGUAGE CENTER
Clinic: Ages 3-18. M-F 9-6.

Stockton, CA 95204. 33 West Alpine Ave, PO Box 4236.
Tel: 209-462-2623. Fax: 209-462-1720.
www1.uop.edu/pharmacy/speechclinicchild.html
Conditions: Primary—S.
Therapy: Lang Speech.
Est 1946. Private.

VENTURA COLLEGE
EDUCATIONAL ASSISTANCE CENTER
Day — Coed Ages 16 and up

Ventura, CA 93003. 4667 Telegraph Rd.
Tel: 805-654-6300. TTY: 805-642-4583. Fax: 805-648-8915.
www.venturacollege.edu/eacenter   E-mail: vceac@vcccd.net
Nancy Latham, MS, Coord.
Focus: Spec Ed. **Conditions:** Primary—ADD ADHD Ap B BI CP D Dx IP LD MD MS ON S.
Col Prep. Gen Acad. Pre-Voc. Voc. Ungraded. Courses: Read Math Lang_ Arts Computers Adaptive_Phys_Ed Braille. Man_Arts & Shop.
Enr: 926. **Staff:** 25 (Full 11, Part 14). Prof 16. Admin 4.
Summer Prgm: Day. Educ.
Est 1976. State.

The college's learning disabilities program provides a full curriculum for students who have a diagnosed learning disability. A high-tech center for the disabled teaches pupils with various disabilities word processing skills and ways to use assistive devices and specialized software. The program also includes job development and placement services.

VIA CENTER
Day — Coed Ages 6-21

Berkeley, CA 94710. 2126 6th St.
Tel: 510-848-1616. Fax: 510-848-1632.
E-mail: viacenter@comcast.net
Nicole Heare, Exec Dir.
Focus: Spec Ed. **Conditions:** Primary—ADD ADHD Ap Asp Au BD BI C

CD CP ED Ep MS OCD ON PDD PW S TS. Sec—B D Db DS MR.
Gen Acad. Ungraded. Courses: Read Math Lang_Arts. On-Job Trng.
Therapy: Art Dance Hydro Lang Movement Occup Phys Recreational Speech.
Est 1988. Private. Nonprofit.

VIA REHABILITATION SERVICES
SPEECH, HEARING AND LEARNING CENTER

Clinic: All Ages. M-F 8:30-4:30.

Santa Clara, CA 95050. 2851 Park Ave.
Tel: 408-243-7861. Fax: 408-243-0452.
www.viaservices.org
Kay R. Walker, EdD, Pres. **Leon Clinton,** COO. **Patricia Yee,** MS, CCC-SLP, Clin Dir.
   Focus: Rehab. Treatment. **Conditions:** Primary—Ap D S. Sec—ADD ADHD Asp Au DS Dx LD MR PDD.
   Therapy: Hear Lang Speech.
   Staff: 4 (Full 3, Part 1). Educ 1. Admin 1.
   Rates 2003: $600 (Learn Evaluation); $90 (Hear Evaluation); $50 (Therapy)/ses.
   Est 1980. Private. Nonprofit.

Persons with articulation, language, fluency, voice and hearing disorders receive evaluation and treatment at this clinic. The center's staff of speech-language pathologists diagnoses specific communicative disorders, determines whether or not treatment is advisable, and designs individualized care programs. Evaluations measure articulation, receptive and expressive language, comprehension and memory, voice and fluency. Other services include audiometric screenings and evaluation and treatment of learning disabilities.

The center operates for five weeks over the summer to assist students in maintaining the progress they made during the school year.

VILLA ESPERANZA SERVICES

Day — Coed Ages 1½-15

Pasadena, CA 91107. 2116 E Villa St.
Tel: 626-449-2919. Fax: 626-449-2850.
www.villaesperanzaservices.org
   E-mail: info@villaesperanzaservices.org
Dottie Cebula Nelson, MSW, CEO. **Casey Gregg,** Adm.
   Focus: Spec Ed. **Conditions:** Primary—Au CP DS Ep MR PDD. Sec—Ap Asp B Bl C D Db ON SB.
   Gen Acad. Pre-Voc. Ungraded. Courses: Read Math.
   Therapy: Dance Lang Music Occup Speech. **Psychotherapy:** Parent.
   Enr: 50. Day Males 35. Day Females 15. **Staff:** 43 (Full 36, Part 7).
   Rates 2003: Day $108/day. Schol 4 ($2800). State Aid.

Summer Prgm: Day. Educ. Rec.
Est 1961. Private. Nonprofit.

Villa Esperanza specializes in providing services for children with developmental disabilities. The school enrolls individuals with Down syndrome, cerebral palsy, epilepsy, mental retardation, autism and other learning handicapping conditions. Programming combines classroom work with recreation, speech therapy, language development and behavior modification. A team-teaching approach promotes expertise in academics, play/social skills and independent living. The program also includes speech-language and occupational therapy services. Parents may receive individual counseling.

VISION CARE CLINIC OF SANTA CLARA VALLEY

Clinic: All Ages. M-S 9-5; Eves M-Th 5-7.

San Jose, CA 95124. 2730 Union Ave, Ste A.
Tel: 408-377-1150. Fax: 408-377-1152.
www.visiondiva.com
Vivian Liane Rice, OD, Dir.
    Conditions: Primary—ADD ADHD BI Dx LD. Sec—As Au B BD C CD CP D
    ED Ep IP MD MR MS OCD ON Psy S SB Sz TB.
    Therapy: Visual.
    Staff: 15.
    Est 1973. Private. Inc.

This clinic provides therapy for visually related learning disabilities, as well as perceptual testing and training. Individuals with handicapping conditions in addition to optic disorders may also receive services.

VISTA DEL MAR
CHILD AND FAMILY SERVICES

Res — Coed Ages 10-17; Day — Coed 7-18
Clinic: Ages Birth-21. M-S 8:30-5; Eves M-S 5-8.

Los Angeles, CA 90034. 3200 Motor Ave.
Tel: 310-836-1223. Fax: 310-204-4134.
www.vistadelmar.org   E-mail: admissions@vistadelmar.org
Gerald Zaslaw, MSW, Pres. **Stacy Lurie,** Adm.
    Focus: Spec Ed. Treatment. **Conditions:** Primary—ADD ADHD Ap Au BD
    CD ED OCD Psy Sz. **IQ 70 and up.**
    Gen Acad. Pre-Voc. Gr PS-12. Courses: Read Math Lang_Arts Life_Skills.
    Therapy: Hear Lang Phys Speech. **Psychotherapy:** Fam Group Indiv
    Parent.
    Staff: 103 (Full 77, Part 26).
    Est 1908. Private. Nonprofit.

Vista Del Mar and its divisions—Reiss-Davis Child Study Center, Home-SAFE Child Care and Julia Ann Singer Center—care for children in southern California who are experiencing emotional distress or the consequences of abuse, neglect or abandonment.

The agency provides a continuum of services, among them an on-grounds nonpublic school and residential, day treatment, outpatient and community-based programs for children and their families.

Vista Del Mar maintains a sliding scale for clinical services, and no children are refused treatment due to the inability to pay.

WESTVIEW SCHOOL

Day — Coed Ages 11-18

Los Angeles, CA 90025. 2000 Stoner Ave.
Tel: 310-478-5544. Fax: 310-473-5235.
www.westviewschool.com   E-mail: contact@westviewschool.com
Judy Gordon, BA, MA, Exec Dir.
  Focus: Spec Ed. **Conditions:** Primary—ADD ADHD Anx Dx ED LD. Sec—Dc Dg OCD SP. **IQ 80 and up.**
  Col Prep. Gen Acad. Gr 6-12. Courses: Read Math Lang_Arts Computers Studio_Art Music Drama Film.
  Therapy: Speech. **Psychotherapy:** Indiv.
  Enr: 100. Day Males 70. Day Females 30. **Staff:** 35 (Full 25, Part 10).
  Rates 2004: Day $27,000/sch yr (+$4000). State Aid.
  Summer Prgm: Day. Educ. Day Rate $3500. 6 wks.
  Est 1990. Private. Nonprofit.

A college prep program emphasizing precision teaching based upon social learning principles, Westview offers personalized instruction for children with learning disabilities, attentional disorders and mild emotional disturbances. In addition to college preparation, the program places significant emphasis on therapeutic support and the building of self-esteem. Students who remain at Westview through grade 12 earn a high school diploma upon completion of standard course requirements.

The school does not tolerate physical aggression or drug usage in its pupils. The usual length of stay is one to seven years.

WHITE MEMORIAL MEDICAL CENTER
PEDIATRIC REHABILITATION PROGRAM

Clinic: Ages Birth-18. M-F 8-5.

Los Angeles, CA 90033. 1720 Cesar E Chavez Ave.
Tel: 323-260-5836. Fax: 323-260-5786.
www.whitememorial.com/content/services/rehab/index.asp
  Conditions: Primary—Ap S.
  Therapy: Hear Lang Occup Phys Speech. **Psychotherapy:** Group.
  Staff: Prof 6.
  Est 1974. Private. Nonprofit.

WIDE HORIZONS RANCH

Res — Males Ages 9-18

Oak Run, CA 96069. 27442 Oak Run to Fern Rd.
Tel: 530-472-3223. Fax: 530-472-3223.
E-mail: janwidehorizons@juno.com
Gene Anderson, Dir. **Jan Anderson,** Admin.
   Focus: Spec Ed. Treatment. **Conditions:** Primary—ADD ADHD Anx Au BD
      Dx ED LD OCD ODD PTSD S. Sec—As C Ep Psy Sz. **IQ 80 and up.**
   Col Prep. Gen Acad. Pre-Voc. Voc. Gr 1-12. Courses: Read Math Lang_
      Arts Sci Soc_Stud Computers Studio_Art. Man_Arts & Shop. On-Job
      Trng. Culinary_Arts.
   Therapy: Hear Lang Milieu Speech. **Psychotherapy:** Fam Group Indiv.
   Enr: 12. Res Males 12. **Staff:** 18 (Full 17, Part 1). Admin 2.
   Rates 2004: Res $4858/mo. State Aid.
   Private. Nonprofit.

Situated on a 167-acre working cattle ranch, Wide Horizons conducts a year-round educational program for adolescent boys with severe emotional disturbances, attentional disorders and a history of neglect or abuse. The Ranch maintains a clinical, therapeutic, highly structured program to help children deal with academic, emotional, social and behavioral problems that cannot be adequately addressed in the home. Boys participate in all of the Ranch's working activities.

WINGS LEARNING CENTER

Day — Coed Ages 5-12
Clinic: Ages 1-12. M-F 9-4:30.

San Mateo, CA 94401. 49 N San Mateo Dr.
Tel: 650-342-8753. Fax: 650-342-8763.
www.wingslearningcenter.org   E-mail: info@wingslearningcenter.org
Irma E. Valasquez, Exec Dir. **Sherry Hartwig,** Adm.
   Focus: Spec Ed. **Conditions:** Primary—ADHD Ap Apr Asp Au MR OH.
      Sec—ADD.
   Gen Acad. Gr K-4. Courses: Read Math Lang_Arts.
   Therapy: Music Occup Percepual-Motor Play Speech.
   Enr: 8. Day Males 5. Day Females 3. **Staff:** 7 (Full 6, Part 1). Educ 2. Admin
      2.
   Rates 2003: Day $180/day. $100 (Clinic)/ses. Schol 1 ($7000).
   Est 2000. Private. Nonprofit.

Wings addresses the academic and social needs of children with autism and communication disorders, making it possible for them to interact, learn and live with typically developing children. The center seeks to create a learning environment where children can learn academic, social and interactive skills at an appropriately challenging pace. Wings also serves as a training facility for professionals interested in working with special-needs children.

YGNACIO LEARNING CENTER

Clinic: All Ages. M-Th 8-6; Eves by Appt.

Walnut Creek, CA 94598. 200 La Casa Via.
Tel: 925-937-7323. Fax: 925-935-3281.
E-mail: sandy@ricksandy.net
Sue E. Caputi, MEd, Co-Dir. **Sandra L. Mitchell,** MA, MEd, Co-Dir. **Cindy M. Gonzales,** MA, Co-Dir.
  Focus: Spec Ed. **Conditions:** Primary—ADD ADHD Dc Dg Dx LD. **IQ 85 and up.**
  Gen Acad. Ungraded. Courses: Read Math Lang_Arts Study_Skills.
  Staff: 5 (Full 2, Part 3).
  Rates 2003: Clinic $56/hr. Schol avail.
  Est 1979. Private. Nonprofit.

This center offers academic and psychometric evaluations and an individualized remediation program to learning-disabled students. Treatment is usually one to two years in length.

YOUTH HOMES

Res — Coed Ages 6-17

Walnut Creek, CA 94596. 1291 Oakland Blvd, PO Box 5759.
Tel: 925-933-2627. Fax: 925-933-5824.
www.youthhomes.org
Stuart McCullough, BA, Exec Dir.
  Conditions: Primary—BD ED. Sec—CD.
  Therapy: Speech. **Psychotherapy:** Fam Group Indiv Parent.
  Enr: 24. **Staff:** 40 (Full 35, Part 5).
  Est 1965. Private. Nonprofit. **Spons:** United Way.

Youth Homes operates four group homes in Contra Costa County with three distinct programs for abused, delinquent and disturbed children. One of the facilities is a short-term shelter; two homes lodge older teens preparing for independent living; and another home treats young adolescents, preparing them to return home or to a foster program.

COLORADO

AIM HOUSE

Res — Males Ages 17½-25

Boulder, CO 80307. PO Box 3492.
Tel: 303-554-0011. Fax: 303-554-0022.
www.aimhouse.com   E-mail: admissions@aimhouse.com
Daniel Martin Conroy, BA, Exec Dir. **Kelly Corn,** Adm.
   Focus: Treatment. **Conditions:** Primary—ADD ADHD Asp Dx PTSD. Sec—
      BD Bl Bu Db ED OCD ODD S SP TS. **IQ 90 and up.**
   Voc. On-Job Trng.
   Therapy: Art Movement Music Play. **Psychotherapy:** Fam Group Indiv.
   Enr: 24. Res Males 24. **Staff:** 12 (Full 6, Part 6). Prof 7. Admin 3.
   Rates 2004: Res $5000/mo (+$500). $150 (Therapy)/hr.
   Est 1999. Private.

This individualized, live-in mentoring program serves male adolescents who are having difficulty with the transition to adulthood. The structured living environment features a personalized program that includes group and private therapy, one-on-one coaching, wilderness experiences, access to academic institutions, vocational internships, volunteer opportunities, tutoring and planned study sessions, and peer support.

ANCHOR CENTER FOR BLIND CHILDREN

Day — Coed Ages Birth-5

Denver, CO 80205. 3801 Martin Luther King Blvd.
Tel: 303-377-9732. Fax: 303-377-9744.
www.anchorcenter.org   E-mail: info@anchorcenter.org
Alice Applebaum, Exec Dir.
   Focus: Spec Ed. **Conditions:** Primary—B.
   Gen Acad. Ungraded.
   Therapy: Hear Lang Music Occup Phys Speech. **Psychotherapy:** Indiv.
   Enr: 250. **Staff:** 18 (Full 5, Part 13).
   Est 1982. Private. Nonprofit.

Anchor Center maintains infant, toddler and preschool programs for children who are blind and visually impaired. The facility strives to maximize the child's independence and foster integration into neighborhood school programs for kindergarten and subsequent grades. All programs provide interdisciplinary evaluations, individual therapy and opportunities for interaction with sighted peers.

Children not enrolled at the center may participate in outreach services, and the facility collaborates closely with local school districts.

BRECKENRIDGE OUTDOOR EDUCATION CENTER

Res — Coed Ages 8 and up

Breckenridge, CO 80424. PO Box 697.
Tel: 970-453-6422. Fax: 970-453-4676.
www.boec.org   E-mail: boec@boec.org
Richard N. Cook, Exec Dir.
   Focus: Treatment. **Conditions:** Primary—ADD ADHD Au BD BI CP Dx ED
      Ep LD MD MR MS ON SB Sz. Sec—B CD D OCD.
   Therapy: Recreational.
   Rates 2004: Res $110/day.
   Summer Prgm: Res. Rec. 2 wks.
   Est 1976. Nonprofit.

The BOEC offers outdoor learning experiences to people of all abilities, including people with disabilities, those with serious illnesses and injuries, and "at-risk" populations. The goal of the program is to provide clients the opportunity to learn new skills, experience natural areas, challenge themselves and work together to enhance the health and self-confidence necessary to expand human potential.

CENTER FOR HEARING, SPEECH AND LANGUAGE

Clinic: All Ages. M-F 8-5, S 9-1.

Denver, CO 80220. 4280 Hale Pky.
   Nearby locations: Colorado Springs.
Tel: 303-322-1871. TTY: 303-322-1871. Fax: 303-399-3411.
www.chsl.org   E-mail: info@chsl.org
Jill Wayne, MA, CCC-A, Exec Dir.
   Focus: Treatment. **Conditions:** Primary—Ap D S. Sec—ADD ADHD Dx LD.
   Therapy: Hear Lang Speech.
   Private.

The center provides diagnostic testing, audiological services and therapy for all communicational disorders (including hearing, speech, language and learning problems). Lip reading and ASL sign language classes are available. A satellite office is located at 1329 N. Academy Blvd., Colorado Springs 80909.

CEREBRAL PALSY OF COLORADO
CREATIVE OPTIONS CENTER FOR EARLY EDUCATION

Day — Coed Ages Birth-5

Denver, CO 80222. 2180 S Hudson St.
Tel: 303-691-9668. Fax: 303-691-9618.
www.cpco.org   E-mail: creativeopts@cpco.org
Judy I. Ham, Exec Dir. **Wendy Edwards,** Educ Dir. **Patty Fradl,** Med Dir. **Lori Medina-Anderson,** Adm.
   Focus: Spec Ed. Treatment. **Conditions:** Primary—ADD ADHD Ap As Au

BI CP Dx Ep IP LD MD MR MS ON S SB. Sec—B BD C CD D ED OCD Psy Sz TB.
Gen Acad. Gr PS.
Therapy: Hear Lang Occup Phys Speech.
Enr: 115. **Staff:** 31 (Full 26, Part 5).
Est 1949. Private. Nonprofit.

Creative Options comprises three distinct programs: infant care (ages six weeks to 12 months); toddler care (ages 12 months to three years); and preschool (ages 3-5). The infant and toddler programs provide early intervention and education services for children who are experiencing delays or are at risk of developing them. Offerings include center-based parent and child play groups, home-based therapy, consultations pertaining to childcare and community services, and community outreach services.

Providing half- and full-day programs, the preschool operates classes throughout the community. Children with special needs receive screening, assessment and direct support, and the center also offers education, health, family and community services. Parental involvement and parent education are integral to the program.

THE CHILDREN'S HOSPITAL
AUDIOLOGY, SPEECH PATHOLOGY,
AND LEARNING SERVICES

Clinic: Ages Birth-21. M-F 8-5:30.

Denver, CO 80218. 1056 E 19th Ave.
Tel: 303-861-6800. Fax: 303-764-8220.
www.thechildrenshospital.org/pro/cs
Deborah Hayes, PhD, Chair.
    Focus: Treatment. **Conditions:** Primary—ADD ADHD BI Dx LD S. Sec—CP SB.
    Therapy: Hear Lang Speech.
    Staff: 40.
    Private.

Comprehensive diagnosis and treatment of communicative and learning disorders, as well as social work support services, are provided at the hospital. The facility also offers augmentative communication and computer-enhanced learning programs.

CHILDREN'S HOSPITAL
NEUROTRAUMA REHABILITATION CENTER

Clinic: Ages Birth-21. M-S 8-5.

Denver, CO 80218. 1056 E 19th Ave.
Tel: 303-861-3960. Fax: 303-861-6066.
www.thechildrenshospital.org
Dennis Matthews, MD, Dir.
    Focus: Rehab. Treatment. **Conditions:** Primary—BI CP MD MS ON S. Sec—IP SB.

Therapy: Chemo Hear Lang Occup Phys Speech. **Psychotherapy:** Fam Group Indiv Parent.
Staff: 126 (Full 117, Part 9).
Est 1956. Private. Nonprofit.

The center provides total evaluation services and treatment for children and adolescents with acquired and developmental disorders. The facility responds to the multiple physical and emotional needs of a diverse patient population whose disabilities range in severity. Recommendations for specific intervention and therapies are made. Many patients begin their physical recovery while still in the acute phase of their illness or injury.

COLORADO SCHOOL FOR THE DEAF AND THE BLIND

Res — Coed Ages 5-21; Day — Coed 3-21

Colorado Springs, CO 80903. 33 N Institute St.
Tel: 719-578-2100. TTY: 719-578-2101. Fax: 719-578-2239.
www.csdb.org   E-mail: csdbsupt@csdb.org
Barbara Meese, Adm.
   Focus: Spec Ed. **Conditions:** Primary—B D DS MR. Sec—Ap As BD BI C CP Dx ED Ep IP LD MD MS ON S SB TB. **IQ 40 and up.**
   Col Prep. Gen Acad. Pre-Voc. Voc. Gr PS-12. Courses: Read Math Lang_ Arts. Man_Arts & Shop. On-Job Trng.
   Therapy: Hear Lang Occup Phys Speech. **Psychotherapy:** Fam Group Indiv.
   Enr: 244. **Staff:** 89 (Full 79, Part 10).
   Est 1874. State. Nonprofit.

This state school provides academic education and vocational training for children who are blind, deaf or both. Programs extend from early intervention through a transitional program. Among the school's services are outreach and counseling. There is no fee for students enrolling from Colorado, while students from other states may attend upon payment of tuition.

COMMUNITY REACH CENTER

Clinic: All Ages.

Thornton, CO 80260. 8931 Huron Street.
Tel: 303-853-3500. Fax: 303-426-9384.
www.communityreachcenter.org
   E-mail: info@communityreachcenter.org
Richard L. Doucet, MA, Exec Dir.
   Conditions: Primary—ED. Sec—Anx CD Mood ODD Sz.
   Est 1957. Private. Nonprofit.

DAYBREAK GIRLS' HOME

Res — Females Ages 12-19

Denver, CO 80236. 3804 W Princeton Cir.
Tel: 303-789-2987.
www.beaconcenter.org
Kathy Wendell, Dir. **Julie Bellum,** Intake.
    Focus: Trng. Treatment. **Conditions:** Primary—BD ED. Sec—LD.
    Gen Acad. Pre-Voc. Voc. Gr 6-12. Courses: Read Math Lang_Arts.
    Therapy: Speech. **Psychotherapy:** Fam Group Indiv.
    Enr: 18. **Staff:** 17 (Full 11, Part 6).
    Est 1970. Private. Nonprofit.

    This home provides several services for emotionally disturbed adolescents, including individual, group, family and couples counseling; vocational counseling and assessment; support groups; and aftercare and follow-up counseling. An on-grounds school offers educational programs. Girls who exhibit assaultive behavior or have a high risk of suicide are not accepted.

DENVER ACADEMY

Day — Coed Ages 6-18

Denver, CO 80222. 4400 E Iliff Ave.
Tel: 303-777-5870. Fax: 303-777-5893.
www.denveracademy.org   E-mail: admissions@denveracademy.org
James E. Loan, BS, MA, Dir. **Daniel A. Loan,** Adm.
    Focus: Spec Ed. **Conditions:** Primary—LD. Sec—Dx. **IQ 90 and up.**
    Col Prep. Gen Acad. Gr 1-12. Courses: Read Math Lang_Arts Span Computers Studio_Art Music Drama.
    Psychotherapy: Parent.
    Enr: 424. Day Males 312. Day Females 112. **Staff:** 69.
    Rates 2003: Day $16,300/sch yr (+$50). Schol avail.
    Summer Prgm: Day. Educ. Rec. Day Rate $450. 5 wks.
    Est 1972. Private. Nonprofit.

    Denver Academy's curriculum is designed to meet the needs of children of normal intelligence with learning, motivational or behavioral problems. Classes are highly structured and personalized. Specific programs are developed for each student with the ultimate aim of mainstreaming him or her into a regular classroom situation, providing college preparatory training, or both.

DEVEREUX CLEO WALLACE

Res — Coed Ages 5-21

Westminster, CO 80021. Westminster Campus, 8405 Church Ranch Blvd.
    Nearby locations: Colorado Springs.
Tel: 303-466-7391. Fax: 303-466-0904.

www.devereux.org   E-mail: info@devereux.org
Focus: Spec Ed. Trng. Treatment. **Conditions:** Primary—ADHD BD LD ODD Psy PTSD Sz. **IQ 55 and up.**
Gen Acad. Voc.
Therapy: Milieu. **Psychotherapy:** Fam Group Indiv Parent.
Private.

See Also Page 1025

EL PUEBLO BOYS' AND GIRLS' RANCH
Res — Coed Ages 10-18

Pueblo, CO 81006. 1 El Pueblo Ranch Way.
Tel: 719-544-7496. Fax: 719-544-7705.
www.elpuebloboysandgirls.org
Patty Erjavec, Pres. **Courtney Montoya,** Adm.
Focus: Rehab. Treatment. **Conditions:** Primary—BD CD ED OCD Psy. Sec—MR. **IQ 70 and up.**
Therapy: Occup Recreational Speech. **Psychotherapy:** Fam Group Indiv Parent.
Enr: 100. Res Males 82. Res Females 18. **Staff:** 42 (Full 41, Part 1).
Est 1961. Private. Nonprofit.

El Pueblo provides residential treatment for emotionally and behaviorally disturbed adolescents, particularly those with conduct disorder and those who have been acting out sexually. Treatment consists of psychotherapy, academic and vocational education, and daily living and recreational activities.

Residents attend local public academic and vocational schools, as well as job-training programs. A work component includes part-time jobs in the community, work-study in area high schools, and daily chores and agricultural work at the ranch. The program makes allowances for health and religious needs, and El Pueblo stresses interaction with the resident's family.

EXCELSIOR YOUTH CENTERS
Res — Females Ages 11-18

Aurora, CO 80014. 15001 E Oxford Ave.
Tel: 303-693-1550. Fax: 303-693-8309.
www.excelsioryc.org   E-mail: info@excelsioryc.org
William C. Gregory, MSW, Exec Dir. **Terry Hoffman,** Adm.
Focus: Spec Ed. Treatment. **Conditions:** Primary—BD CD ED LD OCD. Sec—As Ep MR ON Psy Sz. **IQ 70 and up.**
Col Prep. Gen Acad. Pre-Voc. Voc. Gr 6-12. Courses: Read Math Lang_ Arts Sci Computers. Shelt_Workshop. On-Job Trng.
Therapy: Occup Speech. **Psychotherapy:** Fam Group Indiv Parent.
Enr: 170. Res Females 170.
Est 1973. Private. Nonprofit.

Emotionally and behaviorally disturbed girls receive rehabilitation and treatment at the center. General academics and prevocational training are offered, as are music, dance, drama, art, physical education and home economics. Excelsior cannot accept psychotic or pregnant girls. The usual duration of treatment is 12 to 18 months.

FOREST HEIGHTS LODGE

Res — Males Ages 4-14
Clinic: All Ages. M-F 8-5.

Evergreen, CO 80439. 4761 S Forest Hill Rd, PO Box 789.
Tel: 303-674-6681. Fax: 303-674-6805.
www.forestheightslodge.org
 E-mail: lindaclefisch@forestheightslodge.org
Linda Clefisch, LCSW, Exec Dir. **J. Gary May,** MD, Med Dir.
  Focus: Treatment. **Conditions:** Primary—ED. Sec—Ap BD Dx LD S. **IQ 80 and up.**
  Gen Acad. Courses: Read Math Lang_Arts Sci Soc_Stud. Man_Arts & Shop.
  Therapy: Milieu Play Recreational Speech. **Psychotherapy:** Fam Group Indiv.
  Enr: 24. Res Males 24. **Staff:** 19 (Full 14, Part 5).
  Rates 2003: Res $223/day.
  Est 1955. Private. Nonprofit.

Located in the Rocky Mountains 30 miles west of Denver, Forest Heights provides year-round treatment for moderately to severely emotionally disturbed boys. The on-grounds school is conducted on both individualized and group bases and aims at therapeutic intervention as well as remediation toward mainstreaming the child into the public school programs appropriate to his needs and abilities. Therapy is reality oriented, with a wide range of individual, family and group services.

GOODWILL INDUSTRIES

Day — Coed Ages 18 and up

Denver, CO 80221. 6850 N Federal Blvd.
Tel: 303-650-7700. Fax: 303-650-7749.
www.goodwilldenver.org   E-mail: info@goodwilldenver.org
Tim Welker, Pres.
  Focus: Trng. **Conditions:** Primary—Au Bl D Ep OH. Sec—ADD ADHD Ap As B BD CD CP Dx ED LD MD MR MS OCD Psy Sz. **IQ 40 and up.**
  Voc. Shelt_Workshop. On-Job Trng.
  Enr: 100. **Staff:** 22 (Full 13, Part 9).
  Est 1918. Private. Nonprofit.

Goodwill Industries of Denver offers evaluation, assessment and training for physically, mentally and emotionally disabled young adults and adults. The young adult program's objective is to render the individual employable. Vocational training, job placement assistance and follow-along are available. The center, which accepts persons from all Denver area school districts, tailors its services to meet the individual needs of the student.

GRAND JUNCTION REGIONAL CENTER FOR DEVELOPMENTAL DISABILITIES

Res — Coed All Ages

Grand Junction, CO 81501. 2800 D Rd.
Tel: 970-245-2100. Fax: 970-255-5714.
www.cdhs.state.co.us
Sharon Jacksi, Dir.
Focus: Trng. Treatment. **Conditions:** Primary—ED MR. **IQ 0-73.**
Pre-Voc. Voc. Shelt_Workshop. On-Job Trng.
Therapy: Hear Lang Occup Phys Speech. **Psychotherapy:** Indiv.
Est 1919. State. Nonprofit.

HAVERN CENTER

Day — Coed Ages 5-13

Littleton, CO 80123. 4000 S Wadsworth Blvd.
Tel: 303-986-4587. Fax: 303-986-0590.
www.haverncenter.org   E-mail: nmann@haverncenter.org
Sr. Barbara Schulte, MA, Dir.
Conditions: Primary—LD. **IQ 85 and up.**
Gen Acad. Gr K-8. Courses: Read Math Lang_Arts.
Therapy: Lang Occup.
Est 1966. Private. Nonprofit.

HOPE CENTER

Day — Coed Ages 2½ and up

Denver, CO 80205. 3400 Elizabeth St.
Tel: 303-388-4801. Fax: 303-388-0249.
www.hopecenterinc.org
George E. Brantley, Exec Dir.
Conditions: Primary—MR.
Gen Acad. Ungraded.
Therapy: Lang Occup Speech. **Psychotherapy:** Indiv.
Est 1968. Private. Nonprofit.

LARADON

Res — Coed Ages 9 and up; Day — Coed All Ages

Denver, CO 80216. 5100 Lincoln St.
Tel: 303-296-2400. Fax: 303-296-0737.
www.laradon.org
Timothy C. Hall, BA, MA, Exec Dir. **Lori Brown,** Adm.
　Focus: Spec Ed. Treatment. **Conditions:** Primary—Au MR. Sec—ADD
　　ADHD Ap As B BI CD CP D Dx ED Ep LD MD MS OCD ON Psy S Sz.
　　IQ 25-75.
　Gen Acad. Pre-Voc. Voc. Gr PS-PG. Courses: Read Math Lang_Arts Life_
　　Skills. Shelt_Workshop. On-Job Trng.
　Therapy: Art Hear Lang Movement Music Occup Phys Speech. **Psycho-**
　　therapy: Fam Group Indiv Parent.
　Enr: 300. **Staff:** 125.
　Est 1948. Private. Nonprofit.

Educational and vocational training for mildly to severely developmentally disabled children and adults is provided year-round at Laradon. Vocational rehabilitation for brain-injured individuals, as well as academic and independent living skills instruction, is provided. Counseling and outpatient services are available, and the length of treatment varies.

MOUNT ST. VINCENT HOME

Res — Coed Ages 6-13; Day — Coed 3-13

Denver, CO 80211. 4159 Lowell Blvd.
Tel: 303-458-7220. Fax: 303-477-7559.
www.msvhome.org   E-mail: kidsfirst@msvhome.org
Sr. Amy Willcott, SLC, Exec Dir. **Kirk Ward,** LCSW, Clin Dir. **Kerry Swenson,**
Adm.
　Focus: Treatment. **Conditions:** Primary—ADD ADHD BD CD Dx ED LD
　　OCD Psy Sz. Sec—Ap As Au B BI Ep S. **IQ 70 and up.**
　Gen Acad. Gr PS-8. Courses: Read Math Lang_Arts Lib_Skills Sci Soc_
　　Stud Studio_Art Music Adaptive_Phys_Ed.
　Therapy: Lang Occup Speech. **Psychotherapy:** Fam Group Indiv Parent.
　Enr: 65. **Staff:** 42 (Full 33, Part 9).
　Est 1883. Private. Nonprofit. Roman Catholic.

Mount St. Vincent provides academic and therapeutic remediation for emotionally disturbed children. Individual and group psychotherapy, a warm, structured environment, a specialized school program and family counseling are provided. Recreation and a special summer curriculum are also offered. Children occasionally spend time at a mountain lodge during the summer and on weekends during the winter.

NAMAQUA CENTER

Res and Day — Coed Ages 3-13
Clinic: All Ages. M-F 8-5; Eves M-F 5-7.

Loveland, CO 80537. 1327 W Eisenhower Blvd.
Tel: 970-669-7550. Fax: 970-663-2907.
www.namaqua.com   E-mail: info@namaqua.com
Cyndi Dodds, MS, Exec Dir. **Cheryl Ziegler,** PsyD, Clin Dir. **Chris Gray,**
Intake.
   Focus: Treatment. **Conditions:** Primary—BD ED Mood OCD ODD Psy
   PTSD. Sec—ADD ADHD As BI CP Dx Ep LD. **IQ 80-120.**
   Gen Acad. Ungraded. Courses: Read Math Lang_Arts.
   Therapy: Art Milieu Occup Play Recreational Speech. **Psychotherapy:**
   Fam Group Indiv Parent.
   Enr: 28. Res Males 15. Res Females 8. Day Males 3. Day Females 2. **Staff:**
   61 (Full 55, Part 6).
   Rates 2004: Res $225/day. Day $100/day. Sliding-Scale Rate $65-85/hr
   (Clinic). State Aid.
   Est 1976. Private. Nonprofit.

The center provides year-round education and care for severely emotionally disturbed
children. The typical length of treatment is three to 14 months.

NBA TENNYSON CENTER FOR CHILDREN
AT COLORADO CHRISTIAN HOME

Res and Day — Coed Ages 5-12
Clinic: All Ages. M-F 9-5; Eves M-Th 5-8.

Denver, CO 80212. 2950 Tennyson St.
Tel: 303-433-2541. Fax: 303-433-9701.
www.tennysoncenter.org   E-mail: info@cchtccf.org
Mark Palmer, CEO.
   Conditions: Primary—BD ED. Sec—ADD ADHD CD LD. **IQ 80 and up.**
   Gen Acad. Gr K-8. Courses: Read Math Lang_Arts Sci Soc_Stud.
   Therapy: Lang Recreational Speech. **Psychotherapy:** Fam Group Indiv.
   Enr: 115. **Staff:** 132.
   Est 1904. Private. Nonprofit. **Spons:** National Benevolent Association.

This facility provides a year-round program for children with severe emotional
problems. Each child receives individual therapy, while strong emphasis is placed upon
family therapy. A structured cottage system, a school and work program, and a recreational program are part of the therapeutic environment at the center.

PIKES PEAK MENTAL HEALTH CENTER

Clinic: Ages 1-18. M-F 8-5.

Colorado Springs, CO 80910. 220 Ruskin Dr.

Tel: 719-572-6100. Fax: 719-572-6199.
www.ppmhc.org
Christine Ely, PhD, Dir. **Fred Michel,** MD, Med Dir.
>**Focus:** Treatment. **Conditions:** Primary—ADD ADHD BD CD ED Mood
>   OCD Psy PTSD SP Sz. Sec—B D.
>**Therapy:** Play. **Psychotherapy:** Fam Group Indiv Parent.
>**Staff:** 271 (Full 216, Part 55). Prof 236. Admin 35.
>Private. Nonprofit.

PPMH offers therapy, mentoring, home-based services, respite and skill-building services for children and families. Addiction and crisis services are available for adults through the Lighthouse Assessment Center.

SAN LUIS VALLEY COMPREHENSIVE
COMMUNITY MENTAL HEALTH CENTER

Clinic: All Ages. M-F 8-5; Eves T-Th 5-8.

Alamosa, CO 81101. 8745 County Rd 9 S.
Tel: 719-589-3671. Fax: 719-589-9136.
www.slvmhc.org   E-mail: info@slvmhc.org
Mary E. Young, PhD, Assoc Dir. **Gregory Caesar,** MD, Med Dir.
>**Focus:** Treatment. **Conditions:** Primary—ADD ADHD Anx BD CD ED
>   Mood OCD ODD Psy PTSD Sz. Sec—Asp Au MR PDD.
>**Voc.** On-Job Trng.
>**Therapy:** Art Play. **Psychotherapy:** Fam Group Indiv Parent.
>Private. Nonprofit.

This center provides diagnosis and treatment for a full range of mental health conditions. Offerings include educational, parental and personal counseling. When appropriate, the facility will make referrals. Residents of the six counties of San Luis Valley may receive services. Fees are determined along a sliding scale.

TRAILHEAD WILDERNESS SCHOOL

Res — Coed Ages 12-18

Georgetown, CO 80444. PO Box 797.
Tel: 303-569-0767. Fax: 303-569-0120.
www.trailheadwildernessschool.com   E-mail: dventimiglia@msn.com
David Ventimiglia, BS, Co-Dir. **Lori Ventimiglia,** BS, Co-Dir. **Julie Hanks,**
    Adm.
>**Focus:** Treatment. **Conditions:** Primary—ADD ADHD BD CD Dx ED Mood
>   PTSD. Sec—Anx As. **IQ 70 and up.**
>**Gen Acad.** Gr K-12. Courses: Read Math Lang_Arts Environ_Sci Life_
>   Skills.
>**Therapy:** Milieu Music Recreational. **Psychotherapy:** Fam Group Indiv.
>**Enr:** 18. Res Males 18. **Staff:** 25 (Full 15, Part 10). Prof 10. Educ 3. Admin
>   5.
>**Rates 2003:** Res $250/day.

Est 1996. Private. Inc.

This wilderness program provides therapeutic opportunities that incorporate back-country living, peak ascents, therapeutic games and initiatives to challenge students in effective communication, self-analysis, healthy competition and teamwork, and conflict resolution. Trailhead seeks to build self-confidence and develop in the boys and girls a sense of accomplishment and self-worth. Individual, group and family psychotherapy is provided on a regular basis.

UNIVERSITY OF NORTHERN COLORADO
SPEECH-LANGUAGE PATHOLOGY AND AUDIOLOGY CLINIC

Clinic: All Ages. M-F 8-5.

Greeley, CO 80639. Gunter Hall 1400, Box 140.
Tel: 970-351-2012. Fax: 970-351-1601.
www.unco.edu/cmds/clinic.htm
    Conditions: Primary—Ap D LD S.
    Est 1952. State. Nonprofit.

CONNECTICUT

AHLBIN REHABILITATION CENTERS MEDICINE

Clinic: All Ages. M-F.

Bridgeport, CT 06610. 226 Mill Hill Ave.
Tel: 203-366-7551.
www.bridgeporthospital.org/Ahlbin/index.asp
   Conditions: Primary—C OH. Sec—BD.
   Gen Acad. Ungraded.
   Therapy: Lang Phys Speech.
   Staff: Prof 53.
   Est 1936. Private. Nonprofit.

AMERICAN SCHOOL FOR THE DEAF

Res — Coed Ages 8-21; Day — Coed 3-21

West Hartford, CT 06107. 139 N Main St.
Tel: 860-570-2300. TTY: 860-570-2222. Fax: 860-570-2301.
www.asd-1817.org   E-mail: chris.thorkelson@asd-1817.org
Harvey J. Corson, EdD, Exec Dir. **Cindy Paluch,** Adm.
   Focus: Spec Ed. **Conditions:** Primary—BD BI CP D ED IP LD MR.
   Col Prep. Gen Acad. Pre-Voc. Voc. Gr PS-12. Courses: Read Math Lang_
      Arts Soc_Stud Computers Life_Skills. Man_Arts & Shop. On-Job Trng.
   Therapy: Hear Lang Occup Phys Speech. **Psychotherapy:** Indiv Parent.
   Enr: 236. **Staff:** 185.
   Rates 2003: No Fee.
   Summer Prgm: Day. Educ. Rec.
   Est 1817. Private. Nonprofit.

   Children who are deaf or deaf with other special needs take part in a total communication program that emphasizes language growth and development. The school offers academic, vocational, residential, counseling and support programs. Three separate summer sessions will accept students from other schools. Outpatient services are available, as is home-based counseling for deaf and hard-of-hearing infants and their families. The duration of treatment ranges widely. Outreach and support services are offered on a fee-for-service basis to deaf and hard-of-hearing students in other placements.
   Connecticut families with children participating in the regular programs incur no fee.

ARC GREENWICH
YOUTH SERVICES DIVISION

Day — Coed Ages Birth-3

Greenwich, CT 06831. 50 Glenville St.

Tel: 203-531-1880. Fax: 203-531-6213.
www.arcgreenwich.org
Jon F. Doidge, Exec Dir. **Laurel Ross,** Dir.
  Focus: Treatment. **Conditions:** Primary—Ap Au Bl CP Ep IP MD MR MS
    ON S SB. Sec—As B BD C CD D ED OCD Psy Sz TB.
  Therapy: Hear Lang Occup Phys Speech. **Psychotherapy:** Fam Group
    Parent.
  Enr: 451. **Staff:** 34 (Full 13, Part 21).
  Est 1952. Private. Inc.

ARC conducts various services and supports for families of children with special
needs. The Youth Services Division comprises three departments. High-risk infants and
those with suspected or confirmed developmental delays may receive early intervention
services through age 3. At home or at fully integrated community daycare or education
programs, the facility provides developmental assessments, educational experiences and
therapeutic services of all types.

A second program provides support and assistance services for special-needs children and their families. The final component, the Greenwich Autism Program, features
consultation to schools and other programs serving children with autism; in-home and
after-school behavioral programming and support; respite care; and seminars, parent
training and support.

BEN BRONZ ACADEMY

Day — Coed Ages 7-21
Clinic: Ages 7 and up. M-Th 3-5.

West Hartford, CT 06107. 139 N Main St, Rm 101.
Tel: 860-236-5807. Fax: 860-233-9945.
www.tli.com   E-mail: tli@tli.com
Aileen Stan-Spence, PhD, Exec Dir. **Susan Sharp,** PhD, Head.
  Focus: Spec Ed. **Conditions:** Primary—Dc Dg Dx LD. Sec—ADD ADHD
    Anx ED OCD ODD ON SB SP TS. **IQ 90 and up.**
  Col Prep. Gen Acad. Pre-Voc. Gr 2-PG. Courses: Read Math Lang_Arts
    Sci Computers Soc_Stud Typing Study_Skills. Man_Arts & Shop.
  Therapy: Lang Occup Phys Speech. **Psychotherapy:** Group Indiv.
  Enr: 60. Day Males 40. Day Females 20. **Staff:** 30 (Full 25, Part 5). Prof 26.
    Educ 26.
  Rates 2003: Day $36,000/sch yr. Clinic $75/hr. Schol avail. State Aid.
  Summer Prgm: Day. Educ. Ther. Computers. 1-4 wks.
  Est 1985. Private. Inc. **Spons:** Learning Incentive.

The academy offers individualized academic programs for learning-disabled students
of average to above-average intelligence. The program stresses cognitive abilities, language skills and independence training. Most subjects incorporate computers. Students
work on problem solving and are taught to use strategies that facilitate their own learning. All pupils must take part in a structured study hall, except for those who prove they
have acquired independent study skills or who maintain an "A" average. Parents participate in the program, and therapy and counseling are available.

An on-site clinic concentrates on academic remediation and skill improvement for
both children and adults not enrolled in the day school program. The clinic also empha-

sizes independence and socialization skills. Classes are small and all work is individualized. A summer half-day program provides classes for learning-disabled, gifted and remedial children.

CEDARHURST SCHOOL

Day — Coed Ages 13-21

Hamden, CT 06517. 871 Prospect St.
Tel: 203-764-9314. Fax: 203-764-9321.
http://cedarhurst.yale.edu
Mary Donovan-Canas, Dir.
>   **Focus:** Spec Ed. **Conditions:** Primary—BD CD ED OCD Psy Sz. Sec—ADD ADHD LD. **IQ 90 and up.**
>   **Col Prep. Gen Acad. Pre-Voc.** Gr 7-12. Courses: Read Math Lang_Arts Fr Span Sci Soc_Stud Psych Computers Typing Life Skills. Man_Arts & Shop. On-Job Trng.
>   **Psychotherapy:** Group.
>   **Enr:** 56. Day Males 28. Day Females 28. **Staff:** 17. (Full 17).
>   **Est 1960.** Private. **Spons:** Yale University.

Cedarhurst School, an affiliate of the Yale Department of Psychology, offers a special education program to students with moderate to severe emotional disturbances. The school serves partial hospital patients hospitalized at Yale New Haven Hospital, as well as commuting day students referred by local school districts. A complete junior/senior high school curriculum is offered in small classroom groups, with an emphasis on individualized instruction.

CHAPEL HAVEN

Res — Coed Ages 18 and up

Westville, CT 06515. 1040 Whalley Ave.
Tel: 203-397-1714. Fax: 203-392-3698.
www.chapelhaven.org   E-mail: jlefkowitz@chapelhaven.org
Betsy Parlato, MS, Exec Dir. **Judith S. Lefkowitz,** Adm.
>   **Focus:** Spec Ed. **Conditions:** Primary—ADD ADHD Au Dx LD MR OH. Sec—BI CP ED OCD Psy Sz. **IQ 60-90.**
>   **Pre-Voc. Voc.** Ungraded. Courses: Read Math Lang_Arts Life_Skills Sex_Ed. On-Job Trng.
>   **Therapy:** Art Lang Phys Recreational Speech. **Psychotherapy:** Group Indiv Parent.
>   **Enr:** 29. Res Males 17. Res Females 12. **Staff:** 80 (Full 40, Part 40).
>   **Rates 2004:** Res $43,000/yr. State Aid.
>   **Summer Prgm:** Res & Day. Educ. Rec. 4 wks.
>   **Est 1972.** Private. Nonprofit.

Chapel Haven offers residential and community living programs for young adults with cognitive disabilities. These programs are designed to teach skills and mature behaviors necessary for independent living.

Residents attend classes in practical academics such as math and language arts. Other activities explore the community's resources and develop the resident's awareness of self. Once adjusted to the environment, each resident may spend part of his or her day in a daily volunteer placement or a part-time paid position. Job-seeking skills, job placement, job maintenance and consumer education are provided.

Recreational activities include field trips, dances, sports activities, craft classes and annual events. Individual and crisis counseling is available at all times. Regular meetings deal with interpersonal problems, values clarification, decision making and other related matters. Psychological, speech, language and hearing therapies are available in the community as needed. The usual length of residential treatment is two years.

As residents demonstrate the ability to perform all activities of daily living at a high standard, staff members assist them in finding their own apartments. At that time, clients may continue to receive life skills training, vocational support and social opportunities through Chapel Haven's community programs.

CHARLOTTE HUNGERFORD HOSPITAL PSYCHIATRIC SERVICES

Clinic: Ages 2-17. M-F 8:30-5; Eves W Th 5-9.

Torrington, CT 06790. 1061 E Main St.
Tel: 860-489-3391.
www.charlottesweb.hungerford.org
  Conditions: Primary—BD ED. Sec—ADHD.
  Therapy: Play. **Psychotherapy:** Fam Group Indiv.
  Private.

THE CHILD GUIDANCE CLINIC OF GREATER BRIDGEPORT

Clinic: Ages Birth-18.

Bridgeport, CT 06604. 180 Fairfield Ave.
Tel: 203-394-6529. Fax: 203-394-6534.
www.cgcgb.org
  Conditions: Primary—ED.
  Psychotherapy: Fam Group Indiv.
  Est 1925.

CHILD GUIDANCE CLINIC OF SOUTHERN CONNECTICUT

Clinic: Ages Birth-18. M-F 9-5; Eves M-Th 5-9.

Stamford, CT 06905. 103 W Broad St.
Tel: 203-324-6127. Fax: 203-348-9378.
www.childguidancect.org

Larry Rosenberg, PhD, Dir. **Sanders Stein,** MD, Med Dir.
    Focus: Treatment. **Conditions:** Primary—ADD ADHD Anx Bu CD ED Mood
    OCD PTSD SP. Sec—Ap Asp Au BD BI Dx LD PDD S.
    Therapy: Speech. **Psychotherapy:** Fam Group Indiv.
    Staff: 30. Prof 20.
    Rates 2003: Sliding-Scale Rate $5-110/ses.
    Est 1955. Private. Nonprofit.

Child Guidance offers diagnosis and treatment for a full range of emotional and developmental disturbances, including autism. The clinic also conducts a learning-disability evaluation and treatment program and a child abuse, sexual abuse and domestic violence program. Parental counseling is available.

THE CHILDREN'S CENTER

Res — Coed Ages 7-18; Day — Coed 12-18

Hamden, CT 06517. 1400 Whitney Ave.
Tel: 203-248-2116. Fax: 203-248-2572.
www.childrenscenterhamden.org
    E-mail: info@childrenscenterhamden.org
Eugene Roddy, EdD, Dir. **Candace Ward-McKinlay,** PhD, Prin.
    Conditions: Primary—BD CD ED LD OCD Psy Sz. Sec—Ap As CP Dx Ep
    MR OH. **IQ 79 and up.**
    Gen Acad. Pre-Voc. Ungraded. Courses: Read Math Lang_Arts. On-Job
    Trng.
    Therapy: Lang Speech. **Psychotherapy:** Fam Group Indiv.
    Enr: 147. **Staff:** 165.
    Est 1833. Private. Nonprofit.

Mildly to severely disturbed and abused children receive treatment and special education services at the center. Foster care and group homes are available, and eligible students are enrolled in community schools. Work experience is an important part of the program, with vocational activities provided. An alcohol program provides residential treatment for 45 days, followed by a combination of aftercare services.

THE CHILDREN'S HOME OF CROMWELL

Res — Coed Ages 9-18; Day — Coed 8-18
Clinic: Ages 8-18. By Appt.

Cromwell, CT 06416. 60 Hicksville Rd.
Tel: 860-635-6010. Fax: 860-635-3425.
www.childhome.org   E-mail: info@childhome.org
David E. Jacobsen, PsyD, CEO. **Steve Hodge,** MS, COO.
    Focus: Spec Ed. Treatment. **Conditions:** Primary—ADHD BD ED LD ON
    SP. Sec—Dx MR.
    Gen Acad. Pre-Voc. Ungraded. Courses: Read Math Lang_Arts Soc Sci
    Studio_Art.
    Therapy: Hear Lang Speech. **Psychotherapy:** Fam Group Indiv.

Enr: 87. Res Males 42. Res Females 29. Day Males 8. Day Females 8.
Staff: 140 (Full 120, Part 20). Prof 32. Educ 10. Admin 6.
Est 1900. Private. Nonprofit. Evangelical Covenant.

Family therapy, parenting skills training and intensive therapy with the child are emphasized in this program. Students receive diagnostic testing, special education and tutoring at the on-grounds school. Music, health and physical education, prevocational education and after-school clubs are part of the curriculum. Other therapies include milieu, recreation, art and play. The facility also provides spiritual life education according to the faith of the resident. Alternative home placement referrals are made when necessary. The usual length of treatment is 15 to 24 months.

COMMUNITY CHILD GUIDANCE CLINIC

Day — Coed Ages 3-13
Clinic: Ages Birth-18. M-F 9-5; Eves T Th 5-8.

Manchester, CT 06040. 317 N Main St.
Tel: 860-643-2101. Fax: 860-645-1470.
www.ccgcinc.org   E-mail: cj@ccgcinc.org
Clifford Johnson, MSW, Exec Dir. **Peter Francis,** Educ Coord. **C. Lynn Helman,** MD, Med Dir.
Focus: Spec Ed. Treatment. **Conditions:** Primary—Asp Au BD ED MR. Sec—LD.
Gen Acad. Pre-Voc. Ungraded. Courses: Read Math Lang_Arts.
Therapy: Chemo Lang Occup Speech. **Psychotherapy:** Fam Group Indiv.
Enr: 40. Day Males 30. Day Females 10. **Staff:** 19. Prof 11. Educ 7. Admin 1.
Rates 2003: Day $32,000/yr.
Summer Prgm: Day. Educ. Ther. 4 wks.
Est 1958. Private. Nonprofit.

Community Child Guidance Clinic offers psychiatric outpatient services and a school for children with emotional and learning disabilities and autism. The school program provides an intensive educational experience designed to mainstream children into public schools. Parental counseling and individual and group therapies are available. The school serves a 14-town area in Connecticut.

COMMUNITY MENTAL HEALTH AFFILIATES

Clinic: Ages Birth-18.

Bristol, CT 06010. 300 Main St.
Tel: 860-583-9954. Fax: 860-585-6811.
www.cmhacc.org
Conditions: Primary—BD ED.
Psychotherapy: Fam Group Indiv.
Staff: Prof 28.
Est 1975. Private.

CONNECTICUT CHILDREN'S MEDICAL CENTER SPEECH-LANGUAGE PATHOLOGY AND AUDIOLOGY CARE CENTER

Clinic: Ages Birth-21. M-F 8-5.

Hartford, CT 06103. 282 Washington St.
Tel: 860-545-9670. Fax: 860-545-9662.
www.ccmckids.org/services/speechhearing.asp
Cheryl Archer, Dir.
  Conditions: Primary—D LD S.
  Gen Acad. Gr PS-12.
  Therapy: Hear Lang Occup Phys Speech. **Psychotherapy:** Fam Group
    Indiv.
  Staff: Prof 11.
  Private.

CONNECTICUT COLLEGE CHILDREN'S PROGRAM

Day — Coed Ages Birth-6

New London, CT 06320. Box 5215.
Tel: 860-439-2920. Fax: 860-439-5317.
E-mail: bldem@conncoll.edu
Sara Radlinski, PhD, Dir.
  Focus: Treatment. **Conditions:** Primary—ADD ADHD Ap Apr Ar As Asp Au
    B BI CF CP D Db DS ED Ep LD MD MR MS Nf ODD ON PDD S SB TB.
  Gen Acad. Gr PS.
  Therapy: Hear Lang Occup Phys Speech.
  Enr: 115. **Staff:** 24 (Full 8, Part 16). Prof 13. Educ 7. Admin 3.
  Rates 2004: Day $25,000/sch yr. State Aid.
  Summer Prgm: Day. Educ. Ther. Day Rate $120/day.
  Est 1972. Private. Nonprofit.

This Connecticut College program provides training for undergraduate students interested in working with developmentally delayed children. The early intervention treatment plans are family oriented and provide parental counseling sessions. The usual duration of treatment is 18 months.

THE CONNECTICUT INSTITUTE FOR THE BLIND OAK HILL

Res and Day — Coed Ages 6-21

Hartford, CT 06112. 120 Holcomb St.
Tel: 860-242-2274. Fax: 860-242-3103.
www.ciboakhill.org   E-mail: eddya@ciboakhill.org
Patrick Johnson, PhD, Exec Dir. **Anna M. Eddy,** Dir. **Joann Diaz,** MD, Med Dir.

Focus: Spec Ed. **Conditions:** Primary—ADHD Au B BD. Sec—BI C CP D ED Ep IP LD MR ON S SB.
Pre-Voc. Ungraded. Courses: ADL. Shelt_Workshop. On-Job Trng.
Therapy: Hear Lang Music Occup Phys Recreational Speech.
Enr: 58. Res Males 21. Res Females 11. Day Females 26. **Staff:** 33 (Full 30, Part 3).
Rates 2003: Res $123,826/yr. Day $57,488/yr. State Aid.
Est 1893. State.

Oak Hill serves students who are severely to profoundly multi-handicapped. The year-round educational program includes vocational training, orientation and mobility, and personal management. Classes use data-based teaching technology. Classes generally involve eight students and three or four staff members, depending on the students' needs. There are a variety of living arrangements, from traditional dormitories to community residences. The agency operates approximately 60 group homes for multi-handicapped adults. Respite services are also available.

CONNECTICUT JUNIOR REPUBLIC

Res and Day — Males Ages 12-16

Litchfield, CT 06759. Goshen Rd, PO Box 161.
Tel: 860-567-9423. Fax: 860-567-9792.
www.ctjuniorrepublic.org   E-mail: info@ctjuniorrepublic.org
John F. Boyd, MS, Exec Dir.
　Focus: Spec Ed. Treatment. **Conditions:** Primary—ADD ADHD BD CD ED. IQ 80 and up.
　Gen Acad. Pre-Voc. Voc. Ungraded. Courses: Read Math Lang_Arts Sci. Man_Arts & Shop.
　Therapy: Speech. **Psychotherapy:** Fam Group Indiv.
　Enr: 94. Res Males 84. Day Males 10. **Staff:** 68 (Full 49, Part 19).
　Est 1904. Private. Nonprofit.

This center is a group-care facility for boys with emotional and behavioral problems. Within the 209-acre community, staff members design individualized treatment programs.

Academic classes are divided into three groups—lower elementary, intermediate and advanced—with students placed accordingly. Remedial reading, speech therapy, and art and computer courses are part of the program.

All boys spend a scheduled portion of the day in one of seven prevocational classes: appliance repair and maintenance, culinary arts, general crafts, power mechanics, woodworking, agriculture, and graphic arts and printing. The extensive agricultural program addresses land conservation and development, animal husbandry and horticulture.

The athletic and activities program includes many individual and team sports, as well as a diversified range of special-interest groups. Residents also participate in cultural, recreational and educational events in the local area. Facilities include a town hall, a school, a gymnasium and indoor swimming pool, a farm, industrial shops, an athletic field and a fishing brook.

A family home for six boys aids in the transition from group living to independent community life. Aftercare services assist residents with readjustment problems. The usual length of treatment is 12 months, and the facility generally restricts enrollment to residents of Connecticut.

COUNTY HEARING AND BALANCE

Clinic: All Ages. M-F 8:30-5.

Waterford, CT 06385. 167 Parkway N.
Nearby locations: Groton, Norwich, Old Lyme, Old Saybrook.
Tel: 860-443-6944. Fax: 860-442-7906.
www.countyhearingandbalance.com
   Focus: Treatment. **Conditions:** Primary—Ap S.
   Therapy: Hear Lang Speech.
   Est 1967. Private. Nonprofit.

DEVEREUX GLENHOLME SCHOOL

Res and Day — Coed Ages 5-18

Washington, CT 06793. 81 Sabbaday Ln.
Tel: 860-868-7377. Fax: 860-868-7413.
www.theglenholmeschool.org
   E-mail: admissions@theglenholmeschool.org
Gary L. Fitzherbert, MEd, Exec Dir. **Kathi Fitzherbert,** Adm.
   Focus: Spec Ed. **Conditions:** Primary—Asp ED. Sec—ADD ADHD Anx Ap As BD Db Dc Dg Dx Ep LD Mood OCD ODD PTSD SP TS. **IQ 90 and up.**
   Gen Acad. Ungraded. Courses: Read Math Lang_Arts Soc_Stud Sci Computers.
   Therapy: Lang Milieu Occup Play Recreational Speech. **Psychotherapy:** Fam Group Indiv Parent.
   Enr: 104. Res Males 59. Res Females 35. Day Males 6. Day Females 4.
      Staff: 105 (Full 95, Part 10). Prof 42. Educ 18. Admin 15.
   Rates 2004: Res $86,505/yr. Day $35,475/yr. State Aid.
   Est 1967. Private. Nonprofit. **Spons:** Devereux Foundation.

Glenholme's year-round program is designed for children who have social, emotional and learning disabilities. An environmental milieu combined with individual, group and family therapy is provided to assist each child in acquiring social skills. Asperger's Syndrome is a specialty of the Glenholme program. A therapeutic educational program offers instruction in both self-contained and departmental classes. Small-group and individualized instruction is provided in all content areas and focuses on language development and expressive skills. The 100-acre campus provides facilities for a wide range of residential activities, which are instructional in nature.

See Also Page 1025

EAGLE HILL SCHOOL

**Res — Coed Ages 10-16; Day — Coed 6-16
Clinic: All Ages. M-Th 8-6.**

Greenwich, CT 06831. 45 Glenville Rd.
Tel: 203-622-9240. Fax: 203-622-0914.
www.eaglehillschool.org   E-mail: r.griffin@eaglehill.org
Mark J. Griffin, BA, MA, MEd, PhD, Head. **Rayma-Joan Griffin,** Adm.
   Focus: Spec Ed. **Conditions:** Primary—Dx LD. Sec—ADD ADHD. **IQ 95-135.**
   Gen Acad. Ungraded. Courses: Read Math Lang_Arts Computers Sci Hist Study_Skills.
   Therapy: Lang Speech. **Psychotherapy:** Fam Group Indiv Parent.
   Enr: 205. Res Males 20. Res Females 10. Day Males 115. Day Females 60. **Staff:** 80 (Full 75, Part 5).
   Rates 2004: Res $52,100/sch yr (+$500). Day $40,750/sch yr. Schol avail. State Aid.
   Summer Prgm: Day. Educ. Day Rate $2200. 5½ wks.
   Est 1975. Private. Nonprofit. **Spons:** Eagle Hill Foundation.

Eagle Hill is designed to assist the student with a specific learning disability. The program presents language instruction from its most simple components to its most complex. Individualized programs are designed that utilize individual and small-group tutorials, as well as content area classes. The school's structured program serves pupils of average to high intelligence. Interscholastic athletics and extracurricular programs are offered, and mainstreaming the student into a regular school setting is the overall program goal.

Other Eagle Hill schools operate in Southport and in Hardwick, MA.

See Also Pages 1026-7

EAGLE HILL-SOUTHPORT

Day — Coed Ages 6-16

Southport, CT 06490. 214 Main St.
Tel: 203-254-2044. Fax: 203-255-4052.
www.eaglehillsouthport.org   E-mail: info@eaglehillsouthport.org
Leonard Tavormina, BA, MA, Head.
   Focus: Spec Ed. **Conditions:** Primary—ADD ADHD Dc Dg Dx LD. Sec—Anx CF Ep Mood OCD SP TS. **IQ 90 and up.**
   Gen Acad. Ungraded. Courses: Read Math Lang_Arts.
   Therapy: Lang. **Psychotherapy:** Group Indiv.
   Enr: 107. Day Males 90. Day Females 17. **Staff:** 48 (Full 36, Part 12). Prof 32. Educ 29. Admin 12.
   Rates 2004: Day $32,400/sch yr. Schol 15 ($121,700).
   Summer Prgm: Day. Educ. Day Rate $2100. 5 wks.
   Est 1984. Private. Nonprofit.

Eagle Hill provides a structured, linguistically based language arts program for children with language-learning disabilities. Each student receives individual or small-group tutorial instruction in mathematics, literature, writing, language arts, science and social studies. Athletics and extracurricular activities are also offered. Other campuses are located in Greenwich and in Hardwick, MA.   **See Also Page 1029**

EASTER SEAL REHABILITATION CENTER OF GREATER WATERBURY

Day — Coed Ages Birth-5

Waterbury, CT 06708. 22 Tompkins St.
Tel: 203-754-5141. Fax: 203-757-1198.
www.eswct.com
  Conditions: Primary—D LD MR OH.
  Pre-Voc. Voc. Shelt_Workshop. On-Job Trng.
  Therapy: Hear Phys Speech.
  Private.

ELIZABETH IVES SCHOOL FOR SPECIAL CHILDREN

Day — Coed Ages 5-21

North Haven, CT 06473. 70 State St.
Tel: 203-234-8770. Fax: 203-234-7238.
E-mail: eliz.ives.sch@snet.net
Linda Zunda, MS, MFT, Dir.
  Focus: Spec Ed. **Conditions:** Primary—DS ED MR. Sec—ADD ADHD Ap Asp Au BD Bl Dc Dg Dx LD ODD ON Psy PTSD S SP Sz TS. **IQ 60 and up.**
  Col Prep. Gen Acad. Pre-Voc. Voc. Ungraded. Courses: Read Math Lang_ Arts. On-Job Trng.
  Therapy: Lang Speech. **Psychotherapy:** Group Indiv.
  Enr: 15. Day Males 13. Day Females 2. **Staff:** 7. (Full 7).
  Rates 2004: Day $36,500/sch yr.
  Summer Prgm: Day. Educ. Day Rate $2600. 4 wks.
  Est 1963. Private. Nonprofit.

The Elizabeth Ives School offers a therapeutic academic program for children with emotional disturbances and neurological disabilities. Students are grouped according to ability, and the school maintains a student-teacher ratio of 2:1. Boys and girls choose from various therapeutic, prevocational and vocational services.

ST. VINCENT'S SPECIAL NEEDS SERVICES FEROLETO CHILDREN'S DEVELOPMENT CENTER

Res — Coed Ages 3-21; Day — Coed Birth-21

Trumbull, CT 06611. 95 Merritt Blvd.

Tel: 203-375-6400. Fax: 203-380-1190.
www.stvincentsspecialneeds.org   E-mail: feroleto.child.dev@snet.net
Barry Buxbaum, BA, MS, Pres. **Larry Kaplan,** MD, Med Dir.
 Focus: Spec Ed. Treatment. **Conditions:** Primary—Ap Bl CP ON PDD S
  SB. Sec—ADD ADHD Ar As Asp Au B C CF D Db DS Ep HIV IP LD MD
  MR MS Nf.
 Gen Acad. Pre-Voc. Courses: Life_Skills.
 Therapy: Hear Lang Movement Occup Percepual-Motor Phys Play Speech.
 Enr: 70. **Staff:** 65 (Full 52, Part 13). Prof 29. Educ 10.
 Est 1955. Private. Nonprofit.

Serving southern Connecticut, Feroleto Center treats children with cerebral palsy and orthopedic disabilities, as well as those experiencing speech and language difficulties. The program offers a certified educational curriculum for physically handicapped and multi-handicapped children, providing individualized care with a favorable staff-client ratio. Options include early intervention (ages 6wks-3), a preschool (ages 3-5) and a special education school (ages 3-21). In addition, the center offers various therapies and nursing support services. A split programming option, which enables a boy or girl to attend the special education school for part of the week and a public school for the remainder, is also available.

Among auxiliary services are orthopedic, speech and hearing evaluations; therapy; and parent education. The program also operates for part of the summer, thus allowing for continuation of classroom stimulation and therapy schedules.

FORMAN SCHOOL

Res and Day — Coed Ages 13-20

Litchfield, CT 06759. 12 Norfolk Rd, PO Box 80.
Tel: 860-567-8712. Fax: 860-567-3501.
www.formanschool.org   E-mail: admissions@formanschool.org
Mark B. Perkins, BA, MA, Head. **Beth A. Rainey,** Adm.
 Focus: Spec Ed. **Conditions:** Primary—ADD ADHD Dc Dg Dx LD. **IQ 105
  and up.**
 Col Prep. Gen Acad. Gr 9-12. Courses: Read Math Lang_Arts Sci Comput-
  ers Hist Fine_Arts.
 Enr: 162. Res Males 112. Res Females 35. Day Males 11. Day Females 4.
  Staff: 73.
 Rates 2003: Res $39,500/sch yr. Day $31,500/sch yr. Schol avail.
 Est 1930. Private. Nonprofit.

Forman conducts a structured, traditional college preparatory curriculum featuring special language and math training programs designed to meet the needs of secondary school students with learning differences or dyslexia. Extracurricular activities include studio/performing arts projects, required competitive athletics, community service involvement and a mandatory work program.

THE FOUNDATION SCHOOL

Day — Coed Ages 3-21

Orange, CT 06477. 719 Derby-Milford Rd.
Tel: 203-877-1426. Fax: 203-799-4797.
  Conditions: Primary—LD.
  Gen Acad. Ungraded. Courses: Read Math Lang_Arts. Man_Arts & Shop.
    On-Job Trng.
  Est 1966. Private. Nonprofit.

GENGRAS CENTER

Day — Coed Ages 3-21

West Hartford, CT 06117. 1678 Asylum Ave.
Tel: 860-232-5616. Fax: 860-231-6795.
www.sjc.edu
Bernard Lindauer, EdD, Dir.
  Focus: Spec Ed. Trng. **Conditions:** Primary—ADD ADHD Au Dx LD MR
    ON S. Sec—B BD D ED. **IQ 45-110.**
  Gen Acad. Pre-Voc. Voc. Gr K-12. Courses: Read Math Lang_Arts Comput-
    ers Sci Soc_Stud Life_Skills. On-Job Trng.
  Therapy: Hear Lang Occup Phys Speech. **Psychotherapy:** Fam Group
    Indiv Parent.
  Enr: 137. **Staff:** 33 (Full 28, Part 5).
  Est 1963. Private. Nonprofit. Roman Catholic. **Spons:** St. Joseph College.

Gengras is a state-approved, private special education facility serving special-needs children and young adults. The program includes individualized assessment, planning, and the coupling of academic and vocational instruction with behavioral, social and emotional support tailored to the individual's needs. Instructional methodology and programmatic intervention focus upon the child's developmental progression and problem-solving skills. Music, art, computer, library and a structured athletic program complement academics.

The center also serves as a training facility for St. Joseph College students majoring in special education.

GESELL INSTITUTE OF HUMAN DEVELOPMENT

Clinic: Ages 2½-9. M-F 9-5.

New Haven, CT 06511. 310 Prospect St, 2nd Fl.
Tel: 203-777-3481. Fax: 203-776-5001.
www.gesellinstitute.org   E-mail: gesell.inst@worldnet.att.net
Jacqueline Haines, BS, Dir.
  Focus: Treatment. **Conditions:** Primary—ADD ADHD Dx LD. Sec—ED. **IQ
    90 and up.**
  Therapy: Speech Visual. **Psychotherapy:** Fam Group Indiv.

Est 1950. Private. Nonprofit.

Continuing the work of Dr. Arnold Gesell, who founded the Yale Clinic of Child Development in 1911, the institute's main emphasis is on research and clinical work in child development and education. The staff works on creating developmental examinations for preschoolers and school-age children, researching novel approaches to vision and perception and investigating biochemical variations.

There is also a diagnostic service that utilizes the knowledge gained through research. After administering developmental and psychological evaluations, staff members conduct parental consultations.

GRAY LODGE

Res — Females Ages 12-18

Hartford, CT 06105. 105 Spring St.
Tel: 860-522-9363. Fax: 860-525-6800.
Sandra Sunderland, JD, Exec Dir.
  Focus: Spec Ed. Treatment. **Conditions:** Primary—ADD Anx BD CD ED LD Mood OCD ODD PTSD SP. Sec—ADHD Dx Psy Sz. **IQ 70-120.**
  Col Prep. Gen Acad. Pre-Voc. Gr 5-12. Courses: Read Math Lang_Arts Eng Sci Soc_Stud Studio_Art.
  Therapy: Speech. **Psychotherapy:** Fam Group Indiv.
  Enr: 18. Res Females 18. **Staff:** 24 (Full 18, Part 6). Prof 12. Educ 8. Admin 2.
  Rates 2003: Res $144/day.
  Est 1851. State. Nonprofit.

Special education is provided at this facility for adolescent girls with emotional and social disturbances. Residents are offered group, individual and family therapy, as well as life skills training. The usual length of treatment is two years.

GREENWICH HOSPITAL
HEARING, SPEECH AND LANGUAGE CENTER

Clinic: All Ages. M-F 8-5.

Greenwich, CT 06830. 5 Perryridge Rd.
Tel: 203-863-3240. Fax: 203-863-4730.
  Focus: Treatment. **Conditions:** Primary—Ap D Dx LD S. Sec—ADD ADHD Au BI CP MR MS.
  Therapy: Hear Lang Speech.
  Private.

The center conducts hearing evaluations, including impedance audiometry and Brainstem Evoked Response testing. Staff also provide language, speech and voice evaluations. Other services include hearing aid evaluations and the lending and dispensation of hearing aids. In addition, there is a parent-infant training program.

GROVE SCHOOL

Res and Day — Coed Ages 12-18

Madison, CT 06443. 175 Copse Rd, PO Box 646.
Tel: 203-245-2778. Fax: 203-245-6098.
www.groveschool.org   E-mail: info@groveschool.org
Richard L. Chorney, BA, MS, Pres. **Callie Greenbaum,** Prin. **Kathy Kimmel,** Adm.

Focus: Spec Ed. **Conditions:** Primary—Asp BD ED Mood OCD Psy Sz. Sec—Dx LD. **IQ 90 and up.**

Col Prep. Gen Acad. Pre-Voc. Gr 6-PG. Courses: Read Math Sci Hist Computers. Man_Arts & Shop. On-Job Trng.

Therapy: Chemo Hear Lang Phys Speech. **Psychotherapy:** Fam Group Indiv Parent.

Enr: 104. Res Males 57. Res Females 42. Day Males 5. **Staff:** 26.

Rates 2003: Res $70,800/yr (+$1500). Day $54,400/yr (+$500).

Est 1934. Private. Inc.

A psychiatrically oriented boarding school, Grove offers treatment for emotionally disturbed adolescents. The program provides habit patterning, remedial teaching, psychotherapy, graded responsibilities, creative work and socialized noncompetitive play. A treatment plan is individually designed and utilizes reading and mathematics laboratories for remedial and developmental instruction. Courses are available in creative arts, cooking, photography, art, music, higher mathematics, science, computer science and journalism. The program is year-round, with therapeutic and academic work offered during the summer months. Students can earn a high school diploma, and many graduates go on to college.

Grove conducts a therapeutic program that addresses positive lifestyles and focuses on the mind-body connection. Issues covered in this program include sexuality, smoking cessation, yoga, nutrition and the formation of healthy relationships.

The school's arts program features dance, drama, photography and excursions to art exhibitions. A complete noncompetitive sports program on the 90-acre campus emphasizes participation and body development. Off-campus activities include skiing, sailing, scuba diving, mountain climbing, fishing, camping and theater arts.

Transitional dormitories are designed for older adolescents not yet ready to return home. Counseling services are provided, and the usual length of treatment is 18 to 24 months. Mentally retarded, delinquent and violent acting-out youngsters are not accepted.

HIGH ROAD STUDENT LEARNING CENTER

Day — Coed Ages 5-21

Wallingford, CT 06492. 29 Village Ln.
Tel: 203-284-0441. Fax: 203-265-6335.
www.highrdstudentlearningcenter.prodigybiz.com
E-mail: studentlearn.ctr@snet.net
Ellyn Lerner, PhD, Exec Dir. **Karin Bertero,** BA, MS, Educ Dir. **Carol Revill,** Adm.

Focus: Spec Ed. **Conditions:** Primary—ADD ADHD Anx Ap Apr As Asp

Au BI C CP Dg Dx Ep IP LD MD MR MS OCD ON PDD S SB SP TS.
Sec—B CD D Db ED Psy Sz.

Col Prep. Pre-Voc. Voc. Gr 1-12. Courses: Read Math Lang_Arts Sci Computers Soc_Stud Music Drama Life_Skills. On-Job Trng.

Therapy: Hear Lang Occup Phys Speech.

Enr: 86. Day Males 59. Day Females 27. **Staff:** 42 (Full 37, Part 5). Educ 24. Admin 7.

Rates 2003: Day $178/day.

Summer Prgm: Day. Educ. Soc_Skills. Day Rate $145/day. 6 wks.

Est 1977. Private. **Spons:** KIDS 1.

High Road serves students facing learning, language and social challenges. Each pupil follows an individualized educational program based upon his or her assessed needs. Small classes and a favorable faculty-student ratio facilitate progress. Elements of the center's program include a transitional component, integrated computer technology, a behavior management system and related services, and a summer program that can accept pupils from other schools.

Occupational and physical therapy incurs an additional fee.

INSTITUTE OF LIVING
THE GRACE S. WEBB SCHOOL

Day — Coed Ages 5-18

Hartford, CT 06106. 200 Retreat Ave.
Nearby locations: Cheshire.
Tel: 860-545-7238. Fax: 860-545-7037.
www.instituteofliving.org   E-mail: gjohnson@harthosp.org
Surrey Hardcastle, BS, MA, Dir. **Robert Sahl,** MD, Med Dir. **Gary F. Johnson,** Adm.

Focus: Spec Ed. **Conditions:** Primary—AN Anx Asp Au Bu ED Mood OCD ODD PDD Psy PTSD PW SP Sz TS. Sec—ADD ADHD Ap Apr Ar As B BD BI C CD CP D Db Dc Dg DS Dx Ep HIV LD MD MS Nf ON S SB. **IQ 60 and up.**

Gen Acad. Pre-Voc. Gr K-12. Courses: Read Math Lang_Arts Sci Health Life_Skills. On-Job Trng.

Therapy: Chemo Lang Occup Speech. **Psychotherapy:** Fam Group Indiv Parent.

Enr: 170. **Staff:** 95 (Full 85, Part 10).

Rates 2003: Day $215-275/day. State Aid.

Summer Prgm: Day. Educ. Rec. 4 wks.

Est 1822. Private. Nonprofit. **Spons:** Hartford Hospital.

The school's primary emphasis is the diagnosis, treatment and education of children in the Greater Hartford area who have emotional disturbances. Children with learning disabilities and perceptual disorders may also enroll in the program. Boys and girls have access to a range of diagnostic and assessment services, and the Institute of Living provides such ancillary services as clinical case management, outreach, and community-based educational and behavioral consultations.

The Grace S. Webb School accepts students in grades K-12, and the institute operates two satellite schools. The Webb School at Cheshire (725 Jarvis St., Cheshire 06410; 203-

272-8395) serves children in grades K-8, while the Webb School at West Hartford (11 Wampanoag Dr., West Hartford 06117; 860-714-9250) enrolls boys and girls in grades 7-12.

INTENSIVE EDUCATION ACADEMY

Day — Coed Ages 6-21

West Hartford, CT 06117. 840 N Main St.
Tel: 860-236-2049. Fax: 860-231-2843.
www.intensiveeducationacademy.org
Sr. Helen Dowd, CSJ, Exec Dir.
Focus: Spec Ed. **Conditions:** Primary—LD.
Gen Acad. Pre-Voc. Gr K-12. Courses: Read Math Lang_Arts Sci Computers Soc_Stud Studio_Art Music.
Therapy: Lang Occup Speech. **Psychotherapy:** Fam.
Enr: 50. Day Males 38. Day Females 12. **Staff:** 21 (Full 17, Part 4).
Summer Prgm: Day. Educ. 6 wks.
Est 1971. Private. Nonprofit.

IEA serves children who have learning disabilities. The school, which maintains a low student-teacher ratio, attempts to help children gain confidence, recognize their strengths and weaknesses, and set and reach realistic goals. Activities such as music, art, cooking and drama supplement academics and promote leadership qualities and organizational skills development.

LAKE GROVE AT DURHAM

Res — Coed Ages 8-21

Durham, CT.
Contact: 3390 Rte 112, PO Box 786, Medford, NY 11763.
Tel: 631-205-1950. Fax: 631-205-9439.
www.lgstc.org   E-mail: lgtcadmissions@lgstc.org
Albert A. Brayson II, MEd, Pres. **John M. De Figueiredo,** MD, Med Dir.
Focus: Trng. Treatment. **Conditions:** Primary—ED. Sec—BD BI LD MR.
Gen Acad. Pre-Voc. Voc. Gr 4-12. Ungraded. Courses: Read Math Lang_Arts. Man_Arts & Shop. Shelt_Workshop. On-Job Trng.
Therapy: Chemo Hear Lang Occup Phys Speech. **Psychotherapy:** Fam Group Indiv.
Est 1985. Private. Nonprofit.

THE LEARNING CLINIC

Res and Day — Coed Ages 6-21

Brooklyn, CT 06234. Rte 169, PO Box 324.
Tel: 860-774-1036. Fax: 860-774-1037.

www.thelearningclinic.org   E-mail: admissions@thelearningclinic.org
Raymond W. DuCharme, PhD, Exec Dir. **Katie McGrady,** PsyD, Clin Dir.
Laurie Bell, Adm.
   Focus: Spec Ed. Treatment. **Conditions:** Primary—ADD ADHD Anx Asp
      BD Dc Dg Dx ED LD Mood OCD PDD PTSD SP TS. **IQ 85 and up.**
   Gen Acad. Pre-Voc. Gr K-12. Courses: Read Math Lang_Arts Soc_Skills.
      On-Job Trng.
   Therapy: Art Chemo Milieu Music Recreational Speech. **Psychotherapy:**
      Fam Group Indiv Parent.
   Enr: 65. **Staff:** 32. Educ 23. Admin 2.
   Rates 2003: Res $143/day. Day $134/day. Schol 1. State Aid.
   Summer Prgm: Res & Day. Educ. Ther. 6-12 wks.
   Est 1980. Private. Nonprofit.

TLC offers various educational, therapeutic and medical services to pupils of average to above-average IQ who have not previously achieved to potential due to mood or behavioral disorders, learning disabilities, attentional disorders, Asperger's syndrome or Tourette's syndrome. Instructors formulate individualized educational programming and prepare daily lessons for each student. The clinic does not accept violent individuals.

The TLC Country School provides a full residential and day program for elementary and secondary pupils. The research-based, therapeutic approach seeks to improve learning skills, mood and attention span. Clearly defined goals are a program characteristic.

For an additional daily fee, students at the school may participate in a social skills workshop that operates at the end of the regular school day. The boarding program includes such activities as horseback riding, canoeing, fishing, skiing and wilderness camping. All pupils go on occasional field trips.

THE MID-FAIRFIELD CHILD GUIDANCE CENTER

Clinic: Ages Birth-18. M-F 8:30-5; Eves M-W 5-8, Th 5-6.

Norwalk, CT 06851. 100 East Ave.
Tel: 203-299-1315. Fax: 203-299-0015.
www.mfcgc.org
Stuart Greenbaum, MA, MSW, Exec Dir. **Andrew Lustbader,** MD, Med Dir.
   Focus: Treatment. **Conditions:** Primary—ADD ADHD Au BD CD Dx ED LD
      Mood OCD Psy Sz. Sec—MR.
   Therapy: Art Movement Recreational. **Psychotherapy:** Fam Group Indiv
      Parent.
   Staff: 19 (Full 15, Part 4). Prof 15. Admin 4.
   Rates 2003: Sliding-Scale Rate $5-125/ses.
   Summer Prgm: Day. Ther. 6 wks.
   Est 1957. Private. Nonprofit.

Diagnosis and treatment are offered to children and their families at Mid-Fairfield, and psychological evaluations are made when needed. Treatment services include play, couples, family, child and parent, and group therapies. A preschool therapeutic program is offered to children under age 6. Also available are emergency psychiatric services, a sexual and physical abuse treatment program, extended day treatment and preventive services.

All fees are based upon the client's ability to pay. The center serves Wilton, Westport, Weston, Norwalk, Darien and New Canaan.

ST. FRANCIS CARE BEHAVIORAL HEALTH
Res and Day — Coed Ages 4-21

Hartford, CT 06112. 500 Blue Hills Ave.
Tel: 860-342-0480.
www.stfranciscare.org
　　Conditions: Primary—BD ED Mood OCD Psy Sz TS. Sec—ADD ADHD Dx LD. **IQ 74 and up.**
　　Gen Acad. Gr K-12. Courses: Read Math Lang_Arts Sci.
　　Therapy: Hear Lang Occup Speech. **Psychotherapy:** Fam Group Indiv Parent.
　　Enr: 225. **Staff:** 70.
　　Ther.
　　Private. Nonprofit. **Spons:** Saint Francis Hospital and Medical Center.

SFCBH's educational program designs individualized educational plans for its clients. These plans are behavioral-objective in approach and emphasize providing the student with opportunities to learn in a nonthreatening environment that allows for achievement and success.

　　Adolescents who will be hospitalized for at least five days and who intend to pursue a formalized secondary education participate in the Adolescent Service Educational Program. A psycho-educational team conducts core subject and specific individualized remedial instruction. Family involvement is strongly encouraged in SFCBH's educational programs.

ST. FRANCIS HOME FOR CHILDREN
Res — Males Ages 8-18; Day — Coed 6-15

New Haven, CT 06511. 651 Prospect St.
Tel: 203-777-5513. Fax: 203-777-0644.
Peter T. Salerno, MBA, Exec Dir. **Ivan Torrence Tate, Sr.,** Prgm Dir. **Enid Peterson,** MSW, Clin Dir. **Tammy Paglia,** Adm.
　　Focus: Treatment. **Conditions:** Primary—ADD ADHD BD CD ED Mood. Sec—As Dx OCD. **IQ 70 and up.**
　　Gen Acad. Gr PS-12. Courses: Read Math Lang_Arts. Man_Arts & Shop.
　　Therapy: Speech. **Psychotherapy:** Fam Group Indiv.
　　Enr: 77. Res Males 52. Day Males 17. Day Females 8. **Staff:** 108 (Full 92, Part 16). Prof 24. Educ 8. Admin 12.
　　Rates 2004: Res $57,159/yr. Day $13,300-36,200/yr. State Aid.
　　Est 1962. Private. Nonprofit. Roman Catholic.

　　St. Francis accepts mildly emotionally disturbed and socially disordered youths. Borderline personalities who tend mostly toward acting out their difficulties through hostility and aggression, stealing, abnormal fears, school phobia, depression and neurotic anxiety receive treatment in anticipation of a return to their own homes or to foster homes. A structured living setting offers a protected therapeutic environment to identify problems in social interaction and to contribute to effective treatment and growth.

The usual duration of treatment is nine to 18 months. St. Francis Home does not accept handicapped, mentally retarded, drug or alcohol addicted, or severely acting-out individuals.

SARAH

Day — Coed Ages 16 and up

Guilford, CT 06437. 246 Goose Ln, Ste 101.
Tel: 203-458-4040. Fax: 203-458-4050.
www.sarah-inc.org   E-mail: info@sarah-inc.org
Stephen E. Morris, Exec Dir.
   Focus: Trng. Treatment. **Conditions:** Primary—MR. Sec—ADD ADHD Ap As Au B BD BI C CD CP D Dx ED Ep IP LD MD MS OCD ON Psy S SB Sz TB.
   Staff: 100.
   Est 1957. Private. Nonprofit.

This organization for individuals with developmental disabilities provides advocacy and day services as recreational opportunities, vocational training, job placement, elderly enrichment and respite care. SARAH serves Connecticut's central shoreline area.

SARAH has two sister agencies that provide residential services. SARAH Seneca is located in Branford and SARAH Tuxis is located in Guilford.

SETON ACADEMY

Day — Coed Ages 11-21

Westport, CT 06880. 47 Long Lots Rd.
Tel: 203-341-4506. Fax: 203-227-9526.
Susan D. Steneck, PhD, Dir. **Thomas Smith,** MD, Med Dir.
   Focus: Spec Ed. **Conditions:** Primary—ADD ADHD Anx Asp BD Dc Dg Dx ED LD Mood OCD ODD PDD Psy PTSD SP Sz TS. Sec—AN Ap B Bu D Ep MR S. **IQ 80 and up.**
   Gen Acad. Gr 6-12. Courses: Read Math Lang_Arts Sci Computers Soc_ Stud Studio_Art Music.
   Therapy: Art Milieu Music. **Psychotherapy:** Group Indiv Parent.
   Enr: 32. Day Males 15. Day Females 17. **Staff:** 10 (Full 9, Part 1).
   Rates 2004: Day $250/day.
   Summer Prgm: Day. Educ. Ther. Day Rate $250/day. 6 wks.
   Est 1898. Private. Nonprofit. Roman Catholic. **Spons:** Hall-Brooke Behavioral Health Services.

Seton provides an individualized educational program for students with emotional disorders or learning or adjustment problems. The academy attempts to mainstream the student and works closely with home school systems. Educational services are also available to students hospitalized at the Hall-Brooke Hospital with more severe adjustment and psychiatric problems, including psychosis. An individualized program for each patient includes group, family and individual treatment.

SOUTHERN CONNECTICUT STATE UNIVERSITY CENTER FOR COMMUNICATION DISORDERS

Res — Males Ages Birth-21
Clinic: All Ages. M-F 8-5; Eves M-F 5-7.

New Haven, CT 06515. 501 Crescent St.
Tel: 203-392-5954. Fax: 203-392-5968.
www.southernct.edu/departments/communicationdisorders
Kevin M. McNamara, Dir.
   Focus: Rehab. Treatment. **Conditions:** Primary—Ap Apr Asp Au Bl S.
      Sec—ADD ADHD AN Anx As B BD Bu C CD CP D Db Dc Dg DS Dx ED
      Ep HIV IP LD MD Mood MR MS Nf OCD ON PDD Psy PTSD PW SB SP
      Sz TB.
   Therapy: Hear Lang Speech.
   Staff: 27 (Full 12, Part 15). Prof 26. Admin 1.
   Rates 2003: Clinic $10-50/ses.
   State.

Diagnosis and treatment of speech, language, voice and fluency, as well as audiological evaluation, are among the services offered at the center.

TUTORING AND COUNSELING CENTER OF CONNECTICUT

Clinic: Ages 4 and up. M-S 9-5; Eves M-S 5-6:30.

Bridgeport, CT 06604. 893 Clinton Ave.
Tel: 203-333-2611.
Beverly Larson Smith, MS, Dir.
   Focus: Spec Ed. **Conditions:** Primary—DS ED MR OH. Sec—ADD ADHD
      As BD Bl Bu C Dc Dg Dx LD S. **IQ 60 and up.**
   Gen Acad. Ungraded. Courses: Read Math Lang_Arts.
   Therapy: Lang Occup Percepual-Motor Speech. **Psychotherapy:** Fam
      Group Indiv Parent.
   Staff: 10. (Part 10). Prof 10. Educ 10.
   Rates 2003: Sliding-Scale Rate $35-50/ses.
   Est 1952. Private.

Bridgeport provides a program of psychological, educational, family and speech therapies, as well as academic tutoring. Diagnostic, academic, career and psycho-educational testing, in addition to family and individual therapy, is available. The center also offers educational and career counseling.

UNITED SERVICES
CHILD GUIDANCE CENTER

Clinic: Ages Birth-18. M-F 9-5; Eves M-Th 5-9.

Dayville, CT 06241. 1007 N Main St, PO Box 839.
Tel: 860-774-2020. Fax: 860-774-0826.
www.unitedservicesct.org   E-mail: mail@unitedservicesct.org
Diane L. Manning, MBA, Pres. **Karen B. King,** MSW, Prgm Dir. **J. Patel,** MD, Med Dir.
   Focus: Rehab. Treatment. **Conditions:** Primary—BD CD ED OCD Psy Sz. Sec—B D MR. **IQ 60-110.**
   Psychotherapy: Fam Group Indiv Parent.
   Staff: 17. (Full 17). Prof 16. Admin 1.
   Rates 2001: Clinic $90-150/ses. Sliding-Scale Rate $10-150/session.
   Est 1964. Private. Nonprofit.

This center provides diagnosis, evaluation and treatment (including psychological testing and psychopharmacology) through a multidisciplinary approach. Individual, group and family counseling and therapy are offered. Crisis intervention and educational and support services are available, as are evaluation and treatment for victims of sexual abuse. Other services provided either through the center or by contractual arrangement include alcohol and drug abuse prevention, educational and early intervention programs. The usual duration of treatment is three to 12 months.

Branches of the center operate at 132 Mansfield Ave., Willimantic 06226; 233 Rte. 6, Columbia 06237; and 303 Putnam Rd., Wauregan 06387.

VILLA MARIA EDUCATION CENTER

Day — Coed Ages 5-14

Stamford, CT 06903. 161 Sky Meadow Dr.
Tel: 203-322-5886. Fax: 203-322-0228.
www.villamariaedcenter.org   E-mail: mshogan@optonline.net
Sr. Carol Ann, OSF, MA, Exec Dir. **Dana L. Hogan,** Adm.
   Focus: Spec Ed. **Conditions:** Primary—Dc Dg Dx LD. Sec—ADD ADHD. **IQ 90 and up.**
   Gen Acad. Gr 1-8. Courses: Read Math Lang_Arts Sci Computers Soc_Stud Studio_Art Music Study_Skills.
   Therapy: Lang Occup Phys Speech.
   Enr: 76. Day Males 40. Day Females 36. **Staff:** 29 (Full 24, Part 5).
   Rates 2003: Day $25,750/sch yr. Schol 15 ($15,000). State Aid.
   Est 1973. Private. Nonprofit. Roman Catholic.

Founded as an after-school and summer program, the center eventually instituted a full-time day school for children with specific learning disabilities in the areas of language arts, math and perception. The program utilizes a holistic approach within the context of a small, highly structured learning environment. The individualized, experiential program is flexible enough to accommodate pupils of varying learning styles, personalities, interests and levels of learning.

The nongraded educational program serves students of average to above-average intelligence who are emotionally sound and motivated to learn, but who have not achieved to potential in traditional school settings. In addition to language arts and math courses (in which a 5:1 teacher-student ratio is maintained), Villa Maria offers science, social studies, music, art, computer, language development, study skills, and auditory and visual perception in small groupings based primarily on grade level.

In addition to academics, the school places significant emphasis on the child's emotional and social growth. A formal social skills program, operated along with a guidance program and the student council, provides opportunities for strengthening relationships and developing communicational and leadership skills, responsibility and integrity.

WATERFORD COUNTRY SCHOOL

Res and Day — Coed Ages 10-18

Quaker Hill, CT 06375. 78 Hunts Brook Rd, PO Box 408.
Tel: 860-442-9454. Fax: 860-442-2228.
www.waterfordcountryschool.org
David B. Moorehead, MA, MSW, Exec Dir.
   Focus: Spec Ed. Treatment. **Conditions:** Primary—BD ED. Sec—As BI CD
      CP Dx Ep LD MD MR MS OCD ON Psy TB. **IQ 80 and up.**
   Gen Acad. Pre-Voc. Voc. Ungraded. Courses: Read Math Lang_Arts.
      Shelt_Workshop. On-Job Trng.
   Therapy: Lang Speech. **Psychotherapy:** Fam Group Indiv Parent.
   Enr: 76. **Staff:** 106.
   Est 1922. Private. Nonprofit.

Located on a 350-acre campus, Waterford serves students with mild to severe emotional and learning problems through year-round treatment. Diagnostic-prescriptive techniques are used in the on-grounds school to match each child's program with his or her needs and abilities. Tutorial speech and reading assistance is provided, and there is an opportunity for work experiences both on grounds and in the community. A day school is available for students not requiring intensive residential care. Psychiatric and psychological services are integrated into the entire program and are available on individual, group and crisis bases. Some children attend nearby public schools.

The recreational program includes sports, social activities and hobbies. Arts, crafts, music, farming, horseback riding, swimming and physical education are part of this program. Outpatient and counseling services are available. The usual length of treatment is 14 months, and nonambulatory, blind, deaf and severely acting-out students are not accepted.

DELAWARE

ADVOSERV

Res and Day — Coed Ages 8 and up

Bear, DE 19701. 4185 Kirkwood-St Georges Rd.
Tel: 302-834-7018. Fax: 302-836-2516.
www.advoserv.com
Greg Harrison, MA, Dir. **Dennis Reardon,** Adm.
   Focus: Treatment. **Conditions:** Primary—Au BD CD ED MR OCD Psy.
      Sec—ADD ADHD Dx LD OH.
   Gen Acad. Pre-Voc. Ungraded. Courses: Read Math Lang_Arts.
   Est 1969. Private.

The facility provides both residential and day services for children, adolescents and adults. One part of the program serves individuals with developmental disabilities such as autism, mental retardation and mental health issues, while another part addresses the needs of those with severe emotional disturbances and conduct disorders. AdvoServ also offers intensive treatment for behavioral problems. Emphasis is placed on educational achievement as an alternative to behavioral difficulties and an integral factor in the pupil's future success.

Residents live in several area group homes. Living arrangements accommodate varying degrees of independence.

AdvoServ conducts similar programs in Florida and New Jersey.

CEDARS ACADEMY

Res — Coed Ages 10-18

Bridgeville, DE 19933. PO Box 103.
Tel: 302-337-3200. Fax: 302-337-8496.
www.cedarsacademy.com
Mary-Margaret Pauer, BS, MEd, Exec Dir.
   Focus: Spec Ed. **Conditions:** Primary—ADD ADHD. Sec—Ar As Db. **IQ**
      110 and up.
   Col Prep. Gr 5-12. Courses: Read Math Lang_Arts Sci Hist Studio_Art
      Music Health.
   Enr: 40. Res Males 32. Res Females 8. **Staff:** 15 (Full 14, Part 1). Prof 14.
      Educ 14.
   Rates 2004: Res $34,100/sch yr (+$500).
   Summer Prgm: Res. Educ. Rec. Res Rate $7050. 7 wks.
   Est 1989. Private. **Spons:** Aspen Education Group.

Students who attend Cedars tend to encounter difficulties in focusing, sequencing and organization. The main program focus is social and behavior recognition. The traditional college preparatory curriculum features all standard subjects.

CENTREVILLE SCHOOL

Day — Coed Ages 4-14

Centreville, DE 19807. 6201 Kennett Pike.
Tel: 302-571-0230. Fax: 302-571-0270.
www.centrevilleschool.org   E-mail: information@centrevilleschool.org
  Focus: Spec Ed. **Conditions:** Primary—ADD ADHD Dx LD. **IQ 100 and up.**
  Gen Acad. Ungraded. Courses: Read Math Lang_Arts Computers Sci Soc_
    Stud Studio_Art Music.
  Therapy: Lang Occup Speech.
  Enr: 120. **Staff:** 28 (Full 20, Part 8).
  Est 1974. Private.

Centreville provides an elementary program for children of average to above-average intelligence who have learning disabilities. To facilitate individualized instruction, the school limits classes of younger students to six or seven; as pupils get older, the maximum class size increases to ten. Instructors teach children strategies to compensate for their learning disabilities, and the program emphasizes self-esteem development. Centreville's teaching approach provides each pupil with a team of specialists that work together to ameliorate areas of weakness and build on existing strengths.

Reading forms the foundation of the curriculum. At all grade levels, a specialized and systematic reading course is integral to the school day. Computers are an important learning tool for writing and review. In addition to the core subjects, the school offers a varied arts program that includes drawing, painting, sculpture, building, acting and singing. Students improve fitness and life skills in physical education classes.

DELAWARE GUIDANCE SERVICES
FOR CHILDREN AND YOUTH

Clinic: Ages 3-18. M-F 8:30-5; Eves M-Th 5-8.

Wilmington, DE 19806. 1213 Delaware Ave.
  Nearby locations: Dover; Lewes; Newark; Seaford.
Tel: 302-652-3948. Fax: 302-652-8297.
www.delawareguidance.org
Bruce Kelsey, LCSW, Exec Dir. **Carl Chenkin,** PhD, Clin Dir. **Deborah May-**
  broda, Intake.
  Focus: Treatment. **Conditions:** Primary—ADD ADHD Anx BD CD ED.
    Sec—MR.
  Psychotherapy: Fam Group Indiv Parent.
  Staff: 150 (Full 92, Part 58). Prof 55. Admin 28.
  Rates 2004: Clinic $85/ses.
  Est 1953. Private. Nonprofit.

The clinic offers outpatient psychiatric and psychological services for children with emotional disturbances and their families. The following services are available: comprehensive assessment; psychological and psychiatric evaluation; individual, group and family counseling; parent education; adult counseling; family and school liaison work; and, when necessary, medication.

In addition to the Wilmington location, DGS offers services through the following centers: 103 Mont Blanc Blvd., Dover 19904 (302-678-3020); 1208 Drummond Plz., Bldg. 1, Newark 19711 (302-455-9333); and 224 Coastal Hwy., Lewes 19958 (302-645-5338); and 8893 Middleford Rd., Ste. 303, Seaford 19973 (302-262-3505).

EDUCATIONAL SERVICE

Clinic: Ages 3-18. M-Sa 9-5, Su 12-5; Eves M-F 6-8:30.

Wilmington, DE 19803. 1701 Augustine Cut-Off, Ste 11.
Tel: 302-655-6283. Fax: 302-655-6284.
www.educationalservice.org E-mail: tmm@educationalservice.org
Tina Maida Masington, BA, Dir. **Sue Richle,** Adm.
    Focus: Spec Ed. **Conditions:** Primary—ADD ADHD Dc Dg Dx LD. Sec—MR. **IQ 75 and up.**
    Col Prep. Gen Acad. Gr PS-12. Courses: Read Math Lang_Arts.
    Staff: 91 (Full 2, Part 89).
    Rates 2003: Clinic $34-50/hr.
    Est 1935. Private. Inc.

Students with such learning disabilities as dyslexia, dyscalculia, dysgraphia and attentional disorders receive remedial tutoring at this clinic. One-on-one tutorials are available in reading, language arts, mathematics, other academic disciplines and test preparation. The facility also offers job-related tutorial support for its adult clients. Ancillary services include diagnostic and educational testing, parental counseling and contracted tutorial services to schools.

Summer services comprise one-on-one tutorials, diagnostic testing services and various small workshops. Offerings focus upon such areas as math skills, word analysis, reading comprehension, study and test-taking skills, speed-reading and SAT preparation.

JOHN G. LEACH SCHOOL

Day — Coed Ages 3-21

New Castle, DE 19720. Landers Ln.
Tel: 302-429-4055. Fax: 302-429-4057.
http://issm.doe.state.de.us/profiles/EntitySearch.ASPx
John J. Jadach, Prin.
    Conditions: Primary—B MR OH.
    Gen Acad. Gr PS-12. Courses: Read Math Lang_Arts. Man_Arts & Shop. Shelt_Workshop.
    Therapy: Hear Lang Music Occup Phys Speech. **Psychotherapy:** Indiv.
    Est 1951. State. Nonprofit.

JOHN S. CHARLTON SCHOOL

Day — Coed Ages 3-21

Dover, DE 19934. 278 Sorghum Mill Rd.
Tel: 302-697-3103. Fax: 302-697-4998.
Pamela A. Atchison, Prin.
   Focus: Spec Ed. Conditions: Primary—Au MR. IQ 15-50.
   Therapy: Occup Phys Speech.
   Enr: 170. Day Males 119. Day Females 51. Staff: 90. Prof 39. Educ 34.
      Admin 2.
   Rates 2003: No Fee.
   State.

The school accepts all ambulatory, trainable mentally retarded and autistic children of Kent County. Students receive speech, occupational and physical therapy, as well as meet with the school's psychologists. Charlton operates 217 days over a 12-month period.

MARGARET S. STERCK SCHOOL
DELAWARE SCHOOL FOR THE DEAF

Res — Coed Ages 6-21; Day — Coed Birth-21

Newark, DE 19713. 620 E Chestnut Hill Rd.
Tel: 302-454-2301. TTY: 302-454-2301. Fax: 302-454-3493.
www.christina.k12.de.us/sterck
Edward H. Bosso, Jr., Dir.
   Conditions: Primary—D.
   Col Prep. Gen Acad. Pre-Voc. Voc. Ungraded. Courses: Read Math Lang_
      Arts. Man_Arts & Shop. On-Job Trng.
   Est 1929. State. Nonprofit.

THE MARY CAMPBELL CENTER

Res — Coed Ages 16 and up; Day — Coed 3 and up

Wilmington, DE 19803. 4641 Weldin Rd.
Tel: 302-762-6025. Fax: 302-762-4206.
www.marycampbellcenter.org
Jerry Spilecki, Exec Dir.
   Conditions: Primary—MR OH. IQ 50 and up.
   Gen Acad. Ungraded. Courses: Read Math Lang_Arts.
   Therapy: Hear Hydro Occup Phys Speech.
   Est 1976. Private. Nonprofit.

OPPORTUNITY CENTER

Day — Coed Ages 18 and up

Wilmington, DE 19802. 3030 Bowers St.
Tel: 302-762-0300. Fax: 302-762-8797.
www.oppctr.com
    Conditions: Primary—MR.
    Voc. Shelt_Workshop. On-Job Trng.
    Est 1957. Private. Nonprofit.

THE PILOT SCHOOL

Day — Coed Ages 5-14

Wilmington, DE 19803. 100 Garden of Eden Rd.
Tel: 302-478-1740. Fax: 302-478-1746.
www.familyeducation.com/de/pilotschool   **E-mail: pilotskool@aol.com**
Kathleen B. Craven, MEd, Dir.
    Focus: Spec Ed. **Conditions:** Primary—ADD ADHD Dx LD. **IQ 90 and up.**
    Gen Acad. Gr K-8. Courses: Read Math Lang_Arts Computers Sci Soc_
      Stud Lib_Skills.
    Therapy: Lang Music Occup Phys Speech. **Psychotherapy:** Fam Parent.
    Enr: 163. Day Males 122. Day Females 41. **Staff:** 49 (Full 48, Part 1).
    Rates 2003: Day $18,226/sch yr. Schol avail. State Aid.
    Est 1957. Private. Nonprofit.

A private day school for children of normal ability who are experiencing learning problems, Pilot School offers and individualized program with instruction in small groups and prescriptive teaching. The core of instruction is in language arts and mathematics; however, basic skills weaknesses in auditory, visual-perceptual and memory areas are also addressed. The school tailors each child's program to his or her level of ability and particular learning needs. The student-teacher ratio is approximately 5:1. Reading consultants work with the classroom teacher and the individual child.

The school's program also includes a full range of therapeutic and support services.

DISTRICT OF COLUMBIA

ARMY AUDIOLOGY AND SPEECH CENTER
Clinic: All Ages. M-F 7:45-4:30.

Washington, DC 20307. Walter Reed Army Medical Center, 6825 Georgia
  Ave NW.
Tel: 202-782-3501.
www.wramc.amedd.army.mil/departments/aasc
Col. David W. Chandler, PhD, Dir.
  Focus: Treatment. **Conditions:** Primary—Ap S.
  Therapy: Hear Lang Speech.
  Staff: 34.
  Est 1945. Federal. **Spons:** Walter Reed Army Medical Center.

Military personnel and dependents may receive aural rehabilitation, diagnostic speech
pathology, clinical audiology services and a special treatment program for stuttering.
AASC also conducts research.

COLUMBIA LIGHTHOUSE FOR THE BLIND
Clinic: All Ages. M-F by Appt.

Washington, DC 20036. 1120 20th St NW, Ste 750 S.
  Nearby locations: Riverdale, MD.
Tel: 202-454-6400. **Fax:** 202-454-6401.
www.clb.org   **E-mail:** info@clb.org
Dale T. Otto, Pres. **Heidi Bowie,** MD, Med Dir.
  Focus: Rehab. Treatment. **Conditions:** Primary—B.
  Therapy: Visual. **Psychotherapy:** Parent.
  Staff: 28.
  Summer Prgm: Res & Day. Educ. Rec. Res Rate $0. Day Rate $0. 1-2 wks.
  Est 1900. Private. Nonprofit.

Columbia Lighthouse helps individuals who are blind or visually impaired to attain or
maintain independence at home, school, work and in the community. Offerings include
early intervention services, training and consultation, summer camps, career placement
services, comprehensive low-vision care and various rehabilitation services.

The facility also coordinates services through a nearby office in Riverdale, MD (6200
Baltimore Ave., Ste. 100, 20737; 240-737-5100).

DEVEREUX CHILDREN'S CENTER OF WASHINGTON
Res and Day — Coed Ages 6-12

Washington, DC 20007. 3050 R St NW.
Tel: 202-282-1200. **Fax:** 202-282-1219.

Focus: Spec Ed. Trng. Treatment. **Conditions:** Primary—ADD Anx CD LD ODD PTSD.
Therapy: Lang Milieu Occup Recreational Speech. **Psychotherapy:** Fam Group Indiv.
Private.

See Also Page 1025

EPISCOPAL CENTER FOR CHILDREN

Day — Coed Ages 5½-12

Washington, DC 20015. 5901 Utah Ave NW.
Tel: 202-363-1333. Fax: 202-537-5044.
Alan C. Korz, MA, MSW, Exec Dir. **Harold Plotsky,** MD, Med Dir.
    Focus: Spec Ed. Treatment. **Conditions:** Primary—ADD ADHD Anx Dx ED LD Mood OCD ODD PTSD PW SP. Sec—BD. **IQ 80 and up.**
    Gen Acad. Ungraded. Courses: Read Math Lang_Arts.
    Therapy: Art Chemo Lang Milieu Music Occup Play Recreational Speech.
    Psychotherapy: Fam Group Indiv Parent.
    Enr: 60. Day Males 48. Day Females 12. **Staff:** 63 (Full 47, Part 16).
    Rates 2003: Day $39,690/sch yr. Schol 2 ($21,000). State Aid.
    Est 1959. Private. Nonprofit. **Spons:** United Way.

The Episcopal Center, which operates from September through July, offers therapeutic educational experiences for moderately to severely emotionally disturbed children and emphasizes relationships in small-group living.

Placement in an individualized academic program is arranged once the child is admitted to the center. Reading, art therapy, music therapy, a workshop and athletics supplement the educational program.

Parents are expected to be involved in the treatment process and to participate in casework. The usual length of treatment is two to three years. Psychotic and mentally retarded children are not accepted.

HOSPITAL FOR SICK CHILDREN

Day — Coed Ages Birth-21

Washington, DC 20017. 1731 Bunker Hill Rd NE.
Tel: 202-832-4400. TTY: 202-832-7848. Fax: 202-529-1646.
www.hfscsite.org
Deborah T. Zients, COO. **Robert Blake,** Med Dir.
    Conditions: Primary—Ap As Au B BI C CP D Ep IP MD MR MS ON S SB.
    Therapy: Hear Lang Occup Phys Speech. **Psychotherapy:** Fam Indiv.
    Staff: Prof 35.
    Est 1888. Private. Nonprofit.

HOWARD UNIVERSITY
CHILD DEVELOPMENT CENTER

Clinic: Ages Birth-18. M-F 8:30-4:30.

Washington, DC 20060. 525 Bryant St NW, Ste 100.
Tel: 202-806-6973.TTY: 202-806-6973. Fax: 202-806-7940.
www.huhosp.org/patient_care/child_dev.htm
  Conditions: Primary—Ap B Bl C CP D Dx Ep IP LD MD MR MS ON S SB.
  Therapy: Hear Lang Speech. **Psychotherapy:** Indiv.
  Private.

KENDALL DEMONSTRATION ELEMENTARY SCHOOL

Day — Coed Ages Birth-15

Washington, DC 20002. 800 Florida Ave NE.
Tel: 202-651-5031.TTY: 202-651-5031. Fax: 202-651-5101.
http://clerccenter.gallaudet.edu/kdes
  E-mail: admissions.kdes@gallaudet.edu
Marilyn Farmer, Prin.
  Conditions: Primary—D.
  Gen Acad. Pre-Voc. Gr PS-8. Courses: Read Math Lang_Arts. Man_Arts &
  Shop.
  Therapy: Occup Phys.
  Est 1856. Federal. Nonprofit. **Spons:** Gallaudet University.

THE KINGSBURY CENTER

Day — Coed Ages 5-16
Clinic: All Ages. M-F 9-5.

Washington, DC 20008. 5000 14th St NW.
Tel: 202-722-5555. Fax: 202-722-5533.
www.kingsbury.org   E-mail: center@kingsbury.org
Carolyn Atkinson Thornell, BA, MA, Exec Dir.
  Focus: Spec Ed. Treatment. **Conditions:** Primary—ADD ADHD Dx LD.
  Sec—As ED Ep SB. **IQ 90 and up.**
  Gen Acad. Ungraded. Courses: Read Math Lang_Arts.
  Therapy: Hear Lang Occup Phys Speech. **Psychotherapy:** Fam Group
  Indiv Parent.
  Enr: 121. Day Males 88. Day Females 33. **Staff:** 61 (Full 46, Part 15).
  Rates 2004: $1500-2400 (Evaluation)/ses.
  Summer Prgm: Day. Educ. Rec. Ther. 6 wks.
  Est 1938. Private. Nonprofit.

  The Kingsbury Center offers complete diagnostic testing services, as well as individual and small-group remedial tutoring, to individuals of all ages. The center also con-

ducts psycho-educational and neuropsychological evaluations for both students enrolled in the day school program and other clients. Tutors trained in diagnostic prescriptive teaching methods provide remediation to clients with learning difficulties based on their learning style.

The Kingsbury Day School offers intensive intervention for students of average and above average intelligence with learning disabilities. Occupational therapy, speech and language therapy and psychotherapy are available on site and are integrated with classroom learning. Students enrolled in the day school program either advance to another appropriate school or return to the community.

THE LAB SCHOOL OF WASHINGTON

Day — Coed Ages 5-19

Washington, DC 20007. 4759 Reservoir Rd NW.
Tel: 202-965-6600. Fax: 202-965-5105.
www.labschool.org
Sally L. Smith, BA, MA, Dir. **Susan F. Feeley,** Adm.
  Focus: Spec Ed. **Conditions:** Primary—ADD ADHD Dc Dg Dx LD. **IQ 90 and up.**
  Col Prep. Gen Acad. Gr K-12. Courses: Read Math Lang_Arts Span Studio_Art Film Drama Music Dance.
  Therapy: Lang Occup Speech. **Psychotherapy:** Group Indiv.
  Enr: 328. Day Males 213. Day Females 115. **Staff:** 92.
  Rates 2003: Day $22,000-23,600/sch yr.
  Summer Prgm: Day. Educ. Rec. Ther. Day Rate $2100. 5 wks.
  Est 1967. Private. Nonprofit.

The Lab School is designed for elementary and secondary students of average or above intelligence who have moderate to severe learning disabilities. Students spend half the day in classrooms in individualized prescriptive programs and half the day learning academic skills through the art forms (graphics, woodwork, ceramics, music, dance, drama, filmmaking and photography).

History, geography, civics and academic readiness skills are taught through a method called Academic Clubs. Commercial enterprises, a restaurant program, swimming, driver education and sex education are features of the junior high program. High school students earn academic credit in a college preparatory program, graduating with high school diplomas. Tutoring, diagnostic services, and speech and language therapy are available to persons of all ages.

The summer program combines academics, recreation, and speech-language and occupational therapy. Scholarships are available for summer students only. In addition, the Lab School provides a night school program and career guidance services for adults with learning disabilities.

LT. JOSEPH P. KENNEDY INSTITUTE

Day — Coed Ages Birth-21
Clinic: All Ages. M-F 8:30-4:30.

Washington, DC 20017. 801 Buchanan St NE.
Tel: 202-529-7600. Fax: 202-529-2028.
www.kennedyinstitute.org
Michael D. Ward, BA, Pres. **Belindia Boyer & Moses Washington,** Adms.
   Focus: Spec Ed. **Conditions:** Primary—Ap Au B BI C CP Ep IP MR S SB.
   Sec—ADD ADHD As BD D Dx ED LD. **IQ 20-80.**
   Gen Acad. Pre-Voc. Voc. Ungraded. Courses: Read Math Lang_Arts. Man_
   Arts & Shop. On-Job Trng.
   Therapy: Hear Lang Occup Phys Speech. **Psychotherapy:** Group Indiv
   Parent.
   Enr: 150. **Staff:** 34 (Full 31, Part 3).
   Rates 2003: Day $31,600/yr. Clinic $50-80/ses. State Aid.
   Est 1959. Private. Nonprofit. Roman Catholic.

The Kennedy Institute's Center for Family Support and Early Childhood provides an individualized setting and all types of services for at-risk children from birth through age 6. The center provides families with the tools necessary to minimize the possibility that developmental delays will occur. In addition, young children in the program receive early treatment to lessen long-term impact.

The Center for School and Youth Services educates children and adolescents ages 7-21 with developmental disabilities. Other areas of disability served include learning and language disabilities and mild to moderate hearing impairments. The program supplements academic and vocational training with a variety of related services, such as crisis intervention.

The institute's Employment Services Program offers job training, work experiences and placements for adults with developmental disabilities. Other services include therapies, advocacy opportunities and continuing education.

MODEL SECONDARY SCHOOL FOR THE DEAF

Res and Day — Coed Ages 14-21

Washington, DC 20002. 800 Florida Ave NE.
Tel: 202-651-5031. TTY: 202-651-5031. Fax: 202-651-5109.
http://clerccenter.gallaudet.edu/mssd
   E-mail: admissions.mssd@gallaudet.edu
Marilyn Farmer, Prin.
   Conditions: Primary—D.
   Gen Acad. Gr 9-12. Courses: Read Math Lang_Arts. Man_Arts & Shop.
   Staff: Prof 84.
   Est 1969. Private. Nonprofit. **Spons:** Gallaudet University.

NATIONAL CHILDREN'S CENTER

Res — Coed Ages 8 and up; Day — Coed 1 and up

Washington, DC 20011. 6200 2nd St NW.
  Nearby locations: Silver Spring, MD.
Tel: 202-722-2300. Fax: 202-722-2383.
www.nccinc.org
Arthur Ginsberg, MHA, Exec Dir. **S. Otesia Barr,** MD, Med Dir.
  Focus: Treatment. **Conditions:** Primary—Au MR. Sec—ADD ADHD As CP
    D ED Ep LD MD ON S. **IQ 20-80.**
  Therapy: Hear Lang Occup Phys Speech. **Psychotherapy:** Fam Group
    Indiv.
  Staff: 129 (Full 127, Part 2).
  Est 1958. Private. Nonprofit.

  NCC offers care to individuals with mental retardation and other developmental disabilities. Services include educational diagnosis and prescription; casework; and psychological, psychiatric and language development.
  NCC operates four other Washington, DC area campuses, as well as a Maryland campus in Silver Spring.

ST. JOHN'S COMMUNITY SERVICES

Res — Coed Ages 18 and up; Day — Coed All Ages

Washington, DC 20007. 2201 Wisconsin Ave NW, Ste C-150.
Tel: 202-237-6500. Fax: 202-237-6352.
www.sjcs.org
Thomas F. Wilds, Pres.
  Conditions: Primary—Au MR.
  Pre-Voc. Voc. Ungraded. Courses: Read Math Lang_Arts. Shelt_Workshop.
    On-Job Trng.
  Therapy: Hear Lang Occup Phys Speech. **Psychotherapy:** Fam Indiv.
  Est 1882. Private. Nonprofit.

SCOTTISH RITE CENTER
FOR CHILDHOOD LANGUAGE DISORDERS

Clinic: Ages Birth-18. M-F 8:30-5.

Washington, DC 20009. 1630 Columbia Rd NW.
Tel: 202-939-4703. Fax: 202-939-4717.
Tommie Robinson, Jr., PhD, Dir.
  Conditions: Primary—S.
  Therapy: Speech.
  Private. **Spons:** Children's National Medical Center.

UNIVERSITY OF THE DISTRICT OF COLUMBIA SPEECH AND HEARING CLINIC

Clinic: All Ages. M-F 9-4.

Washington, DC 20008. 4200 Connecticut Ave NW, Bldg 41, Rm 306.
Tel: 202-274-6162. Fax: 202-274-6350.
M. Eugene Wiggins, MS, Dir.
  Focus: Treatment. **Conditions:** Primary—D S.
  Therapy: Hear Lang Speech.
  Staff: 4. Prof 2. Admin 2.
  Rates 2003: No Fee.
  Est 1971. Federal. Nonprofit.

Among the features of this clinic for individuals with communicative disorders are the identification, the evaluation and the treatment of speech, language and hearing disorders.

WALTER REED ARMY MEDICAL CENTER CHILD AND ADOLESCENT PSYCHIATRY SERVICE

Clinic: Ages Birth-18. M-F 7:30-4:30.

Washington, DC 20307. Bldg 6, 2nd Fl.
Tel: 202-782-5945. Fax: 202-782-8387.
www.wramc.amedd.army.mil
  Focus: Treatment. **Conditions:** Primary—ADD ADHD BD CD ED Mood
    OCD Psy Sz. Sec—Ap As Au B Bl C CP D Dx Ep IP LD MD MR MS ON
    S SB TB.
  Therapy: Art Chemo Hear Lang Occup Phys Speech. **Psychotherapy:**
    Fam Group Indiv Parent.
  Staff: 12 (Full 6, Part 6).
  Rates 2004: No Fee.
  Federal.

Diagnostic, therapeutic and counseling services for children of military members and their families are offered at this facility.

FLORIDA

ALL CHILDREN'S HOSPITAL
SPEECH-LANGUAGE-HEARING CENTER

Clinic: All Ages. M-Th 8-5:30, F 8-4.

St Petersburg, FL 33701. 801 6th St S.
Tel: 727-898-7451.
www.allkids.org
Conditions: Primary—S.
Therapy: Hear Lang Speech.
Staff: Prof 9.
Private.

ALPERT JEWISH FAMILY &
CHILDREN'S SERVICE

Clinic: Ages 6-21. By Appt.

West Palm Beach, FL 33417. 4605 Community Dr.
Tel: 561-684-1991. Fax: 561-684-5366.
www.jfcspb.org
Neil P. Newstein, LCSW, Exec Dir. **Elaine Rotenberg,** PhD, Clin Dir. **Phyllis Hoffman,** Adm.
    Focus: Treatment. **Conditions:** Primary—ED LD Sz. Sec—Ap Au MR S. **IQ 45 and up.**
    Therapy: Art Play. **Psychotherapy:** Fam Group Indiv Parent.
    Est 1974. Private. Nonprofit. **Spons:** Jewish Federation of Palm Beach County.

AJFCS provides social services to children and youth with emotional and family problems. Services include a Jewish Big Brother and Big Sister program. Fees vary according to the child's needs and sliding scales may apply.

ARC-RIDGE AREA

Res — Coed Ages 18 and up; Day — Coed 16 and up

Avon Park, FL 33825. 120 E College Dr.
Tel: 863-452-1295.
    Conditions: Primary—MR.
    Pre-Voc. Voc. Gr PS-PG. Shelt_Workshop. On-Job Trng.
    Est 1957. Private. Nonprofit.

ATLANTIS ACADEMY

Day — Coed Ages 5-18

Miami, FL 33176. 9600 SW 107th Ave.
Tel: 305-271-9771. Fax: 305-271-7078.
www.atlantisacademy.com   E-mail: info@atlantisacademy.com
Steve Roth, BA, MA, Dir. **Patricia Giner,** Adm.
   Focus: Spec Ed. **Conditions:** Primary—ADD ADHD Dx LD. Sec—ED Ep
   OCD ON SB. **IQ 72-140.**
   Gen Acad. Gr K-12. Courses: Read Math Lang_Arts.
   Enr: 150. Day Males 110. Day Females 40. **Staff:** 32 (Full 30, Part 2).
   Rates 2002: Day $10,900-12,400/sch yr (+$550).
   Summer Prgm: Day. Educ. Rec. Day Rate $1800. 5 wks.
   Est 1976. Private. Nonprofit.

Atlantis structures a student's academic program according to his or her diagnosed strengths and weaknesses. Instruction is provided in the basic skill areas of reading, writing, speaking, listening, science, math and social studies. Training is also provided in fine- and gross-motor control, auditory and visual perception, discrimination and memory.

BAPTIST HOSPITAL
SPEECH AND HEARING CENTER

Clinic: All Ages. M-F 8-4:30.

Pensacola, FL 32501. 1717 North E St, Ste 236.
   Nearby locations: Gulf Breeze.
Tel: 850-434-4957. Fax: 850-469-7490.
Martha McDowell-Fleming, MS, Dir.
   Focus: Treatment. **Conditions:** Primary—Ap S. Sec—ADD ADHD Apr Au
   CP.
   Therapy: Hear Speech.
   Staff: 7 (Full 6, Part 1).
   Est 1952. Private. Nonprofit. **Spons:** Baptist Health Care.

This hospital-based clinic offers care for individuals who have difficulty hearing or speaking. Services include speech, language, voice and hearing evaluations and treatment, as well as hearing aid evaluation, dispensation, repair and follow-up. Following an initial clinical evaluation of each new patient, staff members design an appropriate course of treatment.

A branch of the center provides outpatient services at Baptist Medical Park, 9 Mile Rd., and at Gulf Breeze Hospital, 1110 Gulf Breeze Pky., Gulf Breeze 32561.

BARBARA KING'S CENTRE
FOR EDUCATIONAL SERVICES

Clinic: All Ages. M-S 8-5; Eves M-Th 5-9.

Tampa, FL 33607. 5005 W Laurel St, Ste 100.
Tel: 813-874-3918. Fax: 813-874-3575.
E-mail: bking33@mindspring.com
Barbara King, MA, Dir.
 Focus: Spec Ed. **Conditions:** Primary—ADD ADHD Dx LD. Sec—ED. **IQ 85 and up.**
 Staff: 7 (Full 3, Part 4). Educ 6. Admin 1.
 Rates 2001: Clinic $50-55/hr. Schol avail.
 Est 1986. Private. Inc.

This program is designed to remediate learning disabilities in a structured learning environment. Individualized instruction teaches techniques for compensation through a multisensory approach. Educational therapy and tutorial support are available, and attention is given to developing communicational and study skills. Students undergo evaluative standardized testing prior to enrollment.

BEACON COLLEGE

Res — Coed Ages 18 and up

Leesburg, FL 34748. 105 E Main St.
Tel: 352-787-7660. Fax: 352-787-0721.
www.beaconcollege.edu   E-mail: admissions@beaconcollege.edu
Stephanie Knight, Adm.
 Focus: Spec Ed. **Conditions:** Primary—ADD ADHD Dx LD. **IQ 90-100.**
 Gen Acad. Gr PG. Courses: Read Math Lang_Arts.
 Enr: 65. Res Males 40. Res Females 25. **Staff:** 23 (Full 15, Part 8).
 Est 1989. Private. Nonprofit.

This college offers high school graduates with diverse learning styles a college degree program. The school provides tutorial support through a mentoring program, and helps students to identify their interests and set realistic academic and career goals. The Field Placement Program allows juniors and seniors the opportunity to experience the workplace and develop employment skills while making career decisions. Beacon offers degrees in both human services and liberal studies.

THE BERTHA ABESS CHILDREN'S CENTER

Day — Coed Ages 3-21

Miami, FL 33137. 5801 Biscayne Blvd.
Tel: 305-756-7116. Fax: 305-756-9335.
www.baccinc.org   E-mail: info@baccinc.org
Carolyn Jenkins-Jaeger, MS, Exec Dir.
 Conditions: Primary—ED. Sec—BD. **IQ 90 and up.**

Gen Acad. Pre-Voc. Gr PS-12. Courses: Read Math Lang_Arts. Man_Arts & Shop.
Therapy: Art Music Occup Speech. **Psychotherapy:** Fam Group Indiv.
Est 1962. Private. Nonprofit.

THE BISHOP-ETON SCHOOL

Day — Coed Ages 5-18

Tampa, FL 33603. 5120 Mendenhall Dr.
Tel: 813-870-1148. Fax: 813-879-1288.
www.bishopeton.org
Scott Corwin, Exec Dir.
    Focus: Spec Ed. Treatment. **Conditions:** Primary—ADD ADHD Dx LD. Sec—As CP D Ep OCD OH. **IQ 85 and up.**
    Col Prep. Gr 1-12. Courses: Read Math Lang_Arts Computers Sci Hist Study_Skills.
    Therapy: Lang Occup Phys Speech. **Psychotherapy:** Fam Indiv Parent.
    Enr: 70. Day Males 35. Day Females 35. **Staff:** 21 (Full 14, Part 7).
    Summer Prgm: Day. Educ. Rec.
    Est 1988. Private. Nonprofit.

Offering remedial, regular and accelerated sections, Bishop-Eton operates a multisensory, experiential program. Those students requiring prescriptive one-on-one instruction take part in a special therapeutic program that utilizes Orton-Gillingham methods and materials. Reading and math labs provide enrichment and help students improve in these areas. Pupils develop better study habits and attitudes through a continuous study skills program and an after-school study period. Activities such as music, drama, art, student government and sports round out the program.

BOLESTA CENTER

Day — Coed Ages Birth-14
Clinic: Ages Birth-14. M-F 8-5.

Tampa, FL 33614. 7205 N Habana Ave.
Tel: 813-932-1184. TTY: 813-935-7944. Fax: 813-932-9583.
www.bolesta.com   E-mail: bolesta@gte.net
Pamela Sullins, RN, Exec Dir. Marcus Rose, MSP, Clin Dir.
    Focus: Rehab. **Conditions:** Primary—D S.
    Therapy: Hear Lang Speech. **Psychotherapy:** Fam.
    Enr: 25. Day Males 14. Day Females 11. **Staff:** 6. Prof 4. Admin 2.
    Rates 2004: Day $280/mo. Clinic $70/ses.
    Est 1962. Private. Nonprofit.

The center's year-round program utilizes residual hearing and follows the theory of acoupedics (teaching through hearing) in order to develop normal speech and language as early as possible. Early detection and intervention and the full-time use of amplification are emphasized, and rehabilitative training for cochlear implant patients is available.

Children are placed in regular schools from kindergarten (if possible) and receive daily tutoring in language and speech. Parents must participate in weekly therapy sessions and daily carryover activities.

BREVARD LEARNING CLINIC
Clinic: Ages 5 and up. M-F 7:30-5; Eves M-Th 5-7.

Melbourne, FL 32901. 1900 S Harbor City Blvd, Ste 231.
  Nearby locations: Rockledge.
Tel: 321-676-3024. Fax: 321-676-3064.
E-mail: blcmelfl@hbrandon.com
Barbara C. Jeffers, BA, MA, Exec Dir. **Mary S. Kellogg,** BA, MA, Dir.
  Focus: Spec Ed. **Conditions:** Primary—ADD Dx LD. Sec—ADHD Db. **IQ 90 and up.**
  Gen Acad. Courses: Read Math Lang_Arts.
  Therapy: Lang.
  Staff: 7 (Full 4, Part 3). Educ 7.
  Rates 2003: Clinic $45-50/hr. Schol avail. State Aid.
  Est 1983. Private. Inc.

This clinic provides intellectual, academic and social evaluations; clinical, multisensory, Lindamood-based teaching; and test preparation. Students receive instruction in individual hourly sessions at least twice a week. Audiovisual equipment, computers, games, texts and a library are also available. Another branch of the facility is located at 975 Eyster Blvd., Rockledge 32955.

CENTER ACADEMY
Day — Coed Ages 8-19
Clinic: Ages 4-21. M-S 9-5.

Pinellas Park, FL 33782. 6710 86th Ave N.
  Nearby locations: Bradenton; Fort Lauderdale; Jacksonville; Orlando; Palm Harbor; St Petersburg; Tampa; London, England.
Tel: 727-541-5716. Fax: 727-544-8186.
www.centeracademy.com   E-mail: infopp@centeracademy.com
Andrew P. Hicks, PhD, Dir. **Lisa Stetler,** Intake.
  Focus: Spec Ed. **Conditions:** Primary—ADD ADHD Dx LD. **IQ 75-130.**
  Col Prep. Gen Acad. Gr 3-12. Courses: Read Math Lang_Arts.
  Therapy: Art Chemo Dance. **Psychotherapy:** Fam Group Indiv Parent.
  Enr: 90. Day Males 70. Day Females 20. **Staff:** 9 (Full 4, Part 5). Prof 6. Educ 2. Admin 1.
  Rates 2003: Day $8000-12,000/sch yr. Schol avail.
  Summer Prgm: Day. Educ. Ther. Day Rate $695. 5 wks.
  Est 1968. Private. Inc.

Enrolling children with attentional disorders, motivational problems and learning disabilities, the academy formulates educational programs for each student following consultation between neuropsychologists and school educators. In addition to improving motivation and self-esteem, the school teaches lifelong learning strategies for pupils to employ. Following assessment, instructors develop an academically appropriate curriculum for the child that addresses processing deficits. Staff members continually evaluate the student's progress and needs.

In addition to its Pinellas Park location, the academy maintains campuses in Tampa, Jacksonville, Orlando, Fort Lauderdale, St. Petersburg, Palm Harbor and Bradenton. The school also operates a relocation service in London, England (92 St. John's Hill, Battersea, SW11 1SH).

CENTRAL FLORIDA SPEECH AND HEARING CENTER

Clinic: All Ages. M-Th 8:30-5:30, F 8-12.

Lakeland, FL 33805. 710 E Bella Vista St.
Tel: 863-686-3189. TTY: 863-686-3189. Fax: 863-682-1348.
www.cfshc.org   E-mail: info@cfshc.org
L. Gay Ratcliff, MS, Pres. Susan R. Snover, Adm.
  Focus: Rehab. Conditions: Primary—Ap D S. Sec—ADD ADHD Au BI CP LD MR PDD.
  Therapy: Hear Lang Speech. Psychotherapy: Group Parent.
  Staff: 32 (Full 20, Part 12).
  Rates 2003: Clinic $100/hr.
  Est 1960. Private. Nonprofit. Spons: United Way.

Evaluation and therapy for speech, language, voice, tongue thrust and audiological problems are provided at the center. Lip-reading classes, a preschool program, industrial consultation, hearing tests and therapy for aphasics are offered. Affiliations with community agencies are maintained for referrals. Mobile therapy and a mobile test unit are available. Fees are based on a sliding scale.

COMMUNITY OF LANDMARK

Res — Coed Ages 18 and up

Opa Locka, FL 33055. 20000 NW 47th Ave.
Tel: 305-626-6219. Fax: 305-628-7201.
www.dcf.state.fl.us/institutions/landmark
Michael S. Mayfield, Admin.
  Focus: Trng. Treatment. Conditions: Primary—MR.
  Pre-Voc. Voc. Ungraded. Man_Arts & Shop. Shelt_Workshop. On-Job Trng.
  Therapy: Hear Lang Occup Phys Speech. Psychotherapy: Indiv.
  Est 1967. State.

CONKLIN CENTERS FOR THE BLIND

Res — Coed Ages 16 and up; Day — Coed Birth-6

Daytona Beach, FL 32114. 405 White St.
Tel: 386-258-3441. Fax: 386-258-1155.
www.conklincenter.org   E-mail: info@conklincenter.org
Robert T. Kelly, MEd, Int Exec Dir.
 Focus: Trng. **Conditions:** Primary—B. Sec—ADD ADHD Ap As BD BI C
  CD CP D Dx ED Ep IP LD MD MR MS OCD ON Psy S SB Sz. **IQ 30 and
  up.**
 Voc. Ungraded. Courses: Read Math Lang_Arts. On-Job Trng. Supported_
  Employment.
 Therapy: Hear Lang Occup Phys Speech. **Psychotherapy:** Fam Indiv
  Parent.
 Enr: 64. **Staff:** 32.
 Rates 2004: Res $86,100/yr. Day $58,725/yr. $50 (Therapy)/hr. Schol avail.
  State Aid.
 Est 1979. Private. Nonprofit.

This facility provides year-round vocational training, placement and supported living arrangements for youths and adults with visual impairments and multiple handicaps. Conklin also emphasizes independent living skills.

DANIEL

Res — Coed Ages 5-17

Jacksonville, FL 32216. 4203 Southpoint Blvd.
Tel: 904-296-1055. Fax: 904-296-1953.
www.danielkids.org   E-mail: info@danielkids.org
James D. Clark, LCSW, Pres. **Sue McCain,** Adm.
 Focus: Treatment. **Conditions:** Primary—BD ED. Sec—LD.
 Psychotherapy: Fam Group.
 Enr: 24. Res Males 12. Res Females 12. **Staff:** 52 (Full 47, Part 5).
 Est 1884. Private. Nonprofit.

This agency provides treatment services that stress the remediation of problems that have resulted in developmentally impaired skills and behavioral control. The basic treatment modality is milieu therapy in an open, nonsecure group setting.

Three distinct phases constitute the treatment plans: intake, residential and aftercare. A comprehensive assessment process during intake establishes suitability for admission based on clinical, educational and group psychological criteria. The residential phase affords opportunities for learning to cope with life situations. Upon discharge from residence, student and family continue treatment in aftercare to assist in readjustment to family and community life. Casework, group work, family therapy and an educational program round-out treatment programs. Rates are based on a sliding scale.

DAVID LAWRENCE CENTER
CHILDREN'S SERVICES PROGRAM

Res — Coed Ages 12-17; Day — Coed 5-18
Clinic: All Ages. M-F 9-5.

Naples, FL 34116. 6075 Golden Gate Pky.
Tel: 239-455-8500. Fax: 239-455-6561.
www.davidlawrencecenter.org   E-mail: info@dlcmhc.com
Dave Schimmel, BA, MS, CEO.
   Focus: Treatment. **Conditions:** Primary—ADD ADHD BD CD ED OCD Sz.
      IQ 80 and up.
   Gen Acad. Pre-Voc. Ungraded. Courses: Read Math Lang_Arts.
   Psychotherapy: Fam Indiv Parent.
   Enr: 46. Res Males 10. Res Females 6. Day Males 18. Day Females 12.
      Staff: 28 (Full 22, Part 6).
   Est 1969. Private. Nonprofit.

   This program provides intervention, outpatient and residential therapy services for children and adolescents with emotional and behavioral problems. The focus of the center is to improve behavior and communication skills, and ultimately to reunite the family. Fees are determined along a sliding scale.

THE DEPAUL SCHOOL OF NORTHEAST FLORIDA

Day — Coed Ages 6-14

Jacksonville, FL 32211. 6620 Arlington Expy.
   Nearby locations: Neptune Beach.
Tel: 904-724-0102. Fax: 904-726-9630.
www.depaulschool.com   E-mail: info@depaulschool.com
Gayle Florence Cane, EdD, Pres. **Diane Hoffman,** Adm.
   Focus: Spec Ed. **Conditions:** Primary—ADD ADHD Dc Dg Dx LD. **IQ 90**
      and up.
   Gen Acad. Gr 1-8. Courses: Read Math Lang_Arts Soc_Stud Computers
      Sci.
   Therapy: Speech. **Psychotherapy:** Parent.
   Enr: 153. Day Males 101. Day Females 52. **Staff:** 25 (Full 24, Part 1).
   Rates 2003: Day $6650/sch yr (+$250). Schol 17 ($20,000). State Aid.
   Summer Prgm: Day. Educ. Rec. Rem. Day Rate $750. 4 wks.
   Est 1980. Private. Nonprofit.

   This school uses a structured, multisensory method of teaching dyslexic children, including repetition and drills. Emphasis is placed on returning the child to a conventional classroom setting, usually after two to three years. DePaul aims to establish a firm educational foundation and to build upon this base, enhancing the child's self-esteem as he or she becomes successful in an academic environment. A summer session and tutoring are also available. A second campus is located at 407 3rd St., Neptune Beach 32266.

DEVEREUX FLORIDA TREATMENT CENTER

Res — Coed Ages 5-17; Day — Coed 5-19

Viera, FL 32940. 8000 Devereux Dr.
Tel: 321-242-9100. Fax: 321-242-1573.
www.devereuxfl.org
  Focus: Treatment. **Conditions:** Primary—ADD ADHD Au CD ED OCD Psy
    Sz. Sec—BD Dx LD MR. **IQ 40 and up.**
  Col Prep. Gen Acad. Pre-Voc. Gr K-12. Courses: Read Math Lang_Arts.
    On-Job Trng.
  Therapy: Chemo Lang Speech. **Psychotherapy:** Fam Group Indiv.
  Enr: 191. Res Males 74. Res Females 37. Day Males 54. Day Females 26.
    Staff: 50 (Full 47, Part 3).
  Est 1988. Private. Nonprofit. **Spons:** Devereux Foundation.

The Devereux Foundation's Florida Treatment Network serves severely emotionally disturbed and developmentally impaired children and adolescents and their families. A full continuum of care is offered, including intensive residential treatment services, open community-based residential treatment services, day treatment services, group home services and therapeutic foster care. Children and adolescents enter at the level appropriate to their needs and move between levels of care as their condition improves.

See Also Page 1025

DORIS A. SANDERS LEARNING CENTER

Day — Coed Ages 5-22

Lakeland, FL 33801. 1201 Enchanted Dr.
Tel: 863-499-2980. Fax: 863-603-6326.
www.pcsb.k12.fl.us/dslc
April Sumner, Prin.
  Focus: Spec Ed. **Conditions:** Primary—ADD ADHD Asp Au B BD BI C CP
    D DS Ep MR OCD PW S TS. Sec—ED OH. **IQ 0-70.**
  Gen Acad. Pre-Voc. Ungraded. Courses: Read Math Lang_Arts. Man_Arts
    & Shop. On-Job Trng. Agriculture.
  Enr: 110. Day Males 70. Day Females 40. **Staff:** 65. Prof 37. Educ 21.
  Rates 2003: No Fee.
    State.

Sanders Learning Center conducts a program designed to socialize profoundly, severely and moderately mentally retarded children of the Lakeland area. Programs emphasize self-help, social, sensorimotor and communicative skills. An extensive vocational program comprises manual arts, on-the-job training and agricultural work.

THE DUVALL HOME

Res — Coed All Ages

Glenwood, FL 32722. 3395 Grand Ave, PO Box 220036.

Tel: 386-734-2874. Fax: 386-734-5504.
www.duvallhome.org   E-mail: administration@duvallhome.org
W. Blake Davis, BS, Admin.
   Focus: Treatment. **Conditions:** Primary—MR. Sec—As Au B Bl C CP D Ep
      ON S SB. **IQ 0-55.**
   Therapy: Occup Phys.
   Enr: 240. Res Males 123. Res Females 117. **Staff:** 271 (Full 245, Part 26).
   Est 1945. Private. Nonprofit. **Spons:** Presbyterian Special Services.

This facility provides residential care for trainable and profoundly retarded children
and adults. This care within a group setting offers training in life skills and social behavior within a homelike atmosphere. In addition, the home provides 24-hour nursing care
for both ambulatory and nonambulatory residents, as well as dormitory and group home
living options.

Residents also participate in many recreational and community activities, including
swimming, sports and choir. Volunteer groups conduct an extensive arts and crafts program. Foster grandparents add individual attention and a personal feeling of caring for
children. The length of treatment varies, and Duvall provides life care for many of its
residents. Limited respite care is available.   **See Also Page 1028**

EASTER SEALS MIAMI-DADE
CHILD DEVELOPMENT CENTER
AND DEMONSTRATION SCHOOL

Day — Coed Ages Birth-22
Clinic: All Ages. M-F 7-6.

Miami, FL 33125. 1475 NW 14th Ave.
Tel: 305-325-0470. Fax: 305-325-0578.
www.miami.easter-seals.org
Joan L. Bornstein, PhD, Pres. **Ronni Waldman,** MS, Dir. **Landa Naya,** Adm.
   Focus: Spec Ed. **Conditions:** Primary—ADD ADHD Asp Au D Dc Dg DS
      LD PDD PW SB SP TS. Sec—As BD Bl C CP Dx Ep MR S. **IQ 70 and
      up.**
   Gen Acad. Gr PS-12. Courses: Read Math Lang_Arts. Culinary_Arts.
   Therapy: Hear Lang Occup Phys Speech. **Psychotherapy:** Fam Group
      Indiv.
   Enr: 196. **Staff:** 57. (Full 57).
   Rates 2003: Day $8600/sch yr. Schol avail. State Aid.
   Summer Prgm: Day. Educ. Day Rate $800/4-wk ses. 8 wks.
   Est 1967. Private. Nonprofit.

The Demonstration School and Child Development Center provide an educational
program for children with language and learning disabilities. Through a learning center
approach using various modalities, the school aims at developing the abilities and skills
that will enable students to achieve success. A two-month summer session is available.

ECKERD YOUTH ALTERNATIVES

Res — Coed Ages 10-17

Brooksville, FL.
Contact: 100 N Starcrest Dr, PO Box 7450, Clearwater, FL 33758.
   Nearby locations: Floral City; Clewiston; Milton; Silver Springs.
Tel: 727-461-2990. Fax: 727-442-5911.
www.eckerd.org   E-mail: admissions@eckerd.org
Karen V. Waddell, BA, Pres. Francene Hazel, Dir.
   Focus: Treatment. **Conditions:** Primary—BD CD ED Mood ODD. Sec—
      ADD ADHD LD. **IQ 70 and up.**
   Gen Acad. Pre-Voc. Ungraded. Courses: Read Math Lang_Arts Sci Soc_
      Stud.
   Therapy: Speech. **Psychotherapy:** Fam Group Indiv.
   Summer Prgm: Res. Ther. Res Rate $180. 2 wks.
   Est 1968. Private. Nonprofit.

The Eckerd outdoor program offers therapeutic treatment to emotionally disturbed children by providing a camp setting as an alternative to institutionalization.

The year-round program utilizes reality therapy, Rogerian techniques and group therapy. Small-group living in the wilderness environment encourages the acquisition of new skills while promoting discipline and responsibility. Each group must construct their shelter, cut wood, repair equipment and perform other tasks necessary for their stay in the forest. Such experiences provide the children with the opportunity to develop academic skills at their own pace and in relation to each project they endeavor. When sufficient progress is made, children are transferred into the transition classroom in preparation for their return to the mainstream.

In addition to Florida, Eckerd conducts outdoor therapeutic treatment programs in the following states: Georgia, New Hampshire, North Carolina, Rhode Island, Tennessee and Vermont (see separate listings).

FLORIDA SCHOOL FOR THE DEAF AND THE BLIND

Res — Coed Ages 5-21; Day — Coed 3-21

St Augustine, FL 32084. 207 N San Marco Ave.
Tel: 904-827-2200. TTY: 904-827-2221. Fax: 904-827-2218.
www.fsdb.k12.fl.us   E-mail: gillespiek@mail.fsdb.k12.fl.us
Elmer Dillingham, MEd, Pres. Cindy Slagle, Adm.
   Focus: Spec Ed. **Conditions:** Primary—B D. Sec—Apr As BI C CP ED Ep
      LD MD MR MS Nf ON S SB TB.
   Col Prep. Gen Acad. Voc. Gr PS-12. Courses: Read Math Lang_Arts. Man_
      Arts & Shop. On-Job Trng.
   Therapy: Hear Lang Occup Phys Speech. **Psychotherapy:** Fam Group
      Indiv.
   Enr: 750.
   Rates 2003: No Fee.
   Summer Prgm: Res & Day. Rec. 2 wks.
   Est 1885. State. Nonprofit.

Hearing- and visually impaired children who are residents of Florida take part in a free educational program that includes vocational training, general academics and remedial instruction. The school awards both standard and special diplomas while preparing its graduates for a wide range of professional careers and trades.

Although FSDB enrolls children with mild secondary handicaps, the school cannot accept students who are homebound or hospitalized, autistic, severely emotionally disturbed or profoundly mentally retarded. The trainable mentally retarded may not take part in the program unless the child has dual sensory impairments.

FLORIDA STATE UNIVERSITY
SPEECH AND HEARING CLINIC

Clinic: All Ages. M-F 8-5.

Tallahassee, FL 32306. 107 Regional Rehabilitation Ctr.
Tel: 850-644-2238. Fax: 850-644-8994.
www.comm.fsu.edu/commdis/clinic.html
   Conditions: Primary—Ap D Dx LD S.
   Therapy: Hear Lang Speech.
   Est 1969. State. Nonprofit.

GATEWAY SCHOOL

Day — Coed Ages 11-21

Orlando, FL 32808. 4000 Silver Star Rd.
Tel: 407-296-6449. Fax: 407-521-3309.
www.gateway.ocps.net   E-mail: sappt@ocps.net
Patricia Taylor, Prin.
   Focus: Spec Ed. **Conditions:** Primary—BD CD ED. Sec—ADD ADHD Dx LD MR. **IQ 70 and up.**
   Gen Acad. Pre-Voc. Voc. Gr 6-12. Courses: Read Math Lang_Arts Music. Man_Arts & Shop. On-Job Trng.
   Therapy: Lang Occup Speech. **Psychotherapy:** Group Indiv.
   Enr: 200. **Staff:** 83.
   Rates 2004: No Fee.
   Est 1958. County. Nonprofit.

A facility of the Orange County Public School System, Gateway offers a highly individualized program for emotionally disturbed, learning-disabled and language-impaired children. Academics and therapies in art, music and gross-motor coordination are featured in the curriculum. The school provides counseling and therapy for students and their parents within the curriculum.

HARBOR SCHOOL

Day — Coed Ages 6-15

Casselberry, FL 32707. 3955 Red Bug Rd.
Tel: 407-699-9502. Fax: 407-699-8022.
www.harborschool.net   E-mail: harborsch@aol.com
Mark R. Brown, BS, Exec Dir.
  Focus: Spec Ed. **Conditions:** Primary—ADD ADHD LD. **IQ 90 and up.**
  Gen Acad. Gr 1-8. Courses: Read Math Lang_Arts Sci Soc_Stud Studio_
    Art Music.
  Therapy: Hear Lang Speech. **Psychotherapy:** Fam Parent.
  Enr: 45. Day Males 39. Day Females 6. **Staff:** 9 (Full 7, Part 2).
  Rates 2004: Day $9600/yr. Schol avail. State Aid.
  Summer Prgm: Day. Educ. Day Rate $875. 5 wks.
  Est 1971. Private. Nonprofit.

A full curriculum emphasizing basic academic skills is provided at this school for pupils of average or above-average intelligence who have learning disabilities or attentional difficulties. Students work at their own pace in classes with a student-teacher ratio of 8:1. Field trips, conferences and counseling are aspects of the program. Parents receive daily reports, in addition to a comprehensive report every nine weeks. Family involvement is required.

HEALTHSOUTH SEA PINES REHABILITATION HOSPITAL PEDIATRIC/ADOLESCENT PROGRAM

Res — Coed Ages Birth-18
Clinic: Ages Birth-18. M-F 8-6.

Melbourne, FL 32901. 101 E Florida Ave.
Tel: 321-984-4600. Fax: 321-984-4627.
  Conditions: Primary—Ap As BI C CP IP LD MD MS ON S SB. **IQ 55 and**
  up.
  Pre-Voc. Voc.
  Therapy: Hear Lang Occup Phys Speech. **Psychotherapy:** Fam Group
  Indiv.
  Staff: Prof 174.
  Est 1987. Private. Inc.

HEARING AND SPEECH CENTER OF FLORIDA

Clinic: All Ages. M-F 9:30-5:30.

Miami, FL 33173. 9425 SSW 72nd St.
Tel: 305-271-7343. Fax: 305-271-7949.
www.hearingandspeechcenter.org
Lillian Poms, Exec Dir.
  Conditions: Primary—D S.

Therapy: Hear Lang Speech.
Est 1936. Private. Nonprofit.

HENDERSON MENTAL HEALTH CENTER

Res — Coed Ages 10-18; Day — Coed 7-18
Clinic: Ages Birth-21. M-S 8-5; Eves M-S 5-8.

Fort Lauderdale, FL 33319. 4720 N State Rd 7.
   Nearby locations: Hollywood; Lauderhill; Pembroke Pines; Pompano
   Beach.
Tel: 954-486-4005.
www.hendersonmhc.org
Steven Ronik, CEO. **Bhagi Sahas,** MD, Med Dir.
   Focus: Treatment. **Conditions:** Primary—ADD ADHD ED OCD Psy Sz.
      Sec—BD CD. **IQ 70 and up.**
   Therapy: Speech. **Psychotherapy:** Fam Group Indiv Parent.
   Enr: 52. Res Males 12. Day Males 20. Day Females 20.
   Est 1953. Private. Nonprofit.

Open to residents of Broward County, this community mental health center offers case management, psychosocial assessments, psychiatric evaluation and follow-up, therapy and psychosocial rehabilitation. In addition, the center conducts both residential and day treatment programs. Henderson also maintains youth programs for prevention and early intervention, in-home counseling and other outreach, in addition to programs for the severely emotionally disturbed.

Twelve branches operate throughout Broward County.

HOPE CENTER

Res and Day — Coed Ages 18 and up

Miami, FL 33130. 666 SW 4th St.
Tel: 305-545-7572. Fax: 305-325-0382.
www.hopecenterhc.org   E-mail: info@hopecenterhc.org
Sherwin Rosenstein, MSW, CEO.
   Focus: Spec Ed. **Conditions:** Primary—MR. Sec—CP Ep OH. **IQ 30-69.**
   Voc. Shelt_Workshop. On-Job Trng.
   Psychotherapy: Group.
   Enr: 160. Res Males 50. Res Females 50. Day Males 30. Day Females 30.
      Staff: 92. (Full 92). Prof 15.
   Rates 2003: Res $2000/mo. Day $700/mo. State Aid.
   Est 1955. Private. Nonprofit.

The center provides facilities for individuals with developmental disabilities. Services, which are geared toward training and education, emphasize independence and normalization. Students participate in a variety of special activities, including educational field trips, physical education, art, music and computer. A halfway house and apartment facilities are also part of the program.

Vocational counseling is available. The center cannot accept individuals with severe emotional problems.

HOPE HAVEN CHILDREN'S CLINIC AND FAMILY CENTER DOWN SYNDROME CENTER

Clinic: Ages Birth-21. M-F 9-4.

Jacksonville, FL 32207. 4600 Beach Blvd.
Tel: 904-346-5100. Fax: 904-346-5111.
www.hope-haven.org   E-mail: lauraw@hope-haven.org
Laura Watts, MEd, Dir.
　　Focus: Treatment. **Conditions:** Primary—DS. Sec—ADHD Au S.
　　Therapy: Occup Phys Speech.
　　Staff: 10 (Full 8, Part 2).
　　Rates 2003: $75 (Evaluation)/ses. Schol avail.
　　Est 1996. Private. Nonprofit.

DSC provides evaluations and consultations using an interdisciplinary team model that includes education, occupational and physical therapies, and speech and medical development. The educationally focused approach helps staff assess the child's strengths and potential to maximize the child's learning experiences. The center also offers assistance in school placement and Individual Education Plan preparation.

KILLIAN OAKS ACADEMY

Day — Coed Ages 5-13

Miami, FL 33176. 10545 SW 97th Ave.
Tel: 305-274-2221.
Mercedes Ricon, Head.
　　Focus: Spec Ed. **Conditions:** Primary—Dx LD. Sec—ADD ADHD S. **IQ 85 and up.**
　　Gen Acad. Gr K-8. Courses: Read Math Lang_Arts Sci Soc_Stud Studio_ Art Music.
　　Therapy: Speech.
　　Enr: 113. **Staff:** 19 (Full 17, Part 2).
　　Est 1970. Private. Inc.

Killian Oaks provides an academic program, based on a modified open classroom concept, for children with disabilities in the areas of language development, reading and verbal behavior. Each student receives three hours of language arts instruction a day, with his or her progress evaluated continually. The school attempts to mainstream children into regular schools as soon as possible, typically after two to three years.

THE KURTZ CENTER
FOR COGNITIVE DEVELOPMENT

Clinic: Ages 5 and up. M-F 8:30-5:30.

Winter Park, FL 32789. 1201 Louisiana Ave, Ste C.
Tel: 407-740-5678. Fax: 407-740-0523.
www.learningdisabilities.com
   E-mail: ld-request@learningdisabilities.com
Gail Kurtz, BS, Dir. **Patty Weick,** Adm.
   Focus: Treatment. **Conditions:** Primary—ADD ADHD Anx Ar As Asp Au
      BD BI Db Dc Dg Dx ED Ep LD PTSD SP. Sec—Ap DS MR Nf OCD ON
      PDD S TS. **IQ 70 and up.**
   Gen Acad. Ungraded. Courses: Read Math Lang_Arts.
   Therapy: Occup Percepual-Motor. **Psychotherapy:** Fam Group Indiv
      Parent.
   Staff: 11 (Full 7, Part 4).
   Rates 2003: $75 (Treatment); $125 (Evaluation); $175 (Psychotherapy)/ses.
   Est 1986. Private. Inc.

   This center serves persons with mild to severe learning, attention and language difficulties by means of several multisensory programs, among them Lindamood-Bell, NeuroNet, Fast ForWord, Interactive Metronome, Belgau, PACE and Brain Gym.

LA AMISTAD RESIDENTIAL TREATMENT CENTER

Res and Day — Coed Ages 6-18

Maitland, FL 32751. 1650 Park Ave N.
Tel: 407-647-0660. Fax: 407-647-3060.
www.lamistad.com   E-mail: laamistadintake@aol.com
Vickie Lewis, CEO. **Karl Sieg,** MD, Med Dir. **Karen Klecic,** Adm.
   Focus: Treatment. **Conditions:** Primary—ADD ADHD Anx Asp BD ED LD
      Mood OCD ODD Psy PTSD SP Sz. Sec—Bu TS. **IQ 70 and up.**
   Gen Acad. Pre-Voc. Gr 1-12. Courses: Read Math Lang_Arts Computers.
      On-Job Trng.
   Therapy: Art Milieu Music Occup Play Recreational Speech. **Psychotherapy:** Fam Group Indiv Parent Equine.
   Enr: 78. Res Males 27. Res Females 27. Day Males 12. Day Females 12.
      Staff: 75. Prof 30. Educ 5. Admin 13.
   Summer Prgm: Res & Day. Educ. Rec. Ther.
   Est 1970. Private. Nonprofit. Nondenom Christian. **Spons:** Universal Health
      Services.

   La Amistad provides a long-term treatment community for children, adolescents and young adults with a wide range of emotional disturbances and psychiatric diagnoses. An on-campus school provides credits that are transferable to other schools. Clinical services include milieu, group and individual psychotherapies, and vocational, occupational and family therapies. Specialized treatment programs focus upon dual diagnosis, sexual abuse and personality disorders.   **See Also Page 1039**

LAVOY EXCEPTIONAL CENTER

Day — Coed Ages 3-22

Tampa, FL 33607. 4410 W Main St.
Tel: 813-872-5285. Fax: 813-872-5291.
Ina J. Helmick, MA, Admin.
 Focus: Spec Ed. Conditions: Primary—Au MR. Sec—B D ED ON S.
 Pre-Voc. Voc. Ungraded. Courses: Read Math Lang_Arts. Man_Arts &
  Shop. On-Job Trng.
 Therapy: Hear Lang Occup Phys Speech.
 Enr: 125. Staff: 65.
 Rates 2003: No Fee.
 Est 1953. State.

This public school admits students who have mental and orthopedic handicaps, visually impairments and autism. The educational program is oriented toward developing prevocational and vocational skills. Custodial care is not available.

LEARNING TO ACHIEVE

Day — Coed Ages 6-12

Hudson, FL 34667. 12401 Yorktown Ln.
Tel: 727-815-3481.
E-mail: dvostello@earthlink.net
Deborah M. Vostello, BA, Dir.
 Focus: Spec Ed. Conditions: Primary—ADD ADHD Dc Dg Dx.
 Gen Acad. Ungraded. Courses: Read Math Lang_Arts.
 Est 1993. Private.

LIGHTHOUSE POINT ACADEMY

Day — Coed Ages 6-17

Lighthouse Point, FL 33064. 3701 NE 22nd Ave.
 Nearby locations: Coconut Creek.
Tel: 954-941-3680. Fax: 954-942-0119.
www.nbps.org
Philip E. Morgaman, Pres. Michael A. Rossi, BA, MA, EdD, Head. Sandi
 Trentacoste, Adm.
 Focus: Spec Ed. Conditions: Primary—ADD ADHD Dx LD. IQ 95 and up.
 Col Prep. Gr 3-12. Courses: Read Math Lang_Arts Sci Computers Soc_
  Stud Studio_Art Music.
 Therapy: Speech.
 Enr: 218. Day Males 148. Day Females 70. Staff: 27. (Full 27). Educ 27.
 Rates 2003: Day $16,650-22,380/sch yr.
 Est 1978. Private. Inc. Spons: North Broward Preparatory Schools.

The academy uses a multisensory approach in small, highly personalized classes. Each student uses computers extensively and may choose from a variety of enrichment courses. A mainstreaming program with the affiliated North Broward School enables students to attend classes at both schools while making use of the shared facilities.

The upper school operates (grades 6-12) at 7600 Lyons Rd., Coconut Creek 33073.

MACDONALD TRAINING CENTER

Res — Coed Ages 18-56; Day — Coed 18-59

Tampa, FL 33607. 5420 W Cypress St.
Tel: 813-870-1300. Fax: 813-872-6010.
www.macdonaldcenter.org
Jim Freyvogel, Pres.
    Conditions: Primary—MR. **IQ 5 and up.**
    Pre-Voc. Voc. Courses: Read Math Lang_Arts. Shelt_Workshop. On-Job Trng.
    Therapy: Hear Lang Speech.
    Private.

MAILMAN CENTER FOR CHILD DEVELOPMENT

Day — Coed Ages Birth-3
Clinic: Ages Birth-21. M-F 8:30-5; Eves W 5-7.

Miami, FL 33101. 1601 NW 12th Ave, Ste 4049, PO Box 016820.
Tel: 305-243-6631. Fax: 305-243-6059.
http://pediatrics.med.miami.edu
F. Daniel Armstrong, PhD, Dir. **Jeffrey Brosco,** MD, PhD, Med Dir.
    Focus: Treatment. **Conditions:** Primary—ADD ADHD AN Anx Ap Apr Ar As Asp Au BD BI Bu C CD CF CP D Db Dc Dg DS Dx ED Ep HIV IP LD MD Mood MR MS Nf OCD ODD ON PDD Psy PTSD PW S SB SP Sz TB TS.
    Therapy: Hear Lang Occup Phys Speech. **Psychotherapy:** Fam Indiv.
    Est 1970. Private. **Spons:** University of Miami.

Comprehensive diagnostic evaluation and related treatment and management services for children with developmental disabilities, including mental retardation, are provided at the Mailman Center of the University of Miami. The center houses the Debbie Institute, which conducts services for severely impaired infants, toddlers and preschoolers.

MARIAN CENTER
SERVICES FOR DEVELOPMENTALLY HANDICAPPED
AND MENTALLY RETARDED

Res — Coed Ages 6 and up; Day — Coed 2 and up

Opa Locka, FL 33054. 15701 NW 37th Ave.
Tel: 305-625-8354. Fax: 305-625-0744.
www.mariancenterschool.org   E-mail: mail@mariancenterschool.org
Tom Horan, PhD, Exec Dir.

Focus: Spec Ed. Treatment. **Conditions:** Primary—MR. Sec—OH.
Voc. Ungraded. Courses: Read Math Lang_Arts Computers. Shelt_Workshop. On-Job Trng.
Enr: 125. Res Males 16. Res Females 16. Day Males 48. Day Females 45.
Staff: 31.
Est 1964. Private. Nonprofit. Roman Catholic.

Marian Center offers a variety of programs for children and adults with developmental disabilities. The preschool provides sensorimotor training, academics, and social and language development for both developmentally disabled and nondisabled children. A day school program offers an alternative to public schools through small classes, self-care training and a general academic curriculum that includes music and physical education. The work activities center offers prevocational experiences and social services to developmentally disabled young adults. The supported employment program places clients in competitive jobs within the community and offers the support of a job coach.

The residential program serves a limited number of boys and girls enrolled in the day school, as well as adults in the workshop program. The five-day boarding schedule allows residents to spend weekends with their families.

Applicants for center services must be ambulatory.

MORNING STAR SCHOOL

Day — Coed Ages 5-16

Jacksonville, FL 32211. 725 Mickler Rd.
Tel: 904-721-2144. Fax: 904-721-1040.
www.morningstar-jax.com   E-mail: taschliman@juno.com
Teri L. Aschliman, EdD, Prin.

Focus: Spec Ed. **Conditions:** Primary—ADD ADHD Asp Dx LD. Sec—Apr BI CP Dg ED MR S. **IQ 80 and up.**
Gen Acad. Ungraded. Courses: Read Math Lang_Arts.
Therapy: Speech.
Enr: 114. **Staff:** 19 (Full 14, Part 5).
Rates 2003: Day $5000/sch yr.
Est 1958. Private. Nonprofit. Roman Catholic.

This school's program accepts learning-disabled, mildly emotionally disturbed and educable mentally retarded children. The curriculum is designed to facilitate the development of academic and motor skills, promoting appropriate social, behavioral and personal relationships, as well as spiritual growth.

The preschool emphasizes self-care, readiness activities and group interaction. Academic areas, perceptual training and self-control are stressed in the primary grades. Intermediate-level and junior high students continue academic training, and the program emphasizes the development of self-directiveness and familiarization with careers and related skill demands.

The school is located on the grounds of an adjoining parochial school, affording students part-time placement in regular classes. All students enroll on a trial basis for one month. Deaf, blind, severely physically or emotionally handicapped, and trainable mentally retarded children are ineligible for admission.

MORNING STAR SCHOOL

Day — Coed Ages 6-15

Tampa, FL 33612. 210 E Linebaugh Ave.
Tel: 813-935-0232. Fax: 813-932-2321.
www.tampa-morningstar.org
Jeanette Friedheim, MA, Prin.

   Focus: Spec Ed. **Conditions:** Primary—ADD ADHD Dx LD. Sec—Ap Asp BD Ep ON S.
   Gen Acad. Gr 1-8. Courses: Read Math Lang_Arts Sci Soc_Stud Fine_Arts.
   Therapy: Lang Speech.
   Enr: 79. Day Males 56. Day Females 23. **Staff:** 16 (Full 13, Part 3).
   Rates 2003: Day $7100/sch yr (+$425-575). Schol avail. State Aid.
   Est 1958. Private. Nonprofit. Roman Catholic.

Morning Star enrolls children who are unable to function in a regular classroom due to learning disabilities or related difficulties. During the primary years (ages 6-9), pupils attend self-contained classes, while departmentalization and ability grouping takes place in the intermediate (ages 9-12) and junior high (ages 12-16) divisions. The individualized curriculum strives to develop maximum efficiency in academics and motor skills connected with those areas. Applicants should possess average or above-average intelligence and must have a current psychological evaluation.

MORTON F. PLANT HOSPITAL
BARRETT REHABILITATION CENTER

Clinic: All Ages. M-F 8-6.

Clearwater, FL 33516. 430 Pinellas St.
Tel: 727-462-7031. Fax: 727-461-8258.
www.mortonplant.com

   Conditions: Primary—Ap D LD S.
   Therapy: Hear Lang Occup Phys Speech. **Psychotherapy:** Fam Group Indiv.
   Staff: Prof 5.
   Est 1961. Private. Nonprofit.

NORTHVIEW COMMUNITY

Res — Coed All Ages

Pensacola, FL 32514. 10050 Hill View Rd.
Tel: 850-474-0666. Fax: 850-474-0290.
Ruthie Andrews, Admin.
   Focus: Trng. Treatment. **Conditions:** Primary—Bl CP MD ON SB.
   Gen Acad. Gr K-12. Courses: Read Math Lang_Arts.
   Therapy: Hear Occup Phys Speech. **Psychotherapy:** Fam Group Indiv.
   Est 1942. Private. Nonprofit. **Spons:** New Horizons of Northwest Florida.

NOVA UNIVERSITY
RALPH J. BAUDHUIN PRESCHOOL

Day — Coed Ages 2-5

Fort Lauderdale, FL 33314. 3301 College Ave.
Tel: 954-262-7100. Fax: 954-262-3936.
www.nova.edu/msi/baudhuin   E-mail: baudhuin@nova.edu
Michele Kaplan, MA, Dir.
   Focus: Spec Ed. **Conditions:** Primary—Au. Sec—B D Db. **IQ 80 and up.**
   Gen Acad. Gr PS. Courses: Read Math Lang_Arts.
   Therapy: Lang Occup Phys Speech. **Psychotherapy:** Fam Parent.
   Enr: 150. **Staff:** 75. Admin 2.
   Rates 2003: No Fee.
   Summer Prgm: Day. Educ.
   Private. Nonprofit.

Baudhuin Preschool provides programming for children with autism. Preschoolers receive full funding from the county school district. The summer session serves only children enrolled in the school-year program.

PACE-BRANTLEY HALL SCHOOL

Day — Coed Ages 5-18

Longwood, FL 32779. 3221 Sand Lake Rd.
Tel: 407-869-8882. Fax: 407-869-8717.
www.pacebrantleyhall.org   E-mail: pabhschool@yahoo.com
Jacqueline Egli, BA, MA, Exec Dir. **Barbara Winter,** Adm.
   Focus: Spec Ed. **Conditions:** Primary—ADD ADHD Dx LD. **IQ 80 and up.**
   Col Prep. Gen Acad. Pre-Voc. Gr 1-12. Courses: Read Math Lang_Arts
     Span Ger Sci Govt Econ Studio_Art. Man_Arts & Shop. On-Job Trng.
   Therapy: Lang Speech. **Psychotherapy:** Fam Indiv.
   Enr: 147. Day Males 111. Day Females 36. **Staff:** 42 (Full 38, Part 4). Educ
     25. Admin 4.
   Rates 2003: Day $12,000/sch yr (+$600-800/sch yr). Schol 10 ($13,000).
   Summer Prgm: Day. Educ. Rec. Day Rate $325-600/3-wk ses. 6 wks.

Est 1972. Private. Nonprofit.

PACE-Brantley Hall provides a full ungraded curriculum for the child with learning disabilities whose needs are not met in a traditional school environment. Following a series of diagnostic tests, the school determines the child's potential for learning. The program's multisensory approach provides remediation while seeking to strengthen confidence and self-esteem. Slow learners and pupils with problems arising from neurological disorders are not accepted.

PALADIN ACADEMY

Day — Coed Ages 5-18

Delray Beach, FL 33445. 600 N Congress Ave, Ste 560.
Nearby locations: Fort Lauderdale; Hollywood; Miami; Pembroke Pines.
Tel: 561-265-1340. Fax: 561-265-6520.
www.paladinacademy.org　E-mail: lon.adams@nlcinc.com
Lonnie Adams, BS, MEd, EdS, Dir.
　　Focus: Spec Ed. **Conditions:** Primary—ADD ADHD Dc Dg Dx LD. Sec—Asp. **IQ 80-130.**
　　Col Prep. Gen Acad. Gr K-12. Courses: Read Math Lang_Arts Sci Soc_Stud.
　　Therapy: Occup Speech.
　　Enr: 30. Day Males 20. Day Females 10. **Staff:** 8 (Full 7, Part 1).
　　Rates 2003: Day $16,000/sch yr (+$1300). State Aid.
　　Summer Prgm: Day. Educ. Rec. Day Rate $300/wk.
　　Est 1980. Private. Inc. **Spons:** Nobel Learning Community.

The academy seeks to identify learning strengths and weaknesses and to develop individual prescriptive programs to remediate learning problems, dyslexia and attention deficit disorder intensively and in as short a time as possible. The program concentrates on reading, writing, language and arithmetic. Paladin conducts testing and adjusts programs to reflect the child's progress, which testing measures every four months. An Orton-Gillingham program is also available, and the program for attentionally disordered pupils includes individualized behavior management programs. The facility provides parental support groups at no additional charge.

PALM BEACH HABILITATION CENTER

Res — Coed Ages 18 and up; Day — Coed 16 and up

Lake Worth, FL 33461. 4522 S Congress Ave.
Tel: 561-965-8500. Fax: 561-433-5248.
www.pbhab.com　E-mail: postman@pbhab.com
Tina Philips, Pres.
　　Focus: Trng. **Conditions:** Primary—Au B CP D ED Ep MR ON SB Sz. Sec—ADD ADHD Ap As BD BI C CD Dx IP LD MD MS OCD Psy TB. **IQ 25 and up.**
　　Pre-Voc. Voc. Ungraded. Shelt_Workshop. On-Job Trng.
　　Est 1959. Private. Nonprofit.

The center offers vocational training, work adjustment, occupational skills training, job placement, supported and sheltered employment, and supported independent living services for individuals with mental, emotional and physical disabilities. PBHC provides the following: vocational evaluation, employee development training, supported employment, job placement, work services, an adult skills acquisition program, computer training, food service training, case management, group and transitional homes, supported living and a recreational program. The center places primary emphasis on work evaluation and training, with the goal being competitive community employment.

PERSONAL ENRICHMENT
THROUGH MENTAL HEALTH SERVICES

Res — Coed Ages 6-17; Day — Coed 13-17

Pinellas Park, FL 34666. 11254 58th St N.
Tel: 727-545-6477. Fax: 727-545-6464.
www.pemhs.org   E-mail: info@pemhs.org
   Conditions: Primary—ED LD. Sec—Ap As B BD Bl D Dx Ep MR ON S TB. **IQ 69 and up.**
   Gen Acad. Pre-Voc. Voc. Ungraded. Courses: Read Math Lang_Arts. Man_ Arts & Shop. Shelt_Workshop. On-Job Trng.
   Therapy: Hear Lang Occup Phys Recreational Speech. **Psychotherapy:** Fam Group Indiv.
   Enr: 33. Res Males 21. Res Females 12.
   Rates 2004: No Fee.
   Est 1981. Private. Nonprofit.

This facility specializes in helping severely emotionally disturbed youths who need ongoing, long-term day treatment or residential care. The following are among the services offered for children and adolescents: emergency intake and stabilization; screening, assessment and diagnosis; intensive adolescent day treatment; residential treatment; family counseling and parental skills training; individualized educational services; self-help support groups; special programs for chronic, psychotic and aggressive populations; behavior modification; psychiatric treatment and nursing care; and walk-in crisis counseling. The usual length of stay is nine months to one year.

PRIMROSE CENTER

Day — Coed Ages 18 and up

Orlando, FL 32806. 2733 S Ferncreek Ave.
Tel: 407-898-7201. Fax: 407-898-2120.
Mary van Buren, Exec Dir.
   Focus: Trng. Treatment. **Conditions:** Primary—MR.
   Pre-Voc. Voc. Ungraded. Courses: Read Math. Shelt_Workshop.
   Est 1952. Private. Nonprofit.

THE PROGRESSIVE SCHOOL

Day — Coed Ages 4-14

West Palm Beach, FL 33406. 1950 Prairie Rd.
Tel: 561-642-3100. Fax: 561-969-1950.
www.progressiveschool.org   E-mail: progsch@fdn.com
Richard J. Vermaas, MA, Dir. **Jennifer Lynn,** Adm.
   Focus: Spec Ed. **Conditions:** Primary—LD. Sec—ADD ADHD Asp Au Dc
   Dg Dx MR. **IQ 75-125.**
   Gen Acad. Gr PS-8. Courses: Read Math Lang_Arts Span Sci Soc_Stud
   Computers Studio_Art Music.
   Enr: 120. Day Males 70. Day Females 50. **Staff:** 19 (Full 16, Part 3). Prof
   15. Admin 4.
   Rates 2003: Day $4725-7497/sch yr (+$500). Schol ($25,000). State Aid.
   Summer Prgm: Day. Educ. Rec. Day Rate $1040. 8 wks.
   Est 1937. Private. Inc. **Spons:** Educational Services of America.

This structured school accommodates boys and girls with varying learning styles.
Students progressing at the appropriate grade level take part in small classes that focus
on individual needs; pupils who are working two to three years below grade level take
part in self-contained classes; and those with more severe learning disabilities utilize the
school's highly individualized learning resource laboratories.

The school reinforces positive behavior and teaches the organizational skills necessary for academic success. Students with learning disabilities engage in various school
activities with boys and girls who are not.

ROYAL PALM SCHOOL

Day — Coed Ages 3-22

Lantana, FL 33462. 6650 Lawrence Rd.
Tel: 561-649-6580. Fax: 561-649-6849.
www.palmbeach.k12.fl.us/royalpalmschool
Revia S. Lee, MEd, Prin.
   Focus: Spec Ed. Treatment. **Conditions:** Primary—Au B Bl CP D ED ON S
   SB. Sec—Ap MR.
   Pre-Voc. Gr PS-12. Courses: Read Math Lang_Arts Adaptive_Phys_Ed.
   Man_Arts & Shop. On-Job Trng.
   Therapy: Hear Lang Occup Phys Speech. **Psychotherapy:** Indiv Parent.
   Enr: 350. **Staff:** 106.
   Rates 2004: No Fee.
   Est 1942. State. Nonprofit.

Royal Palm provides year-round education for children with physical special needs
and mental retardation, with emphasis placed on community living skills, personal and
home management, community access and applied academics. A program of music,
physical and vocational education, developmental reading and speech therapy seeks to
meet the needs of the individual. Other offerings include an adaptive physical education
program and a variety of civic organizations.

SPEECH AND HEARING CENTER

Clinic: All Ages. M-F 8:30-5.

Jacksonville, FL 32206. 1128 Laura St.
Tel: 904-355-3403. TTY: 904-355-3403. Fax: 904-355-4149.
www.shcjax.org   E-mail: shc@shcjax.org
Amy Ernharth, MEd, Exec Dir.
 Focus: Treatment. **Conditions:** Primary—D S.
 Therapy: Hear Lang Speech.
 Staff: 8 (Full 3, Part 5).
 Rates 2003: No Fee.
 Est 1948. Private. Nonprofit.

This center provides diagnostic, evaluative and therapeutic services for children and adults with speech, hearing and language impairments. Fees vary according to services rendered. Duration of treatment varies.

STEP BY STEP
EARLY CHILDHOOD EDUCATION AND THERAPY CENTER

Day — Coed Ages Birth-5

Naples, FL 34116. 5860 Golden Gate Pky.
Tel: 941-455-9525. Fax: 941-455-2844.
Jean Mekeel, Dir.
 Focus: Spec Ed. **Conditions:** Primary—Au Bl CP ED MR. Sec—Ap B C D Ep LD S SB.
 Gen Acad. Gr PS.
 Therapy: Hear Lang Occup Phys Speech Aqua. **Psychotherapy:** Fam Group.
 Enr: 125. **Staff:** 32 (Full 28, Part 4). Prof 10. Educ 9. Admin 2.
 Est 1976. Private. Nonprofit.

Step by Step is an early developmental intervention program. Specialists implement an individualized educational plan that includes the areas of socialization, language, self-help, cognitive, fine- and gross-motor, and self-awareness skills. Goals for individual achievement are periodically revised based upon the child's progress. Parent training is an integral part of both therapy and the education program. The preschool program seeks to ease the transition to public schools.

SUNRISE COMMUNITY

Res — Coed All Ages; Day — Coed 21 and up

Miami, FL 33173. 9040 Sunset Dr.
Tel: 305-596-9040. Fax: 305-598-8240.
www.sunrisegroup.org   E-mail: info@sunrisegroup.org
Leslie W. Leech, Jr., MS, Pres.
 Focus: Trng. Treatment. **Conditions:** Primary—Au Bl CP MR ON SB.

Sec—ADD ADHD Ap As B BD C CD D Dx ED Ep IP LD MD MS OCD Psy S Sz TB.
Voc. Shelt_Workshop. On-Job Trng.
Therapy: Hear Lang Occup Phys Speech. **Psychotherapy:** Group Indiv Parent.
Est 1965. Private. Nonprofit.

Sunrise Community provides residential services, supported living arrangements, developmental training, supported employment opportunities, adult day programs and therapeutic programming for individuals with developmental disabilities. The program's goal is to maximize independence, personal choice and feeling of inclusion in the community for its clients, regardless of the extent of their support needs.

In addition to the Florida location, Sunrise also conducts programs in Connecticut, Tennessee, Virginia, Alabama and Georgia.

TAMPA BAY ACADEMY

Res and Day — Coed Ages 4-18

Riverview, FL 33569. 12012 Boyette Rd.
Tel: 813-677-6700. TTY: 813-677-2502. Fax: 813-671-3145.
www.tampabay-academy.com   E-mail: dsk@tampa.yfcs.com
   Focus: Spec Ed. Treatment. **Conditions:** Primary—ADD ADHD BD CD D ED OCD Psy Sz. Sec—Dx LD. **IQ 65 and up.**
   Gen Acad. Pre-Voc. Gr K-12. Courses: Read Math Lang_Arts. On-Job Trng.
   Therapy: Speech. **Psychotherapy:** Fam Group Indiv Parent.
   Enr: 96. **Staff:** 220 (Full 190, Part 30).
   Est 1988. Private. Inc.

A comprehensive psychiatric treatment center, the academy provides year-round medically directed psychiatric care for children and adolescents who need 24-hour structured care and therapy but are not in an acute state. A three-dimensional structure, which encompasses therapy, education and milieu treatment, is employed to help each individual. Therapy addresses emotional and behavioral needs individually, in groups and as family units, while the educational program offers academic and vocational courses. Community life at the academy fosters overall emotional and social development. The usual length of treatment is three to nine months.

TAMPA DAY SCHOOL

Day — Coed Ages 5-14
Clinic: Ages 5-14. M-F.

Tampa, FL 33625. 12606 Henderson Rd.
Tel: 813-269-2100. Fax: 813-963-7843.
www.tampadayschool.com   E-mail: tds@tampadayschool.com
Lois Delaney, MA, Dir.
   Conditions: Primary—ADD ADHD LD. **IQ 90 and up.**
   Gen Acad. Ungraded. Courses: Read Math Lang_Arts.
   Therapy: Lang Percepual-Motor.

Est 1969. Private. Inc. **Spons:** Florida Children's Center.

THRESHOLD

Res — Coed All Ages; Day — Coed 3-5

Winter Park, FL 32792. 3550 N Goldenrod Rd.
Tel: 407-671-7060. Fax: 407-671-6005.
www.threshold.ws
Teena Willard, Pres. **Veda Vyas,** MD, Med Dir.
  Conditions: Primary—Au.
  Pre-Voc. Gr PS. Courses: Read Math Lang_Arts. Shelt_Workshop. On-Job
    Trng.
  Est 1976. Private. Nonprofit.

UCP OF SOUTH FLORIDA

Res and Day — Coed All Ages

Miami, FL 33174. 10899 SW 4th St.
Tel: 305-325-1080. Fax: 305-325-1313.
www.ucpsouthflorida.org   E-mail: info@ucpsouthflorida.org
Joseph A. Aniello, EdD, Pres.
  Conditions: Primary—Au CP DS MR ON S SB.
  Gen Acad. Pre-Voc. Voc. Courses: Read Math Lang_Arts. Man_Arts &
    Shop. Shelt_Workshop. On-Job Trng.
  Therapy: Music.
  Est 1948. Private. Nonprofit.

UNITED CEREBRAL PALSY OF NORTHWEST FLORIDA

Res and Day — Coed Ages 18 and up

Pensacola, FL 32501. 2912 N "E" Street.
Tel: 850-432-1596. Fax: 850-432-1930.
www.ucpnwfl.org   E-mail: information@ucpnwfl.org
Stephen Bennett, Pres.
  Focus: Trng. **Conditions:** Primary—Au B Bl CP D MR ON S SB.
  Pre-Voc. Voc. Ungraded. Courses: Read Math. Shelt_Workshop. On-Job
    Trng.
  Therapy: Hear Phys Speech. **Psychotherapy:** Fam Group.
  Enr: 84. Res Males 10. Res Females 8. Day Males 34. Day Females 32.
    Staff: 47 (Full 29, Part 18).
  Rates 2004: No Fee.
  Est 1953. Private. Nonprofit. **Spons:** United Cerebral Palsy Association.

This facility provides services for individuals with cerebral palsy and other severe physical disabilities. Two day programs—one in Pensacola and the other in Fort Walton Beach—emphasize daily living skills, community inclusion, physical therapy, academic training and socialization. UCP also operates five residential housing facilities. Residents have access to 24-hour care in a homelike environment that includes participant-directed activities and training opportunities. In addition, supported living and supported employment programs provide training and assistance for individuals with disabilities who wish to live and work in the community.

UNIVERSITY OF FLORIDA SPEECH AND HEARING CLINIC
Clinic: All Ages. M-F 8-5.

Gainesville, FL 32611. 435 Dauer Hall.
Tel: 352-392-2041. TTY: 352-392-2041. Fax: 352-846-2189.
http://web.csd.ufl.edu/speech.html
Betsy P. Vinson, BA, MMS, Dir.
  Focus: Treatment. **Conditions:** Primary—Ap Apr CP D DS Dx LD S. Sec—ADD ADHD Au Bl Dc Dg IP MD MR MS ON SB.
  Therapy: Hear Lang Speech. **Psychotherapy:** Parent.
  Staff: 19 (Full 4, Part 15). Prof 18. Admin 1.
  Rates 2003: Clinic $30/hr. Schol 25.
  Est 1945. State. Nonprofit.

This teaching clinic offers evaluation and therapy for speech, language, augmentative communication and hearing problems. All client services are provided by students under the supervision of faculty members and doctoral students. Fees vary according to the services provided, and there is no charge for therapy if the patient fits the clinic's research protocol.

UNIVERSITY OF SOUTH FLORIDA
DEPARTMENT OF COMMUNICATION
SCIENCES AND DISORDERS
COMMUNICATION DISORDERS CENTER
Clinic: All Ages. M-F 8:30-6.

Tampa, FL 33620. 4202 Fowler Ave, Bldg PCD 1017.
Tel: 813-974-9844. Fax: 813-974-0822.
www.cas.usf.edu/csd/clinic/clinic_page.htm
  E-mail: sgraham@chuma1.cas.usf.edu
Arthur Guilford, PhD, CCC-SLP, Supv. **Sandra Graham,** PhD, CCC-SLP, Dir.
  Focus: Treatment. **Conditions:** Primary—Ap D S. Sec—Apr Asp Au Bl CP Dx IP LD OH.
  Therapy: Hear Lang Speech.
  Staff: 33 (Full 30, Part 3). Prof 33.
  Rates 2003: Sliding-Scale Rate $10-350/sem.
  Est 1969. State.

Master's-level students under the supervision of certified faculty provide comprehensive speech, language and audiological evaluation services at the clinic. Group and individual therapy sessions are also available. In addition, faculty and graduate students jointly conduct clinical research pertaining to the diagnosis and treatment of communicational disorders.

UNIVERSITY OF SOUTH FLORIDA MEDICAL CENTER GENETICS CLINIC

Clinic: All Ages. M Th 8-5.

Tampa, FL 33606. 1 Davis Blvd, Ste 604.
Tel: 813-233-2720. Fax: 813-233-2734.
Boris Kousseff, MD, Med Dir.
   Focus: Treatment. Conditions: Primary—Au B Bl C CP D DS Ep IP MD MR ON S SB. Sec—As BD CD ED MS OCD Psy Sz TB. IQ 10-120.
   Staff: 6 (Full 4, Part 2). Admin 2.
   State.

The clinic provides evaluations, diagnosis, management and treatment of genetic disorders in infants, children and adolescents. Services also include prenatal diagnoses of genetic disorders and physician and genetic counseling services.

VANGUARD SCHOOL

Res — Coed Ages 11-18; Day — Coed 12-18

Lake Wales, FL 33853. 2249 Hwy 27 N.
Tel: 863-676-6091. Fax: 863-676-8297.
www.vanguardschool.org   E-mail: vanadmin@vanguardschool.org
James R. Moon, MBA, Pres. Melanie Anderson, Adm.
   Focus: Spec Ed. Conditions: Primary—Dx LD. Sec—ADD ADHD Bl. IQ 80 and up.
   Col Prep. Gen Acad. Pre-Voc. Gr 5-PG. Courses: Read Math Lang_Arts. Man_Arts & Shop. Shelt_Workshop.
   Therapy: Lang Speech.
   Enr: 134. Res Males 66. Res Females 55. Day Males 9. Day Females 4.
      Staff: 28.
   Rates 2004: Res $34,750/sch yr (+$1000). Day $19,150/sch yr. Schol avail.
   Est 1966. Private. Nonprofit.

Through its prescription for learning, Vanguard prepares students with learning disabilities, learning problems and related school adjustment difficulties for either high school graduation or the return to a less specialized program.

Students with communication problems participate in a curriculum that emphasizes language development and includes speech therapy and auditory training. Those with reading disabilities may participate in one-on-one sessions with reading specialists. Career and vocational orientation stressing practical learning is available for high school students.

Situated three miles north of Lake Wales, the campus occupies a 75-acre tract that include a swimming pool, tennis courts, an industrial/practical arts center and a gymnasium.

VANGUARD SCHOOL OF COCONUT GROVE

Day — Coed Ages 6-14

Coconut Grove, FL 33133. 3939 Main Hwy.
Tel: 305-445-7992. Fax: 305-441-9255.
www.vanguardschool.com   E-mail: vangcg@aol.com
John R. Havrilla, BS, MS, Dir.
  Focus: Spec Ed. **Conditions:** Primary—ADD ADHD Dx LD.
  Gen Acad. Ungraded. Courses: Read Math Lang_Arts Sci Computers Soc_ Stud Studio_Art Music.
  Enr: 80. Day Males 55. Day Females 25. **Staff:** 14. (Full 14). Prof 12. Educ 12. Admin 2.
  Rates 2004: Day $12,800-13,335/sch yr (+$1000). Schol avail. State Aid.
  Est 1968. Private. Nonprofit.

Vanguard offers a nontraditional education for students with atypical learning patterns or difficulties in the visual or auditory processing of information. Education is individualized and classes consist of a maximum of 10 students. The program stresses the development of homework skills, social and organizational skills, and the ability to think, write and communicate. The goal is to return pupils to traditional schools.

See Also Page 1053

WOODLAND HALL ACADEMY

Day — Coed Ages 6-20

Tallahassee, FL 32308. 5746 Centerville Rd.
Tel: 850-893-2216. Fax: 850-893-2440.
www.dyslexia-add.org   E-mail: dri@dyslexia-add.org
Patricia K. Hardman, BS, MAT, PhD, CEO. **Stacy A. Fabrega,** BA, MA, Dir.
  Amber S. Mitchell, BA, Prin.
  Focus: Spec Ed. **Conditions:** Primary—ADD ADHD Dc Dg Dx LD. **IQ 90 and up.**
  Col Prep. Gen Acad. Gr 1-12. Courses: Read Math Lang_Arts Sci Computers Hist Study_Skills.
  Enr: 50. Day Males 28. Day Females 22. **Staff:** 15. Educ 9. Admin 4.
  Summer Prgm: Day. Educ.
  Est 1975. Private. Nonprofit. **Spons:** Dyslexia Research Institute.

Woodland Hall, a division of the Dyslexia Research Institute, accepts only those children diagnosed with dyslexia, attention deficit disorder or a related learning difference who possess average or above-average intelligence. Math, reading, language, sensorial and perceptual skills are emphasized in the primary classes. A basic college preparatory curriculum is followed in the highly structured, nongraded advanced program.

Parental involvement is an integral part of Woodland's program. In addition to academics, the program emphasizes positive self-concept development, self-control, organizational skills, and acceptable social and behavioral adjustment. Pupils may undergo diagnostic testing and may attend one-on-one tutorial sessions. Foster family placement is also available.

GEORGIA

THE ACHIEVEMENT ACADEMY

Day — Coed Ages 6-15

Columbus, GA 31904. 5700 River Rd.
Tel: 706-660-0050. Fax: 706-660-0056.
www.achacad.org
Beth Sawyer, MEd, Dir.
    Focus: Spec Ed. **Conditions:** Primary—ADD ADHD Dx LD. **IQ 85 and up.**
    Gen Acad. Gr 1-8. Courses: Read Math Lang_Arts.
    Enr: 50. Day Males 30. Day Females 20. **Staff:** 11. (Full 11).
    Rates 2004: Day $8450/sch yr (+$450). Schol avail.
    Est 1984. Private. Nonprofit.

Children with specific learning disabilities, ADD and ADHD receive intensive, specialized instruction at the academy. After administering and evaluating tests, faculty members begin setting specific goals for each child. The goal-oriented approach seeks to minimize frustration while also providing encouragement for the student. Pupils return to a traditional school setting after an average of years.

ANNANDALE VILLAGE

Res and Day — Coed Ages 18 and up

Suwanee, GA 30024. 3500 Annandale Ln.
Tel: 770-945-8381. Fax: 770-945-8693.
www.annandale.org   E-mail: administration@annandale.org
Patricia M. Brown, Exec Dir.
    Focus: Treatment. **Conditions:** Primary—BI DS MR OH. Sec—Au CP D
    ED Ep Sz.
    Pre-Voc. Voc. Ungraded. Courses: Life_Skills. Man_Arts & Shop. Shelt_
    Workshop. On-Job Trng.
    Therapy: Hydro Music Recreational. **Psychotherapy:** Group Indiv.
    Enr: 94. Res Males 46. Res Females 43. Day Males 2. Day Females 3.
    Staff: 56 (Full 52, Part 4).
    Rates 2004: Res $29,800-31,500/yr. Day $477-1144/mo.
    Est 1969. Private. Nonprofit.

Situated on a 124-acre tract, Annandale provides a home community for ambulatory individuals with developmental disabilities, mental retardation or head injuries. Programs and services, which include goal-oriented work and recreational activities, professional guidance and support, residential living, respite services, a day program and skilled nursing, emphasize the development of a well-rounded, productive lifestyle.

The facility offers consistent case management services in an effort to meet individual needs and promote personal growth, achievement and adjustment.

ATLANTA AREA SCHOOL FOR THE DEAF

Day — Coed Ages 3-21

Clarkston, GA 30021. 890 N Indian Creek Dr.
Tel: 404-296-7101. TTY: 404-296-7101. Fax: 404-299-4485.
www.aasd.k12.ga.us
Lillian Blakesley, PhD, Dir. **Donald Galloway,** Adm.
   Focus: Spec Ed. **Conditions:** Primary—D. Sec—ADD ADHD Asp Au MR
     ON PDD.
   Col Prep. Gen Acad. Pre-Voc. Voc. Gr PS-12. Courses: Read Math Lang_
     Arts Sci Computers. On-Job Trng.
   Therapy: Hear Lang Occup Phys Speech.
   Enr: 200. **Staff:** 63 (Full 60, Part 3).
   Rates 2003: No Fee.
   Est 1972. State.

AASD provides an academic program for deaf and hearing-impaired children; children with one or more handicapping conditions may enroll. Vocational and educational counseling is available, as is a career education program. In addition, the school offers comprehensive diagnostic and assessment services to local educational agencies.

ATLANTA SPEECH SCHOOL
ORAL SCHOOL

Day — Coed Ages Birth-10

Atlanta, GA 30327. 3160 Northside Pky NW.
Tel: 404-233-5332. Fax: 404-266-2175.
www.atlantaspeechschool.org   E-mail: erajtar@atlspsch.org
Ellen Rajtar, MS, Coord.
   Focus: Spec Ed. **Conditions:** Primary—D. Sec—ADD Apr As CF Db Nf. **IQ
     85 and up.**
   Gen Acad. Ungraded. Courses: Read Math Lang_Arts.
   Therapy: Hear Lang Speech.
   Enr: 33. Day Males 21. Day Females 12. **Staff:** 18. (Full 18).
   Rates 2003: Day $14,025/sch yr (+$60). Clinic $150/hr. Schol avail. State
     Aid.
   Summer Prgm: Day. Educ. Rec. Ther. Day Rate $1800. 6 wks.
   Est 1938. Private. Nonprofit.

This branch of Atlanta Speech School consists of three main components: a special school, a parent-infant program, and a resource program that provides one-on-one assistance for hearing-impaired children from regular school settings. Psycho-educational evaluations for hearing-impaired children are also available. A primary goal of the program is to develop residual hearing, both for better understanding of others and for further developing the child's own speech. The school program incorporates FM amplification systems.

Atlanta Speech School operates a children's cochlear implant center that, in conjunction with the Oral School, offers speech and auditory training to children being considered for implants and to those who have already received implants. Classroom teachers and members of the cochlear implant staff work together to maximize the benefits of the implant.

Other offerings of the facility include educational consultation and placement services as well as learning disabilities and speech/language/audiology clinics that offer diagnostic and remedial services.

ATLANTA SPEECH SCHOOL
WARDLAW SCHOOL

Day — Coed Ages 5-12

Atlanta, GA 30327. 3160 Northside Pky NW.
Tel: 404-233-5332. TTY: 404-233-5332. Fax: 404-266-2175.
www.atlantaspeechschool.org   E-mail: mdemko@atlspsch.org
Maureen Demko, MEd, Co-Coord. **Sondra Mims,** MA, CCC-SLP, Co-Coord.
   Gale Shafer, Adm.
   Focus: Spec Ed. **Conditions:** Primary—Dc Dg Dx LD. Sec—ADD ADHD S.
      IQ 90 and up.
   Gen Acad. Gr K-6. Courses: Read Math Lang_Arts.
   Therapy: Lang Occup Speech.
   Enr: 181. Day Males 114. Day Females 67. **Staff:** 41 (Full 37, Part 4).
   Rates 2003: Day $16,243/sch yr (+$150). Clinic $150/hr. Schol avail.
   Summer Prgm: Day. Educ. Rec. Rem. Day Rate $900-1800. 3-6 wks.
   Est 1938. Private. Nonprofit.

The Wardlaw School, a division of the Atlanta Speech School, integrates individualized remediation within a comprehensive school program. Oral communication, language comprehension, vocabulary developments and conversational skills are key components of the program. To allow for individualized programming, class size is kept small. Classes are nongraded and instructional groupings are based on age, social maturity and general cognitive and skill levels.

The Wardlaw School uses a collaborative model incorporating language-based instruction throughout the curriculum. Speech-language pathologists work with the classroom teacher to design and implement the classroom curriculum, then work individually with children as needed. Reading specialists are also part of the teaching staff.

In addition to the Wardlaw School, the Atlanta Speech School has a mainstream preschool program, and educational programs for children who are deaf or hard of hearing or who have speech or language delays or disorders. Other offerings of the facility include educational consultation and placement services as well as learning disabilities and speech/language/audiology clinics that offer diagnostic and remedial services.

THE AUGUSTA SCHOOL

Day — Coed Ages 6-14

Augusta, GA 30907. 3685 Old Petersburg Rd.
Tel: 706-736-1238.
   Focus: Spec Ed. **Conditions:** Primary—ADD ADHD Dx LD.
   Gen Acad. Gr K-8. Courses: Read Math Lang_Arts.

Therapy: Lang Speech.
Enr: 50. Day Males 36. Day Females 14. **Staff:** 13 (Full 10, Part 3).
Schol avail.
Est 1991. Private. Nonprofit.

This school provides diagnosis, education and therapy for children with average to above-average intelligence who have learning difficulties. Augusta employs the Orton-Gillingham approach, and classes have a maximum of 10 children at all grade levels.

THE BEDFORD SCHOOL

Day — Coed Ages 7-14

Fairburn, GA 30123. 5665 Milam Rd.
Tel: 770-774-8001. Fax: 770-774-8005.
www.thebedfordschool.org   E-mail: bedfordschool@aol.com
Betsy E. Box, Dir.
    Focus: Spec Ed. **Conditions:** Primary—Dx LD. Sec—ADD ADHD As Asp
      Bl Db Dc Dg Ep OCD TS. **IQ 90 and up.**
    Gen Acad. Gr 1-9. Courses: Read Math Lang_Arts.
    Therapy: Speech.
    Enr: 126. Day Males 92. Day Females 34. **Staff:** 24 (Full 17, Part 7).
    Rates 2003: Day $11,900-12,200/sch yr (+$200). Schol avail.
    Summer Prgm: Res. Educ. Res Rate $3475-3975. 5 wks.
    Est 1982. Private. Nonprofit.

The goal of this school for pupils with learning disabilities is to remediate and return children to a mainstream classroom setting. Class size does not exceed 12 students, and Bedford groups children according to skill level. An activity period includes classes such as art, music, computer and social values.

Extracurricular activities include soccer, basketball, volleyball, track and field, cheerleading, yearbook, newspaper and karate. Individual speech and language therapy, hot lunches and after-school care are all available for an additional fee.

BRANDON HALL SCHOOL

Res — Males Ages 13-19; Day — Coed 10-19
Clinic: All Ages. M-S 8-5; Eves M-S 5-8.

Atlanta, GA 30350. 1701 Brandon Hall Dr.
Tel: 770-394-8177. Fax: 770-804-8821.
www.brandonhall.org   E-mail: admissions@brandonhall.org
Paul R. Stockhammer, BA, MEd, Pres. **Steve Boyce,** Adm.
    Focus: Spec Ed. **Conditions:** Primary—ADD ADHD Dx LD. **IQ 85 and up.**
    Col Prep. Gr 4-PG. Courses: Read Math Lang_Arts Sci Hist Studio_Art
      Drama.
    Psychotherapy: Indiv.
    Enr: 155. Res Males 59. Day Males 71. Day Females 25. **Staff:** 39.
    Rates 2003: Res $40,500-42,500/sch yr (+$1000). Day $26,000/sch yr
      (+$1000).

Summer Prgm: Res & Day. Educ. Res Rate $4600. Day Rate $2400. 6 wks.
Est 1959. Private. Nonprofit.

This school stresses college preparatory academic skills, independent study habits, and personal self-discipline for underachieving, learning-disabled and other bright students with different learning styles. Reconstruction of basic skills and acceleration of course work are available. All seniors receive SAT preparation. The middle school program (grades 4-8) features one-on-one and small-group (five or fewer students) instruction; upper school classes do not exceed twelve pupils. Sports and clubs supplement the curriculum.

CENTER FOR THE VISUALLY IMPAIRED

Day — Coed Ages Birth-18
Clinic: Ages 5 and up. M-F by Appt.

Atlanta, GA 30308. 739 W Peachtree St NW.
Tel: 404-875-9011. Fax: 404-607-0062.
www.cviatlanta.org   E-mail: info@cviatlanta.org
Susan B. Green, BFA, MSEd, Exec Dir. **LaDella Holmes-Reddick,** Adm.
  Focus: Spec Ed. Rehab. **Conditions:** Primary—B. Sec—Ap Asp Au D Db DS ED LD MR ON PDD S.
  Therapy: Art Dance Movement Music Phys Recreational. **Psychotherapy:** Fam Group Parent.
  Enr: 195. **Staff:** 9 (Full 6, Part 3). Educ 9. Admin 1.
  Summer Prgm: Day. 7 wks.
  Est 1973. Private. Nonprofit.

CVI provides evaluation and training in all areas of daily living. Areas addressed include mobility, communicational skills, and personal and home management. Vocational education and job placement are an important aspect of the program. The facility maintains a complete early intervention program and operates a developmental preschool, and it also offers group therapy and counseling for parents of very young blind children.

CHATHAM ACADEMY

Day — Coed Ages 6-18

Savannah, GA 31406. 4 Oglethorpe Professional Blvd.
Tel: 912-354-4047. Fax: 912-354-4633.
www.roycelearningcenter.com/ca.htm
  E-mail: info@roycelearningcenter.com
Kathleen Burke, EdD, Exec Dir. **Carolyn M. Hannaford,** MEd, Prin.
  Focus: Spec Ed. **Conditions:** Primary—ADD ADHD Dx LD. **IQ 75 and up.**
  Col Prep. Gen Acad. Pre-Voc. Gr 1-12. Courses: Read Math Lang_Arts.
  Therapy: Lang Speech. **Psychotherapy:** Parent.
  Enr: 85. Day Males 67. Day Females 18. **Staff:** 20 (Full 18, Part 2).
  Rates 2004: Day $9012-9312/sch yr. Schol 28 ($68,000).
  Summer Prgm: Day. Educ. Rec. Day Rate $700. 5 wks.

Est 1978. Private. Nonprofit. **Spons:** Royce Learning Center.

This school provides special education for students with learning disabilities, ADHD or both. Chatham's program includes all the necessary course work for a high school diploma. Students usually spend two to three years at the academy.

THE COTTAGE SCHOOL

Day — Coed Ages 11-18

Roswell, GA 30075. 700 Grimes Bridge Rd.
Tel: 770-641-8688. Fax: 770-641-9026.
www.cottageschool.org   E-mail: tcs@cottageschool.org
Jacque Digieso, PhD, Exec Dir.
  Focus: Spec Ed. **Conditions:** Primary—ADD ADHD Dx LD. **IQ 75-115.**
  Col Prep. Gen Acad. Pre-Voc. Gr 6-12. Courses: Read Math Lang_Arts
    Eng Fr Span Sci Soc_Stud Studio_Art. Man_Arts & Shop. On-Job Trng.
  Enr: 156. Day Males 106. Day Females 50. **Staff:** 48.
  Rates 2004: Day $13,750-16,250/sch yr. Schol avail.
  Summer Prgm: Day. Educ. Life_Skills. Day Rate $900. 6 wks.
  Est 1985. Private. Nonprofit.

This school offers individualized educational programming for adolescents with a history of learning difficulties. The program features an academic curriculum, pre-vocational programming, and attention to study skills and social skills development. Vocational, educational and parental counseling are available, as is career development assistance.

DEVEREUX GEORGIA TREATMENT NETWORK

Res — Coed Ages 10-21

Kennesaw, GA 30156. 1291 Stanley Rd NW, PO Box 1688.
Tel: 770-427-0147. Fax: 770-423-1502.
www.devereuxga.org   E-mail: georgia@devereux.org
Mario Bolivar, LCSW, Exec Dir. **Yassar Kanawati,** MD, Med Dir.
  Focus: Spec Ed. Treatment. **Conditions:** Primary—ADD ADHD Anx BD CD
    ED Mood OCD ODD Psy PTSD Sz. Sec—Db Dx LD MR S. **IQ 55 and
    up.**
  Gen Acad. Pre-Voc. Voc. Ungraded. Courses: Read Math Lang_Arts. Man_
    Arts & Shop. Shelt_Workshop. On-Job Trng.
  Therapy: Art Chemo Music Recreational Speech. **Psychotherapy:** Fam
    Group Indiv Parent.
  Enr: 185.
  Est 1973. Private. Nonprofit. **Spons:** Devereux Foundation.

Serving youth with moderate to severe emotional disturbances and their families, Devereux Georgia offers a variety of treatment programs. Conducted on a 36-acre tract, the residential program admits children whose level of functioning ranges from mild mental retardation to superior intelligence. The individualized program is divided into pre-adolescent (ages 10-13) and adolescent (ages 14-18) divisions. Specialty programs include mental health, sexually reactive disorders (for males only) and sexual trauma recovery (for females only). Psychiatric, psychological, educational, vocational, recreational and aftercare planning services are provided. Project Plus, Devereux's assisted living program, prepares young adults ages 17-21 for an independent adulthood. The program provides educational and vocational instruction, while also addressing money management and social skills.

A wrap-around services program provides individualized care, supervision and treatment on an in-home basis for boys and girls ages 5-18. The therapeutic foster care program also offers in-home services, including case management services and crisis intervention, for individuals ages 3-18.

Devereux seeks to discharge boys and girls to the least restrictive possible environment with skills that improve the likelihood of future success. The average length of stay is 12 to 14 months.   **See Also Page 1025**

ECKERD YOUTH ALTERNATIVES

Res — Males Ages 10-17

Blakely, GA.
Contact: 100 N Starcrest Dr, PO Box 7450, Clearwater, FL 33758.
   Nearby locations: Suches.
Tel: 727-461-2990. Fax: 727-442-5911.
www.eckerd.org   E-mail: admissions@eckerd.org
Karen V. Waddell, BA, Pres. **Francene Hazel,** Dir.
   Focus: Treatment. **Conditions:** Primary—BD CD ED Mood ODD. Sec—
      ADD ADHD LD. **IQ 70 and up.**
   Gen Acad. Pre-Voc. Ungraded. Courses: Read Math Lang_Arts Sci Soc_
      Stud.
   Therapy: Speech. **Psychotherapy:** Fam Group Indiv.
   Summer Prgm: Res. Ther. Res Rate $180. 2 wks.
   Est 1968. Private. Nonprofit.

The Eckerd outdoor program offers therapeutic treatment to emotionally disturbed children by providing a camp setting as an alternative to institutionalization.

The year-round program utilizes reality therapy, Rogerian techniques and group therapy. Small-group living in the wilderness environment encourages the acquisition of new skills while promoting discipline and responsibility. Each group must construct their shelter, cut wood, repair equipment and perform other tasks necessary for their stay in the forest. Such experiences provide the children with the opportunity to develop academic skills at their own pace and in relation to each project they endeavor. When sufficient progress is made, children are transferred into the transition classroom in preparation for their return to the mainstream.

In addition to Georgia, Eckerd conducts outdoor therapeutic treatment programs in the following states: Florida, New Hampshire, North Carolina, Rhode Island, Tennessee and Vermont (see separate listings).

THE FRAZER CENTER
CHILDREN'S PROGRAM

Day — Coed Ages Birth-5

Atlanta, GA 30307. 1815 Ponce de Leon Ave NE.
Tel: 404-377-3836. Fax: 404-373-0058.
www.thefrazercenter.org
Cynthia Byrd Turner, Exec Dir. **Amy Morris,** MSW, Dir. **Andrea McFarland,**
Coord.
> **Focus:** Spec Ed. **Conditions:** Primary—Au Bl CP Ep IP MD MR MS ON
> SB. Sec—Ap As B C D ED LD PTSD S. **IQ 0-70.**
> **Gen Acad.** Gr PS.
> **Therapy:** Hear Lang Occup Phys Speech. **Psychotherapy:** Fam Parent.
> **Enr:** 120.
> **Rates 2003:** Day $797-866/mo (+$75-100/yr). Schol avail. State Aid.
> **Est 1949.** Private. Nonprofit.

The center provides educational services for both typically developing young children and those with special needs. Children must exhibit developmental delays to enter the program. The center maintains a low child-staff ratio, and teachers and instructors focus on different developmental stages within each of the classrooms. Frazer also offers parent play groups, parent education classes and parent counseling.

In addition to children's programming, the center conducts an adult program for individuals with mental retardation. This program focuses on vocation, recreation, education and family resources.

GABLES ACADEMY

Res — Coed Ages 12-18; Day — Coed 9-18

Stone Mountain, GA 30083. 811 Gordon St.
Tel: 770-465-7500. Fax: 770-465-7700.
www.gablesacademy.com   E-mail: info@gablesacademy.com
James D. Meffen III, MSEd, Head.
> **Focus:** Spec Ed. **Conditions:** Primary—ADD ADHD Asp Au Bl Dc Dg Dx
> PDD. **IQ 90 and up.**
> **Col Prep. Gen Acad. Pre-Voc. Voc.** Gr 4-12. Courses: Read Math Lang_
> Arts Study_Skills. On-Job Trng.
> **Therapy:** Occup Percepual-Motor Speech. **Psychotherapy:** Group Indiv.
> **Enr:** 34. Res Males 11. Res Females 2. Day Males 18. Day Females 3.
> **Staff:** 8 (Full 5, Part 3).
> **Rates 2004:** Res $32,000/sch yr. Day $12,000/sch yr. $50 (Therapy)/ses.
> Schol 10 ($60,000).
> **Summer Prgm:** Res & Day. Educ. Rec. Res Rate $3400. Day Rate $975-
> 1545. 6 wks.
> **Est 1961.** Private. Nonprofit.

Gables offers a full curriculum for children who have specific learning deficits. The emphasis is on strengthening basic skills through increased proficiency of learning. Each student receives individualized corrective or remedial instruction, in conjunction with larger group instruction.

In addition to conventional physical education, the academy conducts an outdoor challenge program that addresses self-confidence, coordination and problem solving skills. The curriculum also includes a fine arts program that comprises visual, literary and performing arts activities.

Gables schedules group and individual counseling sessions as needed.

GEORGIA SCHOOL FOR THE DEAF

Res — Coed Ages 4-21; Day — Coed 3-21

Cave Spring, GA 30124. 232 Perry Farm Rd SW.
Tel: 706-777-2200. TTY: 706-777-2200. Fax: 706-777-2204.
www.gsdweb.org
Winfield McChord, Jr., Dir. **Thelma Twyman,** RN, Med Dir. **P. Paulette Bragg,** Adm.
   Focus: Spec Ed. **Conditions:** Primary—D. Sec—CP ED MR S. **IQ 55-109.**
   Gen Acad. Voc. Gr PS-12. Courses: Read Math Lang_Arts. On-Job Trng.
   Therapy: Hear Lang Occup Phys Speech.
   Enr: 109. Res Males 55. Res Females 37. Day Males 9. Day Females 8.
      Staff: 119 (Full 110, Part 9). Prof 36. Admin 3.
   Rates 2004: No Fee.
   Summer Prgm: Res & Day. Educ. Rec. Res Rate $50. 1 wk.
   Est 1846. State. **Spons:** Georgia Department of Education.

The Georgia School provides children with impaired hearing traditional academic instruction, a computer-assisted reading laboratory and a comprehensive vocational program. Staff employ complete audiological and educational services to develop an individualized educational plan for each pupil. Graduates who qualify may attend college.

Students also participate in intramural sports, varsity athletics and cultural enrichment activities. Program participants must be residents of Georgia.

GOTTLIEB VISION GROUP

Clinic: All Ages. M-W 8-5, Th 11:30-6:30, F 9-4.

Stone Mountain, GA 30083. 5462 Memorial Dr, Ste 101.
Tel: 404-296-6000. Fax: 404-296-3600.
www.gottliebvisiongroup.com   E-mail: gvgroup@bellsouth.net
Daniel D. Gottlieb, OD, Dir.
   Focus: Treatment. **Conditions:** Primary—B. Sec—Asp Au BI CP Dg Dx IP LD MD MR MS ON PDD SB.
   Therapy: Percepual-Motor Visual.
   Staff: 11.
   Est 1975. Private. Inc.

This program offers comprehensive diagnosis and treatment, vision therapy and visual rehabilitation for those who are visually impaired or who have visual disorders associated with physical disabilities, learning disabilities or dyslexia. On-site rehabilitation and outpatient services are available to these clients, as well as to individuals who have developed vision problems due to a stroke or an accident.

GRACEWOOD STATE SCHOOL AND HOSPITAL

Res — Coed All Ages

Gracewood, GA 30812. 100 Myrtle Dr, Bldg 8.
Tel: 706-790-2030. Fax: 706-790-2025.
www.state.ga.us/departments/dhr/mhmrsa
  Focus: Spec Ed. Trng. **Conditions:** Primary—MR. **IQ 0-70.**
  Pre-Voc. Voc. Ungraded. On-Job Trng.
  Therapy: Hear Lang Occup Phys Speech. **Psychotherapy:** Fam Indiv.
  Staff: Prof 165.
  Est 1921. State. Nonprofit.

HILLSIDE HOSPITAL

Res — Coed Ages 7-18

Atlanta, GA 30306. 690 Courtenay Dr NE, PO Box 8247.
Tel: 404-875-4551. Fax: 404-875-1394.
www.hside.org   E-mail: residential@hside.org
Teresa Stoker, MEd, CEO. **Jennifer Gould,** MD, Med Dir. **Lori Hogeman,**
  Adm.
  Focus: Treatment. **Conditions:** Primary—ADHD BD CD ED Mood OCD
    Psy PTSD Sz. Sec—AN Anx Ap As Asp Au B Bu CP D Dx Ep LD MR Nf
    ON PDD PW S TB TS. **IQ 55 and up.**
  Gen Acad. Pre-Voc. Gr K-12. Courses: Read Lang_Arts. Shelt_Workshop.
    On-Job Trng.
  Therapy: Art Chemo Dance Hear Lang Milieu Phys Recreational Speech.
    Psychotherapy: Fam Group Indiv Parent.
  Enr: 67. Res Males 47. Res Females 20. **Staff:** 195 (Full 170, Part 25).
  Rates 2003: Res $326/day. State Aid.
  Est 1888. Private. Nonprofit.

Hillside offers year-round treatment for emotionally and behaviorally disordered adolescents. The program is designed to work with students on a long-term basis and place them back in a home setting. Parents must attend bimonthly meetings under the supervision of the psychiatric social worker. Students are expected to accept responsibility for their own actions and to solve various behavioral problems that do not allow them to function successfully either at home or at school.

A school operates on campus in conjunction with the public school system and employs reality therapy aimed at mainstreaming students. The curriculum emphasizes English, math and reading, and vocational training is also available. Advanced students attend public schools. The usual length of treatment is two years.

THE HOWARD SCHOOL

Day — Coed Ages 3-18

Atlanta, GA 30306. 1246 Ponce de Leon Ave.
Tel: 404-377-7436. Fax: 404-377-0884.
www.howardschool.org
Sandra N. Kleinman, EdD, Exec Dir. **Keren Schuller,** Adm.
  Focus: Spec Ed. **Conditions:** Primary—ADHD Dx LD.
  Col Prep. Gen Acad. Gr K-12. Courses: Read Math Lang_Arts Computers
    Sci Soc_Stud Studio_Art Music Drama.
  Therapy: Lang Speech. **Psychotherapy:** Fam Group Indiv.
  Enr: 110. Day Males 87. Day Females 23. **Staff:** 34 (Full 25, Part 9).
  Est 1950. Private. Inc.

Enrolling students with language-learning disabilities and differences, Howard conducts an individualized program that accounts for variations in learning style and manner of expression. The program attempts to sufficiently develop pupils' independent learning skills so that they are capable of success in traditional academic environments. Students build basic skills in reading and math while also developing higher-level thinking skills and learning self-advocacy strategies.

Classes typically comprise ten or fewer pupils, and instructors have master's degrees in either learning disabilities or the content areas in which they teach. Support teachers assist in lower and middle school classes, and speech-language pathologists collaborate with instructors in the classroom. In addition to the standard subjects, the curriculum includes art, music, drama, physical education and technology.

Learning profile assessments, language-communication-speech services, specialized tutoring and professional development are among the school's community outreach services.

THE LEARNING CENTER

Day — Coed Ages 3-22

Milledgeville, GA 31061. 435 E Walton St.
Tel: 478-445-2649. Fax: 478-445-2655.
Patricia J. Wolf, MSW, Dir.
  Focus: Spec Ed. **Conditions:** Primary—Au ED.
  Gen Acad. Gr PS-12. Courses: Read Math Lang_Arts.
  Therapy: Hear Phys Speech. **Psychotherapy:** Fam Group Indiv Parent.
  Enr: 130. **Staff:** 40. (Full 40).
  Rates 2004: No Fee.
  Est 1973. State.

This center, a member of the Georgia Psychoeducational Network, serves severely emotionally disturbed and autistic children. A preschool program offers psychological evaluations, home and school intervention services, and individualized programming in the areas of behavior, socialization, communicational, cognitive development and self-help skills.

The curriculum emphasizes developmental therapy and basic academics. Programs are arranged so that children may be enrolled in regular classes at least on a part-time basis. Additional services include counseling, individual training and referrals. The center serves a seven-county area.

LULLWATER SCHOOL

Day — Coed Ages 5-15

Decatur, GA 30030. 705 S Candler St.
Tel: 404-378-6643. Fax: 404-377-0879.
www.lullwaterschool.org   E-mail: lullwater@mindspring.com
Joan K. Teach, PhD, Dir. **Mary Frances Thompson,** Adm.
   Focus: Spec Ed. **Conditions:** Primary—ADD ADHD Dx LD. Sec—As CD ED Ep MR OCD S. **IQ 80 and up.**
   Col Prep. Gen Acad. Gr K-8. Courses: Read Math Lang_Arts Span Sci Soc_Stud Studio_Art Music.
   Therapy: Hydro Music Recreational.
   Enr: 65. Day Males 30. Day Females 35. **Staff:** 12 (Full 10, Part 2).
   Rates 2003: Day $9450-9850/sch yr. Schol avail.
   Summer Prgm: Day. Day Rate $900. 4 wks.
   Est 1973. Private. Nonprofit.

Lullwater offers cognitive learning and social training to nontraditional learners who often have attentional disorders or learning disabilities. Instruction is individualized and classes are limited to 15 students. Art, music, Spanish and frequent field trips round out the curriculum and provide enrichment. The school also offers an extended-day program.

MILL SPRINGS ACADEMY

Day — Coed Ages 6-18

Alpharetta, GA 30004. 13660 New Providence Rd.
Tel: 770-360-1336. Fax: 770-360-1341.
www.millsprings.org   E-mail: sfitzgerald@millsprings.org
Robert W. Moore, BA, Head. **Lavone R. Rippeon,** MBA, Admin. **Sheila Fitzgerald,** Adm.
   Focus: Spec Ed. **Conditions:** Primary—LD.
   Col Prep. Gr 1-12. Courses: Read Math Lang_Arts Sci Computers Hist.
   Therapy: Lang Speech. **Psychotherapy:** Group.
   Enr: 265. **Staff:** 56 (Full 50, Part 6).
   Rates 2003: Day $15,930/sch yr. Schol avail.
   Summer Prgm: Day. Educ. Rec.
   Est 1981. Private. Nonprofit.

Psychological and diagnostic evaluations form the basis of individualized prescriptive programs at the academy. Serving those who have failed to achieve to potential in traditional settings, Mill Springs generates learning strategies based upon psycho-educational evaluations, previous school records, diagnostic skills assessments and communications with professionals who have dealt with the pupil previously. Within a structured setting, children receive instruction in age-appropriate groupings. An extended-day program offers hiking, gardening, fishing, sports, and arts and crafts to children ages 6-14.

NORTHEAST GEORGIA SPEECH CENTER

Day — Coed Ages 3-5
Clinic: All Ages. M-F 8:30-5.

Gainesville, GA 30503. 621 E Spring St, PO Box 1482.
Tel: 770-534-5141. Fax: 770-534-5141.
www.nega.net/resource/s/speechcenter.htm
   E-mail: negasc@bellsouth.net
Diane M. Brower, MEd, CCC-SLP, Exec Dir.
   Focus: Treatment. **Conditions:** Primary—S. Sec—Ap Au B BI CP D LD MR.
   Gen Acad. Gr PS.
   Therapy: Hear Lang Speech.
   Staff: 4. (Full 4). Prof 2. Educ 1. Admin 1.
   Rates 2001: Day $55/day. Clinic $100/hr. Schol avail. State Aid.
   Summer Prgm: Day. Ther. Lang_Enrich.
   Est 1970. Private. Nonprofit. **Spons:** Junior League.

The center provides evaluation and treatment of speech, language and hearing problems. Diagnostic evaluations and rehabilitation for stuttering, articulation, delayed speech and language problems, and aphasia and laryngectomy patients are available, as are pure-tone audiometric screenings. The facility also maintains a preschool program, Therapeutic Language for Children, that offers services for speech- and language-delayed children (including those with attentional disorders and hearing impairments) ages 3-5.

NORTHWEST GEORGIA REGIONAL HOSPITAL
DEVELOPMENTAL SERVICES UNIT

Res — Coed Ages 5 and up

Rome, GA 30161. 1305 Redmond Rd, Unit 403.
Tel: 706-295-6246. Fax: 706-802-5454.
www.state.ga.us/departments/dhr/mhmrsa
   Focus: Treatment. **Conditions:** Primary—MR. **IQ 0-50.**
   Pre-Voc. Ungraded.
   Therapy: Chemo Hear Lang Occup Phys Speech. **Psychotherapy:** Indiv.
   Est 1971. State. Nonprofit.

READING SUCCESS

Clinic: Ages 4 and up. M-S 3-7.

Martinez, GA 30907. 4434 Columbia Rd.

Nearby locations: Aiken, SC; Lexington, SC.
Tel: 706-863-8173. Fax: 706-863-4523.
www.readingsuccess.com   E-mail: tutorme706@aol.com
Sandra Mashburn, BS, MEd, Dir.
> **Focus:** Spec Ed. **Conditions:** Primary—ADD ADHD Ap Apr As Asp C Dc
> Dg Dx LD MD MS PW SP TS. **IQ 79 and up.**
> **Gen Acad.** Courses: Read Math Lang_Arts.
> **Therapy:** Lang.
> **Staff:** 12 (Full 2, Part 10). Prof 12. Educ 12.
> **Rates 2003:** Clinic $37/hr.
> **Est 1975.** Private. Inc.

This year-round clinic provides diagnosis and remediation of reading and learning disabilities. Students receive organizational and study skills training, as well as educational counseling. Other branches operate at Hahn Village, Aiken, SC 29801 (803-648-7323), and at Whiteford Baptist Church, 501 Whiteford Way, Lexington, SC 29072 (803-553-7449).

RIDGEVIEW INSTITUTE

Res and Day — Coed Ages 6 and up

Smyrna, GA 30080. 3995 South Cobb Dr.
Tel: 770-434-4567.
www.ridgeviewinstitute.com/index.html
Robert M. Fink, CEO. **James D. Vargo,** MD, Med Dir.
> **Conditions:** Primary—BD ED. Sec—ADD Anx CD Mood.
> **Col Prep. Gen Acad. Pre-Voc.** Courses: Read Math Lang_Arts.
> **Therapy:** Play. **Psychotherapy:** Fam Group Indiv.
> **Est 1976.** Private. Nonprofit.

THE SCHENCK SCHOOL

Day — Coed Ages 6-14

Atlanta, GA 30327. 282 Mt Paran Rd NW.
Tel: 404-252-2591. Fax: 404-252-7615.
www.schenck.org   E-mail: office@schenck.org
Gena Calloway, MEd, Dir. **Kait Paden,** Adm.
> **Focus:** Spec Ed. **Conditions:** Primary—Dx LD. Sec—ADD ADHD. **IQ 100
> and up.**
> **Gen Acad.** Gr 1-8. Courses: Read Math Lang_Arts.
> **Enr:** 150. **Staff:** 52. Educ 36. Admin 11.
> **Rates 2003:** Day $16,300-17,200/sch yr. Schol avail.
> **Summer Prgm:** Day. Educ. Rec. 6 wks.
> **Est 1959.** Private. Nonprofit.

Schenck provides remedial training in a day school framework for children with dyslexia and other language disabilities. The educational program enables students to continue study in their basic school subjects while receiving concentrated instruction in reading, writing and spelling. Complete testing of students is conducted three times a year, and individual tutoring is available. The usual duration of treatment is two to three years.

A six-week summer session offers an educational program for both current Schenck pupils and students not enrolled during the academic year.

SHEPHERD'S HILL FARM

Res — Coed Ages 13-17

Martin, GA 30557. 2200 Price Rd.
Tel: 706-779-5766. Fax: 706-779-5736.
www.shepherdshillfarm.org   E-mail: shepherdshillfarm@alltel.net
Trace Embry, Dir. **Rebecca E. Bombet,** Adm.

Focus: Rehab. Treatment. **Conditions:** Primary—ADD ADHD AN Anx Asp BD Bu CD ED Mood OCD ODD PDD PTSD SP. Sec—Ar As Db Dx Ep HIV TS. **IQ 90-109.**

Gen Acad. Ungraded. Courses: Read Math Lang_Arts. On-Job Trng.

Psychotherapy: Fam Group Indiv Parent Equine.

Enr: 10. Res Males 6. Res Females 4. **Staff:** 12 (Full 10, Part 2). Educ 3. Admin 4.

Rates 2004: Day $39,000/yr.

Est 1994. Private. Inc.

The facility offers an outdoor residential therapy services and junior and senior high school academics for adolescents struggling with behavioral issues. Among other available programs are Next Step, a transitional program designed to help boys and girls with their transition back to society; equine therapy; Bible-based parenting classes; a ropes course; and individual and group therapy.

SOUTH CENTRAL FULTON MENTAL HEALTH CENTER

Day — Coed All Ages
Clinic: All Ages. M-F 9-3.

Atlanta, GA 30342. 215 Lakewood Way SW.
Tel: 404-624-0610.
www.myfultoncountyga.com

Focus: Trng. **Conditions:** Primary—MR. **IQ 0-55.** On-Job Trng.

Therapy: Hear Lang Phys Speech. **Psychotherapy:** Fam Indiv.

Est 1970. County. Nonprofit.

SPEECH, HEARING, AND REHABILITATION
ENTERPRISES OF COASTAL GEORGIA

Clinic: All Ages. M-F 8:30-5.

Brunswick, GA 31520. 228 Starling St.
Tel: 912-264-3141. Fax: 912-264-6190.
  Conditions: Primary—Ap D S.
  Therapy: Hear Lang Speech.
  Staff: Prof 2.
  Est 1965. Private. Nonprofit.

UNIVERSITY OF GEORGIA SPEECH AND HEARING CLINIC

Clinic: All Ages. M-F 8-5.

Athens, GA 30602. 593 Aderhold Hall.
Tel: 706-542-4598. TTY: 706-583-8280. Fax: 706-542-5877.
www.coe.uga.edu/csdclinic   E-mail: jharvey@coe.uga.edu
Carol Ann Raymond, MEd, EdS, MBA, Dir.
  Focus: Rehab. Treatment. **Conditions:** Primary—Ap Apr Asp Au Bl CP D
    DS MR. Sec—Dg Dx Ep MD MS SB.
  Therapy: Hear Lang Speech.
  Staff: 7 (Full 6, Part 1). Prof 6. Admin 1.
  Rates 2003: $200 (Evaluation); $30 (Treatment)/ses.
  State.

  The UGA Speech and Hearing Clinic provides comprehensive services for individuals of all ages. Among service options are prevention, assessment and treatment of speech, language, swallowing and hearing disorders. Various services pertaining to audiology and speech-language pathology are available. The clinic serves as a training site for university graduate students who are pursuing a master's degree in speech-language pathology.

VALDOSTA STATE UNIVERSITY
SPEECH AND HEARING CLINIC

Clinic: All Ages. M-F 8-5:30.

Valdosta, GA 31698. Special Education & Communication Disorders Bldg.
Tel: 912-333-5932. Fax: 912-219-1335.
Karla Hull, PhD, Supv.
  Focus: Treatment. **Conditions:** Primary—D S.
  Therapy: Hear Lang Speech.
  Staff: 5.
  Est 1962. State. Nonprofit.

  This clinic at VSU offers services in speech pathology and audiology. Operating on a year-round basis, the clinic provides diagnostic screening and evaluation to area public schools, as well as a neonatal hearing screening program. Services are also available to area nursing homes. Clinic staff conduct community workshops in such areas as hearing conservation and the training of audiometric technicians.

HAWAII

ASSETS SCHOOL
Day — Coed Ages 5-18

Honolulu, HI 96818. 1 Ohana Nui Way.
Tel: 808-423-1356. Fax: 808-422-1920.
www.assets-school.net   E-mail: info@assets-school.net
Lou Salza, BA, MEd, Head.
  Focus: Spec Ed. **Conditions:** Primary—Dx. Sec—Ap BD Bl CP ED Ep S.
    IQ 90 and up.
  Col Prep. Gen Acad. Gr K-12. Courses: Read Math Lang_Arts Span Japan
    Computers Studio_Art Ceramics Music Drama.
  Therapy: Lang Speech. **Psychotherapy:** Fam Indiv.
  Enr: 400. **Staff:** 65.
  Rates 2003: Day $11,755-15,230/sch yr.
  Summer Prgm: Day. Educ. Computers Arts. Day Rate $1200. 5 wks.
  Est 1955. Private. Nonprofit.

The ASSETS School for gifted students and dyslexic children of average to superior
intelligence offers a program consisting of intensive academic remediation, acceleration
and enrichment in the mornings, followed by a departmentalized course of study in the
afternoons. ASSETS also works at improving a child's self-concept through daily group
counseling and ongoing individual counseling. Both initial diagnostic evaluations and
continuous diagnostic and prescriptive services are available.

Additional programs include "Super Saturday" and a full-day enrichment program
for the gifted. The school works in close conjunction with the Special Education Department of the University of Hawaii and utilizes both student teachers and field work placements as supplements to the faculty. A night school is available for adult dyslexics, and
comprehensive testing services are open to community residents age 2 and up.

EASTER SEALS HAWAII
SULTAN EARLY INTERVENTION PROGRAM
Day — Coed Ages Birth-3

Honolulu, HI 96813. 710 Green St.
Tel: 808-536-3764. Fax: 808-521-4491.
www.eastersealshawaii.org   E-mail: info@eastersealshawaii.org
Takayo Inatsuka, Prgm Mgr.
  Focus: Treatment. **Conditions:** Primary—OH. Sec—As B Bl C CP D IP MD
    MR MS S SB.
  Therapy: Hear Lang Occup Phys Speech. **Psychotherapy:** Fam Parent.
  Enr: 75. Day Males 50. Day Females 25. **Staff:** 10 (Full 3, Part 7).
  Rates 2004: No Fee.
  Summer Prgm: Day. Ther. 6 wks.
  Est 1948. Private. Nonprofit.

This school provides a program of early intervention for families with special-needs children. Through evaluations and individualized programs, Sultan strives to develop the skills of infants and preschoolers with special needs, thus enabling them to achieve to potential. Parents and children receive counseling, education and individualized therapy in a trans-disciplinary system. The school conducts a six-week summer session.

HAWAII CENTER FOR THE DEAF AND THE BLIND

Res — Coed Ages 9-20; Day — Coed 3-20

Honolulu, HI 96815. 3440 Leahi Ave.
Tel: 808-733-4999. TTY: 808-733-4999. Fax: 808-733-4824.
Sydney S. Freitas, Admin. **Michael Sia,** MD, Med Dir. **Harry Hayler,** Adm.
　Focus: Spec Ed. **Conditions:** Primary—B D. Sec—Ap MR OH.
　Col Prep. Gen Acad. Pre-Voc. Voc. Gr PS-12. Courses: Read Math Lang_
　　Arts. Man_Arts & Shop.
　Therapy: Hear Lang Occup Phys Speech. **Psychotherapy:** Indiv.
　Enr: 50. Res Males 8. Res Females 5. Day Males 20. Day Females 17.
　　Staff: 25.
　Rates 2004: No Fee.
　Summer Prgm: Res & Day. Educ. Rec. Ther.
　State.

This state-supported center provides education for blind and deaf children. Braille and other special skills needed to function in an integrated public school class are taught. A program specifically designed for multi-handicapped deaf students is also available.

HORIZONS ACADEMY OF MAUI

Day — Coed Ages 6-17

Haiku, HI 96708. PO Box 1308.
Tel: 808-575-2954. Fax: 808-575-9180.
www.horizonsacademy.org   E-mail: hacademy@maui.net
Timothy J. Irvin, BS, MBA, Exec Dir. **Sue Stone,** BA, MA, Prgm Dir.
　Focus: Spec Ed. **Conditions:** Primary—ADD ADHD Dc Dg Dx LD OCD SP.
　　Sec—Au BD ED MR ODD S TS. **IQ 75-130.**
　Gen Acad. Pre-Voc. Gr K-11. Courses: Read Math Lang_Arts Soc_Stud
　　Hist. On-Job Trng.
　Therapy: Lang Occup Speech Visual. **Psychotherapy:** Fam Group Indiv.
　Enr: 32. Day Males 14. Day Females 18. **Staff:** 15.
　Rates 2004: Day $11,800-12,600/sch yr (+$150). $16-49 (Tutoring); $51-70
　　(Therapy)/hr. Schol 14 ($70,000). State Aid.
　Summer Prgm: Day. Educ.
　Est 1993. Private. Nonprofit.

In a small-class setting, Horizons conducts an individualized program for students with learning disabilities. Staff develop an educational plan for each pupil, then regularly assess achievement to ensure that progress is being made. Ongoing adaptation of the program occurs as necessary. The academy addresses behavioral issues by providing instruction in social skills, problem solving, impulse control and anger management.

UNIVERSITY OF HAWAII-MANOA
SPEECH AND HEARING CLINIC

Clinic: All Ages. M-F 8-4:30.

Honolulu, HI 96822. 1410 Lower Campus Dr.
Tel: 808-956-8279. Fax: 808-956-5482.
www.hawaii.edu/spauh/clinic.htm
   Conditions: Primary—Ap D S.
   Therapy: Hear Lang Speech.
   Staff: Prof 9.
   Est 1936. State. Nonprofit.

VARIETY SCHOOL OF HAWAII

Day — Coed Ages 5-13

Honolulu, HI 96816. 710 Palekaua St.
Tel: 808-732-2835. Fax: 808-732-4334.
Duane Yee, MAT, Dir.
   Focus: Spec Ed. **Conditions:** Primary—ADD ADHD Asp Au Dc Dg Dx LD PDD. Sec—BD CD ED OCD S.
   Gen Acad. Ungraded. Courses: Read Math Lang_Arts Sci Computers Soc_ Stud Studio_Art Music Adaptive_Phys_Ed.
   Therapy: Lang Occup Speech. **Psychotherapy:** Fam Group.
   Enr: 50. Day Males 35. Day Females 15. **Staff:** 25.
   Rates 2003: Day $17,000-18,500/sch yr. Schol avail.
   Summer Prgm: Day. Educ. Rec. 6 wks.
   Est 1961. Private. Nonprofit.

This school was established to meet the educational needs of children with mild autism or a learning disability attributable to neurological dysfunction. The program seeks to develop individual readiness, then successfully place each child in a traditional school setting.

Class work is highly individualized. Gross-motor training, visual-motor perceptual training, and speech and language therapies are planned to meet the needs of each pupil. A required program for parents attempts to assist in understanding and solving everyday problems in the home.

The summer session accepts children not enrolled in the regular program. Sessions before and after regular school hours are also available.

IDAHO

ADULT AND CHILD DEVELOPMENT CENTER
INFANT TODDLER PROGRAM

Day — Coed Ages Birth-3

Twin Falls, ID 83301. 803 Harrison St.
Tel: 208-736-2182.
>   **Focus:** Treatment. **Conditions:** Primary—Ap B BI C CP D IP MD MS ON S
>   SB. **IQ 0-70.**
>   **Therapy:** Hear Lang Occup Phys Speech. **Psychotherapy:** Fam Group
>   Indiv.
>   **Enr:** 200. **Staff:** 31.
>   **Rates 2004:** No Fee.
>   **Est 1970.** State. Nonprofit.

The purpose of the ACDC is to provide free habilitative services for individuals with developmental disabilities. Staff members train family members to incorporate therapies into the child's daily routine. Emphasis is placed on providing services within the child's natural environment.

ADULT/CHILD DEVELOPMENT CENTER

Day — Coed All Ages

Idaho Falls, ID 83402. 2475 Leslie Ave.
Tel: 208-525-7223. Fax: 208-525-7176.
www.healthandwelfare.idaho.gov   E-mail: nuckolsk@idhw.state.id.us
Karen Nuckols, Dir.
>   **Focus:** Rehab. Treatment. **Conditions:** Primary—CP MR. **IQ 0-50.**
>   **Pre-Voc. Voc.** Ungraded. Man_Arts & Shop. Shelt_Workshop. On-Job Trng.
>   **Therapy:** Hear Lang Occup Phys Speech. **Psychotherapy:** Fam Group
>   Indiv.
>   **Est 1969.** State.

ASCENT

Res — Coed Ages 13-17

Naples, ID 83847. PO Box 230.
Tel: 208-267-3626. Fax: 208-265-8096.
www.cedu-ascent.com
Scott Hess, BA, MA, Prgm Dir.
>   **Conditions:** Primary—BD. Sec—ADHD LD Mood ODD.
>   **Gen Acad.**
>   **Psychotherapy:** Group Indiv.

Staff: Prof 9.
Est 1992. Private. Inc. **Spons:** CEDU Education.

CLEARVIEW HORIZON

Res — Females Ages 13-20

Sandpoint, ID 83864. 6368 Kaniksu Shores Rd.
Tel: 208-263-5894.
www.clearviewhorizon.com
Mary L. Thielbahr, MA, MS, Dir. **Anabel White,** Adm.
  Focus: Treatment. **Conditions:** Primary—ADD ADHD AN Anx Ap Asp BD
    Bu Dc Dg Dx ED LD Mood OCD PTSD SP.
  Col Prep. Gen Acad. Gr 7-Col. On-Job Trng.
  Therapy: Art Dance Milieu Music Phys Play Recreational. **Psychotherapy:**
    Fam Group Indiv Parent.
  Enr: 10. Res Females 10. **Staff:** 10 (Full 5, Part 5). Prof 3. Educ 1. Admin 1.
  Rates 2003: Res $4500/mo (+$800/yr). Schol 1 ($54,000).
  Est 1997. Private. Inc.

This year-round transitional residence is designed as a practical skills learning opportunity for adolescent girls to undergo emotional, academic and physical growth. The program helps girls deal with unplanned pregnancies, adoption and abandonment issues, sexual and physical abuse, and eating disorders. Clearview also provides individual and group therapy and access to support groups.

COMMUNICARE

Res — Females Ages 18 and up

Meridian, ID 83642. 40 W Franklin Rd, Ste F.
Tel: 208-888-1155. Fax: 208-888-1156.
Tom Whittemore, Admin.
  Focus: Trng. Treatment. **Conditions:** Primary—MR.
  Therapy: Hear Lang Occup Phys Speech. **Psychotherapy:** Indiv.
  Est 1980. Private. Inc.

DEVELOPMENTAL DISABILITIES PROGRAM

Day — Coed All Ages

Lewiston, ID 83501. 2604 16th Ave, PO Drawer B.
  Nearby locations: Grangeville; Moscow (ID); Orofino.
Tel: 208-799-3460. Fax: 208-799-3328.
Vicki Malone, MSW, Prgm Dir.
  Focus: Treatment. **Conditions:** Primary—B Bl CP D Ep MR ON PDD S SB.
    Sec—Ap IP LD MD.

Gen Acad. Gr PS-PG. Courses: Life_Skills.
Therapy: Hear Lang Occup Phys Speech.
Enr: 263. Day Males 184. Day Females 79. **Staff:** 32 (Full 13, Part 19). Prof 21. Educ 7. Admin 2.
Rates 2004: No Fee.
Est 1969. State.

Diagnostic and therapeutic multidisciplinary services are provided for the developmentally disabled at this center. The programs strive to enable the child to develop to potential, reduce his or her level of dependency, and prevent institutionalization.

Branch centers operate at 200 S. Almond, Moscow 83843; 105 N. Myrtle St., Grangeville 83530; and Givens Hall, P.O. Box 672, Orofino 83544.

ECHO SPRINGS TRANSITION STUDY CENTER

Res — Coed Ages 18-24

Bonners Ferry, ID 83805. Rte 1, Box 2730.
Tel: 208-267-1111. Fax: 208-267-1122.
www.echo-springs.com E-mail: echo@coldreams.com
Doug Kim-Brown, Dir. **Rhea Verbanic,** Adm.
   Focus: Spec Ed. **Conditions:** Primary—ADD ADHD Anx As Db Dx OCD PTSD TS. Sec—Asp Bu Ep HIV Mood SP. **IQ 90 and up.**
   Gen Acad. Gr 12-Col.
   Enr: 8. Res Males 5. Res Females 3. **Staff:** 11 (Full 4, Part 7). Prof 10. Admin 1.
   Rates 2003: Res $42,000/yr.
   Est 1993. Private. Inc.

This year-round transition program admits pupils throughout the year. It is a two-phase program that offers students life skills training with increasing independence and autonomy as they progress through the 12-month program (all clients must commit to at least a one-year stay). During the first phase, the focus is on identifying the individual's values, goals, strengths and weaknesses under the guidance and mentoring of professionals. During the second phase (which lasts six to eight months), students live independently, applying the principles learned in phase one while continuing to meet with Echo Springs faculty at least five times per week.

ELK MOUNTAIN ACADEMY

Res — Males Ages 14-18

Clark Fork, ID 83811. PO Box 411.
Tel: 208-266-1122. Fax: 208-266-0508.
www.elkmountainacademy.org E-mail: info@elkmountainacademy.org
Carl Olding, MA, Exec Dir. **Loretta Olding,** Adm.
   Focus: Treatment. **Conditions:** Primary—ADD ADHD BD OCD. Sec—Dx ED SP.
   Gen Acad. Gr 7-12. Courses: Read Math Lang_Arts.
   Psychotherapy: Fam Group Indiv.

Enr: 25. Res Males 25. **Staff:** 24 (Full 22, Part 2).
Rates 2003: Res $46,800/yr.
Est 1994. Private. Nonprofit.

Based on the Twelve-Step Program, this therapeutic boarding school treats boys for an average of one year. The program emphasizes academic success, spiritual awareness, the ability to deal with social and emotional obstacles, and strategies to overcome addictive behavior.

GLACIER MOUNTAIN ACADEMY

Res — Coed Ages 13-17

Sandpoint, ID 83864. 301 N 1st Ave.
Tel: 208-290-6745. Fax: 208-265-8712.
E-mail: glacierm@micron.net
  Focus: Spec Ed. **Conditions:** Primary—ADD ADHD As BD CD ED OCD
    Psy Sz. Sec—Dx LD. **IQ 85 and up.**
  Col Prep. Gen Acad. Gr 7-12. Courses: Read Math Lang_Arts Sci Hist.
  Psychotherapy: Fam Group Indiv Parent.
  Enr: 8. Res Males 4. Res Females 4. **Staff:** 7 (Full 4, Part 3).
  Est 1995. Private. Inc.

Glacier Mountain is a coeducational academic outdoor program for behaviorally at-risk teenagers. The program offers behavioral and emotional modification, individual and group counseling, substance abuse assessments and counseling and a certified academic program. Additional programs for developing organizational skills, anger management, self-esteem building, leadership, team building, life skills, and decision-making skills are also available.

IDAHO ELKS REHABILITATION HOSPITAL

Day — Coed Ages 1 and up

Boise, ID 83702. 600 North Robbins Rd.
Tel: 208-489-4522. Fax: 208-344-8883.
www.idahoelksrehab.org
Joseph P. Caroselli, Admin.
  Conditions: Primary—BI MD OH.
  Gen Acad. Gr PS-6.
  Therapy: Hear Occup Phys.
  Est 1947. Private. Nonprofit. **Spons:** Elks Association.

IDAHO SCHOOL FOR THE DEAF AND THE BLIND

Res — Coed Ages 9-21; Day — Coed 3-21
Clinic: Ages Birth-21. M-F 8-4.

Gooding, ID 83330. 1450 Main St.
Tel: 208-934-4457. TTY: 208-934-4457. Fax: 208-934-8352.
www.isdb.state.id.us   E-mail: info@isdb.state.id.us
Harv Lyter, Actg Supt.
  Focus: Spec Ed. Conditions: Primary—B D. Sec—Ap MR OH.
  Gen Acad. Pre-Voc. Voc. Gr PS-12. Courses: Read Math Lang_Arts. Man_
    Arts & Shop. Shelt_Workshop. On-Job Trng.
  Therapy: Hear Lang Movement Phys Speech.
  Enr: 100. Staff: 121 (Full 116, Part 5).
  Rates 2003: No Fee.
  Est 1906. State.

A full academic program, remedial courses, and business, secretarial and vocational
training are provided by this state school for deaf and blind children. Students with
secondary handicaps are accepted. Hearing, language, physical and speech therapies;
psychological evaluations and counseling; and parental counseling are also offered. The
school features a program specifically for multi-handicapped deaf students.

IDAHO STATE SCHOOL AND HOSPITAL

Res — Coed All Ages

Nampa, ID 83687. 3100 11th Ave N.
Tel: 208-442-2812. Fax: 208-467-1929.
www.healthandwelfare.idaho.gov
Barbara Hancock, Dir.
  Focus: Trng. Treatment. Conditions: Primary—MR.
  Pre-Voc. Ungraded.
  Therapy: Chemo Hear Lang Occup Phys Speech. Psychotherapy: Fam
    Group Indiv.
  Est 1918. State.

IDAHO YOUTH RANCH

Res — Males Ages 8-18, Females 12-18; Day — Coed 13-18

Boise, ID 83704. 7025 Emerald St.
Tel: 208-377-2613. Fax: 208-377-2819.
www.youthranch.org   E-mail: iyr@youthranch.org
Mike Jones, MS, Pres.
  Conditions: Primary—BD. Sec—LD. IQ 80 and up.
  Gen Acad. Ungraded. Courses: Read Math Lang_Arts. Man_Arts & Shop.
  Psychotherapy: Fam Group Indiv.
  Staff: Prof 30.
  Est 1952. Private. Nonprofit.

ROCKY MOUNTAIN ACADEMY

Res — Coed Ages 14-17

Naples, ID 83847. Box 230.
Tel: 208-267-7522. Fax: 208-267-3232.
www.rockymtnacademy.com   E-mail: rma@cedu.com
Pamela Broker, Head. **Claudia Peterson,** Adm.
   Focus: Spec Ed. **Conditions:** Primary—BD ED. Sec—LD.
   Col Prep. Gen Acad. Pre-Voc. Voc. Gr 9-12. Courses: Read Math Lang_
      Arts Span Sci Govt. Man_Arts & Shop.
   Psychotherapy: Fam Group.
   Enr: 150. Res Males 100. Res Females 50. **Staff:** 69 (Full 65, Part 4).
   Est 1982. Private. Inc. **Spons:** CEDU.

The academy's 24-month program combines emotional growth with academic instruction for troubled adolescents and young adults. The program stresses healthy daily living and personal responsibility, and it is supported by counseling, experiential education and a wilderness challenge program. College preparatory academics and vocational application are emphasized.

Rocky Mountain's wilderness program includes training in outdoor living, use of map and compass, first aid, rock and mountain climbing, cross-country skiing, conservation, geology, botany and extended backpacking trips.

The academy is part of the CEDU Family of Services.

SUWS ADOLESCENT AND YOUTH TREATMENT PROGRAMS

Res — Coed Ages 11-17

Shoshone, ID 83352. 911 Preacher Creek Rd.
Tel: 208-886-2565. Fax: 208-886-2041.
www.suws.com   E-mail: suwsfield@suws.com
Kathy Rex, BS, Exec Dir. **Mike Ervin,** Adm.
   Focus: Treatment. **Conditions:** Primary—ADD ADHD Anx Ap As Asp BD
      Bu CD Dc Dg Dx ED LD Mood OCD ODD PTSD SP TS. **IQ 85 and up.**
   Therapy: Music Recreational Speech. **Psychotherapy:** Fam Group Indiv
      Parent.
   Enr: 100. **Staff:** 70 (Full 28, Part 42). Prof 10. Educ 1. Admin 2.
   Rates 2004: Res $410/day (+$750/ses).
   Summer Prgm: Res. Educ. Rec. Ther. Res Rate $5000. 3 wks.
   Est 1981. Private. Inc. **Spons:** Aspen Education Group.

SUWS treatment programs specialize in helping troubled and defiant teens with such behavioral and emotional problems as anxiety disorder, chemical dependency or substance abuse, mood disorders, oppositional defiant disorder, specific developmental disorders or learning differences. Individualized treatment plans, flexible length of stay and experiential learning opportunities help students develop self-esteem as they learn the value of helping others.

WARM SPRINGS COUNSELING CENTER AND TRAINING INSTITUTE
Clinic: All Ages. M-F 8-5; Eves by Appt.

Boise, ID 83712. 740 Warm Springs Ave.
Tel: 208-343-7797. Fax: 208-343-0064.
www.childrenshomesociety.com
Kara L. Craig, MA, CEO. **Becky Yancey,** CSW, Supv.
   Focus: Trng. Treatment. **Conditions:** Primary—ADD ADHD Au BD CD Dx ED LD OCD Psy Sz. Sec—BI. **IQ 60 and up.**
   Therapy: Speech. **Psychotherapy:** Fam Group Indiv Parent.
   Est 1908. Private. Nonprofit. **Spons:** Children's Home Society of Idaho.

Warm springs designs its outpatient psychotherapy services to assist children, adolescents and their families with problems in living, communication, social adjustment education and family crises. Staff prescribe psychotropic medications when indicated, as an adjunct to supportive services.

ILLINOIS

THE ACHIEVEMENT CENTERS
Day — Coed Ages 3-18
Clinic: Ages 3-18. M-S 7-4; Eves M-S 4-9.

La Grange Highlands, IL 60525. 6425 S Willow Springs Rd.
Tel: 708-579-9040. Fax: 708-579-5872.
www.acaciaacademy.com   E-mail: info@acaciaacademy.com
Kathryn Fouks, MSEd, Dir. **Eileen Petzold,** Adm.
  Focus: Spec Ed. **Conditions:** Primary—ADD ADHD Dc Dg Dx LD. Sec—
    Anx Ap Asp Au BD ED MR S SP TS. **IQ 65 and up.**
  Col Prep. Gen Acad. Pre-Voc. Gr PS-12. Courses: Read Math Lang_Arts
    Sci Soc_Stud Computers Fine_Arts Drama.
  Therapy: Lang Occup Percepual-Motor Phys Play Recreational Speech.
  Enr: 100. Day Males 65. Day Females 35. **Staff:** 40 (Full 30, Part 10). Prof
    36. Admin 4.
  Rates 2003: Clinic $30-60/hr.
  Est 1970. Private. Inc.

Offering a range of diagnostic and tutorial services, this facility consists of three programs. The Achievement Center provides academic testing, psycho-educational diagnosis, psychological projective testing, and ACT and SAT exam preparation in a clinic setting. Acacia Academy offers a full elementary and secondary academic program. Acacia enrolls boys and girls with learning disabilities, autism, emotional or behavioral disorders, attentional disorders; slow learners; and accelerated or gifted students who wish to address skills in a particular subject area.

Through preschool, kindergarten and daycare programs, the Early Achievement Center conducts developmentally appropriate instruction that features daily opportunities in art, music, literature and other activities. Flexible weekly schedules are organized around a central theme, and field trips and exhibits enrich the program.

ADULT AND CHILD REHABILITATION CENTER
Clinic: All Ages. M-F 8-5.

Woodstock, IL 60098. 708 Washington St.
Tel: 815-338-1707. Fax: 815-338-1786.
E-mail: acrc-aa@ameritech.net
Susan K. Martino, BS, RN, CEO. **B. B. Neuchiller,** MD, Med Dir.
  Focus: Rehab. **Conditions:** Primary—Ar Bl CP DS MD ON SB. Sec—Ap
    As Asp Au C Ep IP MS.
  Therapy: Lang Occup Phys Speech.
  Staff: 25 (Full 10, Part 15).
  Est 1949. Private. Nonprofit.

The primary purpose of the rehabilitation center is to provide direct services for children and adults in McHenry and Boone counties. Services are offered to anyone in need, regardless of the individual's ability to pay. Physical, speech and occupational therapies are provided at the center through the agency's Home Health Care Program. Homebound patients in McHenry County can also receive the services of registered nurses and home health aides.

ALEXANDER GRAHAM BELL ELEMENTARY SCHOOL

Day — Coed Ages 3-15
Clinic: Ages 3-15. M-F 8:30-3:15.

Chicago, IL 60618. 3730 N Oakley St.
Tel: 773-534-5150. Fax: 773-534-5163.
www.cps.k12.il.us
Robert A. Guercio, Prin.
    Focus: Spec Ed. **Conditions:** Primary—D. Sec—B LD. **IQ 75-135.**
    Gen Acad. Gr PS-8. Courses: Read Math Lang_Arts.
    Therapy: Hear Lang Speech.
    Staff: Prof 74.
    Est 1917. Municipal. Nonprofit.

BEACON THERAPEUTIC
DIAGNOSTIC AND TREATMENT CENTER

Day — Coed Ages 3-21
Clinic: Ages 3-18. M-F.

Chicago, IL 60643. 1912 W 103rd St.
Tel: 773-298-1243. Fax: 773-298-1078.
www.beacon-therapeutic.org   E-mail: beacon@beacon-therapeutic.org
Susan Reyna-Guerrero, LCSW, Pres. **Neal Spira,** MD, Med Dir.
    Focus: Spec Ed. **Conditions:** Primary—ADD ADHD Anx BD CD Dc Dg Dx ED LD Mood MR OCD PTSD S. Sec—Ap Asp Au Bl. **IQ 50-120.**
    Gen Acad. Pre-Voc. Voc. Gr K-12. Courses: Read Math Lang_Arts Sci Soc_Sci Studio_Art Music. On-Job Trng.
    Therapy: Lang Milieu Movement Speech. **Psychotherapy:** Fam Group Indiv.
    Enr: 150. Day Males 122. Day Females 28. **Staff:** 75 (Full 70, Part 5). Prof 30. Educ 20. Admin 4.
    Rates 2004: Day $140/day.
    Summer Prgm: Day. Educ. Ther. Day Rate $140/day. 7 wks.
    Est 1968. Private. Nonprofit.

Beacon Therapeutic is a multi-service agency that provides behavioral and educational services for high-risk children and adolescents with multiple special needs. Local public schools place elementary and secondary students in Beacon's special education programs. These pupils' severe disabilities and attendant needs cannot be properly addressed in a public school setting. The goal of the educational program is to increase function to the point that the boy or girl can successfully return to a less restrictive school setting or to an employment or vocational situation.

Also available through the agency is outpatient programming for children who are experiencing emotional or behavioral problems at home or in the community.

BEVERLY FARM FOUNDATION

Res and Day — Coed Ages 18 and up

Godfrey, IL 62035. 6301 Humbert Rd.
Tel: 618-466-0367. Fax: 618-466-3652.
www.beverlyfarm.org   E-mail: cmark@beverlyfarm.org
Martha Warford, MPA, Exec Dir. **Tanin Parich,** MD, Med Dir. **Cindy Mayhew,** Adm.
  Focus: Treatment. **Conditions:** Primary—Au Bl CP DS Ep MR OH. Sec— Ap As B BD C D Db ED IP MD MS OCD Psy S SB Sz. **IQ 0-80.**
  Gen Acad. Pre-Voc. Voc. Ungraded. Courses: Read Math Lang_Arts. Man_ Arts & Shop. Shelt_Workshop. On-Job Trng.
  Therapy: Hear Hydro Occup Phys Speech. **Psychotherapy:** Indiv Equine.
  Enr: 400. **Staff:** 600 (Full 550, Part 50). Prof 40. Educ 12. Admin 30.
  Rates 2003: Res $1200/mo. State Aid.
  Est 1897. Private. Nonprofit.

The foundation provides a home environment for mildly to profoundly retarded individuals, offering lifetime care. A scholastic training program offers individualized classwork that includes vocational training. Programming stresses self-care programs, motor and behavioral development, and social rehabilitation.

BREHM PREPARATORY SCHOOL

Res and Day — Coed Ages 11-21

Carbondale, IL 62901. 1245 E Grand Ave.
Tel: 618-457-0371. Fax: 618-529-1248.
www.brehm.org   E-mail: admissions@brehm.org
Richard G. Collins, PhD, Exec Dir. **Donna Collins,** Adm.
  Focus: Spec Ed. **Conditions:** Primary—ADD ADHD Dc Dg Dx LD. Sec— Anx Ap Apr Asp Bl CP ED Ep Mood OCD TS. **IQ 90-130.**
  Col Prep. Gen Acad. Pre-Voc. Gr 6-PG. Courses: Read Math Lang_Arts Computers Sci Soc_Stud Studio_Art Health.
  Therapy: Lang Speech.
  Enr: 80. Res Males 47. Res Females 27. Day Males 6. **Staff:** 56. (Full 56).
  Rates 2003: Res $43,780/sch yr (+$800). Day $27,000/sch yr (+$800). State Aid.
  Est 1982. Private. Nonprofit.

Brehm offers a program of general academics for pupils with learning disabilities highlighted by microcomputers, laboratory science and course work required for college entrance. Remedial work, study habits and social skills are also stressed. A total curricular approach encourages students to utilize new skills in their daily living experiences.

The school administers psycho-educational diagnostic evaluations to determine individual program emphases. College and vocational counseling are also available for 12th graders and postsecondary students.

CARLE CLINIC ASSOCIATION
CHILD DISABILITY CLINIC

Clinic: Ages Birth-21. W 7:15-5.

Urbana, IL 61801. 602 W University Ave.
Tel: 217-383-3100. Fax: 217-383-4468.
Annette Lansford, MD, Dir. **Annette Lansford,** MD, Med Dir.
   Focus: Treatment. **Conditions:** Primary—ADD ADHD Anx Ap Apr As Asp Au B BD BI C CD CP D DS Dx ED Ep LD MD Mood MR OCD ON PDD PW S SB TS.
   Staff: 11 (Full 6, Part 5).
   Rates 2003: $2000 (Evaluation)/ses.
   Est 1976. Private.

A multidisciplinary team evaluates children with multiple handicaps. The primary focus is diagnostic, with appropriate treatment recommendations provided.

CENTER FOR SPEECH AND LANGUAGE DISORDERS

Clinic: Ages 1½ and up. T-S 9-4; Eves T-F by Appt.

Elmhurst, IL 60126. 195 W Spangler Ave, Ste B.
   Nearby locations: Chicago.
Tel: 630-530-8551. Fax: 630-530-5909.
www.csld.com   E-mail: info@csld.com
Phyllis Kupperman, MA, CCC-SLP, Dir. **Christina Rees,** MA, CCC-SLP, Co-Clin Mgr. **Karen Supel,** MA, CCC-SLP, Co-Clin Mgr.
   Focus: Treatment. **Conditions:** Primary—Au PDD S. Sec—ADD ADHD Dx ED LD OCD.
   Therapy: Lang Occup Speech. **Psychotherapy:** Group.
   Staff: 16 (Full 14, Part 2).
   Est 1979. Private. Nonprofit.

CLSD provides speech and language evaluations and therapy for children with autism and pervasive developmental disorder. Services include comprehensive speech and language evaluations, individual therapy, social language group treatment, occupational evaluation and therapy services, cotreatment using both speech and occupational therapies, social motor group treatment and support groups. A sliding fee scale is available.
   A second center operates at 430 W. Erie St., Ste. 206, Chicago 60610.

CENTER ON DEAFNESS

Res and Day — Coed Ages 6-21

Northbrook, IL 60062. 3444 Dundee Rd.
Tel: 847-559-0110. TTY: 847-559-7493. Fax: 847-559-8199.
www.centerondeafness.org
Robert Van Dyke, MA, CEO. **Dorothy Eulass,** Adm.
  Focus: Spec Ed. **Conditions:** Primary—D. Sec—Ap BD CD ED LD MR
    OCD Psy Sz. **IQ 50-100.**
  Gen Acad. Pre-Voc. Gr K-12. Courses: Read Math Lang_Arts Soc_Stud.
    Shelt_Workshop. On-Job Trng.
  Psychotherapy: Fam Group Indiv.
  Enr: 22. Res Males 9. Res Females 7. Day Males 5. Day Females 1. **Staff:** 8
    (Full 7, Part 1).
  Rates 2003: Res $72,580/sch yr. Day $26,790/sch yr. State Aid.
  Summer Prgm: Res & Day. Educ. Ther. Res Rate $199/day. Day Rate $119/
    day. 7 wks.
  Est 1973. Private. Nonprofit.

Diagnosis and treatment, in addition to prevocational education, tutoring, counseling
and parent-infant education, are provided for hearing-impaired individuals. The school
serves deaf children and adolescents who have been excluded from public schools due
to behavioral or emotional problems or mental illness. The usual duration of treatment
is three years.

CHADDOCK

Res — Coed Ages 12-21

Quincy, IL 62301. 205 S 24th St.
Tel: 217-222-0034. Fax: 217-222-3865.
www.chaddock.org   E-mail: admissions@chaddock.org
Gene Simon, MDiv, MEd, EdD, Pres. **Andrew Greening,** MSW, Clin Dir.
  Lanny Stiles, DO, Med Dir.
  Focus: Spec Ed. Treatment. **Conditions:** Primary—BD CD ED ODD PTSD.
    Sec—ADD ADHD LD OCD. **IQ 65 and up.**
  Gen Acad. Voc. Ungraded. Courses: Read Math Lang_Arts. Man_Arts &
    Shop. On-Job Trng.
  Therapy: Milieu Play Speech. **Psychotherapy:** Fam Group Indiv.
  Staff: 164 (Full 143, Part 21). Prof 22. Educ 9. Admin 9.
  Est 1853. Private. Nonprofit. United Methodist.

This agency offers four residential programs on its 30-acre main campus: residential
treatment, a group home, independent living, and integrative attachment therapy for
youth with reactive attachment disorder.

CHICAGO ASSOCIATION FOR RETARDED CITIZENS
Res — Coed Ages 18 and up; Day — Coed 6-21

Chicago, IL 60655. 10444 S Kedzie Ave.
Tel: 773-429-0203. Fax: 773-429-0480.
www.chgoarc.org   E-mail: relations@chgoarc.org
Kristin MacRae, Pres. Regina Brown, Adm.
  Focus: Spec Ed. Conditions: Primary—Asp Au DS MR PDD. Sec—ADHD
    Ap As B BD BI C CP D ED Ep IP LD MD MS ON S SB. IQ 0-50.
  Pre-Voc. Voc. Ungraded. Shelt_Workshop. On-Job Trng.
  Therapy: Hear Hydro Lang Occup Phys Speech. Psychotherapy: Fam
    Indiv.
  Enr: 130. Day Males 80. Day Females 50. Staff: 90 (Full 84, Part 6). Prof
    29. Educ 16. Admin 2.
  Summer Prgm: Day. Educ. Rec. 7 wks.
  Est 1964. Private. Nonprofit.

CARC operates three schools, six vocational training centers, two early intervention programs and several residential group homes in Chicago, as well as programs offering placement in competitive jobs, support for independent apartment living, respite care, foster care, and family support and outreach services. Two of the schools operate afternoon programs to assist working parents.

CHICAGO LIGHTHOUSE FOR PEOPLE
WHO ARE BLIND OR VISUALLY IMPAIRED
Day — Coed Ages Birth-21

Chicago, IL 60608. 1850 W Roosevelt Rd.
Tel: 312-666-1331. TTY: 312-666-8874. Fax: 312-243-8539.
www.thechicagolighthouse.org
James M. Kesteloot, MA, Exec Dir. Mary Zabelski, MA, Educ Dir.
  Focus: Treatment. Conditions: Primary—B SB. Sec—As Au BD BI CP D
    ED Ep IP MR MS S.
  Pre-Voc. Voc. Ungraded. Courses: Adaptive_Phys_Ed.
  Therapy: Hear Lang Music Occup Phys Speech Visual.
  Enr: 34. Day Males 22. Day Females 12. Staff: 30 (Full 21, Part 9).
  Rates 2004: No Fee.
  Est 1906. Private. Nonprofit.

The development center at the Lighthouse operates two programs for blind, multi-disabled children. The home-based program provides infant stimulation and parental support for children from birth to age 3. Teacher/therapists visit the children in their homes once a week. Children ages 3-21 receive individual instruction in language, sensory awareness, physical therapy, education and socialization. A deaf-blind program and a low-vision clinic are also available.

CHILDREN'S HABILITATION CENTER

Res — Coed Ages Birth-22

Harvey, IL 60426. 121 W 154th St.
Tel: 708-339-6095. Fax: 708-596-2258.
www.childhabcenter.com
Janice Kurth, Admin.
  Focus: Spec Ed. Treatment. **Conditions:** Primary—MR. **IQ 0-60.**
  Gen Acad. Ungraded.
  Therapy: Hear Lang Occup Phys Speech. **Psychotherapy:** Fam Indiv.
  Est 1971. Private. Inc.

CHILD'S VOICE SCHOOL

Day — Coed Ages 3-9

Wood Dale, IL 60191. 180 Hansen Ct.
Tel: 630-595-8200. TTY: 630-595-8200. Fax: 630-595-8282.
www.childsvoiceschool.com   E-mail: info@childsvoiceschool.com
Michele Wilkins, EdD, Exec Dir.
  Focus: Spec Ed. **Conditions:** Primary—D. Sec—S. **IQ 100-135.**
  Gen Acad. Gr PS-2. Courses: Read Math Lang_Arts Sci Soc_Stud.
  Therapy: Hear Lang Music Speech. **Psychotherapy:** Fam Group Parent.
  Enr: 31. **Staff:** 26 (Full 24, Part 2). Educ 16. Admin 5.
  Rates 2003: Day $144/day. Schol 4 ($100,000).
  Est 1996. Private. Nonprofit.

This oral school teaches hearing-impaired children to speak. The school provides individualized instruction using speech therapy, auditory training, language development and knowledge of technological advances (such as cochlear implants). The program goal is to mainstream the child into his or her local school with minimal support.

Funding from the student's sending school district frequently covers tuition fees.

CLARE WOODS ACADEMY

Day — Coed Ages 3-21

Bartlett, IL 60103. 801 W Bartlett Rd.
Tel: 630-289-4221. Fax: 630-540-2817.
Samuela Bovelli, BS, MEd, Exec Dir. **Ann Craig,** BS, MEd, MAT, Prin.
  Focus: Spec Ed. **Conditions:** Primary—Au ED LD MR. Sec—ADD ADHD
    Ap As BI CD CP Dx Ep MD MS ON S.
  Gen Acad. Pre-Voc. Voc. Gr K-12. Courses: Read Math Lang_Arts Studio_
    Art Music Adaptive_Phys_Ed. On-Job Trng.
  Therapy: Art Lang Occup Speech. **Psychotherapy:** Group.
  Enr: 140. **Staff:** 88 (Full 81, Part 7). Admin 2.
  Summer Prgm: Day. Educ. Rec. Ther. 5 wks.
  Est 1968. Private. Nonprofit. Roman Catholic.

Conducted by the Sisters of St. Joseph, the academy offers remedial and functional academics for boys and girls with mild to moderate mental retardation. Children may also have a learning disability or an emotional disturbance. An adaptive physical education program is part of the curriculum. Applicants must be ambulatory and toilet trained.

During both the school-year and summer programs, Clare Woods offers one-on-one instruction for an additional fee.

CLEARBROOK

Res — Coed Ages 18 and up; Day — Coed Birth-3, 16 and up

Arlington Heights, IL 60005. 1835 W Central Rd.
Tel: 847-870-7711. TTY: 847-870-2239. Fax: 847-870-7741.
www.clearbrook.org   E-mail: bobrien@clearbrook.org
Carl La Mell, Pres. **Tracy Martin,** Adm.
Focus: Rehab. Trng. Treatment. **Conditions:** Primary—DS MR. Sec—Anx Asp Au B BD BI CP D ED Ep LD ON PW S.
Voc. Shelt_Workshop. On-Job Trng.
Therapy: Hear Lang Occup Phys Speech. **Psychotherapy:** Fam Indiv.
Staff: 476 (Full 372, Part 104).
Rates 2003: Res $30,000/yr. Day $1200/mo. Schol avail. State Aid.
Est 1956. Private. Nonprofit.

Clearbrook conducts programs for mentally, emotionally, physically and learning-disabled individuals. The CHILD Program treats children under age 3 who have developmental delays and specific disabilities. An interdisciplinary, family-focused approach is evident.

The Take-A-Break respite program matches trained volunteers with families of young children with special needs. Volunteers provide regular scheduled time for parents to receive relief from their daily responsibilities. Compuplay uses technology as a learning and teaching tool for young children. Lekotek is part of a national network of resources that utilizes play to develop cognitive, physical and social skills. The program also makes specially adapted toys available for home loan.

Clearbrook House is a full-time community living facility for mentally retarded adults requiring minimal supervision. Located in Arlington Heights, it is designed to offer levels of support and supervision that are commensurate with the needs of the individual. Developmental training and employment services are also offered to help participants acquire new skills, experiences and opportunities.

THE COVE SCHOOL

Day — Coed Ages 5-21

Northbrook, IL 60062. 350 Lee Rd.
Tel: 847-562-2100. Fax: 847-562-2112.
www.coveschool.org   E-mail: csward@coveschool.org
Phillip D. Jackson, Exec Dir. **Carol Sward,** Prin.
Focus: Spec Ed. **Conditions:** Primary—Dc Dg Dx LD. Sec—ADD ADHD

Anx Apr Asp Bl Db OCD TS. **IQ 90 and up.**
Col Prep. Gen Acad. Voc. Gr K-12. Courses: Read Math Lang_Arts Sci
   Computers Soc_Stud Studio_Art Music.
Therapy: Lang Occup Speech. **Psychotherapy:** Indiv.
Enr: 150. Day Males 102. Day Females 48. **Staff:** 76 (Full 68, Part 8).
Rates 2003: Day $29,500/sch yr. Schol 2 ($30,000). State Aid.
Summer Prgm: Day. Educ. Rec. Day Rate $3000. 6 wks.
Est 1947. Private. Nonprofit.

The nation's first school designed exclusively for children with learning disabilities,
Cove provides students having various learning problems with a specially designed educational environment. The program, which consists of elementary, junior high and high
school divisions, utilizes an integrated academic program to develop children's critical
thinking, language and study skills. Teachers attempt to formulate an appropriate learning strategy for the pupil.

Social workers at the school provide individual and group counseling for those experiencing social and emotional problems. Cove's seeks to help each student develop the
academic, language, social and practical skills necessary for the successful return to a
traditional classroom.

DEPAUL UNIVERSITY READING AND LEARNING LAB

Clinic: Ages 5-18. M-Th 9-5, S 9-3; Eves M-Th 5-6:30.

Chicago, IL 60614. 2320 N Kenmore Ave, Ste SAC-220.
Tel: 773-325-7745. Fax: 773-325-4673.
E-mail: kliston@depaul.edu
Kathleen M. Liston, MS, Dir.
   Focus: Spec Ed. **Conditions:** Primary—Dx LD.
   Gen Acad. Gr K-12. Courses: Read Math Lang_Arts.
   Staff: 20. Admin 5.
   Rates 2004: Sliding-Scale Rate $75-385/quar.
   Private. Roman Catholic.

The clinic provides diagnostic and remedial services for children at the elementary
and secondary levels who are interested in improving their skills in reading and learning. Ongoing services are provided through periodic evaluation and continued programming.

DEVELOPMENTAL SERVICES CENTER
CHILDREN'S SERVICES

Clinic: Ages Birth-5. M-F 8-5.

Champaign, IL 61820. 1304 W Bradley Ave.
Tel: 217-359-0287. TTY: 217-359-0288. Fax: 217-356-9851.
www.dsc-illinois.org
Dale A. Morrissey, Exec Dir. Bette Chapman, Dir.
   Focus: Spec Ed. Treatment. **Conditions:** Primary—Ap Apr Ar As Asp Au

B Bl C CP D Db DS Ep IP LD MD MR MS ON PDD PW S SB TB. Sec—
ADD ADHD BD CD Dx ED HIV OCD Psy PTSD Sz.
Therapy: Hear Lang Occup Percepual-Motor Phys Play Speech. **Psycho-therapy:** Fam Group Indiv Parent.
Staff: 16 (Full 15, Part 1). Prof 15. Admin 1.
Rates 2003: No Fee.
Est 1972. Private. Nonprofit.

The center provides early identification and intervention programs for children under age 5 with developmental delays, as well as those considered at risk of experiencing a developmental delay. DSC's program comprises therapeutic services for children who may have epilepsy, cerebral palsy, autism, mental retardation or other disabling conditions. Family support services, including parental counseling, are integral to the program.

In addition to its early intervention services, the children's division manages a respite program for children under age 13.

EASTER SEALS CENTRAL ILLINOIS

Day — Coed All Ages

Decatur, IL 62526. 2715 North 27th St.
Tel: 217-429-1052. Fax: 217-423-7605.
www.easterseals-ci.org   E-mail: info@easterseals-ci.org
Jan Kelsheimer, Pres.
    Conditions: Primary—Au B BD CP D DS LD MR OH. Sec—Ar.
    Therapy: Phys Speech.
    Staff: Prof 3.
    Est 1949. Private. Nonprofit.

EASTER SEALS CHILDREN'S DEVELOPMENT CENTER

Day — Coed Ages Birth-12

Rockford, IL 61103. 650 N Main St.
Tel: 815-965-6745. TTY: 815-965-6770. Fax: 815-965-6021.
www.il-rk.easter-seals.org   E-mail: escdc@il-rk.easter-seals.org
Stephen Guedet, MPA, Pres.
    Conditions: Primary—OH. Sec—Au B BD CP ED LD MD MR PDD S SB.
    Therapy: Art Lang Occup Phys Play Speech. **Psychotherapy:** Fam Indiv.
    Staff: Prof 15.
    Est 1968. Private. Nonprofit.

EASTER SEALS DUPAGE

Clinic: Ages Birth-21. M-F 8-6.

Villa Park, IL 60181. 830 S Addison Ave.
Tel: 630-620-4433. TTY: 630-620-4436. Fax: 630-620-1148.
www.dupage.easterseals.com
Mary Alice D'Arcy, Exec Dir. **Sue Rusco,** Clin Dir.
   Focus: Treatment. **Conditions:** Primary—Au BI CP IP MD MS ON S SB.
     Sec—B D MR.
   Therapy: Hear Lang Occup Phys Speech.
   Staff: 49 (Full 38, Part 11).
   Est 1952. Private. Nonprofit. **Spons:** National Easter Seals.

The center provides evaluation and consultation in the disciplines of physical therapy, occupational therapy, speech therapy and audiology. Treatment programs include speech classes, a language stimulation program, a multi-handicapped infant program, a voice clinic, social services, parental discussion groups and workshops. The facility also maintains an integrated daycare center on its premises.

EASTER SEALS OF BOURBONNAIS

Day — Coed Ages Birth-21
Clinic: All Ages. M-S 9-4.

Bourbonnais, IL 60914. 22 Heritage Dr, Ste 108.
Tel: 815-932-0623. Fax: 815-928-7334.
Derra Condotti, Exec Dir.
   Focus: Rehab. **Conditions:** Primary—Ap Au BI CP IP MD MR MS ON S
     SB. Sec—ADD ADHD B D.
   Therapy: Hear Lang Occup Phys Play Speech.
   Enr: 40. Day Males 21. Day Females 19. **Staff:** 4 (Full 1, Part 3). Admin 1.
   Est 1957. Private. Nonprofit.

Governed by a volunteer board of directors, the facility provides various therapies for individuals with disabilities. An equipment loan service and a stroke club are also available. In addition, the center conducts Lekotek, a play intervention program serving children from birth to age 8. Features of the program include computer resource services, integrated and developmental play groups, classroom services and a parent support group.

EASTER SEALS OF LASALLE AND BUREAU COUNTIES

Day — Coed Ages Birth-21
Clinic: All Ages. M-F 8-5.

Ottawa, IL 61350. 1013 Adams St.
Tel: 815-434-0857. Fax: 815-434-2260.
E-mail: pflad@il-lb.easter-seals.org
Pamela A. Flad, Pres. **Paula Williamson,** Prgm Dir. **Dirk Steinert,** MD, Med Dir.

Focus: Treatment. **Conditions:** Primary—DS OH. Sec—Ap Apr Ar As Asp Au B BI C CP D Dx ED Ep IP LD MD MR MS ODD PDD PW S SB. **IQ 50 and up.**
Therapy: Hear Lang Movement Occup Percepual-Motor Phys Play Speech. **Enr:** 96. **Staff:** 35.
Rates 2003: Clinic $120/hr. Schol avail. State Aid.
Est 1947. Private. Nonprofit.

The center offers outpatient care and treatment for handicapped children, as well as inclusive preschool and daycare programs. Various clinical services are also available.

EASTER SEALS-UCP

Clinic: All Ages. M-F 8-5.

Peoria, IL 61603. 507 E Armstrong Ave.
 Nearby locations: Bloomington; Hudson.
Tel: 309-686-1177. Fax: 309-686-7722.
www.easterseals-ucp.org E-mail: sthompson@easterseals-ucp.org
Stephen R. Thompson, MS, Pres. **Andrew Morgan,** MD, Med Dir. **Julie Matthews,** Intake.
 Focus: Rehab. **Conditions:** Primary—ADD ADHD Ap Apr Asp Au B BI CP D DS Dx Ep IP LD MD MR MS ON PDD PW S SB. Sec—Anx As BD C CD ED HIV Mood Nf OCD Psy SP Sz TS. **IQ 70-100.**
 Therapy: Hear Lang Occup Percepual-Motor Phys Speech. **Psychotherapy:** Fam Group Parent.
 Staff: 100 (Full 60, Part 40). Prof 60. Admin 7.
 County. Nonprofit.

The center serves children and adults with developmental delays and disabilities. Clients may receive case management services; occupational, speech, language, physical and developmental therapies; and counseling. The center also offers services during the summer. Fees are determined along a sliding scale.
Easter Seals-UCP provides services out of three locations: the Peoria Center on East Armstrong Avenue; the Bloomington Center at 1505 Eastland Dr., Ste. 110, Bloomington 61701 (309-663-8275); and the Timber Pointe Outdoor Center, 20 Timber Pointe Ln., Hudson 61748 (309-365-8021). Clients come from Peoria, Tazewell, Woodford, Fulton, McLean and Livingston counties.

EASTERN ILLINOIS UNIVERSITY
SPEECH-LANGUAGE-HEARING CLINIC

Clinic: All Ages. M-F 8-5.

Charleston, IL 61920. 600 Lincoln Ave.
Tel: 217-581-2712. Fax: 217-581-7105.
www.eiu.edu/~commdis/services.html E-mail: csldh@eiu.edu
Gail Richard, PhD, Supv. **Frank E. Goldacker,** MS, Dir.
 Focus: Rehab. **Conditions:** Primary—S.

Therapy: Hear Lang Speech.
Staff: 12. Prof 12.
Rates 2004: $25-150 (Evaluation); $150-200 (Therapy)/ses.
Est 1948. State. Nonprofit.

Clients of the clinic receive diagnostic and therapeutic services for speech, language and hearing disorders from college students who are training under the direct supervision of certified faculty. Parental counseling and follow-up services are also available.

EDUCATIONAL SERVICES OF GLEN ELLYN

Clinic: Ages 5 and up.

Glen Ellyn, IL 60137. 444 N Main St.
Tel: 630-469-1479.
Elizabeth Siebens, MA, Dir.
  Focus: Trng. **Conditions:** Primary—ADD ADHD Dx LD. Sec—S. **IQ 75 and up.**
  Therapy: Lang Occup. **Psychotherapy:** Indiv.
  Staff: 30 (Full 2, Part 28).
  Summer Prgm: Day. Educ. 1 wk.
  Est 1988. Private. Nonprofit.

Educational Services offers one-on-one tutoring, in addition to diagnostic testing for children and adults with learning disabilities. The facility evaluates each student's needs and, in many cases, consults with his or her school teacher before designing a suitable tutorial program. Tutoring sessions, which address various subject areas and basic academic skills, are held at the center. Older clients may also receive tutoring in job-seeking skills, support during college or vocational training programs, and on-the-job support.

The week-long summer program, which focuses on basic skills development, consists of five one-and-a-half-hour sessions.

ELIM CHRISTIAN SCHOOL

Res and Day — Coed Ages 3-21

Palos Heights, IL 60463. 13020 S Central Ave.
Tel: 708-389-0555. Fax: 708-389-0671.
www.elimcs.org   E-mail: info@elimcs.org
Bill Lodewyk, MA, Exec Dir. **Mike Otte,** MS, Educ Dir. **Carol Runge,** Adm.
  Focus: Spec Ed. Trng. **Conditions:** Primary—ADD ADHD As Au Bl CP Dx LD MR ON SB. Sec—Ep. **IQ 25-95.**
  Pre-Voc. Ungraded. Courses: Read Math Lang_Arts Studio_Art Music. Shelt_Workshop. On-Job Trng.
  Therapy: Hear Lang Occup Phys Speech. **Psychotherapy:** Fam Group Indiv Parent.
  Enr: 214. Res Males 28. Res Females 14. Day Males 117. Day Females 55.
    Staff: 150 (Full 80, Part 70). Prof 47. Educ 34. Admin 4.
  Rates 2003: Res $241/day. Day $122/day. State Aid.
  Summer Prgm: Res & Day. Educ. Ther. 6 wks.

Est 1948. Private. Nonprofit. Christian Reformed.

In a rural setting, Elim provides training, education and various therapies for boys and girls with moderate to mild retardation, learning disabilities, orthopedic special needs and multiple impairments. Generally, those with a primary psychiatric or behavioral disability are not accepted.

A workshop and rehabilitation center is available for those over age 16. Production activities, recreational and daily living skills, and practical academics are included in the training programs. Long-term sheltered work placement and on-the-job training is available.

ESPERANZA COMMUNITY SERVICES

Day — Coed Ages 5-21

Chicago, IL 60622. 520 N Marshfield Ave.
Tel: 312-243-6097. Fax: 312-243-2076.
E-mail: gorgol520@aol.com
Barbara Belletini-Fields, MS, Exec Dir. **Joseph Gorgol,** Prin.
  Focus: Spec Ed. **Conditions:** Primary—Asp Au BD ED Mood MR PDD S. Sec—ADD ADHD Anx Apr As BI C CP Db Dc Dg Dx Ep LD OCD ON TS. **IQ 20-75.**
  Gen Acad. Pre-Voc. Voc. Ungraded. Courses: Read Math Lang_Arts Sci Soc_Stud Studio_Art Music. Shelt_Workshop. On-Job Trng.
  Therapy: Art Dance Hear Hydro Lang Movement Music Occup Percepual-Motor Phys Recreational Speech. **Psychotherapy:** Fam Group.
  Enr: 65. **Staff:** 36 (Full 29, Part 7). Prof 10. Educ 6. Admin 7.
  Rates 2003: Day $112/day.
  Summer Prgm: Day. Educ. Rec. Ther. Vocational. 6 wks.
  Est 1969. Private. Nonprofit.

Esperanza serves children who have been formally excluded from public schools due to either mental retardation or emotional problems. The program is based on the educational and therapeutic approaches formulated by Rudolph Steiner, emphasizing the education of the whole child. Painting, sculpture, theater, eurhythmy, fairy-tale readings and creative workshops augment the curriculum. Basic academics, in addition to self-help skills, therapies and physical education, are also offered.

GOLDIE B. FLOBERG CENTER

Res and Day — Coed Ages 1 and up

Rockton, IL 61072. 58 W Rockton Rd, PO Box 346.
Tel: 815-624-8431. Fax: 815-624-8461.
www.goldiefloberg.org
Dan J. Pennell, Pres.
  Focus: Rehab. Trng. **Conditions:** Primary—MR. Sec—ADD BD LD PDD Psy PTSD Sz. **IQ 10-50.**
  Gen Acad. Gr 1-12. Courses: Read Math Lang_Arts.
  Therapy: Hear Lang Occup Phys Recreational Speech. **Psychotherapy:**

Indiv.
Staff: Prof 70.
Est 1924. Private. Nonprofit.

GOOD SHEPHERD CENTER

Day — Coed Ages Birth-3

Flossmoor, IL 60422. 2220 Carroll Pky.
Tel: 708-957-5700. Fax: 708-957-5739.
E-mail: gscbrendan@aol.com
   Conditions: Primary—MR. **IQ 20-100.**
   Therapy: Hear Lang Occup Phys Speech.
   Staff: Prof 9.
   Est 1963. Private. Nonprofit.

HARTGROVE HOSPITAL

Res — Coed Ages 3 and up; Day — Coed 6 and up

Chicago, IL 60624. 520 N Ridgeway Ave.
Tel: 773-722-3113. Fax: 773-722-6361.
www.hartgrovehospital.com   E-mail: hgrove5@aol.com
   Conditions: Primary—BD ED.
   Gen Acad. Ungraded. Courses: Read Math Lang_Arts.
   Therapy: Art Dance Music Recreational. **Psychotherapy:** Fam Group Indiv.
   Staff: Prof 35.
   Est 1962. Private. **Spons:** Universal Health Services.

HOLY TRINITY SCHOOL FOR THE DEAF

Day — Coed Ages 3-15

Chicago, IL 60612. 1900 W Taylor St.
Tel: 312-243-8186. Fax: 312-243-8479.
www.copeace.pvt.k12.il.us/deaf.htm
Phyllis Winter, MEd, Prin.
   Focus: Spec Ed. **Conditions:** Primary—D. **IQ 85 and up.**
   Gen Acad. Gr K-8. Courses: Read Math Lang_Arts Sci Soc_Stud.
   Therapy: Lang Speech.
   Staff: 7.
   Rates 2003: Day $4000/sch yr (+$400/mo). Schol avail.
   Est 1957. Private. Nonprofit. Roman Catholic. **Spons:** Children of Peace
      School.

Elementary education for deaf and hard-of-hearing students is provided at Holy Trinity. The program emphasizes an individual approach that uses a total communication

method of instruction. Parents are involved both in the structuring of the program and in communicative skills for use in the home. Speech and language services are also available. Children are mainstreamed into traditional schools.

THE HOPE SCHOOL

Res — Coed Ages 5-21

Springfield, IL 62705. 50 Hazel Ln, PO Box 5810.
Tel: 217-585-5437. Fax: 217-786-3356.
www.thehopeschool.org E-mail: info@thehopeschool.org
Joseph E. Nyre, PhD, Pres. **Jerie Beth Karkos,** MD, Med Dir. **Ann Muenstermann,** Adm.
Focus: Spec Ed. **Conditions:** Primary—Au Bl LD MR ON PDD. Sec—ADD ADHD B CP D Db DS Ep IP MD MS S SB. **IQ 0-50.**
Voc. Ungraded. Courses: Adaptive_Phys_Ed Life_Skills. On-Job Trng.
Therapy: Lang Occup Phys Recreational Speech.
Enr: 98. **Staff:** 320.
Est 1957. Private. Nonprofit.

Located on a 25-acre, wooded campus in the central part of the state, Hope conducts an individualized residential program that serves children and young adults with multiple disabilities. Programs include a school; occupational, physical, recreational and speech therapy services; a vocational program that operates both on and off campus; assistive technology services; and nursing and medical services. In addition to the campus facility, Hope maintains six community homes. Family involvement is integral to the program.

HOWE DEVELOPMENTAL CENTER

Res — Coed Ages 18 and up

Tinley Park, IL 60477. 7600 W 183rd St.
Tel: 708-614-4000. Fax: 708-532-7189.
www.dhs.state.il.us/mhdd/dd
Focus: Treatment. **Conditions:** Primary—MR. **IQ 20-35.**
Gen Acad. Ungraded. Courses: Read Math. Shelt_Workshop.
Therapy: Chemo Hear Lang Occup Phys Speech. **Psychotherapy:** Fam Group Indiv.
Est 1972. State. Nonprofit. **Spons:** Howe Association for the Retarded.

ILLINOIS SCHOOL FOR THE DEAF

Res — Coed Ages 6-21; Day — Coed Birth-21

Jacksonville, IL 62650. 125 Webster Ave.
Tel: 217-479-4200. Fax: 217-479-4209.
www.morgan.k12.il.us/isd E-mail: dhsrsp1@dhs.state.il.us

Joan Forney, EdS, Supt. **Carolyn Eilering,** Actg Adm.
  Focus: Spec Ed. **Conditions:** Primary—D. Sec—ADD ADHD CP Dx ED LD MR ON S.
  Col Prep. Gen Acad. Pre-Voc. Voc. Gr K-12. Courses: Read Math Lang_ Arts Sci Soc_Stud. Man_Arts & Shop. On-Job Trng.
  Therapy: Hear Lang Occup Phys Speech.
  Staff: 259.
  Rates 2004: No Fee.
  Est 1839. State.

An academic program that includes remedial courses and vocational training serves deaf and hard-of-hearing children who reside in Illinois. The school stresses social and emotional growth and development, in addition to optional educational programming. Other offerings include parent-infant services, adult evaluations, extracurricular activities, outreach and various special services.

ILLINOIS SCHOOL FOR THE VISUALLY IMPAIRED

Res and Day — Coed Ages 5-21

Jacksonville, IL 62650. 658 E State St.
Tel: 217-479-4400. TTY: 217-479-4415. Fax: 217-479-4412.
www.morgan.k12.il.us/isvi   E-mail: isvi@dhs.state.il.us
Marjorie Olson, Int Supt.
  Conditions: Primary—B.
  Col Prep. Gen Acad. Pre-Voc. Voc. Ungraded. Courses: Read Math Lang_ Arts. Man_Arts & Shop. On-Job Trng.
  Therapy: Lang Occup Phys Speech.
  Est 1849. State. **Spons:** Illinois Department of Human Services.

JACK MABLEY DEVELOPMENTAL CENTER

Res — Coed Ages 18 and up

Dixon, IL 61021. 1120 Washington Ave.
Tel: 815-288-8300. TTY: 815-288-8361. Fax: 815-288-7275.
E-mail: dhsddfl@dhs.state.il.us
Sharon DeBerry, Dir. **Steven Kouris,** MD, Med Dir.
  Focus: Trng. **Conditions:** Primary—MR. Sec—Anx Asp Au B CP D Ep Mood ON PDD Psy S. **IQ 0-69.**
  Voc. Shelt_Workshop. On-Job Trng.
  Therapy: Hear Lang Occup Phys Recreational Speech. **Psychotherapy:** Group Indiv.
  Enr: 108. Res Males 73. Res Females 35. **Staff:** 26 (Full 25, Part 1).
  Est 1918. State. Nonprofit. **Spons:** Dixon Association for Retarded Citizens.

Severely mentally retarded, deaf and deaf-blind residents of Illinois partake of therapeutic treatments and prevocational training at this state-operated facility. The center calculates fees along a sliding scale.

JEWISH CHILDREN'S BUREAU OF CHICAGO

Res — Coed Ages 6-23; Day — Coed All Ages
Clinic: All Ages. M-F 8:45-5; Eves T-Th 5-9.

Chicago, IL 60606. 216 W Jackson Blvd, Ste 800.
   Nearby locations: Buffalo Grove; Hazel Crest; Northbrook; Skokie.
Tel: 312-444-2090. Fax: 312-855-3754.
www.jcbchicago.org
Robert B. Bloom, PhD, Exec Dir. **Shelley Weiss,** Adm.
   Focus: Spec Ed. Treatment. **Conditions:** Primary—Au CD ED OCD Psy
      Sz. Sec—BD BI CP Dx LD MD MR MS. **IQ 60 and up.**
   Gen Acad. Pre-Voc. Gr 1-12. Courses: Read Math Lang_Arts Studio_Art
      Music Drama. On-Job Trng.
   Therapy: Chemo Hear Occup Phys Speech. **Psychotherapy:** Fam Group
      Indiv Parent.
   Enr: 70. **Staff:** 250 (Full 210, Part 40).
   Est 1893. Private. Nonprofit. Jewish. **Spons:** Jewish Federation of Metro-
      politan Chicago.

The Jewish Children's Bureau is a child welfare agency that provides a full range of
services for children and their families. Counseling is available on an outpatient basis
to children living in their own homes, and the agency offers several placement options
for dependent and neglected children and for emotionally disturbed youths and young
adults. Placement services include regular foster care, specialized foster care, and intensive and transitional group home care. Facilities provide a full range of psychotherapeutic, educational, respite and advocacy services for the disabled. In addition, the bureau
serves pregnant adolescents and operates a preschool for children with autism.
   Branches of the clinic are located at 3344 N. Peterson Ave., 60659; 6014 N. California
Ave., 60659; 1250 Radcliffe St., Ste. 202, Buffalo Grove 60089; 3649 W. 183rd St., Ste.
123, Hazel Crest 60429; 555 Revere Dr., Northbrook 60062; and 5050 Church St., 2nd
Fl., Skokie 60077.

JOSEPH ACADEMY

Day — Coed Ages 8-21

Niles, IL 60714. 7530 N Natchez Ave.
Tel: 847-588-2990. Fax: 847-588-2950.
www.josephacademy.org   E-mail: information@josephacademy.org
Michael Schack, MBA, MA, Exec Dir. **Heather Elliott,** Prin.
   Focus: Spec Ed. **Conditions:** Primary—ADD BD CD ED LD. Sec—ADHD
      Dc Dg Dx Mood MR OCD. **IQ 60-120.**
   Gen Acad. Gr 4-12. Courses: Read Math Lang_Arts Sci Soc_Stud. Man_
      Arts & Shop.
   Psychotherapy: Fam Group Indiv Parent.
   Enr: 90. Day Males 80. Day Females 10. **Staff:** 31 (Full 27, Part 4). Prof 29.
      Admin 2.
   Rates 2004: No Fee.
   Est 1983. Private. Nonprofit.

This therapeutic day school enrolls children with behavioral disorders and learning disabilities. The behavioral program follows the Boys' Town model. Academic credit is given for work-study program. Frequent academic field trips are available.

An interscholastic sports program includes football, soccer, volleyball, basketball, bowling and softball. Among other organizations are girls' club, chess club and student council. All funding and transportation is provided by the sending school district.

KEMMERER VILLAGE

Res — Coed Ages 8-18; Day — Coed Birth-21

Assumption, IL 62510. RR 1, Box 12C.
Tel: 217-226-4451. Fax: 217-226-3511.
www.kv-web.org
Michael A. Havera, MPA, Exec Dir. **Steve Linscott,** Intake.
   Focus: Spec Ed. Treatment. **Conditions:** Primary—BD CD ED LD. **IQ 70-120.**
   Gen Acad. Pre-Voc. Ungraded. Courses: Read Math Lang_Arts Computers Sci Studio_Art Life_Skills. Man_Arts & Shop.
   Therapy: Speech. **Psychotherapy:** Fam Group Indiv Parent.
   Enr: 90. Res Males 25. Res Females 25. Day Males 20. Day Females 20.
      Staff: 40 (Full 38, Part 2).
   Est 1914. Private. Nonprofit. Presbyterian.

Located on a rural 20-acre farm, this former orphanage now provides residential and foster care, aftercare, individualized educational programs and family services for neglected children and those with learning disabilities, social/emotional maladjustment and behavioral disorders. Residents are generally victims of child abuse and family breakup, runaways and children who cannot live with their natural parents. Such children live in cottages housed according to level of behavior.

Boys and girls may take part in academic programming at Fergusson Educational Center. Kemmerer also offers vocational and educational counseling, as well as athletic and work opportunities. Mainstreaming is a goal of the program, and the average stay is 14 months.

LAMBS FARM

Res and Day — Coed Ages 18 and up

Libertyville, IL 60048. Rtes 176 & I-94, PO Box 520.
Tel: 847-362-4636. Fax: 847-362-0742.
www.lambsfarm.org   E-mail: info@lambsfarm.org
Dianne Yaconetti, Pres. **Eugene Salzberg,** MD, Med Dir. **Mary Carroll,** Adm.
   Focus: Treatment. **Conditions:** Primary—MR.
   Voc. Shelt_Workshop. On-Job Trng.
   Therapy: Lang Occup Speech.
   Enr: 238. Res Males 92. Res Females 90. Day Males 32. Day Females 24.
      Staff: 202 (Full 142, Part 60).
   Rates 2003: No Fee.

Est 1961. Private. Nonprofit.

The purpose of this facility is to provide goal-oriented, comprehensive and coordinated habilitation services for mentally retarded adults in order to maximize their life skills at home, at work and in the community. To achieve this goal, Lambs Farm provides vocational, residential and supportive program services.

Residential services include an intermediate care facility and 12 group homes, while the vocational program features developmental training, occupational skills training, vocational evaluation and community placement. Support services consist of case management, social services, and leisure and recreational programs.

LAWRENCE HALL YOUTH SERVICES

Res — Coed Ages 8-18; Day — Coed 8-21

Chicago, IL 60625. 4833 N Francisco Ave.
Tel: 773-769-3500. Fax: 773-769-3882.
www.lawrencehall.org   E-mail: info@lawrencehall.org
Mary Hollie, BS, MSW, CEO. **Dr. D'Agostino,** MD, Med Dir. **Debbie Podmore,**
Intake.
   Focus: Spec Ed. Treatment. **Conditions:** Primary—ADD ADHD BD CD ED.
      Sec—MR OCD Psy S. **IQ 65-105.**
   Gen Acad. Pre-Voc. Voc. Gr 1-12. Courses: Read Math Lang_Arts. Man_
      Arts & Shop. On-Job Trng.
   Therapy: Art Dance Music Recreational Speech. **Psychotherapy:** Fam
      Group Indiv Parent.
   Enr: 600. **Staff:** 300. Prof 150.
   Rates 2003: Res $228-244/day. Day $136/day.
   Est 1868. Private. Nonprofit. Episcopal.

This comprehensive community-based agency is the site of a structured preventative and therapeutic program for high-risk and severely disturbed youth. Individual treatment plans utilize strength-based intervention techniques. Vocational assessment and training, transitional services and wraparound services are available to the client's family support system.

THE LEARNING CLINIC

Clinic: All Ages. M-Th by Appt.

Homewood, IL 60430. 18656 Dixie Hwy.
Tel: 708-799-3089.
   Focus: Treatment. **Conditions:** Primary—Dx LD.
   Therapy: Lang Speech.
   Staff: 10 (Full 2, Part 8).
   Est 1981. Private.

Remediation at this clinic teaches the client how to reach his or her academic potential and how to develop a learning plan for future success. Therapy helps individuals develop increased self-esteem by accepting their learning differences. The facility also serves as a liaison between learning-disabled persons and schools or employers.

LT. JOSEPH P. KENNEDY SCHOOL
FOR EXCEPTIONAL CHILDREN

Res — Coed Ages 6 and up; Day — Coed 3-21

Tinley Park, IL 60477. 18350 Crossing Dr.
Tel: 708-342-5202. Fax: 708-342-2579.
Rosemary Kern, MEd, Dir. **Patti O'Brien,** Adm.
    Focus: Spec Ed. **Conditions:** Primary—Asp Au Bl MR PDD. Sec—ADD ADHD Anx BD Dx ED LD ON S.
    Gen Acad. Pre-Voc. Voc. Ungraded. Courses: Read Math Lang_Arts. Shelt_Workshop. On-Job Trng.
    Therapy: Lang Phys Speech.
    Staff: 61. Prof 12. Educ 7. Admin 1.
    Rates 2003: Day $108/day.
    Est 1949. Private. Nonprofit. Roman Catholic.

The school provides comprehensive year-round special education and vocational training for mildly to moderately retarded children and adolescents. A program for nonacademic students that emphasizes the development of life skills is also offered. Individualized programming includes speech therapy, art, shop experience, home economics, music and physical education.

LIGHTED WAY ASSOCIATION
CHILDREN'S DEVELOPMENTAL CENTER

Day — Coed Ages Birth-21

La Salle, IL 61301. 941 6th St.
Tel: 815-224-1345. Fax: 815-224-4759.
E-mail: lightway@theramp.net
Polly Ann Rimmele, BA, Dir.
    Focus: Treatment. **Conditions:** Primary—Au MR. Sec—OH.
    Pre-Voc. Ungraded. Courses: Read Math Lang_Arts Life_Skills.
    Therapy: Hear Lang Music Occup Phys Speech.
    Staff: 20.
    Rates 2004: No Fee.
    Est 1957. Private. Nonprofit.

This center provides a coordinated program of diagnostic evaluation, treatment, education and rehabilitation for children with physical and mental disabilities. The program emphasizes self-help and daily living skills, socialization and therapy.

LINCOLN PARK HEARING CENTER

Clinic: All Ages. M-S 8-5; Eves T Th 5-7.

Chicago, IL 60614. 550 W Webster Ave.
Tel: 773-883-3711.
   Focus: Treatment. **Conditions:** Primary—Ap D S.
   Therapy: Hear Lang Speech.
   Private.

MARKLUND CHILDREN'S HOME

Res — Coed Ages Birth-21

Bloomingdale, IL 60108. 164 S Prairie Ave.
Tel: 630-529-2871. Fax: 630-529-3266.
www.marklund.org
Joel Rusco, Pres. **Lisa Lipira,** Exec Dir.
   Focus: Rehab. Treatment. **Conditions:** Primary—MR. Sec—OH.
   Therapy: Music Occup Phys Speech.
   Enr: 90. Res Males 40. Res Females 50. **Staff:** 120 (Full 100, Part 20).
   Est 1956. Private. Nonprofit.

This home offers medical, educational and habilitative developmental programs for children with severe disabilities or multiple handicaps. Each child follows a daily program plan of individualized activities specifically designed to meet developmental and physical needs. Children typically reside at Marklund for an extended period of time.

MENTAL HEALTH CENTERS OF CENTRAL ILLINOIS

Res and Day — Coed Ages 3-17

Springfield, IL 62702. 710 N 8th St.
Tel: 217-525-1064. Fax: 217-525-9047.
www.mhcci.org   E-mail: mentalhealth@mhsil.com
Brian A. Allen, MPA, Pres.
   Conditions: Primary—BD ED.
   Pre-Voc. Voc. Shelt_Workshop. On-Job Trng.
   Therapy: Occup Recreational.
   Est 1925. Private. Nonprofit.

MISERICORDIA HOME-SOUTH

Res — Coed Ages Birth-21

Chicago, IL 60632. 2916 W 47th St.
Tel: 773-254-9595. Fax: 773-254-6856.
www.misericordia.com

Sr. Rosemary Connelly, Dir.
  Conditions: Primary—Bl CP MR ON SB.
  Gen Acad. Ungraded.
  Therapy: Hear Occup Phys Speech. **Psychotherapy:** Indiv.
  Staff: Prof 28.
  Est 1921. Private. Nonprofit.

MOSAIC LIVING CENTER

Res and Day — Coed All Ages

Chicago, IL 60626. 7464 N Sheridan Rd.
Tel: 773-338-0200. Fax: 773-338-5122.
www.mosaiclivingcenter.com
  E-mail: mchancay@mosaiclivingcenter.com
Scott Swanson, Exec Dir. **Monica Chancay,** Adm.
  Focus: Rehab. **Conditions:** Primary—MD MR SB. Sec—Ap As B Bl C CP
    D DS Dx Ep ON S. **IQ 0-40.**
  Therapy: Hear Lang Occup Phys Recreational Speech.
  Enr: 150. **Staff:** 96. Prof 32. Educ 26. Admin 18.
  Est 1969. Private.

Mosaic seeks to provide a home environment for children with developmental disabilities and adults with accompanying medical problems. The residential program admits both ambulatory and nonambulatory patients, offering a small living situation in which the individual can develop at his or her own pace. Individualized planning is utilized to improve self-image and help each person realize his or her potential.

NORTH CENTER FOR HANDICAPPED CHILDREN

Day — Coed Ages 6 and up

Chicago, IL 60641. 5104 W Belmont Ave.
Tel: 773-777-4111. Fax: 773-777-6390.
Lucia Alexandra, MA, Dir. **Deena DeNosaque,** Prin.
  Focus: Rehab. Trng. Treatment. **Conditions:** Primary—Bl DS MR. Sec—
    ADD ADHD Anx Ap As Au BD C CP D Db ED Ep IP ON PDD S. **IQ 5-55.**
  Col Prep. Gen Acad. Pre-Voc. Gr K-12. Courses: Read Math Lang_Arts
    Sci.
  Therapy: Hydro Lang Occup Phys Recreational Speech.
  Enr: 31. Day Males 15. Day Females 16. **Staff:** 34 (Full 22, Part 12). Prof
    29. Admin 5.
  Est 1968. Private. Nonprofit.

North Center offers a range of services for children and adults with moderate to profound mental retardation, including speech, physical and occupational therapy; life skills training; prevocational training; recreational programming; and family support services. Young people under age 21 pay no fee for services.

NORTHERN ILLINOIS UNIVERSITY
SPEECH-LANGUAGE-HEARING CLINIC

Clinic: All Ages. M-F 8-4:30.

DeKalb, IL 60115. Dept of Communicative Disorders.
Tel: 815-753-1481. Fax: 815-753-1664.
Anne D. Davidson, MA, Dir.
 Focus: Rehab. **Conditions:** Primary—S. Sec—ADD ADHD Ap Apr Asp Au
 Bl CP D Dc Dg DS Dx LD MR PDD TS.
 Therapy: Hear Lang Speech.
 Staff: 15.
 Est 1959. State.

NIU's Speech-Language-Hearing Clinic provides speech, language and hearing evaluations, therapy and counseling for individuals with hearing impairments.

PAULSON REHABILITATION CENTER

Clinic: All Ages. M-F 8-5; Eves M-F 5-9.

Willowbrook, IL 60521. 619 Plainfield Rd.
Tel: 630-856-8200. Fax: 630-856-8212.
www.bolingbrookmedcenter.net/services/rehab/paulsonrehabnetwork.asp
 Conditions: Primary—Ap As Au B Bl C CP D Dx IP LD MD MR MS ON S
 SB.
 Therapy: Hear Occup Phys.
 Est 1986. Private.

PEORIAREA BLIND PEOPLE'S CENTER

Clinic: Ages 1 and up. M-F 8-4; Eve W 4-8.

Peoria, IL 61605. 2905 W Garden St.
Tel: 309-637-3693.
Mabel Van Dusen, Exec Dir.
 Focus: Spec Ed. **Conditions:** Primary—B. Sec—Ar As BD Bl C CD CP D
 ED Ep IP MD MR MS OCD Psy S Sz.
 Therapy: Speech.
 Staff: 1. (Full 1).
 Est 1956. Private. Nonprofit.

The center provides a variety of educational, counseling, rehabilitative and specific services for residents of the Peoria area. Services are offered in conjunction with a support network for the blind and visually impaired and their families.

PHILIP J. ROCK CENTER AND SCHOOL

Res — Coed Ages 3-21

Glen Ellyn, IL 60137. 818 DuPage Blvd.
Tel: 630-790-2474. TTY: 800-771-1232. Fax: 630-790-4893.
www.project-reach-illinois.org/prc.html
  E-mail: prc@project-reach-illinois.org
Christine D. Lechnick, BA, MEd, Chief Admin. **Peggy Whitlow,** MEd, Educ
  Dir. **Arlene Beaton,** MD, Med Dir.
  Focus: Spec Ed. **Conditions:** Primary—B D.
  Pre-Voc. Voc. Ungraded. Courses: Studio_Art Music. On-Job Trng.
  Therapy: Hear Lang Occup Phys Speech.
  Enr: 18. Res Males 12. Res Females 6. **Staff:** 60.
  Rates 2004: No Fee.
  State. **Spons:** Illinois Advocates for the Deaf-Blind.

This facility provides educational and residential services for deaf-blind students. PRC stresses a multidisciplinary team approach for a highly intensive and individualized educational program. All phases of the student's life, from personal hygiene and grooming to mobility and vocational skills, are developed and individualized.

QUINCY SCHOOL FOR THE HANDICAPPED

Day — Coed Ages 3-21

Quincy, IL 62305. 4409 Maine St, PO Box 3646.
Tel: 217-223-0413. Fax: 217-223-0461.
www.twi.org/services/school.htm
Michael Rein, MA, Exec Dir.
  Focus: Spec Ed. **Conditions:** Primary—MR. Sec—ADD B BI CP D OH. **IQ**
  0-35.
  Gen Acad. Ungraded. Shelt_Workshop.
  Therapy: Hear Lang Occup Phys Speech. **Psychotherapy:** Fam Group
  Indiv Parent.
  Enr: 17. Day Males 14. Day Females 3. **Staff:** 15 (Full 9, Part 6).
  Est 1971. Private. Nonprofit. **Spons:** Transitions of Western Illinois.

This school serves severely to profoundly retarded children who have not had their needs adequately met in public school systems. Individualized programs correspond with each child's requirements and capabilities, and parental involvement plays a major role at the school. Counseling, respite care and referral services are also available.

RAY GRAHAM ASSOCIATION
FOR PEOPLE WITH DISABILITIES

Res — Coed Ages 3 and up; Day — Coed All Ages

Downers Grove, IL 60515. 2801 Finley Rd.
Tel: 630-620-2222. TTY: 630-628-2352. Fax: 630-628-2350.

www.ray-graham.org   E-mail: raygrahamassociation@aol.com
Cathy Ficker Terrill, Pres.
 Conditions: Primary—Au CP MR.
 Pre-Voc. Voc. Gr K-12. Shelt_Workshop.
 Therapy: Hear Lang Occup Phys Speech. **Psychotherapy:** Indiv.
 Est 1951. Private. Nonprofit.

THE READING GROUP

Clinic: All Ages. M-S 9-6.

Urbana, IL 61801. 6 Lincoln Sq.
Tel: 217-367-0914.
www.readinggroup.org   E-mail: info@readinggroup.org
Marilyn Kay, MEd, Exec Dir.
 Focus: Spec Ed. **Conditions:** Primary—ADD ADHD Dg Dx. Sec—LD.
 Staff: 14 (Full 1, Part 13). Educ 12. Admin 2.
 Rates 2003: Clinic $55-60/hr.
 Summer Prgm: Day. Educ. Day Rate $475. 5 wks.
 Est 1972. Private. Nonprofit.

Individual and small-group instruction is provided at this clinic. Programs include training for those with dyslexia, for gifted students with learning differences and for individuals with attentional disorders. The facility also features workshops for parents and teachers.

REHABILITATION INSTITUTE OF CHICAGO

Res and Day — Coed All Ages
Clinic: All Ages.

Chicago, IL 60611. 345 E Superior St.
Tel: 312-238-1000.
www.ric.org   E-mail: webmaster@ric.orgric.org
Wayne M. Lerner, DPH, Pres. **Elliot Roth,** MD, Med Dir.
 Conditions: Primary—Ar As Bl C CP MS ON S.
 Therapy: Art Lang Music Occup Phys Recreational Speech.
 Est 1954. Private.

ROCVALE CHILDREN'S HOME

Res — Coed Ages 6-21

Rockford, IL 61103. 4450 N Rockton Ave.
Tel: 815-654-3050. Fax: 815-654-3073.
Jim Hamilton, Pres. **William Hutt,** MD, Med Dir. **Diane Nelson,** Intake.
 Conditions: Primary—Asp Au DS MR PDD. Sec—ADD ADHD Ar As B Bl

CD CP D Db ED Ep LD Mood OCD ODD ON PW S.
Therapy: Hear Lang Phys Speech.
Enr: 50. Res Males 39. Res Females 11. **Staff:** 120 (Full 90, Part 30). Prof 10. Admin 8.
Rates 2003: No Fee.
Est 1906. Private. Nonprofit.

RocVale provides specialized, individualized programs for children and adolescents with developmental disabilities. The facility employs an approach to diagnosis, evaluation and program planning through a team of professionals. Each team member focuses on identifying the developmental needs of each individual.

Residents attend public school programs. The team assists each resident in attaining his or her highest level of functioning, insuring a smooth transition to his or her natural home, a foster home, a community living facility or a sheltered workshop. Counseling services are available. Children must be free of serious psychiatric and severe behavioral problems.

SAINT XAVIER UNIVERSITY
LUDDEN SPEECH AND LANGUAGE CLINIC

Clinic: All Ages. M-Th 8:30-5, S 8:30-12:30; Eves M-Th 5-7.

Chicago, IL 60655. 3700 W 103rd St.
Tel: 773-298-3561. Fax: 773-779-9061.
www.sxu.edu/comm_sci/clinic
   Focus: Treatment. **Conditions:** Primary—Ap S. Sec—BI CP D LD MR.
   Therapy: Lang Speech.
   Staff: 7 (Full 4, Part 3).
   Est 1959. Private. Nonprofit. Roman Catholic.

Ludden Clinic serves as a training program in speech pathology for undergraduate students. Clinically certified speech pathologists and students under direct supervision provide speech and language therapies for clients with communicative disorders involving phonology/articulation, language, aphasia/stroke, stuttering, voice, auditory processing or hearing impairment.

SHRINERS HOSPITAL

Res — Coed Ages Birth-18
Clinic: Ages Birth-18. M-F 8:30-5.

Chicago, IL 60707. 2211 N Oak Park Ave.
Tel: 773-622-5400. TTY: 773-385-5419. Fax: 773-385-5453.
www.shrinershq.org/shc/chicago/index.html
A. James Spang, MA, Admin. **John P. Lubicky,** MD, Med Dir. **Paula Canham,** Adm.
   Focus: Rehab. Treatment. **Conditions:** Primary—CP IP MD ON SB. Sec—ADD ADHD Ap As Au B BD BI C CD D Dx ED Ep LD MR OCD Psy Sz.
   Therapy: Hear Occup Phys Recreational Speech. **Psychotherapy:** Fam

Group Indiv Parent.
Enr: 60. **Staff:** 260.
Rates 2004: No Fee.
Est 1926. Private. Nonprofit.

Impaired children, especially those with orthopedic handicaps, receive free treatment at this specialized hospital. Rooms for parents and parent teaching are offered. Orthopedic clinics are also conducted, and there is a spinal cord injury program that provides care and rehabilitation.

SONIA SHANKMAN ORTHOGENIC SCHOOL

Res — Coed Ages 6-20

Chicago, IL 60637. 1365 E 60th St.
Tel: 773-702-1203. Fax: 773-702-1304.
http://orthogenicschool.uchicago.edu
   E-mail: bll@yoda.bsd.uchicago.edu
Bennett L. Leventhal, MD, Dir. **Thomas Shoaf,** MD, Med Dir. **D. Patrick Zimmerman,** Adm.
   Focus: Spec Ed. **Conditions:** Primary—Anx Asp Au ED Mood OCD ODD Psy PTSD SP Sz TS. Sec—ADD ADHD Ar As BD CD Db Dx LD. **IQ 80 and up.**
   Col Prep. Gen Acad. Pre-Voc. Voc. Ungraded. Courses: Read Math Lang_ Arts Sci. Man_Arts & Shop. On-Job Trng.
   Therapy: Art Speech. **Psychotherapy:** Fam Group Indiv Parent.
   Enr: 42. Res Males 21. Res Females 21. **Staff:** 75 (Full 67, Part 8). Educ 12. Admin 2.
   Rates 2004: Res $103,500/yr. State Aid.
   Est 1930. Private. Nonprofit. **Spons:** University of Chicago.

The school is affiliated with the University of Chicago. Severely emotionally disturbed children of average intelligence and above receive individualized attention within small groups. Life activities are planned after results of repeated psychiatric and psychological evaluation and staff conferences. Milieu therapy is the basis of rehabilitation and includes both individual therapy and group work. Classroom groups are small, with each student working at a suitable pace. Individualized teaching enables students to reach educational goals similar to those instituted in public schools.

Sonia Shankman maintains close cooperation with the university's Laboratory Schools and appropriate departments of the university. Children enrolled at the school may use the swimming pool of the Laboratory Schools. School is in session year-round, with home and parent visits arranged according to the child's emotional needs. Parents receive monthly reports and attend conferences concerning their child's progress. Length of treatment varies.

SOUTHERN ILLINOIS UNIVERSITY CLINICAL CENTER

Clinic: All Ages. M-F 8-4:30; Eves M-Th 4:30-8.

**Carbondale, IL 62901. Wham Educational Bldg, Rm 141, Mail Code 4602.
Tel: 618-453-2361. Fax: 618-453-6126.
www.siu.edu/offices/clinical   E-mail: clinctr@siu.edu
Brenda Gilbert,** PhD, Dir.

Focus: Treatment. **Conditions:** Primary—ADD ADHD Anx Au BD CD Dx ED Mood OCD ODD PTSD SP. Sec—Ap Ar As B Bl CF CP D Db DS Ep HIV IP LD MD MR MS ON S SB.

Therapy: Hear Lang Phys Speech. **Psychotherapy:** Fam Group Indiv Parent.

Staff: 21 (Full 6, Part 15). Prof 13. Educ 1. Admin 1.

Est 1959. State. Nonprofit.

The Clinical Center provides a wide variety of services for both the general public and university students and staff members. Offerings include reading, therapy, social work, psychological evaluation and counseling services. The staff consists of professionals and student diagnosticians and therapists.

STREAMWOOD BEHAVIORAL HEALTH CENTER

Res — Coed Ages 12-21

**Streamwood, IL 60107. 1360 E Irving Park Rd.
Tel: 630-736-2740. Fax: 630-736-2741.
www.streamwoodhospital.com
Mary Carol Costigan,** LCSW, Prgm Dir. **Mike Gara,** PsyD, Clin Dir. **Joe McNally,** MD, Med Dir. **Fran Babych,** Intake.

Focus: Treatment. **Conditions:** Primary—ADD ADHD Anx BD ED Mood ODD Psy PTSD Sz. Sec—Dx LD MR. **IQ 55 and up.**

Col Prep. Gen Acad. Pre-Voc. Voc. Gr 6-12. Courses: Read Math Lang_ Arts.

Therapy: Recreational Speech. **Psychotherapy:** Fam Group Indiv.

Enr: 74. Res Males 54. Res Females 20. **Staff:** 135 (Full 121, Part 14).

Est 1983. Private. **Spons:** Ardent Health Services.

This therapeutic program for behaviorally and emotionally troubled adolescents is conducted in a safe, structured environment. Treatment comprises clinical and academic components, and it focuses on the identification of each adolescent's resources, the development of problem-solving skills and improved interpersonal relations. Family members also learn how to resolve conflicts and develop more effective means of communication. The usual length of stay at Streamwood is nine to eighteen months, after which time the center aims to reintegrate adolescents into their homes, schools and communities.

SUMMIT SCHOOL

Day — Coed Ages 6-21

Dundee, IL 60118. 611 E Main St.
Tel: 847-428-6451. Fax: 847-428-6419.
www.summitinc.org   E-mail: scarl@summitdundee.org
Sharon Carl, BA, MA, MSEd, Prin.
    Focus: Spec Ed. **Conditions:** Primary—LD. Sec—ED.
    Gen Acad. Pre-Voc. Voc. Gr PS-12. Courses: Read Math Lang_Arts Com-
        puters Studio_Art Adaptive_Phys_Ed. Man_Arts & Shop. On-Job Trng.
    Therapy: Lang Occup Speech. **Psychotherapy:** Group Indiv.
    Staff: 35. (Full 35).
    Est 1968. Private. Nonprofit.

Summit accepts children of normal to superior intelligence who have learning difficulties. Individualized learning and coordinated motor, language and speech instruction
form the foundation of the program. The school day ends early for those students who
are being mainstreamed. Social skills and self-advocacy training is a secondary emphasis of the program.

SWEDISH COVENANT HOSPITAL
SPEECH-LANGUAGE PATHOLOGY

Clinic: All Ages. M-F 7:30-5:30, S 8-12.

Chicago, IL 60625. 5145 N California Ave.
Tel: 773-878-8200. Fax: 773-878-6152.
www.swedishcovenant.org
    Conditions: Primary—Ap S.
    Therapy: Lang Speech. **Psychotherapy:** Group.
    Private.

THE THERAPLAY INSTITUTE

Clinic: Ages Birth-12. M-S by Appt.

Wilmette, IL 60091. 3330 Old Glenview Rd, Ste 8.
Tel: 847-256-7334. Fax: 847-256-7370.
www.theraplay.org   E-mail: info@theraplay.org
Gayle Christensen, Exec Dir. **Jodi Rubin,** MS, Clin Coord. **Phylis Booth,** MA,
    Med Dir.
    Focus: Treatment. **Conditions:** Primary—ADD ADHD Anx Au BD ED
        PTSD. Sec—B D MR.
    Therapy: Speech. **Psychotherapy:** Fam Group Indiv.
    Staff: 10 (Full 5, Part 5). Prof 7. Admin 3.
    Rates 2003: Clinic $120-140/ses.
    Est 1969. Private. Nonprofit.

The Theraplay model uses play activities to simulate healthy interaction between parent and child by focusing on the following areas: structure, engagement, nurture, challenge and playfulness. These elements are employed in combinations geared to the specific needs and problems of the child and his or her parents. Short-term treatment and parental involvement are characteristics of the program.

Theraplay works effectively with children diagnosed with autism or pervasive developmental disorder, attentional disorders, attachment disorders, adjustment disorders, anxiety disorders, behavioral problems or depression.

TRINITY SCHOOL
Day — Coed Ages 3-21

Mokena, IL 60448. 11600 Francis Rd.
Tel: 708-479-0028. Fax: 708-479-0354.
www.trinity-services.org   E-mail: cshields@trinity-services.org
Tony DiVittorio, Dir.
   Focus: Spec Ed. **Conditions:** Primary—Au MR. Sec—ADD ADHD Asp B BD CP D DS Ep LD PW S TS.
   Gen Acad. Ungraded.
   Therapy: Lang Occup Speech.
   Enr: 27. Day Males 18. Day Females 9. **Staff:** 25 (Full 23, Part 2). Admin 2.
   Rates 2003: No Fee.
   Summer Prgm: Day. Educ. 6 wks.
   Est 1950. Private. Nonprofit. **Spons:** Trinity Services.

All children at the school have a developmental disability, such as mental retardation, autism or cerebral palsy. Program emphasis is to help the boy or girl function in society as independently as possible. As children have varying developmental levels, Trinity works with each child individually. Boys and girls learn to interact with one another and with other members of the community.

UNIVERSITY OF CHICAGO
CHILD AND ADOLESCENT PSYCHIATRY CLINIC
Clinic: Ages Birth-18. M-S 7-6.

Chicago, IL 60637. 5841 S Maryland Ave, MC 3077.
Tel: 773-702-4453. Fax: 773-702-9929.
www.psychiatry.uchicago.edu/clinical
Bennett L. Leventhal, MD, Dir. **Willie Watson,** Intake.
   Focus: Treatment. **Conditions:** Primary—ED. Sec—BD BI Ep LD MR. **IQ 60 and up.**
   Therapy: Speech. **Psychotherapy:** Fam Group Indiv.
   Staff: 48 (Full 38, Part 10). Prof 40. Admin 8.
   Rates 2003: Clinic $70-200/ses. State Aid.
   Est 1954. Private.

This clinic treats those with emotional disturbances and psychological problems through a program of psychiatric evaluations and psychological, neuropsychological and learning disabilities testing. Medication management and individual and group psychotherapy are also available.

UNIVERSITY OF ILLINOIS-CHICAGO
CHILDREN'S HABILITATION CLINIC

Clinic: Ages Birth-21. M-F 8:30-5.

Chicago, IL 60612. 1801 W Taylor St, 2 N.
Tel: 312-996-7202. Fax: 312-413-3445.
http://uillinoismedcenter.org/content.cfm/peds_habilitation
Miriam Kalichman, MD, Dir.
   Conditions: Primary—Au CP MR ON SB.
   Therapy: Chemo Hear Lang Occup Phys Speech. **Psychotherapy:** Indiv.
   Staff: Prof 13.
   Est 1956. State. Nonprofit.

UNIVERSITY OF ILLINOIS-CHICAGO
DIVISION OF SPECIALIZED CARE FOR CHILDREN

Clinic: Ages Birth-21. M-F by Appt.

Springfield, IL 62794. 2815 W Washington St, Ste 300, PO Box 19481.
Tel: 217-793-2340. Fax: 217-793-0773.
www.uic.edu/hsc/dscc   E-mail: dscc@uic.edu
Charles N. Onufer, BA, MD, Dir.
   Focus: Rehab. **Conditions:** Primary—B Bl C CP D Ep IP MD MS ON SB.
      Sec—DS S.
   Therapy: Occup Phys Speech.
   Staff: 300. Prof 106. Admin 42.
   Rates 2003: No Fee.
   Est 1937. State. Nonprofit.

An official state agency, DSCC provides care coordination and financial assistance for children with chronic health impairments and physical disabilities. Thirteen regional offices coordinate services throughout the state.

In addition, the agency operates the Children's Habilitation Clinic, which operates on the campus of the University of Illinois at Chicago. The clinic offers comprehensive diagnostic services to children with complex disabling conditions and provides ongoing rehabilitation and developmental management for individuals age 21 and younger.

UNIVERSITY OF ILLINOIS-CHICAGO
INSTITUTE FOR JUVENILE RESEARCH

Day — Coed Ages 4-18
Clinic: Ages Birth-18. M-F 8:30-5.

Chicago, IL 60612. 1747 W Roosevelt Rd, Mail Code 747.
Tel: 312-413-5664. Fax: 312-413-1036.
www.psych.uic.edu
Patrick H. Tolan, PhD, Dir. **Michael Naylor,** MD, Med Dir.
   Focus: Treatment. **Conditions:** Primary—Au BD CD ED Mood. Sec—BI.
   Therapy: Hear. **Psychotherapy:** Fam Group Indiv.
   State.

The clinic provides individual, family and group intervention for mildly to severely disturbed children and adolescents. Consultations with other agencies and schools are also conducted.

WALTER S. CHRISTOPHER SCHOOL

Day — Coed Ages 7-13

Chicago, IL 60632. 5042 S Artesian Ave.
Tel: 773-535-9375. Fax: 773-535-9567.
www.christopher.cps.k12.il.us
Adrienne Watkins, Prin.
   Focus: Spec Ed. **Conditions:** Primary—As BI C CP Ep IP MD MS ON SB.
      Sec—ADD ADHD B D Dx ED LD MR S.
   Gen Acad. Gr 2-8. Courses: Read Math Lang_Arts. Man_Arts & Shop.
   Therapy: Hear Lang Occup Phys Speech. **Psychotherapy:** Indiv Parent.
   Enr: 252. **Staff:** 71 (Full 65, Part 6).
   Rates 2004: No Fee.
   Est 1925. Municipal.

This city school provides an educational program for both nondisabled children and those with health and physical disabilities, mental retardation, cerebral palsy and speech defects. Physical and occupational therapies, psychological evaluations, general academics, remedial courses and language therapy. All referrals are processed by the Bureau of Physically Handicapped Children of the Chicago Board of Education.

WARREN G. MURRAY DEVELOPMENTAL CENTER

Res — Coed Ages 3 and up

Centralia, IL 62801. 1535 W McCord St.
Tel: 618-532-1811. Fax: 618-532-8171.
www.callforhelpinc.org/html/347.htm
   Conditions: Primary—BD ED MR. **IQ 0-67.**
   Pre-Voc. Ungraded.
   Therapy: Hear Lang Occup Phys Speech. **Psychotherapy:** Indiv.
   Est 1964. State. Nonprofit.

WESTERN ILLINOIS UNIVERSITY
SPEECH-LANGUAGE-HEARING CLINIC

Clinic: All Ages.

Macomb, IL 61455. 121 Memorial Hall.
Tel: 309-298-1955. Fax: 309-298-2400.
www.wiu.edu/users/micom/wiu/csd/csd.htm
Robert W. Quesal, PhD, Dir.
  Conditions: Primary—D S.
  Therapy: Hear Lang Speech.
  State.

WILLIAM W. FOX DEVELOPMENTAL CENTER

Res — Coed Ages 14 and up

Dwight, IL 60420. 134 W Main St.
Tel: 815-584-3347. TTY: 815-584-3368. Fax: 815-584-3723.
  Focus: Treatment. **Conditions:** Primary—MR. Sec—As Au B BD BI C CP
  D ED Ep IP MD MS ON S SB. **IQ 0-50.**
  Therapy: Hear Lang Occup Phys Speech. **Psychotherapy:** Indiv.
  Est 1965. State. Nonprofit.

This center is one of more than a dozen area residential facilities serving persons
with developmental disabilities. Each resident of Fox Center follows an individualized
program of daily care and training designed to promote total development and a greater
degree of independence. Each living unit provides a program suited to the needs and
abilities of its residents. Twenty-four-hour medical and nursing care and supervision are
available.

INDIANA

ABILITIES SERVICES

Clinic: Ages Birth-3. M-F 8-4:30.

Crawfordsville, IN 47933. 1237 Concord Rd.
   Nearby locations: Frankfort; Lafayette.
Tel: 765-362-4020. Fax: 765-364-1100.
www.asipages.com   E-mail: abilities@wico.net
Steve Gooch, Exec Dir.
   Focus: Trng. Treatment. **Conditions:** Primary—MR ON S.
   Voc. Shelt_Workshop. On-Job Trng.
   Therapy: Hear Lang Occup Phys Speech.
   Staff: 10 (Full 2, Part 8).
   Rates 2004: No Fee.
   Private. Nonprofit.

Early intervention and home training services are provided for infants up to age 3 who are at risk or who display developmental delays. Parental involvement is encouraged through meetings, workshops and conferences. Offerings for adults include work activity centers and vocational services.

Branch facilities operate at 950 McKinley Ave, Frankfort 46041, 321 E. Clinton St., Ste. 7, Frankfort 46041 and 323 Columbia St., Ste. 2A, Lafayette 47901.

ANN WHITEHILL
DOWN SYNDROME PROGRAM

Clinic: Ages Birth-18. M 8-5.

Indianapolis, IN 46202. 702 Barnhill Dr, Rm 1601.
Tel: 317-274-4846. Fax: 317-278-0126.
Charlene Davis, MSN, RN, Coord.
   Focus: Treatment. **Conditions:** Primary—DS MR. Sec—ADD ADHD Anx
      Ap Apr As Asp Au B BD Bl C CD CP D Dx ED Ep IP LD MD Mood MS Nf
      OCD ODD ON Psy PTSD PW S SB SP Sz TS.
   Staff: 6. (Full 6).
   Est 1984. State. Nonprofit. **Spons:** James Whitcomb Riley Hospital for Children.

This program provides care for children with Down syndrome. Services include pediatric medical and surgical specialists, physical therapy, occupational therapy, speech/language therapy, nutrition counseling, pediatric hearing specialists, pediatric ophthalmology, genetic evaluation and counseling, developmental screenings and referrals to early intervention programs. The program also sponsors a weeklong overnight camping experience for children ages 8-21.

ARC OPPORTUNITIES

Day — Coed All Ages

Howe, IN 46746. 235 W 300 N.
Tel: 260-463-2653. Fax: 260-463-2046.
www.arcopportunities.org   E-mail: info@arcopportunities.org
Debra D. Seman, MA, Exec Dir. **Anne Patka,** Intake.
　Focus: Rehab. **Conditions:** Primary—MR. Sec—S. **IQ 20-79.**
　Voc. Shelt_Workshop.
　Therapy: Hear Speech. **Psychotherapy:** Fam Indiv.
　Enr: 80. **Staff:** 25 (Full 23, Part 2).
　Rates 2003: No Fee.
　Est 1966. Private. Nonprofit.

ARC aims to protect and support individuals with disabilities and to develop their
potential within a unique community. They offer an early stimulation program and
pre- and postpsychometric testing in addition to a wide range of therapeutic treatments.
Vocational and personal counseling are also available.

BALL STATE UNIVERSITY
SPEECH-LANGUAGE AND AUDIOLOGY CLINICS

Clinic: All Ages. M-F 8-5.

Muncie, IN 47306. 1700 University Ave.
Tel: 765-285-8160. Fax: 765-285-5623.
www.bsu.edu/csh/spa/slpclinic/slpclinic.html
　E-mail: sppathaud@gw.bsu.edu
Mary Jo Germani, PhD, Chair.
　Focus: Treatment. **Conditions:** Primary—D S.
　Therapy: Hear Lang Speech.
　Staff: 16. (Full 16).
　Est 1945. State.

These two clinics, operated by the BSU Department of Speech Pathology and Audiology, provide diagnosis and therapy for speech, language and hearing disorders, in addition to teacher training. Parental counseling is also available. Fees are determined along
a sliding scale.

BARTHOLOMEW SPECIAL SERVICES COOPERATIVE

Day — Coed Ages 5-18

Columbus, IN 47201. 703 Washington St.
Tel: 812-376-4460. Fax: 812-376-4204.
www.bcsc.k12.in.us/bssc
　Conditions: Primary—ED MR.
　Gen Acad. Pre-Voc. Voc. Gr K-12. Courses: Read Math Lang_Arts. Man_
　Arts & Shop. Shelt_Workshop. On-Job Trng.

Therapy: Hear Lang Occup Phys Speech.
Federal. **Spons:** Special Education Advisory Community.

BONA VISTA COMPREHENSIVE
REHABILITATION CENTER
Clinic: All Ages. M-F 8-4:30.

Peru, IN 46970. 105 S Benton St.
  Nearby locations: Kokomo.
Tel: 765-473-6744. Fax: 765-473-6749.
www.bonavista.org   E-mail: bonavist@bonavista.org
Jill Dunn, MA, Exec Dir. **Ron Marrs,** MD, Med Dir.
  Focus: Rehab. **Conditions:** Primary—Ap Apr Ar Asp Au B Bl CF CP D DS
    Ep IP MD MR MS ON S SB TS. Sec—ADD ADHD C CD Dx ED LD OCD
    PW Sz. **IQ 0-90.**
  Voc. Shelt_Workshop.
  Therapy: Hear Lang Occup Phys Speech. **Psychotherapy:** Group.
  Staff: 352 (Full 250, Part 102). Prof 36. Educ 7.
  Est 1958. Private. Nonprofit.

A work activity center, Bona Vista employs trainable to moderately retarded adolescents and adults for subcontracted work from local industries. The work consists of simple assembly and packaging jobs, as well as the mailing and the collating of large catalogs for area industries.

Living skills classes held during the work day provide instruction in money management and self-grooming and help with reading and writing. Recreational activities arranged by Bona Vista include swimming and bowling. Preschool classes, therapy programs and community activities are also offered.

A second location operates at 1220 E. Laguna St., P.O. Box 2496, Kokomo 46904.

BONA VISTA REHABILITATION CENTER
Clinic: All Ages. M-F 8-4:30.

Kokomo, IN 46904. 1220 E Laguna St.
  Nearby locations: Peru (IN).
Tel: 765-457-8273. Fax: 765-456-3503.
www.bonavista.org   E-mail: administration@bonavista.org
Jill S. Dunn, MA, Pres.
  Focus: Rehab. Trng. **Conditions:** Primary—Au CP MR. Sec—Ap As B BD
    Bl C D Dx ED Ep IP LD MD MS ON S SB.
  Voc. Shelt_Workshop. On-Job Trng.
  Therapy: Hear Lang Occup Phys Speech. **Psychotherapy:** Fam Group.
  Staff: 400 (Full 250, Part 150).
  Est 1958. Private. Nonprofit.

Bona Vista provides total rehabilitation services for individuals with physical and mental disabilities. Programs for children include infant follow-along and stimulation, developmental evaluation, a care and share group, and a preschool program. Occupational, physical, speech and hearing therapies are available on an outpatient basis.

Vocational services consist of evaluation, supported employment, job placement and a sheltered workshop. Bona Vista also offers residential training in housekeeping, meal planning and preparation, money management and social relations for men and women age 18 and up.

Bona Vista operates five satellite offices, three in Kokomo and two in Peru.

BRIDGEPOINTE GOODWILL INDUSTRIES AND EASTER SEAL SOCIETY

Clinic: Ages 2-11. By Appt.

Clarksville, IN 47131. 1329 Applegate Ln, PO Box 2117.
Tel: 812-283-7908. Fax: 812-283-6248.
Caren L. Marshall, MSW, Exec Dir.
    Focus: Treatment. **Conditions:** Primary—Ap Bl CP IP MD MS ON S SB. Sec—ADD ADHD Au B D Ep MR.
    Therapy: Hear Lang Occup Phys Speech.
    Staff: 33 (Full 27, Part 6).
    Est 1957. Private. Nonprofit. **Spons:** National Easter Seals.

Bridgepointe offers comprehensive and interdisciplinary evaluation and treatment to persons with physical disabilities. A full range of therapies is available to children and adults with physical, developmental and learning disabilities. Services provided are medical, rehabilitative and educational in nature. Specialized programs address individual needs.

CAREY SERVICES

Res — Coed Ages 18 and up; Day — Coed Birth-21
Clinic: Ages Birth-18. M-F 8-5; Eves M-F 5-8.

Marion, IN 46953. 2724 S Carey St.
Tel: 765-668-8961. Fax: 765-664-6747.
www.careyservices.com   E-mail: info@careyservices.com
Mark R. Draves, MA, Exec Dir.
    Focus: Rehab. Treatment. **Conditions:** Primary—Ap Asp Au Bl CP DS Dx Ep LD MR ON S SB. Sec—B BD D ED PW Sz TS.
    Pre-Voc. Voc. Ungraded. Shelt_Workshop. On-Job Trng.
    Therapy: Hear Lang Occup Percepual-Motor Phys Play Speech. **Psychotherapy:** Fam Group.
    Enr: 485. Res Males 40. Res Females 45. Day Males 200. Day Females 200. **Staff:** 290 (Full 260, Part 30). Educ 65. Admin 16.
    Rates 2003: No Fee.
    Est 1954. Private. Nonprofit.

The agency offers three distinct programs providing preschool/infant and adult services, including vocational/functional skills and placement. The Early Head Start program offers comprehensive child and family development services to income-eligible families with a child age 3 or younger. First Steps provides early intervention in the form of various therapeutic services for children from birth to age 3 who have delays or disabilities, or who are at risk of a delay because of a medical or biological condition. Capabilities provides rehabilitative services designed specifically to treat children from infancy through age 21 who have neurological, developmental or rehabilitative issues. Length of treatment varies.

CHILD-ADULT RESOURCE SERVICES

Day — Coed Ages Birth-5

Greencastle, IN 46135. 608 Tennessee St.
Tel: 765-653-2454.
www.cars-services.com
  Conditions: Primary—MR.
  Pre-Voc. Voc. Gr PS. Courses: Read Math Lang_Arts. Shelt_Workshop. On-Job Trng.
  Therapy: Hear Lang Occup Phys Speech.
  Est 1969. Private. Nonprofit.

CHILDREN FIRST CENTER

Day — Coed Ages Birth-5

Auburn, IN 46706. 1752 Wesley Rd, PO Box 166.
Tel: 260-925-3865. Fax: 260-925-3892.
www.childrenfirstcenter.org   E-mail: cfc@childrenfirstcenter.org
  Conditions: Primary—Au CP Ep MR OH.
  Gen Acad. Gr PS.
  Therapy: Hear Lang Phys Speech. **Psychotherapy:** Fam Group.
  Est 1971. Private. Nonprofit. **Spons:** Dekalb County Parent Group for Handicapped Children.

CHILDREN'S BUREAU

Res — Coed Ages 6-21

Indianapolis, IN 46204. 615 N Alabama St, Rm 426.
Tel: 317-264-2700. Fax: 317-264-2714.
www.childrensbureau.org   E-mail: info@childrensbureau.org
Ron D. Carpenter, Pres.
  Conditions: Primary—ED. Sec—BD.
  Gen Acad. Courses: Read Math Lang_Arts.
  Psychotherapy: Fam Group Indiv.
  Staff: Prof 41.
  Est 1851. Private. Nonprofit.

CHRISTIAN HAVEN

Res — Coed Ages 6-18; Day — Coed 10-18

Wheatfield, IN 46392. 12501 North State Rd 49.
Tel: 219-956-3125. Fax: 219-956-4128.
www.christianhaven.org   E-mail: proatis@christianhaven.org
Patrick Oatis, Exec Dir.
  Conditions: Primary—BD ED. Sec—ADD ADHD CD Mood MR ODD PTSD.
  Gen Acad. Voc. Ungraded. Courses: Read Math Lang_Arts. Man_Arts &
    Shop. Shelt_Workshop. On-Job Trng.
  Therapy: Art Play Recreational. **Psychotherapy:** Fam Group Indiv.
  Staff: Prof 29.
  Est 1951. Private. Nonprofit.

CROSSROAD

Res and Day — Coed Ages 6-21

Fort Wayne, IN 46805. 2525 Lake Ave.
Tel: 260-484-4153. Fax: 260-484-2337.
www.crossroad-fwch.org
Imogene Nusbaum-Snyder, MA, Pres. **Margaret Boerger,** RN, Med Dir.
  Focus: Spec Ed. Treatment. **Conditions:** Primary—AN Anx Asp BD Bu CD
    ED Mood OCD ODD PDD Psy PTSD SP Sz TS. Sec—ADD ADHD As BI
    C CF CP D Db Dx Ep HIV LD MR MS ON S. **IQ 60 and up.**
  Gen Acad. Pre-Voc. Ungraded. Courses: Read Math Lang_Arts Soc_Stud
    Health Life_Skills. On-Job Trng.
  Therapy: Hear Play Recreational. **Psychotherapy:** Fam Group Indiv.
  Enr: 84. Res Males 35. Res Females 35. Day Males 7. Day Females 7.
    Staff: 145 (Full 139, Part 6). Prof 34. Educ 21. Admin 10.
  Est 1883. Private. Nonprofit. United Church of Christ.

This year-round facility provides residential treatment, alternative education, day
treatment, foster care, and outpatient and home-based therapy. Residential services
cover a broad continuum that ranges from locked secure programs to independent living.
Psychotherapy services are offered to both children and their families, and education is
available at an on-grounds school. The usual length of treatment is nine months. Residential diagnostic programming is available.

DEVELOPMENTAL SERVICES

Day — Coed Ages Birth-3, 16 and up

Columbus, IN 47202. 2920 10th St, PO Box 1023.
Tel: 812-376-9404. TTY: 812-378-2850. Fax: 812-378-2849.
www.dsiservices.org   E-mail: dsinc@nsonline.net
Bill Hadar, Exec Dir.
  Focus: Rehab. Trng. **Conditions:** Primary—ADD ADHD Au BI CP Dx Ep

IP LD MR SB. Sec—Ap As B BD C CD D ED MD MS OCD ON Psy S Sz TB.
Pre-Voc. Voc. Ungraded. Shelt_Workshop. On-Job Trng.
Therapy: Lang Occup Speech. **Psychotherapy:** Indiv.
Staff: 331.
Est 1975. Private. Nonprofit.

This agency provides educational, residential and vocational rehabilitation services for individuals with developmental disabilities. Programs include infant/toddler services, residential group living, sheltered employment, supported employment, semi-independent living support, habilitation training, supported living services, epilepsy services and occupational therapy. The facility provides services for individuals living in Brown, Bartholomew, Decatur, Jackson, Jennings, Jefferson, and Switzerland counties.
DSI bases fees for respite care on a sliding scale.

DUNN MENTAL HEALTH CENTER

Res — Coed Ages 18 and up
Clinic: All Ages. M-F.

Richmond, IN 47375. PO Box 487.
 Nearby locations: Connersville; Rushville; Winchester.
Tel: 765-983-8045. Fax: 765-983-8019.
www.dunncenter.org   E-mail: info@dunncenter.org
 Conditions: Primary—BD ED.
 Psychotherapy: Fam Group Indiv.
 Est 1962. Private. Nonprofit.

EASTER SEALS CROSSROADS REHABILITATION CENTER

Day — Coed All Ages
Clinic: All Ages. M-F 8-6.

Indianapolis, IN 46205. 4740 Kingsway Dr.
Tel: 317-466-1000. TTY: 317-479-3232. Fax: 317-466-2000.
www.eastersealscrossroads.org
 E-mail: info@eastersealscrossroads.org
James J. Vento, MA, Pres. **Janine Sheppard,** MD, Med Dir. **Anne Marie House,** Adm.
 Focus: Rehab. **Conditions:** Primary—ADD ADHD B D DS ON PDD. Sec—Ap As Asp Au BI C CP Dx ED Ep IP LD MD MR MS S SB TB.
 Pre-Voc. Voc. Ungraded. Shelt_Workshop. On-Job Trng.
 Therapy: Hear Lang Occup Phys Speech.
 Staff: 137 (Full 120, Part 17). Prof 118. Educ 3.
 Est 1936. Private. Nonprofit.

Programming is available at Easter Seals Crossroads for individuals with all types of special needs. Physical restoration forms the core of most patients' rehabilitation programs, with speech, physical and occupational therapies emphasized. Specialty programs address driver evaluations and training, handwriting skills and augmentative communications.

Vocational services for adults are evaluation, supported employment, adjustment, job-seeking skills and a subcontractual workshop. Emphasis is on evaluation, communication, counseling, socialization, paid work and adjustment to independent or semi-independent living.

Other programs include a therapeutic adult day center, assistive technology, deaf community services and case management.

EVANSVILLE ARC

Day — Coed Ages Birth-5

Evansville, IN 47724. 615 W Virginia St, PO Box 4089.
Tel: 812-428-4500. Fax: 812-421-8537.
www.evansvillearc.org   E-mail: info@evansvillearc.org
Deidra Conner, Exec Dir.
   Conditions: Primary—MR.
   Pre-Voc. Voc. Shelt_Workshop. On-Job Trng.
   Therapy: Occup Phys Speech.
   Est 1954. Private. Nonprofit.

FOUR RIVERS RESOURCE SERVICES

Day — Coed All Ages

Linton, IN 47441. PO Box 249.
   Nearby locations: Loogootee; Lyons; Sullivan; Washington.
Tel: 812-847-2231. Fax: 812-847-8836.
www.frrs.org   E-mail: frrs@frrs.org
Stephen Sacksteder, Exec Dir.
   Focus: Trng. Treatment. **Conditions:** Primary—B D DS MR S. Sec—Au Bl
   CP Ep LD MD MS ON Sz TS.
   Voc. Shelt_Workshop. On-Job Trng.
   Enr: 308. Day Males 164. Day Females 144. **Staff:** 300 (Full 200, Part 100).
   Rates 2004: No Fee.
   Est 1986. Private. Nonprofit.

At-risk infants receive developmental and early intervention care at home. Services for adults include work evaluation, sheltered workshop, habilitation training, supported employment and job placement programs.

Centers are located in Daviess County (2212 E. National Hwy., Washington 47501); Greene County (175 S. Wine St., P.O. Box 141, Lyons 47443); Martin County (500 N. Oak St., Loogootee 47553); and Sullivan County (424 E. Hartley, Sullivan 47882).

GIBAULT

Res — Males Ages 8-18, Females 12-18; Day — Coed 8-18

Terre Haute, IN 47802. 6301 S Hwy 41, PO Box 2316.
Tel: 812-299-1156. Fax: 812-299-0118.
www.gibault.org   E-mail: zach.pies@gibault.org
James M. Sinclair, MSSW, JD, Exec Dir. Cathi Swander, Adm.
  Focus: Treatment. Conditions: Primary—ADD ADHD BD CD Dx ED LD
    OCD. Sec—As Ep. IQ 70 and up.
  Gen Acad. Pre-Voc. Gr 1-12. Courses: Read Math Lang_Arts. Man_Arts &
    Shop.
  Therapy: Hear Lang Occup Speech. Psychotherapy: Fam Group Indiv
    Parent.
  Enr: 136. Res Males 124. Day Males 12. Staff: 198 (Full 151, Part 47). Educ
    15.
  Rates 2003: Res $93-270/day. Day $60-85/day.
  Est 1921. Private. Nonprofit. Roman Catholic.

Gibault serves delinquent boys with mild emotional disturbances through a reality-oriented milieu treatment program. An on-grounds school emphasizes remedial reading and mathematics, with the goal of mainstreaming into community schools. Counseling supplements the academic program and is also reality oriented, helping boys accept responsibility for their behavior. A unit treatment team overseeing aspects of the program that directly affect boys during treatment monitors adjustment and progress. Length of stay varies according to the individual's needs.

Gibault also offers a specialized and intensive treatment program for adolescent sex offenders. Intensive Sexual Intervention Systems (ISIS) is a staff-secured treatment unit with separate and isolated educational, recreational and therapeutic programs.

HAMILTON CENTER

Day — Coed Ages Birth-18

Terre Haute, IN 47804. 620 8th Ave.
Tel: 812-231-8323. Fax: 812-231-8400.
www.hamiltoncenter.org
  Conditions: Primary—BD ED.
  Psychotherapy: Fam Group Indiv.
  Est 1971. Private. Nonprofit.

HEARING AND SPEECH CENTER
OF ST. JOSEPH COUNTY

Clinic: All Ages. M-F 8-4:30.

South Bend, IN 46617. 711 E Colfax Ave.
Tel: 574-234-3136. TTY: 574-234-3136. Fax: 574-234-8177.
www.uhs-in.org   E-mail: hbrown@uhs-in.org

Heather L. Brown, MS, MPA, Dir.
  Focus: Treatment. **Conditions:** Primary—Apr D S. Sec—Au DS MR.
  Therapy: Hear Lang Speech.
  Staff: 9 (Full 3, Part 6).
  Private. Nonprofit. **Spons:** United Health Services.

Speech, language, fluency and voice evaluations and therapy are provided at the center. Also available are hearing tests, hearing aid evaluations and dispensing services, and aural rehabilitation. The facility also offers sign language interpreting services. Fess are based along a sliding scale.

INDIANA SCHOOL FOR THE BLIND

Res and Day — Coed Ages 3-21

Indianapolis, IN 46240. 7725 N College Ave.
Tel: 317-253-1481. Fax: 317-251-6511.
http://isb.butler.edu   E-mail: jdurst@isb.state.in.us
James Durst, Supt.
  Focus: Spec Ed. **Conditions:** Primary—B.
  Col Prep. Gen Acad. Pre-Voc. Voc. Gr PS-12. Courses: Read Math Lang_
    Arts Braille Computers Studio_Art Music Adaptive_Phys_Ed Life_Skills.
    Man_Arts & Shop. Shelt_Workshop. On-Job Trng. Horticulture.
  Therapy: Art Hear Lang Movement Music Occup Phys Speech. **Psycho-
    therapy:** Group Indiv.
  Enr: 186. **Staff:** 200. Prof 51. Educ 45. Admin 3.
  Summer Prgm: Res & Day. Educ. Rec. 1 wk.
  Est 1847. State.

Education for blind and visually impaired children, including the multiply handicapped, is provided through this state school. Specialized classes include orientation and mobility, vocational education, music instruction, braille and specially adapted computer technology. Also available are experiences and opportunities to participate in recreational activities, on- and off-campus jobs, scouting, creative dance and ham radio, as well as involvement in competitive speech, track and field, wrestling, cheerleading and swimming.

After graduation, students enter the work force or continue their education at colleges or technical schools. The school is free for residents of Indiana.

INDIANA SCHOOL FOR THE DEAF

Res — Coed Ages 3-21; Day — Coed 1-21

Indianapolis, IN 46205. 1200 E 42nd St.
Tel: 317-924-4374. Fax: 317-923-2853.
www.deafhoosiers.com
George Stailey, Supt. **Deb Robarge,** Med Dir. **Gary Mowl,** Adm.
  Focus: Spec Ed. **Conditions:** Primary—D.
  Col Prep. Gen Acad. Pre-Voc. Voc. Gr PS-12. Courses: Read Math Lang_
    Arts. Man_Arts & Shop. On-Job Trng.

Therapy: Hear Lang Occup Phys Play Speech. **Psychotherapy:** Indiv.
Enr: 310.
Rates 2003: No Fee.
Summer Prgm: Res & Day. Educ. 2 wks.
Est 1844. State. Nonprofit.

The school provides a full academic program for deaf and hard of hearing children who are residents of Indiana. A vocational program that includes manual arts and on-the-job training serves older students. Various therapeutic treatments and recreational activities are integral to the child's development.

INDIANA STATE UNIVERSITY
ROWE CENTER FOR COMMUNICATIVE DISORDERS

Clinic: All Ages. M-F 8-5.

Terre Haute, IN 47809. School of Education, Rm 410.
Tel: 812-237-2800. Fax: 812-237-8137.
http://web.indstate.edu/soe/cdse/rowectr.html
  Conditions: Primary—Ap S. **IQ 60 and up.**
  Therapy: Hear Lang Speech.
  Est 1865. State.

KIDS KAMPUS

Day — Coed Ages 6wks-12
Clinic: All Ages. M-S 8-5.

Huntington, IN 46750. 435 Campus St.
Tel: 260-356-0123. Fax: 260-358-9512.
www.kidskampus.org   E-mail: kk@pathfinderservices.org
Carla MacDonald, MSW, MBA, Admin. **Duane Hougendobler,** MD, Med Dir.
  Carol Bledsoe, Intake.
  Focus: Treatment. **Conditions:** Primary—Au BI CP Ep IP MD MR MS ON SB. Sec—ED LD S.
  Therapy: Hear Lang Occup Phys Speech. **Psychotherapy:** Indiv.
  Enr: 83. Day Males 54. Day Females 29. **Staff:** 8 (Full 6, Part 2).
  Est 1966. Private. Nonprofit. **Spons:** Pathfinder Services.

Services available at the center include infant stimulation and an integrated preschool. The facility's approach prevents special-needs children from feeling isolated.

LEAGUE FOR THE BLIND & DISABLED

Day — Coed Ages Birth-18

Fort Wayne, IN 46816. 5821 S Anthony Blvd.
Tel: 260-441-0551. TTY: 260-441-0551. Fax: 260-441-7760.

www.the-league.org   E-mail: the.league@verizon.net
David Nelson, Pres.
  Conditions: Primary—B.
  Col Prep. Gen Acad. Pre-Voc. Voc. Gr PS-12.
  Psychotherapy: Fam Group.
  Staff: Prof 4.
  Est 1950. Private. Nonprofit.

LOGAN

Res — Coed Ages 18 and up; Day — Coed Birth-18+

South Bend, IN 46617. 1235 N Eddy St.
Tel: 574-289-4831. Fax: 574-234-2075.
www.logancenter.org   E-mail: logan@logancenter.org
  Conditions: Primary—MR.
  Pre-Voc. Voc. Ungraded. Shelt_Workshop.
  Therapy: Occup Speech. **Psychotherapy:** Group.
  Est 1950. Private. Nonprofit.

LOGANSPORT STATE HOSPITAL
JAYNE ENGLISH TREATMENT CENTER

Res — Coed Ages 14 and up

Logansport, IN 46947. 1098 S State Rd 25.
Tel: 219-722-4141. TTY: 219-732-0069. Fax: 219-735-3414.
www.lshonline.org
  Focus: Treatment. **Conditions:** Primary—ADD ADHD Au CD ED MR OCD
    Psy Sz. Sec—Ep. **IQ 35-70.**
  Pre-Voc. Voc. Ungraded. Courses: Read Math. Shelt_Workshop.
  Therapy: Chemo Hear Lang Occup Speech. **Psychotherapy:** Group.
  Enr: 48. Res Males 36. Res Females 12. **Staff:** 60.
  Est 1968. State. Nonprofit.

This center accepts individuals with mild or moderate mental retardation who also exhibit symptoms of mental illness. The patient's family and parents are encouraged to participate in treatment as programs strive to train or modify the patient's behavior so that he or she may return to a home or a community setting. The unit does not accept custodial or nonambulatory cases.

LUTHERWOOD

Res and Day — Coed Ages 6-21

Indianapolis, IN 46219. 1525 N Ritter Ave.
Tel: 317-359-5467. Fax: 317-322-4095.

www.lutheranfamily.org/lutherwood.htm
Beth Eiler, Dir.
    Conditions: Primary—BD ED. **IQ 65 and up.**
    Gen Acad. Gr K-12. Courses: Read Math Lang_Arts.
    Therapy: Recreational. **Psychotherapy:** Group Indiv.
    Staff: Prof 21.
    Est 1893. Private. Nonprofit. **Spons:** Lutheran Child and Family Services.

MANITOU TRAINING CENTER

Day — Coed Ages 18 and up

Rochester, IN 46975. 1690 Lucas St.
Tel: 574-223-6963. Fax: 574-223-3933.
E-mail: manitoucenter1690@yahoo.com
Jodi Smith, Dir.
    Focus: Trng. **Conditions:** Primary—Ap Au Bl CP Ep MR ON S SB. **IQ 0-75.**
    Pre-Voc. Voc. Shelt_Workshop. On-Job Trng.
    Therapy: Hear Lang Occup Speech.
    Est 1967. Private. Nonprofit.

MARIAN DAY SCHOOL

Day — Coed Ages 6-14

Evansville, IN 47711. 700 Herndon Dr.
Tel: 812-422-5346. Fax: 812-422-5345.
www.mariandayschool.com   E-mail: mariandayschool@hotmail.com
Beverly Williamson, MS, Dir.
    Focus: Spec Ed. **Conditions:** Primary—ADHD LD MR. Sec—ED.
    Gen Acad. Pre-Voc. Gr K-8. Courses: Read Math Lang_Arts Soc_Stud
        Studio_Art. Man_Arts & Shop.
    Therapy: Hear Phys Speech. **Psychotherapy:** Fam Indiv.
    Enr: 36. Day Males 20. Day Females 16. **Staff:** 9 (Full 7, Part 2). Educ 5.
    Rates 2003: Day $3600/sch yr. Schol avail.
    Est 1958. Private. Nonprofit. Roman Catholic.

Marian provides a parochial school special education program for children with learning disabilities and mild mental handicaps. Pupils are mainstreamed into the general classes at St. Theresa School. A portion of the school day is allotted to individual study so that students may fully participate in all of the activities at St. Theresa, among them physical education, computer, music, art, lunch and prayer time.

MARSHALL-STARKE DEVELOPMENT CENTER

Day — Coed All Ages

Plymouth, IN 46363. 1901 Pidco Dr.
Tel: 574-936-9400. Fax: 574-936-4537.
http://starkeunited.org/support
Michael Lintner, Dir.
   Conditions: Primary—Au BI CP Ep MR SB.
   Pre-Voc. Voc. Ungraded. Shelt_Workshop. On-Job Trng.
   Therapy: Hear Lang Phys Speech.
   Est 1976. Private. Nonprofit.

MEMORIAL HOSPITAL OF SOUTH BEND
MEMORIAL REGIONAL REHABILITATION CENTER

Res — Coed All Ages
Clinic: All Ages. M-F 7:30-4:30.

South Bend, IN 46601. 615 N Michigan St.
Tel: 574-647-7312. Fax: 574-647-6775.
www.memorialsb.org/services/Rehab
   Conditions: Primary—Ap As BI CP MD MS ON S SB.
   Therapy: Chemo Hear Lang Occup Phys Speech.
   Est 1887. Private. Nonprofit.

NEW HOPE SERVICES

Day — Coed Ages Birth-3, 16 and up

Jeffersonville, IN 47130. 725 Wall St.
   Nearby locations: Austin; Scottsburg.
Tel: 812-288-8248. Fax: 812-288-1206.
www.newhopeservices.org   E-mail: info@newhopeservices.org
James A. Bosley, MA, MBA, Pres.
   Focus: Trng. Treatment. **Conditions:** Primary—MR. Sec—BD BI ED LD ON
      S.
   Pre-Voc. Voc. Ungraded. Shelt_Workshop. On-Job Trng.
   Therapy: Hear Lang Occup Phys Speech. **Psychotherapy:** Parent.
   Enr: 350. **Staff:** 200 (Full 150, Part 50).
   Rates 2004: No Fee.
   Est 1960. Private. Nonprofit.

   Year-round education, vocational evaluation and training are provided for individuals with developmental disabilities at New Hope. The school offers a developmental preschool, therapy, an early intervention program and parent education. Activities, job placement and training in daily living skills are available for adults through the center.

Satellite offices are located at 2277 W. Frontage Rd., Austin 47102 and 1642 W. McClain Ave., Scottsburg 47170.

NEW HORIZONS REHABILITATION

Res — Coed Ages 18 and up; Day — Coed All Ages
Clinic: Ages Birth-3. M-F 8-4:30.

Batesville, IN 47006. 237 Six Pine Ranch Rd, PO Box 98.
Tel: 812-934-4528. TTY: 812-934-4528. Fax: 812-934-2522.
www.nhrehab.org   E-mail: mdausch@venus.net
Marie E. Dausch, BS, Exec Dir. **Carly Langferman,** Adm.
  Focus: Rehab. Trng. **Conditions:** Primary—Asp Au B D DS MR. Sec—BD
    BI CP ED Ep LD MD MS OCD ON S SB TB. **IQ 25-95.**
  Gen Acad. Ungraded. Shelt_Workshop. Job Placement.
  Therapy: Lang Occup Speech.
  Enr: 294. **Staff:** 97 (Full 82, Part 15).
  Rates 2004: No Fee.
  Est 1968. Private. Nonprofit.

Serving a five-county area of southeastern Indiana, New Horizons Rehabilitation provides early intervention programs for infants who have any at-risk condition that affects development. Adult services include day programs, community training, residential habilitation and sheltered workshops.

NEW HORIZONS YOUTH MINISTRIES

Res — Coed Ages 13-17

Marion, IN 46953. 1002 S 350 E.
Tel: 765-668-4009. Fax: 765-662-1407.
www.nhym.org   E-mail: admissions@nhym.org
Tim Blossom, MDiv, LCSW, Exec Dir. **Kellie Blossom,** Adm.
  Focus: Treatment. **Conditions:** Primary—ADD ADHD AN Anx As BD Bu
    ED Mood OCD PTSD. Sec—Db Ep TS. **IQ 90 and up.**
  Col Prep. Gen Acad. Gr 9-12. Courses: Read Math Lang_Arts Bible.
  Therapy: Milieu. **Psychotherapy:** Fam Group Indiv Parent.
  Enr: 106. Res Males 64. Res Females 42. **Staff:** 135 (Full 116, Part 19).
    Prof 36. Educ 24. Admin 13.
  Rates 2004: Res $6000/mo. Schol 78 ($166,556).
  Summer Prgm: Res. Educ. Ther. Res Rate $13,808. 10 wks.
  Est 1971. Private. Nonprofit. Nondenom Christian.

Providing treatment and special education in a Christian environment, NHYM accepts adolescents with behavioral disorders and mild emotional disturbances. Students attend classes at New Horizons Academy, a therapeutic boarding school, while also taking part in individual and group counseling sessions three to four times per week.

NOBLE OF INDIANA

Day — Coed All Ages

Indianapolis, IN 46219. 7701 E 21st St.
Tel: 317-375-2700. Fax: 317-375-2719.
www.nobleofindiana.org
Michael R. Howland, BA, MA, JD, Pres.
   Conditions: Primary—MR. Sec—B.
   Pre-Voc. Voc. Courses: Read Math Lang_Arts. Man_Arts & Shop. Shelt_
      Workshop. On-Job Trng.
   Therapy: Occup Phys Speech.
   Est 1953. Private. Nonprofit.

OPPORTUNITY ENTERPRISES

Day — Coed Ages Birth-3

Valparaiso, IN 46383. 2801 Evans Ave.
Tel: 219-464-9621. Fax: 219-548-7543.
www.oppent.org   E-mail: oppent@oppent.org
Sally Gaff, BA, Exec Dir.
   Focus: Treatment. **Conditions:** Primary—MR. Sec—Au B Bl CP D Ep ON
      PDD S SB.
   Therapy: Hear Lang Occup Phys Speech.
   Enr: 185. **Staff:** 15 (Full 11, Part 4). Prof 13. Admin 2.
   Rates 2004: No Fee.
   Summer Prgm: Day. Educ. Ther.
   Est 1972. County. Nonprofit. **Spons:** The Arc.

   Children of Porter County who exhibit developmental delays, at-risk conditions, or
physical or mental handicaps are provided home-based services through this program.
The early intervention staff instructs parents in administering individualized educational
and therapeutic programs in the home. Center-based play and learning groups (for toddlers) and a parent support group meet weekly. Consultation and therapy are provided by
speech and language pathologists and by physical specialists.

PEAK COMMUNITY SERVICES

Res — Coed Ages Birth-5; Day — Coed -

Logansport, IN 46947. PO Box 10.
Tel: 574-753-4104. Fax: 574-753-9861.
www.peakcommunity.com   E-mail: peak@peakcommunity.com
Stephen R. Brundage, Exec Dir.
   Focus: Trng. **Conditions:** Primary—MR. Sec—B Bl CP D ED Ep ON S SB.
   Pre-Voc. Voc. Ungraded. Courses: Life_Skills. Shelt_Workshop. On-Job
      Trng.
   Therapy: Hear Lang Occup Phys Speech. **Psychotherapy:** Parent.

Enr: 127. **Staff:** 57 (Full 49, Part 8).
Est 1955. Private. Nonprofit.

PCS maintains two facilities, Woodlawn Center and Pulaski Developmental Services, that serve persons with mental retardation and developmental delays. Integrated infant and preschool programs at both sites emphasize developmental activities. In addition, both centers provide adults with a variety of vocational, developmental and residential services.

PORTER-STARKE COUNSELING CENTERS

Res — Males Ages 11-19; Day — Coed 5-17
Clinic: All Ages. M-F 8-5, S 8-12; Eves M-F 5-8.

Valparaiso, IN 46383. 601 Wall St.
 Nearby locations: Knox; Portage.
Tel: 219-531-3500. Fax: 219-462-3975.
www.porterstarke.org
Lee E. Grogg, MSW, MBA, CEO. **Peggy Murphy,** Adm.
 Conditions: Primary—BD ED.
 Therapy: Chemo Speech. **Psychotherapy:** Fam Group Indiv.
 Est 1975. Private. Nonprofit.

Porter-Starke is an advocacy and outpatient treatment facility that offers individual, group and family counseling, in addition to mental health and chemical dependency services. The centers also offer intensive therapeutic day programs for school-age children and residential training programs for adolescent males. The usual length of treatment is three to six months. Branches operate at 3349 Willowcreek Rd., Portage 46368 and 1003 Edgewood Dr., Knox 46534.

RAINBOW'S END CHILD CARE

Day — Coed Ages Birth-12

Corydon, IN 47112. 310 S Capitol Ave.
Tel: 812-738-1979. Fax: 812-738-1985.
www.brsinc.org/YouthAndChildren.html
Lisa Worden, Dir.
 Conditions: Primary—MR.
 Therapy: Lang Occup Speech.
 Private. **Spons:** Blue River Services.

RILEY HOSPITAL AUDIOLOGY AND SPEECH CLINIC

Clinic: All Ages. M-F 8-5.

Indianapolis, IN 46202. 702 Barnhill Dr.
Tel: 317-274-8592. Fax: 317-274-6680.

Terese Stevens, RN, Dir.
  Conditions: Primary—D S.
  Therapy: Hear Lang Speech.
  Staff: Prof 43.
  Federal.

RISE

Day — Coed Ages 16 and up

Angola, IN 46703. 1600 Wohlert St.
Tel: 260-665-9408. Fax: 260-665-1012.
Joyce A. Hevel, MS, OTR, Exec Dir.
  Focus: Trng. **Conditions:** Primary—CP MD MR MS OH. Sec—D Ep S SB.
  IQ 30 and up.
  Voc. Shelt_Workshop. On-Job Trng.
  Therapy: Hear Lang Occup Speech.
  Enr: 220. **Staff:** 35 (Full 30, Part 5).
  Rates 2004: No Fee.
  Est 1965. Private. Nonprofit.

RISE provides employment services for disabled individuals. Work evaluation, sheltered work and job placement are available, as are physical education, recreation and adult day activity. The program also includes social services and vocational training.

SILVERCREST CHILDREN'S DEVELOPMENT CENTER

Res — Coed Ages Birth-22

New Albany, IN 47151. 1809 Old Vincennes Rd, PO Box 99.
Tel: 812-945-5287. Fax: 812-941-9232.
Dennis J. Tomasallo, EdS, Dir. **Lea Marlow,** MD, Med Dir.
  Focus: Treatment. **Conditions:** Primary—OH. Sec—ADD ADHD Ap As Asp
  Au B BD Bl C CD CP D Dc Dg Dx ED Ep IP LD MD MR MS ODD PDD S
  SB TS. **IQ 0-90.**
  Therapy: Hear Hydro Lang Milieu Occup Phys Recreational Speech. **Psy-**
  chotherapy: Fam Indiv.
  Enr: 70. Res Males 35. Res Females 35. **Staff:** 170. Prof 74. Educ 40.
  Admin 8.
  Rates 2003: No Fee.
  Est 1974. State. **Spons:** Indiana Department of Health.

This program for Indiana residents provides assessment, diagnosis and remediation for children with a minimum of two handicaps. Each child is helped to become as independent as possible through special education and therapeutic services, including parent training and public school consultations.

SOUTHERN INDIANA RESOURCE SOLUTIONS

Day — Coed Ages Birth-3

Boonville, IN 47601. 1579 S Folsomville Rd.
Tel: 812-897-4840. Fax: 812-897-0123.
www.sirs.org
Kelly C. Mitchell, CEO.
  Conditions: Primary—MR.
  Pre-Voc. Voc. Shelt_Workshop. On-Job Trng.
  Therapy: Lang Occup Phys Play Speech.
  Staff: Prof 40.
  Est 1968. Private. Nonprofit.

SOUTHWESTERN INDIANA MENTAL HEALTH CENTER

Day — Coed Ages 5-12

Evansville, IN 47713. 415 Mulberry St.
Tel: 812-423-7791. Fax: 812-422-7558.
www.southwestern.org
John K. Browning, Pres. **Willard Whitehead III,** Med Dir.
  Conditions: Primary—ED. Sec—BD.
  Gen Acad. Ungraded. Courses: Read Math Lang_Arts.
  Therapy: Recreational. **Psychotherapy:** Fam Group Indiv.
  Staff: Prof 6.
  Est 1971. Private. Nonprofit.

STONE BELT ARC

Res — Coed Ages 4 and up; Day — Coed 18 and up

Bloomington, IN 47408. 2815 E 10th St.
Tel: 812-332-2168. Fax: 812-323-4610.
www.stonebelt.org
Leslie Green, CEO.
  Focus: Trng. Treatment. **Conditions:** Primary—Au CP MR. Sec—ADD
    ADHD Ap B BD BI CD D Dx ED Ep IP LD MD MS OCD ON Psy S SB
    Sz. **IQ 0-75.**
  Therapy: Speech. **Psychotherapy:** Fam Group Indiv.
  Enr: 1000. **Staff:** 450.
  Summer Prgm: Day. Rec. Ther. Day Rate $180/wk. 8 wks.
  Est 1958. Private. Nonprofit.

Located on the Indiana University campus, this center serves children and adults with developmental disabilities through an educational-developmental program. The residential program serves state residents through group homes and independent living arrangements. Day services consist of a variety of vocational programs.

The supported employment program provides job-seeking, job-training and support services, while the placement assistance program serves individuals with less intensive training needs, such as resume writing and interviewing instruction. Vocational evaluation services help staff match job skills to available employment and training opportunities. Habilitation services focus upon functional skills and vocational training. All of the center's programs emphasize community access to transportation, employment and recreation.

TRADEWINDS REHABILITATION CENTER

Res — Coed Ages 20-35; Day — Coed All Ages

Gary, IN 46406. 5901 W 7th Ave, PO Box 6308.
Tel: 219-949-4000. TTY: 219-949-0879. Fax: 219-944-8134.
www.lakenetnwi.net/org/tradewinds
Jon Gold, Exec Dir. **Vernita Johnston,** Intake.
   Focus: Rehab. **Conditions:** Primary—ADD ADHD AN Anx Ap Apr Ar As Asp Au B BD BI Bu C CD CF CP D Db Dc Dg DS Dx ED Ep IP MD Mood MR MS Nf OCD ODD ON PTSD PW SB TB. Sec—LD S.
   Gen Acad. Gr PS-K. Shelt_Workshop. On-Job Trng.
   Therapy: Hear Lang Movement Occup Phys Speech.
   Enr: 270. **Staff:** 17 (Full 10, Part 7). Prof 8. Educ 1. Admin 1.
   Summer Prgm: Day. Rec.
   Est 1967. Private. Nonprofit.

Serving northwest Indiana, TradeWinds provides a variety of rehabilitative services for children and adults with disabilities. Offerings include therapy, hearing evaluations, a sheltered workshop, vocational evaluations, employment training and placement, work adjustment, job coaching and adult residential services.

WERNLE CHILDREN'S HOME SCHOOL

Res — Males Ages 6-21

Richmond, IN 47375. 2000 Wernle Rd, PO Box 1386.
Tel: 765-966-2506. Fax: 765-962-4210.
www.wernle.org   E-mail: admissions@wernle.org
Darrell Gordon, MSA, JD, CEO. **Becky Abbott,** Adm.
   Focus: Spec Ed. Treatment. **Conditions:** Primary—ADD ADHD Anx BD CD Db ED Mood OCD Psy PTSD. **IQ 58 and up.**
   Pre-Voc. Gr 1-12. Courses: Read Math Lang_Arts Sci Computers Soc_ Stud.
   Therapy: Milieu Play Recreational. **Psychotherapy:** Fam Group Indiv Parent.
   Enr: 41. Res Males 41. **Staff:** 111. Prof 16. Educ 5. Admin 7.
   Rates 2003: Res $78,475/yr.
   Est 1879. Private. Nonprofit. Evangelical.

Wernle offers year-round residential care, including medical, psychological and psychiatric services. Individual, group and family therapy options, as well as supportive counseling and life skills training, are important features of the program.

Individualized educational services promote academic development and prepare students for mainstreaming into public schools.

WORTHMORE ACADEMY
Day — Coed Ages 5-19

Indianapolis, IN 46220. 3535 Kessler Blvd E.
Tel: 317-251-6516. Fax: 317-251-6516.
www.worthmoreacademy.org   E-mail: bjackson@worthmoreacademy.org
Brenda Jackson, BS, MS, Dir.
   Focus: Spec Ed. **Conditions:** Primary—ADD ADHD Anx Ap Apr Asp Au Bl
      Dc Dg Dx LD MR ODD PDD S. Sec—AN Ar As BD Bu CD CP Db ED Ep
      Mood OCD SP TS.
   Gen Acad. Gr K-12. Courses: Read Math Lang_Arts Sci Soc_Stud.
   Enr: 25. Day Males 20. Day Females 5. **Staff:** 6 (Full 4, Part 2).
   Rates 2004: Day $800/mo.
   Summer Prgm: Day. Educ. Day Rate $2500. 6 wks.
   Est 1988. Private. Inc.

Worthmore serves children with specific learning disabilities, among them dyslexia, attentional disorders, autism and auditory processing difficulties. After-school tutoring is available to all students, and the academy also conducts a six-week summer program.

IOWA

AREA RESIDENTIAL CARE

Res — Coed Ages 11 and up; Day — Coed 27 and up

Dubuque, IA 52001. 1170 Roosevelt St Ext.
Nearby locations: Mason City.
Tel: 563-556-7560.
E-mail: aresidentialcare@aol.com
  Focus: Spec Ed. Trng. **Conditions:** Primary—MR. **IQ 0-80.**
  Gen Acad. Pre-Voc. Voc. Ungraded. Courses: Read Math Lang_Arts. Man_
    Arts & Shop. Shelt_Workshop. On-Job Trng.
  Therapy: Hear Lang Occup Phys Speech. **Psychotherapy:** Indiv.
  Est 1968. Private. Nonprofit.

CENTER ASSOCIATES

Clinic: All Ages. M-F.

Marshalltown, IA 50158. 9 N 4th Ave.
Tel: 641-752-1585. Fax: 641-752-9665.
www.centerassoc.com   E-mail: info@centerassoc.com
Michael Bergman, MS, CEO.
  Conditions: Primary—BD ED.
  Psychotherapy: Fam Indiv.
  Est 1957. Private. Nonprofit.

CHILDSERVE

Res — Coed Ages Birth-21

Johnston, IA 50131. 5406 Merle Hay Rd, PO Box 707.
Tel: 515-727-8750. Fax: 515-727-8757.
www.childserve.org
Lloyd C. Vander Kwaak, BA, MPA, Pres. **Sayeed Hussain,** MD, Med Dir. **Mary**
  Goodrich & Monica Roth, Adms.
  Focus: Treatment. **Conditions:** Primary—Apr As Au BI C CP DS Ep IP MD
    MR MS ON PW SB. Sec—Ap Asp B BD D Db Dx ED LD PDD S.
  Therapy: Hear Lang Music Occup Phys Recreational Speech.
  Enr: 100. Res Males 60. Res Females 40. **Staff:** 423 (Full 344, Part 79).
    Prof 101. Educ 22. Admin 69.
  Est 1928. Private. Nonprofit.

  Formerly the Convalescent Home for Children, this organization in central Iowa provides residential and community care for special-needs children and their families. Medically fragile children in need of specialized nursing care and therapy receive 24-hour care through the Habilitation Center, while children with mental retardation who require nursing care, behavioral support and therapy engage in an active treatment program at the center that focuses on helping them reach growth and developmental milestones. A third residential option features supported group home living for children with mental retardation who stand to benefit from daily care and support, living skills instruction, behavior management and therapy. The first two programs operate at the Habilitation Center in Johnston; group homes are located throughout the community.

ChildServe's community program offers seven distinct services to children with special healthcare needs in a dozen counties surrounding Ames and Des Moines. These services relate to home care, therapy, adaptive equipment, respite care, supported community living, case management and childcare.

COMPREHENSIVE SYSTEMS

Res and Day — Coed All Ages

Charles City, IA 50616. 1700 Clark St, PO Box 457.
Tel: 641-228-4842. Fax: 641-228-4675.
www.compsystems.org   E-mail: jbrown@compsystems.org
Jack Brown, Exec Dir. **Laura Wallace,** Adm.
  Focus: Treatment. **Conditions:** Primary—MR. Sec—Asp Au B CP D Db Ep OH.
  Voc. Shelt_Workshop. On-Job Trng.
  Therapy: Hear Occup Phys Speech.
  Enr: 300. Res Males 100. Res Females 120. Day Males 50. Day Females 30. **Staff:** 500 (Full 250, Part 250). Prof 35. Admin 100.
  Est 1970. Private. Nonprofit.

An interdisciplinary approach, individually prescribed, is employed at Comprehensive Systems for dependent to profoundly retarded individuals. Comprising six facilities, the center offers therapeutic education and training, medical support and treatment, planned recreational programs and parent consultation.

Educational services are provided by the local school district at attendance centers and by Comprehensive Systems at the Elma Work Activity Center. Special education, therapy, recreation and medical supervision are offered at both the Comprehensive and the Developmental centers. Secondary special education, work experience, placement and rehabilitation are provided through the work activities center.

Care and maintenance for younger ambulatory residents in the areas of eating, dressing, self-care training and play activities are designed through two units. A developmental care cottage serves nonambulatory children requiring nursing care. Foster grandparents are assigned both to the children in the units and to those in the cottage, sharing daily activities with them.

EASTER SEALS IOWA

Day — Coed Ages Birth-5

Des Moines, IA 50313. 401 NE 66th Ave.
Tel: 515-289-1933. TTY: 515-289-4069. Fax: 515-289-1281.

www.ia.easterseals.com
Donna Elbrecht, CEO.
  Conditions: Primary—MR OH.
  Staff: Prof 20.
  Est 1926. Private. Nonprofit.

EDUCATIONAL RESOURCE ASSOCIATES

Clinic: Ages 2 and up. M-S 7-5; Eves M-S 5-10.

West Des Moines, IA 50265. 1721 25th St.
Tel: 515-225-8513. Fax: 515-225-3831.
www.eduresources.info
Judy K. Hintz, MS, Dir.
  Conditions: Primary—LD.
  Col Prep. Gen Acad. Pre-Voc. Courses: Read Math Lang_Arts.
  Therapy: Lang Speech.
  Est 1983. Private. Inc.

GLENWOOD RESOURCE CENTER

Res — Coed All Ages
Clinic: All Ages. M-F 8-4:30.

Glenwood, IA 51534. 711 S Vine St.
Tel: 712-527-4811. Fax: 712-527-2307.
www.dhs.state.ia.us/institutions/glenwood.asp
  E-mail: wcampbe@dhs.state.ia.us
  Focus: Spec Ed. Rehab. Trng. Treatment. **Conditions:** Primary—MR.
  Gen Acad. Pre-Voc. Voc. Ungraded. Shelt_Workshop.
  Therapy: Chemo Hear Hydro Lang Occup Phys Recreational Speech. **Psy-chotherapy:** Group Indiv.
  Staff: Prof 649.
  Est 1876. State. Nonprofit.

HOPE HAVEN AREA DEVELOPMENT FOUNDATION

Res — Coed Ages 6 and up

Burlington, IA 52601. 1819 Douglas Ave.
Tel: 319-754-4689. Fax: 319-752-1672.
www.hopehavencorp.com
Cynthia Thomas, Exec Dir.
  Focus: Rehab. **Conditions:** Primary—As Au CP DS Ep MR OH. Sec—ADHD Anx B CD D Db Dx ED Mood OCD Psy PW Sz TS.
  Voc. Shelt_Workshop. On-Job Trng.

Enr: 350. **Staff:** 200 (Full 100, Part 100).
Est 1974. Private. Nonprofit.

Hope Haven operates a number of residential care facilities and group homes for individuals with mental retardation and other developmental disabilities.

IOWA BRAILLE AND SIGHT SAVING SCHOOL

Res — Coed Ages 5-21; Day — Coed Birth-21

Vinton, IA 52349. 1002 G Ave.
Tel: 319-472-5221. Fax: 319-472-4371.
www.iowa-braille.k12.ia.us
Dennis Thurman, MEd, Supt.
  Conditions: Primary—B.
  Col Prep. Gen Acad. Pre-Voc. Voc. Ungraded. Courses: Read Math Lang_
    Arts. Man_Arts & Shop. Shelt_Workshop. On-Job Trng.
  Est 1852. State.

LUTHERAN SERVICES IN IOWA

Res — Males Ages 7-18, Females 10-18

Waverly, IA 50677. 106 16th SW, PO Box 848.
Tel: 319-352-2630. Fax: 319-352-0773.
www.lsiowa.org
Jane A. Hartman, MSW, Pres.
  Focus: Treatment. **Conditions:** Primary—BD ED LD. Sec—ADD ADHD
    Mood OCD Psy. **IQ 85 and up.**
  Gen Acad. Pre-Voc. Ungraded.
  Therapy: Art Music Play Recreational. **Psychotherapy:** Fam Group Indiv.
  Enr: 109. Res Males 82. Res Females 27.
  Est 1864. Private. Nonprofit. Lutheran.

Lutheran Services, which was created through the integration of Bremwood Lutheran Services and Lutheran Social Service of Iowa (LSS), is Iowa's largest social service provider. Located statewide, LSI's programs specialize in bringing and keeping families together, service coordination and senior adult services. LSI is affiliated with the Lutheran services in America and the three Iowa Synods of the ELCA.

MENTAL HEALTH CENTER OF NORTH IOWA

Clinic: All Ages. M-F 8-5; Eve M 5-8.

Mason City, IA 50401. 235 S Eisenhower Ave.
Tel: 515-424-2075. Fax: 515-424-9555.
www.mhconi.org   E-mail: mhc@mhconi.org
  Conditions: Primary—BD ED.

Psychotherapy: Fam Group Indiv.
Est 1957. Private. Nonprofit.

NORTH CENTRAL HUMAN SERVICES

Res — Coed Ages 6mos and up; Day — Coed 3-26

Forest City, IA 50436. 102 W Park St.
    Nearby locations: Belmond; Nevada (IA).
Tel: 641-585-5450. Fax: 641-585-4522.
www.nchs-fc.org
Brent Aberg, MHA, MBA, Exec Dir. **Gay Jean Knudtson,** Adm.
    Focus: Treatment. **Conditions:** Primary—MR. Sec—B BD BI CP D Ep OH.
    Voc. On-Job Trng.
    Therapy: Hear Lang Occup Phys Recreational Speech. **Psychotherapy:**
        Fam Group Indiv.
    Enr: 92.
    Est 1969. Private. Nonprofit.

Individuals who are severely or profoundly mentally retarded or developmentally disabled receive long-term care at this facility. While residential-based services are NCHS' focus, the agency also provides home- and community-based and vocational offerings. Services take place in the least restrictive environment possible.

ORCHARD PLACE

Res and Day — Coed Ages 5-18
Clinic: Ages 5-18. M-F 8-5.

Des Moines, IA 50315. 925 SW Porter Ave.
Tel: 515-285-6781. Fax: 515-287-9695.
www.orchardplace.org
Earl P. Kelly, EdD, CEO. **Donner Dewdney,** MD, Med Dir. **Leslie Held,** Adm.
    Focus: Treatment. **Conditions:** Primary—ADD ADHD AN Anx Asp Bu CD
        ED Mood ODD Psy PTSD SP Sz. Sec—Au B BD D Db Dx HIV LD MR
        OCD S TS. **IQ 80 and up.**
    Gen Acad. Ungraded. Courses: Read Math Lang_Arts.
    Therapy: Milieu Play Recreational. **Psychotherapy:** Fam Group Indiv.
    Enr: 103. **Staff:** 260.
    Rates 2001: Res $350/day. Day $75/day. Schol avail. State Aid.
    Est 1962. Private. Nonprofit.

Providing various individualized mental health services for emotionally troubled children and their families, Orchard Place seeks to enable clients to function responsibly in society. Children, who must have a current diagnosis of emotional or behavioral difficulties or both, choose from the following programs: psychiatric residential care, subacute crisis stabilization, intensive outpatient treatment, family-centered services, foster care and respite.

Affiliated with Orchard Place since 1996, the Des Moines Child Guidance Center serves individuals from infancy through age 18. Community-based mental health services, intensive outpatient treatment and school-based programs are their main offerings.

Established in 1983, the PACE program—which operates out of over two dozen counties in the metropolitan area—offers a continuum of services to help youths ages 5-25 develop social, academic and functional life skills.

RIVER HILLS SCHOOL

Day — Coed Ages Birth-21

Cedar Falls, IA 50613. 2700 Grand Blvd.
Tel: 319-268-7775. Fax: 319-268-1828.
www.aea267.k12.ia.us/riverhills/rhhome.html
  E-mail: riverhills@aea267.k12.ia.us
Doug Penno, PhD, Prin.
  Conditions: Primary—MR.
  Pre-Voc. Voc. Courses: Read Math Lang_Arts. Man_Arts & Shop. Shelt_ Workshop. On-Job Trng.
  Therapy: Hear Lang Occup Phys Speech.
  State.

ST. LUKE'S HOSPITAL
OUTPATIENT REHABILITATION CLINIC

Clinic: All Ages. M-F 8-5.

Cedar Rapids, IA 52406. 1026 A Ave NE, PO Box 3026.
Tel: 319-369-7279. Fax: 319-369-8186.
www.stlukescr.org
Theodore W. Peterson, MBA, OTR, Mgr. Paul J. Guidos, MD, Med Dir.
  Focus: Trng. Treatment. Conditions: Primary—ADD ADHD Ap Au Bl CP D Dx IP LD MD MS ON S SB. Sec—As B BD C CD ED Ep MR OCD Psy Sz TB.
  Therapy: Hear Lang Occup Phys Speech Aqua.
  Staff: 15 (Full 12, Part 3).
  Private. Nonprofit. Spons: Iowa Health System.

St. Luke's provides diagnostic and treatment services in occupational therapy, physical therapy, speech pathology and audiology. The Children's Therapy Center coordinates services using a team approach.

SMOUSE SCHOOL

Day — Coed Ages Birth-12

Des Moines, IA 50312. 2820 Center St.

Tel: 515-242-8210. Fax: 515-242-8219.
www.dmps.k12.ia.us/schools/1Smouse/index.htm
Susie Guest, Prin.
  Conditions: Primary—OH.
  Gen Acad. Gr PS-6.
  Therapy: Lang Occup Phys Speech.
  Staff: Prof 25.
  Est 1931. Municipal.

UNIVERSITY OF IOWA
WENDELL JOHNSON SPEECH AND HEARING CLINIC

Clinic: All Ages.

Iowa City, IA 52242. 119 SHC.
Tel: 319-335-8736. Fax: 319-335-8851.
www.shc.uiowa.edu/wjshc/mainclinsrvs.html
Linda Louko, Dir.
  Conditions: Primary—D S.
  Therapy: Hear Lang Speech.
  State.

UNIVERSITY OF NORTHERN IOWA
ROY EBLEN SPEECH & HEARING CLINIC

Clinic: All Ages. M-F 8-5.

Cedar Falls, IA 50614. 230 Communication Arts Center.
Tel: 319-273-2542. Fax: 319-273-6384.
www.uni.edu/comdis/clinic.html
Theresa Kouri, PhD, Dir.
  Conditions: Primary—D S.
  Therapy: Hear Lang Speech.
  Est 1950. State.

WOODWARD RESOURCE CENTER

Res — Coed All Ages

Woodward, IA 50276. 1251 334th St.
Tel: 515-438-2600. Fax: 515-438-3140.
Michael J. Davis, PhD, Supt.
  Focus: Treatment. **Conditions:** Primary—MR. Sec—Anx Asp Au B BD Bl
    CD CP D Db DS Ep Mood OCD ON PDD S SB.
  Gen Acad. Ungraded. Courses: Read Math Life_Skills. Shelt_Workshop.
    On-Job Trng.

Therapy: Hear Lang Occup Phys Speech. **Psychotherapy:** Indiv.
Enr: 285.
Est 1917. State.

Serving individuals with mental retardation in a 47-county area of northern Iowa, Woodward offers programs of specialized treatment, training, habilitation and care. In addition, the facility is a resource center, assisting communities in their programs through technical advice and staff training. Woodward also provides nursing and developmental, educational, vocational habilitation, recreational, short-term treatment, social, psychological, medical and clinical services.

KANSAS

ARROWHEAD WEST CHILD SERVICES
Day — Coed Ages Birth-3

Dodge City, KS 67801. 401 Edgemore St.
Tel: 620-225-5177. Fax: 620-227-2072.
www.arrowheadwest.org   E-mail: jennifer@arrowheadwest.org
Jennifer Tassett, BS, Mgr.
    Focus: Treatment. **Conditions:** Primary—Asp Au BI CP DS IP MR ON
    PDD S SB. Sec—Ap B D Dx Ep LD MD MS Nf PW.
    Gen Acad. Gr PS.
    Therapy: Hear Lang Occup Percepual-Motor Phys Play Speech. **Psycho-**
    therapy: Fam.
    Enr: 175. Day Males 106. Day Females 69. **Staff:** 17 (Full 11, Part 6). Prof
    7. Educ 5. Admin 3.
    Rates 2004: No Fee.
    Est 1976. Private. Nonprofit.

Serving children who are disabled or developmentally at risk, this facility provides evaluations and early intervention services for young children. Admission priority is given to those living in Arrowhead West's service area.

BERT NASH COMMUNITY MENTAL HEALTH CENTER
Clinic: All Ages. M-F 8:30-5:30; Eves M-Th 5:30-9.

Lawrence, KS 66044. 200 Maine St.
    Nearby locations: Baldwin City; Eudora.
Tel: 785-843-9192. Fax: 785-843-6744.
www.bertnash.org
Sandra J. Shaw, PhD, CEO.
    Focus: Treatment. **Conditions:** Primary—ADD ADHD BD CD Dx ED OCD
    Psy Sz. Sec—Au MR. **IQ 80 and up.**
    Therapy: Speech. **Psychotherapy:** Fam Group Indiv Parent.
    Staff: 175.
    Est 1950. Private. Nonprofit.

The center provides psychiatric diagnoses and treatment for emotional and behavioral problems. In addition, consultation and mental health education are conducted with other agencies, institutions and individuals. Clients must be residents of Douglas County.

Branch offices operate at 814 High St., Baldwin City 66006 and 314 E 8th St., Eudora 66025.

THE CAPPER FOUNDATION

Day — Coed All Ages

Topeka, KS 66604. 3500 SW 10th Ave.
  Nearby locations: Kansas City.
Tel: 785-272-4060. Fax: 785-272-7912.
www.capper.org   E-mail: abilities@capper.org
Jim Leiker, MS, Pres. **Annie Swanson,** Intake.
  Focus: Trng. Treatment. **Conditions:** Primary—BI CP IP MD OH. Sec—Ap
    As B C D Dx Ep LD MR S.
  Therapy: Lang Phys Speech.
  Staff: 78.
  Rates 2004: Day $125/wk. $50 (Training)/hr.
  Est 1920. Private. Nonprofit.

Located in a residential section of Topeka and serving primarily children, The Capper Foundation is an educational organization that teaches independent living skills to individuals with physical disabilities, while also training those who live and work with children with disabilities. The facility individualizes its educational, therapeutic, recreational and work-related services to help clients realize their potentials. Offerings include an infant-toddler program, an integrated preschool, pediatric therapies, recreation and assistive technology services.

Assistive technology services include resources, evaluations, consulting services and training in the areas of augmentative communication, computer access and applications, mobility, rehabilitative engineering and educational technology. The center provides short-term student placements that allow for intensive evaluation, and each student's family and school district personnel receive programming and training. Staff members travel to surrounding areas performing evaluative and consulting services for students who require special technology and augmentative communication in school settings.

A satellite office operates at 211 W. Armour Rd., Kansas City 64111.

CRAWFORD COUNTY MENTAL HEALTH CENTER

Day — Coed Ages 3 and up
Clinic: All Ages. M-F 8-5.

Pittsburg, KS 66762. 911 E Centennial Dr.
Tel: 620-231-5130. Fax: 620-235-7101.
www.crawfordcohd.org/frames2.htm
  Conditions: Primary—BD ED.
  Staff: Prof 12.
  Est 1964. County.

FORT HAYS STATE UNIVERSITY
GENEVA HERNDON SPEECH-LANGUAGE-HEARING CLINIC

Clinic: All Ages. M-F 8:30-5.

Hays, KS 67601. Albertson Hall, Rm 131, 600 Park St.
Tel: 785-628-5366. Fax: 785-628-5271.
www.fhsu.edu/commdis/herndon.shtml   E-mail: infoslp@fhsu.edu
Marla S. Staab, MS, CCC-SLP, Coord.
   Focus: Rehab. Treatment. **Conditions:** Primary—Ap D S. Sec—Au B ED
      LD MR OH.
   Therapy: Hear Lang Speech.
   Staff: 10.
   Est 1954. State. Nonprofit.

Geneva Herndon Clinic offers comprehensive screening, diagnostic and therapeutic
services for individuals with speech, language and hearing disorders. Services are rendered by advanced university students under the supervision of or in conjunction with
professional staff members. The clinic also offers a six-week evening aural rehabilitation
program for the hearing-impaired.

HEARTSPRING

Res — Coed Ages 5-21
Clinic: All Ages. M-F 8-5.

Wichita, KS 67226. 8700 E 29th St N.
Tel: 316-634-8700. Fax: 316-634-0555.
www.heartspring.org
Gary Singleton, Pres. **Cara Rapp,** Adm.
   Focus: Spec Ed. **Conditions:** Primary—Ap Asp Au BI CP D MR ON PDD
      SB. Sec—ADD ADHD Anx B BD Dx ED Ep OCD ODD.
   Gen Acad. Pre-Voc. Gr K-12. Courses: Read Math Lang_Arts Life_Skills.
      Shelt_Workshop. On-Job Trng.
   Therapy: Hear Lang Occup Phys Speech. **Psychotherapy:** Indiv.
   Enr: 40.
   Rates 2004: Res $21,000/mo. $85 (Therapy)/ses. Schol avail. State Aid.
   Summer Prgm: Day. Ther. Day Rate $200. 2 wks.
   Est 1934. Private. Nonprofit.

The school serves pupils with mental retardation who often have one or more accompanying disorders, among them autism, orthopedic and neurological conditions, visual
and hearing problems, and attentional disorders. An interdisciplinary team of professionals designs and implements each student's program in the areas of behavior management, communication and health.

In addition to its school program, Heartspring operates a hearing center that provides
comprehensive diagnostic hearing evaluations for adults and pediatric patients. The
hearing center places particular emphasis on the treatment of multi-handicapped and
difficult-to-test individuals.   **See Also Page 1034**

HIGH PLAINS MENTAL HEALTH CENTER

Clinic: All Ages. M-F 8-5; Eves M W Th 5-9.

Hays, KS 67601. 208 E 7th St.
Tel: 785-628-2871. Fax: 785-628-1438.
www.highplainsmentalhealth.com
   Conditions: Primary—BD ED.
   Therapy: Music.
   Est 1964. Private. Nonprofit.

IROQUOIS CENTER FOR HUMAN DEVELOPMENT

Clinic: Ages 5-18. M-F 8-5; Eves T-Th 5-7.

Greensburg, KS 67054. 610 E Grant Ave.
Tel: 620-723-2272. Fax: 620-723-3450.
www.irqcenter.com
C. **Sheldon Carpenter,** MS, Exec Dir. **Vergie Anderson,** Clin Dir. **Luis Alonzo,** MD, Med Dir.
   Focus: Treatment. **Conditions:** Primary—ADD ADHD AN Anx Asp Au BD Bu CD ED Mood OCD PDD Psy PTSD SP Sz TS. Sec—Ap B D Db Dc DS Dx LD MR ON S.
   Therapy: Milieu Play. **Psychotherapy:** Fam Group Indiv Parent.
   Staff: 65 (Full 43, Part 22). Prof 10. Admin 10.
   Rates 2003: Sliding-Scale Rate $5-110.
   Est 1968. Private. Nonprofit.

This center for individuals with emotional and behavioral problems offers a range of evaluation, referral and treatment services. Iroquois can provide mental health services for individuals with handicaps. A sliding-scale fee structure accounts for the client's ability to pay.

KANSAS ELKS TRAINING CENTER
FOR THE HANDICAPPED

Res and Day — Coed Ages 18 and up

Wichita, KS 67211. 1006 E Waterman St.
Tel: 316-383-8700. Fax: 316-383-8883.
www.ketch.org
   Conditions: Primary—BI CP LD MR. **IQ 40 and up.**
   Shelt_Workshop. On-Job Trng.
   Therapy: Hear Speech. **Psychotherapy:** Group Indiv.
   Est 1964. Private. Nonprofit.

KANSAS NEUROLOGICAL INSTITUTE

Res and Day — Coed Ages 3 and up

Topeka, KS 66604. 3107 W 21st St.
Tel: 785-296-5389. Fax: 785-296-7923.
www.srskansas.org/kni
Ray Dalton, Supt.
   Conditions: Primary—MR.
   Pre-Voc. Voc. Ungraded.
   Therapy: Hear Lang Occup Phys Speech. Psychotherapy: Indiv.
   Est 1959. State.

THE KANSAS STATE SCHOOL FOR THE BLIND

Res — Coed Ages 3-21; Day — Coed Birth-21

Kansas City, KS 66102. 1100 State Ave.
Tel: 913-281-3308. Fax: 913-281-3104.
www.kssb.net   E-mail: info@kssb.net
   Conditions: Primary—B.
   Col Prep. Gen Acad. Pre-Voc. Voc. Ungraded. Courses: Read Math Lang_
      Arts. Man_Arts & Shop. Shelt_Workshop. On-Job Trng.
   Therapy: Music Occup Phys Speech.
   Staff: Prof 49.
   Est 1867. State.

KANSAS STATE SCHOOL FOR THE DEAF

Res and Day — Coed Ages 3-21

Olathe, KS 66061. 450 E Park St.
Tel: 913-791-0573. TTY: 913-791-0573. Fax: 913-791-0577.
www.ksdeaf.org
Robert Maile, PhD, Supt. Carolyn Darst, Adm.
   Focus: Spec Ed. Conditions: Primary—D MR. Sec—ADD ADHD Ar As CP
      Ep OH. IQ 70-110.
   Col Prep. Gen Acad. Pre-Voc. Voc. Gr PS-12. Courses: Read Math Lang_
      Arts. Man_Arts & Shop. On-Job Trng.
   Therapy: Hear Lang Occup Phys Speech. Psychotherapy: Indiv.
   Enr: 140. Res Males 35. Res Females 16. Day Males 46. Day Females 43.
      Staff: 174 (Full 173, Part 1). Educ 63. Admin 10.
   Rates 2004: No Fee.
   Est 1861. State.

   Comprehensive academic and vocational training programs for individuals with hearing impairments are provided by the school. Adaptive programming for the multi-handicapped hearing-impaired student is provided, as are specialized classes at all levels for
speech and language development. Counseling is available to parents.

Kansas

KANSAS STATE UNIVERSITY
SPEECH AND HEARING CENTER

Clinic: All Ages. M-F 8-5.

Manhattan, KS 66506. 107 Leasure Hall.
Tel: 785-532-6879. Fax: 785-532-5505.
www.ksu.edu/humec/fshs/centers/speech.htm
Robert Garcia, MBA, AuD, Prgm Dir. **Julie Schraeder,** BS, MA, Clin Dir.
  Focus: Treatment. **Conditions:** Primary—Ap D S. Sec—Bl CP ED Ep MD
   MR MS ON SB.
  Therapy: Hear Lang Speech.
  Est 1946. State. Nonprofit.

The center provides a clinical program for speech, language and hearing disorders, in addition to undergraduate and graduate training in speech pathology and audiology. Facilities include six therapy suites and one audiological testing suite.

LAKEMARY CENTER
CHILDREN'S RESIDENTIAL PROGRAM

Res — Coed Ages 6-21

Paola, KS 66071. 100 Lakemary Dr.
Tel: 913-557-4000. Fax: 913-557-4910.
www.lakemaryctr.org   E-mail: lakemary@lakemaryctr.org
Bill Craig, PhD, Pres. **Earl Kilgore,** Dir.
  Focus: Spec Ed. Treatment. **Conditions:** Primary—Au ED MR PDD. Sec—
   ADD ADHD Ap As BD Bl CD CP D Dx Ep LD OCD Psy S Sz.
  Pre-Voc. Voc. Gr 1-12. Courses: Read Math Lang_Arts. Shelt_Workshop.
   On-Job Trng.
  Therapy: Chemo Hear Lang Occup Phys Speech. **Psychotherapy:** Fam
   Group Indiv.
  Enr: 95. **Staff:** 125.
  Est 1969. Private. Nonprofit.

This center, located on a 34-acre campus, offers diagnostic services, education, training and residential programs for children with mental retardation, autism or pervasive developmental disorder.

Lakemary provides a family-style living experience. A variety of environmental experiences aids the children in living as independently as their potentials will allow. Daily living and self-care skills, therapy, language development, arts and crafts, and recreational activities are part of the program. By using intensive therapy and personalized education, goals are set to help each child toward normalization. The center's approach assists children with their home and community relationships.

All residents have some type of developmental disability, and the majority have one or more concurrent psychiatric disorders that require ongoing treatment. Kansas University Medical Center and Miami County Mental Health Center supply necessary psychiatric services and outpatient psychotherapy. The year-round program features a residential staff that provides 24-hour supervision.

LARNED STATE HOSPITAL
YOUTH SERVICES

Res — Coed Ages 6-17

Larned, KS 67550. RR 3, Box 89.
Tel: 620-285-2131. Fax: 620-285-4357.
www.srskansas.org/LSH/Units.html
   Conditions: Primary—ED. Sec—BD LD MR.
   Gen Acad. Pre-Voc. Voc. Gr K-12. Courses: Read Math Lang_Arts. Man_
   Arts & Shop. On-Job Trng.
   Therapy: Lang Speech.
   Est 1914. State. Nonprofit.

MENTAL HEALTH CENTER OF EAST CENTRAL KANSAS

Day — Coed Ages 9-17
Clinic: Ages Birth-17. M-F.

Emporia, KS 66801. 1000 Lincoln St.
Tel: 620-343-2211. Fax: 620-342-1021.
www.mhceck.com
John G. Randolph, PhD, Exec Dir. **Masferrer Mauricio,** MD, Med Dir.
   Conditions: Primary—BD ED.
   Psychotherapy: Fam Group Indiv.
   Staff: Prof 3.
   Private.

PARSONS STATE HOSPITAL AND TRAINING CENTER

Res — Coed All Ages

Parsons, KS 67357. 2601 Gabriel, PO Box 738.
Tel: 620-421-6550. Fax: 620-421-3623.
www.pshtc.com
Gary J. Daniels, PhD, Supt.
   Conditions: Primary—MR.
   Gen Acad. Pre-Voc. Courses: Read Math Lang_Arts. Man_Arts & Shop.
   Shelt_Workshop. On-Job Trng.
   Therapy: Hear Lang Occup Phys Speech. **Psychotherapy:** Group Indiv.
   Staff: Prof 468.
   Est 1903. State. Nonprofit.

PAWNEE MENTAL HEALTH SERVICES

Clinic: All Ages. M-F 8-5; Eves M W 5-7, T Th 5-9.

Manhattan, KS 66502. 2001 Claflin Rd.
Tel: 785-587-4300.
www.pawnee.org
   Conditions: Primary—ED. Sec—ADD BD.
   Psychotherapy: Fam Group Indiv.
   Staff: Prof 14.
   Est 1967. County.

SAINT FRANCIS ACADEMY

Res — Coed Ages 8-20

Salina, KS 67402. 509 E Elm St.
   Nearby locations: Ellsworth; Hays.
Tel: 785-825-0541. Fax: 785-825-2502.
www.st-francis.org   E-mail: info@st-francis.org
Rev. Edward Fellhauer, Pres.
   Focus: Treatment. **Conditions:** Primary—CD Dx ED LD OCD. Sec—BD
      MR. **IQ 75-120.**
   Voc. Man_Arts & Shop. Shelt_Workshop.
   Therapy: Speech. **Psychotherapy:** Fam Group Indiv Parent.
   Enr: 207. Res Males 167. Res Females 40.
   Est 1945. Private. Nonprofit.

   The academy operates a system of psychiatric hospitals, residential treatment centers
and well-being programs in several Kansas locations. Saint Francis does not accept psychotic individuals or victims of severe brain trauma. Treatment generally lasts three to
four months.

SUNFLOWER DIVERSIFIED SERVICES

Day — Coed Ages Birth-5

Great Bend, KS 67530. Westport Addition, PO Box 838.
Tel: 620-792-1321. Fax: 620-792-4709.
www.srskansas.org/hcp/css/CDDOCENTRALKS.HTML
Jim Johnson, Dir.
   Conditions: Primary—Ap As Au B Bl CP D ED Ep IP LD MD MR MS ON S
      SB.
   Est 1971. State. Nonprofit.

UNITED METHODIST YOUTHVILLE

Res — Coed Ages 10-18

Newton, KS 67114. 900 W Broadway, PO Box 210.
Tel: 316-283-1950. Fax: 316-283-9540.
www.youthville.org
John Francis, Pres.
  Conditions: Primary—BD. Sec—ED.
  Gen Acad. Ungraded. Courses: Read Math Lang_Arts.
  Therapy: Milieu.
  Staff: Prof 47.
  Est 1927. Private. Nonprofit. **Spons:** Combined Conferences East and West Kansas United Methodist Church.

UNIVERSITY OF KANSAS MEDICAL CENTER
HARTLEY FAMILY CENTER

Day — Coed Ages Birth-3

Kansas City, KS 66160. 3901 Rainbow Blvd.
Tel: 913-588-5750. TTY: 913-588-5750. Fax: 913-588-5752.
www.kumc.edu/hfc E-mail: jgideon@kumc.edu
  Focus: Treatment. **Conditions:** Primary—D.
  Therapy: Hear Lang Occup Phys Speech. **Psychotherapy:** Fam.
  Staff: 4 (Full 3, Part 1).
  Est 1948. State. Nonprofit.

Diagnostic evaluations and training of graduate students in speech pathology, audiology and deaf education are provided at the center, as are playgroups and community education. Early childhood classes for deaf children under age 3 emphasizing a communication method are based on the parent and child's needs. Parental counseling and follow-up services are also available.

UNIVERSITY OF KANSAS
SCHIEFELBUSCH SPEECH-LANGUAGE-HEARING CLINIC

Clinic: All Ages. M-F 8-5.

Lawrence, KS 66045. 1200 Sunnyside Ave, 2101 Haworth Hall.
Tel: 785-864-4690. TTY: 785-864-5094. Fax: 785-864-5094.
www.lsi.ku.edu/splh/clinic.htm E-mail: clincoln@ku.edu
Jane R. Wegner, PhD, CCC-SLP, Dir.
  Focus: Treatment. **Conditions:** Primary—S. Sec—Apr Asp Au Bl CP DS Dx MR MS PDD.
  Therapy: Hear Lang Speech.
  Staff: 12.
  State.

The clinic offers diagnostic evaluations, as well as group and individual therapy. Audiological services include hearing testing, hearing aid fitting, a hearing conservation program, tympanometry, hearing aid repair, ear molds and consultation. Schiefelbusch also offers a language-acquisition preschool.

WICHITA CHILD GUIDANCE CENTER

Clinic: Ages Birth-18. M-F.

Wichita, KS 67214. 415 N Poplar St.
Tel: 316-686-6671. Fax: 316-686-1094.
www.wichitawellness.org/wcgc.html
Walter Thiessen, Exec Dir. **Ken Kassebaum,** MD, Med Dir.
  Conditions: Primary—BD ED.
  Psychotherapy: Fam Group Indiv.
  Staff: Prof 25.
  Est 1930. Private. Nonprofit.

WYANDOT CENTER
FOR COMMUNITY BEHAVIORAL HEALTHCARE

Clinic: All Ages. M-F.

Kansas City, KS 66117. 757 Armstrong Ave, PO Box 171578.
Tel: 913-233-3300. Fax: 913-233-3375.
www.wyandotcenter.org   E-mail: howard_p@wmhci.org
  Conditions: Primary—BD ED. Sec—ADD Mood.
  Est 1953. Private. Nonprofit.

KENTUCKY

BINGHAM CHILD GUIDANCE CENTER

Res — Coed Ages 2-17; Day — Coed 6-17
Clinic: Ages Birth-16. M-F 8-6.

Louisville, KY 40202. 200 E Chestnut St.
Tel: 502-852-6941. Fax: 502-852-1071.
www.binghamchildguidancecenter.com
Allan M. Josephson, MD, CEO.
  Focus: Treatment. **Conditions:** Primary—ADD ADHD Anx Au BD CD ED
    Mood OCD ODD PDD PTSD SP Sz. Sec—BI CF OH.
  Therapy: Art Speech. **Psychotherapy:** Fam Group Indiv.
  Staff: 41. Prof 17. Admin 3.
  Est 1913. Nonprofit.

Diagnosis and treatment of emotionally disturbed children are provided through the Department of Psychiatry and Behavioral Sciences, University of Louisville School of Medicine. The Ackerly Child Psychiatric Inpatient Service provides diagnostic assessment and treatment and short-term care for children ages 2-17. The Bingham Child Guidance Clinic offers counseling and therapy on an outpatient basis to emotionally disturbed children, adolescents and their families. The Keller Child Psychiatry Research Center conducts research and a partial hospitalization program.

CARDINAL HILL OF NORTHERN KENTUCKY

Clinic: All Ages. M-F 8-5:30; Eves M-Th 5:30-7.

Florence, KY 41042. 31 Spiral Dr.
Tel: 859-525-1128. Fax: 859-525-0351.
www.cardinalhill.org
Cynthia Williams, JD, Exec Dir. **Douglas Goderwis,** MD, Med Dir.
  Focus: Rehab. **Conditions:** Primary—D DS LD MR ON PDD S.
  Therapy: Hear Lang Occup Phys Speech. **Psychotherapy:** Group Parent.
  Staff: 49. Prof 33. Admin 16.
  Est 1923. Private. Nonprofit. **Spons:** Kentucky Easter Seals Society.

A comprehensive outpatient rehabilitation facility, this center provides an array of services designed to increase independence for children and adults with disabilities. Offerings include audiology services, developmental intervention for young children, occupational therapy, physical therapy, speech-language therapy and adult daycare.

CARDINAL HILL REHABILITATION CENTER

Clinic: Ages Birth-21. M-F 8-6.

Louisville, KY 40299. 9810 Bluegrass Pky.

Tel: 502-584-9781. TTY: 502-568-1229. Fax: 502-589-2409.
www.chhs-lou.org
Susan Eisenback, BS, Exec Dir.
  Focus: Rehab. Treatment. **Conditions:** Primary—ADD ADHD Ap Ar
    Asp Au Bl CP D Dg DS Dx IP LD MD MS ON PDD PW S SB TS. Sec—
    CF Ep OCD.
  Therapy: Hear Lang Occup Phys Speech.
  Staff: 40 (Full 36, Part 4). Prof 28. Admin 12.
  Rates 2004: Clinic $120/ses.
  Est 1958. Private. Nonprofit. **Spons:** Easter Seals of Louisville.

The facility provides diagnosis and treatment of physical and developmental disabilities. Rehabilitation programs include developmental intervention, audiological services, assistive technology and sensory integration. CHRC offers a range of therapeutic services, as well as a preschool for children diagnosed with specific learning disabilities.

CARDINAL HILL REHABILITATION HOSPITAL

Res — Coed All Ages; Day — Coed Birth-5
Clinic: All Ages. M-F 8:30-4.

Lexington, KY 40504. 2050 Versailles Rd.
Tel: 859-254-5701. Fax: 859-281-1365.
www.cardinalhill.org
Kerry Gillihan, Exec Dir. **William Lester,** MD, Med Dir.
  Focus: Rehab. **Conditions:** Primary—ADD Apr Asp Bl CF CP Dx IP LD
    MD MR MS Nf ON PDD S SB. Sec—Ap B C D.
  Therapy: Hear Lang Occup Phys Speech. **Psychotherapy:** Fam Indiv
    Parent.
  Enr: 148. **Staff:** 550.
  Rates 2003: Clinic $25/ses. State Aid.
  Est 1950. Private. Nonprofit. **Spons:** National Easter Seal Society.

Cardinal Hill is a rehabilitation hospital providing services for people with brain and spinal cord injuries, strokes, musculoskeletal injuries and multiple disabilities. A developmental stimulation program is available for disabled infants and preschoolers on an outpatient basis. Also offered are vocational, educational, parental and personal counseling.

CARRITAS PEACE CENTER

Res and Day — Coed All Ages

Louisville, KY 40205. 2020 Newburg Rd.
Tel: 502-451-3330. Fax: 502-473-1797.
www.caritas.com
  Conditions: Primary—Au BD Bl Dx ED LD. **IQ 60 and up.**
  Gen Acad. Gr PS-12. Courses: Read Math Lang_Arts.
  Therapy: Chemo Hear Occup Phys Speech. **Psychotherapy:** Fam Group
    Indiv.

Est 1952. Private. Nonprofit. **Spons:** Sisters of Charity of Nazareth Health Care Corporation.

CEDAR LAKE LODGE

Res — Coed Ages 18 and up

LaGrange, KY 40031. 3301 Jericho Rd.
Tel: 502-222-7157. Fax: 502-222-7150.
www.cedarlake.org
H. James Richardson, Jr., BA, MEd, Pres. Jason Squires, BS, MBA, Admin.
   Focus: Treatment. **Conditions:** Primary—MR. Sec—Au BI CP D LD ON S.
   Voc. Shelt_Workshop.
   Therapy: Hear Lang Occup Phys Speech. **Psychotherapy:** Indiv.
   Enr: 76.
   Est 1970. Private. Nonprofit.

Cedar Lake operates three long-term residential facilities for the mentally retarded a licensed intermediate care facility, a supervised community residence and supported apartments. The intermediate care program provides therapy, social services, a work activity center, medical services and recreational opportunities.

CHILDREN'S HOME OF NORTHERN KENTUCKY

Res — Males Ages 7-17

Covington, KY 41011. 200 Home Rd, Devou Park.
Tel: 859-261-8768. Fax: 859-291-2431.
www.chnk.org   E-mail: chnk@fuse.net
Kathy Stephens, MSSW, CEO.
   Focus: Treatment. **Conditions:** Primary—BD ED. **IQ 70 and up.**
   Psychotherapy: Fam Group Indiv.
   Enr: 36. Res Males 36. **Staff:** 65.
   Rates 2004: No Fee.
   Est 1882. Private.

This residential program serves boys who have been removed from their families due to abuse or neglect. Various treatment groups, individual counseling and family therapy help boys address individual issues of self-esteem and victimization, as well as sexual abuse/offender issues. The home also offers an in-home counseling program, an after-school program and adoption home studies.

The state pays program fees for referred boys.

CHRISTIAN CHURCH HOMES
WOODLAWN CHILDREN'S CAMPUS

Res — Coed Ages 6-18

Danville, KY 40423. 1151 Perryville Rd, PO Box 45.
Tel: 859-236-5507. Fax: 859-236-7044.
www.cchk.org   E-mail: contact@cchk.org
Lee Martin, Jr., MDiv, LCSW, Exec Dir.
  Focus: Treatment. **Conditions:** Primary—B D Dx ED LD OCD S. Sec—As
    BD CD Ep Psy Sz. **IQ 75 and up.**
  Therapy: Lang Speech. **Psychotherapy:** Fam Indiv.
  Est 1884. Private. Inc.

Moderately to severely disturbed children may participate in Woodlawn Children's Campus, a residential treatment program. Offered within a therapeutic milieu, program activities are structured to meet the specific needs of the child and feature special education, on-campus classrooms, individual tutoring and recreation. In addition, Woodlawn's program includes psychiatric, pharmacological and nutritional counseling, all available on an as-needed basis.

Community Youth Homes of Danville, which accommodates up to eight boys and eight girls ages 6-12, offers a highly structured program that serves emotionally disturbed children with significant mental health problems. In-house psychiatric services are available, as is a special-education component for those whose educational or behavioral needs are beyond the capabilities of the public school system.

Another program, Sanders Center, is a short-term treatment facility that serves children in crisis, specifically those at risk of hospitalization or out-of-home placement. Trained residential care workers and mental health associates provide care on a 24-hour daily basis. The center places significant emphasis on meeting the needs of the child through a combination of family and community resources.

THE DE PAUL SCHOOL

Day — Coed Ages 8-14

Louisville, KY 40205. 1925 Duker Ave.
Tel: 502-459-6131. Fax: 502-458-0827.
www.depaulschool.org   E-mail: dpinfo@depaulschool.org
Anthony R. Kemper, Head. **Peggy Woolley,** Adm.
  Focus: Spec Ed. **Conditions:** Primary—ADD ADHD Dx LD. **IQ 100 and up.**
  Gen Acad. Ungraded. Courses: Read Math Lang_Arts Computers Sci
    Soc_Stud.
  Therapy: Lang.
  Staff: 42. (Full 42).
  Est 1970. Private. Nonprofit.

This school provides diagnosis and remediation of dyslexia and other specific learning differences. The program focused upon the acquisition of basic skills and the development of independent learning skills. Faculty members also address difficulties with social skills and self-esteem. Students, who must possess at least average intelligence, spend an average of three to four years at de Paul.

DIOCESAN CATHOLIC CHILDREN'S HOME

Res — Coed Ages 6-14

Fort Mitchell, KY 41017. 75 Orphanage Rd, PO Box 17007.
Tel: 859-331-2040. Fax: 859-344-5022.
www.dcchome.org
Sr. Jean Marie Hoffman, Exec Dir.
   Conditions: Primary—BD ED. **IQ 65 and up.**
   Gen Acad. Ungraded.
   Therapy: Recreational. **Psychotherapy:** Fam Group Indiv.
   Staff: Prof 12.
   Est 1960. Private. Nonprofit.

EASTER SEALS WEST KENTUCKY
CHILD DEVELOPMENT CENTER

Day — Coed Ages 1-5
Clinic: All Ages. M-F 8-5.

Paducah, KY 42002. 2229 Mildred St.
Tel: 270-444-9687. Fax: 270-444-0655.
www.eswky.easter-seals.org   E-mail: info@ky-ws.easter-seals.org
Kenneth Lucas, MA, Pres.
   Focus: Rehab. **Conditions:** Primary—ADD ADHD Ap Apr Ar As Asp Au
      B Bl C CF CP D DS Dx ED Ep IP MD MR MS Nf ODD ON PTSD PW S
      SB. Sec—LD. **IQ 25 and up.**
   Therapy: Hear Lang Occup Phys Speech. **Psychotherapy:** Group.
   Enr: 60. **Staff:** 27 (Full 24, Part 3). Prof 13. Educ 8. Admin 6.
   Est 1952. Private. Nonprofit.

The Child Development Center offers speech and language therapies, early intervention and infant stimulation. Physical and speech therapies are available in the early intervention/infant program. Comprehensive diagnostic audiological services are provided for all ages, including a program for hearing-impaired preschoolers and their families.

EASTERN KENTUCKY UNIVERSITY
SPEECH-LANGUAGE-HEARING CLINIC

Clinic: All Ages. M-Th 9-6.

Richmond, KY 40475. 245 Wallace Bldg.
Tel: 859-622-4444. Fax: 859-622-4443.
www.specialed.eku.edu
Peggy Lindsey, PhD, Co-Dir. **Cindy W. Reeves,** MS, Co-Dir.
   Focus: Treatment. **Conditions:** Primary—Apr D S. Sec—Ap Asp Au LD
      MR.
   Therapy: Hear Lang Speech.

Est 1970. State.

Housed within the university's Department of Special Education, College of Education, the facility offers evaluations of speech, language and hearing conditions, as well as clinical follow-up treatment.

FRANKFORT HABILITATION

Day — Coed Ages 16 and up

Frankfort, KY 40601. 3755 Lawrenceburg Rd.
Tel: 502-227-9529. Fax: 502-227-7191.
Terry R. Shockley, BS, Exec Dir.
    Focus: Trng. **Conditions:** Primary—ADD ADHD B BI CP D Dx ED Ep IP LD MD MR MS ON Sz. Sec—Ap As BD C CD OCD Psy S.
    Voc. Shelt_Workshop.
    Enr: 90. **Staff:** 25.
    Est 1972. Private. Nonprofit.

Individuals with disabilities receive vocational evaluation, training and sheltered employment at the center. Staff design individualized, prescribed programs for clients to gain work skills, self-confidence and appropriate behaviors and thereby increase the probability of employment.

HINDMAN SETTLEMENT SCHOOL

Day — Coed Ages 6-14

Hindman, KY 41822. 71 Hindman Settlement Rd, PO Box 844.
Tel: 606-785-5475. Fax: 606-785-3499.
www.hindmansettlement.org   E-mail: hss@tgtel.com
Mike Mullins, Exec Dir.
    Focus: Treatment. **Conditions:** Primary—Dx LD. **IQ 90 and up.**
    Enr: 30. Day Males 23. Day Females 7. **Staff:** 6 (Full 5, Part 1).
    Summer Prgm: Res & Day. Educ. Res Rate $3000. Day Rate $2000. 6 wks.
    Est 1902. Private. Nonprofit.

Utilizing the Orton-Gillingham method, the school remediates dyslexia in children from the Appalachian region. The East Kentucky Tutorial Program, conducted by Hindman School, provides after-school one-on-one tutoring with a phonetic-linguistic approach. Parent volunteers receive training that enables them to tutor children in Knott County and five surrounding counties.

The summer school provides an intense, structured remedial setting for eight hours each weekday. It features one-on-one tutoring in reading and three-to-one tutoring in math for students ages 6-20. Many of the summer session's participants attend public school during the regular academic year.

HUGH E. SANDEFUR TRAINING CENTER

Day — Coed Ages 18 and up

Henderson, KY 42420. 1449 Corporate Ct.
Tel: 270-827-2401. Fax: 270-827-9575.
www.hesandefur.com
Tracy D. Payne, Exec Dir.
    Focus: Trng. **Conditions:** Primary—ADD ADHD B BI C CD CP D Dx ED
      Ep LD MD MR MS OCD ON Psy SB Sz. Sec—As BD S.
    Voc. Shelt_Workshop.
    Psychotherapy: Parent.
    Enr: 135. **Staff:** 20.
    Est 1967. Private. Nonprofit.

The center provides vocational evaluation and training, work adjustment, and long-term or transitory employment for individuals with disabilities. The training and educational advantages offered enable persons disabled by physical or mental conditions to enter suitable employment. Enrollment is limited to ambulatory and mobile nonambulatory persons, free from contagious diseases, with a diagnosed physical, mental or emotional disorder. Applicants must possess basic self-care skills, and the center does not accept violent or destructive persons.

J. U. KEVIL MEMORIAL FOUNDATION

Day — Coed Ages Birth-3, 16 and up

Mayfield, KY 42066. 1900 S 10th St, PO Box 345.
Tel: 270-247-5396. Fax: 270-247-1233.
www.jukevil.com   E-mail: mail@jukevil.com
Larry G. Knight, BS, MA, Exec Dir.
    Focus: Trng. Treatment. **Conditions:** Primary—ADD ADHD Ap As Au B BD
      BI C CD CP D Dx ED LD MD MR MS OCD ON Psy S SB Sz. Sec—Ep.
    Voc. Shelt_Workshop.
    Therapy: Hear Lang Phys Speech.
    Enr: 175. **Staff:** 25.
    Rates 2004: No Fee.
    Est 1968. Private. Nonprofit.

The center maintains an infant and toddler intervention program for children under age 3 who exhibit one or more delayed developmental skill areas. This program provides an array of therapies and family support systems that aid in the development of gross- and fine-motor, speech and language, social and emotional, self-help and cognitive skills.

The center's vocational component (for those ages 16 and up) consists of work services, vocational evaluations, and vocational adjustment and habilitative services. Supported employment and competitive job placement services are also available.

KENTUCKY SCHOOL FOR THE DEAF

Res — Coed Ages 5-21; Day — Coed Birth-4

Danville, KY 40423. 303 S 2nd St.
Tel: 859-239-7017. TTY: 859-239-7017. Fax: 859-239-7006.
www.ksd.k12.ky.us   E-mail: pbruce@ksd.k12.ky.us
William A. Melton, Jr., MS, Admin. **Fran Martin,** Prin.
  Focus: Spec Ed. **Conditions:** Primary—D.
  Col Prep. Gen Acad. Pre-Voc. Voc. Gr K-12. Courses: Read Math Lang_
    Arts. Man_Arts & Shop. On-Job Trng.
  Enr: 183. **Staff:** 154. (Full 154). Prof 46. Educ 40. Admin 15.
  Rates 2004: No Fee.
  Summer Prgm: Day. Educ. 3 wks.
  Est 1823. State.

Academic and vocational education are offered to deaf and hard-of-hearing children who are residents of Kentucky. Students receive educational counseling and take training classes with a certified speech-language pathologist.

THE LANGSFORD CENTER

Clinic: Ages 5 and up. M-F 9-6.

Louisville, KY 40205. 1810 Sils Ave.
  Nearby locations: Prospect; Cincinnati, OH.
Tel: 502-473-7000. Fax: 502-459-8522.
www.langsfordcenter.com   E-mail: info@langsfordcenter.com
G. Stephen McCrocklin, BA, Dir. **Claudia R. Chervenak,** MEd, Clin Dir.
  Focus: Treatment. **Conditions:** Primary—Dx LD MR. Sec—ADD ADHD Ap
    Au. **IQ 80 and up.**
  Staff: 30 (Full 13, Part 17). Educ 25. Admin 5.
  Rates 2003: Clinic $65/ses. Schol avail.
  Est 1992. Private. Inc.

Langsford offers research-based, multisensory learning programs for individuals with learning disabilities, dyslexia and central auditory processing disorders. Staff utilize the Lindamood-Bell and Nancibell approaches in teaching phonological awareness, phonics, reading comprehension, spelling and math.
    Other centers operate at 5956 Timber Ridge Dr., Ste. 101, Prospect 40059, and 4158 Crossgate Ln., Cincinnati, OH 45236.

LEXINGTON HEARING & SPEECH CENTER

Day — Coed Ages Birth-7

Lexington, KY 40502. 162 N Ashland Ave.
Tel: 859-268-4545. TTY: 859-268-4545.
www.lhscky.org
Carol Hustedde, Dir.

Conditions: Primary—D S.
Gen Acad. Gr PS-K.
Therapy: Lang Speech.
Est 1960. Private. Inc.

LOUISVILLE DEAF ORAL SCHOOL

Day — Coed Ages Birth-9
Clinic: Ages Birth-15. M-F 8-4.

Louisville, KY 40203. 111 E Kentucky St.
Tel: 502-636-2084. Fax: 502-636-9171.
www.ldos.org
Mona K. McCubbin, MS, Exec Dir. **Rebecca Blondeau,** MS, Educ Dir. **Alan Nissen,** MD, Med Dir.
  Focus: Spec Ed. **Conditions:** Primary—D.
  Gen Acad. Gr PS-3. Courses: Read Math Lang_Arts.
  Therapy: Hear Lang Occup Phys Speech.
  Enr: 120. **Staff:** 40 (Full 38, Part 2).
  Rates 2003: Day $10,500/sch yr. Clinic $80/hr. Schol avail.
  Est 1948. Private. Nonprofit. **Spons:** Heuser Hearing Institute.

Children from birth to age 9 who have a hearing loss serious enough to require amplification and educational intervention may enroll at the school. Functioning as both a teaching and a diagnostic center, LDO School provides daily activities that promote language, speech, listening and cognitive development. The school, which is part of the Heuser Hearing Institute, serves as a regional center for cochlear implant evaluation and postimplant rehabilitation.

MARYHURST

Res — Coed Ages Birth-21

Louisville, KY 40223. 1015 Dorsey Ln.
Tel: 502-245-1576. Fax: 502-245-4737.
www.maryhurst.org   E-mail: info@maryhurst.org
Judith Lambeth, MRE, MSSW, Pres.
  Focus: Spec Ed. Treatment. **Conditions:** Primary—BD ED. Sec—ADD ADHD AN Anx Bu OCD Psy PTSD Sz. **IQ 55 and up.**
  Gen Acad. Pre-Voc. Ungraded. Courses: Read Math Lang_Arts Studio_Art Drama Bus. On-Job Trng.
  Therapy: Art Speech. **Psychotherapy:** Fam Group Indiv.
  Staff: 237 (Full 193, Part 44). Educ 16. Admin 28.
  Est 1843. Private. Nonprofit. Roman Catholic.

Maryhurst provides a year-round educational program in a residential treatment setting for severely emotionally disturbed adolescent girls. Social services, family group conferences, and specialized counseling and testing are available. Community resources are utilized and aftercare services are offered. Community-based treatment programs include supervised independent apartment living, treatment foster care, a community-based group home, intensive in-home services, and an after-school and summer program.

MURRAY STATE UNIVERSITY
SPEECH AND HEARING CLINIC
Clinic: All Ages. M-F 8-4:30.

Murray, KY 42071. 125 Alexander Hall Bldg.
Tel: 270-762-2446. Fax: 270-762-3963.
   Focus: Treatment. **Conditions:** Primary—Ap D S.
   Therapy: Hear Lang Speech.
   Staff: 6.
   Est 1968. State. Nonprofit.

Speech, language and hearing evaluations and rehabilitative services are offered at Murray State University Speech and Hearing Clinic.

OUR LADY OF BELLEFONTE
SPEECH AND LANGUAGE PATHOLOGY SERVICES
Clinic: All Ages. M-F 8-5.

Ashland, KY 41101. St Christopher Dr.
Tel: 606-833-2273. Fax: 606-324-1186.
www.careyoucantrust.com/svs_speech_language.asp
   Conditions: Primary—D S.
   Therapy: Hear Lang Speech.
   Staff: Prof 16.
   Est 1971. Nonprofit.

PIONEER VOCATIONAL/INDUSTRIAL SERVICES
Day — Coed Ages 16-65

Danville, KY 40423. 590 Stanford Rd, PO Box 1396.
Tel: 859-236-8413. TTY: 859-236-1251. Fax: 859-238-7115.
www.pioneerservices.org   E-mail: pioneer@pioneerservices.org
Jack Godbey II, Exec Dir.
   Conditions: Primary—Ap As B BD BI C CP D Dx ED Ep IP LD MD MR MS ON S SB.
   Pre-Voc. Voc. Courses: Read Math Lang_Arts. Shelt_Workshop. On-Job Trng.
   Therapy: Chemo Hear Phys Speech. **Psychotherapy:** Fam Group Indiv.
   Staff: Prof 7.
   Est 1967. Private. Nonprofit.

REDWOOD SCHOOL AND REHABILITATION CENTER

Day — Coed All Ages
Clinic: All Ages. M-F 6:30-6.

Fort Mitchell, KY 41017. 71 Orphanage Rd.
Tel: 859-331-0880. Fax: 859-331-6177.
www.redwoodrehab.org
Barbara H. Howard, MA, Exec Dir.
  Focus: Spec Ed. Trng. Treatment. **Conditions:** Primary—ADD ADHD As Au
    B BI CP D Dx Ep LD MD MS OCD ON S SB. Sec—MR.
  Pre-Voc. Voc. Ungraded. Courses: Read Math Lang_Arts Studio_Art Music
    Health. Shelt_Workshop. On-Job Trng.
  Therapy: Hear Lang Occup Phys Speech. **Psychotherapy:** Parent.
  Enr: 581. **Staff:** 100.
  Summer Prgm: Day. Educ. Rec.
  Est 1953. Private. Nonprofit.

Redwood provides comprehensive training programs, special education and therapeutic intervention for multi-handicapped individuals. Programming emphasizes communication and motor skills, as well as socialization and self-help skills. The center also
offers a complete counseling program. Services for multiply handicapped adults are
provided through the Adult Work Activity Center, which assists in the development of
skills to enhance independence in living.

SHEDD ACADEMY

Res and Day — Coed Ages 6-20

Mayfield, KY 42066. 401 S 7th St, PO Box 493.
Tel: 270-247-8007. Fax: 270-247-0637.
www.sheddacademy.org   E-mail: shedd@apex.net
  Focus: Spec Ed. Treatment. **Conditions:** Primary—ADD ADHD Dx LD. **IQ
    80 and up.**
  Col Prep. Gen Acad. Pre-Voc. Voc. Gr 1-PG. Courses: Read Math Lang_
    Arts Sci Computers Hist.
  Therapy: Hear Lang Occup Speech. **Psychotherapy:** Fam Group Indiv
    Parent.
  Enr: 30. Res Males 17. Res Females 8. Day Males 3. Day Females 2. **Staff:**
    18. (Full 18).
  Summer Prgm: Res & Day. Educ. 5-7 wks.
  Est 1974. Private. Nonprofit.

The academy provides a treatment program to remediate children with dyslexia,
learning disabilities, hyperkinesis, aphasia and attention deficit disorder. Teaching methods are based on the latest multisensory, structured-language research. Students learn
techniques of study to be successful in the classroom and to gain personal independence.
A cooperative education program assists students in defining career objectives.

STEWART HOME SCHOOL

Res — Coed Ages 6 and up

Frankfort, KY 40601. 4200 Lawrenceburg Rd.
Tel: 502-227-4821. Fax: 502-227-3013.
www.stewarthome.com   E-mail: info@stewarthome.com
J. Barry Banker, BA, MBA, Pres. **Sandra Bell,** BA, Dir.
 Focus: Spec Ed. **Conditions:** Primary—MR.
 Gen Acad. Pre-Voc. Voc. Ungraded. Courses: Read Math Studio_Art Music
  Drama Journ. Shelt_Workshop.
 Staff: 130.
 Est 1893. Private. Inc.

SHS provides care and training, including lifetime care, for mentally retarded children and adults. All residents have an active, individually planned program that includes recreation, academics, vocational training, job placement, self-care and social skills. A community-based sheltered workshop is also available.   **See Also Pages 1050-1**

SUMMIT ACADEMY

Day — Coed Ages 5-14

Louisville, KY 40243. 11508 Main St.
Tel: 502-244-7090. Fax: 502-244-3371.
www.summit-academy.org
Margaret Thornton, MEd, Exec Dir.
 Focus: Spec Ed. **Conditions:** Primary—ADD ADHD Apr As Asp BI CP Dc
  Dg Dx Ep LD PDD. Sec—Anx Mood OCD SP TS. **IQ 80 and up.**
 Gen Acad. Gr PS-8. Courses: Read Math Lang_Arts Lib_Skills Sci Computers Soc_Stud Studio_Art Music Drama.
 Therapy: Occup Speech. **Psychotherapy:** Fam Group Indiv Parent.
 Enr: 128. Day Males 95. Day Females 33. **Staff:** 38 (Full 34, Part 4). Educ
  24. Admin 11.
 Rates 2004: Day $11,520/sch yr. $35 (Speech Therapy); $60 (Occup
  Therapy)/ses. Schol avail.
 Summer Prgm: Day. Educ. Rec. Day Rate $150/wk. 12 wks.
 Est 1992. Private. Nonprofit.

The academy serves children with learning disabilities, as well as those who are at risk of developing learning disabilities. Each child receives intensive instruction in a small classroom setting. Staff use annual standardized testing results as a complement to ongoing performance assessments and criterion-referenced testing. Extracurricular activities include soccer, basketball, drama, art, chess club and environmental club.

UNIVERSITY OF KENTUCKY CHILDREN'S HOSPITAL CHILD NEUROLOGY PROGRAM

Clinic: Ages Birth-18. M-F 8:30-5:30.

Lexington, KY 40536. Kentucky Clinic L409.
Tel: 859-323-5661. Fax: 859-323-5943.
www.mc.uky.edu/neurology/child.asp   E-mail: baumann@uky.edu
Robert J. Baumann, MD, Dir.
  Focus: Treatment. **Conditions:** Primary—Ap Bl CP Ep IP MD MS OH.
    Sec—ADD ADHD Asp Au Dx LD MR SB.
  Staff: 4. (Full 4).
  State.

The program provides evaluation and treatment for children with diagnosed or suspected neurological conditions.

WENDELL FOSTER'S CAMPUS FOR DEVELOPMENTAL DISABILITIES

Res — Coed Ages 6 and up
Clinic: All Ages. M-F 7:30-4.

Owensboro, KY 42302. 815 Triplett St.
Tel: 270-683-4517. Fax: 270-683-0079.
www.wendellfostercenter.org
Joe Gamble, CEO.
  Conditions: Primary—Au CP DS MR OH. Sec—D LD S.
  Therapy: Hear Hydro Lang Occup Phys Recreational Speech. **Psycho-
    therapy:** Group Indiv.
  Enr: 63.
  Est 1947. Private. Nonprofit.

Wendell Foster provides a full program of treatment, care and education for persons with cerebral palsy and other developmental disabilities. The program includes various therapies and special speech training, as well as prevocational training opportunities.

WOODBRIDGE ACADEMY

Day — Coed Ages 6-17

Lexington, KY 40507. 251 W 2nd St.
Tel: 859-252-3000.
www.woodbridgeacademy.com   E-mail: info@woodbridgeacademy.com
Betsy Goldsworthy, MA, Exec Dir. George A. Goldsworthy, Adm.
  Focus: Spec Ed. **Conditions:** Primary—ADD ADHD Dx LD. Sec—CD ED
    OCD. **IQ 70 and up.**
  Col Prep. Gen Acad. Pre-Voc. Gr 1-12. Courses: Read Math Lang_Arts.
    On-Job Trng.
  Therapy: Occup. **Psychotherapy:** Fam Parent.

Enr: 40. Day Males 25. Day Females 15. **Staff:** 17 (Full 8, Part 9).
Est 1987. Private. Nonprofit.

Woodbridge Academy is a small private school that serves individuals with learning disabilities, dyslexia, attentional disorders and other perceptual disabilities that have prevented them from succeeding in traditional school settings. Since many of its pupils do not respond to the textbook/lecture teaching method, the school utilizes a hands-on approach that requires children to take an active role in their education. Computers and multimedia technologies are integral parts of the program.

LOUISIANA

BRIGHTON ACADEMY

Day — Coed Ages 5-14

Baton Rouge, LA 70809. 9150 Bereford Dr.
Tel: 225-923-2068. Fax: 225-923-2208.
www.brighton-academy.org   E-mail: info@brighton-academy.org
Carole Risher, MS, Prin. **Kathy Whatley,** Adm.
  Focus: Spec Ed. **Conditions:** Primary—Dg Dx LD. Sec—ADD ADHD Dc.
    IQ 90 and up.
  Gen Acad. Ungraded. Courses: Read Math Lang_Arts Computers Linguis-
    tics.
  Psychotherapy: Fam.
  Enr: 138. Day Males 100. Day Females 38. **Staff:** 29. Educ 21. Admin 6.
  Rates 2003: Day $7425/sch yr (+$675). Schol 20 ($40,000).
  Summer Prgm: Day. Educ. Day Rate $800. 4 wks.
  Est 1972. Private. Nonprofit. **Spons:** Dyslexia Association of Greater Baton
    Rouge.

The academy specializes in remediation of dyslexia. A structured teaching approach presents basic linguistic and mathematical symbols and skills, extending to a full curriculum as the child progresses. Involvement of parents is extensive, as they participate in tutoring, carpentry and fundraising. The usual duration of treatment is four years, and Brighton does not accept children with primary emotional problems.

CHILDREN'S HOSPITAL

Res — Coed Ages Birth-21
Clinic: Ages Birth-21. M-F 8-5.

New Orleans, LA 70118. 200 Henry Clay Ave.
Tel: 504-899-9511. Fax: 504-896-3934.
www.chnola.org   E-mail: info@chnola.org
Steve Worley, Pres. **Alan Robson,** MD, Med Dir.
  Conditions: Primary—ADD ADHD As B BI C CP D Dx Ep IP LD MD MS
    ON S SB TB.
  Therapy: Chemo Hear Lang Music Occup Phys Recreational Speech. **Psy-
    chotherapy:** Fam Group Indiv Parent.
  Est 1955. Private. Nonprofit.

This full-service pediatric hospital provides a wide variety of services for children with all types of handicaps and disabilities. Orthopedic therapy, speech pathology and rehabilitative surgery are available, as are academic classes conducted to help the child keep up with his or her peers. An emergency care center is staffed 24 hours per day. Medical and surgical subspecialty services are available.

The facility operates in cooperation with the LSU and Tulane schools of medicine, the State Department of Health and the Orleans Parish School Board.

CHINCHUBA INSTITUTE

Day — Coed Ages 1½-18
Clinic: All Ages. M-F 8-5.

Marrero, LA 70072. 1131 Barataria Blvd.
Tel: 504-340-9261. TTY: 504-340-9261. Fax: 504-340-9263.
www.chinchuba.org   E-mail: info@chinchuba.org
Virginia LeCompte, Exec Dir. **Lois B. Thibodaux,** MEd, CCC, Prin.
   Focus: Spec Ed. **Conditions:** Primary—D S.
   Gen Acad. Gr PS-12. Courses: Read Math Lang_Arts Sci Soc_Stud.
   Therapy: Hear Lang Speech. **Psychotherapy:** Parent.
   Enr: 37. Day Males 28. Day Females 9. **Staff:** 17 (Full 16, Part 1).
   Est 1890. Private. Nonprofit.

This school for hearing-impaired children employs the auditory/oral method in offering training in speech and language development, as well as academics. The program includes a mainstreaming component for students in grades K-12, and a reverse mainstreaming preschool for children with normal hearing ages 2-5.

COLUMBIA DEVELOPMENTAL CENTER

Res — Coed Ages 3-21

Columbia, LA 71418. PO Box 1559.
Tel: 318-649-2385. Fax: 318-649-2868.
   Focus: Trng. Treatment. **Conditions:** Primary—BI MR. Sec—B CP Ep. **IQ 0-25.**
   Therapy: Hear Lang Occup Phys Speech. **Psychotherapy:** Fam Indiv.
   Enr: 25. **Staff:** 55.
   Est 1970. State. Nonprofit.

Columbia provides short-term residential training in a controlled environment for ambulatory individuals with mental retardation. Emphasis is on self-help training, with the objective of returning the individual to community life. The center also provides motor development, feeding, toileting, language development and stimulation, and recreational therapy. Educational programs include a day developmental center. Parental training is available and the length of stay varies.

DEPAUL-TULANE BEHAVIORAL HEALTH CENTER
RESIDENTIAL TREATMENT CENTER

Res — Coed Ages 5-17

New Orleans, LA 70118. 1040 Calhoun St.
Tel: 504-899-8282. Fax: 504-897-5775.
www.tuhc.com
Robert D. Lancaster, MD, Med Dir.
   Conditions: Primary—BD ED.
   Psychotherapy: Fam Group Indiv.
   Est 1861. Private. Nonprofit.

EVANGELINE CHRISTIAN HOME FOR GIRLS

Res — Females Ages 12-17

Lafayette, LA 70503. 605 S College Dr.
Tel: 337-266-9686. Fax: 337-232-6877.
www.evangelhouse.com   E-mail: admissions@evangelhouse.com
Mark D. Barrentine, BA, MSW, LCSW, Exec Dir.
   Focus: Treatment. **Conditions:** Primary—ADD ADHD Anx BD Dx ED Mood
      OCD PTSD SP. Sec—Bu Db HIV.
   Col Prep. Gen Acad. Voc. Gr 6-12. Courses: Read Math Lang_Arts.
   Therapy: Art Milieu Music. **Psychotherapy:** Fam Group Indiv Parent.
   Enr: 11. Res Females 11. **Staff:** 7 (Full 5, Part 2).
   Rates 2003: Res $27,000/yr.
   Est 1995. Private. Nonprofit. Nondenom Christian.

Evangeline's clinical program addresses behavior problems, substance abuse, family problems, poor school performance, and legal problems for troubled adolescent girls. The home provides professional Christian counseling, a structured home and school environment, and a Biblically based coping skills curriculum in a group home setting in which girls typically remain for 12 to 18 months.

EVERGREEN PRESBYTERIAN MINISTRIES

Res — Coed Ages 14 and up

Bossier City, LA 71172. 4400 Viking Dr, PO Box 72360.
Tel: 318-742-8440. Fax: 318-752-5448.
www.epmi.org
   Conditions: Primary—MR.
   Courses: Read Math Lang_Arts. Shelt_Workshop. On-Job Trng.
   Therapy: Hear Lang Occup Phys Speech. **Psychotherapy:** Group Indiv.
   Est 1959. Private. Nonprofit.

GABLES ACADEMY

Day — Coed Ages 6-21

Baton Rouge, LA 70817. 15333 Jefferson Hwy.
Tel: 225-752-9231. Fax: 225-756-3533.
www.gablesacademybr.com   E-mail: gablesbr@bellsouth.net
Susan C. Kramer, MEd, Dir.
   Focus: Spec Ed. **Conditions:** Primary—ADD ADHD Dg Dx LD. Sec—Asp
      OCD.
   Gen Acad. Gr 1-12. Courses: Read Math Lang_Arts Sci Computers Soc_
      Stud Studio_Art Music.
   Therapy: Lang Speech. **Psychotherapy:** Group Indiv.
   Enr: 125. **Staff:** 16 (Full 15, Part 1).
   Rates 2003: Day $5775/sch yr. Schol 5 ($6,000).

Summer Prgm: Day. Educ. Day Rate $175/crse. 7 wks.
Est 1975. Private. Inc.

The academy offers a full curriculum for children with learning disabilities and attentional disorders, and for children who require individualized instruction to succeed academically. Students in grades 1-8 receive daily instruction in such areas as reading, writing, spelling, mathematics, science, social studies and physical education. The curriculum for grades 9-12, which leads to a high school diploma, features a variety of electives and enrichment activities. The school provides speech therapy and counseling for an additional fee. Gables does not accept children whose primary difficulty is behavioral.

HOLY ANGELS RESIDENTIAL FACILITY

Res — Coed Ages 14-25

Shreveport, LA 71106. 10450 Ellerbe Rd.
Tel: 318-797-8500. Fax: 318-798-0159.
Sr. Conchetta, Dir.
  Focus: Trng. Treatment. **Conditions:** Primary—MR.
  Pre-Voc. Voc. Ungraded. Shelt_Workshop. On-Job Trng.
  Therapy: Hear Lang Occup Phys Speech. **Psychotherapy:** Fam Group Indiv.
  Est 1965. Private. **Spons:** Sisters of Our Lady of Sorrows.

LEESVILLE DEVELOPMENTAL CENTER

Res — Males Ages 12-59; Day — Males 18-59, Females 21-59

Leesville, LA 71446. 401 W Texas St, PO Box 131.
Tel: 337-239-2687. Fax: 337-238-3723.
Ronald G. Williams, Admin. **Rene Veillon,** MD, Med Dir. **Jim W. Weeks,** Intake.
  Focus: Treatment. **Conditions:** Primary—BD MR. Sec—ADD ADHD Anx BI CD CP ED Ep Mood OCD PDD Psy PW Sz TS. **IQ 25-69.**
  Voc. Man_Arts & Shop. On-Job Trng.
  Therapy: Hear Lang Occup Phys Speech. **Psychotherapy:** Group Indiv.
  Enr: 47. **Staff:** 113 (Full 109, Part 4). Prof 96. Admin 9.
  Rates 2003: Res $224/day.
  Est 1964. State.

Mentally retarded individuals receive short-term self-help, prevocational training and educational services. Social, recreational, therapeutic and medical services are also available at the facility. Leesville's objective is to facilitate the client's return to an independent or semi-independent living situation within the community.

LOUISE S. DAVIS DEVELOPMENTAL CENTER

Res and Day — Coed Ages 6-65

New Orleans, LA 70128. 11110 Lake Forest Blvd.
Tel: 504-245-1002. Fax: 504-242-7080.
   Conditions: Primary—MR.
   Therapy: Hear Lang Occup Phys Speech. Psychotherapy: Fam Group
      Indiv.
   Est 1945. Private. Nonprofit.

LOUISIANA PHYSICAL THERAPY
OUTPATIENT CLINIC

Clinic: All Ages. M-F 8-5.

Lafayette, LA 70501. 1340 Surrey St.
Tel: 337-235-2411. Fax: 337-235-8037.
www.mshcg.com/therapy.php
   Conditions: Primary—OH.
   Therapy: Hear Lang Occup Phys Speech. Psychotherapy: Indiv.
   Staff: Prof 22.
   Est 1956. Private. Nonprofit. Spons: LHC Group.

LOUISIANA SCHOOL FOR THE DEAF

Res — Coed Ages 3-21; Day — Coed Birth-21

Baton Rouge, LA 70821. 2888 Brightside Ln, PO Box 3074.
Tel: 225-769-8160. TTY: 225-769-8160. Fax: 225-757-3424.
www.lalsd.org   E-mail: bprickett@lalsd.org
Bill Prickett, MEd, EdD, Supt. Beth Forester, Prin. Connie Greenlee, Adm.
   Focus: Spec Ed. Conditions: Primary—D. Sec—MR.
   Col Prep. Gen Acad. Pre-Voc. Voc. Gr PS-12. Courses: Read Math Lang_
      Arts Sci Soc_Stud. Man_Arts & Shop. On-Job Trng.
   Therapy: Hear Lang Occup Phys Speech. Psychotherapy: Fam Group
      Indiv Parent.
   Enr: 475. Staff: 356 (Full 331, Part 25).
   Rates 2003: No Fee.
   Est 1852. State. Nonprofit.

   Designed for deaf and hearing-impaired children who are unable to progress normally
in a public school setting because of a language and communication handicap, the
school provides course offerings comparable to a public school curriculum. Provisions
are also made for deaf-blind children and deaf children with other handicaps, such as
mental retardation or a specific learning disability. Counseling is also available.

LOUISIANA SCHOOL
FOR THE VISUALLY IMPAIRED

Res and Day — Coed Ages 3-21

Baton Rouge, LA 70821. 1120 Government St, PO Box 4328.
Tel: 225-342-8694. Fax: 225-342-1885.
www.lsvi.org
Janet Ford, Supt. Mitzi Jones, Adm.
  Focus: Spec Ed. Conditions: Primary—B. Sec—ADD ADHD Ap As BD CD
    CP Dc Dg Dx ED LD MR. IQ 50-130.
  Gen Acad. Pre-Voc. Ungraded. Courses: Read Math Lang_Arts Music
    Life_Skills.
  Therapy: Hear Lang Occup Phys Speech.
  Enr: 50. Res Males 20. Res Females 21. Day Males 5. Day Females 4.
    Staff: 88.
  Rates 2003: No Fee.
  Est 1852. State.

LSVI's educational program for students with visual impairments includes both classroom activities and extended-day options. Staff members formulate an individualized educational program for each child to enable the individual to reach academic potential. The spectrum of available educational services ranges from daily living skills instruction to socialization to college-bound academic programs. LSVI also offers vocational programs. Students must be a resident of Louisiana.

LOUISIANA STATE UNIVERSITY
HEALTH SCIENCES CENTER
DEPARTMENT OF COMMUNICATION DISORDERS

Clinic: All Ages. M-F 8:30-5.

New Orleans, LA 70112. 1900 Gravier St.
Tel: 504-568-4348. Fax: 504-568-4249.
Barbara Wendt-Harris, PhD, Co-Dir. Silvia Davis, Co-Dir.
  Focus: Treatment. Conditions: Primary—Ap Au D S. Sec—B Bl CP ED Ep
    MD MR MS OH.
  Therapy: Hear Lang Speech.
  Staff: 11.
  Est 1968. State. Nonprofit.

Screening, diagnostic and therapeutic services are provided at this center for individuals who have speech, language and hearing disorders. Individual and group therapies are offered. Additional services include pupil appraisal evaluations and family counseling. The center fits and dispenses assistive communication devices.

LOUISIANA STATE UNIVERSITY
SPEECH AND HEARING CLINIC

Clinic: All Ages. M-F 8:30-5.

Baton Rouge, LA 70803. 144 Music & Dramatic Arts Bldg.
Tel: 225-578-9054. Fax: 225-578-2995.
www.lsu.edu/comd
Paul R. Hoffman, PhD, Supv.
   Focus: Treatment. **Conditions:** Primary—Ap Apr S.
   Therapy: Hear Lang Speech.
   Staff: 10. Prof 8. Admin 2.
   Est 1925. State.

Language, speech and hearing disorders are diagnosed and treated at the clinic, which also provides student training in speech pathology and audiology. Services include diagnostic evaluation and management training, as well as rehabilitation services. Fees vary according to the service provided.

LOUISIANA TECH UNIVERSITY
SPEECH AND HEARING CENTER

Clinic: All Ages. M-Th 8-4:30.

Ruston, LA 71272. PO Box 3165.
Tel: 318-257-4764. Fax: 318-257-4492.
www.latech.edu   E-mail: cdans@ltparts.latech.edu
J. Clarice Dans, PhD, Dir. **Angie Sherman,** PhD, Coord.
   Focus: Trng. **Conditions:** Primary—Ap Apr D S. Sec—B BD BI CP Dx LD
      MD MR MS OH. **IQ 25 and up.**
   Therapy: Hear Lang Speech.
   Staff: 10 (Full 9, Part 1).
   Est 1954. State. Nonprofit.

Among the center's services are full auditory evaluations and treatment of speech, language and hearing disorders. Offerings are combined with parental counseling and aftercare. The center also dispenses hearing aids.

THE MCMAINS CHILDREN'S
DEVELOPMENTAL CENTER

Clinic: Ages Birth-18. M-F 7:30-4:30.

Baton Rouge, LA 70808. 1805 College Dr.
Tel: 225-923-3420. Fax: 225-922-9316.
Janet Ketcham, MSW, Exec Dir.
   Focus: Treatment. **Conditions:** Primary—ADD ADHD Ap CP Dx LD ON S.
      Sec—Au.
   Therapy: Hear Lang Occup Phys Speech. **Psychotherapy:** Group Indiv

Parent.
Staff: 25 (Full 12, Part 13).
Est 1954. Private. Nonprofit. **Spons:** Capital Area United Way.

In addition to standard treatments, this cerebral palsy unit provides orthopedic and pediatric examinations and diagnostic services, psychological testing, and social and prosthetic services. The educational program offers individualized outpatient treatment two times per week. Many children attend special education classes operated by the East Baton Rouge School Board.

MENTAL HEALTH CENTER
OF CENTRAL LOUISIANA

Clinic: Ages 6-17. M-F 8-4:30; Eves Th 4:30-8.

Alexandria, LA 71306. PO Box 7473.
Tel: 318-484-6850. Fax: 318-484-6844.
Claudia Lawson, LCSW, Mgr. **John McDaniel,** LCSW, Clin Mgr. **John Smith,** MD, Med Dir.
Focus: Treatment. **Conditions:** Primary—ADHD ED OCD Psy Sz. Sec— Asp BD CD PTSD SP TS. **IQ 56 and up.**
Therapy: Play. **Psychotherapy:** Fam Group Indiv Parent.
Staff: 12 (Full 10, Part 2).
Rates 2003: Clinic $70/ses.
State. Nonprofit.

The clinic offers a wide range of therapeutic services, including crisis intervention and individual, family and group therapy. Emphasis is placed on the treatment of children and parents of children with severe emotional disturbances. The center determines fees along a sliding scale.

METROPOLITAN DEVELOPMENTAL CENTER

Res — Coed Ages 11-64

Belle Chasse, LA 70037. 251 F Edward Hebert Blvd.
Tel: 504-394-1200. Fax: 504-398-9200.
www.dhh.state.la.us/offices/?ID=126
Robert Sanders, Dir.
Conditions: Primary—MR. **IQ 0-62.**
Pre-Voc. Voc. Ungraded. Courses: Read Math Lang_Arts. Shelt_Workshop. On-Job Trng.
Therapy: Hear Lang Occup Phys Speech. **Psychotherapy:** Fam Group Indiv.
Est 1967. State. Nonprofit.

NEW ORLEANS SPEECH AND HEARING CENTER

Clinic: All Ages. M-F 8:30-5.

New Orleans, LA 70115. 1636 Toledano St.
Tel: 504-897-2606. Fax: 504-891-6048.
www.noshc.org   E-mail: noshc@hotmail.com
Lesley Jernigan, MS, Exec Dir.
>   **Focus:** Treatment. **Conditions:** Primary—Ap Apr D S. Sec—ADD ADHD
>   Asp Au BD BI CP DS Dx ED Ep LD MR OH.
>   **Therapy:** Hear Lang Speech.
>   **Staff:** 17 (Full 15, Part 2). Prof 12. Admin 5.
>   **Rates 2004:** Clinic $40/ses. State Aid.
>   **Est 1930.** Private. Nonprofit.

Children and adults who have speech and hearing problems receive diagnostic and treatment services through the center. Communicative disorders such as cleft palate and lip, stuttering, speech and language disorders associated with strokes, and reading and articulation problems are treated. The center offers complete audiology services, including hearing aid dispensation. Referrals are made to public and private schools for standard or special education.

NORTHWEST LOUISIANA DEVELOPMENTAL CENTER

Res — Coed All Ages

Bossier City, LA 71111. 5401 Shed Rd.
Tel: 318-742-6220. Fax: 318-741-7303.
www.dhh.state.la.us
Josye Ned, Dir.
>   **Focus:** Trng. **Conditions:** Primary—MR. **IQ 0-35.**
>   **Pre-Voc.** Ungraded. Shelt_Workshop. On-Job Trng.
>   **Therapy:** Hear Lang Occup Phys Speech. **Psychotherapy:** Indiv.
>   **Est 1973.** State.

PARKMEADOW HIGH SCHOOL

Day — Coed Ages 13-19

Baton Rouge, LA 70816. 12108 Parkmeadow Ave.
Tel: 225-291-2524. Fax: 225-291-8587.
www.park-meadow.org
Gary Kinchen, MS, Prin.
>   **Focus:** Spec Ed. **Conditions:** Primary—Dx LD. Sec—ADD ADHD Dc Dg.
>   **IQ 90 and up.**
>   **Col Prep.** Gr 8-12. Courses: Read Math Lang_Arts Sci Computers Soc_
>   Stud.
>   **Enr:** 86. Day Males 62. Day Females 24. **Staff:** 12 (Full 8, Part 4). Educ 10.
>   Admin 2.

Rates 2003: Day $5450-7515/sch yr (+$500). Schol 3 ($3000).
Est 2002. Private. Nonprofit. **Spons:** Dyslexia Association of Greater Baton Rouge.

This specialized school for students with dyslexia and related learning disabilities combines a college preparatory curriculum with enrichment programs in athletics, the arts and technology. Parkmeadow pupils, who are of average to above-average intelligence, fulfill course requirements in English, math, science and social studies, and also choose from various electives.

RUSTON DEVELOPMENTAL CENTER

Res — Coed Ages 12 and up

Ruston, LA 71270. PO Box 907.
Tel: 318-247-3721. Fax: 318-247-8908.
www.dhh.state.la.us   E-mail: jjohnson@dhhmail.dhh.state.la.us
    Focus: Trng. Treatment. **Conditions:** Primary—Mood MR. Sec—As B CD CP D ED Ep OCD ON Psy S Sz. **IQ 19-70.**
    Therapy: Chemo Hear Lang Occup Phys Speech. **Psychotherapy:** Indiv.
    Enr: 98. Res Males 84. Res Females 14. **Staff:** 57 (Full 51, Part 6).
    Rates 2001: Res $210/day.
    Est 1959. State.

Ruston, a specialized unit of the Louisiana Health and Human Resources Administration, provides therapies and habilitation for individuals with mild to profound levels of mental retardation. Services include behavioral intervention; occupational and physical therapies; leisure-time activities; and training in communication, socialization and self-help skills. The average length of stay is one to two years.

ST. MARY'S RESIDENTIAL TRAINING FACILITY

Res — Coed Ages 3-21

Alexandria, LA 71306. PO Drawer 7768.
Tel: 318-445-6443. Fax: 318-449-8520.
www.stmarys-rts.com
Sr. Mary Coleman, Admin. **Rodney Richmond,** Adm.
    Focus: Treatment. **Conditions:** Primary—MR. Sec—ADD ADHD Ap As B BD Bl C CD CP D Dx ED Ep IP LD MD MS OCD ON Psy S SB TB. **IQ 20-59.**
    Pre-Voc. Ungraded. Man_Arts & Shop. On-Job Trng.
    Therapy: Hear Lang Occup Phys Speech. **Psychotherapy:** Fam Group Indiv.
    Enr: 152. Res Males 83. Res Females 69. **Staff:** 174.
    Est 1954. Private. Nonprofit. Roman Catholic.

St. Mary's provides a residential program for ambulatory, trainable mentally retarded children and young adults. Clients must submit current medical, social, educational and psychological evaluations at the time of application. The school then schedules an interview and reviews a recommendation for residential care made by an agency or a qualified professional.

St. Mary's maintains a favorable staff-student ratio, and classes average eight to 10 students. Health care, dietetic, speech pathology, social and psychological services, as well as physical therapy, occupational therapy and recreation, are part of the overall program.

SHRINERS HOSPITAL

Res — Coed Ages Birth-18

Shreveport, LA 71103. 3100 Samford Ave.
Tel: 318-222-5704. Fax: 318-424-7610.
www.shrinershq.org
Garry Kim Green, MBA, MHA, Admin.
   Conditions: Primary—OH. Sec—Ar CP SB.
   Therapy: Recreational.
   Est 1922. Private.

UNIVERSITY OF LOUISIANA AT LAFAYETTE
SPEECH, LANGUAGE AND HEARING CENTER

Clinic: All Ages. M-F 8-5.

Lafayette, LA 70504. Hebrard Blvd, PO Box 43170.
Tel: 337-482-6490. Fax: 337-482-6490.
Holly L. Damico, Dir.
   Focus: Treatment. **Conditions:** Primary—Ap Apr Asp Au D Dx PDD S.
   Sec—BI CP ED OH.
   Therapy: Hear Lang Speech. **Psychotherapy:** Fam Group.
   Staff: 9. Prof 8. Admin 1.
   Est 1949. State.

The center offers diagnosis, treatment and referral for speech, language and hearing problems, as well as counseling. The center specializes in language literacy for children who have reading, language and learning difficulties. Infant and toddler communication development and adult services are also available. Fees are determined along a sliding scale.

WOMEN AND CHILDREN'S HOSPITAL
KID'S TEAM

Clinic: Ages Birth-18. M-F 7:30-5.

Lake Charles, LA 70605. 4150 Nelson Rd, Ste D-2A.
Tel: 337-475-4020. Fax: 337-475-4720.
www.women-childrens.com   E-mail: deidre.ardoin@triadhospitals.com

Deidre Ardoin, MS, RPT, Mgr. **Floyd Guidry,** MD, Med Dir.
 Focus: Rehab. **Conditions:** Primary—Ap Ar Au B BI CF CP D DS HIV IP
 MD ON PDD S SB. Sec—ADD ADHD Apr As BD C CD Dx ED Ep LD
 Mood MS OCD ODD Psy Sz TB.
 Therapy: Hear Hydro Lang Movement Occup Percepual-Motor Phys
 Speech.
 Staff: 8 (Full 7, Part 1). Prof 5. Admin 3.
 Est 1985. Private. **Spons:** Triad Hospitals.

This pediatric rehabilitation center utilizes a multidisciplinary approach, employing
physical therapists, speech pathologists and physicians. Kid's Team provides wheelchair
and seating clinics, as well as neonatal intensive care unit follow-up clinics.

MAINE

ELAN SCHOOL

Res — Coed Ages 12-20

Poland Spring, ME 04274. PO Box 578.
Tel: 207-998-4666. Fax: 207-998-4660.
www.elanschool.com   E-mail: info@elanschool.com
Sharon Terry, Exec Dir.
  Conditions: Primary—BD ED. Sec—LD. **IQ 90 and up.**
  Col Prep. Gen Acad. Gr 7-12. Courses: Read Math Lang_Arts.
  Psychotherapy: Group Indiv.
  Staff: Prof 28.
  Est 1970. Private. Inc.

ELIZABETH LEVINSON CENTER

Res — Coed Ages Birth-20

Bangor, ME 04401. 159 Hogan Rd.
Tel: 207-941-4400. TTY: 207-941-4409. Fax: 207-941-4412.
E-mail: carol.trottier@state.me.us
Carol A. Trottier, LICSW, Dir. **John Farquhar, Jr.,** MD, Med Dir.
  Focus: Trng. **Conditions:** Primary—MR. Sec—As B CP D Ep LD ON S. **IQ 0-35.**
  Therapy: Hear Lang Music Occup Phys Recreational Speech. **Psychotherapy:** Indiv.
  Enr: 10. Res Males 6. Res Females 4. **Staff:** 45 (Full 42, Part 3). Prof 10. Admin 5.
  Rates 2003: No Fee.
  Est 1971. State. Nonprofit.

  Serving children with severe and profound mental retardation from around the state, the center provides respite care, short-term evaluation, contracted and residential training, and various individual therapies. Emphasis is placed on motor development, self-help and social skills.

KENNEBEC VALLEY MENTAL HEALTH CENTER

Clinic: All Ages. M-F 8-4:30.

Waterville, ME 04901. 67 Eustis Pkwy.
Tel: 207-873-2136. TTY: 207-626-3614. Fax: 207-872-4522.
www.kvmhc.org
  Conditions: Primary—BD ED. Sec—ADHD AN Anx Bu Mood.
  Psychotherapy: Fam Group Indiv.
  Est 1960. Private. Nonprofit.

MAY CENTER FOR CHILD DEVELOPMENT

Day — Coed Ages 2-8

Freeport, ME 04032. 95 US Rte 1.
Tel: 207-865-1993. Fax: 207-865-6369.
www.mayinstitute.org   E-mail: information@mayinstitute.org
Denise Gobeil, Dir. **Mia Crewell,** Med Dir.
  Focus: Spec Ed. **Conditions:** Primary—ADD ADHD Asp Au BD ED MR PDD.
  Gen Acad. Gr PS-2. Courses: Lang_Arts.
  Therapy: Lang Occup Phys Speech. **Psychotherapy:** Parent.
  Enr: 28. Day Males 26. Day Females 2. **Staff:** 19 (Full 14, Part 5). Educ 19. Admin 2.
  Private. Nonprofit. **Spons:** May Institute.

The educational program at May—which includes training in play/motor, self-care and social skills—accommodates children with autism ages 2-8. School-based consultations and family support round out the center's services.

MID-COAST SPEECH AND HEARING CENTER

Clinic: All Ages. M-F 8:30-4.

Rockport, ME 04856. c/o Penobscot Bay Medical Ctr, 6 Glen Cove Dr.
Tel: 207-230-6380. Fax: 207-230-6378.
E-mail: hkosmo@nehealth.org
Helen Kosmo, MA, CCC-SLP, Mgr.
  Focus: Rehab. Treatment. **Conditions:** Primary—Ap Apr Asp Au D DS S. Sec—ADD ADHD BI CP Dx LD MR SB.
  Therapy: Hear Lang Speech.
  Staff: 8. Prof 6. Admin 1.
  Rates 2003: Clinic $38-110/ses.
  Est 1977. Private. Nonprofit. **Spons:** Penobscot Bay Medical Center.

Persons with communicative disorders receive outpatient treatment, evaluation and counseling services at Mid-Coast. Fees are determined along a sliding scale.

NEW HORIZONS WILDERNESS PROGRAM FOR YOUNG WOMEN

Res — Females Ages 13-18

Orrington, ME 04474. PO Box 186.
Tel: 207-992-2424. Fax: 207-992-2525.
www.daughtersatrisk.com   E-mail: nhwp@earthlink.net
Jacqueline Danforth, Exec Dir. **Eilean MacKenzie,** Clin Dir. **Audrey Peavey,** Adm.
  Focus: Treatment. **Conditions:** Primary—ADD ADHD Anx BD CD ED LD Mood OCD PTSD SP. Sec—Ap As Asp B BI Bu D Db Dc Dg Dx Ep HIV

MD PDD S TS.
Therapy: Art Dance Movement Phys Play Recreational. **Psychotherapy:**
Fam Group Indiv Parent.
Enr: 90. Res Females 90. **Staff:** 38 (Full 22, Part 16). Educ 3. Admin 6.
Rates 2003: Res $398/day (+$3855/ses).
Est 2000. Private. Inc.

Through a six- to nine-week outdoor experience, New Horizons provides a therapeutic program for young women who typically have difficulties with self-expression, body image and self-esteem. Candidates for enrollment usually lack respect for themselves and others, display low motivation, and struggle with depression, academic performance and relationships. During each session, private tutors work as liaisons between girls and their school systems.

THE SPURWINK SCHOOL

Res and Day — Coed Ages 4-20
Clinic: Ages Birth-20. M-F 8-4.

Portland, ME 04103. 899 Riverside St.
Nearby locations: Randolph.
Tel: 207-871-1200. **TTY:** 207-871-1233. **Fax:** 207-871-1232.
www.spurwink.org   E-mail: info@spurwink.org
Peter M. McPherson, MEd, MSW, Exec Dir. **Jessica Oesterheld,** MD, Med
Dir. **Jim Northrop,** Adm.
Focus: Spec Ed. **Conditions:** Primary—ADD ADHD Au BD CD ED MR
OCD Psy Sz. Sec—Ap Bl D Dx Ep LD ON S SB. **IQ 40 and up.**
Gen Acad. Pre-Voc. Voc. Ungraded. Courses: Read Math Lang_Arts. Man_
Arts & Shop. Shelt_Workshop. On-Job Trng.
Therapy: Hear Lang Milieu Occup Speech. **Psychotherapy:** Fam Group
Indiv Parent.
Enr: 216. **Staff:** 808 (Full 780, Part 28).
Est 1960. Private. Nonprofit.

Spurwink offers year-round residential and day services for children, adolescents and adults who have a developmental disability or autism, or who are functionally limited by an emotional or behavioral disturbance. Programs are community based, with residential locations emphasizing a natural home setting. Day treatment takes place in small classes, where eclectic teaching methods focus on a dynamic understanding of the personality and social development of the students. The usual duration of treatment is two years.

SUMMIT ACHIEVEMENT

Res — Coed Ages 13-17

Stow, ME 04037. 69 Deer Hill Road.
Tel: 207-697-2020. **Fax:** 207-697-2021.
www.summitachievement.com
E-mail: admissions@summitachievement.com
Christopher Mays, Exec Dir. **Adam Tsapis,** Adm.

Focus: Treatment. **Conditions:** Primary—ADD ADHD Anx BD CD ED LD OCD ODD. Sec—Mood PTSD. **IQ 90 and up.**
Col Prep. Gen Acad. Gr 9-12. Courses: Read Math Lang_Arts.
Therapy: Recreational. **Psychotherapy:** Fam Group Indiv Parent.
Enr: 32. Res Males 24. Res Females 8. **Staff:** 35. Prof 21. Educ 3. Admin 4.
Rates 2004: Res $325/day (+$145/ses). State Aid.
Est 1995. Private. Inc.

This adventure-based treatment program has three basic components: therapy, which includes weekly individual sessions, weekly facilitated phone calls between student and family, and daily group counseling; traditional classroom academics three days per week; and wilderness expeditions four days a week.

Students who enroll at Summit have experienced difficulty in their family, school or personal lives. Typical program duration is six to eight weeks.

SWEETSER

Res — Coed Ages 5-20; Day — Coed 3-18
Clinic: All Ages. M-F 9-6; Eves M-Th 6-8.

Saco, ME 04072. 50 Moody St.
Tel: 207-294-4889. Fax: 207-294-4420.
www.sweetser.org   E-mail: info@sweetser.org
Carlton D. Pendleton, MEd, Pres. Jami Ream, Intake.
    Focus: Treatment. **Conditions:** Primary—ADD ADHD BD CD Dx ED LD OCD Psy. Sec—MR.
    Gen Acad. Pre-Voc. Gr K-12. Courses: Read Math Lang_Arts Studio_Art Music. Man_Arts & Shop. On-Job Trng.
    Therapy: Lang Speech. **Psychotherapy:** Fam Group Indiv Parent.
    Enr: 120.
    Est 1870. Private. Nonprofit.

This year-round facility provides residential and educational programs, day treatment, home-based family services, and case management and crisis intervention for children with behavioral health issues and their families. Services address emotional disturbances, mental illnesses, behavioral disorders and learning disabilities. Sweetser's school program features an average class size of eight students. The organization operates therapeutic group homes in many Maine communities, and outpatient clinic sites are located along the Maine coast.

TRI COUNTY MENTAL HEALTH SERVICES

Res — Coed Ages Birth-21
Clinic: Ages Birth-21. M-S 8-6; Eves by Appt.

Auburn, ME.
Contact: PO Box 2008, Lewiston, ME 04240.
Tel: 207-784-4110. TTY: 207-783-4678. Fax: 207-783-4679.
http://home.gwi.net/~tcmhs
G. Dean Crocker, MSW, Mgr.

Focus: Treatment. **Conditions:** Primary—CD ED OCD Psy Sz. Sec—ADD
ADHD Ap B BD Bl D Dx LD MR ON S.
Therapy: Chemo. **Psychotherapy:** Fam Group Indiv Parent.
Staff: 20 (Full 19, Part 1).
Est 1951. Private. Nonprofit.

Multidisciplinary team treatment is provided at Tri County for children with mental
health treatment needs. Individual, group and family therapies are available, as is home
behavior management. The average duration of treatment is three months to two years.

UCP OF MAINE

Res — Coed Ages 7-12; Day — Coed Birth-20
Clinic: Ages Birth-20. M-F 7:30-5:30.

Bangor, ME 04401. 700 Mt Hope Ave, Ste 320.
Tel: 207-941-2952. Fax: 207-941-2955.
E-mail: office@ucpofmaine.org
Bobbi Jo Yeager, BS, Exec Dir.
Focus: Spec Ed. Rehab. Trng. Treatment. **Conditions:** Primary—ADD
ADHD Anx Asp Au B BD CD D Dc Dg DS Dx ED LD Mood MR Nf OCD
ODD ON PTSD PW SB SP. Sec—Ap Apr Ar As Bl Bu C CP Db Ep IP
MD MS Psy S TB TS. **IQ 30 and up.**
Gen Acad. Gr PS.
Therapy: Hear Milieu Occup Percepual-Motor Phys. **Psychotherapy:** Fam
Group Indiv.
Enr: 400. **Staff:** 100. Admin 9.
Est 1959. Private. Nonprofit.

The center provides services for children with developmental disabilities and delays.
An infant development program includes home visits, preschool classes, therapy groups
and respite daycare. Among services to parents are peer counseling by other parents of
children with special needs, individual counseling with social workers, and parent meetings. A monthly medical clinic offers specialized care.

UNIVERSITY OF MAINE
CONLEY SPEECH AND HEARING CENTER

Clinic: All Ages.

Orono, ME 04469. 336 Dunn Hall.
Tel: 207-581-2006.
www.umaine.edu/comscidis/clinic/conley.htm
Susan K. Riley, MS, Dir.
Conditions: Primary—S.
Therapy: Lang Speech.
State.

THE WARREN CENTER FOR COMMUNICATION & LEARNING

Clinic: Ages Birth-21. M-F 8-4:30.

Bangor, ME 04401. 175 Union St.
Tel: 207-941-2850. TTY: 207-941-2833. Fax: 207-941-2852.
www.warrencenter.org   E-mail: info@warrencenter.org
Mary E. Poulin, BA, Admin Dir. **MaryBeth B. Richards,** BS, MS, CCC-SLP,
Prgm Dir.
Focus: Rehab. Treatment. **Conditions:** Primary—Ap Apr D S. Sec—Asp Au
CP MS ON PDD.
Therapy: Hear Lang Speech.
Staff: 16 (Full 13, Part 3). Prof 10. Admin 6.
Est 1960. Private. Nonprofit.

Warren Center offers detection, evaluation and rehabilitation of speech and hearing problems. Scheduled according to individual needs, therapy sessions are supplemented by counseling. Parental counseling and training are also part of the program, as is a comprehensive program for hearing-impaired children under age 5. Fees are determined along a sliding scale.

MARYLAND

ANNE ARUNDEL COUNTY MENTAL HEALTH CLINIC ADOLESCENT AND FAMILY SERVICES

Clinic: Ages 5-18. M-F 8-5, S by Appt; Eves M-W 5-8:30.

Glen Burnie, MD 21061. 407 S Crain Hwy, Ste.
Tel: 410-222-6785. Fax: 410-222-6888.
www.aahealth.org
Roger Messick, LCSW, Supv.
   Conditions: Primary—BD CD ED OCD Psy Sz.
   Therapy: Chemo. **Psychotherapy:** Fam Group Indiv.
   Staff: 68.
   County.

The clinic provides evaluation and treatment services for psychotic, neurotic and emotionally disturbed children and adolescents. Medication intervention and individual, family and group therapy are among the clinic's offerings. Residents of Anne Arundel County only are accepted.

THE ARC OF MONTGOMERY COUNTY

Day — Coed All Ages

Rockville, MD 20852. 11600 Nebel St.
Tel: 301-984-5777. Fax: 301-816-2429.
www.arcmontmd.org   E-mail: info@arcmontmd.org
Fred Baughman, MEd, Exec Dir.
   Conditions: Primary—MR. Sec—Au BD LD PDD S.
   Therapy: Occup Phys Speech.
   Staff: Prof 19.
   Est 1958. Private. Nonprofit. **Spons:** The Arc.

ASSOCIATED CATHOLIC CHARITIES

Res — Coed Ages Birth-14; Day — Coed Birth-4

Baltimore, MD 21201. 320 Cathedral St.
Tel: 410-547-5490.
www.catholiccharities-md.org   E-mail: info@catholiccharities-md.org
Harold A. Smith, BS, MSW, Exec Dir.
   Conditions: Primary—BD ED.
   Gen Acad. Gr PS. Courses: Read Math Lang_Arts.
   Therapy: Occup Phys Recreational Speech. **Psychotherapy:** Fam Group
    Indiv.
   Est 1923. Private. Nonprofit.

THE BENEDICTINE SCHOOL

Res and Day — Coed Ages 5-21

Ridgely, MD 21660. 14299 Benedictine Ln.
Tel: 410-634-2112. Fax: 410-634-2640.
www.benschool.com   E-mail: benadmis@juno.com
Sr. Jeanette Murray, OSB, MA, Dir. **Nancy McCloy**, MA, Educ Dir. **Cindy Thornton**, Adm.

Focus: Spec Ed. **Conditions:** Primary—DS MR. Sec—ADD ADHD Ap As Asp Au BD CP ED Ep LD OCD ON PDD S. **IQ 50-79.**

Pre-Voc. Voc. Ungraded. Courses: Read Math Lang_Arts Adaptive_Phys_ Ed. Shelt_Workshop. On-Job Trng.

Therapy: Hear Lang Occup Phys Speech. **Psychotherapy:** Fam Group Indiv.

Enr: 102.

Est 1959. Private. Nonprofit. Roman Catholic.

Located on a 600-acre campus in Caroline County, Benedictine serves children and young adults with mild to severe retarded, autism or multiple handicaps. The school conducts a ten-month program, as well as an extended school year. Benedictine's approach is to create a supportive therapeutic environment that assists the individual with reaching his or her potential. Ultimately, the program seeks to either prepare the client for gainful employment upon graduation or secure the person's transfer to an appropriate, less restrictive educational or vocational environment; to help the client become a contributing member of his or her family unit and community; and to encourage the individual to participate in community leisure activities.

Benedictine employs educational, social and vocational tasks to achieve its program goals. Vocational training includes work in the following areas: laundry, greenhouse, indoor and outdoor maintenance, food service, clerical training, service station, car wash, screen printing, contract work, print shop and industrial training. Academics range from functional skills instruction to GED preparation.

In addition to its school program, the facility provides many related services for its target population. Among Benedictine's offerings are residential, psychological, social work, communication and medical services. In addition, clients may participate in counseling, vocational and prevocational services, adaptive physical education and aquatics, leisure education training, psychiatric services and transitional services.

CHELSEA SCHOOL

Day — Coed Ages 10-18

Silver Spring, MD 20910. 711 Pershing Dr.
Tel: 301-585-1430. Fax: 301-585-5865.
www.chelseaschool.edu   E-mail: information@chelseaschool.edu
Timmothy O'Connor, MS, Head. **Dale Frengel**, Adm.

Focus: Spec Ed. **Conditions:** Primary—Dx LD. Sec—ADHD Dc Dg S. **IQ 90 and up.**

Col Prep. Gen Acad. Gr 5-12. Courses: Read Math Lang_Arts Span Sci Soc_Stud Computers Studio_Art Music.

Therapy: Lang Occup Speech.

Enr: 115. Day Males 80. Day Females 35. **Staff:** 40 (Full 36, Part 4). Educ 24. Admin 7.
Rates 2003: Day $31,018/sch yr. $90-102 (Therapy)/hr. Schol avail. State Aid.
Summer Prgm: Day. Educ. Rec. Ther. Counseling. Day Rate $1675-2200. 5 wks.
Est 1976. Private. Nonprofit.

This school provides a full middle through high school curriculum for students with learning disabilities who possess average to above-average intelligence. The program supports students in a highly structured environment that teaches academic and social skills and further develops self-confidence. Small classes and tutorials assist in meeting these goals. Diagnostic assessments and counseling services are available.

For older high schoolers, Chelsea offers a careers program that provides information and counseling on career choices. The program includes some on-the-job training in the form of internships and work-study opportunities.

THE CHILDREN'S GUILD

Res — Males Ages 12-18; Day — Coed 3-21

Baltimore, MD 21234. 6802 McClean Blvd.
Tel: 410-444-3800. Fax: 410-426-0612.
www.childrensguild.org
Andrew L. Ross, PhD, Pres.
   Conditions: Primary—ED. Sec—BD LD S.
   Gen Acad. Gr PS-12. Courses: Read Math Lang_Arts.
   Therapy: Lang Occup Speech. **Psychotherapy:** Fam Group Indiv.
   Est 1953. Private. Nonprofit. **Spons:** United Way.

CHIMES SCHOOL

Day — Coed Ages 6-21

Baltimore, MD 21236. 3515 Taylor Ave.
Tel: 410-427-0920. Fax: 410-427-0913.
www.chimes.org   E-mail: dashmore@chimes.org
Doris A. Ashmore, MSEd, Prin. **Maureen McGrellis,** Adm.
   Focus: Spec Ed. **Conditions:** Primary—Au DS MR. Sec—ADD ADHD Ap BD BI CD CP ED Ep Mood OCD ODD ON Psy Sz. **IQ 25-70.**
   Gen Acad. Pre-Voc. Voc. Ungraded. Courses: Read Math Lang_Arts. Shelt_Workshop. On-Job Trng.
   Therapy: Lang Speech. **Psychotherapy:** Group Indiv.
   Enr: 69. Day Males 47. Day Females 22. **Staff:** 44 (Full 43, Part 1). Educ 28. Admin 5.
   Rates 2004: Day $30,000/sch yr.
   Est 1947. Private. Nonprofit.

Chimes offers a comprehensive educational program for children and young adults with mental retardation or developmental disabilities. The curriculum provides each child with the opportunity to develop to his or her potential in the areas of basic academic skills and prevocational training. Programming comprises recreational activities and training in speech and language development, practical living skills and sequential motor development.

The school also provides social work and counseling services for both students and their families in individual and group settings.

EDGEMEADE

Res and Day — Males Ages 12-18

Upper Marlboro, MD 20772. 13400 Edgemeade Rd.
Tel: 301-888-1333. Fax: 301-888-1343.
James Filipczak, PhD, Exec Dir. **Donald Taylor,** MD, Med Dir. **Cindy J. Spiller,** Adm.
   Focus: Spec Ed. Treatment. **Conditions:** Primary—ED. Sec—LD MR S. **IQ 70 and up.**
   Col Prep. Gen Acad. Pre-Voc. Gr 7-12. Courses: Read Math Lang_Arts Studio_Art Music. Man_Arts & Shop.
   Therapy: Lang Speech. **Psychotherapy:** Fam Group Indiv.
   Enr: 75.
   Est 1959. Private. Nonprofit. **Spons:** Maryland Center for Youth and Family Development.

Edgemeade is designed to serve the severely emotionally disturbed child or adolescent in need of structured therapeutic programs. Day and residential programs include psychotherapy and prevocational and special education allowing students to earn a high school diploma. The program centers around a therapeutic community model, allowing the integration of individual and specific treatment and educational interventions. A substance abuse counseling and education program for youngsters who are drug experimenters, users or dealers is also available. The usual length of treatment averages 12 to 18 months.

THE FORBUSH SCHOOL

Day — Coed Ages 3-21

Towson, MD 21285. 6501 N Charles St, PO Box 6815.
Tel: 410-938-4400. Fax: 410-938-4421.
E-mail: jtruscello@sheppardpratt.org
James J. Truscello, MA, Educ Dir. **Peter Kahn,** MD, Med Dir. **Thomas F. Monahan,** Adm.
   Focus: Spec Ed. **Conditions:** Primary—Asp Au BD CD ED OCD Psy. Sec—ADD ADHD Dx LD ODD.
   Col Prep. Gen Acad. Pre-Voc. Voc. Gr PS-12. Courses: Read Math Lang_ Arts Sci Computers. Man_Arts & Shop. On-Job Trng.
   Therapy: Chemo Lang Occup Speech. **Psychotherapy:** Fam Group Indiv

Parent.
Enr: 210. Day Males 110. Day Females 100. **Staff:** 195 (Full 180, Part 15).
Prof 23.
Rates 2004: Day $47,500/sch yr. State Aid.
Est 1968. Private. Nonprofit. **Spons:** Sheppard Pratt Health System.

A therapeutic educational program with psychotherapy for severely emotionally disturbed and (for an additional fee) autistic children is provided at Forbush, part of the Sheppard Pratt Health System. The school provides individual psychotherapy and family counseling, in addition to a broad curriculum that includes courses in the areas of studio art, industrial arts, technology and computers. Peer mediation is integral to the program. The usual length of stay at the school is two years.

FRANCIS X. GALLAGHER SERVICES

Res — Coed Ages 5-19

Timonium, MD 21093. 2520 Pot Spring Rd.
Tel: 410-252-4005. Fax: 410-560-3495.
Conditions: Primary—MR.
Private.

FREDERICK READING CENTER

Clinic: Ages 5 and up. Eves M-Th 5-9.

Frederick, MD 21704. 2785 Lynn St.
Tel: 301-662-1051.
E-mail: tutoring@starpower.net
Lavonne Steffy-Radonovich, MSEd, Pres.
Focus: Spec Ed. **Conditions:** Primary—ADD Dg Dx LD. Sec—ADHD Au Dc MR SP. **IQ 60 and up.**
Psychotherapy: Fam Group Parent.
Staff: 3.
Rates 2003: Sliding-Scale Rate $10-40/ses. Schol 2.
Est 1988. Private. Nonprofit.

FRC provides students with different learning styles assistance in overcoming their learning difficulties. Services include diagnostic assessments and tutoring, educational consulting and advocacy.

THE FROST SCHOOL

Day — Coed Ages 6-21

Rockville, MD 20853. 4915 Aspen Hill Rd.
Tel: 301-933-3451. Fax: 301-933-3330.
www.frostcenter.com   E-mail: chobbes@frostcenter.com

Sean McLaughlin, MA, Dir. **Carol Hobbes,** Adm.
  Focus: Spec Ed. **Conditions:** Primary—BD CD ED Mood OCD ODD Psy
    PTSD SP Sz TS. Sec—ADD ADHD AN Asp Au Dx LD.
  Col Prep. Gen Acad. Voc. Gr 1-12. Courses: Read Math Computers Soc_
    Stud. On-Job Trng.
  Therapy: Lang Occup Speech. **Psychotherapy:** Fam Group.
  Enr: 61. **Staff:** 40 (Full 38, Part 2).
  Rates 2001: Day $36,000/yr. Sliding-Scale Rate $20-110/ses. State Aid.
  Est 1976. Private. Nonprofit. **Spons:** Family Foundation.

The Frost School offers education and counseling for severely emotionally disturbed youngsters. Traditional academic courses such as English, math, social studies and science are integrated with daily counseling sessions. Parents and siblings participate in family and group sessions once a week.

The Frost Counseling Center, an affiliate of the school, offers outpatient psychological services, including therapy and evaluation, for children and their families.

GATEWAY SCHOOL

Day — Coed Ages 3-12

Baltimore, MD 21215. 5900 Metro Dr.
Tel: 410-318-6780. Fax: 410-318-6759.
www.hasa.org   E-mail: gateway@hasa.org
Jill Berie, MS, Dir.
  Focus: Spec Ed. **Conditions:** Primary—Ap Apr Asp Au D ON PDD S.
    Sec—ADD ADHD Anx As BD BI C CP Db Dc Dg Dx ED Ep IP LD MD
    Mood MR MS Nf OCD PTSD PW SB SP TB TS. **IQ 70-120.**
  Gen Acad. Ungraded. Courses: Read Math Lang_Arts Sci Soc_Stud.
  Therapy: Lang Occup Phys Play Speech. **Psychotherapy:** Indiv Parent.
  Enr: 47. Day Males 39. Day Females 8. **Staff:** 35 (Full 30, Part 5). Prof 14.
    Educ 9. Admin 5.
  Rates 2004: Day $42,660/sch yr. Clinic $80-90/ses. Schol 3 ($62,000).
    State Aid.
  Summer Prgm: Day. Educ. Day Rate $94/day. 3 wks.
  Est 1957. Private. Nonprofit. **Spons:** Hearing and Speech Agency.

Gateway offers special education for children with moderate to severe speech, language or communication disabilities. The school provides small, self-contained classes and operates a 10-month program, plus an optional extended program during July.

GOOD SHEPHERD CENTER

Res and Day — Females Ages 13-18

Halethorpe, MD 21227. 4100 Maple Ave.
Tel: 410-247-2770. Fax: 410-247-3242.
www.goodshepherdcenter.org   E-mail: info@goodshepherdcenter.org
  Conditions: Primary—ED. Sec—BD Dx LD.
  Gen Acad. Pre-Voc. Gr 8-12. Courses: Read Math Lang_Arts.

Psychotherapy: Fam Indiv.
Staff: Prof 76.
Est 1864. Private. Nonprofit. **Spons:** Sisters of Good Shepherd.

HANNAH MORE SCHOOL

Day — Coed Ages 11-21

Reisterstown, MD 21136. 12039 Reisterstown Rd.
Tel: 410-526-5000. Fax: 410-526-7631.
www.hannahmore.org   E-mail: hms-information@hannahmore.org
Mark Waldman, BS, MEd, Pres. **Paul I. Kaplan,** BA, MSW, JD, Clin Dir. **Carolyn Martin,** Adm.
  Focus: Spec Ed. **Conditions:** Primary—ADD ADHD AN Anx Asp Au BD Bu CD Dg Dx ED LD Mood OCD PDD Psy PW SP Sz TS. Sec—Ap B D Db HIV.
  Gen Acad. Pre-Voc. Voc. Gr 6-12. Courses: Sci Computers Soc_Stud Studio_Art Music Life_Skills. Man_Arts & Shop. On-Job Trng.
  Therapy: Chemo Lang Occup Speech. **Psychotherapy:** Fam Group Indiv.
  Enr: 155. Day Males 90. Day Females 65. **Staff:** 130 (Full 105, Part 25).
  Rates 2003: Day $48,000/sch yr. State Aid.
  Est 1977. Private. Nonprofit.

The school conducts a psycho-educational program consisting of academics, vocational education, counseling programs and a behavioral management system. The program provides each student with individual goals and objectives that are regularly monitored and revised to meet the child's emotional and educational needs.

Hannah More conducts a comprehensive program for middle and high school students diagnosed with pervasive developmental disorder. During the middle school years, each self-contained classroom features a teacher and a teacher assistant. Pragmatic language, leisure and life skills supplement standard course work. The high school program comprises two models: The first is similar to the middle school program, as it continues the use of self-contained classrooms, while the second approach serves students identified with Asperger's syndrome or with pervasive developmental disorder who have functioned academically close to grade level. Students in the latter section participate in a departmentalized curriculum. Activities outside the classroom such as recreational opportunities and various types of therapy round out the program.

The school also provides special education at the middle and high school levels for students with such emotional disabilities as depression, schizophrenia, anxiety, and mood, behavior and personality disorders. Many pupils with emotional disabilities have also been diagnosed with chronic mental illnesses. While students may enroll for anywhere from six months to six years, the average length of stay is three years.

In addition to its traditional high school program, Hannah More also offers a vocational high school program with classes in horticulture, culinary arts, communications, building trades and automotive repair.

THE HARBOUR SCHOOL

Day — Coed Ages 6-21

Annapolis, MD 21401. 1277 Green Holly Dr.
  Nearby locations: Owings Mills.
  Tel: 410-974-4248. Fax: 410-757-3722.
  www.harbourschool.org   E-mail: mail@harbourschool.org
Linda J. Jacobs, EdD, Exec Dir. **Yvonne Callaway,** Adm.
  Focus: Spec Ed. **Conditions:** Primary—ADD ADHD Ap Asp Au BI Dx LD
    PTSD PW S SP TS. Sec—ED Mood OCD. **IQ 70 and up.**
  Col Prep. Gen Acad. Pre-Voc. Voc. Gr 1-12. Courses: Read Math Lang_
    Arts. Man_Arts & Shop. On-Job Trng.
  Therapy: Art Dance Lang Occup Phys Recreational Speech. **Psychother-**
    apy: Fam Group Indiv Parent.
  Enr: 257. Day Males 170. Day Females 87. **Staff:** 164 (Full 155, Part 9).
    Educ 39. Admin 7.
  Rates 2003: Day $28,700/sch yr (+$200). $80 (Occup Therapy)/wk. State
    Aid.
  Est 1982. Private. Nonprofit.

  Children who have been diagnosed with learning problems receive personalized instruction in reading, math and language arts at this school. Other academic subjects are taught in a group setting. The program emphasizes social skill development at all grade levels. High school programming seeks to ease the student's transition into college or a career, and graduates earn a high school diploma. Counseling, speech and psychological services, and occupational therapy are available, and the usual length of treatment is three years.

  Harbour also operates a branch at 11251 Dolfield Blvd., Owings Mills 21117.

THE IVYMOUNT SCHOOL

Day — Coed Ages 4-21

Rockville, MD 20854. 11614 Seven Locks Rd.
Tel: 301-469-0223. Fax: 301-469-0778.
www.ivymount.org
Janet Wintrol, MEd, Dir.
  Focus: Spec Ed. **Conditions:** Primary—Au MR. Sec—Ap CP LD OH.
  Pre-Voc. Voc. Ungraded. Courses: Read Math Lang_Arts. On-Job Trng.
  Therapy: Hear Lang Music Occup Phys Speech. **Psychotherapy:** Fam
    Group.
  Enr: 200. Day Males 130. Day Females 70. **Staff:** 141 (Full 129, Part 12).
  Est 1961. Private. Nonprofit.

  Ivymount provides therapeutic education for children with developmental disabilities. Through early diagnosis and individualization of programs geared to the child's learning style, the school believes that the student will grow toward social and emotional health, developing to his or her intellectual potential. The areas emphasized are sensorimotor functioning, visual/auditory perception and processing, language development, academic skills, functional living skills, social behavior and emotional development.

THE JEMICY SCHOOL

Day — Coed Ages 6-14

Owings Mills, MD 21117. 11 Celadon Rd.
Tel: 410-653-2700. Fax: 410-653-1972.
www.jemicyschool.org   E-mail: info@jemicyschool.org
Ben Shifrin, Head. **Sarah Morse,** Adm.
  Focus: Spec Ed. **Conditions:** Primary—Dg Dx LD. Sec—ADD ADHD Dc.
    IQ 100 and up.
  Col Prep. Gr 1-8. Courses: Read Math Lang_Arts Sci Environ_Sci Soc_
    Stud Computers Studio_Art Music Dance Drama Woodworking.
  Therapy: Speech.
  Enr: 156. Day Males 92. Day Females 64. **Staff:** 68 (Full 63, Part 5). Admin
    8.
  Rates 2003: Day $22,700/sch yr. Schol 20 ($245,000).
  Summer Prgm: Day. Educ. Rec. 6 wks.
  Est 1973. Private. Nonprofit.

Jemicy works with above-average to gifted students with dyslexia and language-based learning differences. Employing a variety of proven research-based, multisensory teaching techniques, faculty work with students in small groups and individually as needed. A strong arts and athletic program complement the core curriculum.

JEWISH FAMILY SERVICES

Clinic: All Ages. M-F 8:30-5; Eves M W Th 5-9.

Baltimore, MD 21215. 5750 Park Heights Ave.
  Nearby locations: Columbia; Owings Mills.
Tel: 410-466-9200. Fax: 410-664-0551.
www.jfs.org   E-mail: jfs@jfs.org
Barbara Gradet, MSW, LCSW, CEO.
  Focus: Treatment. **Conditions:** Primary—ADD ADHD BD CD ED OCD Psy
    Sz. Sec—MR.
  Therapy: Speech. **Psychotherapy:** Fam Group Indiv Parent.
  Staff: 80.
  Est 1856. Private. Nonprofit. Jewish. **Spons:** Associated Jewish Community
    Federation of Baltimore.

This multiservice agency assists families in the community of Greater Baltimore with outpatient treatment and counseling. Individual, family and marital therapies are offered, with particular attention given to the specific problems that arise at different life stages. Supportive services include foster care, appropriate referrals and various workshops in family life education. Fees vary according to income.

JFS maintains district offices in Owings Mills and Columbia.

JEWISH SOCIAL SERVICE AGENCY

Clinic: All Ages. M-F 9-5; Eves M-Th 5-9.

Rockville, MD 20852. 6123 Montrose Rd.
  Nearby locations: Gaithersburg; Washington, DC; Fairfax, VA.
Tel: 301-881-3700. TTY: 301-984-5662. Fax: 301-770-0901.
www.jssa.org   E-mail: info@jssa.org
Joan de Pontet, LCSW-C, Exec Dir. **Lisa Fribush,** Intake.
  Focus: Treatment. **Conditions:** Primary—ADD ADHD D ED OCD. **IQ 85 and up.**
  Therapy: Speech. **Psychotherapy:** Fam Group Indiv.
  Est 1893. Private. Nonprofit.

Residents of the Metropolitan Washington area with physical, developmental or learning disabilities are offered assisted referrals, individual counseling, specialized counseling for the deaf, and support groups for family members. The agency determines its fees along a sliding scale.

LAUREL HALL SCHOOL

Day — Coed Ages 6-21

Hagerstown, MD 21742. 13218 Brook Lane Dr, PO Box 1945.
Tel: 301-733-0330. Fax: 301-733-4038.
www.brooklane.org/psspecia.html
Catherine Byers, Dir.
  Focus: Spec Ed. **Conditions:** Primary—ADD ADHD AN Anx Asp BD Bu ED Mood OCD Psy PTSD SP Sz TS. Sec—As Dc Dg Dx Ep MR.
  Gen Acad. Gr 1-12. Courses: Read Math Lang_Arts.
  Therapy: Art Speech. **Psychotherapy:** Fam Group Indiv Parent Substance_Abuse.
  Enr: 80. **Staff:** 58 (Full 50, Part 8). Educ 11. Admin 3.
  Rates 2004: Day $137/day.
  Summer Prgm: Day. Educ. Ther. Day Rate $137/day. 6 wks.
  Est 1945. Private. Nonprofit. Mennonite. **Spons:** Brook Lane Health Services.

Lauren Hall, which is part of Brook Lane Health Services, includes among its offerings inpatient and partial hospitalization services. The school provides special education for individuals diagnosed as emotionally disturbed who require a highly structured and individualized setting, in addition to psychiatric support services. All boys and girls receive group therapy and individual therapy. Additionally, students may receive substance abuse counseling, art therapy or family therapy. Psychological services and medical management are provided as needed.

LINWOOD CENTER

Res and Day — Coed Ages 7-21
Clinic: Ages 7-21. M-Su 9-5; Eves M-Su 5-11.

Ellicott City, MD 21043. 3421 Martha Bush Dr.
Tel: 410-465-1352. Fax: 410-461-1161.
www.linwoodcenter.org   E-mail: admin@linwoodcenter.org
William Moss, Exec Dir. **Scott Hagaman,** MD, Med Dir. **Karen Spence,** Adm.
   Focus: Spec Ed. **Conditions:** Primary—Asp Au PDD.
   Voc. Ungraded. Courses: Read Math Lang_Arts. Man_Arts & Shop.
   Therapy: Art Lang Occup Recreational Speech. **Psychotherapy:** Indiv.
   Enr: 48. Res Males 15. Res Females 2. Day Males 29. Day Females 2.
      Staff: 60 (Full 58, Part 2). Educ 20. Admin 4.
   Rates 2004: Res $107,000/yr. Day $35,000/yr. Clinic $95/ses. State Aid.
   Est 1955. Private. Inc.

Linwood provides full-day and residential special education and related services for students with autism.

LOYOLA COLLEGE
MCMANUS-MOAG SPEECH AND HEARING CENTER

Clinic: Ages 10mos and up. T-F 9-5.

Baltimore, MD 21212. 5911 York Rd, Ste 100.
Tel: 410-617-1200. Fax: 410-617-5022.
www.loyola.edu/Clinics/Margaret.html
Janet Simon-Schreck, MS, Dir.
   Conditions: Primary—Ap S.
   Therapy: Hear Lang Speech.
   Est 1962. Private. Nonprofit.

THE MARYLAND SCHOOL FOR THE BLIND

Res — Coed Ages 7-21; Day — Coed Birth-21
Clinic: All Ages. M-F by Appt.

Baltimore, MD 21236. 3501 Taylor Ave.
Tel: 410-444-5000. TTY: 410-319-5703. Fax: 410-319-5719.
www.mdschblind.org   E-mail: info@mdschblind.org
Elaine Sveen, EdS, Pres. **Debbie Badawi,** MD, Med Dir. **Ruth Ann Hynson,** Adm.
   Focus: Spec Ed. **Conditions:** Primary—B. Sec—ADD ADHD Ap Apr As Asp Au Bl CP D Ep LD MD MR MS Nf ON PDD S. **IQ 10 and up.**
   Gen Acad. Pre-Voc. Voc. Gr PS-PG. Courses: Read Math Lang_Arts. Man_Arts & Shop. On-Job Trng.
   Therapy: Hear Lang Music Occup Phys Recreational Speech. **Psychotherapy:** Fam Group Indiv Parent.

Enr: 184. Res Males 71. Res Females 56. Day Males 31. Day Females 26.
 Staff: 368 (Full 346, Part 22). Prof 97. Educ 56. Admin 9.
Rates 2004: No Fee.
Summer Prgm: Res & Day. Educ. Ther. 4 wks.
Est 1853. Private. Nonprofit.

Educational opportunities for children who are blind or visually impaired and have additional impairments are available through MSB, which offers a curriculum parallel-ing that of public schools. Students who are incapable of fulfilling academic require-ments for graduation enter an independence or developmental skills program.

Maryland residents attend free of charge, while out-of-state pupils pay tuition charges.

MARYLAND SCHOOL FOR THE DEAF

Res — Coed Ages 4-21; Day — Coed Birth-21

Frederick, MD 21705. 101 Clarke Pl, PO Box 250.
 Nearby locations: Columbia.
Tel: 301-360-2000. TTY: 301-360-2001. Fax: 301-360-1400.
www.msd.edu   E-mail: msdsupt@msd.edu
James Tucker, Supt. **Kate Baker,** Adm.
 Focus: Spec Ed. **Conditions:** Primary—D. Sec—ADD ADHD OH. **IQ 60
  and up.**
 Col Prep. Gen Acad. Pre-Voc. Voc. Gr PS-12. Courses: Read Math Lang_
  Arts Computers Studio_Art. Man_Arts & Shop. On-Job Trng.
 Therapy: Dance Hear Lang Occup Phys Speech. **Psychotherapy:** Fam
  Group Indiv.
 Enr: 512. **Staff:** 456.
 Rates 2004: No Fee.
 Est 1868. State.

MSD provides education for severely and profoundly deaf children using a total com-munication concept of language development that involves manual, auditory and oral approaches. The educational program includes general studies, with college preparation and a prevocational program offering work-study. A preschool and parental counseling program helps teach parents and children to communicate, through teacher/counselors, in the home. Students usually enroll from preschool through high school. Multi-handi-capped deaf children may not attend the school. The school is free to Maryland resi-dents, while out-of-state children may attend by paying tuition.

Another campus for pupils in grades K-8 operates in Columbia (P.O. Box 894, 21044).

MCKUSICK-NATHANS INSTITUTE OF GENETIC MEDICINE
GREENBERG CENTER FOR SKELETAL DYSPLASIAS

Clinic: All Ages. T 8:30-5 by Appt.

Baltimore, MD 21287. 600 N Wolfe St, Blalock 1008.
Tel: 410-614-0977. Fax: 410-614-2522.

www.hopkinsmedicine.org/greenbergcenter   E-mail: deedee@jhmi.org
Victor McKusick, MD, Dir. **Julie Hoover-Fong,** MD, Med Dir.
   Focus: Treatment. **Conditions:** Primary—B D Db DS LD MR ON PDD S.
   Staff: 15. Prof 12. Admin 3.
   Private. **Spons:** John Hopkins Hospital.

The Greenberg Center for Skeletal Dysplasias is a centralized genetics clinic that utilizes a multidisciplinary approach to the diagnosis and treatment of individuals with skeletal dysplasias and their families. Staff at the center educate parents and families about the patient's condition.

MT. WASHINGTON PEDIATRIC HOSPITAL

Day — Coed Ages Birth-18
Clinic: Ages Birth-18. M-F 8:30-5.

Baltimore, MD 21209. 1708 W Rogers Ave.
Tel: 410-578-8600. Fax: 410-466-1715.
www.mwph.org
Sheldon J. Stein, MBA, Pres.
   Focus: Rehab. Treatment. **Conditions:** Primary—ADD ADHD Ap As BI CD
      CP Dx Ep IP LD MD MS ON S SB TB. Sec—B C D ED MR.
   Therapy: Hear Lang Occup Phys Speech. **Psychotherapy:** Fam Group
      Indiv Parent.
   Staff: 199.
   Est 1922. Private. Nonprofit.

This pediatric hospital offers a continuum of comprehensive specialty and rehabilitative services to medically fragile children whose needs surpass short-term care. Seven distinct programs meet a full range of health care needs. A pediatric pulmonary rehabilitation program serves individuals with chronic lung diseases such as asthma and also assists ventilator-dependent children. Physical rehabilitation is available for children with arthritis, spinal cord injuries, burns, orthopedic conditions, traumatic brain injuries and neuromuscular diseases. Rehabilitation of chronic illness consists of short-term multidisciplinary intervention for youths with such medical conditions as diabetes, failure to thrive, renal diseases, gastrointestinal dysfunctions and other chronic diseases. Children who have sustained traumatic brain injuries or who have severe central nervous system birth defects that are unlikely to improve significantly may take part in the continuing care program.

Other programs provide short-term respite care for children with physical disabilities; short-term home-based nursing and rehabilitative services for those with acute and chronic illnesses and physical disabilities; and outpatient services that include comprehensive evaluations, rehabilitative services, and psychological and neuropsychological assessments and treatment.

No patients are refused services due to inability to pay. A branch of Mt. Washington operates at 3001 Hospital Dr., Cheverly 20785.

NEW HEIGHTS LEARNING AND TRAINING CENTER

Clinic: Ages 6 and up. M-F 8-6:30.

Towson, MD 21204. 305 W Chesapeake Ave, Ste 208.
Tel: 410-821-8808. Fax: 410-821-5880.
www.newheights.qpg.com   E-mail: nhltc@aol.com
M. Therese Kelly, BA, MLA, Dir.
    Focus: Trng. Treatment. **Conditions:** Primary—ADD ADHD Asp Au Dc Dg
    Dx LD. **IQ 100 and up.**
    Gen Acad. Ungraded. Courses: Read Math Lang_Arts.
    Therapy: Lang Percepual-Motor Speech.
    Staff: 6.
    Rates 2004: Clinic $70/hr.
    Summer Prgm: Day. Educ.
    Est 1991. Private. Inc.

New Heights provides diagnostic, intervention and remedial services for children and adults. After determining a plan, NHLTC works one-on-one with its students. Speech and language therapies are available, and the center utilizes the following methods: Fast ForWord, Lindamood-Bell Learning Process4s, Orton-Gillingham and Phono-Graphix.

NORBEL SCHOOL

Day — Coed Ages 4-18

Elkridge, MD 21075. 6135 Old Washington Rd.
Tel: 410-796-6700. Fax: 410-796-7661.
www.norbelschool.org   E-mail: info@norbelschool.org
Eric Isselhardt, PhD, Head. **Frank Pugliese,** Adm.
    Focus: Spec Ed. **Conditions:** Primary—ADD ADHD Dc Dg Dx LD. **IQ 90**
    and up.
    Col Prep. Gen Acad. Voc. Gr PS-12. Courses: Read Math Lang_Arts.
    Therapy: Phys Speech.
    Enr: 92. Day Males 83. Day Females 9. **Staff:** 43 (Full 39, Part 4). Educ 33.
    Admin 10.
    Rates 2003: Day $17,500-19,000/sch yr.
    Est 1980. Private. Nonprofit.

Norbel is a private school for boys and girls who have one or more of the following: specific learning disabilities, language-based disabilities and attentional disorders. Students must possess average or above-average intelligence. Instruction utilizes multisensory, cross-curricular, experiential methodologies that account for the pupil's strengths and needs.

THE PATHWAYS SCHOOLS

Day — Coed Ages 9-21

Silver Spring, MD 20902. 1106 University Blvd W.

Tel: 301-649-0778. Fax: 301-649-2598.
www.pathwayschools.org   E-mail: info@pathwayschools.org
Rev. Sharon F. Peters, MDiv, Exec Dir. **Helen C. Williams,** MA, EdD, Educ Dir.
  Dottie Slavcoff, Adm.
  Focus: Spec Ed. **Conditions:** Primary—ED. Sec—LD. **IQ 65 and up.**
  Gen Acad. Pre-Voc. Gr 4-12. Courses: Read Math Lang_Arts Sci Soc_
    Stud. On-Job Trng.
  Therapy: Lang Occup Recreational Speech. **Psychotherapy:** Fam Group
    Indiv.
  Enr: 150. Day Males 102. Day Females 48. **Staff:** 110 (Full 98, Part 12).
  Est 1982. Private. Nonprofit.

Pathways' seven schools utilize a holistic approach to the remediation of emotional deficits. The facility comprises two middle schools that serve students ages 9-14 as well as five secondary programs: one focusing on general academics, another on work-entry skills development, two on helping pupils return to the public school system, and a fifth focusing on community-based living skills. The curriculum at each site combines academics, therapy, life and transitional skills, field trips and recreational activities. Counseling and parental support groups are also available.

REGIONAL INSTITUTE FOR CHILDREN
AND ADOLESCENTS-SOUTHERN MARYLAND

Res — Coed Ages 12-17; Day — Coed 11-17

Cheltenham, MD 20623. 9400 Surratts Rd.
Tel: 301-372-1800. Fax: 301-372-1906.
Audrey Chase, LCSW, CEO. **Caroline Jones,** Adm.
  Focus: Treatment. **Conditions:** Primary—ADD ADHD BD CD ED LD Psy
    Sz. Sec—OCD. **IQ 70 and up.**
  Gen Acad. Pre-Voc. Gr 6-12. Courses: Read Math Lang_Arts. Man_Arts &
    Shop.
  Therapy: Speech. **Psychotherapy:** Fam Group Indiv.
  Enr: 78.
  Est 1983. State. Nonprofit.

RICA provides residential and day services for severely emotionally disturbed adolescents, with an emphasis on family treatment. Educational counseling is available. The usual duration of treatment is 18 months.

THE RIDGE SCHOOL OF MONTGOMERY COUNTY

Res and Day — Coed Ages 12-18

Rockville, MD 20850. 14901 Broschart Rd.
Tel: 301-251-4525. Fax: 301-251-4588.
www.potomacridge.com
Charles Maust, EdD, Prin. **Connie Hartman,** Adm.
  Focus: Spec Ed. **Conditions:** Primary—ADD ADHD BD CD Dx ED LD
    Mood OCD PTSD SP. **IQ 50 and up.**

Gen Acad. Gr 6-12. Courses: Read Math Lang_Arts.
Therapy: Art Dance Music Occup Recreational Speech. **Psychotherapy:** Fam Group Indiv Parent.
Enr: 116. Res Males 60. Res Females 20. Day Males 20. Day Females 16. **Staff:** 55. Prof 27. Admin 2.
Summer Prgm: Res & Day. Educ. 4 wks.
Private. Nonprofit. Seventh-day Adventist. **Spons:** Adventist HealthCare.

The Ridge School addresses the educational and social-emotional needs of students in treatment at Potomac Ridge Residential Treatment Center, Potomac Ridge Partial Hospital Program (PHP) and Chesapeake Acute Care Unit. In addition, the school serves day pupils from the local community. Ridge provides an individualize learning environment in which boys and girls also learn effective strategies for use in other settings.

RIDLEY AND FILL
SPEECH AND LANGUAGE ASSOCIATES
Clinic: All Ages. M-F 9-5.

Bethesda, MD 20814. 4915 Auburn Ave, Ste 201.
Tel: 301-652-8997. Fax: 301-652-6073.
Donna Ridley, MEd, CCC, Co-Dir. **Michelle Fill,** MS, CCC, Co-Dir.
Focus: Treatment. **Conditions:** Primary—Ap Dx LD S. Sec—ADD ADHD.
Therapy: Lang Speech.
Staff: 10 (Full 9, Part 1). Prof 9. Admin 1.
Est 1980. Private.

This facility provides individual and small-group speech and language therapy. The Phono-Graphix program and other reading programs are also utilized. Staff members coordinate the individual program with the curriculum at the school the child attends. Fees vary according to the program selected.

ST. ELIZABETH SCHOOL
Day — Coed Ages 11-21

Baltimore, MD 21218. 801 Argonne Dr.
Tel: 410-889-5054. Fax: 410-889-2356.
www.stelizabeth-school.org   E-mail: inforeq@stelizabeth-school.org
Christine Manlove, EdD, Exec Dir.
Focus: Spec Ed. **Conditions:** Primary—Asp Au Bl DS MR. Sec—ADD ADHD Anx Ap Apr As BD CP Dc Dg Dx ED Ep LD Mood OCD ON PW S SB TS. **IQ 25-89.**
Gen Acad. Pre-Voc. Voc. Ungraded. Courses: Read Math Lang_Arts Life_ Skills. Man_Arts & Shop. On-Job Trng.
Therapy: Art Lang Occup Phys Speech. **Psychotherapy:** Fam Group Indiv Parent.
Enr: 125. Day Males 80. Day Females 45. **Staff:** 126 (Full 117, Part 9). Prof 48. Educ 25. Admin 22.
Rates 2003: Day $41,161/sch yr. $100 (Therapy)/hr. State Aid.

Est 1961. Private. Nonprofit. Roman Catholic.

Operating 11 months a year, the school provides education, counseling, vocational training and placement for middle and high school students with special needs. Pupils who complete program requirements earn a certificate of completion from their local school systems or a high school diploma from St. Elizabeth. Physically aggressive students are not accepted.

THE SUMMIT SCHOOL

Day — Coed Ages 6-15

Edgewater, MD 21037. 664 E Central Ave.
Tel: 410-798-0005. Fax: 410-798-0008.
www.thesummitschool.org   E-mail: info@thesummitschool.org
Jane Snider, EdD, Dir. **Kathleen Heefner,** Adm.
    Focus: Spec Ed. **Conditions:** Primary—Dc Dg Dx LD. **IQ 90 and up.**
    Gen Acad. Gr 1-8. Courses: Read Math Lang_Arts Sci Soc_Stud.
    Therapy: Occup Speech.
    Enr: 100. Day Males 69. Day Females 31. **Staff:** 42 (Full 35, Part 7). Educ
       31. Admin 7.
    Rates 2004: Day $23,000/yr. Schol 19 ($94,800).
    Summer Prgm: Day. Educ. Rec. Day Rate $1400. 4 wks.
    Est 1989. Private. Nonprofit.

Summit provides an elementary program that addresses learning difficulties and provides academic challenge. The curriculum employs a multisensory teaching approach that introduces and reinforces auditory, visual, tactile and kinesthetic skills.

SYLVAN LEARNING CENTER

Clinic: Ages 5-18.

Baltimore, MD 21202. 1001 Fleet St.
Tel: 888-338-2283.
www.educate.com
PhD,
    Conditions: Primary—Dx LD.
    Gen Acad. Gr K-12. Courses: Read Math Lang_Arts.
    Est 1979. Private. Inc. **Spons:** Educate, Inc.

TAYLOR HEALTH SYSTEM

Res — Coed Ages 5-17; Day — Coed 12-17
Clinic: All Ages. M-F 9-5; Eves M-F 5-8.

Ellicott City, MD 21041. 4100 College Ave, PO Box 396.
Tel: 410-465-3322. TTY: 410-461-8264. Fax: 410-461-7075.

www.taylorhealth.com   E-mail: ktaylor@sheppardpratt.org
Barbara Merke, LCSW, Admin. **Bruce T. Taylor,** MD, Med Dir.
    Focus: Treatment. **Conditions:** Primary—ED Mood OCD Psy Sz. Sec—
    ADD ADHD As CP Dx Ep LD OH. **IQ 65 and up.**
    Therapy: Chemo Occup Speech. **Psychotherapy:** Fam Group Indiv.
    Enr: 120. Res Males 60. Res Females 60. **Staff:** 207.
    Est 1907. Private. Inc.

The child and adolescent programs at this hospital utilize a specialized, multi-modality treatment approach that addresses both the psychiatric disturbance and the patient's developmental needs. Program goals include the resolution of acute symptomatology, the development of more functional behaviors, and the acquisition of more effective coping and communicational skills. The facility aims to enable the patient to function safely and adequately outside of the hospital. Services include inpatient, outpatient, crisis, respite and partial hospitalization.

TOWSON UNIVERSITY
SPEECH-LANGUAGE-HEARING CLINIC

Clinic: All Ages. M-F 8:30-5.

Towson, MD 21252. Van Bokkelen Hall, 8000 York Rd.
Tel: 410-830-3095. Fax: 410-704-4131.
www.towson.edu/asld/clinic.htm   E-mail: pmoore@towson.edu
Karen Pottash, MA, CCC-SLP, Admin.
    Focus: Treatment. **Conditions:** Primary—S. Sec—Ap Au Bl MR.
    Therapy: Hear Lang Speech.
    County.

The clinic offers diagnostic and treatment services for speech, language and hearing disorders. Hearing aid evaluations and dispensations, counseling and referrals are also available. A training program for speech pathologists and audiologists is offered. The clinic maintains a sliding fee scale according to need.

THE TREATMENT AND LEARNING CENTERS

Day — Coed Ages 2-14
Clinic: All Ages. M-F 8-5, S 8-2; Eves T-Th 5-7:30.

Rockville, MD 20850. 9975 Medical Center Dr.
Tel: 301-424-5200. TTY: 301-424-5203. Fax: 301-424-8063.
www.ttlc.org   E-mail: info@ttlc.org
Richard J. Pavlin, Exec Dir. **Theresa Petrungaro,** MS, Admin Dir.
    Focus: Spec Ed. **Conditions:** Primary—ADD ADHD Ap Apr Asp Au Dg Dx
    LD PDD S. Sec—Anx CD D ON SP TS.
    Gen Acad. Gr PS-8. Courses: Read Math Lang_Arts Computers Studio_Art
    Music Drama. On-Job Trng.
    Therapy: Hear Lang Occup Percepual-Motor Phys Speech. **Psychother-**
    apy: Fam Indiv.

Enr: 100. Day Males 55. Day Females 45. **Staff:** 170 (Full 145, Part 25). Prof 54. Educ 40.
Rates 2004: Day $19,368/sch yr. Schol avail.
Summer Prgm: Day. Educ. Ther. Day Rate $2175. 6 wks.
Est 1950. Private. Nonprofit.

TLC conducts a range of programs for children and adults with special needs. The Katherine Thomas School provides instruction for elementary students with learning and language disabilities. Another program, psycho-educational testing and tutoring, addresses the needs of both children and adults with such learning problems as attentional disorders and learning disabilities.

Speech-language, occupational and physical therapies are available on an outpatient basis, and TLC also operates a hearing clinic that provides comprehensive hearing evaluation, counseling, and hearing aid sales and services. The Outcomes Neuro Rehab Center, for adults and transitioning youth with neurological impairments and learning disabilities, consists of programs in vocational evaluation, work adjustment training, speech-language therapy, job placement and supported employment. The facility also conducts an annual summer camp, Camp Littlefoot, for children ages 3-12 who can benefit from language-intensive instruction.

UCP CENTRAL MARYLAND
DELREY CHILD DEVELOPMENT CENTERS

Day — Coed Ages 2-21

Baltimore, MD 21228. 18 Delrey Ave.
Tel: 410-744-3151. Fax: 410-744-8467.
www.ucp-cm.org   E-mail: dlemonthompson@ucp-cm.org
Mimi M. Wang, MEd, Prin. **George A. Lentz, Jr.,** MD, Med Dir. **Dorothy Lemon-Thompson,** Adm.
Focus: Spec Ed. **Conditions:** Primary—CP ON SB. Sec—S.
Gen Acad. Ungraded. Courses: Read Math Lang_Arts.
Therapy: Hear Lang Occup Phys Speech. **Psychotherapy:** Fam Parent.
Enr: 64. Day Males 36. Day Females 28. **Staff:** 46 (Full 44, Part 2). Educ 26. Admin 1.
Rates 2003: Day $32,153/sch yr. State Aid.
Summer Prgm: Day. Educ. Rec. Ther. 5 wks.
Est 1964. Private. Nonprofit.

Delrey serves children with physical disabilities and their families through two Baltimore-area child development centers. A preschool program aims to prepare children educationally, physically and emotionally for entrance into the public school system. In addition, Delrey provides educational programs and functional therapies for children and young adults up to age 21.

VILLA MARIA SCHOOL

Res and Day — Coed Ages 3-14

Timonium, MD 21093. 2300 Dulaney Valley Rd.

Tel: 410-252-6343.
www.catholiccharities-md.org/children/villarschoolmain.htm
E-mail: villamar@catholiccharities-md.org
Mark Greenberg, MSW, Admin. **Joseph O'Leary,** MD, Med Dir. **Andrea Commarata,** Adm.
Focus: Spec Ed. Treatment. **Conditions:** Primary—CD ED OCD Psy Sz. Sec—BD Dx LD. **IQ 70 and up.**
Gen Acad. Pre-Voc. Ungraded. Courses: Read Math Lang_Arts Soc_Stud Sci Studio_Art Music. Man_Arts & Shop.
Therapy: Lang Occup Speech. **Psychotherapy:** Fam Group Indiv Parent. **Enr:** 86.
Est 1981. Private. Nonprofit. **Spons:** Catholic Charities.

Villa Maria assists emotionally disturbed children who have been unable to reach their potentials in the community. Treatment programs address the psychodynamic and ecological factors relating to the child's social, emotional and intellectual difficulties. A therapeutic team approach provides individual therapy and behavior modification. The goal is to return the child to a less restrictive environment and ultimately return him or her to the family. Parental involvement is vital and family therapy is offered.

The center's educational component provides academic, prevocational and tutorial services for those students not attending local public schools. After-school/extended-day treatment and diagnostic/crisis school placement are also available. A limited number of day students may enroll, and the usual duration of treatment is 10 to 12 months.

THE WOODBOURNE CENTER

Res — Males Ages 8-18, Females 9-16

Baltimore, MD 21239. 1301 Woodbourne Ave.
Tel: 410-433-1000. Fax: 410-433-1459.
www.woodbourne.org
Stanley E. Weinstein, Pres. **Wendol Williams,** MD, Actg Med Dir.
Conditions: Primary—BD ED.
Gen Acad. Ungraded. Courses: Read Math.
Therapy: Art. **Psychotherapy:** Fam.
Est 1798. Private. Nonprofit.

MASSACHUSETTS

ACADEMY OF PHYSICAL AND SOCIAL DEVELOPMENT

Day — Coed Ages 5-16

Newton, MA 02458. 425R Watertown St.
Tel: 617-969-2200. Fax: 617-244-4906.
www.academynewton.com   E-mail: academynewton@aol.com
Ken Barringer, MA, Dir.
   Conditions: Primary—ED. Sec—LD.
   Est 1954. Private. Inc.

AMEGO

Res and Day — Coed Ages 11 and up

Mansfield, MA 02048. 115 Plymouth St.
Tel: 508-261-1000. Fax: 508-261-1042.
www.amegoinc.org   E-mail: bbrown@amegoinc.org
Barbara L. Brown, EdD, Pres.
   Conditions: Primary—Au MR. Sec—ADD ADHD BI Ep.
   Pre-Voc. Voc. Ungraded. Courses: Read Math Lang_Arts Life_Skills.
   Therapy: Speech.
   Enr: 62.
   Est 1971. Private. Nonprofit.

Amego serves adolescents and adults who have been diagnosed with autistic, mental retardation or both, and whose special needs require an intensive year-round program.

A student's individual educational or treatment plan identifies goals that relate to increased independent life skills. Behavior management, precision teaching and errorless learning are primary techniques. The curriculum emphasizes social, communicative and vocational skills. Amego also offers recreational and educational activities in the community.

ARLINGTON SCHOOL

Day — Coed Ages 12-20

Belmont, MA 02478. 115 Mill St.
Tel: 617-855-2124. Fax: 617-855-2757.
http://mcleanhospital.org/Child/arlington_school.html
Kenneth R. McElheny, MA, Dean. **Suzanne Loughlin,** Clin Dir.
   Focus: Spec Ed. **Conditions:** Primary—ADD ADHD ED LD OCD Psy Sz.
   Sec—Dx. **IQ 100 and up.**
   Col Prep. Gen Acad. Gr 8-12. Courses: Read Math Lang_Arts Fr Span Sci
   Computers Studio_Art Music Photog.
   Enr: 40. Day Males 24. Day Females 16. **Staff:** 12 (Full 9, Part 3). Educ 9.

Admin 1.
Rates 2004: Day $36,000/sch yr. State Aid.
Summer Prgm: Day. Educ. Day Rate $9190. 8 wks.
Est 1961. Private. Nonprofit. **Spons:** McLean Hospital.

Arlington School is a comprehensive secondary school for moderately to severely emotionally disturbed and learning-disabled individuals from surrounding communities. The school emphasizes individualized attention while gearing its program to meet each student's ability level. The program's goal is to facilitate the pupil's return to his or her public or private school system. The student's home school district typically pays tuition fees.

Students may elect a course of study stressing either college or career preparation. The traditional academic curriculum includes foreign language and creative arts classes. Career exploration classes are available. Graduates move on to employment, two- and four-year colleges, and vocational training schools.

THE ASSOCIATION FOR COMMUNITY LIVING

Res — Coed All Ages

Springfield, MA 01104. 1 Carando Dr.
Tel: 413-732-0531. Fax: 413-732-1168.
www.theassn.org
Donald Fletcher, Dir.
   Conditions: Primary—MR.
   Pre-Voc. Ungraded.
   Therapy: Hear Lang Occup Phys Speech.
   Est 1952. Private. Nonprofit.

AUBURN FAMILY INSTITUTE

Clinic: Ages 3-21. M-F 7-6, S 7-1; Eves M T Th 6-10.

Auburn, MA 01501. 6 South Ter.
Tel: 508-832-4297. Fax: 508-832-2768.
E-mail: drallenfrank@aol.com
Allen F. Johnson, MSW, PhD, Dir.
   Focus: Treatment. **Conditions:** Primary—ADD ADHD AN Anx Asp Au BD
      Bu CD Dx ED HIV LD Mood MS OCD ON PDD Psy PTSD SB SP Sz.
      Sec—Ap As B Bl C CP D Db Ep IP MD MR Nf PW S TB TS.
   Psychotherapy: Fam Group Indiv Parent.
   Staff: 1. (Full 1).
   Rates 2003: Clinic $70/hr.
   Est 1977. Private.

Among the many programs offered at Auburn Family Institute, emphasis is placed on family therapy, individual counseling, psychotherapy and parental guidance. Counseling usually lasts a few months, although some treatments may take longer.

AVKO DYSLEXIA RESEARCH FOUNDATION

Clinic: Ages 6 and up. M-Su 9-5; Eves M-Su 5-9.

Clio, MA 48420. 3084 W Willard Rd.
Tel: 810-686-9283. Fax: 810-686-1101.
www.avko.org   E-mail: avkoemail@aol.com
Don McCabe, PhB, MA, Dir.
  Focus: Treatment. Conditions: Primary—ADD ADHD Dg Dx LD. Sec—Ap
    Au DS.
  Staff: 4 (Full 3, Part 1).
  Rates 2004: No Fee.
  Est 1974. Nonprofit.

AVKO delivers free daily tutoring to children and adults at the reading clinic. Instructors employ various techniques to systematically teach poor readers and poor spellers.

BAIRD CENTER

Res and Day — Males Ages 10-15

Plymouth, MA 02360. Great Outlook Way.
Tel: 508-224-8041. Fax: 508-224-7787.
E-mail: bairdcenter@aol.com
Christine Coffin, MA, Dir.
  Focus: Treatment. Conditions: Primary—Asp BD ED LD Mood SP TS.
    Sec—Bl Ep S. IQ 75-115.
  Gen Acad. Pre-Voc. Ungraded. Courses: Read Math Lang_Arts Sci Soc_
    Stud. On-Job Trng.
  Therapy: Milieu Occup Speech. Psychotherapy: Fam Group Indiv.
  Enr: 52. Res Males 32. Day Males 20. Staff: 30.
  Rates 2003: Res $90,053/yr. Day $37,423/sch yr. State Aid.
  Est 1974. Private. Nonprofit. Spons: Home for Little Wanderers.

The center provides short-term reality-based treatment for adolescent boys who display behavioral, emotional or school-related difficulties. The facility's goal is to return students to their families and local school districts. An educational program is available and public facilities are used. The usual length of treatment is 10 to 18 months. Family involvement is required in both day and residential programs. A group home is available to aid the transition back to home and community.

BEACON HIGH SCHOOL

Day — Coed Ages 15-22

Brookline, MA 02446. 74 Green St.
Tel: 617-232-1958.
www.beaconhighschool.org
Nancy C. Lincoln, BA, Dir.
  Focus: Spec Ed. Conditions: Primary—ADD ADHD Anx Bu Dc Dg Dx ED

Mood OCD PTSD SP. Sec—LD. **IQ 95 and up.**
Gen Acad. Ungraded. Courses: Read Math Lang_Arts.
Therapy: Art Milieu. **Psychotherapy:** Fam Group Indiv.
Enr: 53. Day Males 23. Day Females 30. **Staff:** 18. (Full 18).
Rates 2003: Day $45,000/yr. State Aid.
Est 1971. Private. Nonprofit.

Beacon is an alternative, 11-month school for emotionally disturbed students. In addition to traditional academics, courses in anthropology, political science, computers, video, carpentry and photography are offered. Students are evaluated twice a semester in each course, and recommendations for further study are submitted to counselors.

THE BERKSHIRE CENTER
COLLEGE INTERNSHIP PROGRAM

Res — Coed Ages 18-28

Lee, MA 01238. 18 Park St, PO Box 160.
Tel: 413-243-2576. Fax: 413-243-3351.
www.berkshirecenter.org   E-mail: gshaw@berkshirecenter.org
Michael McManmon, MA, MA, EdD, Exec Dir. **Gary Shaw,** Adm.
   Focus: Spec Ed. Trng. **Conditions:** Primary—ADD ADHD Asp Dc Dg Dx
      LD PDD. Sec—Anx As Bl C CP D Db ED Mood OCD TS. **IQ 70-130.**
   Voc. Courses: Read Math. On-Job Trng.
   Therapy: Milieu. **Psychotherapy:** Group Indiv.
   Enr: 63. Res Males 42. Res Females 21. **Staff:** 23 (Full 11, Part 12). Prof 8.
      Educ 6. Admin 4.
   Rates 2004: Res $30,000/sch yr. State Aid.
   Summer Prgm: Res. Educ. Rec. Ther. Voc. Res Rate $5515. 8 wks.
   Est 1984. Private. Inc.

CIP offers a variety of postsecondary programming for young adults with learning differences, including academic classes, tutoring, individual and group counseling, case management, vocational internships, culinary services and recreational activities.

BERKSHIRE HILLS MUSIC ACADEMY

Res — Coed Ages 18-30

South Hadley, MA 01075. 48 Woodbridge St.
Tel: 413-540-9720. Fax: 413-534-3875.
www.berkshirehills.org   E-mail: info@berkshirehills.org
Greg A. Williams, MM, Dean. **Michaela Doran,** Adm.
   Focus: Spec Ed. **Conditions:** Primary—ADD ADHD Asp Bl Dc Dg DS Dx
      LD MR. Sec—Anx As Au B C CP Db ED Mood OCD ON PDD. **IQ 55 and
      up.**
   Pre-Voc. Voc. Gr PG. Courses: Read Math Lang_Arts Music. On-Job Trng.
   Psychotherapy: Group.
   Enr: 24. Res Males 14. Res Females 10. **Staff:** 40 (Full 14, Part 26). Prof
      14. Educ 12. Admin 6.

Rates 2004: Res $38,000/sch yr (+$1500). State Aid.
Summer Prgm: Res. Educ. Rec. Res Rate $800/wk. 2 wks.
Est 2001. Private. Inc.

This postsecondary school enrolls young adults with strong musical aptitude who have learning, cognitive or developmental disabilities. Academy graduates may enroll in a one-year extension program, Music in Careers, to gain fieldwork experience and training, in addition to support in apartment living. The summer program encourages potential candidates for the school (ages 16-25) to try out a variety of musical activities.

BERKSHIRE MEADOWS

Res — Coed All Ages

Housatonic, MA 01236. 249 N Plain Rd.
Tel: 413-528-2523. Fax: 413-528-0293.
www.berkshiremeadows.org   E-mail: berkshiremeadows@jri.org
Liisa Kelly, MA, Prgm Dir. **Dennis Tresp,** MD, Med Dir.
  Focus: Spec Ed. **Conditions:** Primary—MR. Sec—Ap As Au B Bl C CD CP
    D ED Ep IP MD MS OCD ON Psy S SB Sz.
  Pre-Voc. Ungraded. Courses: ADL Life_Skills. On-Job Trng.
  Therapy: Chemo Hear Hydro Lang Occup Phys Speech. **Psychotherapy:**
    Indiv.
  Enr: 55. **Staff:** 130.
  Rates 2004: Res $158,000/yr. State Aid.
  Est 1979. Private. Nonprofit. **Spons:** Justice Resource Institute.

The year-round program at this facility provides a normal living environment for children and adults with multiple disabilities while promoting their involvement in the community. Services include academic and therapeutic programs, prevocational training and Activities of Daily Living. A day program for adults concentrates on life skills, employment skills and on-the-job training, and independence.

BEVERLY SCHOOL FOR THE DEAF

Day — Coed Ages 3-22

Beverly, MA 01915. 6 Echo Ave.
Tel: 978-927-7070. Fax: 978-927-6536.
www.beverlyschoolforthedeaf.org
  E-mail: markcarlson@beverlyschoolforthedeaf.org
Mark E. Carlson, MEd, MBA, Exec Dir. **Jane S. Kelly,** MEd, Educ Dir.
  Focus: Spec Ed. **Conditions:** Primary—D. Sec—ED LD MR S. **IQ 70 and
    up.**
  Gen Acad. Pre-Voc. Voc. Ungraded. Courses: Read Math Lang_Arts.
    Shelt_Workshop. On-Job Trng.
  Therapy: Hear Lang Occup Phys Speech.
  Enr: 34. Day Males 21. Day Females 13. **Staff:** 26 (Full 25, Part 1).
  Rates 2004: Day $36,570/sch yr.
  Summer Prgm: Day. Educ. 6 wks.

Est 1876. Private.

The school's educational program for deaf and hard-of-hearing children emphasizes social/emotional growth and development. Counseling is available, and a summer session for preschoolers and kindergartners will accept enrollment from the regular program only.

BOSTON COLLEGE CAMPUS SCHOOL

Day — Coed Ages 3-21

Chestnut Hill, MA 02167. Campion Hall, Rm 197.
Tel: 617-552-3460. Fax: 617-552-0812.
www.bc.edu/bc_org/avp/soe/campsch   E-mail: ricciato@bc.edu
Philip DiMattia, Dir.
  Conditions: Primary—OH.
  Gen Acad. Ungraded. Courses: Read Math Lang_Arts. Shelt_Workshop.
  Therapy: Hear Occup Phys Speech.
  Est 1970. Private. Nonprofit.

THE BOSTON INSTITUTE FOR ARTS THERAPY

Clinic: All Ages. M-F 8-5; Eves M-F 5-7:30.

Boston, MA 02125. 90 Cushing Ave.
Tel: 617-288-5858. Fax: 617-288-6262.
www.biat.org   E-mail: artstherapy@biat.org
Phillip Speiser, MA, PhD, Exec Dir. **Karen Wise,** MEd, Clin Dir.
  Focus: Treatment. **Conditions:** Primary—ADD ADHD Au BD CD ED S.
    Sec—Ap As B BI C CP D Dx Ep IP LD MD MR MS OCD ON Psy SB Sz
    TB.
  Therapy: Art Dance Music Speech. **Psychotherapy:** Fam Group Indiv.
  Staff: 23 (Full 17, Part 6).
  Est 1982. Federal. Nonprofit.

The institute uses art, dance and music therapies as a means for social, emotional and developmental progress. Focus is on communication and self-esteem enhancement.

BOUNDARIES THERAPY CENTER

Clinic: All Ages. M-F 8-5; Eves M-Th 5-8.

Acton, MA 01720. 518 Great Rd.
Tel: 978-263-4878.
www.boundariestherapy.com
Peter Musliner, MD, Co-Dir.
  Conditions: Primary—BD ED LD. Sec—ADD Anx CD Mood.
  Therapy: Play. **Psychotherapy:** Fam Group Indiv.
  Est 1975. Private.

BRANDON RESIDENTIAL TREATMENT CENTER
AND DAY SCHOOL

Res and Day — Males Ages 7-16

Natick, MA 01760. 27 Winter St.
Tel: 508-655-6400. Fax: 508-650-9431.
www.brandonschool.org   E-mail: info@brandonschool.org
Timothy M. Callahan, EdD, Exec Dir. **Patricia Kelley,** Adm.
  Focus: Spec Ed. Treatment. **Conditions:** Primary—BD ED LD. Sec—ADD
    ADHD Anx CD Dx Mood OCD ODD PTSD. **IQ 70-135.**
  Gen Acad. Pre-Voc. Gr 1-12. Courses: Read Math Lang_Arts Sci Soc_Stud
    Computers. On-Job Trng. Culinary_Arts.
  Therapy: Art Music Play Recreational. **Psychotherapy:** Fam Group Indiv
    Parent.
  Enr: 85. Res Males 75. Day Males 10. **Staff:** 198. Educ 40. Admin 8.
  Rates 2003: Res $288/day. Day $143/day. State Aid.
  Est 1967. Private. Nonprofit.

Located on a 35-acre campus, this facility offers residential and day services for
young and adolescent boys with emotional and behavior problems. The learning environment approximates that of a public school, but Brandon's small enrollment allows
for additional supports and structure. The program seeks to improve students' academic
and social skills, to develop more appropriate behavioral controls, and to improve self-
esteem levels. Psychotherapists and graduate clinical interns administer psychotherapy
and family services.

Brandon's residents live in one of seven community residences located in Natick,
Framingham, Milford and Ashland. The residential program offers two levels of
treatment, ranging from more restrictive to less restrictive. All residents utilize group
meetings, family-style meals, study halls and privilege levels. Acute services, including diagnostic services, emergency placements, and programs for children with sexual
compulsions and fire-setting issues, are also available.

THE BRIEN CENTER

Clinic: All Ages. M-F 9-5.

Pittsfield, MA 01201. 333 East St.
Tel: 413-499-0412. Fax: 413-448-2198.
www.mhsab.com
Marjorie Cohan, MS, Exec Dir. **Carlos Carrera,** MD, Med Dir.
  Conditions: Primary—ED.
  Therapy: Play. **Psychotherapy:** Fam Group Indiv.
  Private.

BRIGHTSIDE FOR FAMILIES AND CHILDREN

Res — Males Ages 5-17, Females 5-12
Clinic: All Ages.

West Springfield, MA 01089. 2112 Riverdale St.
Tel: 413-788-7366. Fax: 413-827-4250.
www.sphs.com/pages.asp?id=508
   Conditions: Primary—BD ED. Sec—ADHD LD.
   Gen Acad. Ungraded. Courses: Read Math Lang_Arts. Man_Arts & Shop.
   Therapy: Recreational. **Psychotherapy:** Fam Group Indiv.
   Est 1881. Private. Nonprofit. **Spons:** Sisters of Providence Health System.

CADMUS LIFESHARING ASSOCIATION

Res — Coed Ages 18 and up

Great Barrington, MA 01230. PO Box 46.
Tel: 413-528-1307. Fax: 413-528-0114.
www.cadmuslife.org   E-mail: cadmus@bcn.net
   Focus: Trng. **Conditions:** Primary—MR. Sec—Ap Au BD Bl ED Ep.
   Therapy: Lang Occup Speech. **Psychotherapy:** Fam Parent.
   Enr: 65. **Staff:** 26 (Full 16, Part 10).
   Summer Prgm: Res. Rec. 2 wks.
   Est 1972. Private. Nonprofit.

The association provides individual, ongoing training in homemaking, crafts and horticulture at eight separate households. Candidates for admission are individuals with mental retardation who can benefit from a community living setting. The horticultural program includes the maintenance of an apple orchard and a garden, landscaping of the grounds, and produce drying, canning and freezing. All adults must choose an area of expertise and participate in the upkeep of the home and the garden. Residents may also pursue remunerative employment with a local recycling company.

A recreational program features horseback riding, swimming and hiking. Cadmus also conducts a recreational summer camp.

CARDINAL CUSHING CENTER
AT BRAINTREE

Day — Coed Ages 8-22

Braintree, MA 02184. 85 Washington St.
Tel: 781-848-6250. Fax: 781-848-0640.
www.coletta.org   E-mail: plarson@coletta.org
Patricia A. Larson, BA, MSEd, Exec Dir.
   Focus: Spec Ed. **Conditions:** Primary—MR PDD. Sec—Ap Au BD CP ED
      Ep ON S TB.
   Pre-Voc. Voc. Ungraded. Courses: Read Math Lang_Arts. Shelt_Workshop.
      On-Job Trng.

Therapy: Hear Lang Music Occup Speech. **Psychotherapy:** Indiv.
Enr: 54.
Rates 2003: Day $50,966/yr.
Est 1948. Private. Nonprofit.

Located 15 minutes from Boston on a four-acre site, this school offers a year-round academic program for moderately to severely retarded children and young adults. Students acquire functional daily living skills for home and community living and take part in practical academic, prevocational, vocational and recreational programs. The curriculum includes social studies, science, music, physical education, drama, industrial arts and perceptual-motor development.

CARDINAL CUSHING SCHOOL AND TRAINING CENTER

Res and Day — Coed Ages 8-21

Hanover, MA 02339. 400 Washington St.
Tel: 781-826-6371. Fax: 781-826-1559.
www.coletta.org/cushingschool.html   E-mail: lsauer@coletta.org
Lawrence Sauer, Exec Dir.
  Focus: Spec Ed. Trng. **Conditions:** Primary—MR. Sec—As BD BI CP Dx ED Ep LD OH. **IQ 45-85.**
  Gen Acad. Pre-Voc. Voc. Ungraded. Courses: Read Math Computers Life_ Skills. Shelt_Workshop. On-Job Trng.
  Therapy: Occup Phys Speech. **Psychotherapy:** Group Indiv.
  Est 1947. Private. Nonprofit. Roman Catholic. **Spons:** St. Coletta's of Massachusetts.

The center offers education and vocational training within a therapeutic milieu atmosphere for children and adults with mild to severe retardation. The 11-month program includes functional academics, music, arts, crafts, and fine- and gross-motor therapy, as well as crisis intervention, respite care and counseling. The goal is to teach the skills and provide the experience necessary for students to integrate into the community to the best of their abilities.

CARROLL CENTER FOR THE BLIND

Res — Coed Ages 14 and up; Day — Coed 3 and up

Newton, MA 02458. 770 Centre St.
Tel: 617-969-6200. Fax: 617-969-6204.
www.carroll.org   E-mail: dinarosen@carroll.org
Rachel Rosenbaum, MA, Pres.
  Focus: Spec Ed. Trng. Treatment. **Conditions:** Primary—B. Sec—ADD ADHD As Au BD BI C CD CP D Dx ED Ep IP LD MD MR MS OCD ON Psy S SB Sz.
  Gen Acad. Ungraded. Man_Arts & Shop.
  Therapy: Speech Visual. **Psychotherapy:** Fam Group Indiv.
  Staff: 20.
  Summer Prgm: Res. Educ. Rec. Voc.

Est 1947. Private. Nonprofit.

The center's range of year-round services provided for visually impaired children and adults includes the following: orientation and mobility, available both at home and at school; assistance to teachers and parents with the instruction of students who are blind or visually impaired; low-vision training and evaluations that feature various technical devices; a loan program enabling individuals to try out adaptive devices at school; and computer device training and evaluation. Summer programs include a youth-in-transition camp designed to foster increased independence and a career development camp.

THE CARROLL SCHOOL

Day — Coed Ages 7-15

Lincoln, MA 01773. 25 Baker Bridge Rd.
Tel: 781-259-8342. Fax: 781-259-8852.
www.carrollschool.org   E-mail: admissions@carrollschool.org
Phillip Burling, Actg Head. **Veronica I. Kenney,** Adm.
   Focus: Spec Ed. **Conditions:** Primary—Dx LD. **IQ 95 and up.**
   Col Prep. Gen Acad. Gr 2-9. Courses: Read Math Lang_Arts Sci Computers Soc_Stud Studio_Art Film Woodworking Outdoor_Ed.
   Enr: 229. Day Males 132. Day Females 97. **Staff:** 106 (Full 100, Part 6).
   Rates 2004: Day $29,500/sch yr. Schol avail. State Aid.
   Summer Prgm: Day. Educ. Rec. Day Rate $3950-4450. 5 wks.
   Est 1967. Private. Nonprofit.

The school specializes in the education of children with average to superior intelligence who have been diagnosed with dyslexia or a specific language disability in one or more of the following areas: reading, writing and organizational skills.

The objective of the program is to develop academic and social growth so that students may reenter a regular school environment. Children are grouped according to language competency and age, as well as by physical and emotional maturity. Employing an adaptation of the Orton-Gillingham method, Carroll helps students acquire skills in reading, writing and speaking. The curriculum also includes math, science, social studies, art, film/video, woodworking, physical education and an Outward Bound-type program.

The five-week summer program combines morning academics with various afternoon recreational opportunities.

CEREBRAL PALSY OF MASSACHUSETTS CHILDREN'S DEVELOPMENTAL CENTER

Day — Coed Ages 3-7
Clinic: Ages 3-7. M-F 9-3.

Quincy, MA 02169. 43 Old Colony Ave.
Tel: 617-479-7980. Fax: 617-479-3398.
Thomas J. Zukauskas, Exec Dir. **Louis P. Tozzi,** MEd, Dir. **Marylin Augustine,** MD, Med Dir.
   Focus: Spec Ed. **Conditions:** Primary—Asp Au Bl CP IP LD MD ON SB. Sec—ADD ADHD Ap Apr As B BD D Dg Dx ED Ep MR.

Gen Acad. Gr PS.
· **Therapy:** Dance Hear Lang Music Occup Percepual-Motor Phys Speech Visual.
Enr: 8. Day Males 6. Day Females 2. **Staff:** 14.
Summer Prgm: Day. Educ. Rec. Ther. 6 wks.
Est 1952. Private. Nonprofit.

Serving 45 communities and towns, this organization includes the following: a walk-in clinic providing diagnostic evaluations and treatments for individuals with disabilities; a preschool program for multiply handicapped children ages 3-7; therapy; and social services.

The agency also sponsors an adult class that involves arts and crafts, education, recreation and socialization.

THE CHILDREN'S STUDY HOME

Res — Males Ages 6-18, Females 13-18; Day — Coed 6-18

Springfield, MA 01109. 44 Sherman St.
Tel: 413-739-5626. Fax: 413-732-5457.
www.studyhome.org   E-mail: smccafferty@studyhome.org
Steve McCafferty, Exec Dir. **Allen Zippin,** BA, MEd, Educ Dir. **Janet Stabile,** Clin Dir.

Focus: Spec Ed. **Conditions:** Primary—ADD ADHD BD CD ED. Sec—Anx Mood OCD PTSD. **IQ 75-129.**
Gen Acad. Pre-Voc. Voc. Gr K-12. Courses: Read Math Lang_Arts Sci Hist. Man_Arts & Shop. On-Job Trng.
Therapy: Milieu. **Psychotherapy:** Fam Group Indiv Parent.
Enr: 85. Res Males 20. Day Males 53. Day Females 12. **Staff:** 51.
Rates 2003: No Fee.
Est 1865. Private. Nonprofit.

This multiservice agency specializes in four areas: residential treatment, special education, community-based services and family support services. The residential program serves children and adolescents with emotional and behavioral challenges. Psychological counselors, social workers, nurses, psychiatrists and psychologists provide daily support and individual treatment plans. The special education programs offer traditional academic programming, life skills and a vocational training curriculum. The home schedules therapy and family counseling on a regular basis.

Community-based programs assist families who are considered to be at risk or who are homeless. The aim of the program is to assist the family in reaching economic independence. In cooperation with the Department of Social Services, the home provides an array of programs designed to educate and support families in crisis. These services offer supervision and instruction to help families function healthily and independently.

Sending school districts pay program fees.

CLARKE SCHOOL FOR THE DEAF

Res — Coed Ages 5-18; Day — Coed 4-18
Clinic: All Ages. M-F 8:30-6.

Northampton, MA 01060. 47 Round Hill Rd.
Tel: 413-584-3450. TTY: 413-584-3450. Fax: 413-584-8273.
www.clarkeschool.org   E-mail: info@clarkeschool.org
Dennis Gjerdingen, MS, Pres.
  Focus: Spec Ed. **Conditions:** Primary—D.
  Gen Acad. Gr PS-12. Courses: Read Math Lang_Arts.
  Therapy: Hear Lang Speech.
  Summer Prgm: Res. Educ. Rec.
  Est 1867. Private. Nonprofit.

The educational program for profoundly deaf children at the Clarke School utilizes an auditory and oral method of instruction. The program seeks to prepare and assist students to enter schools with hearing children. Parent-infant, preschool and outreach programs are available. During the summer, Clarke offers theme-oriented, camplike programs to hearing-impaired students and their siblings.

CLEARWAY SCHOOL

Day — Coed Ages 9-18

West Newton, MA 02465. 61 Chestnut St.
Tel: 617-964-6186. Fax: 617-964-5680.
Mary Ryan, AB, Admin. **Margot Flouton,** Educ Dir.
  Focus: Spec Ed. **Conditions:** Primary—ADD ADHD Dc Dg Dx LD. Sec—
    Asp ED S. **IQ 85 and up.**
  Gen Acad. Pre-Voc. Ungraded. Courses: Read Math Lang_Arts Studio_Art
    Music Photog Woodworking. On-Job Trng.
  Therapy: Lang Speech.
  Enr: 25. Day Males 15. Day Females 10. **Staff:** 13 (Full 8, Part 5).
  Rates 2003: Day $26,941/sch yr.
  Est 1975. Private. Nonprofit.

Clearway's highly individualized program features regularly scheduled one-on-one tutorials as well as speech and language services. The curriculum incorporates vocational offerings (including a community-based work-study program) and numerous electives. Vocational and educational counseling are integrated into the student's routine, and therapy is also available. Some students attend the school for one or two years and then return to a public school setting, while others remain at Clearway until they graduate.

CLINICAL AND SUPPORT OPTIONS

Clinic: All Ages. M-S 8-5; Eves W Th 5-8.

Greenfield, MA 01301. 215 Shelburne Rd, PO Box 1365.
Tel: 413-774-1000. Fax: 413-774-1197.

www.csoinc.org   E-mail: info@csoinc.org
Timothy Diehl, MEd, Dir. **Michael LaVarnway,** MD, Med Dir.
Focus: Treatment. **Conditions:** Primary—ADD ADHD AN Anx Bu CD ED
Mood OCD ODD PTSD SP. Sec—BD Dc Dg Dx MR Psy Sz TS.
Psychotherapy: Fam Group Indiv Parent.
Staff: 175 (Full 70, Part 105). Prof 114. Admin 35.
Rates 2004: Sliding-Scale Rate $40-90/ses.
Est 1955. Private. Nonprofit.

CSO offers crisis intervention, as well as services for the chronically mentally ill and victims of emotional and psychological trauma. The clinic also provides psychotherapy for those dealing with domestic violence. The usual duration of treatment is four to 10 sessions.

COMMONWEALTH LEARNING CENTER

Clinic: Ages 6 and up. M-S 10-5; Eves M-S 5-7.

Needham, MA 02494. 123 Highland Ave.
Nearby locations: Danvers; Needham; Sudbury.
Tel: 781-444-5193. Fax: 781-444-6916.
www.commlearn.com   E-mail: info@commlearn.com
Lisa M. Brooks, MEd, Dir.
Focus: Spec Ed. **Conditions:** Primary—ADD ADHD Dc Dg Dx LD. Sec—S.
IQ 85 and up.
Gen Acad. Ungraded. Courses: Read Math Lang_Arts.
Staff: 39 (Full 12, Part 27). Educ 32. Admin 7.
Rates 2003: Clinic $60/hr. Sliding-Scale Rate $5-50/ses.
Est 1988. Private. Nonprofit. **Spons:** Stratford Foundation.

CLC's program provides alternative curricula, tailored to the learning style of the individual, for persons with learning disabilities, attentional disorders, dyslexia and other learning problems. Programs offered include Orton-Gillingham, Lindamood-Bell and Project Read. Math instruction is offered at elementary and advanced levels. Additional offerings include study skills and exam preparation for pupils.

CONCORD FAMILY & YOUTH SERVICES

Res — Females Ages 12-19; Day — Coed 12-19
Clinic: All Ages. M-F 8:30-6; Eves W Th 6-9.

Acton, MA 01720. 380 Massachusettes Ave.
Tel: 978-263-3006. Fax: 978-263-3088.
www.cfys.org   E-mail: cafas@cafas.org
Conditions: Primary—BD Dx ED LD.
Col Prep. Gen Acad. Pre-Voc. Courses: Read Math Lang_Arts.
Therapy: Speech. **Psychotherapy:** Fam Group Indiv.
Staff: Prof 74.
Est 1976. Private. Nonprofit.

CORNERSTONES SCHOOL

Res — Coed Ages 6-12; Day — Coed 6-13

Ipswich, MA 01938. 35 Mitchell Rd.
 Nearby locations: Beverly; Haverhill.
Tel: 978-356-9321. Fax: 978-948-7851.
www.hes-inc.org/scar_crnrstns.htm   E-mail: lsuggs@hes-inc.org
Lesli Suggs, MSW, LICSW, Dir.
 Conditions: Primary—ADD ADHD Anx Asp BD CD Dc Dg Dx ED LD Mood
 OCD Psy PTSD SP Sz TS. Sec—AN Bu D Db HIV. **IQ 68 and up.**
 Gen Acad. Ungraded.
 Therapy: Art Dance Milieu Movement Music Occup Percepual-Motor Play
 Recreational Speech. **Psychotherapy:** Fam Group Indiv Parent.
 Private. **Spons:** Health & Education Services.

THE CORWIN-RUSSELL SCHOOL
AT BROCCOLI HALL

Day — Coed Ages 11-19

Sudbury, MA 01776. 142 North Rd.
Tel: 978-369-1444. Fax: 978-369-1026.
www.corwin-russell.org   E-mail: brochall@corwin-russell.org
Jane Jakuc, MEd, Head. **Kristen Call,** Adm.
 Focus: Spec Ed. **Conditions:** Primary—ADD ADHD Asp Dx LD. Sec—Anx
 Db ED Mood OCD. **IQ 100 and up.**
 Col Prep. Gen Acad. Gr 7-12. Courses: Read Math Lang_Arts Fr Span Sci
 Soc_Stud Studio_Art Performing_Arts Fine_Arts Music Study_Skills.
 Therapy: Lang.
 Enr: 45. Day Males 31. Day Females 14. **Staff:** 20 (Full 14, Part 6).
 Rates 2003: Day $28,400/sch yr. State Aid.
 Est 1997. Private. Nonprofit.

 This college preparatory school enrolls high-potential students with various learning styles. The school provides multi-modal, imaginative instruction in all traditional academic areas, as well as foreign language study, career education and social service opportunities. Classes consist of no more than eight students, and tutoring is available for advancing skills and organizational assistance.

 A visual and performing arts program, an outdoor challenge experience and a varied after-school program complement academics. Study partnerships with area museums, colleges and performance centers; a career exploration week; and a drama intersession are also available.

COTTAGE HILL ACADEMY

Res — Females Ages 13-19

Baldwinville, MA 01436. 38 Hospital Rd, PO Box 38.

Tel: 978-652-1100. Fax: 978-652-1185.
Jon Hogue, EdD, Admin. **Ludmilla Tonkonogy,** MD, Med Dir. **Jean Lindquist,** Adm.
> **Focus:** Spec Ed. Treatment. **Conditions:** Primary—ADD ADHD AN Anx Ar As BD Bu CD Dx ED LD Mood OCD ODD PTSD SP. Sec—Db Ep HIV Psy. **IQ 70-135.**
> **Gen Acad.** Ungraded. Courses: Read Math Lang_Arts Sci Hist Fine_Arts Woodworking. Man_Arts & Shop. Culinary_Arts.
> **Therapy:** Art Dance Milieu Music Play Recreational. **Psychotherapy:** Fam Group Indiv.
> **Enr:** 48. Res Females 48. **Staff:** 66 (Full 51, Part 15). Prof 17. Educ 7. Admin 3.
> **Rates 2004:** Res $389/day.
> **Est 1970.** Private. Nonprofit. **Spons:** You Inc.

Serving girls with behavioral and other emotional disorders, Cottage Hill offers special education classes and intensive treatment. Integrated milieu therapy, as well as group and family counseling services, is essential the program.

COTTING SCHOOL/HOPE HOUSE

Res — Coed Ages 19-26; Day — Coed 3-22

Lexington, MA 02421. 453 Concord Ave.
Tel: 781-862-7323. Fax: 781-861-1179.
www.cotting.org   E-mail: admissions@cotting.org
David W. Manzo, MEd, Pres. **Lynda G. Kabbash,** MD, Med Dir. **Janine Brown-Smith,** Adm.
> **Focus:** Spec Ed. Trng. **Conditions:** Primary—LD OH. Sec—ADD ADHD Ap As B Bl C CP D Db Dx Ep IP MD MR MS S SB TB. **IQ 70 and up.**
> **Col Prep. Gen Acad. Pre-Voc. Voc.** Ungraded. Courses: Read Math Lang_ Arts Computers Music Drama. Man_Arts & Shop. On-Job Trng.
> **Therapy:** Hear Lang Occup Phys Speech. **Psychotherapy:** Fam Group Indiv Parent.
> **Enr:** 128. Res Males 4. Res Females 4. Day Males 56. Day Females 64. **Staff:** 122 (Full 72, Part 50). Prof 61. Educ 33. Admin 20.
> **Rates 2004:** Res $45,000/yr. Day $39,500-46,000/sch yr.
> **Est 1893.** Private. Nonprofit.

Cotting's objective is to provide the necessary educational, vocational and medical training programs for children and adolescents with communication deficits, medical disabilities, moderate to severe learning disabilities, multiple physical disabilities and posttraumatic head and spinal cord injuries.

The program includes individualized academic, prevocational, vocational and enrichment experiences. Comprehensive therapy and medical support services are available on site, as are vision and dental clinic services.

HOPE House is a transitional residential program that provides living assistance for postgraduate-age individuals with learning or physical disabilities. Components of this program are diagnostic evaluation and goal setting, work-related internships (when appropriate), vocational training and job placement. **See Also Pages 1022-3**

CRYSTAL SPRINGS SCHOOL

Res — Coed Ages 3-22

Assonet, MA 02702. 38 Narrows Rd, PO Box 372.
Tel: 508-644-3101. Fax: 508-644-2008.
Charles B. Young, BS, CEO. **Kenneth Piva,** DO, Med Dir. **Cheryl Tsimprea-Andrade,** Adm.

Focus: Spec Ed. Treatment. **Conditions:** Primary—MR. Sec—As Au B Bl C CP D Db DS Ep IP MD ON SB TS.

Pre-Voc. Ungraded. Courses: Life_Skills.

Therapy: Lang Occup Phys Speech.

Enr: 48. Res Males 22. Res Females 26. **Staff:** 208 (Full 127, Part 81). Prof 25. Educ 9. Admin 14.

Rates 2003: Res $139,471-163,986/yr.

Est 1953. Private. Nonprofit. **Spons:** Institute for Developmental Disabilities.

This school offers an educationally based program for students with severe to profound developmental disabilities who have accompanying medical, physical and behavioral disabilities. Pre-academic, prevocational and life skills programs are offered. Services include psychological assessments and family services. Physical, occupational, speech and language evaluations, and therapies are available. A 24-hour self-contained behavioral development unit serves students with severe behavioral disorders.

DEARBORN ACADEMY

Day — Coed Ages 5-22

Arlington, MA 02174. 34 Winter St.
Tel: 781-641-5992. Fax: 781-641-5997.
www.dearbornacademy.org
Howard Rossman, PhD, Dir.

Conditions: Primary—BD ED LD.

Gen Acad. Pre-Voc. Ungraded. Courses: Read Math Lang_Arts. Man_Arts & Shop. Shelt_Workshop. On-Job Trng.

Psychotherapy: Fam Group Indiv.

Est 1919. Private. Inc. **Spons:** Schools for Children.

DEVEREUX MASSACHUSETTS

Res — Males Ages 6-22, Females 13-22; Day — Coed 6-22

Rutland, MA 01543. 60 Miles Rd, PO Box 219.
Tel: 508-886-4746. Fax: 508-886-4773.
www.devereuxma.org   E-mail: ma_admissions@devereux.org
Stephen Yerdon, LICSW, Exec Dir. **Donna Daunais,** Adm.

Focus: Spec Ed. Treatment. **Conditions:** Primary—ADD Anx Asp ED LD Mood PDD Psy TS. Sec—As BD Bl Dx Ep HIV MR OCD S SP Sz. **IQ 60 and up.**

Gen Acad. Pre-Voc. Voc. Ungraded. Courses: Read Math Lang_Arts. Man_
Arts & Shop. On-Job Trng.
Therapy: Chemo Lang Milieu Music Occup Recreational Speech. **Psycho-
therapy:** Fam Group Indiv Parent.
Enr: 160. Res Males 118. Res Females 27. Day Males 14. Day Females 1.
Staff: 170 (Full 149, Part 21). Educ 31. Admin 21.
Rates 2004: Res $102,746-125,017/yr. Schol avail. State Aid.
Est 1965. Private. Nonprofit. **Spons:** Devereux Foundation.

Located on a 213-acre site, Devereux in Massachusetts offers treatment for emotionally disturbed, neurologically impaired children and young adults through both a
residential treatment center and an acute treatment center. Devereux seeks to develop or
restore the client's skills, confidence and potential by using an interdisciplinary approach
that encompasses individually prescribed therapeutic treatment and educational, prevocational, vocational and recreational programs. Treatment includes individual, group,
family and sex-abuse therapy. An academic program provides individualized small- and
large-group instruction, and a career development center is an integral part of the educational program. Students are mainstreamed as soon as possible, and the usual length of
treatment is 12 to 18 months. **See Also Page 1025**

DOCTOR FRANKLIN PERKINS SCHOOL

Res — Coed Ages 3 and up; Day — Coed 4-16

Lancaster, MA 01523. 971 Main St.
Tel: 978-365-7376. Fax: 978-368-8861.
www.perkinschool.org   E-mail: blossom@perkinschool.org
Charles P. Conroy, EdD, Exec Dir. **Laura Beckman-Devik,** BA, MA, Clin Dir.
Michelle Brady, Adm.
Focus: Spec Ed. Treatment. **Conditions:** Primary—ADD ADHD ED LD
OCD Sz. Sec—BD CD Dx MR Psy. **IQ 80 and up.**
Gen Acad. Pre-Voc. Voc. Ungraded. Courses: Read Math Lang_Arts
Studio_Art Music.
Therapy: Lang Occup Speech. **Psychotherapy:** Fam Group Indiv Parent.
Enr: 155.
Est 1896. Private. Nonprofit.

Perkins provides year-round, 24-hour care to clients who are coping with varying
degrees of trauma, behavioral disturbances, psychiatric disturbance, family dysfunction
and previous failed placements. Individuals may have deficits in self-care, community
awareness and interpersonal skills. Residential services are available in a continuum of
settings, with the goal being normalization and successful community living. Treatment
programs seek to improve the client's behavioral controls and insight, interpersonal relationships, and life and leisure skills.
Year-round educational programming is available to both residents and day students.
The curriculum features course work in the traditional disciplines, a young children's
readiness class, computer training, prevocational training, job skills instruction, art,
music, physical education, swimming, a therapeutic riding program and fitness instruction.

EAGLE HILL SCHOOL
Res and Day — Coed Ages 13-19

Hardwick, MA 01037. 242 Old Petersham Rd, PO Box 116.
Tel: 413-477-6000. Fax: 413-477-6837.
www.ehs1.org   E-mail: admission@ehs1.org
Peter John McDonald, BS, MEd, PhD, Head. **Dana Harbert,** Adm.
  Focus: Spec Ed. **Conditions:** Primary—ADD LD. **IQ 90 and up.**
  Col Prep. Gen Acad. Gr 8-12. Courses: Read Math Lang_Arts Sci Computers Hist Studio_Art Film Journ.
  Therapy: Lang Speech. **Psychotherapy:** Indiv.
  Enr: 150. **Staff:** 57 (Full 52, Part 5).
  Rates 2004: Res $42,530/sch yr (+$3000). Day $30,100/sch yr (+$500). State Aid.
  Summer Prgm: Res. Educ. Rec. Res Rate $5950 (+$500). 6 wks.
  Est 1967. Private. Nonprofit.

One of the few independent schools designed for the adolescent diagnosed with specific learning disabilities, attention deficit disorder or both, Eagle Hill accepts only students of average or above-average intelligence who are free of primary emotional and behavioral difficulties. The college preparatory program allows faculty to take advantage of the pupil's strengths while also providing remediation of learning deficits. An important aspect of the curriculum is the Pragmatics Program, which assists students with their verbal and nonverbal communicational skills. Specialized training in perceptual speech and language development is also available. In addition, the residential program facilitates the development of organizational, time management and social skills.

Activities include interscholastic team sports, intramural athletics, skiing, computers, student council, newspaper, literary magazine, ecology club, a campus radio station and community service.

EMERSON COLLEGE
ROBBINS SPEECH, LANGUAGE AND HEARING CENTER
Clinic: All Ages. M-F 9-5.

Boston, MA 02116. 120 Boylston St.
Tel: 617-824-8323. Fax: 617-824-8733.
Betsy Micucci, MA, CCC-SLP, Dir.
  Focus: Treatment. **Conditions:** Primary—D S. Sec—Ap.
  Therapy: Hear Lang Speech.
  Staff: 14. Admin 1.
  Rates 2003: $150 (Evaluation); $25 (Treatment)/ses.
  Est 1955. Private. Nonprofit.

Clients with speech, language and hearing disorders obtain diagnoses and treatment at the center. Clinical staff conduct a preschool program for children with hearing impairments three mornings per week, as well as a parental therapy group once a week.

EUNICE KENNEDY SHRIVER CENTER

Clinic: All Ages. M-F 9-5.

Waltham, MA 02154. 200 Trapelo Rd.
Tel: 781-642-0001. TTY: 800-764-0200.
www.umassmed.edu/shriver
  Conditions: Primary—ED LD MR. **IQ 30-90.**
  Therapy: Hear Lang Phys Speech. **Psychotherapy:** Fam Group Indiv.
  Staff: Prof 19.
  Est 1969. Private. Nonprofit.

EVERGREEN CENTER

Res — Coed Ages 6-22

Milford, MA 01757. 345 Fortune Blvd.
Tel: 508-478-2631. Fax: 508-634-3251.
www.evergreenctr.org   E-mail: services@evergreenctr.org
Robert F. Littleton, Jr., MEd, Exec Dir. **Nancy K. Manske,** Adm.
  Focus: Treatment. **Conditions:** Primary—Au BD BI CP ED Ep MR PTSD.
    Sec—Ap As B C D IP MD MS S SB.
  Voc. Shelt_Workshop.
  Therapy: Hear Lang Occup Phys Speech.
  Staff: 166.
  Est 1982. Private. Nonprofit.

Evergreen provides an integrated learning and living environment for students with severe developmental disabilities. Populations served include individuals with mental retardation, autism, physical disabilities, hearing or sight impairments, traumatic brain injury, posttraumatic stress disorder, dual diagnoses or severe behavioral problems. The educational program applies an extensive range of instructional procedures, teaches functional skills and substantiates each student's progress.

The Basic Skills Program teaches functional daily living skills to individuals with such disabilities as autism or severe mental retardation, and to some with physical special needs as well. The Behavior Development Program aids individuals with more challenging behavior problems, such as self-injurious or aggressive behavior, and has the capacity to serve individuals at early stages of academic achievement who are both mentally retarded and emotionally disturbed.

The center's multidisciplinary teaching team provides nursing services, occupational therapy, vocational services, family services, physical therapy, speech therapy and adaptive physical education.

FALL RIVER DEACONESS HOME

Res — Females Ages 13-18

Fall River, MA 02722. 603 Rock St, PO Box 2118.
Tel: 508-674-4847. Fax: 508-730-1167.

www.deaconesshome.org   E-mail: johng@deaconesshome.org
John F. Golden, Exec Dir.
   Focus: Spec Ed. Treatment. **Conditions:** Primary—ADD ADHD AN Anx BD
      Bu CD Dc Dg Dx ED Mood OCD PTSD SP. Sec—MR.
   Gen Acad. Ungraded. Courses: Read Math Lang_Arts.
   Psychotherapy: Fam Group Indiv.
   Enr: 35. Res Females 35. **Staff:** 63 (Full 56, Part 7). Admin 6.
   Rates 2003: Res $100,308/yr.
   Est 1893. Private. Nonprofit.

Girls admitted to Deaconess have generally experienced failures in fundamental development areas and education. Many of the children have been hospitalized for psychiatric reasons, and girls are often impulsive and self-destructive. After acceptance, each student undergoes a period of psychological and educational evaluation, followed by a treatment planning conference.

Residential treatment combines a consistent behavioral approach with individual and group therapy, special education, individual tutoring and vocational programs. Family counseling, permanency planning and clinical services are also part of the cohesive treatment program for children and their families.

FAMILY COUNSELING ASSOCIATES

Clinic: All Ages. M-F 9-5; Eves M-Th 5-8.

Newton, MA 02461. 34 Lincoln St.
Tel: 617-965-6200. Fax: 617-630-0381.
Barry Pomerantz, MSW, Dir.
   Focus: Treatment. **Conditions:** Primary—ADD ADHD Anx ED. Sec—BD
      Dx LD Mood OCD PTSD SP.
   Therapy: Recreational. **Psychotherapy:** Fam Group Indiv Parent.
   Staff: 7 (Full 2, Part 5).
   Rates 2003: Clinic $95/ses.
   Est 1963. State. Nonprofit.

This agency provides substance abuse evaluations and counseling for adolescents and their families. Parental, personal, group and family counseling is also available to adolescents with emotional and behavioral issues. Fees are determined along a sliding scale.

FARR ACADEMY

Day — Coed Ages 12-19

Cambridge, MA 02139. 71 Pearl St.
Tel: 617-492-4922. Fax: 617-547-8301.
E-mail: farracademy@farracademy.org
Thomas F. Culhane, MEd, Exec Dir. **Bonnie K. Culhane,** Dir.
   Focus: Spec Ed. **Conditions:** Primary—ADD ADHD Anx BD Dc Dg Dx ED
      LD Mood PTSD SP. Sec—OCD TS. **IQ 90 and up.**
   Col Prep. Gen Acad. Gr 7-12. Courses: Read Math Lang_Arts Span Sci

Soc_Stud. Man_Arts & Shop.
Psychotherapy: Fam Group Indiv Parent.
Enr: 36. **Staff:** 16 (Full 15, Part 1). Prof 13. Admin 3.
Est 1972. Private. Nonprofit.

The academy provides a therapeutic day school program for students with one or more learning, emotional or behavioral difficulties. Intensive individualized programs aim to develop a student's academic skills while alternatives within the program encourage success in nonacademic areas. The program also includes comprehensive physical education and elective components, as well as frequent overnight weekend camping trips. Homeroom teacher/counselors conduct individual and small-group counseling sessions.

FRANCISCAN CHILDREN'S HOSPITAL
& REHABILITATION CENTER
KENNEDY DAY SCHOOL

Day — Coed Ages 3-22

Brighton, MA 02135. 30 Warren St.
Tel: 617-254-3800. TTY: 617-254-6835. Fax: 617-779-1119.
www.fch.com   E-mail: info@fch.com
   Focus: Spec Ed. Treatment. **Conditions:** Primary—As Bl C CP Ep IP MD ON SB. Sec—ADD ADHD Ap Dx LD MR S.
   Gen Acad. Pre-Voc. Voc. Gr PS-12. Courses: Read Math Lang_Arts Computers Music Adaptive_Phys_Ed.
   Therapy: Hear Lang Music Occup Phys Speech. **Psychotherapy:** Fam Group Indiv Parent.
   Est 1963. Private. Nonprofit.

Kennedy provides a hospital-based day program for children with multiple disabilities or medical challenges in one or more of the following areas: physical/motor, perceptual, language/communication, cognitive/learning and attention/interaction. Hospital services are coordinated with a team approach in designing individualized programs.

The spectrum of integrated offerings includes an augmentative communication team, assistive/computer technology, music therapy (and various other therapies), life skills/vocational training, family resource services, adaptive physical education, audiology, speech-language pathology, psychological services and reading services. The school maintains a 3:1 pupil-staff ratio.

FRANCISCAN CHILDREN'S HOSPITAL
& REHABILITATION CENTER
PEDIATRIC REHABILITATION PROGRAM

Res — Coed Ages 3-16
Clinic: Ages Birth-18. M-S 9-4; Eves M-F 4-7.

Brighton, MA 02135. 30 Warren St.
Tel: 617-254-3800. TTY: 617-254-6835. Fax: 617-779-1119.

www.fch.com/clinical_services/rehabilitation.html
   E-mail: info@fchrc.org
   Focus: Rehab. Treatment. **Conditions:** Primary—As Bl C CP Ep IP MD MS ON SB. Sec—Au BD CD ED OCD Psy Sz.
   Therapy: Hear Lang Occup Phys Speech. **Psychotherapy:** Fam Group Indiv Parent.
   Est 1949. Private. Nonprofit. Roman Catholic.

This program at FCH&RC provides comprehensive inpatient and outpatient programs for children and adolescents who have functional deficits resulting from catastrophic illness or injury. Infants, children and adolescents who have neurological or musculoskeletal impairments are candidates for service. Care focuses on the medical, therapeutic and educational needs of the patient. The interdisciplinary treatment team comprises professionals from various rehabilitation specialties at Franciscan.

FRANCISCAN CHILDREN'S HOSPITAL
EDUCATIONAL RESOURCE CENTER
Clinic: Ages 5-18. M-S 9-4; Eves M-F 4-7.

Brighton, MA 02135. 30 Warren St.
Tel: 617-254-3800. TTY: 617-254-6835. Fax: 617-779-1119.
www.fch.com/family/education_resource.html   E-mail: fch@fch.com
   Focus: Spec Ed. Treatment. **Conditions:** Primary—Dx LD.
   Gen Acad. Gr K-12. Courses: Read Math Study_Skills.
   Est 1949. Private. Nonprofit. Roman Catholic.

The center provides educational evaluations and individualized tutoring for school-age children who are experiencing difficulties in one or more of the following areas: reading, writing or spelling. Evaluators and Orton-Gillingham tutors work with parents and schools to help children overcome obstacles and achieve to potential.

Pupils first undergo a one- or two-day educational evaluation that assesses needs and compares the student's performance to that of his or her peers. This evaluation may include any of the following assessments: phonological awareness, pre-reading skills, decoding, spelling, word recognition, oral reading, reading comprehension, listening comprehension written expression, study and organizational skills, pre-math skills, and math computation and application. Detailed recommendations for placement, instruction and classroom accommodations follow the evaluation.

Tutorials are available to pupils in grades 1-12 who have dyslexia or a learning disability that affects reading, spelling, writing, or expressive and receptive language. Tutors integrate individualized programs, parental input, diagnostic tests and written progress reports.

FRANKLIN MEDICAL CENTER
SPEECH AND HEARING CENTER
Clinic: All Ages. M-F 8-5.

Greenfield, MA 01301. 164 High St.

Tel: 413-773-0211.
www.baystatehealth.com/fmc
> **Focus:** Treatment. **Conditions:** Primary—D S. Sec—Bl CP Dx ED Ep IP
> LD MR OH.
> **Therapy:** Hear Lang Speech.
> **Est 1920.** Private. Inc. **Spons:** Baystate Health System.

The Speech and Hearing Center provides diagnostic and therapeutic services for the identification and the treatment of speech, language and hearing disorders. Evaluation of the child's capabilities and problem areas, development of individualized programs, suggestions for implementation, consultation, and follow-up services are elements of the program. Fees vary according to services provided.

FREDERIC L. CHAMBERLAIN SCHOOL

Res and Day — Coed Ages 11-18

Middleboro, MA 02346. 1 Pleasant St, PO Box 778.
Tel: 508-947-7825. Fax: 508-947-0944.
www.chamberlainschool.org
> **E-mail: admissions@chamberlainschool.org**
William J. Doherty, Exec Dir. **Diane Wilson,** Prgm Dir. **Lawrence H. Mutty,**
Adm.
> **Focus:** Spec Ed. **Conditions:** Primary—ADD ADHD Anx Asp Au BD ED
> LD Mood OCD PTSD. Sec—As CD Dx Ep ODD Psy SP TS. **IQ 95 and**
> **up.**
> **Col Prep. Gen Acad. Pre-Voc. Voc.** Gr 6-12. Courses: Read Math Lang_
> Arts. On-Job Trng.
> **Therapy:** Hear Lang Occup Play Speech. **Psychotherapy:** Fam Group
> Indiv.
> **Enr:** 105. Res Males 59. Res Females 26. Day Males 15. Day Females 5.
> **Staff:** 154 (Full 150, Part 4). Educ 34. Admin 6.
> **Rates 2003:** Res $300/day. Day $216/day.
> **Summer Prgm:** Res & Day. Educ. Rec. Ther. 6 wks.
> **Est 1976.** Private. Nonprofit.

This therapeutic, highly structured boarding and day school, located on a 15-acre, rural campus, provides 24-hour care for students with learning, emotional and psychological special needs. Therapeutic services are coordinated with the school's individualized academic programming. Boys and girls, who typically have experienced significant difficulties in school, at home or in the community, receive individual, group and family counseling, as well as psychiatric therapy.   **See Also Pages 1030-1**

THE GIFFORD SCHOOL

Day — Coed Ages 8-22

Weston, MA 02493. 177 Boston Post Rd.
Tel: 781-899-9500. Fax: 781-899-4515.
www.gifford.org   E-mail: admin@gifford.org

Michael J. Bassichis, LICSW, Exec Dir. **Mary Howard,** Adm.
Focus: Spec Ed. **Conditions:** Primary—ADD ADHD AN Anx Asp BD Bu CD Dc Dg Dx ED LD Mood OCD Psy PTSD PW SP Sz TS. Sec—BI. **IQ 75 and up.**
Col Prep. Gen Acad. Pre-Voc. Ungraded. Courses: Read Math Lang_Arts. Man_Arts & Shop. Culinary_Arts.
Therapy: Lang Milieu Speech.
Enr: 100. Day Males 75. Day Females 25. **Staff:** 70 (Full 60, Part 10). Educ 43. Admin 6.
Rates 2003: Day $36,000/sch yr. State Aid.
Summer Prgm: Day. Educ. Rec. Ther. Day Rate $3800. 3 wks.
Est 1965. Private. Nonprofit.

Gifford offers special education for students with mild to severe social and emotional problems and learning disabilities. Students are assigned to small classroom groups according to their skills, age and peer-group relations. Courses in art, shop and sports are integrated into the curriculum, as is individual tutoring. High school diplomas are awarded to students completing a prescribed course of study.

The clinical staff collaborates with teachers in understanding intellectual, social and emotional factors affecting the student's learning and overall functioning.

GLAVIN REGIONAL CENTER

Res — Coed Ages 18 and up

Shrewsbury, MA 01545. 214 Lake St.
Tel: 508-845-9111. Fax: 508-792-7452.
www.doe.mass.edu/sped/links/COareaofficelist.html
Diane Enochs, Dir.
Conditions: Primary—Au BI CP ED MR. **IQ 0-70.**
Pre-Voc. Voc. Courses: Read Math Lang_Arts. Shelt_Workshop.
Therapy: Hear Lang Occup Phys Speech. **Psychotherapy:** Indiv.
Staff: Prof 27.
Est 1974. State. Nonprofit.

GOULD FARM

Res — Coed Ages 18 and up

Monterey, MA 01245. PO Box 157.
Nearby locations: Lincoln; Waltham.
Tel: 413-528-1804. Fax: 413-528-5051.
www.gouldfarm.org   E-mail: admissions@gouldfarm.org
Brian Snyder, MA, Exec Dir. **John Roberts,** Clin Dir. **Stuart Bartle,** MD, Med Dir. **Donna B. Burkhart,** Adm.
Focus: Rehab. **Conditions:** Primary—Anx BD ED Mood OCD Psy Sz. **IQ 80 and up.**
Voc. On-Job Trng.
Therapy: Milieu Recreational. **Psychotherapy:** Fam Group Indiv.

Enr: 40. Res Males 25. Res Females 15. **Staff:** 40 (Full 35, Part 5). Educ 28.
Admin 6.
Rates 2003: Sliding-Scale Rate $15-170/day.
Est 1913. Private. Nonprofit. **Spons:** William J. Gould Associates.

Gould Farm is a secluded retreat for mildly to severely emotionally disturbed young adults and adults. Located on 650 acres of farm land, the program centers on the work of a community and farm, supplemented with group and individual counseling. Recreational and community events include sports, picnics, concerts and crafts. The usual length of treatment is six to thirty months. Brain-injured, assaultive and mentally retarded individuals are not accepted.

Transitional housing programs in the Boston area are available for long-term transfers from Gould Farm.

HEALTHALLIANCE HOSPITAL
SPEECH, LANGUAGE AND HEARING CENTER

Clinic: All Ages. M-F 8-4:30.

Fitchburg, MA 01420. Burbank Campus, 275 Nichols Rd.
Tel: 978-343-5005. Fax: 978-343-5024.
www.memorialhc.org/ummhc/hospitals/alliance/services/speech.cfm
Paula L. Fagan, Mgr.
    Conditions: Primary—Ap D S.
    Therapy: Hear Lang Speech.
    Staff: Prof 9.
    Private. **Spons:** HealthAlliance.

HILLCREST EDUCATIONAL CENTERS

Res — Males Ages 6-18, Females 6-14

Pittsfield, MA 01201. 788 South St, PO Box 4699.
Tel: 413-499-7924. Fax: 413-443-0143.
www.hillcrestec.org   E-mail: admissions@hillcrestec.org
Gerard E. Burke, MBA, Pres. **David Michelson,** Adm.
    Focus: Spec Ed. Treatment. **Conditions:** Primary—BD CD ED OCD ODD.
    IQ 55-120.
    Gen Acad. Pre-Voc. Ungraded. Courses: Read Math Lang_Arts. Man_Arts
    & Shop. On-Job Trng.
    Therapy: Chemo Hear Lang Occup Phys Speech. **Psychotherapy:** Group
    Indiv.
    Enr: 140. Res Males 120. Res Females 20.
    Est 1985. Private. Nonprofit.

HEC operates four campuses in the Berkshire Mountains: Brookside School in Great Barrington; High Point School and Hillcrest Center in Lenox; and Intensive Treatment Unit in Hancock. The centers offer residential and educational programming aimed at facilitating the social, emotional, intellectual and physical growth of students, enabling them to return to their communities.

Hillcrest delivers services through an interdisciplinary team model wherein educators, psychologists, social workers, nurses, physicians, therapists and other specialists work together with the child-care staff to formulate treatment teams. Each student's individualized plan comprises an educational, a clinical, a rehabilitative, a medical, a recreational and a residential component. The usual length of stay is one to two years.

HOLDEN SCHOOL

Day — Coed Ages 12-21

Charlestown, MA 02129. 8 Pearl St.
Tel: 617-242-3940. Fax: 617-242-1038.
www.holdenschool.com   E-mail: holdenschl@aol.com
Janice I. Brenner, MEd, Exec Dir. **Paul L. Walker,** Adm.
Focus: Spec Ed. **Conditions:** Primary—ADD ADHD BD CD ED LD Mood Psy PTSD SP Sz. Sec—Dc Dg Dx MR. **IQ 75 and up.**
Gen Acad. Gr 6-12. Courses: Read Math Lang_Arts Sci Soc_Stud Health. On-Job Trng.
Therapy: Art.
Enr: 41. Day Males 34. Day Females 7. **Staff:** 19 (Full 17, Part 2).
Rates 2003: Day $198/day.
Est 1976. Private. Nonprofit.

Programs at this school include diagnostic testing, a full academic curriculum, counseling and family involvement. A behavior management system utilizes contracts and frequent rewards. Career counseling and decision-making classes are provided for all students. Staff members network .with families, courts and agencies on behalf of the students. Pupils participate in service learning and in a vocational program that features apprenticeship activities and on-the-job training. The usual length of treatment is two to three school years.

HORACE MANN SCHOOL FOR THE DEAF AND HARD OF HEARING

Day — Coed Ages Birth-22

Allston, MA 02134. 40 Armington St.
Tel: 617-635-8534. TTY: 617-783-3664. Fax: 617-635-6667.
www.boston.k12.ma.us/mann
Patrice DiNatale, BS, MEd, Prin.
Focus: Spec Ed. **Conditions:** Primary—D.
Col Prep. Gen Acad. Pre-Voc. Voc. Gr PS-12. Courses: Read Math Lang_Arts Sci Soc_Stud. Man_Arts & Shop. On-Job Trng.
Therapy: Hear Lang Occup Phys Speech. **Psychotherapy:** Fam Group Indiv Parent.
Enr: 140. **Staff:** 73.
Summer Prgm: Day. Educ. Rec.

Est 1869. Municipal. Nonprofit.

HMS, a part of the Boston public school system, conducts a comprehensive educational program for deaf and hard-of-hearing students. Middle and high school departments offer career and occupational education, as well as work-study in grades 11 and 12.

Specialized instruction is available in art, adaptive physical education and media. Other services include evaluations and counseling.

I. H. SCHWARTZ
CHILDREN'S REHABILITATION CENTER

Day — Coed Ages 3-21

New Bedford, MA 02740. 374 Rockdale Ave.
Tel: 508-996-3391. TTY: 508-996-3397. Fax: 508-996-3397.
www.schwartzcenter.org
    E-mail: kimberlibettencourt@schwartzcenter.org
Barry R. De St. Croix, BS, MS, Exec Dir. **Edward Lund,** MD, Med Dir.
    Focus: Spec Ed. **Conditions:** Primary—Ap Au Bl CP DS IP MR ON PDD
    S. Sec—ADD ADHD B D LD MD MS SB.
    Gen Acad. Ungraded. Courses: Life_Skills.
    Therapy: Hear Hydro Lang Occup Phys Speech.
    Enr: 36. Day Males 21. Day Females 15. **Staff:** 60 (Full 35, Part 25). Prof
    30. Educ 10. Admin 6.
    Rates 2003: No Fee.
    Est 1956. Private. Nonprofit. **Spons:** Cerebral Palsy Council of Greater New
    Bedford.

Schwartz Center provides evaluations and treatment for children with many types of disabilities, including physical handicaps, developmental impairments, medical conditions and communicative disorders. Staff members provide comprehensive treatment through one or more of the center's treatment programs: day school, audiology, occupational therapy, physical therapy, speech and language pathology, and early intervention.

INSTITUTE FOR LEARNING AND DEVELOPMENT

Clinic: Ages 6 and up. M-F 9-5; Eves M-F 5-8.

Lexington, MA 02421. 125 Hartwell Ave.
Tel: 781-861-3711. Fax: 781-861-3701.
www.ildlex.org
Bethany Roditi, MEd, PhD, Co-Dir. **Lynn Meltzer,** PhD, Co-Dir.
    Focus: Spec Ed. Trng. Treatment. **Conditions:** Primary—ADD ADHD Dc
    Dg Dx LD. **IQ 95 and up.**
    Therapy: Lang. **Psychotherapy:** Group Indiv Parent.
    Staff: 8. Admin 2.
    Est 1988. Private. Nonprofit.

The institute provides psychological and educational services for youth and adults with learning, attentional and behavioral difficulties. In addition, gifted individuals may receive educational enrichment at the facility.

THE ITALIAN HOME FOR CHILDREN

Res and Day — Coed Ages 4-14

Jamaica Plain, MA 02130. 1125 Centre St.
Tel: 617-524-3116. Fax: 617-983-5372.
www.italianhome.org
Christopher F. Small, Exec Dir.
    Conditions: Primary—BD ED. Sec—ADHD Anx CD LD Mood ODD PTSD.
    Gen Acad. Ungraded. Courses: Read Math Lang_Arts.
    Therapy: Milieu Occup Speech. **Psychotherapy:** Fam Group Indiv.
    Staff: Prof 59.
    Est 1918. Private. Nonprofit.

THE IVY STREET SCHOOL

Res — Coed Ages 13-22; Day — Coed 5-22

Brookline, MA 02446. 200 Ivy St.
Tel: 617-732-0224. Fax: 617-738-1247.
Joe Collins, MSW, Exec Dir. **Ilene Lieberman**, Adm.
    Focus: Spec Ed. **Conditions:** Primary—Asp BD BI Ep MR OH. Sec—ADD ADHD ED Mood TS.
    Gen Acad. Pre-Voc. Ungraded. Courses: Read Math Lang_Arts ADL Adaptive_Phys_Ed. Man_Arts & Shop. Shelt_Workshop. On-Job Trng.
    Therapy: Art Hear Lang Milieu Movement Music Occup Percepual-Motor Phys Recreational Speech. **Psychotherapy:** Group Indiv Parent.
    Enr: 28. Res Males 18. Res Females 10. **Staff:** 59 (Full 36, Part 23).
    Rates 2003: Res $153,472/yr. Day $51,000/yr. State Aid.
    Est 1903. Private. Nonprofit.

This year-round therapeutic day and residential school addresses the educational and behavioral needs of children and adolescents who have either suffered traumatic brain injuries or experienced other neurologically based difficulties. Ivy Street offers specialized education programs, along with rehabilitative therapies, vocational services, psychotherapy and neurobehavioral management.

JUDGE BAKER CHILDREN'S CENTER

Day — Coed Ages 5-15

Boston, MA 02120. 53 Parker Hill Ave.
Tel: 617-232-8390. Fax: 617-232-8399.
www.jbcc.harvard.edu   **E-mail: info@jbcc.harvard.edu**

Stuart T. Hauser, MD, PhD, Pres.
  Conditions: Primary—BD ED LD.
  Gen Acad. Ungraded. Courses: Read Math Lang_Arts. Man_Arts & Shop.
  Psychotherapy: Fam Group Indiv.
  Est 1917. Private.

KENNEDY-DONOVAN CENTER SCHOOL

Day — Coed Ages 3-22

New Bedford, MA 02740. 19 Hawthorn St.
Tel: 508-992-4756. Fax: 508-999-5367.
www.kdc.org   E-mail: kdc@kdc.org
Heidi J. Bettencourt, BA, MEd, Prgm Dir. **Karen Dobbins,** Adm.
  Focus: Spec Ed. **Conditions:** Primary—Ap Apr As Asp Au B Bl C CP D DS
    Ep IP MD Mood MR MS OCD PDD PTSD PW S SB. Sec—ADD ADHD
    Anx CD Db Dc Dg Dx ED LD SP TS.
  Gen Acad. Pre-Voc. Ungraded.
  Therapy: Lang Occup Speech.
  Enr: 53. **Staff:** 58 (Full 48, Part 10). Prof 38. Educ 33.
  Rates 2003: Day $38,369/yr.
  Est 1969. Private. Nonprofit.

Kennedy-Donovan serves students who are medically fragile or face cognitive, physical or behavioral challenges. The school provides year-round education, therapy and support services, while also maintaining an after-school program.

THE KOLBURNE SCHOOL

Res — Coed Ages 8-22

New Marlborough, MA 01230. 343 New Marlborough-Southfield Rd.
Tel: 413-229-8787. Fax: 413-229-4165.
E-mail: ks01230@aol.com
Jeane K. Weinstein, MA, Exec Dir. **James A. Smith,** MD, Med Dir. **Kathleen
  A. Greco,** Adm.
  Focus: Spec Ed. **Conditions:** Primary—ADD ADHD Asp Au BD Dx ED LD
    Mood OCD PDD Psy SP Sz TS. Sec—Bl CD MR PTSD S. **IQ 60-120.**
  Col Prep. Gen Acad. Pre-Voc. Voc. Gr 3-12. Courses: Read Math Lang_
    Arts Sci Soc_Stud Studio_Art. Man_Arts & Shop. On-Job Trng.
  Therapy: Chemo Hear Lang Occup Phys Speech. **Psychotherapy:** Fam
    Group Indiv.
  Enr: 100. Res Males 90. Res Females 10. **Staff:** 180 (Full 165, Part 15).
    Prof 38. Educ 18. Admin 15.
  Rates 2003: Res $111,472/yr. State Aid.
  Est 1947. Private. Inc.

Kolburne provides comprehensive services for moderately to severely disturbed children who are able to benefit from academic or vocational placement. Special education classes and instruction in all standard areas are supplemented by courses in graphic arts, industrial arts and career awareness. Self-help skills and social skills training are also provided. Religious services are available to each student.

Recreational facilities include fields for soccer, flag football and softball, camping areas, ponds for fishing and ice-skating, a gymnasium and an indoor swimming pool. Trips to fairs, theaters, athletic events, museums and parks are part of regular programming.

LAKE GROVE MAPLE VALLEY SCHOOL

Res — Males Ages 13-21

Wendell, MA.
Contact: 3390 Rte 112, PO Box 786, Medford, NY 11763.
Tel: 631-205-1950. Fax: 631-205-9439.
www.lgstc.org   E-mail: LGTCadmissions@lgstc.org
Albert A. Brayson II, MEd, Pres.
  Focus: Spec Ed. Trng. Treatment. **Conditions:** Primary—ED LD.
  Col Prep. Gen Acad. Pre-Voc. Voc. Gr 7-12. Ungraded. Courses: Read Math Lang_Arts. Man_Arts & Shop. On-Job Trng.
  Therapy: Chemo Lang Speech. **Psychotherapy:** Fam Group Indiv.
  Private.

LAKESIDE SCHOOL

Res and Day — Males Ages 8-16

Peabody, MA 01960. 629 Lowell St.
Tel: 978-535-0250. Fax: 978-535-5630.
E-mail: lakesid@rcn.com
Susan Ankeles-Wilchins, BA, MA, Exec Dir. **Carolyn Joy Terenzoni,** Prgm Dir.
  Focus: Spec Ed. **Conditions:** Primary—ADD ADHD BD ED LD Mood OCD ODD PTSD TS. Sec—CD Dx Psy. **IQ 70-130.**
  Gen Acad. Ungraded. Courses: Read Math Lang_Arts Sci Soc_Stud.
  Therapy: Art Lang Milieu Occup Play Recreational. **Psychotherapy:** Fam Group Indiv Parent.
  Enr: 50. Res Males 25. Day Males 25. **Staff:** 47 (Full 39, Part 8).
  Summer Prgm: Res & Day. Educ. Rec. Ther.
  Est 1969. Private. Inc.

Lakeside is an educational and therapeutic day and residential center that provides remedial and clinical services for boys with emotional or behavioral problems. The average length of treatment is two years. The school does not admit sex offenders.

LANDMARK SCHOOL

Res — Coed Ages 14-20; Day — Coed 7-20

Prides Crossing, MA 01965. 429 Hale St, PO Box 227.
  Nearby locations: Manchester-by-the-Sea.
Tel: 978-236-3000. Fax: 978-927-7268.
www.landmarkschool.org   E-mail: jtruslow@landmarkschool.org
Robert J. Broudo, BA, MEd, Head. **Carolyn Orsini-Nelson,** Adm.
  Focus: Spec Ed. **Conditions:** Primary—Dx LD. **IQ 95 and up.**
  Col Prep. Gen Acad. Gr 2-12. Courses: Read Math Lang_Arts Sci Soc_
    Stud Studio_Art Drama Chorus Dance.
  Therapy: Lang Speech. **Psychotherapy:** Indiv.
  Enr: 414. Res Males 117. Res Females 63. Day Males 162. Day Females
    72. **Staff:** 299 (Full 261, Part 38). Educ 213. Admin 93.
  Rates 2003: Res $36,800-43,800/sch yr. Day $26,600-33,600/sch yr.
  Summer Prgm: Res & Day. Educ. Rem. Res Rate $7200-7600. Day Rate
    $3600-5500. 6 wks.
  Est 1971. Private. Nonprofit.

Landmark accepts intellectually capable and emotionally sound students who have been unable to achieve in school because of a language-based learning disability or dyslexia. Daily one-on-one tutoring in reading, spelling, writing and study skills forms the basis of the program, which aims to return the child to a standard classroom situation through the remediation of skills. In addition to its tutorials, Landmark provides small classes in math, writing, science and social studies, as well as electives in the arts, wood-working, computer science and mechanics. The school provides an extensive athletic program, in addition to student government, yearbook, drama and interest clubs.

Over the summer, the school offers a seamanship program, a marine science program, an adventure ropes course and an academic program that features two daily tutorial sessions. All summer offerings last for six weeks.

Landmark operates two campuses on Boston's North Shore: the elementary and middle school location at 167 Bridge St., P.O. Box 1489, Manchester-by-the Sea 01944, and the high school at the Prides Crossing address.   **See Also Page 1040**

THE LANGUAGE AND COGNITIVE DEVELOPMENT CENTER

Day — Coed Ages 3-13

Jamaica Plain, MA 02130. 11 Wyman St, PO Box 270.
Tel: 617-522-5434. Fax: 617-522-9631.
www.millermethod.org   E-mail: arnmill@aol.com
Arnold Miller, PhD, Dir.
  Conditions: Primary—Au PDD. Sec—BD LD MR.
  Gen Acad. Ungraded. Courses: Read Math Lang_Arts. Man_Arts & Shop.
  Therapy: Movement.
  Est 1973. Private. Nonprofit.

LATHAM SCHOOL

Res — Females Ages 8-22

Brewster, MA 02631. 1646 Rte 6A, PO Box 1879.
Tel: 508-896-5755. Fax: 508-896-8310.
www.lathamcenters.org   E-mail: info@lathamcenters.org
Anne McManus, MA, LCSW, Exec Dir. **Octavia Ossola,** MSW, LICSW, Prgm
  Dir. **Lin Hood-Glidden,** Intake.
  Focus: Spec Ed. Treatment. **Conditions:** Primary—ADD ADHD ED MR
  ODD PTSD. Sec—Asp BD BI CP Mood OCD PDD Sz. **IQ 60-80.**
  Gen Acad. Pre-Voc. Voc. Ungraded. Courses: Read Math Lang_Arts Com-
  puters Sci Soc_Stud. Shelt_Workshop. On-Job Trng.
  Therapy: Lang Occup Phys Recreational Speech. **Psychotherapy:** Group
  Indiv Parent.
  Enr: 34. Res Females 34. **Staff:** 43 (Full 28, Part 15).
  Rates 2004: Res $137,715/yr. State Aid.
  Est 1970. Private. Nonprofit. **Spons:** Latham Centers.

Latham provides a residential, educational and treatment services for girls with both
developmental disabilities and emotional disturbances. The year-round program accommodates children and adolescents who are considered moderately mentally retarded
and who face significant psychiatric illnesses. Extreme social withdrawal and physical
aggression are typical resident behaviors. Referrals, which are usually considered the
final chance for behaviorally demanding girls, come from the client's local school district or a responsible social agency.

The highly structured program combines individualized instruction with a variety of
educational counseling and supplementary services that are not available in the public
sector. Staff members continually monitor achievement levels and update individual
programs as warranted. Students receive individual and group counseling, along with
recreational, physical and language therapies. In addition, the school dispenses a full
range of psychological and psychiatric services as needed.

LEAGUE SCHOOL OF GREATER BOSTON

Res and Day — Coed Ages 3-22

Walpole, MA 02032. 300 Boston Providence Tpke.
Tel: 508-850-3900. Fax: 508-660-2442.
www.leagueschool.com
Herman T. Fishbein, EdD, Exec Dir.
  Conditions: Primary—Asp Au. Sec—MR.
  Pre-Voc. Voc. Courses: Read Math Lang_Arts. Man_Arts & Shop. Shelt_
  Workshop. On-Job Trng.
  Therapy: Art Lang Music Occup Phys Speech.
  Est 1966. Private. Nonprofit.

LEARNING AND DEVELOPMENTAL DISABILITIES EVALUATION AND REHABILITATION SERVICES

Clinic: All Ages. M-F 8-5.

Wellesley, MA 02481. 65 Walnut St.
Tel: 781-449-6074. Fax: 781-237-0968.
www.ladders.org   E-mail: info@ladders.org
Margaret L. Bauman, MD, Dir. **Thomas L. Maloney,** MSN, RN, Clin Coord.
  Focus: Spec Ed. Rehab. Treatment. **Conditions:** Primary—ADD ADHD
    Ap Apr Asp Au Bl CP Dc Dg DS Dx Ep IP LD MD MR Nf ON PDD S SB.
    Sec—As BD C ED.
  Therapy: Occup Phys Speech. **Psychotherapy:** Indiv.
  Staff: 24 (Full 14, Part 10). Prof 20. Admin 3.
  Est 1981. Private. Nonprofit. **Spons:** Massachusetts General Hospital.

This interdisciplinary program provides evaluation and treatment for children and adults with autism, pervasive developmental disorder and related disorders. LADDERS also provides advocacy services, as well as educational training and resources for the community. The program serves as a training facility for graduate students and medical trainees.

THE LEARNING CENTER

Res and Day — Coed Ages 6-22

Waltham, MA 02452. 411 Waverley Oaks Rd, Ste 104.
Tel: 781-893-6000. Fax: 781-893-1171.
www.protestantguild.org/LChome.html
  Conditions: Primary—Au MR.
  Pre-Voc. Voc. Courses: Read Math. Shelt_Workshop. On-Job Trng.
  Therapy: Lang Speech. **Psychotherapy:** Indiv.
  Est 1952. Private. Nonprofit. **Spons:** Protestant Guild for the Blind.

THE LEARNING CENTER FOR DEAF CHILDREN

Res — Coed Ages 4-21

Framingham, MA 01701. 848 Central St.
  Nearby locations: Randolph.
Tel: 508-879-5110. TTY: 508-879-5110.
www.tlcdeaf.org   E-mail: inquiries@tlcdeaf.org
Michael Bello, MA, Exec Dir.
  Focus: Treatment. **Conditions:** Primary—BD D ED Mood OCD ODD
    PTSD. Sec—ADD ADHD Au Bu CD MR Psy SP Sz TS.
  Gen Acad. Pre-Voc. Gr PS-12. Courses: Read Math Lang_Arts.
  Therapy: Hear Lang Occup Phys Speech. **Psychotherapy:** Fam Group
    Indiv.
  Est 1970. Private. Nonprofit.

This residential school provides comprehensive treatment and educational services for deaf children and youth with severe social and emotional difficulties resulting from childhood trauma, mental illness and organic dysfunctions. Students receive individualized care and therapy in an environment in which approximately half of the staff are deaf, and all are proficient in American Sign Language. The program combines a full range of academic and enrichment courses with social and work training skills.

TLC comprises three schools: a comprehensive preschool through high school program in Framingham that serves a majority of the students; Walden School, a therapeutic treatment program for deaf students who also have severe emotional, behavioral or developmental disturbances (at the same Framingham address; 508-626-8581); and a satellite program in Randolph (30 Seton Way, 02368; 781-963-5110) designed to serve the southeastern region of the state.

LEARNING PREP SCHOOL

Day — Coed Ages 8-22

West Newton, MA 02465. 1507 Washington St.
Tel: 617-965-0764. Fax: 617-527-1514.
www.learningprep.org   E-mail: info@learningprep.org
Nancy E. Rosoff, MEd, Dir.
  Focus: Spec Ed. Trng. **Conditions:** Primary—LD PDD. Sec—ADD ADHD Apr As Asp Au Bl CP Db Dc Dg Dx ED IP Mood OCD ON S SP TS. **IQ 75-125.**
  Gen Acad. Pre-Voc. Voc. Gr 2-12. Courses: Read Math Lang_Arts Eng Sci Hist Computers Studio_Art Health. Man_Arts & Shop. On-Job Trng.
  Therapy: Lang Occup Speech. **Psychotherapy:** Group Indiv.
  Enr: 317. Day Males 207. Day Females 110. **Staff:** 121.
  Rates 2003: Day $122/day. State Aid.
  Est 1970. Private. Nonprofit. **Spons:** Little People's School.

Language- and learning-disabled students with secondary handicaps receive academic and work/job training at the school. Children follow an individualized program. The high school level includes work-study opportunities and vocational training that stresses personal responsibility and social skills development.

THE LEDGES

Res — Coed Ages 18 and up

Hopedale, MA 01747. 55 Adin St, PO Box 38.
Tel: 508-473-6520. Fax: 508-478-3054.
www.theledges.org   E-mail: varone@theledges.org
Vincent J. Arone, Sr., PhD, Exec Dir. **Nancy Arone,** MA, Educ Dir. **John Tognazzi,** MD, Med Dir. **Vincent J. Arone, Jr.,** Adm.
  Focus: Treatment. **Conditions:** Primary—Ap As Au Bl C Dx ED Ep MR OCD ON S. Sec—B CD CP D Db MD MS Psy Sz. **IQ 25 and up.**
  Gen Acad. Pre-Voc. Voc. Ungraded. Courses: Read Math Studio_Art Music Home_Ec. Shelt_Workshop. On-Job Trng.

Therapy: Lang Occup Speech. **Psychotherapy:** Group Indiv.
Enr: 36. Res Males 18. Res Females 18. **Staff:** 42 (Full 24, Part 18).
Rates 2004: Res $52,000/yr. State Aid.
Est 1960. Private. Inc.

The Ledges offers a year-round, specially structured program within a homelike environment for individuals with disabilities. The program includes psychotherapy, work activity, vocational evaluation, counseling and functional academics. Community residence and employment opportunities are also available. Length of treatment varies, with lifetime care available. **See Also Page 1041**

LESLEY UNIVERSITY THRESHOLD PROGRAM

Res — Coed Ages 18-26

Cambridge, MA 02138. 29 Everett St.
Tel: 617-349-8181.
www.lesley.edu/threshold/threshold_home.htm
    E-mail: threshold@mail.lesley.edu
Jim Wilbur, BA, MEd, Dir. **Helen McDonald,** Adm.
    Focus: Spec Ed. Trng. **Conditions:** Primary—ADD ADHD Dx LD MR.
    Voc. Gr PG. Courses: Life_Skills.
    Enr: 66.
    Est 1982. Private.

Threshold is a comprehensive, nondegree, campus-based program at Lesley University for highly motivated young adults with diverse learning disabilities and other special needs. In the first year, students further develop life skills such as personal finance and independent living, and they gain exposure to three different vocational options. Students chose to major in either business services, early childhood studies or human services in the second year of study. Pupils earn certificates of completion and six college credits upon completion of the program.

LIGHTHOUSE SCHOOL

Day — Coed Ages 3-22

North Chelmsford, MA 01863. 25 Wellman Ave.
Tel: 978-251-4050. Fax: 978-251-8950.
www.lighthouseschool.org   E-mail: office@lighthouseschool.org
    Conditions: Primary—BD ED LD MR OH.
    Gen Acad. Pre-Voc. Voc. Ungraded. Courses: Read Math Lang_Arts.
        Shelt_Workshop. On-Job Trng.
    Therapy: Occup Speech.
    Est 1967. Private. Nonprofit.

LINDEN HILL SCHOOL

Res — Males Ages 9-16

Northfield, MA 01360. 154 S Mountain Rd.
Tel: 413-498-2906. Fax: 413-498-2908.
www.lindenhs.org   E-mail: office@lindenhs.org
James A. McDaniel, Head. **Sarah Care,** Adm.
  Focus: Spec Ed. **Conditions:** Primary—Dx LD. Sec—ADD ADHD. **IQ 90 and up.**
  Gen Acad. Ungraded. Courses: Read Math Lang_Arts Sci Hist Studio_Art Woodworking.
  Therapy: Lang Occup Speech.
  Enr: 46. Res Males 46. **Staff:** 27 (Full 15, Part 12).
  Rates 2003: Res $38,800/sch yr.
  Summer Prgm: Res & Day. Educ. Rec. Res Rate $4750. 4 wks.
  Est 1961. Private. Nonprofit.

Linden Hill offers a language development program that utilizes the Orton-Gillingham phonics approach and small subject classes. The multisensory approach to learning in all classes is geared to teaching to the boy's strengths to overcome language deficiencies.

Residence of two or three years is typical. Frequent trips to historic and interesting sites, recreation and outdoor activities make use of the attractive campus and environs. A remodeled dairy farm forms the nucleus of the school. Arts and crafts and athletic training are correlated with the reading and writing program.   **See Also Page 1042**

LIPTON CENTER

Day — Coed Ages 12-19
Clinic: All Ages. M-F 9-5; Eve W 5-8.

Leominster, MA 01453. 100 Erdman Way.
  Nearby locations: Ayer; Fitchburg.
Tel: 978-537-3324. Fax: 978-537-3496.
S. Kay Jarvis, MA, Dir. **James Bonner,** MD, Med Dir. **Carolyn Droser,** Adm.
  Focus: Spec Ed. **Conditions:** Primary—ED LD. Sec—ADD ADHD Asp BD Dc Dg Dx Mood OCD ODD PTSD SP Sz TS.
  Gen Acad. Gr 7-12. Courses: Read Math Lang_Arts Sci Health.
  Therapy: Hear Lang Milieu Occup Phys Speech. **Psychotherapy:** Fam Group Indiv.
  Enr: 20. Day Males 12. Day Females 8. **Staff:** 9 (Full 5, Part 4).
  Rates 2003: Day $160/day. State Aid.
  Summer Prgm: Day. Rec. Ther.
  Est 1972. Private. Nonprofit. **Spons:** Community Healthlink.

Lipton Center offers full mental health services for children, adolescents and families who stand to benefit from early and intensive diagnosis, evaluation, treatment and consultation. Services are integrated and comprehensive, with an emphasis on focused, goal-oriented treatment. Lipton Academy provides educational programming for students with learning disabilities in grades 7-12; it focuses on core subjects such as reading, math, science and language arts.

With additional locations in Ayer and Fitchburg, the center serves a broad area of northern and central Massachusetts.

MASSACHUSETTS GENERAL HOSPITAL
LANGUAGE DISORDERS UNIT
READING DISABILITIES CLINIC

Clinic: All Ages. M-Th 9-4.

Boston, MA 02114. Wang Ambulatory Care Ctr, Ste 737.
Tel: 617-726-2764. Fax: 617-724-3952.
Phyllis B. Meisel, BA, Dir. **David Caplan,** PhD, MD, Med Dir.
  Focus: Treatment. **Conditions:** Primary—Dx LD.
  Staff: 6. Prof 5. Admin 1.
  Rates 2003: No Fee.
  Est 1934. Private. Nonprofit.

This unit provides diagnostic and treatment services for children and adults with dyslexia who are experiencing problems in reading, writing, spelling and comprehension. The individualized program features use of the Orton-Gillingham approach.

MASSACHUSETTS HOSPITAL SCHOOL

Res — Coed Ages 3-21; Day — Coed 5-22
Clinic: All Ages. M-F 7-4:30.

Canton, MA 02021. 3 Randolph St.
Tel: 781-828-2440. Fax: 781-821-4086.
www.state.ma.us/dph/hosp/mhs.htm
Philip E. Dould, BS, MAEd, Actg Exec Dir. **Carlton Akins,** MD, Med Dir. **Karen McHugh,** Adm.
  Focus: Rehab. **Conditions:** Primary—BI CP MD ON SB. Sec—Ep.
  Gen Acad. Pre-Voc. Voc. Ungraded. Courses: Read Math Lang_Arts. Man_ Arts & Shop. On-Job Trng.
  Therapy: Hear Lang Music Occup Phys Recreational Speech. **Psychotherapy:** Group Indiv Equine.
  Enr: 119. Res Males 48. Res Females 38. Day Males 18. Day Females 15.
    Staff: 214.
  Rates 2003: Res $770/day. Clinic $106/ses. State Aid.
  Summer Prgm: Day. Educ. Rec. Ther. Res Rate $1600. 6 wks.
  Est 1904. State. Nonprofit.

Situated on 165 acres just outside of Boston in the Blue Hills, this 110-bed facility provides medical, rehabilitative, recreational and educational services to children and young adults who are physically disabled, assisting them in developing their maximum level of independence. The principle patient groups include cerebral palsy, myelodysplasia and spinal cord injuries.

Physical and occupational therapies and social rehabilitation are offered. The hospital provides an accredited academic curriculum and an ungraded certificate program.

Vocational skills and job placement are encouraged through a work-study program with local community businesses. Other programs include noncommunicative speech and language systems, dental, independent living and respite care.

MAY CENTER FOR CHILD AND FAMILY SERVICES

Day — Coed All Ages

Fall River, MA 02720. 178 Pine St.
Tel: 508-678-0041. Fax: 508-324-9002.
www.mayinstitute.org   E-mail: information@mayinstitute.org
Catherine Vieira-Baker, PhD, Dir.
   Focus: Trng. Treatment. **Conditions:** Primary—BD LD MR.
   Private.

MAY CENTER FOR CHILD DEVELOPMENT

Day — Coed Ages 3-22

Chatham, MA 02633. 100 Sea View St, PO Box 708.
Tel: 508-945-1147. Fax: 508-945-2698.
www.mayinstitute.org   E-mail: smiller@mayinstitute.org
Walter P. Christian, PhD, Pres.
   Focus: Spec Ed. **Conditions:** Primary—Au PDD. Sec—LD MR OH.
   Gen Acad. Pre-Voc. Ungraded. Courses: Read Math Lang_Arts.
   Therapy: Lang Speech. **Psychotherapy:** Fam Indiv Parent.
   Enr: 53.
   Est 1955. Private. Nonprofit. **Spons:** May Institute.

May Center provides educational services, supported employment opportunities, parental education and support, and school- and home-based consultations. Various types of therapy are available.

MAY CENTER FOR EARLY CHILDHOOD EDUCATION

Day — Coed Ages 3-12

Arlington, MA 02476. 10 Acton St.
Tel: 781-648-9260. Fax: 781-641-2362.
www.mayinstitute.org   E-mail: info@mayinstitute.org
Tania Treml, MEd, Dir. **Jennifer Gower,** Adm.
   Focus: Spec Ed. **Conditions:** Primary—Au. Sec—LD MR.
   Gen Acad. Gr PS-8. Courses: Read Math Lang_Arts.
   Therapy: Lang Music Phys Speech.
   Enr: 50. **Staff:** 43.
   Rates 2003: Day $52,146/yr. State Aid.
   Private. Nonprofit. **Spons:** May Institute.

This year-round program comprises early intervention, educational and consultative services for children with autism and their families. The early intervention program serves both preschoolers and school-age children. Educational services are integral to the center's program, and school- and home-based consultations are also available.

MAY CENTER FOR EARLY INTERVENTION
SCHOOL AND FAMILY CONSULTATION SERVICES

Day — Coed Ages Birth-5

West Springfield, MA 01089. 1111 Elm St, Ste 2.
Tel: 413-734-0300. Fax: 413-734-0800.
www.mayinstitute.org   E-mail: information@mayinstitute.org
Nancy R. M. Lunden, MSW, LCSW, Dir. **Carol Patten,** Adm.
　　Focus: Spec Ed. **Conditions:** Primary—Apr Asp Au BD CP DS LD MR S.
　　Gen Acad. Ungraded. Courses: Lang_Arts.
　　Therapy: Lang Occup Phys Play Speech. **Psychotherapy:** Group Parent.
　　Enr: 161. **Staff:** 23. (Full 23). Educ 14. Admin 4.
　　Private. Nonprofit. **Spons:** May Institute.

May Center provides home- and community-based early intervention services for young children, in addition to school-based consultation. May addresses the spectrum of pervasive developmental disorders. For parents, the center offers education and support groups. Local school districts generally cover program fees.

MAY CENTER FOR EDUCATION
AND NEUROREHABILITATION

Res and Day — Coed Ages 5-22

Norwood, MA 02062. 1 Commerce Way.
Tel: 781-440-0400. TTY: 781-440-0461.
www.mayinstitute.org   E-mail: info@mayinstitute.org
Jeffrey Skowron, PhD, Dir.
　　Focus: Spec Ed. Rehab. Trng. Treatment. **Conditions:** Primary—BI OH.
　　Col Prep. Gen Acad. Pre-Voc. Voc. Ungraded. Courses: Read Math Lang_
　　Arts. On-Job Trng.
　　Therapy: Lang Occup Phys Speech. **Psychotherapy:** Fam Group Indiv
　　Parent.
　　Enr: 53.
　　Private. Nonprofit. **Spons:** May Institute.

Children, adolescents and young adults with orthopedic and neurological disorders, including acquired or traumatic brain injury, receive various educational and vocational services at this facility. Vocational offerings include on-the-job training and supported employment, and schooling is available at all age levels served. Community reentry programs, parent education and support, and school-based consultation are among the other services. Community-based residences are located in Arlington, Holbrook and Randolph.

MAY CENTER FOR EDUCATION
AND VOCATIONAL TRAINING

Res — Coed Ages 11-22; Day — Coed 5-22

Braintree, MA 02184. 22 Blanchard Blvd.
Tel: 781-849-0223. Fax: 781-849-0597.
www.mayinstitute.org   E-mail: information@mayinstitute.org
Walter P. Christian, PhD, Pres. **Jane Carlson,** PhD, Clin Dir.
  Focus: Spec Ed. Trng. **Conditions:** Primary—Au. Sec—LD MR.
  Gen Acad. Pre-Voc. Voc. Ungraded. Courses: Read Math Lang_Arts. On-
    Job Trng.
  Therapy: Occup Phys Speech. **Psychotherapy:** Fam.
  Enr: 63. Res Males 14. Res Females 8. Day Males 31. Day Females 10.
  Est 1987. Private. Nonprofit. **Spons:** May Institute.

Children age 5 and up participate in the center's educational program, and older students may also take part in a supported employment program. Other services include school-based consultation and family support.

MCAULEY NAZARETH HOME FOR BOYS

Res and Day — Males Ages 6-13

Leicester, MA 01524. 77 Mulberry St.
Tel: 508-892-4886. Fax: 508-892-9736.
E-mail: naz1901@aol.com
Sr. Janet Ballentine, MSW, LICSW, Exec Dir.
  Focus: Spec Ed. Treatment. **Conditions:** Primary—ADD ADHD Asp BD CD
    Dx ED LD Mood OCD ODD ON PTSD SP TS. Sec—Ar As Bl Db Ep HIV
    TB. **IQ 80 and up.**
  Gen Acad. Ungraded. Courses: Read Math Lang_Arts Sci Soc_Stud.
  Therapy: Chemo Lang Milieu Occup Phys Play Recreational Speech. **Psychotherapy:** Fam Group Indiv.
  Enr: 25. Res Males 21. Day Males 4. **Staff:** 36. Prof 16. Educ 7. Admin 3.
  Rates 2003: Res $111,084/yr. State Aid.
  Est 1901. Private. Nonprofit. Roman Catholic. **Spons:** Sisters of Mercy.

McAuley offers a year-round, family-centered program with special education for mildly to severely emotionally disturbed and delinquent boys. Tutoring, casework and family counseling are available. The usual length of treatment is two to three years.

MCLEAN-FRANCISCAN CHILD AND ADOLESCENT
MENTAL HEALTH PROGRAMS

Res — Coed Ages 5-18

Brighton, MA 02135. 30 Warren St.
Tel: 617-779-1677. Fax: 617-779-1654.
www.mclean.harvard.edu/patient/child/kha.php

David Rourke, MS, Prgm Mgr.
  Focus: Treatment. **Conditions:** Primary—ADD ADHD Asp Au BD CD ED
    OCD PDD Psy Sz. **IQ 40-70.**
  Therapy: Occup Speech. **Psychotherapy:** Fam Group Indiv.
  Est 1949. Private. Nonprofit. Roman Catholic. **Spons:** Franciscan Children's
    Hospital/McLean Hospital.

Located on the campus of Franciscan Children's Hospital & Rehabilitation Center, this program provides a continuum of care for children and adolescents who are experiencing acute psychiatric symptoms. A multidisciplinary team offers diagnostic services, treatment planning and ongoing care, each tailored to the individual's specific needs. Services include crisis stabilization, acute residential treatment, psychopharmacology, psychosocial skills training, access to various pediatric subspecialties, and a locked and secure unit.

Prior to admission, each client must undergo a psychiatric diagnosis.

MERCY CENTRE

Day — Coed Ages 6-22

Worcester, MA 01605. 25 W Chester St.
Tel: 508-852-7165. Fax: 508-856-9755.
www.mercycentre.com   E-mail: mercy@mercycentre.com
Doris Dyer, Admin.
  Conditions: Primary—MR. Sec—DS PDD PW S.
  Pre-Voc. Voc. Ungraded. Courses: Read Math Lang_Arts. Shelt_Workshop.
    On-Job Trng.
  Therapy: Lang Music Occup Phys Speech.
  Staff: Prof 28.
  Est 1960. Private. Nonprofit. **Spons:** Catholic Charities.

METROWEST MEDICAL CENTER
CHILD DEVELOPMENT UNIT

Res — Coed Ages 3-15

Natick, MA 01760. Leonard Morse Campus, 67 Union St.
Tel: 508-650-7380.
  Conditions: Primary—ED.
  Therapy: Occup. **Psychotherapy:** Fam.
  Staff: Prof 17.
  Est 1984.

MIDDLESEX COMMUNITY COLLEGE
TRANSITION PROGRAM

Day — Coed Ages 18 and up

Bedford, MA 01730. 590 Springs Rd.
Tel: 781-280-3641. Fax: 781-275-7126.
www.middlesex.mass.edu   E-mail: transition@middlesex.mass.edu
Susan Woods, MEd, Dir.
    Focus: Trng. **Conditions:** Primary—ADD ADHD Dc Dg Dx LD. **IQ 70-89.**
    Voc. On-Job Trng.
    Enr: 40. Day Males 20. Day Females 20. **Staff:** 9 (Full 3, Part 6).
    State.

This two-year noncredit certificate program offers vocational preparation for Massachusetts residents with learning disabilities who are not candidates for enrollment in traditional college programs. Specially designed courses and intensive experience seek to develop independent living, job survival and personal/social skills. Students focusing on office skills training prepare for entry-level employment as clerks, data-entry clerks, file clerks and receptionists; those focusing on business skills training prepare for positions as shipping and receiving clerks, stock clerks, warehouse workers, mailroom clerks, central distribution and facility support. Prospective students must already possess either a high school diploma, a GED or a certificate of completion.

MILL SWAN COMMUNICATION SKILLS CENTER

Day — Coed Ages 3-21

Worcester, MA 01602. 337 Mill St.
Tel: 508-799-3510. Fax: 508-799-8232.
www.wpsweb.com/millswan
Kathleen Dion, Prin.
    Conditions: Primary—CP OH.
    Gen Acad. Courses: Read Math Lang_Arts.
    Est 1961. Municipal.

MORTON HOSPITAL AND MEDICAL CENTER
SPEECH, HEARING AND LANGUAGE CENTER

Clinic: All Ages. M-F 7:30-5; Eves M-Th 5-7.

Taunton, MA 02780. 2007 Bay St, Ste B-100.
Tel: 508-823-3050. TTY: 508-821-4470. Fax: 508-828-5858.
www.mortonhospital.org
Ellen Manchester, MA, Dir.
    Focus: Rehab. **Conditions:** Primary—Ap Apr Asp Au CP D PDD S. Sec—
        ADD ADHD BI Dx LD MR.
    Therapy: Hear Lang Speech.
    Staff: 15 (Full 11, Part 4). Prof 11. Admin 1.

Private. Nonprofit.

The center provides diagnosis and treatment of communicative disorders on inpatient and outpatient bases. Therapeutic services are available for aphasia, articulation, child language problems, laryngectomy, stuttering and voice disorders. Diagnostic services in audiology include assessment of middle ear function; auditory brainstem response testing; infant hearing testing; and hearing aid evaluation, fitting and orientation.

THE NATIONAL BIRTH DEFECTS CENTER

Clinic: Ages Birth-21. M-F 8:30-5.

Waltham, MA 02451. 40 2nd Ave, Ste 520.
Tel: 781-466-9555. Fax: 781-487-2361.
www.thegenesisfund.org/nbdc.htm   E-mail: nbdc@thegenesisfund.org
Murray Feingold, MD, Dir.
    Focus: Treatment. **Conditions:** Primary—ADD ADHD Ap B BI CP D Dx IP
      LD MD MR MS ON S SB TB. Sec—Au.
    Est 1984. Nonprofit. **Spons:** Genesis Fund.

NBDC provides diagnosis and treatment for children born with birth defects, genetic diseases and mental retardation. The center also offers genetic counseling to prospective parents who are concerned about the possibility of genetic diseases occurring in their children.

NAUSET

Res and Day — Coed Ages 18 and up

Hyannis, MA 02601. 895 Mary Dunn Rd.
    Nearby locations: Eastham; Falmouth.
Tel: 508-778-5040. Fax: 508-778-9642.
www.nausetinc.org   E-mail: nausetly@cape.com
Larry R. Thayer, Exec Dir.
    Conditions: Primary—MR. Sec—Ap B BD BI C CP D Dx ED Ep LD ON S.
    Voc. Shelt_Workshop. On-Job Trng.
    Therapy: Lang Occup Phys Speech.
    Enr: 110. **Staff:** 100.
    Est 1968. Private. Nonprofit.

Serving individuals with multiple disabilities, Nauset provides such vocational services as assessment, on-the-job training, supported employment, placement, job coaching and follow-up. Staff members formulate a plan for each client and dictate services based upon the individual's needs. Day habilitation services seek to increase self-sufficiency and enable the client to participate more fully in his or her community.

Nauset also operates supervised residential homes. Shared and supported living opportunities are available throughout Cape Cod. Options range from four-person group homes to cooperative apartments to family placements.

NEARI SCHOOL

Day — Coed Ages 8-22

Holyoke, MA 01040. 70 N Summer St.
Tel: 413-532-1713. Fax: 413-540-1915.
E-mail: sbengis@aol.com
Steven Bengis, EdD, Exec Dir.
  Focus: Spec Ed. **Conditions:** Primary—ADD ADHD AN Anx As BD Bu CD Dc Dg Dx ED HIV LD Mood OCD Psy PTSD SP Sz TS. Sec—MR. **IQ 65-130.**
  Gen Acad. Pre-Voc. Gr K-12. Courses: Read Math Lang_Arts Soc_Stud Studio_Art Music. Man_Arts & Shop.
  Psychotherapy: Group Indiv.
  Enr: 42. Day Males 32. Day Females 10. **Staff:** 35 (Full 31, Part 4). Prof 25. Admin 4.
  Rates 2004: Day $46,000/yr. State Aid.
  Est 1985. Private. Nonprofit. **Spons:** New England Adolescent Research Institute.

The New England Adolescent Research Institute provides year-round educational, clinical, recreational and prevocational services for highly aggressive, abused and abusive children and youth, as well as training opportunities and resources for professionals who work with this at-risk population.

NEARI's special education day school enrolls severely emotionally disturbed young people. A training and consulting center for at-risk children that specializes in the care of sexually abusive students is a component of the school program, as is an after-school prevention program for highly at-risk boys and girls.

THE NEW ENGLAND CENTER FOR CHILDREN

Res — Coed Ages 3-22; Day — Coed 1½-12

Southborough, MA 01772. 33 Turnpike Rd.
Tel: 508-481-1015. Fax: 508-485-3421.
www.necc.org   E-mail: info@necc.org
L. Vincent Strully, Jr., Exec Dir. **Catherine Welch,** Adm.
  Focus: Spec Ed. Treatment. **Conditions:** Primary—ADHD Asp Au ED PDD. Sec—MR OCD TS.
  Gen Acad. Pre-Voc. Voc. Ungraded. Courses: Read Math Lang_Arts Adaptive_Phys_Ed. On-Job Trng.
  Therapy: Hear Lang Occup Phys Speech. **Psychotherapy:** Indiv.
  Enr: 213. Res Males 94. Res Females 29. Day Males 75. Day Females 15. **Staff:** 630 (Full 627, Part 3).
  Rates 2004: Res $145,600-280,500/yr. Day $43,700-77,300/yr.
  Est 1975. Private. Nonprofit.

NECC provides clinical and educational services for children with autism and related disabilities. A continuum of offerings ranges from home-based integrated preschool to day and residential educational programs. The center bases all of its educational and treatment programs on the principles of Applied Behavior Analysis, with the goals of developing maximum independence and increasing social, educational and employment opportunities.

NEW ENGLAND NEUROLOGICAL ASSOCIATES

Clinic: All Ages. M-F 8:35-5.

North Andover, MA 01845. 220 Sutton St.
Tel: 978-687-2321. Fax: 978-685-7265.
www.neneuro.com
  Conditions: Primary—ADD ADHD Ap Au BD Bl Dx ED Ep LD MR S.
  Therapy: Speech. **Psychotherapy:** Fam Indiv.
  Est 1985. Private. Inc.

NEW ENGLAND PEDIATRIC CARE

Res — Coed Ages Birth-22; Day — Coed 3-22

North Billerica, MA 01862. 78 Boston Rd.
Tel: 978-667-5123. Fax: 978-663-5154.
Ellen O'Gorman, Exec Dir.
  Focus: Treatment. **Conditions:** Primary—B Bl CP D IP MR ON S. Sec—As
  Au C Ep MD MS SB.
  Voc. Ungraded. Courses: Read Math Lang_Arts.
  Therapy: Occup Phys Recreational Speech.
  Enr: 80.
  Est 1986. Private. Nonprofit.

This nursing facility treats children whose conditions are medically complex and who have severe cognitive or neurological impairments. Offerings include 24-hour nursing, comprehensive pediatric services, individualized rehabilitation programs, nutritional services, therapeutic recreational programs and social work services.

NEPC also offers a day school program that focuses on the development and maintenance of skills in the areas of sensory stimulation, communication, language, cognition, functional academics, gross and fine motor, prevocational skills, community awareness and aquatics. The educational program is available to multiply handicapped students ages 3-22 who reside at NEPC or live in neighboring communities.

NEW ENGLAND SINAI HOSPITAL
AND REHABILITATION CENTER

Clinic: All Ages. M-F 8:30-5.

Stoughton, MA 02072. 150 York St.
Tel: 781-344-0600. TTY: 781-341-2395. Fax: 781-344-0128.
www.newenglandsinai.org
Saroj Dave, MD, Dir.
  Conditions: Primary—As Bl C CP IP MD MS ON SB.

Therapy: Hear Lang Occup Phys Speech.
Private.

NEW ENGLAND VILLAGE

Res and Day — Coed Ages 18 and up

Pembroke, MA 02359. 664 School St.
Tel: 781-293-5461. Fax: 781-294-8385.
www.newenglandvillage.org   E-mail: info@newenglandvillage.org
Bryan Efron, PhD, Exec Dir. **Judy Andracchio,** Adm.
  Focus: Trng. **Conditions:** Primary—MR. Sec—Ap Au B BI CP D Ep ON S.
  Voc. Shelt_Workshop. On-Job Trng.
  Therapy: Hear Lang Occup Phys Speech. **Psychotherapy:** Group Indiv.
  Enr: 162. **Staff:** 160.
  Est 1972. Private. Nonprofit.

Located on a wooded, 80-acre campus, this facility provides community living
arrangements for young adults and adults with mental retardation and other developmental disabilities. The village's highly individualized environment encourages residents to
cultivate friendships, develop talents and become involved members of the local community.

Day programs assist residents and day participants in developing the skills and
responsibilities necessary to succeed in a work environment. A year-round recreation
and activities program provides such social and learning activities as adult education
courses, fitness classes, community trips, volunteer opportunities, Special Olympics and
dances.

Staff members monitor client programs daily, and the center places emphasis on long-
term relationships between staff and the resident's family.

NORTH SHORE INFANT AND TODDLER PROGRAM

Day — Coed Ages Birth-3
Clinic: Ages Birth-3. M-F 7:30-5; Eves M-F 5-7:30.

Lynn, MA 01902. 103 Johnson St.
Tel: 781-593-2727. Fax: 781-593-2542.
Andrew J. Baumgartner, MA, Exec Dir. **Jennifer Greco,** BSEd, Prgm Dir.
  Focus: Spec Ed. **Conditions:** Primary—ADD ADHD Anx Ap Apr As Asp Au
    B BD BI C CD CP D DS Dx ED Ep HIV IP LD MD MR MS Nf ON PDD
    Psy PTSD PW S SB Sz TB TS. Sec—OCD.
  Therapy: Hear Lang Occup Phys Speech. **Psychotherapy:** Fam Indiv
    Parent.
  Staff: 80 (Full 65, Part 15). Prof 63. Educ 9. Admin 8.
  Rates 2003: No Fee.
  Est 1951. Private. Nonprofit. **Spons:** Cerebral Palsy of Eastern Massachu-
    setts.

This infant developmental program treats children between birth and age 3 with diagnosed conditions or developmental delays, as well as those dealing with biological, medical or environmental factors that may cause developmental delays. The facility formulates an individualized therapeutic plan for each child. Parent education is an integral element of North Shore's services.

NORTHEAST REHABILITATION OUTPATIENT CENTER

Clinic: All Ages. M-F 8-5.

North Andover, MA 01845. 200 Sutton St.
Tel: 978-682-7009. Fax: 978-682-3294.
  Conditions: Primary—Ap Bl C CP IP MD MS ON S SB.
  Therapy: Hear Lang Occup Phys Speech. **Psychotherapy:** Group Indiv.
  Staff: Prof 8.
  Est 1992. Private.

NORTHEASTERN FAMILY INSTITUTE

Res — Coed Ages 12 and up; Day — Coed Birth-18

Danvers, MA 01923. 10 Harbor St.
  Nearby locations: Arlington; Beverly; Dorchester; Fitchburg; Haverhill; Lawrence; Middleton; Peabody; Stoneham; Wakefield; Westboro.
Tel: 978-774-0774. Fax: 978-774-8369.
www.nafi.com   E-mail: nafi@nafi.com
Yitzhak Bakal, Pres.
  Conditions: Primary—BD ED. Sec—MR.
  Gen Acad. Pre-Voc. Voc. Courses: Read Math Lang_Arts. Man_Arts &
    Shop. On-Job Trng.
  Psychotherapy: Fam Group Indiv.
  Est 1974. Private. Nonprofit. **Spons:** North American Family Institute.

NORTHEASTERN UNIVERSITY
SPEECH-LANGUAGE AND HEARING CENTER

Clinic: All Ages.

Boston, MA 02115. 30 Leon St.
Tel: 617-373-2492. TTY: 617-373-8927. Fax: 617-373-8756.
www.bouve.neu.edu/Health/slpa_speechcenter.html
Linda J. Ferrier, MA, MS, PhD, Chair.
  Conditions: Primary—D S.
  Therapy: Hear Lang Speech.
  Est 1967. Private. Nonprofit.

OPPORTUNITY WORKS

Day — Coed Ages 16 and up

Newburyport, MA 01950. 10 Opportunity Way.
Tel: 978-462-6144. Fax: 978-465-5972.
www.opportunityworks.net
Jane Harris-Fale, Exec Dir.
  Focus: Trng. **Conditions:** Primary—MR. **IQ 25 and up.**
  Pre-Voc. Voc. Shelt_Workshop.
  Therapy: Occup.
  Est 1974. Private. Nonprofit.

PEDIATRIC DEVELOPMENT CENTER

Day — Coed Ages Birth-3
Clinic: Ages Birth-3. M-F 8:30-5.

Pittsfield, MA 01201. 388 Columbus Ave Ext.
Tel: 413-499-4537. Fax: 413-448-8223.
E-mail: pdc@berkshire.rr.com
Patricia Hall Pellegrino, MEd, Dir.
  Focus: Treatment. **Conditions:** Primary—ADD ADHD Ap As Au B BI C CP
    D Ep IP ON S SB. Sec—ED OCD.
  Therapy: Hear Lang Occup Phys Speech. **Psychotherapy:** Fam Group
    Indiv Parent.
  Enr: 188. **Staff:** 27 (Full 21, Part 6). Prof 17. Educ 6. Admin 3.
  Est 1982. State. Nonprofit.

This year-round early intervention program serves medically fragile infants and toddlers, as well as those who are considered developmentally at risk. Programming features a full range of therapeutic services administered with a family focus. Massachusetts residents only may receive services at PDC.

PERKINS SCHOOL FOR THE BLIND

Res and Day — Coed Ages 3-22

Watertown, MA 02472. 175 N Beacon St.
Tel: 617-924-3434. Fax: 617-926-2027.
www.perkins.pvt.k12.ma.us
Steven M. Rothstein, MBA, Pres.
  Conditions: Primary—B. Sec—D.
  Col Prep. Gen Acad. Pre-Voc. Voc. Ungraded. Courses: Read Math Lang_
    Arts. Man_Arts & Shop. Shelt_Workshop. On-Job Trng.
  Therapy: Hear Lang Music Occup Phys Speech. **Psychotherapy:** Group
    Indiv.
  Est 1829. Private. Nonprofit.

PROFESSIONAL CENTER FOR CHILD DEVELOPMENT
Day — Coed Ages 3-7

Andover, MA 01810. 32 Osgood St.
Tel: 978-475-3806. Fax: 978-475-6288.
www.theprofessionalcenter.org   E-mail: info@theprofessionalcenter.org
Veryl D. Anderson, RN, Exec Dir. Susan M. Buehler & Jane Howe, Adms.
 Focus: Spec Ed. Rehab. Trng. Conditions: Primary—Bl CP Ep MR ON SB.
  Sec—Ap As B C D ED MD S.
 Gen Acad. Ungraded.
 Therapy: Hear Lang Music Occup Phys Play Speech Visual. Psychother-
  apy: Fam. Counseling: Nutrition.
 Enr: 25. Day Males 20. Day Females 5. Staff: 13 (Full 9, Part 4).
 Rates 2004: Day $21,437/yr. $80 (Therapy)/ses.
 Summer Prgm: Day. Educ. Ther. Day Rate $300. 5 wks.
 Est 1984. Private. Nonprofit.

This developmental preschool program provides coordinated medical, educational, social, psychological and referral services for children with multiple handicaps and their families. The center seeks to prevent deterioration of family units by providing the relief necessary to allow the child to remain at home. Children with a variety of disabilities, many of which require specific monitoring and intervention, enroll at the school. Integrated therapies are an integral part of the program.

The center serves as a training site for students working in various human service professions.

REED ACADEMY
Res — Males Ages 7-13

Framingham, MA 01701. 1 Winch St.
Tel: 508-877-1222. Fax: 508-877-7477.
E-mail: reed.academy@verizon.net
Edward A. Cohen, EdD, Exec Dir. Diane Engel, Adm.
 Focus: Spec Ed. Conditions: Primary—ADD ADHD Anx Asp BD Bl ED LD
  Mood OCD ODD ON PDD PTSD. Sec—As Dx Ep S TS. IQ 65 and up.
 Gen Acad. Ungraded. Courses: Read Math Lang_Arts Studio_Art.
 Therapy: Lang Occup Speech. Psychotherapy: Fam Group Indiv.
 Enr: 24. Res Males 24. Staff: 25. Prof 18. Educ 9.
 Summer Prgm: Res & Day. Rec. Ther. 6 wks.
 Est 1975. Private. Nonprofit.

The five-day residential program focuses on promoting developmental and academic growth, as well as behavioral changes. Enrichment courses, workshop skills, household chores and supervised social activities are part of a highly structured program. All students participate in psychotherapy sessions. The usual length of treatment is two years. A six-week summer camp program emphasizes socialization skills.

RIVERBROOK RESIDENCE

Res — Females Ages 18 and up

Stockbridge, MA 01262. 4 Ice Glen Rd, PO Box 478.
Tel: 413-298-4926. Fax: 413-298-5166.
www.riverbrook.org   E-mail: riverbro@berkshire.net
Joan S. Burkhard, MEd, MSW, Exec Dir. **Heather Murphy,** MS, Prgm Dir. **Margaret Smith,** RN, Med Dir.
  Focus: Treatment. **Conditions:** Primary—MR. Sec—ADD ADHD As B CP Db Ep ON PW S. **IQ 35-75.**
  Pre-Voc. Voc. Ungraded. Courses: Read Math. Shelt_Workshop. On-Job Trng.
  Therapy: Hear Lang Phys Speech. **Psychotherapy:** Indiv Parent.
  Enr: 22. Res Females 22. **Staff:** 24 (Full 16, Part 8).
  Rates 2004: Res $55,000/yr. State Aid.
  Est 1976. Private. Nonprofit.

Riverbrook offers a program specifically designed to meet the needs of women with moderate retardation. Individualized programs vary according to learning strengths and weaknesses, with basic instruction provided in prevocational and vocational skills.

The facility also places emphasis on the development of skills necessary for independent living. As a complement to the educational program, local professionals provide instrumental and choral lessons, dance and art therapy, cooking, sewing and swimming instruction.

Riverbrook carefully reviews each applicant's folder and requires a month's trial stay before granting admission to the program. Lifetime care is available to those residents whose health remains intact. **See Also Page 1047**

RIVERVIEW SCHOOL

Res — Coed Ages 12-23

East Sandwich, MA 02537. 551 Rte 6A.
Tel: 508-888-0489. Fax: 508-888-1315.
www.riverviewschool.com   E-mail: admissions@riverviewschool.org
Richard D. Lavoie, MA, MEd, Pres. **Janet M. Lavoie,** Adm.
  Focus: Spec Ed. **Conditions:** Primary—Dx LD. Sec—BI CP Ep S. **IQ 70-100.**
  Gen Acad. Ungraded. Courses: Read Math Lang_Arts Sci Computers Soc_Stud Studio_Art. Man_Arts & Shop.
  Therapy: Lang Occup Phys Speech.
  Enr: 182. **Staff:** 36 (Full 35, Part 1). Educ 29. Admin 7.
  Summer Prgm: Res. Educ. Rec.
  Est 1957. Private. Nonprofit.

This school provides ungraded secondary and postsecondary instruction for adolescents with learning disabilities and marginal intellectual impairments. The secondary program utilizes a thematic, integrated curriculum that emphasizes language development. Project GROW, the postsecondary component, focuses on independent living and life skills; it is available on both ten- and 12-month bases. GROW participants may also attend vocational programs at Cape Cod Community College.

Riverview's summer program serves students at the middle and high school levels.

ROBERT F. KENNEDY ACTION CORPS

Res — Males Ages 6-17

Lancaster, MA 01523. 220 Old Common Rd.
Tel: 978-365-2803. Fax: 978-368-3066.
www.rfkchildren.org
William Hogan, LICSW, Admin. **Jose Correa,** MD, Med Dir.
  Focus: Spec Ed. Treatment. **Conditions:** Primary—ADD ADHD BD CD ED Mood OCD ODD PTSD. Sec—Ep LD. **IQ 75 and up.**
  Gen Acad. Pre-Voc. Gr 2-11. Courses: Read Math Lang_Arts Sci Soc_ Stud. Man_Arts & Shop.
  Therapy: Lang Occup Recreational Speech. **Psychotherapy:** Fam Group Indiv.
  Enr: 55. Res Males 55. **Staff:** 86. Prof 46. Educ 19. Admin 14.
  Rates 2004: Res $126,990/yr.
  Est 1969. Private. Nonprofit.

Founded by a group of citizens as a memorial to the late Senator, the Action Corps works closely with the Department of Social Services and the Department of Education to care for some of the state's most troubled and disadvantaged children and their families. The agency provides comprehensive educational, clinical and residential services. The usual duration of treatment is 12 to 18 months.

Several programs operate on the Lancaster campus. The Elizabeth Birk Oatis Children's Center is a long-term residential treatment facility that provides stability for boys ages 10-15 who have engaged in unsafe and risky behavior in the past. The adolescent treatment unit serves as a long-term residential program for boys ages 12-17 who have committed less serious crimes than have those children cared for by the Department of Youth Services. Wellington Hall provides residential, educational, recreational, medical, clinical and psychopharmacological services for boys ages 6-12 who are dealing with such issues as attention deficit disorder, posttraumatic stress disorder, aggression, other emotional disorders and, in most cases, learning disabilities. Finally, the Robert F. Kennedy School provides on-campus schooling for boys in residence at RFK.

ST. ANN'S HOME

Res and Day — Coed Ages 6-17
Clinic: All Ages. M-F 9-5; Eves M-Th 5-9.

Methuen, MA 01844. 100A Haverhill St.
Tel: 978-682-5276. Fax: 978-688-4932.
www.st.annshome.org   E-mail: info@st.annshome.org
Denis Grandbois, MSW, MBA, Exec Dir. **Kathleen Lentz,** MD, Med Dir.
  Edward J. O'Brien, Adm.
  Focus: Spec Ed. Treatment. **Conditions:** Primary—ADD ADHD Asp CD ED

Mood ODD PTSD SP. Sec—BD Dx LD. **IQ 80 and up.**
Gen Acad. Ungraded. Courses: Read Math Lang_Arts Sci Soc_Stud Computers Studio_Art Music.
Therapy: Chemo Hear Lang Occup Speech. **Psychotherapy:** Fam Group Indiv.
Enr: 160. Res Males 85. Res Females 20. Day Males 35. Day Females 20. **Staff:** 240.
Rates 2004: Res $112,360/yr. Day $32,499/sch yr. State Aid.
Summer Prgm: Day. Educ. Rec. Ther. 10 wks.
Est 1925. Private. Nonprofit. Roman Catholic. **Spons:** Catholic Social Services.

St. Ann's serves children with moderate to severe emotional problems. The home provides a new environment for the child through therapy, special education and a therapeutic living experience. Younger children live in the main building. Small group homes in the community meet the needs of adolescents. Day treatment is designed for children who need a comprehensive day program, but not residential care. The program centers around a number of small classroom areas with a curriculum structured to meet both the academic and the emotional needs of each child.

An educational program is provided through St. Ann's own school for both day and residential students. Children are placed in small classroom groups. Each group of children engages in activities inside and outside the classroom to learn social living and academic skills necessary for mainstreaming.

The return of the child to his own family and community is the primary goal of treatment at St. Ann's. Therapy and follow-up services are essential components for a successful transition. Children unable to return to their families are placed in foster and adoptive families.

A ten-week summer session accepts enrollment from the day program. Counseling and outpatient services are available. The usual length of treatment is 18 months. Organically impaired, mentally retarded, autistic and seriously self-destructive children are not accepted.

SHRINERS HOSPITAL

Res — Coed Ages Birth-18

Springfield, MA 01104. 516 Carew St.
Tel: 413-787-2000. Fax: 413-787-2009.
www.shrinershq.org
Mark L. Niederpruem, BS, MPA, Admin.
  Conditions: Primary—OH. Sec—CP SB.
  Therapy: Occup Phys.
  Est 1925. Private. Nonprofit.

SOUTH SHORE MENTAL HEALTH CENTERS

Clinic: All Ages. M-F 9-5; Eves M-Th 5-9.

Quincy, MA 02169. 6 Fort St.

Nearby locations: Brewster; Chatham; Hyannis; Plymouth;Wareham.
Tel: 617-847-1950. TTY: 617-847-1922. Fax: 617-786-9894.
www.ssmh.org   E-mail: contactus@ssmh.org
Harry Shulman, MSW, Pres.
  Focus: Treatment. **Conditions:** Primary—BD CD ED MR OCD Psy Sz.
    Sec—ADD ADHD As Au B BI C CP D IP LD MD MS ON S SB.
  Therapy: Hear Lang Occup Phys Speech. **Psychotherapy:** Fam Group
    Indiv Parent.
  Staff: 625.
  Est 1926. State. Nonprofit.

Diagnosis and treatment for children and parents is offered at the center, as are special education and diagnoses of retardation cases. Outpatient and counseling services are available.
  Ten branches operate in Brewster, Chatham, Hyannis, Plymouth, Quincy and Wareham.

SOUTHEAST ALTERNATIVE HIGH SCHOOL

Day — Coed Ages 13-18

Berkley, MA 02779. 132 S Main St.
Tel: 508-822-7728. Fax: 508-824-2083.
  Focus: Spec Ed. **Conditions:** Primary—Dx LD. Sec—BD ED.
  Gen Acad. Pre-Voc. Gr 9-12. Courses: Read Math Lang_Arts Sci Soc_
    Stud. Man_Arts & Shop.
  Therapy: Speech. **Psychotherapy:** Fam Group Indiv.
  Enr: 34. Day Males 23. Day Females 11. **Staff:** 12.
  Est 1952. Private. Nonprofit.

The school provides special education and counseling for students with learning disabilities, dyslexia and mild emotional disturbances. Some vocational training is also available, and the usual length of stay is one to two years.

STETSON SCHOOL

Res — Males Ages 8-18; Day — Males 10-17

Barre, MA 01005. 455 South St, PO Box 309.
Tel: 978-355-4541. Fax: 978-355-6335.
www.stetsonschool.org   E-mail: abfitz@netiplus.com
Kathleen Lovenbury, MA, Exec Dir. **Robert Fitzgerald,** Adm.
  Focus: Treatment. **Conditions:** Primary—ED. Sec—ADD ADHD Anx As
    Asp Au BD BI C CD CP Dg Dx Ep Mood MR OCD Psy PTSD SP Sz TS.
    IQ 60 and up.
  Gen Acad. Pre-Voc. Ungraded. Courses: Read Math Lang_Arts Sci Soc_
    Stud Hist Studio_Art Health. Man_Arts & Shop.
  Therapy: Art Milieu Play Recreational. **Psychotherapy:** Fam Group Indiv
    Parent.
  Enr: 161. Res Males 111. Day Males 50. **Staff:** 300. Prof 50. Educ 47.

Admin 10.
Rates 2003: Res $131,481/yr. State Aid.
Est 1899. Private. Nonprofit.

Stetson serves boys and adolescent males who have a history of sexually abusive behaviors, including sexual acting out and sexually misconduct. Treatment, which takes place in a secure rehabilitative environment, addresses the emotional, behavioral, social, familial and cognitive domains. Structured external behavioral controls are in place to assist the boy with developing self-control, and the multidisciplinary, integrated treatment model incorporates milieu treatment, psychotherapy, academics, health services and recreation. The ultimate program goal is the client's successful reintegration into his community.

STEVENS SPECIALIZED RESIDENTIAL TREATMENT PROGRAMS

Res — Males Ages 12-18

Swansea, MA 02777. 24 Main St.
Tel: 508-679-0183. Fax: 508-679-1950.
www.stevenshome.org   E-mail: info@stevenshome.org
Thomas A. Drooger, MSW, Exec Dir. **Bernie DiLullo,** Intake.
   Focus: Spec Ed. Treatment. **Conditions:** Primary—BD ED ODD. Sec—Anx CD Dx LD OCD PTSD.
   Col Prep. Gen Acad. Pre-Voc. Ungraded. Courses: Read Math Lang_Arts.
   Therapy: Speech. **Psychotherapy:** Fam Group Indiv.
   Enr: 34. Res Males 34. **Staff:** 80 (Full 76, Part 4). Prof 21. Educ 14. Admin 6.
   Rates 2004: Res $350/day. State Aid.
   Est 1938. Private. Nonprofit. **Spons:** Stevens Children's Home.

Stevens Treatment Programs operates a highly structured residential treatment center for emotionally and behaviorally disturbed adolescent males. Among the specialized programs are services for sexual offenders and fire setters. The special education program, which incorporates one-on-one instruction to improve basic academic skills and deal more effectively with behavioral issues, provides a solid foundation for further education.

SWANSEA WOOD SCHOOL

Res — Coed Ages 13-22

Swansea, MA 02777. 789 Stevens Rd.
Tel: 508-672-6560. Fax: 508-672-6595.
www.jri.org/swansea.htm   E-mail: woodschool@jri.org
Stephanie Ward, MEd, Prgm Dir. **Edgardo C. Angeles,** MD, Med Dir. **Maribeth Balzano-August,** Adm.
   Focus: Spec Ed. **Conditions:** Primary—BD ED LD MR. Sec—As BI CP Dx Ep OH. **IQ 60-85.**
   Pre-Voc. Voc. Ungraded. Courses: Read Math Lang_Arts. Man_Arts &

Shop. On-Job Trng.
Therapy: Hear Occup Phys Recreational Speech. **Psychotherapy:** Group Indiv.
Enr: 26. Res Males 15. Res Females 11. **Staff:** 48 (Full 47, Part 1). Prof 15. Educ 6. Admin 4.
Rates 2004: Res $374/day.
Est 1987. Private. Nonprofit. **Spons:** Justice Resource Institute.

Located on six acres of wooded land, Wood School serves clients who are mildly to moderately retarded and emotionally disturbed with accompanying behavioral maladaptations. The school accepts individuals who have been involved with the court system, as well as those who have neurological and physical handicaps of moderate nature. Services include educational, vocational and social skills training, including close interaction with the community. Group and individual counseling is offered, as are specialized groups employed for some behavioral difficulties.

THE TRAUMA CENTER

Clinic: All Ages. M-F 9-5, S by Appt; Eves M-Th 5-9.

Allston, MA 02134. 14 Fordham Road.
Tel: 617-782-6460. Fax: 617-782-6457.
www.traumacenter.org   E-mail: moreinfo@traumacenter.org
Roy Ettlinger, Dir. **Bessel van der Kolk,** MD, Med Dir. **Steve Gordon,** Adm.
  Focus: Treatment. **Conditions:** Primary—ADD ADHD ED Mood ODD PTSD SP. Sec—BD.
  Therapy: Play. **Psychotherapy:** Fam Group Indiv.
  Staff: 61 (Full 11, Part 50). Prof 58. Admin 3.
  Rates 2003: Sliding-Scale Rate $65-100/hr.
  Est 1969. Private. Inc. **Spons:** Arbour Health System.

Inpatient and outpatient services are offered at the center to individuals with psychological difficulties. A 68-bed inpatient facility emphasizes family participation in treatment. Eclectic therapy, psychopharmacological services and electric shock therapy are conducted. Satellite outpatient centers operate in Franklin, Lawrence, Malden, Norton and Lowell.

TUFTS-NEW ENGLAND MEDICAL CENTER
CENTER FOR CHILDREN WITH SPECIAL NEEDS

Clinic: Ages Birth-22. M-F 8:30-5.

Boston, MA 02111. 750 Washington St, Box 334.
Tel: 617-636-7242. Fax: 617-636-5621.
www.nemc.org/ccsn
N. Paul Rosman, MD, Dir. **Carol Curtin,** MSW, LICSW, Clin Dir. **Ellen Perrin,** MD, Med Dir.
  Focus: Treatment. **Conditions:** Primary—ADD ADHD Asp Au BI CP Dx ED Ep LD MR ON PDD S SB TS. Sec—B BD CD D OCD Psy.

Therapy: Hear Lang Phys Speech. **Psychotherapy:** Indiv Parent.
Staff: 20 (Full 5, Part 15).
Est 1894. Private.

CCSN provides care for infants, children and adolescents with developmental, behavioral, learning and neurological disorders. Candidates for treatment are children who have learning problems; difficulties with attention or concentration; or delays in one or more of the following areas: motor, language or physical development. Some clients have very specific, well-defined problems, while others have difficulties that are more complex and extensive in nature.

Care involves an initial evaluation and appropriate follow-up services over the subsequent months and years. As soon as problems are identified, the center helps each family understand the child's difficulties and gives advice about how best to respond. CCSN then recommends a specially designed treatment program. Parents receive information services, and the program includes parent support groups as well.

TUFTS-NEW ENGLAND MEDICAL CENTER DEPARTMENT OF PHYSICAL MEDICINE AND REHABILITATION

Res and Day — Coed Ages Birth-18
Clinic: All Ages. M-F 8-5.

Boston, MA 02111. 750 Washington St, PO Box 387.
Tel: 617-636-5626. Fax: 617-636-5056.
www.nemc.org/rehab
Harry C. Webster, MD, Chief.
  Focus: Rehab. **Conditions:** Primary—BI CP IP MD MS ON PW SB. Sec—MR.
  Therapy: Hear Lang Occup Phys Speech. **Psychotherapy:** Fam Group Indiv.
  Staff: 5 (Full 4, Part 1). Prof 3. Admin 2.
  Est 1958. Private. Nonprofit. **Spons:** Tufts-New England Medical Center.

This department of Tufts-NEMC helps individuals with injuries and diseases improve their health and functioning performance. Staff members work closely with various professionals and with patients and families. Fees vary according to services provided.

UNIVERSITY OF MASSACHUSETTS-AMHERST CENTER FOR LANGUAGE, SPEECH AND HEARING

Clinic: All Ages. M-F 8:30-4:30; Eves by Appt.

Amherst, MA 01003. 17 Arnold House, Box 30410.
Tel: 413-545-2565. Fax: 413-545-0803.
www.umass.edu/sphhs/centers/speech.html
  E-mail: speech-hearing@comdis.umass.edu
Neva L. Frumkin, PhD, CCC-SLP, Dir.
  Focus: Treatment. **Conditions:** Primary—Ap S.

Therapy: Hear Lang Speech.
Staff: 10 (Full 3, Part 7).
State.

Services, including diagnosis and remediation, are provided for communicatively handicapped individuals. Referral and contact sources in psychology, social work and counseling are maintained within the university. Summer services are available.

VALLEY VIEW SCHOOL

Res — Males Ages 11-16

North Brookfield, MA 01535. Oakham Rd, PO Box 338.
Tel: 508-867-6505. Fax: 508-867-3300.
www.valleyviewschool.org   E-mail: valview@aol.com
Philip G. Spiva, AB, MA, PhD, Dir.
    Focus: Trng. **Conditions:** Primary—ADD ADHD Anx ED Mood. Sec—BD CD Dx LD OCD SP. **IQ 90 and up.**
    Col Prep. Gen Acad. Gr 5-12. Courses: Read Math Lang_Arts Computers Studio_Art Drama.
    Therapy: Milieu Speech. **Psychotherapy:** Group Indiv.
    Enr: 54. Res Males 54. **Staff:** 27 (Full 26, Part 1). Educ 11. Admin 8.
    Rates 2003: Res $51,000/yr (+$800-1200).
    Est 1970. Private. Nonprofit.

Located on 215 acres of timberland and fields, Valley View offers a year-round therapeutic environment for adolescent boys with adjustment difficulties. A large percentage of the school's population arrives with a history of oppositional behavior and attentional problems.

A school program emphasizes the remediation of academic and motivational difficulties, encouraging boys to return to a more traditional educational setting. Boys participate in community activities and maintain contact with their families. Activities on campus include organized athletics, creative arts and crafts, computer lab, photography and indoor sports. As an extension of the philosophy of providing boys with a wide variety of success-oriented experiences, travel opportunities are offered both locally and abroad.

Counseling and a full range of psychotherapeutic services are provided. The usual length of treatment is two to three years. Delinquent, substance abusing and overtly psychotic boys are not accepted.

VALLEYHEAD

Res — Females Ages 10-22

Lenox, MA 01240. 79 Reservoir Rd, PO Box 714.
Tel: 413-637-3635. Fax: 413-637-3501.
www.valleyhead.org   E-mail: valleyhd@berkshire.net
Matthew J. Merritt, Jr., BS, JD, Pres. **M. Christine Macbeth,** ACSW, LICSW, Exec Dir. **Steve Hoff,** PsyD, Clin Dir. **Ellen G. Merritt,** Adm.
    Focus: Treatment. **Conditions:** Primary—ADD ADHD ED Mood PTSD SP.

Sec—AN Anx As BD Bl CD Dx Ep LD MR OCD Sz TS. **IQ 65-120.**

Gen Acad. Pre-Voc. Ungraded. Courses: Read Math Lang_Arts Sci Soc_ Stud. On-Job Trng.

Therapy: Art Dance Lang Milieu Music Recreational Speech. **Psychotherapy:** Fam Group Indiv.

Enr: 66. Res Females 66. **Staff:** 90 (Full 80, Part 10). Prof 30. Educ 10. Admin 7.

Rates 2003: Res $99,000/yr (+$1000). State Aid.

Est 1969. Private. Inc.

Located in the Berkshire Hills adjacent to the Pleasant Valley Wildlife Sanctuary, Valleyhead serves adolescent girls with mild to moderate emotional and behavioral problems and learning disabilities. The program encourages learning skills and personal adjustment, with the goal of mainstreaming into a traditional setting.

The school offers an individualized general course of study leading either to a certificate of completion or a diploma. Additional course work is available in business, music and domestic arts. Remedial classes in reading, speech and language supplement both the academic and the nonacademic courses of study. A variety of vocational and prevocational opportunities are available for the students, and a separate vocationally oriented program is also offered.

The summer term is a continuation of the regular school year. Girls attend classes in the morning while also taking advantage of cultural and recreational opportunities in the Berkshires, including theater, concerts and trips. Psychological and psychiatric therapies are provided within the context of a supportive, structured milieu approach. Individual and group counseling is available. The usual length of treatment is 18 months.

Valleyhead is affiliated with Bennington School in Vermont.

WALKER HOME AND SCHOOL

Res and Day — Coed Ages 6-13

Needham, MA 02192. 1968 Central Ave.
Tel: 781-449-4500. Fax: 781-453-0808.
www.walkerschool.org
Richard W. Small, PhD, Exec Dir. **Joseph Cambone,** COO. **Christopher Bellonci,** MD, Med Dir. **Michael Carter,** Intake.

Focus: Spec Ed. Treatment. **Conditions:** Primary—ED. Sec—ADD ADHD AN Anx Ap Apr As Asp BD Bu CD Db Dc Dg Dx Ep HIV LD Mood OCD PDD Psy PTSD S SP TS.

Gen Acad. Pre-Voc. Ungraded. Courses: Read Math Lang_Arts Sci Soc_ Stud Studio_Art.

Therapy: Lang Milieu Occup Speech. **Psychotherapy:** Fam Group Indiv.

Enr: 82. Res Males 27. Res Females 10. Day Males 32. Day Females 13. **Staff:** 200 (Full 170, Part 30). Prof 36. Educ 11. Admin 25.

Rates 2003: Res $91,513-164,534/yr. Day $59,679/yr. State Aid.

Summer Prgm: Res & Day. Educ. Rec. Ther. 7 wks.

Est 1961. Private. Nonprofit.

Located adjacent to the Charles River, Walker School is a day and residential treatment center that serves children with severe emotional, behavioral and learning disorders.

Residential units provide three levels of services: intensive residential, with a goal of stepping down to less restrictive programs; residential services, with a goal of increased community involvement; and acute residential services for children ages 3-10, with a goal of stabilization and assessment at times of crisis. The year-round school includes afternoon activities and summer programs. The treatment approach emphasizes milieu, family, individual and group therapy; specialized pediatric and psychiatric care; and a strong academic curriculum with emphasis on the remediation of language-based learning disabilities. Through its division of Walker Partnerships, Walker offers transition and support services to students, families and educators involved in public school inclusion.

WAYSIDE YOUTH AND FAMILY SUPPORT NETWORK

Day — Coed Ages 12-17
Clinic: All Ages. M-F.

Framingham, MA 01702. 75 Fountain St.
Tel: 508-879-9800. TTY: 508-872-4721. Fax: 508-875-1348.
www.waysideyouth.org   E-mail: wayside_info@waysideyouth.org
Eric L. Masi, EdD, Pres.
   Conditions: Primary—BD ED. Sec—LD.
   Gen Acad. Ungraded.
   Psychotherapy: Fam Group Indiv.
   Staff: Prof 42.
   Est 1977. Nonprofit.

WELDON REHABILITATION HOSPITAL
CHILDREN'S REHABILITATION SERVICES

Clinic: Ages Birth-16. M-F 8-6.

Springfield, MA 01104. 233 Carew St.
Tel: 413-748-6855. Fax: 413-730-6627.
www.mercycares.com
Angela Mansolillo, MA, Prgm Mgr.
   Focus: Rehab. **Conditions:** Primary—ADD ADHD Ap Au B BI CP D Dx IP
   MD MR MS ON SB. Sec—As.
   Therapy: Hear Lang Occup Phys Speech. **Psychotherapy:** Group.
   Staff: 15 (Full 7, Part 8).
   Est 1974. Private. Nonprofit. Roman Catholic. **Spons:** Mercy Medical
   Center.

Utilizing an interdisciplinary approach in a developmentally appropriate setting, this children's program consists of diagnostic evaluations, ongoing therapy sessions in individual and small-group settings, and consultations with local schools and agencies in the design and the adaptation of programs, services, materials and equipment. The pediatric evaluation team offers evaluations, formulation of treatment plans and follow-up services.

A parent-infant program for hearing-impaired children aims to identify, diagnose and habilitate these children as early as possible. Services include hearing assessments, hearing aid fittings, speech and language intervention, sign language instruction, home visits and advocacy.

THE WHITNEY ACADEMY

Res — Males Ages 10-22

East Freetown, MA 02717. PO Box 619.
Tel: 508-763-3737. Fax: 508-763-5300.
www.whitney-info.com   E-mail: rmancini@whitney-info.com
George E. Harmon, MEd, Exec Dir. **Richard Mancini,** Adm.
   Focus: Spec Ed. Treatment. **Conditions:** Primary—BD CD ED MR Psy Sz. Sec—ADD ADHD Dx LD. **IQ 50-80.**
   Gen Acad. Pre-Voc. Voc. Ungraded. Courses: Read Math Lang_Arts Sci Soc_Stud. Man_Arts & Shop. Shelt_Workshop.
   Therapy: Chemo Hear Lang Movement Phys Play Speech. **Psychotherapy:** Fam Group Indiv Parent.
   Enr: 48. Res Males 48. **Staff:** 160 (Full 150, Part 10).
   Est 1986. Private. Nonprofit.

The academy provides year-round care for dually diagnosed children while maintaining a 2:1 staff-student ratio. Patients with mild to moderate retardation and psychiatric diagnoses receive academic training and interdisciplinary treatment. Whitney also conducts a program that serves both sex offenders and victims of sexual offenses. Counseling and individual and group therapies are available, and the average length of stay is three years.

WILLIE ROSS SCHOOL FOR THE DEAF

Day — Coed Ages 3-22

Longmeadow, MA 01106. 32 Norway St.
Tel: 413-567-0374. TTY: 413-567-0374. Fax: 413-567-8808.
www.willierossschool.org   E-mail: labbate@willierossschool.org
Louis E. Abbate, EdD, Exec Dir. **Diane Shaughnessy,** Adm.
   Focus: Spec Ed. **Conditions:** Primary—D. Sec—ED MR.
   Gen Acad. Pre-Voc. Voc. Ungraded. Courses: Read Math Lang_Arts. On-Job Trng.
   Therapy: Hear Lang Occup Phys Speech. **Psychotherapy:** Indiv Parent.
   Enr: 68. **Staff:** 40.
   Rates 2004: Day $29,532/sch yr.
   Summer Prgm: Day. Educ. Day Rate $700. 6 wks.
   Est 1967. Private. Nonprofit.

This school provides a full continuum of services for deaf and hard-of-hearing children who reside in western Massachusetts. WRSD employs a total communication approach and conducts signing in all classes. Emphasis is placed on the development of oral speech and sign language. Staff attempt to maximize residual hearing.

The school's integrated model, incorporating both center-based and public school settings, allows deaf and hard-of-hearing students to share many experiences of regular education with their hearing peers.

WILLOW HILL SCHOOL

Day — Coed Ages 11-19

Sudbury, MA 01776. 98 Haynes Rd.
Tel: 978-443-2581. Fax: 978-443-7560.
www.willowhillschool.org   E-mail: info@willowhillschool.org
Judith Vaillancourt, BA, MA, Head. **Nancy S. Brody,** Adm.
  Focus: Spec Ed. **Conditions:** Primary—ADD ADHD Asp Dg Dx LD. **IQ 90 and up.**
  Col Prep. Gen Acad. Gr 6-12. Courses: Read Math Lang_Arts Sci Soc_ Stud Fine_Arts Dance Drama Outdoor_Ed.
  Enr: 58. Day Males 38. Day Females 20. **Staff:** 26. Educ 17.
  Rates 2003: Day $40,108/sch yr. State Aid.
  Est 1970. Private. Nonprofit.

Willow Hill offers personalized education for students of average to high intelligence who are underachievers, as well as for those who have dyslexia, learning-style differences and attentional difficulties. Small group tutorials and small classes in a college preparatory curriculum are provided, as are courses in art, drama, computer, sports and an outdoor challenge program. Additional opportunities include writing workshops, language training, developmental reading, SAT preparation and a cultural program.

THE WINCHENDON SCHOOL

Res and Day — Coed Ages 13-20

Winchendon, MA 01475. 172 Ash St.
Tel: 978-297-1223. Fax: 978-297-0911.
www.winchendon.org   E-mail: admissions@winchendon.org
J. William LaBelle, BS, MS, MEd, Head. **Richard John Plank,** Adm.
  Focus: Spec Ed. **Conditions:** Primary—LD. Sec—ADD ADHD Dc Dg Dx. **IQ 95 and up.**
  Col Prep. Gr 8-PG. Courses: Read Math Lang_Arts Fr Span Lat Sci Hist Art_Hist Music.
  Enr: 200. Res Males 140. Res Females 50. Day Males 5. Day Females 5. **Staff:** 50. (Full 50).
  Rates 2004: Res $32,250/sch yr (+$2000). Day $20,250/sch yr (+$1250). Schol 45 ($900,000).
  Summer Prgm: Res & Day. Educ. Res Rate $5600. 6 wks.
  Est 1926. Private. Nonprofit.

Through personal attention to the academic capabilities of each student, Winchendon seeks to aid those who have not previously developed sound study habits. A wide range of students is enrolled, from bright underachievers to those with basic learning deficits.

The curriculum is college preparatory, with emphasis on small, student-centered classes. The school offers daily tutorials in English and math, and one-on-one remedial programs are available. Instructors administer grades each day in every course, and counselors provide services daily.

Many sports and interest clubs are among the extracurricular activities. Winchendon's facilities include tennis courts, an outdoor swimming pool, an 18-hole golf course, and a gymnasium and athletic complex.

YOU, INC.

Res — Coed Ages 12-18; Day — Coed 12-21
Clinic: All Ages. M-F 9-5; Eves M-Th 5-9.

Worcester, MA 01604. 81 Plantation St.
Tel: 508-849-5600. Fax: 508-849-5617.
www.youinc.org
Maurice Boisvert, Pres. **Ludmilla Tonkonogy,**
MD, Med Dir.

Conditions: Primary—As BD C D Dx ED LD.

Gen Acad. Pre-Voc. Courses: Read Math Lang_Arts. Man_Arts & Shop. On-Job Trng.

Therapy: Chemo Speech. **Psychotherapy:** Fam Group Indiv.

Est 1970. Private. Nonprofit.

MICHIGAN

ARBOR CIRCLE

Clinic: All Ages. M-F.

Grand Rapids, MI 49505. 1115 Ball Ave NE.
  Nearby locations: Newaygo.
Tel: 616-456-7775. Fax: 616-456-8568.
www.arborcircle.org   E-mail: info@arborcircle.org
  Conditions: Primary—BD ED.
  Psychotherapy: Fam Group Indiv.
  Staff: Prof 55.
  Est 1945. Federal. Nonprofit.

BLOSSOMLAND LEARNING CENTER

Day — Coed Ages 3-26

Berrien Springs, MI 49103. 711 St Joseph Ave.
Tel: 269-473-2600. Fax: 269-471-9788.
www.remc11.k12.mi.us/blc
Pamela Harper, Prin.
  Focus: Spec Ed. **Conditions:** Primary—Au MR. Sec—B D Db.
  Pre-Voc. Ungraded. Courses: Read Math Lang_Arts Life_Skills.
  Therapy: Hear Lang Music Occup Phys Speech. **Psychotherapy:** Indiv.
  Enr: 210. Day Males 109. Day Females 101. **Staff:** 66.
  Rates 2004: No Fee.
  Est 1952. County. Nonprofit.

  Blossomland provides comprehensive educational services for children and young adults with mental retardation and autism. The program emphasizes the development of self-help, daily living and transitional skills. Students must reside in Berrien County to gain admittance.

CARO CENTER

Res — Coed Ages 1 and up

Caro, MI 48723. 2000 Chambers Rd.
Tel: 989-673-3191. Fax: 989-673-6749.
www.michigan.gov/mdch
Rose Laskowski, RN, BSN, Dir.
  Focus: Treatment. **Conditions:** Primary—BI MR. **IQ 0-70.**
  Gen Acad. Ungraded.
  Therapy: Chemo Hear Lang Occup Phys Speech. **Psychotherapy:** Fam Indiv.

Staff: Prof 73.
Est 1913. State.

CENTER FOR HUMAN DEVELOPMENT
Clinic: All Ages. M-S 9-5.

Berkley, MI 48072. 1695 W Twelve Mile Rd, Ste 120.
Tel: 248-691-4744. Fax: 248-691-4745.
Earnest Krug, MD, Dir.
    Focus: Treatment. **Conditions:** Primary—Asp Au Dx ED LD Mood OCD
        ODD PDD Psy PTSD PW TS. Sec—BI MR.
    Therapy: Speech. **Psychotherapy:** Fam Group Indiv.
    Staff: 19.
    Est 1968. Private. Nonprofit. **Spons:** William Beaumont Hospital.

The center conducts a medically based program of study, diagnosis and remediation for those with learning disabilities and other educational and developmental handicaps. A complete physical, visual, audiological, neurological and educational assessment is provided. A psychological evaluation appraises the child's intellectual functioning and potential along with behavioral and emotional status. Family counseling sessions are part of the evaluation process and may continue during treatment if necessary. In addition, a tutorial program offers individual and group instruction classes at the center. Rates are based on a sliding scale.

CENTRAL MICHIGAN UNIVERSITY
SPEECH AND HEARING CLINICS
Clinic: All Ages.

Mount Pleasant, MI 48859. Moore Hall.
Tel: 989-774-3904. Fax: 989-774-2799.
www.chp.cmich.edu/academics/sh_clinics.htm
Renny Tatchell, Chair.
    Conditions: Primary—D S. Sec—BI MR OH.
    Gen Acad. Gr PS.
    Therapy: Hear Lang Speech.
    State.

CHILD GUIDANCE
Res — Coed Ages 7-17
Clinic: Ages Birth-17. M-F 8-5.

Traverse City, MI 49684. 1100 Silver Dr, Ste C.
Tel: 231-947-2255. Fax: 231-947-5982.
www.childguide.us   **E-mail: tctfps@chartermi.net**

Conditions: Primary—BD ED.
Therapy: Art Play.
Est 1929. State.

THE COLEMAN FOUNDATION

Res — Coed Ages 18 and up

Hudson, MI 49247. 313 S Church St.
Tel: 517-448-3101.
www.colemanfdn.org
    Conditions: Primary—MR. **IQ 20-60.**
    Gen Acad. Ungraded. Courses: Read Math Lang_Arts. Shelt_Workshop.
      On-Job Trng.
    Therapy: Hear Lang Speech. **Psychotherapy:** Indiv.
    Est 1931. Private. Nonprofit.

THE DETROIT INSTITUTE FOR CHILDREN

Clinic: Ages Birth-21. M-F 7:30-6.

Detroit, MI 48202. 5447 Woodward Ave.
Tel: 313-832-1100. Fax: 313-832-4223.
www.detroit-children.org
Dianne L. Haas, RN, PhD, Pres. **Eileen Donovan,** MD, Med Dir.
    Conditions: Primary—ADD ADHD Au BI CP Ep IP MD MR MS ON SB.
      Sec—Ap As B BD CD D Dx ED LD S Sz.
    Therapy: Hear Lang Occup Phys Play Speech. **Psychotherapy:** Fam
      Group Indiv Parent.
    Staff: 100.
    Est 1920. Private. Nonprofit.

A clinical facility for physically, developmentally, emotionally and neurologically impaired children and young adults, The Detroit Institute for Children offers diagnostic and medical care, psychotherapy, and physical, occupational and speech therapies. A program of family counseling is provided through caseworkers. Fees are based on the client's ability to pay.

DON BOSCO HALL

Res — Males Ages 12-20, Females 16-20; Day — Coed 7-20

Detroit, MI 48206. 2340 Calvert St.
Tel: 313-869-2200. Fax: 313-869-8220.
www.donboscohall.org
Charles Small, Exec Dir.
    Conditions: Primary—BD ED.

Man_Arts & Shop. On-Job Trng.
Therapy: Recreational. **Psychotherapy:** Fam Group Indiv.
Staff: Prof 35.
Est 1954. Private. Nonprofit.

EASTERN MICHIGAN UNIVERSITY
SPEECH AND HEARING CLINIC

Clinic: All Ages. M-F 8:30-10:30, 1-4.

Ypsilanti, MI 48197. 135 Porter Bldg.
Tel: 734-487-4410. Fax: 734-487-2473.
www.emich.edu/coe/speced/clinic.html
Steven E. Press, MSW, Dir.
   Conditions: Primary—D S.
   Therapy: Hear Lang Speech.
   State.

ERICKSON LEARNING CENTER

Clinic: Ages 5 and up. M-S 8-5; Eves M-S 5-9.

Okemos, MI 48864. 2043 Hamilton Rd.
Tel: 517-347-0122. Fax: 517-347-0288.
www.erickson-learning.org
Caryn Edwards, BS, Dir. **James Edwards,** Adm.
   Focus: Spec Ed. **Conditions:** Primary—ADD ADHD Dc Dg Dx LD S. Sec—
      Asp Au BD BI CD CP Db DS ED Mood MR PDD TS. **IQ 70-135.**
   Gen Acad. Pre-Voc. Voc. Ungraded. Courses: Read Math Lang_Arts Sci.
      On-Job Trng.
   Staff: 66 (Full 3, Part 63). Educ 63. Admin 3.
   Rates 2003: Clinic $35/hr.
   Summer Prgm: Day. Educ. Day Rate $35/hr. 1-2 hrs.
   Est 1986. Private.

   The center uses a variety of multisensory techniques to meet the individual needs
of its clients. Tutoring comprises enrichment, remediation and specialized tutoring for
those with learning disorders such as learning disabilities, dyslexia and attentional disorders. Educational diagnostic evaluations assess auditory and visual processing abilities
and measure such language skills as reading, writing, spelling and receptive vocabulary.
Clients may also receive math evaluations. In addition to its clinical services, the center
provides training for teachers, tutors and parents.

ETON ACADEMY

Day — Coed Ages 6-19

Birmingham, MI 48009. 1755 Melton St.
Tel: 248-642-1150. Fax: 248-642-3670.
www.etonacademy.org
Pete Pullen, Head. **Sharon M. Morey,** Adm.
  Focus: Spec Ed. **Conditions:** Primary—ADD ADHD Dx LD. **IQ 85 and up.**
  Col Prep. Gen Acad. Voc. Gr 1-12. Courses: Read Math Lang_Arts Sci
    Soc_Stud Studio_Art.
  Therapy: Hear Lang Occup Phys Speech.
  Enr: 190. Day Males 125. Day Females 65. **Staff:** 37.
  Rates 2003: Day $15,100-16,750/sch yr. Schol avail.
  Est 1980. Private. Nonprofit.

Eton offers academic instruction to children with dyslexia and related learning problems through individualized lessons and classes of no more than eight students. The program emphasizes the development of mathematics, reading, language, communicative and study skills. Physical movement, physical education, computer instruction, art and curriculum enrichment programs are available. The usual duration of enrollment is three years.

FAMILY AND CHILDREN'S SERVICE OF MIDLAND

Clinic: All Ages. M-F 9-5; Eves M-Th 5-9.

Midland, MI 48640. 1714 Eastman Ave.
Tel: 989-631-5390.
www.fcs-midland.org
  Conditions: Primary—BD ED.
  Psychotherapy: Fam Indiv.
  Est 1925. Private. Nonprofit.

FOUNDATION FOR EXCEPTIONAL CHILDREN

Day — Coed Ages 1-8

Grosse Pointe Farms, MI 48236. 16 Lake Shore Rd.
Tel: 313-885-8660. Fax: 313-882-7675.
www.childrenshomeofdetroit.org/fec
Deborah Moffat, Dir.
  Focus: Spec Ed. Rehab. Trng. Treatment. **Conditions:** Primary—MR.
  Gen Acad. Gr PS.
  Therapy: Hear Music Occup Phys Speech.
  Staff: Prof 4.
  Est 1954. Private. Nonprofit. **Spons:** Children's Home of Detroit.

HAWTHORN CENTER

Res — Coed Ages 5-17
Clinic: Ages 5-17. M-S 8-5.

Northville, MI 48167. 18471 Haggerty Rd.
Tel: 248-349-3000. Fax: 248-349-9552.
www.michigan.gov/mdch
Shobhana Joshi, Dir.
    Focus: Rehab. Trng. Treatment. **Conditions:** Primary—ED Psy Sz.
    Gen Acad. Pre-Voc. Gr PS-12. Courses: Read Math Lang_Arts. Man_Arts
      & Shop. Shelt_Workshop.
    Therapy: Hear Lang Speech. **Psychotherapy:** Fam Group Indiv.
    Enr: 118.
    Est 1956. State. Nonprofit.

Severely disturbed and mentally ill children receive intensive psychiatric treatment within a multidisciplinary setting at Hawthorn that emphasizes special education. Academic and remedial studies feature individual plans of study and extensive tutoring. Outpatient and counseling services are available. The usual length of treatment is six to nine months. Michigan residents only may receive services at the center, and the state determines all fees.

JUDSON CENTER

Res — Coed Ages 9-17

Royal Oak, MI 48073. 4410 W 13 Mile Rd.
    Nearby locations: Ann Arbor; Ecorse; Redford Township; Warren.
Tel: 248-549-4339. Fax: 248-549-8955.
www.judsoncenter.org
Mounir W. Sharobeem, MA, Pres. **Marn G. Myers,** MA, COO. **Gregory Everett,** MSW, Dir.
    Focus: Treatment. **Conditions:** Primary—BD ED. Sec—LD. **IQ 70 and up.**
    Therapy: Art Dance Music Speech. **Psychotherapy:** Fam Group Indiv.
    Enr: 36. Res Males 24. Res Females 12. **Staff:** 30. Prof 8. Admin 2.
    Est 1924. Private. Nonprofit.

The center provides milieu and developmental therapy supported by art therapies. Children receive tutorial aid in addition to attending schools in the community or on grounds. In addition to the main center location in Royal Oak, Judson maintains regional centers at 23750 Elmira, Ste. 103, Redford Township 48239; 12220 13 Mile Rd., Warren 48088; and 4925 Packard Rd., Ste. 200, Ann Arbor 48108. At-risk boys and girls can develop skills for successful employment through the WAY program in Ecorse (360 Salliotte Rd., 48229).

LINCOLN SCHOOL

Day — Coed Ages 5-26

Grand Rapids, MI 49546. 860 Crahen Ave NE.
Tel: 616-771-2762. Fax: 616-771-3311.
http://web.grps.k12.mi.us/sped
Lisa Key, Prin.
> **Focus:** Rehab. Trng. **Conditions:** Primary—MR. **IQ 32-50.**
> **Gen Acad.** Ungraded.
> **Therapy:** Hear Occup Phys Speech.
> **Est 1948.** County. Nonprofit.

LUTHERAN SPECIAL EDUCATION MINISTRIES GREAT LAKES REGION

Day — Coed Ages 5-14

Detroit, MI 48234. 6861 E Nevada Ave.
Tel: 313-368-1220. Fax: 313-368-0159.
www.luthsped.org   E-mail: lsem@luthsped.org
Roger DeMeyere, MSW, Pres. **Kathleen Schroeder,** MS, Dir.
> **Focus:** Spec Ed. **Conditions:** Primary—ADD ADHD Dx LD. Sec—MR. **IQ 70 and up.**
> **Gen Acad. Pre-Voc.** Gr K-8. Courses: Read Math Lang_Arts.
> **Psychotherapy:** Indiv.
> **Staff:** 90.
> **Est 1873.** Private. Nonprofit. Lutheran.

Providing support for children with learning differences in a Christian setting, the agency operates 97 resource rooms and consultation services at Christian elementary and middle schools. It also works with churches to provide Sunday school and Confirmation services for students with learning differences. The National Resource Center works with anyone outside of established regions to enable all students to receive a Christian education.

Additional regional programs operate in Illinois, New York, Minnesota, California and Texas (see separate listing).

THE MANOR FOUNDATION

Res — Coed Ages 6-18

Jonesville, MI 49250. 115 East St, PO Box 98.
Tel: 517-849-2151. Fax: 517-849-2880.
Robert M. Clark, MA, Dir.
> **Focus:** Spec Ed. Trng. Treatment. **Conditions:** Primary—ADD ADHD Au BD CD Dx ED LD MR OCD Psy Sz. Sec—OH. **IQ 50-100.**
> **Gen Acad. Pre-Voc.** Gr 1-12. Courses: Read Math Lang_Arts Life_Skills.
> **Therapy:** Hear Speech. **Psychotherapy:** Fam Group Indiv Parent.

Enr: 118. Res Males 81. Res Females 37. **Staff:** 85.
Rates 2004: Res $139/day. State Aid.
Est 1930. Private. Nonprofit.

Manor provides a structured program, emphasizing reentry into society, for educable individuals with emotional impairments or mental retardation. The special education curriculum stresses reading, spelling, writing and arithmetic supplemented with audio-visual techniques. Speech therapy and individual, group and milieu treatment are provided.

Each boy is assigned a job for a two-week period within the job training program. Once the resident has successfully completed small tasks, staff members delegate jobs assisting in the maintenance of the grounds and arrange contracted work with local industries.

A regular daily physical fitness program includes instruction in wrestling, tumbling, softball, basketball and group games. Counseling services are part of the treatment program for each client. The usual length of treatment is 18 to 24 months.

MICHIGAN SCHOOL FOR THE BLIND

Res and Day — Coed Ages Birth-26
Clinic: All Ages. M-F 8-4.

Flint, MI 48503. 1667 W Miller Rd.
Tel: 810-257-1420.
www.msdb.k12.mi.us/msb/msb.htm   E-mail: msdb_mail@state.mi.us
Kathy Brown, Dir.
    Focus: Spec Ed. **Conditions:** Primary—B. Sec—Ap As BD Bl C CP D Dx
    ED Ep IP LD MD MR MS ON S SB.
    Gen Acad. Pre-Voc. Voc. Gr PS-12. Courses: Read Math Lang_Arts. On-
    Job Trng.
    Therapy: Lang Occup Speech. **Psychotherapy:** Indiv.
    Staff: 12 (Full 7, Part 5).
    Est 1879. State.

This state school provides both academic and prevocational opportunities for visually impaired children, adolescents and young adults. Students participate in a variety of recreational and social activities. An educational program for children who are both deaf and blind is also available. Michigan residents only may enroll at MSB.

MICHIGAN SCHOOL FOR THE DEAF

Res — Coed Ages 6-26; Day — Coed Birth-26

Flint, MI 48503. 1667 W Miller Rd.
Tel: 810-257-1400. Fax: 810-257-1490.
www.msdb.k12.mi.us   E-mail: msdb_mail@michigan.gov
Cecelia A. Winkler, MA, Supt.
    Focus: Spec Ed. **Conditions:** Primary—D. Sec—ADD ADHD AN Anx Ap
    Apr As Au B BD CP Db DS Dx Ep LD MR OCD ON PDD S SB TS. **IQ 70
    and up.**

Col Prep. Gen Acad. Pre-Voc. Gr PS-12. Courses: Read Math Lang_Arts. Man_Arts & Shop.
Therapy: Occup Phys Speech.
Enr: 161. Res Males 74. Res Females 37. Day Males 34. Day Females 16.
Staff: 61 (Full 58, Part 3).
Rates 2003: No Fee.
Est 1854. State.

A full academic program, including remedial courses and vocational training, speech and physical therapies, and psychological evaluation and therapy, is provided for deaf and hearing-impaired children. The school also operates a speech and hearing center and offers a program specifically designed for multi-handicapped deaf children.

MICHIGAN STATE UNIVERSITY
HERBERT J. OYER
SPEECH-LANGUAGE-HEARING CLINIC

Clinic: All Ages. M-F 8:30-5; Eves T Th 5-7:30.

East Lansing, MI 48824. 101 Wilson Rd.
Tel: 517-353-8780. TTY: 517-355-8780. Fax: 517-353-3176.
www.msu.edu/~asc/OyerClinic
Michael W. Casby, PhD, CCC-SLP, Dir.
Focus: Rehab. Treatment. **Conditions:** Primary—Ap D S. Sec—As B BD Bl C CP Dx ED IP LD MD MS ON SB.
Therapy: Hear Lang Speech.
Est 1937. State. Nonprofit.

Diagnostic, therapeutic and consultative services in the areas of speech, hearing and language disorders are offered through the clinic. Therapy programs are designed to fit the individual needs of the patient and usually consist of individual and group work on a weekly basis. Aural-oral habilitation/rehabilitation includes communicational skills, home training, preschool remedial instruction and hearing aid orientation. Special services available through the clinic include a preschool language laboratory, assistive listening devices, spectral analysis of hearing aids, industrial audiology, and otolaryngological and social services.

THE MONTCALM SCHOOL

Res — Males Ages 12-18

Albion, MI 49224. 13725 Starr Commonwealth Rd.
Tel: 517-629-5591. Fax: 517-629-6521.
www.montcalmschool.org   E-mail: info@montcalmschool.org
John P. Weed, MA, Dir.
Focus: Spec Ed. Treatment. **Conditions:** Primary—CD ED.
Pre-Voc. Courses: Read Math Lang_Arts.
Psychotherapy: Fam Group.
Private. Nonprofit. **Spons:** Starr Commonwealth.

Montcalm's specially structured residential program for adolescents with emotional and behavioral problems offers therapeutic and growth experiences as it promotes intellectual development. Individualized treatment and education plans address the needs of each student. Fine arts, athletics and adventure education round out the core curriculum.

The program also provides treatment for substance abuse.

MT. PLEASANT REGIONAL CENTER FOR DEVELOPMENTAL DISABILITIES

Res — Coed All Ages

Mount Pleasant, MI 48858. 1400 W Pickard St.
Tel: 989-773-7921. TTY: 989-772-4270. Fax: 989-772-5093.
www.michigan.gov/mdch   E-mail: sautermic@michigan.gov
Kenneth Longton, BN, Dir. **Jay Hoffman,** DO, Med Dir.
　Focus: Rehab. Trng. Treatment. **Conditions:** Primary—MR. **IQ 1-70.**
　Gen Acad. Ungraded.
　Therapy: Hear Lang Occup Phys Recreational Speech. **Psychotherapy:** Indiv.
　Staff: Prof 81.
　Est 1933. State.

MUNSON MEDICAL CENTER CARLS SPEECH AND HEARING CLINIC

Clinic: All Ages. M-F 8-5.

Traverse City, MI 49684. 1105 6th St.
Tel: 231-935-6455. Fax: 231-935-6646.
www.munsonhealthcare.org   E-mail: speech&hearing@mhc.net
Crystal Feeney, MS, Dir. **James Mackenzie,** MD, Med Dir.
　Focus: Treatment. **Conditions:** Primary—D S. Sec—ADD ADHD Ap Apr Asp Au B BD Bl CP Dc Dg Dx ED Ep LD MR Nf ON PDD.
　Therapy: Hear Lang Speech.
　Staff: 6. (Full 6).
　Est 1964. Private. Nonprofit.

Comprehensive clinical services are provided for individuals with hearing, language, speech and voice communicative disorders. Consultative services are available to families.

NORTHEAST GUIDANCE CENTER

Clinic: Ages Birth-17. M-Th 8:30-5; Eves M W Th 5-9.

Detroit, MI 48225. 20303 Kelly Rd.

Tel: 313-245-7000. Fax: 313-245-7009.
www.negconline.org
Cheryl Coleman, MSW, CSW, Exec Dir. **David Harris,** MD, Med Dir.
    Conditions: Primary—ADD ADHD BD CD ED OCD Psy Sz. Sec—Dx LD.
    IQ 70 and up.
    Psychotherapy: Fam Group Indiv Parent.
    Staff: 40 (Full 35, Part 5).
    Est 1963. Private. Nonprofit.

The center provides a full range of services to diagnose and treat mental health problems of residents of the northeast Wayne County area. Diagnostic services include initial diagnostic interviews in addition to psychological and psychiatric examinations. Treatment services include individual, family and group psychotherapy. A second child and family services branch is located at 5555 Conner Ave., Ste. 2224, 48213, while adult clinics are located at 12800 E. Warren Ave., 48215, and 2670 Chalmers St., 48215.

THE PENRICKTON CENTER FOR BLIND CHILDREN

Res — Coed Ages 1-12; Day — Coed Birth-6

Taylor, MI 48180. 26530 Eureka Rd.
Tel: 734-946-7500. Fax: 734-946-6707.
www.penrickton.com   E-mail: mail@penrickton.com
Kurt M. Sebaly, MEd, Exec Dir. **Kim Stoltenberg,** RN, Med Dir. **Ardie Snider,**
    Adm.
    Focus: Treatment. **Conditions:** Primary—B. Sec—Ap Bl CP D Dx ED Ep IP
    LD MD MR MS ON S SB.
    Therapy: Lang Movement Music Occup Speech.
    Enr: 29. Res Males 13. Res Females 10. Day Males 1. Day Females 5.
    Staff: 33 (Full 16, Part 17).
    Rates 2003: No Fee.
    Est 1952. Private. Nonprofit.

Penrickton provides treatment for legally blind children who may also have another disability. Typical accompanying disorders are orthopedic problems, mental retardation and deafness. All children receive intensive, individualized programming to maximize their development. Penrickton offers training in self-care, motor skills, speech and language acquisition, and orientation and mobility.

REHABILITATION INSTITUTE OF MICHIGAN
VARIETY MYOELECTRIC CENTER

Clinic: Ages Birth-21. M-F 8-5.

Detroit, MI 48201. 261 Mack Blvd.
Tel: 313-745-1195. Fax: 313-745-1242.
Edward Dabrowski, MD, Dir. **Eileen Wilhelm,** Coord. **Lawrence Morawa,** MD,
    Med Dir.
    Focus: Rehab. **Conditions:** Primary—OH. **IQ 50 and up.**
    Therapy: Occup. **Psychotherapy:** Parent.

Staff: 3. (Part 3). Prof 3.
Rates 2003: No Fee.
Est 1976. Private. Nonprofit. **Spons:** Detroit Medical Center.

The Variety Myoelectric Center serves 75 to 100 children daily who suffer from upper-limb deficiencies or amputations due to illness or injury. The center provides orthopedic and rehabilitative care, fits children with prosthetics, and offers therapy and counseling to help each child adjust to and use the prosthesis for everyday activities.

ST. LOUIS CENTER

Res — Males Ages 6-18

Chelsea, MI 48118. 16195 W Old US Hwy 12.
Tel: 734-475-8430. Fax: 734-475-0310.
www.stlouiscenter.org   E-mail: mail@stlouiscenter.org
Rev. Joseph Rinaido, SC, Dir. **Janet Brown,** RN, Med Dir. **Barbara Sheel-Aires,** Adm.
    Focus: Spec Ed. **Conditions:** Primary—MR. Sec—ED.
    Voc. Man_Arts & Shop. Shelt_Workshop. On-Job Trng.
    Therapy: Hear Lang Occup Phys Speech. **Psychotherapy:** Fam Group Indiv Parent.
    Enr: 25. Res Males 25. **Staff:** 35 (Full 25, Part 10). Prof 8. Admin 8.
    Rates 2003: Res $33,600/yr. State Aid.
    Est 1960. Private. Nonprofit. Roman Catholic.

Located on a 180-acre, wooded campus, the center offers a combined program of academic instruction, creative handicrafts, and work and play activities for boys and young men with developmental disabilities.

Testing and evaluative procedures help staff members to determine each student's program. Speech and language therapy is part of daily class activities, and a prevocational work-study program is available for adolescent boys ages 16-18. The center provides additional therapies when they will make a significant contribution to the individual's program.

ST. VINCENT AND SARAH FISHER CENTER

Res — Coed Ages 4-17; Day — Males 12-23, Females 12-21

Farmington Hills, MI 48334. 27400 W 12 Mile Rd.
Tel: 248-626-7527. Fax: 248-626-0865.
www.svsfcenter.org   E-mail: info@svsfcenter.org
Paula Hebert, Pres.
    Conditions: Primary—ED. Sec—BD.
    Therapy: Recreational. **Psychotherapy:** Fam Group Indiv.
    Est 1844. Private. Nonprofit. **Spons:** Daughters of Charity of St. Vincent de Paul.

SLD LEARNING CENTER

Clinic: All Ages. M-F 9-4:30.

Kalamazoo, MI 49007. 504 S Westnedge Ave.
Tel: 269-345-2661. Fax: 269-345-5210.
www.sldread.org   E-mail: sldread@iserv.net
Tom Schrock, BBA, MA, Exec Dir.
   Focus: Spec Ed. Treatment. **Conditions:** Primary—Dx. Sec—LD.
   Gen Acad. Ungraded. Courses: Read Math Lang_Arts.
   Staff: 76. Educ 73. Admin 3.
   Rates 2003: /sesSliding-Scale Rate $23-43.
   Est 1974. Private. Nonprofit.

The center offers individualized instruction and tutoring in the basic skill areas to children of average and above intelligence who suffer from a specific language disability. The tutorial program utilizes the Orton-Gillingham method and a highly structured phonetic system. Diagnostic testing is conducted before and during treatment to measure the student's progress.

A branch of the center operates at 525 Cheshire Dr. NE, Grand Rapids 49505.

STARFISH FAMILY SERVICES

Clinic: All Ages. M-F.

Inkster, MI 48141. 30000 Hiveley St.
Tel: 734-728-3400. Fax: 734-728-3500.
www.sfish.org   E-mail: sfs@sfish.org
Ouida G. Cash, EdD, CEO.
   Conditions: Primary—BD ED.
   Psychotherapy: Indiv.
   Staff: Prof 31.
   Est 1963. Private. Nonprofit.

STARR COMMONWEALTH

Res — Males Ages 10-17

Albion, MI 49224. 13725 Starr Commonwealth Rd.
   Nearby locations: Battle Creek; Detroit; Van Wert, OH.
Tel: 517-629-5591. Fax: 517-629-2317.
www.starr.org   E-mail: info@starr.org
Arlin E. Ness, ACSW, Pres. **Martin Mitchell,** EdD, COO. **Renee Hunt,** Intake.
   Focus: Trng. **Conditions:** Primary—ADD ADHD AN Anx As Asp BD CD
      ED Mood OCD PTSD TS. **IQ 70 and up.**
   Gen Acad. Pre-Voc. Ungraded. Courses: Read Math Lang_Arts. Man_Arts
      & Shop.
   Psychotherapy: Fam Group.
   Enr: 493. Res Males 493. **Staff:** 480 (Full 421, Part 59). Prof 240. Educ 33.

Admin 80.
Est 1913. Private. Nonprofit.

Starr Commonwealth's Albion campus offers group care and community services to boys who have not realized their fullest potentials because of social and behavioral problems. Three treatment programs are conducted through Maple Village, Cedar Village and Lakeview Village. Each village is a self-contained community that affords a total living and learning environment. Other branches operate in Battle Creek (155 Garfield Ave., 49017; 269-968-9287) and Detroit (22390 W. 7 Mile Rd., 48219; 313-794-4447).

In addition, a program for boys is conducted in Ohio (15145 Lincoln Hwy., Van Wert 45891; 419-238-4051). Similar to the Albion location, this program features remedial education and a full intramural sports program. The affiliated Hannah Neil Center for Children, located in Columbus, OH (see separate listing), provides comprehensive care and treatment for children with emotional and behavioral difficulties.

THE UNIVERSITY OF MICHIGAN
COMMUNICATIVE DISORDERS CLINICS

Clinic: Ages 3 and up. M-F 8-5.

Ann Arbor, MI 48109. 1111 E Catherine St.
Tel: 734-764-8440. Fax: 734-647-2489.
www.umich.edu/~comdis   E-mail: ucll@umich.edu
Holly K. Craig, PhD, CCC-SLP, Dir. **Mimi Block,** MS, CCC-SLP, Clin Dir.
   Focus: Treatment. **Conditions:** Primary—LD ON S. Sec—ADD ADHD Ap Bl CP Dx.
   Therapy: Lang. **Psychotherapy:** Group Parent.
   Staff: 12. (Full 12). Admin 4.
   Summer Prgm: Day. Ther.
   Est 1932. State. Nonprofit.

Clinical services are provided for the evaluation and the treatment of language and learning disorders. Residential programs are offered on a six-week basis for the improvement of communication patterns of adults with language disorders secondary to cerebral damage. Speech and language evaluations and therapy are available on an outpatient basis. Children may participate in a summer program that addresses language skills.

VISTA MARIA

Res — Females Ages 11-17

Dearborn Heights, MI 48127. 20651 W Warren Ave.
Tel: 313-271-3050. Fax: 313-271-6250.
www.vistamaria.org
Cameron Hosner, MSA, MBA, Pres. **Jackie Cuschieri,** Intake.
   Focus: Treatment. **Conditions:** Primary—ADD ADHD AN Anx BD Bu CD Dx Mood OCD ODD PTSD Sz. Sec—As Db ED. **IQ 60 and up.**
   Gen Acad. Pre-Voc. Voc. Gr 6-12. Courses: Read Math Lang_Arts. On-Job Trng.
   Therapy: Art Dance Lang Milieu Recreational Speech. **Psychotherapy:**

Fam Group Indiv.
Enr: 160. Res Females 160. **Staff:** 148. Admin 20.
Rates 2004: Res $155-296/day.
Est 1883. Private. Nonprofit.

Vista Maria offers a continuum of residential and community-based programs. There are both short-term emergency shelter and longer-term specialized programs, including an accredited high school program. Residential programs are provided for girls preparing for independent living, and for those who are acting out or who are chronic offenders. The active support and involvement of parents and guardians is an integral part of the program. Supportive services include therapy, remedial and tutorial education, and medical and counseling services. The length of treatment varies.

WAYNE STATE UNIVERSITY
SPEECH AND LANGUAGE CENTER

Clinic: All Ages. M-Th 9-6.

Detroit, MI 48124. 581 Manoogian Hall, 906 W Warren Ave.
Tel: 313-577-3339. Fax: 313-577-8885.
http://sun.science.wayne.edu/~aslp/depart/features.htm
   E-mail: aslp@sun.science.wayne.edu
Kristine V. Sbaschnig, MA, Dir.
   Conditions: Primary—Ap S.
   Therapy: Lang Speech.
   State.

WILLIAM BEAUMONT HOSPITAL
SPEECH AND LANGUAGE PATHOLOGY DEPARTMENT
CENTER FOR CHILDHOOD SPEECH AND LANGUAGE
DISORDERS

Clinic: Ages 1-14. M-F 8-6.

Royal Oak, MI 48073. 4949 Coolidge Hwy.
Tel: 248-655-5695.
   Focus: Treatment. **Conditions:** Primary—Ap Au Bl CP MR S.
   Therapy: Lang Speech. **Psychotherapy:** Fam Group.
   Staff: 16 (Full 11, Part 5).
   Est 1972. Private. Nonprofit.

This center offers a full range of diagnostic and treatment services to children with communication disorders. Special emphasis is given to preschoolers with severe communicative inability related to brain dysfunction and emotional disturbance. A toddler language stimulation program, cognitive retraining for head trauma, a preschool program for speech- and language-impaired children, and high-risk infant stimulation programs are available.

Parental involvement and counseling are integral to each treatment plan. The facility maintains a close coordination with local school districts on an individual basis.

MINNESOTA

ARCHDEACON GILFILLAN CENTER

Res and Day — Coed Ages 6-18

Bemidji, MN 56619. 1741 15th St NW, PO Box 744.
Tel: 218-751-6553. Fax: 218-751-1846.
www.ecsmn.org
Carol Swan, MSW, LICSW, Dir.
   Focus: Spec Ed. Treatment. **Conditions:** Primary—BD CD ED OCD Psy
   Sz. Sec—As Au B Bl D Dx Ep LD S. **IQ 70 and up.**
   Col Prep. Gen Acad. Pre-Voc. Voc. Gr K-12. Courses: Read Math Lang_
   Arts. Man_Arts & Shop. On-Job Trng.
   Therapy: Occup Speech. **Psychotherapy:** Fam Group Indiv Parent.
   Enr: 67. **Staff:** 52 (Full 31, Part 21).
   Est 1965. Private. Nonprofit. Episcopal. **Spons:** Episcopal Community Ser-
   vices.

Located on 40 acres of woods and meadows, the center serves emotionally disturbed
and behaviorally disordered children through reality-oriented group living, therapy and
special education.

An educational program operates in conjunction with the public school district. The
setting at Riverside School makes it possible for students to transfer to Bemidji public
schools. Course work, geared to individuals and small groups, includes social studies,
English, art, science, shop, math and computers. Field trips supplement the curriculum
and encourage growth as students strive to return to community life.

BAR-NONE RESIDENTIAL TREATMENT CENTER

Res — Coed Ages 10-18

Anoka, MN 55303. 22426 St Francis Blvd.
Tel: 763-753-2500. Fax: 763-753-6529.
www.voamn.org
Verlyn R. Wenndt, MSW, Dir. **Dick Pederson,** Intake.
   Focus: Treatment. **Conditions:** Primary—Anx Asp Au BD CD ED Mood MR
   OCD PDD PTSD PW. Sec—ADD ADHD AN As Bl Bu Db DS Dx HIV LD
   ON SP TS. **IQ 60 and up.**
   Gen Acad. Pre-Voc. Ungraded. Courses: Read Math Lang_Arts Computers
   Music. Man_Arts & Shop. Shelt_Workshop. On-Job Trng.
   Therapy: Milieu Occup Speech. **Psychotherapy:** Fam Group Indiv Parent.
   Enr: 80. Res Males 70. Res Females 10. **Staff:** 140. Prof 68. Educ 50.
   Admin 5.
   Rates 2003: Res $160-260/day.
   Est 1961. Private. Nonprofit. **Spons:** Volunteers of America.

Bar-None offers residential programs—ranging from emergency shelter to secure
treatment—for children with autism, psychoses and emotional disturbances.

Shelter services include emergency shelter, stabilization and six-week evaluation for boys and girls who are experiencing a crisis or behavior difficulties. The structured, closely supervised setting facilitates the formulation of realistic treatment and placement plans.

Short-term (two to 10 months) residential treatment accommodates boys with severe behavioral and emotional problems who require a residential intervention to alter irresponsible behavior and thinking patterns. Length of stay varies according to treatment goals and student motivation.

An intensive residential treatment center serves boys who exhibit behavioral or emotional problems, as well as those with cognitive, social, emotional or behavioral delays who also have severe behavioral problems. The program employs cognitive behavior therapy, occupational therapy, social skills training, a work program, recreational activities and special therapy groups to enhance the child's self-esteem and social and self-help skills. A second intensive treatment program provides therapy and training for boys with delays who are sex offenders. Finally, a third intensive treatment program offers a secure environment for court-adjudicated boys with a history of therapeutic and placement failures.

An on-site mental health clinic offers psychiatric assessment, medication management, psychological testing and psychotherapy.

Specialized educational and vocational programming is conducted by the local school district at various sites. As return to the family is the primary goal of each program, parental involvement is highly encouraged.

BISHOP MCNAIRY RECOVERY CENTER

Res — Coed Ages 11-17

Bemidji, MN 56601. 1741 15th St NW, PO Box 744.
Tel: 218-751-6553. Fax: 218-751-1846.
www.ecsmn.org   E-mail: bemidjicam@ecsmn.org
   Focus: Spec Ed. Treatment. **Conditions:** Primary—BD CD ED OCD Psy Sz. Sec—ADD ADHD Dx LD. **IQ 70 and up.**
   Gen Acad. Gr 6-12. Courses: Read Math Lang_Arts Sci Soc_Stud.
   Therapy: Recreational. **Psychotherapy:** Fam Group Indiv Parent.
   Enr: 12. Res Males 6. Res Females 6. **Staff:** 16 (Full 10, Part 6).
   Est 2000. Private. Nonprofit. Episcopal. **Spons:** Episcopal Community Services.

This program treats adolescents who have a chemical dependency diagnosis and a coexisting mental/emotional disorder. Using the results of a thorough evaluation, staff formulate a comprehensive and individualized treatment plan for each patient. The center works closely with the Bemidji School District.

BUSH MEMORIAL CHILDREN'S RESIDENTIAL SERVICES

Res — Coed Ages 5-17

St Paul, MN 55105. 180 S Grotto St.

Tel: 651-225-3680. Fax: 651-224-9510.
www.wilder.org/programs/HealthYouth/Bush.html
    E-mail: dct@wilder.org
Don Turvold, Dir.
    Conditions: Primary—BD ED.
    Gen Acad. Courses: Read Math Lang_Arts.
    Therapy: Recreational. **Psychotherapy:** Fam Group Indiv.
    Staff: Prof 36.
    Est 1957. Private.

COURAGE CENTER

Day — Coed All Ages
Clinic: All Ages. M-Th 7-6, F 7-4.

Golden Valley, MN 55422. 3915 Golden Valley Rd.
Tel: 763-520-0312. TTY: 763-520-0245. Fax: 763-520-0392.
www.courage.org
Eric Stevens, CEO. **Mark Moret,** MD, Med Dir. **Judy Meyer,** Intake.
    Focus: Rehab. **Conditions:** Primary—Ap Apr Ar Bl CP D DS MD MS Nf
        ON S SB. Sec—ADD ADHD Anx As Asp Au B BD C Db Dx Ep IP LD
        MR.
    Therapy: Hear Lang Occup Phys Speech. **Psychotherapy:** Fam Group
        Indiv Parent.
    Staff: 545. Prof 190.
    Est 1973. Private. Nonprofit.

Serving patients with physical disabilities and sensory impairments, the center provides medical examinations, therapy, specialty services and clinics, speech and language treatment, hearing and hearing aid services, and vocational, parental and personal counseling. Various outpatient services are also available. The facility sponsors summer camps at two locations that emphasize outdoor camping experiences in an accessible environment. Courage Center also offers regional day camp opportunities. The facility's program also includes competitive and recreational activities, and social and leisure pursuits.

DISTRICT 518 RESIDENTIAL PROGRAM

Res — Coed Ages 6-21

Worthington, MN 56187. 2011 Nobles St.
Tel: 507-372-2983. Fax: 507-372-2980.
www.isd518.net
Jeff Jorgensen, Dir.
    Focus: Spec Ed. **Conditions:** Primary—Au MD MS OH. Sec—ADHD BD D
        ED Ep MR OCD Psy.
    Gen Acad. Pre-Voc. Gr K-12. Courses: Read Math Lang_Arts. Man_Arts &
        Shop. On-Job Trng.
    Therapy: Hear Lang Occup Phys Speech.

Enr: 13. Res Males 7. Res Females 6.
Est 1959. Municipal. Nonprofit.

This is the only public, tax-supported residential program for students with autism in Minnesota. Pupils with mental retardation and behavioral problems may also enroll. The school program is administered and supervised by the Worthington Independent School District 518. It operates on a regular nine-month school term and includes speech and occupational therapies. Instructors design individual academic programs for the multi-handicapped.

EDITH HATCH EVALUATION CENTER

Res — Coed Ages 5-17

Bemidji, MN 56601. 1741 15th St NW, PO Box 744.
Tel: 218-751-6553. Fax: 218-751-1846.
www.ecsmn.org
  Focus: Treatment. **Conditions:** Primary—ADD ADHD BD CD Dx ED LD. **IQ 60 and up.**
  Gen Acad. Gr K-12. Courses: Read Math Lang_Arts.
  Psychotherapy: Fam Indiv Parent.
  Enr: 12. Res Males 6. Res Females 6. **Staff:** 18 (Full 11, Part 7).
  Private. Nonprofit. Episcopal. **Spons:** Episcopal Community Services.

Edith Hatch provides evaluation and diagnostic services for children and adolescents with emotional disturbances. Patients undergo psychological and academic testing, as well as chemical dependency assessment and basic health screening, over the course of a 35-day program. At the end of the program, staff members compose for each client a full diagnostic report with recommendations and goals for the resident's future.

FAIRVIEW-UNIVERSITY MEDICAL CENTER
PEDIATRIC SPECIALTIES CLINIC

Clinic: All Ages. W 12:30-5.

Minneapolis, MN 55455. 516 Delaware St SE, 4th Fl.
Tel: 612-626-6777.
www.fairview.org
  Conditions: Primary—C CF Db DS MD.
  Therapy: Hear Occup Phys. **Psychotherapy:** Indiv.
  Staff: Prof 4.
  Est 1959. Private.

FRASER SCHOOL

Day — Coed Ages 6wks-6

Minneapolis, MN 55423. 2400 W 64th St.

Tel: 612-861-1688. Fax: 612-861-6050.
www.fraser.org   E-mail: fraser@fraser.org
Diane S. Cross, STM, Exec Dir. **Mary Waters-Cryer,** MA, Dir.
  Focus: Spec Ed. Rehab. **Conditions:** Primary—ADD ADHD As Asp Au B
    BI C CP D DS Ep IP LD MD MR ON PDD PW S SB. Sec—ED.
  Therapy: Music Occup Phys Speech.
  Rates 2003: Day $46-64/day. $35 (Therapy)/ses. Schol avail. State Aid.
  Est 1935. Private. Nonprofit.

Within a fully inclusive environment, Fraser places children in an age-appropriate classroom regardless of their disability or lack thereof. Focus areas include cognition, gross- and fine-motor development, communication, social and emotional development, and social skills development, all provided in a developmentally and individually appropriate curriculum. All pupils participate in music therapy, and occupational, physical and speech/language therapy are available as needed.

GERARD TREATMENT PROGRAMS
AUSTIN CAMPUS

Res — Coed Ages 10-18

Austin, MN 55912. PO Box 715.
Tel: 507-433-1843. Fax: 507-433-7868.
www.nexustreatment.org
Brent Henry, BS, Exec Dir. **Pam Retterath,** MA, Clin Dir. **Loren Nerison,** Adm.
  Focus: Treatment. **Conditions:** Primary—ED. Sec—Au BD BI Dx LD. **IQ 70
    and up.**
  Col Prep. Gen Acad. Pre-Voc. Gr 4-12. Courses: Read Math Lang_Arts Sci
    Soc_Stud.
  Therapy: Milieu Recreational Speech. **Psychotherapy:** Fam Group Indiv.
  Enr: 42. Res Males 26. Res Females 16. **Staff:** 54 (Full 53, Part 1). Prof 32.
    Educ 7. Admin 15.
  Est 1969. Private. Nonprofit. **Spons:** Nexus.

Gerard Treatment Programs offer psychotherapy, special education, and milieu and family therapies in a psychiatric setting for emotionally disturbed adolescents. Each child's treatment program is individually designed and may be supplemented with behavior programming, relationship therapy and a multidisciplinary team approach. Family counseling and consultation with the child's school and parents and involved agencies are provided. The usual length of treatment is nine to 12 months.

GILLETTE CHILDREN'S SPECIALTY HEALTHCARE

Clinic: All Ages. M-F 8-5.

St Paul, MN 55101. 200 E University Ave.
Tel: 651-291-2848. Fax: 651-229-3833.
www.gillettechildrens.com
Margaret E. Perryman, MBA, Pres. **Steven E. Koop,** MD, Med Dir. **Lynn Car-
  pentier,** Adm.

Minnesota

543

Focus: Rehab. Treatment. **Conditions:** Primary—Ap BI CP Ep IP MD ON PW SB. Sec—ADD ADHD B BD D Db Dg Dx TS. **IQ 20 and up.**
Therapy: Hear Lang Occup Phys Speech. **Psychotherapy:** Fam Group Indiv.
Staff: 700 (Full 480, Part 220). Admin 50.
Est 1897. Private. Nonprofit.

Serving orthopedically/neurologically and mentally handicapped children, the hospital utilizes an integrated, multidisciplinary approach. Major programs are available for children with cerebral palsy, spina bifida, brain and spinal cord injuries, orthopedic conditions and epilepsy. Ventilator-dependent patients also receive treatment at the hospital. The programs are intensive, aimed at returning each child to a home or some other permanent placement. Educational, parental and personal counseling are available. The usual duration of treatment is one day to three months.

GROVES ACADEMY

Day — Coed Ages 3-18

St Louis Park, MN 55416. 3200 Hwy 100 S.
Tel: 952-920-6377. Fax: 952-920-2068.
www.grovesacademy.org   E-mail: information@grovesacademy.org
Michael Mongeau, BA, MA, Head. **Debbie Moran,** Adm.
    Focus: Spec Ed. **Conditions:** Primary—ADD ADHD CP Dc Dg Dx ED LD S. **IQ 80 and up.**
    Col Prep. Gen Acad. Pre-Voc. Gr PS-12. Courses: Read Math Lang_Arts Computers Sci Soc_Stud Studio_Art. Man_Arts & Shop.
    Therapy: Lang Speech.
    Enr: 198. Day Males 125. Day Females 73. **Staff:** 49 (Full 40, Part 9).
    Rates 2003: Day $15,400/sch yr. Schol avail.
    Summer Prgm: Day. Educ. Rec. 3-6 wks.
    Est 1972. Private. Nonprofit.

The academy accepts students with learning disabilities and attentional disorders of normal or higher intelligence with the goal of returning them to the educational mainstream. Pupils may also remain through grade 12 and earn a high school diploma at Groves. Individualized instruction and remediation are tailored to each student's learning characteristics.

Prior to admission, staff members conduct a diagnostic assessment of the educational, psychological, social and physical factors of the student's learning disorders. Course offerings include reading, writing, math, science, social studies, art, physical education and computer, and various extracurricular activities supplement class work. The school also offers a basic skills tutorial for children, teens and adults after school. A summer session open to all pupils provides intensive remediation for academic deficits and also includes recreational and social skills programs.

HOME FOR CREATIVE LIVING

Res — Coed All Ages

Windom, MN 56101. 108 9th St.
Tel: 507-831-5033. Fax: 507-831-2612.
  Conditions: Primary—MR.
  On-Job Trng.
  Est 1975. Private. **Spons:** Habilitative Services.

LAURA BAKER SERVICES ASSOCIATION

Res — Coed Ages 4 and up; Day — Coed 4-22

Northfield, MN 55057. 211 Oak St.
Tel: 507-645-8866. Fax: 507-645-8869.
www.laurabaker.org   E-mail: doug@laurabaker.org
Sandra Gerdes, Exec Dir.
  Conditions: Primary—MR. Sec—ED Ep. **IQ 0-70.**
  Gen Acad. Pre-Voc. Voc. Ungraded. Courses: Read Math Lang_Arts.
    Shelt_Workshop.
  Therapy: Hear Lang Music Occup Phys Speech.
  Staff: 90.
  Est 1897. Private. Inc.

Established in 1897 as an experiment in education, today the association comprises a private school, an adult program and a residential center for trainable to severely retarded individuals. The school functions as a tool in helping its residents adapt to society, while also stressing the behaviors, values and skills necessary for daily living.

Residents live in small groups within living units, and each group has a coordinator to ensure that physical, emotional and social needs are met. More independent living arrangements are available, promoting self-sufficiency and responsibility.

All residents enroll in developmental programs. School-age residents attend the private school program, while adults participate in a developmental achievement center and sheltered workshop placement. The private school consists of levels ranging from preprimary to prevocational and facilitates transition to independent living within the community.

On-campus activities include physical education, crafts and training in food service skills. A continuation of the regular program, the six-week summer session offers swimming, fishing, outdoor sports, games, picnics and field trips.

MINNESOTA STATE ACADEMY FOR THE BLIND

Res and Day — Coed Ages 3-21

Faribault, MN 55021. 400 SE 6th Ave, PO Box 68.
Tel: 507-333-4800. Fax: 507-333-4825.
www.msab.state.mn.us   E-mail: info@msab.state.mn.us
Linda Mitchell, Supt. **Wade Karli,** Prin.

Focus: Spec Ed. Trng. **Conditions:** Primary—B. Sec—Au D ED LD MR ON S.
Gen Acad. Pre-Voc. Voc. Gr K-12. Courses: Read Math Lang_Arts Sci Soc_Stud Computers Braille Life_Skills. Man_Arts & Shop. Shelt_Workshop. On-Job Trng.
Therapy: Hear Lang Music Occup Phys Recreational Speech. **Psychotherapy:** Fam Group Indiv.
Enr: 85. **Staff:** 60.
Rates 2004: No Fee.
Summer Prgm: Res & Day. Educ. Rec. Ther. 3-4 wks.
Est 1866. State. Nonprofit.

MSAB provides educational programming for blind or visually impaired children with or without other disabilities. A vocational training program allows students to gain work experience. Length of enrollment varies widely according to the pupil's needs.

MINNESOTA STATE ACADEMY FOR THE DEAF

Res — Coed Ages 5-21; Day — Coed 2-21

Faribault, MN 55021. PO Box 308.
Tel: 507-332-5400. TTY: 507-332-5400. Fax: 507-332-5528.
www.msad.state.mn.us   E-mail: adm@msad.state.mn.us
Linda Mitchell, Supt.
  Focus: Spec Ed. **Conditions:** Primary—D.
  Gen Acad. Gr PS-12. Courses: Read Math Lang_Arts.
  Therapy: Lang Occup Phys Speech. **Psychotherapy:** Indiv.
  Enr: 170. **Staff:** 100.
  Summer Prgm: Res & Day. Educ. 2 wks.
  Est 1863. State. Nonprofit.

MSAD provides an educational program for hard-of-hearing students. Programming emphasizes language and reading skills and adheres to Minnesota guidelines and graduation standards. The Special Education Unit is available to assist students in developing basic living skills and functional academic skills. MSAD also offers a full range of cocurricular activities, and mainstreaming opportunities are available through Faribault Public Schools.

MINNESOTA STATE UNIVERSITY-MOORHEAD SPEECH-LANGUAGE-HEARING CENTER

Day — Coed Ages 3-21
Clinic: All Ages. M-F 8-5.

Moorhead, MN 56563. 1104 7th Ave S.
Tel: 218-477-2286. TTY: 218-477-2286. Fax: 218-477-4392.
E-mail: slhs@mnstate.edu
Nancy Paul, MS, Dir.
  Focus: Treatment. **Conditions:** Primary—S.
  Therapy: Hear Lang Speech.

Staff: 12 (Full 5, Part 7).
Est 1961. State.

MSUM's program provides speech, language and hearing assessment and management services for difficulties caused by all types of disorders.

NORTHWOOD CHILDREN'S SERVICES

Res — Coed Ages 5-17; Day — Coed 1½-17

Duluth, MN 55811. 714 W College St.
Tel: 218-724-8815. Fax: 218-724-0251.
www.nwch.com   E-mail: yeagerj@aol.com
James F. Yeager, EdD, Exec Dir.
    Focus: Spec Ed. Treatment. **Conditions:** Primary—ADD ADHD Au BD CD Dx ED LD OCD ON Psy Sz. Sec—As B Bl C CP D Ep IP MD MS S SB TB. **IQ 70 and up.**
    Gen Acad. Gr PS-12. Courses: Read Math Lang_Arts Music Studio_Art. Man_Arts & Shop. On-Job Trng.
    Therapy: Lang Occup Recreational Speech. **Psychotherapy:** Fam Group Indiv.
    Enr: 119. Res Males 87. Res Females 24. Day Males 6. Day Females 2.
    Rates 2001: Res $149/day. Day $67/day. State Aid.
    Est 1883. Private. Nonprofit.

Northwood serves children who have developmental, behavioral, emotional and learning disabilities. Group living, individual therapy and special education create a therapeutic environment. Staff members emphasize the development of daily living and social skills. In addition to education and therapy, children participate in an extensive recreational program that includes such activities as swimming, canoeing, skiing and community outings. Parents stay involved in the program through contact with the child's social worker, and the usual length of treatment is 10 to 12 months.

In addition to the main facility (which serves up to 40 children), Northwood operates a 48-bed residential unit and three homes. Two of the homes serve as long-term placement areas for youths who cannot be placed in foster or adoptive homes. The remaining home serves as a 35-day evaluation program.

ST. JOSEPH'S HOME FOR CHILDREN

Res — Coed Ages 6-17; Day — Coed 6-12

Minneapolis, MN 55407. 1121 E 46th St.
Tel: 612-827-6241. Fax: 612-827-9321.
www.ccspm.org
Edward McBrayer, BSW, Admin.
    Focus: Treatment. **Conditions:** Primary—BD ED. **IQ 65 and up.**
    Voc. On-Job Trng.
    Therapy: Chemo Hear Lang Occup Phys Speech. **Psychotherapy:** Fam Group.
    Enr: 68. Res Males 24. Res Females 7. Day Males 27. Day Females 10.

Staff: 160 (Full 120, Part 40). Admin 4.
Rates 2001: Res $108/day. Day $62/day. State Aid.
Est 1959. Private. Nonprofit. **Spons:** Catholic Charities.

St. Joseph's conducts developmental, educational and family assessments; psychological testing; and a short-term emergency shelter. The residential program treats children with persistent social and emotional problems, while day treatment helps those with life-adjustment problems and learning disabilities.

Services at the home include educational and vocational programs; arts and crafts; occupational, recreational and music therapy; computer; and sensory integration/dance. The staff also works with the child's parents. The average length of treatment is 11 months.

SOLTREKS

Res — Coed Ages 13-25

Two Harbors, MN 55616. 2346 Hwy 3.
Tel: 218-834-4607. Fax: 218-834-6166.
www.soltreks.com   E-mail: soltreks@cpinternet.com
Lorri Hanna, MA, Exec Dir.
   Focus: Treatment. **Conditions:** Primary—ADD ADHD Anx Asp BD Dc Dg Dx ED LD Mood ON PDD. Sec—As BI CD CP D Db HIV MR MS OCD PTSD. **IQ 90 and up.**
   Therapy: Art Recreational.
   Staff: 4. Prof 3. Admin 1.
   Rates 2003: Res $375/day (+$150/ses). Schol 2 ($4000).
   Summer Prgm: Res. Rec. Ther. Res Rate $8700. 6 wks.
   Est 1997. Private. Inc.

Soltreks offers therapeutic, adventure-based programs throughout the year for teenagers, young adults and their families. Founded upon the need to individualize adventure-based experiences, each program provides customized, focused treks where students can experience greater opportunities for personal development, growth and change. Trek options are One-on-One, Winter Adventure, Summer Adventure and Specialty (which is designed in conjunction with the boy's family).

UNIVERSITY OF MINNESOTA SCHOOL OF DENTISTRY CLEFT PALATE AND CRANIOFACIAL ANOMALIES CLINICS

Clinic: All Ages. T W 8-4:30.

Minneapolis, MN 55455. 6296 Moos Tower.
Tel: 612-625-5945. Fax: 612-626-2900.
www.dentistry.umn.edu   E-mail: molle001@umn.edu
Karlind T. Moller, MA, PhD, Dir. **Kathy Conway,** RN, MS, Med Dir. **Kathy Patka,** Intake.
   Focus: Trng. Treatment. **Conditions:** Primary—S.
   Therapy: Speech.
   Staff: 45 (Full 3, Part 42). Prof 41. Admin 2.

State.

The School of Dentistry offers the following clinics for patients and their families: craniofacial anomalies, cleft lip and cleft palate, skull-base surgery, maxillofacial prosthodontic and speech prosthesis. All clinics provide comprehensive diagnostic, evaluation and treatment planning services.

VISION LOSS RESOURCES

Day — Coed Ages 16 and up

Minneapolis, MN 55403. 1936 Lyndale Ave S.
Tel: 612-871-2222. Fax: 612-872-0189.
www.visionlossresources.com
Steven Fischer, Exec Dir.
  Conditions: Primary—B.
  Col Prep. Gen Acad. Pre-Voc. Voc. Ungraded. Man_Arts & Shop. Shelt_
    Workshop. On-Job Trng.
  Psychotherapy: Fam Group.
  Est 1914. Inc.

WASHBURN CHILD GUIDANCE CENTER

Day — Coed Ages 3-10
Clinic: Ages Birth-18. M-F.

Minneapolis, MN 55404. 2430 Nicollet Ave S.
Tel: 612-871-1454. Fax: 612-871-1505.
www.washburn.org
Steve Lepinski, MA, Exec Dir.
  Conditions: Primary—BD ED.
  Psychotherapy: Fam Group Indiv.
  Est 1883. Private. Nonprofit.

WOODLAND CENTERS

Res — Coed Ages 9-18; Day — Coed 6-16
Clinic: Ages 3-18. M-F 8-5.

Willmar, MN 56201. 1125 SE 6th St, PO Box 787.
  Nearby locations: Benson; Dawson; Litchfield; Montevideo; Olivia.
Tel: 320-235-4613. Fax: 320-231-9140.
www.woodlandcenters.com
Eugene Bonynge, PhD, CEO. **Richard Lee,** PhD, Clin Dir. **David Kerski,** MD, Med Dir.
  Focus: Treatment. **Conditions:** Primary—ADD ADHD Au BD CD ED Mood OCD ON Psy Sz. Sec—Dx LD.

Gen Acad. Gr 1-10.
Therapy: Chemo. **Psychotherapy:** Fam Group Indiv Parent.
Staff: 97. Prof 25. Admin 9.
Rates 2003: Res $300/day.
Est 1958. State. Nonprofit.

Woodland offers comprehensive community mental health programs, including an adolescent day treatment program, chemical dependency counseling and crisis intervention. Inpatient services are provided under contractual arrangements with a community hospital. A youth partial hospitalization program is also available.

WOODLAND HILLS

Res — Coed Ages 12-20; Day — Coed 12-17

Duluth, MN 55803. 4321 Allendale Ave.
Tel: 218-728-7500. Fax: 218-724-7403.
www.woodlandhills.org   E-mail: mail@woodlandhills.org
Richard Quigley, MEd, CEO. **Glenn Dallmann,** Adm.
    Focus: Rehab. Treatment. **Conditions:** Primary—BD CD ED ODD. Sec—
       ADD ADHD Db Dx LD Mood OCD PTSD. **IQ 80-135.**
    Gen Acad. Ungraded. Courses: Read Math Lang_Arts Health.
    Psychotherapy: Fam Group Indiv.
    Enr: 110. **Staff:** 130 (Full 102, Part 28). Educ 34. Admin 6.
    Rates 2004: Res $114-172/day. Day $69/day.
    Est 1909. Private. Nonprofit.

Woodland Hills offers prevention, intervention and rehabilitation services through five programs: Neighborhood Youth Services, which consists of educational, cultural, recreational and service-learning components; intensive day treatment; short-term residential treatment for youth referred by the juvenile justice and social service systems; an open-ended residential treatment center; and a community transition program. All programs emphasize a positive peer culture and help residents learn problem-solving skills and develop living and interpersonal skills. Psychotherapy, family counseling, and educational and vocational guidance services are available.

Students attend school full-time and volunteer for community work. Out-of-state pupils must pay tuition charges, in addition to the program rate. Among recreational options are arts and crafts, creative writing and wood shop, in addition to various sports and games.

MISSISSIPPI

THE BADDOUR CENTER
Res — Coed Ages 18 and up

Senatobia, MS 38668. 3297 Hwy 51 S, PO Box 69.
Tel: 662-562-9666. Fax: 662-562-0638.
www.baddour.org   E-mail: admissions@baddour.org
Steve Dickie, MDiv, MA, Exec Dir. **Tricia Melvin,** MEd, Prgm Dir.
Focus: Trng. Treatment. **Conditions:** Primary—MR. **IQ 40-69.**
Voc. Shelt_Workshop. On-Job Trng.
Therapy: Art Music Recreational. **Psychotherapy:** Fam Group Indiv.
Enr: 173. Res Males 84. Res Females 89. **Staff:** 179 (Full 122, Part 57).
Rates 2003: Res $22,200-23,400/yr.
Est 1978. Private. Nonprofit. Methodist.

Situated on a 120-acre complex, Baddour offers a variety of program options to meet the needs of persons with mild to moderate mental retardation. The center stresses normalization through training and living experiences that allow for choice and maximum independence. The primary objective is to promote the self-sufficiency and self-worth of individuals diagnosed with mental retardation.

Staff members design individualized prescriptive programs to foster mental, spiritual, social, physical and vocational growth. Fourteen group homes offer instruction in independent living skills, socialization skills and money management. On-campus supervised, transitional and apartment living arrangements are also available. In addition, Baddour operates the Buckman Enrichment Center for residents whose age, health or both dictate a slower-paced setting.

An extensive vocational program provides training and employment for both residents and day clients. Individuals without previous work history may receive prevocational training. A work center offers various work opportunities contracted from local and Tennessee-area industries. The center's greenhouse and retail garden center serves residents interested in horticulture. Residents earn wages in accordance with federal guidelines.

Among other center activities are a physical fitness program, a traveling choir, music therapy (including optional instrumental lessons), Special Olympics, drama, adult education and intramural sports.

THE EDUCATION CENTER SCHOOL
Day — Coed Ages 5-21

Jackson, MS 39296. 4080 Old Canton Rd, PO Box 55509.
Tel: 601-982-2812. Fax: 601-982-2827.
www.educationcenterschool.com   E-mail: edcenter@bellsouth.net
Lynn T. Macon, MEd, Prin.
Focus: Spec Ed. **Conditions:** Primary—ADD ADHD Dx ED LD. Sec—BD.
IQ 90 and up.
Gen Acad. Gr 1-12. Courses: Read Math Lang_Arts.
Psychotherapy: Fam Parent.

Enr: 175. **Staff:** 19 (Full 10, Part 9).
Summer Prgm: Day. Educ.
Est 1964. Private.

This center provides special academic instruction in a small-class setting, as well as diagnostic and prescriptive education, for students with learning differences. The program emphasizes the development of reading skills, learning strategies and study skills. Preliminary vocational counseling and screening are also available, as are summer courses, tutoring and evening classes.

HERITAGE SCHOOL

Day — Coed Ages 6-15

Ridgeland, MS 39289. 550 Sunnybrook Rd.
Tel: 601-853-7163.
Lynn Stribling, BS, Dir. **Jo Ann White,** Adm.
  Focus: Spec Ed. **Conditions:** Primary—ADD ADHD Dc Dg Dx LD. Sec—As C CF Db Ep OCD. **IQ 85 and up.**
  Gen Acad. Ungraded. Courses: Read Math Lang_Arts Sci Soc_Stud.
  Enr: 22. Day Males 18. Day Females 4. **Staff:** 5 (Full 4, Part 1).
  Rates 2003: Day $350/mo (+$325/sch yr). State Aid.
  Summer Prgm: Day. Educ. Day Rate $300. 6 wks.
  Est 1971. Private. Nonprofit.

Heritage accommodates children with learning disabilities, attentional disorders and certain other learning differences. Students learn in a classroom featuring individualized self-pacing and participate in programs with large-group discussions. The student-teacher ratio in the classroom is 9:1.

HUDSPETH REGIONAL CENTER

Res — Coed Ages 5 and up

Whitfield, MS 39193. PO Box 127-B.
Tel: 601-664-6000. Fax: 601-354-6945.
John P. Lipscomb, MEd, PhD, Dir. **Suzanne Senter,** MD, Med Dir. **Nancy Hobson,** Adm.
  Focus: Spec Ed. **Conditions:** Primary—MR. Sec—B D S.
  Pre-Voc. Ungraded. Shelt_Workshop. On-Job Trng.
  Therapy: Chemo Hear Hydro Lang Music Occup Phys Recreational Speech. **Psychotherapy:** Indiv.
  Enr: 406. **Staff:** 854.
  Est 1974. State. Nonprofit.

This facility offers comprehensive developmental treatment and training to mentally retarded individuals. A vocational program and various individual therpaies are available. Rates are on a sliding scale.

MAGNOLIA SPEECH SCHOOL

Day — Coed Ages Birth-14

Jackson, MS 39209. 733 Flag Chapel Rd.
Tel: 601-922-5530. TTY: 601-922-5531. Fax: 601-922-5534.
www.oraldeafed.org/schools/magnolia
    E-mail: magnolia@oraldeafed.org
Anne Sullivan, MS, MEd, Dir.
    Conditions: Primary—D.
    Gen Acad. Ungraded. Courses: Read Math.
    Therapy: Hear Lang Speech.
    Est 1956. Private. Nonprofit.

MERIDIAN SPEECH AND HEARING CENTER

Clinic: All Ages. M-F 8:30-4:30.

Meridian, MS 39301. 2203 Hwy 39 N, Ste A, Box 5.
Tel: 601-483-8121. Fax: 601-485-6627.
E-mail: mershc@bellsouth.net
Judy F. Hammack, Exec Dir.
    Focus: Treatment. **Conditions:** Primary—Ap D S. Sec—ADD ADHD Au Bl
        CP MD MR MS ON SB.
    Therapy: Hear Speech.
    Staff: 5. (Full 5).
    Rates 2003: Sliding-Scale Rate $4-38/ses.
    Est 1973. Private. Nonprofit. **Spons:** United Way/Sertoma International.

Meridian is a community-based clinic that satisfies the needs of patients with speech,
language, voice, fluency and hearing disorders with such services as evaluations, therapy, amplification and referrals. Fees are determined along a sliding scale.

MILLCREEK BEHAVIORAL HEALTH SERVICES

Res — Coed Ages 5-21; Day — Coed 5-17

Magee, MS 39111. 900 1st Ave NE, PO Box 1160.
    Nearby locations: Pontotoc.
Tel: 601-849-4221. Fax: 601-849-6107.
www.yfcs.com/facilities/millcreekbhs   E-mail: info.mc-ms@yfcs.com
Margret F. Tedford, Admin. **Rudolph S. Runnels,** MD, Med Dir. **Suzanne
Carter,** Adm.
  · **Focus:** Spec Ed. Rehab. Trng. Treatment. **Conditions:** Primary—Bl Ep MR
        OH. Sec—ADD ADHD CP ED LD MD OCD Psy S SB Sz. **IQ 45 and up.**
    Gen Acad. Pre-Voc. Voc. Ungraded. Courses: Read Math Lang_Arts Com-
        puters. Man_Arts & Shop. On-Job Trng.
    Therapy: Chemo Hear Lang Occup Phys Speech. **Psychotherapy:** Fam
        Group Indiv.

Staff: 475.
Est 1976. Private. Inc. **Spons:** Youth and Family Centered Services.

Formerly Millcreek Rehabilitation Centers. Millcreek provides multidisciplinary evaluation, treatment and schooling for dually diagnosed children. Weekly psychiatric evaluation is available, as are personal, parental, educational and vocational counseling and advocacy programs. The facility seeks to increase each resident's level of functioning in preparation for return to a less restrictive environment.

MISSISSIPPI SCHOOL FOR THE BLIND

Res — Coed Ages 5-20; Day — Coed Birth-5
Clinic: Ages Birth-20. W by Appt.

Jackson, MS 39211. 1252 Eastover Dr.
Tel: 601-984-8200. TTY: 601-984-8097. Fax: 601-984-8230.
www2.mde.k12.ms.us/msb   E-mail: rpridgen@mde.k12.ms.us
Rosie L. T. Pridgen, PhD, Supt. **Claudia Hollingsworth,** Adm.
　　Focus: Spec Ed. **Conditions:** Primary—B. Sec—D MR ON S.
　　Col Prep. Gen Acad. Pre-Voc. Voc. Gr PS-12. Courses: Read Math Lang_
　　　Arts Braille Orientation & Mobility. Man_Arts & Shop. Shelt_Workshop.
　　　On-Job Trng.
　　Therapy: Lang Occup Phys Speech. **Psychotherapy:** Indiv.
　　Enr: 85. **Staff:** 90 (Full 75, Part 15). Prof 35. Admin 11.
　　Rates 2003: No Fee.
　　Est 1848. State.

This state facility provides education at all grade levels for blind children, ranging from home-based preschool through grade 12. Rehabilitative services in orientation and mobility, vocational training and communications are also available. For admittance, students must be from Mississippi and must have a visual disorder as the primary disabling condition.

MISSISSIPPI SOCIETY FOR DISABILITIES
KIDS CLINIC

Clinic: Ages Birth-18. M-F 8:30-4:30.

Jackson, MS 39296. 3226 N State St, PO Box 4958.
Tel: 601-982-7051. Fax: 601-982-1951.
Carla Thompson, CEO.
　　Focus: Treatment. **Conditions:** Primary—Ap S. Sec—MR OH.
　　Therapy: Hear Lang Occup Phys Speech.
　　Staff: 6 (Full 3, Part 3). Prof 5. Admin 1.
　　Rates 2003: Clinic $100/hr.
　　Est 1973. Private. Nonprofit.

KIDS Clinic offers comprehensive habilitative/rehabilitative therapy programs for the remediation of communicative disorders in the areas of language, voice, articulation and fluency.

NORTH MISSISSIPPI REGIONAL CENTER

Res — Coed Ages 5 and up

Oxford, MS 38655. 967 Regional Ctr Dr.
Tel: 662-234-1476. Fax: 662-234-1699.
www.nmrc.state.ms.us   E-mail: staff@nmrc.state.ms.us
Carole B. Haney, JD, Dir. **Eric Dahl,** MD, Med Dir.
   Focus: Treatment. **Conditions:** Primary—MR. Sec—ADD ADHD Ap As Au
   B BD BI C CP D Db DS ED Ep ODD ON Psy PTSD PW S SB Sz TS. **IQ
   0-69.**
   Gen Acad. Pre-Voc. Voc. Ungraded. Courses: Read Math Lang_Arts Life_
   Skills. Shelt_Workshop. On-Job Trng.
   Therapy: Chemo Hear Hydro Lang Music Occup Phys Recreational
   Speech. **Psychotherapy:** Group Indiv.
   Enr: 470. Res Males 270. Res Females 200. **Staff:** 211.
   Est 1972. State. **Spons:** Mississippi Department of Mental Health.

The center provides comprehensive residential and community-based services for mentally retarded and developmentally disabled individuals of north Mississippi. The Diagnostic Services Department uses speech and language, educational, social, medical, psychological, hearing, visual, nutrition and occupational therapy assessments to determine appropriate placement and programming recommendations.

Residential services are available for those who need interdisciplinary treatment in the areas of self-help, communication, socialization, mobility, vocational readiness and behavior management.

Supported employment, case management, work activity centers, supervised apartments and group homes are available through the Department of Community Services. Fees are determined along a sliding scale.

Programs available through the Home and Community Based Services include adult day habilitation, attendant care, specialized medical supplies, physical and occupational therapy, behavior intervention, speech, language and hearing therapy. Prevocational and respite services are also available.

SOUTH MISSISSIPPI REGIONAL CENTER

Res — Coed Ages 5 and up

Long Beach, MS 39560. 1170 W Railroad St.
Tel: 228-868-2923. Fax: 228-865-9364.
www.smrc.state.ms.us
Pamela C. Baker, Dir.
   Conditions: Primary—MR. **IQ 0-70.**
   Therapy: Hear Lang Occup Phys Speech. **Psychotherapy:** Group Indiv.
   Staff: Prof 48.
   Est 1978. State. Nonprofit.

UNIVERSITY OF MISSISSIPPI
SPEECH AND HEARING CENTER

Clinic: All Ages. M-F 8-6.

University, MS 38677. PO Box 1848.
Tel: 662-915-7271. Fax: 662-915-5717.
www.olemiss.edu/depts/speech_and_hearing
   E-mail: umcdshc@olemiss.edu
Virginia Wiggins, MS, CCC-SLP, Dir.
   Focus: Treatment. **Conditions:** Primary—Ap LD S. Sec—BI CP D Dx.
   Therapy: Hear Lang Speech.
   Staff: 11 (Full 10, Part 1).
   Est 1968. State. Nonprofit.

This university-operated clinic conducts evaluation and treatment of all speech, language and hearing disorders.

UNIVERSITY OF SOUTHERN MISSISSIPPI
DUBARD SCHOOL FOR LANGUAGE DISORDERS

Day — Coed Ages 3-14
Clinic: Ages Birth-15. M-F 8-5.

Hattiesburg, MS 39406. 118 College Dr, Ste 10035.
Tel: 601-266-5223. Fax: 601-266-6763.
www.dubard.usm.edu   E-mail: dubard@usm.edu
Maureen K. Martin, BS, MS, PhD, Dir.
   Focus: Spec Ed. **Conditions:** Primary—Ap D LD S. Sec—ADD ADHD Au Dx.
   Gen Acad. Gr PS-4. Courses: Read Math Lang_Arts.
   Therapy: Hear Lang Speech. **Psychotherapy:** Group.
   Enr: 38. Day Males 24. Day Females 14. **Staff:** 11 (Full 10, Part 1).
   Summer Prgm: Day. Educ.
   Est 1962. State. Nonprofit. **Spons:** United Way.

This school offers programs for children with severe speech and language disorders related to deafness, aphasia, auditory processing, apraxia and dyslexia. Elementary education is offered through grade 4. Language, speech, lip reading and oral communication are provided, as are programs specifically designed for the multi-handicapped deaf. There is no fee for the day program and acceptance is determined by eligibility according to Mississippi State Department of Education guidelines. Outpatient services and parental counseling are available.

UNIVERSITY OF SOUTHERN MISSISSIPPI
SPEECH AND HEARING CLINIC

Clinic: All Ages. M-F 8-5.

Hattiesburg, MS 39406. 118 College Dr, PO Box 5092.
Tel: 601-266-5216. Fax: 601-266-5224.
www.usm.edu/shs/clinic.htm   E-mail: speech.hearing@usm.edu
Raymond M. Alexander,
MS, Dir.
   Conditions: Primary—Ap D S.
   Therapy: Hear Lang Speech.
   Est 1955. State.

MISSOURI

AREA HEARING AND SPEECH CLINIC

Clinic: All Ages. M-F 9-4:30.

Joplin, MO 64804. 2311 Jackson Ave.
Tel: 417-781-2311.
  Focus: Treatment. **Conditions:** Primary—D S.
  Therapy: Hear.
  Staff: 4 (Full 3, Part 1).
  Est 1968. Private. Inc.

This clinic serves the therapeutic needs of individuals with communicative disorders who reside in the Joplin area. The program addresses all aspects of communication therapy, including hearing aid dispensation.

AUDRAIN MEDICAL CENTER
DEPARTMENT OF SPEECH PATHOLOGY-AUDIOLOGY

Clinic: All Ages. M-F 8-4.

Mexico, MO 65265. 620 E Monroe St.
Tel: 573-582-5000. Fax: 573-582-3721.
www.audrainmedicalcenter.com
  Conditions: Primary—Ap BI CP D ON S.
  Gen Acad. Gr K-PG. Courses: Lang_Arts.
  Therapy: Hear Lang Speech. **Psychotherapy:** Group.
  Staff: Prof 3.
  Est 1913. County. Nonprofit.

CAPITAL REGIONAL MEDICAL CENTER
PEDIATRIC THERAPY

Clinic: All Ages. M-F 7:30-5:30.

Jefferson City, MO 65102. 1125 Madison St.
Tel: 573-632-5614. Fax: 573-632-5990.
www.crmc.org
Sara Koenigsfeld, Supv. **Jackie Steuber,** Adm.
  Focus: Treatment. **Conditions:** Primary—ADD ADHD Ap Au BI CP Dx IP
  LD MD MR ON S SB. Sec—B D.
  Therapy: Hear Lang Occup Phys Play Speech. **Psychotherapy:** Indiv.
  Staff: 7 (Full 5, Part 2).
  Private. Nonprofit.

The clinic provides assessment, treatment and intervention services for children with special needs. Services address developmental delays, physical disabilities, disability rehabilitation, neurological disorders, speech and language disorders, learning and school difficulties, swallowing dysfunctions and substance abuse. The center emphasizes parental involvement and offers both education and support to parents.

THE CENTER FOR HUMAN SERVICES CHILDREN'S THERAPY CENTER

Day — Coed Ages Birth-3

Sedalia, MO 65301. 1500 Ewing Dr.
 Nearby locations: California (MO); Marshall.
Tel: 660-826-4400. TTY: 660-827-1406. Fax: 660-827-3034.
www.chs-mo.org   E-mail: smergen@chs-mo.org
Roger A. Garlich, Exec Dir.
 Focus: Rehab. Trng. **Conditions:** Primary—Au DS MR ON PDD S. Sec—LD.
 Voc. Shelt_Workshop. On-Job Trng.
 Therapy: Hear Lang Occup Phys Speech. **Psychotherapy:** Indiv Parent.
 Staff: 12 (Full 8, Part 4). Prof 9. Educ 1. Admin 2.
 Rates 2003: No Fee.
 Est 1955. Private. Nonprofit.

This program provides early intervention services for young children with developmental delays. Offerings also include prenatal education, home visits to young families and training services for area preschools. In addition to the Ewing Drive location, the center maintains facilities at another Sedalia address (600 E. 14th St.; 660-826-4400), as well as in Marshall (175 W. Slater St., 65340; 660-886-4261) and California (P.O. Box 287, 65108).

CENTRAL INSTITUTE FOR THE DEAF

Res — Coed Ages 3-12; Day — Coed Birth-12

St Louis, MO 63110. 4560 Clayton Ave.
Tel: 314-977-0000. TTY: 314-977-0091. Fax: 314-977-0023.
www.cid.wustl.edu   E-mail: jepstein@cid.wustl.edu
Robert G. Clark, Exec Dir. **JoEllen Epstein,** MAEd, Prin.
 Focus: Spec Ed. **Conditions:** Primary—D. **IQ 80 and up.**
 Gen Acad. Ungraded. Courses: Read Math Lang_Arts Computers Soc_Stud Studio_Art.
 Therapy: Hear Lang Speech. **Psychotherapy:** Fam Parent.
 Enr: 62. Res Males 5. Res Females 2. Day Males 23. Day Females 32.
 Staff: 39 (Full 30, Part 9).
 Rates 2003: Res $41,580/sch yr. Day $21,525/sch yr. Schol 12 ($290,190). State Aid.
 Summer Prgm: Day. Educ. Day Rate $122/day. 3 wks.
 Est 1914. Private. Nonprofit.

CID offers a variety of instructional styles and learning sequences suited to children with varying degrees of hearing impairment, language-learning ability and academic achievement. The use of a hearing aid or cochlear implant is an important part of the hearing-impaired child's educational and social program.

The CID School provides a broad range of extracurricular activities, academics and nonacademic classes, among them computer, art and physical education. The CID Family Center combines instruction and counseling for parents with an initial nursery school experience for their children. Diagnostic services are available.

CENTRAL MISSOURI STATE UNIVERSITY
WELCH-SCHMIDT CENTER FOR COMMUNICATION DISORDERS

Clinic: All Ages. M-F 8-5.

Warrensburg, MO 64093. Martin Bldg, Rm 34.
Tel: 660-543-4993. Fax: 660-543-8234.
http://comdisorders.cmsu.edu
Carl L. Harlan, PhD, Supv.
   Focus: Treatment. **Conditions:** Primary—Ap Au BI D ON S. Sec—ADD ADHD B CP Dx LD MD MR MS SB.
   Therapy: Hear Lang Speech.
   Staff: 21 (Full 18, Part 3).
   Rates 2004: $45 (Evaluation); $25 (Therapy)/ses.
   State. Nonprofit.

Evaluation and treatment of speech, language and hearing disorders, as well as parental counseling and follow-up services, constitute the program at Welch-Schmidt Center. Clients follow a twice-weekly program that lasts for 13 weeks.

CHILD CENTER OF OUR LADY

Res — Males Ages 5-14; Day — Coed 5-14

St Louis, MO 63121. 7900 Natural Bridge Rd.
Tel: 314-383-0200. Fax: 314-383-6334.
www.ccstl.org/our_lady   **E-mail:** jbausch@ccstl.org
Edward S. Koszykowski, MA, Exec Dir. **Pat Slowiak,** Adm.
   Focus: Treatment. **Conditions:** Primary—ADD ADHD BD CD ED Mood PDD PTSD. Sec—Ap MR. **IQ 70 and up.**
   Gen Acad. Ungraded. Courses: Read Math Lang_Arts.
   Therapy: Art Lang Milieu Occup Recreational Speech. **Psychotherapy:** Fam Group Indiv Parent.
   Enr: 36. Res Males 24. Day Males 12. **Staff:** 52 (Full 48, Part 4). Prof 23. Educ 13. Admin 6.
   Rates 2003: Res $200/day. Day $150/day.
   Est 1947. Private. Nonprofit.

The center offers a comprehensive program of psychiatric services for mildly to severely emotionally disturbed children and their families. Day treatment seeks to provide therapeutic intervention for children who can remain in a home setting and emphasizes educational and adjunctive therapies. Treatment utilizes individual and group dynamics and problem solving to deal with academic and behavioral problems. In addition, individualized academic programming is provided. Adjunctive therapy—including art, music and recreational therapy—helps to remediate perceptual problems.

Residential treatment for boys provides a therapeutic milieu through group activities, individual projects, positive peer culture, behavior modification and psychotherapy.

CHILDREN'S CENTER FOR THE VISUALLY IMPAIRED

Day — Coed Ages Birth-8

Kansas City, MO 64111. 3101 Main St.
Tel: 816-841-2284. Fax: 816-753-7836.
www.ccvi.org   E-mail: ccvikc@crn.org
Mary Lynne Dolembo, MSEd, Exec Dir. **Lisa Sprenger,** Adm.
Focus: Spec Ed. **Conditions:** Primary—B. Sec—ADD ADHD Ap Bl CP D Ep MR OH.
Gen Acad. Gr PS-K. Courses: Read Math Lang_Arts Braille Orientation & Mobility.
Therapy: Hydro Lang Occup Phys Speech Aqua. **Psychotherapy:** Parent.
Enr: 177. Day Males 111. Day Females 66. **Staff:** 41 (Full 23, Part 18).
Rates 2003: Day $325-525/mo. $12 (Therapy)/ses. Schol avail. State Aid.
Summer Prgm: Day. Educ. Rec. Ther. Day Rate $488. 6 wks.
Est 1952. Private. Nonprofit.

CCVI's program features early education and social development for blind and visually impaired children. Services include visual and auditory training; speech and language therapy; occupational, physical and aquatic therapy; orientation and mobility; and braille instruction. An infant intervention program provides home-based instruction for families, and preschool and kindergarten classes held at the center prepare children for inclusion in public or private elementary schools. Itinerant and consulting services comprise services to schools (including assessment and instruction); training on such specialized equipment as closed-circuit television, braillers and computers; developing in-service programs; and providing support for teachers and parents.

CHILDREN'S MERCY HOSPITAL
HEARING AND SPEECH DEPARTMENT

Clinic: Ages Birth-21.

Kansas City, MO 64108. 2401 Gillham Rd.
Tel: 816-234-3677. Fax: 816-234-3291.
www.childrens-mercy.org
Cynthia Jacobsen, PhD, Dir.
Conditions: Primary—D S. Sec—Dx.
Therapy: Lang Speech.
Private.

CHILDREN'S TLC

Day — Coed Ages Birth-8

Kansas City, MO 64111. 3101 Main St.
Tel: 816-756-0780. Fax: 816-756-1677.
www.childrenstlc.org   E-mail: staff@childrenstlc.org
Shirley Patterson, Exec Dir.
  Focus: Treatment. **Conditions:** Primary—Ap As Au Bl C CP D Ep IP LD MD MR MS ON S SB TB.
  Therapy: Hear Lang Occup Phys Speech Aqua. **Psychotherapy:** Fam Group Parent.
  Enr: 150. Day Males 84. Day Females 66. **Staff:** 34 (Full 26, Part 8).
  Est 1947. Private. Nonprofit.

Children's TLC offers pre-academic, social, physical and emotional support to children who are developmentally delayed, autistic or deaf. The center takes an interdisciplinary approach to therapy. A home-based program is also available.

THE CHURCHILL SCHOOL

Day — Coed Ages 8-16

St Louis, MO 63124. 1035 Price School Ln.
Tel: 314-997-4343. Fax: 314-997-2760.
www.churchillschool.org   E-mail: admissions@churchillschool.org
Sandra K. Gilligan, MS, Dir.
  Focus: Spec Ed. **Conditions:** Primary—Dx LD. **IQ 90 and up.**
  Gen Acad. Ungraded. Courses: Read Math Lang_Arts Sci Soc_Stud.
  Enr: 130. Day Males 100. Day Females 30. **Staff:** 57 (Full 55, Part 2).
  Rates 2004:
  Summer Prgm: Day. Educ. 6 wks.
  Est 1978. Private. Nonprofit.

Churchill serves high-potential children with specific learning disabilities. The school's primary goals are to help children achieve to full academic potential and to prepare them for a successful return to a traditional classroom setting as soon as possible. Each student attends a 50-minute daily tutorial, and pupils receive small-group instruction in all other classes.

COLLEGE VIEW STATE SCHOOL

Day — Coed Ages 5-21

Joplin, MO 64801. 1101 N Goetz Blvd.
Tel: 417-629-3044. Fax: 417-629-3259.
  Focus: Spec Ed. Trng. Treatment. **Conditions:** Primary—MR. **IQ 0-40.**
  Voc. Ungraded. Shelt_Workshop. On-Job Trng.
  Therapy: Hear Occup Phys Speech.
  Est 1957. State.

DEVELOPMENT CENTER OF THE OZARKS

Day — Coed All Ages
Clinic: All Ages. M-F 7-6.

Springfield, MO 65802. 1545 E Pythian St.
Tel: 417-829-0800. Fax: 417-865-7603.
www.dcoonline.com   E-mail: jproffitt@dcoonline.com
Allan McKelvy, MSEd, Exec Dir. **Sharon Hailey,** MS, Prgm Dir.
   Focus: Spec Ed. **Conditions:** Primary—Ap Asp BI CP DS IP LD MD ON
      PDD S SB. Sec—ADD ADHD B D Dx Ep MR.
   Gen Acad. Ungraded. On-Job Trng.
   Therapy: Hear Lang Occup Phys Speech. **Psychotherapy:** Fam Group
      Indiv Parent.
   Enr: 275. Day Males 150. Day Females 125. **Staff:** 100 (Full 80, Part 20).
      Educ 30. Admin 12.
   Est 1953. Private. Nonprofit.

DCO provides a variety of therapeutic, educational and habilitative services for infants, children and adults with either physical disabilities, mental retardation or developmental disabilities who reside in a 14-county area of southwest Missouri. Programs seek to promote personal growth and the development of skills that will allow the individual to live in the least restrictive possible environment.

Services include infant stimulation, early education, extended-hours childcare, habilitative training, community integration and supported employment. In addition to various therapies, the center offers both individual and group counseling for families.

EDGEWOOD CHILDREN'S CENTER

Res — Males Ages 3-14, Females 3-17; Day — Coed 3-17

St Louis, MO 63119. 330 N Gore Ave.
Tel: 314-968-2060. Fax: 314-968-8308.
www.eccstl.org   E-mail: info@eccstl.org
   Conditions: Primary—ED. Sec—BD LD.
   Gen Acad. Gr PS-12. Courses: Read Math Lang_Arts.
   Therapy: Art Lang Music Occup Recreational Speech. **Psychotherapy:**
      Fam Group Indiv.
   Staff: Prof 90.
   Est 1834. Private. Nonprofit.

EVANGELICAL CHILDREN'S HOME

Res and Day — Coed Ages 7-17

St Louis, MO 63114. 8240 St Charles Rock Rd.
Tel: 314-593-2999. Fax: 314-593-2994.
www.newbeginnings-ech.org   E-mail: lrees@newbeginnings-ech.org
Michael Brennan, MSW, Exec Dir. **Linda Bock,** MD, Med Dir.

Focus: Spec Ed. Treatment. **Conditions:** Primary—ADD ADHD AN Anx Ap Asp BD Bu CD Db Dc Dg Dx ED HIV LD Mood MR OCD PDD Psy PW S SP Sz TS. **IQ 75 and up.**
Gen Acad. Ungraded. Courses: Read Math Lang_Arts Life_Skills.
Therapy: Art Milieu Speech. **Psychotherapy:** Fam Group Indiv Parent Equine.
Enr: 80. Res Males 20. Res Females 20. Day Males 20. Day Females 20. **Staff:** 26 (Full 23, Part 3). Prof 13. Educ 9. Admin 1.
Summer Prgm: Res & Day. Educ. Rec. Ther. 4 wks.
Est 1858. Private. Nonprofit. United Church of Christ.

Children served by the home typically have experienced severe physical, sexual or emotional abuse or neglect, and many are suicidal or severely depressed. The Family and Personal Counseling Center provides brief, goal-oriented interventions for a full range of issues, including depression, family conflict, troubled relationships, school problems, substance abuse, and loss and grief. Short-term assessments (lasting 14 to 90 days), highly supervised and structured safe intensive units, and less restrictive open residential units are among the program options.

GALLAUDET HEARING IMPAIRED

Day — Coed Ages 5-16

St Louis, MO 63104. 1616 S Grand Blvd.
Tel: 314-771-2894. Fax: 314-776-3884.
www.slps.org/Schools/other_2.htm
Dyanne Anthony, Prin.
Conditions: Primary—D.
Gen Acad. Ungraded. Courses: Read Math Lang_Arts.
Therapy: Hear Lang Occup Phys Speech. **Psychotherapy:** Indiv.
Est 1878. Municipal.

GOOD SHEPHERD SCHOOL FOR CHILDREN

Day — Coed Ages Birth-6

St Louis, MO 63146. 1170 Timber Run Dr.
Tel: 314-469-0606. Fax: 314-469-3294.
www.goodss.org   E-mail: goodshepherd@goodss.org
Corinne C. Esneault, BS, MA, Exec Dir. **Laura Max,** BS, MA, Prgm Dir.
Focus: Treatment. **Conditions:** Primary—Au LD MR S. Sec—CP SB.
Gen Acad. Gr PS-K.
Therapy: Hear Lang Occup Phys Speech. **Psychotherapy:** Fam Group Indiv Parent.
Enr: 105. **Staff:** 33 (Full 17, Part 16).
Est 1967. Private. Nonprofit.

This school provides year-round services for special-needs children in communicational skills; social/psychological development; sensorimotor integration; self-care;

visual and auditory skills; physical development; readiness skills; and academics. Parental involvement is integral to the program.

HAWTHORN CHILDREN'S PSYCHIATRIC HOSPITAL

Res and Day — Coed Ages 6-18

St Louis, MO 63133. 1901 Pennsylvania Ave.
Tel: 314-512-7800. TTY: 314-512-7800. Fax: 314-512-7812.
David Blue, Supt.
    Conditions: Primary—ADD ADHD ED Mood Psy Sz. Sec—BI Dx LD. **IQ 70 and up.**
    Therapy: Chemo Lang Occup Speech. Psychotherapy: Fam Group Indiv.
    Est 1976. State. Nonprofit.

This center supplies inpatient services and day treatment services for emotionally disturbed children and adolescents. The program includes classroom instruction, as well as psychiatric, psychological and social work services. Inpatient and residential programs serve the city of St. Louis, St. Louis County and 31 other counties. Fees are based on a sliding scale according to income.

HOPEWELL CENTER

Clinic: Ages 3-17. M-F 8:30-5.

St Louis, MO 63104. 1504 S Grand.
Tel: 314-531-1770. Fax: 314-531-3072.
www.hopewellcenter.com
Amanda Murphy, PhD, Pres.
    Conditions: Primary—BD ED.
    Gen Acad. Courses: Read Math Lang_Arts.
    Psychotherapy: Fam Group Indiv.
    Staff: Prof 3.
    Est 1979. State. Nonprofit.

JUDEVINE CENTER FOR AUTISM

Res — Coed Ages 5 and up; Day — Coed 3 and up
Clinic: Ages 3 and up. M-F 9-6.

St Louis, MO 63132. 1101 Olivette Executive Pky.
Tel: 314-849-4440. Fax: 314-849-2721.
www.judevine.org   E-mail: judevine@judevine.org
Rebecca Blackwell, MA, Exec Dir.
    Conditions: Primary—Au ED. Sec—Ap BI D LD MR S.
    Gen Acad. Pre-Voc. Ungraded. Courses: Read Math Lang_Arts. Man_Arts & Shop. On-Job Trng.
    Therapy: Lang Speech. Psychotherapy: Group.

Enr: 163.
Est 1971. Private. Nonprofit.

Judevine provides a variety of services for children and adults with autism. The day treatment program utilizes a communication-based approach and has the goal of placing children in public school inclusion programs. Adult day programs feature vocational and daily living skills training leading toward supported employment. Residential services consist of a short-term intensive treatment program, a group home, and eight alternative living homes for those requiring long-term residential care.

Additional services include the following: evaluations, parent and professional training, inclusion support, educational advocacy and consulting, respite care, family and sibling support groups, a 24-hour intensive intervention program, futures planning, communication training, social behavior development, in-home family training, and natural support trainings and consultations.

Another program at Judevine is the training center, which provides three-week sessions for parents, professionals and master trainers that teach participants how to formulate strategies for helping individuals with autism learn and develop at home, at school and in social situations.

KIRKSVILLE REGIONAL CENTER

Clinic: All Ages. M-F 8-5.

Kirksville, MO 63501. 1702 E LaHarpe St.
Tel: 660-785-2500. TTY: 660-785-2500. Fax: 660-785-2520.
www.dmh.missouri.gov/kirksville
    E-mail: mlpowel@mail.dmh.state.mo.us
Lois M. Powell, BSE, MA, Dir.
    Focus: Treatment. **Conditions:** Primary—MR. Sec—Au CP Ep LD. **IQ 0-70.**
    Therapy: Hear Lang Occup Phys Speech.
    Staff: 41.
    State.

Case management services provided at this center include evaluations, therapy, respite care and placements in state- and community-operated alternative living situations. KRC serves individuals from 14 counties of northeast Missouri. Fees are based on the ability to pay.

LOGOS SCHOOL

Day — Coed Ages 11-21

St Louis, MO 63132. 9137 Old Bonhomme Rd.
Tel: 314-997-7002. Fax: 314-997-6848.
www.logosschool.org   E-mail: davidct@logosschool.org
David C. Thomas, PhD, CEO. **Kathy L. Heimburger & Cara C. Meier,** Adms.
    Focus: Spec Ed. **Conditions:** Primary—ADD ADHD AN Anx Asp BD BI Bu
        CD Dc Dg Dx ED LD Mood OCD PDD Psy PTSD SP Sz TS. Sec—Ap Au
        B Db HIV MR ON S. **IQ 65 and up.**
    Col Prep. Gr 7-12. Courses: Read Math Lang_Arts Hist Sci.

Therapy: Art Lang Occup Recreational Speech. **Psychotherapy:** Group Indiv Parent.
Enr: 133. Day Males 103. Day Females 30. **Staff:** 53 (Full 49, Part 4).
Rates 2003: Day $18,280/yr (+$900). Schol ($130,075).
Est 1970. Private. Inc.

This alternative, therapeutic middle and high school offers a complete academic program. The program is designed to assist students and their families with academic and emotional needs that have not been met satisfactorily in the traditional classroom. Logos teaches coping skills, study skills and responsible behaviors, in addition to ways to make healthier choices.

LUTHERAN ASSOCIATION FOR SPECIAL EDUCATION

Day — Coed Ages 6-16

St Louis, MO 63118. 3558 S Jefferson Ave.
Tel: 314-268-1234. Fax: 314-268-1232.
www.lutheranspecialed.org   E-mail: luthsped@cs.com
Norma Speckhard, PhD, Exec Dir.
  Focus: Spec Ed. **Conditions:** Primary—ADD ADHD MR. Sec—Asp Au CP DS Dx ED LD PDD S. **IQ 40 and up.**
  Gen Acad. Ungraded. Courses: Read Math Lang_Arts.
  Enr: 20. **Staff:** 42.
  Rates 2004: Day $5000/sch yr (+$225). Schol avail.
  Est 1956. Private. Nonprofit. Lutheran.

The association conducts an individualized program for mildly retarded, learning-disabled, autistic, cerebral palsied and mildly emotionally disturbed children. Educational emphasis is on the utilization of a resource room, with an objective of mainstreaming all children. Diagnostic and consultative services are available.

MARILLAC

Res and Day — Coed Ages 5-16
Clinic: Ages 5-16. M-F by Appt.

Kansas City, MO 64108. 2826 Main St.
Tel: 816-508-3300. Fax: 816-508-3321.
www.marillac.org   E-mail: marillac@marillac.org
R. Michael Bowen, LCSW, Pres. **Mark Richards,** MA, Admin. **Fran Hirt,** MSE, Prin. **Brian Barash,** MD, Med Dir. **Eric Giovanni,** Adm.
  Focus: Spec Ed. Treatment. **Conditions:** Primary—ADD ADHD Anx Asp Au BD Bu Db Dx ED LD PDD PTSD SP Sz TS. Sec—As CD D Ep HIV Mood OCD Psy PW. **IQ 80 and up.**
  Gen Acad. Gr K-10. Courses: Read Math Lang_Arts Sci Soc_Stud.
  Therapy: Art Lang Music Occup Play Recreational Speech. **Psychotherapy:** Fam Group Indiv Parent.
  Enr: 132. Res Males 73. Res Females 35. Day Males 20. Day Females 4. **Staff:** 100. (Full 100). Educ 10.

Rates 2003: Res $250-370/day. Day $82/day. Sliding-Scale Rate $30-75/ses (Clinic). State Aid.
Est 1897. Private. Nonprofit.

Marillac provides a therapeutic atmosphere of learning for emotionally disturbed children. The program includes individualized prescriptive educational programming, perceptual-motor training, psychotherapy, and a combination of individual and group therapy aimed at mainstreaming. Aftercare services are available for six months to both student and family.

Marillac does not generally accept individuals who are nonambulatory, deaf or blind.

THE METROPOLITAN SCHOOL

Day — Coed Ages 10-21

St Louis, MO 63143. 7281 Sarah St.
Tel: 314-644-0850. Fax: 314-644-3363.
www.metroschool.org   E-mail: info@metroschool.org
Rita M. Buckley, BS, MA, Exec Dir. **Carol Eubanks,** Adm.
   Focus: Spec Ed. **Conditions:** Primary—ADD ADHD Anx Asp CD Dc Dg Dx LD Mood OCD PDD SP TS. Sec—AN Ap Au B BD Bu D Db ED MR ON Psy PTSD PW S Sz.
   Gen Acad. Gr 5-12. Courses: Read Math Lang_Arts Sci Hist Studio_Art Woodworking.
   Therapy: Chemo. **Psychotherapy:** Group.
   Enr: 70. Day Males 55. Day Females 15. **Staff:** 22 (Full 19, Part 3).
   Rates 2003: Day $15,950/sch yr. Schol 18 ($120,000).
   Summer Prgm: Day. Educ. Rec.
   Est 1967. Private. Nonprofit.

Metropolitan provides comprehensive educational services for children with learning disabilities, attention deficit disorder and other special learning needs. The school's program also addresses such issues as self-esteem, personal responsibility and interpersonal skills. An outdoor challenge program complements academics.

Although some students spend all their junior high and high school years at the school, most return to their original school after learning about their disabilities and developing compensating skills, a time period that averages two years.

MID-MISSOURI MENTAL HEALTH CENTER

Res — Coed Ages 6 and up; Day — Coed 6-18

Columbia, MO 65201. 3 Hospital Dr.
Tel: 573-884-1300. Fax: 573-884-1010.
www.modmh.state.mo.us/mid_mo/index.htm
   Conditions: Primary—ED.
   Gen Acad. Courses: Read Math Lang_Arts.
   Staff: Prof 41.
   Est 1967. State.

THE MIRIAM SCHOOL

Day — Coed Ages 4-14

Webster Groves, MO 63119. 501 Bacon Ave.
Tel: 314-968-5225. Fax: 314-968-9338.
www.miriamschool.org   E-mail: jsmith@miriamschool.org
Joan Holland, MEd, Dir. **Jackie Smith,** Adm.
  Focus: Spec Ed. **Conditions:** Primary—ADD ADHD Apr Dc Dg Dx LD.
    Sec—Ap Asp CP D TS. **IQ 90 and up.**
  Gen Acad. Gr PS-8. Courses: Read Math Lang_Arts.
  Therapy: Lang Occup Speech.
  Enr: 92. Day Males 64. Day Females 28. **Staff:** 26.
  Rates 2003: Sliding-Scale Rate $5580-18,360/sch yr (+$100).
  Summer Prgm: Day. Educ. Rec. Day Rate $425. 2 wks.
  Est 1951. Private. Nonprofit. **Spons:** Miriam Foundation.

Miriam School conducts a program for children with normal intellectual potential who evidence mild to moderate learning problems, behavioral problems, or both. Emphasis is on diagnostic-prescriptive teaching with the goal of returning the child to the mainstream of education. The program is highly structured and addresses basic academic skills and appropriate social and classroom behavior.

The school also provides parental classes and a broad community program, serving as a consultant to preschools, daycare centers and public school systems to help children with developmental problems. The usual length of treatment is two to three years.

MISSOURI SCHOOL FOR THE BLIND

Res and Day — Coed Ages 5-21

St Louis, MO 63110. 3815 Magnolia Ave.
Tel: 314-776-4320. Fax: 314-776-1875.
www.msb.k12.mo.us
James Sucharski, PhD, Supt.
  Focus: Spec Ed. **Conditions:** Primary—B. Sec—D Db LD MR ON PDD S.
  Col Prep. Gen Acad. Pre-Voc. Voc. Gr K-12. Courses: Read Math Lang_
    Arts Braille Orientation & Mobility Life_Skills. Man_Arts & Shop. On-Job
    Trng.
  Therapy: Hear Occup Phys Speech. **Psychotherapy:** Indiv.
  Enr: 106. Res Males 27. Res Females 22. Day Males 33. Day Females 24.
    Staff: 175 (Full 172, Part 3). Prof 47. Educ 40. Admin 16.
  Rates 2004: No Fee.
  Est 1851. State.

This program provides comprehensive services for blind, multi-handicapped blind and deaf-blind children that include diagnosis and evaluation, education and prevocational training. Physical, occupational, speech, hearing and visual therapies are also conducted.

OZANAM HOME FOR BOYS

Res and Day — Coed Ages 12-18

Kansas City, MO 64145. 421 E 137th St.
  Nearby locations: Belton; Liberty.
Tel: 816-508-3600. Fax: 816-508-3797.
www.ozanam.org   E-mail: ozanam@crn.org
Douglas Zimmerman, MSW, Pres. **Mark Cederburg,** Adm.
  Focus: Treatment. **Conditions:** Primary—BD CD ED Mood OCD PTSD SP
    Sz. Sec—ADD ADHD B D Dx LD Psy PW S TS. **IQ 70 and up.**
  Col Prep. Gen Acad. Pre-Voc. Voc. Ungraded. Courses: Read Math Lang_
    Arts. Man_Arts & Shop.
  Therapy: Art Chemo Milieu Recreational. **Psychotherapy:** Fam Group
    Indiv Parent.
  Enr: 112. Res Males 52. Res Females 20. Day Males 30. Day Females 10.
    Staff: 126 (Full 100, Part 26). Prof 75. Educ 17. Admin 34.
  Rates 2003: Res $170/day. Day $96/day. $85 (Therapy)/hr. Schol avail.
    State Aid.
  Est 1948. Private. Nonprofit.

Ozanam's year-round treatment program for emotionally disturbed children of average intelligence comprises a full range of services, including individual, group and family psychotherapy. A special-education program is also conducted, and the usual duration of treatment is 6-12 months. The majority of clients come from Missouri and Kansas.

RAINBOW CENTER DAY SCHOOL

Day — Coed Ages 3-21

Blue Springs, MO 64015. 900 NW Woods Chapel Rd.
Tel: 816-229-3869. Fax: 816-229-4260.
www.rainbow-center.org   E-mail: peggy.britton@rainbow-center.org
Marilu W. Herrick, MS, CCC-SLP, Exec Dir.
  Focus: Spec Ed. **Conditions:** Primary—ADD ADHD Ap Asp Au CP DS Dx
    LD MR PDD S. Sec—Apr As BD CD Ep OCD ODD PW TS.
  Gen Acad. Pre-Voc. Ungraded. Courses: Read Math Life_Skills.
  Therapy: Hear Lang Music Occup Phys Speech.
  Enr: 60. Day Males 30. Day Females 30. **Staff:** 35 (Full 15, Part 20). Prof
    15. Admin 5.
  Summer Prgm: Day. Educ. Rec. 8 wks.
  Est 1977. Private. Nonprofit.

This school provides therapeutic intervention within an academic setting for children and young adults with autism, cerebral palsy, Down syndrome, learning disabilities, and other behavioral and developmental disabilities. Individualized programming and a favorable student-teacher ratio are program characteristics. In addition to its school-day programming, Rainbow Center provides before- and after-school care and a summer session.

RANKEN JORDAN
PEDIATRIC REHABILITATION CENTER

Res — Coed Ages Birth-16
Clinic: Ages Birth-16. M-F.

St Louis, MO 63141. 10621 Ladue Rd.
Tel: 314-993-1207. Fax: 314-567-0414.
www.rankenjordan.org
Laureen Tanner, Pres.
   Conditions: Primary—Ap As BI C CP Ep IP MD MS ON S SB TB.
   Therapy: Hear Lang Occup Phys Speech.
   Staff: Prof 61.
   Est 1940. Private. Nonprofit.

RIVENDALE INSTITUTE OF LEARNING

Day — Coed Ages 3-18

Springfield, MO 65807. 1613 W Elfindale Dr.
Tel: 417-864-7921. Fax: 417-864-6024.
E-mail: kerri.duncan@worldnet.att.net
Kerri Duncan, EdS, Dir.
   Focus: Spec Ed. **Conditions:** Primary—ADD ADHD Asp Au BI Dx Ep LD
      PDD S. Sec—ED.
   Gen Acad. Gr K-12. Courses: Read Math Lang_Arts.
   Therapy: Art Lang Music Occup Phys Speech.
   Staff: 14 (Full 10, Part 4). Educ 8. Admin 1.
   Rates 2003: Day $13,200/yr. Schol 2 ($6500).
   Summer Prgm: Day. Educ. Res Rate $1500. 7 wks.
   Est 1986. Private. Inc.

The institute provides an alternative to public education for students with speech and learning problems. Individual instruction is designed to meet each child's needs for development in academic, cognitive, perceptual, language and personal/social areas. Student-teacher ratios do not exceed 8:1 in the general classrooms, or 2:1 in the classes for children with autism.

An after-school program offers diagnosis and remediation for language development and learning disabilities, as well as for all academic areas. An instrumental enrichment program for junior high and high school students supplements traditional course work. In the evenings, remediation services are provided for those age 5 and up. The institute will also accept students for the summer months only.

ST. JOSEPH INSTITUTE FOR THE DEAF

Res — Coed Ages 5-15; Day — Coed Birth-15
Clinic: Ages Birth-3. M-F 8-5.

Chesterfield, MO 63017. 1809 Clarkson Rd.

Tel: 636-532-3211. Fax: 636-532-4560.
www.sjid.org
Deborah S. Wilson, Pres. **Mary T. Gannon,** Prin.
  Focus: Spec Ed. **Conditions:** Primary—D. Sec—ADD ADHD. **IQ 90 and up.**
  Gen Acad. Gr PS-8. Courses: Read Math Lang_Arts Computers Studio_Art.
  Therapy: Hear Lang Speech. **Psychotherapy:** Indiv.
  Enr: 71. Res Males 6. Res Females 8. Day Males 33. Day Females 24.
    Staff: 70 (Full 57, Part 13). Prof 33. Educ 21. Admin 8.
  Rates 2004: Res $24,400/sch yr. Day $19,900/sch yr. Clinic $125/hr. Schol
    avail. State Aid.
  Est 1837. Private. Nonprofit. Roman Catholic. **Spons:** Sisters of St. Joseph
    of Carondelet.

A private Catholic school for severely and profoundly hearing-impaired children, the institute offers an educational program that includes speech, language and regular academic courses, taught through speech reading and auditory-oral development. Children are mainstreamed into regular educational facilities as they progress. Early intervention programs for children (birth to age 3) and counseling for both parents and students are also available. The duration of treatment varies.

ST. LOUIS ASSOCIATION
FOR RETARDED CITIZENS

Res — Coed Ages 18 and up; Day — Coed All Ages

St Louis, MO 63146. 1816 Lackland Hill Pky, Ste 200.
Tel: 314-569-2211. Fax: 314-569-0778.
www.slarc.org
Kathy Meath, BA, MSW, Exec Dir.
  Focus: Trng. Treatment. **Conditions:** Primary—Au MR. Sec—ADD ADHD
    Ap As B BI C CP D Dx Ep IP LD MD MS ON S SB TB.
  Voc. On-Job Trng.
  Therapy: Hear Lang Occup Phys Speech. **Psychotherapy:** Group.
  Est 1950. Private. Nonprofit.

Founded by a small group of parents seeking an organization able to provide programs for their children with mental retardation, St. Louis ARC now meets the needs of children and adults with mental retardation and such disabilities as cerebral palsy, autism and epilepsy. Among the facility's services are housing, childcare, recreation, supported employment, respite care and family support.

ST. LOUIS COUNTY
FAMILY MENTAL HEALTH SERVICES

Clinic: All Ages. M-F 8-5; Eves M T Th 5-7.

Clayton, MO 63105. 111 S Meramec Ave.
Tel: 314-615-0600. TTY: 314-615-8428. Fax: 314-615-6435.

www.stlouisco.com
Alan Reeves, PhD, Prgm Dir.
  Conditions: Primary—ADD ADHD BD CD ED LD MR OCD Psy Sz.
  Therapy: Chemo Speech. **Psychotherapy:** Fam Group Indiv Parent.
  Staff: 33 (Full 30, Part 3).
  Est 1950. County. Nonprofit.

Family Mental Health provides services directed toward both prevention and treatment through three programs. The outpatient component offers diagnosis, evaluation and treatment to children and their families as well as consultation with and crisis services to schools and community agencies. The Children's Clinics Program provides assessment and counseling services, focusing on the early detection and the treatment of emotional and developmental problems. Community Services offers support groups and mental health educational programs.

Branches of this facility are located at 21 Village Sq., Hazelwood 63042; 4548 Lemay Ferry, St. Louis 63129; 78 Clarkson Wilson Ctr, Chesterfield 63017.

SHERWOOD CENTER FOR THE EXCEPTIONAL CHILD

Res — Coed Ages 21 and up; Day — Coed 3-21

Kansas City, MO 64132. 7938 Chestnut St.
Tel: 816-363-4606. Fax: 816-822-1988.
www.sherwoodcenter.org   E-mail: sherwood@crn.org
Deborah L. Wood, MA, Dir.
  Focus: Spec Ed. Treatment. **Conditions:** Primary—Ap Au DS S. Sec—
    ADHD B BD CP D Ep MR. **IQ 35-100.**
  Voc. Ungraded. Courses: Read Math Lang_Arts Computers Adaptive_
    Phys_Ed.
  Therapy: Hear Lang Music Occup Phys Speech. **Psychotherapy:** Parent.
  Enr: 66. Res Males 13. Res Females 3. Day Males 37. Day Females 13.
    Staff: 27 (Full 26, Part 1).
  Summer Prgm: Day. Educ. Rec. 9 wks.
  Est 1974. Private. Nonprofit.

Sherwood applies functional behavior analysis and precision-teaching techniques in its classroom instruction. Emphasis is placed upon speech, language and social skills. Charts of daily and weekly records allow immediate analysis of teaching and behavior management procedures, as well as long-term program analysis and accountability. Additional offerings include a summer program with developmental habilitation training and community-inclusion activities, as well as classroom readiness for public school special education.

SHRINERS HOSPITAL

Res — Coed Ages Birth-18
Clinic: Ages Birth-18. M-F 7-3.

St Louis, MO 63131. 2001 S Lindbergh Blvd.
Tel: 314-432-3600. Fax: 314-432-2930.

www.shrinershq.org
Carolyn P. Golden, RN, Admin. **Perry L. Schoenecker,** MD, Med Dir. **Cindy A. Steiner,** Adm.
  Focus: Rehab. **Conditions:** Primary—OH.
  Therapy: Hear Lang Occup Phys Speech. **Psychotherapy:** Fam.
  Staff: 17 (Full 6, Part 11). Prof 13. Educ 1. Admin 3.
  Rates 2003: No Fee.
  Private. Nonprofit.

Children with orthopedic handicaps and neurological disabilities receive inpatient and clinical care. Treatment for child burn victims and those with spinal cord injury problems is also offered. The hospital provides surgery and therapeutic services, and an in-house teacher offers tutorial services.

SOUTHEAST MISSOURI STATE UNIVERSITY SPEECH AND HEARING CLINIC

Clinic: All Ages. M-F 8-5.

Cape Girardeau, MO 63701. 1 University Plz, MS 2600.
Tel: 573-651-2050. Fax: 573-651-2155.
E-mail: jrenaud@semovm.semo.edu
Joyce Renaud, MA, Coord.
  Focus: Trng. **Conditions:** Primary—Ap Apr D S. Sec—ADD ADHD Asp Au BI CP Dc Dg DS Dx ED IP LD MD MR MS ON PDD SB Sz.
  Therapy: Hear Lang Speech. **Psychotherapy:** Fam Group Parent.
  Staff: 10 (Full 9, Part 1). Prof 8. Admin 2.
  Rates 2004: $75 (Evaluation)/ses. Sliding-Scale Rate $0-150/sem (Treatment).
  State.

The clinic provides diagnostic, treatment and referral services for children and adults with communicative disorders.

SPOFFORD

Res — Coed Ages 4-12

Kansas City, MO 64134. 9700 Grandview Rd, PO Box 9888.
Tel: 816-508-3400. Fax: 816-508-3425.
www.spoffordhome.org   **E-mail: info@spoffordhome.org**
Janine Hron, MS, Pres. **Chan Peck,** MD, Med Dir. **Eric Hansen,** Adm.
  Focus: Treatment. **Conditions:** Primary—AN Anx CD Db ED Mood Psy Sz. Sec—Ap As Au BD BI Dx Ep LD S. **IQ 80 and up.**
  Therapy: Art Play Recreational Speech. **Psychotherapy:** Fam Group Indiv.
  Enr: 49. Res Males 35. Res Females 14. **Staff:** 96 (Full 72, Part 24). Prof 5. Educ 2.
  Rates 2003: Res $87/day. Schol avail. State Aid.
  Summer Prgm: Res. Educ. Rec. Ther. Art.
  Est 1916. Private. Nonprofit. United Methodist.

Spofford provides psychiatric care for emotionally disturbed children through a structured environment. The program includes special education, psychotherapy, arts and crafts, and recreational and pastoral care activities. Families are involved in group and individual therapies and counseling. The usual length of treatment is nine months.

TNC COMMUNITY

Res — Coed Ages 18 and up

Kansas City, MO 64139. 15600 Woods Chapel Rd.
Tel: 816-373-5060. Fax: 816-373-5787.
Scott Litten, Exec Dir.
  Focus: Rehab. **Conditions:** Primary—BI CP Ep IP MD MR MS ON SB.
  Sec—Ap As Asp Au B D DS ED.
  Therapy: Hear Lang Occup Phys Speech. **Psychotherapy:** Indiv.
  Enr: 25. Res Males 13. Res Females 12. **Staff:** 52 (Full 47, Part 5). Admin 3.
  Rates 2003: Res $38,197/yr (+$55/day). State Aid.
  Est 1949. Private. Nonprofit.

Located on an 11-acre site, this center provides comprehensive services for developmentally disabled and mentally retarded adults. A comprehensive program includes physical, occupational and speech therapies; psychological services; life skills training; and 24-hour nursing care.

TRUMAN STATE UNIVERSITY
SPEECH AND HEARING CLINIC

Clinic: Ages 1 and up. M-Th 8:30-5.

Kirksville, MO 63501. Barnett Hall 121.
Tel: 660-785-7414. Fax: 660-785-7424.
www2.truman.edu/comdis
Janet L. Gooch, PhD, Dir. **Melissa S. Passe,** MA, Coord.
  Focus: Trng. **Conditions:** Primary—Ap Au D S. Sec—ADD ADHD Apr As
  Asp B BD BI C CD CP DS Dx ED Ep LD MD MR MS OCD ON PW SB
  Sz TB TS.
  Therapy: Hear Lang Speech.
  Staff: 7 (Full 6, Part 1).
  Est 1960. State.

Persons with speech, language and hearing problems receive diagnostic and therapeutic services at TSU's clinic. Follow-up services are also available.

UNIVERSITY OF MISSOURI
SPEECH AND HEARING CLINIC

Clinic: All Ages. M-F 8-5.

Columbia, MO 65211. 303 Lewis Hall.
Tel: 573-882-3873. Fax: 573-884-8686.
www.umshp.org/csd/clinic.htm
Barbara Brinkman, MA, CCC-SLP, Dir.
   Focus: Treatment. **Conditions:** Primary—D Dx LD S. Sec—Ap CP MR OH.
   Therapy: Hear Lang Speech.
   State.

This clinic provides a full range of speech-language pathology and audiology services.

MONTANA

AFFINITY FOUNDATION

Res — Coed Ages 13-18

Proctor, MT 59929. 1019 Big Meadows Rd.
Tel: 406-849-6301. Fax: 406-849-6042.
www.affinityfoundation.com   E-mail: affinity@centurytel.net
Alan Sullenger, Co-Dir. **Barbara Sullenger,** Co-Dir. **Audrey Hannah,** Adm.
    Focus: Treatment. **Conditions:** Primary—ADD ADHD Anx As BD CD LD
        Mood OCD PTSD. Sec—AN Bu Db Dx ED Ep SP TS.
    Gen Acad. Gr 8-12.
    Psychotherapy: Fam.
    Enr: 15. Res Males 7. Res Females 8. **Staff:** 9 (Full 7, Part 2). Prof 1. Educ
        1. Admin 3.
    Rates 2003: Res $38,400/yr (+$75). Schol 2.
    Est 1999. Private. Nonprofit. Nondenom Christian.

Affinity's Christian, home-based program provides mentoring for boys and girls who are at risk; have low self-esteem; have drug or alcohol dependence; have attentional disorders; are manipulative; are failing in school; have anger management problems; have poor communication skills; or are defiant. Academics are available in the form of an accredited home schooling program that enables students to earn a high school diploma. A progressive-level system promotes maturity development.

CHILD DEVELOPMENT CENTER

Clinic: Ages Birth-21. M-F 8-5.

Missoula, MT 59801. T-214 Ft Missoula Rd.
    Nearby locations: Kalispell.
Tel: 406-549-6413. Fax: 406-542-0143.
www.childdevcenter.org   E-mail: cvolinkaty@childdevcenter.org
Cris Volinkaty, Exec Dir. **Peggy Moses,** Clin Dir. **Ned Vasquez,** MD, Med Dir.
    Focus: Trng. **Conditions:** Primary—Au Bl CP Ep LD MR OH. Sec—B D S
        SB. **IQ 50-100.**
    Staff: 43 (Full 31, Part 12). Prof 35. Admin 8.
    Rates 2003: No Fee.
    Est 1966. Private. Nonprofit.

Comprehensive evaluations, a home training and support program, and respite care are offered by CDC. A family-care project provides families with the equipment and assistance necessary to keep their children in the home. A branch is located at 945 4th Ave. E, Kalispell 59901.

COR ENTERPRISES

Day — Coed Ages 16 and up

Billings, MT 59101. 200 S 24th St.
Tel: 406-248-9115. Fax: 406-245-0606.
www.corenterprises.com   E-mail: cor@corenterprises.com
Tony Cline, MS, CEO. **Leigh Ann Olson,** BS, Voc Dir.
  Focus: Trng. **Conditions:** Primary—ADD ADHD Asp Au BD Bl DS ED MD
    Mood MR MS OCD Psy PTSD PW Sz. Sec—Anx Ar B C CD CF CP D
    Db Dx Ep LD ON S TS. **IQ 50-110.**
  Voc. Shelt_Workshop. On-Job Trng.
  Psychotherapy: Group Indiv.
  Enr: 150. Day Males 60. Day Females 90. **Staff:** 33 (Full 30, Part 3). Prof 6.
    Admin 4.
  Est 1971. Private. Nonprofit.

Vocational evaluation, training and rehabilitation services are offered at COR. Work adjustment training aims at preparing clients for competitive employment, and job placement services are provided. Personal counseling, case management services, and socialization and self-care skills instruction are included in the program. Program participation typically ranges from three months to two years.

DANCING MOON RANCH

Res — Females Ages 11-20

Chinook, MT 59523. PO Box 806.
Tel: 406-357-3614. Fax: 406-357-3604.
www.dancingmoonranch.com
L. Gay Miller, MSW, Pres.
  Focus: Treatment. **Conditions:** Primary—ADD Anx BD CD ED Mood OCD
    PTSD SP.
  Col Prep. Gen Acad. Gr 6-12.
  Therapy: Art Milieu. **Psychotherapy:** Fam Group Indiv Parent.
  Enr: 7. Res Females 7. **Staff:** 5 (Full 1, Part 4). Prof 1. Educ 1. Admin 1.
  Rates 2003: Res $36,500/yr (+$1500/yr).
  Summer Prgm: Res. Educ. Rec. Ther.
  Est 1997. Private. Inc.

This residential facility that integrates therapy into daily activities, focusing on reintegration with the family.

EXPLORATIONS

Res — Coed Ages 12-18

Trout Creek, MT 59874. 119 S Hill Rd, PO Box 1303.
Tel: 406-827-3863. Fax: 406-827-4072.
www.explorationsmt.com   E-mail: explorations@blackfoot.net

Lorne Riddell, Co-Dir. **Penny James-Riddell,** Co-Dir.
  Focus: Treatment. **Conditions:** Primary—ADD ADHD AN Anx Ar As BD
    Bu Db LD Mood OCD SP TS. Sec—Asp Au CD Dc Dg Dx ED ODD PDD
    PTSD. **IQ 80 and up.**
  Col Prep. Gen Acad. Ungraded. Courses: Read Math Lang_Arts. Man_Arts
    & Shop. Shelt_Workshop. On-Job Trng.
  Therapy: Milieu Recreational. **Psychotherapy:** Fam Group Indiv Parent.
  Enr: 17. Res Males 14. Res Females 3. **Staff:** 21 (Full 12, Part 9). Educ 1.
    Admin 2.
  Rates 2004: Res $3500/mo.
  Summer Prgm: Res. Educ. Rec. Res Rate $9400. 12 wks.
  Est 1990. Private. **Spons:** Aspen Education Group.

Explorations conducts a wilderness program and a boarding school for troubled teens. Among the programs offered are Home Base, a boarding school with a family-centered living environment; Wilderness Assessment, a wilderness intervention for troubled teens; Big Sky Summer Programs, an 8-week adventure program offered as an alternative to traditional summer camps; an experiential learning program that combines family-style living, individualized academics, challenging outdoor pursuits and travel; and customized experiences and family experiences for young adults, families, parents and youth.

HOPE RANCH

Res — Females Ages 12-18

Whitefish, MT 59937. PO Box 4480.
Tel: 406-862-7871. Fax: 406-862-5903.
www.hoperanchmt.org   E-mail: exec@hoperanchmt.org
Linda Carpenter, BS, Admin Dir. **Cheryl Anderson,** MS, Clin Dir. **Appel**
  Edwards, Adm.
  Focus: Rehab. Treatment. **Conditions:** Primary—ADD ADHD BD CD Dx
    ED LD Mood OCD.
  Col Prep. Gen Acad. Pre-Voc. Gr 8-12. Courses: Read Math Lang_Arts
    Life_Skills.
  Therapy: Art Dance Occup Phys. **Psychotherapy:** Fam Group Indiv Parent.
  Enr: 26. Res Females 26. **Staff:** 20 (Full 2, Part 18). Prof 17. Educ 3.
  Rates 2003: Res $30,000/yr (+$700).
  Est 1988. Private. Nonprofit. Nondenom Christian.

The ranch serves troubled adolescent girls from various family backgrounds and at differing levels of development, awareness and difficulty. Participants advance through a six-level program that rewards progressive improvement and achievement in the areas of education, life skills, accountability, responsibility, self-confidence, community living, ranch chores, attitude and respect. In a Christian setting, residents learn to take responsibility for all aspects of their lives.

MONTANA CENTER ON DISABILITIES

Clinic: Ages Birth-21. M-F 8-5.

Billings, MT 59101. Montana State Univ-Billings, 1500 University Dr.
Tel: 406-657-2312. TTY: 406-657-2312. Fax: 406-657-2313.
www.msubillings.edu/mtcd
Marsha Sampson, Int Dir.
   Focus: Treatment. Conditions: Primary—OH. Sec—D.
   Therapy: Hear.
   Est 1947. Federal. Spons: Montana State Univ-Billings.

Operated by the university's College of Education and Human Services, this clinic maintains a diagnostic and evaluation unit, an assistive technology unit, and an integrated preschool and respite care facility. The center provides on-site consultation for families and school districts, with emphasis placed upon assessing community resources, computer technology and curricular adaptations. The staff also offers community instruction in such areas as curricular adaptation, integration and parental education.

MONTANA DEVELOPMENTAL CENTER

Res — Coed All Ages

Boulder, MT 59632. 310 W 4th Ave.
Tel: 406-225-4411. Fax: 406-225-4414.
www.dphhs.state.mt.us
Jeff Sturm, Dir.
   Focus: Rehab. Trng. Treatment. Conditions: Primary—MR.
   Pre-Voc. Voc. Ungraded. Courses: Read Math Lang_Arts. Shelt_Workshop.
      On-Job Trng.
   Therapy: Hear Lang Occup Phys Speech. Psychotherapy: Indiv.
   Staff: Prof 33.
   Est 1889. State.

MONTANA SCHOOL FOR THE DEAF AND THE BLIND

Res — Coed Ages 5-21; Day — Coed 2-21

Great Falls, MT 59405. 3911 Central Ave.
Tel: 406-771-6000. Fax: 406-771-6164.
www.sdb.state.mt.us   E-mail: bdenoma@sdb.state.mt.us
Steve Gettel, Supt. Bill Davis, Prin.
   Focus: Spec Ed. Conditions: Primary—B D. Sec—Dx ED MR ON S.
   Col Prep. Gen Acad. Pre-Voc. Voc. Gr PS-12. Courses: Read Math Lang_
      Arts Braille Orientation & Mobility. Man_Arts & Shop. On-Job Trng.
   Therapy: Hear Lang Occup Phys Speech.
   Enr: 75. Res Males 26. Res Females 13. Day Males 21. Day Females 15.
      Staff: 102 (Full 90, Part 12). Prof 51. Educ 35. Admin 4.
   Rates 2004: No Fee.

Est 1893. State.

A state school for both blind and deaf children, this facility provides a full academic program including prevocational training, domestic science, typing, braille and sight-saving classes. The school also offers outreach services to public schools and families in Montana.

STAR MEADOWS ACADEMY

Res — Females Ages 13-17

Whitefish, MT 59937. PO Box 4480.
Tel: 406-862-7871. Fax: 406-862-5903.
www.hoperanchmt.org/starmeadows.htm
   E-mail: hope@hoperanchmt.org
Linda Carpernter, BS, Exec Dir. **Dianna Keane,** MA, Prgm Dir. **Jim Carpenter,** Adm.
   Focus: Spec Ed. Treatment. **Conditions:** Primary—ADD ADHD Anx As BD CD CP Db Dx ED Mood OCD ON PTSD SP. Sec—AN B Bu D Psy PW Sz TS. **IQ 82 and up.**
   Col Prep. Gen Acad. Gr 8-12. Courses: Read Math Lang_Arts Sci Life_Skills. On-Job Trng.
   Therapy: Art Dance Music. **Psychotherapy:** Fam Group Indiv Parent.
   Enr: 26. Res Females 26. **Staff:** 18 (Full 16, Part 2). Prof 10. Educ 4. Admin 3.
   Rates 2004: Res $38,400/yr.
   Est 1999. Private. Nonprofit. Nondenom Christian. **Spons:** Hope Ranch.

Star Meadows provides special education classes for girls with learning disabilities and various emotional disorders. In addition to academics, students take part in a therapeutic treatment program on the 360-acre working ranch. Family retreats, outdoor activities and community service projects round out the program.

THREE RIVERS MONTANA

Res — Coed Ages 13-18

Belgrade, MT 59714. 8977 Dry Creek Rd.
Tel: 406-388-5748. Fax: 406-388-5275.
www.threeriversmontana.org
   E-mail: admissions@threeriversmontana.org
Marylis Filipovich, MSW, Exec Dir. **Cathy Waterman,** MD, Med Dir. **Holli Richardson,** Adm.
   Focus: Treatment. **Conditions:** Primary—ADD ADHD Anx Asp BD Bu CD ED Mood OCD PTSD SP TS. Sec—AN As BI Db Dc Dg Dx Ep OH. **IQ 70 and up.**
   Gen Acad. Gr 9-12. Courses: Read Lang_Arts Sci Soc_Stud Studio_Art.
   Therapy: Milieu Recreational. **Psychotherapy:** Fam Group Indiv Parent.
   Enr: 18. **Staff:** 33 (Full 29, Part 4). Prof 12. Educ 1. Admin 2.
   Rates 2004: Res $385/day. Schol avail.

Est 2003. Private. Nonprofit.

Offering six-week wilderness treatment expeditions throughout the year, Three Rivers Montana serves adolescents with emotional disorders and limited physical disabilities. Accompanied by therapists and field staff, teens explore the wilderness and engage in emotional, mental and physical challenges. Upon admission, participants undergo basic reading and writing assessments in order to track their progress throughout the program. High school students may earn up to six semester credits in such courses as physical education, science, social studies, art and English.

YELLOWSTONE BOYS AND GIRLS RANCH

Res — Males Ages 6-18, Females 12-18; Day — Males 6-18, Females 10-18

Billings, MT 59106. 1732 S 72nd St W.
Tel: 406-655-2100. Fax: 406-656-0021.
www.ybgr.org   E-mail: admin@ybgr.org
Ry Sorensen, BS, CEO. **Ry Sorensen,** BS, COO. **Joseph Rich,** MD, Med Dir. **Rishay Vollertson & Diedra Kracht,** Adms.
> **Focus:** Spec Ed. Treatment. **Conditions:** Primary—ADD ADHD ED Mood PTSD. Sec—As Asp BD Bl CD Dc Dg Dx Ep LD OCD ODD Psy Sz TS. **IQ 70 and up.**
> **Gen Acad. Pre-Voc. Voc.** Gr K-12. Courses: Read Math Lang_Arts Life_ Skills. Man_Arts & Shop. On-Job Trng.
> **Therapy:** Hear Lang Milieu Phys Recreational Speech. **Psychotherapy:** Fam Group Indiv Parent.
> **Enr:** 165. Res Males 80. Res Females 35. Day Males 40. Day Females 10. **Staff:** 250 (Full 235, Part 15). Prof 150. Educ 20. Admin 20.
> **Rates 2004:** Res $300-340/day. Day $43-148/day. State Aid.
> **Est 1957.** Private. Nonprofit.

Offering residential psychiatric treatment, group home and community-based services for children and adolescents, Yellowstone conducts a series of programs that emphasize family involvement, education and pastoral care. Psychotherapy, educational counseling and an on-the-job vocational program are among the many forms of treatment for boys and girls with emotional disturbances, learning disabilities or both. The average duration of treatment is nine to 10 months.

NEBRASKA

ALEGENT HEALTH
IMMANUEL REHABILITATION CENTER

Res — Coed All Ages
Clinic: All Ages.

Omaha, NE 68122. 6901 N 72nd St.
Tel: 402-572-2295. Fax: 402-572-2632.
www.alegent.com
    Conditions: Primary—BI IP MS OH.
    Therapy: Hear Lang Occup Phys Speech. **Psychotherapy:** Group Indiv.
    Est 1898. Private. Nonprofit.

BOYS TOWN NATIONAL RESEARCH HOSPITAL

Clinic: All Ages.

Omaha, NE 68131. 555 N 30th St.
Tel: 402-498-6540.
www.boystownhospital.org
Patrick E. Brookhouser, MD, Dir.
    Conditions: Primary—D. Sec—S.
    Therapy: Hear Lang Speech. **Psychotherapy:** Fam.
    Est 1977. Private. Nonprofit. **Spons:** Girls and Boys Town.

CHILD GUIDANCE CENTER

Clinic: Ages Birth-21. M-F 8-5; Eves M-Th 5-8.

Lincoln, NE 68510. 2444 O St.
Tel: 402-475-7666. Fax: 402-476-9623.
www.childguidance.org
Carol Crumpacker, PhD, Dir. Stephen Paden, MD, Med Dir. Harvey Brindell, Intake.
    Focus: Treatment. **Conditions:** Primary—ADD ADHD AN Anx Asp BD CD ED Mood OCD PDD Psy PTSD SP Sz. Sec—BI D Dx LD MR OH. **IQ 60 and up.**
    Therapy: Art Chemo Hear Play. **Psychotherapy:** Fam Group Indiv Parent.
    Staff: 28. (Full 28). Prof 22. Admin 4.
    Est 1949. Private. Nonprofit.

The center offers individual, group, family and play therapies. There are also special programs for sexually abused children, adolescent sex offenders and adolescents from alcoholic families. Consultations are provided for other agencies and the usual length of treatment is 15 sessions. Fees are determined along a sliding scale.

DR. J. P. LORD SCHOOL

Day — Coed Ages 5-21

Omaha, NE 68131. 330 S 44th St.
Tel: 402-554-6771. Fax: 402-554-1540.
www.ops.org/lord
Michael Dotson, Prin.
 Conditions: Primary—BI C CP IP MS ON S. **IQ 60 and up.**
 Gen Acad. Pre-Voc. Gr K-12. Courses: Read Math Lang_Arts.
 Therapy: Hear Occup Phys Speech.
 Est 1937. Private.

EPWORTH VILLAGE

Res — Males Ages 8-19; Day — Coed 7-19

York, NE 68467. 2119 Division Ave, PO Box 503.
Tel: 402-362-3353. Fax: 402-362-3248.
www.epworthvillage.org   E-mail: tom@epworthvillage.org
Thomas G. McBride, MS, Dir. **Susan Howard,** MD, Med Dir. **Kristi Weber,** Adm.
 Focus: Treatment. **Conditions:** Primary—ADD ADHD Anx BD CD ED Mood OCD Psy PTSD SP Sz TS. Sec—As BI Db Dx Ep LD MR OH. **IQ 70 and up.**
 Gen Acad. Pre-Voc. Voc. Gr 1-12. Courses: Read Math Lang_Arts Sci Soc_Stud Music.
 Therapy: Chemo Hear Lang Occup Phys Speech. **Psychotherapy:** Fam Group Indiv.
 Enr: 72. **Staff:** 149 (Full 119, Part 30). Educ 11. Admin 10.
 Rates 2003: Res $225/day. Day $100/day. State Aid.
 Est 1890. Private. Nonprofit. United Methodist.

Epworth is designed for mildly to severely disturbed adolescents needing care apart from a family or community setting. A treatment-oriented program uses group process combined with casework emphasizing group living, therapy and interaction in cottage and group home living units, with the goal of mainstreaming into family or independent living. An on-grounds remedial and improvement center supplements the education students receive in community schools. Psychological and counseling services are available.

Boys and girls typically receive about five months of treatment per level of care, with the overall stay averaging 11 months.

MADONNA SCHOOL FOR EXCEPTIONAL CHILDREN

Day — Coed Ages 5-21

Omaha, NE 68104. 2537 N 62nd St.
Tel: 402-556-1883. Fax: 402-556-7332.
www.madonnaschool.org   E-mail: madonnaschool@cox.net
Deirdre Milobar, MS, MA, EdD, Prin.
   Focus: Spec Ed. **Conditions:** Primary—ADD ADHD Asp Au Dx ED Ep LD
      MR ON SB. Sec—Ap CD D Mood OCD TS. **IQ 30-75.**
   Pre-Voc. Voc. Ungraded. Courses: Read Math Lang_Arts Sci Soc_Stud
      Home_Ec. Shelt_Workshop. On-Job Trng.
   Therapy: Lang Music Speech.
   Enr: 47. **Staff:** 17. Educ 10. Admin 1.
   Est 1961. Private. Nonprofit. Roman Catholic.

Children with mild or moderate levels of mental retardation or specific severe learning disabilities may enroll at the school. Madonna also can accept students with minimal
emotional disturbances and developmental disorders. Programming emphasizes academic and social adaptation. The school operates a work site used for vocational evaluation: Students above age 15 participate in a community vocational placement.

MUNROE-MEYER INSTITUTE

Clinic: All Ages. M-F 8-4:30.

Omaha, NE 68198. 985450 Nebraska Medical Ctr.
Tel: 402-559-6402. Fax: 402-559-5737.
www.unmc.edu/mmi
Bruce A. Buehler, MD, Dir. **J. Wagner,** Adm.
   Focus: Treatment. **Conditions:** Primary—ADHD Au BI ON SB. Sec—Ap B
      BD CP D Dx LD MR.
   Therapy: Hear Lang Occup Phys Speech. **Psychotherapy:** Fam Group
      Indiv.
   Est 1968. State. **Spons:** University of Nebraska Medical Center.

Munroe-Meyer provides diagnostic assessment and selective therapy for children and
adults with physical, sensory, behavioral and neuro-developmental handicaps. Offerings
include medical, genetic, psychological and behavioral evaluation and counseling, special-education assessment and family social services.
   Special services include behavior management, a media resource center, and an adult
program for individuals with mental retardation and behavioral problems. Fees vary
according to services provided.

NEBRASKA CENTER FOR EDUCATION OF
CHILDREN WHO ARE BLIND OR VISUALLY IMPAIRED

Res — Coed Ages 5-21; Day — Coed Birth-21

Nebraska City, NE 68410. 824 10th Ave, PO Box 129.

Tel: 402-873-5513. Fax: 402-873-3463.
www.ncecbvi.org
Sally Giittinger, Admin.
  Focus: Spec Ed. **Conditions:** Primary—B.
  Gen Acad. Pre-Voc. Voc. Ungraded. Courses: Read Math Lang_Arts. Man_
    Arts & Shop. Shelt_Workshop. On-Job Trng.
  Therapy: Hear Lang Occup Phys Speech. **Psychotherapy:** Indiv.
  Staff: 45.
  Est 1875. State. Nonprofit.

Children who are blind follow a state-sponsored educational program at the center.
Vocational, educational, parental and personal counseling are available, and mainstreaming is a primary goal.

OMAHA HEARING SCHOOL FOR CHILDREN

Day — Coed Ages Birth-8

Omaha, NE 68132. 1110 N 66th St.
Tel: 402-558-1546. Fax: 402-558-1017.
www.oraldeafed.org/schools/omaha   E-mail: ohs@hearingschool.org
Karen Rossi, MA, Dir.
  Focus: Spec Ed. **Conditions:** Primary—D. Sec—As C CP ED MR ON S.
  Gen Acad. Gr PS-3.
  Therapy: Hear Lang Speech.
  Enr: 35. **Staff:** 17 (Full 13, Part 4).
  Rates 2004: Day $10,300-11,890/sch yr. Schol avail. State Aid.
  Summer Prgm: Day. Educ. Rec.
  Est 1952. Private. Nonprofit.

The Omaha Hearing School for Children uses an experience-based approach to
language development for the deaf and the hard of hearing. Individualized speech,
language, auditory training, and cognitive and motor development are also emphasized,
and FM auditory training units are utilized. A preschool for normally hearing children is
housed in the building in order to mainstream the hearing-impaired children on a daily
basis. A parent-infant program for children up to age 3 is also available.

UNIVERSITY OF NEBRASKA-KEARNEY
SPEECH, LANGUAGE, AND HEARING CLINIC

Clinic: All Ages.

Kearney, NE 68849. College of Education Bldg.
Tel: 308-865-8300. Fax: 308-865-8397.
Kenya Taylor, BA, MS, EdD, Dir.
  Conditions: Primary—D S.
  Therapy: Hear Lang Speech.
  Est 1955. State.

UNIVERSITY OF NEBRASKA-LINCOLN
BARKLEY SPEECH-LANGUAGE AND HEARING CLINIC

Clinic: All Ages. M-F 8-5.

Lincoln, NE 68583. 253 Barkley Memorial Ctr, PO Box 830731.
Tel: 402-472-2071. TTY: 402-472-2149. Fax: 402-472-7697.
www.unl.edu/barkley/spath/clinic/slh.html
John E. Bernthal, PhD, Supv. Marilyn Sheffler, PhD, Coord. Kevin Menefee, Adm.

Focus: Trng. Conditions: Primary—Anx Ap Apr Asp Au B BD CD CP D Dc Dg DS Dx ED LD MD Mood MS OCD ODD ON PDD PTSD S SP TS. Sec—ADD ADHD AN Ar As BI Bu C CF Db Ep IP MR Nf Psy PW SB Sz TB.

Therapy: Hear Lang Speech. Psychotherapy: Fam Group Indiv Parent.
Staff: 9 (Full 6, Part 3). Educ 1. Admin 1.
Est 1943. State.

Diagnostic and therapeutic services for all hearing, speech, language and learning problems are available at Barkley. The facility also serves individuals requiring augmentative or alternative modes of communication. Fees are determined along a sliding scale.

UTA HALEE GIRLS VILLAGE

Res — Females Ages 12-18; Day — Coed 12-18

Omaha, NE 68112. 10625 Calhoun Rd, PO Box 12034.
Tel: 402-453-0803. Fax: 402-453-1247.
www.utahalee-cooper.org   E-mail: pmahoney@utahalee-cooper.org
Denis McCarville, Exec Dir.

Focus: Treatment. Conditions: Primary—BD CD ED OCD Psy Sz. Sec— ADD ADHD As LD. IQ 80 and up.
Gen Acad. Gr 7-12. Courses: Read Math Lang_Arts Sci.
Therapy: Hear Occup Phys Speech. Psychotherapy: Fam Group Indiv.
Enr: 60.
Est 1950. Private. Nonprofit.

Uta Halee serves girls who exhibit a variety of self-destructive behaviors and need long-term placement due to severe family conflicts. The basis of the program is structure and role modeling, and family involvement is emphasized. This year-round residential village provides occupational and recreational therapy, special education, religious instruction, vocational counseling and independent living skills training. The average duration of treatment is six to nine months for the residential program and three to four months for the day treatment program.

VILLA MARIE SCHOOL

Res — Coed Ages 6-18

Waverly, NE 68462. 7205 N 112 St, PO Box 109.
Tel: 402-786-3625.
www.lincolndiocese.com/mauve/marian.htm
Conditions: Primary—MR. **IQ 60-85.**
Pre-Voc. Ungraded. Courses: Read Math Lang_Arts.
Therapy: Speech.
Est 1963. Private. Nonprofit.

NEVADA

NEW HORIZONS ACADEMY

Day — Coed Ages 6-18

Las Vegas, NV 89146. 6701 W Charleston Ave.
Tel: 702-876-1181. Fax: 702-365-7807.
www.nhalv.org
Roger D. Gehring, EdD, Exec Dir. **Elsa Borell,** Admin.
  Focus: Spec Ed. **Conditions:** Primary—LD. Sec—ADD ADHD Dc Dg Dx.
  IQ 90 and up.
  Gen Acad. Gr 1-12. Courses: Read Math Lang_Arts Sci Soc_Stud Studio_
  Art Music.
  Psychotherapy: Parent.
  Enr: 100. **Staff:** 20 (Full 18, Part 2).
  Rates 2004: Day $9350/yr (+$750). Schol avail.
  Est 1974. Private. Nonprofit.

New Horizons offers specific educational programs for students with such learning differences as processing difficulties and attentional problems. Classes are multi-aged; the school places children in classes according to academic, social and emotional needs, not simply chronological age. The academy also maintains a program for the gifted.

SPECIAL CHILDREN'S CLINIC

Day — Coed Ages Birth-3
Clinic: Ages Birth-3. M-F 8-5.

Las Vegas, NV 89102. 1161 S Valley View Blvd.
Tel: 702-486-7670. Fax: 702-486-7686.
Karen M. Cummings, MEd, Dir.
  Focus: Treatment. **Conditions:** Primary—MR. Sec—Ap Au B BI C CP D
  ED Ep IP LD MD MS ON S SB.
  Therapy: Hear Lang Occup Phys Speech. **Psychotherapy:** Fam Group.
  Staff: 60 (Full 48, Part 12).
  Rates 2004: No Fee.
  Est 1957. State.

The clinic serves as a regional center that provides comprehensive early intervention diagnostic treatment and follow-up services for families with developmentally delayed and at-risk young children. Diagnostic assessments are performed by a multidisciplinary team.

UNIVERSITY OF NEVADA-RENO
SPEECH AND HEARING CLINIC

Clinic: All Ages. M-F 8-4:30.

Reno, NV 89557. Sch of Medicine, MS 152.
Tel: 775-784-4887. Fax: 775-784-4095.
www.unr.edu/spa   E-mail: martinez@unr.edu
Thomas Watterson, Supv. **Leslie L. Golberg,** Dir. **Stephen C. McFarlane,**
PhD, Med Dir.
   Focus: Rehab. Treatment. **Conditions:** Primary—Ap D S. Sec—As B Bl C
   CP Dx Ep IP LD MD MR MS ON SB.
   Therapy: Hear Lang Speech.
   Staff: 9 (Full 7, Part 2).
   Rates 2003: Clinic $65/ses.
   State.

Complete diagnosis and treatment are conducted in a clinical training setting at the University of Nevada-Reno. The clinic offers treatment for voice disorders, language disorders, articulation/phonological disorders, hearing disorders, cleft palate and fluency disorders.

VARIETY SCHOOL

Day — Coed Ages 3-22

Las Vegas, NV 89101. 2601 Sunrise Ave.
Tel: 702-799-7938. Fax: 702-799-7956.
www.ccsd.net/sssd/special/VarietySchool.html
   Conditions: Primary—As C CP IP MD MR MS ON SB. **IQ 1-130.**
   Col Prep. Voc. Gr PS-PG. Courses: Read Math Lang_Arts. On-Job Trng.
   Therapy: Hear Lang Occup Phys Speech. **Psychotherapy:** Fam Group
   Indiv.
   Est 1953. County.

NEW HAMPSHIRE

CEDARCREST

Res — Coed Ages Birth-16; Day — Coed 3-16

Keene, NH 03431. 91 Maple Ave.
Tel: 603-358-3384. Fax: 603-358-6485.
www.cedarcrest4kids.org   E-mail: info@cedarcrest4kids.org
Cathy Gray, BS, MA, Pres. **Jan McGonagle,** Med Dir. **Peg Knox,** Intake.
  Focus: Treatment. **Conditions:** Primary—CP MR OH. Sec—B Bl D Ep
    Mood S. **IQ 0-60.**
  Gen Acad. Ungraded.
  Therapy: Hear Lang Occup Phys Recreational Speech.
  Enr: 27. Res Males 13. Res Females 13. Day Males 1. **Staff:** 85 (Full 65,
    Part 20). Prof 32. Educ 13. Admin 7.
  Est 1947. Private. Nonprofit.

Cedarcrest provides specialized care and residential services for children with complex medical and developmental needs. Children served range in age from infants to teens and have such disabilities as cerebral palsy; multiple disabilities; complications resulting from premature birth; broncho-pulmonary dysplasia; and other high-risk conditions. Care is available on both long- and short-term bases. The facility offers postoperative care, feeding assessments and comprehensive evaluations. Cedarcrest also functions as a transitional placement between hospital and home, providing both the specialized care required by the child and training for the client's family.

In addition to its medical and therapeutic services, the program conducts an on-site school program for both residents and day students. Residents participate in scheduled recreational activities after school and on weekends. Children take part in various community programs as well.

Cedarcrest will accept individuals with a diagnosis of mental retardation or developmental delay, so long as they also have a medical diagnosis.

CLM BEHAVIORAL HEALTH

Clinic: All Ages. M-F 9-5; Eves M-Th 5-9.

Salem, NH 03079. 44 Stiles Rd.
  Nearby locations: Derry.
Tel: 603-893-3548. Fax: 603-898-4779.
www.clmbehav.org   E-mail: contactus@clmnh.org
Victor Topo, CEO. **Daniel P. Potenza,** MD, Med Dir.
  Conditions: Primary—BD CD ED OCD Psy Sz. Sec—ADD ADHD Au Dx
    LD.
  Psychotherapy: Fam Group Indiv Parent.
  Staff: 43 (Full 29, Part 14).
  Est 1967. Private. Nonprofit.

This comprehensive mental health center provides a full range of treatment services. Screening and assessment, psychological testing, psychiatric evaluations and crisis intervention are offered to children and their families. Individual, family and group counseling, as well as psycho-educational instruction, is provided. Inpatient hospitalization is available to the severely and chronically mentally ill.

A branch office provides services at 44 Birch St., Derry 03038.

COMMUNITY PARTNERS
BEHAVIORAL HEALTH AND DEVELOPMENTAL SERVICES
OF STRAFFORD COUNTY

Clinic: All Ages. M-F 9-5; Eves M-Th 5-8.

Dover, NH 03820. 113 Crosby Rd, Ste 1.
  Nearby locations: Rochester.
Tel: 603-749-4015. Fax: 603-743-3244.
www.dssc9.org
Cathryn BeCallo, MSW, Exec Dir. **Donna Frank-Berchulski,** MSW, Dir. **R. J. Allister,** MD, Med Dir. **Jody Lubaisky,** Adm.
  Focus: Treatment. **Conditions:** Primary—BD CD ED OCD Psy Sz.
  Therapy: Speech. **Psychotherapy:** Fam Group Indiv.
  Staff: 225 (Full 195, Part 30).
  Rates 2001: Sliding-Scale Rate $0-85/hour. State Aid.
  Est 1955. Private. Nonprofit.

A comprehensive mental health center, Community Partners offers community education and consultations, as well as 24-hour emergency services. A team approach is utilized in the diagnosis and the treatment of emotional disturbances. The center also includes a specialized sexual abuse treatment program for individuals and families. The sliding scale fee is only available to Strafford County residents.

Community Partners has three additional locations in Dover, as well as an office at 101 N. Main St., Rochester 03867.

CROTCHED MOUNTAIN REHABILITATION CENTER

Res and Day — Coed Ages 6-21

Greenfield, NH 03047. 1 Verney Dr.
Tel: 603-547-3311. Fax: 603-547-6212.
www.cmf.org   E-mail: info@cmf.org
Michael Terrian, CEO.
  Focus: Rehab. Trng. **Conditions:** Primary—ADD ADHD Au BI CP ED IP LD MD MR MS ON SB. Sec—Ap As B C CD D Ep OCD Psy S Sz. **IQ 50 and up.**
  Gen Acad. Pre-Voc. Voc. Gr K-12. Courses: Read Math Lang_Arts Sci Soc_Stud Studio_Art Music. Man_Arts & Shop. Shelt_Workshop. On-Job Trng.
  Therapy: Hear Lang Occup Phys Speech. **Psychotherapy:** Fam Group Indiv.

Enr: 120.
Est 1936. Private. Nonprofit.

Located atop a mountain in rural southern New Hampshire, this center provides diagnosis, treatment, education and research for multi-handicapped individuals. The center also treats individuals with hearing impairments, physical and learning disabilities, and emotionally disturbances. It has become a pilot model for similar institutions throughout the country.

An academic program includes remedial, general academic and college preparatory courses, as well as vocational training and occupational, physical and speech therapies. Crotched Mountain offers a 12-month behavior management program in conjunction with the academic program.

DARTMOUTH-HITCHCOCK MEDICAL CENTER
SPEECH PATHOLOGY DEPARTMENT

Clinic: All Ages. M-F 7-5:30.

Lebanon, NH 03756. 1 Medical Center Dr.
Tel: 603-650-5978. Fax: 603-650-8908.
Dennis G. Tobin, BS, MEd, MBA, Dir.
   Focus: Treatment. **Conditions:** Primary—S. Sec—BI CP ED LD MD MR MS.
   Therapy: Hear Lang Occup Phys Speech.
   Staff: 42 (Full 33, Part 9).
   Est 1890. Private.

The clinical services of this department deal with a variety of communicative disorders. Special offerings include augmentative evaluation and swallowing evaluation and treatment programs.

EASTER SEALS NEW HAMPSHIRE

Res and Day — Coed All Ages

Manchester, NH 03103. 22 Auburn St.
Tel: 603-623-8863. TTY: 603-623-8863. Fax: 603-625-1148.
http://nh.easterseals.com
Larry J. Gammon, Pres.
   Conditions: Primary—BI LD OH.
   Pre-Voc. Voc. Gr K-12. Courses: Read Math Lang_Arts. Man_Arts & Shop. Shelt_Workshop. On-Job Trng.
   Therapy: Hear Lang Occup Phys Speech. **Psychotherapy:** Fam Group Indiv.
   Staff: Prof 29.
   Est 1921. Private. Nonprofit.

ECKERD YOUTH ALTERNATIVES

Res — Males Ages 10-17

Colebrook, NH.
Contact: 100 N Starcrest Dr, PO Box 7450, Clearwater, FL 33758.
Tel: 727-461-2990. Fax: 727-442-5911.
www.eckerd.org   E-mail: admissions@eckerd.org
Karen V. Waddell, BA, Pres. **Francene Hazel,** Dir.
  Focus: Treatment. **Conditions:** Primary—BD CD ED Mood ODD. Sec—
    ADD ADHD LD. **IQ 70 and up.**
  Gen Acad. Pre-Voc. Ungraded. Courses: Read Math Lang_Arts Sci Soc_
    Stud.
  Therapy: Speech. **Psychotherapy:** Fam Group Indiv.
  Summer Prgm: Res. Ther. Res Rate $180. 2 wks.
  Est 1968. Private. Nonprofit.

The Eckerd outdoor program offers therapeutic treatment to emotionally disturbed
children by providing a camp setting as an alternative to institutionalization.

The year-round program utilizes reality therapy, Rogerian techniques and group
therapy. Small-group living in the wilderness environment encourages the acquisition
of new skills while promoting discipline and responsibility. Each group must construct
their shelter, cut wood, repair equipment and perform other tasks necessary for their
stay in the forest. Such experiences provide the children with the opportunity to develop
academic skills at their own pace and in relation to each project they endeavor. When
sufficient progress is made, children are transferred into the transition classroom in
preparation for their return to the mainstream.

In addition to New Hampshire, Eckerd conducts outdoor therapeutic treatment programs in the following states: Florida, Georgia, North Carolina, Rhode Island, Tennessee and Vermont (see separate listings).

HAMPSHIRE COUNTRY SCHOOL

Res — Males Ages 8-18

Rindge, NH 03461. 122 Hampshire Rd.
Tel: 603-899-3325. Fax: 603-899-6521.
www.hampshirecountryschool.com
  E-mail: hampshirecountry@monad.net
William Dickerman, BA, MA, PhD, Head.
  Focus: Spec Ed. **Conditions:** Primary—Asp LD. Sec—ADD ADHD ED
    OCD SP TS. **IQ 110 and up.**
  Col Prep. Gen Acad. Gr 3-12. Courses: Read Math Lang_Arts Sci Hist.
  Enr: 22. Res Males 22. **Staff:** 21 (Full 18, Part 3). Educ 7. Admin 3.
  Rates 2004: Res $37,000/sch yr (+$1000).
  Est 1948. Private. Nonprofit.

This small boarding school serves high-ability boys with learning disabilities who
have serious difficulties adapting to larger social settings. Classes are small, consisting
of five or six students, and dormitory groups typically consist of six or seven residents.

HCS' activity program includes music lessons, drama, horseback riding, sledding, soccer, canoeing, swimming, tennis and hiking.

THE HUNTER SCHOOL
Res and Day — Males Ages 5-15

Rumney, NH 03266. 768 Doetown Rd, PO Box 600.
Tel: 603-786-3666. Fax: 603-786-2221.
www.hunterschool.org   E-mail: pettee@hunterschool.org
Jeffrey C. Pettee, MEd, Head.
>   **Focus:** Spec Ed. **Conditions:** Primary—ADD ADHD ED ODD TS. Sec—
>   Anx BD Dx Mood OCD. **IQ 90 and up.**
>   **Gen Acad.** Gr K-8. Courses: Read Math Lang_Arts.
>   **Therapy:** Lang Occup Speech. **Psychotherapy:** Group Indiv.
>   **Enr:** 28. Res Males 10. Day Males 18. **Staff:** 18 (Full 13, Part 5). Prof 5.
>   Educ 5. Admin 4.
>   **Rates 2003:** Res $53,233/sch yr. Day $27,864/sch yr. $85 (Therapy)/hr.
>   **Summer Prgm:** Res & Day. Educ. Rec. Ther. Res Rate $7000/wk. Day Rate
> $4400/wk. 6 wks.
>   **Est 1998.** Private. Nonprofit.

Situated on a rural, 137-acre tract, Hunter serves children with attention deficit disorder and, frequently, opposition defiant disorder. Staff formulate an individual education program for the student following an initial comprehensive academic and social assessment. Previous educational experiences, previous testing and input from the pupil's family are all taken into consideration.

Hunter's residential component features such wilderness experiences as hiking, camping and snowshoeing, as well as such athletic options as skiing, swimming, skating and team sports. Nearby Dartmouth College and Plymouth State College provide cultural options, while students may also participate in community-based pursuits and recreational activities.

LAKEVIEW NEURO REHABILITATION CENTER
Res and Day — Coed Ages 8-21

Effingham Falls, NH 03814. 244 Highwatch Rd.
Tel: 603-539-7451. Fax: 603-539-8815.
www.lakeviewsystem.com   E-mail: admitnh@lakeview.ws
Tina M. Trudel, PhD, Exec Dir. **Dennis Badman,** MD, Med Dir. **Susan Bartlett,**
Adm.
>   **Focus:** Rehab. Treatment. **Conditions:** Primary—ADD ADHD Anx Ap Apr
>   Asp Au BD BI CD CP Dc Dg Dx ED Ep LD Mood OCD ON PDD PTSD S
>   TS. Sec—AN As B Bu C D Db DS HIV IP MD MR MS Nf Psy PW SB SP
>   Sz TB.
>   **Gen Acad. Pre-Voc.** Gr 1-12. Courses: Read Math Lang_Arts. Man_Arts &
>   Shop. On-Job Trng.
>   **Therapy:** Hydro Milieu Occup Percepual-Motor Phys Play Recreational

Speech. **Psychotherapy:** Fam Group Indiv Parent.
Enr: 45. Res Males 25. Res Females 20.
Est 1995. Private. Inc.

The individualized treatment program at Lakeview provides services for children and adolescents with neurological and behavioral disorders. Upon admission, boys and girls undergo a comprehensive evaluation to determines the appropriate approach to treatment. Therapeutic services include occupational, physical and recreational therapies, as well as social skills training and psychiatric counseling.

Lakeview's on-site school combines special education classes with independent living and prevocational training.

LUKAS COMMUNITY

Res — Coed Ages 18 and up

Temple, NH 03084. 63 Memorial Hwy, PO Box 137.
Tel: 603-878-4796. Fax: 603-878-4111.
www.lukascommunity.org   E-mail: lukas@monad.net
David A. Spears, Exec Dir.
   Focus: Treatment. **Conditions:** Primary—Au BI DS MR.
   Therapy: Art Dance Movement Music Recreational.
   Enr: 17. Res Males 11. Res Females 6. **Staff:** 11 (Full 9, Part 2). Prof 9.
      Admin 2.
   Rates 2003: Res $30,000/yr.
   Est 1981. Private. Nonprofit.

The therapeutic focus of this community for developmentally disabled individuals is inspired by the teachings of Austrian philosopher and humanitarian Rudolph Steiner. As special emphasis is placed on the value of work, farming, gardening and forestry are integral aspects of community life.

MANCHESTER PROGRAM FOR THE DEAF AND HARD OF HEARING

Day — Coed Ages 3-21

Manchester, NH 03109. 100 Aurore Ave.
Tel: 603-624-6422. TTY: 603-624-6422. Fax: 603-624-6403.
www.mansd.org/greenacres
Jean Dickson, Int Dir.
   Conditions: Primary—D. Sec—Au B LD MR ON S.
   Col Prep. Gen Acad. Voc. Gr PS-12. Courses: Read Math Lang_Arts.
      Man_Arts & Shop.
   Therapy: Lang Occup Speech. **Psychotherapy:** Parent.
   Enr: 38. Day Males 21. Day Females 17. **Staff:** 23 (Full 18, Part 5).
   Summer Prgm: Day. Educ. 5 wks.
   Municipal.

MPDHH utilizes a total communication approach to the education of hearing-impaired students. The program includes resource classes for the deaf, as well as mainstreamed classes with interpreter/tutors within the local public school system.

MENTAL HEALTH CENTER OF GREATER MANCHESTER

Res — Coed Ages 18 and up
Clinic: All Ages. M-F.

Manchester, NH 03103. 401 Cypress St.
Tel: 603-668-4111. Fax: 603-669-1131.
www.mhcgm.org
  Conditions: Primary—BD ED.
  Psychotherapy: Fam Group Indiv.
  Est 1963. Private. Nonprofit.

THE NEW ENGLAND SALEM CHILDREN'S VILLAGE

Res — Males Ages 6-18

Rumney, NH 03266. PO Box 600.
Tel: 603-786-9427. Fax: 603-786-2221.
www.salemchildrensvillage.org   E-mail: info@salemchildrensvillage.org
Jane Merrithew, MSEd, Exec Dir.
  Focus: Treatment. **Conditions:** Primary—ADD ADHD BD Dx ED LD Mood
    PTSD S. Sec—Dc Dg OCD SP TS.
  Therapy: Art Play. **Psychotherapy:** Fam Group Indiv Parent.
  Enr: 12. Res Males 12. **Staff:** 15. (Full 15). Prof 11. Admin 4.
  Est 1978. Private. Nonprofit.

The Children's Village is a group home for children who have experienced difficulties and are unable to live at home for a time. The children typically display mild to moderate emotional handicaps, learning disabilities, predelinquency or behavioral disorders. The home is designed for foster children who have not succeeded in a less restrictive environment. Country living, a whole food diet and a family atmosphere are emphasized as part of the program for development.

Residents attend public schools when possible, or an on-campus private school when the child's educational team sees fit.

NEW ENGLAND SPEECH SERVICES

Clinic: All Ages.

Dover, NH 03820. 745 Central Ave.
Tel: 603-749-2446. Fax: 603-749-3486.
www.nespeech.com   E-mail: ness@rcn.com
Sarah T. Stram, MA, MS, CCC, Dir.
  Conditions: Primary—S.

Therapy: Hear Lang Speech. **Psychotherapy:** Indiv.
Staff: Prof 12.
Est 1986. Private. Inc.

PINE HAVEN BOYS CENTER

Res — Males Ages 6-15

Suncook, NH 03275. River Rd, PO Box 162.
Tel: 603-485-7141. Fax: 603-485-7142.
E-mail: phbc@comcast.net
John B. Vitali, MEd, MA, Exec Dir. Joyce Pollinger, MSW, Clin Dir.
  Focus: Treatment. **Conditions:** Primary—ADD ADHD Dx ED LD ODD
    PTSD SP. Sec—BD MR.
  Gen Acad. Pre-Voc. Ungraded. Courses: Read Math Lang_Arts Sci Soc_
    Stud. Man_Arts & Shop. Shelt_Workshop.
  Therapy: Art Lang Milieu Occup Play Recreational Speech. **Psychother-
    apy:** Fam Group Indiv Parent.
  Enr: 20. Res Males 20. **Staff:** 41 (Full 36, Part 5). Prof 10. Educ 6. Admin 5.
  Est 1968. Private. Nonprofit.

Pine Haven emphasizes school experience for emotionally disturbed boys. Therapeutic intervention, a residential setting and special education help develop emotional,
social and academic skills, with the goal of mainstreaming. Individual and group counseling for students and group meetings for parents are provided. The usual length of
treatment is one to three years.

RICHIE MCFARLAND CHILDREN'S CENTER

Day — Coed Ages Birth-3

Stratham, NH 03885. 11 Sandy Point Rd.
Tel: 603-778-8193. Fax: 603-778-0388.
www.richiemcfarland.org   E-mail: rhalloran@richiemcfarland.org
Peggy Small-Porter, MEd, Exec Dir. Sue Ford, Intake.
  Focus: Treatment. **Conditions:** Primary—ADD ADHD Ap Au B BD BI C CD
    CP D DS Dx ED IP LD MD MR MS ON S SB.
  Therapy: Hear Lang Occup Phys Speech. **Psychotherapy:** Fam Group
    Indiv Parent.
  Est 1971. Private. Nonprofit.

RMCC provides early intervention services (including developmental, therapeutic
and support offerings) for children with an established disability or medical condition
and their families. The center offers in-home speech, occupational and physical therapies, in addition to family counseling and support. Therapeutic playgroups are available
on a weekly basis.

SECOND START
ALTERNATIVE HIGH SCHOOL PROGRAM
Day — Coed Ages 14-18

Concord, NH 03301. 450 N State St.
Tel: 603-225-3318. Fax: 603-226-0842.
www.second-start.org   E-mail: info@second-start.org
James B. Snodgrass, BA, MEd, Exec Dir. **Tom Herbert,** Prgm Dir.
  Focus: Spec Ed. **Conditions:** Primary—ADD BD ED LD. Sec—MR. **IQ 75 and up.**
  Gen Acad. Pre-Voc. Gr 9-12. Courses: Read Math Lang_Arts Eng Sci Soc_Stud Computers. On-Job Trng.
  Enr: 48. Day Males 25. Day Females 23. **Staff:** 12.
  Rates 2003: Day $12,273/sch yr.
  Est 1971. Private. Nonprofit.

This alternative high school program at Second Start serves children with emotional handicaps and mild learning disabilities that have interfered with their functioning in a traditional educational setting. Treatment strives to combine an individual academic and counseling program with group work and small classes. The primary objective is to develop basic academic skills, thereby improving self-image and social development. A transitional employment and training program, which aims to develop positive job-related attitudes and behaviors, is available for an additional fee. Educational counseling and an alcohol and drug abuse program are also offered. The usual duration of treatment for children enrolled in the program is one to two years.

SPAULDING YOUTH CENTER
PROGRAM FOR EMOTIONALLY DISTURBED BOYS
Res and Day — Males Ages 6-16

Tilton, NH 03276. 130 Shedd Rd, PO Box 189.
Tel: 603-286-8901. Fax: 603-286-8650.
www.s-y-c.org
Gary Lavallee, Dir. **Pat Seaward-Salvati,** Adm.
  Focus: Spec Ed. Treatment. **Conditions:** Primary—ADHD BD CD ED LD OCD Psy. **IQ 65 and up.**
  Gen Acad. Pre-Voc. Ungraded. Courses: Read Math Lang_Arts Soc_Stud Computers Sci Studio_Art Outdoor Ed.
  Therapy: Speech. **Psychotherapy:** Fam Group Indiv.
  Staff: 40.
  Est 1958. Private. Nonprofit.

Located on a 380-acre hilltop in central New Hampshire, Spaulding provides year-round education and treatment for boys with serious emotional and learning problems, attentional disorders and posttraumatic stress disorder. Treatment programs emphasize remedial education, counseling, self-management and support to families and schools. All programs are aimed at developing new skills in children so that they may function appropriately at home and in the community.

Opportunities for daily community interaction are available. An on-campus school offers motivating and stimulating learning experiences, and the learning environment is individualized for each student. The school stresses traditional academics along with social skills learning. Recreational activities, sports, clubs, off-campus trips, environmental offerings, social skills classes, and group and individual student meetings round out the child's program. The usual length of treatment is 12 to 18 months.

SPAULDING YOUTH CENTER
PROGRAM FOR NEUROBEHAVIORAL DISORDERS AND AUTISM
Res and Day — Coed Ages 6-21

Tilton, NH 03276. 130 Shedd Rd, PO Box 189.
Tel: 603-286-8901. Fax: 603-286-8650.
www.s-y-c.org
Gary Lavallee, Dir. Pat Seaward-Salvati, Adm.
   Focus: Spec Ed. Treatment. Conditions: Primary—Au BD OH. Sec—ADD BI ED LD MR.
   Gen Acad. Pre-Voc. Voc. Ungraded. Courses: Read Math Lang_Arts Life_ Skills. Shelt_Workshop. On-Job Trng.
   Therapy: Lang Speech. Psychotherapy: Indiv.
   Enr: 20. Res Males 16. Res Females 1. Day Males 2. Day Females 1. Staff: 33.
   Est 1972. Private. Nonprofit.

The autistic program at Spaulding provides intensive, short- and long-term behavioral and nonaversive intervention for autistic and developmentally disabled students on a year-round basis. Individual educational plans are designed to teach children necessary living and socialization skills. Staff members evaluate programs daily to meet each child's changing needs.

The program seeks primarily to help students return to less restrictive settings and have success in community-based programs.

SPECIAL MEDICAL SERVICES
Clinic: Ages Birth-20. M-F 8-4:30.

Concord, NH 03301. 29 Hazen Dr.
Tel: 603-271-4488. Fax: 603-271-4902.
www.dhhs.state.nh.us/dhhs/specialmedsrvcs/default.htm
   Conditions: Primary—As BI C CP D Ep ON S SB.
   Staff: Prof 27.
   State.

NEW JERSEY

ALPHA SCHOOL

Day — Coed Ages 3-21

Lakewood, NJ 08701. Forest Ave & 11th St.
Tel: 732-370-1150. Fax: 732-901-0736.
www.alphaschool.com
Monica Walsh DeTuro, BA, MA, Prin.
   Focus: Spec Ed. Treatment. **Conditions:** Primary—ADD ADHD Anx Asp
      Au BD BI CD DS Dx ED Ep LD Mood MR OCD PDD Psy PW S SP Sz
      TS. Sec—AN Ap Apr As B Bu C CP D Db Dc Dg IP MD MS Nf ON SB.
   Gen Acad. Gr PS-12. Courses: Read Math Lang_Arts Sci Computers Soc_
      Stud Studio_Art Music Health Life_Skills.
   Therapy: Hear Lang Music Occup Percepual-Motor Phys Speech.
   Enr: 165. Day Males 75. Day Females 90. **Staff:** 75 (Full 70, Part 5). Prof
      35. Educ 15. Admin 2.
   Rates 2003: No Fee.
   Est 1980. Private. Inc. **Spons:** RKS Associates.

   The school program is designed to remediate problems in academic achievement,
motor skills, and speech and language in the learning-impaired child. Individualized
educational plans include adaptive physical education and a sensorimotor integration
program. Social counseling is provided, and accepted students enroll at no cost.
   Similar programs are conducted at Harbor School in Eatontown (240 Broad St.,
07724) and at Gateway School in Carteret (60 High St., 07008).

THE ARC EMPLOYMENT CENTER

Day — Coed Ages 16 and up

Lakewood, NJ 08701. 150 Oberlin Ave N.
Tel: 732-363-6677. Fax: 732-901-7540.
www.arcocean.org
Gina Lambusta, BA, Dir.
   Focus: Trng. **Conditions:** Primary—MR. Sec—B BD BI CP D Dx ED Ep LD
      MD MS ON PDD S. **IQ 50-120.**
   Voc. Shelt_Workshop. On-Job Trng.
   Enr: 191. Day Males 114. Day Females 77. **Staff:** 16 (Full 13, Part 3). Prof
      8.
   Est 1955. Private. Nonprofit.

   The center offers rehabilitation and employment assistance for disabled persons.
Evaluation and job training aim at placement of the client in competitive employment.

THE ARC OF SOMERSET COUNTY

Day — Coed Ages Birth-6

Manville, NJ 08835. 141 S Main St.
Tel: 908-725-8544.
www.thearcofsomerset.org   E-mail: bonnies@thearcofsomerset.org
Lou Baldino, Exec Dir.
   Conditions: Primary—LD MR OH.
   Gen Acad. Gr PS.
   Therapy: Occup Phys Speech. **Psychotherapy:** Group Indiv.
   Private.

ARCHWAY PROGRAMS

Day — Coed Ages 3-21

Atco, NJ 08004. 280 Jackson Rd, PO Box 668.
Tel: 856-767-5757. Fax: 856-768-5562.
www.archwayprograms.org   E-mail: info@archwayprograms.org
Douglas Otto, MA, Exec Dir.
   Focus: Spec Ed. **Conditions:** Primary—As Au BI CP DS ED Ep OH. Sec—
      ADD ADHD Ap B BD C CD D Dx IP LD MD MR MS OCD Psy SB Sz.
   Gen Acad. Pre-Voc. Ungraded. Courses: Read Math Lang_Arts. On-Job
      Trng.
   Therapy: Art Hear Lang Occup Phys Speech. **Psychotherapy:** Group Indiv.
   Enr: 201. Day Males 131. Day Females 70. **Staff:** 126.
   Rates 2003: Day $23,000-29,700/yr. State Aid.
   Summer Prgm: Day. Educ. Day Rate $148/day. 7 wks.
   Est 1965. Private. Nonprofit.

Archway offers treatment for boys and girls with autism or learning, language, behavioral or multiple disabilities through highly structured, individual programs of education and therapy. Educational and personal counseling is available to all clients. A special-education program serves preschoolers.

Learning takes place in a small-class setting at four southern New Jersey locations. Each school provides a full complement of related services.

ARTHUR BRISBANE CHILD TREATMENT CENTER

Res — Coed Ages 11-17

Farmingdale, NJ 07727. Rte 524.
Tel: 732-938-7803. Fax: 732-938-3102.
www.state.nj.us/humanservices/pfnurse/Brisbane.htm
   E-mail: judy.gnad@dhs.state.nj.us
   Conditions: Primary—ED.
   Gen Acad. Ungraded. Courses: Read Math Lang_Arts. Man_Arts & Shop.
   Est 1946. State. Nonprofit.

BANCROFT NEUROHEALTH

Res and Day — Coed All Ages

Haddonfield, NJ 08033. 425 Kings Highway E.
Tel: 856-429-0010. Fax: 856-429-4755.
www.bancroft.org   E-mail: inquiry@bancroftneurohealth.org
   Conditions: Primary—Au BI OH. Sec—MR.
   Gen Acad. Pre-Voc. Voc. Courses: Read Math Lang_Arts. Man_Arts &
      Shop.
   Therapy: Occup Phys Speech.
   Est 1973. Private. Nonprofit.

BANYAN SCHOOL

Day — Coed Ages 6-14

Fairfield, NJ 07004. 12 Hollywood Ave.
Tel: 973-439-1919. Fax: 973-439-1396.
www.banyanschool.com
Mary Jo Saunders, MA, Dir.
   Focus: Spec Ed. **Conditions:** Primary—ADD ADHD Dx LD. **IQ 75 and up.**
   Gen Acad. Gr 1-8. Courses: Read Math Lang_Arts Sci Soc_Stud Studio_
      Art Music Drama Life_Skills.
   Therapy: Occup Speech. **Psychotherapy:** Group.
   Enr: 65. **Staff:** 22 (Full 20, Part 2).
   Summer Prgm: Day. Educ. 6 wks.
   Est 1993. Private. Nonprofit.

Banyan offers a highly structured elementary and middle school program for students of average to above-average intelligence with learning disabilities. The elementary program is designed to fully develop basic academic and social skills. The middle school program focuses upon the application of these skills while emphasizing organizational and study techniques. Banyan also provides therapy and assists pupils with social skills development.

BERGEN CENTER FOR CHILD DEVELOPMENT

Day — Coed Ages 5-21

Haworth, NJ 07641. 140 Park St.
Tel: 201-385-4857. Fax: 201-385-4997.
Vincent R. Benfatti, Dir. **Michele Johnson,** Med Dir.
   Focus: Spec Ed. **Conditions:** Primary—Ap ED. Sec—Asp BI OH.
   Gen Acad. Pre-Voc. Gr K-12. Courses: Read Math Lang_Arts. Man_Arts &
      Shop.
   Therapy: Lang Music Occup Speech. **Psychotherapy:** Fam Indiv.
   Enr: 68. **Staff:** 51 (Full 48, Part 3).
   Est 1968. Private.

The center provides special education, prevocational training and language development for multi-handicapped, emotionally disturbed and neurologically impaired children. Parents may receive behavior modification training, counseling and home training. The program includes both individual and family psychotherapy, as well as various other therapies.

BERGEN COUNTY SPECIAL SERVICES
Day — Coed Ages 3-21

Paramus, NJ 07652. 327 E Ridgewood Ave.
Tel: 201-343-6000. Fax: 201-225-9182.
www.bergen.org
John Grieco, EdD, Supt. **Ann Potvin,** Adm.
  Focus: Spec Ed. **Conditions:** Primary—ADD Asp Au BD CP D DS ED LD MD MS ON SB. Sec—MR S.
  Col Prep. Gen Acad. Ungraded. Courses: Read Math Lang_Arts. Man_Arts & Shop. Shelt_Workshop. On-Job Trng.
  Therapy: Hear Lang Occup Phys Recreational Speech. **Psychotherapy:** Indiv.
  Enr: 1377. **Staff:** 450. Prof 368.
  Rates 2003: No Fee.
  Summer Prgm: Day. Educ. 4 wks.
  Est 1972. County.

The agency offers county-wide education services to deaf, hearing-impaired, multiply handicapped, developmentally disabled, emotionally disturbed and autistic children. Both group and individual techniques are employed and emphasis is given to the development of auditory and oral communicational skills. Resource programs are provided for those children whose speech, language, academic, social and emotional abilities qualify them to be mainstreamed. A child study team, a consulting audiologist, and support services and personnel are also available to students.

BERGEN REGIONAL MEDICAL CENTER
BEHAVIORAL HEALTH SERVICES
Res — Coed Ages 5-17
Clinic: Ages 5-17.

Paramus, NJ 07652. 230 East Ridgewood Ave.
Tel: 201-967-4080.
www.bergenregional.com
Linda Villanueva, MD, Med Dir.
  Conditions: Primary—ED.
  Gen Acad. Courses: Read Math Lang_Arts. Man_Arts & Shop.
  Therapy: Art Occup Play Recreational. **Psychotherapy:** Fam Group Indiv.
  Staff: Prof 19.
  Est 1971. County. Nonprofit.

BONNIE BRAE

Res and Day — Males Ages 11-18

Liberty Corner, NJ 07938. 3415 Valley Rd, PO Box 825.
Tel: 908-647-0800. Fax: 908-604-8869.
www.bonnie-brae.org   E-mail: info@bonnie-brae.org
William E. Powers, MHA, MPA, CEO. Donna Crane, MA, Educ Dir. James
P. Rau, MSW, LCSW, Clin Dir. Vanita Braver, MD, Med Dir. Joanne Allen,
Adm.
  Focus: Treatment. Conditions: Primary—ADD ADHD BD CD ED Mood
    OCD ODD PTSD. Sec—HIV TS. IQ 70 and up.
  Gen Acad. Pre-Voc. Voc. Ungraded. Courses: Read Math Lang_Arts Com-
    puters. Man_Arts & Shop. On-Job Trng.
  Therapy: Milieu Occup Speech. Psychotherapy: Fam Group Indiv.
  Enr: 78. Res Males 64. Day Males 14. Staff: 100.
  Rates 2004: Res $685/day. Day $335/day. State Aid.
  Est 1916. Private. Nonprofit.

Bonnie Brae offers comprehensive treatment programs to boys with emotional problems. The facility's treatment team provides clinical, educational and residential services, and the average duration of treatment is 12 to 18 months.

In addition to its main program, Bonnie Brae provides a separate program for adolescent male chemical abusers. This program, utilizing a holistic approach, consists of individual, group and family therapy; academic and vocational special education; career development; therapeutic recreation; life skills training; and specialized substance abuse services. Residents are integrated into ongoing Bonnie Brae programs.

BROOKFIELD SCHOOLS

Day — Coed Ages 5-21

Cherry Hill, NJ 08034. 1009 Berlin Rd.
  Nearby locations: Blackwood; Camden; Jamesburg.
Tel: 856-795-8228. Fax: 856-795-3009.
www.brookfieldschools.org
Dorothy K. Van Horn, MA, Exec Dir. Betsey Westover, PhD, Clin Dir. Barbara
Lilien, Adm.
  Focus: Spec Ed. Conditions: Primary—ADD ADHD Anx Asp BD CD ED
    LD Mood OCD SP TS. Sec—AN Bu Db HIV. IQ 90-135.
  Col Prep. Gen Acad. Pre-Voc. Voc. Gr K-12. Courses: Read Math Lang_
    Arts Sci Soc_Stud. Man_Arts & Shop.
  Therapy: Art Speech. Psychotherapy: Group Indiv Parent.
  Enr: 138. Day Males 110. Day Females 28. Staff: 70 (Full 68, Part 2). Prof
    23. Educ 21. Admin 7.
  Rates 2003: Day $28,652-33,493/sch yr. State Aid.
  Summer Prgm: Day. Educ. 6 wks.
  Est 1975. Private. Nonprofit.

Brookfield Schools accommodate boys and girls who are experiencing personality disorders or adjustment or behavioral problems. Programs are Brookfield Elementary (ages 5-14), which operates at 1000 Atlantic Ave., Camden 08104 (856-966-0025); Brookfield Academy (ages 14-20), which is conducted on the Cherry Hill campus; and Transition to College, a program based at Camden County College (P.O. Box 200, Blackwood 08012; 856-401-2642) that enables students to fulfill their high school graduation requirements while concurrently taking college courses. Pupils enroll from Atlantic, Burlington, Camden, Gloucester and surrounding counties.

CALAIS SCHOOL

Day — Coed Ages 6-21

Whippany, NJ 07981. 45 Highland Ave.
Tel: 973-884-2030. Fax: 973-884-0460.
www.thecalaisschool.org   E-mail: mkopec@thecalaisschool.org
David Leitner, LCSW, Exec Dir. **Diane Manno,** Adm.
   Focus: Spec Ed. **Conditions:** Primary—ADD ADHD Dx ED LD Mood OCD PTSD SP TS. Sec—AN Anx As Asp BD Bu CP Db OH.
   Col Prep. Gen Acad. Pre-Voc. Gr K-12. Courses: Read Math Lang_Arts. On-Job Trng.
   Psychotherapy: Group Indiv.
   Enr: 160. Day Males 126. Day Females 34. **Staff:** 64. Educ 42. Admin 6.
   Summer Prgm: Day. Educ. Rec. Ther. 4 wks.
   Est 1970. Private. Nonprofit.

This school for special-needs children offers a highly structured behavioral modification program and individualized instruction to address the academic, emotional, social and psychological needs of the student. A team of cognitive-behavioral therapists provide both emotional support and cognitive strategies for dealing with stressful situations.

Special programs offered at the school include speech and language therapy (in both diagnostic and remedial formats), therapeutic interventions, prescriptive learning services, prevocational training and transitional education programs.

Computer skills are taught in a computer lab, which is equipped with state-of-the-art computers. Athletic programs are part of each student's curriculum. Basketball, softball, soccer and cross-country are the intramural sports.

A shared program with the Morris County School of Technology is available to eligible Calais students. The summer program is in session in July and enrolls both students from Calais and pupils who attend other special education programs during the regular school year.

CAMBRIDGE SCHOOL

Day — Coed Ages 5-14

Pennington, NJ 08534. 62 S Main St.
Tel: 609-730-9553. Fax: 609-730-9584.
www.thecambridgeschool.org   E-mail: jpeters@thecambridgeschool.org
Deborah C. Peters, BA, MA, Head. **Joan Duggan,** Adm.
   Focus: Spec Ed. **Conditions:** Primary—ADD ADHD Dc Dg Dx. Sec—Anx

Apr Asp IP SP. **IQ 90 and up.**
Gen Acad. Gr K-8. Courses: Read Math Lang_Arts.
Therapy: Art Lang Music Speech. **Psychotherapy:** Fam Indiv Parent.
Enr: 60. Day Males 38. Day Females 22. **Staff:** 21 (Full 13, Part 8). Educ 18.
Admin 4.
Rates 2004: Day $24,380/yr. Schol avail. State Aid.
Est 2001. Private. Inc.

The school provides a specially formulated educational environment for children who have been diagnosed with primary language-based learning differences. Instruction is based on the Orton-Gillingham method, and it incorporates the Wilson Reading and Lindamood-Bell learning processes. The individualized, comprehensive, multisensory and structured curriculum is representative of that found at a traditional elementary and middle school.

CEREBRAL PALSY CENTER
BERGEN COUNTY

Day — Coed Ages 1½-8
Clinic: All Ages. M-F 8-5.

Fair Lawn, NJ 07410. 29-01 Berkshire Rd.
Tel: 201-797-7440. Fax: 201-797-1039.
www.thechildrenstherapycenter.org   E-mail: cgarafola@nac.net
Carolann Garafola, MA, Exec Dir.
Focus: Spec Ed. **Conditions:** Primary—Ap Bl C CP Ep IP MD MR MS Nf
ON SB.
Gen Acad. Ungraded.
Therapy: Lang Occup Phys Speech.
Staff: 67 (Full 35, Part 32). Prof 35. Educ 4. Admin 7.
Rates 2003: Day $250-375/mo. $63 (Clinic)/ses. Sliding-Scale Rate $16-
47/ses (Clinic).
Summer Prgm: Day. Educ. Ther. Day Rate $213/day. 5 wks.
Est 1950. Private. Nonprofit.

The center provides diagnosis and treatment for at-risk infants, and early intervention programs for infants and children with developmental delays, as well as for those with motor, speech and learning disabilities. Services including medical supervision; educational services; and physical, occupational, language and speech therapies are offered for individuals with cerebral palsy and other physical disabilities. The facility also operates a state-approved preschool and a class for those with multiple disabilities.

CEREBRAL PALSY CENTER
OF GLOUCESTER & SALEM COUNTIES

Day — Coed Ages Birth-21

Hurffville, NJ 08080. 610 Hollydell Dr.
Tel: 856-582-5151. Fax: 856-582-5055.

E-mail: cpctr@snip.net
Gracanne H. Ryan, MA, Exec Dir. **Karen Marano,** Adm.
  Focus: Spec Ed. **Conditions:** Primary—Apr BI CP Ep IP MD ON SB.
    Sec—Ap B D DS MR.
  Voc. Ungraded. Courses: Read Math Lang_Arts.
  Therapy: Art Music Occup Percepual-Motor Phys Play Recreational
    Speech.
  Enr: 90. Day Males 57. Day Females 33. **Staff:** 77 (Full 51, Part 26). Educ 9.
    Admin 3.
  Rates 2004: Day $214/day.
  Summer Prgm: Day. Educ. Rec. Ther. Day Rate $214/day. 6 wks.
  Est 1951. Private. Inc.

The Cerebral Palsy Center provides various educational and therapeutic services for children and young adults.

CEREBRAL PALSY LEAGUE

Day — Coed Ages 6mos and up

Union, NJ 07083. 373 Clermont Ter.
Tel: 908-709-1800. Fax: 908-709-1334.
E-mail: cpl.agency@verizon.net
Debra Wolfer, MEd, Exec Dir. **Randye Huron,** MD, Med Dir. **Barbara Gray,**
  Adm.
  Focus: Spec Ed. Trng. **Conditions:** Primary—B BI CP IP MR ON SB.
    Sec—D S.
  Pre-Voc. Courses: Read Math Lang_Arts Life_Skills. Shelt_Workshop. On-
    Job Trng.
  Therapy: Hear Lang Occup Phys Speech. **Psychotherapy:** Fam Group
    Parent.
  Enr: 80. **Staff:** 112.
  Est 1948. Private. Nonprofit.

The league offers therapeutic programs to individuals with multiple handicaps. CPL offers an early intervention program, a preschool (ages 3-5), pediatric and social daycare, and special education classes for children with severe handicaps (ages 3-21). Adults with severe handicaps may participate in a work activity training center that includes vocational training and job placement. In addition, adult medical daycare for adults with developmental disabilities and medical issues is available.

CEREBRAL PALSY OF NORTH JERSEY

Res — Coed Ages 21 and up; Day — Coed Birth-21

Maplewood, NJ 07040. 515 Valley St.
Tel: 973-763-9900. Fax: 973-763-9905.
www.cpnj.org   E-mail: dbishop@cpnj.org
Alan Mucatel, Exec Dir.
  Focus: Spec Ed. Treatment. **Conditions:** Primary—OH. Sec—Ap As Asp

Au B BI C CP D Dx Ep LD MD MR MS PDD S SB.
Gen Acad. Pre-Voc. Gr PS-12. Courses: Read Math Lang_Arts.
Therapy: Hear Hydro Lang Occup Phys Speech.
Enr: 231. Staff: 300. Prof 121. Educ 70. Admin 30.
Est 1953. Private. Nonprofit.

CPNJ provides diagnosis and treatment for individuals with various disabilities, among them cerebral palsy, mental retardation, visual and hearing impairments, speech and language delays, paraplegia, quadriplegia and autism. Utilizing a multidisciplinary team of professionals, the agency offers medical evaluation and therapy. The programs are designed to complement other private and community resources.

Horizon School, serving children and adolescents ages 3-21 who have varying developmental delays, offers a comprehensive educational program that is integrated with physical, occupational and speech therapy. The functional curriculum includes adaptive physical education, job coaching, library skills instruction and local field trips.

Public school children may receive therapeutic treatment at their schools through the Community Therapy Services program. Other offerings include early intervention services, an adult day program, and residential and respite services.

THE CHANCELLOR ACADEMY

Day — Coed Ages 13-18

Pompton Plains, NJ 07444. 157 West Pky, PO Box 338.
Tel: 973-835-4989. Fax: 973-835-0768.
Richard A. Sheridan, PhD, Dir. **James Badavas,** Prin.
   Focus: Spec Ed. **Conditions:** Primary—BD ED.
   Gen Acad. Gr 7-12. Courses: Read Math Lang_Arts Sci.
   Psychotherapy: Fam Group.
   Staff: 33 (Full 27, Part 6). Prof 16. Educ 9. Admin 8.
   Est 1965. Private. Inc.

The programs at Chancellor Academy are aimed at teaching emotionally disturbed and socially maladjusted adolescents who have not been able to accept the traditional public school approach. Opportunities for active participation in student government, work-study and interscholastic athletics are available. Strong academics and daily individual and group counseling are integral parts of the program. Tuition is set by the state.

THE CHILD CENTER

Day — Coed Ages Birth-3

Paramus, NJ 07652. 2 Sears Dr.
Tel: 201-261-2006. Fax: 201-262-1471.
   Focus: Treatment. **Conditions:** Primary—Au MR S.
   Therapy: Hear Lang Occup Phys Speech. **Psychotherapy:** Parent.
   Enr: 120. Staff: 21.
   Rates 2004: No Fee.
   Est 1947. Private. Nonprofit. **Spons:** The Arc.

Center & Home Infant Learning & Development serves infants and toddlers who have mental, physical or sensory difficulties. Immediate support is provided for parents of disabled infants in order to assist in their adjustment.

CHILDREN'S CENTER OF MONMOUTH COUNTY
Day — Coed Ages 3-21

Neptune, NJ 07753. 1115 Green Grove Rd.
Tel: 732-922-0228. Fax: 732-922-8133.
www.ccprograms.com
George Scheer, Exec Dir. **Mary Ellen Smith,** MA, CCP-SLP, Educ Dir.
 Focus: Spec Ed. Trng. Treatment. **Conditions:** Primary—ADHD Ap Au Bl
  CP Ep IP MD MR ON SB.
 Pre-Voc. Ungraded. Courses: Read Math Lang_Arts Life_Skills. Man_Arts &
  Shop. On-Job Trng.
 Therapy: Art Hear Lang Movement Music Occup Phys Speech. **Psycho-
  therapy:** Fam Group Parent.
 Enr: 438. Day Males 303. Day Females 135. **Staff:** 107.
 Est 1990. Private. Inc.

The Children's Center provides educational programs and training in living and pre-vocational skills for multiply handicapped and autistic children. A variety of services includes speech, language, movement, art and music therapies. Parent training and support, as well as family consultation, are also available. In addition to regular classrooms, the school features an exercise room, fully equipped treatment rooms for occupational and physical therapy, an adaptive living skills room and an outdoor recreation area.

THE CHILDREN'S HOME OF BURLINGTON COUNTY
Res and Day — Coed Ages 11-17

Mount Holly, NJ 08060. 243 Pine St.
Tel: 609-267-1550. Fax: 609-261-5672.
www.childrens-home.org   E-mail: kids@chbc.org
Gena M. Palm, MSW, EdD, LCSW, Exec Dir. **Lainie Rogers,** Adm.
 Focus: Treatment. **Conditions:** Primary—ADD ADHD As BD CD Dx ED LD
  ODD. **IQ 70 and up.**
 Gen Acad. Ungraded. Courses: Read Math Lang_Arts Sci Soc_Stud.
 Therapy: Speech. **Psychotherapy:** Fam Group Indiv.
 Enr: 80. **Staff:** 180 (Full 130, Part 50). Prof 37. Educ 32. Admin 20.
 Rates 2004: No Fee.
 Summer Prgm: Res & Day. Educ. Rec. Ther.
 Est 1864. Private. Nonprofit.

The Children's Home provides residential treatment to emotionally disturbed girls and boys. Services include individual, group and family counseling or therapy; educational services and tutoring; community service opportunities; recreational activities; daily living skills; and vocational/career assessments. Only New Jersey residents are accepted.

Also offered at the home is the Mercer House Shelter, a short-term, noncategorical residential facility serving troubled children from Mercer County. Youngsters and their families receive individualized services, including case management, recreational activities and access to educational services.

CHILDREN'S SPECIALIZED HOSPITAL

Res — Coed Ages Birth-21

Mountainside, NJ 07092. 150 New Providence Rd.
Tel: 908-233-3720. Fax: 908-301-5576.
www.childrens-specialized.org
Amy B. Mansue, Pres.
   Conditions: Primary—As BD BI C CP Ep IP MD ON SB TB.
   Therapy: Hear Lang Occup Phys Speech. **Psychotherapy:** Fam Group Indiv.
   Est 1891. Private. Nonprofit.

COLLIER HIGH SCHOOL

Day — Coed Ages 13-18

Wickatunk, NJ 07765. 160 Conover Rd.
Tel: 732-946-4771. Fax: 732-946-3519.
www.collierservices.com/HS/hs.html
   E-mail: jmcmerty@collierservices.com
   Focus: Spec Ed. **Conditions:** Primary—ED.
   Col Prep. Gen Acad. Pre-Voc. Gr 7-12. Courses: Read Math Lang_Arts Sci Hist. Man_Arts & Shop. On-Job Trng.
   Therapy: Speech. **Psychotherapy:** Fam Group Indiv.
   Enr: 150.
   Est 1927. Private. Nonprofit. Roman Catholic. **Spons:** Collier Services.

Emotionally disturbed adolescents follow individualized educational programs and receive year-round individual, group and family counseling at the school. The program highlights both college and career preparation. Various extracurricular activities supplement academic work. The average length of stay is 18 months.

COMMUNITY HIGH SCHOOL

Day — Coed Ages 14-21

Teaneck, NJ 07666. 1135 Teaneck Rd.
Tel: 201-862-1796. Fax: 201-862-1791.
www.communityschoolnj.org
   E-mail: tbraunstein@communityhighschool.org
Dennis Cohen, BA, MA, Prgm Dir. **Toby Braunstein,** MA, Educ. Dir.
   Focus: Spec Ed. **Conditions:** Primary—ADD ADHD Dx LD. **IQ 90 and up.**

Col Prep. Gr 9-PG. Courses: Read Math Lang_Arts Span Computers.
Therapy: Lang Speech. **Psychotherapy:** Indiv.
Enr: 166. Day Males 127. Day Females 39. **Staff:** 80.
Rates 2003: Day $34,096/sch yr.
Est 1967. Private. Nonprofit.

Community School provides a traditional college preparatory program geared to students with learning and attentional difficulties. One-on-one and small-class instruction addresses SAT preparation, remediation, study skills, and tutoring in reading, language and speech. The curriculum includes courses in computers, photography, graphics, industrial arts, typing and driver education. Interscholastic and intramural sports are also available.

An enriched elementary program, conducted at 11 W. Forest Ave. (separately listed), closely resembles that of the high school. **See Also Page 1021**

THE COMMUNITY SCHOOL

Day — Coed Ages 5-14

Teaneck, NJ 07666. 11 W Forest Ave.
Tel: 201-837-8070. Fax: 201-837-6799.
www.communityschoolnj.org
Rita Rowan, Exec Dir. **Isabel Shoukas,** Adm.
  Focus: Spec Ed. **Conditions:** Primary—ADD ADHD Dc Dg Dx LD. Sec—
    Anx Ap Apr As Asp Ep Mood OCD SP. **IQ 90 and up.**
  Gen Acad. Gr K-8. Courses: Read Math Lang_Arts.
  Therapy: Lang Percepual-Motor Speech. **Psychotherapy:** Group.
  Enr: 133. Day Males 121. Day Females 12. **Staff:** 52 (Full 48, Part 4).
  Rates 2003: Day $25,000/sch yr. State Aid.
  Est 1968. Private. Nonprofit.

Community School offers an elementary and junior high school program for students of average to above-average intelligence with specific learning disabilities, attentional disorders, hyperactivity and accompanying mild behavior problems. The curriculum is individualized to meet students' needs and learning styles. Small classes and close supervision are important characteristics of the program. Extracurricular activities and field trips round out the program.

Local sending school districts typically pay tuition costs.

THE COMMUNITY SCHOOL OF FAMILY CONNECTIONS

Day — Coed Ages 7-21

West Paterson, NJ 07424. 665 McBride Ave.
Tel: 973-754-1900. Fax: 973-754-1290.
www.familyconnectionsnj.com   E-mail: fam.connections@att.net
Barney Fabbo, MA, Prin.
  Focus: Spec Ed. **Conditions:** Primary—BD CD ED Mood OCD. Sec—LD
    Sz. **IQ 70-120.**
  Gen Acad. Pre-Voc. Voc. Ungraded. Courses: Read Math Lang_Arts Sci

Soc_Stud Studio_Art Music.
Therapy: Speech. **Psychotherapy:** Fam Group Indiv Parent.
Enr: 50. Day Males 42. Day Females 8. **Staff:** 23 (Full 18, Part 5).
Rates 2001: Day $26,578/sch yr.
Summer Prgm: Day. Educ. Rec. Ther. 6 wks.
Est 1879. Private. Nonprofit.

This school provides individual academic programs and behavior modification within a therapeutic milieu for severely emotionally disturbed children. All children see psychotherapists twice weekly. The school encourages parental participation; in fact, in most cases, parental involvement is a condition of the child's admittance.

Community School conducts a school-to-careers transitional program for older pupils. Another feature of the program is a six-week summer session that provides academic and therapeutic carryover.

COOPER UNIVERSITY HOSPITAL
SPEECH AND HEARING DEPARTMENT

Clinic: All Ages. M-F 8-4:30.

Camden, NJ 08103. 3 Cooper Plz, Ste 511.
Tel: 856-342-3060. Fax: 856-968-8358.
Stephen Nastasi, Admin Dir.
  Focus: Treatment. **Conditions:** Primary—Ap D S. Sec—BI LD MR OH.
  Therapy: Hear Lang Occup Phys Speech.
  Staff: 7 (Full 5, Part 2). Prof 6. Admin 1.
  Est 1961. Private. Nonprofit.

Cooper's Speech and Hearing Department administers diagnostic evaluations, thereby assessing the nature of speech and language disorders. Staff members then prescribe suitable therapy. This initial evaluation consists of articulation and language testing, evaluation of oral-peripheral mechanisms and gross-motor functioning, and audiometric screening.

The therapy program utilizes family members to assist in maintaining therapeutic goals. If therapy is not recommended, referrals are made to agencies who can aid individuals in locating a successful management program. Fees are based on a sliding scale, with the center serving residents of southern New Jersey.

CPC BEHAVIORAL HEALTHCARE

Res — Coed Ages 12-21; Day — Coed 5-21

Neptune, NJ 07753. 3535 Rte 66, Bldg 5, Ste D.
  Nearby locations: Freehold; Matawan; Morganville; Red Bank.
Tel: 732-643-4300. Fax: 732-643-4399.
www.cpcbhc.com
William D. Barry, LCSW, CEO.
  Conditions: Primary—BD ED LD S. Sec—ADHD.
  Gen Acad. Pre-Voc. Ungraded. Courses: Read Math Lang_Arts.
  Therapy: Hear Lang Occup Speech. **Psychotherapy:** Fam Group Indiv.

Staff: Prof 113.
Est 1960. Private. Nonprofit.

CRAIG SCHOOL

Day — Coed Ages 6-19

Mountain Lakes, NJ 07046. 10 Tower Hill Rd.
   Nearby locations: Lincoln Park.
Tel: 973-334-1099. Fax: 973-334-1299.
www.craigschool.org   E-mail: jday@craigschool.org
David Blanchard, Int Head.
   Focus: Spec Ed. **Conditions:** Primary—ADD ADHD Dx LD. Sec—Dc Dg.
      IQ 90-120.
   Col Prep. Gen Acad. Gr 1-12. Courses: Read Math Lang_Arts Sci Comput-
      ers Soc_Stud Studio_Art Health.
   Therapy: Lang Occup Speech.
   Enr: 150. **Staff:** 52 (Full 39, Part 13). Educ 34. Admin 6.
   Rates 2003: Day $22,400-29,000/sch yr.
   Summer Prgm: Day. Educ. Rec. 2-6 wks.
   Est 1980. Private. Nonprofit.

Craig provides an education for children with learning disabilities in a supportive, structured environment. The core curriculum, which is taught in small classes, is supplemented by educational field trips and assemblies. Individual goals and objectives are set for each child and are closely monitored, with parent-teacher conferences held regularly. Social skills and self-esteem are strengthened throughout the program and are reinforced through a mentor system. Consistent, positive behavior management is employed.

The lower school (grades 1-8) operates at the Mountain Lakes address, while the upper school (grades 9-12) occupies quarters at 200 Comly Rd., Lincoln Park 07035.

See Also Page 1024

CUMBERLAND COUNTY GUIDANCE CENTER

Day — Coed Ages 5-17
Clinic: All Ages. M-F 9-5.

Millville, NJ 08332. 2038 Carmel Rd, PO Box 808.
   Nearby locations: Bridgeton; Vineland.
Tel: 856-825-6810. Fax: 856-327-4281.
www.guidancecenter.org   E-mail: ccgc808@aol.com
H. Dieter Hovermann, MA, Dir. **Jorge Priori,** MD, Med Dir.
   Focus: Treatment. **Conditions:** Primary—ED.
   Therapy: Speech. **Psychotherapy:** Fam Group Indiv.
   Staff: 179 (Full 111, Part 68). Admin 8.
   Est 1961. Private. Nonprofit.

The Guidance Center provides outpatient and day treatment services for children with emotional and psychological problems. The partial-care day program features group, individual and family therapy, as well as linkages and joint treatment planning with schools, courts and agencies. Outpatient services include therapy and a program for victims of sexual assault. Clinical fees are determined along a sliding scale.

Branches of the clinic are located in Vineland (80 S. Main Rd., 08360) and Bridgeton (423 Manheim Ave., 08302).

DEVEREUX NEW JERSEY CENTER FOR AUTISM

Res — Coed Ages 14 and up; Day — Coed 5-21

Bridgeton, NJ 08302. 198 Roadstown Rd.
Tel: 856-455-7200. Fax: 856-455-2765.
www.devereuxnewjersey.org
Sue Keffer, Prin.
 Focus: Spec Ed. **Conditions:** Primary—Au. Sec—Anx As BD CP D ED Ep Mood MR OCD ON S.
 Gen Acad. Pre-Voc. Ungraded. Shelt_Workshop. On-Job Trng.
 Therapy: Occup Phys.
 Enr: 53. Res Males 36. Res Females 5. Day Males 11. Day Females 1.
  Staff: 130. Prof 13. Admin 7.
 Rates 2004: Day $220/day. State Aid.
 Summer Prgm: Res & Day. Educ. 6 wks.
 Private. Nonprofit. **Spons:** Devereux Foundation.

Addressing the particular needs of children, adolescents and adults with autism spectrum disorders, the center offers residential, educational and vocational programs. Programs aim to help these individuals better deal with their behaviors, while teaching them life skills. The center works with individual strengths and supports areas that need development through an individualized, behavioral approach.   **See Also Page 1025**

DOROTHY B. HERSH HIGH SCHOOL

Day — Coed Ages 14-21

Tinton Falls, NJ 07712. 1158 Wayside Rd.
Tel: 732-493-3563. Fax: 732-493-3427.
www.arcofmonmouth.org   E-mail: hershhigh@arcofmonmouth.org
Mary Scott, MA, Exec Dir. **Carol A. Padgitt,** MSEd, Prin.
 Focus: Spec Ed. **Conditions:** Primary—DS MR. Sec—ADD ADHD As Au BD CD Dx LD OCD ON PDD S. **IQ 30-85.**
 Pre-Voc. Voc. Ungraded. Courses: Read Math Lang_Arts Studio_Art Music Adaptive_Phys_Ed Health Speech. Shelt_Workshop. On-Job Trng.
 Therapy: Music Occup Phys Speech. **Psychotherapy:** Indiv.
 Enr: 19. Day Males 11. Day Females 8. **Staff:** 15 (Full 11, Part 4).
 Summer Prgm: Day. Educ. 6 wks.
 Est 1949. Private. Nonprofit. **Spons:** Arc of Monmouth.

Hersh High School is an on-site day school that provides academic and vocational training for students ages 14-21 with mental retardation. The school seeks to develop in pupils the skills and attitudes necessary to successfully function within the adult community. Hersh High's curriculum addresses academic skills, independent learning skills, social skills, vocational training, job exposure and employment training, supplemental services and family life education. An extended school year option is available. Tuition charges are generally paid by the sending school district.

EAST MOUNTAIN DAY SCHOOL

Day — Coed Ages 12-19

Belle Mead, NJ 08502. Rte 601, PO Box 147.
Tel: 908-281-1415. Fax: 908-281-1663.
www.carrier.org/educational_services.asp
Gloria Kalina, PhD, Dir.
   Focus: Spec Ed. Conditions: Primary—CD ED OCD Psy Sz. Sec—BD. IQ
      80 and up.
   Col Prep. Gen Acad. Pre-Voc. Gr 7-12. Courses: Read Math Lang_Arts
      Computers Sci Drama.
   Therapy: Speech. Psychotherapy: Fam Group Indiv.
   Enr: 80. Staff: 25.
   Est 1980. Private. Nonprofit. Spons: Carrier Clinic.

This school offers psycho-educational special education at the secondary school level for severely emotionally disturbed boys and girls. The ultimate goal of the school is to return students to their appropriate vocational or high school settings within two years.

A psycho-educational-humanistic approach to learning is utilized, and learning strategies are applied to instruction. Small educational classes emphasize individualized instruction. Positive behaviors are reinforced through a status system. Group counseling with a psychologist, a social worker and a drug counselor is required, and parental support groups are available. Tuition fees are paid by the local school district.

EASTERN CHRISTIAN CHILDREN'S RETREAT

Res and Day — Coed Ages 8 and up

Wyckoff, NJ 07481. 700 Mountain Ave.
Tel: 201-848-8005. Fax: 201-847-9619.
www.eccretreat.org   E-mail: info@eccretreat.org
Jayne Press, Pres.
   Conditions: Primary—MR.
   Pre-Voc.
   Therapy: Hear Occup Phys Speech. Psychotherapy: Indiv.
   Staff: Prof 18.
   Est 1972. Private. Nonprofit.

EDEN INSTITUTE
Day — Coed Ages 3-21

Princeton, NJ 08540. 1 Eden Way.
Tel: 609-987-0099. Fax: 609-987-0243.
www.edenservices.org   E-mail: info@edenservices.org
David L. Holmes, EdD, Pres. **Carol Markowitz,** MEd, Educ Dir.
  Focus: Spec Ed. **Conditions:** Primary—Au. Sec—MR S. **IQ 25-80.**
  Pre-Voc. Ungraded. Courses: Adaptive_Phys_Ed. Shelt_Workshop. On-Job
    Trng.
  Therapy: Lang Speech. **Psychotherapy:** Fam.
  Enr: 53. Day Males 46. Day Females 7. **Staff:** 57 (Full 53, Part 4).
  Summer Prgm: Res & Day. Educ. 8 wks.
  Est 1975. Private. Nonprofit.

Eden offers individual and two-to-one instruction for children with autism ages 3-7; remedial activities in speech, academic and social skills for children ages 7-12; and a prevocational and vocational preparation program for those ages 13-21. The prevocational program trains adolescents with autism to function semi-independently through the development of work habits and self-help and communicational skills.

Eden's Outreach and Support Services Division provides an infant and toddler program, diagnostics, clinical services, consultations and evaluations. A parental training program, parental support groups and in-home respite care are also available.

FAIRLEIGH DICKINSON UNIVERSITY
CENTER FOR PSYCHOLOGICAL SERVICES
Clinic: All Ages. M-F.

Hackensack, NJ 07601. 139 Temple Ave.
Tel: 201-692-2645. Fax: 201-692-2164.
www.fdu.edu/webresources/cps.html
Linda A. Reddy, Dir.
  Conditions: Primary—BD ED. Sec—ADHD Anx Asp TS.
  Therapy: Play. **Psychotherapy:** Fam Group Indiv.
  Staff: Prof 14.
  Est 1961. Private. Nonprofit.

FAMILY RESOURCE ASSOCIATES
Clinic: Ages Birth-8. M-S 9-4.

Shrewsbury, NJ 07702. 35 Haddon Ave.
Tel: 732-747-5310. Fax: 732-747-1896.
Nancy Phalanukorn, Admin.
  Focus: Spec Ed. **Conditions:** Primary—Ap Au BI CP Dx IP LD MD MR ON
    S SB.
  Therapy: Dance Lang Music Occup Phys Speech. **Psychotherapy:** Fam

Group.
Staff: 19 (Full 4, Part 15). Prof 12. Educ 11.
Est 1979. Private. Nonprofit.

Therapeutic and educational services provided at this clinic include recreational programs, parent and staff training workshops, and computer and augmentative communication programs. Programs are also available for siblings and grandparents.

THE FELICIAN SCHOOL FOR EXCEPTIONAL CHILDREN
Day — Coed Ages 5-21

Lodi, NJ 07644. 260 S Main St, PO Box 530.
Tel: 973-777-5355. Fax: 973-777-0725.
E-mail: felicianexcep@hotmail.com
Sr. Mary Ramona Borkowski, BSEd, MA, EdD, Dir. **Kathy Miroddi,** Adm.
  Focus: Spec Ed. **Conditions:** Primary—MR. Sec—Au CD ED. **IQ 0-65.**
  Gen Acad. Pre-Voc. Voc. Ungraded. Courses: Read Math Lang_Arts. On-Job Trng.
  Therapy: Hear Lang Music Occup Phys Speech. **Psychotherapy:** Group Indiv.
  Enr: 137. Day Males 82. Day Females 55. **Staff:** 65 (Full 61, Part 4). Prof 23. Educ 17. Admin 8.
  Est 1971. Private. Nonprofit.

The Felician School provides an educational program designed to offer individualized instruction to cognitively disabled children, as well as those with emotional disturbances and autism. Emphasis is placed on the development of cognitive, language-perceptual, self-help and social skills to prepare students for entrance into a more structured classroom setting.

A prevocational program offers training in specific job skills. Group physical education and individualized physical therapy aid students with neuro-developmental difficulties.

1ST CEREBRAL PALSY OF NEW JERSEY
Day — Coed Ages Birth-21
Clinic: All Ages. T 1-3.

Belleville, NJ 07109. 7 Sanford Ave.
Tel: 973-751-0200. Fax: 973-751-4635.
www.cerebralpalsycenter.org   E-mail: cpcenter@excite.com
Patrick Colligan, Exec Dir. **David Greifinger,** MD, Med Dir.
  Focus: Spec Ed. **Conditions:** Primary—CP Ep IP MD MS ON SB. Sec—ADD Ap Dc Dg Dx LD MR S.
  Pre-Voc. Gr PS-8. Courses: Read Math Lang_Arts.
  Therapy: Lang Occup Percepual-Motor Phys Recreational Speech.
  Enr: 90. Day Males 60. Day Females 30. **Staff:** 60 (Full 56, Part 4).
  Rates 2004: Res $50,856/sch yr.
  Est 1946. Private. Nonprofit.

Services available at the facility such as medical supervision; orthopedic, pediatric and eye clinics; psychological and social services; and physical, occupational and speech therapies are offered for individuals with cerebral palsy and other physical disabilities. Clients are referred by professional agencies, schools, clinics and physicians.

Classroom programs from preschool to an upper school transition program include offerings for educable, trainable and multiply handicapped students. Adult services include training in independent living, a counseling program, orthopedic consultation, social services and housing.

The center provides guidance information and referral services for all clients. Recreational services include scout programs, a sports program, an adult travel group, a teen recreation program and a performing arts workshop. Fees are determined along a sliding scale or by contractual arrangement.

THE FORUM SCHOOL

Day — Coed Ages 3-16

Waldwick, NJ 07463. 107 Wyckoff Ave.
Tel: 201-444-5882. Fax: 201-444-4003.
www.theforumschool.com   E-mail: info@theforumschool.com
Steven Krapes, EdD, Dir.

>**Focus:** Spec Ed. **Conditions:** Primary—ADD ADHD Ap Apr Asp Au Dc Dg Dx ED OCD Psy Sz. Sec—Ep HIV MR SP TS. **IQ 60-130.**
>**Gen Acad. Pre-Voc.** Courses: Read Math Lang_Arts Sci Soc_Stud Studio_Art Music Life_Skills.
>**Therapy:** Art Lang Music Speech.
>**Enr:** 150. Day Males 131. Day Females 19. **Staff:** 103. Prof 36. Educ 26. Admin 2.
>**Rates 2003:** Day $31,403/sch yr. State Aid.
>**Summer Prgm:** Day. Educ. Day Rate $3140. 3½ wks.
>**Est 1954.** Private. Nonprofit.

Forum offers therapeutic education for children diagnosed with one or more of the following conditions: autism, Asperger's syndrome, an emotional disturbance, ADD, ADHD or communicational disorders. The school offers a structured program to meet the student's individual needs. This includes the fostering of emotional, verbal, cognitive, physical and vocational growth. A primary goal is to increase the child's self-esteem while strengthening inner controls.

Through a psycho-educational approach, Forum aims to return students to a public school setting or to the least restrictive environment possible. A summer session is available only to students enrolled in the school-year program.

GARFIELD PARK ACADEMY

Day — Coed Ages 5-20

Willingboro, NJ 08046. 24 Glenolden Ln.
Tel: 609-877-4111. Fax: 609-877-5551.
www.garfieldparkacademy.org

E-mail: gmorse@garfieldparkacademy.org
Gladys Morse, EdD, Exec Dir.
 Focus: Spec Ed. Treatment. **Conditions:** Primary—ADD ADHD AN Anx
  Ap Apr As Asp Au BD Bl Bu C CD CP Dc Dg Dx ED Ep LD MD Mood Nf
  OCD PDD Psy PTSD PW SP Sz TS. Sec—MR. **IQ 65 and up.**
 Col Prep. Gen Acad. Pre-Voc. Gr K-12. Courses: Read Math Lang_Arts Sci
  Soc_Stud. Man_Arts & Shop. On-Job Trng.
 Therapy: Art Lang Movement Music Occup Percepual-Motor Play Recre-
  ational Speech. **Psychotherapy:** Fam Group Indiv Parent.
 Enr: 280. Day Males 200. Day Females 80. **Staff:** 130 (Full 90, Part 40).
  Prof 70. Educ 25.
 Rates 2003: Day $165/day. Schol avail.
 Summer Prgm: Day. Educ. Rec. Ther. Day Rate $165/day. 6 wks.
 Est 1992. Private. Nonprofit.

This family-oriented school serves children with learning and emotional problems. Garfield's behavioral management system, together with its intensive counseling services, allows for effective remediation of psychiatric and behavioral problems. Individual and group therapy is part of the daily program. Art, music, speech and language therapy are also available.

Boys and girls enroll from Burlington, Mercer, Gloucester, Camden and surrounding counties.

GITHENS CENTER

Day — Coed Ages 3-21
Clinic: All Ages. By Appt.

Mount Holly, NJ 08060. 40 Cedar St.
Tel: 609-261-1667. Fax: 609-261-1844.
www.githenscenter.org E-mail: githenscp@aol.com
Kate G. York, BS, MS, Exec Dir.
 Focus: Spec Ed. Treatment. **Conditions:** Primary—CP ON SB. Sec—Ep
  LD MR S.
 Gen Acad. Pre-Voc. Ungraded. Courses: Read Math Lang_Arts.
 Therapy: Lang Occup Phys Speech.
 Enr: 43. **Staff:** 26 (Full 17, Part 9).
 Est 1951. Private. Nonprofit. **Spons:** Burlington County Cerebral Palsy
  Association.

This facility aims to mainstream children with physical disabilities as early as possible into environments that require minimal adaptation. Githens provides educational, therapeutic, medical and recreational services for both children and adults. The educational program develops areas of fine- and gross-motor skills, cognition, self-help skills, feeding, speech and language, auditory and visual perception, and social and emotional growth. After-school and in-home respite services are also available.

Fees vary according to services rendered.

GLENVIEW ACADEMY

Day — Coed Ages 6-21

Fairfield, NJ 07004. 24 Dwight Pl.
Tel: 973-808-9555. Fax: 973-227-8626.
www.glenview.org   E-mail: kgerritz@glenview.org
James E. Perri, BS, Dir. Cherie Stein, Adm.
    Focus: Spec Ed. Conditions: Primary—ADD ADHD BD CD ED LD Mood ODD. Sec—AN Anx As Bl Dx OCD PTSD S SP. IQ 50-120.
    Pre-Voc. Gr 1-12. Courses: Read Math Lang_Arts. Shelt_Workshop. On-Job Trng.
    Therapy: Art Lang Milieu Percepual-Motor Phys Play Speech. Psycho-therapy: Group Indiv.
    Enr: 125. Day Males 104. Day Females 21. Staff: 65 (Full 63, Part 2). Admin 8.
    Rates 2004: Day $220/day.
    Summer Prgm: Day. Educ. Rec. Ther. Day Rate $220/day. 6 wks.
    Est 1986. Private. Inc.

Glenview enrolls boys and girls who have educational disabilities that cannot be adequately addressed in the public schools. The academy's curriculum, which incorporates New Jersey standards, addresses both academic and social/emotional needs of the students. Individual, small-group and multimodal instruction employs diagnostic and direct teaching techniques. In addition to gaining a grounding in the fundamental skills, pupils learn to use technology as a tool and develop problem solving and critical thinking abilities.

THE GRAMON SCHOOL

Day — Coed Ages 13-21

Fairfield, NJ 07004. 24 Dwight Pl.
Tel: 973-808-9555. Fax: 973-227-8626.
www.gramon.org   E-mail: kgerritz@gramon.org
Kalle Gerritz, EdD, Dir.
    Focus: Spec Ed. Conditions: Primary—BD ED OCD Sz. Sec—LD OH. IQ 80 and up.
    Col Prep. Gen Acad. Pre-Voc. Gr 7-12. Courses: Read Math Lang_Arts Computers.
    Therapy: Art Speech. Psychotherapy: Group Indiv.
    Enr: 72. Staff: 27.
    Est 1939. Private.

The school follows a program built around a homelike, nonpressuring atmosphere. Individualized and small-group instruction, participation in small-group activity and flexible curricula, including independent study, are stressed in helping students attain their maximum potentials. Achievement motivation and reality therapy are also utilized.

In addition to a full academic program, activities such as adaptive physical education, computer, prevocational laboratories, counseling, advisory groups and art, are offered.

Swimming, roller skating, interscholastic sports, yearbook and similar co-curricular and extracurricular activities are also available. Special classes for the neurologically impaired and emotionally disturbed are held.

The school also has a companion elementary school, Glenview Academy (for boys and girls ages 6-12).

GREEN BROOK ACADEMY

Day — Coed Ages 11-21

Bound Brook, NJ 08805. 126 Vosseller Ave.
Tel: 732-469-5892. Fax: 732-469-0035.
E-mail: gbainfo@aol.com
Edward J. Dougherty, BA, MA, EdD, Exec Dir. **Louise M. Mancino,** Adm.
  Focus: Spec Ed. **Conditions:** Primary—ED. Sec—ADD ADHD Anx BD Bl Dx LD Mood OCD ODD TS. **IQ 70 and up.**
  Gen Acad. Pre-Voc. Ungraded. Courses: Read Math Lang_Arts Computers Soc_Stud.
  Therapy: Art Speech. **Psychotherapy:** Group Indiv.
  Enr: 72. Day Males 54. Day Females 18. **Staff:** 35 (Full 33, Part 2).
  Rates 2003: Day $34,426/sch yr.
  Summer Prgm: Day. Educ. Day Rate $191.
  Est 1979. Private. Inc.

Green Brook Academy helps emotionally disturbed students return to their schools or complete their formal education and directly enter the job market. The individualized curriculum is developed in cooperation with the district's child study team and approved by the student's parents or legal guardian. The academy also offers a physical education program, vocational guidance, and individual, group and art therapy.

HACKENSACK UNIVERSITY MEDICAL CENTER
JUDY CENTER FOR DOWN SYNDROME

Clinic: All Ages. W 8:30-4.

Hackensack, NJ 07601. 30 Prospect Ave.
Tel: 201-996-5839. Fax: 201-996-0754.
E-mail: fhirschenfang@humed.com
Fred Hirschenfang, MD, Med Dir.
  Focus: Treatment. **Conditions:** Primary—DS MR.
  Therapy: Hear Phys. **Psychotherapy:** Fam Group Indiv Parent.
  Staff: 4. (Full 4). Prof 3. Admin 1.
  State. Nonprofit.

This center provides outpatient evaluation and care for individuals with Down syndrome and their families. Consultation services to families and physicians are also available.

HARBOR SCHOOL

Day — Coed Ages 3-21

Eatontown, NJ 07724. 240 Broad St.
Tel: 732-544-9493. Fax: 732-544-9394.
www.harborschool.com   E-mail: admin@harborschool.com
Ann Gunteski, Prin.

Focus: Spec Ed. **Conditions:** Primary—ADD ADHD Ap Au BI Dx LD S.
Sec—As B BD C CD CP D ED Ep IP MR OCD ON SB TB. **IQ 50-110.**
Pre-Voc. Ungraded. Courses: Read Math Lang_Arts Sci Soc_Stud Studio_
Art Music Health Adaptive_Phys_Ed Life_Skills.
Therapy: Hear Lang Occup Phys Speech.
Enr: 120. Day Males 85. Day Females 35. **Staff:** 70 (Full 64, Part 6).
Private.

The school provides academic instruction for both neurologically impaired and communicatively handicapped children who have specific learning disabilities. In addition to basic academics, the curriculum includes science, social studies, health and prevocational activities. An adaptive physical education program offers swimming instruction. The developmental program provides auditory, visual, perceptual, and gross- and fine-motor training. The New Jersey Department of Education determines annual tuition rates at Harbor.

Similar programs are conducted in Lakewood at Alpha School (Forest Ave. & 11th St., 08071) and at Gateway School, in Carteret (60 High St., 07008).

HOLLEY CHILD CARE AND DEVELOPMENT CENTER

Res — Coed Ages 6-12

Hackensack, NJ 07601. 260 Union St.
Tel: 201-343-8803. Fax: 201-343-8563.
www.ycs.org

Conditions: Primary—ED. Sec—BD.
Gen Acad. Courses: Read Math Lang_Arts.
Therapy: Milieu Play.
Est 1971. Private. Nonprofit. **Spons:** Youth Consultation Service.

HOLMSTEAD SCHOOL

Day — Coed Ages 13-18

Ridgewood, NJ 07450. 14 Hope St.
Tel: 201-447-1696. Fax: 201-447-4608.
www.holmstead.org   E-mail: mail@holmstead.org
Patricia G. Whitehead, MEd, Dir.

Focus: Spec Ed. **Conditions:** Primary—ED. **IQ 115 and up.**
Col Prep. Gen Acad. Gr 8-12. Courses: Read Math Lang_Arts.
Psychotherapy: Fam Group Indiv.

Enr: 77. Day Males 56. Day Females 21. **Staff:** 21 (Full 16, Part 5).
Est 1970. Private. Nonprofit.

Holmstead offers an alternative educational program for adolescents with intellectual ability who are not succeeding in a traditional academic setting because of emotional disturbances. It is primarily a college preparatory program. For individuals with learning disabilities, the school provides remediation and tutorial help in the development of skills and compensatory techniques. Every student takes six subjects within a multidisciplinary curriculum. Adjunct services such as testing and vocational and college counseling, as well as individual psychotherapy, are readily available. The usual duration of treatment is three years.

HUNTERDON DEVELOPMENTAL CENTER

Res — Coed Ages 18 and up

Clinton, NJ 08809. 40 Pittstown Rd, PO Box 4003.
Tel: 908-735-4031. Fax: 908-730-1338.
www.state.nj.us/humanservices/pfnurse/hunterdon.htm
    E-mail: hdcnurses@dhs.state.nj.us
William A. Wall, MEd, CEO.
    Focus: Trng. Treatment. **Conditions:** Primary—MR. Sec—Au B D ED LD ON S. **IQ 1-70.**
    Gen Acad. Pre-Voc. Ungraded. Man_Arts & Shop. Shelt_Workshop.
    Therapy: Chemo Hear Lang Occup Phys Speech. **Psychotherapy:** Indiv.
    Est 1968. State. Nonprofit.

Situated on a 102-acre tract, HDC utilizes an interdisciplinary approach in its year-round care and habilitation of persons with developmental disabilities. Each client follows an individualized habilitation plan designed to meet his or her needs that includes structured activities, educational programming and recreational offerings. The center also provides prevocational and vocational training. Facilities include a 70-bed on-campus hospital as well as 18 residential cottages, all staffed by direct-care and supervisory personnel. The program encourages community involvement.

HUNTERDON LEARNING CENTER

Day — Coed Ages 12-18

Califon, NJ 07830. 37 Hoffmans Crossing Rd.
Tel: 908-832-7200. Fax: 908-832-9772.
www.hunterdonlearning.com
Toby Ray Loyd, MEd, Dir.
    Focus: Spec Ed. **Conditions:** Primary—ADD ADHD BD ED. Sec—Anx Asp Mood OCD TS. **IQ 92-130.**
    Gen Acad. Pre-Voc. Gr 7-12. Courses: Read Math Lang_Arts Sci.
    Therapy: Speech.
    Enr: 76. Day Males 50. Day Females 26. **Staff:** 26 (Full 24, Part 2).
    Rates 2004: Day $30,000/sch yr. Schol 2 ($1000).
    Est 1975. Private. Nonprofit.

Hunterdon focuses on developing personal and social responsibilities in adolescents with special needs. Drawing on therapeutic community concepts, the staff and students work to create a family environment. The development of academic and employable skills is emphasized, and vocational, educational, parental and personal counseling sessions are conducted.

HUNTERDON MEDICAL CENTER
CHILD DEVELOPMENT CENTER

Day — Coed Ages Birth-21
Clinic: All Ages. M-F 8-4:30.

Flemington, NJ 08822. 2100 Wescott Dr.
Tel: 908-788-6396. Fax: 908-788-6370.
www.hunterdonhealthcare.org/services/child_development/
    child_development.asp
    Conditions: Primary—Bl CP Ep OH.
    Therapy: Chemo Hear Lang Occup Phys Speech. **Psychotherapy:** Fam
      Group Indiv.
    Staff: Prof 12.
    Est 1953. Private. Nonprofit.

HUNTERDON MEDICAL CENTER
SPEECH AND HEARING DEPARTMENT
AND CHILD DEVELOPMENT CENTER

Clinic: Ages Birth-21. M-F 8:30-5; Eves T W 5-7.

Flemington, NJ 08822. 2100 Wescott Dr.
Tel: 908-788-6424. Fax: 908-788-6581.
www.hunterdonhealthcare.org/services/child_development/
    child_development.asp
Robert P. Wise, Pres.
    Focus: Rehab. Treatment. **Conditions:** Primary—ADD ADHD Ap Au Dx LD
      PDD S. Sec—B CD CP D ED MR OCD ON Psy.
    Therapy: Lang Occup Phys Speech.
    Staff: 35 (Full 9, Part 26).
    Private. Nonprofit.

The center provides diagnosis and rehabilitation of communicative disorders for individuals of all ages with speech, language and hearing impairments, as well as those with ADHD and PDD. Diagnostic procedures include language and speech evaluation, audiological services and hearing aid evaluation. Speech, occupational and physical therapy are available for children and adolescents.

JCC ON THE PALISADES
THERAPEUTIC NURSERY

Day — Coed Ages 3-5

Tenafly, NJ 07670. 411 E Clinton Ave.
Tel: 201-569-7900. Fax: 201-569-7448.
www.jcconthepalisades.org
Lois Mendelson, PhD, Dir. Anita Miller, MS, OTR, Prgm Coord.
  Focus: Spec Ed. Conditions: Primary—ADD ADHD Ap Asp Au LD PDD S.
    Sec—CD ED.
  Gen Acad. Gr PS-K.
  Therapy: Lang Occup Speech. Psychotherapy: Group Parent.
  Enr: 16. Staff: 10 (Full 8, Part 2). Prof 4. Educ 2. Admin 4.
  Summer Prgm: Day. Educ. Ther. 6 wks.
  Est 1995. Private. Nonprofit.

The nursery offers developmental preschool and kindergarten programs for children with social/communication deficits associated with emotional disturbance, language disorders, learning disabilities, attention deficits and autistic behaviors. Parents are an integral part of the program and are trained to become part of the psycho-educational team through daily participation and meetings with staff and therapists. Many children are mainstreamed by grade 1, while others go on to inclusion classes.

JFK JOHNSON REHABILITATION INSTITUTE
PEDIATRIC REHABILITATION DEPARTMENT

Day — Coed Ages Birth-16
Clinic: All Ages. M-F 8-5:30.

Edison, NJ 08820. 2050 Oak Tree Rd.
Tel: 732-548-7610. Fax: 732-548-7751.
www.njrehab.org
Patricia Munday, EdD, Dir.
  Conditions: Primary—ADD ADHD Ap As Au BD C CD CP D Dx ED Ep IP
    LD MD MS ON PTSD S SB TB. Sec—B MR OCD.
  Therapy: Hear Lang Occup Phys Speech. Psychotherapy: Fam Group
    Indiv.
  Est 1978. Private.

The department provides comprehensive interdisciplinary medical, therapeutic and educational diagnostic and treatment services. Treatment is available in such developmental areas as speech and language, fine and gross motor, sensory integration, cognition, social skills and affective adjustment.

Other offerings include a preschool and primary program for children with autism (You & Me School), as well as child evaluation, medical, prosthetic, orthotic and adaptive equipment, and spina bifida and muscular dystrophy clinics.

KINGSWAY LEARNING CENTER

Day — Coed Ages 5-21
Clinic: Ages Birth-3. M-F 8-4.

Haddonfield, NJ 08033. 144 Kings Hwy W.
  Nearby locations: Moorestown.
Tel: 856-428-8108. Fax: 856-428-7520.
www.kingswaylc.com   E-mail: kingswaylc@aol.com
David J. Panner, MA, Exec Dir. **Nancy Healey,** MA, Educ Dir. **Rolanda Sykes,** Adm.
  Focus: Spec Ed. **Conditions:** Primary—ADD ADHD Dx LD MR. Sec—Ap As B Bl C CP D Db Ep MD MS ON S SB. **IQ 20-70.**
  Gen Acad. Pre-Voc. Ungraded. Courses: Read Math Lang_Arts Sci Soc_ Stud Health Life_Skills. Man_Arts & Shop. Shelt_Workshop.
  Therapy: Hear Lang Occup Phys Speech. **Psychotherapy:** Indiv.
  Enr: 190. Day Males 130. Day Females 60. **Staff:** 100 (Full 60, Part 40). Prof 22. Educ 19. Admin 7.
  Rates 2003: Day $30,000/sch yr. State Aid.
  Summer Prgm: Day. Educ. Ther. Day Rate $4100. 6 wks.
  Est 1970. Private. Nonprofit.

Kingsway provides special education and early intervention services to children with developmental and learning disabilities. The center addresses the academic and therapeutic needs of children from Burlington, Camden, Mercer and Gloucester counties in New Jersey and Philadelphia, PA.

The early intervention program consists of learning and therapeutic services to the families of infants up to age 3 who show delays in reaching developmental milestones or who have received a diagnosis that has designated them at high risk of experiencing delays.

Kingsway's school-age program provides individualized education and therapy for students with developmental and learning disabilities. The elementary school (ages 5-14) consists of special education classes and social skills training. The secondary school (ages 14-21), located at 244 W. Rte. 38, Moorestown 08057, focuses on prevocational training and career assessment.

LAKEVIEW SCHOOL

Day — Coed Ages 3-21
Clinic: All Ages. M W Th 9-3.

Edison, NJ 08837. 10 Oak Dr.
Tel: 732-549-5580. Fax: 732-494-6038.
Lynn Sikorski, BA, MA, Dir. **Louis Pellegrino,** MD, Med Dir. **Maria Freis,** Adm.
  Focus: Spec Ed. **Conditions:** Primary—Ap Apr Bl CP Ep IP MD MS ON SB. Sec—MR.
  Pre-Voc. Ungraded. Courses: Read Math Lang_Arts. Shelt_Workshop.
  Therapy: Lang Occup Phys Speech. **Psychotherapy:** Indiv Parent.
  Enr: 178. Day Males 86. Day Females 92. **Staff:** 148 (Full 85, Part 63).
  Rates 2004: Day $52,740/sch yr. State Aid.

Est 1949. Private. Nonprofit.

Lakeview serves severely and multiply disabled children. The school offers an individualized special education program specific to the learning needs of each student. Individualized therapy and monthly medical clinics in physiatry, orthopedics and pediatrics support educational placement. Psychological assessment for multiply disabled students, comprehensive assessment and training in adaptive technologies for mobility, communication and Activities of Daily Living are also part of the program.

Local sending school districts typically pay tuition costs.

LEHMANN SCHOOL AND TECHNICAL EDUCATION CENTER
Day — Coed Ages 3-21

Lakewood, NJ 08701. 1100 Airport Rd.
Tel: 732-905-7200. Fax: 732-905-1403.
E-mail: luisa.vroman@ladacin.org
Luisa Vromin, Assoc Dir. **Steven Streit,** MD, Med Dir. **Gina Shulman,** Adm.
  Focus: Spec Ed. **Conditions:** Primary—Apr BI CP Ep IP MD MS SB.
    Sec—Ap B D MR.
  Pre-Voc. Ungraded. Courses: Read Math Lang_Arts.
  Therapy: Art Music Occup Phys Recreational Speech.
  Enr: 42. Day Males 21. Day Females 21. **Staff:** 52 (Full 35, Part 17).
  Rates 2003: No Fee.
  Est 1953. Private. Nonprofit. **Spons:** LADACIN Network.

A branch of the LADACIN Network, this year-round educational program serves children and adults with developmental and multiple physical disabilities. Training and vocational preparation are elements of the program.

THE LEWIS SCHOOL AND THE LEWIS CLINIC FOR EDUCATIONAL THERAPY
Day — Coed Ages 5 and up
Clinic: All Ages. M-S 9-5.

Princeton, NJ 08540. 53 Bayard Ln.
Tel: 609-924-8120. Fax: 609-924-5512.
www.lewisschool.org
Marsha Gaynor Lewis, MA, Dir.
  Focus: Spec Ed. Treatment. **Conditions:** Primary—ADD ADHD Dx LD. **IQ 100 and up.**
  Col Prep. Gr K-Col. Courses: Read Math Lang_Arts Sci Hist.
  Therapy: Lang Speech.
  Enr: 150. **Staff:** 37 (Full 31, Part 6).
  Est 1974. Private. Nonprofit.

The Lewis Clinic evaluates and educates individuals with dyslexia. Diagnostic and educational testing services, evaluation of speech pathology, and early childhood screening are available at the facility. The school educates its students in a small, structured classroom setting within a regular school. Study skills instruction complements other academic courses. Faculty members provide personal support in helping students deal with frustration accompanying dyslexia.

High school seniors and college students are offered a demanding course of study. The usual duration of the program is two to three years, with most students going on to public and private schools and colleges. A five-week summer program emphasizes the development of language retraining.

LORD STIRLING SCHOOL

Day — Coed Ages 9-20

Basking Ridge, NJ 07920. 190 Lord Stirling Rd, PO Box 369.
Tel: 908-766-1786. Fax: 908-766-9443.
Joseph E. Gorga, MA, Dir. **Melanie North,** Adm.
  Focus: Spec Ed. **Conditions:** Primary—ED. Sec—ADD ADHD BD Dx LD.
  Gen Acad. Ungraded. Courses: Read Math Lang_Arts.
  Therapy: Speech. **Psychotherapy:** Group Indiv.
  Enr: 50. Day Males 45. Day Females 5. **Staff:** 22 (Full 20, Part 2). Educ 14.
  Admin 3.
  Rates 2003: Day $47,700/sch yr.
  Est 1964. Private. Nonprofit.

Lord Stirling provides a special learning environment for mildly to severely disturbed children, with the goal of mainstreaming. Both individual and group psychotherapy and speech therapy are provided in the program. Parental participation is encouraged. The usual length of treatment is one to three years.

MARIE H. KATZENBACH SCHOOL FOR THE DEAF

Res and Day — Coed Ages Birth-21

Trenton, NJ 08625. PO Box 535.
Tel: 609-530-3100. TTY: 609-530-6620. Fax: 609-530-5791.
www.mksd.org   E-mail: mapmksd@aol.com
Dennis P. Russell, Supt. **Margaret Provost,** Adm.
  Focus: Spec Ed. **Conditions:** Primary—D. Sec—Anx Asp B BD CD CP Db
  DS ED Ep LD Mood MR OCD ON PDD TS. **IQ 65 and up.**
  Col Prep. Gen Acad. Pre-Voc. Voc. Gr PS-12. Courses: Read Math Lang_
  Arts Sci Soc_Stud Health. Man_Arts & Shop. Shelt_Workshop. On-Job
  Trng.
  Therapy: Art Dance Lang Movement Speech. **Psychotherapy:** Group Indiv.
  Enr: 225. **Staff:** 94. Educ 64. Admin 9.
  Rates 2003: Res $36,000-98,000/sch yr. Day $29,000-60,000/sch yr.
  Summer Prgm: Day. Educ. Rec. Day Rate $500. 4 wks.
  Est 1883. State. Nonprofit.

Open only to New Jersey residents, this school provides a complete academic, vocational and social program for children who are deaf. Group and individual counseling,

New Jersey 629

various therapies and special courses in deaf culture are available. Services are also offered to a limited number of children who are deaf and blind.

MATHENY SCHOOL AND HOSPITAL

Res — Coed Ages 3 and up; Day — Coed 3-21

Peapack, NJ 07977. Main St.
Tel: 908-234-0011. Fax: 908-719-2137.
www.matheny.org   E-mail: admissions@matheny.org
Steven Proctor, Pres. Gabor Barabas, MD, Med Dir. Deborah Steube, Adm.
  Focus: Spec Ed. Treatment. Conditions: Primary—CP MD ON SB. Sec—B D Db MR S. IQ 40 and up.
  Pre-Voc. Ungraded. Courses: Read Math Lang_Arts. Shelt_Workshop. On-Job Trng.
  Therapy: Hear Lang Music Occup Phys Speech. Psychotherapy: Indiv.
  Enr: 68. Res Males 30. Res Females 19. Day Males 13. Day Females 6.
    Staff: 350. Educ 25.
  Rates 2003: Res $523/day. Day $333/day.
  Est 1946. Private. Nonprofit.

Founded by Walter and Marguerite Matheny, this year-round school occupies 78 acres in rural New Jersey, providing inpatient services for physically disabled children and young adults. Matheny specializes in the treatment of cerebral palsy and other neurological impairments. Clients receive a combination of services through an interdisciplinary team, including several therapies, comprehensive health care and special education. Short-term comprehensive evaluations are also available.

MERCER SPEECH AND HEARING

Clinic: All Ages. M-F 8-4:30.

Trenton, NJ 08618. 446 Bellevue Ave.
Tel: 609-394-4176. Fax: 609-394-4642.
www.capitalhealth.org/medical_services/speech_pathology.html
  Conditions: Primary—S.
  Therapy: Hear Lang Speech.
  Est 1963. Private. Nonprofit.

THE MIDLAND SCHOOL

Day — Coed Ages 5-21

North Branch, NJ 08876. Readington Rd, PO Box 5026.
Tel: 908-722-8222. Fax: 908-722-6203.
www.midlandschool.org   E-mail: info@midlandschool.org
Philip M. Gartlan, MA, Exec Dir. Barbara Barker, Adm.
  Focus: Spec Ed. Conditions: Primary—ADD ADHD Asp Dc Dx LD MR S.

Sec—Apr As B Bl CP D Db ED Ep Mood OCD ON Psy PW SB TS. **IQ 50-100.**

Gen Acad. Pre-Voc. Ungraded. Courses: Read Math Lang_Arts Sci Soc_Stud Studio_Art Music ADL Adaptive_Phys_Ed. Man_Arts & Shop. Shelt_Workshop. On-Job Trng.

Therapy: Lang Occup Speech. **Psychotherapy:** Group Indiv Parent.

Enr: 244. Day Males 160. Day Females 84. **Staff:** 122. (Full 122). Prof 47. Educ 37. Admin 6.

Private. Nonprofit.

This private rehabilitation center serves the special educational needs of children with learning disabilities, communicative disorders or maladaptive behavior. Midland provides early delineation of problems and careful planning to help these children develop their abilities and work to educational potential.

Midland teaches the child to compensate for his or her special need, to overcome learning difficulties and to discover new capabilities. Counseling is offered to students and their parents and emphasis is placed on the development of the whole child. The school also provides a comprehensive career education program, as well as job training and placement services.

MIDWAY SCHOOL

Day — Coed Ages 5-21

Lumberton, NJ 08048. 111 Municipal Dr, PO Box 587.
Tel: 609-267-5366. Fax: 609-267-5433.
Charles B. Hawn, Jr., Dir.

Conditions: Primary—LD S.

Gen Acad. Pre-Voc. Gr K-12. Courses: Read Math Lang_Arts. Man_Arts & Shop.

Therapy: Lang Occup Phys Speech.

Est 1975. Private. Nonprofit. **Spons:** Learning Disabilities Society.

MILLBURN REGIONAL DAY SCHOOL

Day — Coed Ages 3-21

Millburn, NJ 07041. Spring & Willow Sts.
Tel: 973-376-9430. Fax: 973-912-8887.
www.bergen.org/spserv/millburn.html
June Zabchin, Prgm Dir.

Focus: Spec Ed. **Conditions:** Primary—D MR. Sec—Au Bl CP. **IQ 0-60.**

Pre-Voc. Voc. Ungraded. Courses: Read Math Lang_Arts Studio_Art Music Adaptive_Phys_Ed. Shelt_Workshop. On-Job Trng.

Therapy: Hear Lang Occup Phys Speech. **Psychotherapy:** Group Parent.

Enr: 105. Day Males 60. Day Females 45. **Staff:** 41 (Full 34, Part 7).

Rates 2004: No Fee.

Est 1968. County. Nonprofit.

Operated by the Bergen County Special Services School District, MRDS provides a comprehensive academic, vocational and functional curriculum for deaf and hearing-impaired pupils with multiple disabilities. The school combines its curriculum with an intensive therapy program featuring speech, physical and occupational therapies. Programming promotes independence and seeks to help students achieve to potential. Underlying all school services is an emphasis on total communication: namely, sign language, augmentative communication and assistive computer technology.

MONTCLAIR STATE COLLEGE PSYCHOEDUCATIONAL CENTER

Day — Coed Ages Birth-12
Clinic: All Ages. M-F 9-5.

Upper Montclair, NJ 07043. 1Normal Ave.
Tel: 973-655-4357. Fax: 973-655-5155.
http://cehs.montclair.edu/academic/psychcenter
Antoinette Spiotta, Dir.
   Conditions: Primary—LD S.
   Therapy: Lang Speech.
   State.

MONTGOMERY ACADEMY

Day — Coed Ages 5-21

Gladstone, NJ 07934. PO Box 710.
Tel: 908-234-2840. Fax: 908-234-2817.
Helene Magno, Supv.
   Focus: Spec Ed. **Conditions:** Primary—ADD ADHD Ap Asp Bu Dc Dg Dx LD Mood OCD PDD PTSD PW S SP Sz TS. **IQ 80 and up.**
   Col Prep. Gen Acad. Pre-Voc. Gr K-12. Courses: Read Math Lang_Arts.
   Psychotherapy: Group.
   Private.

MORRISTOWN MEMORIAL HOSPITAL CENTER FOR HUMAN DEVELOPMENT

Clinic: All Ages. M-F 8-5.

Morristown, NJ 07960. 100 Madison Ave.
Tel: 973-971-5000. Fax: 973-290-7164.
Kathleen Selvaggi-Fadden, MD, Dir.
   Focus: Treatment. **Conditions:** Primary—Ap BI CP Dx Ep LD MD MR ON S SB.
   Therapy: Hear Lang Occup Phys Speech. **Psychotherapy:** Fam Group

Indiv.
Est 1986. Private. Nonprofit. **Spons:** Atlantic Health System.

This regional center provides a wide array of evaluation and treatment services for the developmentally disabled, including a neonatal follow-up program that monitors the development of high-risk infants; a child development center that provides evaluations and ongoing treatment; an early intervention program that serves at-risk infants up to age 3; a mental health and behavioral team that offers psychiatric and behavioral services; and a developmental disabilities center that offers comprehensive health care and dental services to local developmentally disabled individuals. In addition, the center provides case management services for families of handicapped and high-risk children in Morris County.

MOUNT SAINT JOSEPH CHILDREN'S CENTER

Res — Males Ages 6-14

Totowa, NJ 07512. 124 Shepherds Ln.
Tel: 973-595-5720. Fax: 973-595-1930.
Sr. Dorothy Sheahan, PhD, Dir. **Jill Pringle,** Adm.
  Focus: Treatment. **Conditions:** Primary—BD CD ED Mood. Sec—ADD ADHD OCD PTSD. **IQ 80 and up.**
  Gen Acad. Ungraded. Courses: Read Math Lang_Arts.
  Therapy: Milieu Speech. **Psychotherapy:** Fam Group Indiv.
  Enr: 42. Res Males 42. **Staff:** 62 (Full 49, Part 13).
  Rates 2004: No Fee.
  Est 1972. Private. Nonprofit. **Spons:** Catholic Family & Community Services.

MSJ combines a nonsectarian, residential treatment facility with an on-site special education school for children classified with emotional or behavioral problems. The center provides for the therapeutic and educational needs of the boys, while also offers counseling and support for their families.

The center's clinical division includes a psychiatric consultant, psychological services, clinical social workers, medical consultants and nurses.

NEW BRIDGE SERVICES

Clinic: All Ages. M-F 9-5; Eves T Th 5-9.

Pompton Plains, NJ 07444. 21 Evans Pl.
Tel: 973-839-2520. Fax: 973-616-0447.
www.newbridge.org   E-mail: cnaughton@newbridge.org
  Conditions: Primary—BD ED.
  Therapy: Play. **Psychotherapy:** Fam Indiv.
  Est 1963. Private. Nonprofit.

NEW LISBON DEVELOPMENTAL CENTER

Res — Coed Ages 13 and up

New Lisbon, NJ 08064. Rte 72, PO Box 130.
Tel: 609-726-1000. Fax: 609-726-1159.
www.peoplefirstnurses.nj.gov/newlisbon.htm
Focus: Rehab. Treatment. Conditions: Primary—BI MR OH. Sec—ADD
ADHD Ap B BD CP D Dx ED Ep LD MS OCD S SB Sz. IQ 2-79.
Gen Acad. Pre-Voc. Voc. Ungraded. Courses: Read Math Lang_Arts.
Shelt_Workshop. On-Job Trng.
Therapy: Chemo Hear Lang Occup Phys Speech. Psychotherapy: Group
Indiv.
Enr: 554.
Est 1914. State. Nonprofit.

This institution, accepting mentally retarded persons with concomitant handicaps, offers an inclusive program of rehabilitation and medical, psychological, psychiatric, remedial and educational services. Lifetime care is provided for individuals who cannot be returned to the community. Fees are based on the ability to pay.

NEWGRANGE SCHOOL

Day — Coed Ages 8-18

Trenton, NJ 08629. 526 South Olden Ave.
Tel: 609-584-1800. Fax: 609-430-3030.
www.thenewgrange.org   E-mail: info@thenewgrange.org
Gordan Sherman, PhD, Exec Dir.
Focus: Spec Ed. Conditions: Primary—LD. Sec—Dx S. IQ 90 and up.
Col Prep. Gen Acad. Gr 2-PG. Courses: Read Math Lang_Arts Computers
Study_Skills. Man_Arts & Shop.
Therapy: Lang Occup Speech. Psychotherapy: Indiv.
Enr: 85. Day Males 59. Day Females 26. Staff: 32.
Est 1977. Private. Nonprofit.

Newgrange provides individualized instruction in the basic skill areas, preparing students for return to a traditional school setting.

NORTH JERSEY DEVELOPMENTAL CENTER

Res — Coed All Ages

Totowa, NJ 07511. 169 Minisink Rd, PO Box 169.
Tel: 973-256-1700. Fax: 973-256-7651.
www.state.nj.us/humanservices/ddd/developcenters.html
Conditions: Primary—MR. IQ 0-83.
Gen Acad. Ungraded. Shelt_Workshop.
Therapy: Chemo Hear Lang Occup Phys Speech. Psychotherapy: Indiv.
Est 1928. State. Nonprofit.

OCEAN MENTAL HEALTH SERVICES

Res — Coed Ages 11-17; Day — Coed 12-25

Bayville, NJ 08721. 160 Rte 9.
Tel: 732-349-5550. Fax: 732-349-0841.
www.ochd.org/resourcedir/omhpd.htm
   Conditions: Primary—BD ED.
   Gen Acad. Pre-Voc. Gr 6-12. Courses: Read Math Lang_Arts.
   Therapy: Art Recreational. **Psychotherapy:** Fam Group Indiv.
   Est 1959. Private. Nonprofit.

PASSAIC COUNTY ELKS
CEREBRAL PALSY TREATMENT CENTER

Day — Coed Ages 3-21

Clifton, NJ 07011. 1481 Main Ave.
Tel: 973-772-2600. Fax: 973-772-5171.
www.passaiccountyelkscpc.org
   E-mail: cphslab@passaiccountyelkscpc.org
William Weiss, EdD, Exec Dir.
   Focus: Treatment. **Conditions:** Primary—Bl CP IP MD MS ON SB. Sec—
      Ap As Au B C D Dx LD MR S. **IQ 25-100.**
   Pre-Voc. Ungraded. Courses: Read Math Lang_Arts Sci Soc_Stud Life_
      Skills. Man_Arts & Shop. Shelt_Workshop. On-Job Trng.
   Therapy: Art Hear Lang Music Occup Phys Speech. **Psychotherapy:** Indiv.
   Enr: 200. Day Males 120. Day Females 80. **Staff:** 200 (Full 160, Part 40).
      Prof 94. Educ 31. Admin 12.
   Rates 2003: Day $47,000/sch yr. State Aid.
   Summer Prgm: Day. Educ. Rec. Ther.
   Est 1947. Private. Nonprofit. **Spons:** Passaic County Elks.

Admitting residents of Northern New Jersey, this center operates almost exclusively for children with multiple disabilities. The center utilizes microcomputer technology for the treatment of severely physically handicapped and speech-impaired individuals. Personal and parental counseling are available. A comprehensive elementary and high school program are offered.

PINELAND LEARNING CENTER

Day — Coed Ages 5-21

Rosenhaym, NJ 08352. PO Box 389.
Tel: 609-451-9363. Fax: 609-451-7186.
Frederick W. Eccleston, MA, Exec Dir.
   Focus: Spec Ed. **Conditions:** Primary—ADD AN Anx Asp BD Bu CD Dx
      ED Mood OCD Sz TS. Sec—Ap As Au Bl C CP D Db DS Ep MR. **IQ 50
      and up.**

Gen Acad. Ungraded. Courses: Read Math Lang_Arts Agriculture Mar_Sci Computer Soc_Stud. On-Job Trng.
Therapy: Lang Speech.
Enr: 108. Day Males 93. Day Females 15. **Staff:** 44 (Full 42, Part 2). Prof 23. Admin 4.
Rates 2003: Day $32,191/sch yr.
Est 1980. Private. Inc.

Enrolling primarily students with emotional or behavioral problems, Pineland conducts a highly structured program at both elementary and secondary levels. The instructional program covers all academic areas and also features a comprehensive computer lab, a marine science program and an agricultural/horticultural program.

PRINCETON CHILD DEVELOPMENT INSTITUTE

Res — Coed Ages 7 and up; Day — Coed 2 and up

Princeton, NJ 08540. 300 Cold Soil Rd.
Tel: 609-924-6280. Fax: 609-924-4119.
www.pcdi.org   E-mail: info@pcdi.org
Lynn E. McClannahan, PhD, Co-Dir. **Patricia J. Krantz,** PhD, Co-Dir.
  Focus: Spec Ed. Treatment. **Conditions:** Primary—Au.
  Gen Acad. Pre-Voc. Voc. Ungraded. Courses: Read Math Lang_Arts. On-Job Trng.
  Therapy: Lang Speech. **Psychotherapy:** Fam Indiv.
  Enr: 40. Res Males 10. Res Females 2. Day Males 15. Day Females 13.
    Staff: 51. Educ 46. Admin 5.
  Summer Prgm: Day. Ther.
  Est 1971. Private. Nonprofit.

The institute designs individualized education and treatment programs for autistic children and provides group home living as well. These programs are developed to encourage the acquisition of reading, math and language arts skills. Psychological and language therapies and home programming are available to enable parents to serve as tutors and therapists. Summer school scholarships are available on a limited basis.

RANCH HOPE

Res and Day — Males Ages 9-16½, Females 14-17

Alloway, NJ 08001. Sawmill Rd, PO Box 325.
  Nearby locations: Williamstown.
Tel: 856-935-1555. Fax: 856-935-5189.
www.ranchhope.org   E-mail: info@ranchhope.org
Rev. David L. Bailey, Exec Dir. **John Dickinson,** Adm.
  Focus: Spec Ed. Treatment. **Conditions:** Primary—ED. Sec—BD CD OCD. IQ 65-125.
  Gen Acad. Pre-Voc. Ungraded. Courses: Read Math Lang_Arts. Man_Arts & Shop.
  Therapy: Speech. **Psychotherapy:** Fam Group Indiv.

Summer Prgm: Day. Educ. Rec. Ther. 6 wks.
Est 1964. Private. Nonprofit.

Ranch Hope is a treatment-oriented home for emotionally disturbed adolescents. The boys' residential treatment center, which is located on the Alloway campus, serves young men experiencing severe emotional or behavioral problems. On a seperate campus in Williamstown, Victory House is a group home for girls, providing academics, couseling and behavior modification. The behavior modification system guides teens toward positive behaviors in their cottages and school. After consistently demonstrating a positive behavior pattern, the child leaves the point system, receiving responsibilities and privileges.

Academic and shop programs are emphasized during the regular school session, and they include history, music, science and four shops: wood, auto, career opportunities and food services. The entire school program is student-project oriented, with an emphasis on hands-on activities. Socialization is stressed during the six-week summer session. Self-confidence and group support are the goals of the outdoor education program, based on the concepts of Outward Bound.

RARITAN BAY MENTAL HEALTH CENTER

Clinic: All Ages. M-F 8:30-4:15; Eves T-Th 4:15-9.

Perth Amboy, NJ 08861. 570 Lee St.
Tel: 732-442-1666. Fax: 732-442-9512.
www.co.middlesex.nj.us/raritanbay
Laurie R. Sneider, MSW, Exec Dir. **Barbara Norris,** LCSW, Clin Dir. **Arnold Jacques,** MD, Med Dir.
Focus: Treatment. **Conditions:** Primary—BD ED. Sec—BI Dx LD MR.
Psychotherapy: Fam Group Indiv Parent.
Staff: 56 (Full 47, Part 9).
Est 1971. County. Nonprofit.

A comprehensive community mental health center, this clinic offers psychiatric evaluations, psychological testing and treatment for children and adults. Fees are determined along a sliding scale. Prospective clients must be residents of Middlesex County.

ROCK BROOK SCHOOL

Day — Coed Ages 5-12
Clinic: Ages Birth-12. M-F 9-6.

Skillman, NJ 08558. 109 Orchard Rd.
Tel: 908-431-9500. Fax: 908-431-9503.
www.rock-brook.org   E-mail: info@rock-brook.org
Mary Caterson, MS, Dir. **Joan Fenster,** MS, Educ Dir.
Focus: Spec Ed. **Conditions:** Primary—ADD ADHD Ap Au D Dx LD ON S. Sec—As CP Ep MD MR SB.
Gen Acad. Ungraded. Courses: Read Math Lang_Arts.
Therapy: Lang Movement Occup Speech. **Psychotherapy:** Parent.
Enr: 70. Day Males 50. Day Females 20. **Staff:** 35 (Full 30, Part 5).

Est 1974. Private. Nonprofit.

Rock Brook takes a team-teaching approach to the treatment of children with language and learning deficits. The school's program offers speech and language remediation, as well as help with academic skills. Outpatient services are available, and the usual duration of treatment is three school years.

THE RUGBY SCHOOL AT WOODFIELD

Day — Coed Ages 5-21

Wall, NJ 07719. Belmar Blvd & Woodfield Ave, PO Box 1403.
Tel: 732-681-6900. Fax: 732-681-4867.
www.rugbyschool.org   E-mail: generalinfo@rugbyschool.org
Donald J. DeSanto, MA, Exec Dir. **Anthony Aquilino,** MEd, Dir. **Rose Snyder,** MA, Prin. **Ed Vidal,** MD, Med Dir.
   Focus: Spec Ed. **Conditions:** Primary—ADD ADHD Anx Asp Dg Dx ED LD Mood OCD ODD PDD PTSD SP TS. Sec—OH. **IQ 60 and up.**
   Col Prep. Gen Acad. Pre-Voc. Voc. Gr 1-12. Courses: Read Math Lang_ Arts Sci Environ_Sci Studio_Art Photog Music Drama. On-Job Trng.
   Therapy: Art Music Occup Recreational Speech. **Psychotherapy:** Fam Group Indiv Parent.
   Enr: 100. Day Males 74. Day Females 26. **Staff:** 70 (Full 55, Part 15).
   Rates 2004: Day $45,720/sch yr.
   Summer Prgm: Day. Educ. Rec. Ther. Day Rate $7700. 6 wks.
   Est 1977. Private. Nonprofit.

Through an intensive academic program, individualized counseling and a structured environment, the Rugby School provides comprehensive academic and vocational programs for young people of normal intelligence with special needs. Specific programs focus upon college preparation, cooperative trade and industry, office occupation, career exploration and health services. Other services include behavior management and full clinical services.

The school maintains small, structured classes to help students develop necessary life and interpersonal skills while they prepare for college or the work force. Faculty tailor instruction to each student's skills, needs and capabilities. The curriculum features specialized programs in photography, music, art, drama, environmental science, ornamental horticulture, creative writing, journalism, cosmetology, comprehensive behavior management and art therapy, as well as workshops, lectures, hands-on activities and one-on-one tutoring sessions. Rugby's summer program admits only currently enrolled students. **See Also Page 1049**

ST. JOHN OF GOD COMMUNITY SERVICES

Day — Coed All Ages

Westville, NJ 08093. 1145 Delsea Dr.
Tel: 856-848-4700. Fax: 856-384-1512.
www.sjogcs.org
   Conditions: Primary—MR.

Pre-Voc. Courses: Read Math Lang_Arts. Man_Arts & Shop. Shelt_Workshop.
Therapy: Hear Lang Occup Phys Speech. **Psychotherapy:** Fam Group Indiv.
Est 1969. Private. Nonprofit.

ST. JOSEPH'S SCHOOL FOR THE BLIND

Res — Coed Ages 5-21; Day — Coed 3-21

Jersey City, NJ 07306. 253 Baldwin Ave.
Tel: 201-653-0578. Fax: 201-653-4087.
www.sjsb.net   E-mail: stjosschbl@aol.com
Herbert Miller, MS, Admin. **Dennis Cruz,** EdM, MSEd, Prin.
  Focus: Spec Ed. **Conditions:** Primary—B. Sec—ADHD As BI C CP Ep LD MR ON S.
  Pre-Voc. Voc. Ungraded. Courses: Read Math Lang_Arts ADL. On-Job Trng.
  Therapy: Hear Music Occup Phys Speech. **Psychotherapy:** Fam Indiv.
  Enr: 63. Res Males 7. Res Females 4. Day Males 28. Day Females 24.
    Staff: 51 (Full 45, Part 6). Educ 29. Admin 9.
  Rates 2004: No Fee.
  Summer Prgm: Res & Day. Rec. Pre-Voc. 4 wks.
  Est 1900. Private. Nonprofit.

Multi-handicapped blind children in the New Jersey area take part in the educational program and receive the training necessary for them to achieve to potential. The basic curriculum addresses language development, Activities of Daily Living, sensorimotor skills, prevocational skills, and personal and social skills.

ST. PATRICK'S SCHOOL

Day — Coed Ages 5-12

West Orange, NJ 07052. 100 Valley St.
Tel: 973-325-4400.
www.ccsnewark.org
Robert Baroska, MEd, MA, Prin.
  Focus: Spec Ed. **Conditions:** Primary—ADD ADHD BD CD ED. **IQ 70-100.**
  Gen Acad. Pre-Voc. Ungraded. Courses: Read Math Lang_Arts.
  Therapy: Occup Speech. **Psychotherapy:** Group Indiv Parent.
  Enr: 59. Day Males 50. Day Females 9. **Staff:** 29 (Full 25, Part 4).
  Est 1964. Private. Nonprofit. **Spons:** Catholic Community Services.

St. Patrick's seeks to help students reach an age-appropriate development, then return them to their home schools with adequate behavioral, social, academic and emotional coping skill levels. The program features structure, incremental learning, corrective feedback and small classes of no more than eight students.

SEARCH DAY PROGRAM

Res — Males Ages 21 and up; Day — Coed 3-21

Ocean, NJ 07712. 73 Wickapecko Dr.
Tel: 732-531-0454. Fax: 732-531-5934.
http://members.aol.com/searchday   E-mail: searchday@aol.com
Katherine Solana, MA, Exec Dir.
  Focus: Spec Ed. Conditions: Primary—Au PDD.
  Gen Acad. Pre-Voc. Ungraded. Courses: Read Math Lang_Arts Adaptive_
    Phys_Ed. Man_Arts & Shop. Shelt_Workshop. On-Job Trng.
  Therapy: Lang Occup Speech. Psychotherapy: Fam Group Indiv.
  Enr: 60.
  Rates 2003: No Fee.
  Est 1971. Private. Nonprofit.

SEARCH is a multiservice agency (school, adult activities and group home) that
provides comprehensive year-round services for individuals with autism, beginning with
preschool-age programs and running through adulthood. A favorable staff-client ratio is
a characteristic of all services.

Speech and language therapy, adaptive physical education, occupational therapy,
behavioral support, daily living skills and transitional planning, job coaching, community work programs, swimming, computer programs, community opportunities, musical
activities, home training, outreach and consultations, and consulting psychologist and
psychiatrist are all available through the agency.

SINAI SPECIAL NEEDS INSTITUTE

Day — Coed Ages 5-21

Teaneck, NJ 07666. 1650 Palisade Ave.
Tel: 201-833-9220. Fax: 201-833-8772.
www.sinaiinstitute.org   E-mail: mail@sinaiedu.org
Laurette Rothwachs, MS, Dean.
  Focus: Spec Ed. Conditions: Primary—ADD ADHD Asp Au Dc Dg DS Dx
    MR PDD. Sec—AN Anx Ap Apr As BD Bl Bu C CD CP D Db ED Ep IP
    MD Mood MS Nf OCD ON PTSD S SB SP TB TS. IQ 60 and up.
  Col Prep. Gen Acad. Pre-Voc. Voc. Gr K-12. Courses: Read Math Lang_
    Arts.
  Therapy: Lang Occup Speech. Psychotherapy: Group Indiv.
  Enr: 120. Day Males 65. Day Females 55. Staff: 83 (Full 71, Part 12). Prof
    73. Admin 10.
  Rates 2004: Day $34,500/sch yr. Schol avail.
  Est 1982. Private. Nonprofit. Orthodox Jewish.

Sinai's programs address the educational, psychological and emotional needs of
Jewish children and young adults with learning disabilities of varying severity. Whenever possible, students are mainstreamed into traditional school classes for a portion of
the day.

THE SISTER GEORGINE SCHOOL

Day — Coed Ages 5-21

Trenton, NJ 08611. 544 Chestnut Ave.
Tel: 609-396-5444. Fax: 609-396-0989.
www.srgeorgineschool.org   E-mail: srgeorgine@aol.com
Sr. Barbara Furst, BS, MA, Prin.
  Focus: Spec Ed. **Conditions:** Primary—ADHD CP DS Dx MR OH. Sec—
    Ap As Au Bl. **IQ 25-55.**
  Voc. Ungraded. Courses: Read Math Lang_Arts. Shelt_Workshop. On-Job
    Trng.
  Therapy: Lang Occup Phys Speech.
  Enr: 18. Day Males 7. Day Females 11. **Staff:** 12. Prof 11. Admin 1.
  Rates 2003: Day $27,000/sch yr. State Aid.
  Est 1969. Private. Nonprofit. Roman Catholic.

Boys and girls with developmental disabilities follow a specially designed curriculum that emphasizes the following: readiness skills, functional academics, life skills, transitional planning, and prevocational and work skills. Class size ranges from four to nine students, and each classroom features both a special education teacher and a full-time teacher assistant. Enrichment opportunities include art, computers, library skills, music, gardening, Special Olympics and field trips. Speech/language, physical and occupational therapies are available.

SOMERSET HILLS

Res and Day — Males Ages 7-14

Middlesex, NJ 08846. 1275 Bound Brook Rd, Ste 1.
Tel: 732-764-8800. Fax: 732-764-8808.
www.somersethillsrtc.org   E-mail: info@somersethillsrtc.org
Jerome P. Amedeo, Exec Dir. **Frank Soltesz,** Adm.
  Focus: Spec Ed. Treatment. **Conditions:** Primary—ADD ADHD Anx Asp
    BD CD ED LD Mood OCD ODD ON PDD Psy PTSD TS. Sec—As Bl Db
    Dc Dg Dx Ep HIV S. **IQ 70-120.**
  Gen Acad. Ungraded. Courses: Read Math Lang_Arts Sci Soc_Stud
    Studio_Art.
  Therapy: Chemo Milieu Occup Phys Play Recreational Speech. **Psycho-
    therapy:** Fam Indiv.
  Enr: 109. Res Males 76. Day Males 33. **Staff:** 145 (Full 123, Part 22).
  Rates 2004: Res $508/day. Day $291/day.
  Summer Prgm: Res. Rec. Ther. 8 wks.
  Est 1971. Private. Inc.

This organization operates two facilities for boys with behavioral disabilities: Somerset Hills Residential Treatment Center, which provides 24-hour care and supervision, and Somerset Hills School, which provides day treatment and schooling.

The residential program includes on-site health services and arrangements for specialized medical care. The school formulates an Individual Educational Plan for each student geared to age-level functioning, maturity and specific learning style. In addition to traditional course work, the school offers counseling and speech/language and occupational therapy. An Orton-Gillingham multisensory remedial reading program is also available to pupils with a language-based reading disability. Residents at Somerset Hills attend a compulsory recreational summer camp.

SUMMIT SPEECH SCHOOL
Day — Coed Ages Birth-5

New Providence, NJ 07974. 705 Central Ave.
Tel: 908-508-0011. TTY: 908-508-0011. Fax: 908-508-0012.
www.summitspeech.com   E-mail: info@summitspeech.com
Pamela A. Paskowitz, PhD, Exec Dir.
   Focus: Spec Ed. **Conditions:** Primary—D.
   Gen Acad. Gr PS. Courses: Read Math Lang_Arts Music.
   Therapy: Hear Lang Occup Phys Speech. **Psychotherapy:** Fam Group
      Indiv.
   Enr: 115. Day Males 60. Day Females 55. **Staff:** 43 (Full 24, Part 19).
   Rates 2003: Day $19,440/sch yr. Schol avail. State Aid.
   Est 1967. Private. Nonprofit. **Spons:** F. M. Kirby Center.

Hearing-impaired students at the Summit receive speech, language, speech reading and auditory training within a nursery school program that employs the auditory-oral method. Pupils at the school do not use sign language. Children too young for the preschool program may participate in a parent-infant early intervention program. Parents also learn how to instill oral skills at home. Nursery school activities include art and music classes, gym and field trips.

THE TITUSVILLE ACADEMY
Day — Coed Ages 5-18

Titusville, NJ 08560. 86 River Dr.
Tel: 609-737-7733. Fax: 609-737-3343.
www.titusac.org   E-mail: titusinfo@titusac.org
Deborah R. Zerbib, Dir.
   Focus: Spec Ed. **Conditions:** Primary—ADD ADHD BD Dx ED LD.
   Col Prep. Gen Acad. Pre-Voc. Gr K-12. Courses: Read Math Lang_Arts
      Computers Sci Soc_Stud Studio_Art Study_Skills.
   Therapy: Speech. **Psychotherapy:** Indiv Parent.
   Enr: 96. **Staff:** 32 (Full 30, Part 2).
   Est 1971. Private.

Titusville provides a highly structured, individualized, noncompetitive academic environment for students with learning and behavioral difficulties. The academy also offers clinical services in an effort to integrate the students social and emotional development with the educational process.

VANTAGE HEALTH SYSTEM

Res — Males Ages 13-17
Clinic: All Ages. M-F.

Dumont, NJ 07628. 2 Park Ave.
Tel: 201-385-4400. Fax: 201-385-9689.
www.vantagenj.org   E-mail: djg@vantagenj.org
Victoria Sidrow, Pres.
   Conditions: Primary—BD ED. Sec—LD.
   Therapy: Art. **Psychotherapy:** Fam Group Indiv.
   Est 1957. Private. Nonprofit.

VOORHEES PEDIATRIC REHABILITATION SERVICES

Res and Day — Coed Ages Birth-21
Clinic: Ages Birth-20. M-F 8-6.

Voorhees, NJ 08043. 1304 Laurel Oak Rd.
Tel: 856-346-3300. Fax: 856-435-4223.
www.forkidcare.com/vprs   E-mail: info@forkidcare.com
   Focus: Rehab. **Conditions:** Primary—Ap Bl C CP Ep IP MD MS ON S SB.
      Sec—Au B BD CD D ED LD MR OCD Psy Sz.
   Therapy: Hear Lang Occup Phys Speech. **Psychotherapy:** Fam Indiv
      Parent.
   Enr: 110. **Staff:** 89 (Full 82, Part 7). Prof 67. Educ 2. Admin 20.
   Private. Inc. **Spons:** Voorhees Pediatric Facility.

This clinic offers occupational, physical, speech therapies; social work; and psychology services on a contractual basis in a variety of educational, medical and home environments. The client base comprises medically fragile and technology dependent infants, children and adolescents.

THE WINSTON SCHOOL

Day — Coed Ages 6-14

Short Hills, NJ 07078. 100 East Ln.
Tel: 973-379-4114. Fax: 973-379-3984.
www.winstonschool.org
Pamela Bloom, MEd, Head.
   Focus: Spec Ed. **Conditions:** Primary—Dx LD. Sec—ADD ADHD. **IQ 90
      and up.**
   Gen Acad. Gr 1-8. Courses: Read Math Lang_Arts Sci Soc_Stud Computers Studio_Art Music.
   Therapy: Lang Occup Speech. **Psychotherapy:** Indiv.
   Enr: 50. Day Males 36. Day Females 14. **Staff:** 22 (Full 16, Part 6).
   Est 1981. Private. Nonprofit.

The Winston School offers assessment and individualized programs to learning-disabled children of average to above-average intelligence. Emphasis on reading and related language arts skills is designed to reduce the disability. Other curricular features include math, science, art, music, computers and physical education. Instructional groups are small (two to four students) and the staff works closely with parents. When a student is ready for reentry into public or private education, usually after two or three years, counseling and assistance are given in placement.

WOODCLIFF ACADEMY

Day — Coed Ages 10-18

Wall, NJ 07753. 1345 Campus Pky.
Tel: 732-751-0240. Fax: 732-751-0243.
www.woodcliff.com   E-mail: mail@woodcliff.com
Elizabeth J. Ferraro, EdD, Supt.
> **Focus:** Spec Ed. **Conditions:** Primary—ADD ADHD Anx Asp Bl C Dc Dg Dx ED Ep LD Mood OCD ON PW S SP Sz TS. **IQ 100 and up.**
> **Col Prep. Gen Acad.** Gr 2-12. Courses: Read Math Lang_Arts Span Sci Computers Soc_Stud Studio_Art Music.
> **Therapy:** Lang Speech. **Psychotherapy:** Group Indiv.
> **Enr:** 75. Day Males 55. Day Females 20. **Staff:** 35. Prof 35. Educ 31.
> **Rates 2003:** Day $36,000/sch yr. State Aid.
> **Summer Prgm:** Day. Educ. Ther. Day Rate $3000.
> **Est 1949.** Private. Nonprofit.

This state-approved school for the handicapped serves pupils with various academic and mild emotional conditions. The academy utilizes applied cognitive behavior modification to encourage more appropriate school behavior. State school districts typically pay tuition costs. The summer program emphasizes skill enhancement and features therapeutic counseling sessions.

NEW MEXICO

ALBUQUERQUE HEARING & SPEECH LANGUAGE CENTER

Clinic: Ages 1 and up. M-F 8:30-5.

Albuquerque, NM 87106. 1011 Buena Vista Dr SE.
Tel: 505-247-4224. Fax: 505-247-1772.
E-mail: aslhc@nm.net
Deanna Earley, MS, CCC-SLP, Exec Dir. **Jackie Bader,** Adm.
Focus: Treatment. **Conditions:** Primary—ADD ADHD Ap Apr Au BI CP D
Dc Dg Dx MR S. Sec—B.
Therapy: Hear Lang Speech.
Staff: 10 (Full 8, Part 2). Prof 7.
Rates 2003: Clinic $80/hr. Schol avail.
Est 1953. Private. Nonprofit.

The center provides complete audiological assessments, hearing aid evaluations and hearing aid dispensation services for individuals with communicative disorders. Other services include a hearing aid bank for low-income adults and scholarship dispensation of children's hearing aids.

BRUSH RANCH SCHOOL

Res — Coed Ages 12-19

Tererro, NM 87573. N Hwy 63, HC 73, Box 33.
Tel: 505-757-6114. Fax: 505-757-6118.
www.brushranchschool.org   E-mail: sweisman@cybermesa.com
Kay C. Rice, MA, Head. **Suzanne Weisman,** Adm.
Focus: Spec Ed. **Conditions:** Primary—ADD ADHD Asp Db Dc Dg Dx LD.
Sec—ED Mood OCD SP TS. **IQ 85 and up.**
Gen Acad. Pre-Voc. Gr 7-12. Courses: Read Math Lang_Arts Sci Comput-
ers Soc_Stud Studio_Art Music Drama Outdoor_Ed. Man_Arts & Shop.
On-Job Trng.
Psychotherapy: Indiv.
Enr: 50. Res Males 30. Res Females 20. **Staff:** 32. (Full 32). Prof 18. Educ
7. Admin 5.
Rates 2004: Res $38,200/sch yr (+$700-800). Schol 3 ($30,000).
Est 1970. Private. Nonprofit.

Located on 283 acres in the Sangre de Cristo Range of the Rocky Mountains, Brush Ranch offers a program for students with cognitive or language-based learning differences or both. The school's objective is to develop pupils' academic, vocational and social skills. Brush Ranch's curriculum addresses the particular needs of each student.

Recreational activities include skiing and snowboarding, horseback riding, a ropes course, backpacking and swimming. The full-time residential staff coordinates evening and weekend programs.

EASTERN NEW MEXICO UNIVERSITY
SPEECH-LANGUAGE-HEARING CLINIC

Clinic: All Ages. M-F 8-5.

Portales, NM 88130. Lea Hall, Sta 3.
Tel: 505-562-2156. Fax: 505-562-2409.
www.enmu.edu
Phillip Million, Dir.
   Focus: Treatment. **Conditions:** Primary—Ap LD S.
   Therapy: Hear Lang Speech.
   State.

LAS CUMBRES LEARNING SERVICES

Res — Coed Ages 18 and up; Day — Coed All Ages

Espanola, NM 87532. 404 Hunter St, PO Box 1362.
Tel: 505-753-4123.
www.lclsinc.com/lclsabout.html
   Conditions: Primary—Au BD ED MR.
   Pre-Voc. Voc. Ungraded. Shelt_Workshop. On-Job Trng.
   Therapy: Hear Lang Occup Phys Speech. **Psychotherapy:** Fam Group
     Indiv.
   Est 1971. Private. Nonprofit.

LOS LUNAS COMMUNITY PROGRAM

Day — Coed All Ages

Los Lunas, NM 87031. 1000 Main St NW, PO Box 1269.
Tel: 505-865-9611. Fax: 505-841-5316.
   Conditions: Primary—MR. **IQ 19-69.**
   Pre-Voc.
   Therapy: Chemo Hear Lang Occup Phys Speech. **Psychotherapy:** Indiv.
   State.

MANDY'S SPECIAL FARM

Res — Females Ages 18 and up

Albuquerque, NM 87105. 346 Clark Rd SW.
Tel: 505-873-1187. Fax: 505-256-8011.
www.mandysfarm.org   E-mail: info@mandysfarm.org
Ruthie Horn Robbins, JD, Pres.
   Focus: Trng. Treatment. **Conditions:** Primary—Au.

Pre-Voc. Voc. Ungraded. Courses: Read Math Lang_Arts. Shelt_Workshop.
Therapy: Occup Phys Speech Aqua. **Psychotherapy:** Equine.
Enr: 6. Res Females 6. **Staff:** 16 (Full 1, Part 15).
Est 2000. Private. Nonprofit.

This residential facility provides education and care for women with autism. The program centers around a farm environment where the women can work and learn. Staffing consists of students working towards degrees in occupational therapy, speech and language pathology, physical therapy and nursing.

NEW MEXICO SCHOOL FOR THE DEAF

Day — Coed Ages Birth-22

Santa Fe, NM 87505. 1060 Cerrillos Rd.
Tel: 505-476-6379. Fax: 505-476-6315.
www.nmsd.k12.nm.us
Ronald Stern, Supt.
   Conditions: Primary—D. Sec—LD.
   Col Prep. Gen Acad. Pre-Voc. Voc. Gr 3-12. Courses: Read Math Lang_
      Arts. Man_Arts & Shop. On-Job Trng.
   Therapy: Occup Phys.
   Est 1887. State.

NEW MEXICO SCHOOL
FOR THE VISUALLY HANDICAPPED

Day — Coed Ages Birth-21

Alamogordo, NM 88310. 1900 N White Sands Blvd.
Tel: 505-437-3505. Fax: 505-439-4411.
www.nmsvh.k12.nm.us   E-mail: info@nmsvh.k12.nm.us
Dianna Jennings, Supt.
   Conditions: Primary—B.
   Col Prep. Gen Acad. Pre-Voc. Voc. Ungraded. Courses: Read Math Lang_
      Arts. Man_Arts & Shop. On-Job Trng.
   Est 1903. State.

NEW MEXICO SPEECH AND LANGUAGE CONSULTANTS

Clinic: All Ages. M-F 8-5.

Roswell, NM 88201. 1000 W 4th St.
Tel: 505-623-8319. Fax: 505-623-8220.
Eileen Grooms, MS, Pres.
   Focus: Treatment. **Conditions:** Primary—Ap S.
   Therapy: Lang Speech.

Staff: 9.
Private. Inc.

The clinic offers programs for individuals with speech, language, fluency and voice disorders. Length of treatment varies according to services provided.

RCI

Day — Coed Ages Birth-3
Clinic: All Ages. M-F 8-5.

Albuquerque, NM 87106. 1023 Stanford Dr NE.
Tel: 505-255-5501. TTY: 505-255-5501. Fax: 505-255-9971.
www.rci-nm.org
John Baldi, Pres. **Karen Lucero,** Prgm Dir. **Anna Lavato,** Intake.
  Focus: Treatment. **Conditions:** Primary—ADD ADHD Ap Au Bl CP Dx IP LD MD MR MS ON S SB. Sec—B D.
  Therapy: Hear Lang Occup Phys Speech. **Psychotherapy:** Indiv.
  Est 1958. Private. Nonprofit.

The facility offers early intervention, as well as diagnostic and therapy treatment services. Physical therapy incorporates neuro-developmental treatment, gait training, wheelchair evaluations, orthotic evaluations and pool therapy. Occupational therapy emphasizes the development of sensorimotor skills, visual functions, fine-motor skills, self-care skills and splinting. Speech and language therapy includes evaluations and treatment of dysphagia/feeding, fluency, voice, augmentative communication, speech and language delay, articulation, aural rehabilitation, and neurogenic speech and language disorders. Home visits are available.

In addition to its children's programs, RCI provides a host of vocational services for adults with disabilities.

SOUTHWESTERN NEW MEXICO SERVICES HELPING CHILDREN AND ADULTS

Res — Coed Ages 18 and up; Day — Coed Birth-3

Silver City, NM 88061. 907 N Pope St.
Tel: 505-388-1976. Fax: 505-538-2339.
  Conditions: Primary—Ap Au B Bl C CP D Dx Ep IP LD MD MR MS ON S SB TB.
  Voc. Man_Arts & Shop. Shelt_Workshop. On-Job Trng.
  Therapy: Hear Phys.
  Private.

UNIVERSITY OF NEW MEXICO
CARRIE TINGLEY HOSPITAL

Res — Coed Ages Birth-21
Clinic: Ages Birth-21. M-F 8-6.

Albuquerque, NM 87102. 1127 University Blvd NE.
Tel: 505-272-5335. Fax: 505-272-4232.
http://hospitals.unm.edu/cth/index.shtml
Barbara Ohm, Exec Dir. **Frederick Sherman,** MD, Med Dir. **Kimmie McKinney,** Int Adm.
  Focus: Rehab. **Conditions:** Primary—ADD ADHD Ap Apr Asp Au BI CP DS IP LD MD MS ON PDD S SB. Sec—As B BD C D Db Dc Dg Dx ED Ep HIV MR Nf PTSD PW TB.
  Therapy: Hydro Lang Occup Percepual-Motor Phys Play Recreational Speech. **Psychotherapy:** Fam Indiv Parent.
  Staff: 160. Prof 80. Educ 2. Admin 20.
  Est 1937. State. Nonprofit.

One of the University of New Mexico Hospitals, Carrie Tingley serves as the state's only inpatient rehabilitation program for children. The hospital also provides a variety of outpatient services for those with orthopedic and neurological diagnoses. Specialty clinics address traumatic brain injury, spina bifida, cerebral palsy, juvenile rheumatoid arthritis, congenital hip deformity, scoliosis, arthrogryposis, club foot, neurology, general orthopedics, specialty pediatrics, and hand, knee and sports medicine concerns.

Inpatients take part in a special education program during the school year, while outpatients may receive school placement assistance. An on-site orthotics and prosthetics shop specializes in children's needs.

UNIVERSITY OF NEW MEXICO
CHILDREN'S PSYCHIATRIC CENTER

Res and Day — Coed Ages Birth-17

Albuquerque, NM 87106. 1001 Yale Blvd NE.
Tel: 505-272-2890. Fax: 505-272-0052.
www.cph.unm.edu
  Conditions: Primary—ED.
  Gen Acad. Courses: Read Math Lang_Arts.
  Therapy: Art Occup Recreational Speech. **Psychotherapy:** Fam Group Indiv.
  Staff: Prof 53.
  Est 1978. State. Nonprofit.

UNIVERSITY OF NEW MEXICO
DEPARTMENT OF COMMUNICATIVE DISORDERS
SPEECH AND HEARING CENTER

Clinic: All Ages. M-F 8-5.

Albuquerque, NM 87131. MSC01 1195, 1 University of New Mexico.
Tel: 505-277-4453. Fax: 505-277-0968.
www.unm.edu/~sphrsci/clinic/clinic.htm
Charlotte Lough, Dir.
   Conditions: Primary—Ap Au Bl D S.
   Therapy: Hear Lang Speech. Psychotherapy: Group.
   State.

UNIVERSITY OF NEW MEXICO
DIVISION OF CHILD AND ADOLESCENT PSYCHIATRY
PROGRAMS FOR CHILDREN AND ADOLESCENTS

Clinic: Ages 2-18. M-F.

Albuquerque, NM 87131. 2400 Tucker NE.
Tel: 505-272-5002.
http://hsc.unm.edu/som/psychiatry/child/clinical.shtml
Sally Ann Torrez, Admin.
   Conditions: Primary—BD ED.
   Psychotherapy: Fam Group Indiv.
   Est 1966. Nonprofit. Spons: University of New Mexico Mental Health
   Center.

NEW YORK

THE ACHIEVEMENT CENTER

Clinic: Ages 4 and up. M-F 8:30-6:30.

Horseheads, NY 14845. 10 Ridge Rd, PO Box 315.
Tel: 607-739-3894. Fax: 607-739-3895.
Laura Satterly-Austin, BS, MS, Dir.
  Focus: Spec Ed. **Conditions:** Primary—ADD ADHD Dx LD. **IQ 75 and up.**
  Staff: 18.
  Est 1978. Private. Nonprofit.

Each student at the center follows an individualized program featuring one-on-one instruction and remediation during after-school hours. In addition to its standard academic course work, the center offers tutorial preparation for high school and college entrance examinations. Summer instruction is available, and the usual duration of treatment is one to two years.

ADELPHI UNIVERSITY
LEARNING DISABILITIES PROGRAM

Res and Day — Coed Ages 17 and up

Garden City, NY 11530. 1 South Ave, Chapman Hall, Lower Level.
Tel: 516-877-4710. Fax: 516-877-4711.
http://academics.adelphi.edu/ldprog E-mail: ldprogram@adelphi.edu
Susan Spencer, MSW, Dir.
  Focus: Spec Ed. **Conditions:** Primary—ADD ADHD Dx LD. Sec—Dc Dg.
  IQ 90 and up.
  Gen Acad. Gr Col-Col. Courses: Read Lang_Arts.
  Therapy: Lang. **Psychotherapy:** Fam Group Indiv Parent.
  Enr: 125. **Staff:** 18. (Full 18).
  Rates 2003: Day $4700/sch yr.
  Est 1979. Private.

Students with learning disabilities, ADHD or both attend regular college classes and may pursue any major in fulfillment of normal degree requirements in this program. Individualized services meet special educational, emotional and social needs. Students receive academic tutoring and individual and group counseling as needed, and equal-access accommodations are also available

ADIRONDACK LEADERSHIP EXPEDITIONS

Res — Coed Ages 13-18

Saranac, NY 12983. 82 Church St.
Tel: 518-897-5011. Fax: 518-897-5017.

www.adirondackleadership.com   E-mail: admissions@adkle.com
Paul Eugene Goddard, PhD, Exec Dir. **Jeff Johnson,** Adm.
  Focus: Treatment. **Conditions:** Primary—ADD ADHD Anx BD ED LD Mood
    ODD. Sec—AN Asp Bu CD OCD PTSD TS. **IQ 80 and up.**
  Therapy: Milieu Play Recreational. **Psychotherapy:** Fam Group Indiv.
  Enr: 27. **Staff:** 28. Prof 3. Admin 7.
  Rates 2004: Res $395/day (+$750/ses).
  Private. **Spons:** Aspen Education Group.

This intensive, short-term character development program seeks to help adolescents develop self-confidence, clarity of purpose and healthy relationships. The forested, mountain setting removes urban distractions and requires participants to acquire new skills and accept responsibility for their choices. Individualized programming, daily group processing, weekly individual and family counseling, experiential activities, written exercises and milieu groups are all part of the student's experience.

Optional psychological and educational testing is available for an additional fee.

ADVOCACY AND RESOURCE CENTER
FAMILY SERVICES DEPARTMENT

Day — Coed All Ages

Plattsburgh, NY 12901. 14 Salmon River Rd.
Tel: 518-561-2514. Fax: 518-561-2529.
  Focus: Treatment. **Conditions:** Primary—ADD ADHD Au BI CP Dx Ep LD
    MD MR MS SB. Sec—As B BD C D ED OCD S Sz TB. **IQ 0-80.**
  Staff: 12. (Full 12).
  Private. Nonprofit.

The center provides community services primarily for individuals with mental retardation. Although children may receive services, the main focus is on adults. Programming is designed to increase the client's level of independence and to promote community integration.

ALBERT EINSTEIN COLLEGE OF MEDICINE
CHILDREN'S EVALUATION AND REHABILITATION CENTER

Clinic: Ages Birth-21. M-F 8:30-6.

Bronx, NY 10461. 1410 Pelham Pky S.
Tel: 718-930-8500. Fax: 718-904-1162.
www.aecom.yu.edu/cerc   E-mail: cerc@aecom.yu.edu
Herbert J. Cohen, MD, Dir.
  Focus: Rehab. Treatment. **Conditions:** Primary—ADD ADHD Au CP D Dx
    LD MD MR ON S SB. Sec—Ep.
  Therapy: Lang Occup Phys Speech. **Psychotherapy:** Parent.
  Staff: 92 (Full 42, Part 50).
  Est 1956. Private. Nonprofit.

CERC is a regional center for the diagnosis and treatment of infants, children and adolescents with a broad range of developmental disabilities. Services including research, education, evaluation and treatment of neuromuscular disorders, mental retardation, autism, speech and language disorders, hearing impairments, learning disabilities and delays in development.

A sliding fee scale is available.

ANDERSON SCHOOL

Res and Day — Coed Ages 5-21

Staatsburg, NY 12580. 4885 Rte 9, PO Box 367.
Tel: 845-889-4034. Fax: 845-889-3104.
www.andersonschool.org   E-mail: info@andersonschool.org
Neil Pollock, BA, MS, Exec Dir. **Kate Haas,** Adm.
  Focus: Spec Ed. **Conditions:** Primary—Au. Sec—ADD ADHD Ap As Asp B BD BI C CD CP D Dx ED Ep LD MR OCD ON Psy SB Sz.
  Pre-Voc. Ungraded. Courses: Read Math Lang_Arts. Man_Arts & Shop. Shelt_Workshop. On-Job Trng.
  Therapy: Chemo Lang Occup Phys Speech. **Psychotherapy:** Indiv.
  Enr: 136. Res Males 109. Res Females 15. Day Males 8. Day Females 4.
  Staff: 450.
  Rates 2004: Res $205/day. Day $34,653/yr.
  Est 1924. Private. Nonprofit.

Anderson provides year-round educational, residential and treatment services for children and adults with autism and other developmental disabilities. The program seeks to prepare students to return to a mainstream school setting, while providing career education opportunities for pupils age 14 and up.

THE ARC
ONEIDA-LEWIS CHAPTER

Res — Coed Ages 18 and up; Day — Coed All Ages

Utica, NY 13501. 245 Genesee St.
  Nearby locations: Lowville; Turin.
Tel: 315-735-6477. Fax: 315-792-4800.
www.thearcolc.org
Angela Z. VanDerhoof, Exec Dir.
  Focus: Rehab. Trng. **Conditions:** Primary—MR. Sec—BI ED Ep S.
  Therapy: Hear Lang Occup Phys Speech.
  Summer Prgm: Day. Rec.
  Est 1954. Private. Inc. **Spons:** NYSARC.

The Arc provides several programs concerned with educating, socializing, training and rehabilitating of mentally retarded and developmentally disabled persons. Assistance is also available in utilizing community resources.

An employment training program prepares individuals with developmental disabilities ages 21 and up for employment or the workshop, with a day training program available for those who do not qualify for inclusion in the workshop program.

ASSOCIATION FOR NEUROLOGICALLY IMPAIRED BRAIN INJURED CHILDREN

Res — Coed Ages 18 and up; Day — Coed 5 and up

Bayside, NY 11360. 212-12 26th Ave.
Tel: 718-423-9550. Fax: 718-423-9838.
E-mail: info@anibic.org
Gerard Smith, Exec Dir. Christine Fisher, Intake.
  Focus: Spec Ed. Trng. Conditions: Primary—ADD ADHD Au BI CP Dx Ep LD OH. Sec—MR. IQ 45-85.
  Gen Acad. Pre-Voc. Voc. Ungraded. Courses: Read Math Lang_Arts. On-Job Trng.
  Therapy: Occup Speech. Psychotherapy: Fam Group Indiv Parent.
  Enr: 165. Res Males 20. Res Females 30. Day Males 65. Day Females 50. Staff: 125.
  Summer Prgm: Day. Rec. 7 wks.
  Est 1958. Private. Nonprofit.

ANIBIC provides individual, family, educational and job counseling, recreational programs, socialization groups, community residence placements, a summer day camp, parental support groups and tutoring. Rates vary according to services rendered.

ASSOCIATION FOR THE HELP OF RETARDED CHILDREN NEW YORK CITY

Res — Coed Ages 9 and up; Day — Coed All Ages
Clinic: All Ages. M-F 9-5; Eves M-F 5-7.

New York, NY 10003. 200 Park Ave S.
Tel: 212-780-2500. Fax: 212-777-5893.
www.ahrcnyc.org   E-mail: sbstein@ahrcnyc.org
Michael Goldfarb, Exec Dir. Susan Pincus, MD, Med Dir.
  Focus: Spec Ed. Treatment. Conditions: Primary—Au BI DS MR PDD. Sec—B BD C CD CP D ED Ep LD ON S. IQ 0-89.
  Gen Acad. Ungraded. Shelt_Workshop. On-Job Trng.
  Therapy: Hear Lang Occup Phys Recreational Speech. Psychotherapy: Fam Group Indiv Parent.
  Est 1949. Private. Nonprofit.

AHRC provides an array of programs for developmentally disabled individuals including, but not limited to the following: early intervention, preschool and school-age education, primary healthcare, vocational training, psychiatric and psychological counseling, social work services, rehabilitation, service coordination, substance abuse treatment, parent and sibling support, residential services and advocacy services.

Families of the disabled may take advantage of educational programs, counseling, support, information and referral, and advocacy services available through the organization. The association also offers recreational camping programs for children and adults with developmental disabilities.

THE ASTOR HOME FOR CHILDREN

**Res — Coed Ages 5-12; Day — Coed 2-12
Clinic: Ages Birth-18. M-F 9-5; Eves by Appt.**

Rhinebeck, NY 12572. 6339 Mill St, PO Box 5005.
Tel: 845-871-1000. Fax: 845-876-2020.
www.astorservices.org
James McGuirk, PhD, Exec Dir. **Alice A. Linder,** MD, Med Dir. **Brendan Sullivan,** Intake.

Focus: Treatment. **Conditions:** Primary—ADD ADHD Anx BD ED Mood OCD ODD PDD Psy PTSD Sz. Sec—Asp Au CD CP Dc Dg Dx Ep HIV SP TS. **IQ 60-130.**
Gen Acad. Ungraded. Courses: Read Math Lang_Arts.
Therapy: Art Chemo Lang Milieu Occup Recreational Speech. **Psychotherapy:** Fam Group Indiv Parent.
Enr: 75. **Staff:** 220 (Full 156, Part 64). Educ 111. Admin 18.
Rates 2003: Res $107-217/day. State Aid.
Summer Prgm: Res & Day. Educ. Rec. Ther.
Est 1952. Private. Nonprofit. **Spons:** Catholic Charities.

Astor offers preventive, consultative and treatment services on long- and short-term bases for emotionally disturbed and mentally ill children and families. Four child guidance centers, four day treatment centers, five head start centers, one residential treatment facility/therapeutic home program, one residential treatment center and one group home are operated.

Residential facilities provide psychiatric, psychological and family services as well as child care and other supportive services. Psychological, group, chemo and speech therapies are available. An alternative placement program includes foster care.

The Astor Learning Center offers specialized education for children in residential treatment and includes an ungraded academic program.

Astor Child Guidance Center is located at 750 Tilden St., Bronx 10467. Diagnostic screening, behavior modification, rehabilitation, and individual, family and group therapies are offered. Educational, clinical and family services are provided at the day treatment centers.

The facility's head start centers provide a developmental preschool program consisting of educational, health and social services for children from low-income families. This program features extensive parental participation.

BEHAVIORAL HEALTH SERVICES NORTH

Res — Coed Ages 4-12; Day — Coed 5-17

Plattsburgh, NY 12901. 63 Broad St.

Tel: 518-563-8000.
www.bhsn.org   E-mail: bblack@bhsn.org
Harry Cook, CEO.
   Conditions: Primary—ED. Sec—AN Anx Bu Mood.
   Gen Acad. Courses: Read Math Lang_Arts.
   Therapy: Play. **Psychotherapy:** Fam Group Indiv.
   Est 1874. Private. Nonprofit.

BETH ISRAEL MEDICAL CENTER
CHILD AND ADOLESCENT PSYCHIATRY SERVICE

Clinic: All Ages. M-F 9-5.

New York, NY 10002. 10 Nathan Perlman Pl.
Tel: 212-420-4135. Fax: 212-420-3936.
Alan Lyman, MD, Dir.
   Focus: Spec Ed. Trng. Treatment. **Conditions:** Primary—ADD ADHD Dc Dg
      Dx ED Mood OCD Psy PTSD SP Sz TS. Sec—As Au BD BI C CD CP Ep
      IP LD MD MR MS ON S SB.
   Therapy: Chemo Speech. **Psychotherapy:** Fam Group Indiv.
   Staff: 16 (Full 9, Part 7). Prof 14. Admin 2.
   Private.

The clinic provides comprehensive testing, evaluation and treatment of psychiatric
and behavioral problems, as well as services for children with learning disabilities.
Parental, personal and educational counseling is available, and the usual duration of
treatment is six months.

BLOCK INSTITUTE

Day — Coed Ages Birth-21

Brooklyn, NY 11214. 376 Bay 44th St.
Tel: 718-946-9700. Fax: 718-714-0197.
www.blockinstitute.org   E-mail: info@blockinstitute.org
Scott L. Barkin, PhD, Exec Dir. **Teresa DelPriore,** Prin.
   Focus: Spec Ed. **Conditions:** Primary—ADD ADHD Apr As Asp Au BI Db
      Dc Dg DS Dx IP LD MR ON PDD PW. Sec—Ap B C CD CP D ED Ep MD
      Mood MS OCD S SB TS. **IQ 0-45.**
   Pre-Voc. Ungraded. Courses: Read Math Lang_Arts Life_Skills. Shelt_
      Workshop.
   Therapy: Hear Hydro Lang Occup Phys Play Speech. **Psychotherapy:**
      Fam Group Indiv Parent.
   Enr: 177. Day Males 112. Day Females 65. **Staff:** 170 (Full 161, Part 9).
      Educ 135. Admin 6.
   Summer Prgm: Day. Educ. Ther.
   Est 1963. Private. Nonprofit.

The institute provides educational and therapeutic services for children and young adults diagnosed with a variety of developmental disabilities and neuromuscular disorders. A nursery program is offered to young children, and a social training program is designed for those with severe retardation or handicaps. Psychological services, as well as occupational and physical therapy, are available. The curriculum emphasizes daily living and self-help skills, and a residential program offers young adults a home setting in the community.

BROOKLYN CENTER FOR
MULTIPLE HANDICAPPED CHILDREN
CONNIE LEKAS SCHOOL

Day — Coed Ages 14-21

Brooklyn, NY 11235. P811K, 2525 Haring St.
Tel: 718-769-6984. Fax: 718-648-7816.
http://schools.nycenet.edu/d75/p811k   E-mail: 75K811@nycboe.net
Rachel Henderson, Prin.
   Focus: Spec Ed. Trng. **Conditions:** Primary—As C CP MD MR ON SB.
   Gen Acad. Ungraded. Courses: Read Math Lang_Arts.
   Therapy: Hear Occup Phys Speech. **Psychotherapy:** Indiv.
   Est 1976. Municipal.

BUFFALO STATE COLLEGE
SPEECH-LANGUAGE-HEARING CLINIC

Clinic: All Ages. M-F 8:30-4:30; Eves M-Th 4:30-7.

Buffalo, NY 14222. 1300 Elmwood Ave.
Tel: 716-878-3530. Fax: 716-878-3526.
www.buffalostate.edu/depts/speech/clinic.htm
   E-mail: joneskb@buffalostate.edu
Karen Bailey Jones, MA, Dir.
   Focus: Treatment. **Conditions:** Primary—Ap S. Sec—ADD ADHD Dx LD.
   Therapy: Hear Lang Speech.
   Staff: 7 (Full 2, Part 5).
   Rates 2004: $50 (Evaluation); $200 (Treatment)/sem. Schol avail.
   Est 1956. State. Nonprofit.

This clinic at BSC offers a wide range of speech, language and hearing services. Graduate and undergraduate students provide diagnostics and therapy under direct supervision of certified staff. Full speech and language therapies are available for children ages 3-5, as well as for school-age children and youths to supplement services provided by public schools.

In addition, the clinic provides services for adults with poststroke trauma, learning and language disabilities, mental retardation, voice problems, hearing impairments and other communicative disorders.

BURKE REHABILITATION HOSPITAL
SPEECH/LANGUAGE & AUDIOLOGY DEPARTMENT
Clinic: All Ages. M-F 8:30-4:30.

White Plains, NY 10605. 785 Mamaroneck Ave.
Tel: 914-597-2500. TTY: 914-597-2580. Fax: 914-946-0866.
www.burke.org   E-mail: web@burke.org
John J. Ryan, Exec Dir. **Marybeth Walsh,** MD, Med Dir.
   Focus: Rehab. Treatment. **Conditions:** Primary—Ap Au Bl LD ON S. Sec—
   ADD ADHD.
   Therapy: Hear Lang Speech.
   Staff: 12.
   Est 1915. Private. Nonprofit.

This department at Burke offers evaluation, diagnosis and treatment for communicative disorders associated with language, articulation, voice and fluency impairments. Clients also choose from a program for hearing-impaired preschoolers, vocational rehabilitation and a full range of consultative services.

CANTALICIAN CENTER FOR LEARNING
Day — Coed Ages Birth-21

Buffalo, NY 14214. 3233 Main St.
Tel: 716-833-5353. Fax: 716-833-0108.
www.cantalician.org
Sr. Mary Patricia Tomasik, CSSF, MS, Exec Dir. **Sr. Mary Francelita Machnica, CSSF,** Prgm Dir.
   Focus: Spec Ed. Treatment. **Conditions:** Primary—B Bl CP MR S. Sec—
   Au D. **IQ 0-65.**
   Pre-Voc. Gr PS-12. Shelt_Workshop. On-Job Trng.
   Therapy: Hear Lang Occup Phys Speech. **Psychotherapy:** Fam.
   Enr: 234. Day Males 176. Day Females 58.
   Est 1956. Private. Nonprofit. Roman Catholic.

CCL provides educational, rehabilitative and occupational services for severely and profoundly mentally retarded and multiply handicapped children. Programming features community management; functional academics; occupational, physical and speech therapy; creative arts; physical education; and home training.
   The basic instructional model uses a behavior management approach with an emphasis on training for independent living.

CAYUGA HOME FOR CHILDREN
Res — Coed Ages 11-17

Auburn, NY 13021. 101 Hamilton Ave, PO Box 865.
Tel: 315-253-5383. Fax: 315-253-7278.
www.cayugahome.org   E-mail: info@cayugahome.org

Edward Myers Hayes, MA, CEO. **Jill Stanton,** BA, Dir. **Grace Plvan,** MSW, Clin Dir.

> **Focus:** Treatment. **Conditions:** Primary—ADD ADHD AN Anx BD Bu CD Db DS SP. Sec—As BI Dx ED Ep HIV LD Mood MR OCD PTSD S TS. **IQ 70 and up.**
>
> **Gen Acad. Pre-Voc. Voc.** Gr 6-10. Courses: Read Math Lang_Arts. On-Job Trng.
>
> **Therapy:** Milieu Play Recreational Speech. **Psychotherapy:** Fam Group Indiv.
>
> **Enr:** 44. Res Males 19. Res Females 25. **Staff:** 43 (Full 32, Part 11). Prof 13. Admin 2.
>
> **Est 1852.** Private. Nonprofit.

Founded as a home for the abandoned and the orphaned, today the Cayuga Home for Children conducts a program for mildly emotionally disturbed and pre-delinquent/delinquent children. Providing structured therapy and intense casework, on campus educational program tutors are also available for those with special educational needs. Some students make the transition into community schools. The usual duration of treatment is 12 months.

THE CENTER FOR DEVELOPMENTAL DISABILITIES

Res and Day — Coed Ages 5-21

Woodbury, NY 11797. 72 S Woods Rd.
Tel: 516-921-7650. Fax: 516-364-4258.
www.centerfor.com
Nick Boba, EdD, Exec Dir.

> **Focus:** Treatment. **Conditions:** Primary—Au MR.
>
> **Voc.** On-Job Trng.
>
> **Therapy:** Art Hear Lang Music Occup Phys Recreational Speech. **Psychotherapy:** Fam Indiv.
>
> **Enr:** 107. **Staff:** 428. Educ 107. Admin 80.
>
> **Rates 2003:** No Fee.
>
> **Summer Prgm:** Res & Day. Educ. Rec. Ther.
>
> **Est 1958.** Private. Nonprofit.

The center provides treatment for children with autism or developmental or communicational disabilities. The facility provides medical, psychiatric, psychological, social, educational, remedial, rehabilitative, childcare and residential placement services.

An educational program emphasizes social and academic skills, as well as speech and language skills. The center also operates a day treatment program and residential facilities for developmentally disabled adults.

THE CENTER FOR DISCOVERY

Res — Coed Ages 5 and up; Day — Coed 3 and up

Harris, NY 12742. Benmosche Rd, PO Box 840.
Tel: 845-794-1400. Fax: 845-791-2022.

www.thecenterfordiscovery.org   E-mail: admissions@sdtc.org
Patrick Dollard, CEO. **Dennis Raymond,** Adm.
  Focus: Spec Ed. **Conditions:** Primary—ADD ADHD Au B CP D Ep MR
    OCD ON PDD SB.
  Therapy: Music Occup Phys Speech. **Psychotherapy:** Equine.
  Staff: 873 (Full 792, Part 81). Educ 143. Admin 38.
  Est 1948. Private. Nonprofit.

The center provides pediatric and adult services for individuals with developmental disabilities and multiple handicaps. The pediatric program, which begins with a pre-school for three- to five-year-olds, accommodates children and adolescents who have been diagnosed with significant disabilities such as autism, pervasive developmental disorder, cerebral palsy, mental retardation, neurological impairment and many other conditions. All students have mild to severe cognitive delays and most have significant language and social impairments. The campus setting allows children to participate year-round in seasonal outdoor, nature-based lessons.

The adult program offers a variety of residential options, designed to address individual needs, in several communities and rural settings. Residences range from apartments to five-person homes to larger, community-based intermediate care facilities (for those in need of more assistance) that implement up-to-date therapeutic interventions, medical services and assistive technologies.

CENTER FOR THE DISABLED

Res — Coed Ages 6 and up; Day — Coed All Ages
Clinic: All Ages. M-F 8:30-4:30.

Albany, NY 12208. 314 S Manning Blvd.
Tel: 518-437-5602. Fax: 518-437-5667.
  Focus: Treatment. **Conditions:** Primary—OH. Sec—CP LD MR.
  Gen Acad. Pre-Voc. Voc. Ungraded. Courses: Read Math Lang_Arts.
    Shelt_Workshop.
  Therapy: Hear Lang Occup Phys Speech. **Psychotherapy:** Group Indiv.
  Enr: 600. **Staff:** 325.
  Summer Prgm: Day. Rec. 6 wks.
  Est 1946. Private. Nonprofit. **Spons:** United Cerebral Palsy.

Limited to individuals with neurological impairments who can profit from intensive therapy and educational programs, the center's services include a diagnostic evaluation clinic for screening and diagnosis, medical services and reevaluation; social services; therapies; a dental care program; and an adaptive physical education and swimming program.

Full educational programming is available to children of school age in self-contained classrooms staffed by interdisciplinary teams of special educators and therapists. CFTD also sponsors adult and teen programs, as well as a six-week summer program conducted at Camp Patches day camp.

CENTRAL ASSOCIATION
FOR THE BLIND AND VISUALLY IMPAIRED
Day — Coed Ages 3-5
Clinic: Ages Birth-18. Th 8-4:30.

Utica, NY 13501. 507 Kent St.
Tel: 315-797-2233. Fax: 315-797-2244.
www.cabvi.org   E-mail: info@cabvi.org
Donald D. LoGuidice, MEd, Pres. **Kathy Beaver,** Adm.
   Focus: Rehab. **Conditions:** Primary—B. Sec—ADD ADHD AN Anx Ap Apr Ar As Asp Au BD Bl Bu C CD CF CP D Db Dc Dg DS Dx ED Ep HIV IP LD MD Mood MR MS Nf OCD ODD ON PDD Psy PTSD PW S SB SP Sz TB TS.
   Therapy: Movement Occup Percepual-Motor Visual. **Psychotherapy:** Fam Group Indiv Parent.
   Enr: 56. **Staff:** 6 (Full 4, Part 2). Admin 1.
   Rates 2004: No Fee.
   Summer Prgm: Day. Ther. 6 wks.
   Est 1929. Private. Nonprofit.

CABVI offers year-round low-vision examinations, visual training, orientation and mobility, and rehabilitation teaching to children in their homes and schools. In addition, school texts and related materials are available. Family and school staff involvement is necessary in determining the special needs of each child. The in-house preschool program includes mobility training, introduction to braille and self-help skills.

Clients with a visual impairment that affects their educational development are accepted regardless of other disabilities.

CENTRAL NEW YORK
DEVELOPMENTAL DISABILITIES SERVICES OFFICE
Res and Day — Coed All Ages
Clinic: All Ages. M-S 9-5.

Rome, NY 13442. 101 W Liberty St, PO Box 550.
Tel: 315-336-2300. Fax: 315-339-5456.
www.omr.state.ny.us
Stephen M. Smits, Dir. **James J. DiCastro,** MD, Med Dir.
   Focus: Treatment. **Conditions:** Primary—Au Bl CP MR. Sec—B C D ED Ep IP ON S SB. **IQ 0-35.**
   Pre-Voc. Ungraded. Shelt_Workshop. On-Job Trng.
   Therapy: Hear Lang Occup Phys Speech. **Psychotherapy:** Fam Indiv.
   Enr: 2450. **Staff:** 2867 (Full 2185, Part 682).
   Est 1854. State.

Central New York DDSO provides residential, educational and habilitative services for severely and profoundly retarded persons. The agency maintains a second office at 800 S. Wilbur Ave., and clients may receive outreach and aftercare services at Seguin Community Services, 416 W. Onondaga St., 13204. Individuals must be residents of

Onondaga, Madison, Cayuga, Oswego, Herkimer, Oneida, Lewis and Cortland counties to receive services. Fees are determined along a sliding scale.

CHILD AND ADOLESCENT TREATMENT SERVICES
Clinic: Ages Birth-21. M-F.

Buffalo, NY 14213. 3350 Main St.
Tel: 716-835-4011. Fax: 716-835-0253.
www.catswny.org
Bonnie L. Glazer, CSW, Exec Dir.
  Conditions: Primary—ED.
  Psychotherapy: Fam Group Indiv.
  Est 1937. Private. Nonprofit.

THE CHILD SCHOOL/LEGACY HIGH SCHOOL
Day — Coed Ages 5-21

Roosevelt Island, NY 10044. 587 Main St.
Tel: 212-223-5055. Fax: 212-223-5031.
www.thechildschool.org   E-mail: tcslegacy@aol.com
Maari de Souza, PhD, Exec Dir. **Sheila Steiner,** Adm.
  Focus: Spec Ed. **Conditions:** Primary—ADD ADHD Anx Ap Asp BD CD
    Dc Dg Dx ED Mood OCD PDD PTSD S SP. Sec—Apr As BI C CP Ep
    MD MS ON SB TS. **IQ 80 and up.**
  Col Prep. Gen Acad. Pre-Voc. Gr K-12. Courses: Read Math Lang_Arts Sci
    Computers Soc_Stud.
  Therapy: Lang Occup Speech. **Psychotherapy:** Indiv.
  Enr: 280. Day Males 165. Day Females 115. **Staff:** 100. Admin 8.
  Rates 2003: Day $22,874/sch yr (+$200-250). State Aid.
  Est 1973. Private. Nonprofit.

The school comprises four divisions: elementary school (grades K-6), middle school (grades 7 and 8), academy (grades 9-12) and Legacy High School (also grades 9-12). Each division addresses the progressive academic, emotional and psychological development of its students. Curricula include physical education, computer science, fine arts and music. Psychological services, speech and language therapy, and occupational therapy are available on an individual or group basis or both in all divisions.

CHILDREN'S EVALUATION AND REHABILITATION CENTER
Clinic: Ages Birth-21. M-F 8:30-5.

Bronx, NY 10461. c/o Albert Einstein College of Medicine of Yeshiva Univ,
  1410 Pelham Pky S.
Tel: 718-430-8500. Fax: 718-892-2296.

www.aecom.yu.edu/cerc   E-mail: cerc@aecom.yu.edu
Herbert J. Cohen, MD, Dir.
  Focus: Rehab. Treatment. **Conditions:** Primary—Au BI CP LD MR ON S
    SB. Sec—B D Ep MD.
  Therapy: Hear Lang Occup Phys Speech. **Psychotherapy:** Fam Group
    Indiv Parent.
  Staff: 127 (Full 64, Part 63).
  Est 1971. State.

Part of New York City's regionalized system of care for children with special needs, CERC offers diagnostic and treatment services to children with a wide range of developmental disabilities. Conditions addressed include neuromuscular disorders, mental retardation, autism, speech and language disorders, hearing impairments, learning disabilities and delays in development. Fees vary according to services provided.

CHILDREN'S HEARING INSTITUTE
Clinic: Ages 2-18. M-F 8-5.

New York, NY 10021. 310 E 14th St.
Tel: 212-614-8380. Fax: 212-614-8259.
www.childrenshearing.org   E-mail: info@childrenshearing.org
  Focus: Treatment. **Conditions:** Primary—D. Sec—LD S.
  Therapy: Hear Lang Speech. **Psychotherapy:** Indiv.
  Staff: 14.
  Est 1983. Private.

CHI offers comprehensive, differential diagnosis and treatment of profoundly deaf children. Emphasis is on cochlear implants, and the institute conducts standard and pediatric audiometric testing, neuropsychological testing, impedance audiometry, electronystagmography, hearing aid evaluations and consultations, voice restoration programs, and speech and language screening examinations. Alaryngeal voice and speech instruction, speech reading, psychometric testing and developmental evaluations are also available.

CHILDREN'S HOSPITAL OF BUFFALO
ROBERT WARNER REHABILITATION CENTER
Clinic: Ages Birth-22. M-F 9-5.

Buffalo, NY 14209. 936 Delaware Ave.
Tel: 716-888-1344. Fax: 716-888-1315.
www.chob.edu/Clinical_Services/robert_warner.html
  Conditions: Primary—ADD Au CP DS MR ON SB.
  Gen Acad. Courses: Read Math.
  Therapy: Hear Lang Occup Phys Speech. **Psychotherapy:** Fam Group
    Indiv.
  Est 1955. Private. Nonprofit.

THE CHILDREN'S SCHOOL
FOR EARLY DEVELOPMENT

Day — Coed Ages Birth-5

Hawthorne, NY 10532. 40 Saw Mill River Rd.
Tel: 914-347-3227. Fax: 914-347-4216.
www.westchesterarc.org/services/educational.html
  E-mail: fporcaro@westchesterarc.org
Frances B. Porcaro, MA, Educ Dir.
  Focus: Spec Ed. Treatment. **Conditions:** Primary—Au MR PDD. Sec—S.
  Gen Acad. Gr PS.
  Therapy: Hear Occup Phys Speech. **Psychotherapy:** Fam.
  Enr: 185. **Staff:** 40.
  Rates 2004: No Fee.
  Est 1963. Private. **Spons:** Westchester ARC.

CSED provides various services for children residing in Westchester County who have developmental delays. Center-based and inclusion classes, among them classes designed specifically for children diagnosed with PDD or autism, are tailored to the individual's particular needs. In addition, the school offers home-based services and full-inclusion parent-child groups for children from birth to age 2 and their families.

THE CHILDREN'S VILLAGE

Res — Males Ages 5-15

Dobbs Ferry, NY 10522. Echo Hills.
Tel: 914-693-0600. Fax: 914-674-1259.
www.childrensvillage.org   E-mail: slieberman@childrensvillage.org
Mona Swanson, MSW, CEO. **Douglas Waite,** MD, Med Dir. **Susan Lieber-man,** Adm.
  Focus: Treatment. **Conditions:** Primary—ADD ADHD BD ED Mood OCD ODD PTSD SP. Sec—LD TS. **IQ 51 and up.**
  Voc. On-Job Trng.
  Therapy: Hear Lang Phys Recreational Speech. **Psychotherapy:** Fam Group Indiv.
  Enr: 300. Res Males 300. **Staff:** 600.
  Summer Prgm: Res. Educ. Rec. Ther.
  Est 1851. Private. Nonprofit.

The Children's Village is a 21-cottage treatment center for mildly emotionally disturbed and psychotic boys. Remedial tutoring, counseling, recreation, crafts and creative arts are offered. Individual treatment is planned after psychological testing and diagnosis. Five group homes and foster homes are available, as are adoption services. The Village also provides training for specialists and research to prevent emotional problems. The usual length of treatment is two years.

THE CHURCHILL SCHOOL AND CENTER
Day — Coed Ages 5-21

New York, NY 10016. 301 E 29th St.
Tel: 212-722-0610. Fax: 212-722-1387.
www.churchillschool.com
Kristine Baxter, BA, MA, Head. **Estella S. Otis,** Adm.
  Focus: Spec Ed. **Conditions:** Primary—LD S. **IQ 85 and up.**
  Gen Acad. Gr K-12. Courses: Read Math Lang_Arts Sci Computers Soc_
    Stud Studio_Art Music Adaptive_Phys_Ed Health.
  Therapy: Lang Occup Speech. **Psychotherapy:** Group Indiv.
  Enr: 396. Day Males 264. Day Females 132. **Staff:** 80.
  Rates 2001: Day $25,600/sch yr.
  Est 1972. Private. Nonprofit.

The school program utilizes individually prescribed educational approaches, including multisensory teaching of reading, writing and spelling, within an informal but structured classroom setting. Specialists in the fields of learning disabilities, speech and language therapy, sensorimotor integration, curriculum development and adaptive physical education provide appropriate remediation and a varied curriculum.

The middle school program (grades 6-8) includes some departmentalization and emphasizes organizational and study skills. A college preparatory high school division commenced operation in the fall of 2000 with three ninth-grade classes.

CLEAR VIEW SCHOOL DAY TREATMENT PROGRAM
Day — Coed Ages 3-21

Briarcliff Manor, NY 10510. 550 Albany Post Rd.
Tel: 914-941-9513. Fax: 914-941-2339.
William T. Barnes, Exec Dir. **Victoria E. Lyons,** MS, Educ Dir. **Elaine K.**
  Haagen, MD, Clin Dir. **Jill Buckley,** Intake.
  Focus: Spec Ed. Treatment. **Conditions:** Primary—AN Anx BD Bu CD ED
    Mood OCD Psy PTSD SP Sz TS. Sec—Ap Asp Au LD MR OH. **IQ 60**
    and up.
  Col Prep. Gen Acad. Pre-Voc. Voc. Gr PS-12. Courses: Read Math Lang_
    Arts Sci Soc_Stud Studio_Art Music. Man_Arts & Shop. On-Job Trng.
  Therapy: Lang Speech. **Psychotherapy:** Fam Group Indiv Parent.
  Enr: 117. Day Males 87. Day Females 30. **Staff:** 95 (Full 92, Part 3).
  Summer Prgm: Day. Educ. Ther. 6 wks.
  Est 1968. Private. Nonprofit. **Spons:** Association for Mentally Ill Children of
    Westchester.

Clear View treats severely emotionally disturbed children. The principle mode of treatment is psycho-educational therapy, with emphases on psychotherapy, conjoint mother-child therapy and family counseling. Children suffering from a variety of developmental disorders are accepted if they also have an emotional disturbance. Students residing in Westchester County who cannot attend public school receive admission priority. The usual duration of treatment is five years.

The summer program serves children enrolled in the regular program only.

CLEARY SCHOOL FOR THE DEAF

Day — Coed Ages Birth-21

Nesconset, NY 11767. 301 Smithtown Blvd.
Tel: 631-588-0530. TTY: 631-588-0530. Fax: 631-588-0016.
www.clearyschool.org
Sr. Catherine Fitzgibbon, CSJ, MS, Supt. **Eileen M. Kelly, CSJ,** Prin.
   Focus: Spec Ed. **Conditions:** Primary—D. Sec—S.
   Col Prep. Gen Acad. Pre-Voc. Voc. Gr PS-12. Courses: Read Math Lang_
     Arts Computers Sci Soc_Stud.
   Therapy: Hear Occup Phys Speech. **Psychotherapy:** Parent.
   Rates 2004: No Fee.
   Summer Prgm: Day. Educ. 6 wks.
   Est 1930. Private. Nonprofit.

Profoundly deaf children from Suffolk and Nassau counties receive a total communication approach to learning that emphasizes the development of the whole child at Cleary. The curriculum includes traditional academic subjects, in addition to speech reading, auditory training, finger spelling and signs. Programming also includes instruction in art, photography, visual perception, cognitive training, vocational job training and visual communication. Students undergo an evaluation each year to determine if they are ready for mainstreaming into regular schools. An infant program provides educational services for parents and their children (birth to age 3).

The State of New York pays all tuition, fees and transportation costs.

COARC
THE STARTING PLACE

Day — Coed Ages 3-5

Hudson, NY 12534. 65 Prospect Ave.
Tel: 518-828-3890. Fax: 518-828-4195.
www.coarc.org   E-mail: info@coarc.org
Barbara Browne, Dir.
   Focus: Spec Ed. **Conditions:** Primary—MR. Sec—BI CP Ep LD MD MS
     ON S SB.
   Gen Acad. Gr PS.
   Therapy: Hear Lang Occup Phys Speech. **Psychotherapy:** Fam Indiv.
   Enr: 30. **Staff:** 20. (Full 20). Educ 15. Admin 2.
   Summer Prgm: Day. Educ.
   Est 1983. Private. Nonprofit. **Spons:** Columbia County Association for
     Retarded Citizens.

The Columbia County Association for Retarded Citizens offers a preschool program to children with developmental disabilities and to those who exhibit severe delays in speech, movement, learning or behavior. Early intervention, diagnosis and treatment are provided. Improvement is directed toward growth in communicational skills; fine- or gross-motor development; self-care; and socialization. Programming is provided to educate both parent and child. Parental counseling is available.

COBB MEMORIAL SCHOOL

Res and Day — Coed Ages 5-21

Altamont, NY 12009. PO Box 503.
Tel: 518-861-6446. Fax: 518-861-5228.
www.timesunion.com/communities/cobbschool
    E-mail: cobbschool1@msn.com
Sr. Mary Thomas, Dir.
    Focus: Spec Ed. Trng. Treatment. **Conditions:** Primary—MR.
    Pre-Voc. Ungraded. Courses: Read Math Lang_Arts.
    Therapy: Hear Lang Occup Phys Speech. **Psychotherapy:** Indiv.
    Est 1962. Private. Nonprofit. **Spons:** Sisters of The Presentation.

CP ROCHESTER

Day — Coed Ages Birth-5
Clinic: Ages Birth-18. M-F 8-6.

Rochester, NY 14623. 3399 Winton Rd S.
Tel: 585-334-6000. Fax: 585-334-2858.
www.cprochester.org
Lucille Brandt, Dir. **Lisa Steen,** Clin Dir. **Elmar Frangenberg,** MD, Med Dir.
    Focus: Treatment. **Conditions:** Primary—CP ON SB. Sec—ADD Ap BI D
        Dx Ep LD MD MR MS S.
    Therapy: Hear Lang Occup Phys Speech.
    Est 1946. Private. Nonprofit.

The center's day program addresses physical, cognitive, speech and language impairments in young children with such individualized educational and therapeutic services as assistive technology, swimming, horseback riding and musical activities. The nursery and kindergarten program prepares children for success in school-age programs while providing opportunities for disabled and nondisabled youngsters to learn together. Home-based intervention is also available.

Pediatric Therapy Services, CP Rochester's outpatient clinic, serves children with chronic and acute therapeutic needs. Services include an adaptive workshop, assistive technology and several forms of therapy.

CRESTWOOD CHILDREN'S CENTER

Res — Coed Ages 5-17; Day — Coed 3-21
Clinic: Ages Birth-21. M-Th 9-5, F 9-3; Eves M T 5-7.

Rochester, NY 14623. 2075 Scottsville Rd.
Tel: 585-429-2700.
www.hillside.com   E-mail: info@hillside.com
Barbara Conradt, Pres. **Elisabeth Hager,** MD, Med Dir. **Nancy Bleichfeld,**
    Adm.
    Focus: Treatment. **Conditions:** Primary—ADD ADHD Asp BD CD Dx ED

LD Mood OCD ODD PDD Psy PTSD SP Sz TS. Sec—AN Ar As Au Bl Bu C CF CP Db Dc Dg Ep HIV OH. **IQ 70 and up.**

Gen Acad. Ungraded. Courses: Read Math Lang_Arts Sci Soc_Stud. On-Job Trng.

Therapy: Art Hear Lang Occup Phys Play Recreational Speech. **Psychotherapy:** Fam Group Indiv.

Enr: 179. Res Males 30. Res Females 5. Day Males 114. Day Females 30. **Staff:** 190 (Full 167, Part 23). Prof 92. Educ 37. Admin 11.

Rates 2004: Res $145-249/day. Day $135/day. Clinic $120/hr. State Aid.

Est 1837. Private. Nonprofit. **Spons:** Hillside Family of Agencies.

Located on a 50-acre campus overlooking the Genesee River, Crestwood treats emotionally disturbed children and their families. Programs include residential and day treatment (ages 3-18), preschool day treatment (ages 3-6), and group home and foster care, as well as outpatient services. Individual, group and family counseling is available, and the usual length of treatment ranges from six to 18 months.

DEVELOPMENTAL DISABILITIES INSTITUTE

Res — Coed Ages 5-21; Day — Coed 13-21

Smithtown, NY 11787. 99 Hollywood Dr.
Tel: 631-366-2900. Fax: 631-366-2997.
www.ddiinfo.org
Peter Pierri, MA, Exec Dir. **Jamie Powell,** MD, Med Dir.

Focus: Spec Ed. **Conditions:** Primary—Asp Au DS MR PDD.
Pre-Voc. Voc. Ungraded. On-Job Trng.
Therapy: Occup Phys Speech. **Psychotherapy:** Indiv Parent.
Staff: 405. (Full 405). Prof 58. Admin 6.
Rates 2004: Res $146,000/yr. Day $35,500/sch yr. State Aid.
Summer Prgm: Day. Educ. Day Rate $5000. 6 wks.
Est 1965. Private. Nonprofit.

DDI's children's day program involve a full-day special education program for those students who display evidence of autism or pervasive developmental disorder. In addition to a highly structured learning experience, the program provides speech and language services, adaptive physical education, occupational and physical therapy, clinical and vocational services. Intensive parent training programs are also available.

The residential program offers intensive education to autistic and autistic-like children whose needs cannot be addressed adequately in typical special education settings. Students in four residences receive highly specialized intervention designed to improve functioning in areas that restrict their participation in normal activities. Children make use of the school's recreational facilities at night and on weekends. DDI schedules small-group trips into the community daily.

DEVEREUX

Res and Day — Coed Ages 5-21

Red Hook, NY 12571. 8192 Old Post Rd.

Tel: 914-758-1899. Fax: 914-758-1817.
www.devereuxny.org
William F. Sullivan, MS, Exec Dir.

> **Focus:** Treatment. **Conditions:** Primary—ADD ADHD Au Bl CP Ep MR ON PW S. Sec—As ED LD. **IQ 35-79.**
> **Pre-Voc. Voc.** Ungraded. Courses: Read Math Lang_Arts Computers Studio_Art Music Life_Skills. On-Job Trng.
> **Therapy:** Hear Lang Occup Phys Speech. **Psychotherapy:** Group Indiv.
> **Enr:** 122. Res Males 70. Res Females 30. Day Males 11. Day Females 11.
> **Est 1987.** Private. Nonprofit. **Spons:** Devereux Foundation.

This center is located in Dutchess County, 100 miles north of New York City in the Mid-Hudson Valley. The facility serves children and adolescents with mild to moderate developmental disabilities in a residential, comprehensive treatment community.

A closely integrated, multi-modal, multidisciplinary approach enables children to attain IEP goals established to improve academic, emotional, developmental, vocational and social development. This least restrictive therapeutic milieu is designed to maximize children's potential and improve the quality of their lives. **See Also Page 1025**

DIAGNOSTIC LEARNING CENTER

Clinic: All Ages. M-Th 9-6; Eve Th 6-9.

Queensbury, NY 12804. 505 Ridge Rd.
Tel: 518-793-0668.
www.learningproblems.com
Jan Bishop, MA, Dir.

> **Focus:** Trng. **Conditions:** Primary—ADD ADHD Bl Dx LD. **IQ 85 and up.**
> **Psychotherapy:** Parent.
> **Staff:** 3 (Full 1, Part 2).
> **Est 1975.** Private. Inc.

This clinic provides diagnosis and remediation for the learning disabled. Individuals who have sustained head injuries are admitted to the center for cognitive testing and retraining. The clinic also offers educational counseling and assists patients with academic placement.

EDENWALD CENTER

Res — Coed Ages 6-18

Pleasantville, NY 10570. Rte 141, PO Box 140.
Tel: 914-769-7150. Fax: 914-769-8505.
www.jccany.org/programs/rts.asp   E-mail: ec@jccany.org
Edward D. Sperling, MSW, MBA, Dir. **Susan Livitsky,** MD, Med Dir.

> **Focus:** Spec Ed. Treatment. **Conditions:** Primary—BD ED. Sec—MR. **IQ 50-79.**
> **Gen Acad. Pre-Voc. Voc.** Gr 1-12. Courses: Read Math. Man_Arts & Shop. Shelt_Workshop. On-Job Trng.
> **Psychotherapy:** Fam Group Indiv Parent.

Enr: 102. Res Males 62. Res Females 40. **Staff:** 50. Educ 17. Admin 13.
Summer Prgm: Res. Educ. Rec. Ther.
Est 1925. Private. Nonprofit. **Spons:** Jewish Child Care Association.

Emotionally disturbed children who are residents of New York City and are approved by the New York City Department of Social Services are eligible for admission into Edenwald. An on-campus school offers an academic program and instruction in manual arts and shop as well as on-the-job training and a sheltered workshop. Psychological and group therapy sessions are available.

EDUCATIONAL LEARNING EXPERIENCE

Day — Coed Ages 5-21

Middletown, NY 10940. 28 Ingrassia Rd.
Tel: 845-341-0700. Fax: 845-341-0788.
www.orangeahrc.org   E-mail: jbcele@warwick.net
Lorraine Tomasi, MS, Educ Dir. **Adriana Lopes,** Adm.
  Focus: Spec Ed. **Conditions:** Primary—Apr Asp Au Bl CP DS Ep MR ON PDD. Sec—ADD ADHD Anx Ap As B BD C CD D Db Dg Dx ED HIV IP LD MD Mood MS Nf OCD PTSD PW S SB TB TS.
  Gen Acad. Ungraded. Courses: Read Math Lang_Arts Sci Soc_Stud Life_Skills.
  Enr: 39. **Staff:** 49 (Full 43, Part 6). Educ 5. Admin 1.
  Rates 2004: Res $23,042/sch yr. State Aid.
  Private. Nonprofit. **Spons:** Orange County Association for the Help of Retarded Citizens.

ELE provides comprehensive services, advocacy and assistance for students with developmental disabilities. Services include adaptive music; adaptive physical education; family counseling and support services; occupational, physical, and speech and language therapy; psychological services; and student counseling. One-on-one tutoring is available for an additional fee.

EDWIN GOULD ACADEMY

Res — Coed Ages 12-20

Chestnut Ridge, NY 10977. 675 Chestnut Ridge Rd.
Tel: 845-573-5000. Fax: 845-578-6824.
www.edwingouldacademy.org
Thomas Webber, PhD, Exec Dir. **Edgar Walker,** Med Dir.
  Conditions: Primary—ED.
  Gen Acad. Pre-Voc. Voc. Gr 7-12. Courses: Read Math Lang_Arts. Man_Arts & Shop. Shelt_Workshop. On-Job Trng.
  Psychotherapy: Group.
  Est 1990. Private. Nonprofit.

ENABLE

Day — Coed All Ages

Syracuse, NY 13208. 1603 Court St.
Tel: 315-455-7591. TTY: 315-455-1794. Fax: 315-455-2494.
www.enablecny.org   E-mail: info@enablecny.org
Sara Wall-Bollinger, MA, Exec Dir. **Carl Crosley,** MD, Med Dir. **Monica
    Cappa,** Intake.
   Focus: Treatment. **Conditions:** Primary—Asp Au Bl CP D MD MR MS ON
    S SB. Sec—ADD ADHD B Dx Ep LD.
   Therapy: Hear Lang Occup Phys Speech Aqua. **Psychotherapy:** Fam
    Group Indiv Parent.
   Staff: 225.
   Summer Prgm: Day. Rec. Ther.
   Est 1948. Private. Nonprofit.

Formerly known as the United Cerebral Palsy Center of Syracuse, Enable provides a
range of services for individuals with cerebral palsy and other developmental and physical disabilities. Services include diagnostic, therapeutic, medical and special education
preschool programs; supported employment services for adults; family support and
home services; and group home or individualized living arrangements.

THE FAMILY FOUNDATION SCHOOL

Res — Coed Ages 13-19

Hancock, NY 13783. 431 Chapel Hill Rd.
Tel: 845-887-5213. Fax: 845-887-4939.
www.thefamilyschool.com   E-mail: info@thefamilyschool.com
   Focus: Spec Ed. **Conditions:** Primary—ADD ADHD ED ODD.
   Col Prep. Gr 7-12.
   Psychotherapy: Group.
   Enr: 230. Res Males 120. Res Females 110. **Staff:** 94.
   Rates 2004: Res $3725/mo. State Aid.
   Est 1982. Private. Inc. **Spons:** Education Plus.

Family Foundation is an emotional growth school based on the 12-step program of
Alcoholics Anonymous. This year-round program helps adolescents who suffer from
arrested development learn social and coping skills and reach their academic potential.
While the school does not offer rehabilitation, assistance with counseling arrangements
is available.

FERNCLIFF MANOR

Res — Coed Ages Birth-21

Yonkers, NY 10710. 1154 Saw Mill River Rd.
Tel: 914-968-4854. Fax: 914-968-4857.
www.ferncliffmanor.com

William Saich, Admin. **Jerome Strachman,** MD, Med Dir. **Sheila Chu,** Adm.
  Focus: Spec Ed. **Conditions:** Primary—DS MR. Sec—ADD ADHD Ap As
    Au B Bl C CP D Db Dc Dg Dx ED Ep HIV IP MD Mood OCD ON Psy
    PTSD PW S SB SP Sz. **IQ 0-69.**
  Gen Acad. Ungraded.
  Therapy: Hear Lang Movement Music Occup Phys Recreational Speech.
    Psychotherapy: Fam Indiv.
  Enr: 53. Res Males 28. Res Females 25. **Staff:** 210 (Full 180, Part 30).
    Educ 17. Admin 15.
  Est 1935. Private. Inc.

Situated in a residential neighborhood, this specialized school offers year-round educational, habilitative, medical and residential services for children with multiple disabilities. Services include special education; occupational, physical and speech therapies; adaptive physical education; and psychological and social services. Personal computers and electronic adaptive devices facilitate the acquisition of academic and communicational skills, as well as the ability to control one's environment. Traditional approaches to fostering growth and development are also utilized.

Ferncliff Manor encourages parents and family members to participate in the child's individualized program. Activities and social events provide children with recreational opportunities and also promote awareness in the community.

FOUR WINDS SARATOGA

Res — Coed Ages 5 and up
Clinic: Ages 5 and up. M-F by Appt.

Saratoga Springs, NY 12866. 30 Crescent Ave.
Tel: 518-584-3600.
www.fourwindshospital.com
  E-mail: info.saratoga@fourwindshospital.com
Robert M. Greenbaum, PhD, CEO.
  Focus: Treatment. **Conditions:** Primary—BD CD ED Mood OCD ODD Psy
    PTSD Sz.
  Therapy: Art Milieu Play. **Psychotherapy:** Fam Group Indiv Parent.
  Private. **Spons:** Four Winds Hospitals.

Four Winds is a psychiatric health system specializing in inpatient and outpatient mental health treatment services for children, adolescents and adults. The treatment services program offers a peer-group community living experience that emphasizes group therapy, psychodrama and behavior modification. Individuals receiving inpatient services reside in individual cottages while being treated by a multidisciplinary team of professionals. A variety of therapeutic modalities is available, including individual, group and family therapy. Community meetings and projects, as well as goal-oriented social and recreational groups, aid in the development of daily living skills.

A second location operates in Katonah (see separate listing).

FOUR WINDS WESTCHESTER

Res — Coed Ages 5 and up
Clinic: Ages 5 and up. M-F by Appt.

Katonah, NY 10536. 800 Cross River Rd.
Tel: 914-763-8151. TTY: 888-639-3098. Fax: 914-763-9598.
www.fourwindshospital.com
E-mail: info.westchester@fourwindshospital.com
Martin A. Buccolo, PhD, CEO. Samuel C. Klagsbrun, MD, Med Dir. Deborah
Oliver Brown, Adm.
Focus: Treatment. Conditions: Primary—BD CD ED Mood OCD ODD Psy
PTSD Sz.
Therapy: Art Milieu Play. Psychotherapy: Fam Group Indiv Parent.
Staff: 600.
Private. Spons: Four Winds Hospitals.

Four Winds is a psychiatric health system specializing in inpatient and outpatient mental health treatment services for children, adolescents and adults. The treatment services program offers a peer-group community living experience that emphasizes group therapy, psychodrama and behavior modification. Individuals receiving inpatient services reside in individual cottages while being treated by a multidisciplinary team of professionals. A variety of therapeutic modalities is available, including individual, group and family therapy. Community meetings and projects, as well as goal-oriented social and recreational groups, aid in the development of daily living skills.

A second location operates in Saratoga Springs (see separate listing).

FRANZISKA RACKER CENTERS
EARLY CHILDHOOD SERVICES

Day — Coed Ages Birth-5

Ithaca, NY 14850. 3226 Wilkins Rd.
Tel: 607-272-5891. Fax: 607-272-0188.
www.rackercenters.org
Conditions: Primary—Ap Au B BD Bl CP D Dx ED IP LD MD MR MS ON
S SB.
Therapy: Hear Lang Occup Phys Speech.
Private.

GATEWAY-LONGVIEW

Res — Coed Ages 9-21; Day — Coed Birth-12

Williamsville, NY 14221. 6350 Main St.
Tel: 716-633-7266. Fax: 716-633-7395.
www.gateway-longview.org   E-mail: info@gateway-longview.org
Conditions: Primary—BD ED.
Gen Acad. Ungraded. Courses: Read Math Lang_Arts. Man_Arts & Shop.
Est 1890. Private. Nonprofit.

GELLER HOUSE

Res — Coed Ages 11-15

Staten Island, NY 10305. 77 Chicago Ave.
Tel: 718-442-7828. Fax: 718-720-0762.
Beryl Kende, MSW, Dir.
  Focus: Treatment. **Conditions:** Primary—ADD ADHD BD CD ED Mood OCD ODD Psy PTSD SP Sz. Sec—Dx HIV.
  Gen Acad. Courses: Math. Man_Arts & Shop.
  Therapy: Chemo Recreational Speech. **Psychotherapy:** Fam Group Indiv.
  Enr: 24. Res Males 12. Res Females 12. **Staff:** 24.
  Est 1972. Private. Nonprofit. **Spons:** Jewish Board of Family and Children's Services.

Geller House is a diagnostic evaluation center providing multidisciplinary diagnoses, as well as short-term treatment and crisis intervention, for children remanded by the family courts or placed through the Administration for Children's Services. The duration of treatment is usually eight weeks. The facility attempts to return children to community living situations or, where required, to prepare them for residential settings.

GEORGE JUNIOR REPUBLIC

Res — Males Ages 12-18

Freeville, NY 13068. 380 Freeville Rd.
Tel: 607-844-6460. Fax: 607-844-4053.
www.georgejuniorrepublic.com
Brad Herman, MSW, Exec Dir. **Mark Glossenger,** MD, Med Dir. **Chris Mac-Cormick,** Adm.
  Focus: Treatment. **Conditions:** Primary—ADD ADHD BD CD ED. Sec—As Dx LD OCD Psy. **IQ 70 and up.**
  Gen Acad. Gr 7-12. Courses: Read Math Lang_Arts. Man_Arts & Shop. On-Job Trng.
  Therapy: Speech. **Psychotherapy:** Fam Group Indiv.
  Enr: 170. Res Males 170. **Staff:** 297 (Full 262, Part 35).
  Rates 2003: Res $155-217/day.
  Est 1895. Private. Nonprofit.

Located on 650 acres of farmland, George Junior Republic offers treatment to emotionally disturbed and socially maladjusted adolescents. Supportive and milieu therapy, counseling, group structures and intensive treatment are the approaches utilized. The Special Services program offers treatment for hard-to-place youth and sexual offenders. There is also an on-campus clinic that serves chemically dependent youth.

The academic program offers basic academic skills in support of vocational skills, general high school and college preparatory courses. A work experience and vocational preparation program provides over 30 different kinds of employment, both indoors and outdoors. A full recreation program is available, and the usual length of treatment is 12 to 18 months.

THE GOW SCHOOL

Res — Males Ages 12-18

South Wales, NY 14139. 2491 Emery Rd, PO Box 85.
Tel: 716-652-3450. Fax: 716-652-3457.
www.gow.org   E-mail: admissions@gow.org
M. **Bradley Rogers, Jr.,** BS, Head. **Robert Garcia,** Adm.
 Focus: Spec Ed. **Conditions:** Primary—Dx. **IQ 90 and up.**
 Gen Acad. Gr 7-12. Courses: Computers Fine_Arts.
 Rates 2004: Res $39,500/sch yr (+$1600).
 Summer Prgm: Res & Day. Educ. Res Rate $5500. Day Rate $3600. 5 wks.
 Est 1926. Private. Nonprofit.

Gow enrolls students of average to above-average intelligence who have specific language difficulties. Classes are small, averaging four to six pupils each. The core of the program is "reconstructive language" and multisensory mathematics, both of which are designed to improve and extend the student's academic ability within a college preparatory setting.

The athletic program features soccer, cross-country, basketball, skiing, lacrosse, boxing, crew, ice hockey and tennis. An Outward Bound-type outdoors program and various clubs and student publications are among other school activities.

GREEN CHIMNEYS

Res — Coed Ages 6-17; Day — Coed 5-17

Brewster, NY 10509. 400 Doansburg Rd, Box 719.
Tel: 845-279-2995. Fax: 845-279-4013.
www.greenchimneys.org   E-mail: info@greenchimneys.org
Joseph Whalen, MS, MBA, Exec Dir. **Martin G. Vigdor,** PhD, Clin Dir. **Myra M. Ross,** Adm.
 Focus: Spec Ed. **Conditions:** Primary—Asp ED. Sec—ADD ADHD As CD Dx Ep LD MR OCD Psy S Sz. **IQ 70 and up.**
 Gen Acad. Pre-Voc. Gr K-12. Courses: Read Math Lang_Arts Sci Hist. Man_Arts & Shop. On-Job Trng.
 Therapy: Art Lang Milieu Music Occup Percepual-Motor Recreational Speech. **Psychotherapy:** Indiv.
 Enr: 174. Res Males 88. Res Females 14. Day Males 63. Day Females 9.
  Staff: 385 (Full 327, Part 58). Educ 75. Admin 32.
 Est 1947. Private. Nonprofit.

Green Chimneys provides a year-round therapeutic milieu for children with emotional, behavioral and educational handicaps. There is a full range of social service, clinical and educational programs, including psychotherapy and diagnostic evaluations. The program incorporates the use of a farm as a therapeutic modality, with animal- and plant-facilitated therapy. Enrollment is limited to children residing in New York State.

THE HALLEN SCHOOL

Day — Coed Ages 5-21

New Rochelle, NY 10801. 97 Centre Ave.
Tel: 914-636-6600. Fax: 914-633-4089.
www.hallenschool.com   E-mail: carol@hallenschool.com
Carol LoCascio, MEd, PhD, Dir. **James Welker,** Adm.
Focus: Spec Ed. **Conditions:** Primary—ADD ADHD Ap Apr Ar As Asp Au B Bl C Dc Dg Dx ED LD Mood Nf OCD ODD PW SP TS. Sec—AN Anx Db.
Col Prep. Gen Acad. Pre-Voc. Gr K-PG. Courses: Read Math Lang_Arts. Man_Arts & Shop. On-Job Trng.
Therapy: Art Lang Occup Speech. **Psychotherapy:** Fam Group Indiv.
Enr: 280. **Staff:** 80. Prof 12. Admin 4.
Rates 2004: Day $26,000/sch yr. State Aid.
Est 1972. Private. Inc.

Hallen provides early diagnosis, remediation and education for children with learning disabilities. The curriculum emphasizes the development of academic skills and emotional growth. Individual and group therapy are integrated with academia and incorporated into the student's weekly schedule. In addition to the prescribed curriculum, the school offers creative art, manual arts, music, business subjects, supportive work and career education. Active participation by parents is stressed, and counseling is available.

THE HANDICAPPED CHILDREN'S ASSOCIATION OF SOUTHERN NEW YORK

Res — Coed Ages 4-21; Day — Coed Birth-5
Clinic: All Ages. M-F 7:30-5.

Johnson City, NY 13790. 18 Broad St.
Tel: 607-798-7117. Fax: 607-798-0074.
www.hcaserves.com   E-mail: hcaserves@hcaserves.com
Steve Sano, Dir.
Focus: Treatment. **Conditions:** Primary—ADD ADHD Ap Au B Bl CP D Dx IP LD MD MS ON S SB. Sec—As BD C CD ED Ep MR OCD Psy Sz TB.
Gen Acad. Gr PS.
Therapy: Hear Lang Occup Phys Speech. **Psychotherapy:** Indiv Parent.
Enr: 250. **Staff:** 60 (Full 52, Part 8).
Est 1947. Private. Nonprofit. **Spons:** United Way.

HCA serves infants and children with developmental delays and such other disabilities as perceptual dysfunction, sensory integrative deficit, trauma, hyperactivity and multiple handicaps. Diagnostic services include developmental assessments, evaluations and treatment, as well as family support services offered by a staff of physical and occupational therapists, audiologists, speech pathologists, nurses, social workers, psychologists and medical consultants. Special and general early intervention services and therapies assist children through age 5.

The association provides individualized residential alternatives and residential habilitation for individuals with developmental disabilities, while also offering monthly weekend respite opportunities. Family support consists of service coordination, social work, advocacy, support systems, information services, family training and counseling regarding consumer's disabilities.

An on-site speech and hearing center provides outpatient diagnostic and treatment services for persons with hearing impairments. Although this clinic treats individuals of all ages, it specializes in the care of infants and children.

HAWTHORNE COUNTRY DAY SCHOOL

Day — Coed Ages Birth-21

Hawthorne, NY 10532. 5 Bradhurst Ave.
 Nearby locations: New York City.
Tel: 914-592-8526. Fax: 914-592-2169.
www.hawthornecountryday.org
Eileen Bisordi, MEd, Exec Dir.
   Focus: Spec Ed. Trng. **Conditions:** Primary—Asp Au MR PDD PW.
   Gen Acad. Pre-Voc. Voc. Ungraded. Courses: Read Math Lang_Arts.
   Est 1976. Private. Nonprofit. **Spons:** Hawthorne Foundation.

HEBREW ACADEMY FOR SPECIAL CHILDREN

Res — Coed Ages 5-21; Day — Coed Birth-21

Brooklyn, NY 11219. 1311 55th St.
Tel: 718-851-6100. Fax: 718-851-7163.
www.hasc.net   E-mail: chayam.hasc@verizon.net
Bernard M. Kahn, MSEd, CEO. **Chaya Miller,** Admin. **Nancy Hershkowitz,**
   RN, Med Dir.
   Focus: Spec Ed. **Conditions:** Primary—DS MR. Sec—ADD ADHD As Asp
      Au BI CP Ep IP LD MD ON S SB.
   Pre-Voc. Ungraded. Courses: Creative_Arts Adaptive_Phys_Ed ADL. Shelt_
      Workshop. On-Job Trng.
   Therapy: Art Dance Hear Lang Music Occup Phys Recreational Speech.
      Psychotherapy: Indiv.
   Enr: 250. Day Males 140. Day Females 110. **Staff:** 283. Prof 80. Educ 25.
      Admin 5.
   Summer Prgm: Res & Day. Educ. Rec. 7 wks.
   Est 1964. Private. Nonprofit. Jewish.

HASC provides educational and clinical services for individuals from infancy through adulthood who exhibit developmental delays. The no-fee early intervention program, for children from birth to age 3, offers year-round evaluations and services at the child's home, a daycare setting or one of HASC's centers. Children ages 3-5 may participate in half- or full-day preschool programs; if the child's school district grants its approval, the preschool incurs no fee.

The school-age educational program (ages 5-21) emphasizes functional skills such as Activities of Daily Living, academic achievement and socialization. In addition, the curriculum includes a prevocational component that incorporates travel training, community integration, socialization techniques, exploration of postgraduate programs, volunteer job experiences, workshop skills and hand-on work experiences. Therapy and psychological services are part of this program.

Over the summer, Camp HASC offers sleep-away and day camp experiences for individuals of all ages who have mental or physical handicaps. The camp synthesizes academic and recreational programming.

HELEN HAYES HOSPITAL

**Day — Coed All Ages
Clinic: All Ages. M-F 8:30-5.**

West Haverstraw, NY 10993. Rte 9W.
Tel: 845-786-4000. TTY: 845-947-3187. Fax: 845-947-3097.
www.helenhayeshospital.org   E-mail: info@helenhayeshospital.org
Magdalena Ramirez, MPA, CEO. **John Pellicone,** MD, Med Dir. **Gina V. Harris,** Adm.
  Focus: Rehab. **Conditions:** Primary—Ap Bl CP Ep LD MD MS ON S SB.
  Therapy: Hear Hydro Lang Occup Phys Recreational Speech. **Psychotherapy:** Indiv.
  Est 1900. State.

Situated just north of New York City overlooking the Hudson River, this rehabilitation hospital provides an array of evaluative, special education, therapeutic and medical services. Infant-toddler and prekindergarten school programs provide early intervention for children with developmental delays, speech and language delays, neurological/orthopedic problems and learning disabilities. Early intervention seeks to develop academic readiness, increase the child's understanding and use of language, improve gross- and fine-motor skills, and promote social skills development.

HENRY VISCARDI SCHOOL

Day — Coed Ages 3-21

Albertson, NY 11507. 201 I U Willets Rd.
Tel: 516-465-1696.
www.hvs.k12.ny.us
  Conditions: Primary—CP MD ON SB.
  Col Prep. Gen Acad. Pre-Voc. Voc. Gr PS-12. Courses: Read Math Lang_ Arts. Man_Arts & Shop. On-Job Trng.
  Therapy: Hear Occup Phys Speech. **Psychotherapy:** Fam Group Indiv.
  Staff: Prof 49.
  Private.

HERBERT G. BIRCH SERVICES

Res — Coed Ages 4 and up; Day — Coed Birth-16

New York, NY 10001. 275 7th Ave, 19th Fl.
  Nearby locations: Flushing.
Tel: 212-741-6522. Fax: 212-242-5874.
www.hgbirch.org
Paul A. Larsen, Pres. **Susan Lee Miller,** COO.
  Focus: Spec Ed. Treatment. **Conditions:** Primary—Au BI MR OH. Sec—Dx
    ED Ep LD S. **IQ 20-100.**
  Gen Acad. Pre-Voc. Ungraded. Courses: Read Math Lang_Arts.
  Therapy: Lang Occup Speech. **Psychotherapy:** Fam Group Indiv.
  Enr: 120.
  Est 1975. Private. Nonprofit.

Birch Services offers educational programs for children who have a wide range of mental, emotional and neurological impairments. The facility attempts to maximize students' cognitive, emotional and communicational skills, thus enabling them to function as independently as possible. After-school recreational activities include swimming, cooking, crafts and music.

The community program provides preschool evaluations and services to children under age 5 with special needs. Skilled professionals, with the support of parents, provide this extra assistance in the home or other locations in the child's community.

Early childhood programs serve preschoolers (ages 3-5) with and without disabilities, in an environment that allows children to grow intellectually, socially and emotionally.

At the affiliated School for Exceptional Children (71-64 168th St., Flushing 11365), students ages 5-16 develop skills in the areas of reading and writing, music, the arts and technology.

HILLSIDE CHILDREN'S CENTER

Res and Day — Coed Ages 3-21

Rochester, NY 14620. 1183 Monroe Ave.
Tel: 585-256-7500. TTY: 585-256-7881.
www.hillside.com   E-mail: info@hillside.com
  Conditions: Primary—BD ED.
  Gen Acad. Pre-Voc. Ungraded. Courses: Read Math Lang_Arts.
  Therapy: Art Dance Play.
  Staff: Prof 118.
  Est 1837. Private. Nonprofit.

HOFSTRA UNIVERSITY
SPEECH-LANGUAGE-HEARING CLINIC

Clinic: All Ages. M-F 9-5, S 8:30-4; Eves M-F 5-9.

Hempstead, NY 11550. Saltzman Community Services Ctr.

Tel: 516-463-5656.
www.hofstra.edu/com/saltzman/sal_speechlanguage.cfm
   E-mail: saltzmancenter@hofstra.edu
Wendy C. Silverman, MS, Dir.
   Conditions: Primary—S.
   Therapy: Hear Lang Speech.
   Staff: Prof 7.
   Est 1950. Private.

THE HOUSE OF THE GOOD SHEPHERD

Res — Males Ages 6-17, Females 12-17; Day — Coed 6-18

Utica, NY 13502. 1550 Champlin Ave.
Tel: 315-733-0436. Fax: 315-732-0772.
www.hgs-utica.com   E-mail: info@hgs-utica.com
William F. Holicky, Jr., MSW, Exec Dir. Susan Blatt, MD, Med Dir. Dawn
   Petrie, Intake.
   Focus: Spec Ed. Treatment. Conditions: Primary—ADD ADHD Anx BD CD
   ED Mood PTSD SP TS. Sec—As D Db LD OCD S. IQ 65-120.
   Gen Acad. Pre-Voc. Gr K-12. Courses: Read Math Lang_Arts Sci Soc_Stud
   Studio_Art Health. Man_Arts & Shop.
   Therapy: Chemo Lang Milieu Occup Play Recreational Speech. Psycho-
   therapy: Fam Group Indiv.
   Enr: 180. Res Males 110. Res Females 60. Day Males 6. Day Females 4.
   Staff: 400 (Full 380, Part 20). Prof 68. Educ 12. Admin 10.
   Est 1871. Private. Nonprofit.

The House provides children and families with the treatment, education and support services designed to help them succeed individually, within the family and as part of the community. Tilton School, the 12-month special education day school that forms an integral part of the overall program, consists of two divisions: an accredited developmental section for children ages 6-12 (grades 1-8) and a life skills division for teens ages 13-18. Educational support services for all students include occupational therapy, speech and language therapy, and a learning center.

Aside from the educational program, HGS operates two group homes, two boarding homes, a residential treatment center and a residential treatment facility. Preventive, aftercare, diagnostic, emergency housing, nonsecure detention and foster care services are also available. Referrals come from public agencies. Both residential and day service programs operate year-round, with the usual duration of treatment being six to 12 months.

HUDSON VALLEY LEARNING CENTER

Clinic: Ages 6 and up. M-F 9-5; Eves W Th F 5-7.

Poughkeepsie, NY 12601. 47 S Hamilton St.
Tel: 845-454-4769. Fax: 845-473-0305.
   Focus: Trng. Conditions: Primary—LD. Sec—Dx.

Staff: 3 (Full 1, Part 2).
Est 1990. Private.

Tutoring at the clinic covers academic subject areas, organizational and study skills, and aspects of written and verbal expression. In addition to remediating deficit areas, the Learning Center attempts to strengthen clients' interest areas, stimulate their desire to read, and help them develop appropriate learning strategies. The program seeks to increase self-confidence while also teaching individuals what they must do to succeed in either school or the workplace.

HUNTER COLLEGE
CENTER FOR COMMUNICATION DISORDERS

Clinic: All Ages. M-F 9-6.

New York, NY 10010. 425 E 25th St.
Tel: 212-481-4467.
www.hunter.cuny.edu/schoolhp/comsc/practicum.htm
    E-mail: comsc@hunter.cuny.edu
F. Scheffler, PhD, Dir.
    Focus: Treatment. **Conditions:** Primary—Ap S.
    Therapy: Hear Lang Speech.
    Staff: 12.
    Municipal.

Serving as a clinical practicum site for graduate students, this center provides diagnostic and therapeutic services for individuals displaying disorders involving speech, voice, fluency, swallowing, language or hearing. Staff members encourage parental observation and participation.

INTERNATIONAL CENTER FOR THE DISABLED

Clinic: Ages 2½-18. M-F 8-6.

New York, NY 10010. 340 E 24th St.
Tel: 212-585-6000. Fax: 212-585-6262.
www.icdrehab.org   E-mail: ldicd@aol.com
Arnold Shapiro, MA, Dir. **Sam Wu,** MD, Med Dir.
    Focus: Rehab. Trng. Treatment. **Conditions:** Primary—ADD ADHD AN Anx Asp Au Bu CD D Dc Dg Dx ED LD Mood OCD ODD PDD PTSD S SP TS. Sec—Ap As BD Bl C CP Ep MD MS ON SB TB. **IQ 70-130.**
    Therapy: Art Hear Lang Occup Phys Speech. **Psychotherapy:** Fam Group Indiv Parent.
    Staff: 21. (Full 21). Prof 15.
    Rates 2003: Sliding-Scale Rate $15-125/ses.
    Est 1917. Private. Nonprofit.

Programs in the areas of speech and language pathology, audiology (including hearing aid dispensation), postlaryngectomy rehabilitation and learning disabilities are available at ICD. Although the center can accommodate individuals with various conditions, clients must be medically stable and must not be mentally retarded.

ITHACA COLLEGE
SIR ALEXANDER EWING SPEECH AND HEARING CLINIC
Clinic: Ages Birth-21. M-F 9-5.

Ithaca, NY 14850. Smiddy Hall.
Tel: 607-274-3714. Fax: 607-274-1137.
www.ithaca.edu/hshp/slpa/DEPTHOMEPAGE/clinic.html
   E-mail: jchambers@ithaca.edu
Christine Cecconi, MA, CCC-SLP, Co-Dir. **John Stephens,** MA, Co-Dir.
   Focus: Rehab. **Conditions:** Primary—Ap D S. Sec—ADD ADHD Asp Au BI
   CP LD MD MR MS ON PDD.
   Therapy: Hear Lang Speech.
   Staff: 14. (Full 14). Prof 12. Admin 2.
   Rates 2003: Clinic $10/hr.
   Private. Nonprofit.

Operating during the college school year, the clinic offers outpatient speech, language and hearing evaluations and therapy services. The facility serves as a laboratory and training program for undergraduate and graduate students who work under the supervision of licensed, certified faculty. No client is refused services due to an inability to pay.

JAWONIO
Day — Coed Ages Birth-21
Clinic: Ages Birth-21. M-F 8:30-4:30; Eves M-Th 4:30-9.

New City, NY 10956. 260 N Little Tor Rd.
Tel: 845-634-4648. TTY: 845-634-4672. Fax: 845-634-7731.
www.jawonio.org   E-mail: jawonio@jawonio.org
   Conditions: Primary—OH. **IQ 50 and up.**
   Gen Acad. Pre-Voc. Gr PS-12. Courses: Read Math Lang_Arts. Shelt_
   Workshop. On-Job Trng.
   Therapy: Hear Lang Occup Phys Speech. **Psychotherapy:** Fam Group
   Indiv.
   Staff: Prof 16.
   Est 1947. Private. Nonprofit.

JULIA DYCKMAN ANDRUS MEMORIAL
Res and Day — Coed Ages 5-14

Yonkers, NY 10701. 1156 N Broadway.
Tel: 914-965-3700. Fax: 914-965-3883.

www.andruschildren.org
Nancy Woodruff Ment, MSW, COO.
    Conditions: Primary—ADD ADHD Asp ED Mood OCD. Sec—BD. **IQ 70 and up.**
    Gen Acad. Pre-Voc. Gr K-9. Courses: Read Math Lang_Arts. Man_Arts & Shop.
    Est 1928. Private. Nonprofit.

THE KARAFIN SCHOOL

Day — Coed Ages 13-21

Mount Kisco, NY 10549. 40-1 Radio Cir, PO Box 277.
Tel: 914-666-9211. Fax: 914-666-9868.
http://users.bestweb.net/~karafin   E-mail: karafinschool@yahoo.com
John E. Greenfieldt, BA, MEd, PhD, Exec Dir. **Bart A. Donow,** Adm.
    Focus: Spec Ed. **Conditions:** Primary—ADD ADHD Anx Asp CD Dc Dg Dx ED LD Mood OCD ODD PDD PTSD SP TS. Sec—Au BD Psy Sz. **IQ 80 and up.**
    Col Prep. Gen Acad. Gr 8-12. Courses: Read Math Lang_Arts Sci Computers Music Studio_Art.
    Therapy: Lang Speech. **Psychotherapy:** Fam Group Indiv.
    Enr: 80. Day Males 50. Day Females 30. **Staff:** 40 (Full 39, Part 1). Prof 26. Admin 2.
    Rates 2003: Day $20,911/sch yr. Schol avail. State Aid.
    Est 1958. Private. Inc.

A school for underachievers and children with learning and emotional disabilities who have been unable to achieve to potential in the regular school environment, Karafin provides a specialized, individualized structure that addresses the particular needs of each child. The goal is to remediate learning handicaps and to develop skills, confidence and motivation so that students are able to make the transition back to a mainstream setting. Karafin devises each student's program after testing by the school and reports and evaluations from psychologists, psychiatrists and neurologists.

Pupils who are mentally retarded or who are substance abusers may not enroll.

KENNEDY CHILD STUDY CENTER

Day — Coed Ages Birth-5
Clinic: Ages Birth-21. M-F 9-5.

New York, NY 10021. 151 E 67th St.
Tel: 212-988-9500. Fax: 212-570-6690.
www.kennedychildstudycenter.org
    E-mail: sclark@kennedychildstudycenter.org
Ann Williams, PhD, Exec Dir.
    Focus: Spec Ed. **Conditions:** Primary—MR. Sec—BI C CP ED Ep OH. **IQ 0-80.**
    Gen Acad. Gr PS.

Therapy: Hear Lang Occup Phys Speech. **Psychotherapy:** Fam Group
Indiv Parent.
Enr: 240. **Staff:** 157 (Full 140, Part 17).
Est 1958. Private. Nonprofit.

Serving mentally retarded and developmentally disabled children, KCSC maintains
an early childhood program offering infant stimulation for youngsters from birth to age
3, as well as a preschool for three- to five-year-olds that aims for placement in community programs. Audiometric testing and language screening are held regularly to assess
each child's progress. The clinic provides evaluations only, while the day school offers
social, psychiatric, psychological and pediatric services in the day program. The facility
does not charge a fee for day services.

The center has an annex at 1028 E. 179th St., Bronx 10460 that serves developmentally disabled infants and preschoolers.

KILDONAN SCHOOL

Res — Coed Ages 11-19; Day — Coed 7-19

Amenia, NY 12501. 425 Morse Hill Rd.
Tel: 845-373-8111. Fax: 845-373-9793.
www.kildonan.org   E-mail: admissions@kildonan.org
Ronald A. Wilson, BS, MS, Head. **Bonnie A. Wilson,** Adm.
  Focus: Spec Ed. **Conditions:** Primary—Dx LD.
  Col Prep. Gr 2-PG. Courses: Read Math Lang_Arts Sci Soc_Stud Studio_
  Art Music. Man_Arts & Shop.
  Therapy: Lang Speech. **Psychotherapy:** Indiv.
  Enr: 141. Res Males 61. Res Females 14. Day Males 58. Day Females 8.
  Staff: 60.
  Rates 2004: Res $38,800-40,800/sch yr (+$1500). Day $23,000-28,000/sch
  yr (+$500). Schol avail.
  Summer Prgm: Res & Day. Educ. Rec. Res Rate $7300. Day Rate $3725-
  5725. 6 wks.
  Est 1969. Private. Nonprofit.

Kildonan is located on a 450-acre estate. The educational program, designed for
dyslexic children, gives students skills for reading and written work while insuring
a continuation of their education. Instruction in basic academics as well as ceramics,
sculpture, silk-screen, painting and drawing is provided. The full athletic program is
aimed at developing increased physical fitness and self-confidence. Soccer, football,
tennis, baseball, horseback riding, skiing and skating are offered. Counseling is available, and the usual duration of remediation is one to two years.

The summer program, Dunnabeck at Kildonan, provides an educational and recreational camp for boys and girls of normal intelligence who have a specific reading, writing or spelling difficulty. Instructors utilize the Orton-Gillingham approach.

See Also Pages 1036-7

KINGSBROOK JEWISH MEDICAL CENTER

Res — Coed Ages Birth-18
Clinic: Ages Birth-18. M-F 9-4; Eve M 4-8.

Brooklyn, NY 11203. 585 Schenectady Ave.
Tel: 718-604-5000. Fax: 718-604-5294.
www.kingsbrook.org   E-mail: info@kjmc.org
Linda Brady, MD, CEO.
  Focus: Rehab. **Conditions:** Primary—ADD ADHD Ap As B Bl C CP D Dx
  Ep IP LD MD MR MS ON S SB.
  Therapy: Hear Lang Occup Phys Speech. **Psychotherapy:** Group Indiv.
  Enr: 32. **Staff:** 36 (Full 30, Part 6).
  Est 1925. Private. Nonprofit.

This pediatric facility houses a 32-bed long-term chronic care unit and an eight-bed acute care unit. Full rehabilitative services for all virtually all conditions that warrant rehabilitation. The program includes infant stimulation and therapeutic services, and the New York City Board of Education maintains an on-site classroom for long-term care patients.

LAKE GROVE SCHOOL

Res — Coed Ages 10-21

Lake Grove, NY.
Contact: 3390 Rte 112, PO Box 786, Medford, NY 11763.
Tel: 631-696-1400. Fax: 631-716-2136.
www.lgstc.org   E-mail: lgsadmissions@lgstc.org
Albert A. Brayson II, MEd, Pres. Norman Alperin, MS, Exec Dir.
  Focus: Spec Ed. **Conditions:** Primary—D ED. Sec—BD CD LD OCD. **IQ
  65 and up.**
  Gen Acad. Pre-Voc. Voc. Ungraded. Courses: Read Math Lang_Arts. Man_
  Arts & Shop. Shelt_Workshop. On-Job Trng.
  Therapy: Chemo Hear Lang Occup Phys Speech. **Psychotherapy:** Fam
  Group Indiv Parent.
  Staff: 45.
  Est 1941. Private. Nonprofit.

The Open Gates program of the Lake Grove School serves hearing-impaired adolescents who are experiencing mild to severe emotional difficulties. The 12-month program focuses on education, therapy, vocational development and socialization. Individualized educational plans stress basic academics in small-group and tutorial settings. Industrial arts, work-study and on-the-job work experiences highlight the vocational program. Students may obtain a high school diploma. Activities include recreation, trips and interscholastic sports.

LANGUAGE AND LEARNING ASSOCIATES

Clinic: Ages 3-21. M-S by Appt.

Harrison, NY 10528. 550 Mamaroneck Ave, Ste 102.
Tel: 914-381-4477.
Rosalind W. Rothman, BS, MA, EdD, Dir.
    Focus: Treatment. **Conditions:** Primary—ADD ADHD Ap Dc Dg Dx LD S.
      Sec—CD ED MR. **IQ 70 and up.**
    Gen Acad. Gr PS-Col.
    Therapy: Lang Speech. **Psychotherapy:** Indiv Parent.
    Staff: 15 (Full 9, Part 6).
    Rates 2003: Clinic $80-90/hr.
    Est 1980. Private.

LLA provides diagnosis and remediation for individuals with speech, language and learning impairments. Services include individualized sessions, school visits, and parent and teacher conferences.

LAVELLE SCHOOL FOR THE BLIND

Day — Coed Ages 3-21

Bronx, NY 10469. 3830 Paulding Ave.
Tel: 718-882-1212. Fax: 718-882-0005.
Angelus Healy, Supt.
    Focus: Spec Ed. **Conditions:** Primary—B.
    Gen Acad. Pre-Voc. Ungraded. Courses: Read Math Lang_Arts Braille.
      Man_Arts & Shop.
    Therapy: Hear Occup Phys Speech. **Psychotherapy:** Indiv.
    Enr: 90.
    Rates 2004: No Fee.
    Est 1904. Private. Nonprofit.

Education of the legally blind at Lavelle consists of an academic program, training in braille techniques, music, manual arts, gymnastics, typing, dramatics and cane travel. Counseling is available. The duration of treatment varies.

LEAGUE FOR THE HARD OF HEARING

Clinic: All Ages. M-F 9-5, S by Appt; Eves by Appt.

New York, NY 10004. 50 Broadway, 6th Fl.
Tel: 917-305-7700. TTY: 917-305-7999. Fax: 917-305-7888.
www.lhh.org
Laurie Hanin, PhD, CCC-A, Exec Dir.
    Focus: Treatment. **Conditions:** Primary—D S. Sec—B.
    Therapy: Hear Lang Speech. **Psychotherapy:** Fam Group Indiv Parent.
    Staff: 48 (Full 36, Part 12).
    Est 1910. Private. Nonprofit.

LHH conducts programs in audiology and communication therapy. Parental, personal, educational and vocational counseling are available, and the usual duration of treatment is one to 10 visits.

LEAGUE TREATMENT CENTER

Day — Coed Ages 2½-21

Brooklyn, NY 11201. 30 Washington St.
Tel: 718-643-5300. Fax: 718-643-0640.
www.leaguetreatment.org   E-mail: office@leaguetreatment.org
Hannah A. Achtenberg-Kinn, MA, Exec Dir. **Aubrey Reese,** Clin Dir. **Polizoes Polizos,** MD, Med Dir.
   Focus: Spec Ed. Treatment. **Conditions:** Primary—ADD ADHD Asp Au BD CD Dc Dg Dx ED Mood OCD Psy PTSD PW SP Sz TS. Sec—Ap Bl Ep MR. **IQ 50-120.**
   Gen Acad. Pre-Voc. Ungraded. Courses: Read Math Lang_Arts. Shelt_ Workshop. On-Job Trng.
   Therapy: Chemo Lang Movement Music Occup Phys Speech. **Psychotherapy:** Fam Group Indiv.
   Enr: 225. Day Males 165. Day Females 60. **Staff:** 97 (Full 93, Part 4).
   Rates 2003: No Fee.
   Summer Prgm: Day. Educ. Ther. 4 wks.
   Est 1953. Private. Nonprofit.

The center comprises five facilities that provide a continuum of service for multiply mentally handicapped preschoolers, school-age children, aging-out students and adults.

A therapeutic nursery emphasizes speech and language development through total communication, as well as providing special education. The day school and the treatment center focus on special education, daily living activities and prevocational skills. In the adult day treatment center the program is geared toward adaptive learning skills and appropriate socialization based on a token economy. A work training program and supported work are available. Special services and therapies are provided as needed. All facilities have multidisciplinary teams involved in assessment, programming and treatment.

LEARNING DISABILITIES ASSOCIATES

Clinic: All Ages. M-S 9-6; Eve T 6-9:30.

Latham, NY 12110. 400 Troy-Schenectady Rd.
Tel: 518-785-4433. Fax: 518-785-4433.
John R. Ouimet, BS, MA, Dir.
   Focus: Spec Ed. **Conditions:** Primary—Ap Dx LD S. Sec—Bl CP ED MR OH. **IQ 75 and up.**
   Gen Acad. Courses: Read Math Lang_Arts.
   Therapy: Hear Lang Speech. **Psychotherapy:** Indiv.
   Staff: 10 (Full 4, Part 6). Prof 10.
   Est 1977. Private. Inc.

The clinic provides diagnosis and treatment for individuals with reading, writing, math, and speech and language disorders. Remediation is performed over a six- to 15-week trial period. Staff members then evaluate the client's progress and recommend either further clinical remediation, school-based remediation or home-based remediation. If necessary, clinicians train parents to administer home remediation.

LEEWAY SCHOOL

Day — Coed Ages Birth-14

Sayville, NY 11782. 335 Johnson Ave.
Tel: 631-589-8060. Fax: 631-589-0908.
Anne Tinder, MS, Exec Dir.
> **Focus:** Spec Ed. **Conditions:** Primary—ADD ADHD Ap Apr Dx LD S.
> Sec—Asp Au ED MR PDD. **IQ 70 and up.**
> **Gen Acad.** Ungraded. Courses: Read Math Lang_Arts Music.
> **Therapy:** Hear Lang Movement Music Occup Phys Play Speech. **Psycho-therapy:** Group Indiv.
> **Staff:** 65 (Full 59, Part 6). Admin 2.
> **Rates 2004:** No Fee.
> **Est 1969.** Private. Nonprofit.

Leeway offers individualized programs and a structured class environment. A multisensory approach to reading is offered with other academics. Social behavior and self-help, health and motor skills are integral parts of the program. The school's early intervention program provides multidisciplinary services for children under age 3. The preschool program emphasizes speech and language development. Counseling and speech training are also available.

LENOX HILL HOSPITAL
CENTER FOR COMMUNICATION DISORDERS

Clinic: All Ages. M-F 9-5; Eves M W 5-8.

New York, NY 10021. 100 E 77th St.
Tel: 212-434-3385. Fax: 212-434-4978.
www.lenoxhillhospital.org/services/meeth.jsp
> **Conditions:** Primary—Ap LD S.
> **Therapy:** Hear Lang Speech.
> **Staff:** Prof 6.
> Private.

LEXINGTON SCHOOL FOR THE DEAF

Day — Coed Ages Birth-21

Jackson Heights, NY 11370. 30th Ave & 75th St.
Tel: 718-899-8800. TTY: 718-899-3030. Fax: 718-899-9846.

Frank G. Bowe, PhD, Supt.
  Focus: Spec Ed. **Conditions:** Primary—D. Sec—Ap B MR OH.
  Col Prep. Gen Acad. Pre-Voc. Voc. Gr PS-12. **Courses:** Read Math Lang_
    Arts. Shelt_Workshop. On-Job Trng.
  Therapy: Hear Lang Occup Phys Speech. **Psychotherapy:** Fam Group
    Indiv Parent.
  Enr: 384. **Staff:** 250.
  Est 1864. State. Nonprofit.

Comprehensive instruction for students who are profoundly deaf consists of the following: an early intervention program serving children from birth to age 3; preschool, elementary, middle school and high school programs; and a program designed for individuals who are deaf and multiple disabled called the Special Education Unit. All programs utilize Mediated Learning, a teaching/learning framework developed by Dr. Reuven Feuerstein that allows students to make meaningful connections across content areas and thus participate more actively in the learning process.

Graduating pupils may earn either a standard or a specialized high school diploma. Career education begins in the elementary grades and culminates in the middle and high school years, when students explore potential careers through formal classes, internships and community service experiences.

Various residential and vocational services are available through the Lexington Center for the Deaf.

LIFELINE CENTER FOR CHILD DEVELOPMENT

Day — Coed Ages 2-18

Queens Village, NY 11427. 80-09 Winchester Blvd.
Tel: 718-740-4300. Fax: 718-217-9566.
www.lifelinecenter.org   E-mail: llifecenter@aol.com
Joseph Zacherman, PhD, Exec Dir. **Sungnai Cho,** MD, Med Dir.
  Focus: Treatment. **Conditions:** Primary—Anx ED Mood OCD ODD Psy
    PTSD SP TS. Sec—ADHD Dc Dg Dx LD MR S Sz. **IQ 55-120.**
  Gen Acad. Pre-Voc. Gr PS-11. **Courses:** Read Math Lang_Arts.
  Therapy: Art Lang Milieu Music Occup Phys Play Speech. **Psychotherapy:**
    Fam Group Indiv.
  Enr: 186. **Staff:** 100 (Full 91, Part 9).
  Rates 2003: No Fee.
  Summer Prgm: Day. Educ. Ther.
  Est 1959. Private. Nonprofit.

Lifeline treats severely emotionally disturbed children through a full range of clinical services. Individual and group therapy are provided for children and parents. A special education component utilizes a therapeutic milieu and individualized programs.

LIFESPIRE

Res and Day — Coed Ages 18 and up

New York, NY 10118. 350 5th Ave, Ste 301.

Tel: 212-741-0100. Fax: 212-242-0696.
www.lifespire.org E-mail: info@lifespire.org
Mark van Voorst, Pres.
> **Focus:** Rehab. Trng. Treatment. **Conditions:** Primary—MR. **IQ 50 and up.**
> **Pre-Voc. Voc.** Shelt_Workshop.
> **Therapy:** Hear Occup Phys Speech. **Psychotherapy:** Fam Indiv.
> **Est 1951.** Federal. Nonprofit.

LIGHTHOUSE INTERNATIONAL

Day — Coed All Ages

New York, NY 10022. 111 E 59th St.
> **Nearby locations:** Queens, Brooklyn, Staten Island, Westchester and Duchess Counties.

Tel: 212-821-9200. TTY: 212-821-9713. Fax: 212-821-9707.
www.lighthouse.org E-mail: info@lighthouse.org
Barbara Silverstone, Pres.
> **Focus:** Spec Ed. Rehab. Treatment. **Conditions:** Primary—B.
> **Gen Acad.**
> **Est 1905.** Private. Nonprofit.

LITTLE VILLAGE SCHOOL

Day — Coed Ages Birth-12

Seaford, NY 11783. 750 Hicksville Rd.
Tel: 516-520-6000. Fax: 516-796-6341.
www.littlevillage.org
Barbara Feingold, PhD, Co-Dir. **Caryl Bank,** PhD, Co-Dir. **Vijaya Atluru,** MD, Med Dir.
> **Focus:** Spec Ed. **Conditions:** Primary—ADD ADHD Ap Apr Asp CF CP Dx Ep LD MR PDD S. Sec—As B BD BI C D ED IP MD MS Nf ON PW SB TB TS. **IQ 19-100.**
> **Pre-Voc.** Ungraded. Courses: Read Math Lang_Arts Adaptive_Phys_Ed.
> **Enr:** 411. Day Males 315. Day Females 96. **Staff:** 184 (Full 88, Part 96).
> **Rates 2004:** No Fee.
> **Summer Prgm:** Day. Educ. Ther.
> **Est 1969.** Private. Nonprofit.

Affiliated with the special education graduate programs at Hofstra and Adelphi universities, the Little Village School groups children in classes of six, nine or 12. The program includes prescriptive teaching, self-help and life skills, gross- and fine-motor training, remediation and therapy. Parental counseling is provided, and outpatient services are available. The usual duration of treatment is three years. There is a special early intervention program for parents and children under age 2 that includes home visitations and therapies.

LIVINGSTON-WYOMING ARC

Day — Coed Ages Birth-12, 18 and up

Mount Morris, NY 14510. 18 Main St.
Tel: 585-658-2828. Fax: 585-658-4109.
www.lwarc.org
Cynthia R. Huether, Exec Dir.
　Conditions: Primary—MR.
　Gen Acad. Gr PS.
　Therapy: Occup Phys Speech.
　Est 1961. Private. Nonprofit. **Spons:** The Arc.

LOCHLAND SCHOOL

Res — Coed Ages 18 and up

Geneva, NY 14456. 1065 Lochland Rd.
Tel: 315-789-5208. Fax: 315-789-4597.
www.lochland.org　E-mail: sbrier@lochland.org
Suzanne Brier, Exec Dir.
　Focus: Spec Ed. Trng. Treatment. **Conditions:** Primary—MR. **IQ 0-50.**
　Pre-Voc. Ungraded. Courses: Read Math Lang_Arts.
　Therapy: Hear Occup Phys Speech. **Psychotherapy:** Indiv.
　Est 1933. Private. Nonprofit.

LONG ISLAND COLLEGE HOSPITAL
STANLEY S. LAMM INSTITUTE
FOR CHILD NEUROLOGY AND DEVELOPMENTAL MEDICINE

Clinic: All Ages. M-F 8-6.

Brooklyn, NY 11201. 110 Amity St.
Tel: 718-780-1211. Fax: 718-780-2849.
www.wehealny.org/directory/lammsite/index.html
Vincent M. Mulvihill, BA, MDiv, MSA, Admin Dir. **Harvey S. Bennett,** MD, Med
　Dir. **Cristobal Amador & Iris Gersten,** Adms.
　Focus: Treatment. **Conditions:** Primary—ADD ADHD Ap Au B BI CP D Dx
　Ep IP LD MD MR MS ON S SB.
　Therapy: Lang Occup Phys Speech. **Psychotherapy:** Fam Group Indiv.
　Staff: 76 (Full 55, Part 21). Educ 40. Admin 4.
　Rates 2004: Clinic $272/ses. Sliding-Scale Rate $54-245/ses.
　Est 1951. Private. Nonprofit. **Spons:** Continuum Health Partners.

In addition to a preschool, the institute conducts a total care program. Offerings
include pediatric, orthopedic, neurological, general medical diagnostic and psychiatric
services, as well as social service counseling, rehabilitation and nutritional therapy.

Imaging procedures, metabolic and genetic studies, routine lab tests and dental care are also available. The institute accepts residents of Brooklyn.

LONG ISLAND COUNSELING CENTER

Clinic: All Ages. M-F 9-5, S 9-2:30; Eves M-Th 5-9.

Elmont, NY 11003. 570 Elmont Rd, Ste 301.
Tel: 516-437-6050.
Roger P. Feldman, MD, Co-Dir.
  Conditions: Primary—BD ED LD.
  Psychotherapy: Fam Group Indiv.
  Staff: Prof 19.
  Est 1958. County.

LONG ISLAND JEWISH MEDICAL CENTER
HEARING AND SPEECH CENTER

Clinic: Ages Birth-21. M-F 8-5; Eves W 5:30-8.

New Hyde Park, NY 11042. 270-05 76th Ave.
Tel: 718-470-8910. Fax: 718-347-8241.
www.northshorelij.com/hearingandspeech
Lynn G. Spivak, PhD, CCC-A, Dir. **Merrill Goodman,** MD, Med Dir.
  Focus: Treatment. **Conditions:** Primary—Ap D S. Sec—Au BI CP IP MD
    MR MS ON SB.
  Therapy: Hear Lang Speech. **Psychotherapy:** Group Indiv.
  Staff: 41 (Full 33, Part 8). Prof 19. Admin 7.
  Private. Nonprofit. **Spons:** North Shore-Long Island Jewish Health System.

  Providing diagnostic and treatment services for individuals with communicative and swallowing disorders, the center accepts referrals from schools, agencies, other medical facilities and the patients themselves. Although treating persons of all ages, the center places a particular emphasis on pediatric care.

THE LOWELL SCHOOL

Day — Coed Ages 5-21

Flushing, NY 11357. 24-20 Parsons Blvd.
Tel: 718-445-4222. Fax: 718-353-6942.
E-mail: tlschool@aol.com
Dede Proujansky, BA, MS, Exec Dir. **Susan Price & Veronica McCue,** Adms.
  Focus: Spec Ed. **Conditions:** Primary—Dx LD S. Sec—ED OCD. **IQ 70
    and up.**
  Gen Acad. Pre-Voc. Gr 1-12. Courses: Read Math Lang_Arts Sci Comput-
    ers Soc_Stud. On-Job Trng.
  Therapy: Art Hear Lang Occup Phys Speech. **Psychotherapy:** Group Indiv.

Enr: 220. **Staff:** 77 (Full 75, Part 2). Prof 35. Educ 35. Admin 7.
Rates 2003: Day $23,319/sch yr. State Aid.
Summer Prgm: Day. Educ. 6 wks.
Est 1968. Private. Nonprofit.

The school emphasizes intensive one-on-one sessions with specialists for building basic reading and math skills, language development and perceptual-motor skills. Each student participates in full academic, art and music programs. Counseling is offered, and Lowell encourages strong parental participation.

The improvement of the student's day-to-day performance and a placement in a less restrictive environment are program goals. Pupils who remain at Lowell through grade 12 typically enter the workforce, attend college or proceed to a vocational training program.

MAIMONIDES MEDICAL CENTER

Clinic: All Ages. M-F 9-5; Eves M W 5-7.

Brooklyn, NY 11219. 4802 10th Ave.
Tel: 718-283-6000.
www.maimonidesmed.org   E-mail: info@maimonidesmed.org
Pamela S. Brier, CEO.
　　Focus: Treatment. **Conditions:** Primary—ADD ADHD Ap Au CP Dx Ep LD MR ON S. Sec—As B C CD D ED OCD Psy SB Sz TB. **IQ 20 and up.**
　　Therapy: Chemo Hear Lang Speech. **Psychotherapy:** Fam Group Indiv Parent.
　　Private.

This center provides year-round comprehensive diagnostic evaluations and individualized treatment services for infants, children and adults with a broad range of developmental disabilities, including care for those who have been dually diagnosed. Maimonides specializes in working with young children suspected of developmental delay. A sliding-scale fee is available to eligible clients and their families.

MAPLEBROOK SCHOOL

Res and Day — Coed Ages 11-21

Amenia, NY 12501. 5142 Rte 22.
Tel: 845-373-9511. Fax: 845-373-7029.
www.maplebrookschool.org   E-mail: mbsecho@aol.com
Roger A. Fazzone, MA, EdD, Pres. **Donna M. Konkolics,** MA, Head. **Jennifer L. Scully,** Adm.
　　Focus: Spec Ed. **Conditions:** Primary—ADD ADHD Ap LD S. Sec—Apr Bl Dc Dg Dx Ep OH. **IQ 70-95.**
　　Gen Acad. Pre-Voc. Ungraded. Courses: Read Math Lang_Arts Span Computers Psych Home_Ec. On-Job Trng.
　　Therapy: Lang Percepual-Motor Speech.
　　Enr: 77. Res Males 33. Res Females 37. Day Males 5. Day Females 2.
　　　　Staff: 70 (Full 55, Part 15). Prof 29. Admin 12.

Rates 2004: Res $37,400-41,950/sch yr. Day $25,900/sch yr. Schol 15
($130,000).
Summer Prgm: Res. Educ. Rec. Res Rate $7000. 6 wks.
Est 1945. Private. Nonprofit.

Predominantly a boarding school, Maplebrook offers academic and social programs
to adolescents who are unable to thrive in traditional school settings or whose learning differences require more individual attention. The program includes individualized
tutorials designed to remediate academic weaknesses, and faculty place emphasis on
multisensory instruction and the development of social skills and self-esteem. CAPS
(The Center for the Advancement of Post Secondary Studies), a postsecondary program
providing either vocational or college programming, is available to students ages 18-21
for an additional fee.

The school does not accept individuals with emotional or behavioral problems.

MARTIN DE PORRES SCHOOL

Day — Coed Ages 7-21

Springfield Gardens, NY 11413. 136-25 218th St.
Tel: 718-525-3414. Fax: 718-525-0982.
www.mdp.org   E-mail: ccristen@mdp.org
Br. Raymond Blixt, Exec Dir. **Ed Dana,** Adm.
  Focus: Spec Ed. **Conditions:** Primary—ADD ADHD Asp BD ED LD. Sec—
    Anx Au BI CD Dx Mood MR OCD PTSD SP TS. **IQ 50 and up.**
  Col Prep. Gen Acad. Pre-Voc. Voc. Gr 1-12. Courses: Read Math Lang_
    Arts Fr Sci Computers Soc_Stud Studio_Art Music Dance. Man_Arts &
    Shop. Shelt_Workshop. On-Job Trng. Culinary_Arts.
  Therapy: Art Dance Hear Milieu Movement Music Occup Phys Speech.
    Psychotherapy: Group Indiv.
  Enr: 306. Day Males 263. Day Females 43. **Staff:** 125 (Full 121, Part 4).
    Prof 87. Educ 35.
  Rates 2004: No Fee.
  Est 1972. Private. Nonprofit. Roman Catholic.

Martin de Porres serves children who have had difficulties in the development of
their educational skills and whose behavior has been severely disoriented and disruptive.
The curriculum offers a blend of academic, affective and practical learning experiences.
Students come from New York City and Nassau County, and the sending school district
pays tuition fees.

THE MARY MCDOWELL CENTER FOR LEARNING

Day — Coed Ages 5-12

Brooklyn, NY 11201. 20 Bergen St.
Tel: 718-625-3939. Fax: 718-625-1456.
www.marymcdowell.org   E-mail: info@mmcl.net
Debbie Zlotowitz, BA, MS, Head. **Deborah Edel,** Adm.
  Focus: Spec Ed. **Conditions:** Primary—ADD ADHD Dc Dg Dx LD. Sec—

OH S TS. **IQ 90 and up.**
Gen Acad. Ungraded. Courses: Read Math Lang_Arts Sci Computers Studio_Art Music.
Therapy: Lang Movement Occup Percepual-Motor Speech. **Psychotherapy:** Indiv Parent.
Enr: 108.
Rates 2003: Day $400/sem. Schol avail.
Est 1984. Private. Nonprofit. Religious Society of Friends.

This Friends school offers education and therapy to children of average to above-average intelligence with learning disabilities. Classes are small and are grouped by skill level and age. Enrichment classes include computers, drama/music, library, movement, science, Spanish and physical education.

Social skills groups are available for an additional fee.

MARYHAVEN CENTER OF HOPE
CHILDREN'S SERVICES

Res and Day — Coed Ages 5-21

Port Jefferson, NY 11777. 450 Myrtle Ave.
Tel: 631-474-3400. Fax: 631-474-4181.
www.maryhaven.org
Robin Dwyer, MSW, Dir. **Arthur Kurtz,** MD, Med Dir. **Miriam Fortunoff,** Intake.
   Focus: Spec Ed. **Conditions:** Primary—Asp Au DS MR PDD. Sec—ADD ADHD Anx Ap Apr As BD CD CP Dc Dg Dx ED Ep LD Mood OCD ON PTSD PW SB TS. **IQ 0-70.**
   Pre-Voc. Voc. Ungraded. Courses: Read Math Lang_Arts. Shelt_Workshop. On-Job Trng.
   Therapy: Dance Lang Occup Percepual-Motor Phys Play Recreational Speech. **Psychotherapy:** Group Indiv.
   Staff: 320 (Full 243, Part 77). Educ 70. Admin 3.
   Rates 2004: No Fee.
   Est 1934. Private. Nonprofit. Roman Catholic.

Maryhaven offers educational, residential, recreational and clinical services to children who are mentally retarded or multiply handicapped. The integrated team of teachers, residential counselors, nurses and clinical professionals maintain a consistent approach while addressing the child's needs.

MERCY OF NORTHERN NEW YORK
BEHAVIORAL HEALTH SERVICES

Clinic: All Ages. M-Th 8-5, F 8-4:30.

Watertown, NY 13601. 218 Stone St.
Tel: 315-782-7445. Fax: 315-779-1184.
Mark Stoddart, Dir.
   Focus: Treatment. **Conditions:** Primary—ADD ADHD BD CD ED Mood

OCD Psy Sz TS. Sec—MR. **IQ 50 and up.**
Psychotherapy: Fam Group Indiv Parent.
Staff: 23 (Full 19, Part 4). Prof 19. Admin 4.
Rates 2001: Clinic $126-147/hr. State Aid.
Est 1971. Private. Nonprofit.

Formerly Genesis Healthcare of New York, Mercy of Northern New York operates an outpatient clinic for children and adults with mental and emotional difficulties. The children's team, serving those under age 19, provides a broad range of services, including group, individual and family therapies. The facility also operates an ADHD clinic and offers continuing day treatment for adults.

MILL NECK MANOR SCHOOL FOR DEAF CHILDREN AND EARLY CHILDHOOD CENTER

Day — Coed Ages Birth-21

Mill Neck, NY 11765. Frost Mill Rd, PO Box 12.
Tel: 516-922-4100. Fax: 516-922-4172.
www.millneck.org   E-mail: info@millneck.org
Mark R. Prowatzke, PhD, Supt. **Francine Atlas Bogdanoff,** Adm.
  Focus: Spec Ed. **Conditions:** Primary—D. Sec—CP ON S. **IQ 50 and up.**
  Col Prep. Gen Acad. Pre-Voc. Voc. Gr PS-12. Courses: Read Math Lang_
    Arts Sci. Man_Arts & Shop. On-Job Trng.
  Therapy: Hear Lang Occup Phys Speech. **Psychotherapy:** Fam Group
    Indiv.
  Enr: 200. **Staff:** 88 (Full 79, Part 9).
  Rates 2004: No Fee.
  Summer Prgm: Day. Educ.
  Est 1951. Private. Nonprofit. Lutheran.

Mill Neck Manor accepts severely to profoundly deaf children who have been evaluated by the assessment team. Services are available for both deaf infants and their families. The school maintains an early childhood center for communicationally delayed and language-delayed preschoolers.

An alternative program for multiply handicapped deaf children offers preparation for independent living. The school is state supported and enrollment is not limited to Lutherans.

MORRISANIA DIAGNOSTIC & TREATMENT CENTER

Day — Coed Ages Birth-18
Clinic: Ages Birth-18.

Bronx, NY 10452. 1225 Gerard Ave.
Tel: 718-960-2777.
www.ci.nyc.ny.us/html/hhc/html/morrisania.html
  Conditions: Primary—BD ED. Sec—MR.
  Gen Acad. Courses: Read Math Lang_Arts. Man_Arts & Shop. On-Job Trng.
  Therapy: Occup.
  Est 1940. Municipal. Nonprofit.

MOUNT ST. URSULA SPEECH CENTER

Clinic: Ages 3-18. M-F 8:30-4:30.

Bronx, NY 10458. 2885 Marion Ave.
Tel: 718-584-7679. Fax: 718-584-7954.
Sr. Bernadette Hannaway, MA, Admin. **Richard Lane,** MD, Med Dir.
  Focus: Trng. **Conditions:** Primary—Ap S.
  Therapy: Hear Lang Speech.
  Staff: 15.
  Rates 2003: Clinic $75/hr.
  Est 1961. Private. Nonprofit.

Serving the needs of children with speech, language and hearing disorders and associated learning disabilities, the center emphasizes early diagnosis and treatment. Children receive treatment either in small groups or individually, according to their needs.

MT. SINAI MEDICAL CENTER
CHILD AND ADOLESCENT PSYCHIATRY CLINIC

Clinic: Ages 5-18. M-F 9-5; Eves M-F 5-7.

New York, NY 10029. 1 Gustave L Levy Pl, Box 1228.
Tel: 212-241-7175. Fax: 212-987-5683.
Edward Greenblatt, PhD, Dir. **Abraham Bartell,** MD, Clin Dir. **Regina Lara,**
  MD, Med Dir. **Joan Dornhoefer,** Intake.
  Focus: Treatment. **Conditions:** Primary—ADD ADHD AN Anx BD Bu CD
    ED Mood OCD Psy PTSD SP Sz TS. Sec—Ap As Asp Au B Bl Db Dx Ep
    LD MR ON PDD PW S. **IQ 65 and up.**
  Psychotherapy: Fam Group Indiv Parent.
  Staff: 9 (Full 6, Part 3). Prof 9.
  Est 1853. Private. Nonprofit.

The clinic offers mental health diagnoses and short- and long-term treatment. Treatments offered include individual, group and parental psychotherapy, as well as educational counseling. Fees are determined along a sliding scale.

MT. SINAI MEDICAL CENTER
COMMUNICATION DISORDERS CENTER

Clinic: All Ages. M-F 8-5.

New York, NY 10029. 1 Gustave Levy Pl.
Tel: 212-241-6153. Fax: 212-831-1816.
  Conditions: Primary—D Dx LD. **IQ 40 and up.**
  Gen Acad. Gr PS-PG. Courses: Read Math Lang_Arts.
  Therapy: Hear Lang Speech. **Psychotherapy:** Fam Group Indiv.
  Staff: Prof 16.
  Private.

NASSAU LEARNING CENTER

Day — Coed Ages 15-21
Clinic: Ages 15 and up. M-F 8-4.

Port Washington, NY 11050. 382 Main St.
  Nearby locations: Deer Park.
Tel: 516-883-3006. Fax: 516-883-0412.
E-mail: jerrystone@nyc.rr.com
Gerald Stone, Prgm Dir.
  Focus: Spec Ed. **Conditions:** Primary—ADD ADHD Dc Dg Dx ED LD.
    Sec—BD CD ODD. **IQ 80 and up.**
  Col Prep. Gen Acad. Gr 9-12. Courses: Read Math Lang_Arts.
  Psychotherapy: Indiv.
  Enr: 90. Day Males 60. Day Females 30. **Staff:** 49 (Full 6, Part 43).
  Rates 2003: $40 (Clinic)/ses.
  Summer Prgm: Day. Educ. 4 wks.
  Est 1970. Private. Nonprofit. **Spons:** Education and Assistance Corporation.

Individual psychotherapy is an integral component of the center's services. The high school level, tutorial-based program specializes in students who are phobic, withdrawn, learning disabled or not functioning in the mainstream. Other services include psycho-educational evaluations; tutorials for all ages; liaison services between family and school; various workshops on family issues; and a program that teaches life skills and provides career planning.

A branch of the clinic is located at 300 Park Ave., Deer Park 11729.

NEW INTERDISCIPLINARY SCHOOL

Day — Coed Ages Birth-5

Yaphank, NY 11980. 430 Sills Rd.
Tel: 631-924-5583. Fax: 631-924-5687.
www.niskids.org   E-mail: info@niskids.org
Helen Wilder, Exec Dir.
  Focus: Spec Ed. **Conditions:** Primary—Au BD BI CD CP ED MD MR ON
    PDD SB Sz. Sec—ADD ADHD Ap As C D Ep IP LD S.
  Gen Acad. Gr PS-K.
  Therapy: Hear Lang Music Occup Phys Play Speech. **Psychotherapy:**
    Fam Group Indiv Parent.
  Enr: 320. Day Males 200. Day Females 120. **Staff:** 104 (Full 96, Part 8).
  Rates 2004: No Fee.
  Summer Prgm: Day. Educ. Rec. Ther. 6 wks.
  Est 1976. Private. Nonprofit. **Spons:** Independent Group Home Living.

NIS provides education for young children with and without disabilities. Therapy is available at the school, at home and in the community. The length of treatment varies according to the child's needs, and there is no fee for residents of Suffolk County.

NEW YORK HOSPITAL CORNELL MEDICAL CENTER HEARING AND SPEECH SERVICE

Clinic: All Ages. M-F 7-5, Sat 8-12; Eves M-F 5-7.

New York, NY 10021. NYPH-WMCCU, Dept of Otorhinolaryngology, Box 101.
Tel: 212-746-2231. Fax: 212-746-2253.
www.nycornell.org/ent
Peg Warren, Admin.
   Focus: Rehab. Treatment. **Conditions:** Primary—Ap D S.
   Therapy: Hear Lang Speech.
   Staff: Prof 5.
   Private. Nonprofit. **Spons:** New York Presbyterian Hospital.

THE NEW YORK INSTITUTE FOR SPECIAL EDUCATION

Res — Coed Ages 5-21; Day — Coed 3-21

Bronx, NY 10469. 999 Pelham Pky.
Tel: 718-519-7000. Fax: 718-231-9314.
www.nyise.org
   Conditions: Primary—B ED LD MR. Sec—BD ON S.
   Col Prep. Gen Acad. Pre-Voc. Ungraded. Courses: Read Math Lang_Arts.
   Man_Arts & Shop. On-Job Trng.
   Therapy: Lang Occup Phys Speech.
   Est 1831. Private. Nonprofit.

NEW YORK PRESBYTERIAN MEDICAL CENTER-COLUMBIA CAMPUS SPEECH AND HEARING DEPARTMENT

Clinic: All Ages. M-F 8:30-5; Eves M-Th by Appt.

New York, NY 10032. 622 W 168th St.
Tel: 212-305-2961. Fax: 212-305-2249.
www.entcolumbia.org/audspdiv.htm
Jaclyn B. Spitzer, PhD, Dir. **Lanny Garth Close,** MD, Med Dir.
   Focus: Rehab. **Conditions:** Primary—Ap D S. Sec—ADD ADHD Au ED LD.
   Therapy: Hear Lang Speech.
   Staff: 18 (Full 14, Part 4). Prof 18.
   Est 1947. Private. Nonprofit.

The department provides diagnosis and treatment of hearing, voice, language, learning and speech disorders. Other services include cochlear implant evaluation, surgery, rehabilitation and follow-up.

NEW YORK SCHOOL FOR THE DEAF

Res — Coed Ages 10-21; Day — Coed 3-21

White Plains, NY 10603. 555 Knollwood Rd.
Tel: 914-949-7310. TTY: 914-949-7310. Fax: 914-949-8260.
www.nysd.k12.ny.us   E-mail: fanwood@nysd.k12.ny.us
John T. Tiffany, PhD, Head.

> **Focus:** Spec Ed. **Conditions:** Primary—D. Sec—ADD ADHD CP Dx LD MD MS OH.
>
> **Col Prep. Gen Acad. Pre-Voc. Voc.** Gr PS-PG. Courses: Read Math Lang_ Arts. Man_Arts & Shop. On-Job Trng.
>
> **Therapy:** Hear Lang Occup Phys Speech. **Psychotherapy:** Indiv.
>
> **Enr:** 155.
>
> **Rates 2004:** No Fee.
>
> **Est 1817.** Private. Nonprofit.

NYSD offers a complete academic program for children who are profoundly deaf, as well as vocational, psychiatric and psychological casework and special training. Career and transition services are available at all grade levels, particularly for pupils age 14 and up.

NEW YORK STATE SCHOOL FOR THE BLIND

Res and Day — Coed Ages 5-21

Batavia, NY 14020. 2A Richmond Ave.
Tel: 585-343-5384. Fax: 585-344-5557.
www.vesid.nysed.gov/specialed/nyssb   E-mail: nyssb@mail.nysed.gov
Jennifer Spas Ervin, MS, Supt. **Suzanne Wheeler,** Adm.

> **Focus:** Spec Ed. **Conditions:** Primary—B. Sec—ADD ADHD Ap As Au BI C CP D Dx ED Ep IP LD MD MR MS ON S SB TB.
>
> **Gen Acad. Pre-Voc.** Gr K-12. Courses: Read Math Lang_Arts Sci Life_ Skills Braille Orientation & Mobility Adaptive_Phys_Ed. Man_Arts & Shop.
>
> **Therapy:** Hear Occup Phys Speech. **Psychotherapy:** Group Parent.
>
> **Enr:** 75.
>
> **Rates 2004:** No Fee.
>
> **Summer Prgm:** Res & Day. Educ. 6 wks.
>
> **Est 1866.** State. Nonprofit.

NYSSB is a state-operated school for students who are legally blind and have accompanying disabilities. The program involves all aspects of educational and personal skills. While focusing on hearing therapy, the school also provides occupational, physical and speech therapy. Tuition fees are paid by the state.

NEW YORK STATE SCHOOL FOR THE DEAF

Res — Coed Ages 5-21; Day — Coed 3-21

Rome, NY 13440. 401 Turin St.
Tel: 315-337-8400. TTY: 315-337-8489. Fax: 315-336-8859.
www.vesid.nysed.gov/specialed/nyssd
Nancy Clark, BS, MS, Supt. Lawrence Glantz, MD, Med Dir. Gordon Baker, Adm.
Focus: Spec Ed. Conditions: Primary—D. Sec—ADD ADHD AN Anx Ap As Asp Au B BD BI Bu CD CP Db Dg DS Dx ED Ep IP LD MD Mood MR OCD ON PDD S TS.
Col Prep. Gen Acad. Pre-Voc. Voc. Gr PS-12. Courses: Read Math Lang_ Arts Sci Soc_Stud Studio_Art Mus. Shelt_Workshop. On-Job Trng.
Therapy: Art Hear Lang Music Occup Phys Recreational Speech. Psychotherapy: Indiv.
Enr: 86. Res Males 43. Res Females 14. Day Males 18. Day Females 11.
Staff: 77 (Full 74, Part 3). Prof 42. Educ 28. Admin 4.
Rates 2003: No Fee.
Summer Prgm: Res & Day. Educ. 6 wks.
Est 1875. State. Nonprofit.

The agency serves as a state facility for children with hearing impairments. It offers a comprehensive educational and residential program. Art, music and recreational therapies complement the hearing therapy program. An academic curriculum at all grade levels and vocational training are available to students.

NEW YORK UNIVERSITY CHILD STUDY CENTER

Clinic: Ages Birth-24. M-F.

New York, NY 10016. 577 1st Ave.
Tel: 212-263-6622. Fax: 212-263-0990.
www.aboutourkids.org   E-mail: services@aboutourkids.org
Harold S. Koplewicz, MD, Dir.
Conditions: Primary—BD ED LD. Sec—ADHD AN Anx Bu Mood TS. Courses: Read Math Lang_Arts.
Psychotherapy: Fam Group Indiv.
Staff: Prof 71.
Est 1998. Municipal. Spons: New York University School of Medicine.

THE NORMAN HOWARD SCHOOL

Day — Coed Ages 11-18

Rochester, NY 14623. 275 Pinnacle Rd.
Tel: 585-334-8010. Fax: 585-334-8073.
www.normanhoward.org   E-mail: info@normanhoward.org
Marcie C. Roberts, Exec Dir. Julie Murray, Adm.

Focus: Spec Ed. **Conditions:** Primary—ADD ADHD Dc Dg Dx LD. Sec—
Asp TS. **IQ 97 and up.**
Col Prep. Gen Acad. Gr 5-12. Courses: Read Math Lang_Arts Sci Comput-
ers Soc_Stud Studio_Art Music Health.
Therapy: Lang Speech.
Enr: 161. Day Males 126. Day Females 35. **Staff:** 78 (Full 70, Part 8).
Rates 2003: Day $22,000/sch yr. Schol 5 ($28,000).
Summer Prgm: Day. Educ. Rec. Day Rate $235. 3 wks.
Est 1980. Private. Nonprofit.

The school offers remedial work to children of average and above intelligence who
suffer from learning disabilities. The curriculum stresses college preparation in the areas
of reading, writing, spelling, math and organizational skills. Visual and auditory teaching
methods, study skills, and educational, college and parental counseling are available.

NORTH SHORE
CHILD AND FAMILY GUIDANCE CENTER

Clinic: Ages Birth-24. M-F 9-5; Eves M-Th 5-9.

Roslyn Heights, NY 11577. 480 Old Westbury Rd.
Tel: 516-626-1971. Fax: 516-626-8043.
www.northshorechildguidance.org
  E-mail: info@northshorechildguidance.org
Marion Levine, ACSW, Exec Dir.
  Conditions: Primary—ADD ADHD Au BD CD Dx ED LD MR OCD ON Psy
  Sz.
  Therapy: Chemo Speech. **Psychotherapy:** Fam Group Indiv Parent.
  Staff: 71 (Full 55, Part 16).
  Est 1914. Private. Nonprofit.

Providing mental health services for children, youth and families in Long Island, the
center offers direct service, training and consultation, and advocacy. Fees are assessed
on a sliding-scale basis. In addition to the Roslyn Heights location, the center serves
clients at facilities in Manhasset and Westbury.

NORTH SHORE LEARNING ASSOCIATES

Clinic: Ages 6-21. M-F 8-5; Eves M-Th 5-9.

Roslyn Heights, NY 11577. 37 Milburn Ln.
Tel: 516-625-1008. Fax: 516-625-1034.
E-mail: drsnlsa@aol.com
Howard S. Boll, EdD, Co-Dir. **Joan Bossis,** EdD, Co-Dir.
  Focus: Treatment. **Conditions:** Primary—ADD ADHD Dc Dg Dx LD. Sec—
  Anx Au BD Bu CD ED Mood OCD SP. **IQ 85 and up.**
  Therapy: Lang Speech. **Psychotherapy:** Fam Indiv Parent.
  Staff: 3 (Full 2, Part 1). Prof 2.
  Rates 2003: Clinic $125/ses.

Est 1980. Private. Inc.

This private practice provides individualized psycho-educational therapy and comprehensive diagnostic testing and consultative services for individuals with learning disabilities, attention deficit disorder, panic attacks and eating disorders. NSLA also offers such dual services as meta-cognitive training, organizational and study skills instruction, and psychoanalytic therapy.

NORTH SHORE UNIVERSITY HOSPITAL
NEUROPSYCHOLOGICAL SERVICES

Day — Coed Ages Birth-5
Clinic: All Ages. M-F 8-6.

Manhasset, NY 11030. 300 Community Dr.
Tel: 516-562-0100.
   Conditions: Primary—ADHD Au BD ED LD OH.
   Therapy: Hear Lang Occup Phys Speech. **Psychotherapy:** Fam Indiv.
   Staff: Prof 43.
   Private.

NORTH SHORE UNIVERSITY HOSPITAL
SPEECH AND HEARING CENTER

Clinic: All Ages. M-S 9-5.

Manhasset, NY 11030. 300 Community Dr.
Tel: 516-562-4600. Fax: 516-562-2404.
www.northshorelij.com
   Conditions: Primary—Ap D LD S.
   Therapy: Hear Lang Speech.
   Est 1969. Private. Nonprofit.

NORTHSIDE CENTER FOR CHILD DEVELOPMENT

Day — Coed Ages 9mos-8
Clinic: Ages 5-17.

New York, NY 10029. 1301 5th Ave.
Tel: 212-426-3400. Fax: 212-410-7561.
www.northsidecenter.org
Thelma Dye, Exec Dir.
   Conditions: Primary—ED LD S.
   Therapy: Art Lang Music Occup Phys Speech. **Psychotherapy:** Fam
      Group Indiv.
   Est 1946. Private. Nonprofit.

OAK HILL SCHOOL

Day — Coed Ages 7-14

Scotia, NY 12302. 39 Charlton Rd.
Tel: 518-399-5048. Fax: 518-399-6140.
E-mail: oakhill12@aol.com
Sylvia K. Johann, EdD, Exec Dir.
  Focus: Spec Ed. Treatment. **Conditions:** Primary—ED. Sec—BD CD OCD.
    IQ 90 and up.
  Gen Acad. Gr 2-8. Courses: Read Math Lang_Arts. Man_Arts & Shop.
  Therapy: Speech. **Psychotherapy:** Fam.
  Enr: 24. Day Males 21. Day Females 3. **Staff:** 12 (Full 9, Part 3).
  Rates 2004: No Fee.
  Summer Prgm: Day. 6 wks.
  Est 1970. Private. Nonprofit.

The Oak Hill program is designed for children who have severe learning problems or behavioral disorders or both. Remedial education in all subjects, combined with field trips, camping and group discussions, aims to improve the child's self-understanding and academic and socializing skills. The usual length of treatment is two to three years, and the sending district pays tuition charges.

OHEL CHILDREN'S HOME AND FAMILY SERVICES

Res — Coed Ages 7-18
Clinic: Ages 10-21. M-F 9-5; Eves M T 5-9.

Brooklyn, NY 11204. 4510 16th Ave.
Tel: 718-851-6300. Fax: 718-851-2772.
www.ohelfamily.org   E-mail: askohel@ohelfamily.org
David Mandel, CEO.
  Focus: Treatment. **Conditions:** Primary—Au BD CD ED OCD Psy Sz.
    Sec—ADD ADHD Dx LD MR OH.
  Therapy: Chemo Lang Speech. **Psychotherapy:** Fam Group Indiv.
  Enr: 27. Res Males 27.
  Rates 2004: No Fee.
  Est 1969. Private. Nonprofit. Jewish.

Located in a residential section of Boro Park, Ohel offers year-round group residences, homes and foster care programs for emotionally and socially disturbed and retarded children and adults. Licensed under Orthodox Jewish auspices, the programs enroll strictly Jewish children. Community Yeshivas and special schools provide educational programs. Counseling and outpatient services are available, and length of treatment varies.

ONTARIO COUNTY MENTAL HEALTH CENTER

Clinic: All Ages. M-F 8:30-5; Eve M 6-8:30.

Canandaigua, NY 14424. 3019 County Complex Dr.
Tel: 585-396-4363. Fax: 585-396-4993.
www.co.ontario.ny.us/mental_health
   E-mail: healthfacilityadm@co.ontario.ny.us1
William M. Swingly, MDiv, MSW, Dir.
   Focus: Treatment. **Conditions:** Primary—ADD ADHD Anx BD CD ED LD
      Mood OCD ODD Psy PTSD SP Sz.
   Therapy: Chemo Play. **Psychotherapy:** Fam Group Indiv.
   Staff: 22 (Full 15, Part 7). Prof 18. Admin 4.
   Rates 2004: Sliding-Scale Rate $6-127/hr.
   Est 1952. County. Nonprofit.

The center provides evaluation, treatment, case management and referral services for residents of Ontario County. A satellite office operates at 28 Seneca St, Geneva 14456.

PARKSIDE SCHOOL

Day — Coed Ages 5-11

New York, NY 10023. 48 W 74th St.
Tel: 212-721-8888. Fax: 212-721-1547.
www.parksideschool.org   E-mail: parkamlt@aol.com
Albina Miller, MA, Co-Dir. **Leslie Thorne,** MA, Co-Dir.
   Focus: Spec Ed. **Conditions:** Primary—ADD ADHD Ap Asp Dx LD. **IQ 80-119.**
   Gen Acad. Ungraded. Courses: Read Math Lang_Arts Sci Soc_Stud
      Studio_Art Music.
   Therapy: Art Lang Music Percepual-Motor Play Speech.
   Enr: 80. Day Males 50. Day Females 30. **Staff:** 54 (Full 42, Part 12).
   Rates 2003: Day $27,000/sch yr. State Aid.
   Summer Prgm: Day. Educ. Rec. Ther. Day Rate $6000. 6 wks.
   Est 1986. Private. Nonprofit.

Parkside enrolls young children with language-based learning difficulties. The curriculum consists of three essential components: direct involvement and active participation in the classroom; supported communication methods, which incorporate such visual cues as sign language, symbols, pictures and photographs; and integrated, thematically organized hands-on learning experiences. Interventions address issues related to the child's social and emotional development, cognition, motor/sensory functioning and communication.

PATHFINDER VILLAGE

Res — Coed Ages 5 and up; Day — Coed 5-21

Edmeston, NY 13335. 3 Chenango Rd.

Tel: 607-965-8377. Fax: 607-965-8655.
www.pathfindervillage.org   E-mail: info@pathfindervillage.org
Edward A. Shafer, EdD, CEO. **Tracey Lindberg,** Adm.
   Focus: Spec Ed. **Conditions:** Primary—DS. Sec—MR.
   Pre-Voc. Voc. Ungraded. Courses: Read Math Lang_Arts Computers
      Studio_Art Adaptive_Phys_Ed Life_Skills.
   Therapy: Hear Lang Occup Phys Speech. **Psychotherapy:** Group Indiv.
   Staff: 140 (Full 120, Part 20).
   Est 1980. Private. Nonprofit.

Pathfinder offers individuals with Down syndrome comprehensive care in a village community. Staff members design an individualized educational program for each student. Components of these programs include basic academics, adaptive physical education, art classes and creative arts programs, behavioral analysis, area field trips, computer training, life skills training, speech pathology and social competency instruction.
   The vocational rehabilitation program aims to develop the person mentally, physically and emotionally, while also helping the individual acquire vocational skills.

PLEASANTVILLE COTTAGE SCHOOL

Res — Coed Ages 7-15

Pleasantville, NY 10570. 1075 Broadway, PO Box 237.
Tel: 914-769-0164. Fax: 914-741-4596.
www.jccany.org   E-mail: pcs@jccany.org
Denis Gufarotti, CSW, Dir.
   Conditions: Primary—ED.
   Col Prep. Gen Acad. Pre-Voc. Voc. Courses: Read Math Lang_Arts. Man_
      Arts & Shop.
   Est 1912. Private. Nonprofit. **Spons:** Jewish Child Care Association.

PROSPECT CHILD AND FAMILY CENTER

Day — Coed Ages 2-21

Queensbury, NY 12804. 133 Aviation Rd.
Tel: 518-798-0170. Fax: 518-798-0533.
www.prospectcenter.com   E-mail: pcfccent@prospectcenter.com
A. Larrie Gouge, MS, Exec Dir. **Guy Lehine,** MD, Med Dir. **Patricia Thompson,** Adm.
   Focus: Spec Ed. **Conditions:** Primary—Ap Asp Au B Bl CP D DS ED IP
      MR Nf ON PDD PW S SB. Sec—ADD ADHD Ep.
   Gen Acad. Ungraded.
   Therapy: Lang Occup Phys Speech.
   Enr: 8. **Staff:** 250 (Full 200, Part 50). Prof 115. Educ 18. Admin 12.
   Summer Prgm: Day. Educ. Ther. 6 wks.
   Est 1950. Private. Nonprofit.

The center accommodates at-risk and developmentally disabled individuals and their families. Diagnostic, treatment and special education services are available at Prospect.

QUEENS CENTERS FOR PROGRESS

Day — Coed All Ages

Jamaica, NY 11432. 81-15 164th St.
Tel: 718-380-3000. Fax: 718-380-0483.
www.ucp-queens.org E-mail: info@queenscp.org
Charles Houston, Exec Dir.
   Conditions: Primary—OH.
   Voc. Courses: Read Math. Shelt_Workshop.
   Therapy: Occup Phys Speech.
   Est 1958. Nonprofit.

QUEENS COLLEGE
SPEECH-LANGUAGE-HEARING CENTER

Clinic: All Ages. M-F 9-5; Eves M-F 5-7.

Flushing, NY 11367. 65-30 Kissena Blvd.
Tel: 718-997-2930. Fax: 718-997-2935.
Patricia McCaul, MS, Coord.
   Focus: Treatment. **Conditions:** Primary—S.
   Therapy: Lang Speech.
   Staff: 12 (Full 9, Part 3).
   State.

This specialized, multidisciplinary augmentative communication center provides all hearing services, including the dispensation of hearing aids.

REHABILITATION CENTER

Res — Coed Ages 5 and up; Day — Coed 6wks and up
Clinic: All Ages. M-F 8:30-4.

Olean, NY 14760. 1439 Buffalo St.
Tel: 716-375-4747. TTY: 716-375-4858. Fax: 716-375-4795.
www.rehabcenter.org
Jim Bellanca, Pres.
   Conditions: Primary—Ap Bl CP Dx LD MD MR MS ON S SB.
   Gen Acad. Pre-Voc. Voc. Ungraded. Shelt_Workshop. On-Job Trng.
   Therapy: Hear Lang Occup Phys Speech. **Psychotherapy:** Fam Group
      Indiv.
   Est 1958.

RITA AND STANLEY H. KAPLAN HOUSE

Res — Males Ages 16-21

New York, NY 10003. 74 St Marks Pl.
Tel: 212-477-1565. Fax: 212-674-2513.
Neil Freedman, Dir.
Focus: Treatment. **Conditions:** Primary—BD CD ED OCD Psy Sz. **IQ 75 and up.**
Therapy: Chemo Occup Speech. **Psychotherapy:** Fam Group Indiv.
Enr: 25. Res Males 25. **Staff:** 20.
Est 1951. Private. Nonprofit. **Spons:** Jewish Board of Family and Children's Services.

Treating severely emotionally disturbed and delinquent older adolescent boys, Kaplan House emphasizes preparation for vocational, social adjustment and independent living. This is accomplished through therapeutic milieu, individual therapy, house counseling, tutoring and job counseling. The average length of treatment is two years.

ROBERT LOUIS STEVENSON SCHOOL

Day — Coed Ages 12-18

New York, NY 10023. 24 W 74th St.
Tel: 212-787-6400. Fax: 212-873-1872.
www.stevenson-school.org
B. H. Henrichsen, Head.
Focus: Spec Ed. **Conditions:** Primary—ADD ADHD Dc Dg Dx LD. Sec— ED.
Col Prep. Gr 7-12. Courses: Read Math Lang_Arts Span Sci Computers Econ Studio_Art.
Therapy: Speech. **Psychotherapy:** Indiv.
Enr: 72. **Staff:** 12. (Full 12).
Rates 2004: Day $32,500/sch yr.
Summer Prgm: Day. Educ. Day Rate $1000/crse. 4 wks.
Est 1908. Private. Nonprofit.

A school for bright underachievers, Robert Louis Stevenson provides personalized instruction in a supportive, structured environment. The major effort is to facilitate growth in independence and personal accountability in preparation for potential college admission. A skills laboratory assists students in overcoming deficiencies in reading, writing and math, and it also helps strengthen organizational and study skills. A variety of counseling services is available.

A strong enrichment program offers courses in creative expression, film, theater and fine arts. Experiential education includes outdoor education and field placement study.

See Also Pages 1044-5

ROCHESTER INSTITUTE OF TECHNOLOGY
NATIONAL TECHNICAL INSTITUTE FOR THE DEAF

Res — Coed Ages 18 and up

Rochester, NY 14623. 52 Lomb Memorial Dr.
Tel: 585-475-6400. TTY: 585-475-6400. Fax: 585-475-5623.
www.rit.edu/ntid   E-mail: ntidmc@rit.edu
T. Alan Hurwitz, Dean.
   Focus: Spec Ed. Conditions: Primary—D.
   Gen Acad. Gr PG.
   Therapy: Hear Lang Speech. Psychotherapy: Indiv.
   Est 1968. Federal. Nonprofit.

Deaf students receive college educations in a hearing environment on the RIT campus. In addition to participating in the NTID program, enrollees may choose from numerous technical and professional courses available through RIT's other seven colleges. Students who have not yet completed a secondary program can be considered for admission if their secondary school authorities feel they will benefit more from the NTID program. Other qualifications include an overall eighth-grade or above achievement level on a standardized achievement test.   **See Also Page 1048**

ROCHESTER MENTAL HEALTH CENTER
CHILDREN AND YOUTH SERVICES

Clinic: Ages Birth-18. M-F 8:30-5.

Rochester, NY 14621. Hart Bldg, 490 E Ridge Rd.
Tel: 585-922-2500. Fax: 585-922-2646.
www.viahealth.org/rgh/rmhc/rmhc-youth.htm
   Conditions: Primary—ED. Sec—BD.
   Gen Acad. Courses: Read Math Lang_Arts.
   Therapy: Play. Psychotherapy: Fam Group Indiv.
   Est 1967. Private. Nonprofit.

ROCHESTER SCHOOL FOR THE DEAF

Res and Day — Coed Ages Birth-21

Rochester, NY 14621. 1545 St Paul St.
Tel: 585-544-1240. Fax: 585-544-0383.
www.rsdeaf.org   E-mail: rsd@rsdeaf.org
Harold Mowl, Jr., PhD, Supt. M. Ellen Gellerstedt, MD, Med Dir. Paul Holmes, Adm.
   Focus: Spec Ed. Conditions: Primary—D. Sec—CP ED LD MR ON S. IQ 65-130.
   Gen Acad. Pre-Voc. Gr PS-PG. Courses: Read Math Lang_Arts Computers Music Dance.
   Therapy: Hear Lang Occup Phys Speech. Psychotherapy: Group Indiv.

Enr: 141. Res Males 15. Res Females 12. Day Males 61. Day Females 53.
   Staff: 98.
Rates 2004: No Fee.
Est 1876. Private. Nonprofit.

Rochester School provides a comprehensive educational program for hearing-impaired children residing in the central-west portion of New York State. Courses of study are arranged as in public schools. Students may enter a vocational program that offers industrial and graphic arts, driver education, computer study, home economics and business science. The program of occupational and educational training provides off-campus work experience for juniors and seniors. Counseling is available. A deaf infant program is conducted for children from birth to age 3 who are suspected of having a hearing loss.

In cooperation with the Hillside Children's Center, the school also provides a comprehensive residential treatment facility for deaf emotionally disturbed adolescents and a school-to-work program for young hearing-impaired adults ages 18-21 who need additional support. Enrollment is restricted to New York State residents.

ROCKLAND CHILDREN'S PSYCHIATRIC CENTER

Res — Coed Ages 11-18; Day — Coed 5-18

Orangeburg, NY 10962. 599 Convent Rd.
Tel: 845-359-7400. Fax: 845-359-3460.
www.omh.state.ny.us/omhweb/facilities/wcpc/facility.htm
   Conditions: Primary—ED.
   Therapy: Hear Occup Recreational Speech.
   Est 1971. State.

SAGAMORE CHILDREN'S PSYCHIATRIC CENTER

Res and Day — Coed Ages 8-18
Clinic: Ages 8-18. M-F 10-5; Eves M-F 5-8.

Dix Hills, NY 11746. 197 Half Hollow Rd.
Tel: 631-673-7700. Fax: 631-673-7816.
Annette Shapiro, Dir.
   Focus: Treatment. **Conditions:** Primary—BD CD ED OCD Psy Sz. Sec—Dx LD. **IQ 75 and up.**
   Therapy: Chemo Hear Lang Speech. **Psychotherapy:** Fam Group Indiv.
   Est 1969. State. Nonprofit.

Serving children and adolescents who reside in the Long Island counties of Nassau and Suffolk only, Sagamore conducts the following behavioral healthcare programs for young people and their families: inpatient hospitalization, day hospitalization, day treatment, outpatient clinical treatment, family care respite, home care, mobile mental health crisis services, information and referral, and community consultation and training. Multidisciplinary teams in the areas of psychiatry, psychology, social work, nursing and education carry out treatment. Fees are based on a sliding scale.

SAINT AGATHA HOME

Res — Coed Ages 8-18

Nanuet, NY 10954. 135 Convent Rd.
Tel: 845-623-3461. Fax: 845-623-6244.
www.nyfoundling.org/agatha.htm
  Conditions: Primary—BD ED MR.
  Gen Acad. Gr 1-12. Courses: Read Math Lang_Arts. Man_Arts & Shop.
    Shelt_Workshop. On-Job Trng.
  Therapy: Lang Play Recreational.
  Est 1884. Private. **Spons:** New York Foundling.

ST. ANNE INSTITUTE

Res and Day — Females Ages 12-18

Albany, NY 12206. 160 N Main Ave.
Tel: 518-437-6500. Fax: 518-437-6555.
www.stanneinstitute.org
Rick Riccio, MA, Exec Dir. **David Pankin,** MD, Med Dir. **Mary Mulchy,** Intake.
  Focus: Spec Ed. Rehab. **Conditions:** Primary—BD ED. Sec—As LD S. **IQ
  80-130.**
  Col Prep. Gen Acad. Pre-Voc. Voc. Gr 7-12. Courses: Read Math Lang_
  Arts Computers. On-Job Trng.
  Therapy: Art Dance Recreational Speech. **Psychotherapy:** Fam Group
  Indiv.
  Enr: 150. Res Females 115. Day Females 35. **Staff:** 123 (Full 111, Part 12).
  Educ 35. Admin 5.
  Rates 2003: Res $45,260/yr. Day $29,300/yr.
  Summer Prgm: Res & Day. Educ. Rec. Ther. 8 wks.
  Est 1887. Private. Nonprofit.

The institute is designed to meet the needs of emotionally and socially handicapped adolescent girls and their families through a comprehensive program of rehabilitative services. Components of the multiservice program include clinical services, therapeutic education, family services, medical and dental services, and aftercare. The academic program offers tutorial help and a remedial and developmental reading program. Students may select major sequences from the fields of business, home economics, science, math, cosmetology, keypunching, art, nursing and trade sewing. The Child Care Department provides long-term, 24-hour coverage.

ST. CABRINI HOME

Res — Coed Ages 12-21

West Park, NY 12493. Rte 9 W.
Tel: 845-384-6500. Fax: 845-384-6001.
www.cabrinihome.com   **E-mail: info@cabrinihome.com**

Conditions: Primary—ED. Sec—BD.
Gen Acad. Pre-Voc. Ungraded. Courses: Read Math Lang_Arts.
Therapy: Art Recreational. **Psychotherapy:** Group Indiv.
Staff: Prof 124.
Est 1890. Private.

ST. CHARLES HOSPITAL
AND REHABILITATION CENTER

Day — Coed Ages Birth-18
Clinic: Ages Birth-21. M-F 8:30-4.

Port Jefferson, NY 11777. 200 Belle Terre Rd.
Tel: 631-474-6267. Fax: 631-474-6144.
www.stcharles.org
   Conditions: Primary—BI C CP IP MD MS ON S SB.
   Therapy: Hear Lang Occup Phys Speech. **Psychotherapy:** Fam Group
      Indiv.
   Est 1907. Private. Nonprofit.

ST. CHRISTOPHER'S

Res — Coed Ages 12-21; Day — Coed 12-18

Dobbs Ferry, NY 10522. 71 Broadway.
Tel: 914-693-3030. Fax: 914-693-8325.
www.sc1881.com   E-mail: info@sc1881.org
   Conditions: Primary—ED. Sec—BD LD.
   Pre-Voc. Ungraded. Courses: Read Math Lang_Arts.
   Therapy: Lang Speech. **Psychotherapy:** Fam Indiv.
   Staff: Prof 50.
   Est 1881. Private. Nonprofit.

ST. FRANCIS DE SALES SCHOOL FOR THE DEAF

Day — Coed Ages Birth-14

Brooklyn, NY 11225. 260 Eastern Pky.
Tel: 718-636-4573. Fax: 718-636-4577.
www.sfdesales.org
Edward McCormack, Dir.
   Conditions: Primary—D.
   Private.

ST. JOSEPH'S SCHOOL FOR THE DEAF

Day — Coed Ages Birth-14

Bronx, NY 10465. 1000 Hutchinson River Pky.
Tel: 718-828-9000. TTY: 718-828-1671. Fax: 718-792-6631.
www.sjsdny.org E-mail: stjosephs@sjsdny.org
Patricia Martin, MSEd, Exec Dir. Steve Sarran, Prin.
Focus: Spec Ed. Conditions: Primary—D.
Gen Acad. Gr PS-8. Courses: Read Math Lang_Arts.
Therapy: Hear Lang Occup Phys Speech.
Enr: 140. Staff: 37. (Full 37).
Rates 2004: No Fee.
Est 1869. Private. Nonprofit.

This state-supported educational program for school-age children emphasizes communicational skills through an aural-oral approach. A parent-infant program provides weekly mother-child participation, individually and in small groups. Personal counseling is available. The school's summer session is open only to pupils enrolled in the school-year program.

ST. JOSEPH'S VILLA OF ROCHESTER

Res — Males Ages 11-17, Females 13-17; Day — Coed 14-18

Rochester, NY 14616. 3300 Dewey Ave.
Tel: 585-865-1550. Fax: 585-865-5219.
www.stjosephsvilla.org
Roger Battaglia, Pres. Mohsen Emami, MD, Med Dir. Jay Gullo, Intake.
Focus: Treatment. Conditions: Primary—ADD ADHD Anx As BD CD ED Mood ODD PTSD. Sec—OCD TS. IQ 70 and up.
Gen Acad. Pre-Voc. Voc. Gr 5-12. Courses: Read Math Lang_Arts. Man_Arts & Shop.
Therapy: Milieu Recreational Speech. Psychotherapy: Fam Group Indiv Parent.
Enr: 160.
Est 1942. Private. Nonprofit.

This mental health agency provides mental health and supportive services for children and their families. St. Joseph's responds to community needs through residential, educational and preventive programs. Children whose behaviors prohibit placement in an open setting are not admitted. The average length of stay is 10 to 12 months.

ST. MARY'S HOSPITAL FOR CHILDREN

Res — Coed Ages Birth-19

Bayside, NY 11360. 29-01 216th St.
Tel: 718-281-8800. Fax: 718-631-7874.
www.stmaryskids.org E-mail: info@stmaryskids.org

Burton Grebin, MD, Pres.
    Focus: Rehab. Treatment. **Conditions:** Primary—As BI C CP Ep IP MD MR MS ON SB TB. Sec—ADD ADHD Ap B BD CD D Dx ED LD OCD S.
    Therapy: Hear Lang Occup Phys Speech. **Psychotherapy:** Fam Group Indiv Parent.
    Enr: 97.
    Est 1870. Private. Nonprofit. Episcopal. **Spons:** St. Mary's Healthcare System for Children.

St. Mary's Hospital, a skilled nursing care facility for children in the New York metropolitan area, provides comprehensive treatment for habilitation and rehabilitation of disabled children. Medical services are organized into a general pediatric program and subspecialty programs that include asthma, birth defects and genetic disorders, palliative care and rehabilitation.

Classroom teaching is made available for children over age 5 by the New York City Board of Education, and children under age 5 may take part in an early education program. A home care program and a medical/social daycare program are also available for children with rehabilitative needs. St. Mary's cannot accept custodial cases.

ST. MARY'S SCHOOL FOR THE DEAF

Res — Coed Ages 5-21; Day — Coed Birth-21

Buffalo, NY 14214. 2253 Main St.
Tel: 716-834-7200. Fax: 716-834-2720.
www.smsdk12.org
William Page Johnson, PhD, Supt.
    Conditions: Primary—D.
    Col Prep. Gen Acad. Pre-Voc. Voc. Gr PS-12. Courses: Read Math Lang_ Arts. Man_Arts & Shop. On-Job Trng.
    Therapy: Hear Lang Occup Phys Speech. **Psychotherapy:** Indiv.
    Spons: Northeast Communication Achievement Center.

ST. URSULA LEARNING CENTER

Day — Coed Ages 6-16

Mount Vernon, NY 10550. 183 Rich Ave.
Tel: 914-664-6656. Fax: 914-663-7948.
Barbara J. Stefanik, BS, MS, Prin.
    Focus: Spec Ed. **Conditions:** Primary—Ap Apr Dx. Sec—Asp. **IQ 70 and up.**
    Gen Acad. Gr 1-8. Courses: Read Math Lang_Arts.
    Therapy: Lang Occup Percepual-Motor Phys Play Speech.
    Enr: 60. **Staff:** 16 (Full 11, Part 5).
    Rates 2003: Res $6500/sch yr (+$100).
    Est 1990. Private. Nonprofit. Roman Catholic.

St. Ursula's elementary-level curriculum includes specialized academic classes for learning-disabled students. Specialists provide speech, occupational and physical therapies, as well as educational counseling for pupils and their families.

ST. VINCENT'S HOSPITAL AND MEDICAL CENTER
CHILD AND ADOLESCENT PSYCHIATRY SERVICE

Clinic: Ages 3-18. M-F 9-5; Eves M-F 5-7.

New York, NY 10011. 144 W 12th St.
Tel: 212-604-8211. Fax: 212-604-8212.
www.svcmc.org/behavioral
  Focus: Treatment. **Conditions:** Primary—ADD ADHD BD CD Dx ED LD OCD Psy Sz. Sec—Au. **IQ 70 and up.**
  Therapy: Chemo Speech. **Psychotherapy:** Fam Group Indiv Parent.
  Staff: 12.
  Est 1849. Private. Nonprofit. Roman Catholic.

The Child and Adolescent Service provides an acute-care psychiatric inpatient unit for children with acute psychiatric symptomatology, an outpatient clinic serving a broad range of psychiatric disorders and a pediatric consultation/liaison program. Comprehensive psychiatric and psychosocial evaluations, together with psychological testing when indicated, are provided for both inpatients and outpatients. Treatment modalities used include individual and group psychotherapy, family therapy, behavioral therapy and pharmacotherapy.

SCHNEIDER CHILDREN'S HOSPITAL
DIVISION OF DEVELOPMENTAL
AND BEHAVIORAL PEDIATRICS

Day — Coed Ages Birth-5
Clinic: Ages 3-21. M-S 8-5; Eves T-Th 5-7:30.

New Hyde Park, NY 11040. 269-01 76th Ave.
Tel: 718-470-3000. Fax: 718-470-9291.
www.schneiderchildrenshospital.org/sch_pat_dev_behave.html
  Conditions: Primary—ADD ADHD AN Ap Au BD Bu D Dx Ep LD ON TS.
  Gen Acad. Gr PS-12. Courses: Read Math Lang_Arts.
  Therapy: Hear Lang Phys Speech. **Psychotherapy:** Fam Group Indiv.
  Staff: Prof 40.
  Private.

SCHOOL FOR LANGUAGE
AND COMMUNICATION DEVELOPMENT

Day — Coed Ages 2-12

Glen Cove, NY 11542. 100 Glen Cove Ave.
Tel: 516-609-2000. Fax: 516-609-2014.
www.slcd.org   E-mail: language@optionline.net
Ellenmorris Tiegerman, PhD, Exec Dir.
  Focus: Spec Ed. **Conditions:** Primary—ADD ADHD Ap Apr Asp Au Dc Dg
    DS Dx ED LD MR ON PDD S. Sec—As Bl CP D Ep OCD. **IQ 59-115.**
  Gen Acad. Gr PS-6. Courses: Read Math Lang_Arts.
  Therapy: Art Dance Hear Lang Movement Music Occup Percepual-Motor
    Phys Play Recreational Speech. **Psychotherapy:** Group Indiv Parent.
  Enr: 200. **Staff:** 160. (Full 160). Prof 51. Educ 30. Admin 17.
  Rates 2003: No Fee.
  Summer Prgm: Day. Educ. Ther.
  Est 1985. Private. Nonprofit. Spons: New York State Education Department.

SLCD provides educational and educare services for children with and without developmental disabilities who have severe language and communication disorders. Services include education, clinical evaluations and therapy. In addition, the program provides full-day childcare and parent education classes. Parents may also learn techniques to facilitate language learning at home by watching the child during the day on a closed-circuit video system.

SCHOOL OF THE HOLY CHILDHOOD

Day — Coed Ages 5 and up
Clinic: All Ages. M-F 8:30-4:30.

Rochester, NY 14623. 100 Groton Pky.
Tel: 585-359-3710. Fax: 585-359-3722.
www.holychildhood.org
Sr. Seraphine Herbst, MA, Exec Dir. **Joseph Incavo,** MD, Med Dir. **Suzanne Caruso,** Adm.
  Focus: Spec Ed. **Conditions:** Primary—Asp Au DS MR PDD. **IQ 30-75.**
  Pre-Voc. Voc. Ungraded. Courses: Read Math Lang_Arts Life_Skills Adaptive_Phys_Ed Home_Ec. Man_Arts & Shop. Shelt_Workshop.
  Therapy: Dance Lang Movement Occup Recreational Speech. **Psychotherapy:** Group Indiv.
  Enr: 116. Day Males 65. Day Females 51. **Staff:** 97 (Full 85, Part 12).
  Rates 2003: Day $1700/sch yr. Schol 13 ($15,000). State Aid.
  Est 1946. Private. Nonprofit.

Founded by the Sisters of St. Joseph of Rochester, this school serves individuals with mental retardation in Monroe County. The school has three separate programs: a children's program for children ages 5-21, an adult program for those ages 18-50 and a clinical program for those of all ages. Intensive education features all basic subjects, and class size averages 10 students. Prevocational and vocational training supplements standard academics. Courses in cooking, sewing, woodworking, weaving and ceramics are part of the curriculum. Emphasis is also placed on physical fitness, exercise and recreation.

In addition to sports-oriented activities, students may also participate in programs designed to enhance perceptual ability and coordination. The school does not accept students who have severe emotional or physical handicaps.

SILVER CREEK MONTESSORI SCHOOL
Day — Coed Ages Birth-5

Silver Creek, NY 14136. 87 Main St.
Tel: 716-934-4274. Fax: 716-934-9129.
www.bflohearspeech.org   E-mail: info@askbhsc.org
Janet Maher, Pres.
   Conditions: Primary—D LD S. Sec—Au ED OH.
   Gen Acad. Gr PS.
   Therapy: Hear Lang Occup Phys Speech. **Psychotherapy:** Fam Group Indiv.
   Staff: 47 (Full 9, Part 38).
   Est 1973. Private. Nonprofit. **Spons:** Buffalo Hearing and Speech Center.

Silver Creek provides individualized instruction in speech, language and auditory training; prereading and special education skills; and fine- and gross-motor and sensory integration skills from one to five days weekly, as prescribed by county and school district guidelines. Offerings consist of three half-day center-based programs—one daily morning and one daily afternoon for preschoolers ages 3-5 and one toddler group three days per week that provides early intervention services for children from birth to age 3—and through related services in the home, in a community setting or both. The usual duration of treatment is one to three years.

STATE UNIVERSITY OF NEW YORK-BINGHAMTON INSTITUTE FOR CHILD DEVELOPMENT
Day — Coed Ages 10mos-12

Binghamton, NY 13902. PO Box 6000.
Tel: 607-777-2829. Fax: 607-777-6981.
http://icd.binghamton.edu   E-mail: icdadmin@binghamton.edu
Raymond G. Romanczyk, PhD, Dir.
   Conditions: Primary—Au ED LD. Sec—Asp MR.
   Gen Acad. Ungraded. Courses: Read Math Lang_Arts.
   Therapy: Lang Speech.
   Est 1974. Private.

STATE UNIVERSITY OF NEW YORK-FREDONIA
HENRY C. YOUNGERMAN CENTER
FOR COMMUNICATION DISORDERS

Clinic: All Ages. M-F 9-4.

Fredonia, NY 14063. W121 Thompson Hall.
Tel: 716-673-3203. Fax: 716-673-3235.
www.fredonia.edu/department/speechpathology
Michele Notte, MS, Dir.
  Focus: Treatment. **Conditions:** Primary—S. Sec—Ap BI CP ED LD MD MR OH.
  Therapy: Hear Lang Speech.
  Staff: 10 (Full 7, Part 3).
  Est 1954. State.

A training facility for professionally supervised student interns in the school's Department of Speech Pathology and Audiology, the center offers various diagnostic and therapeutic services for persons with hearing, speech and language disorders. Audiogical testing services include hearing screenings, hearing aid evaluations, and educational and vocational assessments. Diagnostic evaluations, conducted in conjunction with language, articulation, voice, fluency and speech mechanism function assessments, help the center to determine the nature of the communicative disorder. Treatment consists of one-on-one and small-group sessions and allows for the active participation of parents and other family members.

Disorders treated by the center are the following: phonological and language development problems, aphasia and related neurogenic disorders, hearing impairments, communicative problems of the mentally retarded, cleft palate, articulation and dialect differences, stuttering, auditory processing disorders, and voice disorders and laryngectomy.

STATE UNIVERSITY OF NEW YORK-NEW PALTZ
DEPARTMENT OF COMMUNICATION DISORDERS
SPEECH AND HEARING CENTER

Clinic: All Ages. M-Th 1-6.

New Paltz, NY 12561. 75 S Manheim Blvd, Ste 6.
Tel: 845-257-3600. Fax: 845-257-3605.
www.newpaltz.edu/commdis/org_sphgctr.html
  E-mail: vayos@newpaltz.edu
Stella Turk, MS, Dir.
  Focus: Treatment. **Conditions:** Primary—S.
  Therapy: Hear Lang Speech.
  Staff: 8.
  State. Nonprofit.

The center offers both diagnostic and therapeutic services for children and adults who demonstrate speech, language or hearing difficulties. Speech and language pathologists, along with graduate and upper-level undergraduate students, provide a range of services related to speech and language difficulties that includes screening for speech and language disorders; assessment and treatment; and hearing aid evaluation, fitting and follow-up.

University students, faculty and staff receive services free of charge, while other clients pay a nominal fee.

STATE UNIVERSITY OF NEW YORK-PLATTSBURGH SPEECH AND HEARING CENTER

Clinic: All Ages. M-F 8:30-4:30.

Plattsburgh, NY 12901. 101 Broad St.
Tel: 518-564-2170. Fax: 518-564-5110.
www2.plattsburgh.edu/cds/speechandhearingcenter.cfm
    E-mail: morganmd@plattsburgh.edu
Michael Morgan, MD, Supv. Nancy Allen, Dir.
    Focus: Treatment. Conditions: Primary—Ap Asp Au Bl D DS MR PDD S.
    Therapy: Hear Lang Speech.
    Staff: 9. Admin 1.
    Est 1965. State.

The center serves as an academic training facility and a community service. Pre- and postsurgical evaluations, speech reading, auditory training, hearing aid evaluations, and various speech and hearing therapies are provided. Fees are determined along a sliding scale.

STATE UNIVERSITY OF NEW YORK UPSTATE MEDICAL UNIVERSITY COMMUNICATION DISORDER UNIT

Clinic: All Ages. M-F 8:30-4:30.

Syracuse, NY 13210. Jacobsen Hall, 175 Elizabeth Blackwell St.
Tel: 315-464-4806. Fax: 315-464-5321.
www.upstate.edu/ent/comdis.shtml
Robert J. Shprintzen, PhD, Dir.
    Focus: Treatment. Conditions: Primary—Ap D S.
    Therapy: Hear Lang Speech.
    Staff: 14.
    Est 1963. State. Nonprofit.

This unit offers diagnosis and treatment for speech and language disorders. The facility also renders audiological services that include brainstem evoked response studies, cochlear implant evaluation and rehabilitation, and the treatment of central auditory processing disorders. Treatments are administered by appointment.

STATEN ISLAND MENTAL HEALTH SOCIETY
CHILDREN'S COMMUNITY MENTAL HEALTH CENTER

Day — Coed Ages 5-18
Clinic: Ages Birth-18. M-F 8-5; Eves T Th 5-9.

Staten Island, NY 10301. 669 Castleton Ave.
Tel: 718-442-2225. Fax: 718-442-2289.
www.simhs.org
Nathalie J. Weeks, CSW, MBA, Dir. **Sundar Ramaswamy,** MD, Med Dir.
    Focus: Treatment. **Conditions:** Primary—BD CD ED OCD Psy Sz. Sec—
    ADD ADHD As Dx Ep LD MR.
    Gen Acad. Gr PS-12. Courses: Read Math Lang_Arts. Man_Arts & Shop.
    Therapy: Lang Speech. **Psychotherapy:** Fam Group Indiv Parent.
    Enr: 118. Day Males 59. Day Females 59. **Staff:** 85.
    Summer Prgm: Day. Educ. Ther. 8 wks.
    Est 1952. Private. Nonprofit.

The center has two major outpatient facilities (North Shore and South Shore clinics) that provide diagnosis and treatment of emotional disorders. Emergency psychiatric services are available in affiliation with St. Vincent's Medical Center in Richmond.

Two day treatment centers, conducted in affiliation with the New York City Board of Education, serve emotionally disturbed children. On-site mental health services are available in eight area public schools. In addition, the facility provides individual and family services for teens experiencing difficulties with drugs or alcohol.

STEPHEN GAYNOR SCHOOL

Day — Coed Ages 5-13

New York, NY 10023. 22 W 74th St.
Tel: 212-787-7070. Fax: 212-787-3312.
www.sgaynor.com   **E-mail: info@sgaynor.com**
Yvette Siegel, Educ Dir. **Lilli Friedman,** Adm.
    Focus: Spec Ed. **Conditions:** Primary—Dx LD. **IQ 89 and up.**
    Gen Acad. Ungraded. Courses: Read Math Lang_Arts Computers Music
    Drama. Man_Arts & Shop.
    Therapy: Lang Occup.
    Enr: 118. **Staff:** 52 (Full 50, Part 2).
    Est 1962. Private. Nonprofit.

The focus of this school is to provide an environment in which students with learning disabilities can realize their academic potentials. Groups are small, consisting of eight to 10 students per class, and Stephen Gaynor utilizes a remedial approach that emphasizes multisensory teaching.

THE SUMMIT SCHOOL

Day — Coed Ages 7-21

Jamaica Estates, NY 11432. 187-30 Grand Central Pky.
   Nearby locations: Flushing.
Tel: 718-264-2931. Fax: 718-264-3030.
Judith Gordon, PhD, Dir.
   Focus: Spec Ed. **Conditions:** Primary—ADD ADHD Anx Asp Dc Dg Dx LD
   OCD. Sec—ED TS. **IQ 90 and up.**
   Col Prep. Gen Acad. Pre-Voc. Gr 2-12. Courses: Read Math Lang_Arts Sci
   Soc_Stud Psych. On-Job Trng.
   Therapy: Lang Occup Speech.
   Enr: 290. Day Males 200. Day Females 90. **Staff:** 130 (Full 128, Part 2).
   Prof 59. Educ 50. Admin 4.
   Est 1968. Private. Nonprofit.

Summit provides an individualized academic program commensurate with each student's intellectual ability. The school incorporates learning and organizational strategies into its academic program. The development of social skills and pragmatic language are also important elements of the program.

The lower school campus, serving grades 1-8, operates at 183-02 Union Tpke., Flushing 11366.

SUMMIT SCHOOL

Res and Day — Coed Ages 14-21
Clinic: All Ages. M-S 8:30-5; Eves M-S 5-6:30.

Upper Nyack, NY 10960. 339 N Broadway.
Tel: 845-358-7772. Fax: 845-358-8810.
Bruce Goldsmith, EdD, Exec Dir. **Richard Sitman,** Prin.
   Focus: Treatment. **Conditions:** Primary—BD ED OCD Psy Sz. Sec—ADD
   ADHD Dx LD. **IQ 75 and up.**
   Col Prep. Gen Acad. Pre-Voc. Voc. Gr 9-12. Courses: Read Math Lang_
   Arts Photog Studio_Art. Man_Arts & Shop.
   Therapy: Speech. **Psychotherapy:** Fam Group Indiv Parent.
   Enr: 124. Res Males 77. Res Females 32. Day Males 8. Day Females 7.
   Est 1974. Private. Nonprofit.

Occupying a nine-acre campus overlooking the Hudson River, Summit is 18 miles from New York City and treats children who are learning disabled or emotionally disturbed. The program offers a therapeutic milieu, clinical intervention, academic remediation and psychotherapeutic treatment. Counseling is available and the length of treatment varies.   **See Also Page 1047**

SUNNYVIEW REHABILITATION HOSPITAL

Res and Day — Coed All Ages

Schenectady, NY 12308. 1270 Belmont Ave.
Tel: 518-382-4500. Fax: 518-382-4570.
www.sunnyview.org
Robert J. Bylancik, Pres. **Lynn Nicolson,** MD, Med Dir.
    Focus: Rehab. **Conditions:** Primary—Ap BI MS OH. Sec—Ar As C CP MD
    SB.
    Voc. On-Job Trng.
    Therapy: Hear Lang Occup Phys Speech. **Psychotherapy:** Fam Group
    Indiv.
    Staff: 550 (Full 490, Part 60).
    Est 1928. Private. Nonprofit.

Sunnyview specializes in comprehensive medical rehabilitation and orthopedics.
Emphasis is on increasing mobility and learning self-care skills. Specialty clinics
include amputee, multiple sclerosis, myelodysplasia, cleft palate, scoliosis, spinal cord
and stroke. Vocational rehabilitation is available on both inpatient and outpatient bases.
The hospital integrates tutorial instruction, remedial education and prevocational evaluation services with the rehabilitation program for children.

UCP OF NEW YORK CITY

Day — Coed All Ages
Clinic: All Ages. M-F.

New York, NY 10038. 80 Maiden Ln, 8th Fl.
Tel: 212-683-6700. Fax: 212-685-8394.
www.ucpnyc.org   E-mail: info@ucpnyc.org
    Conditions: Primary—CP ON SB.
    Gen Acad. Pre-Voc. Voc. Courses: Read Math Lang_Arts. Man_Arts &
    Shop. Shelt_Workshop. On-Job Trng.
    Est 1947. Private. Nonprofit.

UCP OF ULSTER COUNTY

Res — Coed Ages 5 and up; Day — Coed Birth-21
Clinic: All Ages. M-F 8:30-4:30.

Kingston, NY 12402. 250 Tuytenbridge Rd, PO Box 1488.
Tel: 845-336-7235. TTY: 845-336-4055. Fax: 845-336-7248.
www.ulster.net/~ucprtc   E-mail: ucprtc@mhv.net
Pamela Carroad, Exec Dir. **Susan Krogstad-Hill,** Educ Dir. **Alfred Frontera,**
    MD, Med Dir.
    Focus: Treatment. **Conditions:** Primary—B BI CP D IP MD MR MS ON S
    SB. Sec—ADD ADHD Dx LD.
    Gen Acad. Pre-Voc. Voc. Ungraded. Courses: Read Math Lang_Arts.

Therapy: Hear Lang Occup Percepual-Motor Phys Recreational Speech.
  Psychotherapy: Fam Group Indiv Parent.
Enr: 191. Res Males 36. Res Females 24. Day Males 78. Day Females 53.
  Staff: 94 (Full 85, Part 9). Prof 40. Educ 38. Admin 16.
Est 1952. Private. Nonprofit.

Services at this center include a free referral service for special-needs preschoolers, an outpatient clinic, and educational and early intervention programs. In addition, the facility maintains a residential program for school-age children with disabilities. The day program is fully funded. Counseling; various therapies; and neurological, audiological and psychological services round out UCP's offerings.

ULSTER COUNTY
COMMUNITY MENTAL HEALTH SERVICES

Clinic: Ages Birth-18. M-F 9-6; Eves M-Th 6-8:30.

Kingston, NY 12401. 239 Golden Hill Ln.
Tel: 845-340-4000. Fax: 845-340-4094.
www.co.ulster.ny.us/mentalhealth
Marshall Beckman, MPA, Dir.
  Focus: Treatment. **Conditions:** Primary—ADD ADHD Au BD CD ED OCD
    Psy Sz. Sec—Dx LD.
  Therapy: Speech. **Psychotherapy:** Fam Group Indiv.
  Staff: 26 (Full 23, Part 3).
  County.

This agency provides outpatient clinical evaluation and treatment of children and adolescents who are seriously emotionally disturbed and their families. Treatment for those who have been sexually abused and for sex offenders is also provided. Treatment generally lasts from 16 to 20 visits.

UNITED CEREBRAL PALSY ASSOCIATION
OF NASSAU COUNTY

Day — Coed All Ages
Clinic: All Ages. M W Th F 8:30-4:30, T 8:30-5.

Roosevelt, NY 11575. 380 Washington Ave.
Tel: 516-378-2000. Fax: 516-378-0357.
www.ucpn.org   E-mail: info@ucpn.org
Robert McGuire, Exec Dir.
  Focus: Rehab. Treatment. **Conditions:** Primary—Ap BI CP DS Ep MR ON
    SB. Sec—PW TS.
  Pre-Voc. Voc. Ungraded. Courses: Read Math Lang_Arts.
  Therapy: Art Hear Lang Occup Percepual-Motor Phys Play Speech. **Psy-chotherapy:** Fam Group Indiv.
  Summer Prgm: Day. Educ. Rec. Ther.
  Est 1948. Private. Nonprofit.

Diagnosis and treatment are provided for developmentally disabled individuals at this facility. Services include therapies, primary medical care, psychological counseling, social services, medical clinics, dentistry, podiatry and orthopedics, as well as developmental education programs for infants and children, vocational rehabilitation, day rehabilitation, adult day treatment and Medicaid service coordination. The center also operates several residential facilities.

UNITED CEREBRAL PALSY ASSOCIATION OF WESTCHESTER COUNTY
Day — Coed Ages 3-21

Rye Brook, NY 10573. 1186 King St.
Tel: 914-937-3800. Fax: 914-937-0967.
www.ucpw.org
Katie Meskell, Exec Dir. **Annabelle Strozza,** MSEd, Dir.
   Focus: Spec Ed. Trng. **Conditions:** Primary—ADD ADHD Ap Au B BI CP D DS Dx IP LD MD MR MS ON S SB. Sec—Apr As C Ep. **IQ 20 and up.**
   Gen Acad. Pre-Voc. Ungraded. Courses: Read Math Lang_Arts. Shelt_ Workshop. On-Job Trng.
   Therapy: Hear Hydro Lang Occup Phys Speech. **Psychotherapy:** Fam Group Indiv Parent.
   Enr: 100. Day Males 55. Day Females 45. **Staff:** 63 (Full 60, Part 3). Prof 13. Educ 11. Admin 1.
   Summer Prgm: Day. Educ. Rec. 6 wks.
   Est 1949. Private. Nonprofit.

UCP/W provides a day training program for children with neurological impairments and related disorders. Programming consists of recreational training, therapeutic education, and psychosocial and prevocational services. Children referred by their school district pay no fee for service.

UNITED CEREBRAL PALSY OF QUEENS CHILDREN'S CENTER SCHOOL
Day — Coed Ages Birth-21

Jamaica, NY 11432. 82-25 164th St.
Tel: 718-374-0002. Fax: 718-380-3214.
www.queenscp.org   E-mail: nglass@queenscp.org
Nancy Glass, BS, MA, Dir.
   Focus: Spec Ed. **Conditions:** Primary—ADD ADHD Ap Asp Au BI CP IP LD MD MR ON PDD S SB. Sec—As B C D Dx ED Ep HIV TB.
   Gen Acad. Ungraded.
   Therapy: Hear Lang Occup Phys Speech. **Psychotherapy:** Fam Indiv Parent.
   Staff: 105 (Full 90, Part 15). Prof 65. Educ 20. Admin 3.
   Rates 2004: No Fee.
   Est 1954. Private. Nonprofit.

The facility provides year-round information, referral, social and psychological services, vocational and rehabilitative therapies, and medical consultations for individuals with cerebral palsy. The center's educational program features a preschool and classes for children ages 5-21.

Counseling and home services are also available.

UPSTATE HOMES FOR CHILDREN AND ADULTS

Res — Coed Ages 5-21; Day — Coed 3-21

Oneonta, NY 13820. 2705 State Hwy 28.
Tel: 607-286-7171. Fax: 607-286-7166.
www.upstatehome.org   E-mail: info@upstatehome.org
Patricia Kennedy, MA, Exec Dir. **Jeff Edelstein,** Adm.
  Focus: Spec Ed. Rehab. Trng. Treatment. **Conditions:** Primary—Asp Au CF CP DS MR OH. Sec—Anx Ap Apr Ar As B Bl C CD D Db ED Ep IP MD MS Nf OCD ODD Psy PTSD PW S SB SP TB TS. **IQ 30-70.**
  Pre-Voc. Voc. Ungraded. Courses: Read Math Lang_Arts Life_Skills. Shelt_ Workshop. On-Job Trng.
  Therapy: Art Chemo Hear Lang Occup Phys Recreational Speech. **Psychotherapy:** Fam Group Indiv Parent.
  Enr: 108. Res Males 40. Res Females 15. Day Males 36. Day Females 17. **Staff:** 64 (Full 62, Part 2).
  Rates 2004: Res $57,436/sch yr. Day $26,000/sch yr. State Aid.
  Summer Prgm: Res & Day. Educ. Ther. Res Rate $11,753. Day Rate $4000. 6 wks.
  Est 1923. Private. Nonprofit.

Located on 105 acres, UHCA provides care and training for severely retarded and multi-handicapped (nonambulatory and ambulatory) children. The home employs an individualized education plan to meet the needs of the children, training them to cope with the demands of everyday life.

The educational program includes all necessary therapies as well as classroom activities supervised by certified special education teachers. The educational program begins with an integrated preschool.

A community residence and day programming are available for adults who are unable to live independently in the community.

VARIETY CHILD LEARNING CENTER

Day — Coed Ages Birth-7

Syosset, NY 11791. 47 Humphrey Dr.
Tel: 516-921-7171. Fax: 516-921-8130.
www.vclc.org   E-mail: info@vclc.org
Judith S. Bloch, MSW, CEO. **Andrea Zukerman,** Adm.
  Focus: Spec Ed. **Conditions:** Primary—ADD ADHD AN Anx Ap Apr Asp Au Bl CD ED LD Mood MR OCD ODD PDD Psy PTSD PW S SP Sz TS. Sec—As C CF CP Ep Nf. **IQ 35-130.**

Gen Acad. Gr PS-2. Courses: Read Math Lang_Arts.
Therapy: Lang Music Occup Percepual-Motor Phys Play Speech. **Psycho-therapy:** Fam Group Indiv.
Enr: 502. **Staff:** 325 (Full 147, Part 178). Prof 191. Educ 72.
Rates 2004: No Fee.
Est 1966. Private. Nonprofit.

VCLC conducts evaluations, an early intervention program (home and center based), a preschool and special-education classes for children in grades K-2 who have learning, language and behavioral disabilities. Family support is also available, and additional programs include social skills training groups (ages 4-14), a Sunday respite and recreational program, research materials and a training center for early childhood personnel.

WESTCHESTER EXCEPTIONAL CHILDREN'S SCHOOL

Day — Coed Ages 5-21

North Salem, NY 10560. Rte 22, RR 1, Box 1.
Tel: 914-277-5533. Fax: 914-277-7219.
Linda M. Murphy, MS, Dir.
   Focus: Spec Ed. **Conditions:** Primary—Asp Au DS ED PW TS. Sec—ADD ADHD Ep LD MR. **IQ 36-100.**
   Pre-Voc. Voc. Ungraded. Courses: Read Math Lang_Arts Adaptive_Phys_ Ed. Shelt_Workshop. On-Job Trng.
   Therapy: Hear Lang Occup Phys Speech. **Psychotherapy:** Fam Group Indiv Parent.
   Enr: 70. **Staff:** 53. (Full 53). Prof 21. Educ 15. Admin 4.
   Rates 2004: No Fee.
   Summer Prgm: Day. Educ. Ther.
   Est 1969. Private. Nonprofit.

A behavioral approach is used to provide therapeutic education for emotionally handicapped children and to prepare them for regular public schools or sheltered workshops. Individualized academics, therapy, prevocational work activities and functional living activities are provided. Enrichment activities such as French, horseback riding, Scouts and a school newspaper are conducted during the school day. The average length of treatment is three years.

WESTERN NEW YORK CHILDREN'S PSYCHIATRIC CENTER

Res and Day — Coed Ages 4-18
Clinic: Ages 4-18.

West Seneca, NY 14224. 1010 East Rd.
Tel: 716-674-9730. Fax: 716-675-6455.
www.omh.state.ny.us/omhweb/facilities/wcpc/facility.htm
   E-mail: westernneryorkcpc@omh.state.ny.us
   Conditions: Primary—ED.
   Gen Acad. Pre-Voc. Courses: Read Math Lang_Arts. Man_Arts & Shop.

On-Job Trng.
Est 1980. State. Nonprofit.

WINDWARD SCHOOL
Day — Coed Ages 6-15

White Plains, NY 10605. 13 Windward Ave.
Tel: 914-949-6968. Fax: 914-949-8220.
www.windward-school.org
James E. Van Amburg, EdD, Head. **Maureen A. Sweeney,** Adm.
  Focus: Spec Ed. **Conditions:** Primary—LD. **IQ 90 and up.**
  Gen Acad. Gr 1-9. Courses: Read Math Lang_Arts Lib_Skills Math Sci
    Computers.
  Enr: 458. Day Males 281. Day Females 177. **Staff:** 161 (Full 144, Part 17).
  Rates 2004: Day $32,500/sch yr (+$220). Schol avail.
  Est 1926. Private. Nonprofit.

The school's language-based curriculum serves students with learning disabilities who possess average to superior intelligence. The program combines small-group basic skills remediation with daily instruction in math, science and social studies. Other courses include computer, art, library skills and physical education. Windward seeks to prepare the pupil for a return to an independent or public school setting.

WINSTON PREPARATORY SCHOOL
Day — Coed Ages 11-19

New York, NY 10011. 126 W 17th St.
Tel: 212-496-8400. Fax: 212-362-0927.
www.winstonprep.edu   E-mail: admissions@winstonprep.edu
Scott Bezsylko, BS, MA, Head. **Erinn Skeffington,** Adm.
  Focus: Spec Ed. **Conditions:** Primary—ADHD Dx LD. **IQ 90 and up.**
  Col Prep. Gen Acad. Gr 6-PG. Courses: Read Math Lang_Arts Sci Hist.
  Therapy: Lang Speech.
  Enr: 140. Day Males 98. Day Females 42. **Staff:** 48.
  Rates 2003: Day $33,450/sch yr (+$40).
  Educ.
  Est 1981. Private.

Winston Prep provides an educational program for students of average to above-average potential with learning differences such as dyslexia, nonverbal learning disabilities and attentional problems. The skills-based curriculum offers intensive, small-group instruction in academics, organizational skills and study strategies. In addition, the program includes a daily one-on-one instructional period.

Studio art and gym are part of the school day, and after-school theater and varsity sports are available. High school students who demonstrate commitment and skill acquisition become eligible for a preparatory honors program. Most graduates go on to attend two- or four-year colleges.

WOMAN'S CHRISTIAN ASSOCIATION HOSPITAL
DEPARTMENT OF SPEECH AND HEARING
Clinic: All Ages. M-F 8:30-5.

Jamestown, NY 14701. 207 Foote Ave.
Tel: 716-664-8194. Fax: 716-664-8418.
www.wcahospital.org
   Focus: Treatment. **Conditions:** Primary—Ap D S. Sec—LD OH.
   Therapy: Hear Lang Speech.
   Staff: 7 (Full 6, Part 1).
   Est 1968. Private. Nonprofit.

Individuals with communicative and swallowing disorders and auditory handicaps receive diagnostic and therapeutic treatment at this facility. Fees vary according to services provided, and parental counseling is available.

THE WOMEN AND CHILDREN'S HOSPITAL OF BUFFALO
SPEECH, LANGUAGE AND HEARING CLINIC
Clinic: Ages Birth-21. M-F 8-4:30.

Buffalo, NY 14209. 936 Delaware Ave.
Tel: 716-878-7371. Fax: 716-888-3834.
www.chob.edu   E-mail: dsnyder@kaleidahealth.org
Stuart Williams, Pres. Linda Brodsky, MD, Med Dir.
   Focus: Rehab. Treatment. **Conditions:** Primary—Ap Apr Asp Au Bl CP D Dx IP LD MD Nf ON PDD S SB. Sec—ADD ADHD As B C DS Ep MR MS PW.
   Therapy: Hear Lang Speech. **Psychotherapy:** Fam Indiv Parent.
   Staff: 27. Prof 12.
   Est 1955. Private. Nonprofit. **Spons:** Kaleida Health.

The clinic provides diagnosis and treatment for those with hearing, language and speech disorders. Short-term intervention services are available, as is an early childhood program for children from birth to age 5.

WOODWARD CHILDREN'S CENTER
Day — Coed Ages 5-21
Clinic: Ages 5-21. M-S 9-3:30; Eve T 4-8.

Freeport, NY 11520. 201 W Merrick Rd.
Tel: 516-379-0900. Fax: 516-379-0997.
www.woodwardchildren.org   E-mail: info@woodwardchildren.org
Robert Ambrose, BA, MSEd, Exec Dir. Alta Harbin, Clin Dir. Susan Spater-Zimmerman, MD, Med Dir.
   Focus: Treatment. **Conditions:** Primary—BD CD ED Mood OCD Psy SP Sz. Sec—Ap Dx LD MR ON S.

Gen Acad. Pre-Voc. Gr K-12. Courses: Read Math Lang_Arts.
Therapy: Lang Speech. **Psychotherapy:** Fam Group Indiv Parent.
Enr: 80. **Staff:** 50. Educ 22. Admin 4.
Summer Prgm: Day. Educ. Ther.
Est 1950. Private. Nonprofit.

Woodward provides psychiatric day treatment for mildly to severely emotionally disturbed children and adolescents. A comprehensive clinical treatment program is offered consisting of personal adjustment training, counseling and psychotherapy, remedial academics and vocational training. Developing adequate strengths as contributing members of society and mainstreaming are the goals of the vocational, educational and clinical teams.

The education division comprises early childhood development, special education classes and prevocational programs. Early childhood development is designed for handicapped children emphasizing communicative skills, physical development, interpersonal relationships and ego growth. The special education program is individualized and therapeutic. Family involvement is required and counseling is provided. The program lasts between two and three years.

YAI NATIONAL INSTITUTE FOR PEOPLE WITH DISABILITIES

Res — Coed Ages 21 and up; Day — Coed All Ages
Clinic: All Ages. M-S By Appt.

New York, NY 10001. 460 W 34th St, 11th Fl.
Tel: 212-273-6100. TTY: 212-290-2787. Fax: 212-273-6590.
www.yai.org   E-mail: link@yai.org
Philip H. Levy, PhD, Pres. **Joel M. Levy,** DSW, Exec Dir. **Jennifer Shaoul,**
Intake.
  Focus: Treatment. **Conditions:** Primary—ADD ADHD Asp Au Bl CP DS
    Dx Ep IP LD MR ON PDD PW SB TS. Sec—Anx Ap Apr Ar As B BD C
    CD CF D Db ED HIV MD Mood MS Nf OCD ODD Psy PTSD S Sz TB. **IQ
    0-110.**
  Voc. On-Job Trng.
  Therapy: Hear Lang Occup Phys Speech. **Psychotherapy:** Fam Group
    Indiv Parent.
  Est 1957. Private. Nonprofit.

YAI is an agency that serves individuals with mental retardation and developmental disabilities through day and evening programs, community-based residences, family assistance and counseling, supervised medical treatment and support services. Programs help patients develop prevocational, vocational, social and basic academic and living skills, the goals being normalization and independence in daily community living. Residents live in satellite apartments and group homes throughout the greater metropolitan area.

A relationship with the New York League allows YAI to provide early childhood services for children from birth to age 5. Also available are family support services, and adult and elderly daycare and treatment programs.

NORTH CAROLINA

THE ACHIEVEMENT SCHOOL

Day — Coed Ages 6-20

Raleigh, NC 27609. 400 Cedarview Ct.
Tel: 919-782-5082. Fax: 919-782-5980.
www.achievementschool-ld.com   E-mail: lsilber@aol.com
Leon D. Silber, EdD, Dir.
  Focus: Spec Ed. **Conditions:** Primary—ADD ADHD Dx LD. Sec—Db Dc
  Dg. **IQ 90 and up.**
  Gen Acad. Pre-Voc. Gr 1-12. Courses: Read Math Lang_Arts Sci Comput-
  ers Soc_Stud Studio_Art. On-Job Trng.
  Psychotherapy: Parent.
  Enr: 120. **Staff:** 34. (Full 34).
  Rates 2003: Day $12,745/sch yr.
  Summer Prgm: Day. Educ. Day Rate $1250. 5 wks.
  Est 1981. Private. Nonprofit.

Students with learning disabilities and attention deficit disorder develop basic academic skills at the school by means of a multisensory, systematic approach. Contracts,
contingent rewards and social reinforcement are used to increase motivation and self-
esteem. The school offers full-day programs, a summer program, hourly tutoring, and
a supervised study hall beginning in grade 6, as well as a program for individuals with
mild educational handicaps.

ALEXANDER YOUTH NETWORK

Res and Day — Coed Ages 5-18

Charlotte, NC 28222. 6220 Thermal Rd, PO Box 220632.
Tel: 704-366-8712. Fax: 704-362-8464.
www.alexandercc.org   E-mail: info@alexanderyouthnetwork.org
  Conditions: Primary—BD ED. Sec—ADD ADHD ODD Psy PTSD.
  Gen Acad. Ungraded. Courses: Read Math Lang_Arts.
  Psychotherapy: Fam Group Indiv.
  Staff: Prof 21.
  Est 1888. Private. Nonprofit.

APPALACHIAN STATE UNIVERSITY
COMMUNICATION DISORDERS CLINIC

Clinic: All Ages. M-F 8-5.

Boone, NC 28608. 114 Duncan Hall.
Tel: 828-262-2185. Fax: 828-262-6766.

www.lre.appstate.edu/programs/cdclinic
Mary Ruth Sizer, MA, CCC-A, Dir.
  Focus: Treatment. **Conditions:** Primary—Ap Bl CP D ON S. Sec—BD Dx
    Ep LD MR.
  Therapy: Hear Lang Speech.
  Staff: 7.
  Est 1968. State. Nonprofit.

Serving as a hands-on clinical experience for Appalachian State students, the clinic
provides speech, language and hearing therapy for area children and adults who have
communication disorders. The facility also acts as a consulting agency to local daycare
centers and public school systems. Fees are determined along a sliding scale.

CAROBELL

Res — Coed All Ages

Hubert, NC 28539. 198 Cinnamon Dr.
Tel: 910-326-7600. Fax: 910-326-9988.
www.carobell.com   E-mail: info@carobell.com
Vanessa Ervin, Pres. **Leon Kea,** MSA, Dir. **Charles R. Martin,** MD, Med Dir.
  Focus: Treatment. **Conditions:** Primary—MR. Sec—ADD ADHD Ap As B
    Bl C CP D Dx Ep IP LD MD MS ON PW S TB.
  Pre-Voc. Ungraded.
  Therapy: Hear Lang Occup Phys Speech Aqua. **Psychotherapy:** Indiv.
  Enr: 38. **Staff:** 23 (Full 18, Part 5). Prof 13. Educ 10. Admin 5.
  Est 1969. Private. Nonprofit.

Within a homelike environment, Carobell offers a developmental program designed to
develop basic self-help skills in individuals with severe or profound mental retardation.

CASWELL CENTER

Res — Coed Ages 16 and up

Kinston, NC 28528. 2415 W Vernon Ave.
Tel: 252-208-4000.
www.caswellcenter.org   E-mail: caswell.center@ncmail.net
Beverly Vinson, Int Dir. **Janet Roberts,** Med Dir.
  Focus: Spec Ed. **Conditions:** Primary—MR PW Sz. Sec—Au B Bl CP D
    Db ED IP MD MS ON SB TS.
  Gen Acad. Pre-Voc. Voc. Ungraded. Courses: Read Math Lang_Arts. Man_
    Arts & Shop. Shelt_Workshop. On-Job Trng.
  Therapy: Chemo Hear Lang Music Occup Phys Recreational Speech. **Psy-
    chotherapy:** Indiv.
  Enr: 450. **Staff:** 1600. Educ 400. Admin 150.
  Est 1911. State. Nonprofit.

Education, training and residential services are provided at Caswell for children and adults with all types of mental retardation. Personal counseling and life care are available, with enrollment limited to residents of eastern North Carolina counties.

CHILD & FAMILY DEVELOPMENT
Clinic: Ages Birth-18. M-F.

Charlotte, NC 28207. 2034 Randolph Rd, Ste 300.
Tel: 704-332-4834. Fax: 704-372-9653.
www.childandfamilydevelopment.com
Sherry Launt, BS, MPH, Dir.
   Conditions: Primary—BD ED LD OH. Sec—ADD ADHD Apr Ar Au Bl CP D DS MD MR S SB.
   Gen Acad. Courses: Read Math Lang_Arts.
   Therapy: Hear Lang Occup Phys Play Speech. **Psychotherapy:** Fam Group Indiv.
   Staff: Prof 18.
   Est 1980. Private. Inc.

THE CHILDREN'S CENTER
FOR THE PHYSICALLY DISABLED
Day — Coed Ages Birth-11

Winston-Salem, NC 27106. 2315 Coliseum Dr.
Tel: 336-727-2440. Fax: 336-727-2873.
E-mail: preavis@wsfcs.k12.nc.us
Mike Britt, Exec Dir.
   Focus: Treatment. **Conditions:** Primary—As Bl C CP IP MD MS ON SB. Sec—B D Dx LD MR S. **IQ 40 and up.**
   Gen Acad. Pre-Voc. Ungraded. Courses: Read Math Lang_Arts.
   Therapy: Hear Lang Occup Phys Speech.
   Enr: 115. **Staff:** 60. (Full 60). Prof 20. Educ 13. Admin 2.
   Summer Prgm: Day. Educ. Rec. Ther.
   Est 1952. Federal. Nonprofit.

The center comprises a day school and a treatment facility for children with orthopedic handicaps and neurological conditions. The program offers therapies in conjunction with an academic curriculum similar to that in the local school system, but modified to meet the particular needs of the handicapped. Computers and adaptive devices enhance communication and learning.

CHILDREN'S DEVELOPMENTAL SERVICES AGENCY
Clinic: Ages Birth-5. M-F 8-5.

Fayetteville, NC 28304. 1211-A Ireland Dr.

Tel: 910-486-1605. Fax: 910-486-1590.
www.ncei.org/ei/itp/cdsa.html   E-mail: ann.crane@ncmail.net
Ann Crane, MS, Dir. Charles Friend, MD, Med Dir. Carol Wilson, Intake.
  Focus: Treatment. Conditions: Primary—ED OH. Sec—Ap As B Bl C CP D
    Dx Ep IP LD MD MR MS S SB.
  Therapy: Hear Lang Phys Speech. Psychotherapy: Fam Indiv.
  Staff: 43 (Full 38, Part 5). Prof 37. Admin 6.
  Est 1968. State.

Evaluation through a multidisciplinary approach is offered for developmentally disabled children. Short-term therapy, counseling or both are available on a limited basis. Fees are determined along a sliding scale. Children come from Cumberland, Sampson, Bladen and Robeson counties.

Separate centers serve the remainder of North Carolina.

COMPREHENSIVE EDUCATIONAL SERVICES

Day — Coed Ages 6-18
Clinic: Ages 6-18. M-Th 1-5; Eves M-Th 5-9.

Charlotte, NC 28226. 6401 Carmel Rd, Ste 101.
Tel: 704-542-6471. Fax: 704-541-2858.
www.ces-tcc.com   E-mail: info@ces-tcc.com
Greg Sieman, MA, Dir. Ginna Gosney, MEd, Educ Dir.
  Focus: Spec Ed. Conditions: Primary—ADD ADHD Dx ED LD Mood ODD
    SP. Sec—Asp Au Bl MR. IQ 70 and up.
  Col Prep. Gen Acad. Pre-Voc. Voc. Gr 1-12. Courses: Read Math Lang_
    Arts. On-Job Trng.
  Enr: 40. Day Males 29. Day Females 11. Staff: 25 (Full 21, Part 4). Prof 12.
    Educ 10. Admin 3.
  Rates 2003: Day $12,200/yr. $45 (Tutoring)/hr.
  Summer Prgm: Day. Educ. Day Rate $900.
  Est 1984. Private. Inc.

The clinic provides educational therapy and diagnostic and consultative services for persons with learning disabilities and attention deficit disorder. CES conducts two distinct programs: a school for students in grades 1-12, and a tutoring center that serves pupils four days per week in the afternoons and evenings. Summer courses and tutoring are also available during the summer months. Vocational, educational and parental counseling, parent workshops and teacher training are components of the program.

CONCERN OF DURHAM
GREENHOUSE PROGRAMS

Res — Coed Ages 12-18

Durham, NC 27707. 1800 Martin Luther King Jr Pky, Ste 204.
Tel: 919-489-5652. Fax: 919-490-6288.
E-mail: concernofdurham@nc.rr.com
Gail Yashar, MS, MSW, Exec Dir. Christopher Smith, MSW, Clin Dir.

Focus: Treatment. **Conditions:** Primary—ADD ADHD Anx Asp BD CD ED Mood OCD PTSD. **IQ 80 and up.**
Psychotherapy: Fam Group Indiv Parent.
Enr: 10. Res Males 5. Res Females 5. **Staff:** 19 (Full 16, Part 3). Prof 17. Admin 2.
Rates 2003: Res $187-220/day. State Aid.
Summer Prgm: Day. Educ. Rec. Ther. Day Rate $87/day. 5 wks.
Est 1979. Private. Nonprofit.

These year-round, community-based group homes—Greenhouse for Boys and Greenhouse for Girls—each provide a structured, homelike environment with clear limits and expectations. A point system enables residents who show responsible and appropriate behavior to earn a greater degree of freedom and privileges. Residents can eventually use the points to visit their families on weekends and holidays.

Boys and girls attend public schools or take part in vocational training or other educational programs during the week and participate in chores, meal planning and preparation, and activity planning. Recreation is an integral part of the program. During the summer, residents may attend school, work, hold volunteer jobs or participate in the Concern of Durham summer program. The summer program comprises academics, therapeutic groups, recreational activities and the arts.

The average length of stay is eight to 18 months, but never longer than three years. Greenhouse is available only to residents of North Carolina, with preference given to those from Durham County.

COVE CREEK CENTER

Res — Males Ages 18-25; Day — Males 16-25

Sugar Grove, NC 28679. Hwy 321 N, PO Box 407.
Tel: 828-297-4175. Fax: 828-297-4176.
www.covecreekfarm.com   E-mail: chris@covecreekfarm.org
Sara Hardy, BS, Pres. **Kevin Hardy,** BS, Head.
  Focus: Spec Ed. Trng. **Conditions:** Primary—ADD ADHD Anx Apr Ar As BD Bu CD Dc Dg Dx ED LD Mood OCD ODD Psy PTSD S SP TS. Sec— AN Ap Asp Au Bl C CF CP Db DS Ep HIV MD MR MS ON PDD PW Sz.
  Col Prep. Gen Acad. Pre-Voc. Voc. Ungraded. Courses: Read Math Lang_ Arts. On-Job Trng.
  Enr: 18. Res Males 12. Day Males 6. **Staff:** 3. (Full 3).
  Rates 2004: Res $2500-3000/mo. Schol avail.
  Summer Prgm: Res. Rec. Ther. 8 wks.
  Est 2002. Private. Nonprofit.

Located on 50 acres of pasture and woodland, the center operates several programs for adolescent males who are struggling with emotional difficulties, attentional disorders or substance abuse. Cove Creek Farm provides a spiritually based, structured and chemical-free living environment for young men ages 18-25. Individual and group sessions with staff and other residents are built into the weekly schedule, as are weekly Alcohol Anonymous and Narcotics Anonymous meetings.

Cove Creek Academy is a day school designed for boys ages 16-25 who require an alternative educational environment. Tutoring and assistance with ADD and ADHD are available, and an on-staff educational consultant devises study plans for the students.

While Cove Creek does not provide on-site psychoanalytic counseling, the facility maintains a relationship with a local psychiatrist who specializes in adolescents and a psychologist who is available for long-term therapy.

A two-month summer wilderness program enrolls boys ages 13-17 who are demonstrating such signs of at-risk behavior as drug or alcohol abuse, problematic behavior, inability to follow parents' rules, and oppositional defiant disorder.

DEVELOPMENTAL EVALUATION CENTER

Clinic: Ages Birth-5. M-F 8-5.

Asheville, NC 28805. 11 Tunnel Rd, Ste D.
Tel: 828-251-6091. Fax: 828-251-6911.
Joyce S. Greene, BA, MPH, Dir.
   Focus: Treatment. **Conditions:** Primary—ADD ADHD Ap Au B Bl CP D Dx
   Ep IP LD MR ON S SB. Sec—As C MD MS TB.
   Therapy: Lang Occup Phys Speech.
   Staff: 19 (Full 14, Part 5).
   Est 1964. State. Nonprofit.

Children considered at risk of experiencing developmental disabilities receive evaluation and therapeutic treatment at the center. A multidisciplinary diagnostic team determines each child's special needs and counsels parents. Referrals and consultations with pediatricians, neurologists, family physicians and educational personnel are included in the services. Fees vary according to services provided, and a sliding scale is available.

DIVISION FOR THE TREATMENT AND EDUCATION
OF AUTISTIC AND RELATED
COMMUNICATION HANDICAPPED CHILDREN

Day — Coed All Ages
Clinic: All Ages.

Chapel Hill, NC 27599. Univ of North Carolina-Chapel Hill, CB 7180.
Tel: 919-966-2174. Fax: 919-966-4127.
www.teacch.com   E-mail: teacch@unc.edu
   Conditions: Primary—Au.
   Gen Acad.
   Psychotherapy: Indiv.
   Est 1972. State.

DOROTHEA DIX HOSPITAL
CHILD PSYCHIATRY OUTPATIENT CLINIC

Clinic: Ages 2-18. M-F 8-5.

Raleigh, NC 27603. 2108 Umstead Dr.

Tel: 919-733-5344. Fax: 919-733-9441.
Karen Poulos, MD, Co-Dir. **Jack Naftel,** MD, Co-Dir.
   Focus: Treatment. **Conditions:** Primary—Anx BD CD ED Mood OCD Psy
      PTSD Sz TS. Sec—ADD ADHD LD.
   Therapy: Speech. **Psychotherapy:** Fam Group Indiv Parent.
   Staff: 27 (Full 12, Part 15).
   Rates 2003: Sliding-Scale Rate $0-86/hr.
   Est 1969. State.

The clinic offers diagnoses and long-term treatment (18 to 24 months) for emotionally disturbed children. Services include child psychotherapy; parental counseling; family, child, adolescent and parent group therapy; psychopharmacological treatment; and school consultations.

The clinic also conducts residential, graduate and undergraduate training in psychiatry, clinical psychology, social work and education of the emotionally disturbed.

DUKE UNIVERSITY MEDICAL CENTER
AUDIOLOGY DEPARTMENT

Clinic: Ages Birth-21. M-F 7:30-5.

Durham, NC 27710. DUMC 3887.
Tel: 919-684-3859. Fax: 919-684-8298.
www.dukespeechandhearing.com
Frank DeRuyter, PhD, Chief. **Gwen O'Grady,** MS, Clin Dir. **Danny O. Jacobs,**
   MD, Med Dir.
   Focus: Rehab. **Conditions:** Primary—Asp Au B D Db DS HIV MD MR MS
      Nf PW SB.
   Therapy: Hear Speech.
   Staff: 37 (Full 31, Part 6). Prof 30. Admin 7.
   Est 1973. Private. Nonprofit.

This department offers complete diagnostic and rehabilitative services for individuals who are hearing impaired. Services include neonatal evoked potentials, visual reinforcement audiometry, diagnostic hearing evaluation, auditory brainstem response, and hearing aid and cochlear implant evaluation and fitting. A sliding fee scale may be arranged.

DUKE UNIVERSITY MEDICAL CENTER
SPEECH AND LANGUAGE PATHOLOGY

Clinic: Ages 1-18. M-F 8-5.

Durham, NC 27710. DUMC 3887.
Tel: 919-684-6271. Fax: 919-684-8298.
www.dukespeechandhearing.com
Frank DeRuyter, PhD, Chief. **Robert W. Anderson,** MD, Med Dir.
   Focus: Treatment. **Conditions:** Primary—Ap BI S. Sec—ADD ADHD As
      Asp Au C CP Ep IP MD MS PDD SB.

Therapy: Hear Lang Speech. **Psychotherapy:** Group.
Staff: 30 (Full 26, Part 4).
Est 1973. Private. Nonprofit.

This facility offers inpatient, rehabilitative, and outpatient diagnostic and treatment services for infants, children and adolescents exhibiting communicative or feeding disorders. Services include infant developmental assessments, a dysphagia diagnostic program, feeding disorders team assessment and management, an interdisciplinary augmentative communication program, a speech/voice disorders program, a cognitive/communicative disorders program, and assessment and treatment of speech and language disorders due to developmental or acquired disorders.

The program places special emphasis upon complex, medically ill infants and children. A sliding fee scale may be arranged.

EAST CAROLINA UNIVERSITY
DEVELOPMENTAL EVALUATION CLINIC
Clinic: Ages Birth-6. M-F 8-5.

Greenville, NC 27858. Irons Bldg, Charles Blvd.
  Nearby locations: Elizabeth City; New Bern; Rocky Mount; Wilmington.
Tel: 252-328-4480. Fax: 252-328-4486.
Gary J. Stainback, PhD, Dir. **Michael Reichel,** MD, Med Dir.
  Focus: Treatment. **Conditions:** Primary—ADD ADHD Ap Au BI CP Dx Ep IP LD MD MR MS ON S SB. Sec—B D.
  Therapy: Hear Lang Occup Phys Speech. **Psychotherapy:** Indiv.
  Staff: 29 (Full 22, Part 7).
  Rates 2004: Sliding-Scale Rate $0-829/session.
  Est 1964. State. Nonprofit.

The clinic, affiliated with the East Carolina University School of Medicine, provides diagnosis and evaluation of developmentally handicapped children, with follow-up services available. All fees are based on a sliding scale. Other centers serving the eastern region of North Carolina are located in Elizabeth City, New Bern, Rocky Mount and Wilmington.

EAST CAROLINA UNIVERSITY
SPEECH-LANGUAGE & HEARING CLINIC
Clinic: All Ages. M-F 8-5.

Greenville, NC 27858. Dept of Communication Sciences & Disorders, Belk Annex.
Tel: 252-328-4405. Fax: 252-328-4469.
www.ecu.edu/csd/clinichome.htm
Betty Smith, PhD, Dir.
  Focus: Treatment. **Conditions:** Primary—D LD S. Sec—ADD ADHD Ap Au BI CP Dx MR.
  Therapy: Hear Lang Speech. **Psychotherapy:** Parent.

Staff: 16 (Full 14, Part 2).
State. Nonprofit.

The clinic offers diagnosis, evaluation and treatment of speech, hearing and language disorders. The facility serves as a training center for ECU students majoring in speech, language and auditory pathology, and all services are provided by student clinicians under direct supervision of certified, state-licensed staff.

EASTER SEALS UCP NORTH CAROLINA

Res and Day — Coed Ages Birth-18

Raleigh, NC 27606. 2315 Myron Dr.
Tel: 919-783-8898. Fax: 919-782-5486.
www.nc.eastersealsucp.com   E-mail: soneal@nc.eastersealsucp.com
C. L. Cochran, MEd, Pres. **Susan O' Neal,** Adm.
  Focus: Spec Ed. Rehab. Trng. Treatment. **Conditions:** Primary—ADD
    ADHD Ap Apr As Asp Au BD Bl C CD CF CP Dx ED Ep HIV IP MD
    Mood MR Nf ON PDD Psy PTSD PW S SB SP Sz TS. Sec—B D Db TB.
  Gen Acad. Ungraded.
  Therapy: Occup Phys Speech.
  Enr: 650. Res Males 50. Res Females 50. Day Males 275. Day Females
    275. **Staff:** 755 (Full 520, Part 235). Prof 250. Educ 60. Admin 60.
  Rates 2003: Res $31,000/yr. State Aid.
  Est 1953. Private. Nonprofit.

The facility offers various programs to children and adults with disabilities and their families, including children's therapy, durable medical equipment dispensation, information and referral, camping and recreation, individual and family support services, and stroke and postpolio support groups.

Day fees are determined along a sliding scale.

EASTERN NORTH CAROLINA
SCHOOL FOR THE DEAF

Res and Day — Coed Ages 5-21

Wilson, NC 27894. Hwy 301N, PO Box 2768.
Tel: 252-237-2450. Fax: 252-237-2450.
www.encsd.net
Henry N. Widmer, Dir.
  Focus: Spec Ed. **Conditions:** Primary—D. Sec—ADD ADHD Au B CP Dx
    LD ON S.
  Gen Acad. Pre-Voc. Voc. Gr 5-12. Courses: Read Math Lang_Arts. Man_
    Arts & Shop. Shelt_Workshop. On-Job Trng.
  Therapy: Hear Lang Occup Phys Speech. **Psychotherapy:** Group Indiv
    Parent.
  Enr: 172. Res Males 63. Res Females 52. Day Males 33. Day Females 24.
    Staff: 146.
  Rates 2004: No Fee.

Summer Prgm: Res & Day. Educ.
Est 1964. State. Nonprofit.

This school for deaf and hearing-impaired students includes vocational, educational, parental and personal counseling in its program. Affiliated preschool centers operate in several nearby locations. ENCSD's summer session serves students enrolled in the academic-year program only.

ECKERD YOUTH ALTERNATIVES

Res — Coed Ages 10-17

Boomer, NC.
Contact: 100 N Starcrest Dr, PO Box 7450, Clearwater, FL 33758.
  Nearby locations: Candor; Elizabethtown; Hendersonville; Lowgap; Manson; Newport.
Tel: 727-461-2990. Fax: 727-442-5911.
www.eckerd.org   E-mail: admissions@eckerd.org
Karen V. Waddell, BA, Pres. **Francene Hazel,** Dir.
  Focus: Treatment. **Conditions:** Primary—BD CD ED Mood ODD. Sec— ADD ADHD LD. **IQ 70 and up.**
  Gen Acad. Pre-Voc. Ungraded. Courses: Read Math Lang_Arts Sci Soc_ Stud.
  Therapy: Speech. **Psychotherapy:** Fam Group Indiv.
  Summer Prgm: Res. Ther. Res Rate $180. 2 wks.
  Est 1968. Private. Nonprofit.

The Eckerd outdoor program offers therapeutic treatment to emotionally disturbed children by providing a camp setting as an alternative to institutionalization.

The year-round program utilizes reality therapy, Rogerian techniques and group therapy. Small-group living in the wilderness environment encourages the acquisition of new skills while promoting discipline and responsibility. Each group must construct their shelter, cut wood, repair equipment and perform other tasks necessary for their stay in the forest. Such experiences provide the children with the opportunity to develop academic skills at their own pace and in relation to each project they endeavor. When sufficient progress is made, children are transferred into the transition classroom in preparation for their return to the mainstream.

In addition to North Carolina, Eckerd conducts outdoor therapeutic treatment programs in the following states: Florida, Georgia, New Hampshire, Rhode Island, Tennessee and Vermont (see separate listings).

GASTON COMPREHENSIVE DAY CENTER

Day — Coed Ages 2-21

Dallas, NC 28034. 1906 Dallas-Cherryville Hwy.
Tel: 704-922-5259. Fax: 704-922-8606.
Julie Gaston, Dir.
  Focus: Spec Ed. Treatment. **Conditions:** Primary—MR.
  Pre-Voc. Voc. Ungraded. Courses: Read Math Lang_Arts.

Therapy: Art Hear Lang Movement Music Occup Phys Recreational Speech.
Enr: 44. Day Males 33. Day Females 11. **Staff:** 24 (Full 23, Part 1). Prof 21. Educ 18. Admin 3.
Rates 2003: Clinic $80/wk.
Summer Prgm: Day. Rec. Day Rate $70/wk.
Est 1969. State.

The center provides year-round developmental and educational treatment for persons with moderate to profound mental retardation. Cognitive and self-help therapy is available.

GATEWAY EDUCATION CENTER

Day — Coed Ages Birth-22

Greensboro, NC 27405. 3205 E Wendover Ave.
Tel: 336-375-2575. Fax: 336-621-1922.
www.guilford.k12.nc.us   E-mail: metzd@guilford.k12.nc.us
Dale J. Metz, BS, MEd, EdD, Exec Dir.
  Focus: Spec Ed. Treatment. **Conditions:** Primary—Au Bl CP IP MD MR MS ON SB. Sec—Ap C S.
  Gen Acad. Pre-Voc. Gr PS-12. Courses: Read Math Lang_Arts Music Studio_Art Adaptive_Phys_Ed. Shelt_Workshop. On-Job Trng.
  Therapy: Hear Hydro Lang Occup Phys Speech. **Psychotherapy:** Group Parent.
  Enr: 304. Day Males 188. Day Females 116. **Staff:** 146.
  Rates 2004: No Fee.
  Est 1950. Municipal. Nonprofit. **Spons:** Greensboro Cerebral Palsy Association.

This program enables orthopedically handicapped, multi-handicapped, autistic and severely mentally handicapped students to reach their physical, mental and social potential. Gateway provides full therapy services, adaptive physical education and after-school care for day school students. Also available are outpatient physical and occupational therapies and an infant stimulation program. The center schedules orthopedic and dental clinics once a month.

THE GUILFORD CENTER

Res — Coed Ages 13 and up; Day — Coed All Ages

Greensboro, NC 27401. Edgeworth Bldg, 232 N Edgeworth St.
  Nearby locations: High Point.
Tel: 336-641-4981. Fax: 336-641-3655.
www.guilfordcenter.com
Leon Shaw, BS, MS, Dir.
  Focus: Trng. **Conditions:** Primary—MR. Sec—Ap As Au B Bl C CP D Dx ED Ep IP LD MD MS S SB. **IQ 0-90.**
  Therapy: Hear Lang Occup Phys Speech. **Psychotherapy:** Fam Group

Indiv.
Enr: 128. Res Males 30. Res Females 28. Day Males 45. Day Females 25.
Staff: 9. Prof 9.
Est 1967. County. Nonprofit.

Serving citizens of Guilford County, the center offers such specialized services as early intervention; treatment for juvenile sex offenders; court liaison care, which provides a transition for those who have had court involvement; and vocational programming for individuals affected by mental illness, developmental disabilities or both. Treatment typically lasts one to two years.

GUILFORD DAY SCHOOL

Day — Coed Ages 6-20

Greensboro, NC 27410. 3310 Horse Pen Creek Rd.
Tel: 336-282-7044. Fax: 336-282-2048.
www.guilfordday.org   E-mail: info@guilfordday.org
Patty L. Fagin, PhD, Exec Dir. **Sandra Gordon,** Adm.
    Focus: Spec Ed. **Conditions:** Primary—ADD ADHD Dc Dg Dx LD. Sec—
      ED Mood OCD ON PTSD SP TS. **IQ 85 and up.**
    Col Prep. Gr 1-12. Courses: Read Math Lang_Arts Sci Soc_Stud.
    Enr: 120. Day Males 96. Day Females 24. **Staff:** 34 (Full 30, Part 4). Prof
      30. Admin 4.
    Rates 2003: Day $12,858-16,588/sch yr. Schol 12 ($39,600).
    Summer Prgm: Day. Educ. Ther. Day Rate $650. 3½ wks.
    Est 1987. Private. Nonprofit.

Guilford enrolls students of average to above-average intelligence who have specific learning disabilities, attentional disorders or both. The individualized approach enables faculty to make appropriate accommodations in light of pupil needs. Among the accommodations provided are extended testing time, use of a computer for written work, use of charts and diagrams as a supplement to lecture, and access to special assistance in the form of a reader or a scribe.

THE HILL CENTER

Day — Coed Ages 5-19

Durham, NC 27705. 3200 Pickett Rd.
Tel: 919-489-7464. Fax: 919-489-7466.
www.hillcenter.org
Sharon Maskel, EdD, Dir. **Wendy Speir,** Adm.
    Focus: Spec Ed. **Conditions:** Primary—ADD ADHD Dx LD. Sec—Ap S. **IQ**
      90 and up.
    Col Prep. Gen Acad. Gr K-12. Courses: Read Math Lang_Arts Spanish.
    Enr: 168. Day Males 118. Day Females 50. **Staff:** 40. Educ 28. Admin 3.
    Rates 2004: Day $12,535/sch yr (+$150). Schol avail.
    Summer Prgm: Day. Educ. Day Rate $2350. 5 wks.
    Est 1977. Private. Nonprofit. **Spons:** Durham Academy.

The center conducts a variety of structured remedial programs for learning-disabled individuals. A half-day academic program includes instruction in reading, writing and math skills, as well as courses in Spanish, algebra and geometry. Students are instructed on a 4:1 student-teacher ratio. Supervised study halls and study skills instruction are offered to students in grades 6 and above. A five-week summer program accepts students already enrolled in the regular academic program as well as those interested in the summer session only.

JOHN UMSTEAD HOSPITAL

Res — Coed Ages 6 and up

Butner, NC 27509. 1003 12th St.
Tel: 919-575-7211. Fax: 919-575-7643.
www.dhhs.state.nc.us/mhddsas/Umstead.htm
Patricia Christian, PhD, Dir.
   Conditions: Primary—ED.
   Courses: Read Math Lang_Arts. Man_Arts & Shop.
   Staff: Prof 147.
   Est 1947. State. Nonprofit.

KANT AND ASSOCIATES

Clinic: Ages 5-18. M-F 10-5; Eves M-F 5-8.

Raleigh, NC 27609. 216 W Millbrook Rd.
Tel: 919-870-0664. Fax: 919-870-5618.
E-mail: offkey2@aol.com
Terri Kant, MEd, Dir.
   Focus: Treatment. **Conditions:** Primary—ADD ADHD Dc Dg Dx LD SP.
      Sec—Anx OCD ODD TS. **IQ 85 and up.**
   Gen Acad. Ungraded. Courses: Read Math Lang_Arts Writing.
   Staff: 5 (Full 2, Part 3). Educ 5.
   Rates 2004: Clinic $290/mo.
   Est 1976. Private.

The clinic serves children with diagnosed learning disabilities, dyslexia, attention deficit disorder and other related diagnoses. Services include consultation, testing, individualized instruction and tutoring.

MENTAL HEALTH SERVICES OF CATAWBA COUNTY

Clinic: All Ages. M-F 8-5.

Hickory, NC 28602. 3050 11th Avenue Dr SE.
Tel: 828-695-5900. Fax: 828-695-4256.
www.co.catawba.nc.us/mentalhealth
   E-mail: johnh@catawbacountync.gov

John Hardy, MSW, Dir.
   Focus: Treatment. **Conditions:** Primary—ADD ADHD Ap Au B BD BI CD
      CP D Dx ED Ep IP LD MD MR MS OCD ON Psy S SB Sz.
   Voc. Shelt_Workshop.
   Therapy: Hear Occup Phys Speech. **Psychotherapy:** Fam Group Indiv
      Parent.
   Staff: 244 (Full 188, Part 56).
   County.

This center provides a variety of services for mentally retarded and developmentally disabled persons. Early childhood intervention services serve children from birth to age 3. Education, therapy and vocational skill development are among the services offered to children and adults. Residential placement, developmental daycare, substance abuse and respite services are additional features.

NORTH CAROLINA SCHOOL FOR THE DEAF

Res — Coed Ages 5-21; Day — Coed Birth-21
Clinic: All Ages. M-F.

Morganton, NC 28655. 517 W Fleming Dr.
Tel: 828-432-5200. TTY: 828-432-5200. Fax: 828-433-4044.
www.ncsd.net   E-mail: ncsd-morgantown@wncsd.dhhs.ncmail.net
Linda Lindsey, Dir. **Janet McDaniel,** Prin.
   Focus: Spec Ed. **Conditions:** Primary—D. **IQ 70-135.**
   Col Prep. Gen Acad. Pre-Voc. Voc. Gr PS-12. Courses: Read Math Lang_
      Arts. Man_Arts & Shop. On-Job Trng.
   Therapy: Lang Occup Speech. **Psychotherapy:** Fam Group Indiv Parent.
   Staff: 232.
   Est 1894. State. Nonprofit.

An institution for deaf children of North Carolina, NCSD does not accept uneducable mentally retarded or severely emotionally disturbed deaf children. The preschool program consists of two classes on campus, eight classes at satellite locations, and an itinerant teacher who works with students and their families in the home. The school emphasizes vocational training, and many graduates attend college.

NORTH CAROLINA STATE UNIVERSITY
DIAGNOSTIC TEACHING CLINIC

Clinic: Ages 3-18. M-F.

Raleigh, NC 27695. 602D Poe Hall.
Tel: 919-515-7061. Fax: 919-513-1687.
www.ced.ncsu.edu/DTC   E-mail: stacy_rush@ncsu.edu
Cathy L. Crossland, EdD, Dir.
   Conditions: Primary—BD LD. Sec—ED.
   Est 1983. State.

OLSON HUFF CENTER FOR CHILD DEVELOPMENT

Clinic: Ages Birth-18. M-F 8-5.

Asheville, NC 28801. 509 Biltmore Ave.
Tel: 828-213-1725. Fax: 828-213-1735.
www.missionhospitals.org/childrens-huff.htm
   E-mail: theresa.emmanuel@msj.org
Helene Cohen, Mgr. **Adrian Sandler,** MD, Med Dir.
   Focus: Rehab. **Conditions:** Primary—ADD ADHD Anx Apr Ar Asp Au BD
      Bl CD CF CP Db Dc Dg DS Dx ED IP LD MD Mood Nf ODD ON PDD
      PW S SB SP TS. Sec—Ap As B C D Ep MR MS TB.
   Therapy: Hear Lang Music Occup Phys Speech. **Psychotherapy:** Fam
      Group Indiv Parent.
   Staff: 25. Prof 22. Admin 1.
   Rates 2003: Clinic $208/hr.
   Est 1995. Private. Nonprofit. **Spons:** Mission Hospitals.

Olson Huff Center provides comprehensive treatment for children with difficulties in development and learning. Ongoing outpatient services include the identification of community resources for children, advocacy for children and their families, and parental counseling.

ORTON ACADEMY

Day — Coed Ages 10-18

Asheville, NC 28804. 6 Colonial Pl.
Tel: 828-258-3499. Fax: 828-258-3499.
E-mail: ortonacademy@main.nc.us
M. Victoria Remishofsky, Prin. **Stan Taylor,** Adm.
   Focus: Spec Ed. **Conditions:** Primary—Dc Dg Dx. Sec—ADD ADHD. **IQ
      90-109.**
   Col Prep. Gr 4-12. Courses: Read Math Lang_Arts. On-Job Trng.
   Therapy: Art Dance Music Percepual-Motor Speech.
   Enr: 32. Day Males 26. Day Females 6. **Staff:** 6 (Full 4, Part 2). Educ 6.
   Rates 2003: Day $8000/sch yr. Schol 2 ($16,000).
   Est 1983. Private.

This college preparatory school serves students of average intelligence who have dyslexia or other learning disabilities. In addition to the academic curriculum, the academy provides a wide range of individual and group therapies.

THE PIEDMONT SCHOOL

Day — Coed Ages 6-13

High Point, NC 27265. 815 Old Mill Rd.
Tel: 336-883-0992. Fax: 336-883-4752.
www.thepiedmontschool.com   E-mail: info@thepiedmontschool.com

Mary Lin Brewer, BS, Dir.
Focus: Spec Ed. **Conditions:** Primary—ADD ADHD Dx LD. **IQ 85 and up.**
Gen Acad. Ungraded. Courses: Read Math Lang_Arts Sci Soc_Stud Computers Studio_Art Music Drama.
Enr: 62. **Staff:** 19 (Full 10, Part 9).
Est 1982. Private. Nonprofit.

Students attend either full- or part-time to receive remedial attention for basic academic skills and work to perform at the level of their academic potentials at this school. The goal is to return the pupil to a regular school in 24 to 36 months. Individualized instruction and a student-teacher ratio of no more than 3:1 are provided for reading, writing, language and math instructions. Full-time students receive instruction in science, social studies, art, drama, physical education, computer studies and social skills in groups of no more than nine children. In addition, Piedmont offers turoring services for older students at six area satellite schools.

PITT COUNTY MEMORIAL HOSPITAL
REGIONAL REHABILITATION CENTER

Res — Coed Ages Birth-18
Clinic: All Ages. M-S 8-6.

Greenville, NC 27835. PO Box 6028.
Tel: 252-816-6600. Fax: 252-816-6625.
www.uhseast.com   E-mail: rehab@mail.ecu.edu
Daniel Moore, MD, Med Dir.
Focus: Rehab. **Conditions:** Primary—ADD ADHD Ap Au B BI CP D IP LD MD MR MS ON S SB. Sec—As C.
Gen Acad. Pre-Voc. Courses: Read Math Lang_Arts.
Therapy: Chemo Hear Lang Occup Phys Speech. **Psychotherapy:** Fam Group Indiv Parent.
Est 1977. County. Nonprofit. **Spons:** University Health Systems of Eastern Carolina.

The center operates an eight-bed inpatient rehabilitation unit, while also providing such outpatient services at the pediatric level as evaluation and therapeutic treatment. Counseling is available. In addition, the facility offers educational programs throughout the school year. Length of care varies according to the patient's needs; however, a typical inpatient stay lasts four to six weeks.

SILBER PSYCHOLOGICAL SERVICES

Clinic: Ages 2-26. M-F 8-6.

Raleigh, NC 27609. 1004 Dresser Ct.
Nearby locations: Cary.
Tel: 919-876-5658. Fax: 919-790-1521.
www.silbersolutions.com
Linda Silber, PhD, Dir.

Focus: Treatment. **Conditions:** Primary—ADD ADHD CD Dx ED LD OCD. Sec—Au Psy Sz. **IQ 60 and up.**
Psychotherapy: Fam Group Indiv Parent.
Private.

SPS provides services for children and young adults who have emotional, behavioral and family problems. Services for students with learning differences are also available. The length of treatment varies.

A branch facility is located at 1340 S.E. Maynard Rd., Ste. 201, Cary 27511.

SOUTHEASTERN REGIONAL MENTAL HEALTH CENTER

Clinic: Ages Birth-18. M-F 8:30-5.

Lumberton, NC 28358. 2003 Godwin Ave, Ste A.
 Nearby locations: Elizabethtown; Fayetteville; Laurinburg; Whiteville.
Tel: 910-738-5261. Fax: 910-738-8230.
www.srmhc.org   E-mail: info@srmhc.org
Stephen Ramey, Dir. **Theresa Bullard,** MD, Med Dir.
 Focus: Treatment. **Conditions:** Primary—ADD ADHD AN Anx Asp Au BD Bu CD ED Mood OCD ODD Psy PTSD SP Sz. Sec—B Bl CP D Db HIV LD MR PW TS.
 Voc. Shelt_Workshop.
 Therapy: Lang Speech. **Psychotherapy:** Fam Group Indiv.
 Staff: 16.
 Est 1964. County.

Diagnostic and treatment services are provided for those with emotional or learning difficulties. An early childhood intervention program includes a therapeutic preschool, parent groups, daycare consultation and in-service training for early childhood educators. Two group homes for children ages 6-17 are also available through the Mental Health Center. Family therapy is the primary treatment approach, with some individual and group counseling available.

STONE MOUNTAIN SCHOOL

Res — Males Ages 11-16

Black Mountain, NC 28711. 126 Camp Elliott Rd.
Tel: 828-669-8639. Fax: 828-669-2521.
www.stonemountainschool.com
 E-mail: info@stonemountainschool.com
Catherine Jennings, Exec Dir. **Paige Thomas,** Adm.
 Focus: Spec Ed. **Conditions:** Primary—ADD ADHD Asp BD Dc Dg Dx LD ODD. Sec—Anx Bl ED OCD. **IQ 80 and up.**
 Gen Acad. Gr 6-12. Courses: Read Math Lang_Arts Sci Soc_Stud.
 Therapy: Hear Lang Milieu Movement Speech. **Psychotherapy:** Group Parent.
 Enr: 60. Res Males 60. **Staff:** 47 (Full 42, Part 5). Prof 13. Educ 10. Admin 10.

Rates 2003: Res $4300/mo.
Est 1980. Private. Inc. **Spons:** Aspen Education Group.

Stone Mountain provides a structured academic and behavioral program in an outdoor environment for students who have exhibited learning disabilities, attention deficit disorder, hyperactivity, or emotional or behavioral problems. The school follows a nationally standardized curriculum, and course work is transferable to other private and public schools.

While earning academic credit, the boys learn life skills by participating in such activities as backpacking, swimming, canoeing, white-water rafting, primitive skills development, basic carpentry and campsite construction.

SUCCESS ORIENTED ACHIEVEMENT REALIZED

Res — Coed Ages 8-18

Balsam, NC 28707. PO Box 388.
Tel: 828-456-3435. Fax: 828-456-3449.
www.soarnc.org   E-mail: admissions@soarnc.org
John Willson, MS, Dir. **Ed Parker,** Adm.
    Focus: Spec Ed. **Conditions:** Primary—ADD ADHD LD. **IQ 80 and up.**
    Gen Acad. Ungraded. Courses: Math Lang_Arts Sci Soc_Stud Studio_Art
        Music.
    Staff: 75 (Full 25, Part 50).
    Summer Prgm: Res. Educ. Rec. Ther. Adventure. Res Rate $1750-3600.
        2-4 wks.
    Est 1974. Private. Nonprofit.

SOAR provides an opportunity for students with learning disabilities and attentional disorders to earn academic credits while using a hands-on approach to learning through a semester program. Academic work is closely coordinated with the student's school to ensure that the school will be able to award semester credits in math, English, American history, biology, physical education and art for graduation credits.

SOAR also conducts expeditions throughout the Southeast, the Florida Keys, the Caribbean, the Colorado Rockies, Alaska and the Desert Southwest. These adventure-based therapeutic programs offer students the opportunity to learn life skills, and an experiential education allows students to learn by doing. Adventure activities include wilderness backpacking, rock climbing, white-water rafting and canoeing, wildlife studies, mountaineering, snorkeling, sailing, cross-country skiing and wilderness medicine. The organization schedules shorter adventures during spring, fall and winter.

SUWS OF THE CAROLINAS

Res — Coed Ages 13-18

Old Fort, NC 28762. 363 Graphite Rd.
Tel: 888-828-9770. Fax: 828-668-7959.
www.suwscarolinas.com   E-mail: admissions@suwscarolinas.com
Graham Shannonhouse, Exec Dir. **Leah Halverson,** Adm.
    Focus: Treatment. **Conditions:** Primary—ADD ADHD Anx As Asp BD Dc

Dg Dx LD Mood OCD ODD PTSD SP.
Rates 2004: Res $415/day (+$950/ses).
Est 1981. Private. Inc. **Spons:** Aspen Education Group.

This therapeutic camping program focuses on clinical intervention and assessment. SUWS uses the outdoors as an alternative to conventional treatment environments, while also engaging students by means of traditional therapeutic methods. Staff specialize in treating students who are experiencing low self-esteem, family conflict, defiant behavior, attention deficit disorder, depression, isolation, drug or alcohol use, negative peer relationships or learning differences.

THOMPSON CHILDREN'S HOME

Res — Coed Ages 6-12; Day — Coed 6-14
Clinic: Ages Birth-18. M-F 8-5.

Charlotte, NC 28212. PO Box 25129.
Tel: 704-536-0375. Fax: 704-531-9266.
www.thompsonchildrenshome.org
Ginny Amendum, Pres. **Cindy Shahan,** MD, Med Dir. **Jodie Hearn,** Adm.
 Focus: Spec Ed. Treatment. **Conditions:** Primary—ADD ADHD Mood OCD ODD PTSD Sz. Sec—BD LD S. **IQ 70-120.**
 Gen Acad. Gr K-6. Courses: Read Math Lang_Arts Sci Soc_Stud Health.
 Therapy: Milieu Music Occup Recreational Speech. **Psychotherapy:** Fam Group Indiv Parent.
 Enr: 22. Res Males 9. Res Females 7. Day Males 5. Day Females 1. **Staff:** 90 (Full 80, Part 10). Educ 6.
 Rates 2004: Res $219/day. Day $109/day.
 Est 1886. Private. Nonprofit.

This home for children with emotional and behavioral disorders conducts year-round residential and day treatment, early childhood services, and a range of community-based programs that includes foster care, group homes and clinical treatment.

The School at Thompson provides individualized occupational, speech, language and recreational therapies and hands-on learning experiences for students in grades K-5. Boys and girls may take part in psychotherapy sessions with licensed therapists or child psychiatrists.

The group home assists adolescents in developing life and career skills. Educational and mental health counseling is available.

UNIVERSITY OF NORTH CAROLINA
CENTER FOR DEVELOPMENT AND LEARNING

Day — Coed Ages Birth-20
Clinic: All Ages. M-F 8-5.

Chapel Hill, NC 27599. CB 7255.
Tel: 919-966-5171. Fax: 919-966-2230.
www.cdl.unc.edu

Melvin D. Levine, MD, Dir.
   Conditions: Primary—BI CP Dx LD MR OH.
   Gen Acad. Ungraded. Courses: Read Math.
   Therapy: Chemo Hear Lang Occup Phys Speech. **Psychotherapy:** Fam
      Group Indiv.
   Est 1962. State. Nonprofit.

UNIVERSITY OF NORTH CAROLINA-GREENSBORO
SPEECH AND HEARING CENTER

Clinic: All Ages. M-F 8-5.

Greensboro, NC 27402. 300 Ferguson Bldg, PO Box 26170.
Tel: 336-334-5939. Fax: 336-334-4475.
www.uncg.edu/csd/center.html   E-mail: cvmccrea@uncg.edu
Vicki McCready, MA, Dir.
   Focus: Treatment. **Conditions:** Primary—Ap Dx S. Sec—ADD Asp Au BI
      CP D DS ED LD MR ON PDD.
   Therapy: Hear Lang Speech.
   Staff: 13 (Full 8, Part 5). Prof 10. Admin 3.
   Rates 2003: Clinic $70/ses.
   Est 1967. Private. Nonprofit.

All types of communication disorders are treated at this center, which serves as a training program in speech-language pathology and audiology for students at UNCG. Clients choose from a broad range of evaluation and treatment services, including hearing aid evaluation and fitting. The center also conducts a preschool language program for language- and learning-disabled children. A sliding fee scale may be applied when appropriate.

WESTERN CAROLINA CENTER

Res — Coed Ages 3 and up; Day — Coed Birth-5
Clinic: All Ages. M-F 8-5.

Morganton, NC 28655. 300 Enola Rd.
Tel: 828-433-2711. Fax: 828-433-2799.
www.westerncarolinacenter.org
J. Iverson Riddle, MD, Dir.
   Focus: Treatment. **Conditions:** Primary—MR. Sec—ADD ADHD Ap As Au
      B BI C CD CP D Dx ED Ep IP LD MD MS OCD ON Psy S SB Sz TB.
   Pre-Voc. Voc. Ungraded. Courses: Read Math. Shelt_Workshop. On-Job
      Trng.
   Therapy: Art Chemo Hear Lang Occup Phys Speech. **Psychotherapy:**
      Fam Group Indiv Parent.
   Enr: 362. Res Males 199. Res Females 154. Day Males 6. Day Females 3.
   Est 1963. State. Nonprofit.

Operating year-round, WCC offers an individualized habilitation plan for mentally retarded and multiply handicapped individuals. An interdisciplinary team sets goals and implements appropriate programs for clients. An infant stimulation unit serves pre-schoolers. Outpatient and counseling services are available, and the center determines both infant stimulation and clinical rates along a sliding scale.

NORTH DAKOTA

ALTRU PEDIATRIC REHABILITATION

Clinic: Ages Birth-21. M-F 8:30-4:30.

Grand Forks, ND 58206. 1300 S Columbia Rd, PO Box 6002.
Tel: 701-780-2428. TTY: 701-780-2307. Fax: 701-780-2599.
www.altru.org   E-mail: contactus@altru.org
Larry Burd, Dir. **Kerstin Sobus,** MD, Med Dir.
   Focus: Rehab. Treatment. **Conditions:** Primary—ADD ADHD Ap Apr Asp
      Au BD BI CP Dg DS Dx IP LD MD MR MS Nf ON PW S SB TS. Sec—AN
      Anx As B Bu C CD D Db ED Ep OCD Psy PTSD SP Sz TB.
   Therapy: Lang Occup Phys Speech.
   Staff: 23 (Full 13, Part 10). Prof 12. Educ 1. Admin 2.
   Rates 2003: No Fee.
   Est 1997. Private. Nonprofit. **Spons:** Altru Health System.

Altru provides comprehensive outpatient services for children and adolescents with
developmental disabilities, learning disabilities, psychological and emotional problems,
communicational disorders and a range of physical disabilities. In addition to physicians
specializing in physical medicine and rehabilitation, pediatrics, pediatric neurology,
pediatric orthopedics, clinical genetics and child psychiatry, the pediatric team also
includes therapists, audiologists, psychologists, speech-language pathologists and various other professionals.

ANNE CARLSEN CENTER FOR CHILDREN

Res and Day — Coed Ages Birth-21

Jamestown, ND 58401. 301 7th Ave NW.
Tel: 701-252-3850.
www.annecenter.org
Dan Howell, Dir.
   Focus: Spec Ed. Rehab. Treatment. **Conditions:** Primary—ADD ADHD Ap
      As Au B BI C CD CP D Dx ED Ep IP LD MD MR MS OCD ON S SB.
   Gen Acad. Pre-Voc. Voc. Gr PS-6. Courses: Read Math Lang_Arts Studio_
      Art Music Adaptive_Phys_Ed Life_Skills. Man_Arts & Shop. Shelt_Work-
      shop. On-Job Trng.
   Therapy: Hear Lang Occup Phys Speech Aqua. **Psychotherapy:** Group
      Indiv Equine.
   Summer Prgm: Day. Educ. 10 wks.
   Est 1941. Private. Nonprofit. **Spons:** Banner Health System.

Children and young adults who are unable to attend public schools due to orthopedic
or neurological disabilities receive academic and prevocational instruction at this facility. In addition to education, the program includes various forms of therapy. There are
special programs for both the autistic and educable, trainable and severely mentally
handicapped persons, as well as services for nonverbal communication. The center also

provides transitional services, community vocational integration, a therapeutic equestrian center, dysphagia intervention, and advanced care for individuals with medically fragile conditions.

DAKOTA BOYS AND GIRLS RANCH

Res — Coed Ages 10-18

Minot, ND 58702. PO Box 5007.
Tel: 701-852-3628. Fax: 701-839-5541.
www.dakotaboysranch.org   E-mail: dakota.boys@sendit.nodak.edu
Gene Kaseman, Pres.
  Conditions: Primary—BD ED.
  Pre-Voc. Gr 7-12. Courses: Read Math Lang_Arts. Man_Arts & Shop.
  Psychotherapy: Fam Indiv.
  Est 1952. Private. Nonprofit.

MINOT INFANT DEVELOPMENT PROGRAM

Day — Coed Ages Birth-3

Minot, ND 58707. 500 University Ave W.
Tel: 701-858-3054. Fax: 701-858-3483.
http://ndcpd.misu.nodak.edu/projects/infant_development
Kathy Lee, Dir.
  Conditions: Primary—B MR OH.
  Therapy: Hear Lang Occup Phys Speech. Psychotherapy: Fam Group
    Indiv.
  Est 1977. State. Nonprofit.

MINOT STATE UNIVERSITY
COMMUNICATION DISORDERS CLINIC

Clinic: All Ages. M-F 8-4:30.

Minot, ND 58707. 500 University Ave W.
Tel: 701-858-3030. Fax: 701-858-3032.
Thomas Linares, PhD, Chrm. Leisa Harmon, MS, CCC-SLP, Clin Coord.
  Focus: Treatment. Conditions: Primary—Ap S. Sec—ADD ADHD Apr As
    Asp Au B BD BI C CD CP D DS Dx ED Ep IP LD MD MR MS OCD ON
    PDD Psy SB Sz TB.
  Therapy: Hear Lang Speech.
  Staff: 12. (Full 12).
  State.

This clinic provides speech, language and hearing evaluations and therapy for individuals of all ages. The program's structure allows for team interaction with specialists from such fields as social work, nursing and psychology.

NORTH DAKOTA SCHOOL FOR THE DEAF

Res and Day — Coed Ages Birth-21

Devils Lake, ND 58301. 1401 College Dr.
Tel: 701-662-9000. TTY: 701-662-9000. Fax: 701-662-9009.
www.state.nd.us/ndsd   E-mail: nd.sd@sendit.nodak.edu
Rocklyn Cofer, MEd, Supt.
  Focus: Spec Ed. **Conditions:** Primary—D. Sec—Ap As BD BI C CP ED Ep
  LD MD MR MS ON S. **IQ 50 and up.**
  Col Prep. Gen Acad. Pre-Voc. Voc. Gr PS-12. Courses: Read Math Lang_
  Arts. Man_Arts & Shop.
  Therapy: Hear Lang Speech. **Psychotherapy:** Fam Group Indiv.
  Enr: 35. Res Males 15. Res Females 8. Day Males 4. Day Females 8. **Staff:**
  50.
  Est 1890. State. Nonprofit.

This state school offers an academic and vocational program for deaf and hearing-impaired children and those with handicaps. Counseling is available.

NORTH DAKOTA VISION SERVICES
SCHOOL FOR THE BLIND

Res — Coed All Ages

Grand Forks, ND 58203. 500 Stanford Rd.
Tel: 701-795-2700. Fax: 701-795-2727.
www.ndvisionservices.com   E-mail: gbornsen@state.nd.us
Carmen Grove Suminski, MA, Supt.
  Focus: Spec Ed. **Conditions:** Primary—B.
  Therapy: Hear Lang Occup Phys Speech. **Psychotherapy:** Indiv.
  Rates 2004: No Fee.
  Est 1908. State. Nonprofit.

Academic and vocational instruction are offered through this state school. The usual duration of treatment is 12 months.

NORTHWEST HUMAN SERVICE CENTER

Clinic: All Ages. M-F 8-6; Eves M T 6-8.

Williston, ND 58802. 316 2nd Ave W, PO Box 1266.
Tel: 701-774-4600. TTY: 701-774-4692. Fax: 701-774-4620.
www.state.nd.us/humanservices/locations/regionalhsc/northwest/
  index.html   E-mail: dhsnwhsc@state.nd.us

Conditions: Primary—B BD D Dx ED LD MR S.
Therapy: Chemo Hear Lang Occup Phys Speech. **Psychotherapy:** Fam
    Group Indiv.
Est 1960. State. Nonprofit.

SPEECH AND HEARING SERVICES

Clinic: All Ages. M-F 8-5.

Jamestown, ND 58401. Jamestown Mall, 300 2nd Ave NE.
Tel: 701-252-4100. Fax: 701-252-4143.
    Focus: Treatment. **Conditions:** Primary—Apr D S. Sec—Ap Au BD BI CP
        DS Dx ED IP LD MD MR MS ON SB.
    Therapy: Hear Lang Speech.
    Staff: 5 (Full 4, Part 1). Prof 3. Admin 2.
    Rates 2003: Clinic $95/ses. Sliding-Scale Rate $0-45/hr.
    Est 1972. Private. Nonprofit. **Spons:** Medcenter One Health Centers.

Speech and Hearing Services specialize in the understanding of human communication, its normal development and its disorders, and also studies disorder prevention.
Complete diagnostic and therapy services in speech and language pathology include
hearing testing, hearing conservation and the sale of hearing aids. Parental counseling
is also offered.

UNIVERSITY OF NORTH DAKOTA
SPEECH, LANGUAGE AND HEARING CLINIC

Clinic: All Ages. M-F 8-5.

Grand Forks, ND 58202. Montgomery Hall, Rm 101, PO Box 8040.
Tel: 701-777-3232. Fax: 701-777-3650.
www.und.edu/dept/cdis
    Conditions: Primary—Ap Au CP D S.
    Therapy: Hear Lang Speech.
    Staff: Prof 8.
    State.

OHIO

ACHIEVEMENT CENTERS FOR CHILDREN
Day — Coed Ages Birth-21

Cleveland, OH 44104. 11001 Buckeye Rd.
  Nearby locations: Lakewood.
Tel: 216-795-7100. Fax: 216-795-0615.
www.achievementcenters.org
Patricia W. Nobili, BA, MS, Exec Dir.
  Focus: Treatment. **Conditions:** Primary—Ap As Asp Au Bl C CP DS IP MD MR ON PDD S SB. Sec—ADHD Anx B D Dx ED Ep LD OCD ODD TB TS. **IQ 50-130.**
  Therapy: Hear Lang Music Occup Phys Speech. **Psychotherapy:** Fam Group Indiv.
  Enr: 94. Day Males 56. Day Females 38. **Staff:** 80. Prof 30. Educ 20. Admin 8.
  Summer Prgm: Res & Day. Rec. 1 wk.
  Est 1940. Private. Nonprofit.

The centers, which primarily enroll children of the Greater Cleveland area, provide comprehensive services including rehabilitation and therapy, family support, home- and center-based education, and recreational programs.

Standard therapeutic treatment is available for those with cerebral palsy and orthopedic and cardiac disorders. The partially sighted, the deaf and the mentally retarded are accepted if they have physical disabilities.

An early intervention program stressing parental involvement, Project Heed, is designed for children under age 3 who have physical disabilities. Services include on-site support for daycare and preschool mainstreaming, therapy, counseling, information and referral, and workshops for parents and professionals. The society also sponsors two Junior Achievement programs for disabled young adults.

The residential summer program, Camp Cheerful, located in Strongville, features swimming, computer experiences, nature activities, horseback riding, and arts and crafts. The society also sponsors the West Side Rehabilitation Center, 14587 Madison Ave., Lakewood 44107. Fees are based on a sliding scale.

ACLD SCHOOL AND LEARNING CENTER
Day — Coed Ages 5-12
Clinic: Ages 5 and up. M-Th 9-6, S 9-12.

Youngstown, OH 44503. 118 E Wood St.
Tel: 330-746-0604. Fax: 330-746-4272.
www.members.aol.com/acld/learningcenter2.htm
Erica Brown, Dir.
  Focus: Spec Ed. **Conditions:** Primary—ADD ADHD Dc Dg Dx LD. Sec—Ap As Asp Au BD CD CP ED Ep MD MR MS OCD PDD TS. **IQ 65 and up.**

Gen Acad. Ungraded. Courses: Read Math Lang_Arts.
Therapy: Percepual-Motor Speech.
Staff: 19 (Full 9, Part 10).
Rates 2003: Day $3150/sch yr. $300 (Evaluation); $25 (Tutoring)/hr. Schol avail.
Summer Prgm: Day. Educ. Day Rate $300. 5 wks.
Est 1972. Private. Nonprofit.

ACLD is a chartered school and tutoring program serving students who have learning disabilities. The center offers diagnostic and remedial services to individuals with auditory, visual and motor dysfunctions in the areas of reading, writing, spelling and math. The program also devotes attention to socialization and independent living skills.

ADRIEL SCHOOL

Res — Coed Ages 11-18; Day — Coed 5-18

West Liberty, OH 43357. 414 N Detroit St, PO Box 188.
Tel: 937-465-0010. Fax: 937-465-8690.
www.adriel.org
Marty Lehman, Pres.
Focus: Spec Ed. Treatment. **Conditions:** Primary—BD BI ED MR ODD PDD PTSD. Sec—LD. **IQ 55-80.**
Gen Acad. Voc. Ungraded. Courses: Read Math Lang_Arts. On-Job Trng.
Therapy: Music Speech. **Psychotherapy:** Fam Group Indiv.
Enr: 69. Res Males 20. Res Females 12. Day Males 25. Day Females 12. Staff: 30.
Rates 2004: Res $215-230/day. Day $80/day.
Est 1957. Private. Nonprofit. Mennonite.

Located on a 65-acre site, Adriel serves slow-learning students who have behavioral and adjustment problems. The goals for all youths include family reunification, independent living or foster care. Upon admission, students move into a classroom setting, with traditional academics taught at a level and a rate individually designed. At the senior high level a work program is offered that teaches job responsibility both in the classroom and in work situations. Arts and crafts, industrial arts, food services, physical education and intramural sports supplement the academic program.

Adriel uses the Teaching Parent Program in a residential setting that stresses emotional and social growth. Individual and group therapies are available.

All students attend Sunday religious services, and chaplain services are available on campus.

AIM FOR THE HANDICAPPED

Day — Coed All Ages

Dayton, OH 45420. 945 Danbury Rd.
Tel: 937-294-4611. Fax: 937-294-3783.
www.aimforthehandicapped.org
    E-mail: aimforthehandicapped@aimforthehandicapped.org

Jo A. Geiger, BS, MA, PhD, Exec Dir.
    Focus: Trng. **Conditions:** Primary—ADD ADHD Ap Asp Au B Bl CP D Dx
      ED Ep IP LD MD MR MS ON PDD S SB. Sec—As BD C OCD ODD TB.
    Therapy: Movement.
    Staff: 6.
    Rates 2003: No Fee.
    Summer Prgm: Day. Ther.
    Est 1958. Private. Nonprofit.

AIM is a national organization whose purpose is to provide a movement education program for disabled individuals. Increased body efficiency is achieved through rhythmical exercises and creative movement. The AIM method is taught by trained, certified volunteer teachers in classroom situations, as well as by trained classroom teachers and institutional and agency staffs.

AKRON SPEECH AND READING CENTER

Clinic: All Ages. M-Th 8-5; Eves M-Th 5-9.

Akron, OH 44333. 700 Ghent Rd.
Tel: 330-666-1161. Fax: 330-665-1862.
Ardath Franck, MA, PhD, Dir.
    Focus: Trng. **Conditions:** Primary—ADD ADHD Dx LD S. Sec—CP ED
      MR. **IQ 85 and up.**
    Gen Acad. Pre-Voc. Ungraded. Courses: Read Math.
    Therapy: Lang Speech. **Psychotherapy:** Indiv.
    Staff: 8 (Full 1, Part 7). Educ 8.
    Rates 2003: Clinic $12/ses.
    Summer Prgm: Day. Educ.
    Est 1950. Private.

A year-round educational center specializing in remedial and developmental reading, the center acts as a supplement to regular education. Students attend individual sessions twice weekly, and they may take courses for high school credit. Individual tutoring and therapy are available. The usual duration of treatment is six to 12 months.

ALEXANDER GRAHAM BELL SCHOOL

Day — Coed Ages 3-12
Clinic: All Ages. M-F 8:30-2:20.

Cleveland, OH 44120. 11815 Larchmere Blvd.
Tel: 216-229-6966. Fax: 216-795-0446.
www.cmsdnet.net/schools/elementary/agbell.htm
Juanita Holt, Prin.
    Focus: Spec Ed. Treatment. **Conditions:** Primary—B D.
    Col Prep. Gen Acad. Gr PS-8. Courses: Read Math Lang_Arts.
    Therapy: Hear Lang Occup Phys Speech.
    Est 1893. Municipal.

BEECH BROOK

Res and Day — Coed Ages 5-12

Cleveland, OH 44124. 3737 Lander Rd.
Tel: 216-831-2255. Fax: 216-831-0436.
www.beechbrook.org
Debra Rex, MA, MEd, Actg Pres. **Thomas Brugger,** MD, Med Dir.
  Conditions: Primary—BD ED. Sec—Au.
  Gen Acad. Ungraded. Courses: Read Math Lang_Arts.
  Therapy: Art Lang Music Occup Phys Speech. **Psychotherapy:** Fam
    Group Indiv.
  Staff: Prof 110.
  Est 1852. Private. Nonprofit.

BELLEFAIRE JCB

Res — Coed Ages 12-23

Shaker Heights, OH 44118. 22001 Fairmount Blvd.
Tel: 216-932-2800. Fax: 216-932-6704.
www.bellefairejcb.org
Adam G. Jacobs, PhD, Exec Dir. **Ivy Boyle,** MD, Med Dir. **Jill Yulish,** Intake.
  Focus: Spec Ed. Treatment. **Conditions:** Primary—ED Psy Sz. Sec—BD
    CD Dx LD MR OCD S. **IQ 70 and up.**
  Col Prep. Gen Acad. Pre-Voc. Voc. Gr 7-12. Courses: Read Math. Man_
    Arts & Shop. On-Job Trng.
  Therapy: Chemo Lang Speech. **Psychotherapy:** Fam Group Indiv Parent.
  Enr: 52.
  Est 1868. Private. Nonprofit.

Located on a 32-acre site, the center provides a full therapeutic program of psychotherapy, special education and group living for severely emotionally disturbed adolescents. Staff members formulate an individualized curriculum for each individual, with an on-campus public school designed to meet specific pupil needs.

An intensive treatment unit offers psychotherapeutic programs in a closed unit when necessary. Individual psychotherapy and family counseling—which are combined with group techniques, life-space interviews and behavior modification—are important aspects of the treatment program. Aftercare services may include placement in agency-operated foster homes. Complete vocational and recreational facilities incorporate the use of a 92-acre campsite. The program also includes the following community services: intensive home-based family therapy, outpatient counseling, partial hospitalization, juvenile justice programs, school counseling and outreach, a school for children with autism, and independent living programs.

The usual length of treatment ranges from one to six months, depending upon program.

See Also Page 1020

BEREA CHILDREN'S HOME AND FAMILY SERVICES

Res and Day — Coed Ages Birth-18
Clinic: Ages Birth-18. M-F 8-5; Eves W F 5-8.

Berea, OH 44017. 202 E Bagley Rd.
Tel: 440-234-2006. Fax: 440-234-8319.
www.bchfs.org   E-mail: information@bchfs.org
  Conditions: Primary—BD ED. IQ 76 and up.
  Col Prep. Gen Acad. Pre-Voc. Voc. Gr 1-9. Courses: Read Math Lang_
  Arts.
  Therapy: Hear Lang Occup Phys Speech. Psychotherapy: Fam Group
  Indiv.
  Est 1864. Private. Nonprofit.

BETTY JANE MEMORIAL REHABILITATION CENTER

Day — Coed Ages 3-5
Clinic: All Ages. M-F 7:30-5:30; Eve Th 5:30-8.

Tiffin, OH 44883. 65 St Francis Ave.
Tel: 419-447-9811. Fax: 419-448-5030.
www.bettyjanecenter.com   E-mail: choicerehab@acctiffin.com
Richard Maye, Exec Dir.
  Focus: Rehab. Conditions: Primary—ADD ADHD Ap Au BD BI CD CP Dx
  ED LD OCD ON Psy. Sec—As C Ep IP MD MR MS SB TB. IQ 75 and
  up.
  Voc. Shelt_Workshop. On-Job Trng.
  Therapy: Hear Lang Occup Phys Speech. Psychotherapy: Fam Group
  Indiv Parent.
  Staff: 140 (Full 49, Part 91).
  Est 1956. Private. Nonprofit.

  This center provides diagnostic rehabilitation services for individuals with most types
of disabilities. Other offerings include various therapies, vocational and prevocational
training, psychological services, and a preschool for the handicapped. A sliding fee scale
is available.

BLICK CLINIC

Res and Day — Coed Ages 18 and up
Clinic: All Ages. M-F 8:30-5; Eves by Appt.

Akron, OH 44303. 640 W Market St.
Tel: 330-762-5425. TTY: 330-762-2284. Fax: 330-762-4019.
www.blickclinic.com   E-mail: blickclinic@nls.net
Ted Brewer, Exec Dir. Gayleen Kolaczewski, MD, Med Dir.
  Focus: Treatment. Conditions: Primary—ADD ADHD Anx Ap Asp Au BD
  BI CD CP DS IP MD Mood MR MS Nf OCD ODD ON PDD Psy PTSD

PW S SB Sz TS. Sec—AN As B Bu C CF D Dx ED Ep LD SP TB. **IQ 20-120.**
Gen Acad. Pre-Voc. Ungraded. Courses: Read Math Lang_Arts.
Therapy: Chemo Hear Lang Occup Phys Speech. **Psychotherapy:** Fam Group Indiv Parent.
Enr: 94. **Staff:** 200 (Full 140, Part 60). Prof 50. Educ 2. Admin 26.
Rates 2003: Res $105-425/day.
Est 1969. Private. Nonprofit.

Blick provides year-round services that address the needs of individuals with acute physical, emotional, behavioral or developmental problems. Offerings are available to individuals from the age of infancy to late adulthood and can take place at the clinic, in the home or school, in sheltered workshops, or in day programs or residential homes.

BOWLING GREEN STATE UNIVERSITY SPEECH AND HEARING CLINIC

Clinic: All Ages. M-F 8-5.

Bowling Green, OH 43403. Dept of Communication Disorders, 200 Health Center Bldg.
Tel: 419-372-2515. Fax: 419-372-8089.
www.bgsu.edu/departments/cdis/cdis_content/clinics/clinic.html
   E-mail: donnaco@bgnet.bgsu.edu
Donna Colcord, MS, Dir.
   Focus: Treatment. **Conditions:** Primary—Ap D S. Sec—BI CP IP MS OH.
   Therapy: Hear Lang Speech.
   Staff: 19 (Full 14, Part 5).
   Est 1948. State. Nonprofit.

The clinic provides diagnostic and treatment services for persons with communicative disorders. Clients with language, articulation, fluency, voice, hearing and cognitive disorders receive treatment. Patients must be ambulatory. Services are available during the academic year and for 10 weeks over the summer.

BUCKEYE RANCH

Res — Coed Ages 10-18; Day — Coed 13-18 Clinic: Ages 6-18. M-F 8-5; Eves M-Th 5-8.

Grove City, OH 43123. 5665 Hoover Rd.
Tel: 614-875-2371. TTY: 614-875-6006. Fax: 614-871-6487.
www.swcs.k12.oh.us/buckeye_ranch_school.htm
Richard E. Rieser, CEO. **Michael Wang,** Prin. **Douglas Wallace,** MD, Med Dir.
June Green, Adm.
   Focus: Treatment. **Conditions:** Primary—ADD ADHD Anx BD D ED Mood OCD ODD PTSD Sz. Sec—Asp Au CD Dx LD SP. **IQ 70 and up.**
   Gen Acad. Pre-Voc. Ungraded. Courses: Read Math Lang_Arts Sci Soc_ Stud Studio_Art. Man_Arts & Shop. On-Job Trng.

Therapy: Art Chemo Music Play Recreational Speech. **Psychotherapy:** Fam Group Indiv.
Enr: 128. Res Males 52. Res Females 28. Day Males 24. Day Females 24.
Rates 2003: Res $250-450/day. Day $160/day. Clinic $93/hr.
Summer Prgm: Day. Rec. Ther. Day Rate $160. 10 wks.
Est 1961. Private. Nonprofit.

Buckeye Ranch provides a continuum of services that includes educational/ prevocational day treatment, partial hospitalization, and open-campus and intensive residential treatment. The prevocational program includes vocational assessment, job skills classes, on-the-job training and paid work experience.

The intensive care center provides an alternative to hospitalization for seriously disturbed boys and girls. It also houses a special treatment program for deaf individuals ages 12-21.

CAMP ALLYN

**Day — Coed Ages 18mos and up
Clinic: All Ages. M-F 9-3.**

Cincinnati, OH 45243. 5650 Given Rd.
Tel: 513-831-4660. Fax: 513-831-5918.
www.steppingstonescenter.org/camp-allyn.htm
 Conditions: Primary—Au Bl CP LD MR MS ON SB.
 Est 1962. Private.

CHILD GUIDANCE & FAMILY SOLUTIONS

Clinic: Ages Birth-18. M-F 8-5; Eves M-Th 5-8.

Akron, OH 44302. 312 Locust St.
 Nearby locations: Barberton; Twinsburg.
Tel: 330-762-0591. Fax: 330-258-0931.
www.cgfs.org   E-mail: cvehlow@cgfs.org
Charles Vehlow, Jr., MSW, Exec Dir. **Thingara Jayakumar,** MD, Med Dir.
Vickie Gordon, Adm.
 Focus: Treatment. **Conditions:** Primary—ADD ADHD Asp Au BD CD ED LD Mood OCD ODD Psy PTSD PW SP Sz TS. Sec—Bu MR.
 Therapy: Art Chemo Speech. **Psychotherapy:** Fam Group Indiv Parent.
 Staff: 165. Prof 64. Educ 8. Admin 27.
 Est 1939. Private. Nonprofit.

CGFS provides diagnosis and treatment of emotional and behavioral disturbances in children. Parental and individual counseling is available. Other Akron branches are located at 1225 Lawton St., 44320 and 681 Canton Rd., 44312; in addition, the center operates branches at 344 4th St. NW, Barberton 44203, and 2057 E. Aurora Rd., Twinsburg 44087.

CHILDHOOD LEAGUE CENTER

Day — Coed Ages Birth-6

Columbus, OH 43085. 670 S 18th St.
Tel: 614-253-6933. Fax: 614-253-6935.
www.childhoodleague.org   E-mail: vickyk@childhoodleague.org
Barbara Acton, MA, Exec Dir. **Vicki Kelly,** BS, OTR, Dir.
  Focus: Spec Ed. **Conditions:** Primary—ADD ADHD Asp Au Bl C CP DS
    MD Mood MR PW SB. Sec—As BD ED Ep OH. **IQ 50-100.**
  Gen Acad. Ungraded.
  Therapy: Art Lang Music Occup Phys Speech. **Psychotherapy:** Fam.
  Enr: 138. **Staff:** 33 (Full 17, Part 16).
  Rates 2003: No Fee.
  Rec. Ther. Day Rate $75. 4 wks.
  Est 1945. Private. Nonprofit.

The center provides intervention for children from birth to age 6 who have developmental delays through an integrated team-based approach, involving speech therapy, language development, physical therapy and occupational therapy. Counseling, home visits and parental education are available services. The usual duration of treatment is one to five years.

CHILDREN'S AID SOCIETY

Res and Day — Coed Ages 5-14

Cleveland, OH 44102. 10427 Detroit Ave.
Tel: 216-521-6511. Fax: 216-521-6006.
www.applewoodcenters.org
  Conditions: Primary—BD ED.
  Gen Acad. Courses: Read Math Lang_Arts.
  Therapy: Recreational. **Psychotherapy:** Fam Group Indiv.
  Staff: Prof 46.
  Est 1832. Private. Nonprofit.

THE CHILDREN'S HOME OF CINCINNATI

Day — Coed Ages 2-18

Cincinnati, OH 45227. 5050 Madison Rd.
Tel: 513-272-2800. Fax: 513-272-2807.
www.thechildrenshomecinti.org
  Conditions: Primary—BD ED.
  Gen Acad. Gr K-12. Courses: Read Math Lang_Arts.
  Therapy: Recreational. **Psychotherapy:** Fam Indiv.
  Staff: Prof 37.
  Est 1864. Private. Nonprofit.

CHILDREN'S HOSPITAL MEDICAL CENTER
PSYCHOLOGY DIVISION

Clinic: All Ages. M-F 8:30-5.

Cincinnati, OH 45229. 3333 Burnet Ave.
Tel: 513-636-4336. Fax: 513-636-7756.
www.cincinnatichildrens.org/svc/dept-div/psychology
Lori J. Stark, PhD, Dir.
  Focus: Treatment. **Conditions:** Primary—ADHD BD BI Dx ED Ep LD MR.
  Psychotherapy: Indiv.
  Staff: 25 (Full 22, Part 3).
  Private. Nonprofit.

The division offers assessment, diagnosis and treatment of children and adolescents with behavioral, emotional and developmental disorders. In many cases, both biological and psychological factors contribute to the patient's condition.

THE CHILDREN'S MEDICAL CENTER

Clinic: Ages 4-18. M-Th 8-6.

Dayton, OH 45404. 1 Children's Plz.
Tel: 937-641-3401. Fax: 937-641-3066.
www.childrensdayton.org   E-mail: huebnerj@childrensdayton.org
James M. Huebner, MEd, Prgm Coord. **Eileen Kasten,** MD, Med Dir. **Brenda Young,** Adm.
  Focus: Treatment. **Conditions:** Primary—ADD ADHD Dc Dg Dx ED LD. **IQ 50 and up.**
  Therapy: Chemo Hear Lang Occup Speech. **Psychotherapy:** Fam Indiv.
  Staff: 11.
  Rates 2003: Clinic $130/hr. State Aid.
  Est 1975. Private. Nonprofit.

This center provides diagnostic evaluation and treatment of speech, language, psychological and sociological problems. Vocational, educational, parental and personal counseling is provided, and attentional disorders are treated.

CHILDREN'S REHABILITATION CENTER

Day — Coed Ages Birth-18

Warren, OH 44484. 885 Howland-Wilson Rd NE.
Tel: 330-856-2107. Fax: 330-856-2107.
www.childrensrehab.org
Robert C. Foster, Exec Dir.
  Conditions: Primary—As BI C CP Dx IP LD MD MR MS ON S SB.
  Therapy: Hear Lang Occup Phys Speech. **Psychotherapy:** Group.
  Staff: Prof 13.
  Est 1957. Private. Nonprofit.

CINCINNATI ASSOCIATION FOR THE BLIND

Day — Coed All Ages

Cincinnati, OH 45202. 2045 Gilbert Ave.
Tel: 513-221-8558. Fax: 513-221-2995.
www.cincyblind.org   E-mail: info@cincyblind.org
Hank Baud, EdD, Exec Dir. **Gina Carroll,** Intake.
   Focus: Rehab. **Conditions:** Primary—B. Sec—Ap Asp Au Bl D Nf ON PDD
   S.
   Therapy: Music. **Psychotherapy:** Fam Group Parent.
   Staff: 37.
   Rates 2003: Sliding-Scale Rate $0-65/ses.
   Est 1911. Private. Nonprofit.

Blind and visually impaired persons in the Greater Cincinnati area are provided individual and family counseling; low-vision service; technology and daily living instruction; and orientation and mobility instruction. Talking book machine and home-based early childhood intervention services are also offered.

CINCINNATI CHILDREN'S HOSPITAL MEDICAL CENTER
DIVISION OF DEVELOPMENTAL DISORDERS

Day — Coed Ages Birth-7
Clinic: Ages Birth-21. M-F 8-5.

Cincinnati, OH 45229. 3333 Burnet Ave.
Tel: 513-636-4688. Fax: 513-636-7361.
www.cincinnatichildrens.org/affiliates/74
   E-mail: barbara.johnson@cchmc.org
Sonya Oppenheimer, MD, Dir.
   Focus: Treatment. **Conditions:** Primary—ADD ADHD Ap Au B Bl CP D DS
   Dx LD MR ON S SB. Sec—C ED Ep MD.
   Therapy: Chemo Hear Lang Occup Phys Speech. **Psychotherapy:** Fam
   Group Indiv Parent.
   Est 1957. Private. Nonprofit.

The center provides diagnosis, comprehensive evaluation, treatment, training and education for infants, children, and adolescents with developmental disorders. Children with mental retardation, neuromuscular disorders, birth defects, autism, attentional disorders and learning disabilities receive diagnostic evaluations, referrals and periodic reevaluations from an interdisciplinary team of professionals. Preschool and laboratory classes for school-age children with autistic-like behavior, mental retardation and severe behavioral disorders—as well as an early intervention program for high-risk infants and their families—are diagnostic and therapeutic in nature.

Among services available are home training, diagnostic therapy, dietary counseling, play interview and diagnosis, behavior modification, dental therapy, infant stimulation and parents' groups. Adolescent programs include gynecological supervision. The center conducts community workshops and provides parental counseling.

CINCINNATI CHILDREN'S HOSPITAL MEDICAL CENTER ORTHOPAEDIC SURGERY DIVISION
Clinic: Ages Birth-21. M-S 8:30-5.

Cincinnati, OH 45229. 3333 Burnet Ave, ML 2017.
Tel: 513-636-4785. Fax: 513-636-3928.
E-mail: sandy.singleton@cchmc.org
Alvin H. Crawford, MD, Dir.
    Focus: Treatment. **Conditions:** Primary—CP MD MS Nf ON SB.
    Staff: 25. Prof 7. Admin 15.
    Private. Nonprofit.

This hospital division diagnoses and treats the full spectrum of orthopedic diseases and conditions in children, including congenital and acquired spinal deformities, neuromuscular spinal disorders, and instability problems associated with dwarfism and dysplasia. Other areas of expertise include scoliosis, sports medicine, neurofibromatosis, cerebral palsy, myelomeningocele, juvenile arthritis and limb deficiency.

CINCINNATI OCCUPATIONAL THERAPY INSTITUTE
Clinic: All Ages. M-F 8-6.

Cincinnati, OH 45242. 4440 Carver Woods Dr.
Tel: 513-791-5688. Fax: 513-791-0023.
www.cintiotinstitute.com   E-mail: coti@cintiotinstitute.com
Elaine Mullin, OTR, Exec Dir.
    Focus: Treatment. **Conditions:** Primary—ADD ADHD Ap Asp Au Bl CP Dg
    Ep IP LD MR ON PDD S. Sec—Anx B CD D ED Mood OCD TS.
    Therapy: Occup.
    Staff: 36 (Full 16, Part 20). Prof 33. Admin 3.
    Rates 2003: Clinic $81/ses.
    Est 1981. Private. Inc.

This occupational therapy clinic specializes in the area of sensory integrative dysfunction. In addition to its regular program, COTI also provides consultations and workshops on incorporating sensory integrative principles into programs for children with learning, behavioral and motor deficits. The usual duration of treatment is six months to two years.

CLEVELAND CLINIC CHILDREN'S HOSPITAL FOR REHABILITATION
Res — Coed Ages Birth-18

Cleveland, OH 44104. 2801 Martin Luther King Jr Dr.
Tel: 216-721-5400. Fax: 216-721-4590.
www.clevelandclinic.org/childrensrehab
    Conditions: Primary—As Au Bl C CP Ep IP MD MS ON SB TB.
    Gen Acad. Courses: Read Math Lang_Arts.

Therapy: Art Hear Lang Music Occup Phys Recreational. **Psychotherapy:** Fam Indiv.
Est 1895. Private. Nonprofit.

CLEVELAND HEARING AND SPEECH CENTER

Clinic: All Ages.

Cleveland, OH 44106. 11206 Euclid Ave.
Tel: 216-231-8787. TTY: 216-231-8787. Fax: 216-231-7141.
www.chsc.org
Bernard P. Henri, PhD, Exec Dir.
    Conditions: Primary—D S. Sec—Ap Asp Au CP DS LD MS ON PDD.
    Courses: Read Lang_Arts.
    Therapy: Hear Lang Speech.
    Staff: Prof 25.
    Est 1921. Private. Nonprofit.

CLEVELAND SIGHT CENTER

Day — Coed Ages Birth-5
Clinic: All Ages. M-F 8:30-4:30.

Cleveland, OH 44106. 1909 E 101st St, PO Box 1988.
Tel: 216-791-8118. Fax: 216-791-1101.
www.clevelandsightcenter.org   E-mail: email@clevelandsightcenter.org
Michael E. Grady, Exec Dir.
    Focus: Treatment. **Conditions:** Primary—B.
    Gen Acad. Gr PS-K.
    Therapy: Hear Lang Music Occup Phys Speech. **Psychotherapy:** Fam Group Indiv.
    Staff: 10 (Full 4, Part 6).
    Summer Prgm: Res & Day. Rec. Ther.
    Est 1906. Private. Nonprofit. **Spons:** Cleveland Society for the Blind.

A parent-infant program for children from birth to age 3 provides speech and occupational therapy and family life education. A preschool program is available for children ages 3-5. Other services include educational and vocational counseling, financial/material assistance, a low-vision clinic, taped and braille books, a sports and camping program, and parent support groups.

CLEVELAND STATE UNIVERSITY
SPEECH AND HEARING CLINIC

Clinic: All Ages. M-F 8-5; Eves T Th 5-8.

Cleveland, OH 44115. 2121 Euclid Ave, Mail Code 429.

Tel: 216-687-3804. Fax: 216-687-6993.
Deanna Laurence, MA, Admin.
   Focus: Rehab. **Conditions:** Primary—Ap Asp Au PDD S. Sec—Bl CP D Dx
      ED IP LD MD MR MS PW.
   Therapy: Hear Lang Speech.
   Staff: 12 (Full 8, Part 4). Prof 8. Admin 1.
   Rates 2004: /hrSliding-Scale Rate $4-35/hr.
   Est 1965. State. Nonprofit.

Located in the Main Building of Cleveland State University, this clinic serves as an integral part of the university's program in Speech Pathology and Audiology and provides services for individuals in Greater Cleveland who have communicative disorders. Specialized hearing testing is available for infants and those unable to be tested by conventional methods.

COLUMBUS HEARING IMPAIRED PROGRAM

Day — Coed Ages Birth-21

Columbus, OH 43224. 1455 Huy Rd.
Tel: 614-365-5977. Fax: 614-365-5941.
www.columbus.k12.oh.us/agbell
John Crerand, Dir.
   Conditions: Primary—D.
   Col Prep. Gen Acad. Pre-Voc. Voc. Gr PS-12. Courses: Read Math Lang_
      Arts. Man_Arts & Shop. On-Job Trng.
   Therapy: Hear Lang Speech.
   Est 1918. Municipal. **Spons:** Alexander Graham Bell School.

CUYAHOGA COUNTY BOARD OF MENTAL RETARDATION AND DEVELOPMENTAL DISABILITIES

Res — Coed Ages 13 and up; Day — Coed All Ages

Cleveland, OH 44114. 1275 Lakeside Ave E.
Tel: 216-241-8230. Fax: 216-861-0253.
www.ccbmrdd.org
Terrence M. Ryan, PhD, Supt. **Janet Derby-Sheldon,** Intake.
   Focus: Spec Ed. **Conditions:** Primary—Asp Au Bl CP DS MR PDD PW SB
      TS. Sec—Ap B CD D ED Ep ON S.
   Pre-Voc. Gr K-12. Courses: Read Math Lang_Arts ADL. Shelt_Workshop.
      On-Job Trng.
   Therapy: Hear Lang Music Occup Phys Speech. **Psychotherapy:** Fam
      Indiv Parent.
   Staff: 1507.
   Rates 2003: No Fee.
   Est 1967. County. Nonprofit.

This agency oversees an educational and vocational training program, supplemented with counseling and therapy, for infants, children and adults with mental retardation and other developmental disabilities. The residential program consists of 56 group homes in 39 communities.

ELEANOR GERSON SCHOOL

Day — Coed Ages 13-21

Cleveland, OH 44114. 2201 Superior Ave E.
Tel: 216-861-6015. Fax: 216-696-6986.
www.applewoodcenters.org E-mail: jdunne@applewoodcenters.org
Jim Dunne, MEd, MSSA, Dir.
  Focus: Spec Ed. **Conditions:** Primary—Anx ED Mood SP. Sec—AN Psy Sz TS.
  Gen Acad. Gr 9-12. Courses: Read Math Lang_Arts Soc_Stud Sci Studio_ Art Health.
  Enr: 50. Day Males 25. Day Females 25. **Staff:** 9. Educ 7. Admin 2.
  Rates 2003: Day $18,000/sch yr. State Aid.
  Est 1984. Private. Nonprofit. **Spons:** Applewood Centers.

Gerson School offers an alternative high school experience for adolescents of average intelligence who, for various personal, behavioral or relationship reasons, have not had success in standard educational settings. The school emphasizes education within a personal and therapeutic milieu to bring about positive growth that accounts for individual needs and abilities.

The school's downtown location gives students access to other education and cultural experiences, among them theater, ballet and other artistic performances.

FAIRFIELD CENTER FOR DISABILITIES AND CEREBRAL PALSY

Day — Coed Ages 18 and up

Lancaster, OH 43130. 681 E 6th Ave.
Tel: 740-653-5501. Fax: 740-653-6046.
Edwin Payne, Exec Dir.
  Focus: Trng. Treatment. **Conditions:** Primary—CP OH.
  Gen Acad. Ungraded.
  Therapy: Hear Lang Occup Phys Speech.
  Private.

FAIRHAVEN

Day — Coed All Ages

Niles, OH 44446. 45 North Rd.
Tel: 330-652-9800. Fax: 330-652-1345.

www.fairhavenpgm.com
Douglas A. Burkhardt, PhD, Supt.
> **Focus:** Spec Ed. Trng. Treatment. **Conditions:** Primary—MR.
> Courses: Read Math Lang_Arts. Man_Arts & Shop. Shelt_Workshop. On-Job Trng.
> **Therapy:** Hear Lang Occup Phys Speech. **Psychotherapy:** Indiv.
> **Staff:** Prof 30.
> **Est 1952.** County. **Spons:** Trumbull County Board of Mental Retardation and Developmental Disabilities.

FILLING MEMORIAL HOME OF MERCY

Res — Coed All Ages

Napoleon, OH 43545. N-160 State Hwy 108.
Tel: 419-592-6451. Fax: 419-599-5178.
www.lutheranhomessociety.org/4-agency.htm
> **Conditions:** Primary—MR.
> **Pre-Voc.** Ungraded. Courses: Read Math Lang_Arts. Shelt_Workshop.
> **Therapy:** Hear Lang Occup Phys Speech. **Psychotherapy:** Indiv.
> **Staff:** Prof 154.
> **Est 1958.** Private. Inc.

GRANT/RIVERSIDE PHYSICAL REHAB CENTERS

Clinic: All Ages. M-F 7:30-6.

Columbus, OH 43220. 4666 Larwell Dr.
Tel: 614-451-2318. Fax: 614-451-1096.
www.grmh.org
> **Focus:** Treatment. **Conditions:** Primary—LD S. Sec—Ap Au.
> **Therapy:** Occup Phys Speech. **Psychotherapy:** Fam Parent.
> **Staff:** 4.
> Private. United Methodist.

Outpatient speech pathology through Grant/Riverside provides individual speech-language therapy. Offerings include programs addressing language, speech and fluency problems. Family education is also available.

Satellite centers operate at 223 E. Town St., 43215; 100 W. 3rd Ave., Ste. 150, 43201; and 10401 Sawmill Pky., Ste. B, Powell 43065.

HALLENBECK PSYCHO-EDUCATIONAL CENTER

Clinic: All Ages. M-Th 1-5, S 9-3; Eves M-Th 5-7.

Willoughby, OH 44094. 4805 Wood St.
Tel: 440-942-3829. Fax: 440-942-3839.

E-mail: p_hallenbeck@hotmail.com
Phyllis N. Hallenbeck, PhD, Dir.
    Focus: Trng. Treatment. **Conditions:** Primary—ADD ADHD BD Dx ED LD.
    Sec—CD MR OCD. **IQ 75 and up.**
    Psychotherapy: Indiv Parent.
    Staff: 2 (Full 1, Part 1). Prof 1. Admin 1.
    Rates 2001: Sliding-Scale Rate $75-90/hour.
    Est 1971. Private. Inc.

Treatment at the center includes comprehensive diagnostic evaluations (personality, intelligence and educational achievement tests); individual marriage and family counseling; individual psychotherapy; academic tutoring; remediation of specific learning disabilities; and biofeedback training.

HANNAH NEIL CENTER FOR CHILDREN

Res — Males Ages 8-12

Columbus, OH 43207. 301 Obetz Rd.
Tel: 614-491-5784. Fax: 614-491-2615.
www.starr.org   E-mail: nocellas@starr.org
    Conditions: Primary—BD ED.
    Gen Acad. Courses: Read Math Lang_Arts.
    Est 1858. Private. Nonprofit. **Spons:** Starr Commonwealth.

THE HATTIE LARLHAM FOUNDATION

Res — Coed Ages Birth-26

Mantua, OH 44255. 9772 Diagonal Rd.
Tel: 330-274-2272. Fax: 330-274-3877.
www.larlham.org
Dennis Allen, Exec Dir. **Stacia Smith,** Intake.
    Focus: Treatment. **Conditions:** Primary—BI CP IP MD MR OH. Sec—Ap
    As B C D Ep MS S SB TB. **IQ 0-70.**
    Gen Acad. Ungraded.
    Therapy: Hear Hydro Lang Occup Phys Recreational Speech. **Psycho-
    therapy:** Fam Parent.
    Enr: 485. **Staff:** 298 (Full 235, Part 63).
    Rates 2004: No Fee.
    Est 1961. Private. Nonprofit.

The foundation provides care for severely retarded, multiply handicapped, nonambulatory individuals and their families. Service settings include a residential facility for children and young adults, adult group and supported living homes, foster homes, an integrated daycare, and the homes of the individual's family or caregiver. The foundation also supports individuals and their families through care management, service coordination, and a free toy and technology lending library.

HEARING, SPEECH & DEAF CENTER
OF GREATER CINCINNATI

Clinic: All Ages. M-F 8:30-5; Eves by Appt.

Cincinnati, OH 45219. 2825 Burnet Ave.
Nearby locations: West Chester.
Tel: 513-221-0527. TTY: 513-221-3300. Fax: 513-221-1703.
www.hearingspeechdeaf.com
Eleanor M. Stromberg, PhD, Exec Dir.
  Focus: Treatment. **Conditions:** Primary—D. Sec—ADD ADHD Ap Apr Asp
    Au BI CP DS Dx MR MS OH.
  Therapy: Hear Lang Speech.
  Staff: 37 (Full 28, Part 9). Prof 23. Admin 8.
  Est 1925. Private.

The center conducts speech, hearing and language evaluations and therapy, while also providing advocacy for deaf individuals. Preschool programs for language-delayed and hearing-impaired children are offered. All fees are determined along a sliding scale.

Branches operate at 4440 Glen Este Withamsville Rd., Ste. 475, 45245, and at 5900 W. Chester Rd., Ste. J, West Chester 45069.

HELP FOUNDATION

Res — Coed Ages 9-22; Day — Coed 3-12

Cleveland, OH 44115. 3622 Prospect Ave E.
Tel: 216-432-4810. Fax: 216-361-2608.
www.helpfoundationinc.org
Daniel J. Rice, MSW, Exec Dir. **Patricia Schwartz,** Adm.
  Focus: Trng. **Conditions:** Primary—Asp Au DS MR PDD. Sec—ADD
    ADHD Anx Ap Apr As B BD BI CD CP D Dx ED Ep LD Mood OCD ON
    Psy PTSD S SB Sz TS. **IQ 15-70.**
  Therapy: Lang Music Speech. **Psychotherapy:** Indiv.
  Enr: 12. Res Males 9. Res Females 3.
  Rates 2003:
  Summer Prgm: Day. Educ. Rec. Res Rate $3200. 8 wks.
  Est 1965. Private. Nonprofit.

A small, residential self-help training program, HELP serves children and adolescents with mental retardation. An intensive program of developing self-help skills and appropriate social behavior is conducted within a homelike atmosphere. Located close to Case Western Reserve and University hospitals, HELP draws on their professionals for extra assistance. Music and speech therapies supplement special education classes.

Through parental involvement, HELP aids the family's adjustment to the child's return home. An eight-week summer session that provides self-help training will accept enrollment for that program only. Outpatient services are available, and the usual length of treatment is four years. Fees are based on a sliding scale.

JULIE BILLIART SCHOOL

Day — Coed Ages 6-14

Lyndhurst, OH 44124. 4982 Clubside Rd.
Tel: 216-381-1191. Fax: 216-381-2216.
www.juliebilliartschool.org   E-mail: info@juliebilliartschool.org
Sr. Agnesmarie, MEd, Prin.

Focus: Spec Ed. **Conditions:** Primary—ADD ADHD Asp Dc Dg Dx LD. Sec—CP. **IQ 80-130.**
Gen Acad. Gr 1-8. Courses: Read Math Lang_Arts Sci Computers Soc_ Stud Relig Music.
Therapy: Art Speech.
Enr: 110. Day Males 70. Day Females 40. **Staff:** 23 (Full 19, Part 4).
Rates 2003: Day $6900/sch yr. Schol 18 ($50,000).
Est 1954. Private. Nonprofit. Roman Catholic.

The school's program is designed for the child with learning disabilities, for those who learn more slowly and for those who have problems in a regular classroom setting. A full scholastic program is provided to meet the needs of each individual. Children with mild cerebral palsy may be accepted, but blind, aphasic and severely disabled children are not accepted.

KENT STATE UNIVERSITY
SPEECH AND HEARING CLINIC

Clinic: Ages Birth-18. M-F 9-5.

Kent, OH 44242. PO Box 5190.
Tel: 330-672-2672. Fax: 330-672-2643.
Carol Sommer, MA, Dir.

Focus: Treatment. **Conditions:** Primary—Ap Apr Asp Au D S. Sec—BI CP LD.
Therapy: Hear Lang Speech.
Staff: 6 (Full 3, Part 3). Prof 6.
Rates 2003: Clinic $60/hr.
Est 1945. State.

The clinic provides diagnostic and therapeutic services for children and adults who present impairments in articulation, language, voice, fluency and hearing. Staff dispense hearing aids and evaluate children with multiple handicaps pertaining to speech, language or hearing.

LAWRENCE SCHOOL

Day — Coed Ages 6-17

Broadview Heights, OH 44147. 1551 E Wallings Rd.
Tel: 440-526-0003. Fax: 440-526-0595.
www.lawrenceschool.org   E-mail: tbeam@lawrenceschool.org

Conditions: Primary—ADHD Dx LD.
Gen Acad. Gr 1-11. Courses: Read Math Lang_Arts.
Est 1982. Private. Nonprofit.

LIMA MEMORIAL HOSPITAL SPEECH AND HEARING CENTER
Clinic: All Ages. M-F 8-4:30.

Lima, OH 45804. 1001 Bellefontaine Ave.
Tel: 419-226-5070. Fax: 419-998-4548.
www.limamemorial.org
Vanessa L. Lee, MA, CCC-SLP, Mgr.
  Conditions: Primary—D S.
  Therapy: Lang Speech.
  Est 1961. Private. Inc.

LOGAN COUNTY BOARD OF MENTAL RETARDATION AND DEVELOPMENTAL DISABILITIES
Day — Coed All Ages

Bellefontaine, OH 43311. 1851 State Rte 47 W, PO Box 710.
Tel: 937-592-0015. Fax: 937-592-5615.
www.co.logan.oh.us/mrdd   E-mail: dcsmrdd@odmrdd.state.oh.us
Joseph F. Mancuso, Supt.
  Focus: Spec Ed. Trng. **Conditions:** Primary—MR. Sec—Ap As B BD BI C
    CP D Dx ED Ep IP LD MD MS ON S SB TB. **IQ 20-97.**
  Pre-Voc. Voc. Ungraded. Courses: Read Math Lang_Arts. Shelt_Workshop.
    On-Job Trng.
  Therapy: Hear Lang Occup Phys Speech.
  Staff: 80.
  Est 1967. County.

A comprehensive program is offered at this center for infants, children and adults with moderate, severe and profound developmental disabilities. Remedial instruction in all academic areas is provided for children, while adults participate in a sheltered workshop that leads to job placement. In addition, Ludlow conducts an early intervention program, a preschool and home-based services. Counseling is also available. Logan County residents only may receive services.

MARBURN ACADEMY
Day — Coed Ages 6-18

Columbus, OH 43229. 1860 Walden Dr.
Tel: 614-433-0822. Fax: 614-433-0812.

www.marburnacademy.org
E-mail: marburnadmission@marburnacademy.org
Earl B. Oremus, MEd, Head. **Scott B. Burton,** Adm.
Focus: Spec Ed. **Conditions:** Primary—ADD ADHD Dc Dg Dx LD. **IQ 90 and up.**
Col Prep. Gen Acad. Pre-Voc. Voc. Gr 1-12. Courses: Read Math Lang_ Arts Sci Soc_Stud Studio_Art Music Drama Life_Skills.
Therapy: Hear Lang Speech.
Enr: 100. Day Males 75. Day Females 25. **Staff:** 29 (Full 28, Part 1).
Rates 2003: Day $15,500/sch yr. Schol 70 ($350,000).
Summer Prgm: Day. Educ. Res Rate $$500-1500. 4 wks.
Est 1981. Private. Nonprofit.

Marburn assists students in strengthening their academic skills and developing strategies for coping with their specific disabilities. Boys and girls with learning disabilities and those who may be prohibited from receiving LD services in the public school system are accepted. Services include vocational, educational, parental, personal and career counseling.

MARIMOR SCHOOL

Day — Coed Ages 6-22

Lima, OH 45801. 2550 Ada Rd.
Tel: 419-221-1262. Fax: 419-225-5184.
www.school.acbmrdd.org
Esther M. Baldridge, Supt. **Peggy Cockerell,** Educ Dir.
Focus: Spec Ed. Trng. **Conditions:** Primary—MR. Sec—BI CP ED ON SB. **IQ 0-55.**
Gen Acad. Ungraded. Courses: Read Math Lang_Arts Studio_Art Music Life_Skills. Shelt_Workshop. On-Job Trng.
Therapy: Hear Lang Occup Phys Speech.
Enr: 174. **Staff:** 90.
Rates 2004: No Fee.
Est 1951. County. Nonprofit. **Spons:** Allen County Board of Mental Retardation/Developmental Disabilities.

Marimor offers a realistic training approach and a sheltered workshop for multi-handicapped retarded and developmentally disabled children and young adults. The program includes speech and language development, physical development, vocational skills training, therapeutic and respite services. Clients must reside in Allen County.

MARY IMMACULATE SCHOOL

Day — Coed Ages 6-14

Toledo, OH 43623. 3837 Secor Rd.
Tel: 419-474-1688. Fax: 419-479-3062.
www.maryimmaculatetoledo.org   E-mail: maryim_miller@nwoca.org
Sr. Mary Alan Miller, SND, BA, MEd, Prin.

Focus: Spec Ed. **Conditions:** Primary—ADD ADHD Asp Dc Dg Dx LD. Sec—As Au ED Ep OCD ODD SP TS. **IQ 85 and up.**
Gen Acad. Ungraded. Courses: Read Math Lang_Arts Sci Soc_Stud Computers Relig Studio_Art Music.
Therapy: Art Movement Music Phys. **Psychotherapy:** Indiv.
Enr: 72. Day Males 42. Day Females 30. **Staff:** 22 (Full 10, Part 12).
Rates 2003: Day $3000/sch yr (+$150). Schol 16 ($16,000).
Est 1960. Private. Nonprofit. Roman Catholic. **Spons:** Sisters of Notre Dame.

Conducted by the Sisters of Notre Dame, Mary Immaculate provides general academic instruction for pupils with learning disabilities and other learning differences, among them ADD and ADHD. Pupils must undergo a psychological evaluation prior to admittance.

MARY MAVEC EUCLID OPPORTUNITY SCHOOL
Day — Coed Ages 5 and up

Euclid, OH 44123. 22101 Lake Shore Blvd.
Tel: 216-731-4666.
Focus: Spec Ed. Trng. **Conditions:** Primary—MR. **IQ 0-50.**
Courses: Read Math Lang_Arts. Shelt_Workshop. On-Job Trng.
Therapy: Hear Occup Phys Speech. **Psychotherapy:** Fam.
Est 1951. Private. Nonprofit.

METROHEALTH MEDICAL CENTER
Clinic: Ages Birth-18. M-F 8-5.

Cleveland, OH 44109. 2500 MetroHealth Dr.
Tel: 216-778-5198. Fax: 216-778-8840.
www.metrohealth.org
Conditions: Primary—BI CP IP ON SB.
Therapy: Hear Lang Occup Phys Speech. **Psychotherapy:** Group Indiv.
Est 1961. County.

MIAMI UNIVERSITY
SPEECH AND HEARING CLINIC
Clinic: All Ages.

Oxford, OH 45056. 2 Bachelor Hall.
Tel: 513-529-2500.
http://casnov1.cas.muohio.edu/spa/Clinic.htm **E-mail: spa@muohio.edu**
Melissa Price, Coord.
Conditions: Primary—D S.

Therapy: Hear Lang Speech.
Est 1952. State. Nonprofit.

MIDDLEBURG EARLY EDUCATION CENTER

Day — Coed Ages 1½-6

Middleburg Heights, OH 44130. 7171 Pearl Rd.
Tel: 440-888-9922. Fax: 440-843-6664.
Marilyn Edwards, BSEd, Dir.
  Focus: Spec Ed. **Conditions:** Primary—ADD ADHD Ap Asp Au BI DS LD
    MR ON PDD S. Sec—As BD CD D Dx ED Ep OCD SB Sz.
  Gen Acad. Gr PS.
  Therapy: Lang Movement Music Occup Speech. **Psychotherapy:** Parent.
  Enr: 101. Day Males 57. Day Females 44. **Staff:** 17 (Full 1, Part 16).
  Rates 2003: Sliding-Scale Rate $68-396/mo.
  Summer Prgm: Day. Educ. Ther. Day Rate $325-470. 7 wks.
  Est 1972. Private. Nonprofit.

This center provides early intervention and therapy for children who are experiencing developmental delays and disabilities. Middleburg also offers field experience and training for students from Cleveland State University and Baldwin-Wallace College.

MOUNT ALOYSIUS

Res — Males Ages 18 and up

New Lexington, OH 43764. 5375 Tile Plant Rd SE, PO Box 598.
Tel: 740-342-3343. Fax: 740-342-4805.
Jean Ann Arbaugh, Dir.
  Focus: Trng. **Conditions:** Primary—MR. **IQ 30-50.**
  Gen Acad. Gr K-6. Courses: Read Math Lang_Arts. Man_Arts & Shop. On-
    Job Trng.
  Therapy: Hear Occup Phys Speech. **Psychotherapy:** Fam Group Indiv.
  Est 1969. Private. Nonprofit.

MOUNT VERNON DEVELOPMENTAL CENTER

Res — Coed Ages 14-22

Mount Vernon, OH 43050. 1250 Vernonview Dr, PO Box 762.
Tel: 740-393-6200. Fax: 740-393-2904.
www.odmrdd.state.oh.us
Timothy J. Elder, Supt.
  Focus: Treatment. **Conditions:** Primary—BI MR ON S.
  Pre-Voc. Ungraded. Courses: Read Math Lang_Arts. Shelt_Workshop.
  Therapy: Hear Lang Occup Phys Speech. **Psychotherapy:** Indiv.

Staff: Prof 72.
Est 1965. State.

NICHOLAS SCHOOL

Day — Coed Ages 5-14

Piqua, OH 45356. 710 S Main St.
Tel: 937-773-6979. Fax: 937-778-2561.
E-mail: nicholasschool@woh.rr.com
Amy Simindinger, Prin.
   Focus: Spec Ed. **Conditions:** Primary—ADD ADHD Asp Au BI CP Dc Dg
      DS Dx MR.
   Gen Acad. Gr K-8. Courses: Read Math Lang_Arts Sci Health.
   Therapy: Percepual-Motor.
   Enr: 16. **Staff:** 8 (Full 7, Part 1).
   Rates 2003: Day $3700/sch yr (+$425). Schol avail.
   Summer Prgm: Day. Day Rate $425. 3 wks.
   Est 1976. Private. Nonprofit.

The school provides a comprehensive educational program of academic and percep-tual-motor skills for children with learning disabilities, developmental disabilities or attentional disorders, as well as for those nondiagnosed children who have not succeeded in traditional settings.

NORTH COAST TUTORING SERVICES

Day — Coed Ages 5-18
Clinic: Ages 5-18. M-Su 8-5; Eves M-Su 5-10.

Chagrin Falls, OH 44022. 120 N Main St.
Tel: 440-247-1622. Fax: 440-247-9049.
www.northcoasted.com   E-mail: caroler@northcoasted.com
Carole Richards, BS, Exec Dir.
   Focus: Spec Ed. **Conditions:** Primary—ADD ADHD Asp BD Dc Dg Dx LD
      PDD S. Sec—Anx Ap Apr Au BI CD CP ED Mood MR OCD SP TS. **IQ 70**
      and up.
   Col Prep. Gen Acad. Pre-Voc. Voc. Gr K-Col. Courses: Read Math Lang_
      Arts. On-Job Trng.
   Staff: 180 (Full 4, Part 176).
   Rates 2003: Clinic $36-40/hr. State Aid.
   Est 1985. Private. Inc.

NCTS provides educational services, employing the RICHARDS READ Systematic Language program, for students with learning disabilities and mild emotional distur-bances. The program addresses systematic phonics, writing, reading comprehension and study skills. One-on-one in-home tutoring is also available in all subjects and at all grade and age levels.

A six-week summer day camp serves children with learning differences ages 6-14.

OESTERLEN SERVICES FOR YOUTH

Res — Coed Ages 12-18
Clinic: Ages 5-20.

Springfield, OH 45503. 1918 Mechanicsburg Rd.
Tel: 937-399-6101. Fax: 937-399-6609.
www.oesterlen.org   E-mail: osfyi@oesterlen.org
Donald L. Warner, LISW, Exec Dir.
   Conditions: Primary—BD ED. Sec—ADHD AN Bu CD Mood OCD ODD
   PTSD Sz.
   Gen Acad. Pre-Voc. Ungraded. Courses: Read Math Lang_Arts. On-Job
   Trng.
   Therapy: Music. **Psychotherapy:** Fam Group Indiv.
   Est 1903. Private. Nonprofit.

OHIO SCHOOL FOR THE DEAF

Res and Day — Coed Ages 5-22

Columbus, OH 43214. 500 Morse Rd.
Tel: 614-728-4030. TTY: 614-728-4033. Fax: 614-995-3447.
www.ohioschoolforthedeaf.org
Edward E. Corbett, Jr., PhD, Supt. **Dawn Henslee,** RN, Med Dir. **Barb Stahl,**
Adm.
   Focus: Spec Ed. **Conditions:** Primary—D.
   Col Prep. Gen Acad. Voc. Gr K-12. Courses: Read Math Lang_Arts. Man_
   Arts & Shop. On-Job Trng.
   Therapy: Hear Lang Occup Speech.
   Enr: 141. **Staff:** 48.
   Rates 2003: No Fee.
   Est 1829. State.

OSD provides educational, vocational and residential services for hearing-impaired students. In addition to basic academic course work, the curriculum includes speech, lip reading, auditory training, and art and physical education. Students may participate in work-study and extracurricular activities.

Career education begins at the third-grade level in preparation for vocational training. The vocational block program offers three years of training in such areas as masonry, printing, business and auto maintenance, along with general academics. Seniors receive on-the-job cooperative experience.

Each hearing-impaired child referred to the school by a local educational agency receives a multifactorial evaluation.

OHIO STATE SCHOOL FOR THE BLIND

Res — Coed Ages 8-21; Day — Coed 5-21
Clinic: Ages 3-18. W 8-4.

Columbus, OH 43214. 5220 N High St.
Tel: 614-752-1152. Fax: 614-752-1713.
http://tlcf.osn.state.oh.us/ohiostate   E-mail: lmazzoli@ossb.oh.gov
Louis A. Mazzoli, EdD, Supt. Jerry Marcom, MA, Prin.
   Focus: Spec Ed. Conditions: Primary—B. Sec—ADD ADHD Anx As BI CP
   D Dx MR OH. IQ 40 and up.
   Col Prep. Gen Acad. Pre-Voc. Voc. Gr K-12. Courses: Read Math Lang_
   Arts Sci. Man_Arts & Shop. Shelt_Workshop. On-Job Trng.
   Therapy: Hear Music Occup Recreational Speech. Psychotherapy: Group
   Indiv.
   Enr: 130. Staff: 137 (Full 127, Part 10). Prof 42. Educ 38. Admin 7.
   Rates 2003: No Fee.
   Est 1837. State. Nonprofit.

Blind children who are residents of Ohio follow a full educational program at this
state school. Educational and personal counseling are available. The school also educates and treats youth with certain learning disabilities and those who suffer from
orthopedic/neurological disabilities. In addition, the school conducts vocational programs, psychotherapy, and occupational, speech and recreational therapy. The usual
duration of treatment is nine months.

OHIO UNIVERSITY
SPEECH AND HEARING CLINIC

Clinic: All Ages. M-F 9-5.

Athens, OH 45701. Grover Center, W181.
Tel: 740-593-1407. Fax: 740-593-0287.
www.ohiou.edu/hearingspeech/clinicfacilities.htm
Davida Parsons, Dir.
   Conditions: Primary—BI D S.
   Therapy: Hear Lang Speech.
   State.

THE OLYMPUS CENTER

Clinic: Ages 5 and up. M-F 8:30-4:30.

Cincinnati, OH 45206. 2230 Park Ave.
Tel: 513-559-0404. Fax: 513-559-0008.
www.olympuscenter.org   E-mail: olympus@fuse.net
Sandy Sanborn Martin, EdD, Dir.
   Focus: Treatment. Conditions: Primary—ADD ADHD Dx LD.
   Therapy: Lang.

Staff: 7 (Full 3, Part 4).
Est 1976. Private. Nonprofit.

Olympus offers diagnostic and consultative services for children, adolescents and adults with learning disabilities. Treatment usually lasts approximately four to six weeks.

OSU MEDICAL CENTER
OSU HARDING HOSPITAL
CHILD AND ADOLESCENT SERVICES

Res — Coed Ages 3-18; Day — Coed 12-18
Clinic: All Ages. M-F 8-5.

Columbus, OH 43210. 1670 Upham Dr.
Tel: 614-293-9600. Fax: 614-293-4763.
www.medicalcenter.osu.edu   E-mail: saveanu.1@osu.edu
Radu Saveanu, MD, COO. **Alan Freeland,** MD, Med Dir.
  Focus: Treatment. **Conditions:** Primary—Anx ED Mood OCD Psy PTSD
    Sz. Sec—ADD ADHD AN As Asp Au B BD BI C CD CP D Db Dx Ep HIV
    IP LD MD MR MS ODD ON PW S SB SP TB TS. **IQ 65 and up.**
  Gen Acad. Ungraded. Courses: Read Math.
  Therapy: Art Milieu Music Occup. **Psychotherapy:** Fam Group Indiv
    Parent.
  Enr: 20. **Staff:** 40 (Full 32, Part 8). Prof 30. Admin 1.
  Est 1916. State. Nonprofit. **Spons:** Ohio State University.

The facility provides inpatient, outpatient and partial hospital treatment for children and adolescents. The Adolescent Integrated Program, serving those ages 12-18, consists of acute inpatient care, partial hospital, and outpatient care. Short-term acute treatment for children ages 4-18 is also available.

REHABILITATION SERVICE OF NORTH CENTRAL OHIO

Day — Coed Ages Birth-6
Clinic: All Ages. M-F by Appt.

Mansfield, OH 44907. 270 Sterkel Blvd.
Tel: 419-756-1133. TTY: 419-756-1133. Fax: 419-756-6544.
www.therehabcenter.org   E-mail: info@therehabcenter.org
James Schaum, Pres.
  Focus: Rehab. **Conditions:** Primary—OH. Sec—Ap Au B BD BI C CP D
    ED Ep IP LD MD MR MS S SB.
  Gen Acad. Pre-Voc. Voc. Ungraded. Courses: Read Lang_Arts. Man_Arts &
    Shop. Shelt_Workshop. On-Job Trng.
  Therapy: Hear Lang Occup Phys Speech. **Psychotherapy:** Fam Group
    Indiv Parent.
  Est 1954. Private. Nonprofit.

The early intervention infant program offers a trans-disciplinary approach to the evaluation and the management of children from birth to age 3 who have learning or developmental disabilities or who are at risk. Kindergarten and nursery services for children ages 3-5 provide educational stimulation, social experiences and therapy appropriate to the physical or language disability. Both these programs aim to increase each child's physical, cognitive, social, emotional and communicational skills. Parental involvement is stressed.

Special medical clinics are offered in the following areas: orthopedic, amputee, neurology, birth defects, pediatric-otologic-diagnostic, and scoliosis. A broad scope of physical and occupational therapies is utilized. Support services consist of psychological, social and parental counseling as well as recreational activities. In addition, vocational evaluation, work adjustment, supported employment, job-seeking skills and projects within industries are offered.

ST. RITA SCHOOL FOR THE DEAF
Res and Day — Coed Ages 6mos-21

Cincinnati, OH 45215. 1720 Glendale-Milford Rd.
Tel: 513-771-7600. TTY: 513-771-7600. Fax: 513-326-8264.
www.srsdeaf.org   E-mail: gernst@srsdeaf.org
Gregory Ernst, Sr., MEd, Exec Dir. **Mary Ann Stansfield**, Adm.
  Focus: Spec Ed. **Conditions:** Primary—D. Sec—Ap Apr S.
  Col Prep. Gen Acad. Pre-Voc. Voc. Gr PS-12. Courses: Read Math Lang_
    Arts Computers Sci Soc_Stud Studio_Art Relig.
  Therapy: Hear Occup Phys Speech.
  Enr: 130. Res Males 9. Res Females 8. Day Males 67. Day Females 46.
    Staff: 84 (Full 78, Part 6).
  Rates 2003: Res $23,388/sch yr. Day $13,388/sch yr. Schol avail. State Aid.
  Est 1915. Private. Nonprofit. Roman Catholic.

A residential private school for deaf and hard-of-hearing children, St. Rita School uses total communication—a combination of the oral method of lip reading and the manual method of communicating through signed gestures and finger spelling—in educating the children.

Out-of-state and physically and educationally handicapped deaf children may enroll. SRSD administers entrance and placement tests measuring basic skills in reading, language and math to all applicants.

ST. RITA'S MEDICAL CENTER
PEDIATRIC AND ADOLESCENT REHABILITATION CENTER
Clinic: Ages Birth-18. M-F 8-5:30.

Lima, OH 45801. 730 W Market St.
Tel: 419-226-9338. Fax: 419-226-9705.
www.stritas.org
Kelley Recker, CCC-SLP, Admin Dir. **Susan Hubbell**, MD, Med Dir.
  Focus: Rehab. **Conditions:** Primary—ADD ADHD Apr Asp Au BI CF CP

181

Dx IP MD ON SB. Sec—Ap MS.
Therapy: Hear Lang Occup Percepual-Motor Phys Speech.
Staff: 14. Prof 9. Admin 5.
Est 1918. Private. Nonprofit. Roman Catholic. **Spons:** Catholic Health Partners.

The center provides an array of services for children with impairments, disabilities and handicaps. Programming includes therapeutic evaluations, feeding evaluations and treatment, sensory integration, praxis tests, infant massage instruction, consultation services for individuals requiring wheelchairs or other adaptive equipment, fabrication of splints for upper and lower extremities, and karate and dance movement classes. Family members take an active role in the child's treatment plan.

ST. VINCENT FAMILY CENTERS

Res — Coed Ages 6-12; Day — Coed 3-12
Clinic: Ages Birth-18. M-F by Appt.

Columbus, OH 43205. 1490 E Main St.
Tel: 614-252-0731. TTY: 614-252-2069. Fax: 614-252-8468.
www.svfc.org
Michelle Ward, LSW, Pres. **Jon Fouts,** ACSW, LISW, Clin Dir. **Rosemary Standish,** LISW, Prgm Dir. **James Christopher,** MD, Med Dir.
Focus: Spec Ed. Treatment. **Conditions:** Primary—BD CD ED. Sec—ADD ADHD CP D Dx LD MD MR OCD Psy S Sz. **IQ 60 and up.**
Gen Acad. Ungraded. Courses: Read Math Lang_Arts.
Therapy: Chemo Hear Lang Movement Music Occup Percepual-Motor Phys Play Recreational Speech. **Psychotherapy:** Fam Group Indiv Parent.
Enr: 97. Res Males 14. Res Females 3. Day Males 65. Day Females 15.
Staff: 140 (Full 135, Part 5). Prof 45. Educ 12. Admin 25.
Summer Prgm: Res & Day. Rec. Ther. 2-8 wks.
Est 1875. Private. Nonprofit. Roman Catholic.

Children with severe emotional disturbances and behavioral disorders, some of whom have hearing impairments, receive treatment at St. Vincent. Staff members design an educational program to assist children in developing appropriate classroom behavior and to continue the child's academic growth, especially when remedial intervention is necessary.

The Clinical Services Department consists of the following: intake services; treatment teams for both extended-day and residential treatment programs; psychological testing services; weekend respite services; preschool and school-age partial hospitalization services; juvenile sex offender services; medication management clinic; research; and program coordination. Adaptive behavior specialists meet with children to promote activities and to provide opportunities for peer relationship development. The overall environment of St. Vincent's is neither permissive nor punitive, but it is highly structured. Prospective clients must be from Ohio and must be medically stable. The usual duration of treatment is six to 12 months.

SOCIETY FOR REHABILITATION

Clinic: All Ages. M-F 8:30-4:30.

Mentor, OH 44060. 9521 Lake Shore Blvd.
Tel: 440-352-8993. Fax: 440-352-6632.
www.societyhelps.org E-mail: info@societyhelps.org
 Conditions: Primary—Ap BI C CP D Dx IP MD MS ON S SB.
 Therapy: Hear Lang Occup Phys Speech. **Psychotherapy:** Fam Group
  Indiv.
 Staff: Prof 19.
 Est 1940. Private. Nonprofit.

SPRINGER SCHOOL AND CENTER

Day — Coed Ages 6-14

Cincinnati, OH 45208. 2121 Madison Rd.
Tel: 513-871-6080. Fax: 513-871-6428.
www.springerschoolandcenter.org E-mail: info@springer.hccanet.org
Shelly Weisbacher, MA, Exec Dir. **Jan Annett,** Adm.
 Focus: Spec Ed. **Conditions:** Primary—Dc Dg Dx LD. Sec—ADD ADHD.
  IQ 90 and up.
 Gen Acad. Ungraded. Courses: Read Math Lang_Arts.
 Therapy: Lang Percepual-Motor Speech. **Psychotherapy:** Group Indiv.
 Enr: 206. **Staff:** 70 (Full 40, Part 30).
 Rates 2003: Day $14,920/sch yr. Schol 50 ($450,000). State Aid.
 Summer Prgm: Day. Educ. Rec.
 Est 1971. Private. Nonprofit.

 Springer provides various services for individuals affected by learning disabilities. The school's comprehensive academic program, which serves elementary-age students, features small-group instruction and diagnostic teaching. Pupils develop the skills and strategies necessary for success in traditional school settings. Individualized student programs may include one or more of the following elements: language therapy, psychotherapy and motor skills training. The center provides information and offers referral services and programs for parents, teachers and students.

SUNSHINE CHILDREN'S HOME OF NORTHWEST OHIO

Res — Coed Ages Birth-23

Maumee, OH 43537. 7223 Maumee-Western Rd.
Tel: 419-865-0251. Fax: 419-865-9715.
www.sunshineincnwo.org E-mail: info@sunshineincnwo.org
John L. Martin, MA, Exec Dir. **Donald I. Cameron,** MD, Med Dir.
 Focus: Treatment. **Conditions:** Primary—MR. Sec—B D ED. **IQ 0-50.**
 Voc. On-Job Trng.
 Therapy: Hear Lang Occup Phys Speech. **Psychotherapy:** Indiv.

Enr: 75. **Staff:** 200.
Est 1949. Private. Nonprofit. Mennonite.

This home offers intensive developmental treatment with a Christian orientation to dependent to profoundly retarded children and adolescents. The majority of residents attend schools and workshops within the county, with the remainder receiving formalized educational stimulation at Sunshine. Transfer to group, foster or natural home settings is emphasized.

TOWNSEND LEARNING CENTERS

Clinic: All Ages. M-S 9-5; Eves M-Th 5-9.

Cleveland, OH 44103. 1667 E 40th St, Ste 1B.
Tel: 440-472-8300.
www.learnwithus.com
   Conditions: Primary—BD Dx ED LD MR ON S.
   Col Prep. Gen Acad. Pre-Voc. Ungraded. Courses: Read Math Lang_Arts.
   Therapy: Lang Speech. **Psychotherapy:** Indiv.
   Staff: Prof 63.
   Est 1969. Private. Inc.

UNIVERSITY OF CINCINNATI MEDICAL CENTER
SPEECH, LANGUAGE, HEARING CLINIC

Clinic: All Ages. M-F 8:30-5; Eve T 5-8.

Cincinnati, OH 45267. Dept of Communication Sciences and Disorders,
   PO Box 670379.
Tel: 513-558-8502. Fax: 513-558-0618.
www.uc.edu/csd/clinic.html   E-mail: phyllis.breen@uc.edu
Phyllis Breen, MA, CCC-SLP, Dir.
   Focus: Treatment. **Conditions:** Primary—D S. Sec—ADD ADHD CP Dx
   LD. **IQ 70 and up.**
   Therapy: Hear Lang.
   State.

This division of the University of Cincinnati Medical Center offers diagnostic services and therapeutic treatment to hearing- and speech-impaired persons. Referrals are made through community agencies and physicians, and by the patients themselves.

WARRENSVILLE DEVELOPMENTAL CENTER

Res — Coed Ages 19 and up

Highland Hills, OH 44128. 4325 Green Rd.
Tel: 216-464-7400. TTY: 216-464-5051. Fax: 216-464-0075.
http://odmrdd.state.oh.us/Includes/Dev_Ctrs/Developmental.htm

E-mail: tlynn@wdc.mr.state.oh.us
Theresa A. Lynn, Supt.
  Focus: Trng. **Conditions:** Primary—MR. Sec—ADD ADHD Ap As Au B BD BI C CD CP D Dx ED Ep IP MD MS OCD ON Psy SB Sz TB. **IQ 0-55.**
  Voc. Shelt_Workshop.
  Therapy: Hear Lang Occup Phys Speech. **Psychotherapy:** Group Indiv.
  Enr: 252. Res Males 177. Res Females 75. **Staff:** 78 (Full 64, Part 14).
  Rates 2004: No Fee.
  Est 1975. State. Nonprofit.

WDC is a residential training facility for moderately, severely and profoundly retarded persons. Services include prevocational and vocational training, leisure and recreational programs, and social and advocacy services. The ultimate goal is for clients to make a successful transition from the facility to the least restrictive possible living environment, such as a group home or a semi-independent supervised apartment.

WDC relies on volunteers to supplement and enhance staff services, and to provide clients with supportive community relationships.

YOUTH DEVELOPMENT CORPORATION OF AMERICA

Res — Coed Ages Birth-18

South Point, OH 45680. 1130 County Rd 18, PO Box 810.
Tel: 740-894-4612. Fax: 740-894-5373.
www.ydca.org
Phillip R. Flesher, BA, MA, Exec Dir.
  Focus: Treatment. **Conditions:** Primary—BD ED.
  Therapy: Chemo Lang Speech. **Psychotherapy:** Fam Group Indiv.
  Enr: 300. **Staff:** 33.
  Est 1982. Private. Nonprofit.

YDCA provides a therapeutic foster care program for children and adolescents. The program places an emphasis on resiliency theory. Length of treatment averages two years.

OKLAHOMA

CARL ALBERT COMMUNITY MENTAL HEALTH CENTER
Clinic: Ages 8-18. M-F 8-5.

McAlester, OK 74502. 1101 E Monroe, PO Box 579.
Tel: 918-426-7800. Fax: 918-426-5642.
George Jones, Dir. Charles Van Tuyl, MD, Med Dir.
 Focus: Treatment. Conditions: Primary—ADHD ED Mood OCD Psy PTSD
  Sz. Sec—Anx BD HIV ODD.
 Psychotherapy: Fam Group Indiv.
 Staff: 11. (Full 11). Prof 9. Admin 2.
 Est 1973. State.

This community mental health center offers individual, group and family treatment through outpatient psychotherapy. Psychological evaluations and consultation to other agencies are also available. The adult inpatient unit is utilized for emergency crisis stabilization. Inpatients generally stay at the center for five to seven days, while the usual length of outpatient treatment is six months.

THE CHILDREN'S CENTER
Res — Coed Ages Birth-18

Bethany, OK 73008. 6800 NW 39th Expy.
Tel: 405-789-6711. Fax: 405-789-0690.
www.thechildrens-center.org   E-mail: info@thechildrens-center.org
Albert Gray, CEO.
 Focus: Spec Ed. Rehab. Treatment. Conditions: Primary—As Bl C CP Ep
  IP MD MR MS ON SB. Sec—ADD ADHD Ap Au B D Dx LD S.
 Gen Acad. Gr PS-12. Courses: Read Math Lang_Arts.
 Therapy: Hear Lang Music Occup Phys Speech Aqua.
 Enr: 76. Res Males 46. Res Females 30. Staff: 108 (Full 90, Part 18).
 Est 1898. Private. Nonprofit.

This center provides 24-hour nursing services to critically ill children with multiple disabilities. Offerings include therapy, as well as infant and developmental stimulation.

DALE ROGERS TRAINING & EMPLOYMENT CENTER
Day — Coed Ages 18 and up

Oklahoma City, OK 73101. 2501 N Utah St.
Tel: 405-946-4489. Fax: 405-943-9710.
www.drtc.org   E-mail: dalerogers@drtc.org
Connie Thrash McGoodwin, Exec Dir.
 Conditions: Primary—MR.

Gen Acad. Pre-Voc. Voc. Ungraded. Courses: Read Math Lang_Arts.
Shelt_Workshop. On-Job Trng.
Therapy: Hear Lang Phys Speech.
Est 1953. Private. Nonprofit.

EDWIN FAIR COMMUNITY MENTAL HEALTH CENTER
Clinic: Ages Birth-18. M-F 8-5.

Ponca City, OK 74601. 1500 N 6th St.
Tel: 580-762-7561. Fax: 580-762-2576.
E-mail: efcmhc@poncacity.net
Geoffrey H. Cowan, Exec Dir. **Alzira Vaidya,** MD, Med Dir.
   Focus: Treatment. **Conditions:** Primary—ADD ADHD ED LD MR. Sec—BI
   Dx. **IQ 50 and up.**
   Psychotherapy: Fam Group Indiv.
   Staff: 12. Prof 10. Admin 2.
   Est 1958. Private. Nonprofit.

Early evaluation and treatment of educational, speech, language, hearing and psychological problems are provided using a team approach. Community consultation and education are also featured. Learning disabilities are diagnosed and remedial work is available. Parental counseling and follow-up services are part of the program, and the center also offers counseling services for clients who have been dually diagnosed with mental illness and mental retardation. Inpatient, partial hospitalization and 24-hour emergency services are available by affiliation with the Ponca City Hospital.

Fees are determined along a sliding scale.

GATESWAY FOUNDATION
Res — Coed Ages 18 and up

Broken Arrow, OK 74012. 116 W Commercial St.
Tel: 918-258-3900. Fax: 918-259-0598.
www.helplinetulsa.net/data/ov0s53hq.htm
   Conditions: Primary—MR.
   Pre-Voc. Voc. Ungraded. Courses: Read Math Lang_Arts. Man_Arts &
   Shop. Shelt_Workshop. On-Job Trng.
   Therapy: Hear Lang Occup Phys Speech. **Psychotherapy:** Indiv.
   Est 1964. Private. Nonprofit.

J. D. MCCARTY CENTER FOR CHILDREN
WITH DEVELOPMENTAL DISABILITIES
Res — Coed Ages Birth-21

Norman, OK 73071. 1125 E Alameda Dr.

Tel: 405-321-4830. Fax: 405-321-4833.
www.jdmc.org   E-mail: greg@jdmc.org
Curtis A. Peters, CEO.
  Focus: Rehab. Treatment. **Conditions:** Primary—Ap Au BI CP MR ON S
    SB. Sec—ADD ADHD As B C CD D ED Ep IP LD MD MS OCD TB.
  Gen Acad. Pre-Voc. Gr K-12. Courses: Read Math Lang_Arts. Shelt_Work-
    shop.
  Therapy: Hear Lang Music Occup Phys Recreational Speech. **Psychother-
    apy:** Fam Group Indiv Parent.
  Staff: 142 (Full 109, Part 33).
  Est 1948. State. Nonprofit.

Any individual under age 21 who resides in Oklahoma is eligible for treatment at this center. Therapy aims at developing maximum independence in the activities of daily living. An accredited special education program is conducted by the Norman Public Schools, and individual instruction is available when needed. The program also includes psychological testing and counseling, weekly interdisciplinary assessments, orthopedic and neurological services, and dental services. Diagnostic x-rays and the construction of adaptive equipment are also available through the center.

JANE BROOKS SCHOOL FOR THE DEAF

Res — Coed Ages 3-14; Day — Coed 6mos-14

Chickasha, OK 73023. PO Box 669.
Tel: 405-224-3500. TTY: 405-224-3500. Fax: 405-224-3501.
E-mail: jbsftd@sbcglobal.net
Carolyne Paradiso, BA, BS, MLS, Dir.
  Focus: Spec Ed. **Conditions:** Primary—D.
  Gen Acad. Gr PS-8. Courses: Read Math Lang_Arts Sci Soc_Stud.
  Therapy: Hear Lang Speech.
  Enr: 14. **Staff:** 12. Prof 7. Educ 4. Admin 1.
  Est 1929. Private. Nonprofit.

Three academic programs—preschool, elementary and junior high—stress language development for deaf children at the Jane Brooks School. Communication skills are stressed through a comprehensive approach that utilizes sign language and speech training.

JOHN A. MORRIS SPEECH AND HEARING CLINIC

Clinic: All Ages. M Th 1-4.

Chickasha, OK 73018. 1727 W Alabama Ave.
Tel: 405-574-1274. Fax: 405-574-1220.
Diane Holland, MS, Dir.
  Focus: Treatment. **Conditions:** Primary—D S. Sec—ADD ADHD LD MR.
  Therapy: Hear Lang Speech.
  Staff: 4 (Full 2, Part 2).
  State. **Spons:** University of Science and Arts of Oklahoma.

This facility offers diagnostic therapeutic treatment to hearing- and speech-impaired persons.

LOGAN COUNTY GUIDANCE CENTER
Clinic: Ages Birth-18. M-F 8-5.

Guthrie, OK 73044. 215 Fairgrounds Rd, Ste A.
Tel: 405-282-3485. Fax: 405-282-5389.
Jay Smith, Admin.
 Conditions: Primary—BD ED LD MR S.
 Therapy: Hear Lang Occup Phys Speech. **Psychotherapy:** Fam Group Indiv.
 Est 1971. County. Nonprofit.

NORTHWEST CENTER FOR BEHAVIORAL HEALTH
Clinic: Ages 8 and up. M-F 8-4:30; Eve T 4:30-8.

Woodward, OK 73801. 1222 10th St, Ste 211.
Tel: 580-256-8615. Fax: 580-256-8643.
www.odmhsas.org/menthealth.htm
Steve Norwood, Exec Dir.
 Conditions: Primary—BD.
 Psychotherapy: Fam Group Indiv.
 Est 1982. State.

OKLAHOMA SCHOOL FOR THE BLIND
Res — Coed Ages 3-21; Day — Coed 2-21

Muskogee, OK 74403. 3300 Gibson St.
Tel: 918-781-8200. Fax: 918-781-8300.
www.osb.k12.ok.us/index.html
Karen Kizzia, MEd, Supt. **Mike Stratton,** MD, Med Dir.
 Focus: Spec Ed. **Conditions:** Primary—B. Sec—BD CP ED Ep LD MR OH. **IQ 50 and up.**
 Col Prep. Gen Acad. Pre-Voc. Voc. Gr PS-12. Courses: Read Math Lang_ Arts. Man_Arts & Shop. Shelt_Workshop. On-Job Trng.
 Therapy: Hear Lang Occup Phys Speech. **Psychotherapy:** Indiv.
 Enr: 138. Res Males 46. Res Females 48. Day Males 22. Day Females 22. **Staff:** 47. (Full 47).
 Rates 2003: No Fee.
 Summer Prgm: Res. Educ. 4 wks.
 Est 1907. State. Nonprofit.

Elementary and secondary educational programs for visually impaired children are available at Parkview. Blind children with mild secondary disabilities are also accepted, and counseling is available.

OKLAHOMA SCHOOL FOR THE DEAF

Res and Day — Coed Ages 2½-21

Sulphur, OK 73086. 1100 E Oklahoma Ave.
Tel: 580-622-3186. Fax: 580-622-4950.
www.osd.k12.ok.us
Larry Hawkins, Supt. **Teresa Ryan,** Med Dir. **Patricia Baldwin,** Adm.
  Focus: Spec Ed. **Conditions:** Primary—D. **IQ 60 and up.**
  Col Prep. Gen Acad. Pre-Voc. Gr PS-12. Courses: Read Math Lang_Arts
    Sci Soc_Stud. Man_Arts & Shop. On-Job Trng.
  Therapy: Hear Lang Phys Speech.
  Enr: 169. Res Males 65. Res Females 55. Day Males 29. Day Females 20.
    Staff: 44.
  Rates 2003: No Fee.
  Est 1912. State. Nonprofit.

Deaf children and adults receive education in academic and vocational work, social and psychological guidance, and physical training. A program for the multiply handicapped and a preschool have been developed.

OKLAHOMA STATE UNIVERSITY
SPEECH-LANGUAGE PATHOLOGY & AUDIOLOGY CLINICS

Clinic: All Ages. M-F 8-5.

Stillwater, OK 74078. 120 Hanner Hall, Hester & Athletic Ave.
Tel: 405-744-6021. TTY: 405-744-8937. Fax: 405-744-7074.
www.cas.okstate.edu/cdis/clinic.html
  Focus: Rehab. Treatment. **Conditions:** Primary—Ap D S.
  Therapy: Hear Lang Speech.
  Staff: Prof 7.
  Est 1960. State. Nonprofit.

OKLAHOMA YOUTH CENTER

Res — Coed Ages 5-18

Norman, OK 73071. 320 12th Ave NE.
Tel: 405-364-9004. Fax: 405-573-3804.
Robert Lee, LCSW-C, Dir. **Peggy Jewell,** MD, Med Dir.
  Focus: Treatment. **Conditions:** Primary—ED. Sec—BD.
  Gen Acad. Gr K-12. Courses: Read Math Lang_Arts.
  Psychotherapy: Fam Group Indiv.

Enr: 40. **Staff:** 78.
Rates 2003: Res $500/day. State Aid.
Summer Prgm: Res. Educ. Ther.
Est 1985. State. Nonprofit.

This state-operated psychiatric hospital for children and adolescents who are emotionally disturbed. School education is provided on site through the Norman Public Schools.

PAULA STANFORD'S HUMAN RESOURCE NETWORK

Clinic: Ages 6 and up. M-Th 9-6.

Oklahoma City, OK 73116. 6520 N Western Ave, Ste 101.
Tel: 405-524-4610. Fax: 405-607-6252.
E-mail: pjstan@coxinet.net
Paula Stanford, MA, Pres. **J. R. Smith,** MD, Med Dir. **Phyllis Duncan,** Adm.
  Focus: Treatment. **Conditions:** Primary—ADD ADHD Dx LD. Sec—AN Anx BD Bu CD Db ED Mood MR OCD ODD PTSD SP. **IQ 65 and up.**
  Psychotherapy: Fam Indiv Parent.
  Staff: 8 (Full 3, Part 5).
  Est 1973. Private. Inc.

This facility provides diagnosis of learning disabilities that relate to academic underachievement in reading, spelling, writing and math. The center makes referrals for those diagnosed with visual, hearing, emotional, physical and chemical disorders, and arranges for specialized tutoring. The network also provides interest and aptitude testing.

THAYNE A. HEDGES
REGIONAL SPEECH AND HEARING CENTER

Clinic: All Ages. Eves M-S 5-8.

Enid, OK 73701. 2615 E Randolph Ave.
Tel: 580-234-3734. Fax: 580-234-3554.
Alan D. Livingston, MA, Exec Dir. **Kathy Chambers,** MA, Clin Dir.
  Focus: Trng. **Conditions:** Primary—Ap S. Sec—ADD ADHD BI CP Dx LD MD MR MS OH.
  Therapy: Dance Hear Hydro Lang Recreational Speech.
  Staff: 16 (Full 14, Part 2). Prof 14. Admin 2.
  Rates 2003: Sliding-Scale Rate $2-50/hr.
  Est 1955. Private. Nonprofit.

Regional Speech and Hearing Center offers diagnosis and therapy to individuals with speech, hearing, reading, language and learning disorders. Educational counseling is available, and the length of treatment varies.

TOWN & COUNTRY SCHOOL

Day — Coed Ages 5-18

Tulsa, OK 74137. 5150 E 101st St.
Tel: 918-296-3113. Fax: 918-298-8175.
www.tandcschool.org E-mail: tcsinfo@tandcschool.org
Gayle Pottle, BS, Exec Dir.
  Focus: Spec Ed. **Conditions:** Primary—ADD ADHD Asp Dc Dg Dx LD TS.
    IQ 100 and up.
  Gen Acad. Gr K-12. Courses: Read Math Lang_Arts Computers Studio_Art
    Music Speech Adaptive_Phys_Ed.
  Therapy: Lang Speech. **Psychotherapy:** Parent.
  Enr: 135. **Staff:** 40 (Full 36, Part 4).
  Rates 2003: Day $6800-7800/sch yr. Schol avail.
  Est 1961. Private. Nonprofit.

The school aids children with learning disabilities, attentional disorders and developmental delays. Town & Country employs an individualized approach and a flexible curriculum that lessens scholastic stress and allows students to think, read, write, communicate and perform more effectively. To gain admittance, pupils must have a primary diagnosis of a learning disability and must have an average or better IQ.

UNIVERSITY OF OKLAHOMA
HEALTH SCIENCES CENTER
CHILD STUDY CENTER

Clinic: Ages Birth-14. M-F 8-5.

Oklahoma City, OK 73117. 1100 NE 13th St, PO Box 26901.
Tel: 405-271-5700. Fax: 405-271-8835.
Mark Wolraich, MD, Dir. **Diana Garvey,** Intake.
  Focus: Treatment. **Conditions:** Primary—ADD ADHD Asp Au Dx ED LD
    MR ON S SB. Sec—B BI CD CP D Ep OCD.
  Therapy: Lang Occup Phys Speech. **Psychotherapy:** Fam Group Indiv.
  Staff: 23. Prof 21. Admin 2.
  Est 1963. State.

The CSC is a training setting for the university that offers multidisciplinary evaluations and treatment for children with neurological, physical, emotional, learning and developmental problems. Therapy, counseling and parental support groups are available.

UNIVERSITY OF OKLAHOMA HEALTH SCIENCES CENTER
JOHN W. KEYS SPEECH AND HEARING CENTER

Clinic: All Ages.

Oklahoma City, OK 73190. 825 NE 14th St.

Tel: 405-271-4214. Fax: 405-271-3360.
Richard Talbott, PhD, Dir.
  Conditions: Primary—Ap BI CP D LD MD MR ON S.
  Gen Acad. Gr PS.
  Therapy: Hear Lang Speech.
  Est 1947. State.

UNIVERSITY OF TULSA
MARY K. CHAPMAN CENTER

Clinic: All Ages. M-F 8-5.

Tulsa, OK 74104. Dept of Communication Disorders, 600 S College Ave.
Tel: 918-631-2504. TTY: 918-631-2504. Fax: 918-631-3668.
www.cas.utulsa.edu/commdis
Paula Cadogan, EdD, Supv. Suzanne J. T. Stanton, Coord.
  Focus: Spec Ed. Conditions: Primary—Ap D S. Sec—ADD ADHD Apr Asp
    Au B BD BI CP Dx ED LD MD MR MS ON PDD.
  Therapy: Hear Lang Speech.
  Staff: 13 (Full 10, Part 3). Prof 7. Admin 1.
  Rates 2003: Clinic $38/hr.
  Est 1953. Private.

  Mary K. Chapman Center houses the university's Department of Communication
Disorders. The professional and clinical staff provide an interdisciplinary approach to
services for clients with speech, language and hearing disorders.

OREGON

BRIDGES ACADEMY

Res — Males Ages 13-17

Bend, OR 97701. 67030 Gist Rd.
Tel: 541-318-9345. Fax: 541-383-4108.
www.bridgesboysacademy.com
 E-mail: information@bridgesboysacademy.com
Bruce Barrett, MBA, Exec Dir. **Erick R. Scheiderman,** Adm.
 Focus: Spec Ed. Treatment. **Conditions:** Primary—ADD ADHD Anx Asp
  BD CD ED LD Mood OCD ODD PDD SP.
 Col Prep. Gen Acad. Gr 7-12. Courses: Read Math Lang_Arts.
 Psychotherapy: Fam Group Indiv Parent.
 Enr: 30. Res Males 30. **Staff:** 18 (Full 6, Part 12). Educ 3.
 Rates 2004: Res $4450/mo (+$1500/yr).
 Est 1997. Private. Inc.

Bridges program for temperamentally challenged boys is based on four specific components: small population size, individually paced education, family involvement and a single-sex student population. The minimum length of enrollment is one year, with some boys requiring additional time to achieve their program goals.

Bridges conducts a year-round, self-paced middle and high school program that promotes credit recovery and transferable credits. Students who remain until graduation may earn a diploma. In addition to academics, the academy offers individual, group and family counseling; experiential learning opportunities; and community living options.

THE CHRISTIE SCHOOL

Res — Coed Ages 8-18

Marylhurst, OR 97036. PO Box 368.
Tel: 503-635-3416. Fax: 503-697-6932.
www.christieschool.org   E-mail: admissions@christieschool.org
Lynne Saxton, Exec Dir. **Chris Larsen,** Adm.
 Focus: Spec Ed. Treatment. **Conditions:** Primary—ADD ADHD BD Dx ED
  LD OCD Psy Sz. Sec—As CD Ep. **IQ 70 and up.**
 Gen Acad. Ungraded. Courses: Read Math Lang_Arts.
 Therapy: Speech. **Psychotherapy:** Fam Group Indiv.
 Enr: 80.
 Est 1859. Private. Nonprofit.

This facility for emotionally disturbed children conducts several programs. An intensive treatment program treats fire setters, runaways and physically aggressive boys and girls in an attempt to later release them to a less restrictive setting. An open residential treatment program is for girls only who have been neglected or sexually or physically abused. It also provides for those with learning disabilities and a lack of socialization skills or low self-esteem. A group home for boys and girls ages 12-18 focuses on the development of independent living skills, while community-based residential treatment combines residential and family/community services for those ages 8-18. In addition, assessment and evaluation services provide immediate security and stability to children in crisis ages 8-18.

The school emphasizes behaviorally oriented therapies and also utilizes milieu therapy and a therapeutic recreational program. Prevocational training and a self-contained school program are available. The average length of treatment is 13 months.

CLATSOP BEHAVIORAL HEALTHCARE

Clinic: All Ages. M-F 8:30-5.

Astoria, OR 97103. 6th St, Ste 103.
Tel: 503-325-5722. Fax: 503-325-8483.
  Conditions: Primary—BD ED.
  Therapy: Speech. **Psychotherapy:** Fam Group Indiv.
  Est 1963. Private. Nonprofit.

DRAGONFLY ADVENTURES

Res — Coed Ages 18 and up

Klamath Falls, OR 97601. 517 N 4th St.
Tel: 541-850-0841. Fax: 541-850-0841.
www.dragonflyadventures.com   E-mail: trips@dragonflyadventures.com
Glenn White, BS, Co-Dir. **Mona Treadway,** BA, Co-Dir.
  Focus: Treatment. **Conditions:** Primary—ADD HIV LD PTSD SP. Sec—
    Anx BD ED Mood OCD ODD.
  Psychotherapy: Group Indiv.
  Enr: 10. **Staff:** 3. Prof 1. Admin 2.
  Rates 2004: Res $2300/mo (+$2000/ses).
  Private. Inc.

Dragonfly Adventures provides two distinct services: an independent living skills program that serves young adults struggling with mental health and emotional challenges, and customized therapeutic wilderness trips for adolescents or young adults. The independent living program provides employment and vocational assistance, educational and career planning, independent living skills instruction, health and nutrition information, community service opportunities, substance abuse education, drug testing services, group therapy and parental support. Perspective clients must have no extensive history of violence and must be willing to adhere to program rules and guidelines.

Wilderness trips enable boys and girls to communicate openly with others, discuss their problems, confront the consequences of their behavior and discover the impact of their decisions. Trip destinations include Sitka, AK; Death Valley, CA; and Rogue River, OR.

EDGEFIELD CHILDREN'S SERVICES

Res and Day — Coed Ages 6-12

Troutdale, OR 97060. 2408 SW Halsey St.
Tel: 503-665-0157. Fax: 503-666-3066.
www.morrisoncenter.org
Jay Bloom, MSW, CEO. **Mona Ozaki,** PhD, Clin Dir. **Ajit Jetmalani,** MD, Med
Dir. **Rachel Byrns,** Intake.
　Focus: Treatment. **Conditions:** Primary—ED. Sec—ADD ADHD Anx BD
　　CD Dx LD OCD Psy PTSD. **IQ 70 and up.**
　Gen Acad. Gr K-6. Courses: Read Math Lang_Arts.
　Therapy: Art Lang Play Speech. **Psychotherapy:** Fam Group Indiv.
　Enr: 44. Res Males 16. Res Females 8. Day Males 14. Day Females 6.
　　Staff: 70 (Full 54, Part 16). Prof 18. Educ 8. Admin 8.
　Rates 2003: Res $245-290/day. Day $117-162/day. State Aid.
　Est 1964. Private. Nonprofit. **Spons:** Morrison Child and Family Services.

In a rural setting, Edgefield treats children with extreme emotional disturbances and offers residential and day treatment. The residential and day treatment programs feature a year-round, on-site educational program. Parents must agree to participate in family therapy and in their child's program. Edgefield does not accept mentally retarded children. The usual length of treatment ranges from nine to 12 months.

EUGENE HEARING AND SPEECH CENTER

Clinic: All Ages. M-F 8-5.

Eugene, OR 97402. 1500 W 12th Ave.
Tel: 541-485-8521. TTY: 541-485-8521. Fax: 541-485-6159.
www.eugenehearingspeech.org　　E-mail: info@eugenehearingspeech.org
Jane Eyre McDonald, Exec Dir.
　Conditions: Primary—D S.
　Courses: Read Math Lang_Arts.
　Therapy: Hear Lang Speech.
　Est 1955. Private. Nonprofit.

HEARING & SPEECH INSTITUTE

Day — Coed Ages 2-5
Clinic: Ages Birth-18. M-F 8-6.

Portland, OR 97239. 3515 SW US Veterans Hospital Rd.
Tel: 503-228-6479. TTY: 503-228-6479. Fax: 503-228-4248.
www.hearingandspeech.org　　E-mail: info@hearingandspeech.org
Donald S. Rushmer, PhD, Exec Dir.
　Focus: Treatment. **Conditions:** Primary—Ap Apr Asp Au D S. Sec—BD DS.
　Therapy: Hear Lang Occup Speech. **Psychotherapy:** Fam Indiv.
　Staff: 32. (Full 32). Prof 20. Admin 6.

Summer Prgm: Day. Ther. 6 wks.
Est 1927. Private. Nonprofit.

The institute offers audiological and speech evaluations, advice and training to individuals with hearing, speech and language disorders. An early intervention preschool is conducted for speech- and language-impaired children ages 2-5.

Affiliated with the Oregon Health Sciences University, this facility provides evaluations for aphasic and dysphasic individuals, hearing aids, esophageal speech training and parent education. The center primarily serves residents of Oregon and Clark County, WA, with fees scaled in accordance with other United Way agencies.

JOSEPHINE COUNTY CLINIC

Clinic: All Ages. M-F 8:30-5; Eve W 5-8.

Grants Pass, OR 97526. 714 NW A St.
Tel: 541-474-5365. Fax: 541-474-5366.
www.co.josephine.or.us/jcmhd/jcmhmain.htm
Joe Adair, MSW, Dir.
   Conditions: Primary—Au BD CP ED MR.
   Therapy: Chemo Speech. **Psychotherapy:** Fam Group Indiv.
   Est 1965. State.

MUSCULAR DYSTROPHY ASSOCIATION

Clinic: All Ages. M-F 8:30-5.

Portland, OR 97239. 4800 SW Macadam Ave, Ste 205.
Tel: 503-223-3177. Fax: 503-223-3026.
www.mdausa.org   E-mail: portlandorservices@mdausa.org
Lynne DiVecchio, Coord.
   Focus: Treatment. **Conditions:** Primary—MD.
   Therapy: Occup Phys Speech. **Psychotherapy:** Fam Group Parent.
   Staff: 6. (Full 6).
   Rates 2003: No Fee.
   Est 1950. Private. Nonprofit.

The clinic, held at Oregon Health Sciences University, is an outpatient facility for residents of Oregon and Clark County, WA. The center diagnoses and evaluates neuromuscular disorders and provides treatment. The clinic also offers a selection of orthopedic equipment and daily living aids.

NORTHSTAR CENTER

Res — Coed Ages 18-24

Bend, OR 97709. PO Box 1370.
Tel: 541-385-8657. Fax: 541-385-0997.

www.northstarcenter.com   E-mail: nstar@northstarcenter.com
Trina Packard, MEd, Exec Dir. **Julie Still,** Adm.
> **Focus:** Treatment. **Conditions:** Primary—ADD ADHD AN Anx As BD Bu
> Dx ED LD Mood OCD PTSD. Sec—Ar Db Dc Dg HIV ODD PDD SP TS.
> **IQ 94-130.**
> **Col Prep. Gen Acad.** Gr 12-PG. Courses: Read Math Lang_Arts.
> **Psychotherapy:** Fam Group Indiv Substance_Abuse.
> **Enr:** 42. Res Males 30. Res Females 12. **Staff:** 38 (Full 35, Part 3). Prof 17.
> Educ 2. Admin 2.
> **Rates 2004:** Res $57,600/yr.
> Private. Inc. **Spons:** Aspen Education Group.

NorthStar is a transitional independent program for young adults that typically enrolls clients for one year; the minimum length of stay is six months. The center provides a sober living environment with recovery support, job coaching and independent living skills instruction. Students who wish to complete high school or engage in college course work may do so in cooperation with Central Oregon Community College: COOO offers a high school diploma, GED test preparation, and two-year degree and transfer programs.

OPEN MEADOW ALTERNATIVE SCHOOLS

Day — Coed Ages 10-18

Portland, OR 97217. 7621 N Wabash.
Tel: 503-978-1935. Fax: 503-978-1898.
www.openmeadow.org
Carole L. Smith, EdM, Exec Dir.
> **Focus:** Spec Ed. **Conditions:** Primary—ADD ADHD Asp BD Dx ED LD.
> **Col Prep. Gen Acad. Pre-Voc.** Gr 6-12. Courses: Read Math Lang_Arts.
> **Enr:** 180. Day Males 90. Day Females 90. **Staff:** 39 (Full 34, Part 5). Educ
> 26. Admin 7.
> **Summer Prgm:** Day. Educ. Rec. Ther.
> **Est 1971.** Private. Nonprofit.

This program emphasizes peer counseling and group interaction. Students share in decisions regarding school rules, personal and group goals, class offerings and course content. Courses such as youth and the law, horticulture and creative writing supplement the basic educational program. The length of treatment ranges from two months to four years.

OREGON SCHOOL FOR THE BLIND

Res and Day — Coed Ages 5-21

Salem, OR 97310. 255 Capitol St NE.
Tel: 503-378-3569. TTY: 503-378-2892. Fax: 503-378-5156.
www.ode.state.or.us   E-mail: ode.frontdesk@state.or.us
Don Ouimet, Dir.
> **Focus:** Spec Ed. **Conditions:** Primary—B. Sec—Au D ED MR ON S.

Gen Acad. Pre-Voc. Gr K-12. Courses: Read Math Lang_Arts Braille. Man_
Arts & Shop. On-Job Trng.
Therapy: Hear Lang Occup Phys Speech. **Psychotherapy:** Group Indiv.
Enr: 53. **Staff:** 40.
Rates 2004: No Fee.
Summer Prgm: Res & Day. Educ. Rec. Ther. 1-4 wks.
Est 1873. State.

The school provides diagnosis and evaluation for visually impaired students at the request of local districts. Direct consultation and a vision clinic are available statewide, and a media center loans books, equipment and aides. The summer program offers academics; computer education; braille, music, and living and work skills instruction; augmentative communication; recreation; respite care; and early childhood education.

OREGON SCHOOL FOR THE DEAF

Res and Day — Coed Ages 5-21

Salem, OR 97303. 999 Locust St NE.
Tel: 503-378-3825. TTY: 503-378-3825. Fax: 503-373-7879.
www.osd.k12.or.us
Jane Mulholland, MEd, MS, Dir.
   Focus: Spec Ed. **Conditions:** Primary—D. Sec—ADD ADHD DS LD MR
   OH.
   Col Prep. Gen Acad. Pre-Voc. Voc. Gr K-12. Courses: Read Math Lang_
   Arts. Man_Arts & Shop. Shelt_Workshop. On-Job Trng.
   Therapy: Hear Lang Occup Phys Speech. **Psychotherapy:** Indiv.
   Enr: 130. **Staff:** 100. (Full 100).
   Rates 2003: No Fee.
   Est 1870. State.

The educational program provides a full range of academic, vocational and transition-related courses and services for students who are deaf or hard of hearing. The school is free to age-eligible Oregon residents who have a diagnosed hearing impairment worthy of special education.

OREGON STATE HOSPITAL
CHILD AND ADOLESCENT TREATMENT SERVICE

Res — Coed Ages 14-18

Salem, OR 97301. 2600 Center St NE, Bldg 40.
Tel: 503-945-7130. TTY: 503-945-2996. Fax: 503-945-2807.
www.dhs.state.or.us/mentalhealth/osh
Sue Zakes, MS, Prgm Dir.
   Focus: Treatment. **Conditions:** Primary—ADD AN Anx Bu ED OCD PTSD
   Sz. Sec—Ap As Asp B BD Bl CD D Db Dc Dg Dx Ep HIV MR ON PDD
   PW SP TS. **IQ 65-120.**
   Gen Acad. Pre-Voc. Voc. Gr 7-12. Courses: Read Math Lang_Arts.
   Therapy: Art Hear Lang Milieu Occup Percepual-Motor Phys Recreational

Speech. **Psychotherapy:** Fam Group Indiv.
Enr: 40. **Staff:** 95. Prof 12. Admin 3.
Est 1976. State.

Statewide psychiatric treatment services for severely emotionally disturbed children and adolescents are provided. Treatment, which usually lasts for nine months, includes personal, parental and educational counseling. Adjunctive therapies are available. The program is affiliated with the Oregon Health Science University's Child Psychiatry Department.

PORTLAND HABILITATION CENTER

Day — Coed Ages 18-65

Portland, OR 97230. 5312 NE 148th Ave.
Tel: 503-261-1266. TTY: 503-408-3036. Fax: 503-256-8665.
www.phcnw.com
John Murphy, Pres.
   Conditions: Primary—MR.
   Pre-Voc. Voc. Shelt_Workshop. On-Job Trng.
   Est 1951. Private. Nonprofit.

PORTLAND STATE UNIVERSITY
SPEECH AND HEARING CLINICS

Clinic: All Ages. M-F 8-5.

Portland, OR 97207. Dept of Communication, PO Box 751.
Tel: 503-725-3533. Fax: 503-725-5385.
www.sphr.pdx.edu/clinics
Ellen Reuler, MA, Dir.
   Focus: Treatment. **Conditions:** Primary—Ap D S. Sec—ADD ADHD Au BI CP Dx LD MR OH.
   Therapy: Hear Lang Speech.
   Staff: 8. (Full 8).
   Est 1964. State. Nonprofit.

Primarily an educational center for speech, language and hearing clinicians, the facility provides outpatient services for the community.

THE RANCH HOUSE

Res — Males Ages 14-17

Portland, OR 97225. 8000 SW Greenhouse Ln.
Tel: 503-292-2531.
www.boysranchhouse.com   E-mail: contact@boysranchhouse.com
Marilyn Siegel, CSW, Co-Dir. **Gabriel Rivera,** Co-Dir.

Focus: Treatment. **Conditions:** Primary—ADD ADHD Anx As Asp BD CD Dc Dg Dx ED LD Mood OCD PTSD. Sec—Db. **IQ 100 and up.**
Psychotherapy: Fam Group Indiv Parent.
Enr: 10. Res Males 10.
Rates 2003: Res $4000/mo (+$1000/ses). $125 (Therapy)/ses. Schol 2.
Est 2001. Private. Inc.

The program assists young men of average or above-average intelligence who have mild to moderate emotional and behavioral issues that may lead to at-risk behavior. The nine-acre tract enables boys to work on the land surrounding the facility and also care for the animals on the ranch. Aftercare, consultation and ongoing psychotherapy are aspects of the program.

THE RIGGS INSTITUTE
LITERACY AND LEARNING CENTER

Clinic: Ages 5 and up. M-S 9-5; Eves M-F 5-8, S by Appt.

Beaverton, OR 97005. 4755 SW Tucker Ave.
Tel: 503-574-2691. Fax: 503-644-5191.
www.riggsinst.org   E-mail: riggs@integraonline.com
Carolyn Miki, MA, Dir.
Focus: Spec Ed. **Conditions:** Primary—ADD ADHD Dg Dx LD.
Gen Acad. Ungraded. Courses: Read Lang_Arts.
Staff: 6. (Part 6). Educ 6.
Rates 2004: Clinic $9-36/ses. Schol avail.
Est 2001. Private. Nonprofit.

Students at Riggs receive multisensory instruction in listening, writing, spelling, reading and grammar. The program teaches the basic sounds of English and sound-spelling relationships to enable boys and girls to spell, blend, read and analyze common words and sentences.

The center offers private one-on-one tutoring or small-group instruction.

SCAR/JASPER MOUNTAIN

Res — Coed Ages 4-12; Day — Coed 6-12

Jasper, OR 97438. 37875 Jasper Lowell Rd.
Tel: 541-747-1235. Fax: 541-747-4722.
www.scar-jaspermtn.org   E-mail: davez@scar-jaspermtn.org
Dave Ziegler, PhD, Exec Dir. **Janine Gordon,** MD, Med Dir.
Focus: Spec Ed. Treatment. **Conditions:** Primary—ADD ADHD AN Anx Asp BD Bu CD ED LD Mood OCD ON PDD PTSD S SP TS. Sec—Ap Apr As Au Bl C CP D Db Dc Dg Dx Ep MD MR MS Nf Psy PW Sz. **IQ 68 and up.**
Gen Acad. Gr PS-8. Courses: Read Math Lang_Arts Sci Studio_Art Music.
Therapy: Art Chemo Dance Lang Milieu Movement Music Percepual-Motor Phys Play Recreational Speech. **Psychotherapy:** Fam Group Indiv Parent.

Enr: 50. Res Males 16. Res Females 18. Day Males 14. Day Females 2.
Staff: 96 (Full 56, Part 40). Prof 33. Educ 20. Admin 14.
Rates 2003: Res $267/day. Day $99/day.
Summer Prgm: Res & Day. Educ. Rec. Ther. Res Rate $267/day. Day Rate
$99/day. 3 wks.
Est 1982. Private. Nonprofit.

The agency's services are built around two residential centers, Jasper Mountain Center and the SAFE Center. Programming features treatment, prevention, education and residential offerings. The agency treats children who are violent or have serious behavioral problems, attachment disturbances or sexualized behaviors. Substance abusers and those with a primary diagnosis of mental retardation are not admitted.

SHRINERS HOSPITAL

Res — Coed Ages Birth-21
Clinic: Ages Birth-21. M-F 8-4:30.

Portland, OR 97239. 3101 SW Sam Jackson Park Rd.
Tel: 503-241-5090. TTY: 800-735-2900. Fax: 503-221-3475.
www.shrinershq.org
C. Thomas D'Esmond, Admin.
   Focus: Treatment. **Conditions:** Primary—CP MD Nf ON SB.
   Therapy: Hear Occup Phys Speech.
   Enr: 40. **Staff:** 311. Prof 61. Educ 2. Admin 14.
   Rates 2004: No Fee.
   Est 1924. Private.

Primarily for orthopedically handicapped children whose parents cannot pay for surgical orthopedic care, hospitalization and treatment, this hospital serves the northwestern United States, western Canada and Alaska. Public elementary and high school teachers are provided as an adjunct to the program, which includes prosthetics, physical therapy and family services.

THOMAS A. EDISON HIGH SCHOOL

Day — Coed Ages 13-18

Portland, OR 97225. 9020 SW Beaverton Hillsdale Hwy.
Tel: 503-297-2336. Fax: 503-297-2527.
www.taedisonhs.org   E-mail: info@taedisonhs.org
Patrick Maguire, BA, MA, Dir.
   Focus: Spec Ed. **Conditions:** Primary—ADD ADHD Asp Dx LD. Sec—ED.
   IQ 90-110.
   Gen Acad. Gr 9-12. Courses: Read Math Lang_Arts.
   Therapy: Speech. **Psychotherapy:** Group Indiv.
   Enr: 65. Day Males 49. Day Females 16. **Staff:** 18.
   Rates 2004: Day $14,290/sch yr.
   Summer Prgm: Day. Educ. Day Rate $745. 5 wks.
   Est 1975. Private. Nonprofit.

Thomas Edison offers an individualized high school program for adolescents who, due to learning disabilities or difficulties, have been unable to succeed in a traditional school setting. The curriculum focuses on reading and study skills, language arts, math, social studies, science and health. Classes are small and a noncompetitive grading system is used. The goal of the program is to return students to a larger high school after two to four years.

WAVERLY CHILDREN'S HOME

Res — Coed Ages 6-18; Day — Coed 3-12
Clinic: Ages Birth-18. M-S 8-5; Eves M-S 5-9.

Portland, OR 97202. 3550 SE Woodward St.
Tel: 503-234-7532. Fax: 503-233-0187.
Robert L. Roy, MSSW, CEO. **Kim Scott,** COO. **Marianne Straumfjord,** MD, Med Dir. **Kerry Blum,** Adm.

Focus: Treatment. **Conditions:** Primary—Asp BD CD ED Mood OCD ODD Psy PTSD SP Sz TS. Sec—ADD ADHD Au BI Dx LD MR.

Therapy: Art Lang Milieu Occup Play Recreational. **Psychotherapy:** Fam Group Indiv Parent.

Enr: 59. **Staff:** 142 (Full 100, Part 42). Prof 43. Educ 7. Admin 5.

Rates 2004: Res $102,200/yr. Day $31,050-33,000/yr. Clinic $90/hr. State Aid.

Summer Prgm: Res & Day. Educ. Rec. Ther.

Est 1887. Private. Nonprofit.

The agency provides care for severely emotionally disturbed and educable mentally impaired children who are residents of Oregon. A program of milieu therapy includes classroom work, language development, behavior modification and family therapy. The agency also provides therapeutic foster care and a range of outpatient mental health services. The usual length of treatment is 16 months.

PENNSYLVANIA

AC-ACLD
KATHARINE DEAN TILLOTSON SCHOOL
Day — Coed Ages 7-21

Pittsburgh, PA 15227. 4900 Girard Rd.
Tel: 412-881-2268. Fax: 412-881-2263.
www.acldonline.org   E-mail: info@acldonline.org
Thomas W. Fogarty, MEd, Pres. **Kathy Donahoe,** EdD, Prgm Dir. **William I. Cohen,** MD, Med Dir.
  Focus: Spec Ed. Treatment. **Conditions:** Primary—ADD ADHD Dx LD OH. Sec—Anx Ap As Asp Bl C CF CP Ep Nf OCD S SB SP TS. **IQ 80-120.**
  Gen Acad. Pre-Voc. Voc. Gr 1-12. Courses: Read Math Lang_Arts. Man_ Arts & Shop.
  Therapy: Lang Occup Phys Speech. **Psychotherapy:** Group Indiv Parent.
  Enr: 120. Day Males 90. Day Females 30. **Staff:** 52 (Full 44, Part 8).
  Rates 2004: Day $28,000/sch yr. State Aid.
  Summer Prgm: Day. Educ. Day Rate $139.
  Est 1972. Private. Nonprofit.

The school offers individualized diagnosis, evaluation and remediation to learning-disabled and brain-damaged children. The program includes individualized educational programs, speech and language therapy, group therapy, behavior management, prevocational classes and adaptive physical education in an effort to address the varied needs of the child.

The program emphasizes a family atmosphere and provides appropriate adult role models. Instructors encourage students to participate in the student council, community service, clubs and activities. Whenever possible, pupils take part in the planning of their individual education programs. The school also provides a phase-in program for students whose progress allows their return to a traditional school setting.

ACHIEVA EARLY INTERVENTION PROGRAM
Day — Coed Ages Birth-3
Clinic: Ages Birth-3. By Appt.

Pittsburgh, PA 15203. 711 Bingham St.
Tel: 412-995-5000. Fax: 412-995-5001.
www.achieva.info   E-mail: contact@achieva.info
Lynda J. Wright, PhD, Dir.
  Focus: Treatment. **Conditions:** Primary—MR.
  Gen Acad. Gr PS.
  Therapy: Hear Lang Occup Phys Speech Visual. **Counseling:** Nutrition.
  Est 1956. Private. Nonprofit.

Achieva conducts a family-centered early intervention program for developmentally delayed children. Individual sessions occur both in community-based centers and in homes. Toddler groups, which require parental participation, are held in the centers. Parental support groups, trained respite care and sitter services, family educational opportunities and advocacy services supplement the infant and toddler program.

THE ACHIEVEMENT CENTER

Day — Coed Ages Birth-21

Erie, PA 16507. 101 E 6th St, PO Box 1506.
Tel: 814-459-2755. Fax: 814-456-4873.
www.achievementctr.org   E-mail: info@achievementctr.org
Rebecca N. Brumagin, Exec Dir.
  Conditions: Primary—ADD ADHD BD BI CD CP ED MD MR MS OCD ODD ON Psy S SB Sz. Sec—Au B D. **IQ 81 and up.**
  Therapy: Hear Lang Occup Phys Recreational Speech. **Psychotherapy:** Group Indiv.
  Staff: 148.
  Est 1923. Private. Inc.

The center provides outpatient medical rehabilitation and recreation therapy for children and young adults of Erie County who have physical and neurological impairments. Services include individualized instruction in cognitive, language, self-help, social, and fine- and gross-motor skills; family counseling; and developmental, psychological, occupational, speech and language, and physical therapy evaluations. An early intervention program assists children with developmental disabilities between birth and age 5.

In addition, the center provides family-based, outpatient, wraparound and respite mental health services for children and teenagers.

ALLEGHENY VALLEY SCHOOL

Res — Coed Ages 6 and up; Day — Coed 21 and up

Coraopolis, PA 15108. 1996 Ewings Mill Rd.
Tel: 412-299-7777. Fax: 412-299-6701.
www.avs.net
Regis G. Champ, BA, MA, Pres. **Carl Culig,** MD, Med Dir. **Theo Lasinski,** Adm.
  Focus: Trng. Treatment. **Conditions:** Primary—DS MR. Sec—Ap Apr As Asp Au B BD BI C CP D Db ED Ep IP MD Mood MS Nf OCD ON PDD Psy PW S SB Sz TS. **IQ 1-75.**
  Voc. On-Job Trng.
  Therapy: Hydro Lang Music Occup Percepual-Motor Phys Recreational Speech.
  Enr: 804.
  Rates 2003: No Fee.
  Est 1960. Private. Nonprofit.

Allegheny Valley School operates facilities for mentally retarded children and adults. Each residential facility is designed to provide comfortable, homelike surroundings while assuring convenience for residents and the proper degree of supervision and medical care. The purpose is to develop daily living skills and to encourage independence through leisure-time activities and a range of decision-making opportunities.

The small number of clients per facility enables residents to become involved in a variety of activities, promoting independence and understanding of the community. Single-family residences provide development in the areas of consumer skills and life management while utilizing community resources such as schools and income-producing jobs. For residents ages 6-21, education is provided by the local school districts, while residents over age 21 attend continuing adult education classes on campus or at various community adult day programs. Day services for residents and clients from the local communities include occupational, physical, recreational, speech and music therapy, as well as medical, psychological and social services and academics.

ALLIED SERVICES
DE PAUL SCHOOL
Day — Coed Ages 6-15

Scranton, PA 18505. Morgan Hwy.
Tel: 570-346-5855. Fax: 570-346-0368.
Tina M. O'Hara, BS, MA, Dir.
   Conditions: Primary—Dx. **IQ 100 and up.**
   Gen Acad. Gr K-8. Courses: Read Math Lang_Arts.
   Therapy: Hear Lang Occup Phys Speech. **Psychotherapy:** Fam Group Indiv.
   Staff: Prof 4.
   Est 1981. Private. Nonprofit.

ARCHBISHOP RYAN SCHOOL
FOR DEAF AND HARD OF HEARING CHILDREN
Day — Coed Ages Birth-14

Norwood, PA 19074. 233 Mohawk Ave.
Tel: 610-586-7044. TTY: 610-586-7044. Fax: 610-586-7053.
E-mail: apryangab01@nni.com
Sr. Margaret Langer, IHM, BA, MA, Prin.
   Focus: Spec Ed. **Conditions:** Primary—ADHD D. **IQ 90-120.**
   Gen Acad. Gr PS-8. Courses: Read Math Lang_Arts Sci Soc_Stud Religion.
   Therapy: Hear Lang Music Speech. **Psychotherapy:** Fam Indiv.
   Enr: 40. **Staff:** 18 (Full 12, Part 6).
   Rates 2004: Day $1450-2900/sch yr (+$100).
   Est 1912. Private. Nonprofit. Roman Catholic.

Archbishop Ryan offers a regular academic program for deaf and hard-of-hearing children and those diagnosed with a central auditory processing disorder. A parent-infant program assists parents in learning to work with the child and preparing him or her for formal education. Speech reading and auditory training enable deaf children to participate in a regular class as soon as possible. Mainstreaming is determined by lip-reading ability, speech intelligibility, parental cooperation and teacher judgment.

BLOOMSBURG UNIVERSITY
SPEECH, LANGUAGE AND HEARING CLINIC
Clinic: All Ages. M-F 8-4.

Bloomsburg, PA 17815. 339 Centennial Hall.
Tel: 570-389-4436. TTY: 570-389-4864. Fax: 570-389-5022.
www.bloomu.edu/academic/aud/clinic.htm
Richard M. Angelo, PhD, EdD, Dir. **Kathy Miller,** Adm.
　　Focus: Rehab. **Conditions:** Primary—ADD Ap Apr Asp Au BI CP D S.
　　Therapy: Hear Lang Speech.
　　Staff: 7.
　　Summer Prgm: Day. Ther.
　　State.

This training clinic provides various diagnostic, therapeutic and counseling services for both children and adults.

THE BRADLEY CENTER
Res — Males Ages 6-17½, Females 10-17½

Pittsburgh, PA 15238. 3710 Saxonburg Blvd.
Tel: 412-767-5306. Fax: 412-767-5409.
www.thebradleycenter.org   E-mail: bcintake@thebradleycenter.org
Dan Hunt, COO. **Melvin Melnick,** MD, Med Dir. **Gary Phillips,** Adm.
　　Focus: Treatment. **Conditions:** Primary—ADD ADHD AN Anx Ap Apr As
　　　　Asp Au B BD BI Bu CD CP D Db Dc Dg Dx ED Ep HIV LD MD Mood MS
　　　　Nf OCD ODD Psy PTSD PW S SP Sz TS. Sec—MR. **IQ 50 and up.**
　　Gen Acad. Gr 1-12.
　　Therapy: Art Chemo Milieu Phys Play Recreational. **Psychotherapy:** Fam
　　　　Group Indiv Parent.
　　Enr: 181. Res Males 128. Res Females 53. **Staff:** 481 (Full 394, Part 87).
　　　　Educ 32.
　　Rates 2004: Res $257-310/day. State Aid.
　　Est 1905. Private. Nonprofit.

Bradley offers a regional network of behavioral healthcare and child welfare services in southwestern Pennsylvania, including residential treatment facilities, school-based support services and a therapeutic foster care program. In addition to the Bradley North location on Saxonburg Boulevard, the center operates two other facilities: Bradley Mt. Lebanon, 2904 Castlegate Ave., 15226 (412-563-5702) and Bradley Robinson, 5180 Campbells Run Rd., 15205.

THE BRIDGE

Res — Coed Ages 14-18; Day — Coed All Ages

Philadelphia, PA 19111. 8400 Pine Rd.
Tel: 215-342-5000. Fax: 215-342-7709.
www.phmc.org/addictionsvs/thebridge.html
   Conditions: Primary—BD ED.
   Col Prep. Gen Acad. Pre-Voc. Courses: Read Math Lang_Arts. On-Job
   Trng.
   Psychotherapy: Fam Group Indiv.
   Staff: Prof 30.
   Est 1971. Private. Nonprofit. **Spons:** Philadelphia Health Management Cor-
   poration.

BRYN MAWR COLLEGE
CHILD STUDY INSTITUTE

Clinic: All Ages. M-F 9-5, S 9-1; Eves M-Th 5-8.

Bryn Mawr, PA 19010. Roberts Rd & Wyndon Ave.
Tel: 610-527-5090. Fax: 610-527-5780.
www.brynmawr.edu/csi   E-mail: amoleski@brynmawr.edu
Leslie A. Rescorla, PhD, Dir. **Nancy DeHaven,** Intake.
   Focus: Treatment. **Conditions:** Primary—ADD ADHD Asp Au BD Dx ED
   LD OCD. Sec—MR.
   Therapy: Lang Speech. **Psychotherapy:** Fam Group Indiv.
   Staff: 50. Prof 20. Admin 3.
   Est 1930. Private. Nonprofit.

CSI is a multidisciplinary mental health agency serving individuals experiencing interpersonal and academic difficulties. Services include psychological tests and interpretations for children and young adults, psychiatric evaluation and treatment for children, a special counseling service for parents of children with emotionally disturbances and mental retardation, and counseling for parents of children with learning problems. In addition, the institute conducts workshops for schools, professionals and parents.

BRYN MAWR HOSPITAL
YOUTH & FAMILY CENTER

Clinic: Ages Birth-18. M-F 8:30-5; Eve T 5-9.

Bryn Mawr, PA 19010. Sumit Grove Ave & Old.
Tel: 610-526-3234.
www.mainlinehealth.org/bm/article_1708.asp
   Conditions: Primary—ADD BD ED.
   Therapy: Chemo Play Speech. **Psychotherapy:** Fam Group Indiv Parent.
   Est 1968. Private. Nonprofit.

CAMPHILL SPECIAL SCHOOL

Res and Day — Coed Ages 5-21

Glenmoore, PA 19343. 1784 Fairview Rd.
Tel: 610-469-9236. Fax: 610-469-9758.
www.beaverrun.org   E-mail: bvrrn@aol.com
Bernard Wolf, BA, Dir. **Richard G. Fried**, MD, Med Dir.
  Focus: Spec Ed. **Conditions:** Primary—MR PDD. Sec—ADD ADHD Ap Au
    BI CP Dx ED Ep LD ON PW S. **IQ 20-75.**
  Pre-Voc. Ungraded. Courses: Read Math Lang_Arts. Man_Arts & Shop.
  Therapy: Art Lang Movement Music Occup Phys Speech.
  Enr: 89. Res Males 48. Res Females 20. Day Males 16. Day Females 5.
    Staff: 90 (Full 80, Part 10). Prof 21. Educ 12. Admin 9.
  Rates 2004: Res $49,000/sch yr. Day $28,000/sch yr. Schol 10 ($160,000).
    State Aid.
  Summer Prgm: Res. Educ. Rec. Res Rate $4900. 4 wks.
  Est 1954. Private. Nonprofit.

Accepting profoundly retarded trainable and educable children, Camphill also provides care for those with Down syndrome, brain injury, autism, pre-psychosis and multiple handicaps. The program includes special education classes, arts, crafts, music, drama and individual therapy and exercises. Results of periodic evaluations determine whether or not a child continues in the program.

In addition to developmentally appropriate cognitive training for each child, Camphill places emphasis on social, artistic and practical skills. Teachers utilize a curriculum adapted from Waldorf education, with its focus on experiential learning through the fine and practical arts.

CARSON VALLEY SCHOOL

Res — Males Ages 9-18, Females 12-18; Day — Coed 7-18

Flourtown, PA 19031. 1419 Bethlehem Pike.
Tel: 215-233-1960. Fax: 215-233-2386.
www.carsonvalleyschool.org   E-mail: info@carsonvalleyschool.org
John Taaffe, MSW, Exec Dir. **Marie O'Donnell**, MD, Med Dir. **Dave Puchalski**,
  Adm.
  Focus: Spec Ed. **Conditions:** Primary—ADD ADHD BD ED LD Mood ODD.
    Sec—Sz.
  Gen Acad. Gr 1-12. Courses: Read Math Lang_Arts.
  Therapy: Art Dance Music Speech. **Psychotherapy:** Fam Group Indiv
    Parent.
  Enr: 190. Res Males 75. Res Females 25. Day Males 50. Day Females 40.
    Staff: 280 (Full 240, Part 40).
  Summer Prgm: Res. Educ. Rec. Ther.
  Est 1917. Private. Nonprofit.

Carson Valley provides the severely emotionally disturbed with residential treatment and therapy, as well as educational, parental and personal counseling. Neither fire setters, children with severe drug or alcohol dependencies, nor severely to profoundly retarded youths are accepted. Average length of stay in the residential treatment program is 14 months, while students may remain in the educational day program for up to 12 years.

CENTER FOR PSYCHOLOGICAL SERVICES
PSYCHOEDUCATIONAL DIVISION

Clinic: All Ages. M-Th 9-5, F 9-1.

Ardmore, PA 19003. 125 Coulter Ave.
  Nearby locations: Paoli.
Tel: 610-642-4873. Fax: 610-642-4886.
www.centerpsych.com   E-mail: ctrpsychsv@aol.com
Moss A. Jackson, PhD, Co-Dir. **Bruce V. Miller,** PhD, Co-Dir.
  Focus: Treatment. **Conditions:** Primary—ADD ADHD BD Dx ED LD OH.
  Psychotherapy: Fam Group Indiv Parent.
  Staff: 18.
  Private.

The center provides psychotherapy, counseling and psycho-educational assessments for students who have experienced educational or emotional difficulties. To evaluate the pupil's strengths and weaknesses, a team of educational, school and clinical psychologists works with children, adolescents and adults to diagnose adjustment issues, attention deficits, and other disorders, learning differences and learning disabilities. Testing addresses the following areas: intellectual, academic, emotional, memory, perceptual and perceptual-motor, learning style, and attention and concentration.

In addition to comprehensive and specific evaluations, the center conducts therapy; maintains support groups; and provides consultation services for parents and adults, school consultations, and in-service training to help teachers, administrators and physicians remain current in the field.

CENTRAL MONTGOMERY
MENTAL HEALTH/MENTAL RETARDATION CENTER

Clinic: All Ages. M F 9-5; Eves M W Th 5-9.

Norristown, PA 19401. 1100 Powell St.
Tel: 610-277-4600. Fax: 610-275-0216.
www.centralmhmr.org   E-mail: central@centralmhmr.org
Clark E. Bromberg, PhD, Dir. **Romani S. George,** MD, Med Dir.
  Conditions: Primary—BD CD ED OCD Psy Sz. Sec—Au.
  Therapy: Chemo Lang Occup Speech. **Psychotherapy:** Fam Group Indiv
    Parent.
  Staff: 88 (Full 63, Part 25).
  Est 1958. Private. Nonprofit.

Central Montgomery MH/MR Center provides outpatient evaluation and treatment for children and adults who have either emotional or personality problems. A day program for preschoolers features reading, math and language arts. The program also includes wraparound services, consisting of highly individualized mental health interventions designed to support an individual under age 21 in his or her home, school or community. In addition, the center conducts the FLECS Program, which provides counseling and seeks to further develop the child's problem-solving and coping skills; the program goal is to improve the child's ability to deal successfully with behavioral, school and family difficulties.

Fees are determined along a sliding scale.

CEREBRAL PALSY ASSOCIATION OF DELAWARE COUNTY
Day — Coed Ages 2-21

Swarthmore, PA 19081. 401 Rutgers Ave.
Tel: 610-328-5955. Fax: 610-328-0495.
www.delctycerebralpalsy.org   E-mail: mail@delctycerebralpalsy.org
William A. Benson, MA, Exec Dir.
  Focus: Spec Ed. **Conditions:** Primary—Au Bl CP IP MR ON S.
  Gen Acad. Pre-Voc. Ungraded. Courses: Read Math Lang_Arts.
  Therapy: Occup Phys Speech.
  Enr: 138. Day Males 76. Day Females 62. **Staff:** 70 (Full 55, Part 15). Prof
    25. Educ 16. Admin 11.
  Rates 2003: No Fee.
  Summer Prgm: Day. Educ. 6 wks.
  Est 1952. Private. Nonprofit.

The agency offers services to individuals with cerebral palsy, mental retardation, and other physical and neurological disorders. Programs include education, early intervention and therapy. A summer learning skills program serves children ages 5-8.

CHILD GUIDANCE RESOURCE CENTERS
Day — Coed Ages Birth-21

Media, PA 19063. 600 N Olive St.
Tel: 610-565-6000. Fax: 610-565-6008.
www.cgrc.org   E-mail: cgrc@cgrc.org
  Conditions: Primary—ED.
  Voc. Courses: Read Math Lang_Arts. Man_Arts & Shop.
  Psychotherapy: Fam Group Indiv.
  Est 1956. Private.

CHILDREN'S HOSPITAL OF PITTSBURGH
DEPARTMENT OF AUDIOLOGY
AND COMMUNICATION DISORDERS
Clinic: Ages Birth-18. M-Th 8:30-5, F 8:30-4:30.

Pittsburgh, PA 15213. 3705 5th Ave, DeSoto Wing, Fl 4A, Ste 418.

Tel: 412-692-5580. TTY: 412-692-5754. Fax: 412-692-5563.
www.chp.edu
Thomas F. Campbell, PhD, Dir.
  Focus: Rehab. Treatment. **Conditions:** Primary—Ap D S. Sec—DS MR
    OH.
  Therapy: Hear Lang Speech.
  Staff: 45 (Full 41, Part 4). Prof 40. Admin 5.
  Private.

  This department's primary concern is the assessment and treatment of communicative disorders of children within the context of the family. Audiologic services include hearing evaluations, habilitative management, and fitting of hearing aids and other assistive listening devices. Communication assessment services include comprehensive diagnostic evaluations in speech, language, voice and fluency.

THE CHILDREN'S INSTITUTE

Res — Coed Ages 1-40; Day — Coed 2-21
Clinic: All Ages. M-F 8-5; Eves M-F 5-8.

Pittsburgh, PA 15217. 6301 Northumberland St.
Tel: 412-420-2400. Fax: 412-420-2200.
www.amazingkids.org   E-mail: afa@the-institute.org
David K. Miles, MS, Pres. **William R. Bauer,** MEd, Educ Dir. **Jamie Calabrese,** MD, Med Dir.
  Focus: Rehab. **Conditions:** Primary—CP IP ON PW. Sec—Ap As Au B BD
    BI C D Dx ED Ep LD MD MR MS S SB.
  Gen Acad. Pre-Voc. Ungraded. Courses: Read Math Lang_Arts. Man_Arts
    & Shop. On-Job Trng.
  Therapy: Art Hear Hydro Lang Occup Percepual-Motor Phys Recreational
    Speech. **Psychotherapy:** Fam Group Indiv.
  Enr: 180. **Staff:** 171 (Full 163, Part 8). Prof 98. Educ 59. Admin 14.
  Rates 2004: Res $510-615/day. Day $77/day. Schol avail. State Aid.
  Est 1902. Private. Nonprofit.

  The institute is a comprehensive rehabilitation center providing coordinated programs for handicapped children and young adults. The program is structured to deal with all special needs of the disabled patient involving multidisciplinary diagnoses, service and follow-up. Educational, medical, social, psychological and prevocational services are offered. The institute offers professional clinical training in many disciplines through affiliation with more than a dozen institutions of higher learning.

CLARION UNIVERSITY
SPEECH AND HEARING CLINIC

Clinic: All Ages. M-F 8-4.

Clarion, PA 16214. Keeling Health Ctr, 840 Wood St.
Tel: 814-393-2326. Fax: 814-393-2206.

Colleen McAleer, BS, MS, PhD, Supv.
  Focus: Treatment. **Conditions:** Primary—Ap D S. Sec—ADD ADHD Au BI
    MR.
  Therapy: Hear Lang Speech. **Psychotherapy:** Group Indiv.
  Staff: 9.
  Rates 2004: No Fee.
  Est 1962. State. Nonprofit.

The Speech and Hearing Clinic at Clarion University includes a classroom, a clinic, and conference rooms and audiological suites. Diagnosis and remediation of communicative disorders are provided, as are parental and personal counseling.

CLELIAN HEIGHTS SCHOOL
FOR EXCEPTIONAL CHILDREN
Res and Day — Coed Ages 5-25

Greensburg, PA 15601. RR 9, Box 607.
Tel: 724-837-8120. Fax: 724-837-6480.
www.clelianheights.org   E-mail: clelian@aol.com
Sr. Rosemary Zaffuto, MSEd, Exec Dir. **Sr. Linda Pettinella, ASCJ,** MSEd,
  Prin.
  Focus: Spec Ed. **Conditions:** Primary—MR. Sec—Au BI CP Dc Ep Mood
    OCD ODD ON PDD. **IQ 30-70.**
  Gen Acad. Pre-Voc. Voc. Ungraded. Courses: Read Math Lang_Arts Sci
    Computers Soc_Stud Music Studio_Art Life_Skills. Man_Arts & Shop.
    Shelt_Workshop. On-Job Trng.
  Therapy: Hear Phys Speech.
  Enr: 121. Res Males 22. Res Females 26. Day Males 51. Day Females 22.
    Staff: 57 (Full 45, Part 12).
  Rates 2003: Res $13,165/sch yr. Day $11,000/sch yr. Schol avail. State Aid.
  Summer Prgm: Res & Day. Educ. Rec.
  Est 1961. Private. Nonprofit. Roman Catholic.

Clelian Heights offers individualized programs of language arts, math, science and self-help skills. Art and music courses are also available. In addition, the school conducts physical education in the areas of gymnastics, calisthenics, swimming, perceptual-motor training and team sports.

Supplementing the educational program are workshops in woodworking, grooming arts, needlecraft, greenhouse, ceramics and domestic arts. The school provides vocational training in the form of custodial work, groundskeeping, food preparation, small-parts assembly, childcare, domestic and commercial laundry, and dishwashing. Field trips and dances are an additional feature of Clelian Heights' program.

COMMUNITY CARE CONNECTIONS
Res and Day — Coed Ages 6-21

Butler, PA 16001. 114 Skyline Dr.
Tel: 724-283-3198. Fax: 724-283-5945.

www.communitycareconnect.org
   E-mail: ccc@communitycareconnect.org
Pat Brennen, BS, Exec Dir.
   Focus: Treatment. Conditions: Primary—ADHD Anx B Bl CP D DS Dx Ep
      IP LD MD Mood MR MS OCD ON PW S SB TS. Sec—As Au C ED.
   Therapy: Lang Movement Music Occup Phys Play Recreational Speech.
   Enr: 300. Staff: 144 (Full 94, Part 50). Prof 21. Admin 5.
   Summer Prgm: Day. Rec. Day Rate $13/hr. 6 wks.
   Est 1972. Private. Nonprofit.

CCC provides services and preventive care for individuals with cerebral palsy and other physically and mentally handicapping conditions. Offerings include educational, recreational, residential, in-home support and adult day services. The center's infant stimulation program is available for developmentally delayed children, with parental involvement being part of the therapy. Residential and day services and training in community skills are provided for adolescents who have been diagnosed with mental retardation. Housing is limited to Butler County residents. In addition, the Pennsylvania Elks Home Service Program sponsors nurses who assist families with educational counseling, referrals and advocacy services.

The center loans the use of specialized equipment at no charge to clients in the three-county area. The length of treatment varies according to services provided.

COMMUNITY COUNSELING CENTER
BEHAVIORAL & EMOTIONAL HEALTHCARE

Clinic: All Ages. M-S 8:30-5; Eves T-F 5-8.

Hermitage, PA 16148. 406 N Buhl Farm Dr.
Tel: 724-981-7141. Fax: 724-981-7148.
www.personal.psu.edu/faculty/w/l/wlm6/CCCBEHC.htm
   Conditions: Primary—BD ED.
   Psychotherapy: Fam Group Indiv.
   Staff: Prof 58.
   Est 1958. Private. Nonprofit.

COMMUNITY COUNTRY DAY SCHOOL

Day — Coed Ages 6-20

Erie, PA 16506. 5800 Old Zuck Rd.
Tel: 814-833-7933. Fax: 814-835-2250.
Aaron B. Collins, Exec Dir.
   Focus: Spec Ed. Conditions: Primary—BD ED. Sec—Ep LD. IQ 75 and
      up.
   Gen Acad. Gr 1-12. Courses: Read Math Lang_Arts. On-Job Trng.
   Therapy: Speech. Psychotherapy: Indiv.
   Enr: 67. Day Males 28. Day Females 39. Staff: 20 (Full 10, Part 10). Educ
      11. Admin 4.
   Summer Prgm: Day. Educ.

Est 1968. Private. Nonprofit.

Personal attention in a structured environment is featured at this school. Each student receives individual instruction in standard courses, and vocational, educational, parental and personal counseling are available. The usual duration of treatment is one year. Fees are based on a sliding scale.

CRAIG ACADEMY

Day — Coed Ages 6-21

Pittsburgh, PA 15206. 751 N Negley Ave.
Tel: 412-361-2801. Fax: 412-361-6775.
www.craigacademy.org E-mail: bmack@craigacademy.org
Roberta Mack, MEd, Prgm Dir. **Dale Hindmarsh,** MD, Med Dir.
  Focus: Spec Ed. Treatment. **Conditions:** Primary—ADD ADHD BD CD ED OCD. Sec—Dc Dg Dx Psy Sz. **IQ 72 and up.**
  Gen Acad. Pre-Voc. Ungraded. Courses: Read Math Lang_Arts Sci Soc_ Stud. Man_Arts & Shop. On-Job Trng.
  Therapy: Chemo Lang Milieu Speech. **Psychotherapy:** Fam Group Indiv Parent.
  Enr: 165. Day Males 131. Day Females 34. **Staff:** 136 (Full 133, Part 3). Educ 44. Admin 5.
  Rates 2003: Day $160/day.
  Est 1966. Private. Nonprofit.

The academy provides comprehensive, family-oriented social, educational and behavioral health services for children with severe emotional disturbances. The elementary program stresses appropriate work habits to enable the child to return to or enter community schools. A psychotherapeutic, rehabilitative secondary program for adolescents emphasizes skills relevant to employment or mainstreaming to public schools.

Vocational evaluation and counseling are available. Treatment typically lasts two to three years.

CROSSROADS SCHOOL

Day — Coed Ages 5-15

Paoli, PA 19301. 1681 N Valley Rd, PO Box 730.
Tel: 610-296-6765. Fax: 610-296-6772.
www.thecrossroadsschool.net
  E-mail: admissions@thecrossroadsschool.net
George B. Vosburgh, BA, MA, Head. **Julia Sadtler,** Adm.
  Focus: Spec Ed. **Conditions:** Primary—Dx LD. Sec—ADD ADHD. **IQ 90 and up.**
  Gen Acad. Gr K-8. Courses: Read Math Lang_Arts.
  Therapy: Lang Speech.
  Enr: 104. Day Males 66. Day Females 38. **Staff:** 42 (Full 38, Part 4). Educ 37. Admin 5.
  Rates 2003: Day $16,590-19,710/sch yr (+$750). Schol 12 ($89,000).

Summer Prgm: Day. Educ. Rec. Day Rate $1300-2100. 5 wks.
Est 1977. Private. Nonprofit.

Crossroads offers individualized programs and remedial work in the areas of reading, language arts and mathematics to bright children with learning differences. The structured program utilizes a language-centered, multisensory, individualized approach. Physical education, music and art programs are a regular part of the weekly schedule. The school's goal is to facilitate academic growth as required to return the student to a traditional school setting.

DELAWARE VALLEY FRIENDS SCHOOL
Day — Coed Ages 12-19

Paoli, PA 19301. 19 E Central Ave.
Tel: 610-640-4150. Fax: 610-296-9970.
www.dvfs.org
Katherine Schantz, Head. **Jeannie Bowman,** Adm.
   Focus: Spec Ed. **Conditions:** Primary—Dc Dg Dx LD. Sec—ADD ADHD.
      IQ 100 and up.
   Col Prep. Gr 7-12. Courses: Read Math Lang_Arts.
   Enr: 164. Day Males 108. Day Females 56. **Staff:** 56 (Full 45, Part 11).
   Rates 2003: Day $24,250/sch yr (+$600/yr). Schol 41 ($225,700).
   Summer Prgm: Day. Educ. Day Rate $2500. 5 wks.
   Est 1986. Private. Nonprofit. Religious Society of Friends.

This Quaker school utilizes multisensory teaching methods while providing college preparation for adolescents with learning disabilities. All students take five major subjects, and the majority take a foreign language. In addition, a variety of electives in art, music, cooking, technology, outdoor education and physical education is available. Academic classes have a maximum of 10 students, and the average class size is under seven. The program also includes educational, personal and college counseling.

THE DELTA SCHOOL
Day — Coed Ages 4-21

Philadelphia, PA 19154. 3515 Woodhaven Rd.
Tel: 215-632-5904. Fax: 215-632-3052.
Marlene Moore, Prin.
   Focus: Spec Ed. **Conditions:** Primary—Dx ED Ep LD MR.
   Gen Acad. Ungraded. Courses: Read Math Lang_Arts Computers Life_
      Skills. Man_Arts & Shop.
   Therapy: Lang Speech. **Psychotherapy:** Group Indiv.
   Enr: 150. Day Males 136. Day Females 14. **Staff:** 35 (Full 33, Part 2).
   Rates 2004: No Fee.
   Est 1958. Private. Nonprofit.

This school provides intensive education for individuals with learning disabilities caused by emotional problems and neurological dysfunctions. A primary focus is placed on building a foundation for learning skills. The secondary program prepares adolescents to return to a traditional academic setting. Psychological and vocational counseling is offered, and community work and work-study programs are available.

THE DEPAUL INSTITUTE

Day — Coed Ages Birth-21

Pittsburgh, PA 15206. 6202 Alder St.
Tel: 412-924-1012. TTY: 412-924-1012. Fax: 412-924-1036.
www.oraldeafed.org/schools/depaul
Dennis Barrett, PhD, Supt.
   Focus: Spec Ed. **Conditions:** Primary—D S. Sec—ADD C CP LD ON
      PTSD.
   Gen Acad. Voc. Gr PS-12. Courses: Read Math Lang_Arts.
   Therapy: Hear Lang Occup Phys Speech.
   Enr: 72. Day Males 45. Day Females 27. **Staff:** 49 (Full 46, Part 3).
   Rates 2003: No Fee.
   Summer Prgm: Day. Educ.
   Est 1908. Private. Nonprofit.

DePaul provides oral and aural education for children with severe to profound hearing loss through the use of the auditory/oral method of communication. DePaul also offers on-site and outreach services in the child's home, as well as on campus.

DEVEREUX BENETO CENTER

Res — Coed Ages 4-18; Day — Coed 6-17

Malvern, PA 19355. 655 Sugartown Rd.
Tel: 610-251-2407. Fax: 610-251-2415.
www.devereuxbeneto.org
Jim Cole, Exec Dir.
   Focus: Spec Ed. Treatment. **Conditions:** Primary—BD CD ED OCD Psy
      Sz. Sec—ADHD. **IQ 70 and up.**
   Gen Acad. Ungraded. Courses: Read Math Lang_Arts Sci Studio_Art
      Music. Man_Arts & Shop.
   Therapy: Lang Speech. **Psychotherapy:** Fam Group Indiv.
   Enr: 265.
   Est 1995. Private. Nonprofit. **Spons:** Devereux Foundation.

The center offers an array of behavioral mental health and educational services for children, adolescents and young adults. In addition to outpatient services, it incorporates the residential treatment programs available at the Brandywine and Mapleton facilities, the acute psychiatric hospital at Mapleton, the day educational facilities of The Devereux Day School and programs in Philadelphia. **See Also Page 1025**

DICKINSON MENTAL HEALTH CENTER

Clinic: All Ages. M-F 8-5; Eves T-Th 5-7.

Ridgway, PA 15853. 110 Lincoln St.
Tel: 814-776-2145. Fax: 814-776-1470.
www.dmhc.org
John W. Yates, LSW, LCSW, Dir.
   Conditions: Primary—BD ED.
   Psychotherapy: Fam Group Indiv.
   Est 1958. Private. Nonprofit.

DIVERSIFIED HUMAN SERVICES
EARLY INTERVENTION PROGRAM

Day — Coed Ages Birth-3

Monessen, PA 15062. Eastgate 8.
Tel: 724-684-9000. Fax: 724-684-5401.
www.sphs.org/dhshome.html   E-mail: earlyinter@sphs.org
Antoinette Tarquinio, MEd, Dir.
   Focus: Treatment. Conditions: Primary—Au BI MR. Sec—CP.
   Therapy: Hear Lang Occup Phys Speech Visual.
   Enr: 42. Day Males 29. Day Females 13. Staff: 6 (Full 3, Part 3).
   Rates 2003: No Fee.
   Est 1963. Private. Nonprofit. Spons: Southeastern Pennsylvania Human
      Services.

Infants and toddlers suspected of having developmental delays receive evaluation and
treatment through this program. DHS combines physical and intellectual evaluation with
a comprehensive review of the family's psychosocial history. Following the evaluation,
staff compose a prescriptive developmental program for the child that focuses upon such
areas as gross-motor skills, fine- and perceptual-motor skills, socialization, communication, emotional development and self-help skills.

Services are rendered both at the center and in the home. Several therapies are available within the context of the program, and the center makes referrals for other services
as they are required.

DR. GERTRUDE A. BARBER CENTER

Day — Coed Ages Birth-21

Erie, PA 16507. 100 Barber Pl.
Tel: 814-453-7661. TTY: 814-459-4211. Fax: 814-454-2771.
www.drbarbercenter.org   E-mail: gabcmain@drbarbercenter.org
John J. Barber, JD, Pres. Julia Karsznia, Adm.
   Focus: Spec Ed. Trng. Conditions: Primary—Asp Au BI CP D DS MD MR
      ON PDD. Sec—ADD ADHD Ap Apr B Ep LD MS S TB.
   Gen Acad. Ungraded. Courses: Read Math Lang_Arts.

Therapy: Art Hear Lang Music Occup Phys Speech.
Enr: 400. **Staff:** 200.
Est 1952. Private. Nonprofit.

The center provides early intervention, specialized and inclusive preschool programs, an approved private school, and therapies and other supports for children from birth through age 21 and their families. (Referring school districts pay tuition fees for students attending the school.) An autism center provides evaluation and treatment for children with the condition. Among the center's offerings for adults are employment training and job placement; day support focusing on recreational, vocational and socialization skills; and a retirement center. Respite care, supported living and community group homes are available, and community support for children and adults with disabilities includes in-home waiver services, behavioral health rehabilitation and specialized clinical support.

The Dr. Gertrude Educational Institute provides training and consultative services for educators, school districts and special-needs professionals.

DON GUANELLA SCHOOL

Res and Day — Males Ages 6-21

Springfield, PA 19064. 1797 S Sproul Rd.
Tel: 610-543-1418. Fax: 610-328-2136.
Dan McCardle, MEd, Admin.
  Focus: Spec Ed. **Conditions:** Primary—MR. Sec—ADD ADHD Au CD CP ED LD ON SB. **IQ 30-70.**
  Pre-Voc. Ungraded. Courses: Read Math Lang_Arts. Shelt_Workshop.
  Therapy: Hear Lang Occup Phys Speech. **Psychotherapy:** Fam Group Indiv.
  Enr: 36. **Staff:** 34 (Full 17, Part 17).
  Est 1960. Private. Nonprofit. Roman Catholic.

Educable and trainable mentally retarded boys receive care and education at this year-round school. Programming emphasizes daily living skills, and residential options consist of independent and group living arrangements. Don Guanella provides group instruction and a sheltered workshop for vocational training.

EASTER SEAL SOCIETY
OF WESTERN PENNSYLVANIA

Day — Coed Ages 2-8

Pittsburgh, PA 15222. 632 Fort Duquesne Blvd.
Tel: 412-281-7244. TTY: 412-232-1710. Fax: 412-281-9333.
www.westernpa.easterseals.com
  E-mail: toutrich@pa-ws.easter-seals.org
Lawrence P. Rager, Jr., Pres. **Karen Sweeny,** Educ Dir.
  Focus: Spec Ed. **Conditions:** Primary—Au BI CP MD ON SB. Sec—B BD S.
  Gen Acad. Ungraded.
  Therapy: Hear Lang Occup Phys Speech. **Psychotherapy:** Fam Parent.

Enr: 70. Day Males 45. Day Females 25. **Staff:** 85 (Full 79, Part 6). Prof 37.
Educ 34. Admin 14.
Rates 2003: No Fee.
Est 1961. Private. Nonprofit.

This Easter Seal school offers a community-based special education program. While education is emphasized, comprehensive therapeutic services based on each child's individual needs are an integral part of the program. Staff include teachers; physical, occupational and speech-language therapists; school nurses; and social workers. The school prepares the young child with a disability for entrance into the public school system or another appropriate school setting.

EASTER SEALS EASTERN PENNSYLVANIA

Day — Coed Ages Birth-10
Clinic: Ages Birth-21. M-F.

Allentown, PA 18104. 1503 N Cedar Crest Blvd, Ste 317.
  Nearby locations: East Stroudsburg.
Tel: 610-289-0114. Fax: 610-289-4282.
www.easterseals-easternpa.org
Nancy L. Teichman, MBA, CEO.
  Focus: Rehab. Treatment. **Conditions:** Primary—Au CP DS IP ON SB.
    Sec—Asp BI C D Ep MR S.
  Therapy: Hear Lang Occup Phys Speech. **Psychotherapy:** Fam.
  Enr: 2700. **Staff:** 88.
  Summer Prgm: Day. Rec. Ther.
  Est 1963. Private. Nonprofit.

The Society provides a spectrum of habilitative and rehabilitative services for disabled individuals from Lehigh, Monroe and Northampton counties. In addition to home- and community-based early intervention programs, the agency offers infant stimulation, a preschool, audiological services, various clinics and support groups, and a therapeutic horseback riding program.

A satellite facility is located at 109 Seven Bridge Rd., East Stroudsburg 18301.

EASTER SEALS SOUTHEASTERN PENNSYLVANIA

Day — Coed Ages 2-8
Clinic: All Ages. M-F 8:30-4:30.

Philadelphia, PA 19131. 3975 Conshohocken Ave.
Tel: 215-879-1000. Fax: 215-879-8424.
www.easterseals-sepa.org
Carl G. Webster, Exec Dir. **Janet Rubien,** MEd, Dir.
  Focus: Spec Ed. **Conditions:** Primary—Ap Asp Au BI CP IP MD MS ON
    SB. Sec—B D ED Ep LD MR S.
  Therapy: Hear Lang Occup Phys Speech. **Psychotherapy:** Fam Group
    Indiv.
  Enr: 110. **Staff:** 49.

Summer Prgm: Day. Rec. Day Rate $54/day. 5 wks.
Est 1936. Private. Nonprofit.

The Society offers school, outpatient and summer programs for disabled individuals. Therapeutic services are available on an outpatient basis to children and adults, and physically disabled children may enroll in a day preschool program. Parental and personal counseling are also available. Children may participate in the six-week camp during the summer; fees for this program are based on a sliding scale.

THE EDUCATION CENTER
AT THE WATSON INSTITUTE

Day — Coed Ages 3-21

Sewickley, PA 15143. 301 Camp Meeting Rd.
Tel: 412-741-1800. Fax: 412-741-1958.
www.dtwatson.org
Raymond B. White, CEO.
  Focus: Spec Ed. **Conditions:** Primary—Au BI CP MD OH.
  Gen Acad. Ungraded. Courses: Read Math Lang_Arts Sci Soc_Stud Music
    Studio_Art.
  Therapy: Hear Lang Occup Phys Speech. **Psychotherapy:** Indiv.
  Enr: 152.
  Est 1920. Private. Nonprofit.

Located on a 67-acre campus in suburban Pittsburgh, the center provides comprehensive, individualized educational services for handicapped children. The emphasis is on short-term enrollment, with the usual duration of treatment being two to five years.

ELWYN

Res — Coed Ages 6 and up; Day — Coed All Ages

Elwyn, PA 19063. 111 Elwyn Rd.
Tel: 610-891-2000. TTY: 215-895-5595. Fax: 610-891-2458.
www.elwyn.org   E-mail: online@elwyn.org
Sandra Cornelius, PhD, Pres. **Heidi Becker-Shore,** Adm.
  Focus: Treatment. **Conditions:** Primary—BI MR. Sec—B CP D ED Ep LD
    ON S.
  Pre-Voc. Voc. Gr K-12. Courses: Read Math Lang_Arts. Shelt_Workshop.
    On-Job Trng.
  Therapy: Hear Lang Occup Phys Recreational Speech. **Psychotherapy:**
    Group Indiv.
  Enr: 1186. Res Males 375. Res Females 259. Day Males 356. Day Females
    196.
  Est 1852. Private. Nonprofit.

Located on a 400-acre campus near Philadelphia, Elwyn provides a network of educational, rehabilitative and employment training services for individuals with mental and physical disabilities. Programs accommodate persons of all ages and include the following: infant stimulation; early intervention; a partially integrated preschool; elementary and secondary education; supported employment; vocational training and placement services; sheltered employment; residential services; programs for deaf, hearing-impaired and blind individuals; and outpatient services, including various therapies.

The facility serves persons with such disabilities as mental retardation, mental illness, neurological impairments, physical disabilities, deafness and hearing impairments, visual impairments, traumatic head injuries and multiple disabilities.

Elwyn maintains a management agreement with The Training School in Vineland, NJ. Elwyn also operates programs in California and Delaware.　　**See Also Page 1032**

ERIE HOMES
FOR CHILDREN AND ADULTS

Res — Coed All Ages

Erie, PA 16504. 226 E 27th St.
Tel: 814-454-1534. Fax: 814-452-6723.
www.ehca.org　　E-mail: info@ehca.org
Paul Carpenedo, MS, Exec Dir. **Philip M. Cacchione,** DO, Med Dir. **Mary Ellen Hughes,** Adm.
　　Focus: Treatment. **Conditions:** Primary—ADD ADHD Asp Au B BD BI CD CP D Db DS ED Ep IP Mood MR OCD ON PW SB TB. Sec—Ap Apr As C Dc Dg Dx HIV MD MS S TS.
　　Therapy: Lang Occup Phys Recreational Speech. **Psychotherapy:** Indiv.
　　Enr: 80. Res Males 41. Res Females 39. **Staff:** 342 (Full 175, Part 167). Admin 27.
　　Rates 2003: Res $267/day.
　　Est 1912. Private. Nonprofit.

These 14 homes for children and adults with severe to profound mental retardation and physical disabilities provide a variety of medically related, therapeutic and habilitative services. Each resident receives specialized services in such areas as nutrition, various therapies, psychological and medical services, aquatic therapy, therapeutic recreation and community access.

Another program of EHCA, Project First Step, assists birth families in finding the necessary community support services and education that will enable infants born medically fragile, developmentally disabled or both to live in a family environment.

FAMILY BEHAVIORAL RESOURCES

Clinic: Ages 4-18. M-F 9-5; Eves T Th 5-7:30.

Greensburg, PA 15601. 531 S Main St.
Tel: 724-850-7300. Fax: 724-850-8011.
E-mail: gbgclinic@msn.com
Suzanne Bailey, MSW, Dir. **Raj Kumar Sarma,** MD, Med Dir.
　　Focus: Treatment. **Conditions:** Primary—ADD ADHD Anx Asp Au BD CD ED Mood OCD PTSD SP Sz TS. Sec—AN Bu CP MR MS ON S.
　　Psychotherapy: Fam Indiv Parent.

Staff: 5 (Full 2, Part 3).
Private. Inc.

FBR is a nonresidential mental health treatment center that provides psychiatric, psychological, social, educational and other related services. The center also operates an autism unit.

FAMILY GUIDANCE CENTER

Clinic: All Ages. M-F 8:30-5:30; Eves M-Th 5:30-9.

Wyomissing, PA 19610. 1235 Penn Ave, Ste 206.
Tel: 610-374-4963. Fax: 610-378-5403.
www.familyguidancecenter.com
Kimberly McConell, MA,, Exec Dir. **Tom Gerhart,** Clin Dir.
  Focus: Treatment. **Conditions:** Primary—ADD ADHD Anx BD CD Dx ED LD Mood OCD ODD ON Psy PTSD SP Sz. Sec—As B C CP D Ep HIV MD MS S SB TB. **IQ 70 and up.**
  Psychotherapy: Fam Group Indiv Parent.
  Staff: 19 (Full 14, Part 5). Prof 17. Admin 2.
  Rates 2004: Sliding-Scale Rate $0-80/ses.
  Est 1902. Private. Nonprofit.

The center provides outpatient treatment that includes individual, couples, group and family therapies. In addition, FGC offers diagnosis and treatment for those who are coping with depression, fear, anxiety, stress, separation and divorce, grief and loss, abuse, and work, health and domestic difficulties. Treatment usually lasts for eight to 10 sessions.

FAMILYLINKS

Res — Coed Ages 13-18; Day — Males 3-18, Females 8-18
Clinic: Ages 3-18. M-F 9-5; Eves M-F 5-9.

Pittsburgh, PA 15206. 250 Shady Ave.
Tel: 412-661-1800. Fax: 412-661-6525.
www.familylinks.org   E-mail: info@familylinks.org
Steve Grimshaw, Exec Dir. **Mary Ann Eppinger,** MD, Med Dir. **Kevin Cronin,** Intake.
  Focus: Treatment. **Conditions:** Primary—ADD ADHD Anx BD Bu ED MR PTSD. Sec—Asp Au CD LD Mood OCD PDD SP.
  Gen Acad. Gr PS-4. Courses: Read Math Lang_Arts.
  Therapy: Chemo Speech. **Psychotherapy:** Fam Group Indiv.
  Enr: 40. Day Males 31. Day Females 9. **Staff:** 403. Prof 300. Educ 5. Admin 8.
  Est 2001. Private. Nonprofit.

Treatment plans, which address the specific needs of each child and family, generally include one or more elements: individual or group therapy, parental counseling, family therapy, play therapy, school consultation and planning, therapeutic preschool, educational remediation or medication. Children and adolescents come to FamilyLinks from southern Allegheny County and, in most instances, have been referred by their local community mental health centers. Fees are determined along a sliding scale.

FRIENDSHIP HOUSE CHILDREN'S CENTER

Res — Coed Ages 6-18; Day — Coed 3-15

Scranton, PA 18505. 1509 Maple St.
Tel: 570-342-8305. Fax: 570-344-1172.
www.friendshiphousepa.org
Robert H. Angeloni, MSW, Pres.
  Conditions: Primary—ED. Sec—BD.
  Gen Acad. Pre-Voc. Gr K-12. Courses: Read Math Lang_Arts. Man_Arts & Shop. On-Job Trng.
  Therapy: Art Music Recreational Speech.
  Est 1871. Private. Nonprofit.

GEORGE JUNIOR REPUBLIC

Res — Males Ages 9-18

Grove City, PA 16127. 233 George Junior Rd, PO Box 1058.
Tel: 724-458-9330. Fax: 724-458-0389.
www.gjrinpa.org   E-mail: lcummings@gjrinpa.org
Richard L. Losasso, MA, MSW, CEO. **Andria Donnatucci,** Adm.
  Focus: Spec Ed. Rehab. Treatment. **Conditions:** Primary—ADD ADHD As BD CD Dx ED SP. Sec—TS. **IQ 70 and up.**
  Col Prep. Gen Acad. Voc. Gr 5-12. Courses: Read Math Lang_Arts. Man_ Arts & Shop. Shelt_Workshop. On-Job Trng.
  Therapy: Art Recreational. **Psychotherapy:** Fam Group Indiv Parent.
  Enr: 490. Res Males 490. **Staff:** 675 (Full 500, Part 175). Prof 151. Educ 80. Admin 26.
  Rates 2004: Res $121-201/day.
  Private. Nonprofit.

This residential treatment facility for delinquent and dependent boys employs a five-step motivational system that rewards positive behavior and penalizes negative conduct. A general residential program, a 90-day intensive treatment program, a special-needs program, drug and alcohol services, diagnostic evaluation, community-based group homes and preventative aftercare are among George Junior's offerings.

GLADE RUN LUTHERAN SERVICES

Res — Coed Ages 6-21

Zelienople, PA 16063. Beaver Rd, PO Box 70.
Tel: 724-452-4453. Fax: 724-452-6576.

www.gladerun.org   E-mail: glade@stargate.net
Charles T. Lockwood, MDiv, Exec Dir. **Victor Adebimpe,** MD, Med Dir. **Laura Carlantonio,** Adm.
　Focus: Spec Ed. Trng. Treatment. **Conditions:** Primary—ADD ADHD AN Anx BD Bu CD ED Mood OCD ODD Psy Sz. Sec—MR.
　Gen Acad. Gr 1-12. Courses: Read Math Lang_Arts.
　Psychotherapy: Fam Group Indiv Parent.
　Staff: 477 (Full 318, Part 159). Educ 56. Admin 69.
　Summer Prgm: Day. Ther.
　Est 1854. Private. Nonprofit. Lutheran.

Located in the hills of western Pennsylvania, Glade Run operates a psychiatric residential treatment program (RTP), single-gender group homes and an emergency shelter for children who have been temporarily removed from their homes.

Designed for boys and girls ages 6-18 who are able to live safely outside the structure of an inpatient hospital setting, the RTP combines daily therapeutic intervention with specialized educational services. Group homes provide a more restrictive environment in which children meet independently with mental health workers. The emergency shelter seeks to identify emotional and psychological needs, while also offering course work in the core academic subjects.

A supervised independent living program for adolescents ages 16-21 teaches basic living skills and offers training workshops.

GREEN TREE SCHOOL

Day — Coed Ages 3-21

Philadelphia, PA 19144. 146 W Walnut Ln, PO Box 25639.
Tel: 215-843-4528. Fax: 215-843-2688.
www.greentreeschool.org   E-mail: admin@greentreeschool.org
Herman Axelrod, BS, MEd, PhD, Dir.
　Focus: Spec Ed. **Conditions:** Primary—Au ED. Sec—BI.
　Gen Acad. Pre-Voc. Gr K-12. Courses: Read Math Lang_Arts. Man_Arts & Shop.
　Therapy: Lang Movement Speech. **Psychotherapy:** Fam Group Indiv.
　Enr: 150. **Staff:** 60.
　Rates 2004: No Fee.
　Summer Prgm: Day. Educ. 6 wks.
　Est 1957. Private. Nonprofit.

Green Tree provides a therapeutic and academic program for children and youths who have been diagnosed with serious emotional disturbances, neurological impairments or both. Many have displayed several behavioral problems that have prevented them from succeeding in traditional settings. In addition to receiving instruction in basic academics, students participate in movement therapy and physical education.

Twice a year, staff members comprehensively evaluate a student's progress and restructure the program accordingly. Parental participation is encouraged at all levels. The usual duration of treatment at Green Tree is three to five years, with pupils going on to a regular public school, a more advanced special school, a vocational facility or a college.

HAMBURG CENTER

Res — Coed Ages 18-84

Hamburg, PA 19526. PO Box 1000.
Tel: 610-562-6001. Fax: 610-562-6201.
www.racc.edu/socialservice/h020.aspx
Jay Willis, Dir.
   Conditions: Primary—MR. **IQ 5-70.**
   Gen Acad. Ungraded.
   Therapy: Chemo Hear Lang Occup Phys Speech. **Psychotherapy:** Indiv.
   Est 1960. State. Nonprofit.

HELPING HANDS SOCIETY

Day — Coed Ages Birth-6
Clinic: Ages 6-12. M-F 9-4:30; Eves T Th 6-9.

Hazleton, PA 18201. 301 Rocky Rd.
Tel: 570-455-4958. Fax: 570-455-4959.
www.helpinghandssociety.org   E-mail: helpinghands@ddisp.net
Mary Beth Koch, MA, Prgm Dir.
   Focus: Spec Ed. **Conditions:** Primary—ADD ADHD Ap Asp Au BI CP Dx
   IP LD MD S SB. Sec—DS MR MS OH.
   Therapy: Hear Lang Occup Percepual-Motor Phys Recreational Speech.
   Psychotherapy: Group.
   Enr: 200. Day Males 150. Day Females 50. **Staff:** 20 (Full 6, Part 14).
   Est 1927. Private. Nonprofit.

Helping Hands provides therapy for those with speech or hearing impairments. The program also includes infant stimulation and a daily class for preschoolers, as well as an academic helper program for school-age children who are experiencing difficulties in traditional subjects, particularly reading.

HILL TOP PREPARATORY SCHOOL

Day — Coed Ages 11-21

Rosemont, PA 19010. 737 S Ithan Ave.
Tel: 610-527-3230. Fax: 610-527-7683.
www.hilltopprep.org   E-mail: admissions@hilltopprep.org
Leslie H. McLeen, EdD, Head. **Lynne F. Little,** Adm.
   Focus: Spec Ed. **Conditions:** Primary—ADD ADHD Dx LD. **IQ 90 and up.**
   Col Prep. Gr 6-12. Courses: Read Math Lang_Arts Sci Hist Studio_Art.
   Man_Arts & Shop.
   Psychotherapy: Group Indiv.
   Enr: 90. Day Males 66. Day Females 24. **Staff:** 42 (Full 38, Part 4).
   Rates 2003: Day $26,975/sch yr. Schol avail.
   Summer Prgm: Day. Educ. Rec. Day Rate $1650. 4 wks.

Est 1971. Private. Nonprofit.

For students of average and above-average intelligence who have learning disabilities, attentional disorders or both, this program offers a college preparatory curriculum leading to a high school diploma. A transitional college program allows students to take college courses at local colleges while continuing academic work in areas of weakness at Hill Top and receiving therapeutic support.

THE HILLSIDE SCHOOL
Day — Coed Ages 5-13

Macungie, PA 18062. 2697 Brookside Rd.
Tel: 610-967-5449. Fax: 610-965-7683.
www.hillsideschool.org   E-mail: office@hillsideschool.org
Linda L. Whitney, MA, Dir.
   Focus: Spec Ed. **Conditions:** Primary—Dc Dg Dx LD. Sec—ADD ADHD ED. **IQ 90 and up.**
   Gen Acad. Gr K-6. Courses: Read Math Lang_Arts.
   Therapy: Lang Speech. **Psychotherapy:** Parent.
   Enr: 126. **Staff:** 31 (Full 28, Part 3). Prof 28. Admin 2.
   Rates 2003: Day $12,500/sch yr. Schol 50 ($360,000).
   Summer Prgm: Day. Educ. Rec.
   Est 1983. Private. Nonprofit.

The Hillside School offers a carefully structured educational program for learning-disabled children of average to above-average intelligence. The student is placed in an individualized program of remedial, developmental and accelerated approaches. The child's social and emotional development is also emphasized. Parents frequently participate in conferences with staff members.

HMS SCHOOL FOR CHILDREN
WITH CEREBRAL PALSY
Res and Day — Coed Ages 2-21

Philadelphia, PA 19104. 4400 Baltimore Ave.
Tel: 215-222-2566. Fax: 215-222-1889.
www.hmsschool.org   E-mail: admin@hmsschool.org
Diane L. Gallagher, MEd, PhD, Dir. **Steven Bachrach,** MD, Med Dir.
   Focus: Spec Ed. **Conditions:** Primary—Bl CP OH. Sec—Ap B D Ep LD MR S.
   Gen Acad. Pre-Voc. Ungraded. Courses: Read Math Lang_Arts Sci Computers Soc_Stud Health Life_Skills.
   Therapy: Dance Hear Lang Movement Music Occup Phys Recreational Speech.
   Enr: 54. Res Males 13. Res Females 7. Day Males 18. Day Females 16.
   Staff: 95 (Full 62, Part 33).
   Summer Prgm: Res & Day. Educ. Rec. Ther. 3-6 wks.
   Est 1882. Private. Nonprofit.

Originally named Home of the Merciful Savior for Crippled Children, HMS School is an educational and habilitation center for children with severe disabilities stemming from cerebral palsy or traumatic brain injury. Emphasis is on assistive technology and computer-assisted instruction, the development of communication systems for non-speaking children, and special education and intensive therapy. Nursing services and medical consultations are also available.

Parents incur no financial charges when state and local education agencies agree to this approved private school placement. The average length of stay is four to six school years. **See Also Page 1029**

HOPE ENTERPRISES

Res — Coed All Ages; Day — Coed 3-All

Williamsport, PA 17703. PO Box 1837.
Tel: 570-326-3745. Fax: 570-326-1258.
www.heionline.org   E-mail: info@heionline.org
James F. Campbell, Pres.
   Conditions: Primary—MR. **IQ** 20-70.
   Pre-Voc. Voc. Ungraded. Man_Arts & Shop. Shelt_Workshop. On-Job Trng.
   Therapy: Hear Occup Phys Speech. **Psychotherapy:** Indiv.
   Est 1952. Private. Nonprofit.

HUMAN SERVICES CENTER

Clinic: All Ages. M-F 8-4; Eves M-Th 4-9.

New Castle, PA 16101. 130 W North St.
Tel: 724-658-3578. Fax: 724-654-6627.
www.humanservicescenter.net
Dennis W. Nebel, PsyD, Exec Dir. **Shoukry Matta,** MD, Med Dir.
   Conditions: Primary—BD ED MR.
   Psychotherapy: Fam Group Indiv.
   Staff: Prof 52.
   Est 1963. Private. Nonprofit.

INSTITUTES FOR THE ACHIEVEMENT
OF HUMAN POTENTIAL

Clinic: Ages Birth-20. M-F 8:30-5.

Wyndmoor, PA 19038. 8801 Stenton Ave.
Tel: 215-233-2050. Fax: 215-233-1530.
www.iahp.org   E-mail: institutes@iahp.org
Janet Doman, BS, Dir. **Neil Harvey,** MA, MSEd, PhD, Dean. **Coralee Thompson,** MD, Med Dir. **Harriet Pinsker,** Adm.
   Focus: Rehab. **Conditions:** Primary—ADD ADHD Ap Au B Bl CP D DS Dx

Ep LD MR ON S. Sec—BD CD ED OCD Psy Sz.
Therapy: Hear Lang Occup Phys Speech. **Psychotherapy:** Fam Parent.
Staff: 115. (Full 115). Prof 62. Educ 9. Admin 40.
Est 1955. Private. Nonprofit.

The institutes provide services for brain-injured children and their families with the goal of physical, intellectual and social growth resulting in normality. The staff develops and teaches treatment techniques to parents who then use these procedures to promote the child's development at home. Individuals must have mild, moderate, severe or profound brain injury to receive care at the facility.

Other locations include the European Institute in Fauglia, Italy, as well as sister organizations in Tokyo, Japan, and Rio de Janeiro and Barbacena, Brazil.

IRENE STACY COMMUNITY MENTAL HEALTH CENTER

Day — Coed Ages 6-18
Clinic: All Ages. M-Th 9-6, F 9-3; Eves M Th 6-9.

Butler, PA 16001. 112 Hillvue Dr.
Tel: 724-287-0791. Fax: 724-287-2730.
www.drddesigns.com/bmha
Roger Kelly, Dir.
  Focus: Treatment. **Conditions:** Primary—BD BI ED LD MR.
  Gen Acad. Gr 1-12. Courses: Read Math Lang_Arts.
  Therapy: Chemo Hear Lang Speech. **Psychotherapy:** Fam Group Indiv.
  Staff: Prof 6.
  Est 1959. Private. Nonprofit. **Spons:** Butler County Mental Health Association.

THE JANUS SCHOOL

Day — Coed Ages 6-19

Mount Joy, PA 17552. 205 Lefever Rd.
Tel: 717-653-0025. Fax: 717-653-0696.
www.janus.pvt.k12.pa.us   E-mail: sjasin@janus.pvt.k12.pa.us
Douglas Atkins, MEd, Dir. **Staci Jasin,** Adm.
  Focus: Spec Ed. **Conditions:** Primary—ADD ADHD Dx LD.
  Gen Acad. Gr 1-12. Courses: Read Math Lang_Arts Sci Soc_Stud Study_ Skills.
  Enr: 80. **Staff:** 27 (Full 24, Part 3).
  Est 1991. Private. Nonprofit.

Janus offers an intensive remedial academic program for students diagnosed with a specific learning disability. Pupils typically take part in the program for an average of three years before transitioning back into their local school systems.

JOHN PAUL II CENTER FOR SPECIAL LEARNING

Day — Coed Ages 3-21

Shillington, PA 19607. 1092 Welsh Rd.
Tel: 610-777-0605. Fax: 610-777-0682.
www.jp2center.org   E-mail: jp2center@comcast.net
Mary A. Adams, MEd, Prin.
  Focus: Spec Ed. **Conditions:** Primary—As Asp Au BI CP DS Ep IP MD
    MR MS Nf ON PDD PW SB. **IQ 0-79.**
  Pre-Voc. Ungraded. Courses: Read Math Lang_Arts. On-Job Trng.
  Therapy: Lang Music Occup Speech.
  Enr: 30. Day Males 20. Day Females 10. **Staff:** 15 (Full 11, Part 4).
  Rates 2004: Day $2700/sch yr. Schol 15 ($12,000).
  Summer Prgm: Day. Rec. Day Rate $250/wk. 6 wks.
  Est 1982. Private. Nonprofit. Roman Catholic. **Spons:** Catholic Social
    Agency.

The center provides an educational and social program for children and young adults with mental retardation and developmental disabilities. Students age 14 and up may attend a local technical school on a half-day basis. The center conducts a summer program, Camp Discovery, that places emphasis on the development of mental, physical and social skills. A Christian perspective is present in all programming.

KEYSTONE COMMUNITY RESOURCES

Res and Day — Coed Ages 9-18

Scranton, PA 18503. 406 N Washington Ave.
Tel: 570-207-5090. Fax: 570-342-3461.
www.keycommres.org   E-mail: info@keycommres.com
Robert J. Fleese, MSW, Pres. **Ed Cerny,** MA, Clin Dir. **Lisa Cunningham,**
    Adm.
  Focus: Trng. Treatment. **Conditions:** Primary—MR PW. Sec—ADD ADHD
    BD ED LD OH. **IQ 20-75.**
  Voc. Man_Arts & Shop. Shelt_Workshop. On-Job Trng.
  Therapy: Chemo Hear Lang Occup Phys Recreational Speech. **Psycho-
    therapy:** Fam Group Indiv.
  Summer Prgm: Res & Day. Rec.
  Est 1964. Private. Inc.

Keystone serves as the central facility for a network of group homes and a residence/camp in the Pocono Mountains. The facilities, where emphasis is on integrating children and adults into the vocational and social community, treat individuals with all levels of mental retardation and mild physical handicaps. Medical evaluations, group therapy, education, vocational training and placement are integral elements of the program.

Keystone also utilizes public school special education classes and private special education programs. Persons with Prader-Willi syndrome receive specialized residential services. Non-Pennsylvania residents must pay a separate education fee.

Keystone maintains a branch facility at 154 Front St., South Plainfield, NJ 07080.

See Also Page 1038

KIDSPEACE

Res — Coed Ages 6-18; Day — Coed 10-18
Clinic: All Ages. M-S 9-5; Eves M-S 5-9.

Orefield, PA 18069. 5300 KidsPeace Dr.
Nearby locations: Allentown; Bethlehem; Easton; Temple.
Tel: 610-799-8000. TTY: 610-799-8849. Fax: 610-799-8401.
www.kidspeace.org   E-mail: admissions@kidspeace.org
C. T. O'Donnell, MS, Exec Dir. **Lorrie Henderson,** PhD, COO. **Herb Mendel,** MD, Med Dir. **Richard Snyder,** Adm.
   Focus: Spec Ed. Treatment. **Conditions:** Primary—ADD ADHD Anx Asp BD CD Dx ED LD Mood OCD ODD PDD Psy PTSD SP Sz. Sec—MR. **IQ** 70-120.
   Col Prep. Gen Acad. Pre-Voc. Gr 1-12. Courses: Read Math Lang_Arts Sci Soc_Stud Studio_Art Music.
   Therapy: Chemo Hear Lang Milieu Occup Phys Play Recreational Speech. **Psychotherapy:** Fam Group Indiv.
   Enr: 530. Res Males 350. Res Females 180. **Staff:** 2000 (Full 1800, Part 200). Prof 160. Educ 71. Admin 9.
   Rates 2004: Res $220-424/day. Day $130-171/day.
   Est 1882. Private. Nonprofit.

KidsPeace offers a fully integrated continuum of care for socially, emotionally and behaviorally disturbed children and their families. Programs include inpatient psychiatric care, specialized residential services, group homes, intensive treatment family care, diagnostic and shelter care, in-home counseling, day treatment and outpatient mental health clinics. Licensed private schools provide regular and special-education programs.

LANCASTER GENERAL HOSPITAL
LANCASTER CLEFT PALATE CLINIC

Clinic: All Ages. M-F 8-4:30.

Lancaster, PA 17602. 223 N Lime St.
Tel: 717-394-3793. Fax: 717-396-7409.
www.lancastergeneral.org/content/lancastercleftpalateclinic.asp
Julie Fischel, MSEd, Dir.
   Conditions: Primary—S.
   Therapy: Hear Lang Speech.
   Staff: Prof 20.
   Est 1938. Private. Nonprofit.

LANCASTER PREPARATORY SCHOOL

Day — Coed Ages 5-13

Columbia, PA 17512. 3950 Columbia Ave.

Tel: 717-285-9555. Fax: 717-285-9455.
www.lancasterprep.org   E-mail: ksmoker.lps@starband.net
Karen Smoker, MEd, Dir.
   Focus: Spec Ed. **Conditions:** Primary—ADD ADHD Dg Dx LD. Sec—OCD.
   IQ 100 and up.
   Gen Acad. Gr K-8. Courses: Read Math Lang_Arts Sci Soc_Stud.
   Therapy: Lang Speech.
   Enr: 25. **Staff:** 10 (Full 6, Part 4).
   Rates 2003: Day $6,185/sch yr (+$100). $42 (Tutoring)/ses. Schol avail.
   Private. Nonprofit.

Lancaster serves children of average to above-average intelligence with learning disabilities. The school maintains a small class size and offers an individualized educational program for each student. Students must have no emotional difficulties that would interfere with learning, and must be able to function in small groups. LPS strongly encourages parental participation in classroom activities, school administration and extracurricular events.

LAUGHLIN CHILDREN'S CENTER

Clinic: Ages 1½-18. M-S 8:45-4:45; Eves M-Th 4:45-8:30.

Sewickley, PA 15143. 424 Frederick St.
Tel: 412-741-4087. Fax: 412-741-6808.
www.laughlincenter.org
Karen T. Nickell, Exec Dir. **Judy Allison,** Intake.
   Focus: Treatment. **Conditions:** Primary—ED. Sec—BD BI D Dx LD S.
   Therapy: Hear Lang Speech. **Psychotherapy:** Fam Indiv Parent.
   Staff: 42 (Full 15, Part 27).
   Summer Prgm: Day. Rec. Day Rate $175. 1 wk.
   Est 1956. Private. Nonprofit.

Laughlin provides diagnosis and remediation for children with mild emotional problems, in addition to speech, hearing and developmental delays. Preschool screening and counseling for both children and their families are provided. These services supplement the work of schools, they do not replace them. The center assesses fees along a sliding scale.

LEHIGH UNIVERSITY
CENTENNIAL SCHOOL

Day — Coed Ages 6-21

Bethlehem, PA 18017. 2196 Ave C, LVIP I.
Tel: 610-266-6500. Fax: 610-266-7126.
www.lehigh.edu/~insch
Michael George, EdD, Dir.
   Focus: Spec Ed. **Conditions:** Primary—ED. Sec—Au BI. **IQ 50 and up.**
   Gen Acad. Pre-Voc. Ungraded. Courses: Read Math Lang_Arts Adaptive_
   Phys_Ed. Man_Arts & Shop. On-Job Trng.

Therapy: Lang Speech.
Enr: 100. Day Males 90. Day Females 10. **Staff:** 51.
Rates 2003: Day $29,800/sch yr. State Aid.
Est 1962. Private. Nonprofit.

Centennial School offers an educational program to socially and emotionally disturbed children who cannot be served by their local districts. The program includes vocational, educational and partial hospitalization services. Offerings include a physical education program, speech therapy and computer instruction. The usual duration of treatment is two years.

LENAPE VALLEY FOUNDATION
Clinic: All Ages. M-F 8:30-5:30; Eves M-Th 5:30-9.

Doylestown, PA 18901. 500 N West St.
  Nearby locations: Warrington.
Tel: 215-345-5300. Fax: 215-345-5347.
www.buckscounty.org/departments/mental_health
Alan Hartl, Pres.
  Focus: Treatment. **Conditions:** Primary—BD ED MR.
  Therapy: Chemo Speech. **Psychotherapy:** Fam Group Indiv.
County.

LIFE'S WORK OF WESTERN PENNSYLVANIA
Day — Coed Ages 16 and up
Clinic: All Ages. M-F 8-4:30.

Pittsburgh, PA 15219. 1323 Forbes Ave.
Tel: 412-471-2600. Fax: 412-471-3894.
www.lifesworkwpa.org
Everett McElveen, Pres.
  Conditions: Primary—MR.
  Voc. Shelt_Workshop. On-Job Trng.
  Therapy: Speech. **Psychotherapy:** Group Indiv.
  Est 1927. Private. Nonprofit.

LOURDESMONT
GOOD SHEPHERD YOUTH AND FAMILY SERVICES
Res — Females Ages 12-17; Day — Coed 12-17

Clarks Summit, PA 18411. 537 Venard Rd.
Tel: 570-587-4741. Fax: 570-587-5255.
www.lourdesmont.com
John A. Antognoli, EdD, Exec Dir. Judy Neri, MS, COO. Varsha Pandya, MD,

Med Dir. **Mary Lesho,** Adm.
Focus: Treatment. **Conditions:** Primary—BD CD ED. Sec—ADD ADHD As
  C Dx Ep LD OCD ON Psy. **IQ 80-130.**
Gen Acad. Pre-Voc. Gr 7-12. Courses: Read Math Lang_Arts. Man_Arts &
  Shop. On-Job Trng.
Therapy: Chemo Speech. **Psychotherapy:** Fam Group Indiv Parent.
Enr: 126. Res Females 33. Day Males 40. Day Females 53. **Staff:** 89.
Rates 2003: Res $140-193/day. Day $120/day.
Est 1889. Private. Nonprofit. Roman Catholic.

Lourdesmont provides diagnostic assessment on a residential (girls only) and day
(coeducational) basis for emotionally disturbed, adjudicated delinquent and dependent
adolescents. An on-campus school offers remediation in academic courses as well as
electives in business, art and home management. Vocational guidance and testing for
further education, training and job placement are administered. Drug and alcohol abuse
prevention/intervention and an emergency shelter program are available. Counseling,
psychiatric and casework services are provided for students and their families.

A full recreation and activities program is conducted, and summer services are available. Admission is restricted to eastern Pennsylvania counties. Psychotic, mentally
retarded and physically disabled adolescents are not accepted. The average duration of
treatment is six to nine months.

LYCOMING COUNTY CRIPPLED CHILDREN'S SOCIETY
CHILDREN'S DEVELOPMENT CENTER

Day — Coed Ages 3-6
Clinic: Ages Birth-21. F 8-12.

Williamsport, PA 17701. 625 W Edwin St.
Tel: 570-326-0565. Fax: 570-326-7582.
Anthony Perrotta, BS, MPA, Exec Dir.
  Focus: Rehab. Treatment. **Conditions:** Primary—CP IP ON S SB. Sec—D
  LD MR.
  Therapy: Hear Lang Occup Phys Speech.
  Enr: 23. Day Males 16. Day Females 7. **Staff:** 30 (Full 20, Part 10).
  Est 1923. Private. Nonprofit.

This agency provides diagnosis, treatment and rehabilitation services for neurologically and orthopedically handicapped children. A preschool and kindergarten program is
available for moderately to severely speech-delayed children and children with developmental delays. Parental and individual counseling sessions are available, as is a special
preventative nutrition program for pregnant women and nursing mothers and their children. The usual duration of treatment is one year.

A satellite office for the nutrition program operates at 755 Bellefonte Ave., Lock
Haven 17745.

MAIN LINE ACADEMY

Day — Coed Ages 5-21

Bala Cynwyd, PA 19004. 124 Bryn Mawr Ave.
Tel: 610-617-9121. Fax: 610-660-8416.
E-mail: thelabsch@aol.com
June Brown, MA, EdD, Exec Dir.
   Focus: Spec Ed. **Conditions:** Primary—ADD ADHD Dc Dg Dx LD MR.
   Gen Acad. Ungraded. Courses: Read Math Lang_Arts.
   Staff: Prof 11.
   Private.

MARGARET J. KAY & ASSOCIATES

Clinic: All Ages. M-F 8-5.

Lancaster, PA 17601. 2818 Lititz Pike.
Tel: 717-569-6223. Fax: 717-560-9931.
www.margaretkay.com   E-mail: mjk@margaretkay.com
Margaret J. Kay, EdD, Dir. **Kathy Ference,** Adm.
   Focus: Spec Ed. **Conditions:** Primary—ADD ADHD Ap Apr Asp Au Bl CP
   Dc Dg DS Dx Ep LD MD PDD S SB TS. Sec—AN Anx As BD Bu CD ED
   HIV Mood MR MS Nf OCD ON Psy PTSD PW SP Sz TB.
   Gen Acad. Gr K-Col. Courses: Read Math Lang_Arts.
   Therapy: Speech. **Psychotherapy:** Fam Group Indiv Parent.
   Staff: 5.
   Rates 2003: Clinic $150/hr.
   Est 1980. Private.

The facility provides educational, psychological, neuropsychological and career/vocational evaluations. Learning-disabled children and adults receive individualized remedial instruction in a variety of disciplines. Other services offered include Orton-Gillingham tutoring, Wilson Reading System and cognitive therapy for individuals with head injuries.

MARTHA LLOYD COMMUNITY SERVICES

Res and Day — Coed Ages 15 and up

Troy, PA 16947. 190 W Main St.
Tel: 570-297-2185. Fax: 570-297-1019.
www.marthalloyd.org   E-mail: information@marthalloyd.org
Richard MacIntire, CEO. **Todd Boyles,** Adm.
   Focus: Trng. **Conditions:** Primary—Bl LD MR ON PW. Sec—ADD ADHD
   Ap As Asp Au B BD C CP D Db Dx ED Ep IP MD Mood MS OCD ODD
   Psy S SB Sz. **IQ 0-70.**
   Voc. Man_Arts & Shop. Shelt_Workshop.
   Therapy: Hear Lang Music Occup Percepual-Motor Phys Speech. **Psycho-**

therapy: Indiv.
Enr: 265. Res Females 120. Day Males 10. Day Females 135. **Staff:** 300 (Full 200, Part 100). Admin 30.
Rates 2004: Res $26,304/yr. Day $11,367/yr.
Est 1928. Private. Nonprofit.

Martha Lloyd provides choices and lifestyles for individuals 15 and older with mental retardation and developmental disabilities. A variety of integrated services are offered, including residential programs, adult day care, respite care, vocational work center/work experience, school to work, sensory integration, and recreational opportunities. The campus lies on a 25-acre tract in rural north-central Pennsylvania.

See Also Page 1043

MCGUIRE MEMORIAL

Res and Day — Coed Ages 3 and up

New Brighton, PA 15066. 2119 Mercer Rd.
Tel: 724-843-3400. Fax: 724-847-2004.
www.mcguirememorial.org   E-mail: mcgm@mcguirememorial.org
Sr. Mary Thaddeus Markelewicz, Exec Dir. **Pat Sciaretta,** Adm.
    Focus: Spec Ed. Trng. Treatment. **Conditions:** Primary—MR. Sec—As Asp Au B BD BI C CP D DS Ep IP MD Mood Nf ON PDD S SB.
    Pre-Voc. Ungraded.
    Therapy: Hear Lang Occup Phys Speech. **Psychotherapy:** Indiv.
    Enr: 170. Res Males 95. Res Females 75. **Staff:** 395. Prof 131. Educ 30. Admin 3.
    Rates 2003: No Fee.
    Est 1963. Private. Nonprofit.

The facility provides intermediate-level medical and educational care for children and adults with severe mental and physical special needs. Clients receive training and education services that address their medically frail conditions and help them develop to potential. McGuire offers lifetime care and is home to many clients due to the severity of their limitations. Respite services run from preschool age to adult, up to a maximum of 31 calendar days a year.

THE MELMARK HOME

Res and Day — Coed Ages 4 and up

Berwyn, PA 19312. 2600 Wayland Rd.
Tel: 610-353-1726. Fax: 610-353-4956.
www.melmark.org   E-mail: admissions@melmark.org
Joanne Gillis-Donovan, PhD, RN, Pres. **Peter J. McGuiness,** Adm.
    Focus: Spec Ed. Rehab. **Conditions:** Primary—Asp DS MR. Sec—Ap Au B BI C CP D Ep ON PDD S SB. **IQ 2-60.**
    Pre-Voc. Voc. Ungraded. Courses: Read Math Lang_Arts Music. Man_Arts & Shop. Shelt_Workshop. On-Job Trng. Horticulture.
    Therapy: Art Hear Hydro Lang Milieu Movement Music Occup Phys Play

Recreational Speech.
Enr: 250. **Staff:** 450.
Est 1966. Private. Nonprofit.

Melmark provides educational, residential and therapeutic services for children and adults with a diagnosis of autism spectrum disorders, acquired brain injury, mental retardation and other neurological impairments.

MERCY HOSPITAL
SPEECH, LANGUAGE PATHOLOGY DEPARTMENT

Clinic: All Ages. M-F 8:30-5.

Pittsburgh, PA 15219. 1400 Locust St.
Tel: 412-232-8111. Fax: 412-232-7773.
www.mercylink.org
  Conditions: Primary—D Dx LD S.
  Therapy: Hear Lang Speech. **Psychotherapy:** Group.
  Private.

MERCY SPECIAL LEARNING CENTER

Day — Coed Ages 1½-21

Allentown, PA 18103. 830 S Woodward St.
Tel: 610-797-8242. Fax: 610-797-9092.
E-mail: altlmslc@ptd.net
Bridget L. Muehlenkamp, MEd, Prin. **Sue Kustafik,** Adm.
  Focus: Spec Ed. Treatment. **Conditions:** Primary—DS MR. Sec—ADD
    ADHD Ap As Asp Au BD CD CP Dg ED Ep OCD PDD PTSD S.
  Pre-Voc. Voc. Ungraded. Courses: Read Math Lang_Arts Life_Skills. On-
    Job Trng.
  Therapy: Music Occup Speech.
  Enr: 99. Day Males 62. Day Females 37. **Staff:** 23. Educ 9. Admin 3.
  Rates 2003: Day $2300-3650/sch yr. Schol ($10,000).
  Est 1954. Private. Nonprofit. Roman Catholic. **Spons:** Catholic Social
    Agency.

Serving children with mental retardation and developmental disabilities from Lehigh, Northampton, Bucks and Monroe counties, Mercy Special Learning Center conducts individualized education programs and a range of therapeutic services. Speech, occupational and physical therapy services are available, as are self-help skills and vocational enrichment opportunities.

Boys and girls gather daily for religious teachings and prayer. A fine arts program features choir and dance classes and performances.

MILL CREEK SCHOOL

Day — Coed Ages 12-20

Philadelphia, PA 19139. 111 N 49th St.
Tel: 215-471-2169.
www.pennhealth.com/pahosp/psychiatry/mill_creek.html
  Conditions: Primary—ED. Sec—BD. **IQ 90 and up.**
  Col Prep. Gen Acad. Pre-Voc. Gr 7-12. Courses: Read Math Lang_Arts. Man_Arts & Shop.
  Est 1971. Private. Nonprofit. **Spons:** University of Pennsylvania Health System.

NORTHWESTERN HUMAN SERVICES OF PHILADELPHIA

Day — Coed Ages Birth-5

Philadelphia, PA 19119. 27 E Mount Airy Ave.
  Nearby locations: 30 locations in PA, VA & DC.
Tel: 215-438-3233. Fax: 215-843-3257.
www.nhsonline.org   E-mail: contact@nhsonline.org
Diane Connolly, Exec Dir.
  Conditions: Primary—MR.
  Gen Acad. Ungraded.
  Therapy: Hear Lang Occup Phys Speech. **Psychotherapy:** Group Indiv.
  Est 1968. Private. Nonprofit.

NORTHWESTERN HUMAN SERVICES OF PHILADELPHIA WOODHAVEN CENTER

Res and Day — Coed Ages 10 and up

Philadelphia, PA 19154. 2900 Southampton Rd.
Tel: 215-671-5000. Fax: 215-671-5038.
  Conditions: Primary—MR. **IQ 0-70.**
  Gen Acad. Pre-Voc. Ungraded. Courses: Read Math Lang_Arts. Man_Arts & Shop. Shelt_Workshop. On-Job Trng.
  Therapy: Chemo Hear Lang Occup Phys Speech. **Psychotherapy:** Group Indiv.
  Est 1973. Private.

OUR LADY OF CONFIDENCE DAY SCHOOL

Day — Coed Ages 5-21

Willow Grove, PA 19090. 314 N Easton Rd.
Tel: 215-657-9311. Fax: 215-657-9312.
www.ourladyofconfidence.com   E-mail: mail@ourladyofconfidence.com
Sr. Francis Christi, SSJ, BS, MA, Prin.
  Focus: Spec Ed. **Conditions:** Primary—Bl MR. Sec—ADHD. **IQ 20-75.**
  Pre-Voc. Ungraded. Courses: Life_Skills.
  Therapy: Hear Lang Occup Phys Speech. **Psychotherapy:** Indiv.
  Enr: 120. Day Males 57. Day Females 63. **Staff:** 24 (Full 18, Part 6). Prof
    24. Educ 24.
  Rates 2003: Day $1250-2500/sch yr (+$75).
  Est 1954. Private. Nonprofit. Roman Catholic.

The emphasis of this school is on growth in the areas of spiritual, physical, academic, social and vocational development. Independent living skills training is provided. Children must be either trainable or educable mentally retarded to be accepted for enrollment.

High school educational services take place at 6301 N. 2nd St., Philadelphia 19120.

OVERBROOK SCHOOL FOR THE BLIND

Res — Coed Ages 7-21; Day — Coed 3-21

Philadelphia, PA 19151. 6333 Malvern Ave.
Tel: 215-877-0313. Fax: 215-877-2709.
www.obs.org
Bernadette M. Kappen, PhD, Dir.
  Conditions: Primary—B.
  Gen Acad. Pre-Voc. Voc. Ungraded. Courses: Read Math Lang_Arts.
    Shelt_Workshop. On-Job Trng.
  Therapy: Occup Phys Speech.
  Est 1832. Private. Nonprofit.

THE PATHWAY SCHOOL

Res — Coed Ages 12-21; Day — Coed 5-21

Norristown, PA 19403. 162 Egypt Rd.
Tel: 610-277-0660. Fax: 610-539-1493.
www.pathwayschool.org
William O'Flanagan, PhD, Pres. **Louise Robertson,** Adm.
  Focus: Spec Ed. **Conditions:** Primary—Anx Asp Au Bl Dx LD Mood ON
    TS. Sec—ADD ADHD ED OCD S. **IQ 70-120.**
  Col Prep. Gen Acad. Pre-Voc. Voc. Gr K-12. Courses: Read Math Lang_
    Arts Sci Studio_Art Music. Man_Arts & Shop. On-Job Trng.
  Therapy: Lang Occup Speech. **Psychotherapy:** Fam Group Indiv.

Enr: 180.
Est 1961. Private. Nonprofit.

Located on a suburban campus near Valley Forge Park, Pathway provides habilitative services for children who have varying degrees of learning and behavioral problems. A total team approach that includes the cooperative participation of parents provides an individualized program of educational, social and emotional involvement.

Pathway also offers career education and individually prescribed speech, language, reading and math programs, in addition to off-campus work experience. Individual and group psychotherapy sessions are conducted.

PENN FOUNDATION

Clinic: All Ages. M-F 8-5; Eves M-Th 5-9.

Sellersville, PA 18960. 807 Lawn Ave, PO Box 32.
Tel: 215-257-6551. Fax: 215-257-9347.
www.pennfoundation.org
John Goshow, MSW, Pres. **James Showalter,** MD, Med Dir.
    Focus: Treatment. **Conditions:** Primary—ADD ADHD Anx Au BD CD ED
      Mood OCD Psy PTSD SP Sz. Sec—MR ODD.
    Psychotherapy: Fam Group Indiv Parent.
    Staff: 13 (Full 8, Part 5).
    Rates 2003: /sesSliding-Scale Rate $70-125.
    Est 1956. Private. Nonprofit.

This community mental health agency serves children and their families, with emphasis placed on a family systems approach. Penn offers outpatient treatment for a wide range of emotional disturbances, as well as services for those with drug and alcohol problems. The foundation also provides case management services for individuals with mental handicaps and mental retardation.

PENNSYLVANIA SCHOOL FOR THE DEAF

Day — Coed Ages 2-21

Philadelphia, PA 19144. 100 W School House Ln.
Tel: 215-951-4700. TTY: 215-951-4703. Fax: 215-951-4708.
www.psd.org   E-mail: info@psd.org
Joseph E. Fischgrund, MA, Head.
    Focus: Spec Ed. **Conditions:** Primary—D.
    Gen Acad. Pre-Voc. Ungraded. Courses: Read Math Lang_Arts Sci Soc_
      Stud.
    Therapy: Hear Lang Movement Occup Play Speech. **Psychotherapy:**
      Group Indiv.
    Enr: 200. **Staff:** 180 (Full 156, Part 24).
    Summer Prgm: Day. Educ. Rec. Ther.
    Est 1820. Private. Nonprofit.

Located on a rural 33-acre area, this school offers a vocational and academic program to children who are unable to make normal progress in public schools because of hearing impairments. Teaching is geared to the individual and emphasizes residual hearing. Outpatient services and counseling are available. The duration of treatment varies.

PHELPS SCHOOL

Res and Day — Males Ages 12-18

Malvern, PA 19355. 583 Sugartown Rd, PO Box 476.
Tel: 610-644-1754. Fax: 610-644-6679.
www.phelpsschool.org   E-mail: admis@phelpsschool.org
Norman Phelps, Jr., BA, MA, Head. **F. Christopher Chirieleison,** Adm.
  Focus: Spec Ed. **Conditions:** Primary—ADD ADHD Dc Dg Dx LD. Sec—S.
    IQ 80-125.
  Col Prep. Gen Acad. Pre-Voc. Gr 7-PG. Courses: Read Math Lang_Arts
    Span Sci Soc_Stud Econ. Man_Arts & Shop.
  Therapy: Speech. **Psychotherapy:** Indiv.
  Enr: 143. Res Males 125. Day Males 18. **Staff:** 28. (Full 28).
  Rates 2003: Res $25,000/sch yr (+$1500). Day $15,500/sch yr (+$200).
    Schol avail.
  Summer Prgm: Res & Day. Educ. Res Rate $4000. Day Rate $3000. 5 wks.
  Est 1946. Private. Nonprofit.

Phelps offers an intensive diagnostic, remedial and guidance program to boys who are underachieving or who have a specific learning disability such as dyslexia or attention deficit disorder. Phelps features small classes and individualized scheduling. Other program opportunities are English as a Second Language, industrial arts, oceanography and driver education. Graduates enter a wide variety of colleges and vocational schools.

All students participate in an afternoon activity program that includes such sports as soccer, baseball, basketball, golf, bowling, tennis, cross-country and lacrosse, as well as farm work, riding, arts and crafts, wood shop, powerlifting, photography, drama and computers.

PINNACLEHEALTH
SPEECH AND HEARING CENTER

Clinic: All Ages. M-F 8-4:30.

Harrisburg, PA 17110. 2601 N 3rd St.
Tel: 717-782-4350. Fax: 717-782-6408.
  Focus: Treatment. **Conditions:** Primary—D S.
  Therapy: Hear Lang Speech. **Psychotherapy:** Parent.
  Staff: 15 (Full 12, Part 3).
  Est 1965. Private. Nonprofit.

Located in the Memorial Building of Polyclinic Hospital, this center provides diagnostic and rehabilitative services for individuals with communication disorders, including hearing impairments, speech problems, language delay or dysfunction, and voice problems.

Evaluations, therapy and counseling are available to the speech and language impaired, while the hearing-impaired receive audiologic and hearing evaluations, hearing aid orientation, speech reading, counseling and hearing screening services. When necessary, the center makes appropriate referrals for medical, psychological and educational services.

THE QUAKER SCHOOL AT HORSHAM

Day — Coed Ages 6-14

Horsham, PA 19044. 318 Meetinghouse Rd.
Tel: 215-674-2875.
www.quakerschool.org   E-mail: info@quakerschool.org
Terry T. Bergman, BA, MEd, EdD, Head.
  Focus: Spec Ed. **Conditions:** Primary—ADD ADHD Dx LD. Sec—Ap Dc Dg. **IQ 85 and up.**
  Gen Acad. Gr 1-8. Courses: Read Math Lang_Arts Sci Computers Soc_ Stud Studio_Art Woodworking.
  Therapy: Occup Speech. **Psychotherapy:** Group.
  Enr: 70. Day Males 45. Day Females 25. **Staff:** 30 (Full 29, Part 1).
  Rates 2003: Day $19,950/sch yr. Schol 15.
  Summer Prgm: Day. Educ. Rec. Day Rate $1700. 5 wks.
  Est 1982. Private. Nonprofit. Religious Society of Friends.

The school offers a varied academic program to children with different learning styles of average or above-average intelligence. A teacher and a teacher assistant work with a group of no more than eight children. Speech and occupational therapy supplement the educational program, and the average length of stay is three years. Students of all faiths are admitted.

QUDC SCHOOL OF SPECIAL EDUCATION

Day — Coed Ages 4½-16

Levittown, PA 19056. 2477 Trenton Rd.
Tel: 215-945-6090. Fax: 215-945-7320.
www.qudaycenter.org   E-mail: office@qudaycenter.org
Clara Chirchirillo, MEd, Prin.
  Focus: Spec Ed. **Conditions:** Primary—BI MR. **IQ 35-75.**
  Pre-Voc. Ungraded. Courses: Read Math Lang_Arts Relig.
  Therapy: Hear Lang Occup Speech.
  Enr: 32. Day Males 18. Day Females 14. **Staff:** 14 (Full 8, Part 6).
  Est 1980. Private. Roman Catholic.

Individualized educational programs and religious training are features of this school. Mentally retarded and brain-injured students are integrated with nondisabled students in all religious functions, assemblies and social activities. Integration occurs in the regular classroom environment when the pupil reaches an appropriate learning level.

REHABILITATION SPECIALISTS

Clinic: All Ages. M-F 8-4:30.

Pittsburgh, PA 15202. 35 N Balph Ave.
Tel: 412-761-6062. Fax: 412-761-7336.
www.rehabspecialists.net   E-mail: rehab.specialists@verizon.net
Kathleen R. Helfrich-Miller, PhD, CCC, Pres.
   Focus: Treatment. **Conditions:** Primary—Ap S. Sec—Au CP D LD MR MS.
   Therapy: Hear Lang Speech.
   Staff: 15 (Full 11, Part 4). Prof 13. Admin 2.
   Rates 2003: Clinic $96/ses.
   Est 1979. Private. Inc.

Individuals of all ages receive speech, language, hearing and swallowing therapies at this facility. Treatment typically lasts one to two years, depending upon the disorder being treated.

ROSEHILL SCHOOL

Res — Coed Ages 10 and up

Chester Heights, PA 19017. 320 Llewelyn Rd, PO Box 298.
Tel: 610-459-2389. Fax: 610-459-8595.
William Fager, Dir.
   Focus: Spec Ed. Trng. **Conditions:** Primary—MR. **IQ 20-85.**
   Pre-Voc. Ungraded.
   Therapy: Hear Lang Occup Phys Speech. **Psychotherapy:** Indiv.
   Staff: Prof 4.
   Est 1927. Private.

ROYER-GREAVES SCHOOL FOR BLIND

Res and Day — Coed Ages 5-21

Paoli, PA 19301. 118 S Valley Rd, PO Box 1007.
Tel: 610-644-1810. Fax: 610-644-8164.
Carol T. Dale, BA, Exec Dir.
   Focus: Spec Ed. Trng. **Conditions:** Primary—B D. Sec—ADD ADHD Au BI CP ED Ep LD MR OH.
   Pre-Voc. Voc. Ungraded. Courses: Life_Skills. Shelt_Workshop.
   Therapy: Hear Lang Music Occup Phys Speech. **Psychotherapy:** Indiv.
   Enr: 23. **Staff:** 21 (Full 16, Part 5).
   Summer Prgm: Res & Day. Educ. Rec. Ther. 5 wks.
   Est 1921. Private. Nonprofit.

Multi-handicapped visually impaired students receive education and training at this residential school, which is located on a country estate. Community life and academics are combined in an individualized program. Royer-Greaves places particular emphasis on helping students attain the greatest degree of independence possible.

ST. ANTHONY SCHOOL PROGRAMS

Day — Coed Ages 5-21

Pittsburgh, PA 15227. 2718 Custer Ave.
Tel: 412-882-1333. Fax: 412-882-1668.
www.stanthonyschoolprograms.com   E-mail: anthexdi@nauticom.net
Tom O'Toole, MSW, MBA, Exec Dir. **Lisa George,** BA, MA, Educ Dir.
 Focus: Spec Ed. **Conditions:** Primary—Au MR.
 Gen Acad. Ungraded. Courses: Read Math Lang_Arts. On-Job Trng.
 Therapy: Occup Speech. **Psychotherapy:** Indiv.
 Enr: 80. **Staff:** 40.
 Rates 2003: Day $4500-6650/sch yr.
 Est 1953. Private. Nonprofit. Roman Catholic.

Mentally retarded children and adolescents who live within the six counties of the Diocese of Pittsburgh are accepted into the educational and vocational programs offered at St. Anthony.

ST. EDMOND'S HOME FOR CHILDREN

Res — Coed Ages Birth-21

Rosemont, PA 19010. 320 S Roberts Rd.
Tel: 610-525-8800. Fax: 610-525-2693.
Mary O'Neill, MEd, LSW, Exec Dir.
 Focus: Treatment. **Conditions:** Primary—MR. Sec—B CP D ON S.
 Therapy: Hear Lang Music Occup Phys Recreational Speech. **Psychotherapy:** Indiv.
 Enr: 40. Res Males 20. Res Females 20. **Staff:** 120.
 Est 1916. Private. Nonprofit. Roman Catholic. **Spons:** Catholic Social Services of Philadelphia.

St. Edmond's, administered by the Sisters of Mercy, provides services for children with mental retardation.

ST. JOSEPH CENTER FOR SPECIAL LEARNING

Day — Coed Ages 5-21

Pottsville, PA 17901. 2075 W Norwegian St.
Tel: 570-622-4638. Fax: 570-622-3420.
E-mail: altssjc@ptd.net
Julia Leskin, Prin.
 Focus: Spec Ed. **Conditions:** Primary—ADD ADHD Ap Apr Ar As Asp Au BD Bl C CD CP Dc Dg DS Dx ED Ep IP LD MD MR MS Nf OCD ON

PDD PW SB Sz TB TS. **IQ 0-78.**
Pre-Voc. Ungraded. Courses: Read Math.
Therapy: Phys Speech.
Enr: 17. Day Males 7. Day Females 10. **Staff:** 8 (Full 5, Part 3).
Rates 2003: Day $1650-2450/sch yr (+$60). Schol 17.
Est 1955. Private. Nonprofit. Roman Catholic.

Sponsored by the Diocese of Allentown for children, adolescents and young adults with mental retardation and other developmental disabilities in Schuylkill County, this school provides academic instruction and educational activities nine months per year. The curriculum consists of educational, developmental and spiritual elements. Serving to enhance the basic program are the following offerings: adaptive physical education, speech and language therapy, medical services, psychological evaluations, vocational services and nursing services. SJC also provides instruction in such practical skills areas as computer literacy, cooking and music.

Tuition assistance allows individuals whose families are unable to afford St. Joseph's fees to attend the school.

ST. JOSEPH'S CENTER

Res — Coed All Ages; Day — Coed 21 and up
Clinic: All Ages. M-F 8:30-4:30; Eves W-F 4:30-8.

Scranton, PA 18509. 2010 Adams Ave.
Tel: 570-342-8379. Fax: 570-342-6080.
www.stjosephscenter.org   E-mail: wecare@stjosephscenter.org
Sr. Therese O'Rourke, IHM, BS, MA, Pres. **Peter Cognetti,** MD, Med Dir. **Mary Ellen Desiderio,** Adm.
Focus: Treatment. **Conditions:** Primary—Asp MR. Sec—ADD Anx Ap Ar As Au B BD BI CP D DS ED Ep IP MD MS ON PDD PW S. **IQ 19-40.**
Therapy: Hear Hydro Lang Music Occup Phys Recreational Speech. **Psychotherapy:** Indiv Parent.
Enr: 156. Res Males 66. Res Females 43. Day Males 27. Day Females 20. **Staff:** 83 (Full 69, Part 14).
Est 1890. Private. Nonprofit. Roman Catholic.

Severely to profoundly mentally retarded, multi-handicapped children and adults from Pennsylvania enroll at the center. An interdisciplinary approach emphasizing self-help skills aids in emotional, physical, psychological and social development. The extensive application of assistive communicative devices and micro-switches, in addition to the use of computers, maximizes participants' independence and environmental control.

Parents take an active role in habilitation plans and activities. There is no religious restriction for admission.

ST. KATHERINE DAY SCHOOL

Day — Coed Ages 4½-21

Wynnewood, PA 19096. 930 Bowman Ave.
Tel: 610-667-3958. Fax: 610-667-3625.

E-mail: apkath01@nni.com
Margaret Devaney, MS, Prin.
Focus: Spec Ed. **Conditions:** Primary—MR. Sec—ADD ADHD Dx LD OH.
IQ 45-70.
Pre-Voc. Voc. Ungraded. Courses: Read Math Lang_Arts. On-Job Trng.
Therapy: Music Occup Phys Speech. **Psychotherapy:** Indiv Parent.
Enr: 140. **Staff:** 30 (Full 26, Part 4).
Rates 2003: Day $1450-2900/sch yr (+$500). Schol 30 ($11,500).
Est 1953. Private. Inc. Roman Catholic.

This day school offers education and vocational training to youth with mental retardation. Speech, physical and occupational therapy complement the academic program. Counseling is also available for parents.

ST. LUCY DAY SCHOOL FOR CHILDREN WITH VISUAL IMPAIRMENTS

Day — Coed Ages Birth-14

Upper Darby, PA 19082. 130 Hampden Rd.
Tel: 610-352-4550. Fax: 610-352-4582.
www.stlucydayschool.org   E-mail: aplucy01@nni.com
Sr. M. Margaret Fleming, IHM, MEd, Prin.
Focus: Spec Ed. **Conditions:** Primary—B. Sec—LD. **IQ 80 and up.**
Gen Acad. Pre-Voc. Gr PS-8. Courses: Read Math Lang_Arts Computers
Music Adaptive_Phys_Ed Braille Orientation & Mobility.
Therapy: Lang Occup Speech.
Enr: 25. Day Males 12. Day Females 13. **Staff:** 12 (Full 11, Part 1). Prof 5.
Admin 1.
Rates 2003: Day $1450-2900/sch yr (+$500). Schol avail.
Est 1955. Private. Nonprofit. Roman Catholic.

Infants receive visual and motor stimulation through individual developmental programs. Intense instruction in regular and special curricular areas is provided for school-age children, and part-time mainstreaming takes place for grades 1-8. Parental guidance and support are offered.

SARAH REED CHILDREN'S CENTER

Res — Coed Ages 5-18; Day — Coed 3-18

Erie, PA 16506. 2445 W 34th St.
Tel: 814-838-1954. Fax: 814-835-2196.
www.sarahreed.org
Conditions: Primary—BD ED.
Gen Acad. Gr K-12. Courses: Lang_Arts.
Psychotherapy: Fam Group Indiv.
Staff: Prof 47.
Est 1871. Private. Nonprofit.

SCHREIBER PEDIATRIC REHAB CENTER

Clinic: Ages Birth-21. M-F 8-5:30; Eves M W Th 5:30-8, T 5:30-7.

Lancaster, PA 17603. 625 Community Way.
Tel: 717-393-0425. TTY: 717-393-1503. Fax: 717-392-7107.
www.schreiberpediatric.org   E-mail: schreiber@wideworld.net
William F. Jefferson, MS, Pres.
  Focus: Rehab. **Conditions:** Primary—Ap Au Bl CP Dx IP LD MD MR ON S
  SB. Sec—B D.
  Therapy: Lang Music Occup Phys Speech.
  Staff: 56 (Full 37, Part 19).
  Est 1936. Private. Nonprofit.

Serving Lancaster County, the center provides a wide range of rehabilitative services
for individuals with disabilities, including physical, occupational and speech therapies;
social services; and recreational activities such as camping, swimming, basketball, karate
and gymnastics. The Preschool Development Program accepts children ages 2½-5.

Shreiber assesses its fees along a sliding scale; no client is refused treatment due to
an inability to pay.

SCRANTON COUNSELING CENTER

Clinic: All Ages. M-F 8:30-4:30; Eve T Th 7-9.

Scranton, PA 18503. 326 Adams Ave.
Tel: 570-348-6100. Fax: 570-969-8955.
Edward F. Heffron, EdD, Exec Dir. **A.C. Patel,** MD, Med Dir.
  Focus: Treatment. **Conditions:** Primary—ADD ADHD AN Anx Asp Au Bu
  CD ED Mood MR OCD Psy PTSD PW SP Sz TS. Sec—BD.
  Therapy: Art Chemo Hear Music Occup Speech. **Psychotherapy:** Fam
  Group Indiv.
  Staff: 383 (Full 252, Part 131).
  Est 1947. Private. Inc.

The center provides comprehensive services for all residents of southern Lackawanna
County. Services includes community-based therapy and management services, therapeutic staff support, mobile therapy and behavior consultancy, and specialized family
home-based treatment service.

Outpatient treatment includes play therapy, activity groups, behavior management,
and individual and family therapy. The mental retardation component of the center
provides opportunity for the mentally retarded individual to lead as normal a life as possible. Supportive services are offered to parents of the retarded, to assist in maintaining
the family as a cohesive unit.

Emergency and crisis intervention services are conducted on a 24-hour basis.

Fees for services are based on a sliding scale.

SCRANTON STATE SCHOOL FOR THE DEAF

Res — Coed Ages 5-21; Day — Coed Birth-21

Scranton, PA 18509. 1800 N Washington Ave.
Tel: 570-963-4546. TTY: 570-963-4546. Fax: 570-963-4544.
http://ns.neiu.k12.pa.us/WWW/SSSD
William O'Neill, Actg Supt.
   Focus: Spec Ed. Conditions: Primary—D. Sec—CP LD MR.
   Col Prep. Gen Acad. Pre-Voc. Voc. Gr PS-12. Courses: Read Math Lang_
      Arts Life_Skills. Man_Arts & Shop. On-Job Trng.
   Therapy: Hear Lang Speech. Psychotherapy: Indiv.
   Enr: 120. Staff: 52 (Full 48, Part 4).
   Est 1882. State. Nonprofit.

The total communication method of instruction is utilized for the education of the deaf. The school also offers vocational, audiological and psychological evaluations, computer-assisted instruction and a career resource center. A parent-infant program is available, as is parental counseling. Deaf adult educational courses are offered each semester.

SHRINERS HOSPITAL

Res — Coed Ages Birth-18

Erie, PA 16505. 1645 W 8th St.
Tel: 814-875-8700. Fax: 814-875-8756.
www.shrinershq.org
Richard W. Brzuz, Admin.
   Conditions: Primary—OH. Sec—CP SB.
   Courses: Read Math Lang_Arts.
   Est 1927. Private. Nonprofit.

SHRINERS HOSPITAL

Res and Day — Coed Ages Birth-18
Clinic: Ages Birth-18. M-F 8-4.

Philadelphia, PA 19140. 3551 N Broad St.
Tel: 215-430-4000. Fax: 215-430-4126.
www.shrinershq.org
Sharon J. Rajnic, RN, MHA, Admin. Randal Betz, MD, Med Dir. Jusy Wessell, Intake.
   Focus: Rehab. Conditions: Primary—CP ON SB.
   Therapy: Occup Phys Recreational. Psychotherapy: Fam Group Indiv
      Parent.
   Staff: 300.
   Rates 2003: No Fee.
   Est 1926. Private. Nonprofit.

Shriners provides surgery and rehabilitation for children with orthopedic disabilities or spinal cord injuries. Group and individual therapies, in addition to recreational opportunities, are provided. Inpatient (59-bed capacity) and outpatient services are available free of charge.

SOUTHWOOD PSYCHIATRIC HOSPITAL

Res — Males Ages 5-18; Day — Males 8-18

Pittsburgh, PA 15241. 2575 Boyce Plaza Rd.
Tel: 412-257-2290. Fax: 412-257-0374.
www.yfcs.com/facilities/southwoodhospital
   E-mail: info.southwoodhospital@yfcs.com
Lynne M. Struble, BSN, MSN, CEO. **Craig A. Taylor,** MD, Med Dir.
   Focus: Spec Ed. Treatment. **Conditions:** Primary—ADD ADHD Anx Asp Au BD CD Dc Dg DS Dx ED LD Mood MR OCD PDD Psy PTSD SP Sz TS. Sec—Ap S.
   Col Prep. Gen Acad. Gr K-12. Courses: Read Math Lang_Arts Sci Soc_ Stud.
   Therapy: Lang Milieu Play Recreational Speech. **Psychotherapy:** Fam.
   Enr: 80. Res Males 74. Day Males 6.
   Rates 2003: Day $15,300/sch yr.
   Summer Prgm: Res & Day. Educ. Res Rate $800. 3 wks.
   Est 1984. Private. **Spons:** Youth and Family Centered Services.

Southwood's inpatient care services include residential treatment, community and family-based services and a private academic school that serves both individuals in residence at Southwood and approved day students. The residential program utilizes cognitive behavioral therapy, encourages family involvement and incorporates a wide range of therapeutic services.

Two of the hospital's residential programs are located at the main campus in Pittsburgh, while two site locations are in Washington County. One of the residential units at the main campus specializes in the treatment of boys who are dually diagnosed with mild to moderate mental retardation and mental illness.

STRATFORD FRIENDS SCHOOL

Day — Coed Ages 5-13

Havertown, PA 19083. 5 Llandillo Rd.
Tel: 610-446-3144. Fax: 610-446-6381.
www.stratfordfriends.org   E-mail: gvare@stratfordfriends.org
Sandra Howze, EdM, Dir. **Nancy D'Angelo,** Adm.
   Focus: Spec Ed. **Conditions:** Primary—Dx LD. **IQ 100 and up.**
   Gen Acad. Gr K-6. Courses: Read Math Lang_Arts Sci Soc_Stud Studio_ Art Music Drama.
   Therapy: Speech.
   Enr: 70. Day Males 46. Day Females 24. **Staff:** 26 (Full 15, Part 11). Educ 20. Admin 6.

Rates 2004: Day $20,300/sch yr.
Summer Prgm: Day. Educ. Rec. Day Rate $3400. 5 wks.
Est 1976. Private. Nonprofit. Religious Society of Friends.

The school tailors its academic program to pupils' individual needs while maintaining a 5:1 student-teacher ratio. Quaker values and traditions are incorporated into the learning process. The school also offers an at-risk program for five-year-olds, after-school tutoring for non-Stratford Friends students, an extended-day program, summer school, an auditory training program and, for an additional fee, a teacher training program.

TEMPLE UNIVERSITY
SPEECH-LANGUAGE AND HEARING CENTER

Clinic: All Ages. M-F 9-5.

Philadelphia, PA 19122. 110 Weiss Hall, 13th St & Cecil B Moore Ave.
Tel: 215-204-7543. TTY: 215-204-7543. Fax: 215-204-8543.
www.temple.edu/commsci/clinic.htm
Barbara Mastriano, PhD, Dir.
  Conditions: Primary—S.
  Therapy: Hear Lang Speech.
  Est 1952. State. Nonprofit.

THREE RIVERS YOUTH

Res — Coed Ages 12-21

Pittsburgh, PA 15212. 2039 Termon Ave.
Tel: 412-766-2215. Fax: 412-766-2212.
www.threeriversyouth.org E-mail: info@threeriversyouth.org
Peggy B. Harris, BA, MPA, CEO.
  Focus: Treatment. **Conditions:** Primary—BD CD ED.
  Therapy: Speech. **Psychotherapy:** Fam Group Indiv.
  Enr: 41. Res Males 8. Res Females 33.
  Est 1970. Private. Nonprofit.

TRY provides community-based care and treatment for high-risk youth and their families. An intensive treatment unit offers a highly structured facility for adolescents needing behavior control and stabilization in a high-impact treatment environment. Services include a group home, counseling and support, and a home-based program for pregnant and parenting teens; two residential teen parent programs; educational and vocational services; shelter and crisis counseling for runaway youths; a transitional living program for homeless children; and in-home services for families.

UNITED CEREBRAL PALSY
OF WESTERN PENNSYLVANIA

Clinic: Ages Birth-3. M-F 8:30-4:30.

Greensburg, PA 15601. 1 Corporate Cir, Ste 2000.
Nearby locations: Ford City; Indiana (PA); Spring Church.
Tel: 724-832-8272. Fax: 724-837-8278.
www.ucpwpa.org   E-mail: ucp@ucpwpa.org
Jane L. Hurd, Exec Dir. **Debra Forsha,** Prgm Dir.
  Focus: Treatment. **Conditions:** Primary—Ap Apr Asp Au B Bl CP D Ep IP
    MD MR MS Nf ON PDD PW S SB. Sec—As BD C ED LD TB.
  Therapy: Hear Lang Occup Phys Speech Visual.
  Staff: 18 (Full 14, Part 4).
  Rates 2003: No Fee.
  Est 1952. Private. Nonprofit.

This home-based program includes individualized and small-group education and
therapeutic services. Family involvement is highly encouraged, and parent support
groups and training are offered.

Other offices are located at 206 5th Ave., Ste. B, P.O. Box 52, Ford City 16226; R.D.
7, Box 353A, Greensburg 15601; 1820 State Rte. 56, Spring Church 15601; and 2273
Philadelphia St, Indiana 15701.

UPMC HEALTH SYSTEM
JOHN MERCK PROGRAM

Res — Coed Ages 3 and up; Day — Coed 6-16
Clinic: All Ages. M-F 9-5.

Pittsburgh, PA 15213. 3811 O'Hara St, Ste 112.
Tel: 412-246-5100.
Martin J. Lubetsky, MD, Dir.
  Focus: Treatment. **Conditions:** Primary—ADD ADHD Au CD ED LD MR
    OCD Psy Sz. Sec—Ap B BD Bl CP D Dx Ep ON S SB.
  Therapy: Hear Lang Occup Phys Speech. **Psychotherapy:** Fam Group
    Indiv Parent.
  Private. Nonprofit. **Spons:** University of Pittsburgh.

This program specializes in the psychiatric evaluation and treatment of behavioral and
emotional problems in children, adolescents and adults with developmental disabilities.
A short-term, intensive approach is designed to assist the individuals in adjusting to his
or her environment.

The principle program goal is the development of a comprehensive, individualized
treatment plan that addresses both the primary psychiatric or behavioral problems and
the individual's developmental needs. A multidisciplinary team recommends a combination of therapies for each client. John Merck's offerings consist of inpatient hospitalization, residential treatment, partial hospitalization, a day program, outpatient services,
wraparound services, vocational training and supported employment. In addition, persons of all ages may receive community-based services.

THE VANGUARD SCHOOL
AND PEDIATRIC THERAPY CENTER

Day — Coed Ages 3-21
Clinic: All Ages. M-Su by Appt.

Paoli, PA 19301. 1777 N Valley Rd, PO Box 730.
Tel: 610-296-6700. Fax: 610-640-0132.
www.vanguardschool-pa.org
Ernest E. Brattstrom, Jr., MS, Head. **Tim Lanshe,** MEd, Educ Dir. **Kathleen M. Wilkins,** PhD, Clin Dir. **Donna M. Annechino,** Adm.
   Focus: Spec Ed. Treatment. **Conditions:** Primary—Asp Au BI ED ON PDD S. Sec—ADD ADHD Anx Ap As Dc Dg Dx Ep LD Mood OCD PTSD PW SP TS. **IQ 60 and up.**
   Col Prep. Gen Acad. Pre-Voc. Voc. Ungraded. Courses: Read Math Lang_ Arts Lib_Skills Span Computers Hist Studio_Art Music Adaptive_Phys_ Ed. Man_Arts & Shop. Shelt_Workshop. On-Job Trng.
   Therapy: Lang Music Occup Percepual-Motor Phys Play Recreational Speech. **Psychotherapy:** Fam Parent.
   Enr: 200. Day Males 125. Day Females 75. **Staff:** 122 (Full 107, Part 15). Admin 10.
   Rates 2003: Day $34,000/sch yr. State Aid.
   Summer Prgm: Day. Educ. Rec. Ther. 5 wks.
   Est 1959. Private. Nonprofit.

Consisting of lower, middle and upper schools, Vanguard occupies a 53-acre campus. The educational program serves students with serious emotional and learning adjustment problems and stresses language development, affective-cognitive learning and vocational experience. As part of its counseling program, the school conducts PACE, a series of structured group activities designed to promote behavior change and self-esteem improvement. Vanguard shares its campus with Crossroads School.

The Pediatric Therapy Center is the clinical branch of the school. School-aged children may receive individual and group therapy, evaluations, and psycho-educational and skills training through the center. Other clinical and tutorial services are available to the individuals of all ages.

WESLEY ACADEMY

Day — Coed Ages 9-21

Pittsburgh, PA 15241. 243 Johnston Rd.
Tel: 412-833-6444. Fax: 412-831-8868.
www.wesleyinstitute.org
Nancy Hill, Dir. **William Law,** MD, Med Dir. **Melissa Garvin,** Adm.
   Focus: Spec Ed. **Conditions:** Primary—ADD ADHD AN Anx BD Bu Dx Mood OCD PTSD SP. Sec—ED. **IQ 90-130.**
   Col Prep. Gen Acad. Gr 4-12. Courses: Read Math Lang_Arts Fr Span Sci Computers Soc_Stud Drama.
   Enr: 130. Day Males 70. Day Females 60. **Staff:** 26. (Full 26). Educ 16. Admin 3.

Rates 2004: Day $13,000/sch yr.
Est 1965. Private. Nonprofit. **Spons:** Wesley Institute.

The academy provides an educational alternative for students who require more individualized attention and emotional support than is normally available in public school. Offering both full- and part-time programs, Wesley utilizes a full academic curriculum to develop self-esteem, personal responsibility, mutual respect and social adjustment. The curriculum is individualized to address students' special needs and to challenge their particular capabilities.

WEST CHESTER UNIVERSITY
SPEECH AND HEARING CLINIC

Clinic: All Ages. M-Th 9-5; Eves M-Th 5-7.

West Chester, PA 19383. 201 Carter Dr, Ste 300B.
Tel: 610-436-3401. Fax: 610-436-3388.
Cheryl Gunter, PhD, CCC-SLP, Coord.
 Focus: Treatment. **Conditions:** Primary—Ap D S. Sec—BI CP LD MR.
 Therapy: Hear Lang Speech.
 Staff: 6.
 State.

WCU's Speech and Hearing Clinic serves primarily as a student training facility, with a complete range of therapeutic and diagnostic services provided during the fall and spring semesters for clients with communicative disorders.

WESTERN PENNSYLVANIA SCHOOL
FOR BLIND CHILDREN

Res and Day — Coed Ages 2-21

Pittsburgh, PA 15213. 201 N Bellefield St.
Tel: 412-621-0100. Fax: 412-621-4067.
www.wpsbc.org
Janet Simon, MA, PhD, Exec Dir.
 Focus: Spec Ed. **Conditions:** Primary—B. Sec—OH S.
 Pre-Voc. Gr PS-12. Courses: Math Life_Skills. Man_Arts & Shop. Shelt_
 Workshop.
 Therapy: Hydro Lang Occup Phys Speech. **Psychotherapy:** Fam Indiv.
 Staff: 270.
 Rates 2003: No Fee.
 Est 1887. Private.

An independently operated residential school for legally blind students from the 33 counties of western Pennsylvania, this school stresses functional skills. Integrated and clinical therapies augment the educational focus. The majority of students have severe disabilities in addition to visual impairment. The facility is completely adapted for both the physically handicapped and the blind.

WESTERN PENNSYLVANIA SCHOOL
FOR THE DEAF

Res and Day — Coed Ages 2-21

Pittsburgh, PA 15218. 300 E Swissvale Ave.
Tel: 412-371-7000. Fax: 412-244-4223.
www.wpsd.org
Donald Rhoten, MEd, Supt. **Deborah Fell,** Adm.
   Focus: Spec Ed. **Conditions:** Primary—D. Sec—MR OH. **IQ 40 and up.**
   Col Prep. Gen Acad. Pre-Voc. Gr PS-12. Courses: Read Math Lang_Arts
     Sci Computers. Man_Arts & Shop. On-Job Trng.
   Therapy: Art Hear Lang Occup Phys Speech. **Psychotherapy:** Group Indiv.
   Enr: 190. Res Males 40. Res Females 37. Day Males 60. Day Females 53.
     Staff: 183 (Full 169, Part 14). Prof 81. Educ 65. Admin 10.
   Rates 2004: No Fee.
   Summer Prgm: Res & Day. Educ. Rec. 1 wk.
   Est 1869. Private. Nonprofit.

This schools serves hearing-impaired individuals who are residents of western Pennsylvania. In addition to its academic program, the school provides a complete after-school program that includes sports, clubs and activities for students of all ages; support services; a learning center that includes a mini aviary, tropical rain forest and mini-max theater; and a TV studio and video production department where students use digital technology to produce videos and daily news programs.

A training program for teachers and a parent-teacher association are integral parts of the program for the education of the deaf.

WHITE HAVEN CENTER

Res — Coed Ages 9 and up

White Haven, PA 18661. RR 2, Box 2195.
Tel: 570-443-4200. Fax: 570-443-4209.
www.dpw.state.pa.us   E-mail: tcurran@dpw.state.pa.us
Tom Curran, Dir.
   Focus: Trng. Treatment. **Conditions:** Primary—MR. **IQ 20-70.**
   Gen Acad. Ungraded. Shelt_Workshop.
   Therapy: Chemo Hear Lang Occup Phys Speech. **Psychotherapy:** Fam
     Indiv.
   Est 1961. State.

WOODS SERVICES

Res — Coed Ages 5 and up

Langhorne, PA 19047. Rte 213, PO Box 36.
Tel: 215-750-4000. Fax: 215-750-4591.

www.woods.org   E-mail: admissions@woods.org
Robert G. Griffith, EdD, Pres. **Harry Getz,** MD, Med Dir. **Gail Martino,** Adm.
   Focus: Spec Ed. Rehab. Trng. Treatment. **Conditions:** Primary—ADD
      ADHD Anx As Asp Au BD BI CD CP Db Dc Dg DS Dx ED Ep LD Mood
      MR OCD ODD PDD PTSD PW SB SP TS. Sec—B D MD ON S.
   Gen Acad. Pre-Voc. Voc. Gr K-12. Courses: Read Math Lang_Arts Life_
      Skills. Shelt_Workshop. On-Job Trng.
   Therapy: Lang Occup Phys Speech. **Psychotherapy:** Fam Group Indiv.
   Enr: 850. **Staff:** 1800.
   Rates 2004: Res $68,785-160,000/yr.
   Est 1913. Private. Nonprofit.

The agency offers a full range of residential, educational, therapeutic, rehabilitative and medical services to children and adults with developmental disabilities and emotional disorders. School-age individuals enroll in a 12-month, licensed school program, while adults participate in various habilitative and vocational programs. Woods also provides specialized, highly structured residential treatment settings for individuals with a dual diagnosis, an emotional disorder or both; these persons often exhibit severe aggression or self-injurious behavior.

In addition, Woods operates similarly highly structured programs that serve individuals displaying challenging behaviors, Prader-Willi syndrome, Rett syndrome, muscular dystrophy, multi-handicapping conditions, traumatic brain injury and other neurological disorders.   **See Also Page 1054**

WORDSWORTH ACADEMY

Res and Day — Coed Ages 5-21

Fort Washington, PA 19034. Pennsylvania Ave & Camp Hill Rd.
Tel: 215-643-5400. Fax: 215-643-0595.
www.wordsworth.org   E-mail: info@wordsworth.org
Jo-Ann Pierie, MEd, Dir. **Debbie Lacks,** Clin Dir. **James Luebbert,** MD, Med
   Dir.
   Focus: Spec Ed. **Conditions:** Primary—Dx LD. Sec—BD ED OH. **IQ 90-
      130.**
   Gen Acad. Pre-Voc. Voc. Ungraded. Courses: Read Math Lang_Arts. Man_
      Arts & Shop. On-Job Trng.
   Therapy: Art Chemo Lang Music Recreational Speech. **Psychotherapy:**
      Fam Group Indiv.
   Enr: 490. Res Males 90. Res Females 40. Day Males 240. Day Females
      120.
   Summer Prgm: Res & Day. Educ. Rec. Ther.
   Est 1952. Private. Nonprofit.

Formerly The Matthews School, this remedial school is for children having serious difficulty, especially with reading, in an ordinary school setting. Instruction in all subjects, geared to building reading and math skills, begins at the student's present level of achievement. Residents are housed in a residential treatment unit.

Psychotherapy, speech and vision therapy, family therapy, counseling and diagnostic services are available. Clinical services are recommended on an individual basis as needed.

A remedial summer school and a recreational summer camp program are also offered.

RHODE ISLAND

ECKERD YOUTH ALTERNATIVES

Res — Males Ages 10-17

Exeter, RI.
Contact: 100 N Starcrest Dr, PO Box 7450, Clearwater, FL 33758.
Tel: 727-461-2990. Fax: 727-442-5911.
www.eckerd.org   E-mail: admissions@eckerd.org
Karen V. Waddell, BA, Pres. **Francene Hazel,** Dir.
  Focus: Treatment. **Conditions:** Primary—BD CD ED Mood ODD. Sec—
    ADD ADHD LD. **IQ 70 and up.**
  Gen Acad. Pre-Voc. Ungraded. Courses: Read Math Lang_Arts Sci Soc_
    Stud.
  Therapy: Speech. **Psychotherapy:** Fam Group Indiv.
  Summer Prgm: Res. Ther. Res Rate $180. 2 wks.
  Est 1968. Private. Nonprofit.

The Eckerd outdoor program offers therapeutic treatment to emotionally disturbed children by providing a camp setting as an alternative to institutionalization.

The year-round program utilizes reality therapy, Rogerian techniques and group therapy. Small-group living in the wilderness environment encourages the acquisition of new skills while promoting discipline and responsibility. Each group must construct their shelter, cut wood, repair equipment and perform other tasks necessary for their stay in the forest. Such experiences provide the children with the opportunity to develop academic skills at their own pace and in relation to each project they endeavor. When sufficient progress is made, children are transferred into the transition classroom in preparation for their return to the mainstream.

In addition to Rhode Island, Eckerd conducts outdoor therapeutic treatment programs in the following states: Florida, Georgia, New Hampshire, North Carolina, Tennessee and Vermont (see separate listings).

THE GRODEN CENTER

Res — Coed Ages 12-21; Day — Coed 3-21

Providence, RI 02906. 86 Mt Hope Ave.
Tel: 401-274-6310. Fax: 401-421-3280.
www.grodencenter.org   E-mail: grodencenter@grodencenter.org
Gerald Groden, PhD, Co-Dir. **June Groden,** PhD, Co-Dir.
  Focus: Spec Ed. Treatment. **Conditions:** Primary—Au. Sec—ADD ADHD
    BD CD ED LD MR PDD.
  Gen Acad. Pre-Voc. Ungraded. Courses: Read Math Lang_Arts. Shelt_
    Workshop. On-Job Trng.
  Therapy: Hear Lang Occup Phys Speech. **Psychotherapy:** Fam Indiv
    Parent.
  Enr: 79. Res Males 10. Res Females 2. Day Males 49. Day Females 18.
    Staff: 97 (Full 90, Part 7).

Est 1976. Private. Nonprofit.

Comprehensive treatment programs are available to children and young adults with autism and behavioral disorders at the center. Early intervention, day, residential, workshop and Saturday recreational programs are components of the center. The curriculum focuses on the development of cognitive, social and affective, self-help, verbal and nonverbal communication, and fine- and gross-motor skills. Improving a student's daily skills, ability for self-control and ability to learn in other curricular areas are the program's primary objectives. This is accomplished through positive procedures such as relaxation, imagery and social skills acquisition.

Additional services include family therapy, parental education, respite services and a social skills program. Groden does not accept children with severe physical or medical disabilities.

HAMILTON SCHOOL AT WHEELER
Day — Coed Ages 6-14

Providence, RI 02906. 216 Hope St.
Tel: 401-421-8100. Fax: 401-751-7674.
www.wheelerschool.org   E-mail: onlineinquiry@wheelerschool.org
Jonathan Green, MEd, Dir. **Barbara Staples,** BS, MS, Med Dir. **Jeanette Epstein,** Adm.
  Focus: Spec Ed. **Conditions:** Primary—Dc Dg Dx LD. Sec—ADD ADHD.
  Gen Acad. Gr 1-8. Courses: Read Math Lang_Arts.
  Enr: 68. Day Males 48. Day Females 20.
  Rates 2004: Day $26,975/sch yr. Schol 20 ($175,000).
  Summer Prgm: Day. Educ. Day Rate $950-1890. 3-6 wks.
  Est 1988. Private. Nonprofit. **Spons:** Wheeler School.

Located on the campus of The Wheeler School, Hamilton enrolls elementary students with language-based learning differences. Staff teach compensatory strategies as children develop fundamental academic skills.

HARMONY HILL SCHOOL
Res and Day — Males Ages 8-18

Chepachet, RI 02814. 63 Harmony Hill Rd.
Tel: 401-949-0690. TTY: 401-949-4130. Fax: 401-949-2060.
www.harmonyhillschool.org
Terrence J. Leary, MEd, Pres. **Donald Jackson,** Adm.
  Focus: Spec Ed. **Conditions:** Primary—ADD ADHD Asp BD CD ED LD Mood ODD SP TS. Sec—Anx As Dc Dg Dx Ep MR MS OCD ON PDD Psy PTSD S. **IQ 70 and up.**
  Gen Acad. Pre-Voc. Gr 2-12. Courses: Read Math Lang_Arts Sci Soc_Stud Music Health. On-Job Trng.
  Therapy: Art Lang Milieu Music Phys Play Recreational Speech. **Psychotherapy:** Fam Group Indiv Parent.
  Enr: 89. Res Males 62. Day Males 27. **Staff:** 149 (Full 137, Part 12). Prof

30. Educ 11. Admin 20.
Rates 2004: Res $114,000-119,000/yr. Day $42,000/yr.
Summer Prgm: Res & Day. Educ. Rec. Ther.
Est 1976. Private. Nonprofit.

The school provides residential, community and day treatment programs for behaviorally disordered and learning-disabled youngsters who cannot receive treatment within the local educational system or through community-based mental health programs. Harmony Hill's objective is to successfully return students to their communities.

The program features education, group activities, and peer and counselor support systems. Special offerings include a diagnostic program for a limited number of moderately to severely behaviorally disordered individuals and, for an additional fee, a program for sex offenders. The average length of treatment is 18 months.

See Also Page 1033

HASBRO CHILDREN'S HOSPITAL
CHILD DEVELOPMENT CENTER

Clinic: Ages Birth-21. M-F 8-4.

Providence, RI 02903. 593 Eddy St.
Tel: 401-444-5685. Fax: 401-444-6115.
www.lifespan.org/Services/ChildHealth/CDC
Michael E. Msall, MD, Dir.
  Focus: Treatment. **Conditions:** Primary—ADD ADHD Ap Au B Bl CP D DS Dx IP LD MD MR ON S SB. Sec—As CD ED Ep.
  Therapy: Lang Speech. **Psychotherapy:** Fam Group Parent.
  Staff: 38 (Full 21, Part 17).
  Est 1966. Private. Nonprofit.

The CDC provides interdisciplinary evaluation and treatment for children and youths with developmental, communicative, learning and genetic disorders. Medical, surgical and diagnostic services, along with psychological counseling and occupational, motor, speech and physical therapies, are also available. Fees vary according to services provided.

KENT COUNTY ARC
J. ARTHUR TRUDEAU MEMORIAL CENTER

Day — Coed All Ages

Warwick, RI 02886. 3445 Post Rd.
Tel: 401-739-2700. TTY: 800-745-5555. Fax: 401-737-8907.
Mary Madden, Exec Dir.
  Conditions: Primary—Au MR PDD. Sec—OH.
  Pre-Voc. Voc. Shelt_Workshop. On-Job Trng.
  Therapy: Lang Occup Phys Speech.
  Staff: Prof 298.
  Est 1964. Private. Nonprofit.

MEETING STREET

Day — Coed Ages Birth-21
Clinic: All Ages. M-Th 8:30-4:45, F 8-3; Eves by Appt.

East Providence, RI 02914. 667 Waterman Ave.
Tel: 401-438-9500. TTY: 401-438-3690. Fax: 401-438-3760.
www.meetingstreet.org   E-mail: askmeetingstreet@meetingstreet.org
John M. Kelly, BS, Pres.
  Focus: Spec Ed. **Conditions:** Primary—Ap Apr Bl CP IP MD MR MS Nf
   ON SB. Sec—B D ED.
  Gen Acad. Pre-Voc. Voc. Gr PS-12. Courses: Math Lang_Arts. On-Job
   Trng.
  Therapy: Art Hear Lang Music Occup Percepual-Motor Phys Play Speech.
   Psychotherapy: Indiv.
  Enr: 160. **Staff:** 180.
  Summer Prgm: Day. Educ. Rec. Ther.
  Est 1946. Private. Nonprofit.

The center provides educational and functional assessments for children with disabilities. Comprehensive early intervention services for infants, young children and their parents are available. Clients may also receive technology-related services and help with assistive devices. Clinical rates are determined along a sliding scale.

Meeting Street offers educational, developmental and therapeutic services to children, adolescents and young adults ages 3-21. Prevocational training supplements educational programming for secondary students ages 14-21.

RHODE ISLAND SCHOOL FOR THE DEAF

Day — Coed Ages 3-21

Providence, RI 02908. 1 Corliss Park.
Tel: 401-222-3825. TTY: 401-222-3888. Fax: 401-222-6998.
www.rideaf.net   E-mail: info@rideaf.net
John F. Plante, MEd, Int Dir. **Robert Raphael,** Adm.
  Focus: Spec Ed. **Conditions:** Primary—D. Sec—ADD ADHD Asp BD C CD
   CP DS ED MR ON PDD PTSD. **IQ 65-130.**
  Col Prep. Gen Acad. Pre-Voc. Gr PS-12. Courses: Read Math Lang_Arts.
   On-Job Trng.
  Therapy: Hear Lang Occup Speech. **Psychotherapy:** Fam Group Indiv
   Parent.
  Enr: 112. **Staff:** 68 (Full 64, Part 4). Admin 18.
  Rates 2004: No Fee.
  Summer Prgm: Day. Day Rate $0. 4 wks.
  Est 1877. State. Nonprofit.

The school provides a full range of diagnostic services, as well as prescribed direct services such as occupational therapy, physical therapy, speech therapy, auditory training and adaptive physical education. The school provides many opportunities for cooperative mainstreaming. Parents may engage in an active Parent-Teacher League and family members may take free sign language classes.

Rhode Island residents attend free of charge, while out-of-state students must pay tuition.

SARGENT REHABILITATION CENTER

Day — Coed Ages 3-21
Clinic: Ages Birth-21. M-F 8-4:30.

Warwick, RI 02818. 800 Quaker Ln.
Tel: 401-886-6600. Fax: 401-886-6632.
E-mail: sargctr@aol.com
Marilyn F. Serra, MS, CCC-SLP, Dir. **Nedo Nora,** MD, Med Dir.
   Focus: Rehab. Treatment. **Conditions:** Primary—ADD ADHD Ap Asp Au Bl
   LD ON PDD S. Sec—D Dx ED OCD.
   Gen Acad. Pre-Voc. Voc. Ungraded. Courses: Read Math Lang_Arts. Man_
   Arts & Shop. On-Job Trng.
   Therapy: Hear Lang Occup Phys Play Speech. **Psychotherapy:** Fam
   Group Indiv Parent.
   Enr: 45. Day Males 32. Day Females 13. **Staff:** 60 (Full 37, Part 23). Prof
   21. Educ 16. Admin 12.
   Rates 2003: No Fee.
   Summer Prgm: Day. Educ.
   Est 1917. Private. Nonprofit.

The Sargent Center's school program specializes in the treatment of learning disabilities, including neurological disorders, aphasia, head injury, language-learning disability and inter-sensory processing disorders. Development of speech and language, gross- and fine-motor control, and perceptual and sensorimotor skills are integrated into the program. The program combines individual and group therapies with intensive, small-class instruction.

Parents are strongly encouraged to take part in the program and to participate in a psycho-educational group. Social services at the center help integrate school learning experiences with home life.

Sargent offers specialized programs in independent living training, vocational evaluation, community integration, and job training and placement at the secondary level.

SOUTH CAROLINA

ANDERSON-OCONEE
SPEECH AND HEARING SERVICES

Clinic: All Ages. M-F 9-5.

Anderson, SC 29621. 106 Dostak Dr.
Tel: 864-226-2477. Fax: 864-226-2477.
E-mail: shclinic@aol.com
Dick Brandon, Dir.
   Focus: Treatment. **Conditions:** Primary—Ap D S. Sec—ED LD MR OH.
   Therapy: Hear Lang Speech.
   Staff: 9 (Full 3, Part 6).
   Est 1967. Private. Nonprofit.

Anderson-Oconee offers speech, voice, hearing and language evaluations to individuals with speech or hearing impairments. The facility conducts rehabilitative treatments on both individual and group bases.

A satellite program operates at 409 E. North 1st St., Seneca 29678.

CAMPERDOWN ACADEMY

Day — Coed Ages 5-14

Greenville, SC 29615. 501 Howell Rd.
Tel: 864-244-8899. Fax: 864-244-8936.
www.camperdown.org
Dana Blackhurst, Head.
   Focus: Spec Ed. **Conditions:** Primary—Dx LD. **IQ 100 and up.**
   Gen Acad. Gr K-8. Courses: Read Math Lang_Arts. Man_Arts & Shop.
   Therapy: Lang.
   Est 1986. Private. Nonprofit.

CHARLES WEBB CENTER

Day — Coed Ages Birth-10

Charleston, SC 29407. 1611 Evergreen St.
Tel: 843-852-5545. Fax: 843-852-5570.
Tricia Burgess, Dir.
   Focus: Trng. Treatment. **Conditions:** Primary—BI CP MD MS ON SB.
   Therapy: Hear Lang Occup Phys Speech. **Psychotherapy:** Fam Group
      Indiv.
   Est 1939. Private. Nonprofit.

CHEROKEE CREEK BOYS SCHOOL

Res — Males Ages 12-15

Westminster, SC 29693. 198 Cooper Rd.
Tel: 864-647-1885. Fax: 864-647-4930.
www.cherokeecreek.net   E-mail: info@cherokeecreek.net
Beth Black, Pres. **Kathy Whitmire,** MEd, Exec Dir. **Chery Smart,** LCSW, Clin Dir.
   Focus: Spec Ed. **Conditions:** Primary—ADD ADHD BD CD Dc Dg Dx ED Mood OCD SP. **IQ 90 and up.**
   Gen Acad. Gr 6-8. Courses: Read Math Lang_Arts Sci.
   Therapy: Lang Percepual-Motor Phys Play Recreational. **Psychotherapy:** Fam Group Indiv Parent.
   Staff: 17 (Full 16, Part 1). Educ 2. Admin 3.
   Rates 2003: Res $57,600/sch yr.
   Est 2003. Private. Inc.

Boys of middle school age who are struggling emotionally, personally or socially receive treatment at Cherokee Creek. The program offers opportunities for academic success, personal growth, social responsibility, physical challenge, and moral and spiritual exploration.

COASTAL CENTER SCDDSN RESIDENTIAL FACILITY

Res — Coed All Ages

Ladson, SC 29456. 9995 Miles Jamison Rd.
Tel: 843-873-5750. Fax: 843-821-5800.
Ronald Lofts, Dir. **Steve Lewes,** MD, Med Dir.
   Focus: Rehab. **Conditions:** Primary—MR. Sec—Ap Au B CF CP D Dx ED LD Mood MS OCD ODD Psy PTSD PW S SB Sz. **IQ 10-68.**
   Gen Acad. Pre-Voc. Voc. Ungraded. Courses: Read Math Lang_Arts. Shelt_Workshop. On-Job Trng.
   Therapy: Hear Lang Occup Phys Speech. **Psychotherapy:** Fam Group Indiv.
   Enr: 196. **Staff:** 453. Prof 91. Admin 8.
   Est 1968. State. Nonprofit.

Habilitation training, therapy and counseling are provided at this center for children and adults who have moderate to profound levels of retardation.

EDUCATION RX ASSOCIATES

Clinic: All Ages. M-S 8-5; Eves by Appt.

Myrtle Beach, SC 29577. 4703 Hwy 17 Bypass S.
Tel: 843-293-1411. Fax: 843-293-1412.
Alice D'Antoni-Phillips, EdD, Pres.
   Focus: Treatment. **Conditions:** Primary—ADD ADHD Dx LD. Sec—BD ED

MR OH. **IQ 85 and up.**
Psychotherapy: Fam Parent.
Staff: 5 (Full 2, Part 3).
Est 1980. Private. Inc.

This facility offers diagnostic educational evaluation, academic therapy, counseling, neuropsychological testing, school placement and remedial and accelerated tutoring. SAT preparation, college placement and career counseling are also available.

GEORGETOWN COUNTY BOARD OF DISABILITIES AND SPECIAL NEEDS CHILD DEVELOPMENT CENTER

Day — Coed Ages Birth-6

Georgetown, SC 29442. 902 Highmarket St, PO Box 1471.
Tel: 843-546-8228. Fax: 843-546-1617.
www.schsp.org/georgetown
    Conditions: Primary—Au MR. **IQ 0-85.**
    Gen Acad. Pre-Voc. Gr PS-K. Courses: Read Math.
    Therapy: Hear Lang Phys Speech.
    Est 1977. Private. Nonprofit.

GLENFOREST SCHOOL

Day — Coed Ages 6-18

West Columbia, SC 29169. 1041 Harbor Dr.
Tel: 803-796-7622. Fax: 803-796-1603.
www.glenforest.org   E-mail: administration@glenforest.org
Glenda Sternberg, PhD, Head.
    Focus: Spec Ed. **Conditions:** Primary—ADD ADHD Dg Dx LD.
    Col Prep. Gen Acad. Gr 1-12.
    Therapy: Lang Speech.
    Staff: 25 (Full 23, Part 2).
    Rates 2003: Day $14,225-16,669/yr. Schol 5 ($15,750).
    Summer Prgm: Day. Educ. Day Rate $1795-2300. 3-6 wks.
    Est 1983. Private. Nonprofit.

Glenforest's programs are designed for students of average to above-average intelligence who have a learning disabilities or an attentional disorder, as well as those who have not achieved to potential in traditional classroom settings. The school uses such educational methods as direct instruction, multisensory teaching, computerized teaching and the Orton-Gillingham method.

HIDDEN TREASURE CHRISTIAN SCHOOL

Day — Coed Ages 5-20

Taylors, SC 29687. 500 W Lee Rd.
Tel: 864-235-6848. Fax: 864-233-6366.
www.hiddentreasure.org   E-mail: jmccormick@hiddentreasure.org
John J. McCormick, EdD, Admin. **Deborah Bastoni,** Adm.
  Focus: Spec Ed. **Conditions:** Primary—ADD ADHD Anx Ap Apr As Asp Au
    BD Bl C CD CP Dc Dg DS Dx ED Ep LD MR MS Nf OCD ODD ON PDD
    PW S SB TS. Sec—B D Db. **IQ 40-120.**
  Col Prep. Gen Acad. Pre-Voc. Gr K-12. Courses: Read Math Lang_Arts Sci
    Computers Hist Music Speech Life_Skills. Shelt_Workshop.
  Therapy: Speech.
  Enr: 91. Day Males 55. Day Females 36. **Staff:** 27 (Full 21, Part 6).
  Rates 2004: Sliding-Scale Rate $6500-12,500/sch yr.
  Est 1981. Private. Nonprofit. Baptist.

  HTCS serves children with a range of special needs, among them physical, mental
and learning disabilities, attention deficit disorder, autism, cerebral palsy and aphasia. In
addition to special education services, the school offers the following programs: vocational training, physical therapy, occupational therapy, speech therapy, infant stimulation, and creative and nurturing skills.

HOLLIS DEVELOPMENTAL CENTER

Day — Coed Ages Birth-5

Greenville, SC 29607. 1700 Ridge Rd.
Tel: 864-288-2390. Fax: 864-281-9772.
Cathryn Brown, Dir.
  Focus: Trng. **Conditions:** Primary—Bl CP MR. **IQ 20-70.**
  Gen Acad. Ungraded.
  Therapy: Hear Lang Occup Phys Speech.
  Staff: Prof 6.
  Est 1970. Private. Nonprofit. **Spons:** Greenville Association for the
    Retarded.

MIDLANDS REGIONAL CENTER

Res — Coed Ages 1 and up
Clinic: All Ages. M-F 9-4:30.

Columbia, SC 29203. 8301 Farrow Rd.
Tel: 803-935-7502. Fax: 803-935-7678.
James G. Christian, EdD, Dir.
  Focus: Rehab. Trng. Treatment. **Conditions:** Primary—Au MR. **IQ 0-68.**
  Voc. Ungraded. Shelt_Workshop. On-Job Trng.
  Therapy: Hear Lang Occup Phys Speech. **Psychotherapy:** Indiv.

Staff: Prof 15.
Est 1956. State.

ORANGEBURG COUNTY DISABILITIES AND SPECIAL NEEDS BOARD KAPABLE KIDS EARLY INTERVENTION PROGRAM

Day — Coed Ages Birth-6

Orangeburg, SC 29116. 1785 Magnolia Dr, PO Box 1812.
Tel: 803-536-1170. Fax: 803-531-8317.
Charles A. Norman, BA, MA, Exec Dir.
   Focus: Treatment. **Conditions:** Primary—Au MR S. Sec—BI CP ED Ep OH. **IQ 0-70.**
   Therapy: Lang Speech.
   Enr: 60. **Staff:** 5. (Full 5). Educ 4.
   Rates 2003: No Fee.
   Est 1966. County.

Services through OCDSNB include home-based early intervention, special instruction and service coordination. In addition to its childhood offerings, the facility provides vocational programs for adults.

PEE DEE REGIONAL CENTER

Res — Coed All Ages
Clinic: All Ages. M-F 8:30-5.

Florence, SC 29502. 714 National Cemetery Rd, PO Box 3209.
Tel: 843-664-2600. Fax: 843-664-2656.
www.state.sc.us/ddsn
David Goodell, Dir.
   Focus: Trng. Treatment. **Conditions:** Primary—MR.
   Pre-Voc. Voc. Ungraded. Shelt_Workshop. On-Job Trng.
   Therapy: Hear Lang Occup Phys Speech. **Psychotherapy:** Indiv.
   State.

PEE DEE SPEECH AND HEARING CENTER

Clinic: All Ages. M-F 8:30-5.

Florence, SC 29503. 153 N Baroody St.
Tel: 843-662-7802. Fax: 843-662-5601.
   Focus: Treatment. **Conditions:** Primary—Ap D Dx LD S. Sec—BI CP ED OH.
   Therapy: Hear Lang Speech.
   Staff: 14 (Full 12, Part 2).

Est 1968. Private. Nonprofit.

Pee Dee provides diagnosis and remediation for speech, language and hearing disorders.

PINE GROVE

Res — Coed Ages 5-18

Elgin, SC 29045. 1500 Chestnut Rd.
Tel: 803-438-3011. Fax: 803-438-8611.
Carl E. Herring, Dir. **Anita Gotwals,** Adm.
    Focus: Spec Ed. **Conditions:** Primary—Au Bl ED MR.
    Gen Acad. Ungraded.
    Therapy: Art Lang Music Occup Speech. **Psychotherapy:** Group Indiv.
    Enr: 38. Res Males 30. Res Females 8. **Staff:** 70.
    Rates 2004: Res $7000-12,000/mo.
    Est 1970. Private. Inc.

Located on 32 acres of wooded land, Pine Grove treats severely emotionally disturbed and autistic children. Emphasizing behavior modification and communication development, the school conducts an intensive academic program. Parents are offered behavior modification training and must participate in the child's program.

SANDHILLS SCHOOL

Day — Coed Ages 6-15

Columbia, SC 29209. 1500 Hallbrook Dr.
Tel: 803-695-1400. Fax: 803-695-1214.
www.sandhillsschool.org   E-mail: info@sandhillsschool.org
Anne M. Vickers, MEd, Dir. **Thrace Mears,** Adm.
    Focus: Spec Ed. **Conditions:** Primary—ADD ADHD Dc Dg Dx LD. **IQ 100 and up.**
    Gen Acad. Gr 1-8. Courses: Read Math Lang_Arts Sci Soc_Stud Studio_ Art Music.
    Therapy: Lang Speech. **Psychotherapy:** Indiv.
    Enr: 55. **Staff:** 21 (Full 18, Part 3).
    Rates 2004: Day $14,350/sch yr. Schol avail.
    Summer Prgm: Day. Educ. Day Rate $2000. 5 wks.
    Est 1975. Private. Nonprofit.

Sandhills offers a curriculum of individualized instruction to students with dyslexia, attention deficit disorder and other learning disabilities. Each child attends a session of one-on-one language development instruction daily. Extracurricular activities include soccer, softball and basketball teams; interest clubs; and a student council.

One-on-one educational therapy is available during after-school hours for students not enrolled in the school full-time. A five-week summer school, which consists of small-group and individual instruction, is also open to students from other schools.

SOUTH CAROLINA SCHOOL FOR THE DEAF AND BLIND

Res — Coed Ages 4-21; Day — Coed 2½-21

Charleston, SC.
Contact: 355 Cedar Spring Rd, Spartanburg, SC 29302.
  Nearby locations: Conway; Florence.
Tel: 864-577-7521. Fax: 864-585-3555.
www.scsdb.k12.sc.us   E-mail: lmackechnie@scsdb.k12.sc.us
Sheila Breitweiser, BS, MS, EdD, Pres.
  Focus: Spec Ed. **Conditions:** Primary—B D. Sec—ADD ADHD Anx Ap Ar
    As BD Bl C CD CP Db Dc Dg DS Dx ED Ep IP LD MD MR MS Nf OCD
    ODD ON PW S SB SP. **IQ 25 and up.**
  Col Prep. Gen Acad. Pre-Voc. Voc. Gr PS-12. Courses: Read Math Lang_
    Arts Sci Soc_Stud Studio_Art Music Braille. Shelt_Workshop. On-Job
    Trng. Culinary_Arts.
  Therapy: Hear Lang Occup Phys Speech. **Psychotherapy:** Indiv.
  Enr: 431. **Staff:** 401 (Full 383, Part 18). Educ 179. Admin 12.
  Summer Prgm: Res & Day. Rec. 1 wk.
  Est 1849. State.

SCSDB is a specialized instructional and resource center. It provides statewide services for children and adults who are deaf or blind or who have multiple sensory disabilities. The school also assists their families and professionals who work with this population. Programs serve preschool, elementary, middle school and high school students. Vocational and postsecondary programming is also available, as are various outreach and support services.

In addition to the campus in Charleston, SCSDB operates regional centers at 900 4th Ave., Conway 29526 (843-248-8100), and 300 Rainbow Dr., Ste. 102, Florence 29501 (843-665-9705). Separately listed under Spartanburg (the main campus) are other regional campuses in Spartanburg, Columbia and Rock Hill.

SOUTH CAROLINA SCHOOL FOR THE DEAF AND BLIND

Res — Coed Ages 4-21; Day — Coed 2½-21

Spartanburg, SC 29302. 355 Cedar Spring Rd.
  Nearby locations: Columbia; Rock Hill.
Tel: 864-577-7521. Fax: 864-585-3555.
www.scsdb.k12.sc.us   E-mail: lmackechnie@scsdb.k12.sc.us
Sheila Breitweiser, BS, MS, EdD, Pres.
  Focus: Spec Ed. **Conditions:** Primary—B D. Sec—ADD ADHD Anx Ap Ar
    As BD Bl C CD CP Db Dc Dg DS Dx ED Ep IP LD MD MR MS Nf OCD
    ODD ON PW S SB SP. **IQ 25 and up.**
  Col Prep. Gen Acad. Pre-Voc. Voc. Gr PS-12. Courses: Read Math Lang_
    Arts Sci Soc_Stud Studio_Art Music Braille. Shelt_Workshop. On-Job
    Trng. Culinary_Arts.
  Therapy: Hear Lang Occup Phys Speech. **Psychotherapy:** Indiv.
  Enr: 431. **Staff:** 401 (Full 383, Part 18). Educ 179. Admin 12.
  Summer Prgm: Res & Day. Rec. 1 wk.
  Est 1849. State.

SCSDB is a specialized instructional and resource center. It provides statewide services for children and adults who are deaf or blind or who have multiple sensory disabilities. The school also assists their families and professionals who work with this population. Programs serve preschool, elementary, middle school and high school students. Vocational and postsecondary programming is also available, as are various outreach and support services.

In addition to the main campus in Spartanburg, SCSDB operates regional centers at 100 Executive Center Dr., Ste. A-13, Columbia 29210 (803-896-9710), and 197 Piedmont Blvd., Ste. 202, Rock Hill 29732 (803-366-2890). Separately listed under Charleston are other regional campuses in Charleston, Conway and Florence.

SOUTH CAROLINA STATE UNIVERSITY SPEECH-LANGUAGE-HEARING CLINIC

Clinic: All Ages. M-F 9-5; Eves 5-7:30.

Orangeburg, SC 29117. Old Dawn Ctr, 300 College St NE.
Tel: 803-536-8074. Fax: 803-536-8593.
www.scsu.edu/spa/services.htm
Harriette Gregg, MEd, Dir.
  Focus: Rehab. Treatment. **Conditions:** Primary—Ap D S. Sec—Au.
  Therapy: Hear Lang Speech.
  Staff: Prof 10.
  Est 1967. State. Nonprofit.

THE SPEECH, HEARING & LEARNING CENTER

Clinic: All Ages. M-Th 8:30-6, F 9-1.

Greenville, SC 29601. 29 N Academy St.
Tel: 864-331-1400. Fax: 864-331-1416.
www.shlcgreenville.org   E-mail: info@shlcgreenville.org
Stephen T. Guryan, MA, BSEd, Exec Dir.
  Focus: Treatment. **Conditions:** Primary—ADD ADHD D Dx LD S.
  Therapy: Hear Lang Speech. **Psychotherapy:** Group Indiv Parent.
  Staff: 21 (Full 13, Part 8).
  Est 1948. Private. Nonprofit.

The center offers a full range of habilitative and rehabilitative services to those with speech, language, hearing and learning impairments. Audiological services consist of hearing and hearing aid evaluations and selection and auditory training. Speech and language services address problems in articulation, stuttering, cleft palate, cerebral palsy, language and voice. Individuals with learning disabilities receive diagnosis and evaluation, as well as psychological testing for general mental ability.

The center also provides testing and guidance for gifted children.

TRIDENT ACADEMY

Day — Coed Ages 5-19

Mount Pleasant, SC 29464. 1455 Wakendaw Rd.
Tel: 843-884-7046. Fax: 843-884-1483.
www.tridentacademy.com   E-mail: admissions@tridentacademy.com
Myron C. Harrington, Jr., BA, BS, Head.
  Focus: Spec Ed. **Conditions:** Primary—ADD ADHD Dc Dg Dx LD. **IQ 90 and up.**
  Col Prep. Gen Acad. Gr K-PG. Courses: Read Math Lang_Arts Bus Computers.
  Therapy: Lang Speech.
  Enr: 152. Day Males 113. Day Females 39. **Staff:** 50. Educ 42. Admin 8.
  Rates 2004: Day $13,600-18,880/sch yr. Schol avail.
  Summer Prgm: Day. Educ. Rem. Day Rate $800. 6 wks.
  Est 1972. Private. Nonprofit.

Trident is a college preparatory school for students with dyslexia and related academic problems. The academy is organized into lower and upper divisions. Small classes in basic academics are supplemented by individual language development training to develop skills in reading comprehension, written expression, spelling, vocabulary and math computation. Language development training features the multisensory techniques of the Orton approach. A wide variety of interscholastic athletics is available, as are such extracurricular activities as publications and special interest clubs.

YORK PLACE

Res — Coed Ages 6-14

York, SC 29745. 234 Kings Mountain St.
Tel: 803-684-4011. Fax: 803-684-8002.
www.yorkplace.org
  Focus: Treatment. **Conditions:** Primary—ADHD ED Mood ODD. Sec—Au LD. **IQ 70 and up.**
  Gen Acad. Ungraded. Courses: Read Math Lang_Arts.
  Therapy: Chemo Hear Lang Phys Recreational Speech. **Psychotherapy:** Fam Group Indiv.
  Enr: 36.
  Rates 2001: Res $198-335/day. Schol avail. State Aid.
  Est 1969. Private. Nonprofit. Episcopal.

York Place provides year-round residential treatment and a high-management group home for children with serious emotional disturbances, with the treatment goal of restoration to a family setting. Residential treatment serves boys and girls ages 6-14 who require intensive services in an out-of-home placement due to such primary diagnoses as oppositional defiant disorder, ADHD, mood disorder and posttraumatic stress disorder.

The facility cannot accept children with severe physical conditions that interfere with treatment.

SOUTH DAKOTA

BLACK HILLS CHILDREN'S HOME

Res and Day — Coed Ages 4-13

Rapid City, SD 57702. 24100 S Rockerville Rd.
Tel: 605-343-5422. Fax: 605-343-1411.
www.chssd.org   E-mail: mcfarland@chssd.org
Tim Fitzgerald, Dir.
   Conditions: Primary—ADD ADHD BD CD Dx ED LD Mood PTSD.
   Gen Acad. Ungraded. Courses: Read Math Lang_Arts.
   Therapy: Milieu Recreational. **Psychotherapy:** Fam Group Indiv.
   Est 1893. Private. Nonprofit. **Spons:** Children's Home Society.

CHILDREN'S CARE HOSPITAL AND SCHOOL

Res and Day — Coed Ages Birth-21
Clinic: Ages Birth-21.

Sioux Falls, SD 57105. 2501 W 26th St.
Tel: 605-782-2300. Fax: 605-782-2301.
www.cchs.org   E-mail: cchs@cchs.org
   Conditions: Primary—ADD ADHD As Au BI C CF CP DS Ep MD MR ON S
      SB. Sec—D.
   Gen Acad. Pre-Voc. Ungraded. Courses: Read Math Lang_Arts. Man_Arts
      & Shop. Shelt_Workshop. On-Job Trng.
   Therapy: Hear Lang Occup Phys Speech.
   Staff: Prof 209.
   Est 1952. Private. Nonprofit.

COMMUNITY COUNSELING SERVICES

Clinic: All Ages. M-F 8-5; Eve M-Th 5-7.

Huron, SD 57350. 357 Kansas Ave SE.
   Nearby locations: Madison.
Tel: 605-352-8596. Fax: 605-352-7001.
www.ccs-sd.org   E-mail: info@ccs-sd.org
Duane R. Majeres, MS, Exec Dir.
   Conditions: Primary—BD ED LD MR.
   Therapy: Chemo Occup. **Psychotherapy:** Fam Group Indiv Parent.
   Staff: 25 (Full 17, Part 8).
   Est 1960. Private. Nonprofit.

Psychological evaluation and educational consultation with schools are the chief components of this program. CCS conducts an ongoing behavior modification program in conjunction with local public schools. Educational, parental and individual counseling are also part of the program. Fees are determined along a sliding scale.

A branch office operates in Madison.

NORTHEASTERN MENTAL HEALTH CENTER

Clinic: All Ages. M-F 8-6.

Aberdeen, SD 57402. 703 3rd Ave SE, PO Box 550.
Tel: 605-225-1014.
www.nemhc.org
Mike Forgy, Exec Dir.
  Conditions: Primary—BD ED.
  Gen Acad. Pre-Voc. Courses: Read Math Lang_Arts.
  Psychotherapy: Fam Group Indiv.
  Staff: Prof 57.
  Est 1958. County. Nonprofit.

SIOUX FALLS CHILDREN'S HOME

Res and Day — Coed Ages 4-13

Sioux Falls, SD 57101. 801 N Sycamore Ave, PO Box 1749.
Tel: 605-334-6004. Fax: 605-335-2776.
www.chssd.org
Dennis Daugaard, Exec Dir. **Mike McFarland,** Clin Dir.
  Focus: Treatment. **Conditions:** Primary—ADD ADHD BD CD Dx ED LD Mood PTSD. Sec—OCD. **IQ 70 and up.**
  Gen Acad. Ungraded. Courses: Read Math Lang_Arts.
  Therapy: Lang Speech. **Psychotherapy:** Fam Group Indiv.
  Enr: 77. Res Males 45. Res Females 17. Day Males 14. Day Females 1.
  Est 1893. Private. Nonprofit. **Spons:** Children's Home Society.

SFCHS provides residential treatment for children with severe emotional, learning and behavioral disorders. The program emphasizes emotional development, social skills, academics and family therapy. The multidisciplinary approach incorporates psychology, social work, child psychiatry, child care, special education and nursing. An effort is made to deal with all aspects of the child's development, including follow-up counseling. The average length of treatment is one year.

SFCHS does not accept seriously handicapped or developmentally disabled children.

SIOUX VOCATIONAL SERVICES

Res and Day — Coed Ages 14 and up

Sioux Falls, SD 57105. 1406 S Minnesota Ave.
Tel: 605-274-1331. Fax: 605-338-0259.
www.siouxvocational.org

Anne Rieck-McFarland, Pres.
  Focus: Trng. **Conditions:** Primary—Asp Au BI CP Ep IP MD MR MS ON SB TS. Sec—ADD ADHD As B C CD D Dx ED LD OCD Psy S Sz.
  Voc. Shelt_Workshop. On-Job Trng.
  Therapy: Lang Occup Phys Speech. **Psychotherapy:** Indiv.
  Enr: 330.
  Est 1966. Private. Nonprofit.

SVS, which serves citizens with a wide range of disabilities (including both single and multiple diagnoses), provides prevocational evaluation, training and employability development services in such activities as mailings; assembly of materials; custodial services; food services; bakery work; pallet building/sawing; recycling; vehicle, grounds and building maintenance; and office support. Clients earn wages in accordance with federal guidelines.

Among residential accommodations are agency-owned homes, supported living homes and supervised apartments. Independent and community living services include evaluation and training.

SVS professionals provide various medical and therapeutic services.

SKY RANCH FOR BOYS

Res — Males Ages 10-18

Camp Crook, SD 57724. Sky Ranch Ln.
Tel: 605-797-4422. **Fax:** 605-797-4425.
www.skyranchfoundation.org   **E-mail:** slouks@starband.net
Scott Louks, MEd, Exec Dir.
  Focus: Treatment. **Conditions:** Primary—ADD ADHD BD Dx. Sec—CD ED.
  Gen Acad. Pre-Voc. Voc. Gr 3-12. Courses: Read Math Lang_Arts Sci Computers Health Aviation. Man_Arts & Shop.
  Psychotherapy: Group Indiv.
  Enr: 42. Res Males 42. **Staff:** 39. (Full 39). Prof 7. Educ 4. Admin 2.
  Est 1960. Private. Nonprofit. **Spons:** Sky Ranch Foundation.

Boys with emotional and behavioral disorders receive residential treatment and engage in an educational program at this facility. Residents may take part in a flight program and may also pursue the GED. Educational counseling is also provided for students with learning disabilities such as ADD, ADHD and dyslexia. The usual length of stay is six to twelve months. No psychotic or mentally retarded youths or fire setters are accepted for enrollment.

SOUTH DAKOTA DEVELOPMENTAL CENTER

Res — Coed Ages 10 and up

Redfield, SD 57469. 17267 W 3rd St.
Tel: 605-472-2400. **Fax:** 605-472-4216.
www.state.sd.us/dhs/redfield/page1.htm
  E-mail: infosddc@dhs-rf.state.sd.us
Ted Williams, MBA, Dir.

Focus: Treatment. **Conditions:** Primary—MR. Sec—ADD ADHD As Au B BD BI C CD CP D Dx ED Ep IP LD MD MS OCD ON Psy S SB Sz.
Gen Acad. Pre-Voc. Ungraded. Courses: Read Math. Shelt_Workshop.
Therapy: Chemo Hear Occup Phys Recreational Speech. **Psychotherapy:** Group Indiv.
Enr: 195.
Rates 2001: Res $230/day.
Est 1902. State. Nonprofit.

SDDC is a habilitation program aimed at returning the individual to his or her community. Staff utilize an interdisciplinary approach in developing individualized prescriptive program plans. The center emphasizes behavior management, life skills training and medication management.

SOUTH DAKOTA SCHOOL FOR THE BLIND AND VISUALLY IMPAIRED

Res — Coed Ages 5-21; Day — Coed Birth-21

Aberdeen, SD 57401. 423 17th Ave SE.
Tel: 605-626-2580. TTY: 605-626-2580. Fax: 605-626-2607.
www.sdsbvi.sdbor.edu
Marjorie A. Kaiser, EdD, Supt.
   Focus: Spec Ed. **Conditions:** Primary—B. Sec—Ap Au BI CP ED Ep LD MR ON S.
   Gen Acad. Pre-Voc. Gr PS-12. Courses: Read Math Lang_Arts Sci Soc_ Stud Braille. Man_Arts & Shop. On-Job Trng.
   Therapy: Hear Lang Occup Phys Speech.
   Enr: 31. Res Males 16. Res Females 10. Day Males 2. Day Females 3.
      Staff: 21 (Full 20, Part 1).
   Summer Prgm: Res & Day. Educ. Rec. 6 wks.
   Est 1900. State. Nonprofit. **Spons:** South Dakota Board of Regents.

Offering a regular academic program and a functional skills program, this state school stresses independence while emphasizing ADL, special skills and community interaction. This school is free for state residents. Nonresidents may attend for a fee.

SOUTH DAKOTA SCHOOL FOR THE DEAF

Res — Coed Ages 2½-21; Day — Coed Birth-21
Clinic: Ages Birth-21. M-F 8-4:30; Eve T 6-8:30.

Sioux Falls, SD 57103. 2001 E 8th St.
Tel: 605-367-5200. TTY: 605-367-5200. Fax: 605-367-5209.
www.sdsd.sdbor.edu   E-mail: sdsd@sdsd.sdbor.edu
Jon C. Green, PhD, Supt. Judy Bakkene, Adm.
   Focus: Spec Ed. **Conditions:** Primary—D. Sec—ADD ADHD AN Anx Ap As Asp Au B BD BI C CD CP Dx ED Ep LD MR OCD ODD PW TS. **IQ** 70-130.
   Gen Acad. Pre-Voc. Voc. Gr K-12. Courses: Read Math Lang_Arts. On-Job

Trng.
Therapy: Hear Lang Occup Percepual-Motor Phys Speech. **Psychotherapy:** Indiv.
Enr: 65. Res Males 3. Res Females 8. Day Males 35. Day Females 19.
Staff: 52 (Full 48, Part 4).
Rates 2004: Res $28,299/sch yr. Day $20,214/sch yr.
Summer Prgm: Res & Day. Educ. Rec. 2 wks.
Est 1880. State.

The school provides an early childhood program for families whose children have been diagnosed as deaf or hard of hearing. The educational program (grades K-12) includes occupational and physical therapies and sign language training for children and families. Early home intervention is available to parents who reside in South Dakota.

UNIVERSITY OF SOUTH DAKOTA
SPEECH AND HEARING CENTER

Clinic: All Ages. M-F 8-5.

Vermillion, SD 57069. 414 E Clark St.
Tel: 605-677-5474. Fax: 605-677-5767.
www.usd.edu/dcom/shcenter.cfm   E-mail: dcom@usd.edu
Teri James Bellis, Dir.
Focus: Treatment. **Conditions:** Primary—Ap D S.
Therapy: Hear Lang Speech.
Staff: Prof 7.
Est 1954. State.

TENNESSEE

ADVENT HOME YOUTH SERVICES

Res — Males Ages 12-16

Calhoun, TN 37309. 900 County Rd 950.
Tel: 423-336-5052. Fax: 423-336-8224.
www.adventhome.org   E-mail: info@adventhome.org
Blondel E. Senior, PhD, Exec Dir.

Focus: Spec Ed. Rehab. Trng. Treatment. **Conditions:** Primary—ADD ADHD BD CD ED LD Mood OCD. **IQ 15 and up.**
Gen Acad. Gr 6-10. Courses: Read Math Lang_Arts Sci Bible. On-Job Trng.
Enr: 28. Res Males 28. **Staff:** 28. Prof 15. Educ 6. Admin 6.
Rates 2003: Res $28,200/yr (+$135). Schol 20.
Est 1985. Private. Nonprofit. Seventh-day Adventist.

Advent Home provides an alternative to school suspension and dismissal, accepting students who do not function well in the traditional classroom and need more tutoring and remedial support than is available in a traditional classroom. To aid families, Advent Home also conducts weekend parent training sessions.

BEACON SCHOOL

Res and Day — Coed Ages 6-22

Greeneville, TN 37744. PO Box 188.
Tel: 423-787-8708. Fax: 423-639-7171.
www.holstonhome.org   E-mail: fredadavis@holstonhome.org
Freda G. Davis, Dir.

Focus: Spec Ed. Treatment. **Conditions:** Primary—ADD ADHD Asp Au BD BI CD CP DS Dx ED LD Mood MR MS OCD ON PDD Psy PTSD PW S SP Sz TS. Sec—AN Anx Ap Apr As Bu C Db Dc Dg Ep HIV IP MD Nf SB TB. **IQ 25 and up.**
Col Prep. Gen Acad. Pre-Voc. Voc. Gr K-12. Courses: Read Math Lang_Arts Soc_Stud Life_Skills. On-Job Trng.
Therapy: Lang Milieu Movement Occup Percepual-Motor Phys Play Recreational Speech. **Psychotherapy:** Fam Group Indiv Parent Substance_Abuse.
Enr: 99. Res Males 54. Res Females 9. Day Males 33. Day Females 3.
Staff: 30 (Full 24, Part 6). Prof 15. Educ 12. Admin 3.
Rates 2003: Day $70/day. State Aid.
Est 1895. Private. Nonprofit. United Methodist. **Spons:** Holston United Methodist Home for Children.

Students at the school begin their educational experience with a needs assessment. The pupil then progresses through one-on-one and small-group opportunities in the classroom, in counseling, in spiritual guidance and in recreational activities. Beacon aims to successfully return every child to a public school or a less intensive day program.

BENTON HALL SCHOOL

Day — Coed Ages 6-19

Franklin, TN 37069. 2420 Bethlehem Loop Rd.
Tel: 615-791-6467. Fax: 615-791-6522.
www.bentonhall.org   E-mail: info@bentonhall.org
Walt Murphy, MA, Prin.
Focus: Spec Ed. **Conditions:** Primary—ADD ADHD Anx As Asp CP Db DS
    Dx ED Ep Mood OCD TS. Sec—Au MR ON SP. **IQ 70 and up.**
Gen Acad. Gr 1-12. Courses: Read Math Lang_Arts Span Computers
    Studio_Art Music.
Therapy: Art Lang Occup Phys Speech. **Psychotherapy:** Group.
Enr: 90. Day Males 60. Day Females 30. **Staff:** 16 (Full 14, Part 2). Admin 4.
Rates 2003: Day $8300/sch yr (+$150). Schol 10 ($50,000).
Est 1978. Private. Nonprofit.

Enrolling boys and girls with various special needs, Benton Hall offers a highly individualized program designed to accommodate particular learning styles. In addition to academics, the school addresses the social, behavioral and emotional development of the student.

BILANDY ACADEMY

Res — Males Ages 7-17

Dickson, TN 37055. 222 Church St.
Tel: 615-446-3900. Fax: 615-446-1633.
E-mail: bilandyedu@jacksonacademy.com
Ted J. Gorzny, MS, MAEd, CEO. Kim Stringfield, Adm.
Focus: Spec Ed. **Conditions:** Primary—ADD ADHD BD ED. **IQ 70 and up.**
Gen Acad. Pre-Voc. Voc. Gr 1-12. Courses: Read Math Lang_Arts.
Therapy: Hear Lang Music Recreational Speech. **Psychotherapy:** Fam
    Group Indiv Parent.
Enr: 60. Res Males 60. **Staff:** 110 (Full 100, Part 10). Prof 23. Educ 6.
    Admin 8.
Private. Nonprofit. **Spons:** Jackson Academy.

Based on the campus of Jackson Academy, this year-round school serves emotionally troubled boys who are aggressive, acting-out, or simply in need of a highly structured and therapeutic environment. The educational program operates on a six weeks on, one week off basis.

THE BODINE SCHOOL

Day — Coed Ages 6-18

Germantown, TN 38139. 2432 Yester Oaks Dr.
Tel: 901-754-1800. Fax: 901-751-8595.
www.bodineschool.org   E-mail: info@bodineschool.org

Rene Friemoth Lee, PhD, Dir.
  Focus: Spec Ed. **Conditions:** Primary—Dx LD. Sec—ADD ADHD. **IQ 95 and up.**
  Col Prep. Gen Acad. Gr 1-12. Courses: Read Math Lang_Arts Sci Soc_ Stud.
  Therapy: Lang Speech.
  Enr: 75. **Staff:** 20 (Full 15, Part 5).
  Rates 2004: Day $10,100-12,100/sch yr. Schol avail.
  Summer Prgm: Day. Educ. Ther. Day Rate $575. 4 wks.
  Est 1972. Private. Nonprofit.

This school offers elementary and secondary programs for children with dyslexia. The goal of both programs is to remediate language-based learning disabilities to the degree that students are able to return to traditional educational institutions. Using specialized teaching methods, Bodine develops an individualized educational plan for each pupil that encourages the student to progress at a suitable pace.

The full curriculum includes math, social studies and science, as well as computer, physical education, library and art. As a complement to academics, students gain exposure to a range of cultural experiences through art classes, field trips, and interaction with visiting artists and speakers. Leadership skills—which boys and girls develop through participation in community service, student government and community activities—are integral to the program.

THE CAMELOT SCHOOLS

Res and Day — Coed Ages 5-17

Kingston, TN 37763. 183 Fiddler's Ln.
Tel: 865-376-2296. Fax: 865-376-1850.
Randy Yeager, BS, Exec Dir. **Tammy Kropp,** Prin. **Ryan K. Peters,** MS, Clin Dir. **Pradumna Jain,** MD, Med Dir. **Lisa Yeary,** Adm.
  Focus: Treatment. **Conditions:** Primary—ADD ADHD AN Anx Ap As Asp Au BD Bu CD Db Dc Dg Dx ED LD Mood OCD ODD PDD Psy PTSD S SP Sz TS. **IQ 70 and up.**
  Gen Acad. Pre-Voc. Gr K-12. Courses: Read Math Lang_Arts Sci Soc_Stud Choir Drama Studio_Art.
  Therapy: Lang Milieu Play Speech. **Psychotherapy:** Fam Group Indiv Parent.
  Enr: 41. Res Males 9. Res Females 22. Day Males 10. **Staff:** 32. Prof 20. Educ 4.
  Rates 2004: Day $85-180/day. State Aid.
  Est 1972. Private. Inc.

Camelot is a year-round, open-setting facility that emphasizes personality and behavioral development using process therapy and insight, reality-oriented therapy. Comprehensive evaluation, assessment and diagnosis are provided in a homelike atmosphere in addition to individual, group, family and milieu therapies. Special educational, vocational and independent living skills training programs are also available.

Recreational opportunities include swimming, tennis, basketball, football, and arts and crafts. Children attend an on-grounds school during their stay at Camelot, the length of which is usually three to six months. Nonambulatory, blind, psychotic and physically assaultive children are not appropriate for enrollment in this program.

Affiliated programs are located in Texas and Illinois.

CHILD AND FAMILY TENNESSEE

Res — Coed Ages 12-18
Clinic: All Ages. M-S 8:30-5; Eves M-F 5-9.

Knoxville, TN 37915. 901 Summit Hill Dr.
Tel: 865-524-7483. Fax: 865-524-4790.
www.child-family.org
Kate Oday, Exec Dir.
    Focus: Treatment. **Conditions:** Primary—ED. Sec—BD Dx LD.
    Voc. On-Job Trng.
    Therapy: Chemo Speech. **Psychotherapy:** Fam Group Indiv.
    Est 1929. Private. Nonprofit.

Child and Family Tennessee uses a behavior modification and eclectic approach in treating both child and family while providing a structured, homelike environment for the resident. Family involvement in counseling is required. Each resident participates in weekly peer group and individual psychotherapy sessions. Therapeutically oriented individual foster care is used when it is more appropriate than group home placement. Outpatient, independent living, in-home treatment and follow-up services are also available. The usual length of treatment is six months.

CURREY INGRAM ACADEMY

Day — Coed Ages 6-17

Brentwood, TN 37027. 6544 Murray Lane.
Tel: 615-507-3242. Fax: 615-507-3170.
www.curreyingram.org
Kathleen G. Rayburn, BS, MS, Head. **Kathleen H. Boles,** Adm.
    Focus: Spec Ed. **Conditions:** Primary—ADD ADHD Dc Dg Dx LD. **IQ 90 and up.**
    Col Prep. Gr K-12. Courses: Read Math Lang_Arts Span Sci Soc_Stud Studio_Art Music Drama.
    Therapy: Lang.
    Enr: 256. Day Males 186. Day Females 70. **Staff:** 110 (Full 99, Part 11).
    Rates 2004: Day $19,580-22,915/sch yr. Schol avail.
    Est 1968. Private.

Currey Ingram offers a full-scope curriculum for children with learning differences. The campus has a diagnostic center, a community and family outreach center. University partnerships and enrichment programs aid in the learning process.

EAST TENNESSEE CHILDREN'S HOSPITAL REHABILITATION CENTER

Clinic: Ages Birth-21. M-F 7:30-5:30; Eve T 5:30-7.

Knoxville, TN 37919. 8042 Gleason Rd.
Tel: 865-690-8961. Fax: 865-693-3941.
www.etch.com   E-mail: care@etch.com
Anne Woodle, BS, MS, Exec Dir. **Nadine Trainer,** MD, Med Dir.
  Focus: Rehab. **Conditions:** Primary—ADD ADHD Ap Apr Ar As Au B Bl C
    CF CP DS Ep IP LD MD MS Nf ON PDD PW S SB TS. Sec—Anx BD CD
    D Db Dc Dg Dx ED HIV MR OCD ODD Psy SP Sz TB.
  Therapy: Hear Lang Occup Phys Speech. **Psychotherapy:** Group Indiv
    Parent.
  Staff: 51. Prof 40. Admin 11.
  Est 1948. Private. Nonprofit.

Serving the counties of eastern Tennessee, this department of Children's Hospital provides physician-directed evaluation and treatment services to children with a wide range of special needs, including developmental delays, rehabilitative needs and neuro-muscular disorders, as well as muscular and skeletal diseases. Physical, occupational, speech and language therapies are provided and are based on a team approach to develop the child's individualized treatment plan. The center also provides home and educational programs, nutrition, social work, nursing, and recreational and socialization activities. The facility combines these programs with parental training, advocacy and support for comprehensive, family-focused programming. The facility operates year-round.

Day treatment for medically fragile children is also available.

EAST TENNESSEE STATE UNIVERSITY SPEECH, LANGUAGE AND HEARING CLINIC

Clinic: All Ages. M-F 8-5.

Johnson City, TN 37614. Dept of Communicative Disorders, PO Box 70640.
Tel: 423-439-4355. Fax: 423-439-4607.
www.etsu.edu/cpah/commdis/cdisclnc.htm
Jennifer Borsch, Dir.
  Conditions: Primary—D S.
  Therapy: Hear Lang Speech.
  Staff: Prof 5.
  Est 1960. State.

EASTER SEALS
MCWHORTER FAMILY CHILDREN'S CENTER

Day — Coed Ages Birth-5
Clinic: Ages Birth-18. M-F 8-6.

Nashville, TN 37215. 2001 Woodmont Blvd.
Tel: 615-312-6300. Fax: 615-312-6385.
www.tn.easterseals.com
Amy Harris-Solomon, MA, Dir.
   Focus: Spec Ed. Rehab. **Conditions:** Primary—ADD ADHD Ap Apr Ar As
      Asp Au CP DS Dx Ep LD MR ON PDD S SB.
   Gen Acad. Gr PS-K.
   Therapy: Hydro Milieu Occup Phys Speech.
   Enr: 45. **Staff:** 24 (Full 21, Part 3). Educ 9. Admin 5.
   Rates 2003: Day $650-780/mo. $50-85 (Clinic)/ses. State Aid.
   Private. Nonprofit.

The learning center draws on a number of resources and facilities to provide comprehensive services for children and adults with disabilities and their families. Programs cover the spectrum of rehabilitation, health and wellness, and educational care for the family, and McWhorter sponsors intergenerational programs between senior adults and young children who use the facilities. Each program offers ongoing training for caregivers, favorable staff-to-client ratios and developmentally appropriate learning activities.

ECKERD YOUTH ALTERNATIVES

Res — Males Ages 10-17

Deerlodge, TN.
Contact: 100 N Starcrest Dr, PO Box 7450, Clearwater, FL 33758.
Tel: 727-461-2990. Fax: 727-442-5911.
www.eckerd.org   E-mail: admissions@eckerd.org
Karen V. Waddell, BA, Pres. **Francene Hazel,** Dir.
   Focus: Treatment. **Conditions:** Primary—BD CD ED Mood ODD. Sec—
      ADD ADHD LD. **IQ 70 and up.**
   Gen Acad. Pre-Voc. Ungraded. Courses: Read Math Lang_Arts Sci Soc_
      Stud.
   Therapy: Speech. **Psychotherapy:** Fam Group Indiv.
   Summer Prgm: Res. Ther. Res Rate $180. 2 wks.
   Est 1968. Private. Nonprofit.

The Eckerd outdoor program offers therapeutic treatment to emotionally disturbed children by providing a camp setting as an alternative to institutionalization.

The year-round program utilizes reality therapy, Rogerian techniques and group therapy. Small-group living in the wilderness environment encourages the acquisition of new skills while promoting discipline and responsibility. Each group must construct their shelter, cut wood, repair equipment and perform other tasks necessary for their stay in the forest. Such experiences provide the children with the opportunity to develop academic skills at their own pace and in relation to each project they endeavor. When sufficient progress is made, children are transferred into the transition classroom in preparation for their return to the mainstream.

In addition to Tennessee, Eckerd conducts outdoor therapeutic treatment programs in the following states: Florida, Georgia, New Hampshire, North Carolina, Rhode Island and Vermont (see separate listings).

FORTWOOD MENTAL HEALTH CENTER
Clinic: All Ages. M-F 8:30-5; Eve T 5-7.

Chattanooga, TN 37403. 1028 E 3rd St.
Tel: 423-266-6751. Fax: 423-763-4650.
www.fortwoodcenter.org   E-mail: info@fortwoodcenter.org
  Conditions: Primary—BD ED.
  Psychotherapy: Fam Group Indiv.
  Staff: Prof 56.
  Est 1947. Private. Nonprofit.

HARRIETT COHN CENTER
Res and Day — Coed All Ages

Clarksville, TN 37040. 511 8th St.
Tel: 931-920-7200. Fax: 931-920-7202.
www.centerstone.org/history/harriett_cohn.shtml
  Conditions: Primary—BD ED.
  Col Prep. Gen Acad. Pre-Voc. Voc. Ungraded. Courses: Read Math Lang_
    Arts. Man_Arts & Shop.
  Therapy: Chemo. **Psychotherapy:** Fam Group.
  Est 1959. Private. Nonprofit. **Spons:** Centerstone.

HIGH HOPES
Day — Coed Ages Birth-6
Clinic: Ages Birth-6. M-F 8-5.

Brentwood, TN 37024. 7100 Sharondale Ct, PO Box 1956.
Tel: 615-661-5437. Fax: 615-309-8342.
www.highhopesinc.org   E-mail: rhensley@highhopesnash.org
Rinne Hensley, Exec Dir. Carolyn Roark, Adm.
  Focus: Treatment. **Conditions:** Primary—ADD ADHD Apr Asp Au BI CP
    DS LD MR ON PDD S SB. Sec—Ap BD C D ED Ep IP.
  Therapy: Hear Lang Music Occup Phys Speech.
  Enr: 40. **Staff:** 23 (Full 10, Part 13).
  Rates 2004: Day $2400-4800/yr. $350 (Evaluation); $126 (Therapy)/ses.
    Schol avail. State Aid.
  Est 1984. Private. Nonprofit.

Young children from the middle Tennessee area who have special needs such as Down syndrome, cerebral palsy, speech and language disorders, autism and other developmental delays receive a full range of services through the facility. In addition to classroom activities for children through age 6, High Hopes offers occupational, physical, and speech and language therapies. The year-round program emphasizes learning through play and addresses the needs of both child and family.

THE KING'S DAUGHTERS' SCHOOL

Res and Day — Coed Ages 7-22

Columbia, TN 38401. 412 W 9th St.
Tel: 931-388-3810. Fax: 931-388-0405.
www.tkds.org   E-mail: info@tkds.org
Charlotte G. Battles, Exec Dir. **Janice Hight,** MD, Med Dir.
  Focus: Spec Ed. **Conditions:** Primary—Asp Au DS MR. Sec—CD CP OCD ODD PW. **IQ 40-74.**
  Voc. Ungraded. Courses: Read Math Lang_Arts. Shelt_Workshop. On-Job Trng.
  Therapy: Hear Lang Phys Speech. **Psychotherapy:** Group Indiv.
  Enr: 85. Res Males 53. Res Females 29. Day Males 1. Day Females 2.
    Staff: 120. Prof 32. Educ 25. Admin 7.
  Summer Prgm: Res & Day. Educ. Rec.
  Est 1955. Private. Nonprofit.

The school serves individuals with developmental disabilities such as mental retardation, autism and Prader-Willi syndrome. Students may also have a dual diagnosis. The Total Lifestyles Program, the core program of KDS, is a year-round boarding school that emphasizes education and independence. Under 24-hour supervision, pupils follow specialized plans that are tailored to their academic and social needs and abilities. Independent living skills training, vocational/employment opportunities, leisure and recreational activities, behavioral analysis and modification, social/adaptive behavior training and cognitive behavior therapy are all elements of the program.

In addition to the main residential program, an adult home program offers year-round residential services to a limited number of mentally-challenged adults over age 22. Residents receive vocational and employment services with close supervision. Clients learn practical work skills in a structured setting that focuses on long-term needs. Many of the participants in the adult program first enrolled in the children's program.

KIWANIS CENTER FOR CHILD DEVELOPMENT

Day — Coed Ages Birth-3
Clinic: Ages Birth-18. M-F 8-4:30.

Jackson, TN 38305. 32 Garland Dr.
Tel: 731-668-9070. Fax: 731-668-6549.
Ron Kwasigroh, MBA, Dir. **David Roberts,** MD, Med Dir. **Claire Moss,** Adm.
  Focus: Rehab. **Conditions:** Primary—Au BI CP MR OH. Sec—B D LD S.
  Therapy: Hear Hydro Lang Occup Phys Speech. **Psychotherapy:** Group

Indiv.
Est 1969. County. Nonprofit. **Spons:** West Tennessee Healthcare.

Kiwanis Center conducts a program of early intervention and stimulation for children with developmental delays. Staff members design individualized development programs for each child in the areas of self-help, socialization, language, percepto-cognition, and fine and gross motor. The center's health clinic enables clients to receive pediatric speech, occupational and physical therapy, as well as hydrotherapy. Another aspect of the program is educational training for parents; this training is available both at the center and at home.

MEMPHIS ORAL SCHOOL FOR THE DEAF

Day — Coed Ages Birth-8

Memphis, TN 38105. 711 Jefferson Ave.
Tel: 901-448-8490. TTY: 901-448-1574. Fax: 901-448-8495.
www.oraldeafed.org/schools/memphis   E-mail: ekenworthy@utmem.edu
Elizabeth Farrar, BA, JD, Exec Dir. **Teresa Patterson Schwartz,** BA, Prin.
  Focus: Spec Ed. **Conditions:** Primary—D. **IQ 90 and up.**
  Gen Acad. Gr PS-8.
  Therapy: Hear Lang Movement Music Speech.
  Enr: 26. Day Males 15. Day Females 11. **Staff:** 13. (Full 13).
  Rates 2003: Day $16,000/yr. Schol avail. State Aid.
  Summer Prgm: Day. Educ. Ther. Day Rate $675. 4 wks.
  Est 1959. Private. Nonprofit.

Memphis School provides auditory-oral education, family training, speech and language therapy, audiology services and specialized instruction for young children with hearing impairments. Tuition fees are determined along a sliding scale.

MIDDLE TENNESSEE STATE UNIVERSITY
SPEECH-LANGUAGE-HEARING CLINIC

Clinic: All Ages. M-Th 7:30-4.

Murfreesboro, TN 37132. Boutwell Dramatic Arts Bldg, Rm 232, Box 364.
Tel: 615-898-2661. Fax: 615-898-5826.
www.mtsu.edu/~comm_dis/clinic/clinic.html   E-mail: cshaw@mtsu.edu
Elizabeth Smith, MA, CCC-SLP, Coord.
  Focus: Treatment. **Conditions:** Primary—Au D LD S. Sec—ADD ADHD Dx.
  Therapy: Hear Lang Speech.
  Est 1968. State. Nonprofit.

The clinic offers speech, language and hearing evaluations and therapy for individuals with hearing, articulation, voice, stuttering, language and other communicative disorders. MTSU students, faculty and staff may receive services free of charge. The clinic operates during the university's academic year; clients typically make approximately 25 visits during the course of a semester.

MID-SOUTH ARC

Clinic: All Ages. M-F 8:30-4:30.

Memphis, TN 38111. 3485 Poplar Ave, Ste 225.
Tel: 901-327-2473. Fax: 901-327-2687.
www.arcmidsouth.net   E-mail: msarc@arcmidsouth.net
Carlene I. Leaper, Exec Dir.
   Conditions: Primary—Au CP DS MD MR.
   Pre-Voc. Voc. Ungraded. On-Job Trng.
   Est 1950. Private. Inc.

ORANGE GROVE CENTER

Res — Coed Ages 14 and up; Day — Coed 5 and up

Chattanooga, TN 37404. 615 Derby St.
Tel: 423-629-1451. Fax: 423-624-1294.
Michael L. Cook, MS, Exec Dir.
   Focus: Trng. Treatment. **Conditions:** Primary—MR. Sec—B Bl CP D ED
      Ep ON SB.
   Pre-Voc. Voc. Ungraded. Courses: Read Math Lang_Arts Studio_Art Music.
      Shelt_Workshop. On-Job Trng.
   Therapy: Art Hear Lang Phys Speech Visual. **Psychotherapy:** Indiv.
   Enr: 803. **Staff:** 335.
   Est 1953. Private. Nonprofit.

Orange Grove is a comprehensive training facility for mentally retarded children and adults. An interdisciplinary team formulates and monitors an individual program plan for each client.

Educational programs for school-age children include basic self-help skills training where needed and classes for those whose academic needs may lead toward vocational preparation and eventual independence. Certified special education teachers are responsible for each classroom, with supportive services provided by specialists and assistants.

Adult day services for those not yet demonstrating vocational readiness are available for individuals whose disabilities may be severe. Vocational services consist of a continuum of programs: comprehensive work evaluation, prevocational classes, a work activity center, a sheltered workshop, work stations in industry, placement services and follow-along support.

Professionals direct special services that include a wide range of medical, psychological and physical therapies. The center also offers services to individuals with hearing and visual impairments.

Residential services emphasizing independent living skills are available in group home settings. Staff members make every effort to provide a normal living environment utilizing recreational and home facilities. Available activities include sports and such crafts as woodworking and ceramics.

PATHWAYS CHILDREN AND YOUTH SERVICES

Clinic: Ages 3-18. M-F 8-5.

Jackson, TN 38301. 238 Summar Dr.
Tel: 731-935-8333. Fax: 731-935-8327.
Kelly Yenawine, Exec Dir. Nat Winston, MD, Med Dir. Charlotte Hall, Adm.
  Focus: Treatment. Conditions: Primary—Anx BD CD ED Mood OCD Psy
    PTSD SP Sz. Sec—MR. IQ 70 and up.
  Therapy: Art Chemo. Psychotherapy: Fam Group Indiv Parent.
  Staff: 29 (Full 27, Part 2). Prof 26. Admin 3.
  Rates 2003: Clinic $90/hr. Sliding-Scale Rate $10-75/hr.
  Est 1957. Private. Nonprofit.

A comprehensive mental health center, this facility offers inpatient and outpatient services, partial hospitalization, emergency services, consultation and education, rehabilitation and aftercare. Parental and personal counseling is also available.

PENINSULA VILLAGE

Res — Coed Ages 13-18

Louisville, TN 37777. 2340 Jones Bend Rd, PO Box 100.
Tel: 865-970-3255. Fax: 865-970-1875.
www.peninsulavillage.org
Don Vardell, BA, MS, Admin.
  Conditions: Primary—ADD ADHD BD Mood Psy. Sec—LD. IQ 80 and up.
  Col Prep. Gen Acad. Pre-Voc. Ungraded. Courses: Read Math Lang_Arts.
  Psychotherapy: Fam.
  Est 1986. Private. Inc.

REGIONAL INTERVENTION PROGRAM

Day — Coed Ages Birth-5

Nashville, TN 37215. 3411 Belmont Blvd.
Tel: 615-963-1177. Fax: 615-963-1178.
www.ripnetwork.org   E-mail: mail@ripnetwork.org
Katherine Driskill Kanies, MA, MLS, Dir.
  Focus: Treatment. Conditions: Primary—BD CD ED OCD Psy Sz. Sec—
    ADD ADHD Ap As Au B BI C CP D Dx Ep IP LD MD MR MS ON S SB
    TB.
  Psychotherapy: Parent.
  Staff: 19 (Full 12, Part 7).
  Rates 2004: No Fee.
  Est 1969. State. Nonprofit. Spons: Middle Tennessee Mental Health Institute.

RIP is a state-supported program that trains parents of preschool-age children with behavioral and developmental challenges in positive behavior management and teaching techniques. Parents and other family members serve as primary teachers and therapists for their own children, and as principal trainers of other parents and children. A professional resource staff supports the program.

Families incur no monetary fees for service; parents later pay with their time and skills for a period of time equal to that spent enrolled in the program. The average length of treatment for a family is six months.

SCENIC LAND SCHOOL

Day — Coed Ages 4-14

Chatanooga, TN 37405. 1130 Mountain Creek Rd.
Tel: 423-877-9711. Fax: 423-876-0398.
www.sceniclandschool.org   E-mail: ecard@sceniclandschool.org
Eileen A. Card, BFA, MEd, Head. Michele McRae, Adm.
  Focus: Spec Ed. Conditions: Primary—ADD ADHD Anx Apr As Asp Au Bl
    CF CP Db Dc Dg Dx ED SB SP TS. IQ 80 and up.
  Col Prep. Gen Acad. Ungraded. Courses: Read Math Lang_Arts Sci Soc_
    Stud Studio_Art Keyboarding.
  Therapy: Lang Percepual-Motor Speech.
  Enr: 34. Day Males 26. Day Females 8. Staff: 13 (Full 10, Part 3). Prof 12.
  Rates 2003: Day $10,500/yr (+$100). Sliding-Scale Rate $50-80 (Therapy)/
    hr. Schol 15 ($55,000). State Aid.
  Summer Prgm: Day. Educ. Rec. Day Rate $900. 4 wks.
  Est 1968. Private. Nonprofit.

SLS operates individualized learning programs for pupils with learning differences. In addition, Scenic Land maintains an after-school reading tutorial program and an assessment center to aid in diagnosing students with dyslexia and other learning disabilities. Prospective students must have a diagnosed learning disability.

SOUTHEAST MENTAL HEALTH CENTER

Clinic: Ages 5-18. M-Th 8-4:30, F 8-3:30, S 9-1; Eves M W 4:30-8.

Memphis, TN 38181. 3810 Winchester Rd, PO Box 18720.
Tel: 901-369-1420. Fax: 901-369-1433.
Gene Lawrence, CEO. Debra Dillon, MS, RN, Dir. Laurie Powell, MSW,
  LCSW, Clin Supv. Lalitha Vaddadi, MD, Med Dir.
  Focus: Treatment. Conditions: Primary—ADD ADHD Anx BD CD ED
    Mood OCD Psy PTSD Sz. Sec—AN Au B Bl Bu CP D Dx MD MS S.
  Therapy: Chemo Speech. Psychotherapy: Fam Group Indiv Parent.
  Staff: 18 (Full 14, Part 4). Prof 15. Admin 3.
  Rates 2003: Sliding-Scale Rate $4-150/ses.
  Est 1975. Private. Nonprofit.

The center provides a variety of individual, group and family counseling services for children. Parents are actively involved in the treatment process, as the facility strives for the improvement of parenting skills and the resolution of family conflicts. Clients undergo individual psychological and educational assessments, as necessary, to identify the strengths and weaknesses of the child and to help determine appropriate treatment strategies.

The agency also functions as a resource center that supplies the public with information about mental health issues. Duration of treatment ranges from three months to several years.

SUSAN GRAY SCHOOL FOR CHILDREN

Day — Coed Ages Birth-3

Nashville, TN 37203. Vanderbilt Univ, Peabody Box 40, 230 Appleton Pl.
Tel: 615-322-8200. Fax: 615-322-8236.
www.kc.vanderbilt.edu/kennedy/sgs   E-mail: kc@vanderbilt.edu
Ruth Wolery, PhD, Dir.
   Focus: Spec Ed. Treatment. **Conditions:** Primary—Au BI CP DS Ep IP MR ON S SB. Sec—B D.
   Gen Acad. Gr PS.
   Therapy: Occup Phys Speech.
   Enr: 72. **Staff:** 40.
   Rates 2004: No Fee.
   Est 1968. Private. Nonprofit. **Spons:** Vanderbilt University.

Conducted by Vanderbilt's John F. Kennedy Center for Research on Human Development, the school provides year-round early intervention and early education services for infants and toddlers with developmental delays. The program offers services in homes, classrooms, and community childcare centers for children with and without developmental disabilities.

Susan Gray School also provides a setting for training future teachers and researchers, and for demonstrating educational models serving young children with special needs. In addition, the school supports research on developmental disabilities and related aspects of human development.

TENNESSEE SCHOOL FOR THE BLIND

Res and Day — Coed Ages 3-21

Donelson, TN 37214. 115 Stewarts Ferry Pike.
Tel: 615-231-7300. Fax: 615-871-9312.
www.tsb.k12tn.net
James A. Oldham, MEd, Supt. **Elaine Brown,** Adm.
   Focus: Spec Ed. **Conditions:** Primary—B. Sec—ADD ADHD Ap As BI C CP D Dx ED Ep IP LD MD MR ON S SB.
   Col Prep. Gen Acad. Pre-Voc. Voc. Gr PS-12. Courses: Read Math Lang_ Arts Computers. Man_Arts & Shop. Shelt_Workshop. On-Job Trng.
   Therapy: Lang Occup Phys Speech. **Psychotherapy:** Group Indiv.
   Enr: 176. Res Males 67. Res Females 48. Day Males 31. Day Females 30.
   Staff: 186 (Full 183, Part 3). Prof 54. Educ 43. Admin 8.

Rates 2004: No Fee.
Summer Prgm: Res & Day. Educ. 2-4 wks.
Est 1844. State. Nonprofit.

This state school accepts children who are blind or multi-handicapped and provides them with an educational program and vocational training. A summer session will accept enrollment from the regular program. Pupils typically remain at the school until graduation.

TENNESSEE SCHOOL FOR THE DEAF

Res and Day — Coed Ages 4-21

Knoxville, TN 37920. 2725 Island Home Blvd.
Tel: 865-594-6022. Fax: 865-579-2484.
http://tsdeaf.org   E-mail: tsd@tsdeaf.org
Alan J. Mealka, Supt.
   Conditions: Primary—D.
   Col Prep. Gen Acad. Pre-Voc. Voc. Gr PS-12. Courses: Read Math Lang_
      Arts. Man_Arts & Shop. On-Job Trng.
   Therapy: Hear Phys Speech. **Psychotherapy:** Indiv.
   State.

UNIVERSITY OF TENNESSEE
BOLING CENTER FOR DEVELOPMENTAL DISABILITIES

Clinic: All Ages. M-F 8-5.

Memphis, TN 38105. 711 Jefferson Ave.
Tel: 901-448-6511. TTY: 901-448-4677. Fax: 901-448-3844.
www.utmem.edu/bcdd   E-mail: wwilson@utmem.edu
Frederick B. Palmer, MD, Dir. William M. Wilson, MA, Clin Coord. David B.
   Kube, MD, Med Dir.
   Focus: Treatment. **Conditions:** Primary—ADD ADHD Apr Asp Au B Bl CP
      D Dc Dg DS Dx Ep LD MR Nf ON PDD PW S SB TS. Sec—BD CD ED
      OCD Psy.
   Therapy: Chemo Hear Lang Occup Phys Speech. **Psychotherapy:** Fam
      Group Indiv Parent.
   Staff: 52 (Full 45, Part 7). Prof 29. Educ 8. Admin 8.
   Est 1957. State.

Services at the clinic include diagnostic evaluation and treatment of individuals with mental retardation and other developmental disabilities. Also available are behavioral counseling, psychotherapy, medical therapy for clients with ADHD, speech-language therapy and treatment of inborn metabolic disorders. Fees vary according to family size and income level, services rendered and time involved.

UNIVERSITY OF TENNESSEE-KNOXVILLE HEARING AND SPEECH CENTER

Day — Coed Ages 9mos-18
Clinic: All Ages. M-F 8-5.

Knoxville, TN 37996. 1600 Peyton Manning Pass.
Tel: 865-974-5451. Fax: 865-974-4639.
www.uthearingandspeech.org   E-mail: valentin@utk.edu
Ann Michael, BA, MA, PhD, CCC-SLP, Dir. **Carol Sheridan,** BS, MA, CCC-SLP, Coord.
   Focus: Treatment. **Conditions:** Primary—Ap Apr Asp Au BI CP D DS Dx LD MR MS PDD S SB.
   Therapy: Hear Lang Speech. **Psychotherapy:** Group Parent.
   Staff: 27 (Full 17, Part 10). Admin 5.
   Rates 2003: Sliding-Scale Rate $0-70/hr.
   Est 1953. State.

The UT Hearing and Speech Center offers diagnostic and treatment services for clients with a variety of disorders resulting in speech, language and hearing disorders or differences. A pediatric language clinic serves infants and toddlers with developmental disabilities, while an aural-oral program addresses the needs of infants, toddlers, preschoolers and other children with hearing impairments or cochlear implants. Diagnostic and treatment services are also offered to adolescents and adults who have problems with communication skills.

WAVES EARLY INTERVENTION PROGRAM

Day — Coed Ages Birth-3

Franklin, TN 37064. 435 Main St, Ste A.
Tel: 615-794-9602. Fax: 615-791-9179.
www.wavesinc.com
Susan Van Horn, BS, Prgm Coord.
   Focus: Spec Ed. **Conditions:** Primary—Apr Asp Au B BI C CP D DS IP MD MR Nf ON PDD PW S SB. Sec—As ED Ep.
   Therapy: Hear Lang Occup Percepual-Motor Phys Play Speech.
   Enr: 55. Day Males 35. Day Females 20. **Staff:** 16 (Full 3, Part 13). Prof 14. Admin 2.
   Rates 2003: No Fee.
   Est 1987. Private. Nonprofit.

This program serves children in Williamson County who have any type of developmental delay. Services consist of early intervention, developmental assessments, and community education and support. Home-based services are available to children who can be better served by remaining in their homes. The program operates year-round.

WEST TENNESSEE SCHOOL FOR THE DEAF

Res and Day — Coed Ages 3-13
Clinic: Ages Birth-21. M-F 8-4:30.

Jackson, TN 38301. 100 Berryhill Dr.
Tel: 731-423-5705. Fax: 731-423-6470.
www.wtsd.tn.org
Barbara M. Bone, MS, Supt.
   Focus: Spec Ed. **Conditions:** Primary—D.
   Gen Acad. Gr PS-6. Courses: Read Math Lang_Arts.
   Therapy: Hear Lang Phys Speech.
   Enr: 61. Res Males 7. Day Males 28. Day Females 26. **Staff:** 16.
   Rates 2004: No Fee.
   Est 1986. State.

Program services at the school include education, diagnostic testing for students referred by local school districts, educational consultations and a home-based parent-infant program (Tennessee Infant Parent Services) serving children up to age 4.

TEXAS

ABILENE STATE SCHOOL

Res — Coed Ages 6 and up

Abilene, TX 79604. PO Box 451.
Tel: 325-692-4053.
www.dads.state.tx.us/services/stateschools/Abilene/index.html
  Conditions: Primary—MR.
  Pre-Voc. Ungraded. Courses: Read Math Lang_Arts. Shelt_Workshop. On-Job Trng.
  Therapy: Hear Lang Occup Phys Speech. **Psychotherapy:** Group Indiv.
  Est 1901. State. Nonprofit.

AMARILLO COLLEGE
ACCESS LEARNING CENTER

Day — Coed Ages 16 and up

Amarillo, TX 79109. 2200 S Washington St.
Tel: 806-371-5434. Fax: 806-371-5423.
www.actx.edu/~access/learncent.html   E-mail: hamblin-ag@actx.edu
Ann Hamblin, MEd, Dir.
  Focus: Treatment. **Conditions:** Primary—Dx LD OH.
  Gen Acad. Ungraded. Courses: Read Math Lang_Arts.
  Staff: 24 (Full 4, Part 20). Prof 24. Educ 24.
  Rates 2003: Clinic $45/ses. State Aid.
  Est 1987. State.

Postsecondary students are offered academic assistance within a community college setting. Services include deficient academic skill assessment, development of an educational plan and small-group instruction. Course work consists of English, reading, math, spelling, study skills and English as a Second Language. Instruction consists of 15 hour-long classes.

ARBOR ACRE PREPARATORY SCHOOL

Day — Coed Ages 4-14

Dallas, TX 75232. 8000 S Hampton Rd.
Tel: 972-224-0511. Fax: 972-224-0511.
Mary E. Cunningham, BA, MEd, Dir.
  Focus: Spec Ed. **Conditions:** Primary—ADD ADHD Dc Dg Dx LD. Sec—As Db ED OH.
  Gen Acad. Gr PS-8. Courses: Read Math Lang_Arts Sci Hist.
  Therapy: Art Lang.

Enr: 40. Day Males 35. Day Females 5. **Staff:** 10 (Full 8, Part 2).
Rates 2003: Day $3800/sch yr ($100-150). Sliding-Scale Rate $2720-3260.
Summer Prgm: Day. Educ. Day Rate $500. 6 wks.
Est 1969. Private. Nonprofit.

Arbor Acre enrolls students with learning disabilities in a small-classroom environment that enables them to progress at an appropriate rate. Programming addresses the child's academic, social and emotional needs.

AUSTIN CHILD GUIDANCE CENTER

Clinic: Ages Birth-17. M-F 9-6; Eves M-Th 6-7.

Austin, TX 78751. 810 W 45th St.
Tel: 512-451-2242. Fax: 512-454-9204.
www.austinchildguidance.org
Donald J. Zappone, PhD, Exec Dir. **Michael Hastie,** Clin Dir. **Rebecca Calhoun,** Intake.
  Conditions: Primary—ADD BD CD ED Mood OCD Psy Sz.
  Psychotherapy: Indiv Parent.
  Staff: 30 (Full 20, Part 10).
  Est 1951. Private. Nonprofit.

ACGC provides mental health services for children who are experiencing such difficulties as emotional problems resulting from the breakup of the child's family, sexual abuse, physical abuse or neglect, school adjustment problems, ADD, family communication problems, extreme aggression, depression, experimentation with drugs or alcohol, and poor decision-making skills. The center seeks to improve the client's functioning at home, at school and in the community.

A multidisciplinary team of psychiatrists, psychologists, social workers and counselors administers such services as psychiatric and psychological assessments; individual, family and group counseling; parental and public education; outdoor experiential activities; professional staff trainings; and program evaluation and research projects. ACGC provides some services free of charge, with rates for the remaining services based upon a sliding scale.

AUSTIN STATE HOSPITAL
CHILD AND ADOLESCENT PSYCHIATRIC SERVICES

Res — Coed Ages 4-18

Austin, TX 78751. 4110 Guadalupe St.
Tel: 512-452-0381. Fax: 512-419-2512.
www.mhmr.state.tx.us/hospitals/austinsh/austinsh.html
Jacqueline Hughes, Dir.
  Conditions: Primary—ED. Sec—ADD LD Mood MR PTSD.
  Gen Acad. Pre-Voc. Voc. Ungraded. Courses: Read Math Lang_Arts. Man_ Arts & Shop.
  Therapy: Lang Milieu Music Occup Recreational Speech. **Psychotherapy:** Fam Group Indiv.

Staff: Prof 40.
Est 1966. State.

AUTISTIC TREATMENT CENTER

Res — Coed Ages 4 and up; Day — Coed 3 and up

Dallas, TX 75243. 10503 Forest Ln, Ste 100.
Tel: 972-644-2076. Fax: 972-644-5650.
www.atcoftexas.org   E-mail: csylvester@atcoftexas.org
Anna Hundley, Exec Dir. Carolyn Garver, PhD, Dir. Misty McClure, Adm.
　Focus: Treatment. **Conditions:** Primary—Au B D. Sec—ADD ADHD CD ED
　　MR Psy S. **IQ 0-70.**
　Gen Acad. Pre-Voc. Voc. Ungraded. Courses: Read Math Lang_Arts Life_
　　Skills. Shelt_Workshop. On-Job Trng.
　Therapy: Lang Occup Phys Speech. **Psychotherapy:** Indiv.
　Enr: 55. Res Males 38. Res Females 12. Day Males 3. Day Females 2.
　　Staff: 63 (Full 60, Part 3).
　Rates 2003: Res $165/day. Day $65/day. State Aid.
　Summer Prgm: Day. Educ. Day Rate $65/day. 12 wks.
　Est 1976. Private. Nonprofit.

Children with autism and developmental delays receive long-term, highly structured care at the center. The facility's program consists of an early intervention program; a developmental day school; residential services in group homes, transitional living settings and supported apartments; and vocational services. These services are designed to help students live as independently as possible.

ATC operates a branch facility in San Antonio at 16111 Nacogdoches Rd., 78247.

AVONDALE HOUSE

Res — Coed Ages 4-30; Day — Coed 3-22

Houston, TX 77027. 3611 Cummins Ln.
Tel: 713-993-9544. Fax: 713-993-0751.
www.avondalehouse.org
Barbara F. Boyett, MA, Exec Dir.
　Focus: Trng. **Conditions:** Primary—ADD ADHD Au PDD. Sec—B D ED
　　MR S. **IQ 20-69.**
　Pre-Voc. Ungraded. Courses: Life_Skills.
　Therapy: Speech.
　Enr: 59. Res Males 14. Res Females 4. Day Males 34. Day Females 7.
　　Staff: 43 (Full 39, Part 4). Prof 8. Educ 6. Admin 8.
　Rates 2003: Res $4850/mo. Day $1850/mo. $70 (Speech Therapy)/hr. State
　　Aid.
　Est 1976. Private. Nonprofit.

Children with autism or pervasive developmental disorder receive educational and vocational training at Avondale. The school program offers students speech, behavior, social, prevocational and limited academic instruction. Residents live in one of three area group homes.

THE BATTIN CLINIC

Clinic: All Ages. M-F 9-5.

Houston, TX 77027. 4545 Post Oak Pl, Ste 375.
　　Nearby locations: Nassau Bay.
Tel: 713-621-3072. TTY: 713-621-3073. Fax: 713-621-6020.
E-mail: rhrb@pdq.net
R. Ray Battin, PhD, Dir.
　　Focus: Treatment. **Conditions:** Primary—ADD ADHD Ap BD Bl D Dx ED LD S. Sec—CP MR.
　　Therapy: Hear Lang Speech. **Psychotherapy:** Fam Group Indiv.
　　Staff: 4 (Full 3, Part 1). Prof 3. Admin 1.
　　Rates 2003: Clinic $100-150/hr.
　　Est 1959. Private. Inc.

Primarily treating children and adolescents, The Battin Clinic provides psycholinguistic/psycho-educational evaluation and therapy. Comprehensive testing involves examination of intellectual, visual, auditory and emotional functioning, academic achievement, visual-motor coordination, speech and psycholinguistic/learning skills. Initial evaluations usually last four to five hours, and parent conferences are held to discuss the results.

A branch of the clinic operates in Nassau Bay (18100 Upper Bay Blvd., 77058).

BAYTOWN OPPORTUNITY CENTER

Day — Coed Ages 16 and up

Baytown, TX 77521. 1507 W Baker Rd.
Tel: 281-427-0545.
　　Conditions: Primary—MR OH.
　　Pre-Voc. Voc. Ungraded. Shelt_Workshop. On-Job Trng.
　　Est 1954. Private. Nonprofit. **Spons:** United Way of Baytown.

BRAZOS VALLEY REHABILITATION CENTER

Clinic: All Ages. M-F 8-5.

Bryan, TX 77802. 1318 Memorial Dr.
Tel: 979-776-2872. Fax: 979-776-1456.
www.east-texas.easterseals.com
Cheryl Allen, MBA, OTR, Exec Dir.
　　Focus: Treatment. **Conditions:** Primary—Bl CP IP MD MS ON SB. Sec—Ap As B C D Dx LD MR S.
　　Therapy: Hear Lang Occup Phys Speech. **Psychotherapy:** Fam Equine.

Staff: 15 (Full 13, Part 2).
Est 1957. Private. Nonprofit. **Spons:** National Easter Seal Society.

Brazos Valley serves persons with physical disabilities through programs of physical, occupational, speech and hearing therapies. Psychological and social services, as well as parental counseling, are also available. Fees are determined along a sliding scale.

BRENHAM STATE SCHOOL

Res — Coed Ages 6 and up
Clinic: All Ages. M-F 8-5.

Brenham, TX 77833. 4001 Hwy 36 S.
Tel: 979-836-4511. Fax: 979-277-1865.
www.mhmr.state.tx.us/schools/brenhamss/brenhamss.html
Richard Browder, EdD, Supt.
    Focus: Trng. Treatment. **Conditions:** Primary—MR. Sec—Ap As B BD Bl C CP D Dx ED IP LD MD MS ON S SB.
    Gen Acad. Pre-Voc. Voc. Ungraded. Courses: Read Math Lang_Arts. Shelt_Workshop. On-Job Trng.
    Therapy: Hear Lang Occup Phys Speech. **Psychotherapy:** Fam Group Indiv.
    Enr: 400.
    Est 1969. State.

Brenham provides transitional residential services in the least restrictive manner possible for moderately to profoundly retarded children and adults. Individual programs are designed to give each resident the opportunity to reach his or her potential. Education and training classes include language development, supportive therapy, recreation, arts and crafts, music and special programs for individuals with orthopedic handicaps.

The facility offers outreach services in communities where limited or no programs or services exist for persons with developmental disabilities. These include education and training classes, daycare, work activity centers, and diagnostic and evaluation services. Counseling services are available, and fees are based on a sliding scale. Enrollment is restricted to a 14-county area.

THE BRIARWOOD SCHOOL

Day — Coed Ages 5-21

Houston, TX 77077. 12207 Whittington Dr.
Tel: 281-493-1070. Fax: 281-493-1343.
www.briarwoodschool.org   E-mail: info@briarwoodschool.org
Yvonne Streit, BA, Exec Dir. Carole C. Wills, BBA, Prin. Priscilla Mitchell, Adm.
    Focus: Spec Ed. **Conditions:** Primary—ADD ADHD LD. **IQ 100 and up.**
    Col Prep. Gen Acad. Pre-Voc. Voc. Gr K-12. Courses: Read Math Lang_Arts Studio_Art Drama. On-Job Trng.
    Therapy: Lang Occup Speech. **Psychotherapy:** Fam Parent.
    Enr: 300. Day Males 200. Day Females 100. **Staff:** 91 (Full 85, Part 6).

Rates 2004: Day $12,995/sch yr (+$300-1150). Schol avail.
Summer Prgm: Day. Rec. Day Rate $90-145/wk. 4 wks.
Est 1967. Private. Nonprofit.

Originally founded for children with learning problems, the school now provides instruction for both children with learning differences and those with developmental delays. Briarwood conducts two programs for children of average to above-average intelligence who have learning difficulties: the lower school serves elementary pupils in grades K-6, while the middle/upper school accepts the same population in grades 7-12. The curriculum at the middle/upper school level provides a college preparatory program for students who are planning to continue their education after high school, as well as a basic educational program for those who are better suited to an alternative curriculum.

The special school operates with an 8:1 pupil-teacher ratio. Geared to the developmentally delayed child, the program serves individuals ages 5-21 and includes art, visual and auditory perception, gross motor, recreation, vocational training and language development.

BURTIS & NOEL SPEECH-LANGUAGE CENTER

Clinic: Ages 1½-18. M-S 9-5; Eves M-Th 5-7.

Dallas, TX 75230. 5925 Forest Ln, Ste 517.
Tel: 972-661-5157. Fax: 972-661-5173.
E-mail: burtisnoel@aol.com
Marguerite Burtis, MS, Pres.
   Focus: Treatment. **Conditions:** Primary—ADD ADHD Ap Apr Asp Au Bl
      Dc Dg Dx LD PDD S. Sec—Anx As B BD C CD CP D Db ED Ep IP MD
      Mood MR MS Nf OCD ON SB TB TS.
   Gen Acad. Ungraded. Courses: Read Math Lang_Arts.
   Therapy: Lang Speech.
   Staff: 3.
   Rates 2003: Clinic $90/ses.
   Est 1993. Private. Inc.

This pediatric speech-language pathology practice provides evaluation, diagnosis, treatment, consultation and academic support for disorders involving articulation, fluency, and oral and written language. These disorders may be secondary to medically diagnosed conditions such as apraxia, attention deficit disorder, pervasive developmental disorder, hearing impairment, mental retardation and neurological impairment.

CALLIER CENTER FOR COMMUNICATION DISORDERS

Clinic: All Ages. M-F 8-4:30.

Dallas, TX 75235. 1966 Inwood Rd.
Tel: 214-905-3000. Fax: 214-905-3022.
www.callier.utdallas.edu
Ross J. Roeser, PhD, Dir.
   Conditions: Primary—D S. Sec—Ap Bl LD.
   Courses: Read Math Lang_Arts.

Therapy: Lang Speech.
Est 1964. State. **Spons:** University of Texas-Dallas.

CAPLAND CENTER FOR COMMUNICATION DISORDERS
Clinic: All Ages. M-F 8-5.

Port Arthur, TX 77642. 3049 36th St.
Tel: 409-983-1651. Fax: 409-983-1043.
Carol Hebert, MS, CCC-SLP, Exec Dir.
    Focus: Treatment. **Conditions:** Primary—Ap S. Sec—BI CP D ED MR OH.
    Therapy: Hear Lang Speech.
    Staff: 5.
    Schol avail.
    Est 1953. Private. Nonprofit.

Formerly the Sunnyside Speech and Hearing Center, Capland offers diagnosis and treatment for speech and language disorders. A group language-stimulation program serves nonverbal and significantly language-delayed preschoolers.

CENTER FOR HEALTH CARE SERVICES
MENTAL RETARDATION CLINICAL SERVICES
Day — Coed All Ages

San Antonio, TX 78201. 3031 W IH 10.
Tel: 210-731-1300. Fax: 210-731-1315.
www.center-for-healthcare.org
    Conditions: Primary—MR OH. **IQ 0-50.**
    Pre-Voc. Voc. Ungraded. Shelt_Workshop. On-Job Trng.
    Staff: Prof 60.
    Federal.

THE CENTER FOR HEARING AND SPEECH
Day — Coed Ages 2-6
Clinic: Ages Birth-18. M-S 8-5.

Houston, TX 77019. 3636 W Dallas St.
Tel: 713-523-3633. TTY: 713-874-1173. Fax: 713-523-8399.
www.centerhearingandspeech.org
    E-mail: info@centerhearingandspeech.org
Dianne Foutch, MA, Exec Dir. Mickey Castillo, Adm.
    Focus: Spec Ed. **Conditions:** Primary—D S.
    Gen Acad. Ungraded. Courses: Read Math Lang_Arts.
    Therapy: Art Hear Lang Music Occup Play Speech.
    Enr: 23. **Staff:** 31 (Full 24, Part 7). Prof 12. Educ 4. Admin 3.

Est 1947. Private. Nonprofit.

An oral program for hearing-impaired children is offered through this center. Medical, otological and audiological information is required before admission. School and psychological reports are required if the child has been enrolled elsewhere. The center also offers speech therapy and before- and after-school care. Fees are based on a sliding scale.

THE CENTER SERVING
PERSONS WITH MENTAL RETARDATION

Res — Coed Ages 18 and up; Day — Coed 3-21

Houston, TX 77019. 3550 W Dallas St.
Tel: 713-525-8400. Fax: 713-523-0340.
www.cri-usa.org   E-mail: agarms@cri-usa.org
Alan Garms, MSW, Exec Dir. **Lizette Irvin,** Adm.
    Focus: Rehab. Trng. **Conditions:** Primary—DS MR. Sec—Au B CD CP D
    ED Ep ON S. **IQ 30-70.**
    Voc. Man_Arts & Shop. Shelt_Workshop. On-Job Trng.
    Therapy: Hear Lang Music Occup Phys Speech. **Psychotherapy:** Fam
    Group Indiv.
    Enr: 885. Res Males 140. Res Females 145. Day Males 375. Day Females
    225. **Staff:** 320. Prof 42. Educ 12. Admin 12.
    Rates 2003: Res $1700/mo. Day $20/day. Schol avail. State Aid.
    Est 1950. Private. Nonprofit.

The center provides comprehensive community service programs for children, adolescents and adults with mental retardation or multiple handicaps. Clients may have mild emotional disturbances, controlled epilepsy or ambulatory orthopedic disabilities in conjunction with mental retardation.

The residential program is restricted to older men and women capable of working in the community or in a sheltered setting. Day program range from preschool classes to an adult sheltered workshop. CRI also provides training in horticulture, food services and building maintenance. In addition, the center offers vocational, parental, personal and independent living counseling.

CHILD & FAMILY GUIDANCE CENTERS

Clinic: All Ages. M-F 8-4:30; Eves M-Th 4:30-8.

Dallas, TX 75235. 8915 Harry Hines Blvd.
Tel: 214-351-3490. Fax: 214-352-0871.
www.childrenandfamilies.org
Brandy Wismer, CEO.
    Conditions: Primary—BD ED.
    Therapy: Play. **Psychotherapy:** Fam Group Indiv.
    Staff: Prof 38.
    Est 1923. Private. Nonprofit.

CHILD STUDY CENTER

Day — Coed Ages 1-7
Clinic: Ages Birth-21. M-F 8-5; Eves M Th 5-7:30.

Fort Worth, TX 76102. 1300 W Lancaster Ave.
Tel: 817-336-8611. Fax: 817-390-2941.
www.cscfw.org   E-mail: info@cscfw.org
Joyce Elizabeth Mauk, MD, Pres.
  Conditions: Primary—ADD ADHD Au BD ED LD MR.
  Therapy: Hear Lang Occup Phys Speech. **Psychotherapy:** Fam Group
    Indiv.
  Est 1961. Private. Nonprofit.

CLIFFWOOD SCHOOL

Day — Coed Ages 5-20

Houston, TX 77235. 10050 Woodwind Dr, PO Box 35679.
Tel: 713-667-4649. Fax: 713-721-4801.
www.cliffwoodschool.org
Donna R. Weinberg, BA, Dir.
  Focus: Spec Ed. **Conditions:** Primary—Au CP D LD SP TS. Sec—ADD
    ADHD Asp Dc Dg Dx OCD. **IQ 70 and up.**
  Col Prep. Gen Acad. Gr K-12. Courses: Read Math Lang_Arts Sci Soc_
    Stud.
  Enr: 70. Day Males 40. Day Females 30. **Staff:** 15. (Full 15). Educ 13.
    Admin 2.
  Rates 2003: Day $8700-9000/sch yr.
  Summer Prgm: Day. Educ. Day Rate $720. 3 wks.
  Est 1978. Private. Nonprofit.

Cliffwood provides a structured educational environment that emphasizes the strengthening of skills through re-teaching of reading, language arts and mathematics. The language-based curriculum follows a multisensory approach. Individualized programs are designed to promote academic achievement, as well as social and aesthetic development. Field trips, films and lectures by community professionals highlight the curriculum.

CORPUS CHRISTI STATE SCHOOL

Res — Coed Ages 6 and up

Corpus Christi, TX 78469. 902 Airport Rd, PO Box 9297.
Tel: 361-888-5301. Fax: 361-844-7910.
www.dads.state.tx.us/services/stateschools/CorpusChristi/index.html
  Conditions: Primary—MR.
  Pre-Voc. Ungraded. Shelt_Workshop.
  Therapy: Hear Lang Occup Phys Speech. **Psychotherapy:** Fam Group

Indiv.
Staff: Prof 698.
Est 1970. State.

CRISMAN PREPARATORY SCHOOL

Day — Coed Ages 5-14

Longview, TX 75601. 2455 N Eastman Rd.
Tel: 903-758-9741. Fax: 903-758-9767.
www.crismanprep.org   E-mail: nchurch@crismanprep.org
Nancy Church, BS, MEd, Dir.
   Focus: Spec Ed. **Conditions:** Primary—ADD ADHD Dx LD S. Sec—Ep. **IQ 85 and up.**
   Gen Acad. Gr K-8. Courses: Read Math Lang_Arts Sci Soc_Stud Studio_ Art Health.
   Therapy: Lang Percepual-Motor Speech.
   Enr: 44. Day Males 35. Day Females 9. **Staff:** 15 (Full 10, Part 5).
   Summer Prgm: Day. Educ. 3 wks.
   Est 1970. Private. Nonprofit.

CPS provides students with learning differences with specialized courses, small classes, flexible schedules, frequent evaluations of progress, multisensory activities and the opportunity to receive instruction for each subject at the level on which they function. The school's staff remains flexible in the choice of methods, materials and placement for each child. Pupils in all grades attend classes in art, computer and physical education, as well as foundational academic courses. Each subject area emphasizes strong reading and writing skills at all grade levels.

Middle school students may take part in an interscholastic sports program. Other extracurricular activities include drama and yearbook.

DALLAS ACADEMY

Day — Coed Ages 13-19

Dallas, TX 75218. 950 Tiffany Way.
Tel: 214-324-1481. Fax: 214-327-8537.
www.dallas-academy.com   E-mail: mail@dallas-academy.com
Jim Richardson, MS, Head. **Marta Pappan,** Adm.
   Focus: Spec Ed. **Conditions:** Primary—ADD ADHD Dc Dg Dx LD. **IQ 90-109.**
   Gen Acad. Gr 7-12. Courses: Read Math Lang_Arts Drafting.
   Therapy: Lang Music.
   Enr: 150. **Staff:** 29 (Full 27, Part 2).
   Rates 2003: Day $11,000/sch yr. Schol avail.
   Est 1965. Private. Nonprofit.

Dallas Academy's program is designed to meet the needs of young people who have learning disabilities, including dyslexia. It offers a junior high program and a four-year academic program leading to a high school diploma. Specialized training is provided in the areas of reading, writing, spelling and mathematics for students who have difficulty in these skill areas.

DEVEREUX TEXAS

Res — Coed Ages 13-22

League City, TX 77573. 1150 Devereux Dr.
Tel: 281-335-1000. Fax: 281-554-6290.
www.devereuxtexas.org
Focus: Treatment. **Conditions:** Primary—ADD AN Anx BD Bu CD Mood Psy PTSD TS. **IQ 70 and up.**
Psychotherapy: Fam Indiv.
Est 1992. Private. Nonprofit. **Spons:** Devereux Foundation.

See Also Page 1025

DEVEREUX TEXAS

Res — Coed Ages 6-16

Victoria, TX 77902. 120 David Wade Dr, PO Box 2666.
Tel: 361-575-8271. Fax: 361-575-6520.
www.devereuxtexas.org
Focus: Treatment. **Conditions:** Primary—ED. Sec—BD Dx LD.
Gen Acad. Pre-Voc. Gr 1-11. Courses: Read Math Lang_Arts.
Therapy: Milieu Play Recreational. **Psychotherapy:** Fam Group Indiv.
Staff: Prof 82.
Est 1959. Private. Nonprofit. **Spons:** Devereux Foundation.

See Also Page 1025

DIAGNOSTIC & REMEDIAL READING CLINIC

Clinic: All Ages. M-F 8-5; Eves M-Th 6-8.

San Antonio, TX 78216. 503 E Ramsey Rd.
Tel: 210-341-7417.
www.thewellnessweb.com/austinreading.html
Lola H. Austin, BS, MA, PhD, Dir.
Focus: Treatment. **Conditions:** Primary—ADD ADHD Dc Dg Dx LD. **IQ 75 and up.**
Therapy: Lang Speech. **Psychotherapy:** Fam Group Indiv.
Staff: 14. Prof 9. Educ 9.
Est 1976. Private.

Academic remediation and comprehensive educational, psychological and neuropsychological diagnostic testing are provided at the clinic. Psychotherapy and counseling sessions are available upon request.

EASTER SEAL REHABILITATION CENTER

Day — Coed Ages Birth-3
Clinic: All Ages. M-F 8-5.

San Antonio, TX 78229. 2203 Babcock Rd.
Tel: 210-614-3911. Fax: 210-616-0443.
www.east-texas.easterseals.com
Linda Tapia, MS, Exec Dir.
  Focus: Rehab. **Conditions:** Primary—ADD ADHD Ap As Asp Au B BI C
    CD CP D Dx ED Ep IP LD MD Mood MR MS OCD ODD ON PDD Psy
    PW S SB Sz. Sec—BD.
  Therapy: Hear Lang Occup Phys Speech.
  Staff: 100 (Full 85, Part 15).
  Est 1925. Private. Nonprofit.

The center provides early intervention services; outpatient occupational, physical and speech therapies; a vocational adult closed head-injury program; and a program for the those with chronic mental illnesses. Clients incur no fee for the early intervention program, and the center utilizes a sliding scale for clinical services.

EASTER SEALS-CENTRAL TEXAS

Clinic: All Ages. M-F 8-5.

Austin, TX 78705. 919 W 28½ St.
Tel: 512-478-2581. Fax: 512-476-1638.
www.centraltx.easterseals.com   E-mail: eastersealstx@eastersealstx.com
Kevin Coleman, Pres. **Brian Buck,** MD, Med Dir.
  Focus: Treatment. **Conditions:** Primary—Ap BI C CP Dx IP LD ON S SB.
    Sec—BD MR.
  Voc. Shelt_Workshop.
  Therapy: Hear Lang Occup Phys Speech. **Psychotherapy:** Group.
  Staff: 105 (Full 60, Part 45).
  Est 1947. Private. Nonprofit. **Spons:** National Easter Seal Society.

Easter Seals provides a comprehensive treatment program for children and adults with various disabilities. Programming includes evaluation and remediation services. Direct intervention involves occupational therapy, speech therapy, physical therapy, audiology and social services. Children from birth to age 3 may receive early childhood intervention services.

In addition to restorative services, the center provides therapeutic and instructional swimming, respite and employment programs.

A sliding scale assists clients with financial difficulties.

EASTER SEALS
GREATER NORTHWEST TEXAS

Clinic: Ages 3 and up. M-F 8-5.

Fort Worth, TX 76104. 508 S Adams St, Ste 200.
Tel: 817-536-8693. TTY: 817-536-8693. Fax: 817-536-5214.
www.easterseals-fw.org   E-mail: mail@easterseals-fw.org
Frances G. Kragle, BS, Pres. **Elaine Logan,** Adm.
  Focus: Rehab. **Conditions:** Primary—Ap Ar Bl CP DS Ep MD MS PDD S
    SB. Sec—ADD ADHD Au Db LD MR.
  Therapy: Lang Occup Phys Speech.
  Staff: 17 (Full 14, Part 3). Prof 4. Admin 13.
  Rates 2003: Sliding-Scale Rate $5-30/ses.
  Est 1947. Private. Nonprofit.

Easter Seals helps individuals with disabilities or other special needs and their families achieve maximum independence. Offerings include comprehensive outpatient medical rehabilitation services, including physical, occupational and speech-language therapy (evaluations and treatment); adult audiology; care coordination; client advocacy; durable medical equipment loan; CLASS Medicaid waiver program case management; epilepsy services providing education programs, case management, emergency assistance for anti-seizure medications, low-cost laboratory and advocacy; adult day services for frail elderly; and job training and employment services for adults with disabilities.

EASTER SEALS RIO GRANDE VALLEY

Clinic: All Ages. M-F 8-5.

McAllen, TX 78505. 1217 Houston St, PO Box 489.
Tel: 956-631-9171. Fax: 956-631-7566.
www.easterseals-rgv.org
Patricia Rosehlund, Exec Dir. **Hiram Tavarez,** MD, Med Dir.
  Focus: Rehab. **Conditions:** Primary—Au CP IP MD MS ON PDD S SB.
  Therapy: Lang Occup Phys Speech.
  Staff: 63.
  Est 1952. Private. Nonprofit. **Spons:** National Easter Seal Society.

This center offers comprehensive outpatient rehabilitation to children and adults of Rio Grande Valley regardless of their ability to pay. Additional services include inclusive childcare and professional development programs for rehabilitation professionals.

ECI KEEP PACE

Clinic: Ages Birth-3. M-F 7:30-5.

Houston, TX 77067. 11920 Walters Rd.
Tel: 281-397-4000. Fax: 281-397-4003.
www.ecikeeppace.org   E-mail: greitmeier@hcde-texas.org
Georgan Reitmeier, MS, Prgm Dir. **Carmen Martinez,** Intake.

Focus: Treatment. **Conditions:** Primary—Ap Au B BD BI C CD CP D ED Ep IP LD MD MR MS OCD ON Psy S SB Sz TB.
Therapy: Hear Lang Occup Phys Speech. **Psychotherapy:** Fam Group Indiv Parent.
Staff: 75 (Full 55, Part 20).
Rates 2003: No Fee.
Est 1982. County. Nonprofit.

This infant program provides free early intervention services for children from birth to age 3 who have some type of developmental delay or who are at risk of experiencing a delay due to premature birth or parental exposure to drugs or alcohol. Children served typically trail their peers in sitting, walking, talking, learning or social skills. A staff of various professionals administers services in homes and daycare centers.

EL PASO BRIDGES ACADEMY

Day — Coed Ages 6-14

El Paso, TX 79902. 901 Arizona Ave.
Tel: 915-532-6647. Fax: 915-532-8767.
www.bridgesacademy.org   E-mail: bridgesacademy@sbcglobal.net
Irma Alva Keys, BS, Dir.
   Focus: Spec Ed. **Conditions:** Primary—ADD ADHD Dc Dg Dx. Sec—Anx Asp Au BD CD ED OCD SP. **IQ 80-130.**
   Gen Acad. Gr 1-9. Courses: Read Math Lang_Arts Studio_Art Music Woodworking.
   Therapy: Art Lang Music Percepual-Motor.
   Enr: 66. Day Males 48. Day Females 18. **Staff:** 18 (Full 16, Part 2). Prof 16. Admin 2.
   Rates 2004: Day $5200-7200/sch yr (+$400). Schol 66 ($120,000).
   Est 1979. Private. Nonprofit.

The academy serves learning-disabled children in all academic areas, including specialized therapeutic instruction. Teachers have received training in such methods as Alphabet Phonics, Wilson Reading and Winston Grammar. The school encourages families, teachers, counselors and physicians to work together to provide students with a tailored learning program.

EXCEL ACADEMY

Res — Coed Ages 13-18

Conroe, TX 77304. 12244 Serenity Rose Dr.
Tel: 936-447-4617. Fax: 936-447-6533.
www.excel-boarding-school.com   E-mail: info@excelacademytx.com
Sally Keith, Dir. **Steven Rosenblatt,** MD, Med Dir. **Barbara Potignano,** Adm.
   Focus: Spec Ed. **Conditions:** Primary—ADD ADHD AN Anx As BD Bu CD Db Dc Dg Dx ED LD Mood OCD ODD PTSD SP. **IQ 90 and up.**
   Col Prep. Gen Acad. Gr 7-12. Courses: Read Math Lang_Arts Eng Anat & Physiol.

Therapy: Chemo. **Psychotherapy:** Group.
Enr: 100. Res Males 75. Res Females 25. **Staff:** 21. Educ 6.
Rates 2004: Res $4390/mo.
Est 1995. Private.

Excel offers an academically strong therapeutic program for teenagers with emotional or behavioral special needs. Typical students require a structured setting and engage in self-defeating behaviors such as substance abuse, running away, sexual promiscuity and delinquency. Boys and girls may be dealing with attentional disorders, adoption or attachment issues, childhood trauma, sexual orientation difficulties, depression, eating disorders or lack of personal responsibility.

Academic programming serves junior high and high school students. High school course work includes honors and college preparatory offerings.

THE FAIRHILL SCHOOL

Day — Coed Ages 6-18

Dallas, TX 75248. 16150 Preston Rd.
Tel: 972-233-1026. Fax: 972-233-8205.
www.fairhill.org   E-mail: fairhill@fairhill.org
Jane Sego, MEd, Exec Dir.
  Focus: Spec Ed. **Conditions:** Primary—ADD ADHD Dc Dg Dx. **IQ 90 and up.**
  Col Prep. Gr 1-12. Courses: Read Math Lang_Arts.
  Enr: 235. **Staff:** 40. Educ 32. Admin 4.
  Rates 2004: Day $11,000/yr. Schol 10 ($40,000).
  Summer Prgm: Day. Educ. Rec. 4 wks.
  Est 1971. Private. Nonprofit.

Fairhill enrolls students of average and above intelligence who have been diagnosed with a learning difference. While some pupils complete their high school education and graduate from Fairhill, many others make the transition to a public or private school after recognizing the nature of their learning style and developing appropriate study and organizational skills.

GATEWAY SCHOOL

Day — Coed Ages 12-19

Arlington, TX 76012. 2570 NW Green Oaks Blvd.
Tel: 817-226-6222. Fax: 817-226-6225.
www.gatewayschool.com
Harriet Walber, Exec Dir.
  Focus: Spec Ed. **Conditions:** Primary—ADD ADHD Dc Dg Dx LD.
  Col Prep. Gen Acad. Gr 7-12. Courses: Read Math Lang_Arts Sci Computers Hist Health.
  Enr: 30. **Staff:** 10 (Full 8, Part 2).
  Rates 2004: Day $9800/sch yr.
  Est 1981. Private. Nonprofit.

Gateway offers pupils of average to above-average intelligence with learning differences an alternative education. The school maintains a low student-teacher ratio to provide boys and girls with individualized attention. The school seeks to provide students with alternative learning strategies so that they can successfully return to their local schools.

GULF BEND MENTAL HEALTH
AND MENTAL RETARDATION CENTER

Res — Coed Ages 22 and up
Clinic: All Ages. M-F 8-5.

Victoria, TX 77901. 1502 E Airline Rd, Ste 25.
Tel: 361-575-0611. Fax: 361-578-0506.
www.gulfbend.org
Donald Polzin, Exec Dir. **Robert Lyman,** MD, Med Dir. **Judith Tyler,** Adm.
   Focus: Treatment. **Conditions:** Primary—ADD ADHD Anx BD CD DS ED
      Mood MR OCD ODD Psy PTSD Sz.
   Psychotherapy: Fam Group Indiv Parent.
   Staff: 193.
   Est 1970. State. Nonprofit.

Enrolling clients from Calhoun, DeWitt, Goliad, Jackson, Lavaca, Refugio and Victoria counties, Gulf Bend places primary emphasis on the early diagnosis and evaluation of mental health problems. The program includes a full range of outpatient services, including parental, personal and marital counseling. Short-term adult residential care includes a 90-day treatment and rehabilitation program for alcoholics, as well as apartment living (under limited supervision) and several furnished apartments.

Group homes and work activity centers that provide sheltered work training are available to adults, and placement services are offered to individuals of all ages who have mental health issues. Gulf Bend also provides substance abuse treatment, as well as inpatient crisis intervention and short-term care. The usual duration of treatment is six to nine months.

HAPPY HILL FARM ACADEMY AND HOME

Res — Coed Ages 5-18

Granbury, TX 76048. 3846 N Hwy 144.
Tel: 254-897-4822. Fax: 254-897-7650.
www.happyhillfarm.org   E-mail: info@happyhillfarm.com
Todd L. Shipman, Pres.
   Conditions: Primary—BD ED LD. **IQ 90 and up.**
   Gen Acad. Gr K-12. Courses: Read Math Lang_Arts. Man_Arts & Shop.
      On-Job Trng.
   Est 1975. Private. Nonprofit.

HEALTHSOUTH REHABILITATION CENTER

Clinic: All Ages. M-F 8-5.

Beaumont, TX 77707. 3395 Plaza 10 Blvd, Ste A.
Tel: 409-839-3460. Fax: 409-835-1401.
Lindsay Barry, BS, Dir.
    Focus: Rehab. **Conditions:** Primary—Ap Bl CP IP MD MS ON SB. Sec—
    ADD ADHD As B C D Dx Ep LD MR TB.
    Therapy: Lang Occup Phys Speech. **Psychotherapy:** Fam Group Indiv
    Parent.
    Staff: 10 (Full 9, Part 1).
    Est 1991. Private. Inc. **Spons:** HealthSouth Rehabilitation Hospital of Beau-
    mont.

The hospital's interdisciplinary team offers acute rehabilitation to individuals with orthopedical and neurological handicaps. Counseling, outpatient and occasional inpatient services are available. The center conducts its inpatient rehabilitation at 3340 Plaza 10 Blvd. Fees vary according to services provided.

THE HIGH FRONTIER

Res — Coed Ages 12-18

Fort Davis, TX 79734. PO Box 1325.
Tel: 915-364-2241. Fax: 915-364-2315.
www.sociallearning.org
Barry V. Blevins, Admin.
    Conditions: Primary—ED. Sec—BD.
    Gen Acad. Ungraded. Courses: Read Math Lang_Arts.
    Staff: Prof 24.
    Est 1976. Private. Nonprofit.

HILL SCHOOL OF FORT WORTH

Day — Coed Ages 7-18

Fort Worth, TX 76133. 4817 Odessa Ave.
Tel: 817-923-9482. Fax: 817-923-4894.
www.hillschool.org   E-mail: hillschool@hillschool.org
Greg Owens, MEd, Head. **Judy King,** Adm.
    Focus: Spec Ed. **Conditions:** Primary—ADD ADHD AN Asp Dc Dg Dx LD
    OCD. **IQ 90 and up.**
    Gen Acad. Gr 2-12. Courses: Read Math Lang_Arts Music Life_Skills.
    Therapy: Lang Play Speech. **Psychotherapy:** Group.
    Enr: 223. Day Males 146. Day Females 77. **Staff:** 46 (Full 33, Part 13).
    Rates 2003: Day $9000-10,000/sch yr (+$600). Schol 22 ($135,000).
    Est 1973. Private. Nonprofit.

The school enrolls children of average and above-average intelligence who have learning disabilities. Focusing on academic skills, self-esteem, study skills, self-discipline and social skills, the program seeks to instill a sense of responsibility in the student while also enhancing his or her self-concept. Daily instruction stresses the acquisition of communicative, problem-solving and reasoning skills, as well as self-sufficiency.

HOUSTON LEARNING ACADEMY
Day — Coed Ages 13-18

Houston, TX 77057. 3333 Bering Dr, Ste 200.
   Nearby locations: Humble; Katy; Stafford; Webster.
Tel: 713-974-6658. Fax: 713-975-6666.
Susan McKinney, EdD, Exec Dir. **Mary Welch,** Adm.
   Focus: Spec Ed. **Conditions:** Primary—LD. Sec—ADD ADHD Dx ED. **IQ 95-126.**
   Col Prep. Gen Acad. Gr 7-12. Courses: Read Math Lang_Arts Span.
   Therapy: Lang Speech. **Psychotherapy:** Indiv.
   Enr: 60. Day Males 40. Day Females 20. **Staff:** 38. Educ 18. Admin 6.
   Rates 2003: Day $500/mo. Schol avail.
   Summer Prgm: Day. Res Rate $240. 1½ wks.
   Est 1983. Private. Inc. **Spons:** Nobel Learning Communities.

Comprising six campuses in the Houston area, HLA offers small, structured classes to students of average or above-average ability who have had performance problems in traditional secondary schools. In addition to a college preparatory track, the school maintains a general academic program for those who are not planning to attend college. A career counselor assists pupils with college planning, job placement and career preparation.

In addition to the Bering Drive location, the academy provides services at 13029 Champions Dr., Ste. B-1, 77069; 3964 Bluebonnet Dr., Stafford 77477; 5334 FM 1960 Rd. E, Humble 77346; 17926 Hwy. 3, Ste. 103, Webster 77598; and 180 Applewhite Dr., Katy 77450.

THE HUGHEN CENTER
Res and Day — Coed Ages 5-21
Clinic: All Ages.

Port Arthur, TX 77642. 2849 9th Ave.
Tel: 409-983-6659. Fax: 409-983-6408.
www.hughencenter.org   E-mail: hughen@hughencenter.org
Jeffrey W. Kuchar, Admin. **Martin Haig,** MD, Med Dir.
   Focus: Treatment. **Conditions:** Primary—BI CP IP MD MS ON SB.
   Gen Acad. Pre-Voc. Gr K-12. Courses: Read Math Lang_Arts.
   Therapy: Hear Lang Occup Phys Speech.
   Enr: 52. **Staff:** 45.
   Summer Prgm: Res. Rec. 6 wks.
   Est 1937. Private. Nonprofit.

Children with physical handicaps receive care and education at Hughen. Blind, mentally retarded and other types of disabled children may also enroll at the center, but all clients have primary physical disabilities. The school has two requirements: each child must have a visible orthopedic handicap, and he or she must be treatable, educable and controllable.

Hughen's residential Hebert Program provides a day program for young adults age 18 and up who have physical disabilities.

Hughen offers a wide variety of individualized therapies, in addition to recreational opportunities utilizing community resources. Tuition is free for local children who enroll on a day basis. Boarding facilities serve only from those outside the Greater Port Arthur area. The center offers twelve-month foster care, as well as clinical services one morning a month. Free physical therapy treatments are available for outpatients who are unable to pay.

THE INSTITUTE FOR REHABILITATION AND RESEARCH

Res and Day — Coed Ages 6mos-17
Clinic: All Ages. M-F 9-5.

Houston, TX 77030. 1333 Moursund St.
Tel: 713-799-5000. Fax: 713-797-5289.
www.tirr.org   E-mail: tellmemore@tirr.tmc.edu
Lyn Emerich, MS, Dir. **William Donovan,** MD, Med Dir. **Annette Clark,** Adm.
   Focus: Rehab. **Conditions:** Primary—Ap Apr Ar As BI CP Ep IP MD MS ON S SB. Sec—B D Db.
   Therapy: Hear Music Occup Phys Recreational Speech. **Psychotherapy:** Fam Group Indiv Parent.
   Staff: 428.
   Est 1957. Private. Nonprofit.

Offering comprehensive rehabilitative care for severe physical injuries, TIRR utilizes a team approach to meet the physical, intellectual, emotional and social needs of the patient. Assessment, therapies, counseling and educational services are provided, and treatment also incorporates family participation, re-socialization and follow-up care. Specialized programs address spinal injury, brain injury and pediatric disorders. The average length of stay is 22 days.

JEAN MASSIEU ACADEMY

Day — Coed Ages 3-22

Arlington, TX 76013. 1506 W Pioneer Pkwy, Ste 103.
Tel: 817-460-0396.
www.jeanmassieu.com
Sue Hill, COO.
   Focus: Spec Ed. **Conditions:** Primary—Ap D.
   Gen Acad. Gr PS-12. Courses: Read Math Lang_Arts. On-Job Trng.
   Therapy: Lang Speech.
   Enr: 110. Day Males 54. Day Females 56. **Staff:** 20 (Full 14, Part 6).

Rates 2004: No Fee.
Est 1998. State. Nonprofit.

This charter school offers open enrollment to deaf and hard-of-hearing students. Instruction is primarily in American Sign Language, with mastery emphasized in reading and writing English. Enrichment classes and field trips round out the program.

KEY SCHOOL

Day — Coed Ages 4-18

Fort Worth, TX 76119. 3947 E Loop 820 S.
Tel: 817-446-3738. Fax: 817-496-3299.
www.thekeyschool.com   E-mail: administration@thekeyschool.com
Mary Ann Key, MLA, Dir. **Donna Mills,** Med, Prin.
   Focus: Spec Ed. **Conditions:** Primary—ADD ADHD Asp Bl Dc Dg Dx Ep LD SB. Sec—D S. **IQ 90-120.**
   Gen Acad. Gr K-12. Courses: Read Math Lang_Arts.
   Therapy: Hear Lang Speech.
   Enr: 120. Day Males 95. Day Females 25. **Staff:** 70.
   Rates 2003: Day $15,000/sch yr.
   Summer Prgm: Day. Educ. 4 wks.
   Est 1966. Private. Inc.

This alternative school offers a full academic program for developmental, enrichment and remedial needs. Summer courses include reading, preschool perceptual training, math, grammar, typing, effective writing and SAT preparation. The usual duration of treatment is two years.

LAMAR UNIVERSITY
SPEECH, HEARING AND DEAFNESS CENTER

Clinic: All Ages. M-F 8-5.

Beaumont, TX 77710. PO Box 10076.
Tel: 409-880-8170. TTY: 409-880-2322. Fax: 409-880-2265.
E-mail: shd_center@hal.lamar.edu
Gabriel A. Martin, EdD, Supv.
   Focus: Treatment. **Conditions:** Primary—Ap D S.
   Therapy: Hear Lang Speech.
   Staff: 12. Prof 9. Admin 3.
   State.

Lamar places primary emphasis on training teachers for the communicatively handicapped. Fees vary according to services rendered.

LAUREL RIDGE TREATMENT CENTER

Res and Day — Coed Ages 5-18

San Antonio, TX 78259. 17720 Corporate Woods Dr.
Tel: 210-491-9400. Fax: 210-491-3550.
www.psysolutions.com/facilities/laurelridge
Miriam McClendon, MSW, Dir. **Benigno Fernandez**, MD, Med Dir. **Amy Wood,** Adm.

Focus: Treatment. **Conditions:** Primary—ADD ADHD AN Anx Asp Au BD Bu CD ED LD Mood OCD PDD Psy PTSD SP Sz. Sec—As Db Dx. **IQ 70 and up.**

Gen Acad. Ungraded. Courses: Read Math Lang_Arts.

Therapy: Art Dance Milieu Movement Music Play Recreational. **Psychotherapy:** Fam Group Indiv.

Enr: 120. **Staff:** 303 (Full 203, Part 100). Educ 14. Admin 12.

Est 1983. Private. Inc. **Spons:** Psychiatric Solutions.

Laurel Ridge's behavioral health services include acute programs for children, adolescents and adults, as well as residential treatment for children and adolescents.

Patients undergo a psychiatric evaluation and benefit from case management, discharge planning, and such therapeutic services as individual, group and family therapy. Among other offerings are neurological evaluation, psychological evaluation, speech and language assessment, physical examination, medication management, dietary consultation and formulation of an individualized treatment plan.

LONE STAR EXPEDITIONS

Res — Coed Ages 13-17

Groveton, TX 75845. 1728 FR 5101.
Tel: 936-831-3133. Fax: 936-831-3136.
www.lonestarexpeditions.com   E-mail: sspaw@lonestarexpeditions.com
Scott Spaw, Exec Dir. **Anelle Viola**, Adm.

Focus: Treatment. **Conditions:** Primary—ADD ADHD BD Dg Dx ODD. Sec—Anx As CD ED OCD PTSD. **IQ 80 and up.**

Therapy: Milieu Recreational. **Psychotherapy:** Group Indiv Parent.

Enr: 32. Res Males 16. Res Females 16. **Staff:** 30. (Full 30). Prof 10. Admin 6.

Rates 2004: Res $395/day (+$750/ses).

Est 2002. Private. Inc. **Spons:** Aspen Education Group.

In a wilderness setting, Lone Star provides therapeutic intervention through traditional therapy while emphasizing assessment, intervention and aftercare. The forested, camplike surroundings remove distractions and simplify choices to help students better examine their values and accept responsibility for their decisions. Boys and girls work through their emotional, behavioral and learning issues by developing skills and improving their ability to communicate.

LUTHERAN SPECIAL EDUCATION MINISTRIES
SOUTHCENTRAL REGION
Day — Coed Ages 5-18

Dallas, TX 75214. c/o Zion Lutheran School, 6121 E Lovers Ln.
Tel: 214-405-7954.
www.luthsped.org   E-mail: ggrotjan@luthsped.org
Gayle Grotjan, PhD, Dir.
   Focus: Spec Ed. **Conditions:** Primary—ADD ADHD Ap Apr As Asp Au Bl
      Dc Dg DS Dx Ep LD MR PDD S TS. Sec—Anx B BD C CP D ED MD MS
      Nf SB TB.
   Col Prep. Gen Acad. Gr K-12. Courses: Read Math Lang_Arts.
   Therapy: Lang Speech.
   Enr: 47. **Staff:** 7 (Full 1, Part 6). Prof 6. Educ 6. Admin 1.
   Est 1873. Private. Nonprofit. Lutheran.

Providing support for children with learning differences in a Christian setting, the agency operates 97 resource rooms and consultation services at Christian elementary and middle schools. It also works with churches to provide Sunday school and Confirmation services for students with learning differences. The National Resource Center works with anyone outside of established regions to enable all students to receive a Christian education.

Additional regional programs operate in Michigan (see separate listing), Illinois, New York, Minnesota and California.

MARBRIDGE
Res — Coed Ages 18 and up

Manchaca, TX 78652. PO Box 2250.
Tel: 512-282-1144. Fax: 512-282-3723.
www.marbridge.org   E-mail: info@marbridge.org
R. W. Fullbright, Pres. Kimberly Galusha, MD, Med Dir. Will C. Hoermann,
   Adm.
   Focus: Trng. **Conditions:** Primary—DS MR. Sec—ADD ADHD Asp Au Bl
      CP ED Ep Mood OCD S Sz TS. **IQ 50-70.**
   Gen Acad. Pre-Voc. Voc. Courses: Read Math Lang_Arts Writing Horticulture. On-Job Trng.
   Psychotherapy: Group Indiv.
   Enr: 250. Res Males 175. Res Females 75. **Staff:** 150.
   Rates 2003: Res $2205-3500/mo.
   Summer Prgm: Res. Educ. Rec. Res Rate $500/wk. 8 wk.
   Est 1953. Private. Nonprofit.

Located on a 300-acre working ranch, the facility provides individualized residential care, education and training for young adults and adults with mental retardation. Marbridge offers a full spectrum of services designed to meet specific needs through three distinct programs: Mabee Village, Marbridge Ranch and Marbridge Village. Each program provides a different degree of lifestyle support, guidance and supervision. After assessing each resident's needs in more than a dozen developmental categories, staff consult with family members to tailor an individual program plan to the needs and personal goals of the resident.

A residential work training community, Mabee Village provides a degree of independence for residents who are working toward semi-independent living and community employment, but who require counseling within a safe, structured environment. Supermarkets, Austin's airport, local country clubs and hotels, restaurants and fast-food establishments, and state office buildings are some of the employment sites for Mabee residents.

Ranch clients receive similar training to that offered in the Mabee program. Residents do not, however, work in the community. Instead, they take part in a more supervised and structured day that includes opportunities such as horticultural activities, arts and crafts, sports, music, landscaping, computers, farming, wildlife study and cultural studies.

At Marbridge Villa, program participants engage in many of the same activities as Ranch residents, while receiving a greater level of supervision. This program includes a full schedule of games, classes and other opportunities.

Various activities round out Marbridge's services. Teams and individuals from Mabee Village and the Ranch compete in the annual Special Olympics, and residents also may participate in year-round athletic competition in basketball, bowling, track and softball. The facility schedules visits to local cultural and entertainment events for residents of all three communities. All may embark on periodic special trips to theme parks, camping areas and professional sporting events.

MARY LEE FOUNDATION

Res — Coed Ages 5-12; Day — Coed 18 and up

Austin, TX 78764. 1339 Lamar Square Dr, PO Box 3174.
Tel: 512-443-5777. Fax: 512-444-9949.
www.maryleefoundation.com　E-mail: marylee@maryleefoundation.org
Charlene Crump, Exec Dir.
   Conditions: Primary—ADD BI CD ED LD Mood MR ON Sz. Sec—Anx.
   Gen Acad. Pre-Voc. Voc. Courses: Read Math Lang_Arts. Shelt_Workshop.
      On-Job Trng.
   Therapy: Occup Phys Speech. **Psychotherapy:** Group.
   Staff: Prof 150.
   Est 1963. Private. Nonprofit.

MEADOWVIEW SCHOOL

Day — Coed Ages 6-15
Clinic: Ages 6-15. Eves M-Th 4-7.

Mesquite, TX 75150. 2419 Franklin Dr.
Tel: 972-289-1831. Fax: 972-289-8730.
www.meadowviewschool.com　E-mail: mvschool@flash.net
Beverly Presley, BS, MEd, Dir.
   Focus: Spec Ed. **Conditions:** Primary—LD. Sec—ADD ADHD Dc Dg Dx.
      IQ 90 and up.

Gen Acad. Gr 1-8. Courses: Read Math Lang_Arts Sci Computers Soc_
   Stud.
Therapy: Lang Speech.
Enr: 65. Day Males 50. Day Females 15. **Staff:** 13 (Full 11, Part 2).
Rates 2003: Day $7950/sch yr (+$250). Clinic $35/hr. Schol 14 ($21,000).
Est 1983. Private. Nonprofit.

Meadowview provides a full-day program with individualized instruction in academic areas for children in the elementary grades. The program serves pupils of average to above-average intelligence who have learning differences such as dyslexia, language-processing problems and attention deficit disorder. The average class size is 10 students, and the program includes departmentalized instruction in the standard subjects, as well as a well-developed computer curriculum. Clinical services are available year-round.

Field trips at all grade levels complement classroom instruction, and eighth graders annually embark on a trip to NASA as part of the science curriculum. Students in grades 7 and 8 may play on competitive soccer, basketball and softball teams, and cheerleading is also available. Interested pupils may participate in weekly chapel services and in other spiritual programs.

THE MENNINGER CLINIC
CHILD AND ADOLESCENT SERVICES

Res — Coed Ages 14-18
Clinic: All Ages. M-F 8:30-6.

Houston, TX 77280. 2801 Gessner Dr, PO Box 809045.
Tel: 713-275-5000. Fax: 713-275-5107.
www.menninger.edu   E-mail: info@menninger.edu
   Focus: Treatment. **Conditions:** Primary—CD ED Psy. Sec—Dx LD. **IQ 70
      and up.**
   Voc. Man_Arts & Shop.
   Therapy: Chemo Hear Lang Recreational Speech. **Psychotherapy:** Fam
      Group Indiv.
   Enr: 68. **Staff:** 116.
   Rates 2004: Res $775/day. $1875 (Evaluation)/ses.
   Est 1926. Private. Nonprofit.

The Menninger Clinic offers diagnostic and treatment services for children and adolescents with a wide range of emotional disturbances and learning disabilities. In-depth psychiatric evaluations lasting four to six weeks for inpatients and one week for outpatients are also available. Evaluations consist of psychiatric, psychological, family, educational and medical components and help staff determine treatment recommendations.

Child and Adolescent Services consist of short-term hospital, long-term hospital, residential treatment. The continuum of care model incorporates a variety of therapies at each level. This section maintains its own school, with regular academic and summer sessions both offered. Each child progresses according to an individually designed program.

The Center for Learning Disabilities provides evaluations and tutorial services for those experiencing a variety of school difficulties. Workshops for school districts, parents, teachers and students are part of the program. Teacher training sessions emphasizing multisensory methods of instruction are also available.

Local children and their families receive consultation and treatment services through the outpatient clinic.

MERIDELL ACHIEVEMENT CENTER

Res — Coed Ages 5-18; Day — Coed 5-17

Liberty Hill, TX 78642. PO Box 87.
Tel: 512-528-2100. Fax: 512-515-6710.
www.meridell.com   E-mail: meridell@ev1.net
Gail Oberta, CEO. David Riedel, MD, Med Dir. Jerry Romer, Intake.
   Focus: Treatment. Conditions: Primary—ADD ADHD CD ED Mood ODD
      Psy Sz TS. Sec—BD D Db Dx HIV LD OCD SP. IQ 70 and up.
   Gen Acad. Ungraded. Courses: Read Math Lang_Arts Hist Studio_Art.
      Man_Arts & Shop.
   Therapy: Occup. Psychotherapy: Fam Group Indiv.
   Enr: 112. Staff: 160.
   Est 1961. Private. Inc. Spons: Universal Health Services.

   Meridell provides a psychiatric residential treatment community for severely emotionally disturbed children and adolescents. Specialized treatment programs are designed for sexually abused children, sexual perpetrators and difficult-to-manage patients. The center also maintains an on-campus school. Clinical services include milieu, group and individual psychotherapies; family counseling; and therapy groups for those with drug, alcohol and eating disorders.

MEXIA STATE SCHOOL

Res — Coed Ages 6 and up

Mexia, TX 76667. PO Box 1132.
Tel: 254-562-2821. Fax: 254-562-1444.
E-mail: william.lowry@mhmr.state.tx.us
William H. Lowry, MEd, PhD, Supt. Geoffrey Palter, MD, Med Dir. DiAnne
   Thomas, Adm.
   Focus: Rehab. Conditions: Primary—MR. Sec—ADD ADHD Ap Ar As Au
      B BI CD CP D Db Dc Dg Dx ED Ep LD MD MS OCD ODD ON PDD PW
      S Sz TS. IQ 0-68.
   Pre-Voc. Voc. Ungraded. Courses: Read Math Lang_Arts. Shelt_Workshop.
      On-Job Trng.
   Therapy: Hear Hydro Movement Music Percepual-Motor Phys Recreational
      Speech. Psychotherapy: Group Indiv.
   Enr: 516. Res Males 245. Res Females 271. Staff: 1459. Prof 200. Educ
      150. Admin 50.
   Rates 2003: Res $280/day.
   Est 1946. State. Spons: Texas Department of Mental Health and Mental
      Retardation.

Children and adults with mental retardation who require individualized help with basic care and treatment receive care at the facility. Educational studies cover core subjects such as reading, math and language arts. Rehabilitative services focus on vocational skills development and counseling.

MILAM CHILDREN'S TRAINING CENTER

Day — Coed Ages Birth-21
Clinic: All Ages. M-F 9-2.

Lubbock, TX 79412. 1105 38th St.
Tel: 806-747-2664. Fax: 806-744-7871.
Gary Kimbley, Exec Dir.
   Focus: Trng. Treatment. Conditions: Primary—MR. IQ 0-70.
   Pre-Voc. Ungraded.
   Therapy: Hear Phys Speech.
   Est 1953. Private. Nonprofit.

MISSION ROAD DEVELOPMENTAL CENTER

Res — Coed Ages 3-18

San Antonio, TX 78214. 8706 Mission Rd.
Tel: 210-924-9265. Fax: 210-922-6006.
www.mrdcsat.org
Lora Butler, MEd, Exec Dir. Traci Fritz, Clin Dir. Yolanda Maciel, Adm.
   Focus: Treatment. Conditions: Primary—MR OH. Sec—B BI CP D DS LD.
      IQ 30-79.
   Therapy: Hear Lang Occup Phys Speech. Psychotherapy: Indiv.
   Enr: 106. Staff: 100. Admin 10.
   Est 1947. Private. Nonprofit.

Mission Road provides services for individuals with retardation through a program of academic and vocational training and physical and speech therapies. Activities in the areas of music, swimming and dancing are available, and a workshop provides prevocational experience. School-age children may utilize public school educational and vocational programs. Individuals with severe behavioral disorders are not accepted.

THE MONARCH SCHOOL

Day — Coed Ages 4-18

Houston, TX 77055. 1231 Wirt Rd.
Tel: 713-479-0800. Fax: 713-290-1273.
www.monarchschool.org   E-mail: admissions@monarchschool.org
Marty Webb, EdD, Head. Cordia Anderson, Adm.
   Focus: Spec Ed. Conditions: Primary—ADD ADHD Anx Ap Asp Au Dc Dg
      LD Mood OCD ON PDD PTSD PW S TS. Sec—AN Apr As BD BI CD ED

MR SP. **IQ 70 and up.**
Gen Acad. Voc. Gr PS-12. Courses: Read Math Lang_Arts.
Therapy: Milieu Music.
Enr: 70. Day Males 56. Day Females 14. **Staff:** 34. Educ 22. Admin 5.
Rates 2003: Day $24,000-26,000/sch yr. $60 (Music Therapy)/ses. Schol ($120,000).
Summer Prgm: Day. Educ. Rec. Ther. 5 wks.
Est 1997. Private. Nonprofit.

Monarch provides a therapeutic learning environment for children with neurological differences such as ADD, learning disabilities, pervasive developmental disorders, Asperger's syndrome, Tourette's syndrome, seizure disorder and bipolar disorder. Teachers and psychologists join together in the classroom to work with the student on emotional and behavioral self-regulation, social skills and communication skills. Academics span from the elementary grades through high school.

NEW HORIZONS

Res — Coed Ages 7-17

Goldthwaite, TX 76844. PO Box 549.
Tel: 325-938-5518. Fax: 325-938-5665.
www.newhorizonsinc.com
Del Barnett, Exec Dir.
Conditions: Primary—BD ED. Sec—ADD ADHD Mood.
Private.

NOTRE DAME SCHOOL

Day — Coed Ages 6-21

Dallas, TX 75204. 2018 Allen St.
Tel: 214-720-3911. Fax: 214-720-3913.
www.notredameschool.org   E-mail: notredm@swbell.com
Theresa Francis, MA, Prin.
Focus: Spec Ed. **Conditions:** Primary—DS MR. **IQ 40-70.**
Pre-Voc. Ungraded. Courses: Read Math Relig Music ADL. On-Job Trng.
Enr: 125. Day Males 70. Day Females 55. **Staff:** 32 (Full 26, Part 6).
Rates 2004: Sliding-Scale Rate $2500-4600 (+$175)/sch yr.
Est 1963. Private. Nonprofit. Roman Catholic.

Notre Dame provides mentally handicapped students with a curriculum that emphasizes mathematics, reading, spelling and writing. Music, religion and physical education classes are part of the program at all levels, while independent living skills, job skills and career exploration are important elements in the upper school. Christian values and attitudes prevail.

Area youth volunteers work and interact with the students in their classrooms on a regular basis. Notre Dame pupils engage in regularly scheduled activities with nonhandicapped peers.

OAK HILL ACADEMY

Day — Coed Ages 3-12
Clinic: Ages 3-12. M-Th 3-4.

Dallas, TX 75220. 9407 Midway Rd.
Tel: 214-353-8804. Fax: 214-353-8839.
www.oakhillacademy.org   E-mail: oakhillphq@aol.com
Pam Quarterman, MMS, CCC, Dir.
  Focus: Spec Ed. **Conditions:** Primary—Dx LD S. Sec—ADD ADHD. **IQ 90 and up.**
  Gen Acad. Gr PS-6. Courses: Read Math Lang_Arts Sci Soc_Stud Computers Study_Skills.
  Therapy: Lang Speech.
  Enr: 77. **Staff:** 20 (Full 19, Part 1).
  Rates 2003: Day $6300-10,000/sch yr (+$850).
  Summer Prgm: Day. Educ. Ther.
  Est 1987. Private. Inc.

The academy's program includes reading, writing, spelling and multisensory math. Gross- and fine-motor therapies are available, as is an athletic program for older students.
  A satellite campus is located at 12810 Hillcrest Rd., Ste. B100, 75230.

THE OAKS TREATMENT CENTER

Res — Coed Ages 5-17

Austin, TX 78745. 1407 W Stassney Ln.
Tel: 512-464-0200. Fax: 512-464-0439.
www.theoakstc.com   E-mail: bcathcart@psysolutions.com
Ray Bryant, COO. **Nina Jo Muse,** MD, Med Dir. **Beth Cathcart,** Adm.
  Focus: Treatment. **Conditions:** Primary—Anx BD CD ED Mood OCD ODD Psy PTSD SP Sz. Sec—ADD ADHD Dc Dg Dx Ep LD MR PDD S. **IQ 50 and up.**
  Col Prep. Gen Acad. Pre-Voc. Voc. Gr K-12. Courses: Read Math Lang_Arts Sci Soc_Stud Studio_Art Music. Man_Arts & Shop. Shelt_Workshop. Horticulture.
  Therapy: Art Lang Milieu Music Play Recreational Speech. **Psychotherapy:** Fam Group Indiv.
  Staff: 133. Prof 53. Educ 12.
  Est 1940. Private. Inc. **Spons:** Psychiatric Solutions.

The Oaks specializes in treating troubled children and adolescents through the use of various psychotherapeutic techniques in a highly structured setting. Among the problems addressed are depression, behavioral and personality disorders, drug and alcohol abuse, learning disabilities, eating disorders, and difficulties experienced by runaways and truants.   **See Also Page 1046**

OUR LADY OF THE LAKE UNIVERSITY
HARRY JERSIG CENTER

Clinic: All Ages. M-F 8-5.

San Antonio, TX 78207. 411 SW 24th St.
Tel: 210-434-6711. Fax: 210-436-0824.
http://secs.ollusa.edu/harry_jersig.html
  Focus: Treatment. Conditions: Primary—Ap S. Sec—ADD ADHD Au BI
    CP ED Ep IP MD MR MS ON SB.
  Therapy: Hear Lang Speech.
  Staff: 13. (Full 13).
  Est 1955. Private. Nonprofit. Roman Catholic.

The center provides comprehensive services for individuals with language, speech, hearing and learning disabilities. A preschool program offers language stimulation to children ages 2½-5 who exhibit language delays. Individual therapy, consultative and referral services, and parental counseling are also available.

OVERTON SPEECH AND LANGUAGE CENTER

Clinic: All Ages. M-F by Appt.

Fort Worth, TX 76132. 4763 Barwick Dr, Ste 103.
Tel: 817-294-8408. Fax: 817-294-8411.
www.overtonspeech.net   E-mail: info@overtonspeech.net
Valerie Johnston, MS, CCC-SLP, Dir.
  Focus: Treatment. Conditions: Primary—LD S. Sec—ADD ADHD Apr Dx
    OH.
  Therapy: Lang Speech.
  Staff: 2. (Full 2).
  Rates 2004: Clinic $90/hr.
  Est 1982. Private. Inc.

The clinic provides individualized care for persons with speech, language and learning disorders. Services include family training and speech improvement programs for those with voice projection and enunciation problems.

THE PARISH SCHOOL

Day — Coed Ages 1½-9

Houston, TX 77043. 11059 Timberline Rd.
Tel: 713-467-4696. Fax: 713-467-8341.
www.parishschool.org   E-mail: info@parishschool.org
Bill Clark, MA, CCC-SLP, Pres. Margaret Noecker, MEd, Head. Pollyanna
  Campbell, Adm.
  Focus: Spec Ed. Conditions: Primary—Ap Dx LD S. Sec—ADD. IQ 100
    and up.
  Gen Acad. Gr PS-3. Courses: Read Math Lang_Arts.

Therapy: Lang Speech. **Psychotherapy:** Group.
Enr: 90. **Staff:** 47 (Full 42, Part 5).
Summer Prgm: Day. Educ. Ther. 4 wks.
Est 1983. Private. Nonprofit.

This school provides individualized education plans for children with average or above-average abilities who have poor social interaction skills or minimal delays in language or fine- or gross-motor skills. In addition to the primary conditions served, Parish can accommodate pupils with pervasive developmental disorder, apraxia and coordination disorders. The program promotes the development of language, speech and thinking skills, and the school encourages family involvement. Length of stay averages two to three years.

PSYCHOLOGY CLINIC OF FORT WORTH

Clinic: Ages 10-25. M-Th 9-5; Eves M W 5-7.

Fort Worth, TX 76109. 4200 S Hulen St, Ste 423.
Tel: 817-731-0888. Fax: 817-443-0413.
William Barry Norman, PhD, Dir.
    Focus: Treatment. **Conditions:** Primary—ADD ADHD BD CD Dx ED LD
        Mood OCD Psy SP Sz. **IQ 90 and up.**
    Therapy: Speech. **Psychotherapy:** Fam Indiv Parent.
    Staff: 5 (Full 2, Part 3). Prof 5.
    Rates 2003: Clinic $150/ses.
    Est 1976. Private.

The facility provides evaluation, diagnosis, therapy and treatment for individuals with emotional disturbances who may also have learning disabilities. Clients may receive educational and personal counseling during a treatment period that usually lasts six to eight months. The clinic encourages family intervention as part of each individual's treatment.

READING AND GUIDANCE CENTER

Clinic: Ages 5 and up. M-S 9-5; Eves M-Th 5-9.

Bellaire, TX 77401. 5208 Cedar St.
Tel: 713-667-8531. Fax: 713-666-1247.
Evelyn M. Carson, EdD, Dir.
    Focus: Rehab. **Conditions:** Primary—ADD ADHD As BI Dc Dg Dx LD MR
        OH. Sec—MD. **IQ 80-130.**
    Col Prep. Gen Acad. Pre-Voc. Ungraded. Courses: Read Math.
    Therapy: Lang Speech. **Psychotherapy:** Indiv.
    Staff: 11 (Full 2, Part 9).
    Rates 2003: $150 (Evaluation); $65 (Psychotherapy); $32 (Therapy)/hr.
      State Aid.
    Est 1955. Private. Inc.

Students diagnosed with learning or reading difficulties are assisted in improving basic skills. School dropouts and stroke victims are among those treated.

RICHMOND STATE SCHOOL

Res — Coed Ages 6-65; Day — Coed 18-65

Richmond, TX 77469. 2100 Preston St.
Tel: 281-232-2075.
www.dads.state.tx.us/services/stateschools/Richmond/index.html
   Conditions: Primary—MR. **IQ 0-70.**
   Voc. Ungraded. Courses: Read Math Lang_Arts. Man_Arts & Shop. Shelt_ Workshop. On-Job Trng.
   Therapy: Chemo Hear Lang Occup Phys Speech. **Psychotherapy:** Fam Group Indiv.
   State.

RIVER CITY CHRISTIAN SCHOOL

Day — Coed Ages 4-19

San Antonio, TX 78216. 5810 Blanco Rd.
Tel: 210-384-0297. Fax: 210-384-0446.
www.rivercityfellowship.org   E-mail: rccs@stic.net
Susan Galindo, BS, MA, Prin.
   Focus: Spec Ed. **Conditions:** Primary—ADD ADHD AN Anx Ap As Asp Au BI C CP Dc Dg Dx ED Ep LD Mood MS OCD ON PDD PTSD S SP TS. Sec—Apr B BD Bu CD D Db HIV MD MR Nf PW. **IQ 75 and up.**
   Col Prep. Gen Acad. Pre-Voc. Voc. Gr K-12. Courses: Read Math Lang_ Arts. On-Job Trng.
   Therapy: Lang Movement Music Occup Percepual-Motor Play Speech.
   Enr: 112. Day Males 73. Day Females 39. **Staff:** 23 (Full 19, Part 4). Educ 14. Admin 2.
   Rates 2004: Day $5300/sch yr (+$455). Schol 11 ($25,000).
   Summer Prgm: Day. Educ. Ther. Day Rate $450. 5 wks.
   Est 1990. Private. Nonprofit. **Spons:** River City Fellowship.

The school serves students who have been diagnosed with a learning disability. Upon leaving River City, many students successfully return to a mainstream educational environment. A transitional program for children with autism is also offered. Speech and occupational therapies are available.

RUTHE B. COWL REHABILITATION CENTER

Day — Coed Ages 2-14
Clinic: All Ages. M-F 8-5.

Laredo, TX 78044. 1220 Malinche Ave, PO Box 1620.

Tel: 956-722-2431. Fax: 956-722-7553.
www.ruthebcowlrehabilitationcenter.com
   Conditions: Primary—Ap Au BI CP D Dx IP LD MD MR MS ON S SB.
   Gen Acad. Ungraded.
   Therapy: Hear Lang Occup Phys Speech. **Psychotherapy:** Fam.
   Est 1959. Nonprofit.

SABER ACADEMY

Day — Coed Ages 14-17

Richardson, TX 75080. 811 Canyon Creek Sq.
Tel: 972-231-7040. Fax: 972-231-7043.
E-mail: gerald.rosebure@nlcinc.com
Gerald Rosebure, PhD, Dir. Julie White, Adm.
   Focus: Spec Ed. **Conditions:** Primary—ADD ADHD Anx As Db ED OCD
   SP.
   Col Prep. Gen Acad. Gr 9-12. Courses: Read Math Lang_Arts.
   Enr: 20. **Staff:** 6 (Full 2, Part 4). Prof 6. Educ 6.
   Rates 2003: Day $540/mo. Schol avail.
   Summer Prgm: Day. Educ. Day Rate $270. 2 wks.
   Est 1983. Private. Inc. **Spons:** Nobel Learning Communities.

   Students who attend Saber typically have average to above-average ability, but have
been hindered by learning-style differences. The school offers a selection of accredited,
transferable day, evening and summer high school courses. The high school follows
Texas course requirements for a high school diploma. Fall and spring semesters are
coordinated with the local public school calendar. Various electives prepare students for
future careers.

SABINE VALLEY CENTER

Clinic: All Ages. M-F 8-5.

Longview, TX 75608. 105 Woodbine Pl, Ste C, PO Box 6800.
Tel: 903-757-8194. Fax: 903-757-8294.
www.sabinevalley.org   E-mail: inman.white@sabinevalley.org
Inman White, Exec Dir. J. Chris Webb, MD, Med Dir.
   Focus: Trng. Treatment. **Conditions:** Primary—ADHD Ap Au B BI CP D DS
   MD MR MS ON S SB.
   Therapy: Hear Lang Occup Phys Speech. **Psychotherapy:** Fam Parent.
   Staff: 31 (Full 23, Part 8). Prof 27.
   Est 1981. State. Nonprofit.

   Serving residents of Gregg, Harrison, Rusk, Marion, Panola and Upshur counties,
Sabine Valley offers home-based intervention for infants who exhibit delays in any
area of development. Ancillary services include speech, developmental, occupational
and physical therapies and parental counseling. Other programs available at the center

provide crisis intervention, family and community support, vocational training, respite and substance abuse services.

SAN MARCOS TREATMENT CENTER

Res — Coed Ages 11-17

San Marcos, TX 78666. 120 Bert Brown St.
Tel: 512-396-8500. Fax: 512-754-3883.
www.psysolutions.com/facilities/sanmarcos/index.html
   Conditions: Primary—BD ED. Sec—ADD ADHD AN Anx Asp Bu LD Mood ON Psy PTSD.
   Col Prep. Gen Acad. Pre-Voc. Voc. Ungraded. Courses: Read Math Lang_ Arts. Shelt_Workshop. On-Job Trng.
   Therapy: Art Lang Speech. **Psychotherapy:** Fam Group Indiv.
   Staff: Prof 74.
   Est 1940. Private. **Spons:** Psychiatric Solutions.

THE SETTLEMENT HOME

Res — Females Ages 7-17

Austin, TX 78758. 1600 Peyton Gin Rd.
Tel: 512-836-2150. Fax: 512-836-2159.
www.settlementhome.org   E-mail: info@settlementhome.org
   Conditions: Primary—BD ED.
   Gen Acad. Pre-Voc. Voc. Courses: Read Math Lang_Arts. On-Job Trng.
   Est 1916. Private. Nonprofit.

SHELTON SCHOOL AND EVALUATION CENTER

Day — Coed Ages 3-18
Clinic: Ages 3 and up. M-F 8:30-4.

Dallas, TX 75248. 15720 Hillcrest Rd.
Tel: 972-774-1772. Fax: 972-991-3977.
www.shelton.org
Joyce S. Pickering, BS, MA, CCC, Exec Dir. **Diann Slaton,** Adm.
   Focus: Spec Ed. Treatment. **Conditions:** Primary—ADD ADHD Dc Dg Dx LD. Sec—Anx Ap Apr As D Db OCD TS. **IQ 90 and up.**
   Gen Acad. Gr PS-12. Courses: Read Math Lang_Arts Soc_Stud Computers Studio_Art Drama.
   Therapy: Hear Lang Phys Speech. **Psychotherapy:** Fam Group Indiv.
   Enr: 807. Day Males 527. Day Females 280. **Staff:** 231 (Full 216, Part 15). Prof 170. Admin 61.
   Rates 2004: Day $7770-13,300/sch yr (+$550-975). Schol 120 ($350,000).
   Summer Prgm: Day. Educ. Rec. Ther. 6 wks.

Est 1976. Private. Nonprofit.

Shelton School focuses on individuals who fail to deal with aspects of the written language with normal proficiency despite average to superior intelligence. Students are placed in language therapy and English classes according to their competency in written language skills. Emphasis is placed on reading, writing, spelling, handwriting, vocabulary development and grammatical principles. Science and social studies are taught in sequenced but flexible classroom settings. The remedial curriculum is complemented with offerings in perceptual-motor training, physical education, typing, art, music, aerobic dancing and creative writing, with special emphasis on computer usage and social skills training.

The school's Evaluation Center conducts comprehensive tests designed to assess academic levels, intellectual ability, perceptual-motor development, language skill usage and coping techniques. The center specializes in the diagnosis and the treatment of dyslexia and attention deficit disorder, with and without hyperactivity. Interpretation of results and educational and therapeutic recommendations are imparted to parents in a teaching conference.

SHORKEY CENTER

Clinic: Ages Birth-21. M-F 7:30-5:30.

Beaumont, TX 77701. 855 S 8th St.
Tel: 409-838-6568. Fax: 409-838-1337.
www.shorkeycenter.org
Tanya Goldbeck, MA, Exec Dir. **Peggy Moss,** Adm.
> **Focus:** Spec Ed. Rehab. Treatment. **Conditions:** Primary—ADD ADHD Asp Au BD BI CD CP Dc Dg DS Dx ED Mood ON SB. Sec—As C IP MD MR MS.
> **Gen Acad.** Gr K-12. Courses: Read Math Lang_Arts.
> **Therapy:** Hear Occup Phys Speech Aqua. **Psychotherapy:** Fam Group Indiv Parent.
> **Staff:** 28 (Full 18, Part 10). Educ 9. Admin 7.
> **Rates 2003:** $80 (Therapy)/hr.
> **Est 1944.** Private. Nonprofit.

The center serves orthopedically involved children with mild to severe handicaps and other associated difficulties. Services include physical rehabilitation, occupational rehabilitation, diagnostic evaluations, special counseling and work with parents on special-needs issues. In addition, academic tutoring is available in all subject areas.

SHRINERS HOSPITAL

Res — Coed Ages Birth-18

Houston, TX 77030. 6977 Main St.
Tel: 713-797-1616. Fax: 713-797-1029.
www.shrinershq.org   E-mail: irodriguez@shrinenet.org
Steven B. Reiter, Admin.
> **Conditions:** Primary—Ar CP ON SB.

Gen Acad. Courses: Read Math Lang_Arts.
Therapy: Occup Phys.
Est 1952. Private.

SOUTHWEST ACADEMY LEARNING CENTER

Day — Coed Ages 3-14

Allen, TX 75002. 600 S Jupiter Rd.
Tel: 972-359-6646. Fax: 972-359-8291.
www.southwestacademy.org   E-mail: swacademy@sbcglobal.net
Beverly Dooley, PhD, Exec Dir. **Don Hargrave,** Head.
   Focus: Spec Ed. **Conditions:** Primary—ADD ADHD Dc Dg Dx. **IQ 90 and up.**
   Gen Acad. Gr PS-8. Courses: Read Math Lang_Arts.
   Therapy: Lang Percepual-Motor Speech.
   Enr: 40. Day Males 22. Day Females 18. **Staff:** 18 (Full 12, Part 6). Prof 14. Admin 4.
   Rates 2003: Day $8000-11,000/sch yr (+$900).
   Summer Prgm: Day. Educ. Day Rate $1050. 1 wk.
   Est 1994. Private. Nonprofit.

The academy provides a full-day elementary program for children of average or above-average IQ who have learning difficulties. Using multisensory teaching techniques, instructors facilitate learning through visual, auditory and kinesthetic channels. Training in such practical areas as concentration, self-discipline and study skills is integral to the program. A thorough assessment seeks to uncover the causes of difficulty and to determine the most efficient way to teach the student.

After-school enrichment classes—offered either by the week or by the semester—are available for an additional fee.

SPEECH AND LANGUAGE REMEDIATION CENTER

Clinic: All Ages. M-F 8:30-6.

Houston, TX 77063. 7500 San Felipe St, Ste 875.
Tel: 713-785-6760. Fax: 713-785-9613.
www.speechandlanguagecenter.com
   E-mail: slrc@speechandlanguagecenter.com
Linda Dickerson Young, MA, CCC, Dir.
   Focus: Treatment. **Conditions:** Primary—ADD ADHD Asp Au Dx LD S. Sec—BI MR OH. **IQ 90 and up.**
   Therapy: Lang Speech.
   Staff: 16 (Full 10, Part 6).
   Rates 2003: Clinic $100/hr.
   Est 1973. Private. Inc.

The center provides diagnostic evaluation and remedial therapy of speech and language-based learning disorders. Staff members schedule conferences on a regular basis with parents, schools and teachers regarding improvements in therapy and educational planning. Clients generally receive one-on-one care.

STAR RANCH

Res — Males Ages 7-17

Ingram, TX 78025. 149 Camp Scenic Loop.
Tel: 830-367-4864. Fax: 830-367-2814.
www.starranch.org
Rand Southard, MEd, Exec Dir.
  Focus: Spec Ed. Treatment. **Conditions:** Primary—ADD ADHD BD Dx ED LD OCD. Sec—As Au Bl C CP D Ep IP MD MR MS ON S SB TB. **IQ 70 and up.**
  Gen Acad. Pre-Voc. Gr 1-12. Courses: Read Math Lang_Arts.
  Therapy: Hear Lang Speech. **Psychotherapy:** Indiv Parent.
  Enr: 32. Res Males 32. **Staff:** 30.
  Summer Prgm: Res. Educ. Rec. Res Rate $635/wk. 9 wks.
  Est 1989. Private. Nonprofit. **Spons:** Star Programs.

This residential school serves boys with diagnosed learning disabilities and emotional disturbances. The individualized educational program includes therapy and counseling, while the behavioral side of the program utilizes a reward system designed to reinforce positive behaviors. A variety of noncompetitive clubs and recreational activities is available.

Star Ranch also operates a coeducational summer camp for children with learning differences that combines individualized and small-group instruction with numerous recreational offerings. The camp, which maintains a 3:1 staff-student ratio, seeks to promote emotional, social and physical growth, in addition to reading, writing and language skills development.

SUNSHINE COTTAGE SCHOOL FOR DEAF CHILDREN

Day — Coed Ages Birth-19

San Antonio, TX 78212. 103 Tuleta Dr.
Tel: 210-824-0579. TTY: 210-824-5563. Fax: 210-826-0436.
www.sunshinecottage.org   E-mail: info@sunshinecottage.org
Carolyn Walthall, MEd, Exec Dir. **Blane Trautwein**, MEd, Prin.
  Focus: Spec Ed. **Conditions:** Primary—D. **IQ 90 and up.**
  Gen Acad. Gr PS-12. Courses: Read Math Lang_Arts.
  Therapy: Hear Lang Speech. **Psychotherapy:** Parent.
  Enr: 149. Day Males 81. Day Females 68. **Staff:** 78 (Full 76, Part 2).
  Rates 2003: Day $4365/sch yr. Schol 33 ($84,954).
  Est 1947. Private. Nonprofit.

The educational program for hearing-impaired children at the Sunshine Cottage School employs the oral-auditory method. Students ranging from infant to high school age receive hearing and speech-language therapies. Audiological management and cochlear implant habilitation are among the training programs offered.

TEXAS CHRISTIAN UNIVERSITY
MILLER SPEECH AND HEARING CLINIC

Clinic: All Ages. M-F 8-5.

Fort Worth, TX 76129. Dept of Communication Sciences and Disorders, TCU Box 297450.
Tel: 817-257-7621. Fax: 817-257-5692.
www.csd.tcu.edu/millerclinic.htm   E-mail: w.ryan@tcu.edu
William J. Ryan, BS, MS, PhD, Supv. **Lynn K. Flahive,** MS, Clin Coord.
   Focus: Treatment. **Conditions:** Primary—Ap D S. Sec—Bl ED LD. **IQ 90 and up.**
   Therapy: Hear Lang Speech.
   Staff: 8.
   Private.

This clinic at TCU provides diagnosis and treatment of speech, language and hearing disabilities. Students receive training for work with persons with communication disorders. Individuals with severe reductions in either IQ or functional levels of behavior may not gain acceptance into therapy programs. Services are available to bilingual clients.

TEXAS CHRISTIAN UNIVERSITY
STARPOINT SCHOOL

Day — Coed Ages 6-12

Fort Worth, TX 76129. 2805 Stadium Dr, TCU Box 297410.
Tel: 817-257-7141. Fax: 817-257-7168.
www.sed.tcu.edu
Kathleen S. Cooter, PhD, Dir.
   Focus: Spec Ed. **Conditions:** Primary—Dx LD. Sec—ADD ADHD Dc Dg. **IQ 85 and up.**
   Gen Acad. Ungraded. Courses: Read Math Lang_Arts Sci Studio_Art Music Drama Study_Skills.
   Therapy: Hear Lang Occup Speech. **Psychotherapy:** Group Parent.
   Enr: 54. Day Males 30. Day Females 24. **Staff:** 7. (Full 7). Educ 6. Admin 1.
   Rates 2003: Day $6500/sch yr (+$180). Schol ($10,000).
   Summer Prgm: Day. Educ. Day Rate $200. 2-3 wks.
   Est 1966. Private. Nonprofit.

TCU faculty members and supervised teacher-trainees provide learning-disabled students with a full academic day program, conducted through TCU's School of Education. The curriculum includes the traditional subjects, and Starpoint places particular emphasis on the acquisition of organizational and study skills. The program also includes educational and parental counseling.

TEXAS NEUROREHAB CENTER

Res — Coed Ages 8 and up; Day — Coed 3-21

Austin, TX 78745. 1106 W Dittmar Rd.
Tel: 512-444-4835. Fax: 512-462-6749.
www.texasneurorehab.com   E-mail: smcdaniel@psysolutions.com
Ed Prettyman, CEO. **Nancy Childs,** MD, Med Dir. **Sandra McDaniel,** Adm.
  Focus: Treatment. **Conditions:** Primary—Anx Asp Au BD BI CF CP ED
  Mood MR OCD ODD ON PDD Psy PTSD PW Sz TS. Sec—ADD ADHD
  Ap Apr Ar As C D Db Dc Dg DS Dx Ep LD MD MS Nf S SB SP. **IQ 30-
  100.**
  Gen Acad. Pre-Voc. Voc. Gr PS-12. Courses: Read Math Lang_Arts. Man_
  Arts & Shop. Shelt_Workshop. On-Job Trng.
  Therapy: Lang Milieu Movement Occup Phys Play Recreational Speech.
  Psychotherapy: Fam Group Indiv Parent.
  Private. **Spons:** Psychiatric Solutions.

Texas NeuroRehab provides various medical, psychiatric and behavioral services for children, adolescents and adults with neuropsychiatric or neuro-behavioral problems, brain injury, developmental delays, dual diagnoses (psychiatric issues and chemical dependency) or complex medical issues. A residential program teaches adaptive, compensatory, self-control, self-care and other adaptive skills to adolescents with developmental or behavioral issues or both.

On-site education is integral to the treatment program for clients ages 3-21. Vocational services are also important, with participants learning and further developing—within a community setting—such skills as cooperative work habits, task focus and toleration of stimulation. After developing basic skills, clients may put them to use (often for pay) in a less structured group setting on or off campus.

See Also Page 1046

TEXAS SCHOOL FOR THE BLIND AND VISUALLY IMPAIRED

Res and Day — Coed Ages 6-21

Austin, TX 78756. 1100 W 45th St.
Tel: 512-454-8631. TTY: 512-206-9451. Fax: 512-206-9450.
www.tsbvi.edu
Phil Hatlen, EdD, Supt. **Laura Newton,** PhD, Co-Prin. **Miles Fain,** Co-Prin.
  Kenneth Miller, Adm.
  Focus: Spec Ed. **Conditions:** Primary—B. Sec—Anx BD D Db ED HIV LD
  Mood MR OCD ON PDD S TS.
  Col Prep. Gen Acad. Pre-Voc. Voc. Ungraded. Courses: Read Math Lang_
  Arts Life_Skills Orientation & Mobility. On-Job Trng.
  Therapy: Art Hear Lang Music Occup Phys Recreational Speech. **Psycho-
  therapy:** Group Indiv.
  Enr: 150. **Staff:** 241 (Full 189, Part 52).
  Rates 2004: No Fee.
  Summer Prgm: Res & Day. Educ. Res Rate $0. Day Rate $0. 7 wks.
  Est 1856. State. Nonprofit.

This state facility accepts deaf-blind, partially sighted and blind children with or without multiple handicaps who are residents of Texas. Academic classes through high school, vocational training, and mobility and special skills classes are offered.

TEXAS SCOTTISH RITE HOSPITAL FOR CHILDREN

Res — Coed Ages Birth-18
Clinic: Ages Birth-18. M-F 8-5.

Dallas, TX 75219. 2222 Welborn St.
Tel: 214-559-5000. Fax: 214-559-7642.
www.tsrhc.org   E-mail: tsrh@tsrh.org
J. C. Montgomery, Jr., MPH, Pres.
  Focus: Rehab. Treatment. **Conditions:** Primary—CP MD OH. Sec—BI Dx IP LD MS SB.
  Therapy: Hear Lang Occup Phys Speech. **Psychotherapy:** Fam Group Indiv.
  Rates 2004: No Fee.
  Est 1921. Private. Nonprofit.

The hospital provides orthopedic and limited neurological rehabilitative services for Texas residents of the appropriate age. Inpatient and clinical treatment are available, as are services for children with learning differences such as dyslexia. This facility also offers comprehensive social services.

TEXAS TECH UNIVERSITY HEALTH AND SCIENCES CENTER SPEECH-LANGUAGE-HEARING CLINIC

Clinic: Ages Birth-21. M-F 7:30-5:30.

Lubbock, TX 79430. 3601 4th St.
Tel: 806-743-5678. Fax: 806-743-5670.
E-mail: sherry.sancibrian@ttuhsc.edu
Sherry Sancibrian, MS, Dir. **Diana Puente,** Intake.
  Focus: Rehab. **Conditions:** Primary—ADD ADHD Ap Asp Au Dx LD MR S. Sec—Apr BI CD CP Dg ED IP MD MS ON SB TS.
  Therapy: Hear Lang Speech.
  Staff: 16 (Full 14, Part 2). Prof 13. Admin 3.
  Rates 2003: Clinic $50/ses. Schol avail. State Aid. .
  Est 1938. State.

This Texas Tech clinic provides full services for individuals with communicational disorders. Reading and behavioral problems are common secondary concerns.

TEXAS WOMAN'S UNIVERSITY
SPEECH-LANGUAGE-HEARING CLINIC

Clinic: All Ages. M-Th 9-5.

Denton, TX 76204. PO Box 23775.
Tel: 817-898-2285.
www.twu.edu/hs/comms/gradpgm/slpclin.htm   E-mail: coms@twu.edu
Alfred H. White, PhD, Supv. **Laura Moorer-Cook,** MA, Clin Coord.
   Focus: Treatment. **Conditions:** Primary—Ap Au B BI CP D MR S. Sec—
      ADD ADHD As C Dx ED Ep IP LD MD MS ON SB TB.
   Therapy: Hear Lang Speech.
   Staff: 13.
   Est 1959. State.

   The clinic conducts speech, language and hearing evaluations and therapy for all types of oral communicational disorders, regardless of their cause. TWU graduate students, working under the supervision of licensed and certified speech-language pathologists, provide all clinical services. Fees vary according to services rendered.

UCP OF GREATER HOUSTON

Day — Coed All Ages

Bellaire, TX 77401. 4500 Bissonnet St, Ste 340.
Tel: 713-838-9050. Fax: 713-838-9098.
www.ucphouston.org   E-mail: ucp@ucphouston.org
Elise Coleman Hough, Exec Dir.
   Focus: Rehab. **Conditions:** Primary—ADD ADHD CP Dc Dg Dx LD OH.
      Sec—Ap Au BI IP MR Nf SB.
   Voc. On-Job Trng.
   Therapy: Hear Lang Occup Phys Play Recreational Speech. **Psychotherapy:** Fam Group.
   Staff: 59 (Full 55, Part 4). Admin 8.
   Summer Prgm: Res & Day. Rec. Res Rate $25/day. Day Rate $25/day. 1 wk.
   Est 1946. Federal. Nonprofit. **Spons:** United Way.

   United Cerebral Palsy of Greater Houston offers a wide range of comprehensive programs, including therapy and family support services, to individuals of all ages. Programs include an infant program from birth to age 3, respite care program for all ages, a toy library with assistive technology for those from birth through age 8, the Home of Your Own program, a High School/High Tech program and a family resource center. Services are provided for all disabilities and are either free or are determined along a sliding scale.

UCP OF METROPOLITAN DALLAS

Day — Coed All Ages

Dallas, TX 75325. 8802 Harry Hines Blvd.
Tel: 214-351-2500. Fax: 214-351-2610.
www.ucpdallas.org
   Conditions: Primary—CP. Sec—Au Ep MR.
   Gen Acad. Gr PS.
   Therapy: Occup Phys Speech. **Psychotherapy:** Indiv.
   Staff: Prof 8.
   Est 1953. Private. Nonprofit.

UNIVERSITY OF NORTH TEXAS
SPEECH AND HEARING CENTER

Clinic: All Ages. M-F 8-5.

Denton, TX 76203. PO Box 305010.
Tel: 940-565-2262. TTY: 940-369-7325. Fax: 940-565-4058.
www.sphs.unt.edu/speech.html   E-mail: summers@unt.edu
Kathy Thomas, MS, Dir.
   Focus: Treatment. **Conditions:** Primary—D S. Sec—ADD ADHD Ap Au BI
      CP Dx LD MR OH.
   Therapy: Hear Lang Speech.
   Staff: 24.
   Est 1967. State. Nonprofit.

Offering services during the fall, spring and summer sessions, the clinic provides
diagnoses and treatment for speech, language and hearing problems. UNT's clinic
addresses such speech conditions as fluency, voice, articulatory, developmental language, adolescent and adult language, neuromotor speech and orofacial speech disorders. Among the available hearing services are peripheral/central hearing testing and
screening, brainstem evoked response audiometry, fitting and servicing of conventional
and digital hearing aids, and aural rehabilitation. The center serves as a clinical training
facility for UNT students.

THE UNIVERSITY OF TEXAS AT AUSTIN
SPEECH AND HEARING CENTER

Clinic: All Ages.

Austin, TX 78712. Dept of Communication Science and Disorders.
Tel: 512-471-3841. Fax: 512-232-1804.
http://csd.utexas.edu/facilities.html
Ann Hillis, MA, MBA, Dir.
   Conditions: Primary—D S. Sec—Ap Au CP LD.
   Therapy: Hear Lang Speech.
   Est 1937. State. Nonprofit.

UNIVERSITY OF TEXAS-EL PASO
SPEECH-LANGUAGE PATHOLOGY PROGRAM
SPEECH AND HEARING CLINIC
Clinic: All Ages. M-F 8-5.

El Paso, TX 79902. College of Health Sciences, 1101 N Campbell St.
Tel: 915-747-7250. Fax: 915-747-7207.
E-mail: spchlang@utep.edu
Anthony P. Salvatore, PhD, CCC-SLP, Dir.
  Focus: Treatment. Conditions: Primary—Ap D S. Sec—LD. IQ 90 and up.
  Therapy: Hear Lang Speech.
  Staff: 6 (Full 4, Part 2).
  Est 1971. State.

This facility evaluates and treats speech, language, voice and hearing disorders in children and adults. Fees vary according to services provided.

UNIVERSITY OF TEXAS MEDICAL BRANCH
CENTER FOR AUDIOLOGY AND SPEECH PATHOLOGY
Clinic: All Ages. M-F 8-5.

Galveston, TX 77555. 301 University Blvd.
Tel: 409-772-2711. TTY: 409-772-7493. Fax: 409-747-2185.
www.utmb.edu/casp   E-mail: kpandane@utmb.edu
Deborah L. Carlson, PhD, Dir.
  Focus: Treatment. Conditions: Primary—Ap D S. Sec—ADD ADHD Au BI
    Dx ED LD.
  Therapy: Hear Lang Speech.
  Staff: 19 (Full 17, Part 2). Prof 13. Admin 4.
  State. Nonprofit.

The center prevents, detects and treats communication disorders. Audiological services include hearing aid evaluations and maintenance, central auditory assessments, pediatric audiometry, assistive listening device information, and cochlear implant evaluations and rehabilitation. Speech and language programs feature therapy for voice disorders, cognition, stuttering, motor speech disorders, swallowing, head and neck cancer, aphasia, cleft palate, attentional disorders and learning disabilities.

VIP EDUCATIONAL SERVICES
Clinic: Ages 5 and up. M-F 10-5; Eves M-F 5-7.

Austin, TX 78731. 5900 Balcones Dr, Ste 235.
Tel: 512-345-9274.
E-mail: vip_educational@hotmail.com
Roberta Rosen, MS, Dir.
  Focus: Spec Ed. Conditions: Primary—ADD ADHD Anx As Asp B BI CD

CP D Dc Dg Dx ED Ep LD MD MS Nf OCD PDD S SB SP TS. Sec—OH.
IQ 90 and up.
Gen Acad. Ungraded. Courses: Read Math Lang_Arts Sci Soc_Stud.
Therapy: Lang. **Psychotherapy:** Parent.
Staff: 11 (Full 1, Part 10). Educ 11.
Rates 2003: Clinic $65/hr.
Est 1986. Private.

A year-round diagnostic and remedial facility, the clinic develops learning strategies based on individual strengths and weaknesses. One-on-one tutorials seek to develop learning skills and independence so that future academic success is more likely. A program for underachievers focuses upon organizational skills, verbal and written expression, and logical reasoning skills. The center's team approach allows for referrals to physicians, mental health counselors, and occupational and speech therapists.

WEST TEXAS REHABILITATION CENTER

Clinic: All Ages. M-F 8-5.

Abilene, TX 79605. 4601 Hartford St.
Tel: 325-793-3400. Fax: 325-793-3580.
www.westtexasrehab.org
Larry Evans, Dir.
    Focus: Rehab. **Conditions:** Primary—BI CP IP MD MS ON SB. Sec—Ap As B C D Dx ED LD MR S.
    Therapy: Hear Hydro Lang Occup Phys Speech. **Psychotherapy:** Fam Group.
    Staff: 98 (Full 91, Part 7).
    Est 1953. Private. Nonprofit.

Serving a large rural area between El Paso, Wichita Falls and Dallas-Fort Worth and reaching to the southern border of Texas, WTRC admits patients with various speech and hearing problems and physical disabilities who have been referred by physicians. Service areas include a certified physical therapy, occupational therapy and restoration program, as well as audiological, speech and language, orthotic, psychological and social work services. The center also offers genetic counseling and special integrated rehabilitation programs are offered. WTRC provides services regardless of the ability to pay.

WESTVIEW SCHOOL

Day — Coed Ages 2-12

Houston, TX 77043. 1900 Kersten Dr.
Tel: 713-973-1900. Fax: 713-973-1970.
www.westviewschool.org   E-mail: info@westviewschool.org
Jane Stewart, Dir.
    Focus: Spec Ed. **Conditions:** Primary—Asp Au PDD S.
    Gen Acad. Pre-Voc. Ungraded. Courses: Read Math Lang_Arts Sci Soc_Stud.
    Therapy: Lang Occup Speech.

Enr: 107. Day Males 96. Day Females 11. **Staff:** 29 (Full 10, Part 19).
Rates 2004: Day $6700-10,000/sch yr (+$350). $80 (Therapy)/hr. Schol 12 ($36,000).
Est 1981. Private. Nonprofit.

Westview provides a structured learning environment for children who have been diagnosed with communication disorders, autism or pervasive developmental disorder. Individual and small-group speech and language services are available on site to all students.

THE WINSTON SCHOOL
Day — Coed Ages 6-19

Dallas, TX 75229. 5707 Royal Ln.
Tel: 214-691-6950. Fax: 214-691-1509.
www.winston-school.org   E-mail: amy_smith@winston-school.org
Pamela K. Murfin, BA, MSEd, PhD, Head. **Amy C. Smith,** Adm.
 Focus: Spec Ed. **Conditions:** Primary—ADD ADHD Dc Dg Dx LD.
 Col Prep. Gr 1-12. Courses: Read Math Lang_Arts Span Lat Sci Computers Studio_Art Drama Photog.
 Enr: 219. Day Males 155. Day Females 64. **Staff:** 41 (Full 39, Part 2).
 Rates 2004: Day $13,300-16,886/sch yr. Schol 40 ($430,000).
 Summer Prgm: Day. Educ. Day Rate $1400. 5 wks.
 Est 1975. Private. Nonprofit.

Winston's program provides individual attention, a low student-teacher ratio and small-group instruction for able boys and girls who have learning differences. Pupils develop computer literacy and word processing skills, and course requirements include reading, writing, spelling, grammar, math, social studies, foreign language and the sciences. Students are encouraged to take such electives as drama, art, journalism and photography. Soccer, basketball, football, tennis, golf, baseball and volleyball constitute the sports program.

THE WINSTON SCHOOL SAN ANTONIO
Day — Coed Ages 5-19

San Antonio, TX 78229. 8565 Ewing Halsell Dr.
Tel: 210-615-6544. Fax: 210-615-6627.
www.winston-sa.org   E-mail: wssa@winston-sa.org
Charles J. Karulak, MS, EdD, Head. **Julie A. Saboe,** Adm.
 Focus: Spec Ed. **Conditions:** Primary—ADD ADHD Dc Dg Dx LD. **IQ 90 and up.**
 Col Prep. Gr K-12. Courses: Read Math Lang_Arts Sci Computers Soc_Stud Studio_Art Music Dance Drama.
 Psychotherapy: Parent.
 Enr: 171. Day Males 123. Day Females 48. **Staff:** 43 (Full 35, Part 8).
 Rates 2004: Day $11,850-12,325/sch yr. Schol 43 ($150,000).
 Summer Prgm: Day. Educ. Rec. 5 wks.

Est 1985. Private. Nonprofit.

Winston School San Antonio conducts diagnostic and educational programs for the treatment of learning disabilities. Students follow individualized programs suited to their personal learning styles. Computer-aided instruction, community service projects, sports and extracurricular activities are notable features of the program.

UTAH

ASPEN ACHIEVEMENT ACADEMY

Res — Coed Ages 13-17

Loa, UT 84747. 98 S Main St, PO Box 509.
Tel: 800-283-8334. Fax: 435-836-2477.
www.aspenacademy.com   E-mail: admissions@theaspenacademy.com
Gil Hallows, MA, Exec Dir. **Keith Hooker,** MD, Med Dir. **Penni Torgerson,**
Adm.
Focus: Treatment. **Conditions:** Primary—ADD ADHD CD ED Mood OCD
ODD PTSD. Sec—Bu TS. **IQ 80 and up.**
Gen Acad. Gr 9-12. Courses: Lang_Arts Eng Sci Soc_Stud.
Therapy: Milieu Recreational. **Psychotherapy:** Fam Group Indiv Parent.
Enr: 100. **Staff:** 90 (Full 80, Part 10). Prof 20. Educ 1. Admin 5.
Rates 2004: Res $415/day.
Est 1988. Private. Inc. **Spons:** Aspen Education Group.

The academy offers an outdoor transitional treatment program that focuses on therapy, experiential learning and behavioral change. Set in a wilderness environment, the program is designed to assist individuals who display self-defeating characteristics in making the transition to adulthood.

ASPEN RANCH

Res — Coed Ages 13-18

Loa, UT 84747. 2000 W Dry Valley Rd.
Tel: 435-836-2080. Fax: 435-836-2085.
www.aspenranch.com   E-mail: admin@theaspenranch.com
Elliot Sainer, CEO. **Matthew Alexander,** MBA, Dir. **Becky Brown,** Adm.
Focus: Spec Ed. Rehab. Treatment. **Conditions:** Primary—Anx BD ED
Mood. Sec—AN Asp Au Db Dc Dg Dx OCD PDD Psy PTSD SP Sz TS.
IQ 85 and up.
Col Prep. Gen Acad. Gr 7-12. Courses: Read Math Lang_Arts.
Therapy: Milieu Recreational. **Psychotherapy:** Fam Group Indiv Parent
Equine.
Staff: 121 (Full 105, Part 16). Prof 31. Educ 21.
Rates 2004: Day $6390/mo.
Est 1995. Private. Inc. **Spons:** Aspen Education Group.

The facility provides adolescents with a supportive structure and various therapeutic activities. These goal-oriented activities address specific developmental skill and knowledge deficits, in addition to emotional and behavioral problems.

CEDAR RIDGE

Res — Coed Ages 13-17

Roosevelt, UT 84066. Rte 1, Box 1477.
Tel: 435-353-4498. Fax: 435-353-4898.
www.cedaridge.net   E-mail: admissions@cedaridge.net
Robert Nielson, MS, Prgm Dir. **Mark Mitchell,** MD, Med Dir. **Pamela Nielson,** Adm.
   Focus: Treatment. **Conditions:** Primary—Anx BD ED Mood OCD ODD PTSD. Sec—AN As Bu HIV SP. **IQ 90 and up.**
   Col Prep. Gr 7-12. Courses: Read Math Lang_Arts.
   Therapy: Milieu Recreational. **Psychotherapy:** Fam Group Indiv.
   Enr: 64. Res Males 46. Res Females 18. **Staff:** 66. Prof 23. Educ 14. Admin 5.
   Rates 2003: Res $5500/mo. Day $183/day (+$100/mo).
   Est 1996. Private. Inc.

Cedar Ridge conducts a residential treatment center and a college preparatory academy for high school age students with mild to moderate emotional disorders.

At the center, individual therapy sessions are scheduled weekly, while a group therapy session is held each day. Family workshops, experiential activities, karate training and outdoor recreation are among the therapeutic options.

Students enrolled in the academy take compulsory courses in the core subjects of math, English, science and social studies. In addition, boys and girls receive individualized college counseling and career guidance. Test preparation is available to grade-eligible pupils.

THE CHILDREN'S CENTER

Res — Coed Ages 2-7; Day — Coed 2-5

Salt Lake City, UT 84112. 1855 E Medical Dr.
Tel: 801-582-5534.
www.tccslc.org   E-mail: khansen@tccslc.org
   Conditions: Primary—BD ED.
   Therapy: Lang Speech. **Psychotherapy:** Fam Indiv.
   Est 1962. Private. Nonprofit.

DISCOVERY ACADEMY

Res — Coed Ages 12-17

Provo, UT 84601. 105 N 500 W.
Tel: 801-374-2121. Fax: 801-373-4451.
www.discoveryacademy.com   E-mail: tori@discoveryacademy.com
Jonathan Jones, Head. **Tori Ballard & Barbara Davis,** Adms.
   Focus: Spec Ed. Treatment. **Conditions:** Primary—ADD ADHD Dx LD. Sec—BD ED OCD OH. **IQ 95 and up.**

Col Prep. Gen Acad. Pre-Voc. Gr 6-12. Courses: Read Math Lang_Arts.
   On-Job Trng.
Therapy: Occup Speech. **Psychotherapy:** Fam Group Indiv Parent.
Enr: 80. Res Males 45. Res Females 35. **Staff:** 100 (Full 50, Part 50).
Rates 2004: Res $4650/mo.
Est 1989. Private. Inc. **Spons:** Discovery Foundation.

The academy combines residential treatment with a competency-based tutorial program that allows underachieving, often troubled adolescents to progress at an appropriate pace. Individuals with severe physical, emotional and intellectual handicaps are not accepted, and pupils spend a minimum of one year at Discovery.

HERITAGE SCHOOLS

Res — Coed Ages 12-18

Provo, UT 84604. 5600 N Heritage School Dr.
Tel: 801-226-4600. Fax: 801-226-4641.
www.heritagertc.org   E-mail: info@heritagertc.org
Jerry Spanos, CEO. **Mary Ann Smith,** Adm.
   Focus: Spec Ed. Treatment. **Conditions:** Primary—BD CD ED Sz. Sec—
      OCD Psy. **IQ 70 and up.**
   Gen Acad. Gr 7-12. Courses: Read Math Sci Hist Computers.
   Therapy: Lang Speech. **Psychotherapy:** Fam Group Indiv Parent.
   Enr: 153. **Staff:** 300.
   Est 1984. Private. Nonprofit.

Providing year-round residential services for adolescents who need a structured educational and psychotherapeutic environment, this program uses a multidisciplinary team approach to help residents replace inappropriate patterns of behavior. Individual academic programs are devised, and all students attend school regularly. Progress is evaluated every week, and special arrangements for gifted and learning-disabled residents are available. The program also features counseling, therapy and substance abuse recovery groups.

The center's diagnostic/intensive care unit provides psychological evaluations, assessments, academic assessments, and observation and stabilization services.

INTEGRITY HOUSE

Res — Females Ages 12-17

Cedar City, UT 84720. 465 W 1600 N.
Tel: 435-586-8336. Fax: 435-865-1633.
www.integrityhousertc.com   E-mail: admissions@integrityhousertc.com
Daniel Taylor, Dir. **Gary Munn,** LCSW, Clin Dir.
   Focus: Treatment. **Conditions:** Primary—ADD ADHD BD CD ED Mood.
      Sec—Bu OCD. **IQ 100-120.**
   Col Prep. Gen Acad. Pre-Voc. Gr 6-12. Courses: Read Math Lang_Arts Sci
      Soc_Stud.
   Psychotherapy: Fam Group Indiv Equine.

Enr: 16. Res Females 16. **Staff:** 24 (Full 18, Part 6). Educ 2. Admin 5.
Rates 2003: Res $51,480/yr. Schol avail. State Aid.
Private.

Integrity House serves adolescent girls who are experiencing problems at home, at school or in society, as well as girls dealing with emotional, behavioral or substance abuse issues. The facility houses and treats no more than 12 girls at a time. Each resident participates in a comprehensive program that emphasizes individual improvement, accountability and service.

MOUNTAIN HOMES YOUTH RANCH

Res — Coed Ages 12-25

Vernal, UT 84078. 80 E 100 S.
Tel: 866-781-2450. Fax: 435-781-2442.
www.mhyr.com E-mail: admissions@mountainhomesyouthranch.com
Rob Caldwell, MSW, Dir. **Ladena Sipes,** Adm.
  Focus: Spec Ed. Rehab. Treatment. **Conditions:** Primary—ADD ADHD Anx BD CD Dx ED Mood SP. Sec—As OCD TS. **IQ 80 and up.**
  Gen Acad. Pre-Voc. Voc. Ungraded. Courses: Read Math Lang_Arts Sci Life_Skills Health. Auto_Mechanics Construction.
  Psychotherapy: Indiv.
  Enr: 36. **Staff:** 12. Prof 5. Admin 3.
  Rates 2003: Res $275/day (+$500/ses).
  Est 1994. Private. Inc.

MHYR combines an outdoor ranch experience with professional counseling services. Important components of the program aside from therapy include academics, work ethics, vocational training and communicational skills instruction. Participants may enroll for as little as 42 days, and Mountain Homes' open enrollment enables boys and girls to enter at any time of year. Programming takes place on a 16,000-acre, secure campus.

PROVO CANYON SCHOOL

Res — Coed Ages 12-18

Orem, UT 84059. 1350 E 750 N.
Tel: 801-227-2100. Fax: 801-223-7130.
www.provocanyon.com E-mail: pcsinfo@provocanyon.com
Kreg D. Gillman, PhD, CEO. **Nicholas Pakidko,** Educ Dir. **Steve Nielsen,** Adm.
  Focus: Spec Ed. **Conditions:** Primary—BD ED LD. Sec—ADD ADHD Mood. **IQ 80 and up.**
  Col Prep. Gen Acad. Pre-Voc. Voc. Gr 7-12. Courses: Read Math Lang_Arts Fr Span Ger Studio_Art Bus. Man_Arts & Shop. On-Job Trng.
  Therapy: Recreational. **Psychotherapy:** Fam Group Indiv Substance_Abuse.
  Enr: 245. Res Males 114. Res Females 131. **Staff:** 182 (Full 128, Part 54).

Educ 28.
Rates 2003: Res $315/day.
Est 1971. Private. **Spons:** Universal Health Services.

Provo Canyon provides therapeutic treatment for boys and girls with emotional, behavioral and learning problems. The year-round, highly structured program offers comprehensive education and treatment to help students develop self-awareness, a sense of responsibility and behavior controls. Individual academic programs place students at their appropriate levels. Individual and family therapy sessions are part of the therapeutic program.

REID LEARNING CENTER

Res — Coed Ages 8-20; Day — Coed 5-15
Clinic: Ages 5-25. M-F 8:15-3:30; Eves M W Th 3:30-7.

Salt Lake City, UT 84109. 2965 E 3435 S.
Tel: 801-466-4214. Fax: 801-485-0561.
www.reidschool.com   E-mail: ereid@xmission.com
Mervin R. Reid, PhD, Pres. **Ethna R. Reid,** PhD, Dir.
   Focus: Spec Ed. Trng. Treatment. **Conditions:** Primary—Dx LD. Sec—ADD ADHD As BD BI CD D ED MD Mood MR MS.
   Gen Acad. Courses: Read Math Lang_Arts Sci Computers Soc_Stud.
   Therapy: Art Dance Lang Movement Music Phys Recreational Speech.
   Enr: 184. Res Males 12. Res Females 12. Day Males 80. Day Females 80.
      Staff: 42 (Full 22, Part 20).
   Rates 2003: Res $69/day (+$200/yr). Day $895/mo (+$200/yr). Clinic $30/hr.
   Summer Prgm: Res & Day. Educ. Rec. Res Rate $69/day. Day Rate $32/day.
   Est 1986. Private. Inc.

The center teaches students of all abilities to learn to read, write, and spell; improve comprehension and study skills; increase reading rate; develop visual and auditory sequential memory, association and recall; use a computer efficiently and effectively; and learn mathematics. Reid also offers reading improvement classes for professional adults, classes for nonnative English speakers, instruction to develop higher-level thinking skills, and creative and expository writing classes.

SEPS LEARNING CENTER

Day — Coed All Ages
Clinic: All Ages. M-Th 7-5; Eves M-Th 5-7.

Salt Lake City, UT 84105. 1924 S 1100 E, Ste D.
Tel: 801-467-2122. Fax: 801-467-2148.
www.sepslc.com   E-mail: ava.eva.seps@sepslc.com
AvaJane Pickering, PhD, Admin Dir. **EvaJean Pickering,** PhD, Educ Dir.
   Focus: Spec Ed. **Conditions:** Primary—ADD ADHD Anx Ap Apr BD BI Dc Dg Dx Ep HIV LD TS. Sec—As Asp Au B C CP D Db ED Mood OCD

PTSD S SB SP. **IQ 85 and up.**
Col Prep. Gen Acad. Pre-Voc. Ungraded. Courses: Read Math Lang_Arts.
Therapy: Lang Play Recreational Speech. **Psychotherapy:** Fam.
Enr: 114. Day Males 79. Day Females 35. **Staff:** 37.
Rates 2003: Day $9000/sch yr. Clinic $36/hr.
Summer Prgm: Day. Educ. Rec. Ther. Day Rate $65-78/day.
Est 1974. Private. Inc.

SEPS offers academic remediation for the learning disabled, the attentionally disordered, and the hyperactivity or syndrome disordered, as well as acceleration for the gifted and nondisabled. Individualized programs are designed to meet the needs of each client and feature one-on-one instruction. Special services include life skills and adaptive behaviors training; scientific learning and language therapy; mathematics, foreign language conversation and writing workshops; and workshops designed to assist parents of exceptional children.

SORENSON'S RANCH SCHOOL

Res — Coed Ages 14-18

Koosharem, UT 84744. PO Box 440219.
Tel: 435-638-7318. Fax: 435-638-7582.
www.sorensonsranch.com   E-mail: admissions@sorensonsranch.com
Shane Sorenson, MA, Dir. **Sharon Lopez,** Clin Dir. **J. L. Moss,** Adm.
  Focus: Treatment. **Conditions:** Primary—BD CD ED LD Mood OCD SP.
    Sec—AN As Bu Db TS.
  Col Prep. Gen Acad. Pre-Voc. Voc. Gr 7-12. Courses: Read Math Lang_
    Arts. Man_Arts & Shop.
  Therapy: Milieu Play. **Psychotherapy:** Fam Group Indiv Substance_Abuse.
  Enr: 120. Res Males 70. Res Females 50. **Staff:** 100 (Full 70, Part 30).
    Educ 15. Admin 6.
  Rates 2003: Res $46,800/yr.
  Summer Prgm: Res. Educ. Rec. Ther. Res Rate $3900. 4 wks.
  Est 1982. Private. Inc.

Sorenson's serves students with a history of problems with parents, substance abuse, low or nonexistent self-esteem, learning differences, running away, school dropping out or expulsion, or extreme mental stress. Utilizing professional counseling, group counseling and staff-student relationships, the school aims to help young people function successfully both at home and in society. Parental involvement is preferred but not compulsory.

The school's maintains wilderness and work programs to teach students the importance of loyalty, respect, self-esteem, personal management, respect for property, cleanliness and trustworthiness.

Sorenson's also serves as a licensed residential treatment facility that includes drug and alcohol treatment. Staff develop an individualized treatment plan for each child. Group counseling sessions and intensive one-on-one time with Sorenson staff members is part of treatment.

SUNHAWK ACADEMY

Res — Coed Ages 13-17

St George, UT 84770. 948 N 1300 W.
Tel: 435-656-3211. Fax: 435-656-3213.
www.sunhawkacademy.com   E-mail: info@sunhawkacademy.com
Benjamin Harris, Exec Dir. **Kelly Bawden,** Clin Dir. **Staci L. Bradley,** Adm.
   Focus: Treatment. **Conditions:** Primary—ADD ADHD BD Dx LD OCD
      ODD PTSD. **IQ 85-130.**
   Col Prep. Gen Acad. Gr 7-12. Courses: Read Math Lang_Arts.
   Therapy: Art Milieu Music Play Recreational. **Psychotherapy:** Fam Group
      Indiv Parent.
   Enr: 72. Res Males 50. Res Females 22. **Staff:** 107 (Full 87, Part 20). Educ
      6. Admin 15.
   Rates 2004: Res $4985-7055/mo.
   Est 1996. Private. Inc. **Spons:** Aspen Education Group.

SunHawk provides treatment programs for youth facing emotional, family, social, substance abuse, sexual promiscuity or academic problems. Treatment consists of a therapeutic wilderness program, a residential treatment center, and personal and family development workshops. The academy also offers seminars and an aftercare treatment program.

SUNRISE FAMILY SERVICES

Res — Females Ages 12-17

Orem, UT 84057. 1869 N 285 E.
Tel: 801-221-4650. Fax: 801-705-3307.
www.sunrisefamilyservices.com
   E-mail: info@sunrisefamilyservices.com
Phillip D. McBride, BS, Dir.
   Focus: Treatment. **Conditions:** Primary—ADD ADHD Anx BD CD ED
      Mood OCD PTSD. **IQ 75 and up.**
   Therapy: Milieu Recreational. **Psychotherapy:** Fam Group Indiv.
   Enr: 7. Res Females 7. **Staff:** 12 (Full 8, Part 4). Admin 4.
   Rates 2003: Res $3495/mo.
   Est 2000. Private. Inc.

Sunrise's residential treatment program provides intervention for adolescent girls whose emotional, psychological or behavioral issues have resulted in strained relations at home, poor academic performance or both. The facility may also serve as a transitional setting down from a more acute or specialized treatment program. In a safe environment, girls receive therapeutic support designed to help them better understand and appreciate their roles and responsibilities as a contributing member of family and society.

Weekly family counseling assists parents in learning how to facilitate the girl's continued progress upon her return to the home.

TURN-ABOUT RANCH

Res — Coed Ages 12-18

Escalante, UT 84726. 280 N 300 E, PO Box 345.
Tel: 435-826-4240. Fax: 435-826-4261.
www.turnaboutranch.com
Max Stewart, MFT, LSW, Exec Dir. **Dal Liston,** Adm.
  Focus: Treatment. **Conditions:** Primary—ADD ADHD BD Dx ED LD OCD.
  Psychotherapy: Fam Group Indiv Parent.
  Enr: 30. Res Males 17. Res Females 13. **Staff:** 30 (Full 23, Part 7).
  Rates 2004: Res $310/day.
  Private.

Turn-About offers a short-term, high-impact therapy program for adolescents that emphasizes family values and relationships, in the environment of a real-life cow-calf ranch. The program centers around concepts such as honesty, respect, teamwork and accountability. The ranch operates year-round, and the minimum stay is 80 days.

TURNING POINT OF GRANITA PARK

Res — Males Ages 12-18

Duchesne, UT 84021. PO Box 962.
Tel: 435-646-3079. Fax: 435-646-3527.
www.tpgp.net   E-mail: admissions@tpgp.net
Derrick Cook, MA, Dir. **Ralph Davis,** Adm.
  Focus: Treatment. **Conditions:** Primary—ADD ADHD As Asp Au BD CD
    Dx ED Mood OCD Psy PTSD SP. Sec—AN Anx Bu Db TS.
  Gen Acad. Pre-Voc. Voc. Gr 7-12. Courses: Read Math Lang_Arts Sci Hist
    Soc_Stud Woodworking. Man_Arts & Shop. Shelt_Workshop.
  Psychotherapy: Fam Group Indiv.
  Enr: 30. Res Males 30. **Staff:** 16 (Full 11, Part 5). Prof 4. Admin 6.
  Rates 2003: Res $3900/mo.
  Est 2001. Private. Inc. Nondenom Christian.

Boys at Turning Point follow a highly structured emotional growth program within a stable, organized and supportive environment. Enrollment usually lasts for eight to ten months, depending upon the student's progress. Programmatic components comprise the following: individual and group counseling; daily group counseling; adventure activities and leadership opportunities; service roles; forums for discussing and resolving community issues; measures intended to maintain health and safety; accredited academic instruction; experiential education; and recreational activities such as camping, hiking, swimming, fishing, basketball, soccer and martial arts.

UNIVERSITY OF UTAH
REHABILITATION SERVICES

Res — Coed All Ages
Clinic: All Ages. M-F 8-4:30.

Salt Lake City, UT 84132. 50 N Medical Dr.
Tel: 801-581-2267. Fax: 801-581-2177.
www.med.utah.edu/rehabsvc/index.htm
   Conditions: Primary—BI CP IP MD MS ON SB.
   Therapy: Hear Hydro Lang Occup Phys Speech. **Psychotherapy:** Fam Group Indiv.
   Est 1965. State. Nonprofit.

UNIVERSITY OF UTAH
SPEECH-LANGUAGE-AUDIOLOGY CLINIC

Clinic: All Ages. M-F 8-6:30.

Salt Lake City, UT 84112. 390 S 1530 E, Rm 1201.
Tel: 801-581-3506. Fax: 801-581-7955.
www.health.utah.edu/cmdis/clinic.htm
   E-mail: speechandhearing.clinic@health.utah.edu
Janet Goldstein, MS, CCC-SLP, Dir.
   Focus: Treatment. **Conditions:** Primary—Ap Apr D S. Sec—ADD ADHD Asp Au BD BI CD CP Dx ED Ep LD MD MR MS OCD ON PDD SB.
   Therapy: Hear Lang Speech.
   Staff: 6 (Full 4, Part 2). Prof 4. Admin 2.
   Est 1946. State.

Graduate student clinicians working under the direct supervision of licensed professionals provide diagnosis and treatment of speech and hearing disorders at the facility. Individuals with stuttering, articulation, voice, aphasia and brain injury, delayed language, pragmatics, tongue thrust, language learning and auditory processing problems receive services at the clinic.

The center also offers foreign language accent reduction; aural rehabilitation; augmentative communication; hearing aid evaluation and selection; hearing testing; vestibular assessment; and cochlear implant counseling, evaluation and treatment services. Treatment sessions last 14 weeks during the academic year and eight to 10 weeks over the summer.

UTAH SCHOOLS FOR THE DEAF AND THE BLIND

Res and Day — Coed Ages 5-21

Ogden, UT 84404. 742 Harrison Blvd.
   Nearby locations: Logan; Orem; Salt Lake City.
Tel: 801-629-4700. TTY: 801-629-4701. Fax: 801-629-4896.
www.usdb.org

Lee W. Robinson, EdD, Supt.
   Focus: Spec Ed. **Conditions:** Primary—B D. Sec—ADD ADHD Ap As BD
      BI C CP Dx ED Ep IP LD MD MR MS ON SB. **IQ 70 and up.**
   Gen Acad. Pre-Voc. Gr PS-12. Courses: Read Math Lang_Arts Sci Soc_
      Stud.
   Therapy: Hear Occup Phys Speech. **Psychotherapy:** Indiv.
   Est 1884. State.

This state institution provides separate educational programs for the blind and the deaf. A limited residential program for autistic children is available. In addition, the school operates an extension division and programs for the deaf, the hearing-impaired and the blind on a day basis in Salt Lake City, Logan and Orem. A parent-infant program serves parents and their preschool children on a weekly basis in the home. The usual duration of treatment ranges from two to seventeen years.

UTAH STATE UNIVERSITY
SPEECH-LANGUAGE-HEARING CENTER

Clinic: All Ages. M-F 8-5; Eves M-Th 5-7.

Logan, UT 84322. 1000 Old Main Hill.
Tel: 435-797-1375. Fax: 435-797-0221.
www.coe.usu.edu/comd
James C. Blair, PhD, Supv.
   Focus: Trng. **Conditions:** Primary—Ap D S. Sec—ADD ADHD As B BD BI
      C CD CP Dx ED Ep IP LD MD MR MS OCD ON Psy SB Sz TB.
   Therapy: Hear Lang Speech.
   Staff: 18 (Full 16, Part 2). Prof 16. Admin 2.
   Rates 2003: Sliding-Scale Rate $10-20/ses.
   Est 1946. State. Nonprofit. **Spons:** Utah State University.

This center at Utah State provides evaluations and treatment of speech, language and hearing disorders.

WALKABOUT TREATMENT PROGRAM

Res — Coed Ages 13-17

Lehi, UT 84043. 50 N 200 E.
Tel: 801-766-3933. Fax: 801-766-3932.
www.walkabout-treatment.com   E-mail: mail@walkabout-treatment.com
Rick Meeves, PhD, Exec Dir. **Peter Sundwall,** PhD, Med Dir. **Brad Matheson,**
   Adm.
   Focus: Treatment. **Conditions:** Primary—ADD ADHD Anx Ap Asp BD CD
      Dc Dg Dx ED LD Mood OCD PDD PTSD S.
   Gen Acad. Ungraded. Courses: Read.
   Therapy: Art Milieu Music Phys Recreational. **Psychotherapy:** Fam Group
      Indiv Parent.
   Enr: 32. Res Males 24. Res Females 8. **Staff:** 6 (Full 5, Part 1). Prof 6.
   Rates 2003: Res $340/day.

Est 2001. Private. Inc.

Walkabout helps adolescent boys and girls deal with their emotional and developmental issues by providing various forms of therapy in a wilderness environment. The outdoor experience removes distractions often found in a traditional academic setting. Each boy receives one-on-one counseling time with a trained therapist, while parents are encouraged to participate in a group therapy session at the end of the program.

The program also offers an academic component consisting of English, science and history classes, as well as electives in psychology, physical education and art. Each student may earn two credits during a typical stay.

YOUTH CARE

Res and Day — Coed Ages 11-17

Draper, UT 84020. PO Box 909.
Tel: 801-572-6989. Fax: 801-572-8220.
www.youthcare.com   E-mail: csmith@youthcare.com
Craig Smith, LCSW, Exec Dir. **James A. Miller,** MD, Med Dir. **Randie Riegler,**
Adm.
> **Focus:** Treatment. **Conditions:** Primary—Anx ED Mood OCD ODD PTSD.
> Sec—ADD ADHD AN Asp BD Bu Dc Dg Dx LD PDD Psy SP Sz TS. **IQ**
> **90 and up.**
> **Gen Acad.** Gr 7-12. Courses: Read Math Lang_Arts.
> **Therapy:** Art Chemo Milieu Music Recreational. **Psychotherapy:** Fam
> Group Indiv Substance_Abuse.
> **Enr:** 42. Res Males 21. Res Females 21. **Staff:** 95. Prof 24. Educ 7. Admin
> 9.
> **Rates 2004:** Res $217-407/day. Day $133-277/day.
> **Est 1989.** Private. Inc. **Spons:** Aspen Education Group.

Youth Care provides residential treatment for youths who are experiencing academic, emotional or behavioral difficulties due to such issues as depression, attentional disorders, self-destructive behavior, physical and sexual abuse, social withdrawal, learning disabilities, substance abuse, low self-esteem and family maladjustment.

Two distinct programs serve boys and girls. Youth Care Residential Treatment Program provides a strong therapeutic environment for adolescents in need of intensive programming. In addition to receiving psychiatric sessions and individual, group and family therapy, participants attend school and take part in recreational therapy, behavior modification and, if necessary, substance abuse counseling. Clients for whom a less intense therapeutic and staffing pattern is appropriate enter into the Pine Ridge Academy Residential Treatment Program, which operates in nearby West Jordan. While programmatic components are similar to those in Youth Care, therapy sessions are less frequent. Day treatment is also available through both programs.

A final program enables boys and girls to live with families within the community and attend either Pine Ridge Academy or Youth Care Academy on weekdays. It provides a transition for students who are not quite ready for a return home.

VERMONT

THE AUSTINE SCHOOL AND CENTER FOR THE DEAF AND THE HARD OF HEARING

Res and Day — Coed Ages 5-21

Brattleboro, VT 05301. 60 Austine Dr.
Tel: 802-258-9500. Fax: 802-254-3921.
www.austine.pvt.k12.us   E-mail: epeltier@austine.pvt.k12.us
Ed Peltier, MEd, Pres. **Cyndy Ward,** Adm.

Focus: Spec Ed. **Conditions:** Primary—D. Sec—ADD ADHD Dx LD. **IQ 70 and up.**

Col Prep. Gen Acad. Pre-Voc. Voc. Gr K-12. Courses: Read Math Lang_ Arts Soc_Stud Sci Computers Studio_Art Life_Skills. Man_Arts & Shop. On-Job Trng.

Therapy: Hear Lang Speech. **Psychotherapy:** Indiv Parent.

Enr: 48. **Staff:** 90 (Full 75, Part 15). Prof 40.

Summer Prgm: Res & Day. Rec.

Est 1904. Private. Nonprofit. **Spons:** Vermont Center for the Deaf.

Located on a 175-acre campus, the school offers academic, prevocational and vocational programs for students who are deaf or hard of hearing. Counseling is available and the length of enrollment varies. Many pupils go on to attend similar postsecondary educational programs.

THE BAIRD CENTER FOR CHILDREN AND FAMILIES

Res — Males Ages 6-17, Females 6-13; Day — Coed Birth-21

Burlington, VT 05401. 1138 Pine St.
Tel: 802-863-1326. Fax: 802-658-3117.
www.howardcenter.org
Stephen Dale, Dir.

Conditions: Primary—BD ED. Sec—Au.

Gen Acad. Gr 1-12.

Therapy: Recreational. **Psychotherapy:** Fam Group Indiv.

Staff: Prof 11.

Est 1865. Private. Nonprofit. **Spons:** Howard Center for Human Services.

BENNINGTON SCHOOL

Res — Coed Ages 9-21

Bennington, VT 05201. 192 Fairview St.
Tel: 802-447-1557. Fax: 802-442-1118.
www.benningtonschoolinc.org

E-mail: admissions@benningtonschoolinc.org
Jeff LaBonte, BA, Exec Dir. **Francis X. Moriarty,** EdD, Clin Dir. **Patrick
Ramsey,** Adm.
   Focus: Spec Ed. Treatment. **Conditions:** Primary—ADD ADHD CD Dx ED
      LD OCD. Sec—BD. **IQ 65 and up.**
   Gen Acad. Pre-Voc. Voc. Ungraded. Courses: Read Math Lang_Arts. Man_
      Arts & Shop.
   Therapy: Chemo Lang Occup Phys Speech. **Psychotherapy:** Group Indiv.
   Enr: 115. Res Males 75. Res Females 40.
   Rates 2003: Res $100,341/yr.
   Est 1980. Private.

This school provides year-round educational instruction, behavior management and
clinical services within a therapeutic milieu. Vocational, educational and personal counseling are also offered. Students generally enroll for 12 to 18 months.
   Bennington School is affiliated with Valleyhead in Massachusetts.

BRATTLEBORO RETREAT

Res and Day — Coed Ages 6-18
Clinic: All Ages. M-F 9-5; Eves M W 5-9.

Brattleboro, VT 05302. Anna Marsh Ln, PO Box 803.
Tel: 802-257-7785. TTY: 802-258-3770. Fax: 802-258-3791.
www.retreathealthcare.org
Richard T. Palmisano, CEO. **Frederick Engstrom,** MD, Med Dir. **Michele
Noel,** Adm.
   Focus: Treatment. **Conditions:** Primary—ADHD AN Anx BD Bu CD ED
      Mood OCD ODD PDD Psy PTSD SP Sz TS. Sec—ADD Asp Au B Bl D
      Dx LD MR S. **IQ 60 and up.**
   Col Prep. Gen Acad. Pre-Voc. Gr K-12. Courses: Read Math Lang_Arts
      Sci.
   Therapy: Milieu. **Psychotherapy:** Fam Group Indiv Parent.
   Enr: 96. Res Males 50. Res Females 46.
   Est 1834. Private. Nonprofit. **Spons:** Retreat Healthcare.

Providing inpatient, residential and partial hospitalization programs, this facility
employs a therapeutic milieu for the treatment of child and adolescent psychiatric disorders. Children may receive educational services at the on-campus Meadows School.
Inpatient services include general psychiatric and substance abuse programs.

ECKERD YOUTH ALTERNATIVES

Res — Coed Ages 10-17

Benson, VT.
Contact: 100 N Starcrest Dr, PO Box 7450, Clearwater, FL 33758.
Tel: 727-461-2990. Fax: 727-442-5911.
www.eckerd.org   E-mail: admissions@eckerd.org
Karen V. Waddell, BA, Pres. **Francene Hazel,** Dir.

Focus: Treatment. **Conditions:** Primary—BD CD ED Mood ODD. Sec—ADD ADHD LD. **IQ 70 and up.**
Gen Acad. Pre-Voc. Ungraded. Courses: Read Math Lang_Arts Sci Soc_Stud.
Therapy: Speech. **Psychotherapy:** Fam Group Indiv.
Summer Prgm: Res. Ther. Res Rate $180. 2 wks.
Est 1968. Private. Nonprofit.

The Eckerd outdoor program offers therapeutic treatment to emotionally disturbed children by providing a camp setting as an alternative to institutionalization.

The year-round program utilizes reality therapy, Rogerian techniques and group therapy. Small-group living in the wilderness environment encourages the acquisition of new skills while promoting discipline and responsibility. Each group must construct their shelter, cut wood, repair equipment and perform other tasks necessary for their stay in the forest. Such experiences provide the children with the opportunity to develop academic skills at their own pace and in relation to each project they endeavor. When sufficient progress is made, children are transferred into the transition classroom in preparation for their return to the mainstream.

In addition to Vermont, Eckerd conducts outdoor therapeutic treatment programs in the following states: Florida, Georgia, New Hampshire, North Carolina, Rhode Island and Tennessee (see separate listings).

GREENWOOD SCHOOL

Res — Males Ages 9-15

Putney, VT 05346. 14 Greenwood Ln.
Tel: 802-387-4545. Fax: 802-387-5396.
www.greenwood.org   E-mail: admissions@greenwood.org
John Alexander, Head. **Stewart Miller,** Adm.
  Focus: Spec Ed. **Conditions:** Primary—Dc Dg Dx LD. Sec—ADD ADHD. **IQ 90-130.**
  Gen Acad. Ungraded. Courses: Read Math Lang_Arts Studio_Art. Man_Arts & Shop.
  Therapy: Lang Occup Speech. **Psychotherapy:** Indiv.
  Enr: 40. **Staff:** 20 (Full 17, Part 3). Admin 6.
  Rates 2003: Res $43,400/sch yr (+$1000). Schol avail. State Aid.
  Est 1978. Private. Nonprofit.

The Greenwood School conducts an academic program designed for the language-blocked boy of average to above-average intelligence. All teachers are trained in the Orton-Gillingham approach to remedial language. The school also emphasizes the improvement of peer relationships and a student's self-image. Academics are complemented by a sports program offering soccer, cross-country and downhill skiing, martial arts, baseball and cycling, and by a creative arts program including music, art and drama. Speech and language therapy are available.

KING GEORGE SCHOOL

Res — Coed Ages 14-19

Sutton, VT 05867. 2684 King George Farm Rd.
Tel: 802-467-1200. Fax: 802-467-1041.
www.kinggeorgeschool.com   E-mail: mreinhardt@brownschools.com
Rae Ann Knopf, MSW, Exec Dir. **Mary Reinhardt,** Adm.
   Focus: Spec Ed. **Conditions:** Primary—ADD ADHD AN Anx BD Bu Dc Dg Dx ED LD Mood OCD PTSD SP TS. Sec—Asp.
   Col Prep. Gen Acad. Gr 9-12. Courses: Read Math Lang_Arts Sci Soc_ Stud Visual_Arts Performing_Arts.
   Therapy: Art Dance Milieu Music Phys Recreational. **Psychotherapy:** Fam Group Indiv Parent.
   Enr: 65. Res Males 35. Res Females 30. **Staff:** 54 (Full 52, Part 2). Prof 24. Educ 22. Admin 6.
   Rates 2003: Res $5300/mo (+$2000/yr). Schol avail.
   Est 1940. Private. Inc. **Spons:** Brown Schools.

King George conducts a year-round educational program for motivated students of average or above-average intelligence who are in need of guidance due to emotional issues. Significant emphasis is placed on personal accountability, and each boy and girl assists in the maintenance of the school and must assume various community responsibilities.

Academics are the primary emphasis each morning, as pupils attend two and a half integrated sessions. After lunch, boys and girls receive instruction in a third integrated academic session, then take part in a combination of these activities: visual or performing arts classes, exercise, communicational skills instruction, and directed or individual study time. Recreational and on- and off-campus activities are scheduled on weekends.

NORTHWESTERN COUNSELING AND SUPPORT SERVICES

Clinic: Ages Birth-22. M-F 8-5; Eves T-Th 5-8.

St Albans, VT 05478. 107 Fisher Pond Rd.
Tel: 802-524-6554. Fax: 802-527-7801.
www.ncssinc.org
Ted Mable, EdD, Exec Dir.
   Focus: Rehab. Treatment. **Conditions:** Primary—ADD ADHD Anx Asp Au BD CD Dx ED LD Mood OCD PDD Psy PTSD SP Sz TS. Sec—AN Bu PW.
   Gen Acad. Ungraded. Courses: Read Math Lang_Arts Soc_Stud Hist.
   Therapy: Art Chemo Occup Play Recreational Speech. **Psychotherapy:** Fam Group Indiv Parent.
   Staff: 350. Admin 20.
   Est 1958. Private. Nonprofit.

Diagnosis and therapy for emotional and psychological problems are among NCSS' services, as is learning disabilities diagnosis. Educational studies include reading, math, language arts, social studies and history. Counseling is integral to the program, as are recreational and play therapies. Clients typically attend approximately six sessions.

PINE RIDGE SCHOOL

Res and Day — Coed Ages 13-18

Williston, VT 05495. 9505 Williston Rd.
Tel: 802-434-2161. Fax: 802-434-5512.
www.pineridgeschool.com   E-mail: prs@pineridgeschool.com
Douglas Dague, BS, Head. **Joshua Doyle,** Adm.
   Focus: Spec Ed. **Conditions:** Primary—Dx LD. Sec—ADD ADHD.
   Col Prep. Gen Acad. Gr 7-12. Courses: Read Math Lang_Arts Sci Soc_
      Stud. On-Job Trng.
   Therapy: Lang Speech.
   Enr: 98. Res Males 57. Res Females 31. Day Males 5. Day Females 5.
      Staff: 53.
   Rates 2004: Res $47,300/sch yr (+$1500). Day $35,400 (+$1500).
   Summer Prgm: Res & Day. Educ. Rec. Res Rate $7000. Day Rate $5300.
      6 wks.
   Est 1968. Private. Nonprofit.

Pine Ridge is a school for adolescents of average to above-average intelligence diagnosed with specific learning disabilities. An individualized curriculum provides small-class instruction in the basic skills and daily language training in a one-on-one tutorial setting. A structured program includes activities such as camping, hiking, skiing, sports, arts, crafts, yearbook and community projects.

SPRING LAKE RANCH

Res — Coed Ages 17 and up

Cuttingsville, VT 05738. PO Box 310.
Tel: 802-492-3322. Fax: 802-492-3331.
www.springlakeranch.org
   E-mail: springlakeranch@springlakeranch.org
Phillip Puotinen, MS, Exec Dir. **Edward Mueller,** MD, Med Dir. **Pam Grace,**
   Adm.
   Focus: Treatment. **Conditions:** Primary—Anx Asp ED Mood OCD Psy Sz.
      Sec—ADD ADHD AN Ar As BD Bu C CD Dg Dx Ep LD ODD ON PTSD.
   Voc. On-Job Trng.
   Therapy: Chemo Occup Recreational. **Psychotherapy:** Indiv.
   Enr: 30. Res Males 15. Res Females 15. **Staff:** 40. Admin 8.
   Rates 2003: Res $170/mo. Schol ($200,000).
   Est 1932. Private. Nonprofit.

Spring Lake Ranch is located on a 600-acre farm that provides a self-contained therapeutic community for emotionally disturbed adolescents and adults who do not require constant supervision and who are able to care for their own basic needs. Therapy is reality oriented, with residents operating the farm and participating in construction, forestry and the production of maple syrup. Work projects are basic to the ranch's philosophy. Recreation, limited psychotherapy, drug therapy and counseling are available, as are outpatient drug and alcohol treatment and aftercare.

STERN CENTER FOR LANGUAGE AND LEARNING

Clinic: Ages 5 and up. M-F 8-6.

Williston, VT 05495. 135 Allen Brook Ln.
Tel: 802-878-2332. Fax: 802-878-0230.
www.sterncenter.org   E-mail: learning@sterncenter.org
Blanche Podhajski, PhD, Pres.
   Focus: Spec Ed. **Conditions:** Primary—ADD ADHD Asp Au Bl Dc Dg Dx
      LD PDD. Sec—Anx Ap BD CD DS ED MR OCD OH.
   Gen Acad. Ungraded. Courses: Read Math Lang_Arts Study_Skills.
   Therapy: Speech. **Psychotherapy:** Fam Indiv.
   Staff: 37 (Full 20, Part 17).
   Rates 2003: Clinic $2193/sch yr. Schol 103 ($100,000).
   Est 1983. Private. Nonprofit.

Serving northern New England and northeastern New York, the center provides diagnostic evaluations and one-on-one instructional services for individuals with learning disabilities. Treatment begins with a diagnostic evaluation that assesses cognitive abilities, oral language skills, academic skills and neuropsychological functioning. Remediation consists of intensive instruction utilizing methods and materials that match the student's learning strengths. Regular communication with parents and teachers is integral to the program. Students attend one hour a week for 34 weeks. Other services available through the clinic include counseling and support therapy, educational seminars and a six-week summer program.

UNITED COUNSELING SERVICE
OF BENNINGTON COUNTY

Clinic: All Ages. M-F 8:30-5; Eves M-Th 5-8.

Bennington, VT 05201. 1 Ledge Hill Dr, Box 588.
Tel: 802-442-5491. TTY: 802-442-5491. Fax: 802-442-3363.
www.ucsvt.org   E-mail: ucs@ucsvt.org
Ralph Provenza, Exec Dir.
   Conditions: Primary—BD ED LD MR OH.
   Therapy: Play. **Psychotherapy:** Fam Group Indiv.
   Est 1959. Private. Nonprofit.

VERMONT ACHIEVEMENT CENTER

Day — Coed Ages 6wks-18

Rutland, VT 05702. 88 Park St, PO Box 6283.
Tel: 802-775-2395. Fax: 802-773-9656.
www.vac-rutland.com   E-mail: cbucholt@vac-rutland.com
Joanne H. Mattsson, BA, MA, Exec Dir. **Carl Bucholt,** MA, MEd, Educ Dir.
   Focus: Spec Ed. Treatment. **Conditions:** Primary—BD ED. Sec—ADD
      ADHD Anx Ap Ar Asp Au CD Dc Dg Dx LD Mood MR OCD ODD ON

PDD Psy PTSD S TS. **IQ 70 and up.**
Gen Acad. Gr PS-12. Courses: Read Math Lang_Arts Sci Soc_Stud Studio_Art Adaptive_Phys_Ed. Man_Arts & Shop. On-Job Trng.
Therapy: Lang. **Psychotherapy:** Fam Indiv.
Enr: 50. Day Males 46. Day Females 4. **Staff:** 41 (Full 34, Part 7).
Rates 2003: Day $30,000/sch yr.
Summer Prgm: Day. Rec. Ther. Day Rate $3000. 6 wks.
Est 1937. Private. Nonprofit.

Children with an emotional disturbance who may also have a secondary mental health issue such as obsessive-compulsive disorder, oppositional defiant disorder and Asperger's syndrome receive treatment at VAC. The program focuses on treatment, family support and academic skills. Staff members tailor individual and group therapy, counseling and behavioral training to the student's specific needs.

Beginning at six weeks of age, children may take part in the Early Education and Care Program, which includes prekindergarten instruction and, for boys and girls through age 12, a before- and after-school enrichment program. Pupils in grades 1-12 participate in an aggressive educational program at Sheldon Academy that attempts to keep the student on pace with his or her home school.

WINSTON L. PROUTY CENTER
FOR CHILD DEVELOPMENT

Day — Coed Ages Birth-6

Brattleboro, VT 05301. 10 Oak St.
Tel: 802-257-7852. Fax: 802-258-2413.
Marisa Duncan-Holley, MEd, Exec Dir.
　Focus: Spec Ed. **Conditions:** Primary—ADD ADHD Ap As Au B BI C CP D Dx ED Ep LD MR ON S SB.
　Gen Acad. Gr PS.
　Therapy: Hear Lang Phys Speech. **Psychotherapy:** Fam Group.
　Enr: 115. **Staff:** 23 (Full 19, Part 4).
　Est 1969. Private. Nonprofit.

This facility is named in honor of Winston L. Prouty, late US Senator from Vermont, who cosponsored the Handicapped Children's Early Education Act. The preschool development program provides prescriptive education to ensure success in the regular school setting. Enrollment is restricted to those under age 6. A fully integrated early childhood care program provides center-based, home-based and community support for children throughout Windham County.

VIRGINIA

THE ARC OF THE VIRGINIA PENINSULA

Day — Coed All Ages

Hampton, VA 23666. 51 Battle Rd.
Tel: 757-896-6461. Fax: 757-896-8470.
www.arcvap.org   E-mail: lmilam@arcvap.org
Paul B. Babcock, MS, Pres.
   Conditions: Primary—MR.
   Pre-Voc. Voc. Shelt_Workshop. On-Job Trng.
   Therapy: Recreational.
   Est 1953. Private. Nonprofit. Spons: The Arc.

THE BARRY ROBINSON CENTER

Res — Coed Ages 6-17

Norfolk, VA 23502. 443 Kempsville Rd.
Tel: 757-455-6100. Fax: 757-455-6127.
www.barryrobinson.org   E-mail: admissions@barryrobinson.org
Thomas Pittman, Exec Dir. Charles K. Devitt, MD, Med Dir. Nancy Holcomb,
Adm.
   Focus: Treatment. Conditions: Primary—ADD ADHD Anx BD CD Dc Dg
      Dx ED LD Mood OCD ODD Psy PTSD PW SP Sz TS. Sec—Au MR S. IQ
      80 and up.
   Gen Acad. Pre-Voc. Ungraded. Courses: Read Math Lang_Arts. Man_Arts
      & Shop.
   Therapy: Art Chemo Milieu Music Recreational Speech. Psychotherapy:
      Fam Group Indiv.
   Enr: 72. Res Males 36. Res Females 36. Staff: 82 (Full 63, Part 19). Educ 9.
      Admin 10.
   Est 1933. Private. Nonprofit.

The center serves children and adolescents with emotional disturbances and learning
disabilities. Services offered include individualized psychological counseling and family
therapy, as well as academic, prevocational and recreational instruction. Substance abusers are also accepted, and treatment typically lasts for six to 12 months.

BLACKWATER OUTDOOR EXPERIENCES

Res — Coed Ages 14-28

Midlothian, VA 23113. 13821 Village Mill Dr, Ste B.
Tel: 804-794-8900. Fax: 804-378-2012.
www.blackwateroutdoor-ahc.com
   E-mail: admissions@blackwateroutdoor-ahc.com

Grant Leibersberger, MEd, Prgm Dir. George M. Bright, MD, Med Dir. Craig Taylor, Adm.
  Focus: Treatment. Conditions: Primary—ADD ADHD Anx BD Bu CD Dc Dg Dx ED Mood OCD PTSD SP. IQ 85-125.
  Therapy: Recreational. Psychotherapy: Fam Group Indiv Substance_ Abuse.
  Staff: 8. Admin 3.
  Rates 2003: Res $324/day. Schol avail.
  Est 1980. Private.

This experiential, therapeutic program focuses on personal and group activities. Program goals are self-discovery, personal growth and the establishment of better communication patterns, both interpersonal and within the family system.

Blackwater's 21-day sessions, which operate year-round, each serve a maximum of six students.

CENTRAL VIRGINIA TRAINING CENTER

Res — Coed All Ages

Lynchburg, VA 24505. PO Box 1098.
Tel: 434-947-6000. Fax: 434-947-2140.
www.cvtc.state.va.us
  E-mail: rob.merryman@cvtc.dmhmrsas.virginia.gov
Judy L. Dudley, MA, Dir. Vishnu K. Vyas, MD, Med Dir. Rob Merryman, Adm.
  Focus: Trng. Conditions: Primary—MR.
  Gen Acad. Ungraded. Courses: Read Math.
  Therapy: Hear Lang Occup Phys Speech. Psychotherapy: Indiv.
  Enr: 588. Res Males 318. Res Females 270. Staff: 1675 (Full 1536, Part 139). Prof 114. Admin 69.
  Rates 2004: Res $311/day.
  Est 1910. State. Nonprofit.

This state facility provides residential, educational, training, treatment and health care programs for persons with mental retardation whose needs cannot be met by existing community resources. Services include short- or long-term habilitation for individuals whose complex behavioral, physical or healthcare needs preclude community placement; nursing facility services for individuals who require 24-hour nursing supervision; acute care services for individuals in need of emergency care or hospitalization; and transitional support for community placement.

CHARTERHOUSE SCHOOL

Res — Coed Ages 11-17

Richmond, VA 23230. 3900 W Broad St.
Tel: 804-254-9669. Fax: 804-353-3061.
www.charterhouseschool.org   E-mail: info-charterhouse@umfs.org
Erik Laursen, PhD, Dir. Joyce A. Fenimore, Adm.
  Focus: Spec Ed. Treatment. Conditions: Primary—ADD BD CD Dx ED LD

OCD. Sec—As Ep Psy. **IQ 70 and up.**
Gen Acad. Pre-Voc. Ungraded. Courses: Read Math Lang_Arts Soc_Stud
Health. Man_Arts & Shop.
Psychotherapy: Group Parent.
Enr: 44. Res Males 11. Res Females 33.
Est 1979. Private. Nonprofit. United Methodist. **Spons:** United Methodist
Family Services.

This school offers individualized education to adolescents with severe problems who require a more restrictive environment than usual. Specialized treatment teams, 24-hour peer therapy and individual weekly therapy are provided. A wilderness and therapeutic recreation program is offered, as are parental groups and family counseling.

CHILD DEVELOPMENT CENTER

Clinic: Ages Birth-21. M-F 8-5 by Appt.

Arlington, VA 22201. 3033 Wilson Blvd, Ste 600B.
Tel: 703-228-1620. Fax: 703-228-1133.
 Focus: Treatment. **Conditions:** Primary—ADD ADHD Au Dx LD MR. Sec—
 Anx As B BD BI C CD CP D ED Ep IP MD MS OCD ON Psy S SB Sz TB.
 Staff: 4 (Full 2, Part 2).
 Rates 2004: Sliding-Scale Rate $0-318/ses (Evaluation).
 Est 1958. State.

The center performs evaluations of children whose suspected problem is mental retardation, a learning disability or a behavioral reaction. Other problems considered are brain damage and developmental delays.

Staff summarize findings and formulate goals and plans in conjunction with teachers and other professionals. Parents receive a final interpretation, and the clinic designs long-range and immediate plans for schooling, home care and therapy. Counseling and follow-up services are available.

CUMBERLAND HOSPITAL

Res — Coed Ages 2-22

New Kent, VA 23124. 9407 Cumberland Rd.
Tel: 804-966-2242. Fax: 804-966-5639.
www.cumberlandhospital.com
 Conditions: Primary—ADHD AN Au BI Db MR ON PDD.
 Gen Acad. Pre-Voc. Courses: Read Math Lang_Arts. On-Job Trng.
 Therapy: Hear Lang Occup Phys Speech. **Psychotherapy:** Fam Group
 Indiv.
 Est 1983. Private. Inc. **Spons:** Ardent Health Services.

EASTER SEALS HOME AND COMMUNITY THERAPY PROGRAM

Day — Coed Ages Birth-5
Clinic: Ages Birth-21. M-F 8-6.

Falls Church, VA 22046. 111 N Cherry St.
Tel: 703-534-4596. Fax: 703-534-4957.
http://nca-md.easter-seals.org
Chandra Malson, MEd, CCC-SLP, Dir. **Guido Penaranda,** Coord.
  Focus: Treatment. **Conditions:** Primary—Au CP DS LD MR ON PDD S.
  Therapy: Lang Occup Phys Play Speech.
  Staff: 10. Prof 6. Educ 2. Admin 2.
  Rates 2003: Clinic $125/ses.
  Est 1954. Private. Nonprofit.

Early intervention, which is offered both in the home and at various community locations, comprises therapy and evaluations for children from birth to age 3. Therapists provide team evaluations and treatment for children with varying diagnoses through use of specialized treatment strategies, therapeutic play, and parent education and involvement. Evaluations and treatments constitute the outpatient program. Age-appropriate therapeutic activities focus on development in the areas of motor skills, self-care, sensory processing, cognition and speech.

ELK HILL FARM

Res — Males Ages 11-18; Day — Coed 13-17

Goochland, VA 23063. 1975 Elk Hill Rd, PO Box 99.
  Nearby locations: Richmond; Varina.
Tel: 804-457-4866. Fax: 804-457-2830.
www.elkhill.com   E-mail: elkhill@aol.com
Michael C. Farley, BA, Exec Dir.
  Focus: Treatment. **Conditions:** Primary—BD ED LD. **IQ 80 and up.**
  Gen Acad. Pre-Voc. Voc. Gr 6-12. Courses: Read Math Lang_Arts. Man_ Arts & Shop. On-Job Trng.
  Psychotherapy: Fam Group.
  Staff: 80 (Full 75, Part 5).
  Est 1970. Private. Nonprofit.

Adolescents with emotional, educational and legal problems take part in a program that involves individual, group and family therapy; intensive wilderness challenges; school and vocational programs; and family intervention. The plan works to develop self-esteem and a sense of responsibility and cooperation through a peer-group process.

Activities include white-water canoeing, backpacking, rock climbing and a ropes course. Treatment typically lasts nine to 12 months, and comprehensive aftercare services are available. Additional offices are located at 8151 Warriner Rd., Varina 23231 and 3802 Chamberlayne Ave., Richmond 23227.

FAITH MISSION HOME

Res — Coed Ages 2-15

Free Union, VA 22940. 3540 Mission Home Ln.
Tel: 434-985-2294. Fax: 434-985-7633.
Reuben J. Yoder, Dir. **Merle Miller,** Adm.
  Focus: Trng. **Conditions:** Primary—MR. **IQ 20-70.**
  Pre-Voc. Voc. Ungraded. Courses: Read Math Lang_Arts. Man_Arts &
    Shop. Shelt_Workshop. On-Job Trng.
  Therapy: Hear Lang Occup Phys Speech.
  Enr: 60. Staff: 40.
  Rates 2003: Res $1122/mo. State Aid.
  Est 1965. Private. Nonprofit. Mennonite.

The home accepts ambulatory, educable mentally retarded children. Individuals in need of constant medical care and those with severe emotional disturbances are not admitted. The daily training program consists of eight areas: self-care; arts and crafts; and physical, speech, vocational, social, spiritual and academic therapies.

GRAFTON SCHOOL

Res and Day — Coed Ages 3-21

Winchester, VA 22604. PO Box 2500.
  Nearby locations: Berryville; Midlothian; Rockville, MD.
Tel: 540-869-0300. Fax: 540-542-1722.
www.grafton.org   E-mail: admis@grafton.org
Robert W. Stieg, Jr., BS, Head. **Robert Goshen,** MD, Med Dir. **David Yeater,**
  Adm.
  Focus: Spec Ed. Treatment. **Conditions:** Primary—ADD ADHD Au BD CD
    Dx ED MR Psy. Sec—As B Bl CP D Ep IP LD MD MS OCD ON S SB Sz
    TB. **IQ 25-130.**
  Gen Acad. Pre-Voc. Voc. Ungraded. Courses: Read Math Lang_Arts Soc_
    Stud Studio_Art Music. On-Job Trng.
  Therapy: Lang Occup Speech. **Psychotherapy:** Fam Group Indiv Parent.
  Enr: 277. Res Males 179. Res Females 61. Day Males 33. Day Females 4.
  Est 1958. Private. Nonprofit.

Originally established to provide a homelike situation for children with learning differences, Grafton now also serves individuals with emotional disturbances, mental retardation, autism and behavioral disorders. The behaviorally oriented treatment process assists individuals with educational, prevocational and independent living skills to ease the transition back into the community.

GRAYDON MANOR

Res — Males Ages 7-17, Females 13-17; Day — Coed 11-17
Clinic: All Ages. By Appt.

Leesburg, VA 20175. 801 Children's Center Rd SW.
Tel: 703-777-3485. Fax: 703-777-4887.
www.graydonmanor.org
Bernard J. Haberlein, MA, Pres. Robert E. Smith, Adm.
  Focus: Treatment. Conditions: Primary—ADD ADHD BD ED Mood OCD
    Psy Sz. Sec—Anx Asp CD Dx LD ODD PTSD SP. IQ 70 and up.
  Gen Acad. Gr 6-12. Courses: Read Math Lang_Arts Sci.
  Therapy: Art Recreational. Psychotherapy: Fam Group Indiv Parent.
  Enr: 61. Staff: 139. Admin 9.
  Rates 2003: Res $450/day. Day $180/day. Clinic $70/hr.
  Est 1957. Private. Nonprofit.

  Located on a 136-acre tract, this facility for children with severe emotional and behavioral problems emphasizes the improvement of classroom behavior, academic skills and creative abilities. Graydon Manor conducts psychotherapeutic counseling on individual and group bases. Parents participate in the child's treatment through family therapy and counseling sessions. Home-based programs, therapeutic day schooling, out-patient services and group home programs are also available. The usual duration of treatment is six to eight months.

HAMPTON UNIVERSITY
SPEECH, LANGUAGE AND HEARING CLINIC

Clinic: Ages 2 and up. M-F 9-5.

Hampton, VA 23668. Box 6194.
Tel: 757-727-5435. Fax: 757-727-5765.
www.hamptonu.edu/science/communicativedisorders/clinic.htm
Robert M. Screen, PhD, Supv. Cheryl H. Freeman, MS, Clin Dir.
  Focus: Treatment. Conditions: Primary—Ap Apr S. Sec—Asp Au D LD.
  Therapy: Hear Lang Speech.
  Staff: 5.
  Rates 2003: $45 (Evaulation); 125 (Therapy)/ses.
  Summer Prgm: Day. Ther.
  Private. Nonprofit.

  Hampton provides diagnostic and therapeutic speech and hearing services. Parental counseling is available.

HARRISONBURG-ROCKINGHAM
COMMUNITY SERVICES BOARD

Clinic: Ages 3 and up. M-F 8-6; Eves by Appt.

Harrisonburg, VA 22802. 1241 N Main St.
Tel: 540-434-1941. Fax: 540-434-1791.
www.hrcsb.org
Charlotte V. McNulty, Exec Dir. Nicholas McClean-Rice, MD, Med Dir.
　Focus: Treatment. Conditions: Primary—ADD ADHD Asp Au BD Bu CD
　　ED Mood MR OCD Psy SP Sz TS.
　Therapy: Phys Speech. Psychotherapy: Fam Group Indiv.
　Staff: 28 (Full 20, Part 8). Prof 24. Admin 4.
　Est 1966. Municipal.

HRCSB offers evaluation, diagnosis and treatment for children with emotional disturbances, attentional disorders or mental retardation. Family, group and individual counseling is offered. Substance abuse services are also available. Fees are determined along a sliding scale.

INFANT & TODDLER CONNECTION OF VIRGINIA

Day — Coed Ages Birth-3

Richmond, VA 23219. 1220 Bank St, 9th Fl, PO Box 1797.
Tel: 804-786-3710. TTY: 804-771-5877. Fax: 804-371-7959.
www.infantva.org
Mary Ann Discenza, Coord.
　Conditions: Primary—MR.
　Therapy: Lang Occup Phys Speech.
　Staff: Prof 14.
　County.

THE LEARNING CENTER OF CHARLOTTESVILLE

Day — Coed Ages 6-21
Clinic: Ages 6-21.

Charlottesville, VA 22903. 2132 Ivy Rd.
Tel: 434-977-6006. Fax: 434-977-6009.
www.cvillelearning.org　E-mail: info@cvillelearning.org
Elizabeth A. Cottone, PhD, Exec Dir.
　Focus: Spec Ed. Conditions: Primary—ADD ADHD Dc Dg Dx LD. Sec—
　　Ap Apr Asp BI ED OCD SP. IQ 80 and up.
　Gen Acad. Ungraded. Courses: Read Math Lang_Arts.
　Enr: 85. Staff: 25 (Full 4, Part 21).
　Rates 2003: Clinic $40/hr. Schol avail.
　Summer Prgm: Day. Educ. Day Rate $1600. 5 wks.
　Est 1974. Private. Nonprofit.

The center offers educational and psychological evaluations, one-on-one tutoring, summer and full-day school programs for students ages 6-12, tutor workshops and training seminars.

THE LEARNING RESOURCE CENTER
Clinic: Ages 5 and up. M-Th S 10-5; Eves M-Th S 5-9.

Virginia Beach, VA 23454. 909 First Colonial Rd.
Tel: 757-428-3367. Fax: 757-428-1630.
www.learningresourcecenter.net   E-mail: educateme@earthlink.net
Nancy Harris-Kroll, MSEd, Dir.
  Focus: Spec Ed. Treatment. **Conditions:** Primary—ADD ADHD Anx Asp Au Dc Dg DS Dx ED LD Mood OCD PDD S SP TS. Sec—MR. **IQ 100 and up.**
  Gen Acad. Ungraded. Courses: Read Math Lang_Arts Sci Soc_Stud.
  Staff: 24 (Full 4, Part 20).
  Rates 2004: Clinic $285/mo. Schol avail.
  Est 1981. Private. Inc.

The center provides testing, one-on-one remediation and tutorials in all subject areas. The program seeks to teach pupils learning strategies and increase their self-esteem. Educational and parental counseling is available. Advocacy services are also available to parents of students with special needs. The center conducts six-week summer tutoring sessions for individuals and small groups.

LEARY SCHOOL
Day — Coed Ages 5-21

Alexandria, VA 22312. 6349 Lincolnia Rd.
Tel: 703-941-8150. Fax: 703-941-4237.
www.learyschool.org   E-mail: learyschool@bellatlantic.net
Ed Schultze, Pres.
  Conditions: Primary—BD ED LD.
  Gen Acad. Pre-Voc. Gr K-12. Courses: Read Math Lang_Arts. Man_Arts & Shop. On-Job Trng.
  Therapy: Art Lang Occup Recreational Speech. **Psychotherapy:** Fam Group Indiv.
  Staff: Prof 40.
  Est 1964. Private. Inc. **Spons:** Lincolnia Educational Foundation.

LITTLE KESWICK SCHOOL
Res — Males Ages 10-17

Keswick, VA 22947. PO Box 24.
Tel: 434-295-0457. Fax: 434-977-1892.

www.avenue.org/lks   E-mail: columbuslks@aol.com
Marc J. Columbus, MEd, Head. **Terry Columbus,** MEd, Dir.
   Focus: Spec Ed. **Conditions:** Primary—ADD ADHD Anx Asp Dc Dg Dx ED
      LD Mood OCD ODD PDD PTSD SP TS. Sec—Ep S. **IQ 80 and up.**
   Gen Acad. Pre-Voc. Ungraded. Courses: Read Math Lang_Arts. Man_Arts
      & Shop.
   Therapy: Art Lang Occup Speech. **Psychotherapy:** Fam Group Indiv.
   Enr: 31. Res Males 31. **Staff:** 39 (Full 30, Part 9).
   Rates 2004: Res $55,175/yr (+$7340). Schol 2 ($20,000). State Aid.
   Summer Prgm: Res. Educ. Rec. Ther. Res Rate $5585. 5 wks.
   Est 1963. Private. Inc.

The school emphasizes the remediation of learning disabilities and emotional problems in a homelike setting with a small staff-student ratio. Children have access to full medical and educational facilities of the nearby University of Virginia. Many forms of therapy are available, and the usual duration of treatment is two years. The school operates year-round, with some spaces reserved in the summer session for those not enrolled in the regular program. All pupils undergo a free, 24-hour pre-admission screening prior to admittance.

MEMORIAL CHILD GUIDANCE CLINIC

Clinic: Ages Birth-18. M-F 8:30-5; Eves T-Th 5-7:30.

Richmond, VA 23223. 2319 E Broad St.
Tel: 804-649-1605. Fax: 804-649-2151.
www.mcgcva.com
Mark Hierholzer, Exec Dir. **Edward G. Canada, Jr.,** MSW, Dir. **Vivian Mann,**
   MSW, Clin Dir. **Thresa Simon,** MD, Med Dir. **Melinda Driskill,** Adm.
   Focus: Treatment. **Conditions:** Primary—ADD ADHD Anx BD CD ED OCD
      ODD Psy PTSD Sz. Sec—Au.
   Therapy: Art Play. **Psychotherapy:** Fam Group Indiv Parent.
   Staff: 38. Prof 11. Admin 7.
   Rates 2003: /hrSliding-Scale Rate $6-90/ses.
   Est 1924. Private. Nonprofit.

MCGC is a mental health treatment facility for children, adolescents and families. Psychiatric evaluation and treatment for children with social, emotional or educational difficulties are provided. Secondary concerns are community and preventive psychiatry. Parental counseling, crisis intervention and follow-up services are available.

MORRISON SCHOOL

Day — Coed Ages 6-18

Bristol, VA 24202. 139 Terrace Dr.
Tel: 276-669-2823. Fax: 276-669-2823.
E-mail: morrisonschool101@yahoo.com
Sharon Morrison, EdD, Dir.
   Focus: Spec Ed. **Conditions:** Primary—ADD ADHD Dc Dg Dx. **IQ 90-109.**

Col Prep. Gen Acad. Gr 1-12. Courses: Read Math Lang_Arts.
Enr: 30. Day Males 20. Day Females 10. **Staff:** 9 (Full 5, Part 4).
Rates 2003: Day $6000-8000/sch yr. Schol avail.
Summer Prgm: Day. Educ. Day Rate $700. 5 wks.
Est 1977. Private. Nonprofit. **Spons:** Foundation for Educational and Developmental Opportunity.

Among Morrison's services for students with learning disabilities are full- and part-time day school, preschool, after-school tutoring, summer school, psycho-educational testing and child management consultation. Emphasis is placed on correction of or compensation for the disability, with the goal of returning the pupil to a traditional school program as soon as possible.

THE NEW COMMUNITY SCHOOL

Day — Coed Ages 11-18

Richmond, VA 23227. 4211 Hermitage Rd.
Tel: 804-266-2494. Fax: 804-264-3281.
www.tncs.org   E-mail: info@tncs.org
Julia Ann Greenwood, BA, MA, Head.
  Focus: Spec Ed. **Conditions:** Primary—Dc Dg Dx LD. Sec—ADD ADHD.
    IQ 87 and up.
  Col Prep. Gr 6-12. Courses: Read Math Lang_Arts.
  Therapy: Lang.
  Enr: 93. Day Males 64. Day Females 29. **Staff:** 38 (Full 36, Part 2).
  Rates 2003: Day $16,800-17,800/sch yr. Schol avail.
  Summer Prgm: Day. Educ. Day Rate $200-800. 4 wks.
  Est 1974. Private. Nonprofit.

The program provides clinical remediation and a college-option curriculum specifically designed for dyslexic adolescents. English, math, history and science are offered in conjunction with daily tutoring in language remediation. Emphasis is placed on reading, writing, spelling and written expression as well as academic challenge. A media center and a library provide materials especially designed to aid specific learning problems. Classes are limited to six to eight students, and a 3:1 student-teacher ratio is maintained.

Extracurricular activities include sports, music, drama, journalism, student government and other special interest groups.

Continuous faculty training and professional development are emphasized with weekly in-service programs conducted by outside consultants and school staff. In addition, a teacher-training internship for university graduate students is available.

NEW DOMINION SCHOOL

Res — Coed Ages 11-17

Dillwyn, VA 23936. PO Box 540.
Tel: 434-983-2051. Fax: 434-983-2068.
www.ndsvirginia.com   E-mail: mforman@ndsvirginia.com

Ben Montano, BA, MA, Admin Dir. **Mike Forman,** Adm.
  Focus: Spec Ed. **Conditions:** Primary—ADD ADHD BD CD Dx ED LD
    Mood ODD. Sec—OCD. **IQ 75 and up.**
  Col Prep. Gen Acad. Pre-Voc. Gr 7-12. Courses: Read Math Lang_Arts Sci
    Soc_Stud. Man_Arts & Shop.
  Therapy: Art Milieu Recreational Speech. **Psychotherapy:** Fam Group
    Indiv.
  Enr: 120. Res Males 72. Res Females 48. **Staff:** 78 (Full 72, Part 6). Prof
    35. Educ 11. Admin 5.
  Rates 2003: Res $43,800/yr. State Aid.
  Est 1976. Private. Inc. **Spons:** Three Springs.

On separate campuses, NDS provides group and individual counseling, as well as an educational program, for severely emotionally disturbed, learning-disabled and socially disordered boys and girls. Each group of a maximum of 12 students is responsible for carrying out its own activities. Any member of the group can call for a group meeting to solve group and individual problems at any time during the day. Academic classes are small, and education is regarded as a privilege that students must earn. Regular evaluations assist staff members with assessments of emotional, social and academic progress.

New Dominion does not accept pupils with physical conditions that prevent them from taking part in outdoor activities and wilderness trips, boys who have a violent nature or those requiring constant medication. The usual duration of treatment is 12 to 18 months.

NEW LIFESTYLES

Res — Coed Ages 18-26

Winchester, VA 22604. 230 W Boscawen St, PO Box 64.
Tel: 540-722-4521. Fax: 540-722-0223.
www.newlifestyles.net   E-mail: drcuave@newlifestyles.net
Kenneth L. Cuave, PsyD, Pres. **Pamela Throckmorton,** PsyD, Med Dir.
  Focus: Treatment. **Conditions:** Primary—ADD ADHD Asp Mood OCD
    ODD. Sec—Bl CP Db Ep TS. **IQ 90 and up.**
  Therapy: Art Milieu. **Psychotherapy:** Fam Group Indiv Parent.
  Enr: 10. Res Males 5. Res Females 5. **Staff:** 11 (Full 8, Part 3). Prof 4.
    Admin 2.
  Rates 2004: Res $75,000/yr. Schol avail.
  Est 1985. Private. Inc.

This clinically based, individualized transition program prepares adolescents with emotional disorders or learning disabilities for independent living.

NEW VISTAS SCHOOL

Day — Coed Ages 5-19

Lynchburg, VA 24501. 520 Eldon St.
Tel: 434-846-0301. Fax: 434-528-1004.

www.newvistasschool.org   E-mail: director@newvistasschool.org
Lucy Guggenheimer Ross, Dir.
   Focus: Spec Ed. **Conditions:** Primary—ADD ADHD Dc Dg Dx LD. Sec—
      ED. **IQ 90 and up.**
   Col Prep. Gen Acad. Pre-Voc. Gr K-12. Courses: Read Math Lang_Arts Sci
      Computers Soc_Stud Studio_Art Music Drama Study_Skills. Man_Arts &
      Shop. On-Job Trng.
   Therapy: Lang Speech. **Psychotherapy:** Group.
   Enr: 53. Day Males 30. Day Females 23. **Staff:** 22 (Full 11, Part 11). Educ
      17. Admin 5.
   Est 1986. Private. Nonprofit.

Serving pupils who have not previously had successful school experiences, the
school's small-class and tutorial program features multisensory activities designed to
meet particular learning styles. Structured, individually designed programs enable students to develop social skills and strengthen self-concepts while also improving their
learning skills. Other services of the school include an after-school tutorial program,
psychological evaluations, educational assessments, transitional support, and individual,
group and family counseling.

NORTHERN VIRGINIA TRAINING CENTER

Res — Coed Ages 6 and up
Clinic: Ages 6 and up. By Appt.

Fairfax, VA 22032. 9901 Braddock Rd.
Tel: 703-323-4000. Fax: 703-323-4252.
www.nvtc.state.va.us
Mark Diorio, PhD, Dir. **Leslie Katz,** Adm.
   Focus: Trng. Treatment. **Conditions:** Primary—MR. Sec—Ap B Bl CP D ED
      Ep ON S. **IQ 0-50.**
   Voc. Shelt_Workshop.
   Therapy: Hear Lang Occup Phys Recreational Speech. **Psychotherapy:**
      Indiv.
   Staff: 250.
   Est 1973. State. Nonprofit.

Individuals with a primary diagnosis of severe to profound mental retardation receive
educational and vocational training that encourages the development of self-care skills
and independence. Clients often exhibit such associated conditions as sensory or physical disabilities or extreme maladaptive behaviors. Admission is restricted to Virginia
residents, with preference given to those from northern Virginia; individuals typically
enroll from Fairfax, Arlington, Prince William and Loudoun counties, as well as from
the cities of Alexandria and Falls Church. Fees are based on a sliding scale.

OAKLAND SCHOOL

Res and Day — Coed Ages 8-14

Keswick, VA 22947. Boyd Tavern.

Tel: 434-293-9059. Fax: 434-296-8930.
www.oaklandschool.net   E-mail: oaklandschool@earthlink.net
Carol Smieciuch, MEd, Dir.
   Focus: Spec Ed. **Conditions:** Primary—Dx LD. Sec—ADD ADHD Dg ED.
      IQ 90-130.
   Col Prep. Gen Acad. Gr 3-9. Courses: Read Math Lang_Arts Sci Hist
      Study_Skills.
   Therapy: Lang Speech. **Psychotherapy:** Group Indiv.
   Enr: 85. Res Males 30. Res Females 20. Day Males 20. Day Females 15.
      Staff: 53 (Full 48, Part 5). Educ 13. Admin 4.
   Rates 2003: Res $31,950/sch yr. Day $17,500/sch yr. State Aid.
   Summer Prgm: Res & Day. Educ. Rec. Res Rate $5,975. Day Rate $3,200.
      7 wks.
   Est 1950. Private. Nonprofit.

Oakland accepts children of average to above-average ability with dyslexia or learning disabilities. It provides a full academic curriculum stressing basic skills in one-on-
one and small-class settings, with the goal of mainstreaming students into traditional
classrooms. The school specializes in the teaching of reading, math, written language
and study skills.

Social skills are emphasized, and teachers, residential instructors and psychologists
assist in building and maintaining self-esteem in each child. Children with severe behavioral or emotional problems are not appropriate for either the regular academic year
or the summer session. Oakland also offers a full recreational program, daily physical
education, team sports and horseback riding.

OAKWOOD SCHOOL

Day — Coed Ages 6-14

Annandale, VA 22003. 7210 Braddock Rd.
Tel: 703-941-5788. Fax: 703-941-4186.
www.oakwoodschool.com
Robert C. McIntyre, BA, MA, Exec Dir. **Muriel Jedlicka,** Adm.
   Focus: Spec Ed. **Conditions:** Primary—ADD ADHD Dx LD.
   Gen Acad. Ungraded. Courses: Read Math Lang_Arts Sci Computers Soc_
      Stud Health Study_Skills.
   Therapy: Lang Occup Speech.
   Enr: 113. Day Males 87. Day Females 26. **Staff:** 44 (Full 34, Part 10).
   Rates 2003: Day $21,100/sch yr. Schol 6 ($40,000).
   Est 1971. Private. Nonprofit.

Oakwood provides a comprehensive elementary and middle school academic program for students displaying average to above-average intellectual potential who have
mild to moderate learning disabilities. The nongraded program employs a combination
of traditional, remedial and compensatory strategies using multisensory teaching methods, materials and modifications. Small classes follow a curriculum that emphasizes the
acquisition of strong reading, writing and math skills.

Therapy is available on an as-needed basis, and staff members use ongoing assessments of student progress to monitor program effectiveness. The usual duration of treatment is two to five years.

PARENT EDUCATION-INFANT DEVELOPMENT PROGRAM

Clinic: Ages Birth-3. M-F 8-4:30.

Fredericksburg, VA 22401. 600 Jackson St.
Tel: 540-372-3561. Fax: 540-371-3753.
www.racsb.state.va.us/peid.html
Jill Donaldson, MA, CCC-SLP, Prgm Coord. **Raymond Jones,** MD, Med Dir.
  Focus: Treatment. **Conditions:** Primary—Au B Bl CP D ED IP MD MR MS ON S SB.
  Therapy: Hear Lang Occup Phys Speech.
  Staff: 9 (Full 3, Part 6).
  Rates 2003: Sliding-Scale Rate $0-100/ses.
  Est 1979. State. Nonprofit. **Spons:** Rappahannock Area Community Services Board.

PE-ID's year-round services are directed toward developmentally delayed infants and their families. The treatment offered includes home- and center-based developmental programs, team assessments, and parental training and counseling. Rates vary depending upon the service provided and the family's ability to pay.

PHILLIPS SCHOOLS

Day — Coed Ages 5-21

Annandale, VA 22003. 7010 Braddock Rd.
  Nearby locations: Laurel, MD.
Tel: 703-941-8810. Fax: 703-658-2378.
www.phillipsprograms.org
Sally A. Sibley, PhD, Pres.
  Conditions: Primary—Au BD ED LD MR.
  Gen Acad. Pre-Voc. Gr K-12. Courses: Read Math Lang_Arts. Man_Arts & Shop. Shelt_Workshop. On-Job Trng.
  Therapy: Lang Occup Phys Speech. **Psychotherapy:** Fam Indiv.
  Est 1967. Private. Nonprofit.

THE PINES RESIDENTIAL TREATMENT CENTER

Res — Coed Ages 5-21

Portsmouth, VA 23704. 825 Crawford Pky.
Tel: 757-393-0061. Fax: 757-397-5673.
www.absfirst.com   E-mail: info@absfirst.com
Debra Goldstein, MS, Admin. **Lenard Lexier,** MD, Med Dir. **Debbie Creef,** Adm.
  Focus: Treatment. **Conditions:** Primary—Anx CD ED Mood OCD Sz. Sec—ADD ADHD BD Dx LD MR. **IQ 50 and up.**
  Gen Acad. Pre-Voc. Voc. Ungraded. Courses: Read Math Lang_Arts Span

Computers Sci Soc_Stud. Man_Arts & Shop. On-Job Trng.
Therapy: Lang Speech. **Psychotherapy:** Fam Group Indiv.
Enr: 374.
Est 1986. Private. Inc. **Spons:** Alternative Behavioral Services.

This year-round, comprehensive program serves juvenile sex offenders, as well as children and youth with severe emotional and behavioral disorders. Programming encompasses psychological treatment, educational and vocational services, and training in social skills, leisure skills and independent living skills. Services take place on three campuses.

The Behavioral Studies Program (BSP) consists of multiple units for male sex offenders ages 11-21. Within a highly structured setting, residents are separated according to age, level of emotional maturity, and cognitive capacity. Project Right Track, part of the BSP, provides treatment for males ages 13-18 who have been diagnosed with significant psychosexual disorders and developmental disabilities.

The Pines' Behavioral Studies Girls Program treats adolescent girls ages 12-18 who are psychosexually disturbed. These residents typically exhibit aggressive sexual acting out, hyper arousal or both in response to previous abuse. Girls also usually display moderate levels of aggression and have such psychiatric issues as mood disorder, anxiety disorders and compulsive disorders.

A fourth program, the Young Men's Center, serves males ages 13-17 who have psychiatric and behavioral problems. Clinical treatment focuses upon socially inappropriate aggressive, impulsive and self-destructive acts. The program's goal is improved internal self-control and management of the illness.

REGION TEN COMMUNITY SERVICES BOARD

Day — Coed Ages 16 and up
Clinic: All Ages. M-Th.

Charlottesville, VA 22903. 800 Preston Ave.
Tel: 434-972-1800. Fax: 434-970-2104.
www.regionten.org   E-mail: martham@regionten.org
James R. Peterson, MSW, Exec Dir.
   Conditions: Primary—B BD D ED LD MR ON S.
   Pre-Voc. Voc. Ungraded. Courses: Read Math. Shelt_Workshop. On-Job
      Trng.
   Therapy: Occup. **Psychotherapy:** Group Indiv.
   Est 1967. Private. Nonprofit.

RIVERSIDE SCHOOL

Day — Coed Ages 6-13

Richmond, VA 23235. 2110 McRae Rd, PO Box 3533.
Tel: 804-320-3465. Fax: 804-320-6146.
www.riversideschool.org   E-mail: info@riversideschool.org
Patricia W. DeOrio, BS, Dir. **Julie Wingfield,** MS, Prin.
   Focus: Spec Ed. **Conditions:** Primary—As C Db Dx LD. Sec—ADD ADHD.

IQ 100 and up.
Gen Acad. Gr 1-8. Courses: Read Math Lang_Arts Sci Soc_Stud.
Therapy: Occup Speech. **Psychotherapy:** Indiv.
Enr: 52. **Staff:** 36 (Full 11, Part 25).
Rates 2003: Day $13,850/sch yr.
Summer Prgm: Day. Educ.
Est 1970. Private. Nonprofit.

Riverside modifies its educational program to meet the needs of the dyslexic student body. Teachers administer comprehensive tests at the beginning and the end of each school year, and students attend 45-minute individual tutoring sessions four times per week. Riverside attempts to develop pupils' maturity and academic competence levels enough to successfully return them to mainstream schools. The usual duration of treatment is three years.

RIVERVIEW LEARNING CENTER

Day — Coed Ages 5-17

Chesapeake, VA 23321. PO Box 9247.
Tel: 757-488-7586. Fax: 757-465-8995.
Trudy C. Webb, BS, Coord. **Kim Cease,** Adm.
   Focus: Spec Ed. **Conditions:** Primary—LD. **IQ 90-109.**
   Col Prep. Gr 1-12. Courses: Read Math Lang_Arts.
   Enr: 29. Day Males 16. Day Females 13. **Staff:** 5. (Part 5). Prof 5. Educ 5.
   Rates 2004: Day $4720/sch yr.
   Summer Prgm: Day. 4 wks.
   Est 1982. Private. Nonprofit. Nondenom Christian. **Spons:** StoneBridge School.

The learning center's intervention program, developed by the National Institute for Learning Disabilities, focuses on stimulating each student's area of weakness in perception, language and cognition. Problem solving and organizational skills are also addressed. Riverview is not a tutoring program, but is instead an intensive educational therapy that uses specific techniques to strengthen areas of deficiency. Parents undergo training to enable them to work with children at home.

The center is affiliated with StoneBridge School, a Christian elementary and secondary school.

ST. COLETTA OF GREATER WASHINGTON

Day — Coed Ages 4-22

Alexandria, VA 22314. 207 S Peyton St.
Tel: 703-683-3686. Fax: 703-683-9888.
www.stcoletta.org   E-mail: kpadian@stcoletta.org
Sharon B. Raimo, BA, MA, MEd, Exec Dir. **Janice Corazza,** BA, MEd, Prgm Dir.
   Focus: Spec Ed. Trng. **Conditions:** Primary—Au Bl CP DS MR. Sec—ADD ADHD Ap Apr B BD CF D ED Ep IP MS Nf OCD ODD ON PTSD PW S

SB TS.
Pre-Voc. Voc. Ungraded. Courses: Music Life_Skills Adaptive_Phys_Ed. On-Job Trng.
Therapy: Hear Lang Music Occup Phys Speech Visual. **Psychotherapy:** Group Indiv Parent.
Enr: 164. Day Males 104. Day Females 60. **Staff:** 175 (Full 170, Part 5). Prof 46. Educ 18. Admin 17.
Rates 2003: Day $150/day. Clinic $72-86/hr.
Est 1959. Private. Nonprofit.

This independent school provides educational and therapeutic services for children and young adults with mental retardation, autism and secondary disabling conditions. The school offers a vocational program that includes prevocational training, work adjustment training, career exploration, job placement, on-the-job training and continuing support services.

ST. JOSEPH'S VILLA
DOOLEY SCHOOL

Res and Day — Coed Ages 5-21

Richmond, VA 23227. 8000 Brook Rd.
Tel: 804-553-3200. Fax: 804-553-3259.
www.stjosephsvilla.net   E-mail: helpinghands@stjosephsvilla.net
Paul Miller, BS, MEd, Admin. **Hattie Porter,** Adm.
Focus: Spec Ed. **Conditions:** Primary—ED LD MR.
Col Prep. Gen Acad. Pre-Voc. Voc. Gr K-12. Courses: Read Math Lang_ Arts Sci Soc_Stud Hist Health Life_Skills. On-Job Trng.
Therapy: Speech. **Psychotherapy:** Fam Group Indiv.
Enr: 100. Res Males 8. Res Females 2. Day Males 70. Day Females 20. **Staff:** 35 (Full 30, Part 5).
Est 1970. Private. Nonprofit.

The Dooley School's program educates youths who have a diagnosed learning disability, an emotional disturbance or a behavioral disorder. The educable mentally retarded are also accepted. Educational and therapeutic plans are designed to remediate disabilities and return the child to a regular classroom setting, as well as to teach appropriate social and personal behaviors.

ST. MARY'S HOME
FOR DISABLED CHILDREN

Res — Coed Ages Birth-18

Norfolk, VA 23504. 317 Chapel St.
Tel: 757-622-2208. Fax: 757-627-5314.
www.saintmaryshome.org   E-mail: info@saintmaryshome.org
William M. Jolly, BA, MHA, CEO. **A. A. Shoaibi,** MD, Med Dir.
Focus: Treatment. **Conditions:** Primary—MR OH. **IQ 0-40.**

Therapy: Hear Occup Phys Speech. **Psychotherapy:** Indiv.
Enr: 88. **Staff:** 196 (Full 136, Part 60). Prof 148. Educ 18. Admin 17.
Rates 2003: Res $300/day. State Aid.
Est 1973. Private. Nonprofit.

St. Mary's is an intermediate care facility for severely multi-handicapped children in the state of Virginia. Physical treatment, care and training allow each child to develop to maximum capacity. Special education services are provided by the Norfolk Public Schools. The residential units and all facilities can meet the needs of small children.

SOUTHEASTERN VIRGINIA TRAINING CENTER

Res — Coed Ages 2 and up

Chesapeake, VA 23320. 2100 Steppingstone Sq.
Tel: 757-424-8240. TTY: 757-424-8380. Fax: 757-424-8348.
www.sevtc.state.va.us
    Focus: Trng. Treatment. **Conditions:** Primary—Au MR. Sec—Ap B D ON S.
    Therapy: Hear Lang Occup Phys Speech. **Psychotherapy:** Indiv.
    Est 1974. State. Nonprofit.

This year-round center provides educational training and community placement for severely and profoundly retarded individuals. The center, which serves individuals who are not able to participate in community programs, offers training in self-care, language, independent living, socialization, academic/cognitive skills and motor development. Treatment lasts from one to 10 years.

SOUTHSIDE REGIONAL JUVENILE GROUP HOME

Res — Males Ages 13-18

South Boston, VA 24592. 1166 Huell Matthews Hwy.
Tel: 434-572-8906. Fax: 434-572-1655.
E-mail: srjgh@gcronline.com
Rux D. Cannady, Dir.
    Focus: Treatment. **Conditions:** Primary—BD. Sec—ED.
    Psychotherapy: Fam Group.
    Enr: 12. **Staff:** 11 (Full 7, Part 4). Prof 9. Admin 2.
    Rates 2003: Res $135/day.
    Est 1978. State. Nonprofit.

The home provides long-term residential services for troubled adolescents. Residents are involved in ongoing individual, group and family counseling in a structured environment designed to encourage increased responsibility and individual growth. An integral part of the program is a wilderness program, aimed at teaching and reinforcing new methods of communication, problem solving and stress management. Residents also take part in a monitored public school program that includes support services designed to foster academic success.

SPEECH AND LANGUAGE CENTER
OF NORTHERN VIRGINIA

Day — Coed Ages 2-6
Clinic: Ages 2-6. M-F 9-4.

McLean, VA 22101. 1125 Savile Ln.
Tel: 703-356-2833.
  Focus: Spec Ed. Treatment. **Conditions:** Primary—S.
  Therapy: Lang Speech.
  Staff: 5 (Full 2, Part 3).
  Rates 2004: $175-250 (Evaluation); $45-90 (Therapy)/ses.
  Summer Prgm: Day. Ther. 6 wks.
  Est 1969. Private. Nonprofit. Presbyterian.

Diagnostic and therapeutic services assist preschool- and school-age children who exhibit speech and language problems. The center maintains a developmental preschool that provides a facilitative environment for children with moderate to severe speech and language delays and disorders; this program also features speech and group therapies. The summer session operates along the same lines as the developmental preschool. Free speech, language and hearing screenings are available to preschoolers.

STRATFORD PROGRAM

Day — Coed Ages 11-22

Arlington, VA 22207. 4102 Vacation Ln.
Tel: 703-228-6440. Fax: 703-247-3162.
www.arlington.k12.va.us/schools/stratford
Alvin Crawley, BS, MEd, EdD, Prin.
  Focus: Spec Ed. Trng. **Conditions:** Primary—Au MR. Sec—ADD ADHD
    Asp B BI CP D Dx LD MD OCD ON S Sz TS.
  Pre-Voc. Voc. Gr 6-PG. Courses: Adaptive_Phys_Ed. Shelt_Workshop. On-
    Job Trng.
  Therapy: Hear Lang Occup Phys Speech.
  Enr: 55. Day Males 35. Day Females 20. **Staff:** 42 (Full 32, Part 10). Educ
    14. Admin 1.
  Rates 2004: No Fee.
  Summer Prgm: Day. Rec. 7 wks.
  Est 1960. County.

This program for adolescents and young adults with mental retardation or developmental delays includes adaptive physical education and prevocational offerings.

TIDEWATER CHILD DEVELOPMENT SERVICES

Clinic: Ages Birth-21. M-F 8:15-5.

Norfolk, VA 23510. 830 Southampton Ave, Ste 2093.
Tel: 757-683-8770. Fax: 757-683-9211.

Dennis Kade, PhD, Dir. **Carolyn Burwell,** MD, Med Dir. **Allison Knight,** Adm.
Focus: Treatment. **Conditions:** Primary—ADD ADHD AN Anx Ap Apr Ar
As Asp Au B BD Bl Bu C CD CF CP D Db Dc Dg DS Dx ED Ep IP LD
MD Mood MR MS Nf OCD ON PDD Psy PTSD PW S SB SP Sz TB TS.
Therapy: Lang Play Speech. **Psychotherapy:** Fam Indiv Parent.
Staff: 10 (Full 3, Part 7). Prof 5. Educ 2. Admin 2.
Rates 2003: Sliding-Scale Rate $0-109/hr.
Est 1957. State. Nonprofit.

One of 13 regional clinics serving Virginia residents, the facility offers comprehensive
developmental evaluation for youth with chronic developmental, medical, emotional or
behavioral difficulties. Services include neuropsychological, sociological, psychological, ophthalmologic, otological, audiological, educational, nutritional, and speech-language treatment.

TIMBER RIDGE SCHOOL

Res — Males Ages 11-17

Cross Junction, VA 22604. 1463 New Hope Rd, PO Box 3160.
Tel: 540-888-3456. Fax: 540-888-4511.
www.timber-ridge-school.org   E-mail: trschool@shentel.net
John J. Lamanna, EdD, Dir. **Philip E. Arlotta,** Adm.
Focus: Treatment. **Conditions:** Primary—ADD ADHD BD ED. Sec—CD Dx
LD. **IQ 85-120.**
Gen Acad. Pre-Voc. Voc. Gr 6-12. Courses: Read Math Lang_Arts. Man_
Arts & Shop. On-Job Trng.
Therapy: Speech. **Psychotherapy:** Fam Group Indiv Parent.
Enr: 86. Res Males 86.
Est 1969. Private. Nonprofit.

Timber Ridge places emphasis on the treatment of emotional disorders and the
remediation of learning disabilities. Regular classroom teachers are supported by a staff
psychologist, consulting psychiatrists, learning disabilities specialists, residential counselors and vocational instructors. Children of low-average to above-average intelligence
who are three or more grade levels behind are enrolled.

UNIVERSITY OF VIRGINIA
CHILDREN'S MEDICAL CENTER
KLUGE CHILDREN'S REHABILITATION CENTER

Res — Coed Ages Birth-21
Clinic: Ages Birth-21. M-F 8-5.

Charlottesville, VA 22901. 2270 Ivy Rd.
Tel: 434-924-5161. Fax: 434-924-5559.
Terry Lucas, RN, Admin. **Sydney A. Rice,** MD, Med Dir.
Focus: Rehab. Treatment. **Conditions:** Primary—ADD ADHD Ap Asp Au B
Bl CF CP D Dx Ep IP LD MD MR MS ON S SB. Sec—As BD C ED.

Gen Acad. Ungraded. Courses: Read Math Lang_Arts.
Therapy: Chemo Hear Lang Occup Phys Recreational Speech. **Psycho-therapy:** Indiv.
Staff: 153.
Est 1957. State. Nonprofit.

Kluge serves a diverse population that includes recently injured, developmentally disabled and chronically ill children. The emphasis at the center is on reinforcing the child's strengths and coping skills. In addition to therapy, services include special education, home programs, prosthetics and orthotics, radiology, nutrition and dietary services, an activities program, pediatric dentistry and social services. Consulting services are also available.

UNIVERSITY OF VIRGINIA HEALTH SYSTEM
DIVISION OF CHILD AND FAMILY PSYCHIATRY

Clinic: Ages Birth-18. M-F 8-5.

Charlottesville, VA 22908. 310 Old Ivy Way, PO Box 801076.
Tel: 434-243-6950. Fax: 434-243-6970.
www.healthsystem.virginia.edu
Roger C. Burket, MD, Dir. Jim B. Tucker, MD, Med Dir.
  Conditions: Primary—ADHD BD ED.
  Psychotherapy: Fam Group Indiv.
  Est 1968. State. Nonprofit.

VALLEY COMMUNITY SERVICE BOARD

Clinic: All Ages. M-F 8:30-5; Eves M-Th 5-8.

Staunton, VA 24401. 85 Sangers Ln.
Tel: 540-887-3200. Fax: 540-887-3245.
www.waynesboro.va.us/govgroup
Jerry Thomas, Dir.
  Focus: Treatment. **Conditions:** Primary—BD ED MR.
  Therapy: Speech. **Psychotherapy:** Fam Group Indiv.
  Est 1957. County. Nonprofit.

VIRGINIA HOME FOR BOYS
THE JOHN G. WOOD SCHOOL

Res and Day — Coed Ages 12-18

Richmond, VA 23294. 8716 W Broad St.
Tel: 804-270-6566. Fax: 804-935-7675.
www.boyshome.org/JohnGWood.htm   E-mail: school@boyshome.org
Marlin E. Balsbaugh, Jr., MEd, Exec Dir. Charles A. Shipp, Sr., MEd, Prin.

William Dixon, Adm.
Focus: Spec Ed. **Conditions:** Primary—Anx CD ED OCD. Sec—ADD ADHD D Db Mood. **IQ 70 and up.**
Gen Acad. Voc. Gr 6-12. Courses: Read Math Lang_Arts Sci Soc_Stud Computers Graphic_Arts. On-Job Trng. Culinary_Arts.
Therapy: Art Music Speech. **Psychotherapy:** Fam Group Indiv.
Staff: 9 (Full 8, Part 1).
Rates 2004: Day $104/day.
Summer Prgm: Res & Day. Educ. Rec. Day Rate $30/day.
Est 1846. Private. Nonprofit.

The vocational center provides emotionally disturbed and learning-disabled students with general academics and graphic arts training. Some residents attend public schools in the community.

VIRGINIA REHABILITATION CENTER FOR THE BLIND AND VISUALLY IMPAIRED

Res and Day — Coed Ages 14 and up

Richmond, VA 23227. 401 Azalea Ave.
Tel: 804-371-3151. Fax: 804-371-3092.
www.vrcbvi.org   E-mail: garzadr@dvh.state.va.us
Dennis R. Garza, MS, Dir.
Focus: Rehab. **Conditions:** Primary—B. Sec—ADD ADHD Ap As Au BD BI C CD CP D Dx ED Ep IP LD MD MR MS OCD ON Psy S SB Sz TB.
Col Prep. Gen Acad. Pre-Voc. Gr 9-12. Courses: Read Math Lang_Arts. On-Job Trng.
Therapy: Speech. **Psychotherapy:** Group Indiv.
Staff: 24 (Full 23, Part 1).
Est 1970. State. Nonprofit.

The center serves visually impaired adults during the school year and children during the summer months. Emphasis is placed on personal adjustment and prevocational training. Clients must be independent or must need minimal supervision in personal care, although those with secondary handicaps may enroll.

Children ages 14-21 choose from several programs. Two four-week adjustment programs consist of classes in social skills, vocational exploration, recreation, cooking, and orientation and mobility. For students in their junior or senior year of high school, the facility offers an eight-week college preparatory program. A one-week computer camp for those ages 14-18 is also available.

VIRGINIA SCHOOL FOR THE DEAF AND THE BLIND STAUNTON

Res — Coed Ages 5-22; Day — Coed Birth-22

Staunton, VA 24401. E Beverley St, PO Box 2069.
Tel: 540-332-9000. Fax: 540-332-9042.

www.vsdbs.virginia.gov   E-mail: info@vsdbs.virginia.gov
Nancy C. Armstrong, MA, Supt. **Debbie Burns,** Adm.
  Focus: Spec Ed. **Conditions:** Primary—B D.
  Col Prep. Gen Acad. Pre-Voc. Voc. Gr PS-12. Courses: Read Math Lang_
    Arts. Man_Arts & Shop. On-Job Trng.
  Therapy: Art Hear Lang Occup Phys Speech. **Psychotherapy:** Fam Group
    Indiv Parent.
  Enr: 160. **Staff:** 146. (Full 146).
  Rates 2003: No Fee.
  Summer Prgm: Res & Day. Educ. Rec. Res Rate $0. Day Rate $0.
  Est 1839. State.

This state school has separate programs for the deaf and the blind, each having its own faculty and curriculum. The program for the deaf features early intervention (including parent-infant, toddler and preschool components) as well as elementary and secondary school divisions. Students receive vocational training in such areas as industrial arts, home economics, food services and custodial maintenance. High schoolers further develop vocational skills during a year of on- or off-campus work experience.

A recreation coordinator helps organize intramural programs, field trips and various other social activities and interest clubs. Counseling is available. Enrollment is restricted to residents of Virginia.

VIRGINIA SCHOOL FOR THE DEAF, BLIND AND MULTI-DISABLED AT HAMPTON

Res — Coed Ages 8-21; Day — Coed 3-22
Clinic: Ages 6-22. M-Th; Eves M-Th Su.

Hampton, VA 23661. 700 Shell Rd.
Tel: 757-247-2033. Fax: 757-247-2224.
E-mail: dwhite@vsdbh.org
Darlene M. White, EdD, Supt. **Wilnette Bailey,** Clin Dir. **Ellen R. Scott,** Adm.
  Focus: Spec Ed. **Conditions:** Primary—B D. Sec—Au Bl CP Ep LD MR
    ON S.
  Pre-Voc. Voc. Gr PS-12. Courses: Read Math Lang_Arts. Man_Arts & Shop.
    Shelt_Workshop. On-Job Trng.
  Therapy: Art Hear Lang Music Occup Phys Recreational Speech. **Psycho-**
    therapy: Indiv.
  Enr: 74. Res Males 30. Res Females 16. Day Males 17. Day Females 11.
    Staff: 194 (Full 129, Part 65). Prof 42. Educ 26. Admin 10.
  Rates 2004: No Fee.
  Est 1906. State. Nonprofit.

This state-supported school provides academic and vocational training for children and young adults with visual and hearing impairments. The program consists of education and full therapeutic and medical services. The facility's clinic operates on a 24-hour basis from Sunday evening to Friday at noon. Enrollment is restricted to Virginia residents.

VIRGINIA TREATMENT CENTER FOR CHILDREN

Res and Day — Coed Ages 5-17
Clinic: All Ages. M-F 9-5; Eves T Th 5-8.

Richmond, VA 23298. 515 N 10th St, PO Box 980489.
Tel: 804-828-8822. Fax: 804-828-9879.
www.vcuhealth.org/vtcc   E-mail: dmadikiz@mcvh-vcu.edu
Robert Cohen, PhD, Exec Dir.
   Focus: Treatment. **Conditions:** Primary—ADD ADHD BD ED Mood. Sec—LD. **IQ 75 and up.**
   Gen Acad. Pre-Voc. Ungraded. Courses: Read Math Lang_Arts Computers Studio_Art Music.
   Therapy: Chemo Occup Speech. **Psychotherapy:** Fam Group Indiv.
   Enr: 39. Res Males 12. Res Females 12. Day Males 8. Day Females 7.
   Est 1962. State. **Spons:** Virginia Commonwealth University Health System.

VTCC offers study, evaluation, diagnosis, intensive care and specialized treatment for emotionally disturbed children. The inpatient program offers a residential setting for children who can benefit from short-term, intensive psychiatric treatment. The center is not a custodial or long-term treatment hospital. A therapeutic living experience is designed to stimulate personality growth, and the center also conducts a child and adolescent clinic and a day treatment program. An on-campus school provides educational services. VTCC accepts Virginia residents only.

WOODROW WILSON REHABILITATION CENTER

Res and Day — Coed Ages 15½ and up
Clinic: All Ages.

Fishersville, VA 22939. PO Box 1500.
Tel: 540-332-7390. Fax: 540-332-7132.
www.wwrc.net
Richard S. Luck, EdD, Dir. **Barbie M. Ostrander,** Adm.
   Focus: Rehab. Trng. **Conditions:** Primary—ADD ADHD Ap B BI CP D Dx IP LD MD MS ON S. Sec—As BD C ED Ep MR SB Sz TB.
   Gen Acad. Pre-Voc. Voc. Ungraded. Courses: Read Math Lang_Arts. Man_Arts & Shop. On-Job Trng.
   Therapy: Hear Lang Occup Phys Speech. **Psychotherapy:** Group Indiv.
   Enr: 500. Res Males 250. Res Females 150. Day Males 50. Day Females 50. **Staff:** 400.
   Est 1947. State. Nonprofit. **Spons:** Virginia Department of Rehabilitative Services.

This center provides comprehensive programs designed to prepare individuals with severe disabilities for gainful employment. Services offered are evaluation, physical restoration and rehabilitation, work conditioning and adjustment, vocational training (industrial and business arts), counseling and social development.

Specialized programs include a head trauma program, spinal cord injury rehabilitation, deaf and learning disabilities projects, and a center for independent living. To be considered for admission, a disabled person must have a reasonably good prognosis for benefitting from center services.

ZUNI PRESBYTERIAN HOMES

Res — Coed Ages 18 and up

Zuni, VA 23898. 5279 Homegrown Ln.
Tel: 757-242-6131. Fax: 757-242-6138.
www.phfs.org   E-mail: mcarpent@phfs.org
Mitzi M. Carpenter, MSW, Prgm Dir.

> **Focus:** Trng. **Conditions:** Primary—MR. Sec—ADD ADHD Anx Ap Ar As Asp Au B Bl C CP D Db Dc Dg DS Dx ED Ep HIV LD MD Mood MS OCD ON PDD Psy PW S Sz. **IQ 45-75.**
>
> **Voc.** Shelt_Workshop.
>
> **Enr:** 46. Res Males 21. Res Females 25. **Staff:** 50 (Full 34, Part 16). Prof 5. Admin 2.
>
> **Rates 2004:** Res $400-900/mo.
>
> **Est 1967.** Private. Nonprofit. Presbyterian. **Spons:** Presbyterian Homes & Family Services.

Zuni Presbyterian Homes provides residential and vocational training services for educable and trainable adults with mental retardation. Emphasis is placed on the development of socialization skills, and work adjustment is introduced through various training areas. Residents must have a diagnosis of mental retardation, while all other conditions are evaluated on a case by case basis. Enrollment is not limited to those of the Presbyterian faith. Residency is typically long-term.

WASHINGTON

BENTON FRANKLIN DEVELOPMENTAL CENTER

Day — Coed Ages Birth-3

Richland, WA 99352. 1549 Georgia Ave SE, Ste A.
Tel: 509-735-1062. Fax: 509-737-8492.
Gayle A. Womack, Exec Dir. Sara Zirkle, MD, Med Dir. Cathy Tames, Adm.
  Focus: Spec Ed. Conditions: Primary—Apr Asp Au Bl CP DS IP LD MR
    ON PDD S SB. Sec—ADD ADHD Ap B BD C D ED Ep MD MS PW.
  Gen Acad. Gr PS.
  Therapy: Hear Lang Occup Phys Speech.
  Enr: 150. Staff: 30 (Full 26, Part 4). Prof 15. Educ 4. Admin 3.
  Est 1977. Private. Nonprofit.

Benton Franklin offers therapeutic, educational and support services to children with a wide range of disabilities. Individualized educational programs concentrate on fine- and gross-motor development, language, and self-help and social skills. Parents receive instruction in therapy and educational techniques to implement at home. The center assists in the transition to public schools.

BOYER CHILDREN'S CLINIC

Clinic: Ages Birth-15. M-F 8-5.

Seattle, WA 98112. 1850 Boyer Ave E.
Tel: 206-325-8477. Fax: 206-323-1385.
www.boyercc.org   E-mail: information@boyercc.org
Judith Moore, MA, Exec Dir. F. Curt Bennett, MD, Med Dir.
  Conditions: Primary—Bl CP ON SB.
  Therapy: Hear Occup Phys Speech.
  Est 1947. Private. Nonprofit.

CHILDREN'S INSTITUTE FOR LEARNING DIFFERENCES

Day — Coed Ages 4-15
Clinic: Ages 4-15. M-F 9-5.

Mercer Island, WA 98040. 4030 86th Ave SE.
Tel: 206-232-8680. Fax: 206-232-9377.
www.childrensinstitute.com   E-mail: rhonda@childrensinstitute.com
Trina Westerlund, BA, BS, MEd, Exec Dir. Rhonda Jalali, Prgm Dir.
  Focus: Spec Ed. Conditions: Primary—ADD ADHD Anx Apr Asp Au BD
    Bl Dc Dg DS Dx ED LD Mood MR ON PDD PTSD S SP. Sec—Ap As CP
    Db Ep Nf OCD ODD TS.
  Gen Acad. Pre-Voc. Voc. Gr PS-8. Courses: Read Math Lang_Arts. Man_

Arts & Shop. Horticulture Culinary_Arts.
Therapy: Lang Occup Percepual-Motor Phys Play Speech. **Psychotherapy:** Fam Group Indiv.
Enr: 50. Day Males 36. Day Females 14. **Staff:** 33 (Full 28, Part 5).
Rates 2004: Day $1700-2400/mo. Clinic $86/hr. Sliding-Scale Rate $1200-1700/mo (Day).
Summer Prgm: Day. Educ. Ther. Day Rate $850-1200/2-wk ses. 6 wks.
Est 1977. Private. Nonprofit.

Consisting of the CHILD school (grades PS-6) and New Heights Middle School (grades 7-9), the Children's Institute conducts small individualized academic classes for children with learning differences and emotional and developmental disabilities. Students are grouped according to their academic, social and emotional levels, with a three- to four-year age gap evident in some classrooms. Training workshops educate parents about treatment approaches.

The institute also operates a therapeutic day clinic that offers occupational, speech and language therapies.

FRANCES HADDON MORGAN CENTER

Res — Coed Ages 19-35

Bremerton, WA 98312. 3423 6th St, W 18-4.
Tel: 360-475-3480. Fax: 360-475-3455.
E-mail: fhmcenter@dshs.wa.gov
Carol Kirk, Supt. **June Bredin,** BA, BS, MD, Med Dir.
Focus: Treatment. **Conditions:** Primary—Asp Au MR. Sec—ADHD Ap Apr B BD BI CP D ED Ep OCD ON Psy PTSD PW Sz TS. **IQ 0-51.**
Voc. Shelt_Workshop.
Therapy: Hear Occup Phys Recreational Speech. **Psychotherapy:** Indiv.
Enr: 54. Res Males 38. Res Females 16. **Staff:** 126.
Rates 2003: No Fee.
Est 1972. State. Nonprofit.

Frances Haddon Morgan Center supports teenagers and young adults who have autism and other developmental disorders. Specialization treatment addresses chronic behavioral problems and emotional disorders. Emphasis is on the development of socially adaptive behavior in preparation for moving to a community setting. Training is conducted in small groups, and an interdisciplinary team regularly reviews each client. The center also provides evaluations and respite care services. State residents pay no fee.

HAMLIN ROBINSON SCHOOL

Day — Coed Ages 6-14

Seattle, WA 98168. 10211 12th Ave S.
Tel: 206-763-1167. Fax: 206-762-2419.
www.hamlinrobinson.org   E-mail: hamlinrobinson@aol.com
Barbara Bradshaw, BA, Dir.

Focus: Spec Ed. **Conditions:** Primary—ADD ADHD Dc Dg Dx LD.
Gen Acad. Gr 1-8. Courses: Read Math Lang_Arts Sci Soc_Stud Studio_
Art Music.
Therapy: Lang Speech.
Enr: 100. Day Males 59. Day Females 41. **Staff:** 29 (Full 21, Part 8).
Rates 2003: Day $10,250-11,750/sch yr. Schol avail.
Summer Prgm: Day. 4 wks.
Est 1983. Private. Nonprofit.

The school offers remediation and education to students of average to superior intelligence with dyslexia and related language difficulties. The program focuses on both the educational and the emotional needs of students to build self-esteem and self-confidence. While stress is placed heavily on a multisensory approach to language arts, the school also presents a full curriculum with an emphasis on creative arts.

Additional offerings at Hamlin Robinson include adult services, teacher training, and individual speech and language therapy.

HEARING, SPEECH AND DEAFNESS CENTER
PARENT-INFANT PROGRAM

Clinic: Ages Birth-3. M-F 8:30-5; Eve M 6:30-8:30.

Seattle, WA 98122. 1625 19th Ave.
Tel: 206-323-5770. TTY: 206-323-5770. Fax: 206-328-6871.
www.hsdc.org   E-mail: pip@hsdc.org
Susie Burdick, Exec Dir. **Marlyn Minkin,** Dir.
    Focus: Spec Ed. **Conditions:** Primary—D. Sec—ADD ADHD AN Anx Ap
    Apr Ar As Asp Au B BD Bl Bu C CD CF CP Db Dc Dg DS Dx ED Ep HIV
    IP LD MD Mood MR MS Nf OCD ODD ON PDD Psy PTSD PW S SB SP
    Sz TB TS.
    Therapy: Hear Lang Occup Play Speech. **Psychotherapy:** Fam Group
    Parent.
    Staff: 9 (Full 4, Part 5).
    Rates 2003: No Fee.
    Est 1937. Private. Nonprofit. **Spons:** United Way.

The Parent-Infant Program offers educational and counseling support for families with infants and toddlers who are deaf or hard of hearing. Families participate in three sessions each week: a play group/parent group, a home visit and an individual session at HSDC. The Audiology and Parent-Infant Program staffs work together to provide audiological evaluations, hearing aid fittings and continuing follow-up.

In addition to its normal 12-week quarters, the center offers services for four weeks during the summer.

HOLLY RIDGE CENTER
INFANT-TODDLER PROGRAM

Clinic: Ages Birth-3. M-F 8-5.

Bremerton, WA 98312. 5112 NW Taylor Rd.
Tel: 360-373-2536. TTY: 360-373-2344. Fax: 360-373-4934.
www.hollyridge.org/itp.html   E-mail: itp@hollyridge.org
Kathrin Fortner, Dir.
  Focus: Treatment. **Conditions:** Primary—B BI CP D IP LD MR ON S SB.
    Sec—Au.
  Therapy: Hear Lang Occup Phys Speech. **Psychotherapy:** Fam Parent.
  Staff: 24 (Full 17, Part 7).
  Rates 2004: No Fee.
  Est 1963. Private. Nonprofit. **Spons:** United Way.

Year-round neurodevelopmental and preschool services are available at the facility.

HOPE CLINIC

Clinic: All Ages. M-F 9-5; Eves M W 5-8.

Bellevue, WA 98007. 140th Plaza Bldg, 14030 NE 24th St, Ste 101.
  Nearby locations: Silverdale; Tacoma.
Tel: 425-462-7800. Fax: 425-455-3019.
www.hopecliniconline.com
Theodore S. Kadef, BA, OD, Dir.
  Focus: Treatment. **Conditions:** Primary—ADD ADHD BI Dx LD. **IQ 60 and
    up.**
  Therapy: Lang Occup Speech Visual. **Psychotherapy:** Fam Indiv Parent.
  Staff: 8 (Full 3, Part 5).
  Est 1982. Private.

This clinic offers therapy programs that supplement regular school or work schedules to children and adults with learning disabilities. Preventive medicine, counseling, and speech and language pathology are available in addition to therapies.

Branches of the clinic operate at 9633 Levin Rd., Silverdale 98383 and 3315 South 23rd St., Tacoma 98405.

LAKELAND VILLAGE

Res — Coed Ages 16 and up

Medical Lake, WA 99022. PO Box 200.
Tel: 509-299-1800. TTY: 509-299-1097. Fax: 509-299-1070.
www1.dshs.wa.gov/ddd/region1.shtml
  Conditions: Primary—MR. **IQ 0-70.**
  Gen Acad. Pre-Voc. Voc. Ungraded. Courses: Read Math Lang_Arts. Man_
    Arts & Shop. Shelt_Workshop. On-Job Trng.
  Therapy: Chemo Hear Lang Phys Speech. **Psychotherapy:** Group Indiv.
  State.

LIFE DESIGNS

Res — Coed Ages 18-26

Cusick, WA 99119.
Tel: 509-445-0185. Fax: 509-445-0185.
www.lifedesignsranch.com   E-mail: lifedesignsranch@aol.com
Randy Russell, MS, Exec Dir.
Focus: Trng. **Conditions:** Primary—ADD ADHD Dx ED Mood OCD. Sec—Ar As B D Db. **IQ 90 and up.**
Enr: 13. **Staff:** 7 (Full 2, Part 5). Prof 5. Admin 2.
Rates 2004: Res $4000/mo (+$3500/ses).
Est 1998. Private. Inc.

Life Designs is a small residential leadership training program that teaches young adults practical skills for success in a hands-on living or occupational setting. The working ranch environment helps students develop realistic goals and good habits. Although drug and alcohol abuse is not the program's focus, Life Designs offers support to those who have made a commitment to sobriety.

MARY BRIDGE CHILDREN'S HOSPITAL AND HEALTH CENTER

Clinic: Ages Birth-18. M-F by Appt.

Tacoma, WA 98405. 311 S "L" St.
Tel: 253-403-1419. Fax: 253-403-1247.
www.marybridge.org
Linda Latta, PhD, RN, Admin. **Ted Walkley,** BS, MD, Med Dir.
Focus: Treatment. **Conditions:** Primary—ADD Anx Ap Apr As Asp BD BI C CD CP D Db DS Ep MR Nf OCD ON PDD PW S TS.
Therapy: Hear Lang Occup Percepual-Motor Phys Speech.
Est 1955. Private. Nonprofit. **Spons:** MultiCare Health System.

Serving children from southwest Washington, this outpatient facility features pediatric specialty clinics and a comprehensive developmental services program. The range of services includes complete hearing aid and aural rehabilitation programs, cardiology and cancer centers, and pulmonary and neurology programs.

Mary Bridge also offers contractual speech and hearing services to schools and organizations.

MORNING STAR BOYS' RANCH

Res — Males Ages 10-18
Clinic: Ages 10-18. M-F 9-5; Eves M-F 5-8.

Spokane, WA 99203. PO Box 8087.
Tel: 509-448-1411. Fax: 509-448-1413.
www.morningstarboysranch.org
E-mail: msbr@morningstarboysranch.org

Rev. Joseph M. Weitensteiner, BA, MA, Dir. **Brian Barbour,** Adm.
  Focus: Treatment. **Conditions:** Primary—BD CD ED OCD. **IQ 85 and up.**
  Gen Acad. Pre-Voc. Gr 5-12. Courses: Read Math Lang_Arts.
  Therapy: Lang Speech. **Psychotherapy:** Fam Group Indiv Parent Equine.
  Enr: 23. Res Males 23. **Staff:** 25 (Full 19, Part 6).
  Est 1957. Private. Nonprofit. Roman Catholic.

  MSBR aims to provide an environment for emotionally disturbed and delinquent boys through rehabilitation, education and counseling. The program gives boys the opportunity for new experiences in hobbies, athletics, and other skills and interests. Fees vary according to the family's ability to pay. The usual length of treatment is one year.

NORTHWEST SCHOOL
FOR HEARING-IMPAIRED CHILDREN

Day — Coed Ages 3-14

Seattle, WA 98103. 15303 Westminster Way N, PO Box 31325.
Tel: 206-364-4605. Fax: 206-367-3014.
http://northwestschool.com
Judy Ottren Callahan, Co-Dir.
  Conditions: Primary—D.
  Gen Acad. Gr K-9. Courses: Read Math Lang_Arts.
  Therapy: Hear Lang Speech.
  Est 1979. Private. Nonprofit.

PROVIDENCE CHILDREN'S CENTER

Clinic: Ages Birth-14. M-F.

Everett, WA 98206. 900 Pacific Ave, PO Box 1067.
Tel: 425-258-7311. Fax: 425-258-7618.
www.providence.org/everett/programs_and_services/pavilion/
  e60children.htm
  Conditions: Primary—OH.
  Therapy: Occup Phys Speech. **Psychotherapy:** Indiv.
  Est 1978.

ST. CHRISTOPHER ACADEMY

Day — Coed Ages 13-19

Seattle, WA 98168. 140 S 140th St.
Tel: 206-246-9751. Fax: 253-639-3466.
www.stchristopheracademy.com
  E-mail: jevne@stchristopheracademy.com
Darlene Jevne, MA, Dir.

Focus: Spec Ed. **Conditions:** Primary—ADD ADHD Ap Dx LD. **IQ 80 and up.**
Gen Acad. Gr 9-12. Courses: Read Math Lang_Arts Sci Soc_Stud. Man_ Arts & Shop.
Therapy: Lang. **Psychotherapy:** Indiv.
Enr: 40. **Staff:** 6 (Full 4, Part 2). Educ 4.
Rates 2004: Day $11,650/sch yr.
Summer Prgm: Res. Educ. Rec. Adventure. Res Rate $2500 (+$300)/3-wk ses. Day Rate $600 (+$75)/6-wk ses. 6 wks.
Est 1982. Private. Nonprofit.

The academy offers a full academic program for students with attention deficit disorder and learning disabilities. The curriculum includes art and computer course work, and the high school division features electives and a sports program. Diagnostic services and counseling are available at all grade levels.   **See Also Page 1035**

SECRET HARBOR SCHOOL

Res — Males Ages 11-17

Anacortes, WA 98221. 1809 Commercial Ave, PO Box 440.
Tel: 360-293-5151. Fax: 360-293-0692.
www.secretharbor.org   E-mail: sharbor@secretharbor.org
Brian E. Carroll, MSW, Exec Dir.
   Focus: Spec Ed. **Conditions:** Primary—ADD ADHD CD ED Mood ODD. Sec—BD Dx LD. **IQ 71-120.**
   Gen Acad. Pre-Voc. Courses: Read Math Lang_Arts Hist Computers Sci.
   Therapy: Speech. **Psychotherapy:** Fam Group.
   Enr: 33. Res Males 33. **Staff:** 35 (Full 30, Part 5).
   Est 1949. Private. Nonprofit.

Located on a 6000-acre island, Secret Harbor operates as a combined school, farm and residence for boys with emotional and behavioral problems and learning disabilities. The program includes educational and vocational opportunities, psychotherapy and a therapeutically oriented milieu. Individual tutoring is available during the summer. The usual length of treatment is 8 to 10 months. A small separate cottage program focusing on chemical dependency recovery is also available.

An adjunct to Secret Harbor's island program is the Transition House, located in Anacortes, licensed for six adolescent boys who become part of the Anacortes community but remain a part of the Secret Harbor program. This allows for the continuation of the therapeutic alliance already established on the island with their primary therapist. The length of stay at the Transition House is generally one or two semesters.

SHRINERS HOSPITAL

Res — Coed Ages Birth-18

Spokane, WA 99210. 911 W 5th Ave, PO Box 2472.
Tel: 509-455-7844. Fax: 509-623-0474.
www.shrinershq.org/shc/spokane

Charles Young, MB, Admin. **Ron Ferguson,** MD, Med Dir.
  Focus: Treatment. **Conditions:** Primary—OH. Sec—CP MD SB.
  Therapy: Hear Occup Phys Play Recreational Speech.
  Staff: 140. Prof 52.
  Rates 2003: No Fee.
  Est 1924. Private. Inc.

Shriners treats children who have orthopedic, neuromuscular and arthritic impairments. Postacute burn-scar surgeries are available. The hospital school is part of the Spokane Public School System.

TAMARACK CENTER

Res — Coed Ages 12-17

Spokane, WA 99224. 2901 W Fort George Wright Dr.
Tel: 509-326-8100. Fax: 509-326-9358.
www.tamarack.org   E-mail: info@tamarack.org
Tim Davis, MS, Exec Dir. **Brian Gipstein,** MD, Med Dir. **Christopher Dal Pra,** Adm.
  Focus: Treatment. **Conditions:** Primary—ADD ADHD Anx BD ED Mood OCD Psy PTSD SP Sz. **IQ 80 and up.**
  Therapy: Milieu Recreational. **Psychotherapy:** Fam Group Indiv.
  Enr: 16. Res Males 8. Res Females 8. **Staff:** 32 (Full 19, Part 13). Prof 14. Educ 2. Admin 3.
  Rates 2004: Res $375/day. State Aid.
  Est 1984. Private. Nonprofit.

This residential treatment center offers individual, group and family therapies to assist emotionally disturbed adolescents with independent living. Behavioral programs, psychiatric assessments and medical evaluations are available as needed. Families participate in all aspects of treatment and attend group family functions at the center each month.

TYLER RANCH

Res — Males Ages 6-18

Spokane, WA 99208. 4921 W Rosewood Ave.
Tel: 509-327-6900. Fax: 509-327-2859.
www.tylerranch.com   E-mail: latyler@worldnet.att.net
Jon W. Tyler, Dir.
  Focus: Treatment. **Conditions:** Primary—ADD ADHD LD. Sec—BD CD ED. **IQ 70 and up.**
  Col Prep. Gen Acad. Voc. Gr K-12. Man_Arts & Shop.
  Psychotherapy: Fam Group Indiv.
  Enr: 16. Res Males 16. **Staff:** 7. (Full 7).
  Rates 2003: Res $2500/mo. State Aid.
  Est 1978. Private. Nonprofit.

Tyler Ranch offers a home-style environment with intensive professional services. Full-time houseparents supervise up to six children in three homes located in a quiet residential neighborhood. A child and family therapist, a tutor and a recreational specialist constitute the full-time, on-site professional staff for each house. The goal of the program is to transition boys back to their families by individually tailoring each resident's academic and therapeutic program.

UNIVERSITY OF WASHINGTON
EXPERIMENTAL EDUCATION UNIT

Day — Coed Ages Birth-7

Seattle, WA 98195. Box 357925.
Tel: 206-543-4011. Fax: 206-543-8480.
www.depts.washington.edu/eeuweb
Richard Neel, PhD, Dir. **Jennifer Annable,** MEd, Prin. **Kate Ahern,** Adm.
Focus: Spec Ed. **Conditions:** Primary—Apr Asp Au Bl DS MR ON PDD PW S. Sec—Ap As B C CP D ED Ep HIV IP LD MD MS SB.
Gen Acad. Ungraded. Courses: Read Math Lang_Arts Life_Skills.
Therapy: Hear Lang Occup Phys Speech.
Enr: 200. **Staff:** 21 (Full 14, Part 7). Prof 18. Admin 3.
Rates 2003: No Fee.
Est 1969. State.

The EEU is one of four units of the Center on Human Development and Disability at the University of Washington. It serves as a professional training and applied research center in special education and related disciplines, while also providing services for children and families.

Children receive early childhood educational programs at the center. In addition, undergraduate and graduate students in special education and other disciplines obtain training and experience in the classrooms, under the supervision of master teachers and faculty.

UNIVERSITY OF WASHINGTON
SPEECH AND HEARING CLINIC

Clinic: All Ages. M-F 8-5.

Seattle, WA 98105. 4131 15th Ave NE.
Tel: 206-543-5440. TTY: 206-543-5440. Fax: 206-616-1185.
http://depts.washington.edu/sphsc
Nancy B. Alarcon, MS, CCC-SLP, Dir.
Focus: Treatment. **Conditions:** Primary—Ap S. Sec—ADD ADHD Au Bl CP Dx LD MR OH.
Therapy: Hear Lang Speech. **Psychotherapy:** Group.
Est 1932. State.

This speech and hearing clinic is operated as a part of the Speech and Hearing Science Department's training program for the professions of speech pathology and audiology.

WASHINGTON STATE SCHOOL FOR THE BLIND
Res and Day — Coed Ages 3-21

Vancouver, WA 98661. 2214 E 13th St.
Tel: 360-696-6321. Fax: 360-737-2120.
www.wssb.org   E-mail: admin@wssb.wa.gov
Dean O. Stenehjem, EdD, Supt. Dee Amundsen, Adm.
  Focus: Spec Ed. Conditions: Primary—B.
  Gen Acad. Pre-Voc. Gr K-12. Courses: Read Math Lang_Arts Music Braille. Man_Arts & Shop. On-Job Trng.
  Therapy: Hear Lang Occup Phys Speech. Psychotherapy: Indiv.
  Enr: 69. Res Males 36. Res Females 15. Day Males 9. Day Females 9.
    Staff: 34 (Full 33, Part 1).
  Rates 2004: No Fee.
  Est 1886. State.

School services are provided for visually handicapped children in grades K-12. Services include four residential cottages, on-the-job training, and programs designed for the special learning problems of the visually impaired, the multiply handicapped and the deaf-blind. WSSB's goal is to return the student to a public school setting. The usual duration of treatment is three years.

WASHINGTON STATE UNIVERSITY
SPEECH AND HEARING CLINIC
Clinic: All Ages. M-F 8-5.

Pullman, WA 99164. 133 Daggy Hall.
  Nearby locations: Spokane.
Tel: 509-335-1509. Fax: 509-335-8357.
www.libarts.wsu.edu/speechhearing/clinic/index.html
Carla Jones, MA, CCC-SLP, Coord.
  Focus: Treatment. Conditions: Primary—LD S. Sec—Ap.
  Therapy: Hear Lang Speech.
  Staff: 12 (Full 9, Part 3).
  Est 1955. State. Nonprofit.

This university-run clinic provides evaluation and treatment for patients with speech, language and hearing problems. Hearing aid dispensation is among the services provided.

A branch clinic operates at 310 N. Riverpoint Blvd., P.O. Box 1495, Spokane 99210.

WASHINGTON STATE UNIVERSITY-SPOKANE
UNIVERSITY HEARING AND SPEECH CLINIC
Clinic: All Ages. M-F 8-5.

Spokane, WA 99210. 310 N Riverpoint Blvd, PO Box 1495.
Tel: 509-358-7580. Fax: 509-368-6890.

E-mail: upcd@mail.wsu.edu
Doreen Nicholas, MS, Dir. **Shyla Rodgers,** Adm.
    Focus: Rehab. **Conditions:** Primary—Ap Apr Asp Au BI D DS MD MS ON
      S. Sec—ADD ADHD Dg Dx MR.
    Therapy: Hear Lang Speech.
    Rates 2003: Clinic $50/ses. Schol avail.
    State.

This university clinic specializes in speech pathology and audiology. Staff provide diagnostic evaluations for speech and language development, articulation, cleft palate, cerebral palsy, stuttering, dysphasia and audiological problems. Individual and group therapies are offered. Rehabilitative services include planning and consultation with schools, hospitals, nursing homes and community agencies.

YAKIMA VALLEY SCHOOL

Res — Coed Ages 21 and up

Selah, WA 98942. 609 Speyers Rd.
Tel: 509-698-1300. Fax: 509-697-2230.
www1.dshs.wa.gov/ddd/YVS.shtml
    Conditions: Primary—MR.
    Private.

WEST VIRGINIA

ALLDREDGE ACADEMY

Res and Day — Coed Ages 13-18

Davis, WV 26260. William Ave, PO Box 310.
Tel: 304-259-2262. Fax: 304-259-5803.
www.alldredgeacademy.org   E-mail: info@alldredgeacademy.org
Angie Senic, BS, Dir. **Michelle Goss,** Adm.
  Focus: Spec Ed. Treatment. **Conditions:** Primary—ADD ADHD AN Anx BD
    CD Dc Dg Dx ED Mood OCD Psy SP. Sec—Db MR.
  Col Prep. Gen Acad. Gr 7-12. Courses: Read Math Lang_Arts Eng Sci
    Soc_Stud. Man_Arts & Shop.
  Therapy: Recreational. **Psychotherapy:** Fam Group Indiv.
  Enr: 58. Res Males 51. Res Females 7. **Staff:** 62.
  Rates 2004: Res $288/day. Schol avail.
  Est 1995. Private.

This school for troubled youth uses emotional growth techniques to prepare students
for reentry into mainstream educational settings. The outdoor education program consists of college preparatory academics and individual and family workshops designed to
change mild behavioral and emotional patterns. Depression, substance abuse and low
self-esteem are among the issues addressed in counseling sessions.

DEVELOPMENTAL THERAPY CENTER

Clinic: All Ages. M-F 8-5:30; Eves M-Th 5:30-6:30.

Huntington, WV 25701. 845 4th Ave, Ste 302-A.
Tel: 304-523-1164. Fax: 304-522-2474.
Leslie C. Comer-Porter, MA, CCC-S, Exec Dir.
  Focus: Rehab. **Conditions:** Primary—Ap D ON S. Sec—ADD ADHD Apr
    Asp Au BI CP Dx IP LD MD MR MS PW SB TS.
  Therapy: Hear Lang Occup Phys Speech. **Psychotherapy:** Fam.
  Staff: 16 (Full 14, Part 2). Prof 10.
  Rates 2003: $100 (Evaluation)/hr. State Aid.
  Est 1951. Federal. Nonprofit. **Spons:** United Way.

The clinic provides therapeutic services in the related fields of speech and language,
occupational and physical therapy to infants, children and adults. A sliding fee scale is
available to all clients based on income.

EASTER SEALS REHABILITATION CENTER

Clinic: All Ages. M-F 8-4:30.

Wheeling, WV 26003. 1305 National Rd.

Tel: 304-242-1390. Fax: 304-243-5880.
www.wv.easter-seals.org   E-mail: ateaster@comcast.net
Martha L. Hon, Pres. **Ellen L. Kitts,** MD, Med Dir.
Focus: Rehab. **Conditions:** Primary—Ap Apr Asp Au B D DS Ep IP MD
MR MS Nf ON PDD S SB TB. Sec—ADD BI C CP Dx ED LD OCD PTSD
PW TS.
Therapy: Hear Lang Occup Phys Speech Aqua. **Psychotherapy:** Indiv.
Staff: 38 (Full 15, Part 23).
Est 1938. Private. Nonprofit.

Situated in an urban environment, the center is an outpatient facility that serves people
with disabilities. The clinic, which utilizes a team treatment approach, offers both home-
and center-based infant intervention programs, in addition to school screenings.

MARSHALL UNIVERSITY SPEECH AND HEARING CENTER

Clinic: All Ages. M-F 9-6.

Huntington, WV 25755. Dept of Communication Disorders, 143 Smith Hall.
Tel: 304-696-3640. Fax: 304-696-2986.
www.marshall.edu/commdis/mushc   E-mail: commdis@marshall.edu
Beverly Anawalt Miller, MA, Dir.
Focus: Treatment. **Conditions:** Primary—S. Sec—Ap Apr Asp Au BI CP D
DS Dx LD MD MR MS OH.
Therapy: Hear Lang Speech.
Staff: 12 (Full 11, Part 1). Prof 10. Admin 2.
Rates 2003: Clinic $60/hr. State Aid.
Est 1953. State. Nonprofit.

This university-affiliated program includes therapy. Each client attends approximately
25 sessions per semester.

PRESTERA CENTER

Res — Coed Ages 13 and up; Day — Coed All Ages

Huntington, WV 25705. 3375 US Rte 60 E.
Tel: 304-525-7851. Fax: 304-525-1504.
www.prestera.org   E-mail: prestctr@prestera.org
Conditions: Primary—BD ED.
Therapy: Occup Phys Recreational Speech. **Psychotherapy:** Fam Group
Indiv.
Staff: Prof 50.
Est 1967. Private. Nonprofit.

WEST VIRGINIA REHABILITATION CENTER

Res — Coed Ages 15 and up

Institute, WV 25112. PO Box 1004.
Tel: 304-766-4600. Fax: 304-766-4966.
www.wvdrs.org/pwd_wv_rehabilitation_center.html
   Conditions: Primary—OH. **IQ 50 and up.**
   Pre-Voc. Voc. Courses: Read Math Lang_Arts. Shelt_Workshop.
   Therapy: Hear Lang Occup Phys Speech. **Psychotherapy:** Fam Group
      Indiv.
   Staff: Prof 135.
   State.

WEST VIRGINIA SCHOOLS FOR THE DEAF AND THE BLIND

Res and Day — Coed Ages 3-21

Romney, WV 26757. 301 E Main St.
Tel: 304-822-4800. Fax: 304-822-3370.
Jane K. McBride, MA, Supt. **Steve Davis,** Adm.
   Focus: Spec Ed. **Conditions:** Primary—B D.
   Col Prep. Gen Acad. Pre-Voc. Gr PS-PG. Courses: Read Math Lang_Arts.
      Man_Arts & Shop. Shelt_Workshop.
   Therapy: Art Hear Lang Music Occup Percepual-Motor Phys Speech. **Psy-
      chotherapy:** Fam Indiv.
   Enr: 195. **Staff:** 206. Prof 65. Admin 14.
   Rates 2003: No Fee.
   Est 1870. State. Nonprofit.

Comprehensive educational programs for deaf and blind students, including academic, prevocational and vocational tracks, are conducted at this school. A full range of
extracurricular activities, in addition to diagnostic and counseling services, are available.
Enrollment is limited to residents of West Virginia.

WEST VIRGINIA UNIVERSITY
SPEECH AND HEARING CLINICS

Clinic: All Ages. M-F 9-5.

Morgantown, WV 26506. 805 Allen Hall, PO Box 6122.
Tel: 304-293-4241. Fax: 304-293-7565.
www.wvu.edu/~speechpa
Karen B. Haines, BS, MS, Co-Coord. **Gayle Neldon,** BA, MS, Co-Coord.
   Focus: Treatment. **Conditions:** Primary—D S. Sec—ED MR.
   Therapy: Hear Lang Speech. **Psychotherapy:** Parent.
   Est 1958. State. Nonprofit.

This center provides services for speech-, hearing- and language-impaired individuals. The facility includes seven speech therapy rooms and two audiology suites. Parental counseling is available, and the clinic is open year-round.

WESTBROOK HEALTH SERVICES

Clinic: Ages 3-18. M-S 8:30-5; M-Th 5-9.

Parkersburg, WV 26101. 2121 7th St.
  Nearby locations: Harrisville; Ripley; Spencer.
Tel: 304-485-1721. Fax: 304-485-6710.
www.westbrookhealth.com   E-mail: westbrook@westbrookhealth.com
Jo Ann Powell, MD, Exec Dir. **Holly W. Maynard,** MA, Clin Dir. **Robert Keefover,** MD, Med Dir.
  Focus: Treatment. **Conditions:** Primary—ADD ADHD Asp Au BD CD DS ED MR PDD PTSD SP Sz. Sec—Ap As B Bl C CP D Dx Ep IP LD MD MS OCD ON Psy PW S SB TB TS. **IQ 10 and up.**
  Therapy: Chemo Speech. **Psychotherapy:** Fam Group Indiv Parent.
  Staff: 250.
  Private. Nonprofit.

The center offers diagnosis, consultation and treatment of emotional and psychological problems, as well as educational handicaps. Counseling, parent training and follow-up services are available. There is also a group home for the mentally retarded. Branches are located in Harrisville, Spencer and Ripley.

WISCONSIN

BETHESDA LUTHERAN HOME
Res — Coed Ages 8-18

Watertown, WI 53094. 600 Hoffmann Dr.
Tel: 920-261-3050. Fax: 920-261-8441.
www.blhs.org
David Geske, PhD, CEO.
  Focus: Spec Ed. Treatment. **Conditions:** Primary—MR. Sec—Ap As B BI C CP D Ep IP MD MS ON S SB.
  Gen Acad. Pre-Voc. Voc. Ungraded. Courses: Read Math Lang_Arts. Shelt_Workshop.
  Therapy: Chemo Hear Lang Music Occup Phys Speech. **Psychotherapy:** Indiv.
  Est 1904. Private. Nonprofit. Lutheran.

Bethesda Lutheran Home treats mentally retarded and multi-handicapped children and adults. Priority for admission is given to members of Lutheran congregations. The training program includes ungraded academics, religion, music, vocational training, daily living skills and social adjustment. Physical, speech and occupational therapies and a recreational program are available.

CENTER FOR THE DEAF AND HARD OF HEARING
KELLOGG CHILD AND FAMILY PROGRAM
Day — Coed Ages Birth-3

Brookfield, WI 53005. 3505 N 124th St.
Tel: 262-790-1040. TTY: 262-790-0584. Fax: 262-790-0580.
www.cdhh.org   E-mail: dkerr@cdhh.org
Dorothy Kerr, BA, Exec Dir. **Christine Kometer,** Dir.
  Focus: Trng. **Conditions:** Primary—D.
  Therapy: Hear Lang Music Speech.
  Enr: 45. **Staff:** 32 (Full 27, Part 5).
  Rates 2003: Sliding-Scale Rate $50-150/hr.
  Est 1927. Private. Nonprofit.

This early intervention program serves deaf and hard-of-hearing children and their families. Parents select the communication mode they desire for their child; options are oral communication groups, auditory-verbal therapy and the total communication program. For families, the center provides education and support services and conducts sign language classes.

CENTRAL WISCONSIN CENTER
FOR THE DEVELOPMENTALLY DISABLED

Res — Coed All Ages

Madison, WI 53704. 317 Knutson Dr.
Tel: 608-301-9200. Fax: 608-301-9423.
http://dhfs.wisconsin.gov/dd_cwc
Ted Bunck, PhD, Dir.
   Conditions: Primary—MR. **IQ 0-35.**
   Gen Acad. Ungraded. Shelt_Workshop.
   Est 1959. State.

CHILD AND FAMILY PSYCHOLOGICAL SERVICES

Clinic: All Ages. M-S by Appt; Eves M-S by Appt.

Madison, WI 53719. 437 S Yellowstone Dr, Ste 110.
Tel: 608-288-1882. Fax: 608-288-1892.
Nira Melzer-Busch, BA, MS, Dir.
   Focus: Treatment. **Conditions:** Primary—ADD ADHD Asp BD BI Dc Dg DS
      Dx ED LD Mood OCD ODD PTSD PW SP TS. Sec—As CP Ep MD MR
      MS SB. **IQ 20 and up.**
   Therapy: Speech. **Psychotherapy:** Fam Indiv Parent.
   Staff: 6. (Part 6). Prof 3. Admin 3.
   Rates 2003: Clinic $110-125/ses. Sliding-Scale Rate $50-100/ses. State
      Aid.
   Est 1981. Private.

   The clinic provides assessment, treatment and individual and family therapy for
persons with language and learning disabilities, dyslexia and mental health problems.
Vocational, parental and personal counseling are available, and the facility helps place
children in local public and private schools.

CHILDREN'S HOSPITAL OF WISCONSIN
SPEECH AND HEARING CENTER

Clinic: Ages Birth-21. M-F 8-5:30.

Milwaukee, WI 53226. 8901 W Watertown Plank Rd, 3rd Fl.
Tel: 414-266-2934. Fax: 414-266-6189.
www.chw.org
Susan M. Marks, MS, CCC, Mgr. **David Beste,** MD, Med Dir.
   Focus: Treatment. **Conditions:** Primary—D S. Sec—Ap Au LD MR OH.
   Therapy: Hear Lang Speech.
   Staff: 38 (Full 16, Part 22). Prof 32.
   Est 1965. Private.

This center at CHW provides comprehensive evaluation and treatment services for children with hearing, speech, feeding and language disorders. Common disorders include problems with sound production, fluency, language comprehension, voice, feeding and oral-motor functioning. Parents learn to employ methods that will enhance their child's progress. Assessment and treatment techniques utilized at the center include computer technology and x-ray studies of speech and swallowing mechanisms.

CHILEDA HABILITATION INSTITUTE

Res and Day — Coed Ages 6-18

La Crosse, WI 54601. 1020 Mississippi St.
Tel: 608-782-6480. Fax: 608-782-6481.
www.chileda.org
Donald C. Heidel, MSW, Pres. **Pam Hanson,** MD, Med Dir. **Lynn Kay,** Adm.
   Focus: Spec Ed. Treatment. **Conditions:** Primary—Asp Au Bl CP DS Ep
      MR PDD. Sec—ADHD B BD D Db OCD ODD ON PTSD S. **IQ 0-70.**
   Pre-Voc. Voc. Ungraded. Courses: Read Math Lang_Arts Adaptive_Phys_
      Ed Life_Skills. Shelt_Workshop. On-Job Trng.
   Therapy: Hear Lang Occup Phys Speech. **Psychotherapy:** Fam Group
      Indiv.
   Enr: 60. Res Males 40. Res Females 12. Day Males 6. Day Females 2.
      Staff: 175 (Full 80, Part 95). Prof 26. Educ 13. Admin 6.
   Rates 2004: Res $265/day. Day $114/day. State Aid.
   Est 1973. Private. Nonprofit.

Serving children and young adults with severe mental disabilities such as mental retardation, seizure disorders, cerebral palsy and autism, Chileda utilizes a developmental approach to treatment. Year-round programming focuses on helping children successfully adapt to community living. Group activities and one-on-one lessons build social skills, augment physical coordination, and develop the cognitive abilities necessary for academics and vocational training. Staff members evaluate each client to determine his or her educational and behavioral needs, with emphasis placed on correcting cognitive deficits and behaviors that interfere with daily living.

Residential living promotes interaction between peers and staff. Chileda teaches self-care skills such as toilet training, personal hygiene, eating and domestic skills on an individual basis. Children reside in one of three living units, each of which has a house director and a support team.

EASTER SEALS SOUTHEASTERN WISCONSIN
CHILD DEVELOPMENT CENTER

Day — Coed Ages Birth-3

Milwaukee, WI 53210. 3090 N 53rd St.
Tel: 414-449-4444. Fax: 414-449-4448.
www.easterseals-sewi.org   E-mail: b-3@easterseals-sewi.org
Timothy Biondo, Exec Dir. **Michelle Schaefer,** Dir. **Carrie Cianciola,** Adm.
   Focus: Treatment. **Conditions:** Primary—Ap Apr Asp Au Bl CP DS Ep IP

MD MR MS Nf ON PW S SB. Sec—ADD ADHD As B BD CD D Dx ED HIV LD OCD Psy Sz.
Therapy: Lang Occup Phys Speech.
Enr: 85. **Staff:** 26. Educ 2. Admin 3.
Private. Nonprofit. **Spons:** National Easter Seal Society.

The early intervention program provides speech, physical and occupational therapy and special education to children from birth to age 3 with developmental delays and disabilities. Services are provided in the child's home, at daycare or at the center. An individual service plan is developed for each child to help address his or her social, emotional, cognitive, communicational and physical development.

EAU CLAIRE ACADEMY

Res — Coed Ages 10-18

Eau Claire, WI 54702. 550 N Dewey St, PO Box 1168.
Tel: 715-834-6681. Fax: 715-834-9954.
Charles L. Albrent, Dir. **Judith Kistner,** Adm.
  Focus: Spec Ed. **Conditions:** Primary—ADD ADHD CD ED OCD Sz.
    Sec—As BD Ep ON Psy. **IQ 75 and up.**
  Gen Acad. Ungraded. Courses: Read Math Lang_Arts Sci Soc_Stud. Man_
    Arts & Shop. On-Job Trng.
  Psychotherapy: Fam Group Indiv.
  Enr: 135.
  Est 1967. Private. Inc. **Spons:** Clinicare Corporation.

ECA provides psychotherapy, special education, group living and recreation for severely emotionally and behaviorally disturbed children. An individually designed educational program uses psycho-educational and behavior modification methods of teaching.

A developmental program accommodates students who cannot tolerate a full academic day. Older teens take part in reality education and GED preparation. Counseling and psychotherapy are integral parts of every child's week. Length of stay usually does not exceed one year.

GUNDERSEN LUTHERAN

Clinic: All Ages. M-F 8-5.

La Crosse, WI 54601. 1900 South Ave.
Tel: 608-782-7300. Fax: 608-775-6601.
www.gundluth.org   E-mail: info@gundluth.org
Jeffrey E. Thompson, MD, CEO.
  Focus: Treatment. **Conditions:** Primary—ADD ADHD Ap As Au B BD BI C
    CD CP D Dx ED Ep IP LD MD MR MS OCD ON Psy S SB Sz TB.
  Therapy: Hear Lang Occup Phys Speech. **Psychotherapy:** Fam Group
    Indiv Parent.
  Staff: 54.
  Est 1980. Private. Inc.

Complete evaluation, treatment and planning are provided for children and adults with psychological, medical and developmental disabilities. Follow-up appointments are scheduled as needed. A sliding fee scale is available to patients based on income.

LAD LAKE

Res — Males Ages 10-18; Day — Males 10-21, Females 12-21

Dousman, WI 53118. PO Box 158.
Tel: 262-965-2131. Fax: 262-965-4107.
www.ladlake.org
Gary L. Erdmann, MBA, Exec Dir. **William Buzogany,** MD, Med Dir. **Steven Ellmann,** Adm.
  Focus: Treatment. **Conditions:** Primary—ADD ADHD BD CD ED Mood ODD PTSD. Sec—Anx Asp Au Dx LD MR OCD S Sz TS. **IQ 70 and up.**
  Gen Acad. Pre-Voc. Voc. Gr 4-12. Courses: Read Math Lang_Arts. Man_ Arts & Shop. On-Job Trng.
  Therapy: Art Chemo Occup Recreational Speech. **Psychotherapy:** Fam Group Indiv.
  Enr: 83. **Staff:** 220 (Full 120, Part 100). Prof 47. Educ 40. Admin 8.
  Rates 2004: Res $259/day. Day $73/day. State Aid.
  Est 1903. Private. Nonprofit.

Lad Lake utilizes its rural setting to provide treatment and therapy. In addition to traditional educational programming, the school offers special assistance in reading and speech. Prevocational training, work-study and tutoring for the GED are also available. Family involvement is emphasized through biweekly family therapy sessions, parental education programs and in-home counseling.

Residential programs serve boys only, while supervised independent living and transitional living services are available to both males and females.

MARQUETTE UNIVERSITY
SPEECH AND HEARING CLINIC

Clinic: Ages 2 and up. M-F 9-5.

Milwaukee, WI 53201. 619 N 16th St, PO Box 1881.
Tel: 414-288-7426. Fax: 414-288-3980.
www.marquette.edu/chs/sppa   E-mail: dorothy.wood@marquette.edu
Dorothy H. Wood, BS, MS, Coord.
  Focus: Treatment. **Conditions:** Primary—Ap S.
  Therapy: Hear Lang Speech.
  Staff: 11. (Full 11). Prof 10. Admin 1.
  Rates 2003: $50 (Therapy)/hr.
  Est 1922. Private. Nonprofit. Roman Catholic.

This program is primarily a training facility for aspiring speech therapists at the university. Diagnosis and therapy are conducted by undergraduate and graduate students under direct supervision of certified faculty members. The clinic also maintains a preschool language group for preschoolers with language delays, as well as group therapy for adults with aphasia.

MARSHFIELD CLINIC
CHILD DEVELOPMENT CLINIC

Clinic: Ages Birth-21. M-F 8-5.

Marshfield, WI 54449. 1000 N Oak Ave.
Tel: 715-387-5511. Fax: 715-387-5240.
www.marshfieldclinic.org
L. Rebecca Campbell, MD, Dir.
  Focus: Treatment. **Conditions:** Primary—ADD ADHD Anx Ap Apr Asp Au
    B BD Bl CP D Db Dc Dg Dx ED Ep LD MD Mood MR Nf OCD ODD ON
    PDD PTSD PW S SB SP TS.
  Therapy: Lang Occup Phys Speech. **Psychotherapy:** Fam Indiv.
  Est 1930. Private. Nonprofit.

The Child Development Clinic offers comprehensive care for children with chronic illnesses and disabilities through evaluations, diagnoses, treatments and follow-up services. The clinic has access to dozens of regional centers that include outpatient multi-specialty clinics, pediatric inpatient units, and a range of therapy, support and related services designed to provide coordinated care and management.

MENDOTA MENTAL HEALTH INSTITUTE

Res — Coed Ages Birth-12

Madison, WI 53704. 301 Troy Dr.
Tel: 608-301-1000. Fax: 608-301-1358.
www.dhfs.state.wi.us/mh_mendota   E-mail: mismail@dhfs.state.wi.us
  Conditions: Primary—ED. Sec—BD Sz.
  Gen Acad. Pre-Voc. Gr 1-12. Courses: Read Math Lang_Arts. Man_Arts &
    Shop. Shelt_Workshop. On-Job Trng.
  Therapy: Lang Music Occup Phys Recreational Speech.
  Est 1860. State.

MENOMONEE FALLS CENTER

Day — Coed Ages Birth-3

Menomonee Falls, WI 53051. N88 W17550 Christman Rd.
Tel: 262-251-7110.
  Conditions: Primary—LD MR.
  Gen Acad. Gr PS.
  Therapy: Hear Lang Occup Phys Speech.
  Staff: Prof 4.
  Est 1962. Private. Nonprofit. **Spons:** Lutheran Social Services.

MERITER HOSPITAL
PHYSICAL MEDICINE AND REHABILITATION PROGRAM
Clinic: All Ages. M-F 8-5.

Madison, WI 53715. 202 S Park St.
Tel: 608-267-6173. Fax: 608-267-6687.
Joyce Evers, MS, Dir. **William P. Shannon,** MD, Med Dir.
  Focus: Rehab. **Conditions:** Primary—Ap Asp Au Bl CP IP MD ON S.
   Sec—ADD ADHD B D DS Dx LD MR MS SB.
  Therapy: Hear Lang Occup Phys Speech.
  Rates 2003: Clinic $150-200/hr.
  Est 1963. Private. Nonprofit.

The program evaluates and treats sensorimotor, speech and language, and swallowing difficulties. Occupational therapists utilize activities that incorporate fine-motor skills, hand-eye coordination, perceptual abilities, and the use of sensory information from touch, movement and position.

Meriter maintains an early intervention program for children from birth through age 3, as well as a support clinic (ages 4-18) that provides one or two sessions per week focusing on self-care, sensory deficit treatment, motor and coordination skills, techniques to improve behavioral disorders, sensory integration and developmental assessments. Special services designed for the age 3 and under population include a pediatric follow-up clinic, infant hearing screenings, a developmental clinic, video-fluroscopic swallowing evaluations, feeding therapy and parent training.

NORTHWEST READING CLINIC
Clinic: All Ages. M-S 8:30-5; Eves M-F 5-9.

Eau Claire, WI 54701. 2600 Stein Blvd.
Tel: 715-834-2754.
Ruth E. Harris, MS, Dir.
  Focus: Spec Ed. **Conditions:** Primary—ADD ADHD Asp Bl Dc Dg Dx LD
   PDD SP. Sec—Ap Au BD CD CP ED Mood MR OCD ODD OH. **IQ 50
   and up.**
  Gen Acad. Pre-Voc. Ungraded. Courses: Read Math Lang_Arts Study_
   Skills.
  Therapy: Percepual-Motor. **Psychotherapy:** Fam Parent.
  Staff: 13.
  Rates 2003: $475 (Evaluation); $45 (Therapy)/hr.
  Summer Prgm: Day. Educ. Ther. 10 wks.
  Est 1969. Private. Inc.

This year-round clinic provides diagnostic and remedial services for children and adults with attentional disorders, Asperger's syndrome and specific learning disabilities. Through individually tailored programs, students work to improve their self-concepts and become independent learners. The program for students with attentional disorders includes coping strategies, behavioral modification, parental counseling and school advocacy. Additional services include speed-reading, counseling, and preparation for high school equivalency and college entrance examinations.

OCONOMOWOC DEVELOPMENTAL TRAINING CENTER

Res and Day — Coed Ages 4-21

Oconomowoc, WI 53066. 36100 Genesee Lake Rd.
Tel: 262-567-5515. Fax: 262-569-9962.
www.odtc-wi.com
Jeff Kaphengst, BS, MS, Dir. **Michael Purpura,** Adm.
  Focus: Spec Ed. Treatment. **Conditions:** Primary—BI CP ED MR ON TS.
    Sec—ADD ADHD Ap Au CD Ep LD OCD Psy S Sz. **IQ 35 and up.**
  Gen Acad. Pre-Voc. Voc. Ungraded. Courses: Read Math Lang_Arts Life_
    Skills Adaptive_Phys_Ed. Man_Arts & Shop. Shelt_Workshop. On-Job
    Trng.
  Therapy: Chemo Hear Lang Occup Phys Speech. **Psychotherapy:** Fam
    Group Indiv Parent.
  Est 1975. Private. Inc.

Situated in the lake country of Waukesha County in southeastern Wisconsin, ODTC provides year-round residential care and therapeutic treatment for those dually diagnosed with emotional disturbances and developmental disabilities. Individualized treatment plans help clients develop a positive self-image and those skills necessary to live in a less restrictive environment. Psychotherapy, education, workshop, recreation, living-unit experiences and community participation are all elements of the program. Comprehensive medical services assist individuals with special syndromes and neurological conditions; specific areas of expertise include genetic disorders, seizures and other neurological handicaps.

Oconomowoc also operates several area group homes. Three homes serve young adults with Prader-Willi syndrome: Gatehouse in Hartland, Anthony House in Oconomowoc and Hanson House in Ixonia. Two others—Cheryl House in Summit and Sawyer House in Dousman—board children who are making the transition from the main campus back to the community.

REHABILITATION CENTER OF SHEBOYGAN
EARLY INTERVENTION PROGRAM

Day — Coed Ages Birth-3

Sheboygan, WI 53081. 1305 St Clair Ave.
Tel: 920-458-8261. Fax: 920-458-8361.
www.rcspkg.com
  Conditions: Primary—Au B BI C CP D ED Ep IP MR ON S SB.
  Therapy: Hear Lang Occup Phys Speech. **Psychotherapy:** Group Indiv.
  Staff: Prof 8.
  Est 1990. Private. Nonprofit.

SACRED HEART REHABILITATION INSTITUTE
PEDIATRIC PROGRAM

Clinic: Ages Birth-18. M-F 8-5.

Milwaukee, WI 53201. 2350 N Lake Dr.
Tel: 414-298-6700. Fax: 414-298-6751.
www.columbia-stmarys.com
Susan Hinkle, MS, CEO.
   Focus: Rehab. **Conditions:** Primary—Ap Au Bl CP D Ep LD MR ON S SB.
   Therapy: Hear Lang Occup Phys Speech. **Psychotherapy:** Parent.
   Est 1965. Private. Nonprofit. Roman Catholic. **Spons:** Columbia-St. Mary's.

Children with acquired disabilities such as head injury and stroke, as well as those with such congenital problems as cerebral palsy, Down syndrome and seizure disorders, receive care through the Pediatric Program. The trans-disciplinary center specializes in head-injury rehabilitation. Advocacy and community support are integral to the program, and a free patient support group meets once a month. Fees vary according to the client's ability to pay.

ST. AEMILIAN-LAKESIDE

Res — Males Ages 6-15; Day — Coed 4-18

Milwaukee, WI 53222. 8901 W Capitol Dr.
Tel: 414-463-1880. Fax: 414-463-2770.
www.st-al.org
Teri Zywicki-Nelson, Pres.
   Conditions: Primary—BD ED.
   Pre-Voc. Ungraded. Courses: Read Math Lang_Arts.
   Therapy: Art Recreational. **Psychotherapy:** Fam Indiv.
   Staff: Prof 183.
   Est 1850. Private. Inc.

ST. CHARLES
YOUTH AND FAMILY SERVICES

Res and Day — Coed Ages 6-17
Clinic: All Ages. M-F 9-5; Eves M-F 5-9.

Milwaukee, WI 53214. 151 S 84th St.
Tel: 414-476-3710. Fax: 414-778-5985.
www.st-charles.org
Cathy Connolly, Pres.
   Conditions: Primary—ADD ADHD BD CD ED. **IQ 70 and up.**
   Gen Acad. Pre-Voc. Gr 3-12. Courses: Read Math Lang_Arts. On-Job Trng.
   Therapy: Speech. **Psychotherapy:** Fam Group Indiv Parent.
   Enr: 120. Res Males 48. Res Females 48. Day Males 12. Day Females 12.
      Staff: 86.

Est 1920. Private. Nonprofit. Roman Catholic.

Located in southeastern Wisconsin, St. Charles provides a variety of residential, educational and mental health services for severely emotionally disturbed and socially disordered boys and their families. Individualized care involves treatments designed to strengthen the family unit. Educational services are available, and the program also has job readiness and advocacy components. The usual length of treatment is three to six months.

ST. COLETTA DAY SCHOOL

Day — Coed Ages 8-16

Milwaukee, WI 53208. 1740 N 55th St.
Tel: 414-453-1850.
William A. Koehn, BS, Admin.
  Focus: Spec Ed. **Conditions:** Primary—ADD ADHD DS Dx LD MR. **IQ 50-75.**
  Gen Acad. Pre-Voc. Ungraded. Courses: Read Math Lang_Arts Studio_Art Music.
  Enr: 7. Day Males 3. Day Females 4. **Staff:** 3. Educ 2. Admin 1.
  Est 1956. Private. Nonprofit. Roman Catholic.

Children with mild to moderate mental retardation from the Milwaukee area receive ungraded academic instruction at this school, which limits enrollment to 12 students. Programming stresses social and attitudinal development, as well as life skills training. The sequential development educational program includes reading, math and language arts. The school seeks pupils with sufficient self-care skills and a capacity for academic achievement.

ST. COLETTA SCHOOL

Res and Day — Coed Ages 18 and up

Jefferson, WI 53549. W4955 Hwy 18.
Tel: 920-674-4330. Fax: 920-674-4603.
www.stcolettawi.org
Anthony LoDuca, Pres.
  Conditions: Primary—MR.
  Man_Arts & Shop. Shelt_Workshop. On-Job Trng.
  Therapy: Music Recreational.
  Est 1904. Private. Nonprofit.

ST. FRANCIS CHILDREN'S CENTER

Day — Coed Ages Birth-8

Milwaukee, WI 53217. 6700 N Port Washington Rd.

Tel: 414-351-0450. Fax: 414-351-8845.
www.sfcckids.org   E-mail: klengling@sfcckids.org
Gerry Coon, MS, Exec Dir. **Dori Buschke,** MA, Prin. **Jeri Marcuvitz,** Adm.
  Focus: Treatment. **Conditions:** Primary—ADD ADHD Asp Au DS ED ON
    PDD. Sec—Anx Ap Apr As CP Db Ep LD MD Mood MR Nf OCD SB SP
    Sz TS.
  Gen Acad. Gr PS-3. Courses: Read Math Lang_Arts Sci Soc_Stud.
  Therapy: Hear Lang Occup Percepual-Motor Phys Play Speech Visual.
    Psychotherapy: Fam Group Indiv.
  Staff: 42 (Full 33, Part 9).
  Rates 2003: Day $5000-28,000/sch yr.
  Summer Prgm: Day. Educ. Rec. Ther.
  Est 1969. Private. Nonprofit. **Spons:** Wisconsin Society for Brain-Injured
    Children.

The center offers a comprehensive early childhood program for both typically developing children and those with special needs. There is also a program for children with disorders in the autism spectrum. For children with special needs, the Individualized Family Service Plan or Individualized Education Plan is utilized to specially design an educational program. Educational services are available to children under age 3; therapeutic assessments are available to older students.

ST. ROSE YOUTH AND FAMILY CENTER

Res — Females Ages 8-18; Day — Females 12-18

Milwaukee, WI 53222. 3801 N 88th St.
Tel: 414-466-9450. Fax: 414-466-0730.
www.strosecenter.org
Debra M. Goyette, Actg Pres.
  Focus: Spec Ed. Treatment. **Conditions:** Primary—ADD ADHD BD CD Dx
    ED LD OCD. Sec—Psy Sz. **IQ 70-130.**
  Gen Acad. Pre-Voc. Ungraded. Courses: Read Math Lang_Arts Computers
    Studio_Art Study_Skills.
  Therapy: Lang Occup Speech. **Psychotherapy:** Fam Group Indiv.
  Enr: 50. **Staff:** 54 (Full 44, Part 10).
  Est 1848. Private. Nonprofit.

This facility helps girls develop coping skills through a therapeutic relationship and an educational program. The average length of stay is six to 12 months.

SHEBOYGAN COUNTY OUTPATIENT SERVICES

Clinic: Ages 5-18. M-F 8-5; Eves M-F 5-7.

Sheboygan, WI 53081. 1011 N 8th St.
Tel: 920-459-3155. Fax: 920-459-4353.
www.co.sheboygan.wi.us   E-mail: humansrv@co.sheboygan.wi.us
Miles Tonnacliff, PhD, Dir. **Dan Knoedler,** MD, Med Dir.
  Focus: Treatment. **Conditions:** Primary—ADD AN Anx BD Bu CD ED

Mood MR OCD Psy PTSD SP Sz. Sec—ADHD Ap Apr As Asp Au B Bl C CP D Dg DS Dx Ep HIV IP LD MD MS Nf ON S SB TB TS. **IQ 55 and up.**
Therapy: Chemo Occup Play. **Psychotherapy:** Fam Group Indiv Parent.
Staff: 15. (Full 15). Prof 13. Admin 2.
County. Nonprofit.

The team approach is used in diagnosis and therapy for the emotional and psychological problems of county residents. Individual and group therapies are used. Consultations to schools and community agencies are also conducted. Parents receive counseling, and follow-up services are provided. An alcohol and drug abuse program offers counseling, medication and therapy.

Fees are determined along a sliding scale.

TAYLOR HOME

Res — Males Ages 13-16

Racine, WI 53405. 3131 Taylor Ave.
Tel: 262-553-4100. Fax: 262-553-4021.
E-mail: taylorhm@voyager.net
Dolores Teale, MS, Exec Dir.
    Focus: Treatment. **Conditions:** Primary—BD CD ED. Sec—ADD ADHD Dc Dg Dx LD. **IQ 75 and up.**
    Gen Acad. Ungraded. Courses: Read Math Lang_Arts.
    Therapy: Art Recreational Speech. **Psychotherapy:** Fam Group Indiv Parent.
    Enr: 22. Res Males 22. **Staff:** 31 (Full 18, Part 13). Prof 7. Educ 4. Admin 3.
    Rates 2004: Res $235/day.
    Est 1867. Private. Nonprofit.

Taylor Home conducts a 120-day treatment-oriented program for teenage boys who might otherwise be placed in correction programs or typical residential treatment programs. Following three weeks orientation, boys take part in mandatory home visits, as the facility's goal is the return of each student to a family environment. Therapy is experiential in nature and includes art therapy, role playing and other expressive therapies. An extended academic day addresses educational deficits.

THRESHOLD EARLY INTERVENTION SERVICES

Clinic: Ages Birth-3. M-F 8-4:30.

West Bend, WI 53090. 600 Rolfs Ave.
Tel: 262-338-4430. Fax: 262-338-9453.
www.thresholdinc.org   E-mail: lwittemann@thresholdinc.org
Lori Wittemann, Dir.
    Focus: Rehab. **Conditions:** Primary—Ap Apr Asp Au B Bl CP D DS Ep HIV LD MD MR MS ON PDD PW S SB.
    Therapy: Occup Phys Speech.
    Staff: 15.
    Rates 2003: Sliding-Scale Rate $0-150/mo.

Est 1967. Private. Nonprofit.

A wide range of year-round early intervention services is available to developmentally delayed children of Washington County. Developmental areas include vision, hearing, gross, fine and perceptual motor; cognition; language; self-help; and socialization. Threshold offers services wherever the child spends most of his or her time: in the home, at daycare or in another setting.

TOMORROWS CHILDREN

Res — Coed Ages 5-18

Waupaca, WI 54981. N3066 Tomorrows Ln.
Tel: 715-258-1440. Fax: 715-258-1456.
James R. Weyenberg, Admin. **Randy Kerswill,** MD, Med Dir. **Gregory Heindel,** Intake.
    Focus: Treatment. **Conditions:** Primary—ADD ADHD Anx Asp Au BD CD ED LD Mood MR OCD PDD Psy PTSD SP Sz TS. Sec—AN Ap Bl Bu CP DS Dx Ep MD Nf ON PW. **IQ 40-100.**
    Gen Acad. Pre-Voc. Voc. Gr PS-12. Courses: Read Math. On-Job Trng.
    Psychotherapy: Fam Group Indiv Parent.
    Enr: 31. Res Males 22. Res Females 9. **Staff:** 9.
    Rates 2003: Res $205/day.
    Est 1973. Private. Nonprofit.

Tomorrows Children develops programs for children who have been diagnosed with autism, psychosis or severe emotional disturbance. Treatment aims to teach new behavior and skills to replace those that have been found to be socially maladaptive. Child training, education and parent training are the major components of treatment.

The educational program focuses on prerequisite school behaviors, language, and academic and vocational training. A correspondence curriculum is available to those parents or guardians who are unable to attend parental education sessions.

UNIVERSITY OF WISCONSIN-EAU CLAIRE
CENTER FOR COMMUNICATION DISORDERS

Clinic: All Ages. M-F 9-6.

Eau Claire, WI 54702. 239 Water St.
Tel: 715-836-4185. Fax: 715-836-4846.
www.uwec.edu/cdis/center.htm
Alan J. Gallaher, PhD, Dir.
    Focus: Treatment. **Conditions:** Primary—Ap D S. Sec—MR OH.
    Therapy: Hear Lang Speech.
    Staff: 11 (Full 9, Part 2).
    Summer Prgm: Day. Ther. 8 wks.
    Est 1966. State. Nonprofit.

This outpatient facility provides services including speech, language and hearing therapy. An eight-week summer session accepts students from other programs for enrollment. The duration of treatment varies with the individual.

UNIVERSITY OF WISCONSIN-MADISON
CHILD PSYCHIATRY CLINIC
Clinic: All Ages. M-F 8-6.

Madison, WI 53719. 6001 Research Park Blvd.
Tel: 608-263-6100. Fax: 608-263-0265.
http://psychiatry.wisc.edu/home.htm
Stephen Weiler, MD, Dir.
    Conditions: Primary—Anx BD ED Mood Sz.
    Psychotherapy: Group Indiv.
    Private.

UNIVERSITY OF WISCONSIN-MADISON
SPEECH & HEARING CLINICS
Clinic: All Ages. M-F 8-5.

Madison, WI 53706. 1975 Willow Dr.
Tel: 608-262-3951. Fax: 608-262-6466.
www.comdis.wisc.edu/clinics.html
John Westbury, PhD, Supv.
    Focus: Trng. **Conditions:** Primary—ADD ADHD Ap Asp Au D Dx LD MR S.
    Therapy: Hear Lang Speech.
    Staff: 29 (Full 26, Part 3).
    Rates 2003: Sliding-Scale Rate $50-200/ses (Diagnosis); $25-150/ses
      (Treatment).
    State.

The Department of Communicative Disorder's speech and hearing clinics conduct diagnostic and treatment services designed to meet each client's needs, various types of intervention and therapy, and consultations and counseling for parents and clients. Services are provided by qualified graduate students under the close supervision of clinical staff.

UNIVERSITY OF WISCONSIN-MILWAUKEE
SPEECH AND LANGUAGE CLINIC
Clinic: All Ages. M-Th 9-4:30.

Milwaukee, WI 53201. 2400 E Hartford Ave, PO Box 413.
Tel: 414-229-4025. Fax: 414-229-2620.
E-mail: slsieff@uwm.edu

Mary Lou Gelfer, PhD, Supv. **Sherri L. Sieff,** PhD, CCC-SLP, Coord.
 Focus: Treatment. **Conditions:** Primary—S. Sec—D LD MR ON PDD.
 Therapy: Lang Speech.
 Staff: 9.
 Rates 2003: $85 (Evaluation); $75-150 (Therapy)/sem.
 Est 1946. State.

Serving the university and the surrounding community, the clinic provides speech and hearing services as part of the institution's professional preparation of UWM students in the Department of Communication Sciences and Disorders. Students have completed the necessary course work prior to performing services at the clinic, and certified and licensed speech-language pathologists supervise the pupils closely. Children and adults receive evaluation and treatment services (usually on an individual basis) for communication disorders involving articulation, phonology, language, fluency and voice.

UNIVERSITY OF WISCONSIN-RIVER FALLS
SPEECH-LANGUAGE-HEARING CLINIC

Clinic: All Ages. M-F 8-4:30.

River Falls, WI 54022. B31 Wyman Education Bldg.
Tel: 715-425-3801. Fax: 715-425-3800.
www.uwrf.edu/comm-dis
Paul A. Hayden, PhD, CCC-SLP, Dir.
 Focus: Treatment. **Conditions:** Primary—ADD ADHD Ap D Dx LD S.
  Sec—Au.
 Therapy: Hear Lang Speech.
 Staff: 9 (Full 5, Part 4).
 Est 1960. State. Nonprofit.

Operated by the university's Department of Communicative Disorders, this clinic can adjust its fees based on the client's ability to pay.

UNIVERSITY OF WISCONSIN-STEVENS POINT
CENTER FOR COMMUNICATIVE DISORDERS

Clinic: All Ages. M-F 8-4:30.

Stevens Point, WI 54481. 1901 4th Ave.
Tel: 715-346-4517. Fax: 715-346-2157.
www.uwsp.edu/commd   E-mail: clinccd@uwsp.edu
Cynthia Forster, MA, CCC-SLP, Dir.
 Focus: Treatment. **Conditions:** Primary—Ap D S. Sec—ADD ADHD Au BI
  CP Dx IP LD MD MS ON SB.
 Therapy: Hear Lang Speech.
 Staff: 13 (Full 11, Part 2).
 Rates 2001: $100 (Evaluation); $200 (Treatment)/sem. Schol avail. State
  Aid.
 State.

The center provides speech, language and hearing services for central Wisconsin residents. UWSP undergraduates who are majoring in communicative disorders and graduate students pursuing a master's degree in speech and language pathology and audiology administer treatment at the facility. Services include evaluation, therapy and hearing aid dispensation.

VOCATIONAL INDUSTRIES

Day — Coed Ages 16 and up

Elkhorn, WI 53121. 530 E Centralia St.
Tel: 262-723-4043. Fax: 262-723-4984.
www.vocationalindustries.com   E-mail: vi@vocationalindustries.com
Cindy Simonsen, MSW, Exec Dir.
> **Focus:** Trng. **Conditions:** Primary—MR. Sec—ADHD B BI CP D Ep OCD ON Psy S Sz. **IQ 20 and up.**
> **Therapy:** Occup Phys Speech.
> **Enr:** 300. **Staff:** 75 (Full 55, Part 20).
> **Est 1971.** Private. Nonprofit.

This agency provides vocational rehabilitation services and opportunities for personal growth for cognitively impaired and handicapped persons. It aims to assist clients to become as much a part of the community as possible. Work evaluation, adjustment training and job placement are available, and the agency also provides recreation and socialization, counseling and restorative therapies.

WAISMAN CENTER

Clinic: All Ages. M-F 8-5.

Madison, WI 53705. 1500 Highland Ave.
Tel: 608-263-5776. TTY: 608-263-0802. Fax: 608-263-0529.
www.waisman.wisc.edu
Marsha Mailick Seltzer, PhD, Dir.
> **Focus:** Treatment. **Conditions:** Primary—Ap Au BD BI CP Dx ED Ep IP LD MD MR MS ON S SB. Sec—B D.
> **Therapy:** Chemo Hear Lang Occup Phys Speech. **Psychotherapy:** Fam Group Indiv.
> **Est 1973.** State. Nonprofit. **Spons:** University of Wisconsin-Madison.

The clinical services unit consists of a core developmental disabilities clinic and a number of specialty clinics. Evaluation, diagnosis, treatment, follow-up assistance, and information and referral are the primary elements of this unit.

The special education program provides assessments of learning capabilities, recommendations regarding educational planning, follow-up consultations, and training for graduate and undergraduate students. The early childhood program emphasizes cognitive, language and social development.

WALBRIDGE SCHOOL

Day — Coed Ages 7-14

Madison, WI 53717. 7035 Old Sauk Rd.
Tel: 608-833-1338.
http://userpages.chorus.net/walbridg   E-mail: walbridg@chorus.net
Barbara E. Jull, BS, Prin.

Focus: Spec Ed. **Conditions:** Primary—ADD ADHD Dc Dg Dx LD. Sec—
Asp OCD SP.

Gen Acad. Gr 1-8. Courses: Read Math Lang_Arts.

Enr: 30. Day Males 26. Day Females 4. **Staff:** 11 (Full 5, Part 6). Educ 10.
Admin 2.

Summer Prgm: Day. Educ. Day Rate $250/crse. 4 wks.

Est 1986. Private. Nonprofit.

Walbridge offers an alternative full-day elementary and middle school program that emphasizes multisensory teaching and individualization to address the learning differences of children. Specialized and personalized instruction is geared to children with learning disabilities such as dyslexia and ADHD.

WILLOWGLEN ACADEMY

Res — Coed Ages 10-21; Day — Coed 6-21
Clinic: Ages 6-21. M-F 8-5; Eves M-F 5-8.

Milwaukee, WI 53202. 1744 N Farwell Ave.
Nearby locations: Sheboygan.
Tel: 414-225-4460. Fax: 414-225-4475.
www.willowglen-wi.com
Lin Daley, MSW, Exec Dir. **Joseph O'Grady,** MD, Med Dir. **Jill Karnath**
Lemke, Adm.

Focus: Spec Ed. Treatment. **Conditions:** Primary—ADD ADHD Asp Au ED
Ep LD Mood ODD Psy S Sz. Sec—Anx As BD Bl CD CP D Db DS MR
OCD ON PTSD PW SP TS. **IQ 30-95.**

Pre-Voc. Voc. Ungraded. Courses: Read Math Lang_Arts Life_Skills.

Therapy: Art Lang Milieu Occup Play Recreational Speech. **Psychotherapy:** Fam Group Indiv.

Enr: 155. Res Males 35. Res Females 15. Day Males 81. Day Females 24.
Staff: 150. Prof 70. Educ 16. Admin 4.

Rates 2004: Res $262/day. Day $115-123/day. State Aid.

Est 1973. Private. Inc. **Spons:** Phoenix Care Systems.

Willowglen offers a variety of year-round residential and day treatment and educational settings for autistic, mentally ill, emotionally disturbed and developmentally disabled children, adolescents and young adults. The academy provides a comprehensive, community-based alternative care model.

In addition to the North Farwell Avenue site, Willowglen conducts programs at two other Milwaukee locations (3903 W. Lisbon Ave., 53208 and 3109 Highland Blvd., 53208) and in Sheboygan (W. 1236 County Hwy. FF, 53083).

WISCONSIN CENTER FOR THE BLIND
AND VISUALLY IMPAIRED

Res and Day — Coed Ages 5-21

Janesville, WI 53546. 1700 W State St.
Tel: 608-758-6100. Fax: 608-758-6161.
www.wcbvi.k12.wi.us
Sue Enoch, Dir.

Focus: Spec Ed. **Conditions:** Primary—B. Sec—As BD BI C CP ED Ep IP LD MD MR MS ON S.

Col Prep. Gen Acad. Pre-Voc. Voc. Gr K-12. Courses: Read Math Lang_ Arts. Man_Arts & Shop. On-Job Trng.

Therapy: Hear Lang Occup Phys Speech. **Psychotherapy:** Indiv.

Enr: 65. Staff: 93.

Rates 2003: No Fee.

Est 1848. State.

The school offers a general education curriculum for the visually impaired through grade 12. In addition, it provides intensive instruction in skills that help to minimize the effects of blindness, among them braille instruction and the use of technology. Wisconsin residents only may enroll.

WISCONSIN SCHOOL FOR THE DEAF

Res — Coed Ages 5-21; Day — Coed 3-21

Delavan, WI 53115. 309 W Walworth Ave.
Tel: 262-728-7120. TTY: 877-973-3323. Fax: 262-728-7160.
www.wsd.k12.wi.us   E-mail: information@wsd.k12.wi.us
Alex Slappey, MA, Dir.

Focus: Spec Ed. **Conditions:** Primary—D. Sec—ADD ADHD AN Anx Ap Apr Ar As Asp Au B BD BI Bu C CD CF CP Db Dc Dg DS Dx ED Ep IP LD MD Mood MR MS Nf OCD ODD ON PDD Psy PTSD PW S SB SP Sz TS. **IQ 60 and up.**

Col Prep. Gen Acad. Pre-Voc. Voc. Gr PS-12. Courses: Read Math Lang_ Arts Sci Hist Soc_Stud Life_Skills. Man_Arts & Shop. Shelt_Workshop. On-Job Trng.

Therapy: Hear Lang Occup Phys Play Speech.

Enr: 168. Res Males 65. Res Females 73. Day Males 19. Day Females 11. **Staff:** 160 (Full 150, Part 10). Prof 76. Educ 68. Admin 6.

Rates 2004: No Fee.

State. Nonprofit.

The school provides educational and prevocational programs for students in preschool through 12th grade. A day school setting is provided for the youngest students and children from the local area, and a residential program serves students from all counties in the state of Wisconsin. The school offers innovative learning structures for students that are deaf or hard of hearing and students with multiple disabilities. Classes are taught in American Sign Language to eliminate the need for interpreters. Counseling is available.

The program is free to residents of Wisconsin, while out-of-state students may attend for a fee.

WYALUSING ACADEMY

Res — Coed Ages 10-18

Prairie du Chien, WI 53821. 601 S Beaumont Rd, PO Box 269.
Tel: 608-326-6481. Fax: 608-326-6166.
www.wyalusingacademy.com   E-mail: cteynor@centurytel.net
David J. Hernesman, MEd, Dir. **Michael Kaplan,** MD, Med Dir. **Colleen Teynor,** Adm.

> **Focus:** Spec Ed. **Conditions:** Primary—ADD ADHD Asp BD CD ED LD PDD PTSD. Sec—AN Anx As Bl Bu Db Dx Mood MR Nf ON S TS. **IQ 50-100.**
>
> **Gen Acad. Pre-Voc.** Ungraded. Courses: Read Math Lang_Arts Sci Computers. Man_Arts & Shop. On-Job Trng.
>
> **Therapy:** Lang Recreational Speech. **Psychotherapy:** Fam Group Indiv.
>
> **Enr:** 80. Res Males 55. Res Females 25. **Staff:** 91 (Full 79, Part 12). Prof 29. Educ 19. Admin 8.
>
> **Rates 2003:** Res $222/day.
>
> **Summer Prgm:** Res & Day. Educ. Rec. Res Rate $222/day. Day Rate $175/day.
>
> **Est 1969.** Private. Inc. **Spons:** Clinicare Corporation.

Wyalusing serves dependent, neglected, delinquent and emotionally disturbed youths. Psychiatric consultations are available as needed, and residents may receive speech therapy for an additional fee. On-grounds vocational and academic educational opportunities include auto mechanics, landscaping, building trades, food service, cosmetology, art, family consumer education, independent living skills and business education.

Treatment lasts roughly eight months. The academy does not accept fire setters, the actively psychotic or the schizophrenic.

WYOMING

COMMUNITY ENTRY SERVICES

Res — Coed Ages 16 and up; Day — Coed 14 and up

Riverton, WY 82501. 2441 Peck Ave.
Tel: 307-856-5576. Fax: 307-857-6901.
www.ces-usa.com/riverton.htm
Shawn Griffin, CEO.
  Conditions: Primary—CP Ep LD MR.
  Pre-Voc. Voc. Shelt_Workshop. On-Job Trng.
  Est 1975. Private. Nonprofit.

LARAMIE COUNTY OUTPATIENT MENTAL HEALTH AND SUBSTANCE TREATMENT SERVICES

Clinic: All Ages. M-F 8-5.

Cheyenne, WY 82003. 2526 Seymour Ave, PO Box 1005.
Tel: 307-634-9653. Fax: 307-638-8256.
www.sewmhc.org/locations.htm
  Conditions: Primary—BD ED.
  Psychotherapy: Fam Group Indiv.
  Staff: Prof 40.
  Est 1969. Federal. Nonprofit.

STRIDE LEARNING CENTER

Day — Coed Ages Birth-5

Cheyenne, WY 82007. 326 Parsley Blvd.
Tel: 307-632-2991. Fax: 307-632-6271.
www.stridekids.com   E-mail: info@stridekids.com
Donna Merrill, MEd, Dir.
  Focus: Spec Ed. Conditions: Primary—Au BI C CP Ep IP MD MR MS ON SB. Sec—ADD ADHD Ap As B BD CD D ED OCD Psy S Sz TB.
  Gen Acad. Gr PS.
  Therapy: Hear Lang Occup Phys Speech. Psychotherapy: Fam Group Indiv.
  Enr: 356. Day Males 240. Day Females 116. Staff: 48 (Full 40, Part 8). Prof 20. Educ 4. Admin 2.
  Rates 2003: No Fee.
  Est 1973. Private. Nonprofit.

STRIDE provides early intervention services for preschool-age children with developmental delays. Various types of therapy are available. Families incur no fee for services.

TRINITY WILDERNESS TRAILS

Res — Females Ages 12-17

Powell, WY 82435. 89 Rd 8 RA.
Tel: 307-645-3384. Fax: 307-645-3385.
www.wildernessyouthcamp.com
   E-mail: admissions@wildernessyouthcamp.com
Angie Woodward, Dir. **Scott Pollard,** MD, Med Dir.
   Focus: Rehab. Treatment. **Conditions:** Primary—ADD ADHD Anx BD CD
      ED Mood OCD PTSD. Sec—AN Bu.
   Gen Acad. Ungraded. Courses: Read Math Lang_Arts.
   Therapy: Art Chemo Dance Movement Music Occup Percepual-Motor Phys
      Play Recreational. **Psychotherapy:** Fam Group Indiv Parent Equine.
   Enr: 10. Res Females 10. **Staff:** 5 (Full 1, Part 4). Educ 2.
   Rates 2003: Res $195-300/day.
   Est 2002. Private. Inc. Roman Catholic.

Trinity Wilderness provides treatment for emotionally troubled young women in a wilderness ranch setting. Through animal therapy and individualized care plans, the program fosters an environment in which girls can lead healthier lives, make better decisions and improve their self-esteem. Residents remain at TWT an average of eight to 12 months, with 45 days representing the minimum stay.

UNIVERSITY OF WYOMING
SPEECH AND HEARING CLINIC

Clinic: All Ages. M-F 8-5.

Laramie, WY 82071. 1000 E University Ave, Ross Hall, Rm 30.
Tel: 307-766-6427. TTY: 307-766-6426. Fax: 307-766-6829.
http://uwadmnweb.uwyo.edu/comdis/clinic   E-mail: woodall@uwyo.edu
Lynda D. Coyle, MS, CCC-SLP, Co-Dir. **Teresa Garcia,** MS, CCC-A, Co-Dir.
   Focus: Rehab. Treatment. **Conditions:** Primary—D LD S. Sec—ADD
      ADHD BI CP ED.
   Therapy: Hear Lang Speech. **Psychotherapy:** Group.
   Staff: 15 (Full 11, Part 4).
   Est 1948. State. Nonprofit.

Comprehensive diagnostic and rehabilitative treatments are conducted at this university clinic. Evaluative services take place in a fully equipped diagnostic, clinical setting. The program includes speech, pure-tone, and pre- and post-operative audiometry, as well as pediatric hearing, hearing aid, ABR, speech, voice and language evaluations. Therapeutic sessions are available on both group and individual bases. Fees vary according to the client's income level.

WYOMING SCHOOL FOR THE DEAF

Day — Coed Ages Birth-21

Casper, WY 82609. 539 Payne Ave.
Tel: 307-577-4686. Fax: 307-577-6785.
www.trib.com/WYOMING/NCSD/WSD
  Conditions: Primary—D.
  Gen Acad. Gr PS-12. Courses: Read Math Lang_Arts. Man_Arts & Shop.
   On-Job Trng.
  Therapy: Hear Lang Speech. **Psychotherapy:** Group Indiv.
  State.

WYOMING STATE TRAINING SCHOOL

Res — Coed All Ages

Lander, WY 82520. 8204 State Hwy 789.
Tel: 307-335-6891. Fax: 307-335-6990.
http://wdhfs.state.wy.us/wsts/index.asp   E-mail: wdh-wsts@state.wy.us
  Conditions: Primary—MR.
  Pre-Voc. Voc. Ungraded. Shelt_Workshop. On-Job Trng.
  Therapy: Hear Lang Occup Phys Speech. **Psychotherapy:** Indiv.
  Staff: Prof 75.
  Est 1912. State.

ILLUSTRATED
ANNOUNCEMENTS

INDEX TO ILLUSTRATED ANNOUNCEMENTS

BELLEFAIRE JCB
22001 Fairmount Blvd.
SHAKER HEIGHTS, OH 44118
Tel: 216-932-2800   Fax: 216-932-6704

Helping Children & Preserving Families

Since 1868, Bellefaire Jewish Children's Bureau (Bellefaire JCB) has been working to improve the lives of children and families. Originally an orphanage, Bellefaire JCB has emerged as one of the leading nonprofit mental and behavioral health agencies in the State of Ohio.

Bellefaire JCB is a year-round, comprehensive center for emotionally disturbed children, offering Residential Treatment, Foster Care, Adoption and Outpatient Counseling. Additionally, Monarch School for children with autism and JDN Early Childhood Centers Preschool and Kindergarten are programs offered through Bellefaire JCB's Department of Education and Prevention.

The 32-acre campus is located in suburban Cleveland and features Tudor cottage residences, full athletic and recreation facilities. Also located on the campus is Bellefaire School - a complete accredited SBH educational facility affiliated with the Cleveland Hts./University Hts. Board of Education.

Bellefaire JCB is accredited by the National Academy of Early Childhood Programs, Council on Accreditation of Services for Families and Children, and Joint Commission on Accreditation of Healthcare Organizations. Bellefaire JCB is licensed by the Ohio Department of Mental Health, Ohio Department of Human Services, and Ohio Department of Alcohol & Drug Addiction Services. The Agency is a member of/sponsored by the Child Welfare League of America, Ohio Association of Child Caring Agencies, Jewish Community Federation of Cleveland, United Way Services of Greater Cleveland, and The National Association of Psychiatric Treatment Centers for Children.

Bellefaire JCB does not discriminate on the basis of age, race, sex, disability, national origin, religion, color or sexual orientation in the provision of services or employment practices.

Contact the Bellefaire JCB Intake Department by calling 1-800-879-2522.

COMMUNITY HIGH SCHOOL

1135 Teaneck Rd.
TEANECK, NJ 07666

Toby Braunstein, *Director of Education*
Dennis Cohen, *Director of Program*

Community High School provides a full, rich four year college and career preparatory curriculum for students with learning difficulties. Community High School serves students from New York City, Northern New Jersey, and Rockland County. Transportation from New York City is provided.

Adolescent counseling groups, career counseling, college counseling, SAT preparation, small class groupings, individualized instruction, skilled remediation, additional tutorials in reading language and speech, and wide range of study skills classes are provided. Courses follow the traditional high school curriculum, are completely departmentalized, and include computer programming, photography, video production, computer graphics, graphics, keyboarding, music, drama, and drivers education. Extracurricular activities include theater and music productions, newspaper and yearbook production, a complete intramural athletic program and an interscholastic athletic program.

For admissions contact Toby Braunstein: 201-862-1796.

Cotting School

A day school in Lexington, MA for youth ages 3-22 with medical, communication, physical, and other challenges to learning

Cotting focuses on each student's unique needs and tailors an individualized program, drawing from the wide variety of services we offer under one roof.

- Communication Therapy
- One-on-One Tutoring
- Occupational and Physical Therapy
- Counseling and Career Guidance
- Art, Music, Woodworking & other Enrichment Classes
- Medical, Vision & Dental Clinics
- Adapted Physical Education

The **Intensive Services Program** (ISP) at Cotting School provides comprehensive educational, therapeutic, and rehabilitative services for children ages 3-8 with severe developmental delays, serious physical disabilities, limited communication, and various combinations of sensory limitations and medical difficulties.

Cotting School
453 Concord Avenue
Lexington, MA 02421
(781) 862-7323
www.cotting.org

HOPE House

*Supporting young adults with physical and learning challenges
who strive for independence.*

HOPE House helps young adults acquire necessary independent living skills
in a supportive residential program. The custom built 3-story building includes
private individual suites, a double kitchen, two common living rooms, a recreation area, meeting rooms, and laundry facilities – all fully accessible. Each
client works towards the goals and objectives outlined in his or her Individual
Service Plan encompassing:

- Vocational Support
- Social Skills & Recreation
- Educational Support
- Budgeting and Banking
- Community Activities
- Transition Planning
- Human Rights Training
- Fire & Safety Training
- Cooking Program
- Transportation
- Diversity Awareness

HOPE House is committed to a sense of belonging, a sense of hope, and the
wisdom to plan the future.

HOPE House
451 Concord Avenue
Lexington, MA 02421
(781) 862-7323 x114
www.cottinghopehouse.org

THE CRAIG SCHOOL

10 Tower Hill Rd.
MOUNTAIN LAKES, NJ 07046
www.craigschool.org

David Blanchard, *Interim Headmaster*

The Craig School, located in Mountain Lakes (grades 1-8) and Lincoln Park (grades 9-12), is a coed, day school enrolling 150 students. The School is committed to meeting the educational needs of youngsters of average to above-average ability whose progress has been impeded by dyslexia and related language-based learning disorders. In a structured environment, certified specialist teachers and professionals provide individualized instruction in classes of eight children or fewer.

The majority of students at Craig struggle with decoding, reading comprehension and/or written expression. These issues are addressed with individual or small group instruction coordinated with classroom teaching and based on multisensory, Orton Gillingham methods. The program focuses on developing solid written language skills, improved content acquisition and retention. High school courses are consistent with the standards established by the State of New Jersey. Assistive technology, note-taking and test-taking strategies, and organizational methods are key components of a curriculum orchestrated to prepare the student to become a successful, independent learner.

At all grade levels the social, behavioral and self-advocacy skills that are vital to success in the extended community are addressed through small coaching groups, classroom exercises and a behavior management system designed to build self-esteem. personal integrity, and a concern for others.

A rich blend of activities supplements the academic curriculum including yoga, music classes, improvisational theatre, holiday parties, school trips, and supervised social outings. Middle School students compete with other schools in soccer, basketball and lacrosse and all students may participate in intramural sports. Craig School is accredited by Middle States Association of Schools and Colleges and is a member of the New Jersey Association of Independent Schools.

For admission information, call: 973 334-1295.

HELPING SPECIAL PEOPLE LIVE THEIR DREAMS
FOR OVER 90 YEARS

ARIZONA · CALIFORNIA · COLORADO · CONNECTICUT
FLORIDA · GEORGIA · MASSACHUSETTS · NEW JERSEY
NEW YORK · PENNSYLVANIA · TEXAS · THE DISTRICT OF COLUMBIA

Devereux is the nation's largest independent, nonprofit provider of treatment services for children, adolescents, and adults who have a wide range of emotional, behavioral, and developmental challenges and neurological impairments. Devereux's residential, day, and community-based programs are located in 12 states and the District of Columbia.

Devereux

800-345-1292 · www.devereux.org

EAGLE HILL SCHOOL
GREENWICH

45 Glenville Rd.
GREENWICH, CT 06831
Tel: 203-622-9240   Fax: 203-622-8668

Mark J. Griffin, PhD, *Headmaster*

Founded in 1975, Eagle Hill-Greenwich offers specialized instruction to bright children who, because of a learning disability, are unable to realize their full potential in traditional educational environments. Using a language immersion approach in an ungraded, non-competitive setting, students are provided with individualized and small group instruction. All teachers hold special education certification and receive ongoing supervision and in-service training.

Eagle Hill's main objective is to provide three to four years of intensive, remedial instruction and then to return the child to the educational mainstream. A transitional program is incorporated into the plan to develop the academic skills, study strategies, self-advocacy and risk taking necessary to function independently in a traditional school

setting. Students are placed in a range of prep schools, local independent schools and public programs across the country. Eagle Hill offers a wide variety of activities in addition to the extensive academic programs. The addition of a professional library, a 10,000-volume children's library, and new technology in the computer department enhance the academic program, providing students with a state-of-the-art facility in which to develop their study skills and writing proficiency.

Electives include art, music, drama, photography, computer programming, cooking, newspaper, film classes and community service programs. Full interscholastic and intra-mural sports programs include competition in soccer, cross country, field hockey, basketball, ice hockey, baseball, softball and tennis. Regular physical education classes, karate, jazz dance, aerobics and biking round out the physical activity options.

Eagle Hill-Greenwich is a coed day and five-day residential program for students ages six through sixteen. The residential population at Eagle Hill ranges in ages from 10-16. Most students live within a two hour commute of Greenwich, and go home on weekends. Six "super weekends" are offered for the boarders to develop a sense of community and include camping trips, ski weekends and cultural excursions. The living situation is a warm, family-like setting, with close faculty supervision, guidance and interaction.

Eagle Hill houses a Lower School, ages 6-11, and an Upper School, ages 11½-16. An active Advisor system ensures communication among staff and between school and home, and provides an advocate for the child within the program throughout the child's matriculation. Eagle Hill also runs a separate six week summer school. For information regarding Eagle Hill-Greenwich, please contact Rayma-Joan Griffin, Director of Admissions.

THE DUVALL HOME

3395 Grand Ave., P.O. Box 220036
GLENWOOD, FL 32722
Tel: 386-734-2874; 888-445-4722

Established in 1945, The Duvall Home is a private not-for-profit residential facility that serves developmentally disabled children and adults. There is no age limit and no discrimination as to race, nationality or religion.

The main facility is located in Glenwood, Florida on a lovely 25-acre campus, and it provides a caring and home-like atmosphere. Participation in swimming, crafts, dances, community activities, boy scouts, Special Olympics, Best Buddies and recreation is provided. In addition, nine lovely group homes are located throughout the community offering a smaller family setting, 24-hour supervision and community inclusion. All of the supports of the main facility are available to these group homes as needed.

Twenty-four hour nursing care is provided and physical therapy is available as needed. For further information, contact admissions at the above telephone number or visit our web site at www.duvallhome.org.

EAGLE HILL-SOUTHPORT
214 Main St.
SOUTHPORT, CT 06490
Tel: 203-254-2044   Fax: 203-255-4052
Web: www.eaglehillsouthport.org
E-mail: info@eaglehillsouthport.org

Eagle Hill-Southport is a non-profit school for children with learning disabilities. Serving boys and girls ages 6 to 16 in a supportive, structured, success-oriented program, the 3:1 student/staff ratio allows for individualized instruction to address the learning style and level of each child. The school is transitional and non-graded, designed to reinforce students' skills through tutorials and small group classes that prepare them for return to more traditional placements.

Personalized Interdisciplinary Programs

HMS School for Children with Cerebral Palsy serves children, ages 2 - 21, with multiple disabilities resulting from cerebral palsy or traumatic brain injury. Experienced, compassionate staff and consultants provide strong, comprehensive interdisciplinary programs that include:

Day and Residential Programs
Physical & Occupational Therapies
Special Education
Speech/Language Therapy
Music Therapy
Augmentative Communication Aids
Nursing and Nutrition Services
Medical Support
Therapeutic Recreation
Computer Technology
Environmental Control
Powered Mobility

For more information contact:
Diane L. Gallagher, Ph.D., Director

HMS School
For Children With Cerebral Palsy

4400 Baltimore Ave., Philadelphia, PA 19104
(215)222-2566 • Fax: (215)222-1889
Web Site: www.hmsschool.org
E-Mail: admin@hmsschool.org

FREDERIC L. CHAMBERLAIN SCHOOL

1 Pleasant St.
P.O. Box 778
MIDDLEBOROUGH, MA 02346
Tel: 508-947-7825   Fax: 508-947-0944
E-mail: admissions@chamberlainschool.org

   F. L. Chamberlain School is a private, nonprofit, coeducational residential school for moderately to severely emotionally disturbed adolescents, ages 11-18. Many students have emotional and/or behavioral problems with overlapping learning and communication disorders. Chamberlain was founded in 1976 and has always based its treatment upon interdisciplinary service goals.

   Chamberlain School's philosophy is based upon the belief that all children are capable of achieving success in vital areas of their lives no matter how adverse or traumatic their lives may have been thus far. A strong principle of the School is to protect, engage, and teach children and their families to develop the skills and confidence to manage their own lives to their highest potential.

   The therapeutic treatment goal is to focus upon, contain, and modify maladaptive behavior; promote development of greater competence; and build a stronger and more valued sense of self for academically and emotionally troubled students.

   The therapeutic treatment model is reality-based and geared toward transitioning the stu dent back into a strengthened family unit. The strategies utilized include the provision of intensive clinical intervention and treatment, small-group remedial education, a highly structured residential setting, and a therapeutic management system with positive growth and achievement-oriented, nonpunitive consequences and rewards.

A strong community network of services and family involvement throughout the course of treatment underscores the program's commitment to the best possible outcomes.

Located on a beautiful 11-acre campus between Cape Cod and Boston, F. L. Chamberlain School serves students from a wide geographic area. The School is licensed by the Massachusetts Office for Children and approved by the Massachusetts Department of Education.

F. L. Chamberlain School, a diploma-granting institution, offers an education program designed to meet the specific academic needs of each student. The comprehensive curriculum enables students to benefit from a wide variety of learning experiences in order to build classroom skills and promote social growth. A low student-teacher ratio enables students to receive the individualized attention they require in order to be successful.

The School provides a comprehensive and exciting curriculum tailored to each student's needs. Individual and small-group instruction focuses on traditional subjects required for a high school diploma. Extensive and varied electives include computer lab, drama, TV production, photography, and music. Students may prepare for college placement or take advanced courses in coordination with the local high school. Credit requirements for graduation are determined according to individual academic goals, but each student must achieve standard criteria prior to receiving a high school diploma.

Certified special education teachers assist the students in selecting colleges, filling out applications, and arranging to take the SAT. Teachers take students to area colleges to visit the campuses and interview, if desired.

Extracurricular opportunities include a vocational component that encompasses an apprenticeship program as well as work-study. Students are assessed for job readiness and may then participate in either program according to their career planning goals.

Additional extracurricular activities include both planned activities and free-time activities. Extracurricular and recreational activities are scheduled and supervised by the School day staff and residential staff. Activities may be structured, such as bowling, horseback riding, swimming, and team sports, or they may be supervised free-time activities. Students are allowed to listen to music, read, talk with peers, write letters, or pursue individual interests during supervised free time.

Students participate in a structured daily program that includes sharing in meal preparation and basic living chores. Students are responsible for keeping their rooms and general living areas orderly and clean. The school day runs from 8 a.m. to 3 p.m.

The after-school program includes recreational activities and other commitments for reaching individual goals. After dinner, the students complete homework assignments and then may participate in scheduled evening activities and meetings. Bedtime is variable according to the student's level.

The School is a member of the National Association of Private Schools for Exceptional Children. Chamberlain School is under the direction of the board of the directors of the nonprofit corporation.

Daring to Dream with Elwyn. . .

"When Alice was small, I dreamed of a wonderful school - a special place where she could get the care she needed. It was a safe place with a pool and a great playground and lots of other kids to play with. The teachers knew me personally, and were happy to see me whenever I visited. They saw my daughter's special gifts and defined Alice by her potential, not her limitations. We all shared our hopes that we could develop her talent together - and we did. I saw her on a stage as the princess in the school play, all she could do was smile, but boy, could she smile. Now my daughter's world is safe, her opportunities to learn unlimited by labels."

"When Carla got her first job, my wife and I thought she had everything we could hope for. Then she surprised us and said, Dad, I want a place of my own. After seeing her attain her dream of a job, we suddenly had a new dream to share with her - that our daughter could have an apartment with her friend, Jennifer. We knew it would require help and support, but we also knew where that would come from.

Carla and Jennifer got their apartment. They shopped together, went out to movies, had us over for dinner. Carla made a big bowl of macaroni salad and brought it to the family picnic. She's on her own, but she isn't alone. Someone came to her apartment to help her balance her checkbook, save for a new coat and pay her bills. There will always be someone to look out for her, even after we're gone. And that is a real comfort."

At the different times in the lives of our children, dreams change. At Elwyn we share these changing dreams throughout the lives of those who need us. When we dream together, the dream can become a reality.

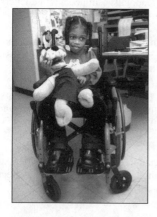

Contact: The Admissions Office
111 Elwyn Road
Elwyn, PA 19063-4699
Phone (610) 891-2000 (800) 345-8111

elwyn

We build lives.

Harmony Hill School, Incorporated

63 Harmony Hill Road ▪ Chepachet, Rhode Island 02814 ▪ (401) 949-0690

Specialized services for behaviorally disordered and learning disabled boys, age eight through eighteen, who cannot be treated within their local educational system or community based mental health programs.

- *Assessment of individual psycho-educational needs*
- *Elementary and secondary level academics with health, physical education, art and technology education*
- *Individual, group and family therapy*
- *Adventure Based therapy*
- *24-hour crisis intervention*
- *Life Skills and Behavioral program to strengthen academic and social behaviors*

Available Programming: Residential Treatment, Sex Offender Treatment, Community Group Homes, Extended Day Program, Work Experience, Diagnostic Day, Transition Programming, Summer Camp, Career Education

We strive to return productive citizens to their communities through effective and innovative treatment.

For more information,
contact President & CEO Terrence J. Leary
(401) 949-0690 ▪ Fax (401) 949-2060
*Or visit our website at **www.harmonyhillschool.org***

lessons of a lifetime

The lessons of a lifetime are taught at Heartspring School with patience, kindness and love to the wonderful and very challenging children we serve.

Heartspring serves children ages 5 -21 with deficits in cognitive, behavioral, communication, physical and emotional skills.

These proven techniques let our children gain confidence in the classroom, independence in the community and peace within themselves. Lessons learned at Heartspring move our students towards lesser restrictive environments.

For information about the lessons of a lifetime, contact Heartspring admissions at (800) 835-1043.

HEARTSPRING

8700 East 29th Street North • Wichita, Kansas 67226
(800) 835-1043 • (316) 634-8700
www.heartspring.org

THE JEVNE OUTDOOR ACADEMY, INC.

c/o St. Christopher Academy
140 S. 140th St.
SEATTLE, WA 98168-3496
Business Office: 206-246-9751
Fax: 253-639-3466
www.jevneranch.com
www.stchristopheracademy.com

Darlene Jevne, *Director*

Summer Adventure at The Jevne Ranch is a program that combines summer school with adventure designed to meet the needs of children age 13-18. It is ideally suited for students with time-management issues, learning differences, ADD/ADHD, special needs or students who learn better by seeing, touching, and/or doing. The Jevne Ranch is located on 400 acres; 30 minutes southeast of Sun Valley, ID, nestled in a land of natural awe-inspiring beauty.

The Jevne Ranch is a working ranch. Everyone gains self-confidence, communication and living skills through hands-on experience. The program is designed to combine creativity, problem solving and sequential thinking by working in small groups, which helps encourage students to develop interpersonal communication skills. For example, a math lesson might entail calculating the number of bales of hay required to feed the cattle; a geometry lesson might challenge a student to set up an irrigation system that reaches every square foot of an entire field.

The Jevne Ranch has a full service furnished bunkhouse, traditional Indian Tee-Pees, hiking, backpacking, water safety, and river rafting to name a few. The individual attention is one of the reasons we attract many teenagers who have never had camping or ranch experience and the ones who love the outdoors.

The Jevne Outdoor Academy, Inc. is an extension of St. Christopher Academy.

Girls' Residence,
Diana Hanbury King-
Founder's House,
Dedicated October 1995

THE KILDONAN SCHOOL

425 Morse Hill Rd.
AMENIA, NY 12501
Tel: 845-373-8111

Ronald A. Wilson, *Headmaster*

Founded in 1969 Kildonan is a well established coeducational boarding and day school for students with learning differences arising from dyslexia. The school offers students grades two through twelve and postgraduate a structured program of one-on-one multisensory Orton-Gillingham tutoring, academic courses, computer literacy, arts, athletics and extracurricular opportunities. Students are accountable for independent work in supervised study halls six days each week. The 450-acre campus, 90 miles north of New York City, provides a relaxed atmosphere. Specific programs such as the all school weekly ski day during the winter term also complement the structured academic schedule.

Language development is the keystone that defines our academic program. Dyslexia is not only a reading or writing difficulty. All language skills are involved to varying degrees: listening, speaking, silent reading comprehension, oral reading, vocabulary, spelling, word retrieval, and expository writing. Often, attention deficits also need to be addressed. The tutorial program approaches language remediation in two stages. First, skills are taught in isolation and tailored to meet the needs of each student. Second, language skills are then integrated in subject matter courses with the ultimate goal of independent learning and confidence in self-expression.

At the high school level, the courses include traditional college preparatory courses in math, science, literature, history, and the arts. Teaching methods are aimed at developing a logical organization of information, critical thinking, and systematic problem solving. Using the principles of careful sequential, multisensory teaching the faculty work closely with the students. The class size ranges from five to twelve students, allowing and encouraging every student to become an active participant in learning. For every course offering there are two levels of study; students are placed in accordance with their reading and writing achievement. Students may enroll at any point during their four years of high school.

The junior high program is designed to prepare students for our high school or another college preparatory high school. Students are introduced to all traditional subject matter and learning strategies—listening comprehension, beginning notetaking, outlining, test taking, and paragraph writing. These strategies and techniques are largely taught and practiced in the classroom. Subject matter assignments are limited to one night each week; tutoring assignments are given five nights each week.

The elementary day program is for students in grades two through six. Their daily schedule includes one-on-one language training, mathematics, science, social studies, computer skills, horseback riding, the arts, music, sports, and one hour of supervised study.

DUNNABECK AT KILDONAN, established in 1955 by Diana Hanbury King, is the oldest summer program in the United States meeting the needs of the dyslexic student ages eight through sixteen. The six-week coed boarding and day program is also designed to help students who are struggling with school work because of specific difficulties with reading, writing, spelling, or math computation, but who do not wish to complete or require a full school year program. All tutoring is one-on-one using the same Orton-Gillingham principles. Students meet daily with their tutors for one hour and complete assignments in supervised study halls. The length of study varies according to the age of the student. Instruction in computer literacy is also included in a student's academic schedule.

The academics are supplemented by daily recreational activity periods of swimming, the arts, and horseback riding. Waterskiing, sailing, canoeing, and camping are integrated into the weekly schedule, and weekends are the times for special events and field trips.

The goal of the program is to bring students closer to grade level functioning in all subjects through an intense focus on the primary academic skills that are required for success at any level of schooling. Through their success at Dunnabeck, students restore their self-confidence and become more motivated and self-directed.

For further information please contact the Office of Admissions.

KEYSTONE COMMUNITY RESOURCES

*the pioneer in urban
residential programming for
persons with mental retardation*

For more information, contact:

KEYSTONE COMMUNITY RESOURCES
406 N. WASHINGTON AVE.
SCRANTON, PA 18503
570-207-5090

OR

KEYSTONE COMMUNITY RESIDENCE
154 FRONT ST.
SOUTH PLAINFIELD, NJ 07080
908-757-1080

- Residences Integrated in the Community
- Fully Licensed
- Well Trained Qualified Staff
- Home Like Atmosphere
- Recreation and Leisure Programs
- Diagnostic and Medical Services

- American Camping Association Accredited Camp
- Vocational-Occupational and Special Education Training
- Cultural Performing Arts Feature
- Cost Efficient Rate
- Prader-Willi Syndrome Programs

- Supported Employment

In the early 1960's, community residences for persons with mental retardation were unheard of. Keystone Community Resources pioneered community living for persons with mental retardation. Since then we've expanded our network of residences in the community to 42 Pennsylvania locations and 5 in New Jersey.

Based on this past experience, we are confident that we can continue to direct our efforts toward the goal of maximizing highest quality service for our residents.

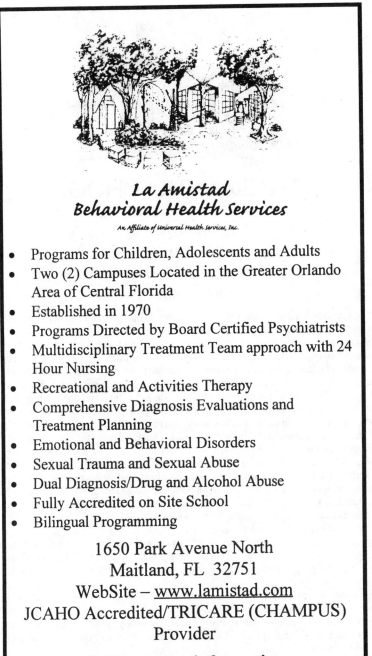

La Amistad
Behavioral Health Services
An Affiliate of Universal Health Services, Inc.

- Programs for Children, Adolescents and Adults
- Two (2) Campuses Located in the Greater Orlando Area of Central Florida
- Established in 1970
- Programs Directed by Board Certified Psychiatrists
- Multidisciplinary Treatment Team approach with 24 Hour Nursing
- Recreational and Activities Therapy
- Comprehensive Diagnosis Evaluations and Treatment Planning
- Emotional and Behavioral Disorders
- Sexual Trauma and Sexual Abuse
- Dual Diagnosis/Drug and Alcohol Abuse
- Fully Accredited on Site School
- Bilingual Programming

1650 Park Avenue North
Maitland, FL 32751
WebSite – www.lamistad.com
JCAHO Accredited/TRICARE (CHAMPUS) Provider

Call for more information
407-647-0660 Fax 407-647-3060

LANDMARK SCHOOL
PRIDES CROSSING, MA
Tel: 978-236-3000
E-mail: jtruslow@landmarkschool.org
Web: www.landmarkschool.org

Robert J. Broudo, MEd, *Headmaster*

The Landmark School, founded in 1971, offers day programs for students age 7-20, in grades 2-12, and boards students age 14-20. Landmark's programs are designed to help students who are of average to superior intelligence, and who have been diagnosed as having a language-based learning disability such as dyslexia.

Landmark offers an intensive ten month academic program as well as six week summer programs that teach to students' *individual* needs. The program core is a *daily,* one-to-one tutorial in all aspects of learning from basic reading, spelling, and handwriting skills, to high school and college preparatory composition and study skills. In addition, there are small group classes in math, social studies, science, and language arts. Electives in art, auto mechanics, computers, chorus, drama, early childhood education, health, music, peer leadership, percussion, photography, physical education, radio and television broadcasting, voice, and woodworking are also offered. A varied athletic program including soccer, basketball, lacrosse, skiing, wrestling, track and field, and tennis provides a supportive, productive, social environment and the opportunity for greater achievement and success. The Landmark Summer Program helps students master reading, writing, spelling, and composition skills in combination with summer activities such as seamanship, marine science, and an adventure ropes course.

The Landmark Preparatory Program offers a secondary school curriculum for students who need a specialized educational environment but do not need an *intensive* remedial program. The program emphasizes study and organizational skills development in a small class setting.

Situated on two beautiful campuses just 25 miles north of Boston, students make supervised trips into Boston to take advantage of its many cultural opportunities. The North Shore is especially rich in historical sights which Landmark students regularly explore, including fishing ports in Gloucester and Rockport and sailing centers in Salem and Marblehead.

Of Landmark graduates, over 85% go on to higher education, with 100% of the Preparatory Program going on to two and four year colleges.

THE LEDGES

P.O. Box 38
HOPEDALE, MA 01747-0038
Tel: 508-473-6520   Fax: 508-478-3054
Web: theledges.org

Vincent J. Arone, Ph.D., *Director*

THE LEDGES is a professionally staffed year-round facility for adults with disabilities. A high quality of life is afforded by a gracious and warm home environment most suitable for happy and fulfilled living.

Work experience is offered in our work activity program, or in supported or community employ. Other programs offered include functional academics, recreational programs, music, arts & crafts, home skills, and a variety of other ancillary programs.

Full residential services are provided and a Registered Nurse oversees the medical needs of all our members. Other services offered are speech therapy, individual and group psychotherapy.

THE LEDGES enrolls people 18 years of age and up. Special provisions accommodate those with physical handicaps or emotional problems. There is no upper age limit and life care is provided.

The aim of the total program is to help the individual approach his or her full capacity in a pleasant and enriched environment.

The facility is located in the town of Hopedale, Massachusetts, just 25 miles southwest of Boston on a 25-acre estate.

LINDEN HILL SCHOOL

"A Home Away From Home"

- Individualized, multi-sensory curriculum in a nurturing setting
- **ESL** Instruction
- Sports, art, music, drama, keyboarding, woodshop, projects, and theme-based trips
- **Co-ed Summer School/Camp Program**

Since 1961 serving the needs of boys ages 9-16 with language-based learning differences in a traditional boarding school with a family atmosphere.

James A. McDaniel, Headmaster
154 South Mountain Rd., Northfield, MA 01360
Contact Us: (866) 498-2906 (toll free)   Fax: (413) 498-2908
Visit us: www.lindenhs.org   Email: office.lindenhs.org

Our kids' faces say it all.

Park Century School...

...an independent day school, offering a comprehensive educational program for bright children, ages 7-14 years old, who have learning disabilities

...an exceptional and unique learning environment, devoted to all aspects of a child's world

2040 Stoner Ave., Los Angeles, CA 90025
Telephone 310-478-5065
parkcentur@aol.com

Genny Shain, M.A. and Gail Spindler, M.A. - Co-Directors

Where Family Matters

*For Over 75 Years, Providing Choices and Lifestyles for Persons
with Developmental Disabilities, in a Loving, Safe and Secure Community.*

Residential ⚮ Adult Day Care ⚮ Vocational Training
Schooling ⚮ Work Experiences ⚮ Physician/RN Care ⚮ Exercise, Fitness
Walking, Hiking, Bicycling ⚮ Dietary ⚮ Greenhouse
Reasonable Fee Structure

MARTHA LLOYD
COMMUNITY SERVICES

190 West Main Street, Troy, PA 16947
For more information, call Todd Boyles at 570.297.2185, ext. 268
www.marthalloyd.org

The Underachieving Adolescent

He (or she) hears repeatedly ... You're so bright. How come you're not doing better?

He's a competent reader, but fails English.

He has a poor self-image, so he either overstates or understates his achievements—academic, artistic, athletic or social.

Adults find him clever and charming, but in school he is restless, unable to concentrate, or sprawls in his chair, passively challenging the establishment with, "What's in it for me?" ...

... From the booklet, "In Support of Parents and Adolescents." For a free copy, write or phone B. H. Henrichsen, Headmaster of the Robert Louis Stevenson School.

A fully accredited, college preparatory, coeducational day secondary school where students and professional staff work in harmony. High academic standards in a low-pressure atmosphere. Expert counseling. Many students willingly commute long distances. Admissions throughout the year.

ROBERT LOUIS STEVENSON SCHOOL
74th Street, New York, NY 10023
(212) 787-6400   Fax (212) 873-1872
an equal opportunity, not-for-profit institution

A DIVISION OF

The Robert Louis Stevenson School,
long established as a secondary school for
gifted, underachieving boys and girls, offers

COLLEGE PREPARATION for ADOLESCENTS with SPECIFIC LEARNING DIFFICULTIES.

For information please call the Headmaster,
ROBERT LOUIS STEVENSON SCHOOL (Est. 1908)
24 West 74th Street, New York, NY 10023
(212) 787-6400 Fax (212) 873-1872

Your Partner for Complex Cases

In Austin, Texas, we can meet all your complex placement needs. At Texas NeuroRehab Center and The Oaks Treatment Center, we remain focused on providing the utmost in clinical excellence. We offer a unique blend of services to help children, adolescents, and adults reach their full potential.

Programs:

Neurobehavioral Program
Neuropsychiatric Program
Medical Rehabilitation
Developmentally Delayed Program
Intensive Residential Treatment
Residential Treatment
Sex Offender Treatment
Dual Diagnosis (Psychiatric/Substance Abuse)

Services:

Behavioral Management Services
Vocational Services
Comprehensive Evaluations
Community Re-Entry
On-Site Approved School
Individual, Group & Family Therapy
Physical, Occupational, & Speech Therapy

Call us at (866)791-5325
for more information about our services.

Texas NeuroRehab Center
1106 West Dittmar Road
Austin TX 78745
www.texasneurorehab.com

The Oaks Treatment Center
1407 West Stassney Lane
Austin TX 78745
www.theoakstc.com

Affiliates of Psychiatric Solutions, Inc.

RIVERBROOK RESIDENCE

4 Ice Glen Road - P.O. Box 478,
Stockbridge, Massachusetts 01262
Tel (413) 298-4926
Fax (413) 298-5166
Web: *www.riverbrook.org*
E-mail: *riverbro@berkshire.net*

A residential facility serving women with developmental disabilities since 1957. Opportunities for vocational, inter-personal, social and creative growth abound. Independent and shared living for women with developmental disabilities within a state of the art integrated community setting.

Guidance and support for developing complete community involvement, provided by professional, creative and dedicated staff.

Riverbrook is licensed by the Massachusetts Department of Mental Retardation

SUMMIT SCHOOL
339 N. Broadway
UPPER NYACK, NY 10960
Tel: 845-358-7772

Bruce Goldsmith, *Executive Director*

Summit serves children and adolescents of average or above average intelligence with serious emotional difficulties, often accompanied by moderate-to-severe learning disabilities. With intensive staff support, children are able to function and participate in group living, group activity programs and classrooms. The program incorporates a thera-peutic milieu, clinical intervention, academic remediation, and a total commitment to the student and his family. Summit's goal is to bring the child to maximum realization of his potential by remediating unsuccessful learning patterns, enriching funds of knowledge, and developing in coordination with personality gains, more productive patterns of study and achievement of skills and knowledge.

The center, occupying a nine-acre campus overlooking the Hudson River and only 18 miles from New York City, is situated in an exclusive residential estate area.

NTID, a college of Rochester Institute of Technology (RIT), is the world's first and largest technological college for students who are deaf or hard-of-hearing.

Get the best of both
RIT/NTID

NTID offers
- more than 30 technological and professional associate degree programs
- more than 200 bachelor's or master's degrees through RIT's seven other colleges

Student success is fostered by access to faculty and staff who use a variety of communication strategies. Qualified students also receive a wide array of support services including
- notetaking
- tutoring
- sign language interpreting
- C-Print® captioning
- on-site audiology and speech pathology

Historically, 92% of deaf and hard-of-hearing graduates who choose to enter the workforce gain employment in
- business
- industry
- government
- education
- other professional fields

National Technical Institute for the Deaf (NTID)
Vice President and Dean: T. Alan Hurwitz, Ed.D.
Public Information Contact: Karen E. Black, Director of Media Relations
Address: 52 Lomb Memorial Drive, Rochester, NY 14623-5604
Voice/TTY: (585) 475-6400
Fax: (585) 475-5623
E-mail: ntidmc@rit.edu

R·I·T ROCHESTER INSTITUTE OF TECHNOLOGY
National Technical Institute for the Deaf

www.rit.edu/NTID

THE RUGBY SCHOOL AT WOODFIELD
Primary, Middle and Secondary Schools

Donald J. DeSanto
Executive Director

PO Box 1403
Belmar Blvd & Woodfield Ave
Wall, New Jersey 07719
www.rugbyschool.org
Tel: (732) 681-6900

More than 27 years after The Rugby School at Woodfield opened its doors to children with special needs, it has become one of the most highly regarded schools of its kind, providing the best educational and treatment approaches to students grades 1 through 12. To help special education students maximize their potential Rugby provides a balanced, comprehensive program with years of experience.

Rugby offers a variety of remedial and academic programs including a one-to-one learning laboratory, behavior management, vocational testing, in-school simulated work experiences, vocational training in a college setting, cooperative industrial education, shepherding, driver's education, college prep, and fast start college credit for seniors.

Rugby affords a full range of professional therapeutic services including speech therapy, occupational therapy, counseling, nursing and medical services. Counseling services are provided by certified psychiatric social workers, clinical psychologists, and psychiatrists who utilize both individual and group counseling techniques along with specialized counseling (family, drug and alcohol, gender issues, anger management and art therapy). Medical services are provided by a nurse practitioner under the guidance of an on-staff medical doctor and psychiatrist.

Located in Wall Township only two miles from the Atlantic Ocean, Rugby is just 5 minutes west of Belmar in Monmouth County, centrally located near the Garden State Parkway, State Highways 33, 34 and 35 and Route 18.

A SPECIAL CHOICE
FOR SPECIAL PEOPLE

STEWART HOME SCHOOL offers progressive education, home community and a full lifestyle for the intellectually disabled child and adult.

- Opportunity for educational progress at any age—minimum age requirement, 6 yrs. No maximum. Academic program when readiness occurs. Individually planned programs daily for all students.

- Opportunity for physical and recreational activities including sports, horseback riding, music, art, ceramics, other crafts and drama.

- Opportunity for vocational training—sheltered workshop, community work, work on campus.

- Opportunity for maximum development of social and self-help skills.

STEWART HOME SCHOOL
ESTABLISHED 1893

Since 1893, STEWART HOME SCHOOL has provided year-round community life for the intellectually disabled child and adult. Eight-hundred-fifty acres serve as a campus for the educational, recreational, vocational and social experiences of the residents and staff. The program is as fine as any available at a substantially lower rate.

Personal interview required for enrollment.

Write for brochure—

STEWART HOME SCHOOL
4200 Lawrenceburg Rd.
Frankfort, KY 40601

John P. Stewart, M.D., *Resident Physician*
Phone: 502-227-4821

www.stewarthome.com

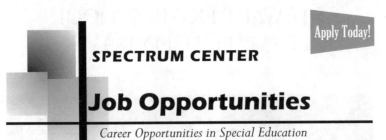

SPECTRUM CENTER

Job Opportunities

Career Opportunities in Special Education

**Check us out at
www.spectrumcenter.org**

SPECTRUM CENTER

2855 Telegraph Suite 312
Berkeley, CA 94705

Phone: 510-845-1321
Fax: 510-845-7841
Email: hr@spectrumcenter.org

Spectrum Center is a non-profit organization in the San Francisco Bay Area committed to providing the highest quality of educational services in the least restrictive environment for students who are "at risk" with challenging behaviors and special educational needs. Our services emphasize outcome based instruction and applied behavior analysis.

We provide an innovative work culture that offers education professionals competitive compensation, a positive, collaborative work environment, support for professional development and excellent opportunities for career advancement including: assistance with completion of credentials, tuition support for higher education, generous curriculum budget, ongoing professional development in curriculum and classroom management and high staff to student ratios.

APPLY TODAY FOR:

- Senior Clinician

- Education Coordinator

- Behavior Analyst

- Special Education Teacher

Contact Janet Medina, Recruitment Manager, for more information on how to apply.

THE VANGUARD SCHOOL OF COCONUT GROVE

3939 Main Hwy.
COCONUT GROVE, FL 33133
Tel: 305-445-7992   Fax: 305-441-9255
Web: www.vanguardschool.com

John R. Havrilla, *Director*

The Vanguard School of Coconut Grove is a non-profit, clinical school offering an individualized program for students with learning difficulties and/or attention deficits. Our primary goal is to return each student to a traditional program. We stress the development of homework skills, social and organizational skills as well as the ability to think, write and communicate.

The school has a full academic program, including reading, language art, math, science and social studies. Special attention is given to handwriting, physical education, computers, art and music.

Recognizing each student's worth, we seek to develop in each student the ability

- To work cooperatively
- To be willing to accept responsibility
- To be considerate of others
- To develop a positive self concept

The Vanguard School of Coconut Grove will provide an individualized program in a positive, nurturing, and structured environment that will enable students to develop academically, socially and personally "to be the best they can be."

The school is accredited by the Association of Independent Schools of Florida and the Dade Association of Academic Nonpublic Schools.

WOODS SERVICES

P.O. BOX 36
LANGHORNE, PA
Tel: 800-782-3646
Fax: 215-750-4591

Woods, a recognized leader in quality services for children and adults with developmental disabilities, is a private, not-for-profit residential facility. We offer a 12-month accredited school for clients under age 21. Adult clients are served by a variety of habilitative and vocational programs. On and off-campus work opportunities are provided for those capable of employment in a supportive environment.

Highly structured programs are offered for people with challenging behaviors including severe aggression and self-injury, Prader-Willi Syndrome, Rett Syndrome, Muscular Dystrophy, multi-handicapping conditions, traumatic brain injury, and other neurological disorders. Nearly half our clients have medical or physical disabilities requiring the use of wheelchairs and other specially adapted equipment.

Founded in 1913 as The Woods Schools, we are fully accredited and licensed and considered one of the best short and long-term care facilities in the mid-Atlantic region. Our 350 acre campus includes 25 client residences, three education and vocational centers, a summer camp, plus community living arrangements.

A staff of over 1400 includes full-time medical, psychological, educational, recreation and dietary personnel. Each client residence is fully staffed.

For complete information contact our Admissions Director at 1-800-782-3646 or Fax at (215) 750-4591. Our mailing address is Langhorne, PA 19047.

ASSOCIATIONS, ORGANIZATIONS AND AGENCIES

INDEX TO ASSOCIATIONS, ORGANIZATIONS
AND AGENCIES

ASSOCIATIONS, ORGANIZATIONS AND AGENCIES

This is a partial listing of organizations in the United States directly or indirectly concerned with the welfare of exceptional children.

ADVOCACY ORGANIZATIONS

ADVOCACY ORGANIZATIONS

GENERAL

ADVOCATES IN ACTION
PO Box 41528, Providence, RI 02940.
Tel: 401-785-2028. Fax: 401-785-2186.
E-mail: aina@aina-ri.org. Web: www.aina-ri.org.

ALLIANCE FOR TECHNOLOGY ACCESS
1304 Southpoint Blvd, Ste 240, Petaluma, CA 94954.
Tel: 707-778-3011. Fax: 707-765-2080.
E-mail: atainfo@ataccess.org. Web: www.ataccess.org.

AMERICAN COUNCIL ON RURAL SPECIAL EDUCATION
Utah State Univ, 2865 Old Main Hill, Logan, UT 84322.
Tel: 435-797 3728.
E-mail: acres@cc.usu.edu. Web: http://extension.usu.edu/acres.

**AMERICAN MEDICAL REHABILITATION PROVIDERS
ASSOCIATION (AMRPA)**
1710 N Street NW, Washington, DC 20036.
Tel: 202-223-1920. Fax: 202-223-1925.
E-mail: czollar@13x.com. Web: www.amrpa.org.

ASSOCIATION FOR CHILDHOOD EDUCATION INTERNATIONAL
17904 Georgia Ave, Ste 215, Olney, MD 20832.
Tel: 301-570-2111. Fax: 301-570-2212.
E-mail: aceihq@aol.com. Web: www.acei.org.

ASSOCIATION OF UNIVERSITY CENTERS ON DISABILITIES
1010 Wayne Ave, Ste 920, Silver Spring, MD 20910.
Tel: 301-588-8252. Fax: 301-588-2842.
Web: www.aucd.org.

CENTER ON HUMAN POLICY
Syracuse Univ, School of Education, 805 S Crouse Ave, Syracuse, NY 13244.
Tel: 315-443-3851. TTY: 315-443-4355. Fax: 315-443-4338.
E-mail: thechp@syr.edu. Web: http://thechp.syr.edu.

CONNECTICUT COALITION FOR INCLUSIVE EDUCATION
PO Box 331053, West Hartford, CT 06110.
Tel: 860-953-8335. Fax: 860-953-8343.
E-mail: arcct@aol.com. Web: www.includeme.org.

CONNECTICUT PARENT ADVOCACY CENTER
338 Main St, Niantic, CT 06357.
Tel: 860-739-3089. TTY: 860-739-3089.
E-mail: cpac@cpacinc.org. Web: www.cpacinc.org.

COUNCIL OF PARENT ATTORNEYS AND ADVOCATES
1321 Pennsylvania Ave SE, Washington, DC 20003.

Tel: 202-544-2210.
E-mail: copaa@copaa.net. Web: www.copaa.net.

CPB/WGBH NATIONAL CENTER FOR ACCESSIBLE MEDIA
125 Western Ave, Boston, MA 02134.
Tel: 617-300-3400. TTY: 617-300-2489. Fax: 617-300-1035.
E-mail: ncam@wgbh.org. Web: http://ncam.wgbh.org.

DISABILITY LAW CENTER
11 Beacon St, Ste 925, Boston, MA 02108.
Tel: 617-723-8455. TTY: 617-227-9464. Fax: 617-723-9125.
E-mail: mail@dlc-ma.org. Web: www.dlc-ma.org.

DISABILITY RIGHTS CENTER
PO Box 2007, Augusta, ME 04338.
Tel: 207-626-2774. Fax: 207-621-1419.
E-mail: advocate@drcme.org. Web: www.drcme.org.

DISABILITY RIGHTS EDUCATION AND DEFENSE FUND
2212 6th St, Berkeley, CA 94710.
Tel: 510-644-2555. Fax: 510-841-8645.
E-mail: dredf@dredf.org. Web: www.dredf.org.

EQUIP FOR EQUALITY
20 N Michigan Ave, Ste 300, Chicago, IL 60602.
Tel: 312-341-0022. Fax: 312-341-0295.
E-mail: contactus@equipforequality.org. Web: www.equipforequality.org.

FAMILY VOICES
2340 Alamo Ave SE, Ste 102, Albuquerque, NM 87106.
Tel: 505-872-4774. Fax: 505-872-4780.
E-mail: kidshealth@familyvoices.org. Web: www.familyvoices.org.

FEDERATION OF FAMILIES FOR CHILDREN'S MENTAL HEALTH
1101 King St, Ste 420, Alexandria, VA 22314.
Tel: 703-684-7710. Fax: 703-836-1040.
E-mail: ffcmh@ffcmh.com. Web: www.ffcmh.org.

FRIENDS OF SPECIAL SCHOOLS
234 Front St, Ste 300, San Francisco, CA 94111.
Fax: 415-982-3543.
Web: www.specialneedschildren.com.

GENETIC ALLIANCE
4301 Connecticut Ave NW, Ste 404, Washington, DC 20008.
Tel: 202-966-5557. Fax: 202-966-8553.
E-mail: information@geneticalliance.org. Web: www.geneticalliance.org.

GEORGIA ADVOCACY OFFICE
100 Crescent Centre Pky, Ste 520, Tucker, GA 30084.
Tel: 404-885-1234.
E-mail: info@thegao.org. Web: www.thegao.org.

THE INCLUSION NETWORK
312 Walnut St, Ste 1160, Cincinnati, OH 45202.

Tel: 513-345-1330. TTY: 513-345-1336. Fax: 513-345-1337.
E-mail: info@inclusion.org. Web: www.inclusion.org.

INSTITUTE FOR COMMUNITY INCLUSION
c/o Univ of Massachusetts-Boston, 100 Morrissey Blvd, Boston, MA 02125.
Tel: 617-287-7645. TTY: 617-287-7597. Fax: 617-287-7664.
Web: www.communityinclusion.org.

THE INSTITUTES FOR THE ACHIEVEMENT OF HUMAN POTENTIAL
8801 Stenton Ave, Wyndmoor, PA 19038.
Tel: 215-233-2050. Fax: 215-233-9312.
E-mail: institutes@iahp.org. Web: www.iahp.org.

IOWA PROTECTION AND ADVOCACY SERVICES
950 Office Park Rd, Ste 221, West Des Moines, IA 50265.
Tel: 515-278-2502. TTY: 515-278-0571. Fax: 515-278-0539.
E-mail: info@ipna.org. Web: www.ipna.org.

KANSAS ADVOCACY AND PROTECTION SERVICES
3745 SW Wanamaker Rd, Topeka, KS 66610.
Tel: 785-273-9661. Fax: 785-273-9414.
E-mail: info@ksadv.org. Web: www.ksadv.org.

KENTUCKY EDUCATION RIGHTS CENTER
106 N Main St, Versailles, KY 40383.
Tel: 859-879-0411. Fax: 859-879-0412.
E-mail: kerc@edrights.com. Web: www.edrights.com.

THE LEGAL CENTER
455 Sherman St, Ste 130, Denver, CO 80203.
Tel: 303-722-0300.
E-mail: tlcmail@thelegalcenter.org. Web: www.thelegalcenter.org.

MARYLAND DISABILITY LAW CENTER
The Walbert Bldg, 1800 N Charles St, 4th Fl, Baltimore, MD 21201.
Tel: 410-727-6352. TTY: 410-727-6387. Fax: 410-727-6389.
Web: www.mdlcbalto.org.

MASSACHUSETTS ASSOCIATION OF SPECIAL EDUCATION PARENT ADVISORY COUNCIL
PO Box 167, Sharon, MA 02067.
Tel: 617-962-4558.
E-mail: info@masspac.org. Web: www.masspac.org.

MOBILITY INTERNATIONAL USA
PO Box 10767, Eugene, OR 97440.
Tel: 541-343-1284. TTY: 541-343-1284. Fax: 541-343-6812.
E-mail: info@miusa.org. Web: www.miusa.org.

NATIONAL ASSOCIATION FOR THE DUALLY DIAGNOSED
132 Fair St, Kingston, NY 12401.
Tel: 845-331-4336. Fax: 845-331-4569.
E-mail: info@thenadd.org. Web: www.thenadd.org.

NATIONAL ASSOCIATION OF PRIVATE SPECIAL EDUCATION CENTERS
1522 K St NW, Ste 1032, Washington, DC 20005.
Tel: 202-408-3338. Fax: 202-408-3340.
E-mail: napsec@aol.com. Web: www.napsec.org.
See Also Display Announcement on Page 1106

NATIONAL CENTER FOR EDUCATION IN MATERNAL AND CHILD HEALTH
Georgetown Univ, Box 571272, Washington, DC 20057.
Tel: 202-784-9770. Fax: 202-784-9777.
E-mail: mchlibrary@ncemch.org. Web: www.ncemch.org.

NATIONAL CENTER FOR HEALTH EDUCATION
375 Hudson St, New York, NY 10014.
Tel: 212-463-4050. Fax: 212-463-4060.
E-mail: nche@nche.org. Web: www.nche.org.

NATIONAL CENTER FOR YOUTH LAW
405 14th St, 15th Fl, Oakland, CA 94612.
Tel: 510-835-8098. Fax: 510-835-8099.
E-mail: info@youthlaw.org. Web: www.youthlaw.org.

NATIONAL COALITION OF ALTERNATIVE COMMUNITY SCHOOLS
1289 Jewett St, Ann Arbor, MI 48104.
Tel: 734-668-9171.
E-mail: ncacs1@earthlink.net. Web: www.ncacs.org.

NATIONAL EDUCATION ASSOCIATION
1201 16th St NW, Washington, DC 20036.
Tel: 202-833-4000. Fax: 202-822-7974.
Web: www.nea.org.

NATIONAL LEAD INFORMATION CENTER
422 S Clinton Ave, Rochester, NY 14620.
Tel: 800-424-5323. Fax: 585-232-3111.
E-mail: hotline.lead@epa.gov. Web: www.epa.gov/lead/nlic.htm.

NATIONAL ORGANIZATION FOR RARE DISORDERS
55 Kenosia Ave, PO Box 1968, Danbury, CT 06813.
Tel: 203-744-0100. TTY: 203-797-9590. Fax: 203-798-2291.
E-mail: orphan@rarediseases.org. Web: www.rarediseases.org.

NATIONAL ORGANIZATION ON DISABILITY
910 16th St NW, Ste 600, Washington, DC 20006.
Tel: 202-293-5960. Fax: 202-293-7999.
E-mail: ability@nod.org. Web: www.nod.org.

NORTH AMERICAN RIDING FOR THE HANDICAPPED ASSOCIATION
PO Box 33150, Denver, CO 80233.
Tel: 303-452-1212. Fax: 303-252-4610.
Web: www.narha.org.

OREGON PARENTS UNITED
22980 Donna Ln, Bend, OR 97701.
Tel: 541-420-2870.
E-mail: opu@peak.org. Web: www.oregonparentsunited.org.

PARENT ADVOCACY COALITION FOR EDUCATIONAL RIGHTS
8161 Normandale Blvd, Minneapolis, MN 55437.
Tel: 952-838-9000. TTY: 952-838-0190. Fax: 952-838-0199.
E-mail: pacer@pacer.org. Web: www.pacer.org.

PEAK PARENT CENTER
611 N Weber St, Ste 200, Colorado Springs, CO 80903.
Tel: 719-531-9400. Fax: 719-531-9452.
E-mail: info@peakparent.org. Web: www.peakparent.org.

PENNSYLVANIA HEALTH LAW PROJECT
924 Cherry St, Ste 300, Philadelphia, PA 19107.
Tel: 215-625-3663. Fax: 215-625-3879.
Web: www.phlp.org.

SINERGIA
15 W 65th St, 6th Fl, New York, NY 10023.
Tel: 212-496-1300. Fax: 212-496-5608.
E-mail: intake@sinergiany.org. Web: www.sinergiany.org.

SOCIETY FOR ADOLESCENT MEDICINE
1916 Copper Oaks Cir, Blue Springs, MO 64015.
Tel: 816-224-8010. Fax: 816-224-8009.
Web: www.adolescenthealth.org.

SPECIAL NEEDS ADVOCATE FOR PARENTS
11835 W Olympic Blvd, Ste 465, Los Angeles, CA 90064.
Tel: 310-479-3755. Fax: 310-479-3089.
E-mail: info@snapinfo.org. Web: www.snapinfo.org.

TASH
29 W Susquehanna Ave, Ste 210, Baltimore, MD 21204.
Tel: 410-828-8274. Fax: 410-828-6706.
Web: www.tash.org.

TRI-STATE RESOURCE AND ADVOCACY CORPORATION
5708 Uptain Rd, Ste 350, Chattanooga, TN 37411.
Tel: 423-892-4774. TTY: 423-892-4774. Fax: 423-892-9866.
E-mail: 4trac@bellsouth.net. Web: www.4trac.org.

UNIVERSITY LEGAL SERVICES
220 I St, Ste 130, Washington, DC 20002.
Tel: 202-547-0198. TTY: 202-547-2657. Fax: 202-547-2622.
Web: www.dcpanda.org.

WASHINGTON PROTECTION AND ADVOCACY SYSTEM
315 5th Ave S, Ste 850, Seattle, WA 98104.
Tel: 206-324-1521. TTY: 206-957-0728. Fax: 206-957-0729.
E-mail: wpas@wpas-rights.org. Web: www.wpas-rights.org.

WISCONSIN COALITION FOR ADVOCACY
16 N Carroll St, Ste 400, Madison, WI 53703.
Tel: 608-267-0214.
Web: www.w-c-a.org.

WISCONSIN FAMILY TIES
16 N Carroll St, Ste 640, Madison, WI 53703.
Tel: 608-267-6888. Fax: 608-267-6801.
E-mail: info@wifamilyties.org. Web: www.wifamilyties.org.

AUTISM

FAMILIES FOR EARLY AUTISM TREATMENT
PO Box 255722, Sacramento, CA 95865.
Tel: 916-843-1536.
E-mail: feat@feat.org. Web: www.feat.org.

NATIONAL ALLIANCE FOR AUTISM RESEARCH
99 Wall St, Princeton, NJ 08540.
Tel: 888-777-6227. Fax: 609-430-9163.
E-mail: naar@naar.org. Web: www.naar.org.

BLINDNESS

AMERICAN COUNCIL OF THE BLIND
1155 15th St NW, Ste 1004, Washington, DC 20005.
Tel: 202-467-5081. Fax: 202-467-5085.
Web: www.acb.org.

AMERICAN FOUNDATION FOR THE BLIND
11 Penn Plz, Ste 300, New York, NY 10001.
Tel: 212-502-7600. Fax: 212-502-7777.
E-mail: afbinfo@afb.net. Web: www.afb.org.

ASSOCIATED SERVICES FOR THE BLIND
919 Walnut St, Philadelphia, PA 19107.
Tel: 215-627-0600. Fax: 215-922-0692.
Web: www.asb.org.

BLIND CHILDREN'S FUND
311 W Broadway, Ste 1, Mt Pleasant, MI 48858.
Tel: 989-799-9966. Fax: 989-799-0015.
E-mail: bcf@blindchildrensfund.org. Web: www.blindchildrensfund.org.

BRAILLE INSTITUTE
741 N Vermont Ave, Los Angeles, CA 90029.
Tel: 323-663-1111. Fax: 323-663-2332.
E-mail: info@brailleinstitute.org. Web: www.brailleinstitute.org.

CHRISTIAN RECORD SERVICES
4444 S 52nd St, Lincoln, NE 68516.
Tel: 402-488-0981. Fax: 402-488-7582.
E-mail: info@christianrecord.org. Web: www.christianrecord.org.

DB-LINK
National Information Clearinghouse on Children Who Are Deaf-Blind, 345 N Monmouth Ave, Monmouth, OR 97361.
Tel: 503-838-8776. Fax: 503-838-8150.
E-mail: dblink@tr.wou.edu. Web: www.dblink.org.

THE FOUNDATION FIGHTING BLINDNESS
11435 Cronhill Dr, Owings Mills, MD 21117.
Tel: 410-568-0150. TTY: 410-363-7139.
E-mail: info@blindness.org. Web: www.blindness.org.

FOUNDATION FOR THE JUNIOR BLIND
5300 Angeles Vista Blvd, Los Angeles, CA 90043.
Tel: 323-295-4555. Fax: 323-296-0424.
E-mail: info@fjb.org. Web: www.fjb.org.

GUIDE DOGS OF AMERICA
13445 Glenoaks Blvd, Sylmar, CA 91342.
Tel: 818-362-5834. Fax: 818-362-6870.
E-mail: mail@guidedogsofamerica.org. Web: www.guidedogsofamerica.org.

JBI INTERNATIONAL
110 E 30th St, New York, NY 10016.
Tel: 212-889-2525. Fax: 212-689-3692.
E-mail: ewertheim@jbilibrary.org. Web: www.jbilibrary.org.

LIGHTHOUSE INTERNATIONAL
111 E 59th St, New York, NY 10022.
Tel: 212-821-9200. TTY: 212-821-9713. Fax: 212-821-9707.
E-mail: info@lighthouse.org. Web: www.lighthouse.org.

NATIONAL ASSOCIATION FOR PARENTS OF CHILDREN WITH VISUAL IMPAIRMENTS
PO Box 317, Watertown, MA 02471.
Tel: 617-972-7441. Fax: 617-972-7444.
E-mail: napvi@perkins.org. Web: www.napvi.org.

NATIONAL ASSOCIATION FOR VISUALLY HANDICAPPED
22 W 21st St, 6th Fl, New York, NY 10010.
Tel: 212-889-3141. Fax: 212-727-2931.
E-mail: staff@navh.org. Web: www.navh.org.

NATIONAL BRAILLE PRESS
88 St Stephen St, Boston, MA 02115.
Tel: 617-266-6160. Fax: 617-437-0456.
E-mail: orders@nbp.org. Web: www.nbp.org.

NATIONAL FEDERATION OF THE BLIND
1800 Johnson St, Baltimore, MD 21230.
Tel: 410-659-9314. Fax: 410-685-5653.
Web: www.nfb.org.

NATIONAL INDUSTRIES FOR THE BLIND
1901 N Beauregard St, Ste 200, Alexandria, VA 22311.

Tel: 703-998-0770. Fax: 703-998-8268.
E-mail: info@nib.org. Web: www.nib.org.

NATIONAL SOCIETY TO PREVENT BLINDNESS
500 E Remington Rd, Schaumburg, IL 60173.
Tel: 847-843-2020. Fax: 847-843-8458.
E-mail: info@preventblindness.org. Web: www.preventblindness.org.

PREVENT BLINDNESS AMERICA
500 E Remington Rd, Schaumburg, IL 60173.
Tel: 847-843-2020. Fax: 847-843-8458.
E-mail: info@preventblindness.org. Web: www.preventblindness.org.

RECORDING FOR THE BLIND & DYSLEXIC
20 Roszel Rd, Princeton, NJ 08540.
Tel: 609-452-0606. Fax: 609-520-7990.
Web: www.rfbd.org.

DIABETES

AMERICAN DIABETES ASSOCIATION
1701 N Beauregard St, Alexandria, VA 22311.
Tel: 703-549-1500. Fax: 703-836-7439.
E-mail: askada@diabetes.org. Web: www.diabetes.org.

JUVENILE DIABETES RESEARCH FOUNDATION INTERNATIONAL
120 Wall St, New York, NY 10005.
Tel: 800-533-2873. Fax: 212-785-9595.
E-mail: info@jdrf.org. Web: www.jdrf.org.

EMOTIONAL DISTURBANCES

AMERICAN ACADEMY OF CHILD AND ADOLESCENT PSYCHIATRY
3615 Wisconsin Ave NW, Washington, DC 20016.
Tel: 202-966-7300. Fax: 202-966-2891.
E-mail: vanthony@aacap.org. Web: www.aacap.org.

AMERICAN ORTHOPSYCHIATRIC ASSOCIATION
2001 N Beauregard St, 12th Fl, Alexandria, VA 22311.
Tel: 703-797-2584. Fax: 703-684-5968.
E-mail: amerortho@aol.com. Web: www.amerortho.org.

AMERICAN PSYCHOLOGICAL ASSOCIATION
750 1st St NE, Washington, DC 20002.
Tel: 202-336-5500. TTY: 202-336-6123. Fax: 202-336-6069.
Web: www.apa.org.

AMERICAN SOCIETY FOR ADOLESCENT PSYCHIATRY
PO Box 570218, Dallas, TX 75357.
Tel: 972-686-6166. Fax: 972-613-5532.
E-mail: info@adolpsych.org. Web: www.adolpsych.org.

AUTISM RESEARCH INSTITUTE
4182 Adams Ave, San Diego, CA 92116.
Tel: 619-281-7165. Fax: 619-563-6840.
Web: www.autism.com/ari.

NATIONAL ALLIANCE FOR THE MENTALLY ILL
2107 Wilson Blvd, Ste 300, Arlington, VA 22201.
Tel: 703-524-7600. Fax: 703-524-9094.
Web: www.nami.org.

NATIONAL ASSOCIATION OF ANOREXIA NERVOSA AND ASSOCIATED DISORDERS
Box 7, Highland Park, IL 60035.
Tel: 847-831-3438. Fax: 847-433-4632.
E-mail: info@anad.org. Web: www.anad.org.

NATIONAL INSTITUTE OF MENTAL HEALTH
6001 Executive Blvd, Rm 8184, MSC 9663, Bethesda, MD 20892.
Tel: 301-443-4513. TTY: 301-443-8431. Fax: 301-443-4279.
E-mail: nimhinfo@nih.gov. Web: www.nimh.nih.gov.

NATIONAL MENTAL HEALTH ASSOCIATION
2001 N Beauregard St, Alexandria, VA 22311.
Tel: 703-684-7722. Fax: 703-684-5968.
E-mail: infoctr@nmha.org. Web: www.nmha.org.

THE NATION'S VOICE ON MENTAL ILLNESS
Colonial Pl 3, 2107 Wilson Blvd, Ste 300, Arlington, VA 22201.
Tel: 703-524-7600. TTY: 703-516-7227. Fax: 703-524-9094.
Web: www.nami.org.

PRADER-WILLI SYNDROME ASSOCIATION
5700 Midnight Pass Rd, Ste 6, Sarasota, FL 34242.
Tel: 941-312-0400. Fax: 941-312-0142.
E-mail: reception@pwsausa.org. Web: www.pwsausa.org.

HIV/AIDS

AIDS NETWORK
600 Williamson St, Madison, Wi 53703.
Tel: 608-252-6540. Fax: 608-252-6559.
E-mail: info@madisonaidsnetwork.org. Web: www.aidsnetwork.org.

LEARNING DISABILITIES

AMERICAN HYPERLEXIA ASSOCIATION
PO Box 335, Flossmoor, IL 60422.
Tel: 773-216-3333.
E-mail: info@hyperlexia.org. Web: www.hyperlexia.org.

ATTENTION DEFICIT DISORDER ASSOCIATION
PO Box 543, Pottstown, PA 19464.

Tel: 484-945-2101. Fax: 610-970-7520.
E-mail: mail@add.org. Web: www.add.org.

**CHILDREN AND ADULTS WITH ATTENTION-DEFICIT/
HYPERACTIVITY DISORDER**
8181 Professional Pl, Ste 150, Landover, MD 20785.
Tel: 301-306-7070. Fax: 301-306-7090.
Web: www.chadd.org.

COUNCIL FOR LEARNING DISABILITIES
PO Box 4014, Leesburg, VA 20177.
Tel: 571-258-1010. Fax: 571-258-1011.
Web: www.cldinternational.org.

LEARNING DISABILITIES ASSOCIATION OF AMERICA
4156 Library Rd, Pittsburgh, PA 15234.
Tel: 412-341-1515. Fax: 412-344-0224.
E-mail: info@ldaamerica.org. Web: www.ldaamerica.org.

NATIONAL CENTER FOR LEARNING DISABILITIES
381 Park Ave S, Ste 1401, New York, NY 10016.
Tel: 212-545-7510. Fax: 212-545-9665.
E-mail: help@ncld.org. Web: www.ncld.org.

**PEOPLE WITH ATTENTIONAL AND DEVELOPMENTAL
DISABILITIES ASSOCIATION**
813 Forrest Dr, Ste 3, Newport News, VA 23606.
Tel: 757-591-9119. Fax: 757-591-8990.
E-mail: amoore@padda.org. Web: www.padda.org.

MENTAL RETARDATION

ALABAMA COUNCIL FOR DEVELOPMENTAL DISABILITIES
RSA Union Bldg, 100 N Union St, PO Box 301410, Montgomery, AL 36130.
Tel: 334-242-3973. Fax: 334-242-0797.
E-mail: addpc@mh.state.al.us. Web: www.acdd.org.

THE ARC
1010 Wayne Ave, Ste 650, Silver Spring, MD 20910.
Tel: 301-565-3842. Fax: 301-565-5342.
E-mail: info@thearc.org. Web: www.thearc.org.

CENTER FOR MENTAL RETARDATION
Keith Bld, 1621 Euclid Ave, Ste 802, Cleveland, OH 44115.
Tel: 216-621-4505. Fax: 216-621-0221.
E-mail: cmr-clev@cmr-cleveland.org. Web: www.cmr-cleveland.org.

MILE HIGH DOWN SYNDROME ASSOCIATION
1899 Gaylord St, Denver, CO 80206.
Tel: 303-797-1699. Fax: 303-336-5669.
E-mail: lindab@mhdsa.org. Web: www.mhdsa.org.

NATIONAL ASSOCIATION FOR DOWN SYNDROME
PO Box 4542, Oak Brook, IL 60522.

Tel: 630-325-9112.
E-mail: info@nads.org. Web: www.nads.org.

NATIONAL ASSOCIATION OF STATE DIRECTORS OF DEVELOPMENTAL DISABILITIES SERVICES
113 Oronoco St, Alexandria, VA 22314.
Tel: 703-683-4202. Fax: 703-683-8773.
Web: www.nasddds.org.

NATIONAL DOWN SYNDROME CONGRESS
1370 Center Dr, Ste 102, Atlanta, GA 30338.
Tel: 770-604-9500. Fax: 770-604-9898.
E-mail: info@ndsccenter.org. Web: www.ndsccenter.org.

NATIONAL DOWN SYNDROME SOCIETY
666 Broadway, New York, NY 10012.
Tel: 212-460-9330. Fax: 212-979-2873.
E-mail: selliott@ndss.org. Web: www.ndss.org.

NATIONAL DOWN'S SYNDROME CONGRESS
666 Broadway, New York, NY 10012.
Tel: 212-460-9330. Fax: 212-979-2873.
E-mail: info@ndss.org. Web: www.ndss.org.

PARCA
1750 El Camino Real, Ste 105, Burlingame, CA 94010.
Tel: 650-312-0730. Fax: 650-312-0737.
E-mail: parca@parca.org. Web: www.parca.org.

SHARING DOWN SYNDROME ARIZONA
745 N Gilbert Rd, Ste 124, Gilbert, AZ 85234.
Tel: 480-926-6500.
E-mail: gina@sharingds.org. Web: www.sharingds.org.

ORTHOPEDIC AND NEUROLOGICAL DISORDERS

ALABAMA HEAD INJURY FOUNDATION
3100 Lorna Rd, Ste 226, Hoover, AL 35216.
Tel: 205-823-3818. Fax: 205-823-4544.
E-mail: info@ahif.org. Web: www.ahif.org.

AMERICAN HEART ASSOCIATION
7272 Greenville Ave, Dallas, TX 75231.
Tel: 800-242-8721.
Web: www.americanheart.org.

AMERICAN JUVENILE ARTHRITIS ORGANIZATION
Arthritis Foundation, 1330 W Peachtree St, Ste 100, Atlanta, GA 30309.
Tel: 404-965-7538.
E-mail: help@arthritis.org. Web: www.arthritis.org.

AMERICAN LUNG ASSOCIATION
61 Broadway, 6th Fl, New York, NY 10006.

Tel: 212-315-8700.
Web: www.lungusa.org.

AMPUTEE COALITION OF AMERICA
900 E Hill Ave, Ste 285, Knoxville, TN 37915.
Tel: 865-524-8772. Fax: 865-525-7917.
Web: www.amputee-coalition.org.

BIRTH DEFECT RESEARCH FOR CHILDREN
930 Woodcock Rd, Ste 225, Orlando, FL 32803.
Tel: 407-895-0802. Fax: 407-895-0824.
Web: www.birthdefects.org.

BRAIN INJURY ASSOCIATION
8201 Greensboro Dr, Ste 611, McLean, VA 22102.
Tel: 703-761-0750. Fax: 703-761-0755.
E-mail: familyhelpline@biausa.org. Web: www.biausa.org.

BRAIN INJURY ASSOCIATION OF AMERICA
8201 Greensboro Dr, Ste 611, McLean, VA 22102.
Tel: 703-761-0750. Fax: 703-761-0755.
Web: www.biausa.org.

CHILD AND ADOLESCENT BIPOLAR FOUNDATION
1187 Wilmette Ave, PO Box 331, Wilmette, IL 60091.
Tel: 847-256-8525. Fax: 847-920-9498.
Web: www.bpkids.org.

**COMMUNICATION INDEPENDENCE FOR THE
NEUROLOGICALLY IMPAIRED**
c/o Kornreich Technology Ctr, 201 I U Willets Rd, Albertson, NY 11507.
Tel: 516-465-1629. Fax: 516-465-3744.
E-mail: cini@cini.org. Web: www.cini.org.

EASTER SEALS
230 W Monroe St, Ste 1800, Chicago, IL 60606.
Tel: 312-726-6200. TTY: 312-726-4258. Fax: 312-726-1494.
Web: www.easter-seals.org.

EPILEPSY FOUNDATION OF AMERICA
4351 Garden City Dr, Landover, MD 20785.
Tel: 301-459-3700. Fax: 301-577-2684.
E-mail: jdeering@efa.org. Web: www.epilepsyfoundation.org.

LOWE SYNDROME ASSOCIATION
222 Lincoln St, West Lafayette, IN 47906.
Tel: 765-743-3634.
E-mail: info@lowesyndrome.org. Web: www.lowesyndrome.org.

THE MAGIC FOUNDATION
6645 W North Ave, Oak Park, IL 60302.
Tel: 708-383-0808. Fax: 708-383-0899.
E-mail: mary@magicfoundation.org. Web: www.magicfoundation.org.

MUSCULAR DYSTROPHY ASSOCIATION
3300 E Sunrise Dr, Tucson, AZ 85718.
Tel: 520-529-2000. Fax: 520-529-5300.
E-mail: mda@mdausa.org. Web: www.mdausa.org.

NATIONAL ATAXIA FOUNDATION
2600 Fernbrook Ln, Ste 119, Minneapolis, MN 55447.
Tel: 763-553-0020. Fax: 763-553-0167.
E-mail: naf@mail.ataxia.org. Web: www.ataxia.org.

NATIONAL HEMOPHILIA FOUNDATION
116 W 32nd St, 11th Fl, New York, NY 10001.
Tel: 212-328-3700. Fax: 212-328-3777.
E-mail: info@hemophilia.org. Web: www.hemophilia.org.

NATIONAL MULTIPLE SCLEROSIS SOCIETY
733 3rd Ave, New York, NY 10017.
Tel: 212-986-3240. Fax: 212-986-7981.
E-mail: info@nmss.org. Web: www.nmss.org.

NATIONAL NEUROFIBROMATOSIS FOUNDATION
95 Pine St, 16th Fl, New York, NY 10005.
Tel: 212-344-6633. Fax: 212-747-0004.
E-mail: nnff@nf.org. Web: www.nf.org.

NATIONAL ORGANIZATION ON FETAL ALCOHOL SYNDROME (NOFAS)
900 17th St NW, Washington, DC 20006.
Tel: 202-785-4585. Fax: 202-466-6456.
E-mail: information@nofas.org. Web: www.nofas.org.

NATIONAL SCOLIOSIS FOUNDATION
5 Cabot Pl, Stoughton, MA 02072.
Tel: 781-341-6333. Fax: 781-341-8333.
E-mail: nsf@scoliosis.org. Web: www.scoliosis.org.

NATIONAL SPINAL CORD INJURY ASSOCIATION
6701 Democracy Blvd, Ste 300-9, Bethesda, MD 20817.
Tel: 301-214-4006. Fax: 301-881-9817.
E-mail: info@spinalcord.org. Web: www.spinalcord.org.

NATIONAL TAY-SACHS AND ALLIED DISEASES ASSOCIATION
2001 Beacon St, Ste 204, Brighton, MA 02135.
Tel: 617-277-4463. Fax: 617-277-0134.
E-mail: info@ntsad.org. Web: www.ntsad.org.

OSTEOGENESIS IMPERFECTA FOUNDATION
804 W Diamond Ave, Ste 210, Gaithersburg, MD 20878.
Tel: 301-947-0083. Fax: 301-947-0456.
E-mail: bonelink@oif.org. Web: www.oif.org.

REHABILITATION INTERNATIONAL
25 E 21st St, New York, NY 10010.
Tel: 212-420-1500. Fax: 212-505-0871.
E-mail: rehabintl@rehab-international.org. Web: www.rehab-international.org.

SPINA BIFIDA ASSOCIATION OF AMERICA
4590 MacArthur Blvd NW, Ste 250, Washington, DC 20007.
Tel: 202-944-3285. Fax: 202-944-3295.
E-mail: sbaa@sbaa.org. Web: www.sbaa.org.

TOURETTE SYNDROME ASSOCIATION
42-40 Bell Blvd, Bayside, NY 11361.
Tel: 718-224-2999. Fax: 718-279-9596.
E-mail: ts@tsa-usa.org. Web: www.tsa-usa.org.

TUBEROUS SCLEROSIS ALLIANCE
801 Roeder Rd, Ste 750, Silver Spring, MD 20910.
Tel: 301-562-9890. Fax: 301-562-9870.
E-mail: info@tsalliance.org. Web: www.tsalliance.org.

UNITED CEREBRAL PALSY ASSOCIATIONS
1660 L St NW, Ste 700, Washington, DC 20036.
Tel: 202-776-0406. TTY: 202-973-7197. Fax: 202-776-0414.
Web: www.ucp.org.

WILLIAMS SYNDROME ASSOCIATION
PO Box 297, Clawson, MI 48017.
Tel: 248-541-3630. Fax: 248-541-3631.
E-mail: info@williams-syndrome.org. Web: www.williams-syndrome.org.

SPEECH AND HEARING DISORDERS

ALEXANDER GRAHAM BELL ASSOCIATION FOR THE DEAF
3417 Volta Pl NW, Washington, DC 20007.
Tel: 202-337-5220. TTY: 202-337-5221. Fax: 202-337-8314.
E-mail: info@agbell.org. Web: www.agbell.org.

AMERICAN CLEFT PALATE-CRANIOFACIAL ASSOCIATION/ CLEFT PALATE FOUNDATION
1504 E Franklin St, Ste 102, Chapel Hill, NC 27514.
Tel: 919-933-9044. Fax: 919-933-9604.
E-mail: info@cleftline.org. Web: www.cleftline.org.

AMERICAN HEARING RESEARCH FOUNDATION
8 S Michigan Ave, Ste 814, Chicago, IL 60603.
Tel: 312-726-9670. Fax: 312-726-9695.
E-mail: blederer@american-hearing.org. Web: www.american-hearing.org.

AMERICAN SOCIETY FOR DEAF CHILDREN
PO Box 3335, Gettysburg, PA 17325.
Tel: 717-334-7922. Fax: 717-334-8808.
E-mail: asdc1@aol.com. Web: www.deafchildren.org.

AMERICAN SPEECH-LANGUAGE-HEARING ASSOCIATION
10801 Rockville Pike, Rockville, MD 20852.
Tel: 301-897-5700. TTY: 301-897-5700. Fax: 301-571-0457.
Web: www.asha.org.

CONFERENCE OF EDUCATIONAL ADMINISTRATORS OF SCHOOLS AND PROGRAMS FOR THE DEAF
PO Box 1778, St Augustine, FL 32085.
Tel: 904-810-5200. Fax: 904-810-5525.
E-mail: nationaloffice@ceasd.org. Web: www.ceasd.org.

CONVENTION OF AMERICAN INSTRUCTORS OF THE DEAF
PO Box 377, Bedford, TX 76095.
Tel: 817-354-8414. TTY: 817-354-8414.
E-mail: caid@swbell.net. Web: www.caid.org.

DEAFNESS RESEARCH FOUNDATION
1050 17th St NW, Ste 701, Washington, DC 20036.
Tel: 800-829-5934.
Web: www.drf.org.

INTERNATIONAL ASSOCIATION OF LARYNGECTOMEES
PO Box 691060, Stockton, CA 95269.
Tel: 866-425-3678. Fax: 209-472-0516.
E-mail: ialhq@larynxlink.com. Web: www.larynxlink.com.

NATIONAL ASSOCIATION OF THE DEAF
814 Thayer Ave, Silver Spring, MD 20910.
Tel: 301-587-1788. TTY: 301-587-1789. Fax: 301-587-1791.
E-mail: nadinfo@nad.org. Web: www.nad.org.

NATIONAL FRATERNAL SOCIETY OF THE DEAF
1118 S 6th St, Springfield, IL 62703.
Tel: 217-789-7429. TTY: 217-789-7438. Fax: 217-789-7489.
E-mail: thefrat@nfsd.com. Web: www.nfsd.com.

NATIONAL INSTITUTE ON DEAFNESS AND OTHER COMMUNICATION DISORDERS
31 Center Dr, Bethesda, MD 20892.
Tel: 301-496-7243. TTY: 301-402-0252. Fax: 301-402-0018.
E-mail: nidcdinfo@nidcd.nih.gov. Web: www.nidcd.nih.gov.

SELF HELP FOR HARD OF HEARING PEOPLE
7910 Woodmont Ave, Ste 1200, Bethesda, MD 20814.
Tel: 301-657-2248. TTY: 301-657-2249. Fax: 301-913-9413.
E-mail: national@shhh.org. Web: www.shhh.org.

STUTTERING FOUNDATION OF AMERICA
3100 Walnut Grove Rd, Ste 603, PO Box 11749, Memphis, TN 38111.
Tel: 901-452-7343. Fax: 901-452-3931.
E-mail: info@stutteringhelp.org. Web: www.stutteringhelp.org.

TELECOMMUNICATIONS FOR THE DEAF
8630 Fenton St, Ste 604, Silver Spring, MD 20910.
Tel: 301-589-3786. TTY: 301-589-3006. Fax: 301-589-3797.
E-mail: info@tdi-online.org. Web: www.tdi-online.org.

PROFESSIONAL ASSOCIATIONS

AMERICAN ACADEMY FOR CEREBRAL PALSY AND DEVELOPMENTAL MEDICINE
6300 N River Rd, Ste 727, Rosemont, IL 60018.
Tel: 847-698-1635. Fax: 847-823-0536.
Web: www.aacpdm.org.

AMERICAN ACADEMY OF OPHTHALMOLOGY
PO Box 7424, San Francisco, CA 94120.
Tel: 415-561-8500. Fax: 415-561-8533.
Web: www.aao.org.

AMERICAN ACADEMY OF PEDIATRICS
141 NW Point Blvd, Elk Grove Village, IL 60007.
Tel: 847-434-4000. Fax: 847-434-8000.
E-mail: kidsdocs@aap.org. Web: www.aap.org.

AMERICAN ASSOCIATION OF CHILDREN'S RESIDENTIAL CENTERS
2020 Pennsylvania Ave NW, Ste 745, Washington, DC 20006.
Tel: 877-332-2272. Fax: 877-362-2272.
E-mail: info@aacrc-dc.org. Web: www.aacrc-dc.org.

AMERICAN COUNSELING ASSOCIATION
5999 Stevenson Ave, Alexandria, VA 22304.
Tel: 703-823-9800. TTY: 703-823-6862. Fax: 703-823-0252.
E-mail: aca@counseling.org. Web: www.counseling.org.

AMERICAN DANCE THERAPY ASSOCIATION
2000 Century Plz, Ste 108, Columbia, MD 21044.
Tel: 410-997-4040. Fax: 410-997-4048.
E-mail: info@adta.org. Web: www.adta.org.

AMERICAN EPILEPSY SOCIETY
342 N Main St, West Hartford, CT 06117.
Tel: 860-586-7505. Fax: 860-586-7550.
E-mail: info@aesnet.org. Web: www.aesnet.org.

AMERICAN OCCUPATIONAL THERAPY ASSOCIATION
4720 Montgomery Ln, PO Box 31220, Bethesda, MD 20824.
Tel: 301-652-2682. Fax: 301-652-7711.
Web: www.aota.org.

AMERICAN PUBLIC HUMAN SERVICES ASSOCIATION
810 1st St NE, Ste 500, Washington, DC 20002.
Tel: 202-682-0100. Fax: 202-289-6555.
E-mail: pubs@aphsa.org. Web: www.aphsa.org.

AMERICAN SCHOOL HEALTH ASSOCIATION
7263 State Rte 43, PO Box 708, Kent, OH 44240.
Tel: 330-678-1601. Fax: 330-678-4526.
E-mail: asha@ashaweb.org. Web: www.ashaweb.org.

ASSOCIATION FOR EDUCATION AND REHABILITATION OF THE BLIND AND VISUALLY IMPAIRED
1703 N Beauregard St, Ste 440, Alexandria, VA 22311.
Tel: 703-671-4500. Fax: 703-671-6391.
E-mail: aer@aerbvi.org. Web: www.aerbvi.org.

CLOSING THE GAP
526 Main St, PO Box 68, Henderson, MN 56044.
Tel: 507-248-3294. Fax: 507-248-3810.
E-mail: info@closingthegap.com. Web: www.closingthegap.com.

COUNCIL FOR EXCEPTIONAL CHILDREN
1110 N Glebe Rd, Ste 300, Reston, VA 22001.
Tel: 703-620-3660. Fax: 703-264-9494.
E-mail: service@cec.sped.org. Web: www.cec.sped.org.

COUNCIL OF ADMINISTRATORS OF SPECIAL EDUCATION
Fort Valley State Univ, 1005 State University Dr, Fort Valley, GA 31030.
Tel: 478-825-7667. Fax: 478-825-7811.
E-mail: lpurcell@bellsouth.net. Web: www.casecec.org.

HELEN KELLER WORLDWIDE
352 Park Ave S, 12th Fl, New York, NY 10010.
Tel: 212-532-0544. Fax: 212-532-6014.
E-mail: info@hki.org. Web: www.hki.org.

INTERNATIONAL DYSLEXIA ASSOCIATION
8600 LaSalle Rd, Ste 382, Baltimore, MD 21286.
Tel: 410-296-0232. Fax: 410-321-5069.
E-mail: info@interdys.org. Web: www.interdys.org.

KURZWEIL EDUCATIONAL SYSTEMS
14 Crosby Dr, Bedford, MA 01730.
Tel: 781-271-0048. Fax: 781-276-0650.
E-mail: info@kurzweiledu.com. Web: www.kurzweiledu.com.

NATIONAL ASSEMBLY OF HEALTH AND HUMAN SERVICE ORGANIZATIONS
1319 F St NW, Ste 402, Washington, DC 20004.
Tel: 202-347-2080. Fax: 202-393-4517.
Web: www.nassembly.org.

NATIONAL ASSOCIATION FOR CHILD DEVELOPMENT
549 25th St, PO Box 1639, Ogden, UT 84401.
Tel: 801-621-8606. Fax: 801-621-8389.
E-mail: info@nacd.org. Web: www.nacd.org.

NATIONAL ASSOCIATION OF DEVELOPMENTAL DISABILITIES COUNCILS
225 Reinekers Ln, Ste 650B, Alexandria, VA 22314.
Tel: 703-739-4400. Fax: 703-739-6030.
E-mail: nacdd@nacdd.org. Web: www.nacdd.org.

NATIONAL BRAILLE ASSOCIATION
3 Townline Cir, Rochester, NY 14623.

Tel: 585-427-8260. Fax: 585-427-0263.
E-mail: nbaoffice@nationalbraille.org. Web: www.nationalbraille.org.

REGISTRY OF INTERPRETERS FOR THE DEAF
333 Commerce St, Alexandria, VA 22314.
Tel: 703-838-0030. TTY: 703-838-0459. Fax: 703-838-0454.
Web: www.rid.org.

RECREATIONAL ORGANIZATIONS

AMERICAN ASSOCIATION OF ADAPTED SPORTS PROGRAMS
PO Box 538, Pine Lake, GA 30072.
Tel: 404-294-0070. Fax: 404-294-5758.
E-mail: adaptedsports@aaasp.org. Web: www.aaasp.org.

AMERICAN CAMPING ASSOCIATION
5000 State Rd 67 N, Martinsville, IN 46151.
Tel: 765-342-8456. Fax: 765-342-2065.
E-mail: psmith@acacamps.org. Web: www.acacamps.org.

AMERICAN MUSIC THERAPY ASSOCIATION
8455 Colesville Rd, Ste 1000, Silver Spring, MD 20910.
Tel: 301-589-3300. Fax: 301-589-5175.
E-mail: info@musictherapy.org. Web: www.musictherapy.org.

AMERICAN THERAPUTIC RECREATION ASSOCIATION
1414 Prince St, Ste 204, Alexandria, VA 22314.
Tel: 703-683-9420. Fax: 703-683-9431.
Web: www.atra-tr.org.

BOY SCOUTS OF AMERICA
1325 W Walnut Hill Ln, PO Box 152079, Irving, TX 75015.
Tel: 972-580-2000. Fax: 972-580-2502.
Web: www.scouting.org.

BOYS & GIRLS CLUBS OF AMERICA
1230 W Peachtree St NW, Atlanta, GA 30309.
Tel: 404-487-5700.
E-mail: info@bgca.org. Web: www.bgca.org.

GIRL SCOUTS OF THE USA
420 5th Ave, New York, NY 10018.
Tel: 212-852-8000. Fax: 212-852-6517.
E-mail: mevans@girlscouts.org. Web: www.girlscouts.org.

NATIONAL ARTS AND DISABILITY CENTER
Tarjan Center for Developmental Disabilities, 300 UCLA Medical Plz, Ste 3310, Los Angeles, CA 90095.
Tel: 310-794-1141. Fax: 310-794-1143.
Web: www.nadc.ucla.edu.

NATIONAL DISABILITY SPORTS ALLIANCE
25 W Independence Way, Kingston, RI 02881.
Tel: 401-792-7130. Fax: 401-792-7132.
E-mail: info@ndsaonline.org. Web: www.ndsaonline.org.

NATIONAL THERAPEUTIC RECREATION SOCIETY
National Recreation and Park Association, 22377 Belmont Ridge Rd
Arlington, VA 20148.
Tel: 703-858-0784. Fax: 703-858-0794.
E-mail: ntrsnrpa@nrpa.org. Web: www.nrpa.org.

SOCIETY FOR THE ADVANCEMENT OF TRAVEL FOR THE HANDICAPPED
347 5th Ave, Ste 610, New York, NY 10016.
Tel: 212-447-7284. Fax: 212-725-8253.
E-mail: info@sath.org. Web: www.sath.org.

SPECIAL OLYMPICS
1325 G St NW, Ste 500, Washington, DC 20005.
Tel: 202-628-3630. Fax: 202-824-0200.
Web: www.specialolympics.org.

SPECIAL RECREATION FOR DISABLED INTERNATIONAL
701 Oaknoll Dr, Iowa City, IA 52246.
Tel: 319-337-7578.
E-mail: john-nesbitt@uiowa.edu.

UNITED STATES ASSOCIATION FOR BLIND ATHLETES
33 N Institute St, Colorado Springs, CO 80903.
Tel: 719-630-0422. Fax: 719-630-0616.
E-mail: njomantas@usaba.org. Web: www.usaba.org.

USA DEAF SPORTS FEDERATION
102 N Krohn Pl, Sioux Falls, SD 57103.
Tel: 605-367-5760. Fax: 605-367-4979.
E-mail: homeoffice@usadsf.org. Web: www.usadsf.org.

VSA ARTS
1300 Connecticut Ave NW, Ste 700, Washington, DC 20036.
Tel: 202-628-2800. Fax: 202-737-0725.
E-mail: info@vsarts.org. Web: www.vsarts.org.

WHEELCHAIR SPORTS, USA
1668 320th Way, Earlham, IA 50072.
Tel: 515-833-2450. Fax: 515-833-2450.
E-mail: wsusa@aol.com. Web: www.wsusa.org.

REHABILITATIVE ORGANIZATIONS

AMERICAN ACADEMY OF PHYSICAL MEDICINE AND REHABILITATION
1 IBM Plz, Ste 2500, Chicago, IL 60611.
Tel: 312-464-9700. Fax: 312-464-0227.
E-mail: info@aapmr.org. Web: www.aapmr.org.

COMMISSION ON ACCREDITATION OF REHABILITATION FACILITIES
4891 E Grant Rd, Tucson, AZ 85712.
Tel: 520-325-1044. Fax: 520-318-1129.
Web: www.carf.org.

GUIDE DOG FOUNDATION FOR THE BLIND
371 E Jericho Tpke, Smithtown, NY 11787.
Tel: 631-265-2121. Fax: 631-361-5192.
E-mail: guidedog@guidedog.org. Web: www.guidedog.org.

GUIDING EYES FOR THE BLIND
611 Granite Springs Rd, Yorktown Heights, NY 10598.
Tel: 914-245-4024. Fax: 914-245-1609.
E-mail: info@guidingeyes.org. Web: www.guidingeyes.org.

LEADER DOGS FOR THE BLIND
PO Box 5000, Rochester, MI 48308.
Tel: 248-651-9011. TTY: 248-651-3713. Fax: 248-651-5812.
E-mail: leaderdog@leaderdog.org. Web: www.leaderdog.org.

NATIONAL AMPUTATION FOUNDATION
40 Church St, Malverne, NY 11565.
Tel: 516-887-3600. Fax: 516-887-3667.
E-mail: info@nationalamputation.org. Web: www.nationalamputation.org.

NATIONAL CLEARINGHOUSE OF REHABILITATION TRAINING MATERIALS
Oklahoma State Univ, 206 W 6th St, Stillwater, OK 74078.
Tel: 405-744-2000. Fax: 405-744-2001.
E-mail: seefelj@okstate.edu. Web: www.nchrtm.okstate.edu.

NATIONAL REHABILITATION INFORMATION CENTER
4200 Forbes Blvd, Ste 202, Lanham, MD 20706.
Tel: 301-459-5900. TTY: 301-459-5984. Fax: 301-459-4236.
E-mail: naricinfo@heitechservices.com. Web: www.naric.com.

WELFARE ORGANIZATIONS

CHILD WELFARE LEAGUE OF AMERICA
440 1st St NW, 3rd Fl, Washington, DC 20001.
Tel: 202-638-2952. Fax: 202-638-4004.
Web: www.cwla.org.

THE COORDINATING CENTER
8258 Veteran's Hwy, Ste 13, Millersville, MD 21108.
Tel: 410-987-1048. Fax: 410-987-1685.
E-mail: bmccord@coordinatingcenter.org.. Web: www.coordinatingcenter.org.

**MASSACHUSETTS CITIZENS FOR CHILDREN/
PREVENT CHILD ABUSE MASSACHUSETTS**
14 Beacon St, Ste 706, Boston, MA 02108.
Tel: 617-742-8555. Fax: 617-742-7808.
Web: www.masskids.org.

PREVENT CHILD ABUSE CALIFORNIA
4700 Roseville Rd, Ste 102, North Highlands, CA 95660.
Tel: 916-244-1923. Fax: 916-244-1950.
E-mail: ctroyano@capcsac.org. Web: www.pca-ca.org.

PREVENT CHILD ABUSE CONNECTICUT
Wheeler Clinic, Plainville Business Ctr, 74 East St, Plainville, CT 06062.
Tel: 860-793-3375. Fax: 860-793-3370.
E-mail: pcact@wheelerclinic.org. Web: www.wheelerclinic.org.

PREVENT CHILD ABUSE FLORIDA
111 N Gadsden St, Ste 200, Tallahassee, FL 32301.
Tel: 850-921-4494. Fax: 850-921-9070.
Web: www.ounce.org.

PREVENT CHILD ABUSE GEORGIA
1720 Peachtree St NW, Ste 600, Atlanta, GA 30309.
Tel: 404-870-6565. Fax: 404-870-6541.
E-mail: dougm@preventchildabusega.org.
Web: www.preventchildabusega.org.

PREVENT CHILD ABUSE ILLINOIS
528 S 5th St, Ste 211, Springfield, IL 62701.
Tel: 217-522-1129. Fax: 217-522-0655.
E-mail: rharley@preventchildabuseillinois.org.
Web: www.preventchildabuseillinois.org.

PREVENT CHILD ABUSE INDIANA
9130 E Otis Ave, Indianapolis, IN 46216.
Tel: 317-542-7002. Fax: 317-542-7003.
E-mail: generalinfo@pcain.org. Web: www.pcain.org.

PREVENT CHILD ABUSE IOWA
431 E Locust St, Ste 202, Des Moines, IA 50309.

Tel: 515-244-2200. Fax: 515-280-7835.
E-mail: pcaia@pcaiowa.org. Web: www.pcaiowa.org.

PREVENT CHILD ABUSE METRO WASHINGTON
PO Box 57194, Washington, DC 20037.
Tel: 202-223-0020. Fax: 202-296-4046.
E-mail: pcamw@juno.com. Web: www.pcamw.org.

PREVENT CHILD ABUSE MINNESOTA
1821 University Ave W, Ste 202S, St Paul, MN 55104.
Tel: 651-523-0099. Fax: 651-523-0380.
E-mail: pcamn@pcamn.org. Web: www.pcamn.org.

PREVENT CHILD ABUSE NEW HAMPSHIRE
NEW HAMPSHIRE CHILDREN'S TRUST FUND
91-93 N State St, Concord, NH 03301.
Tel: 603-224-1279.
E-mail: info@nhctf.org. Web: www.nhctf.org.

PREVENT CHILD ABUSE NORTH CAROLINA
3344 Hillsborough St, Ste 100D, Raleigh, NC 27607.
Tel: 919-829-8009. Fax: 919-832-0308.
E-mail: info@preventchildabusenc.org. Web: www.preventchildabusenc.org.

PREVENT CHILD ABUSE NORTH DAKOTA
418 E Rosser, Ste 110, PO Box 1213, Bismarck, ND 58502.
Tel: 701-223-9052. Fax: 701-355-4362.
Web: www.stopchildabusend.com.

PREVENT CHILD ABUSE SOUTH CAROLINA
1712 Hampton St, Columbia, SC 29201.
Tel: 803-733-5430. Fax: 803-744-4020.
E-mail: pcasc@pcasc.org. Web: www.pcasc.org.

PREVENT CHILD ABUSE TENNESSEE
1120 Glendale Ln, Nashville, TN 37204.
Tel: 615-383-0994. Fax: 615-383-6089.
E-mail: crsnodgrass@earthlink.net. Web: www.pcat.org.

PREVENT CHILD ABUSE TEXAS
12701 Research Blvd, Ste 303, Austin, TX 78759.
Tel: 512-250-8438. Fax: 512-250-8733.
E-mail: pcatx@preventchildabusetexas.org.
Web: www.preventchildabusetexas.org.

PREVENT CHILD ABUSE UTAH
2955 Harrison Blvd, Ste 104, Ogden, UT 84403.
Tel: 801-393-3366. Fax: 801-393-7019.
E-mail: aerickson@preventchildabuse.info.
Web: www.preventchildabuse.info.

PREVENT CHILD ABUSE VIRGINIA
4901 Fitzhugh Ave, Ste 200, Richmond, VA 23230.
Tel: 804-359-6166. Fax: 804-359-5065.
E-mail: mail@pcav.org. Web: www.preventchildabuseva.org.

PREVENT CHILD ABUSE WYOMING
1908 Thomas Ave, Cheyenne, WY 82001.
Tel: 307-637-8622. Fax: 307-635-7755.
E-mail: info@pcawyoming.org. Web: www.pcawyoming.org.

YMCA OF THE USA
101 N Wacker Dr, Chicago, IL 60606.
Tel: 312-977-0031. Fax: 312-977-4809.
Web: www.ymca.net.

YWCA USA
1015 18th St NW, Ste 1100, Washington, DC 20036.
Tel: 202-467-0801. Fax: 202-467-0802.
E-mail: info@ywca.org. Web: www.ywca.org.

FEDERAL AGENCIES

THE ACCESS BOARD
1331 F St NW, Ste 1000, Washington, DC 20004.
Tel: 202-272-0080. TTY: 202-272-0082. Fax: 202-272-0081.
E-mail: info@access-board.gov. Web: www.access-board.gov.

FEDERATION FOR CHILDREN WITH SPECIAL NEEDS
1135 Tremont St, Ste 420, Boston, MA 02120.
Tel: 617-236-7210. Fax: 617-572-2094.
E-mail: fcsninfo@fcsn.org. Web: www.fcsn.org.

HEATH RESOURCE CENTER—NATIONAL CLEARINGHOUSE ON POSTSECONDARY EDUCATION FOR INDIVIDUALS WITH DISABILITIES
American Council on Education, 1 Dupont Cir NW, Ste 800, Washington, DC 20036.
Tel: 202-939-9320. Fax: 202-833-4760.
E-mail: heath@ace.nche.edu.

NATIONAL COUNCIL ON DISABILITY
1331 F St NW, Ste 850, Washington, DC 20004.
Tel: 202-272-2004. TTY: 202-272-2074. Fax: 202-272-2022.
E-mail: mquigley@ncd.gov. Web: www.ncd.gov.

NATIONAL EYE INSTITUTE
2020 Vision Pl, Bethesda, MD 20892.
Tel: 301-496-5248. Fax: 301-402-1065.
E-mail: 2020@b31.nei.nih.gov. Web: www.nei.nih.gov.

NATIONAL DISSEMINATION CENTER FOR CHILDREN WITH DISABILITIES
PO Box 1492, Washington, DC 20013.
Tel: 202-884-8200. Fax: 202-884-8441.
E-mail: nichcy@aed.org. Web: www.nichcy.org.

NATIONAL LIBRARY SERVICE FOR THE BLIND AND PHYSICALLY HANDICAPPED
1291 Taylor St NW, Washington, DC 20542.
Tel: 202-707-5104. TTY: 202-707-0744. Fax: 202-707-0712.
E-mail: nls@loc.gov. Web: www.lcweb.loc.gov/nls.

STATE AGENCIES

ALABAMA

DEPARTMENT OF HUMAN RESOURCES
50 Ripley St, PO Box 304000, Montgomery, AL 36130.
Tel: 334-242-9500. Fax: 334-242-0939.
E-mail: ogapi@dhr.state.al.us. Web: www.dhr.state.al.us.

DEPARTMENT OF PUBLIC HEALTH
201 Monroe St, PO Box 303017, Montgomery, AL 36130.
Tel: 334-206-5200. Fax: 334-206-2008.
Web: www.adph.org.

ALASKA

DEPARTMENT OF HEALTH AND SOCIAL SERVICES
Office of Children's Services, 550 W 8th St, Ste 304, Anchorage, AK 99501.
Tel: 907-269-3900. Fax: 907-269-3901.
E-mail: ocs@health.state.ak.us. Web: www.hss.state.ak.us/ocs.

DEPARTMENT OF HEALTH AND SOCIAL SERVICES
350 Main St, PO Box 110601, Juneau, AK 99811.
Tel: 907-465-3030. TTY: 907-586-4265. Fax: 907-465-3068.
Web: www.hss.state.ak.us.

ARIZONA

DEPARTMENT OF HEALTH SERVICES
Office for Children with Special Health Care Needs, 150 N 18th Ave, Ste 330,
Phoenix, AZ 85007.
Tel: 602-542-1860. Fax: 602-542-2589.
Web: www.hs.state.az.us/phs/ocshcn.

ARKANSAS

DEPARTMENT OF HUMAN SERVICES
Donaghey Plaza W, PO Box 1437, Little Rock, AR 72203.
Tel: 501-682-8650.
Web: www.state.ar.us/dhs.

CALIFORNIA

DEPARTMENT OF DEVELOPMENTAL SERVICES
1600 9th St, PO Box 944202, Sacramento, CA 94244.
Tel: 916-654-1897. TTY: 916-654-2054. Fax: 916-654-2167.
Web: www.dds.ca.gov.

DEPARTMENT OF EDUCATION
1430 "N" St, Sacramento, CA 95814.
Tel: 916-319-0827.
Web: www.cde.ca.gov.

DEPARTMENT OF HEALTH SERVICES
Children's Medical Services Branch, PO Box 997413, Sacramento, CA 95899.
Tel: 916-327-1400. Fax: 916-327-1106.
Web: www.dhs.ca.gov/org/pcfh/cms.

DEPARTMENT OF SOCIAL SERVICES
744 P St, Sacramento, CA 95814.
Tel: 916-445-6951.
Web: www.dss.cahwnet.gov/cdssweb.

COLORADO

DEPARTMENT OF EDUCATION
201 E Colfax Ave, Denver, CO 80203.
Tel: 303-866-6600. Fax: 303-830-0793.
E-mail: harkness_l@cde.state.co.us. Web: www.cde.state.co.us.

DEPARTMENT OF PUBLIC HEALTH AND ENVIRONMENT
4300 Cherry Creek Dr S, Denver, CO 80246.
Tel: 303-692-2000. TTY: 303-691-7700.
E-mail: cdphe.information@state.co.us. Web: www.cdphe.state.co.us.

CONNECTICUT

DEPARTMENT OF CHILDREN AND FAMILIES
550 Hudson St, Hartford, CT 06105.
Tel: 860-550-6300. Fax: 860-566-7947.
Web: www.state.ct.us/dcf.

DEPARTMENT OF MENTAL RETARDATION
460 Capitol Ave, Hartford, CT 06106.
Tel: 860-418-6000. TTY: 860-418-6079. Fax: 860-418-6001.
E-mail: dmrct.co@po.state.ct.us. Web: www.dmr.state.ct.us.

DEPARTMENT OF PUBLIC HEALTH
410 Capitol Ave, PO Box 340308, Hartford, CT 06134.
Tel: 860-509-8000. TTY: 860-509-7191.
Web: www.dph.state.ct.us.

DELAWARE

DEPARTMENT OF EDUCATION
John G Townsend Bldg, PO Box 1402, Dover, DE 19903.
Tel: 302-739-4601. Fax: 302-739-4654.
E-mail: dedoe@doe.k12.de.us. Web: www.doe.state.de.us.

DEPARTMENT OF HEALTH AND SOCIAL SERVICES
Division of Developmental Disabilities Services, 1056 S Governor's Ave, Ste 101, Dover, DE 19904.
Tel: 302-744-9600. Fax: 302-744-9632.
E-mail: dhssinfo@state.de.us. Web: www.state.de.us/dhss/irm/dhss.htm.

HEALTH AND SOCIAL SERVICES
Division of Public Health, PO Box 637, Dover, DE 19903.
Tel: 302-741-2980. Fax: 302-741-2995.
Web: www.state.de.us/dhss.

DISTRICT OF COLUMBIA

DEPARTMENT OF HEALTH
825 N Capitol St NE, Washington, DC 20002.
Tel: 202-442-5999. Fax: 202-442-4788.
E-mail: doh@dc.gov. Web: www.dchealth.dc.gov.

FLORIDA

DEPARTMENT OF EDUCATION
Turlington Bldg, 325 W Gaines St, Tallahassee, FL 32399.
Tel: 850-245-0505. Fax: 850-245-9667.
E-mail: commissioner@fldoe.org. Web: www.fldoe.org.

DEPARTMENT OF HEALTH
Children's Medical Services, 4052 Bald Cypress Way, Bin A06, Tallahassee, FL 32399.
Tel: 850-245-4200. Fax: 850-488-3813.
E-mail: childrensmedicalservices@doh.state.fl.us.
Web: www.doh.state.fl.us/cms.

GEORGIA

DEPARTMENT OF EDUCATION
2054 Twin Towers E, Atlanta, GA 30334.
Tel: 404-656-2800. Fax: 404-651-6867.
E-mail: askdoe@doe.k12.ga.us. Web: www.gadoe.org.

DEPARTMENT OF HEALTH AND HUMAN RESOURCES
Division of Public Health, 2 Peachtree St NW, Atlanta, GA 30303.
Tel: 404-657-2700.
E-mail: gdphinfo@dhr.state.ga.us.
Web: www.ph.dhr.state.ga.us/programs/specialneeds.

HAWAII

DEPARTMENT OF HEALTH
1250 Punchbowl St, PO Box 3378, Honolulu, HI 96801.

Tel: 808-586-4400. Fax: 808-586-4444.
Web: http://mano.icsd.hawaii.gov/doh.

IDAHO

DEPARTMENT OF EDUCATION
650 W State St, PO Box 83720, Boise, ID 83720.
Tel: 208-332-6800. Fax: 208-334-4664.
Web: www.sde.state.id.us/dept.

DEPARTMENT OF HEALTH AND WELFARE
450 W State St, PO Box 83720, Boise, ID 83720.
Tel: 208-334-5500.
Web: www.healthandwelfare.idaho.gov.

ILLINOIS

DEPARTMENT OF HUMAN SERVICES
100 S Grand Ave E, Springfield, IL 62762.
Tel: 217-557-1601. TTY: 217-557-2134.
Web: www.dhs.state.il.us.

INDIANA

DEPARTMENT OF HEALTH
2 N Meridian St, Indianapolis, IN 46204.
Tel: 317-233-1325.
Web: www.in.gov/isdh.

DEPARTMENT OF HEALTH
2 N Meridian St, Indianapolis, IN 46204.
Tel: 317-233-1325.
Web: www.in.gov/isdh.

IOWA

DEPARTMENT FOR THE BLIND
524 4th St, Des Moines, IA 50309.
Tel: 515-281-1333. TTY: 515-281-1355. Fax: 515-281-1263.
Web: www.blind.state.ia.us.

KANSAS

DEPARTMENT OF EDUCATION
120 SE 10th Ave, Topeka, KS 66612.
Tel: 785-291-3097. TTY: 785-296-8583. Fax: 785-296-6715.
E-mail: ztorrey@ksde.org. Web: www.kansped.org.

DEPARTMENT OF HEALTH AND ENVIRONMENT
Special Health Services, 1000 SW Jackson St, Ste 220, Topeka, KS 66612.

Tel: 785-296-1313. Fax: 785-296-8616.
E-mail: jkendall@kdhe.state.ks.us. Web: www.kdhe.state.ks.us/shs.

DEPARTMENT OF HEALTH AND ENVIRONMENT
Services for Children with Special Health Care Needs, 1000 SW Jackson St, Ste 220, Topeka, KS 66612.
Tel: 785-291-3368. Fax: 785-296-6553.
E-mail: info@kdhe.state.ks.us. Web: www.kdhe.state.ks.us/shs.

KENTUCKY

DEPARTMENT OF EDUCATION
500 Mero St, Frankfort, KY 40601.
Tel: 502-564-4770. TTY: 502-564-4970. Fax: 502-564-6721.
Web: www.kde.state.ky.us.

LOUISIANA

DEPARTMENT OF HEALTH AND HOSPITALS
Children's Special Health Services, 325 Loyola Ave, Rm 607, New Orleans, LA 70112.
Tel: 504-568-5055. Fax: 504-568-7529.
E-mail: cshsweb@dhh.la.gov. Web: www.oph.dhh.state.la.us/childrensspecial.

DEPARTMENT OF SOCIAL SERVICES
PO Box 3776, Baton Rouge, LA 70821.
Tel: 225-342-0286. Fax: 225-342-8636.
E-mail: ann.williamson@dss.state.la.us. Web: www.dss.state.la.us.

MAINE

DEPARTMENT OF BEHAVIORAL AND DEVELOPMENTAL SERVICES
40 State House Station, Augusta, ME 04333.
Tel: 207-287-4200. TTY: 207-287-2000. Fax: 207-287-4268.
E-mail: mhmrsa@state.me.us. Web: www.state.me.us/bds.

DEPARTMENT OF HEALTH AND HUMAN SERVICES
Bureau of Child and Family Services, 221 State St, Station 11, Augusta, ME 04333.
Tel: 207-287-5060. TTY: 207-287-5048. Fax: 207-287-5282.
Web: www.state.me.us/dhs/bcfs.

MARYLAND

DEPARTMENT OF EDUCATION
200 W Baltimore St, Baltimore, MD 21201.
Tel: 410-767-0600.
Web: www.msde.state.md.us.

MASSACHUSETTS

COMMISSION FOR THE BLIND
48 Boylston St, Boston, MA 02116.
Tel: 617-727-5550. Fax: 617-626-7685.
Web: www.mass.gov/mcb.

DEPARTMENT OF MENTAL RETARDATION
500 Harrison Ave, Boston, MA 02118.
Tel: 617-727-5608. TTY: 617-624-7783. Fax: 617-624-7577.
E-mail: dmr.info@state.ma.us. Web: www.dmr.state.ma.us.

DEPARTMENT OF PUBLIC HEALTH
250 Washington St, Boston, MA 02108.
Tel: 617-624-6000. TTY: 617-624-6001.
Web: www.mass.gov/dph.

MICHIGAN

DEPARTMENT OF COMMUNITY HEALTH
320 S Walnut St, Lansing, MI 48913.
Tel: 517-241-2112. Fax: 517-241-3700.
Web: www.michigan.gov/mdch.

DEPARTMENT OF EDUCATION
PO Box 30008, Lansing, MI 48909.
Tel: 517-373-4213. Fax: 517-241-0197.

MINNESOTA

DEPARTMENT OF EDUCATION
1500 Hwy 36 W, Roseville, MN 55113.
Tel: 651-582-8200. Fax: 651-582-8202.
Web: www.education.state.mn.us.

DEPARTMENT OF HEALTH
Children with Special Health Needs, 85 E 7th Pl, PO Box 64882, St Paul, MN 55164.
Tel: 651-215-8956. Fax: 651-215-9988.
E-mail: mcshnweb@health.state.mn.us.
Web: www.health.state.mn.us/divs/fh/mcshn.

MISSISSIPPI

DEPARTMENT OF HEALTH
Children's Medical Program, PO Box 1700, Jackson, MS 39215.
Tel: 601-987-3965. Fax: 601-987-5560.
Web: www.msdh.state.ms.us.

DEPARTMENT OF MENTAL HEALTH
1101 Robert E Lee Bldg, 239 N Lamar St, Jackson, MS 39201.

Tel: 601-359-1288. TTY: 601-359-6230. Fax: 601-359-6295.
Web: www.dmh.state.ms.us.

MISSOURI

DEPARTMENT OF HEALTH AND SENIOR SERVICES
PO Box 570, Jefferson City, MO 65102.
Tel: 573-751-6400. Fax: 573-751-6041.
E-mail: info@dhss.mo.gov. Web: www.dhss.state.mo.us.

DEPARTMENT OF MENTAL HEALTH
PO Box 687, Jefferson City, MO 65101.
Tel: 573-751-4122. TTY: 573-526-1201. Fax: 573-751-8224.
E-mail: dmhmail@dmh.mo.gov. Web: www.dmh.missouri.gov.

MONTANA

DEPARTMENT OF PUBLIC HEALTH AND HUMAN SERVICES
Child and Family Services Division, 1400 Broadway, PO Box 8005, Helena, MT 59604.
Tel: 406-444-5900. Fax: 406-444-5956.
E-mail: cfsd@state.mt.us. Web: www.dphhs.state.mt.us.

NEBRASKA

COMMISSION FOR THE BLIND AND VISUALLY IMPAIRED
4600 Valley Rd, Ste 100, Lincoln, NE 68510.
Tel: 402-471-2891. Fax: 402-471-3009.

DEPARTMENT OF EDUCATION
Special Populations Office, PO Box 94987, Lincoln, NE 68509.
Tel: 402-471-2471. Fax: 402-471-5022.
Web: www.nde.state.ne.us.

DEPARTMENT OF HEALTH AND HUMAN SERVICES
PO Box 95044, Lincoln, NE 68509.
Tel: 402-471-2306.
Web: www.hhs.state.ne.us.

NEVADA

BUREAU OF FAMILY HEALTH SERVICES
3427 Goni Rd, Ste 108, Carson City, NV 89706.
Tel: 775-684-4285. Fax: 775-684-4245.
E-mail: jwright@nvhd.state.nv.us. Web: www.health2k.state.nv.us/bfhs.

DEPARTMENT OF EDUCATION
700 E 5th St, Carson City, NV 89701.
Tel: 775-687-9200. Fax: 775-687-9101.
Web: www.doe.nv.gov.

DEPARTMENT OF HUMAN RESOURCES
Kinkead Bldg, 505 E King St, Rm 600, Carson City, NV 89701.
Tel: 775-684-4000. Fax: 775-684-4010.
Web: www.hr.state.nv.us.

NEW HAMPSHIRE

DEPARTMENT OF HEALTH AND HUMAN SERVICES
105 Pleasant St, Concord, NH 03301.
Tel: 603-271-8140.
Web: www.dhhs.state.nh.us.

DEVELOPMENTAL DISABILITIES COUNCIL
The Concord Ctr, 10 Ferry St, Ste 315, Concord, NH 03301.
Tel: 603-271-3236. Fax: 603-271-1156.
Web: www.state.nh.us/nhddc.

NEW JERSEY

DEPARTMENT OF HEALTH AND SENIOR SERVICES
Services For Children With Special Health Care Needs, PO Box 364, Trenton, NJ 08625.
Tel: 609-777-7778. Fax: 609-292-9288.
Web: www.state.nj.us/health/fhs/scservic.htm.

NEW MEXICO

DEPARTMENT OF EDUCATION
Education Bldg, Santa Fe, NM 87501.
Tel: 505-827-6541. Fax: 505-827-6791.
Web: www.ped.state.nm.us/seo.

DEPARTMENT OF HEALTH
1190 S St Francis Dr, Santa Fe, NM 87502.
Tel: 505-827-2613. Fax: 505-827-2530.
Web: www.health.state.nm.us.

NEW YORK

OFFICE OF MENTAL HEALTH
44 Holland Ave, Albany, NY 12229.
Tel: 518-474-4403. Fax: 518-486-6749.
Web: www.omh.state.ny.us.

NORTH CAROLINA

DEPARTMENT OF HEALTH AND HUMAN SERVICES
Division of Public Health, 1330 St Mary's St, 1915 Mail Service Ctr, Raleigh, NC 27699.

Tel: 919-733-7081. Fax: 919-715-3104.
Web: www.dhhs.state.nc.us.

NORTH DAKOTA

DEPARTMENT OF HUMAN SERVICES
600 E Boulevard Ave, Dept 325, Bismarck, ND 58505.
Tel: 701-328-2310. TTY: 701-328-3480. Fax: 701-328-2359.
E-mail: dhseo@state.nd.us. Web: www.state.nd.us/humanservices.

OHIO

DEPARTMENT OF EDUCATION
25 S Front St, Columbus, OH 43215.
Tel: 614-995-1545. Fax: 614-644-3133.
E-mail: contact.center@ode.state.oh.us. Web: www.ode.state.oh.us.

DEPARTMENT OF HEALTH
246 N High St, PO Box 118, Columbus, OH 43216.
Tel: 614-466-3543.
Web: www.odh.state.oh.us.

DEPARTMENT OF MENTAL RETARDATION AND DEVELOPMENTAL DISABILITIES
1810 Sullivant Ave, Columbus, OH 43223.
Tel: 614-466-0129. Fax: 614-644-5013.
E-mail: ken.ritchey@dmr.state.oh.us/dmr. Web: www.odmrdd.state.oh.us.

REHABILITATION SERVICES COMMISSION
400 E Campus View Blvd, Columbus, OH 43235.
Tel: 614-438-1200. TTY: 614-438-1200. Fax: 614-438-1257.
Web: www.rsc.ohio.gov.

OKLAHOMA

DEPARTMENT OF EDUCATION
2500 N Lincoln Blvd, Ste 316, Oklahoma City, OK 73105.
Tel: 405-521-3301. Fax: 405-521-6205.
Web: www.sde.state.ok.us.

DEPARTMENT OF HUMAN SERVICES
PO Box 25352, Oklahoma City, OK 73125.
Tel: 405-521-3076. Fax: 405-521-4158.
E-mail: fssinquiries@okdhs.org. Web: www.okdhs.org/fssd.

DEPARTMENT OF MENTAL HEALTH AND SUBSTANCE ABUSE SERVICES
1200 NE 13th St, PO Box 53277, Oklahoma City, OK 73152.
Tel: 405-522-3908. Fax: 405-522-3650.
Web: www.odmhsas.org.

OREGON

COMMISSION FOR THE BLIND
535 SE 12th Ave, Portland, OR 97214.
Tel: 503-731-3221. Fax: 503-731-3230.
E-mail: ocbmail@cfb.state.or.us. Web: www.cfb.state.or.us.

DEPARTMENT OF EDUCATION
255 Capitol St NE, Salem, OR 97310.
Tel: 503-378-3569. TTY: 503-378-2892. Fax: 503-378-5156.
E-mail: ode.frontdesk@ode.state.or.us. Web: www.ode.state.or.us.

PENNSYLVANIA

DEPARTMENT OF HEALTH
Health & Welfare Bldg, PO Box 90, Harrisburg, PA 17108.
Tel: 717-783-5436. Fax: 717-772-0323.
Web: www.dsf.health.state.pa.us.

DEPARTMENT OF LABOR AND INDUSTRY
Office for the Deaf & Hard of Hearing, 1521 N 6th St, Harrisburg, PA 17102.
Tel: 717-783-4912. TTY: 717-783-4912. Fax: 717-783-4913.
E-mail: kpuckett@dli.state.pa.us. Web: www.dli.state.pa.us.

RHODE ISLAND

DEPARTMENT OF CHILDREN, YOUTH AND FAMILIES
101 Friendship St, Providence, RI 02903.
Tel: 401-528-3502.
Web: www.dcyf.state.ri.us.

DEPARTMENT OF EDUCATION
255 Westminster St, Providence, RI 02903.
Tel: 401-222-4600. Fax: 401-222-6178.
Web: www.ridoe.com.

DEPARTMENT OF HEALTH
3 Capitol Hill, Providence, RI 02908.
Tel: 401-222-2231. Fax: 401-222-6548.
Web: www.healthri.org.

SOUTH CAROLINA

DEPARTMENT OF HEALTH AND ENVIRONMENTAL CONTROL
Division of Children With Special Health Care Needs, Mills-Jarrett Complex,
PO Box 101106, Columbia, SC 29201.
Tel: 803-898-0784. Fax: 803-898-0613.
E-mail: priceld@dhec.sc.gov. Web: www.scdhec.net/hs/mch/cshcn.

VOCATIONAL REHABILITATION DEPARTMENT
1410 Boston Ave, PO Box 15, West Columbia, SC 29171.

Tel: 803-896-6500. Fax: 803-896-6529.
E-mail: info@scvrd.state.sc.us. Web: www.scvrd.net.

SOUTH DAKOTA

DEPARTMENT OF EDUCATION
700 Governors Dr, Pierre, SD 57501.
Tel: 605-773-7228. Fax: 605-773-6139.
E-mail: mary.stadick@state.sd.us. Web: www.state.sd.us/doe.

DEPARTMENT OF HEALTH
Children's Special Health Services, 615 E 4th St, Pierre, SD 57501.
Tel: 605-773-4749. Fax: 605-773-5942.
E-mail: doh.info@state.sd.us. Web: www.state.sd.us/doh.

TENNESSEE

DEPARTMENT OF HEALTH
Children's Special Services, Cordell Hull Bldg, 3rd Fl, Nashville, TN 37247.
Tel: 615-741-3111. Fax: 615-741-2491.
Web: www2.state.tn.us/health/mch/css.htm.

TEXAS

COUNCIL FOR DEVELOPMENTAL DISABILITIES
6201 E Oltorf St, Ste 600, Austin, TX 78741.
Tel: 512-437-5415. TTY: 512-437-5431. Fax: 512-437-5434.
E-mail: txddc@tcdd.state.tx.us. Web: www.txddc.state.tx.us/index.asp.

DEPARTMENT OF ASSISTIVE AND REHABILITATIVE SERVICES
4800 N Lamar Blvd, 3rd Fl, Austin, TX 78756.
Tel: 512-377-0500. Fax: 512-377-0682.
Web: www.dars.state.tx.us.

DEPARTMENT OF STATE HEALTH SERVICES
Children with Special Health Care Needs Division, 1100 W 49th St, Austin,
TX 78756.
Tel: 512-458-7111. TTY: 512-458-7708. Fax: 512-458-7417.
Web: www.tdh.state.tx.us/cshcn.

EDUCATION AGENCY
W B Travis Bldg, 1701 N Congress Ave, Austin, TX 78701.
Tel: 512-463-9734. Fax: 512-463-9838.
Web: www.tea.state.tx.us.

UTAH

DEPARTMENT OF HEALTH
Children with Special Health Care Needs, 44 N Medical Dr, PO Box 144610,
Salt Lake City, UT 84114.

Tel: 801-584-8284. Fax: 801-584-8488.
Web: www.health.utah.gov/cshcn.

OFFICE OF EDUCATION
PO Box 144200, Salt Lake City, UT 84114.
Tel: 801-538-7500. Fax: 801-538-7521.
Web: www.usoe.k12.ut.us.

VERMONT

DEPARTMENT OF HEALTH
Children With Special Health Needs Program, 108 Cherry St, PO Box 70,
Burlington, VT 05402.
Tel: 802-863-7200. Fax: 802-865-7754.
Web: www.healthyvermonters.info/hi/cshn/cshn.shtml.

VIRGINIA

DEPARTMENT FOR THE BLIND AND VISION IMPAIRED
397 Azalea Ave, Richmond, VA 23227.
Tel: 804-371-3140. TTY: 804-371-3140. Fax: 804-371-3390.
Web: www.vdbvi.org.

DEPARTMENT OF HEALTH
Children with Special Health Care Needs Program, 109 Governor St,
Richmond, VA 23218.
Tel: 804-864-7706.
E-mail: nancy.bullock@vdh.virginia.gov.
Web: www.vahealth.org/specialchildren.

WASHINGTON

DEPARTMENT OF HEALTH
Office of Maternal and Child Health, PO Box 47835, Olympia, WA 98504.
Tel: 360-236-3571. Fax: 360-586-7868.
E-mail: cshcn.support@doh.wa.gov. Web: www.doh.wa.gov/cfh/mch.

DEPARTMENT OF SOCIAL AND HEALTH SERVICES
PO Box 45130, Olympia, WA 98504.
Tel: 360-902-8400. Fax: 360-902-7848.
Web: www.dshs.wa.gov.

SUPERINTENDENT OF PUBLIC INSTRUCTION
Old Capitol Bldg, PO Box 47200, Olympia, WA 98504.
Tel: 360-725-6000. Fax: 360-753-6712.
Web: www.k12.wa.us.

WISCONSIN

DEPARTMENT OF HEALTH AND FAMILY SERVICES
Children with Special Health Care Needs Program, 1 W Wilson St, Madison, WI 53701.
Tel: 608-267-2945. Fax: 608-267-3824.
E-mail: webmaildph@dhfs.state.wi.us.
Web: www.dhfs.wisconsin.gov/dph_bfch/cshcn.

DEPARTMENT OF PUBLIC INSTRUCTION
Division for Learning Support: Equity & Advocacy, 125 S Webster St, PO Box 7841, Madison, WI 53707.
Tel: 608-266-1649. Fax: 608-267-3726.
Web: www.dpi.state.wi.us.

WYOMING

DEPARTMENT OF EDUCATION
Hathaway Bldg, 2nd Fl, 2300 Capitol Ave, Cheyenne, WY 82002.
Tel: 307-777-7675. Fax: 307-777-6234.
Web: www.k12.wy.us.

DEPARTMENT OF HEALTH
2300 Capitol Ave, Rm 117, Cheyenne, WY 82002.
Tel: 307-777-7656. Fax: 307-777-7439.
E-mail: wdh@state.wy.us. Web: http://wdhfs.state.wy.us.

CLASSIFIED LISTINGS

ADVOCACY ORGANIZATIONS

NATIONAL ASSOCIATION OF PRIVATE SPECIAL EDUCATION CENTERS
Washington, DC
See Display Announcement on Page 1106

EDUCATIONAL CONSULTANTS

LESLIE GOLDBERG & ASSOCIATES, LLC
Needham, MA—Tel: 617-969-5151.
Hingham, MA—Tel: 781-749-2074.
E-mail: info@edconsult.org. Web: www.edconsult.org.
Schools, Colleges, LD Supports, Crisis Interventions, Therapeutic Programs.

National Association of Private Special Education Centers

NAPSEC is a nonprofit association whose mission is to ensure access for individuals to private special education as a vital component of the continuum of appropriate placements and services in American education.

National Representation
NAPSEC advocates for the rights of individuals with disabilities and their families.

Nationwide Membership
NAPSEC represents private special education facilities throughout the U.S., by providing a wide array of membership services.

Free Referral Service
NAPSEC provides information on potential placement options to parents and professionals who need an appropriate private special education and/or therapeutic setting for their child, family member, or client.

For additional information, contact:
Sherry L. Kolbe, Executive Director & CEO
NAPSEC, 1522 K Street, NW, Suite 1032, Washington, DC 20005
Phone: 202-408-3338   Fax: 202-408-3340
E-mail: napsec@aol.com   Web Site: www.napsec.org

NAPSEC

Serving Individuals with Disabilities and Their Families Since 1971

INDEX
OF PROGRAMS

INDEX OF PROGRAMS

Programs are referenced by page number. Boldface page numbers refer to the optional Illustrated Announcements of programs that subscribe for space. To facilitate the use of this section, refer to the index preceding the Announcements. Illustrated Announcement cross-references also appear at the end of the free editorial listings of subscribing programs.

Yes, send me the most recent editions of:

Title	Price	Qty	Total
The Handbook of Private Schools	$99.00		
Directory for Exceptional Children	$75.00		
Guide to Summer Camps and Summer Schools	$45.00		
Schools Abroad of Interest to Americans	$45.00		

Subtotal		
MA addresses add 5% sales tax		
Shipping	$7.00	
+$1.50/add'l book		
TOTAL		

Domestic shipping is $7.00, plus $1.50 for each additional book. Non-US shipping quoted on request.

All prices in $US.

☐ Check or money order enclosed (payable on a US bank)

☐ Bill me (organizations only)

☐ Visa ☐ MasterCard ☐ American Express ☐ Discover

Card # _____ Exp. Date _____

Card Holder_____

Signature _____

First Name _____ Last Name _____

Company Name _____

Street Address (no P.O. Boxes, please) _____

City _____ State _____ Zip _____

Country _____ Postal Code _____

E-mail _____

Daytime phone _____ DEC04

PORTER SARGENT PUBLISHERS, INC.

300 Bedford St. Ste. 213 Manchester, NH 03101 USA
Tel: 800-342-7470 Fax: 603-669-7945
orders@portersargent.com www.portersargent.com